NOTE TO THE STUDENT:

This text was created to provide you with a high-quality educational resource. As a publisher specializing in college texts for business and economics, our goal is to provide you with learning materials that will serve you well in your college studies and throughout your career.

The educational process involves learning, retention, and the application of concepts and principles. You can accelerate your learning efforts by utilizing the supplements accompanying this text:

The **STUDY GUIDE,** prepared by the author is designed to help you better your performance in your Cost Accounting course. The guide includes objectives, definitions, and true/false, fill-in-the-blank, and matching questions. Answers to all questions are included in the Study Guide, providing verification of responses as well as explanation as to why the statement is true or false.

Ramblewood Manufacturing, by Leland Mansuetti and Keith Weidkamp, both of Sierra College, is a computerized simulation that can be used with your Cost Accounting course. This software is available on both 5.25″ and 3.5″ disks.

These learning aids are designed to improve your performance in the course by highlighting key points in the text and providing you with assistance in mastering basic concepts. Check your local bookstore or ask the manager to place an order for you today.

We at Irwin sincerely hope that this text package will assist you in reaching your goals both now and in the future.

About the Author

L. Gayle Rayburn is currently president of the Management Accounting Section of the American Accounting Association, which is an international organization of over 1,800 professors interested in teaching and research in the field of management accounting. Rayburn has served in other capacities in numerous professional accounting organizations, including Secretary-Treasurer, National Program Representative, and Southeast Regional Director, Management Accounting Section. She has also served on the Personal Testing Subcommittee, American Institute of Certified Public Accountants and the Committee on Research, National Association of Accountants. She is also a member of Beta Alpha Psi and Beta Gamma Sigma. She is an academic associate of the Goldratt Institute and a Certified Jonah in the theory of constraint.

L. Gayle Rayburn's tenure on the Board of Regents of the Institute of Certified Management Accountants, which has responsibility for the CMA examination, gives her insight into the trends experienced in professional examinations as well as the knowledge and problem solving techniques a student needs for successful completion of certification examinations. Not only is the author a CMA, she is also a CPA, CIA, and Certified Cost Analyst. This book is listed as a suggested reference for studying for the CMA, CPA, and CIA examinations. Problems prepared by Rayburn have appeared on CPA and CMA examinations.

Rayburn received a Ph.D. in Accounting from Louisiana State University, where she was named to their university-wide Alumni Hall of Distinction. She has both public and industrial accounting experience. She is the author of over 120 published professional articles in leading accounting and business journals.

In addition to this book, which is translated and published in Spanish, by diciones Centrum Tecnicas y Cientificas of Madrid, Spain, as *The Contabilidad de costos.1 Biblioteca Master Centrum,* Rayburn is the author of *Financial Tools for Effective Marketing Administration* (1976) published by American Management Association and reprinted as part of AMACOM's Executive Books series (1981).

COST ACCOUNTING
Using a Cost Management Approach

Letricia Gayle Rayburn
Professor of Accountancy
Memphis State University

Fifth Edition

IRWIN

Homewood, IL 60430
Boston, MA 02116

Sponsoring editor:	Jeff Shelstad
Developmental editor:	Carolyn Nowak
Developmental editor, supplements:	Nancy Lanum
Marketing manager:	John E. Biernat
Project editor:	Jean Lou Hess
Production manager:	Ann Cassady
Designer:	Diane Beasley
Art coordinator:	Mark Malloy
Compositor:	Weimer Incorporated
Typeface:	10/12 Times Roman
Printer:	Von Hoffmann Press

Photo credit:
The Pyramid Arena
Memphis, Tennessee

Architectural, Engineering Design and Project Management by
Rosser Fabrap International
Atlanta, Georgia

Photo Composition by
Charlie Reynolds
Color Retouching
Memphis, Tennessee

Library of Congress Cataloging-in-Publication Data

Rayburn, Letricia Gayle.
    Principles of cost accounting: using a cost management approach/
Letricia Gayle Rayburn.—5th ed.
      p.   cm.
    Includes bibliographical references and index.
    ISBN 0-256-08649-4   ISBN 0-256-10809-9 (International ed.)
    1. Cost accounting. 2. Managerial accounting. I. Title.
HF5686.C8R364   1993
657′.42—dc20   92–18559

Printed in the United States of America

1 2 3 4 5 6 7 8 9 0 VH 9 8 7 6 5 4 3 2

THE IRWIN SERIES IN UNDERGRADUATE ACCOUNTING

To
Doug, Beverly, and Mike

Preface

Organization of Book

Cost accounting shapes the future of companies as well as nations. Efficient cost management systems provide superior information for improved decision making. Managers are then able to more efficiently allocate resources and measure and control operations. With a superior cost management system, a company can dominate world commerce, becoming more profitable.

This book tries to take account of the needs of its customers—the students, the teachers, and the employers. It is designed to develop critical thinking and communication skills by encouraging professors to teach students how to think. Its emphasis on the cost management approach recognizes that product costing for inventory valuation and income determination is only one of cost accounting's many purposes—certainly not its primary purpose. It further emphasizes that methods of determining product cost must reflect the current manufacturing and service environment. This book's discussion and illustrations of activity-based management and costing emphasize continuous improvement.

Because the text is adaptable, it can be used by instructors with different teaching objectives and instructional methods. The book's organization allows instructors a great deal of flexibility in selecting chapters to meet the objectives of their course. Instructors can skip chapters or rearrange the sequence of chapters because each chapter is self-contained. Adopters of previous editions reported using this book after a first course in managerial accounting by skipping chapters or changing the sequence. End-of-the-chapter materials covering topics from more than one chapter are clearly labeled to allow flexibility.

This book identifies concepts and principles of cost accounting in a clear, concise, and straightforward manner. Discussions are supported by extensive examples.

The first chapters discuss cost accounting concepts concerned with cost collection—factors that influence such managerial decisions as sales price determination. Product costing concepts are covered first because the author believes students can more easily grasp and appreciate cost-volume-profit analysis, budgeting, and short-run decision making *after* they study product costing. Students who have completed a management accounting course prior to enrolling in cost accounting are able to obtain a higher conceptual understanding *after* a detailed study of product costing. The last part of the book emphasizes the application of cost principles in cost management analysis and quantitative tools for decision making.

This book can be used in a cost or management accounting course in which students have had a minimum of one course in accounting principles or financial accounting. An orientation to accounting terminology and the financial reporting systems is a helpful prerequisite. It is not necessary for students to have completed a course in managerial or cost accounting before using this book.

To aid the student, each chapter begins with measurable objectives that focus on important areas of coverage. Each chapter also includes a list of important terms and concepts.

The mix of assignment material includes questions that review concepts and procedures, exercises that review the direct applications of the basic concepts, problems of varying difficulty that enhance the learning process and cover the concepts in greater depth, and relevant cases that illustrate the practical problems associated with concept implementation. The cases are thought-provoking and designed to stimulate class discussion.

This book contains such a variety of problems and cases that there is sufficient material to challenge students who have had previous courses in management accounting or an extensive background in accounting and related fields. The fifth edition contains extensive material concerned with activity-based management and costing for both manufacturing and marketing activities. Its discussion on service industry costing recognizes the need to accurately determine the cost of providing services in an expanding service-oriented environment.

The chapter sequence does not undermine the mix and match possibilities for selecting course content. Chapters in the book are grouped into six major topic modules which include the following features.

Part I Cost Accounting Concepts

Chapter 1 Cost Accounting in the New Automated Manufacturing Environment—Today and Tomorrow discusses the impact of automation on cost accounting and growth of Activity-Based Management, Life-Cycle Costing, and Target Costing. The danger of integrating cost data with the financial accounting system is presented. A clear distinction is made between cost accounting as needed for financial reporting and cost accounting for supporting decision making and performance evaluation.

Chapter 2 Production, Marketing, and Administrative Cost Flows presents the basic concepts, emphasizing the flow of costs through inventory accounts until they are disposed of as expenses on the income statement. The discussion uses volume-related cost drivers to apply overhead. Cost of goods manufacturing statements using actual and applied overhead trace the manufacturing inventory flow. The chapter further discusses the impact of computer-integrated manufacturing on cost mix, labor-based application rates, and quality control. An appendix illustrates inventory costing for students with an inadequate foundation in these concepts.

Chapter 3 Cost Behavior and Cost Estimation discusses the relationship of fixed and variable behavior patterns, unit and total costs, and relevant range. Students are encouraged to learn to apply regression analysis technology and understand the criteria for its analysis rather than memorizing its mathematical foundations. The regression analysis discussion includes criteria for regression analysis, effect of outlier observations, relevant range and linearity, and cost functions and linearity. An appendix contains learning curve theory.

Chapter 4 Activity-Based Costing and Volume-Based Cost Assignments first compares various capacity levels since many students have trouble understanding how capacity relates to application rates for overhead. Illustrations of the direct, step, and linear algebra methods of allocating service costs reflect volume-related cost drivers. The impact of product diversity and volume diversity emphasize the importance of activity-based management. The concluding illustrations apply materials acquisition and handling costs on nonvolume-related cost drivers.

Part 2 Product Cost Allocation and Accumulation Procedures

Chapter 5 Job Order Costing illustrates job order costing and compares it to process costing and operation costing. Internal control surrounding basic documents such as material requisitions and job order sheets prevents miscosting. An appendix illustrates factory ledger and home office ledger accounts.

Chapter 6 Process Costing: Weighted-Average and FIFO introduces process costing in a rather unique way as students are encouraged to think of a snowball gathering snow (cost) as it travels from one department to another. This analogy communicates the essence of how costs accumulate in a process system. Process costing is placed in this chapter sequence because it is difficult to cover this topic before the student has seen how product costing works. A discussion of the impact of flexible manufacturing and Just-in-time process costing questions the future use of equivalent units. An appendix illustrates completed and not transferred inventory.

Chapter 7 Process Costing: Addition of Materials and Lost Units presents additional complexities encountered in process costing systems when concentrated mixtures are diluted and units lost.

Chapter 8 Joint Product and By-Product Costing discusses the necessity of allocating joint costs on physical or market bases for financial reporting. A different cost analysis results when managers are deciding whether to process further.

Part 3 Cost Data for Performance Evaluation

Chapter 9 Flexible Budgeting and the Budgeting Process compares a fixed (static) and a flexible (variable) budget. Discussions emphasize determining the cost of acquired resources not utilized. The information flow outlines the interrelationships between production-related budgets.

Chapter 10 Nonmanufacturing Budgets, Forecasted Statements, and Behavioral Issues discuss the role of cash budgets in cash management. The chapter exposes students to the use of budgets for performance evaluation and the resulting behavioral implications.

Chapter 11 Standard Costs for Materials and Labor and Chapter 12 Standard Costs and Variances for Factory Overhead first present the calculations for material, labor, and overhead variances and then emphasize finding the responsible factor for the variance and taking corrective action. The chapter emphasizes the importance of managers monitoring efficiency and volume variances to prevent excess inventory. By placing standard costing later in the textbook, students have prior exposure to product costing and can understand that standard costs can be used for both job order and process systems.

Part 4 Cost Accounting/Cost Management for Decision Making

Chapter 13 Cost-Volume-Profit Analysis discusses the contribution margin concept and breakeven analysis with emphasis on the manipulation of the cost-volume-profit formula. This helps the student understand the usefulness of differentiating between fixed and variable costs and see how the pieces fit together. However, if instructors prefer to introduce cost-volume-profit analysis earlier, they can present Chapter 13 before Chapter 3.

Chapter 14 Performance Evaluation and Segment Analysis illustrates ROI, residual income, and other short-run measures of evaluating performance. The chapter illustrates the dangers of evaluating only short-term results and emphasizes the use of multiple performance measures, including throughput and nonfinancial evaluations.

Chapter 15 Transfer Pricing in Multidivisional Companies presents the objective of alternative transfer pricing models. The chapter discusses the related behavioral implications of transfer pricing (i.e., internal competition, suboptimization, and other dysfunctional behavior).

Chapter 16 Decision Models and Cost Analysis under Uncertainty presents decision models, including differential analysis and cost studies under uncertainty. Payoff tables are introduced using probabilities in deciding whether to investigate variances from standards or budgets. The expected value of investigating variances in a two-state environment are compared to the present value of the extra costs of not investigating.

Chapter 17 Capital Budgeting outlines discounted cash flow models as well as the payback and unadjusted return on investment alternative models. Aftertax analysis of equipment replacement is demonstrated through use of the total-cost and differential-cost approaches.

Chapter 18 Capital Budgeting—Additional Topics illustrates sensitivity analysis in cash flow and economic life estimates and inflation in the capital budgeting process. The impact of automation on traditional capital budgeting models and the improvements needed in these models are discussed.

Chapter 19 Activity-Based Management for Marketing Cost Standards uniquely presents setting marketing standards on activity-based costing drivers. The chapter outlines the steps to implementing ABC for marketing activities. This chapter demonstrates the diversity of contexts in which cost accounting concepts and decision making techniques apply.

Chapter 20 Variable Costing illustrates the use of variable (direct) costing for internal use and includes a numerical example of how variable (direct) costing can lead to poor pricing practices. The chapter presents the dangers of an absorption costing system showing phantom profits.

Part 5 Selected Topics for Further Study

Chapter 21 Product Quality and Inventory Management in a JIT Environment discusses the impact of JIT, decreased setup times, and shorter lead times on the validity of EOQ. The chapter presents various methods of recording material waste and the importance of selecting inventory controls that match the value of inventory.

Chapter 22 Payroll Accounting and Incentive Plans demonstrates the basic entries for labor distribution, payroll tax, and indirect or fringe benefits. The chapter illustrates incentive compensation plans and the impact of JIT on these plans.

Chapter 23 The Use of Costs in Pricing Decisions provides a sound economic foundation for the product pricing discussion and follows that foundation with an integrated discussion of cost influences on product price. The chapter discusses the role of social responsibility in pricing.

Chapter 24 Revenue Variances, Material Mix and Yield Variances, and Labor Mix and Yield Variances presents price, volume, quantity, and mix variances for revenue and production. The chapter illustrates market size and market share variances as a breakdown of the sales quantity variance.

Chapter 25 Behavioral and Ethical Factors in Accounting Control illustrates potential suboptimization which is likely to occur when managers are rewarded with a bonus for meeting profit objectives. The relationship between Theory X, Theory Y, and Theory Z to the accounting controls employed is presented. An appendix presents the code of ethics of management accountants to give students a better understanding of the important, complex role cost accountants assume. The discussion includes cases involving misconduct to expose students to the "real world environment" of cost accounting.

Part 6 Quantitative Models for Planning and Control

Chapter 26 Gantt Charts, PERT, and Decision Tree Analysis explains quantitative concepts in a straightforward manner with relevant examples. PERT-cost analysis is illustrated in choosing when to crash. Variance analysis and PERT-cost is demonstrated. The roll-back concept is used in decision tree analysis.

Chapter 27 Linear Programming and the Cost Accountant defines the role of the cost accountant in applying linear programming with emphasis on understanding the effect of constraints and developing the objective function.

Strengths of Fourth Edition Retained

The chapter sequence continues to allow instructors flexibility in their chapter material; however, chapters do not exist in isolation. The topics flow evenly through the chapters. Using different costs for different purposes remains a strong emphasis. This focus helps students understand the importance of professional judgment in choosing the most appropriate cost concept for specific situations.

Cost concepts and cost accumulation topics are covered first. This is most appropriate since with robotics and automated manufacturing causing such a change in cost mix and behavior, contribution margin will have lessened significance. The idea that accounting exists to provide useful information is reinforced and an integral part of each chapter. Not only do readers learn how information is produced in cost accounting systems, but they are encouraged to examine how it can be used by management.

Unlike many other cost accounting texts which virtually ignore marketing and distribution costs, this book contends that evaluating segment performance only on production costs provides inaccurate estimates of relative profitability. The fifth edition expands the chapter on distribution and marketing costs, which has been included since the textbook's first edition, to demonstrate the role of activity-based cost drivers to evaluate marketing performance.

Deficiencies of traditional capital budgeting models and performance measures continue to be emphasized. Quantitative elements continue to be integrated into the text rather than included in supplements or appendices. This helps students understand quantitative applications more easily and see how they can be used effectively.

A detailed outline in Chapter 12 shows the relationships between the two-, three-, and four-variance methods for overhead variances so that students quickly realize that they aren't learning complete different variance sets. This understanding of relationships allows students to evaluate which method they prefer and to better understand why the four-variance method is generally preferred.

The book includes many well written exercises, problems, and cases designed to improve the students' writing and critical thinking skills. The book's numerous decision-making cases encourage students to understand the interrelationship of other disciplines with cost accounting. The textbook is also designed to increase students' thinking power by including several capstone cases which test the students' understanding and knowledge of cost accounting systems. Several of these do this by asking students to evaluate a present system, some of which managers have failed to update when they automated their factories. Rayburn wrote and tested them in class so she can see first hand what areas are not clear enough in their first draft form before they appear revised in the text.

The end of chapter material continues to be representative of the text coverage and gives sufficient practice in applications. There are no distractions in the problem material which undermine successful completion in this student-oriented text. The cases are very interesting and provide an opportunity for the professor to discuss some of the ideas presented in the cases in more detail and from a different perspective. CPA/CMA/CIA multiple choice questions have been retained in all relevant chapters.

Changes in Content and Pedagogy of Fifth Edition

Many changes have been made to the content of the fifth edition to reflect the changing nature of cost accounting and the impact of automation, JIT, quality control, and other new manufacturing techniques on the needs for cost management information.

Major changes to the content of the fifth edition are:

1. Extensive discussion and illustration of activity-based costing encourages students to use non-volume based cost drivers when product and volume

diversity exist. Steps to implementing activity-based management to marketing activities also emphasize the appropriateness of non-volume based cost drivers for nonmanufacturing activities.

2. While the clear, concise writing structure has been retained, most of the materials have been revised to a more active writing style to reflect the exciting, changing nature of cost accounting. By removing some of the nice but not needed prose, the readability is enhanced without losing content.

3. Rather than have a separate chapter discussing the benefits of new cost management tools, these topics are integrated in relevant chapters. This better reflects the impact of these changes.

4. Importance of nonfinancial measures of performance and multiple measures of performance are given increased coverage. The book presents alternative measures of performance evaluation.

5. Coverage of the text has been broadened to include more of the conceptual framework and decision-making analysis underlying the treatment of cost accounting procedures.

6. Various concepts have been revised and reorganized so that there are now 27 chapters which represents ample text and assignment material for a two-term semester course (or three-quarter course).

7. Includes Market Size and Market Share Variances as a breakdown of the Sales Quantity Variance, which recognizes the various types of variable analyses available.

8. Code of ethical conduct for management accountants moved to a chapter appendix later in the chapter sequence so professors can insert where they deem most appropriate in their courses.

9. Job order costing is introduced later in the chapter sequence so students have a better grasp of cost concepts. This enables them better to compare job order and process costing.

10. Learning curve theory is placed in an appendix to cost behavior (Chapter 3) which allows professors more flexibility in course content.

11. The more liberal use of graphics and flowcharts is useful in helping students step from a procedural level of thinking to higher levels of thought in developing more refined abstract reasoning skills.

Supplements to the Fifth Edition

Supplements for Students

Student Guide by Rayburn which is keyed to each chapter of the book. This workbook provides a detailed outline of each chapter, a review of the important new terms and concepts, matching questions containing true-false questions, completion questions, and exercises. Answers to all questions are included in the Study Guide, which provides verification of responses as well as explanation as to why the statement is true or false. Since the student workbook is prepared by the textbook author there is a strong carryover to the textbook material.

List of Key Figures prepared by the textbook author provides check figures for each exercise, problem, and case; these lists are provided in quantity to the instructors for distribution.

Videos The Richard D. Irwin Managerial/Cost Accounting video series contains six 15-minute segments covering capital budgeting, the design of a cost accounting system, process and job order costing, and service and activity based costing. Prepared by Pacific Lutheran University in Seattle, Washington, the videos are free upon adoption.

Supplements for Instructors

Solutions Manual by Rayburn. Detailed solutions to all questions, exercises, problems, and cases in the textbook. Comments on alternative teaching approaches and solutions are included.

Solution Transparencies Overhead transparencies of solutions are designed for easy viewing in the classroom.

Test Bank by Rayburn. Supplementary test material including true or false and multiple-choice questions, short-answer problems, and more comprehensive problems. Outlines for each chapter indicate the relationship of test material to specific problems and exercises in the textbook.

Irwin's Computerized Testing Software This improved microcomputer version of the Test Bank allows editing of questions; provides up to 99 different versions of each test; and allows question selection based on type of question, level of difficulty, or learning objective. This software is available on 5.25″ and 3.5″ disks.

Solution Transparencies Overhead transparencies of solutions are designed for easy viewing in the classroom and are available for every exercise and problem in the text.

Contents in Brief

Contents

COST
ACCOUNTING
CONCEPTS

CHAPTER

1

Cost Accounting in the New Automated Manufacturing Environment—Today and Tomorrow

CHAPTER OBJECTIVES

After studying this chapter, you should be able to:

1. Contrast cost accounting and financial accounting.

2. Discuss the role of cost accountants and their interaction with various players in the new automated environment of manufacturing.

3. Recognize the changes cost management concepts are making to traditional accounting systems.

4. Identify the professional certifications available for cost accountants.

Introduction

As you study cost accounting, you will find many ways to use cost analysis in personal decision making. For example, assume you earn $15,000 annually, and you question whether to further your formal education. If you decide to return to school, you must give up your job and its $15,000 salary, which is an opportunity cost. This sacrifice of the lost salary, in addition to costs of tuition and books, must be matched against the future benefits of having increased your education.

While you are applying cost accounting to personal decisions, corporate executives are using cost data to chart successful futures for their companies. Adapting cost accounting systems to better meet management's needs is crucial to an organization's survival when competing in global markets. Global competitors now have relatively free access to markets around the world. As a result, domestic markets on virtually every continent face greater challenges from foreign competition. With increased reliance on global markets, companies need to not only respond quickly to changing market conditions but also tailor products to different consumer tastes and demands.

Note the direct link between cost accounting practices and corporate goals. In today's automated environment, cost accountants use their management control systems to support and reinforce manufacturing strategies. Thus, you will discover that as a cost accountant you play more of an influencing role than an informing role.

What Is Cost Accounting? (L.O. 1)

Cost accounting identifies, defines, measures, reports, and analyzes the various elements of direct and indirect costs associated with producing and marketing goods and services. Cost accounting also measures performance, product quality, and productivity. Cost accounting is broad and extends beyond calculating product costs for inventory valuation, which government reporting requirements

largely dictate. However, accountants do not allow external reporting requirements to determine how they measure and control internal organizational activities. In fact, cost accounting's focus is shifting from inventory valuation for
financial reporting to costing for decision making.

The main objective of cost accounting is communicating financial information
to management for planning, controlling, and evaluating resources. Cost accounting supplies information that enables management to make more informed decisions. Thus, modern cost accounting is often called **management accounting**
because managers use accounting data to guide their decisions.

Cost Management Systems

Managers distribute resources to meet organizational goals. Because of limited
resources, managers should rely on cost data in deciding which actions provide
optimal returns to the company. In arriving at these decisions, they can use cost
management information to direct day-to-day operations and supply feedback to
evaluate and control performance.

Comparison of Cost Accounting with Financial Accounting

Financial accountants prepare information for external parties on the status of
assets, liabilities, and equity. Financial accounting also reports results of operations, changes in owners' equity, and cash flow for an accounting period. Creditors, present owners, potential owners, employees, and the public at large use
financial accounting reports in decision making. Both external financial accounting and internal management analysis require cost information. Cost data are
developed for inventory valuation and income determination, which are concerns
of financial accounting.

However, cost information used for external reporting is usually irrelevant for
actual management decision making. When results from reported production activity require more than one day to reach manufacturing managers, corrective
action is not likely to occur and effectiveness is lost. It is usually better to provide incomplete, perhaps less precise, data to managers quickly than to provide
complete information too late to affect any of their decisions or actions. Thus,
an organization needs two different accounting systems with different degrees of
completeness and timeliness.

Cost Defined

Cost measures the economic sacrifice made to achieve an organization's goal.
For a product, cost represents the monetary measurement of resources used, such
as material, labor, and overhead. For a service, cost is the monetary sacrifice
made to provide the service. Accountants generally use cost with other descriptive terms, such as *historical, product, prime, labor,* or *material.* Each of these
terms defines some characteristic of the cost measurement process or an aspect
of the object being measured.

Different Costs for Different Purposes. Cost systems are designed to collect,
summarize, and report costs for the purpose of product costing, inventory valuation, or operational control/performance measurement. These various purposes influence the collecting, summarizing, and reporting process. Thus,

accountants use different costs for different purposes as the type, purpose, and nature of a cost outline its usage. Cost accountants use professional judgment in choosing the most appropriate cost concept for specific situations.

Roles of Controller and Cost Accountant (L.O. 2)

Although **controller** is the common title given to the chief accounting officer and manager of the accounting department in a company, other titles are also used. Controllers play a significant role in planning and controlling activities by helping managers in the decision-making process. A controller designs systems to prepare internal reports for management and external reports for the public and government. The controller's functions also include analyzing profitability and establishing budgets. In addition, the controller may prepare special managerial revenue and cost analyses. For example, controllers compare the cost of making parts with their purchase cost.

As a member of the controller's department, a **cost accountant** is responsible for collecting product costs and preparing accurate and timely reports to evaluate and control company operations. Cost accountants assemble, classify, and summarize financial and economic data on the production and pricing of goods or services. Cost accountants have greater responsibilities in a manufacturing company than in a retail firm that purchases ready-for-sale merchandise.

A controller's duties differ significantly from those of a treasurer. A **treasurer** primarily manages cash. A treasurer's duties include arranging short-term financing, maintaining banking and investor relationships, investing temporary excess funds, and supervising customer credit and collection activities.

Planning and Control Activities

Cost accountants play an important role in coordinating external and internal data so managers can formulate better plans and control activities. In the planning phases, cost accounting helps management by providing budgets reflecting cost estimates of material, labor, technology, and robotics. Managers use cost accounting data in product pricing, marketing, make-or-buy, and capital budgeting decisions. A company uses cost accounting reports in selecting the best methods of attaining goals when reviewing alternative courses of action.

Control activities involve monitoring production processes and reporting variations from budgets and plans. Cost accountants issue progress reports that summarize activities to show how efficiently various divisions are performing. While planning activities are future oriented, control activities concern the present. By comparing actual results with the budget amounts, they identify areas of deviation where problems may be developing. Cost accounting, then, provides **feedback,** or information about current performance designed to encourage needed changes. However, control reports can result in a change in performance only if management takes the initiative. A control report by itself cannot cause the change.

Cost Analysis. Cost accountants obtain cost information from a variety of sources. Some of this information, such as vendor invoices, become the basis for journal entries. Similarly, they use engineering time and motion studies, timekeepers' records, and planning schedules from production supervisors in cost analysis. Cost analysis techniques include breakeven analysis, comparative cost analysis, capital expenditure analysis, and budgeting techniques. After determining what is actually happening, accountants should identify available alternatives. Professional judgment is then needed to apply and interpret the results of each costing technique. For example, although breakeven analysis indicates the capacity at which operations become profitable, it assumes a static condition in which sales prices and expenses are constant. However, such factors do not remain constant in the real world. For instance, inflation, supply, and demand cause sales prices and expenses to vary.

Cost-Benefit Approach. In accounting there is a direct relationship between the amount of time and funds management is willing to spend on cost analysis and the degree of reliability desired. If a company wants detailed records with a high degree of accuracy, managers should provide additional time and money for compiling and maintaining cost information. However, managers should only use cost analysis and control techniques when the anticipated benefits in helping achieve management goals exceed the cost. This is the primary criterion for choosing among alternative accounting approaches and is the **cost-benefit approach.**

CIM's Impact on Cost Accounting Tasks

In **computer-integrated manufacturing (CIM),** digital control links the entire factory together—from design to production. CIM removes the barrier between accounting, engineering, and manufacturing. Rather than separating these functions, a new **networking form of organization** brings together all functions to promote team-based management. Such a firm recognizes **cross-functional processes** that cut across many organizational areas.

Traditionally, manufacturing personnel have been separated from marketing/salespersons. Manufacturing personnel receive the responsibility of cost control under the assumption that cost is best controlled where it occurs. In turn, because marketing personnel are responsible for increasing sales, their tasks include new product introductions and advertising. However, separating responsibility for cost and revenue does not always lead to increased profitability. Separating responsibility fails to recognize the interdependencies between decisions made by one company division on the performance of another division.

Traditional factories group machines by functions. Parts travel great distances in these factories because all grinding machines and drilling machines are in one location. Improved factory layout eliminates wasted space by bringing together operators who sequentially process a product, allowing greater cross-functional decision making and coordination. Cost accountants play a significant role in integrating the innovative efforts of these employees with the company's long-term strategies and goals.

This networking system encourages accounting, manufacturing, engineering, design, testing, quality control, and marketing to work closely together throughout the product development stage. Tasks are performed in parallel, not in sequence. The traditional cycle is to design first and to perform cost accounting, manufacturing, and quality control functions later. Such tools as **computer-aided design (CAD)** and **computer-aided manufacturing (CAM)** apply computer technology to any or all aspects of the production process from design to fabrication. These tools facilitate closer interaction between personnel. Integrated manufacturing systems better prepare companies to compete in global markets.

What Cost Accountants Do

Within this network, cost accountants work closely with many people in other departments. In meeting the information needs of other departments, cost accountants gather, report, and analyze cost data. They also collect all costs of making goods or providing services. They use such cost data for income measurement and inventory valuation. These data also help management plan and make operating decisions. As part of their jobs, cost accountants interpret results, report them to management, and provide analyses that assist decision making in the following departments:

1. *Manufacturing.* Cost accountants work closely with production personnel to measure and report manufacturing costs. The efficiency of the production departments in scheduling and transforming material into finished units is evaluated for improvements.

2. *Engineering.* Cost accountants and engineers translate specifications for new products into estimated costs. By comparing estimated costs with projected sales prices, they help management decide whether manufacturing will be profitable.

3. *Systems design.* Cost accountants are becoming more involved in designing CIM systems and data bases corresponding to cost accounting needs. The ideal is for cost accountants, engineers, and systems designers to develop a flexible production process responding to changing market needs.

4. *Treasurer.* The treasurer uses budgets and related accounting reports developed by cost accountants to forecast cash and working capital requirements. Detailed cash reports indicate when there will be excess funds to invest.

5. *Financial accounting.* Cost accountants work closely with financial accountants who use cost information in valuing inventory for external reporting and income determination.

6. *Marketing.* Marketing involves the product innovation stage, the manufacturing planning stage, and the sales process. The marketing department develops sales forecasts to facilitate preparing a product's manufacturing schedule. Cost estimates, competition, supply, demand, environmental influences, and the state of technology determine the sales price.

7. *Personnel.* Personnel administers the wage rates and pay methods used in calculating each employee's pay. This department maintains adequate labor records for legal and cost analysis purposes.

Standards of Ethical Conduct

An essential ingredient of these interactions with other departments is for cost accountants to ask questions that management wants answered. Cost accounting is designed to serve managerial purposes—to help management do a better job than could be done without it. To be successful, accountants equip themselves to meet changing cost accounting needs. Also, they must meet the standards of ethical conduct presented in the appendix to Chapter 25 as they interact with other departments.

Automation and Cost Management Concepts (L.O. 3)

Traditional cost accounting models were based on the mass production of a mature product with known characteristics and a stable technology. With automation, the labor content in manufacturing processes diminishes while other costs increase. Automated manufacturing usually requires large investments in engineering design and in new processes.

Estimated product costs influence new product introduction decisions, product design, and the marketing efforts given a product line. Product costs also play an important role in setting prices. Distorted product cost information may cause a company to follow an unprofitable strategy. However, many companies continue to use conventional product costing systems that fail to recognize this shift in cost structure. As a result, traditional cost systems do not cost products correctly for decision-making purposes. Changes in production operations require an updating of cost accounting systems.

The cost management concept developed in response to deficiencies in traditional cost accounting. A new approach addressing this need, **cost management** combines familiar costing techniques with new methods of monitoring economic performance against plans. Instead of focusing attention on what occurred, cost management emphasizes the future impact of economic conditions.

The traditional cost accounting model assumes each company mass produces few standardized items. Mass production was a primary means of cost savings; however, automation reduces the cost of changing manufacturing from one product line to another. Thus, with automation, companies can manufacture many small batches of various products in a short time. Such changes create a need for new types of cost accounting systems. The following pages summarize some of the major changes to which cost accounting systems must adapt as manufacturers move toward the factory of the future.

Flexible Manufacturing Systems

Flexible manufacturing systems result from the use of computer-controlled production processes, including CAD/CAM, programmable machine tools, and robots. Flexible manufacturing reduces setup or changeover times, allowing companies to efficiently manufacture a wide variety of products in small batches. A **product life cycle** is the time between designing and introducing a new product and removing it from the market because of insufficient demand. Product life cycles are getting shorter and the rate of engineering change is increasing; it appears that this rate will continue to increase. Manufacturing one product and then another requires the frequent moving of equipment. Machine tools that are self-contained and shock-resistant offer advantages because today machine mobility is increasingly important.

Flexible manufacturing systems shift the emphasis from large-scale manufacturing processes of standard products to highly automated job shop environments. Job shops manufacture items in small batches for specific customers.

Thus, a company is better equipped to alter product lines as product life cycles become shorter. Computer-controlled machine tools also improve product quality and reliability when properly organized and arranged. Combining these tools with computer scheduling and reporting leads to shorter production runs, lower inventory levels, and lower overall costs.

Zero Defect Program

In addition to purchasing flexible machines easily adaptable to changing markets, effective managers emphasize quality in all manufacturing stages. Rather than waiting to inspect items at the end of the production line or striving to stay within acceptable tolerance limits, eliminating all waste is their goal. Waste is anything other than the minimum amount of labor, machine, materials, and facilities. Cost accountants are adopting the **zero defects** concept, whose performance standard is to *do it right the first time.* Operators, not the inspector, become responsible for zero defects. Operators stop the manufacturing process to take immediate corrective action on discovery of an error or defect.

Nonvalue-Added Time

A companywide operating philosophy to remove waste identifies and eliminates nonvalue activities. **Nonvalue-added time** represents the time a part is delayed, moved, or inspected. It is *waste time* because no value is created for a customer when the product is not being processed. Inefficiencies in production cause nonvalue-added activities. **Throughput time** is value-added time plus nonvalue-added time. Throughput time represents the interval between starting a part in manufacturing and shipping it in a finished state to a customer. To increase profits, cost accountants must be alert to finding ways to reduce throughput time.

Just-In-Time Concept

The **Just-In-Time (JIT) management philosophy** minimizes throughput time by emphasizing continuous improvements. JIT reduces inventories by achieving a continuous production process. In a JIT setting, employees keep on hand only the inventory needed in production until the next order arrives. Having fewer goods on hand requires less warehouse space and storage equipment, and reduces inventory holding cost, while realizing gains in productivity.

Pull Rather than Push System

The essence of JIT is a **pull system,** rather than a **push system.** Using a pull system, managers realize that it is better not to produce than to manufacture unnecessary parts resulting in excessive inventories. The factory production line operates on a demand-pull basis. The demand created by downstream workstations initiates activity at each workstation. Producing goods only for stock is in sharp contrast with the demands of CIM and JIT pull production and delivery systems. Under JIT, when marketing receives a sales order, manufacturing pulls a sales order through its process. Sales, not production, generate funds for the company. A pull system operates most efficiently where schedules are sufficiently level so a manufacturing process can react to the pull signals.

Activity-Based Management

Today, cost accountants recognize that manufacturing and providing services are related activities. Thus, they direct attention to the cost of these activities. The **activity-based management** system links resource consumption to the activities a company performs and costs the activities to products or customers. Activity-based management uses **activity-based costing** (also called **transaction-based costing**) to measure and control these relationships. Activity-based costing (ABC) results from the belief that products consume activities; product design determines which activities the products consume. An **activity** is a process or procedure causing work. Examples include moving parts, performing engineering change orders, and establishing vendor relations. ABC is a cost planning system emphasizing an ongoing process of improvement. ABC encourages an identification of value- and nonvalue-added activities so nonvalue-added activities are eliminated.

Life-Cycle Costing

Combining activity-based management and life-cycle costing illustrates the impact of alternative product designs on product costs. **Life-cycle costing** tracks and collects the costs attributable to each product or service from its initial research and development to final marketing to customers—thus, the term *cradle to grave costing*. Life-cycle costing recognizes that the design stage holds great promise for supporting low-cost production. By the time new products enter the production stage, opportunities to economize are limited. In addition to production costs, life-cycle costing studies preproduction and postproduction costs. For example, accountants estimate the cost of furnishing spare parts and services for the product involved.

Spending more effort in estimating costs in the preproduction stages reduces the number of parts and promotes the use of standard parts across the production lines, also lowering costs. Using standard parts lowers material costs because it creates possibilities for more aggressive volume buying. Also, when manufacturers use rigidly specified equipment designed to make only one product, this product is expensive because the specialized equipment often becomes worthless at the end of the life cycle.

Target Costing

Life-cycle costing encourages **target costing,** an approach that compares costs to date with target costs, beginning from the design stage to the completion of a product. This approach classifies functional areas of a new product by use and value. Each functional area then receives a target cost. A target cost should be established for all activities of a new product's life cycle. Initially, accountants use rough cost estimates to determine whether the product's general drawing fits the target cost. Engineers make design changes if the cost of general drawings is not within the target cost.

Change in Performance Evaluation

The adoption of JIT, life-cycle costing, and other innovative management techniques requires an analysis of current performance evaluation systems. Often traditional labor productivity measures become irrelevant. The use of a single short-term profit measure, such as net income, may not reflect the ability of managers, especially those receiving bonuses for rapid profit improvement. Short-term profits are not reliable indicators of good management because profits can increase solely due to acquiring another company, deferring maintenance, or cutting out research and other discretionary expenses. Thus, manufacturers that successfully compete in the global market use multiple methods for measuring performance and improving productivity, quality, and cost visibility as discussed in Chapter 14.

Goal Congruence. These performance measures should encourage managers to achieve overall organizational goals. To do this, a company breaks down its goals into subgoals for individual managers. These subgoals should be consistent with the company's overall goals. Such **goal congruence** is an ideal that is difficult to achieve, for individuals bring their own aspirations into the company and try to fulfill their own goals as much as possible. Individual employees adopt management's goals as long as the resulting benefits outweigh the required sacrifices. For example, an important personal goal of individual employees is to earn enough money to meet their families' physical and social needs. This may conflict with the goals of the company, because higher employee salaries mean lower company profits. In addition, managers often increase their functional responsibilities and the number of employees reporting to them to obtain power and prestige. The result is an inefficient organizational structure.

Rather than having only one dominant goal, an organization is more likely to have many operating subgoals that yield overall goals. Because multiple goals exist, accountants may have difficulty determining the enterprise's true overall goals. Top managers may inaccurately hand down what each personally considers are the company's goals. Thus, the accountant may not know if an action is congruent with overall goals or not. To help overcome these communication problems while also recognizing that goal congruence is difficult to achieve, managers should agree on company goals. After they carefully explain these goals, employees can better understand their responsibility in goal achievement. Managers should try to set company goals that also satisfy employee goals.

Professional Organizations (L.O. 4)

Several organizations in the private sector have professional certifying examinations for cost accountants. This book includes problems from these examinations. Other organizations influencing cost accounting development, such as the Cost Accounting Standards Board and the Internal Revenue Service, are agencies of the federal government.

Professional Certifications

Institute of Management Accountants (IMA). Formerly the National Association of Accountants, the IMA established the Institute of Certified Management Accountants which administers the **Certified Management Accountant (CMA)** examination. Candidates must pass a series of uniform national examinations that include four parts: economics, finance, and management; financial accounting and reporting; management reporting, analysis, and behavioral issues; and decision analysis and information systems. The CMA exam tests cost accounting knowledge extensively. Test dates are in June and December. Candidates must meet specific experience and education requirements.

American Institute of Certified Public Accountants. The American Institute of Certified Public Accountants prepares, administers, and grades the **Certified Public Accountant (CPA)** examination. Test dates are in May and November. Beginning in May 1994, the CPA examination will consist of four parts: auditing; business law and professional responsibility; accounting and reporting (taxation, managerial-cost, and governmental and not-for-profit organizations); and financial accounting and reporting. The exam also has certain experience and education requirements.

The Institute of Internal Auditors. The Institute of Internal Auditors develops the **Certified Internal Auditing (CIA)** exam that consists of the following four parts: principles of internal auditing, internal auditing techniques, principles of management, and disciplines related to internal auditing. The last part heavily tests cost accounting. This certification program also has experience and education requirements.

Society of Cost Estimating and Analysis. Enhancing the efficiency and effectiveness of cost and pricing activities in proprietary industry, not-for-profit organizations, and governments is a goal of the Society of Cost Estimating and Analysis. The **Certified Cost Estimator/Analyst** designation is a certification by the society that an individual is of high estimating or analysis accomplishment and capability. To receive this designation, applicants meet education and/or job experience criteria and pass a written examination.

Government Agencies

Cost Accounting Standards Board. The U.S. Congress created the Cost Accounting Standards Board (CASB) in 1970 to promulgate cost accounting standards designed to achieve uniformity and consistency for government agencies in cost-type negotiated contracts. The standards are used in pricing, administration, and settlement of negotiated defense contracts and subcontracts with relevant federal agencies.

Internal Revenue Service. The Internal Revenue Service (IRS) is interested in cost accounting practices because of their impact on income determination for tax purposes. Regulations regarding costs to be included in inventory, asset capitalization criteria, allowable depreciation methods and rates, indirect costs, and transfer pricing are among those issued by the IRS.

Summary

This chapter defines cost accounting and explains the functions of cost accountants and their relationships with other departments in an organization. Cost accountants are important members of the management team because their role extends far beyond accumulating product costs for inventory valuation. They have flexibility in preparing cost accounting analyses and reports in a manner that best meets the company's planning and control needs. Thus, modern cost accounting systems better reflect the manufacturing processes that actually occur on the factory floor. Also, market-driven accounting practices enable companies to better meet global competition.

Automation technology is changing long runs that manufacture standardized products for inventory to shorter production runs suitable for changing products. Traditional systems closely monitored direct labor costs in the mass production of a few standardized items. However, large-scale production of an item with unchanging specifications will be the exception in the future, rather than the rule.

Modern methods for costing products, such as activity-based management, trace the costs of resources by the activities needed to produce individual products. In a transaction-related ABC system, units that originate the activities are charged for their costs. ABC identifies activities that add value and encourages the use of designs that reduce the demand for high-cost activities. Identification and elimination of waste emphasize continuous improvement, thus lowering product cost.

Important Terms and Concepts

cost accounting, 2
management accounting, 3
cost, 3
controller, 4
cost accountant, 4
treasurer, 4
feedback, 4
cost-benefit approach, 5
computer-integrated manufacturing (CIM), 5
networking form of organization, 5
cross-functional processes, 5
computer-aided design (CAD), 5
computer-aided manufacturing (CAM), 5
cost management, 7
flexible manufacturing systems, 7
product life cycle, 7

zero defects, 8
nonvalue-added time, 8
throughput time, 8
just-in-time (JIT) management philosophy, 8
pull system, 8
push system, 8
activity-based management/costing (transaction-based costing), 9
activity, 9
life-cycle costing, 9
target costing, 9
goal congruence, 10
Certified Management Accountant, 10
Certified Public Accountant, 11
Certified Internal Auditor, 11
Certified Cost Estimator/Analyst, 11

Problem for Self-Study

Guidelines for Internal Reporting (L.O. 1)

Accounting is the process of measuring and reporting financial information about an economic entity, such as a business enterprise. Accounting serves as the communication process of business by supplying information that permits informed judgments and decisions by users of the data. The accounting process provides financial data for a wide range of parties who study the data for many purposes. For example, accounting supplies management with significant financial and economic data useful for decision making. Managers need reliable information to make sound decisions involving the allocation of scarce resources. Decision making always involves alternatives, even if they entail taking no action or delaying action. Thus, accounting information is useful in choosing from among alternative courses of action because it provides the bases for predicting each alternative's financial results. To fulfill this responsibility, data are presented in the manner best meeting the needs of individual readers.

Required:

With this in mind, set up a structure of reports for a medium-sized manufacturing company. Explain which general principles would guide you in developing reports for different levels of management; for example, top, middle, and lower levels.

Solution to Problem for Self-Study

Guidelines for Internal Reporting

Top Management

1. Give reports that include a complete and readily comprehensible summary of overall aspects of operations.
2. Provide accounting and budget reports that pinpoint high and low efficiency levels throughout the firm.
3. Provide historical data that are valuable in gaining insight into the future.
4. Round to nearest hundred dollars—no need for pennies.
5. Simplify reports by combining similar items as prepaid insurance, prepaid rent, and prepaid taxes into one category of prepaid expenses.
6. Emphasize planning budget and performance reporting.

Middle Management
(These managers may be in charge of major subdivisions. Although more concerned with operations than top management, they also have some important planning functions.)

1. Summarize operations on accounting and budget reports.
2. Reflect day-to-day operations by providing reports with less detail than for lower-level management.

Lower Level Management

1. Distribute reports primarily concerned with coordination and control.
2. Give control reports designed to help control current operations.
3. Prepare reports principally concerned with control of production and costs.
4. Provide *detailed* information that carries a message to operators in such a manner that action will be taken.
5. Prepare reports that are simple, understandable, and limited to items having a direct bearing on the supervisor's operational responsibilities.

Miscellaneous Rules of Reporting for All Levels of Management

1. Prepare external reports according to generally accepted accounting principles, and internal reports that meet managers' specific needs.
2. Consider an executive's background—a former controller may prefer tabulated and detailed data; an engineer may prefer graphic presentation and highly summarized data.
3. Tailor to organization structure.
4. Design to implement the management exception principle—include a basis for evaluation of performance.
5. Provide only essential information.
6. Adapt to the needs and personal preferences of the primary user.
7. Prepare and present promptly.

8. Convey constructive tone rather than implied criticism.

9. Standardize where feasible.

10. Provide accurate, simple, and understandable reports.

11. Follow cost-benefit approach for internal reports.

12. Show dollar variances and the percentage of variance for reports containing budgeted cost.

13. Prepare daily or weekly reporting showing budgeted and actual labor by hours or number of workers.

14. Prepare monthly reports for the plant manager and top managers showing the results by operations in total for the month.

Review Questions

1. Discuss the types of information needed for controlling a company.

2. Define cost accounting. How does it differ from financial accounting?

3. Support your agreement or disagreement with the statement: "Different costs should be used for different purposes."

4. Explain why the accounting system that is most valuable to management is one that raises questions, not answers questions.

5. Compare and contrast the duties of the controller, treasurer, and cost accountant.

6. Who should be involved in designing a cost accounting system so it meets management's needs?

7. Define the term *feedback*. What role does cost accounting play in providing feedback to management?

8. Discuss the relationship of the cost accountant and other departments within the company.

9. Discuss the impact of professional accounting organizations on the development of cost accounting theory.

10. Explain why cost accounting professionals should support and encourage senior executives to approach problems by asking, "What can we do about it?" rather than, "What happened?" What impact does this approach to problem analysis have on developing cost data that are meaningful?

Cases

C1–1 Determining Cost Information Needed (L.O. 1)

Since Joe Toone, a friend of your family, recently learned that you are a cost accounting student, he seeks your advice. Toone has just finished high school, graduating in the top third of his class. However, his grades were not high enough for a scholarship. His family has limited resources, and it will be a financial strain for him to major in accounting at the state college 100 miles from his home.

However, Toone has an opportunity to attend a vocational school in his hometown. He believes that with the accounting courses he takes at the vocational school, he can become a cost clerk or bookkeeper with a local company.

Toone also has received a job offer as a machine operator from a local manufacturing company. There he could receive on-the-job training while earning wages.

Required:

a. In advising Toone, which cost information would be helpful?

b. Which factors are pertinent to the decision? Can they be quantified?

C1–2 Cost Information Needs of Production Managers (L.O. 2)

For several years Lestor Manufacturing Company has produced various lines of motors. Various other firms within the geographical area also produce similar motors. All these firms, including Lestor Company, belong to a national association of motor manufacturers.

Lestor's recently appointed plant manager is eager to use cost information in planning and controlling operations.

Required:

Discuss the areas in which cost information benefits production managers and supervisors of profit and cost centers.

C1–3 Evaluating Cost Reduction Plan (L.O. 2)

Under Tilly Company's continuing education program with a local university, all top and middle managers attend a managerial cost seminar. After hearing the session on cost reduction programs, one of the vice presidents began to actively search for ways to cut costs in the company. He became alarmed when he found that the company is furnishing styrofoam coffee cups costing $0.005 each to employees. Department heads request these cups from purchasing. The company absorbs the cost, without billing each department.

On further investigation, the vice president discovered that each department has its own coffee pot. Employees pay a quarter for every cup of coffee they drink. This coffee fund buys the department's coffee, cream, and sugar. The vice president decides that it is too expensive for the company to furnish the coffee cups and orders the purchasing department to bill individual departments for the cost of the cups.

As a result, all employees become hostile and decide to take their coffee breaks in the company cafeteria. Previously, they stayed in their departments, and if they were behind schedule, they drank coffee at their desks. Due to the distance of many departments from the cafeteria, it takes some of the employees 20 to 30 minutes to get to the cafeteria, drink their coffee, and return to their desks.

Required:

Evaluate the effectiveness of the vice president's cost reduction plan.

C1–4 Problems in Information System (L.O. 3)

After looking at a pile of reports on his desk, the vice president of Jahn, Inc., remarked to one of the supervisors reporting to him, "I take several reports home every night; I just don't have time at the office to read and study all the reports I receive. But I often can't even complete all the pages at home." The vice president then picked up a report on the top of the pile and said, "See this report? You should also have received a copy yesterday. It will take me two hours tonight to wade through all this."

Further conversation revealed that with the introduction two years ago of the company's computer system, the amount of management data increased significantly. The vice president even remarked, "I almost wish for the good old days when one of the major problems was obtaining management control information."

Before the computer system was installed, systems designers studied the old manual system to determine how best to accomplish the conversion. Because most top managers were unfamiliar with computer design or occupied with pressing operational problems, they did not help design the reports. The top managers contacted by the system designers generally gave the following comment, "Give me the computer run, and then I will figure out exactly how to use it." One top manager, who did help the system designers, suggested that an exception report print any actual cost that exceeded the year-to-date budget by 10 percent.

Required:

Discuss problems inherent in the information system.

C1–5 Information Needs for Production and Marketing (L.O. 2)

New York Manufacturing Company was organized 30 years ago. The president started with the company as a supervisor and has served in various managerial capacities. The vice president of marketing joined the company last year after serving as an administrator in another industry. A vice president of production and a vice president of accounting/finance have each been with the company 10 years.

The company has 1,000 employees producing and selling detergents and other household cleaning products. All production occurs with two labor shifts working six days a week in one plant. The company performs all research activities for new product development in this plant facility. Several marketing offices occupy neighboring sites.

Required:

a. Contrast the information needs of the president and the vice president of marketing.
b. Discuss the important information needs of the production, marketing, and accounting/finance vice presidents in controlling operations.
c. Design a report format for the vice president of production and the vice president of marketing. Suggest possible items that should be included in each area.

C1–6 Meaning of the Term *Cost* (L.O. 1)

You are a partner in the consulting firm of Ernest, Inc. One of your clients has asked your assistance in explaining the term *cost* as used in accounting. The client relates the following incidents using the term *cost.*

1. A sales supervisor in a large automobile dealership encourages a prospective customer to buy a new car by agreeing to sell at the dealership's *cost.* When the customer again asked what the price would be, the sale supervisor assured the customer of only paying *cost* by signing the agreement. Further, the dealership would not be making any profit from the sale.
2. The owner of Jones Furniture Store is explaining to the company's banker why company income is down by stating, "My *costs* this year increased 25 percent. Because revenues did not increase this much, income is lower."
3. In viewing an income statement, the client notices that *cost* of goods sold is deducted from sales to give gross margin.

Required:

Determine in these incidents whether *cost* is correctly used and what connotation it has.

C1–7 Cost Accounting for Agricultural Operations (L.O. 2)

The Southern Cotton Company owns and operates several cotton plantations and a cotton gin for extracting raw cotton. Raw cotton is sold and shipped to other companies for further processing.

Fortunately, Southern is located in a geographical area in which operations can continue throughout most of the year. The climate allows regularity of employment. However, this does require careful planning to use a minimum of equipment efficiently. Employees plant fields in rotation so they can harvest cotton at a fairly regular rate throughout the year. This allows a regular pace of cotton gin operations.

These strategic plans require careful review by agricultural experts who are also continually experimenting with various methods of planting, cultivating, fertilizing, and harvesting.

Every three years, employees carefully plow and harrow the fields before planting. Annually, employees cultivate all fields to free them of weeds until the cotton has grown high enough to shade out the weed growth. Southern uses an irrigation system as required and adds liquid nutriments to the irrigation water for fertilizing.

Southern extracts cotton hulls from the raw cotton and sells them to nurseries. Nurseries use the hulls to keep weeds out of their clients' flower beds. Southern uses the remaining cotton hulls as supplementary fuel in heating its boilers.

Required:

List the major cost accounting problems the company has with this cotton planting and processing operation. Suggest an appropriate solution for each of these.

C1–8 Cost-Benefit Analysis of Accounting Data (L.O. 2)

Because the market for one of its major products is facing a decline, management of Lillian, Inc., has asked all office personnel to keep detailed records of both their time and supplies incurred in accounting for the cost of each customer's order. Management is also concerned that monthly $60 to $70 of office supplies are wasted, thrown away too soon, or taken home by employees. Management believes that this new policy of record-keeping will help cut waste and theft.

The office manager has drawn up a policy that requires employees to prepare a daily inventory. At the end of each day, employees count paper clips, envelopes, microcomputer disks, accounting paper, and pencils. Then each employee uses this balance for the next day's beginning balance. The ending daily count is subtracted from the total to yield the cost of supplies used for the day. The supply cost is then allocated to the customers served during the day based on the estimated time that employees worked on specific customers' accounts. The controller then costs the time employees worked on customers' accounts using the payroll cost data. The final report shows both the cost of employees' time and office supplies used for each customer served. Also, the internal auditor examines, on a random basis, the employees' office supply records.

Required:

Evaluate Lillian management's approach to reducing costs.

C1–9 Cost Information Needed (L.O. 1)

Having had experience in metal handling, Sam Miller decided to invest a part of his savings, form his own company, and be his own boss. He realizes that his company will have to be small, especially at first. However, Miller believes that his savings will be large enough to provide an initial down payment for equipment and supplies. He has talked with a local banker and received the bank's backing to borrow limited funds for working capital.

Miller's analysis of the market reveals that the concern for energy conservation will encourage consumers to install woodburning fireplaces. He has designed self-contained units with enough flue pipe to reach an 8-foot ceiling. Some models will include a reducer and a grate along with brass ornaments. Other lower-priced models will not include these items. The more expensive models will include glass paneled doors. Prices of the fireplaces will range from $500 to $800, depending on the model. Miller will employ two people who can install the fireplaces. Customers can either have the fireplaces delivered or pick them up at the factory.

After investigating the vacant buildings available, Miller secured a lease on a building. The building is adequate for initial production.

Miller plans to start operations with five employees and gradually hire another five. At the end of the first year, 10 employees will work one shift. His long-range plans include adding enough employees for a second shift in two to three years.

Miller and an engineer have drawn up plans for two standard styles of fireplace-heaters. They expect to complete three more plans before operations begin next month.

Miller has not yet hired a full-time engineer. The part-time engineer will prepare plans for custom-made fireplace-heaters for an additional fee.

Miller does not know how much advertising to use; however, he realizes he will have to compete with several fireplace firms in his city. He plans to advertise custom work in designing and installing fireplace-heaters for new homes. Also, Miller plans to emphasize the standard models for older homes that already have flues. He has talked with several local residential building contractors and is considering giving them a discount to get customers.

Miller realizes the importance of maintaining adequate accounting records, but he is reluctant to spend much of his time in detailed cost analysis. He believes he can more profitably spend his time in production activities. He questions if checkbook stubs and a few other records will be sufficient for tax return and management purposes.

Required:

List the types of records Miller needs for internal and for external purposes and explain why each is necessary.

C1–10 Cost Accounting Requirements for a Service Agency (L.O. 1)

Even though the volume of revenues has been steadily rising at the Treadwell Advertising Agency, its costs have been increasing at a faster rate. Thus, the ratio of profit to net revenue has decreased.

Treadwell's principal source of revenue is commissions earned for placing advertisements in various communications media, such as television, magazines, and newspapers. Publishers and other communications companies bill Treadwell at a scheduled rate less a 12 percent commission. Treadwell in turn bills its clients at the full scheduled rate in addition to any special artwork or research requested by the client. To make a profit, Treadwell's costs must be less than the 12 percent commission.

At present, there are three departments: copy, art, and production. Each department has its own facilities with production having more equipment because it is responsible for conducting the mechanical aspects of the jobs, such as obtaining engravings, plates, printing, and photographs. Its staff salaries include those for the administrator, account executive, copywriters, artists, and production personnel. The account executive is the principal contact person between the agency and the client. Periodically, it must make outside purchases of mechanical and artwork items such as engravings and photographs for its clients.

Treadwell is now having problems with several clients who expect special artwork and research without an additional charge. Service charges are made based on the staff hours required to develop pamphlets, folders, or booklets. Treadwell adds to this hourly charge a flat 5 percent for an estimate of the cost of any supplies required. However, because one of its large clients complained so bitterly last month over its service charge, Treadwell dropped part of the fee. Treadwell management made the charge elimination because it recognizes that a large part of its costs are for creative skills. These skills are difficult to quantify, and all artists and writers have dry spells in which productivity is less than normal.

The company tries to accumulate the direct costs involved on jobs for which service charges are made. However, Treadwell readily admits that these records lack accuracy. Also, there has never been any continuous costing of its services. Treadwell only has a general idea of which client services are more profitable than others.

Required:

Describe the accounting information the company needs. How should top and middle managers each use this information?

C1–11 Relationship between Planning and Controlling Activities (L.O. 1)

Planning is the process of establishing a predetermined course of action. Plans provide the basis for control, becoming the yardstick by which actual performance is measured.

This necessarily requires establishing goals and the means to attain them. In doing this, an organization defines goals in terms of its task environment. This involves setting goals around the purpose for the existence of the organization. Yet, many organizations fail to distinguish between planning and controlling activities but also to fully understand the process.

Required:

a. To what extent can planning and controlling activities be considered the same function?
b. Some organizations only perform planning and controlling functions at the beginning or end of their accounting period. Do you think this is a wise approach?
c. Compare the planning functions in a newly formed organization versus the planning functions in an organization that has been in existence for some time.
d. From which ingredients are plans made?
e. Why are plans adjusted?

2

Production, Marketing, and Administrative Cost Flows

After studying this chapter, you should be able to:

1. Identify the components of production, marketing, and administration costs.

2. Demonstrate the flow of manufacturing costs through the inventory account as reflected on a cost of goods manufactured statement.

3. Understand the effect of automation on volume-based overhead application rates.

4. Cost material inventory using FIFO, LIFO, or average costing methods.

Introduction

A market-driven philosophy demands rapid cost information beginning from the product conception to its final distribution, service, and follow-up. Managers use product cost information for a variety of strategic decisions, including pricing, accepting or rejecting sales orders, and selecting which products to make. If accounting systems generate inaccurate cost data, companies may sell their products for less than cost. Without accurate costs, product designers may select designs that fail to add value. This chapter describes the procedure for tracking cost flows that lead to effective decisions. The cost of goods manufactured statement shows an overview of cost flows.

Manufacturing Inventory Accounts (L.O. 1)

Accurate cost information is important whether a company engages in retailing, manufacturing, or service operations. Each of these industries has the same basic financial statements; these normally consist of the statement of financial position (balance sheet) and related statements of income, retained earnings, and cash flow. However, a significant difference occurs in the inventory account titles each industry uses. Retailers and other merchandising companies sell goods in substantially the same physical form in which they purchased them. A retailer generally has only one inventory account, called *Merchandise Inventory,* which shows finished goods available for sale.

A manufacturing company converts materials into finished goods and generally has four inventory accounts: Direct Materials Inventory, Factory Supplies Inventory, Work in Process Inventory; and Finished Goods Inventory. Direct Materials shows the cost of materials available for processing; Work in Process, the cost of uncompleted goods; and Finished Goods, the cost of completed goods.

EXHIBIT 2–1

WALTHER RETAIL COMPANY
Statement of Financial Position
As of December 31, 19X1

Assets

Current assets:	
Cash	$ 20,000
Accounts receivable	75,000
Merchandise inventory . . .	183,000
Total current assets . . .	$278,000

EXHIBIT 2–2

WELLS MANUFACTURING COMPANY
Statement of Financial Position
As of December 31, 19X1

Assets

Current assets:		
Cash		$ 20,000
Accounts receivable		75,000
Direct materials inventory	$ 32,000	
Factory supplies inventory	6,000	
Work in process inventory	31,000	
Finished goods inventory	114,000	183,000
Total current assets		$278,000

A service organization furnishes intangible services rather than tangible goods and may have a Direct Materials Inventory.

Corresponding to a manufacturer's work in process, professional service organizations may have unbilled work consisting of costs incurred for clients. Service organizations do not have finished goods inventories. However, the flow of costs through inventory accounts until costs finally appear as expenses on the statement of income is important to all companies. Exhibit 2–1 illustrates the current asset section of a statement of financial position for a retailer. Exhibit 2–2 shows a manufacturer's typical current assets. The four manufacturing inventory accounts often are grouped into one inventory caption on a statement of financial position. However, Exhibit 2–2 details them for illustrative purposes.

A retail company buys a finished product, places a price tag on it, and displays it for sale. The retailer has an invoice from the supplier as evidence of what the product costs. In contrast, production accounting is more involved because the manufacturer accumulates the costs of materials, labor, and overhead to determine product costs. Through the application of labor, machinery, equipment, and other productive elements, manufacturers convert raw materials into finished products.

Direct Materials Inventory or Materials Inventory, an asset account shown in Exhibit 2–2, reports raw material on hand, which will become a part of the finished product. **Factory Supplies Inventory** represents supplies to be used in factory maintenance, repair, and cleaning.

A **Work in Process Inventory** account collects costs incurred in manufacturing a finished product. At any statement of financial position date, some units are usually only partially completed. At the end of a period, the Work in Process Inventory account shows the production costs of these semifinished units. Goods in Process Inventory is another name for this account. A **Finished Goods Inventory** account accumulates the cost of finished products until sold. At their sale, their cost is transferred to a Cost of Goods Sold account. A finished product is sold (1) to another manufacturer, who further refines it or uses it as a component of a product; (2) to a wholesaler or retailer for resale; or (3) directly to the final consumer.

Production, Marketing, and Administrative Costs (L.O. 1)

All costs fall into one of three general classifications: production, marketing, and administrative. **Production cost** includes the direct material, direct labor, and factory overhead incurred to produce a good or service. Product engineering and design costs occurring before manufacturing are also production costs. **Marketing costs** result from selling and delivering products and include the costs of promoting sales and retaining customers, as well as transportation, warehousing, and other distribution costs. **Administrative costs** result from directing and controlling the company and for general activities such as personnel and legal functions. They include management and financial accounting salaries, clerical costs, telephone and telex costs, and rental fees. Both production and marketing functions incur administrative costs.

Even though production costs are generally treated as **product costs** and included in either work in process or finished goods inventories, marketing and administrative costs are generally treated as **period costs.** Period costs are charged against revenue in each accounting period. Product costs do not become the *cost of sales* charged against revenue until the sales of the product on which costs were incurred.

Direct Material

Direct material is any raw material that becomes an identifiable part of the finished product. For example, in manufacturing men's shirts, the fabric is direct material. Accountants separately record and trace all direct material required in manufacturing to specific products. Companies buy direct materials in various forms. They buy some direct material in a finished state and assemble the component parts into their final product. In the manufacture of television sets, companies often purchase electronic components, cabinets, and TV tubes. Workers assemble these components into finished appliances. Other companies purchase direct material in a raw state and apply labor, machinery, and equipment to change it into another form. Sugar processors, for instance, cut and cook raw sugar cane before it becomes a finished product. In either case, receipt of direct material costing $55,000 requires the following entry:

Direct Materials Inventory	55,000	
Cash or a liability account		55,000

This entry records the actual use of direct material costing $39,000 in production:

Work in Process Inventory	39,000	
Direct Materials Inventory		39,000

Direct Labor

Direct labor costs are the wages earned by workers who transform the material from its raw state to a finished product. For example, the wages paid to shirt factory workers who cut fabric and sew the pieces are direct labor costs. Only the wages earned by those workers involved in the physical manufacture of the product are direct labor costs. This entry records direct labor wages of $10,000:

```
Work in Process Inventory  . . . . . . . . . . . . . . . . . . . . . . . . . . . . .   10,000
    Payroll Payable  . . . . . . . . . . . . . . . . . . . . . . . . . . . . . . . . . . .            10,000
```

Factory Overhead

Factory overhead is sometimes called *manufacturing overhead* or *factory burden*. Even though the term *indirect manufacturing overhead* better describes this cost element, this book uses the briefer term *factory overhead.* Factory overhead includes all production costs other than direct material and direct labor. The emphasis here is on the term *production costs;* factory overhead excludes marketing and administrative expenses. For example, a salesperson's salary is a marketing expense; salaries earned by top management, the controller, and the financial accountant are usually administrative expenses. However, an inventory control clerk or timekeeper's wage is factory overhead.

Examples of Factory Overhead. Factory overhead includes various production costs. For example, operating, repair, and janitorial supplies used in the factory are **indirect materials** and are a part of factory overhead costs. Production operations use indirect materials. Because indirect materials are not physically identified in the finished product, they are not direct material.

Indirect materials include small, insignificant items of material costs. Since it may be difficult to determine the amount of thread used in a shirt, it may be impractical to account for the cost of the thread as a direct material. Also, the cost of the thread is relatively small in relation to the cost of all other raw materials. One of the considerations in classifying direct material is the ease of associating the material cost with the finished product. The trade-off in accounting is between how much it costs to collect information and the cost of the item.

Plant superintendents do not actually work on the product, so their salaries are not charged as a direct labor cost. Instead, the plant superintendent's salary is usually a part of the **indirect labor** costs and charged to factory overhead. Other skilled and unskilled workers, such as janitors, repairers, and supervisors, are involved in production. The results of their efforts, however, are not as easily traceable to the finished product. Consequently, they are usually called indirect labor, and their earnings become a part of factory overhead.

In addition to indirect material and indirect labor, factory overhead includes such costs as rent, taxes, insurance, and depreciation on manufacturing facilities. Factory overhead also includes other occupancy costs such as light, heat, and power used in manufacturing facilities. In addition, the wage and salary payments called direct labor costs may not include employee benefits. Employers pay not only the gross wages an employee earns but also employee benefits, such as social security, unemployment compensation, vacation and holiday pay, sick pay, and life and hospitalization insurance. These expenditures for employee benefits have become an increasingly significant part of total payroll costs. Even though employee benefit costs that relate to direct labor workers are direct labor costs, many companies have found it easier to treat all employee benefit costs as indirect costs that are later costed to all products. Some companies expense retirement benefits, such as pension and profit-sharing costs, as period costs rather than apply their costs to products, even though conceptually they are part of labor cost.

Prime and Conversion Costs

Direct material and direct labor comprise the **prime cost** of a product. Usually accountants can measure these two cost elements easily and accurately. Managers maintain accurate records showing the cost of material used in manufacturing a specific product or service. Clock cards or other time records report the time that each worker spends on a job. Multiplying the worker's basic wage rate by the time indicated determines the direct labor cost. Direct labor and factory overhead costs are called **conversion costs** or *processing costs*. Operations converting raw material into a finished product incur both direct labor and factory overhead costs.

Application of Factory Overhead (L.O. 1)

On completion of a product, clerks transfer the accumulated costs in Work in Process to the Finished Goods Inventory account. The amount transferred is the sum of the three factory cost elements: direct material, direct labor, and factory overhead. They obtain actual direct material and direct labor costs by adding the direct material and the labor costs charged as shown earlier in the entries debiting Work in Process. Determination of factory overhead costs is more complicated because the cost accountant cannot calculate total actual factory overhead costs for an accounting period until it ends. For example, accountants cannot determine the total cost of a product finished on the fifth day of a month until after the monthly accounting period ends when cost is based on actual factory overhead. This delay can cause many problems.

In addition, actual factory overhead costs may vary considerably from month to month; so, the value assigned to inventory can fluctuate considerably when using actual costs. For example, suppose a New England company manufactures desks in January and June. This company incurs fuel expense in January to heat the factory, but not in June. However, it is unreasonable to sell a desk manufactured in June at a different price from a similar one made in January. The company assigns estimated overhead to units manufactured so desks produced in January bear the same dollar amount of overhead as those manufactured in June.

To provide timely product costing data and to decrease fluctuations in overhead costs assigned to inventory, a company estimates its overhead costs for an attainable volume to arrive at a factory overhead application rate. Then accountants use this rate to assign factory overhead to different departments and jobs. Much professional judgment and care enter in the calculation of the factory overhead application rate; it is not simply a guess. As illustrated in a later chapter, detailed budgets support each estimated factory overhead item. For example, if management budgets $75,000 in factory overhead costs for the year and estimates that total machine-hours will be 1,500, the factory overhead application rate is as follows:

$$\frac{\$75,000 \text{ estimated factory overhead}}{1,500 \text{ estimated machine-hours}} = \$50 \text{ per machine-hour}$$

For every machine-hour used to finish a product, the factory overhead cost is applied at $50 per machine-hour. Accountants do not enter the $75,000 budgeted factory overhead in the journal or ledger as it is used for determining the application rate. Note also that we are using very few digits in our illustrations to keep them simple. For instance, $75,000 is entirely too small to represent a realistic factory overhead for a manufacturing company.

In a highly automated factory, machine-hours may be the most accurate overhead application basis because many factory overhead costs, such as repairs and maintenance, depreciation, insurance, and property taxes, relate to machine utilization. Machine-hours is one basis for applying factory overhead; other commonly used bases include work cells, machine setups, direct labor-hours, and units of production. A **work cell** is a product-oriented work center that includes the machines and tools necessary to efficiently produce a family of parts. As you learn later, the appropriateness of the basis depends on whether the environment is labor-paced or machine-paced and whether it reflects the factor that causes the cost to occur. Each department may have its own specific factory overhead application rate, or accountants may use a plantwide rate.

Accountants must apply indirect costs included in factory overhead to the product at various stages of production to reflect the full cost of production. A journal entry can be made for each overhead application. For example, when finishing a product on the fifth day of the month, a journal entry applying $50 for every machine-hour charged to the product or job is appropriate. However, this practice involves much time and effort and is not practical. A simpler approach is to separately record the amount of **factory overhead applied** for each job on its cost sheet (as illustrated in Chapter 5). Then accountants prepare a summary entry at the end of the accounting period for the total factory overhead applied to each job finished during the period. At the end of each accounting period, factory overhead must also be applied to the partially finished units remaining in Work in Process Inventory. All production during the period, whether or not completed at the end of each accounting period, must receive an overhead application for the period.

Entry to Apply Overhead

The entry to record applied overhead in an actual cost system involves a debit to Work in Process Inventory and a credit to Factory Overhead Control. Assume that 1,440 machine-hours were incurred on all jobs and the factory overhead application rate is $50 per machine-hour. The following journal entry should be made:

Work in Process Inventory	72,000	
Factory Overhead Control (1,440 hours × $50		
factory overhead application rate = $72,000)		72,000

Control Account. The Factory Overhead Control account is the same as any control account, such as the Accounts Receivable Control account used in financial accounting. In addition, Factory Overhead Control is a suspense or clearing account designed to accumulate actual and applied overhead. Accountants charge actual factory overhead costs to Factory Overhead Control as costs accrue throughout the accounting period. Factory Overhead Control is a general ledger account supported by a subsidiary ledger that details various factory overhead costs. The subsidiary ledger listing the separate cost items is necessary for management planning and control purposes. Management would not be able to analyze the details of factory overhead cost without in-depth accounting for each cost.

Assume that annual actual manufacturing overhead is $72,500 consisting of such cost items as supplies, indirect labor, depreciation, and rent. In this example, the production accounts involved would appear as follows at the end of the accounting period after posting the entry to apply overhead:

Work in Process Inventory

Actual direct material	39,000
Actual direct labor	10,000
Applied manufacturing overhead	72,000

Factory Overhead Control

Actual—factory supplies	5,000	*Applied*	72,000
indirect labor	33,000	($50 × 1,440 actual machine hours)	
depreciation	28,000		
other factory overhead	6,500		
Total actual overhead	72,500		

Factory Overhead Applied Account. An acceptable practice some companies use is to accumulate applied overhead in a separate Factory Overhead Applied account. They debit Factory Overhead Control for actual costs and credit Factory Overhead Applied for the estimated applied overhead when debiting Work in Process Inventory. When using a separate Factory Overhead Applied account, the transaction flow would appear as follows (Work in Process Inventory is not affected):

Suspense **Factory Overhead Control**			*Suspense* **Factory Overhead Applied**	
Actual	72,500		*Applied*	72,000

Overhead was applied to job or work orders for a total of $72,000 using the applied overhead rate of $50 per machine hour. Even though the Factory Overhead Control account shows only one credit entry for $72,000, overhead is applied to each product and the $72,000 is a total for the year. Chapter 5 illustrates subsidiary records detailing the overhead application.

Disposition of Under- or Overapplied Overhead

The debit balance of $500 in the Factory Overhead Control account indicates that the actual overhead costs incurred exceeded the amount of overhead applied to production for the period. Overhead is underapplied or underabsorbed when this occurs. If the overhead applied to production is greater than total actual factory overhead costs incurred, the credit balance in a Factory Overhead Control account indicates that factory overhead has been overapplied or overabsorbed. Cost accountants periodically analyze actual factory overhead costs to determine the reasons for the over- or underabsorption.

Accountants close Factory Overhead Control accounts at year-end. If the amount necessary to close the Factory Overhead Control account is not significant, they close the over- or underapplied amount into the Cost of Goods Sold account. When the amount is significant, either in relation to the total cost of goods sold, total operating income, or some other test of materiality, accountants distribute the over- or underapplied overhead between inventory and cost of sales based on the relative proportion of units sold and units remaining in inventory. For practical reasons, accountants prorate the over- or underapplied balance only when the amount materially affects inventory valuations.

Manufacturing Inventory Flows (L.O. 2)

Exhibit 2–3 illustrates the flow of costs through the four inventory accounts, Factory Supplies, Direct Materials, Work in Process, and Finished Goods. Exhibits 2–4 and 2–7 illustrate the cost of goods manufactured statement using the dollar amounts assumed for these T accounts. Accountants charge Work in Process for direct materials issued from the storeroom to a production department.

Accountants charge Factory Overhead Control for supplies and insignificant materials as indirect material. The Factory Overhead Control account is a general ledger cost control account. Actual factory costs such as indirect material, indirect labor, insurance, and depreciation are charged as debits to this account. This account collects only factory-related costs. Depreciation, insurance, and rent on the office building and office equipment are not part of factory overhead. Instead, an Administrative Expense control account accumulates these costs.

Cost of Goods Manufactured Statement Using Applied Overhead

Cost accountants are primarily responsible for preparing the **cost of goods manufactured statement** illustrated in Exhibit 2–4. The *statement of manufacturing costs* or, more briefly, the *manufacturing statement* is another name for this statement. The purpose of the cost of goods manufactured statement is to support the statement of income by summarizing all production costs for an accounting period. These production costs consist primarily of the three elements discussed previously—direct material, direct labor, and factory overhead.

As shown in Exhibit 2–4, the beginning balance of direct materials inventory on January 1, 19X1, is $16,000. Adding net material purchases gives $71,000 direct material available for use in production. Not all of the direct material was used, since there is an ending inventory on December 31, 19X1, of $32,000. Direct material used was $39,000.

The cost of goods manufactured statement next lists direct labor of $10,000. As illustrated earlier, overhead was applied at the rate of $50 per machine-hour throughout the period, giving a total of $72,000 absorbed. Because Exhibit 2–4 shows applied factory overhead totaling $72,000, the statement does not also show actual overhead. When the cost of goods manufactured statement shows applied overhead, rather than actual overhead, it is usually advisable to verify and tie in actual costs as well. In Exhibit 2–5, cost of goods sold receives the $500 underapplied overhead reconciling amount. Accountants prorate significant over- or underapplied amounts between inventories and cost of sales.

Adding the beginning balance of Work in Process to the total manufacturing cost for the period gives the amount of costs put in production during the period. The resulting manufacturing costs to account for represent costs that are

EXHIBIT 2–3   Inventory Account Flow

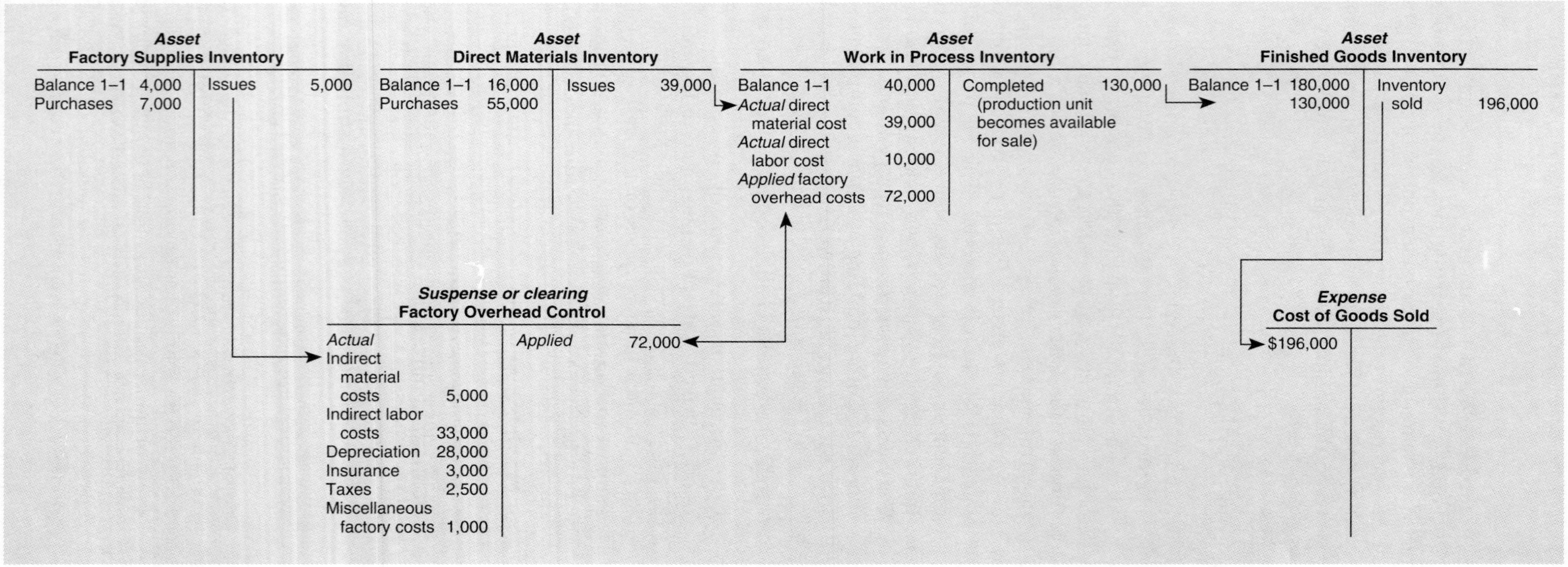

Asset
Factory Supplies Inventory

Balance 1–1	4,000	Issues	5,000
Purchases	7,000		

Asset
Direct Materials Inventory

Balance 1–1	16,000	Issues	39,000
Purchases	55,000		

Asset
Work in Process Inventory

Balance 1–1	40,000	Completed (production unit becomes available for sale)	130,000
Actual direct material cost	39,000		
Actual direct labor cost	10,000		
Applied factory overhead costs	72,000		

Asset
Finished Goods Inventory

Balance 1–1	180,000	Inventory sold	196,000
	130,000		

Expense
Cost of Goods Sold

$196,000	

Suspense or clearing
Factory Overhead Control

Actual		*Applied*	72,000
Indirect material costs	5,000		
Indirect labor costs	33,000		
Depreciation	28,000		
Insurance	3,000		
Taxes	2,500		
Miscellaneous factory costs	1,000		

EXHIBIT 2–4   Cost of Goods Manufactured Statement Using Applied Overhead

WELLS MANUFACTURING COMPANY
Cost of Goods Manufactured Statement
For the Year Ended December 31, 19X1

Direct materials inventory, January 1, 19X1	$16,000	
Add: Net material purchases	55,000	
Direct materials available for use	71,000	
Less: Direct materials inventory, December 31, 19X1	32,000	
Direct materials used		$39,000
Direct labor		10,000
Factory overhead costs applied:		72,000
Total manufacturing costs for the period		121,000
Add: Work in process inventory, January 1, 19X1		40,000
Manufacturing costs to account for		161,000
Less: Work in process inventory, December 31, 19X1		31,000
Cost of goods manufactured		$130,000

associated with either goods manufactured or goods remaining unfinished. Accountants then subtract the ending balance in Work in Process Inventory, which represents the cost of incomplete units at the end of the accounting period, to arrive at the cost of finished goods manufactured and completed during the period.

Manufacturer's Statement of Income

Exhibit 2–5 illustrates a statement of income for a manufacturer. The income statement picks up the cost of goods manufactured shown in Exhibit 2–4 and adds the cost to the beginning balance in finished goods inventory to arrive at the cost of goods available for sale. Some units remain unsold, since there is an ending balance in the finished goods inventory. The Finished Goods Inventory ending balance on December 31, 19X1, is deducted from the cost of goods available for sale to determine the Cost of Goods Sold. Underapplied overhead is added and overapplied overhead is deducted from Cost of Goods Sold as illustrated for the $500 underapplied factory overhead in Exhibit 2–5. Subtracting Cost of Goods Sold from Sales yields gross margin. Accountants deduct marketing and administrative expenses from gross margin to arrive at income before taxes. Net income results from then deducting income taxes. The manufacturer's statement of income and cost of goods manufactured can be combined into one statement, but such a statement may be long and somewhat difficult to read. In practice, accountants often report only the cost of goods sold and not the cost of goods manufactured on the statement of income.

Retailer's Statement of Income

The statement of income for a retailer appears in Exhibit 2–6. One difference between a manufacturer's income statement and a retailer's income statement lies in the terminology used. Because retailers buy only finished goods, *Merchandise Inventory* is their inventory account. *Purchases* are the goods retailers buy. Regardless of the number of inventory accounts used or their titles, the essential factor is understanding that costs flow through inventory accounts until their final disposition as income statement expenses.

EXHIBIT 2–5

WELLS MANUFACTURING COMPANY
Statement of Income
For the Year Ended December 31, 19X1

Net sales		$299,500
Less: Cost of goods sold:		
Finished goods inventory, January 1	$180,000	
Add: Cost of goods manufactured	130,000	
Cost of goods available for sale	310,000	
Less: Finished goods inventory, December 31	114,000	
Cost of goods sold	196,000	
Add: Underapplied factory overhead	500	196,500
Gross margin		103,000
Marketing and administrative expense:		
Less: Marketing expense		38,000
Administrative expense		35,000
Total		73,000
Income before taxes		30,000
Income taxes		10,000
Net income		$ 20,000

EXHIBIT 2–6

WALTHER RETAIL COMPANY
Statement of Income
For the Year Ended December 31, 19X1

Net sales	$299,500
Less: Cost of goods sold:	
Merchandise inventory, January 1	240,000
Add: Net purchases	139,500
Cost of goods available for sale	379,500
Less: Merchandise inventory, December 31	183,000
Cost of goods sold	196,500
Gross margin	103,000
Marketing and administrative expenses:	
Less: Marketing expense	38,000
Administrative expense	35,000
Total	73,000
Income before taxes	30,000
Income taxes	10,000
Net income	$ 20,000

Cost of Goods Manufactured Statement Using Actual Overhead

Alternatively, Exhibit 2–7 illustrates using actual overhead instead of applied overhead on the cost of goods manufactured statement. For illustrative purposes, Exhibit 2–7 lists only a few items of actual factory overhead. Analysis of

EXHIBIT 2–7   Cost of Goods Manufactured Statement Using Actual Overhead

WELLS MANUFACTURING COMPANY
Cost of Goods Manufactured Statement
For the Year Ended December 31, 19X1

Direct materials inventory, January 1, 19X1		$16,000	
Add: Net material purchases		55,000	
Direct materials available for use		71,000	
Less: Direct materials inventory, December 31, 19X1		32,000	
Direct materials used			$39,000
Direct labor			10,000
Factory overhead costs:			
Factory supplies, January 1, 19X1		$ 4,000	
Add: Purchases		7,000	
Supplies available for use		11,000	
Less: Factory supplies, December 31, 19X1		6,000	
Indirect materials used		5,000	
Indirect labor		33,000	
Depreciation		28,000	
Insurance		3,000	
Taxes		2,500	
Miscellaneous		1,000	
Total factory overhead costs			72,500
Total manufacturing costs for the period			121,500
Add: Work in process inventory, January 1, 19X1			40,000
Manufacturing costs to account for			161,500
Less: Work in process inventory, December 31, 19X1			31,000
Cost of goods manufactured			$130,500

inventory flow for factory supplies reveals that $5,000 of indirect materials (factory supplies) were actually used and charged to overhead. Actual factory overhead costs total $72,500. There is no adjustment to cost of goods sold for over- or underapplied overhead on the income statement when using actual factory overhead only.

Statement Equations. The following equations will help you understand the cost flow on the cost of goods manufactured statement and the statement of income. (Note these equations correspond to lines on the cost of goods manufactured statement and statement of income.)

On Cost of Goods Manufactured Statement.

$$\text{Direct materials inventory, beginning balance} + \text{Net material purchases} = \text{Direct materials available for use}$$

$$\text{Direct materials available for use} - \text{Direct materials inventory, ending balance} = \text{Direct materials used}$$

$$\text{Direct materials used} + \text{Direct labor} + \text{Factory overhead} = \text{Total manufacturing costs for the period}$$

$$\text{Total manufacturing costs for the period} + \text{Work in process inventory, beginning balance} = \text{Manufacturing costs to account for}$$

$$\text{Manufacturing costs to account for} - \text{Work in process inventory, ending balance} = \text{Cost of goods manufactured}$$

E X H I B I T   2–8

Retail Accounting		**Manufacturing Accounting**	
Merchandise inventory:		Raw material inventory:	
	Beginning inventory		Beginning inventory
Plus:	Net purchases	Plus:	Net material purchases
Equals:	Available for sale	Equals:	Available for use
Minus:	Ending inventory	Minus:	Ending inventory
Equals:	Cost of goods sold	Equals:	Raw material used

Manufacturing Accounting		**Manufacturing Accounting**	
Work in process inventory:		Finished goods inventory:	
	Beginning inventory		Beginning inventory
Plus:	Cost of direct material, direct labor, and overhead	Plus:	Cost of goods manufactured
Equals:	Manufacturing costs to account for	Equals:	Available for sale
Minus:	Ending inventory	Minus:	Ending inventory
Equals:	Cost of goods manufactured	Equals:	Cost of goods sold

On Statement of Income.

$$\text{Beginning finished goods inventory} + \text{Cost of goods manufactured} = \text{Cost of goods available for sale}$$

Cost of goods available for sale − Ending finished goods inventory = Cost of goods sold

Net sales − Cost of goods sold = Gross Margin

Gross margin − Operating expenses = Net income

Inventory Physical Flow

Note the similarity between the flow of costs through a retailer's merchandise inventory and a manufacturer's inventory accounts. Exhibit 2–8 illustrates the similarity in all inventory accounts. A retailer buys finished goods and makes them available for sale. A manufacturer buys direct materials and adds labor and overhead to produce finished goods for sale. In summary, net purchases, as presented in the cost of goods sold section of a retailer's income statement, is equivalent to the cost of goods manufactured as presented on a manufacturer's income statement. As a reminder, finished goods is usually the only inventory sold. Because the raw material (including direct materials and factory supplies) in a manufacturing company is not generally ready for sale, the total of beginning materials inventory and net purchases represents the materials available for use. Manufacturers do not usually buy partially completed products from the work in process inventory or items from the finished goods inventory from an outside supplier. Instead, they produce this inventory using direct material, direct labor, and overhead.

Volume-Related Cost Drivers (L.O. 3)

Although in estimating the $50 factory overhead application rate, we expressed activity volume in machine-hours, this may not be the **cost driver** or factor that causes the activity to occur. For example, if many factory overhead costs relate to labor, the most accurate application basis is either direct labor-hours or direct

EXHIBIT 2–9   Determination of Factory Overhead Rates

Estimated total factory overhead	$75,000
Estimated machine-hours for period	1,500 hours
Estimated material costs for period	$60,000
Estimated units to be produced in the period	500
Estimated direct labor costs for period @ $15 per hour . . .	$18,750
Estimated direct labor-hours for period	1,250 hours

labor-dollars. Accountants ensure they properly apply costs by analyzing the components of factory overhead. It is helpful for managers to visualize the route of a product as it travels through different factory processes. Then they can consider the causes or cost of the benefits received in each process the product goes through.

The overriding principle is to apply overhead costs to products and other objects based on the causes of costs or the benefits received rather than some arbitrary basis. Increasingly, accountants expect **nonvolume-related** (also known as **nonunit-related**) activities such as numbers of inspections, setups, or scheduling transactions to be the factors that drive overhead cost. However, in introducing overhead application methods, it is easier to use **volume-related (unit-related) application bases** for illustration. Thus, we express activity in these five terms based on the data in Exhibit 2–9 and compare the different rates: (1) machine-hours, (2) direct materials cost, (3) units of production, (4) direct labor costs or dollars, (5) direct labor-hours. (Chapter 4 illustrates activity-based management using both volume-related and nonvolume-related application bases.)

Machine-Hours

As illustrated earlier, the calculation using machine-hours as a base for applying factory overhead is as follows, given the data from Exhibit 2–9.

$$\frac{\$75,000 \text{ estimated factory overhead}}{1,500 \text{ estimated machine-hours}} = \$50 \text{ per machine-hour}$$

Some companies have a fixed relationship between direct labor and machine-hours; for instance, one direct labor worker is stationed at each machine. If this is true, the company can use either direct labor-hours or direct labor costs (if all workers in the department receive approximately the same wage per hour) rather than machine-hours as the application base. This may be easier because wage and labor-hour data are already computed.

Direct Materials Cost

Direct materials cost is an appropriate base if there is a logical relationship between direct materials usage and overhead costs. This occurs if each product involves about the same material costs or if the same amount of material is applied per hour. Also, if many of the overhead costs result from material handling, direct materials is a valid basis. The formula for computing the overhead application rate with direct materials cost as the base, using the data from Exhibit 2–9, is as follows:

$$\frac{\$75,000 \text{ estimated factory overhead}}{\$60,000 \text{ estimated material costs}} = 125 \text{ percent of material cost}$$

Units of Production

Companies that manufacture only one product or have a simple production process use the unit of production base. Firms manufacturing more than one product, however, find another base is more appropriate because units produced rarely receive equal manufacturing effort. Rather than relying strictly on the unit of production basis, a company may assign points to the units produced to obtain a better apportionment of overhead. Also, nonmanufacturing organizations use variations; for example, a healthcare institution uses the number of beds. A marketing company may use the number of sales calls or miles traveled by salespersons, and colleges and universities may use the number of students enrolled in different programs.

The formula for determining the factory overhead rate using the units of production data in Exhibit 2–9 is as follows:

$$\frac{\$75,000 \text{ estimated factory overhead}}{500 \text{ estimated units}} = \$150 \text{ per unit}$$

Direct Labor Cost

When using direct labor cost as a base for applying factory overhead, we assume that higher-paid workers are incurring a larger share of factory overhead than are lower-paid workers. Such a condition exists if the more highly paid, better-trained workers operate the more expensive and more sophisticated machinery and plant facilities. Direct labor cost is appropriate if overhead costs include many employee benefits based on a percentage of employees' base pay. The rate using direct labor costs as the application base is as follows:

$$\frac{\$75,000 \text{ estimated factory overhead}}{\$18,750 \text{ estimated direct labor costs}} = 400 \text{ percent of direct labor costs}$$

Weaknesses of Labor Cost Base. Some factory overhead costs such as heat, light, power, insurance, rent, and taxes represent amounts of resources consumed over time. For instance, assume the relationship of overhead to labor costs is 400 percent as just illustrated; this is typical in an automated factory. Under these circumstances, labor-based application rates give the false impression that a causal relationship exists between the incurrence of direct labor and overhead costs. Another basis, such as machine-hours or work cells, would be more appropriate in this situation.

The use of direct labor costs as an application base when factory overhead is time-related has additional weaknesses. Because most companies do not pay the same rate per hour to all direct labor workers, cost centers using higher-paid workers receive more applied factory overhead. However, much of their factory overhead may result merely from the use of the facilities. For example, assume that actual wages paid amounted to $15.30 per hour and that actual hours were 1,250 as budgeted. Total factory overhead applied would be $15.30 × 1,250 hours = \$19,125 × 400 percent = \$76,500 factory overhead applied. If, instead, actual wages paid equaled the \$15 budgeted, factory overhead applied is \$15 × 1,250 hours = \$18,750 × 400 percent = \$75,000. Thus, the cost center applies more dollars of overhead by paying a higher labor rate than planned. In turn, a comparison of this larger amount of \$76,500 applied factory overhead to \$75,000 actual factory overhead results in overapplied factory overhead if actual factory overhead followed the expected behavior pattern.

Departmental rates based on direct labor dollars do overcome part of this weakness as long as workers within each department receive an hourly rate that is in the same range. Also, rather than use actual direct labor dollars, Chapter 12 introduces the use of standard or budgeted direct labor rates. Another weakness in applying factory overhead on the basis of actual direct labor dollars is that an inefficient use of direct labor causes an excessive amount of applied factory overhead.

Direct Labor-Hours

If many factory overhead costs relate to the use of labor-hours, as in labor-paced manufacturing settings, direct labor-hours is an appropriate base. However, the use of direct labor-hours may require additional computations, because someone must compute these hours for each job using information on labor time tickets. Using the data from Exhibit 2–9, we compute the application rate using direct labor-hours as the base as follows:

$$\frac{\$75,000 \text{ estimated factory overhead}}{1,250 \text{ estimated direct labor-hours}} = \$60 \text{ per direct labor-hour}$$

The following example illustrates an inherent weakness in using actual direct labor-hours as an application base: Assume workers took three hours to produce each unit when two and one-half hours of direct labor were budgeted to finish each product unit. The standard of two and one-half direct labor-hours would be a better basis for applying factory overhead than would applying overhead on the additional inefficient one-half hour of labor per unit.

Impact of Computer-Integrated Manufacturing (L.O. 3)

In the past, the focus of cost control has been on labor in most industries. However, computer-integrated manufacturing (CIM) has reduced the direct-labor component. CIM promotes cross-training in which employees set up production runs, inspect production, operate, repair and maintain machinery, and enter accounting data.

Cost Mix

Traditionally, overhead averaged only 50 to 60 percent of direct labor cost. However, this traditional cost mix is changing along with an emphasis on controlling overhead. Overhead is usually 400 to 500 percent of direct labor costs in CIM. In today's automated factories, direct labor costs are usually less than 10 percent of the total production cost, while overhead is more than 30 percent of total cost. Although the proportion of these elements can vary significantly from industry to industry, typically material is 40 to 50 percent of cost, labor 10 to 30 percent, and overhead 30 to 40 percent.

The composition of overhead is also changing as factories automate. New overhead cost categories are emerging. For example, indirect labor includes manufacturing technicians, equipment maintenance labor, and machine operators who were all formerly direct laborers. Existing overhead categories, such as equipment maintenance, utilities, and manufacturing supplies, are becoming increasingly significant. The extensive use of capital equipment in automated factories causes depreciation to increase regardless of production volumes.

Eliminate Direct Labor Category. Many highly automated work cells are likely to eliminate their direct labor cost category entirely if robots replace direct labor. Organizations in which labor is a very low percentage of product cost may give labor low visibility as a separate cost element by combining it with overhead. Such systems record labor costs in overhead accounts, and apply overhead costs on a new base, such as machine-time or process-time.

Labor-Based Application Rate

Direct labor has been an acceptable basis for overhead application in the past because manufacturing processes were highly labor intensive. Some managers continue to support direct labor as an application basis because they believe that reducing direct labor is essential for ongoing cost improvements. Applying overhead on direct labor creates strong proautomation incentives. However, more managers believe direct labor-hours and direct labor costs are not good predictors of the value added to a product because of changes in cost mix. A basic flaw is that a direct labor application base does not correctly represent the amount of resources consumed by the product during the routing process in many computer-aided manufacturing systems. Thus, in today's automated environment, applying overhead on direct labor often distorts true manufacturing cost performance and distracts management attention from ballooning overhead, staff, and other indirect costs. The accounting system may encourage managers to monitor the absorption of overhead, rather than to eliminate waste. For example, if the overhead rate is 600 percent of direct labor, the costing system implies to product designers that direct labor is very expensive. Thus, a design change reducing direct labor cost by $1 for a product results in an apparent savings of $6 in overhead. However, in reality, a design change reducing labor usually results in increased overhead because of engineering change activities.

Quality Control

More companies are realizing that to be competitive they must change from the conventional produce-and-rework-if-defective routine to a zero defects concept. Material costs also change dramatically as a result of the new emphasis on quality throughout the manufacturing process. With emphasis on reducing scrap and rework costs, material utilization increases, with yields approaching 100 percent. However, the implementation of total quality control involves a companywide commitment from top management down to factory employees. Elimination of defects involves coordinated group efforts.

Summary

Direct material, direct labor, and factory overhead are the three factory cost elements incurred. Many different costs make up factory overhead because this category includes all manufacturing costs other than direct material and direct labor. Production cost components are changing in today's automated factory because overhead is a large portion of the product costs. The composition of manufacturing costs has changed because much of the overhead in a machine-paced environment relates to machine operations. New labor categories are evolving: Personnel once engaged in machine fabrication and assembly work are now categorized as manufacturing and engineering technicians, process control specialists, and equipment maintenance technicians.

Direct labor has been an acceptable basis for overhead application in the past because manufacturing processes were highly labor intensive. However, many of today's highly automated companies report labor costs as low as 3 percent, compared with the traditional labor cost of 10 to 30 percent. Factories of the future expect labor cost ratios to be as low as 1 percent of the cost of sales. Yet, if product costing systems fail to reflect this shift in cost structure, managers will make decisions based on misleading product cost data. The greater the competition in a company's market, the higher is the cost of making incorrect decisions. Thus, alert cost accountants monitor the accumulation of product cost data to ensure they accurately reflect resources used.

Important Terms and Concepts

direct materials inventory, 21
factory supplies inventory, 21
work in process inventory, 22
finished goods inventory, 22
production costs, 22
marketing costs, 22
administrative costs, 22
product costs, 22
period costs, 22
direct materials, 22
direct labor, 23
factory overhead, 23
indirect materials, 23

indirect labor, 23
prime cost, 24
conversion costs, 24
work cell, 25
factory overhead applied, 25
cost of goods manufactured
    statement, 27
cost driver, 32
nonvolume-related (nonunit-related)
    activities, 33
volume-related (unit-related)
    application bases, 33

Appendix 2A Inventory Costing Methods (L.O. 4)

Costing material differs somewhat from costing labor and overhead because the accountant must choose an inventory costing method. The primary goal is to achieve a proper matching of costs and revenues. The residual inventory values on the statement of financial position also receive some consideration. The following briefly describes several actual inventory costing methods.

FIFO Inventory Method

The first-in, first-out (FIFO) method assumes that the first costs incurred are the first costs issued, regardless of the physical flow. Accountants cost material issues at the unit cost of the oldest supply on hand. The ending inventory

EXHIBIT 2A–I

MATERIAL LEDGER CARD—FIFO—PERPETUAL INVENTORY											

Item: Material A

Item description

Reorder point 40   Reorder quantity 60

Receipts				Issued					Balance		
Date	Quantity	Amount	Unit Cost	Date	Req. No.	Job No.	Quantity	Amount	Quantity	Amount	Unit Cost
Jan. 1	Balance								40	$ 88.00	$2.20
Jan. 7	60	$150.00	$2.50						60	150.00	2.50
				Jan. 9	112	84	64	$148.00	36	90.00	2.50
Jan. 18	60	152.40	2.54						60	152.40	2.54
				Jan. 22	113	86	75	189.06	21	53.34	2.54
Jan. 24	60	156.00	2.60						60	156.00	2.60

EXHIBIT 2A–2

MATERIAL LEDGER CARD—LIFO—PERPETUAL INVENTORY											

Item: Material A

Item description

Reorder point 40   Reorder quantity 60

Receipts				Issued					Balance		
Date	Quantity	Amount	Unit Cost	Date	Req. No.	Job No.	Quantity	Amount	Quantity	Amount	Unit Cost
Jan. 1	Balance								40	$ 88.00	$2.20
Jan. 7	60	$150.00	$2.50						60	150.00	2.50
				Jan. 9	112	84	64	$158.80	36	79.20	2.20
Jan. 18	60	152.40	2.54						60	152.40	2.54
				Jan. 22	113	86	75	185.40	21	46.20	2.20
Jan. 24	60	156.00	2.60						60	156.00	2.60

January 9 issues:
60 units @ $2.50 = $150.00
4 units @ 2.20 =   8.80
$158.80

January 22 issues:
60 units @ $2.54 = $152.40
15 units @ 2.20 =   33.00
$185.40

comprises the most recent costs of material or production of goods. Exhibit 2A–1 illustrates a material ledger card using FIFO under a **perpetual inventory system.** A perpetual system records each transaction to make available a book balance of the quantity of material on hand.

A disadvantage of using the FIFO inventory costing method is that a rise in material price matched by a corresponding increase in sales price tends to inflate income. Conversely, a decline in material price and sale price deflates income. This occurs because in periods of increasing costs and sales prices, the costs

EXHIBIT 2A–3

MATERIAL LEDGER CARD—MOVING AVERAGE											
Item: **Material A**									Reorder point 40	Reorder quantity 60	
			Item description								
Receipts				**Issued**					**Balance**		
Date	Quantity	Amount	Unit Cost	Date	Req. No.	Job No.	Quantity	Amount	Quantity	Amount	Unit Cost
Jan. 1	Balance								40	$ 88.00	$2.200
Jan. 7	60	$150.00	$2.50						100	238.00	2.380
				Jan. 9	112	84	64	$152.32	36	85.68	2.380
Jan. 18	60	152.40	2.54						96	238.08	2.480
				Jan. 22	113	86	75	186.00	21	52.08	2.480
Jan. 24	60	156.00	2.60						81	208.08	2.569

charged against revenue come from the older, lower-priced inventory on hand, while the newer, higher-priced stock make up ending inventory. Cost of sales receives the lower cost and the new higher cost remains in inventory. Companies pay income taxes on the artificially inflated profits that result. The advantage of FIFO is that it produces an ending inventory valuation which approximates current replacement costs. However, most companies currently rely on the income statement rather than the statement of financial position for performance evaluation.

LIFO Inventory Method

Using the last-in, first-out (LIFO) method of inventory valuation, the price of the latest items purchased or produced is the first cost assigned to units issued or sold. The materials in ending inventory are costed at prices in existence at a much earlier date since they represent the cost of the oldest stock on hand. Exhibit 2A–2 illustrates the use of LIFO with a perpetual inventory method.

The LIFO inventory method has the advantage of matching current inventory costs with current revenues; this provides a more proper matching on the income statement. In a period of increasing prices, a tax savings results because the cost of goods used or sold is priced at the higher material costs of the latest inventory on hand. When prices are rising, the lower-priced, oldest inventory on hand comprises the ending inventory valuation, which does not reflect a current valuation. If a company experiences a decline in material prices, the reverse is true because accountants cost material used at the latest, lower-priced inventory. Ending inventory, on the other hand, is valued at the older, higher-priced inventory in a deflationary period.

Average Costing Methods

Instead of using FIFO or LIFO costing, variations of the average costing inventory method are available. Some of these are most appropriate for perpetual inventory systems, while others are used with a **periodic inventory system.** A periodic system updates the quantity of each material item only when a physical inventory occurs.

These methods assume that the cost of materials on hand at the end of an accounting period is the weighted-average of the cost of the inventory on hand at the beginning of the period and the cost of the materials purchased during the period. Companies holding goods for a long period of time often use average methods that tend to even out the effects of net increases and decreases in costs. Average cost methods balance abnormally low and abnormally high material prices, giving stable cost figures. Although several methods are available, we only discuss the moving-average cost method with a perpetual inventory procedure.

Moving-Average Method. The moving-average method allows the issues to be costed out currently at the average unit cost of the goods on hand as of the withdrawal date. A new unit cost is calculated after each purchase. However, some companies follow the practice of making moving-average computations monthly. The established unit costs move upward or downward as new material purchases are made at higher or lower prices. Exhibit 2A–3 illustrates a material ledger card for Material A using the moving-average method. For example, adding the $152.40 cost of the January 18 purchase to the $85.68 balance on hand gives the following $2.480 unit cost:

$$\frac{\$152.40 + \$85.68}{96} = \frac{\$238.08}{96} = \$2.480$$

Problem for Self-Study

Using Manufacturing Statement Format to Find Unknown Balances

Leeks Manufacturing Company's net sales for the year ended October 31, 19X2, was $345,000 with a gross margin of $19,000. Ending inventory for work in process was 60 percent of beginning work in process inventory. Factory overhead applied was 25 percent of direct labor cost. Total current manufacturing cost was $300,000.

A count at year-end showed the following balances in ending inventory on October 31, 19X2:

Direct materials	$18,000
Work in process	?
Finished goods	70,000

An analysis of the records showed the following data:

Net direct material purchases	50,000

Beginning inventories on November 1, 19X1:

Direct materials	15,000
Work in process	?
Finished goods	90,000

Required:

Prepare a combined statement of cost of goods manufactured and partial income statement for the year ended October 31, 19X2.

Solution to Problem for Self-Study

Leeks Manufacturing Company

Note:

You may find it helpful to first insert the figures supplied by the problem data in a manufacturing statement format before computing any balances.

LEEKS MANUFACTURING COMPANY
Statement of Cost of Goods Manufactured
and Partial Income Statement
For the Year Ended October 31, 19X2

Net sales			$345,000
Cost of goods sold:			
Direct materials inventory, November 1, 19X1	$15,000		
Purchases of direct material	50,000		
Direct materials available for use	$65,000		
Less: Direct materials inventory, October 31, 19X2	18,000		
Direct materials used		$ 47,000	
Direct labor		202,400	
Applied factory overhead		50,600	
Total current manufacturing costs		$300,000	
Add: Work in process inventory, November 1, 19X1		15,000	
Manufacturing costs to account for		$315,000	
Less: Work in process inventory, October 31, 19X2		9,000	
Cost of goods manufactured		$306,000	
Add: Finished goods inventory, November 1, 19X1		90,000	
Cost of goods available for sale		$396,000	
Less: Finished goods inventory, October 31, 19X2		70,000	
Cost of goods sold			326,000
Gross margin			$ 19,000

Supporting computations

Let X = beginning work in process inventory . . . $300,000 + X - .6X = \$306,000$
$$+ .40X = 6,000$$
$$X = \$ 15,000$$
Beginning work in process inventory

$$60\% \times \$15,000 = \$ 9,000$$
Ending work in process inventory

1:4 relationship for factory overhead and direct labor
$253,000 ÷ 5 parts = $50,600 × 4 = $202,400 direct labor

Review Questions

1. Discuss the production inventory accounts. How do these accounts differ from merchandiser's inventory accounts?

2. Why do many companies use applied rates for factory overhead as opposed to actual factory overhead rates?

3. Are wages paid to a timekeeper in a factory a prime cost or a conversion cost?

4. Discuss the basic component parts of inventory flow. (*Hint:* A model may be helpful.)

5. Define the primary production cost elements.

6. Classify the following costs as either production, marketing, or administrative costs:

   a. Materials used to make finished units.
   b. Wages of production workers.
   c. Property taxes on factory building.
   d. Financial accounting salaries.
   e. Warehousing and handling costs.
   f. Factory rent.
   g. Depreciation on the sales executive's office.
   h. Insurance on factory machinery.
   i. Advertising.
   j. Production superintendent's wages.

7. Contrast direct and indirect material; direct and indirect labor.

8. Which common element of total cost do prime costs and conversion costs share?

9. When would it be most appropriate to use the direct labor cost basis as the means of applying factory overhead?

10. Under which conditions would it be appropriate to use direct material costs as an application base?

11. Which of the following are examples of period rather than product costs for a manufacturing company?

    a. Advertising campaign.
    b. Insurance on factory machines.
    c. Depreciation of factory building.
    d. Wages of salespersons.
    e. Factory machinery repairs.
    f. Wages of machine operators.

CPA/CMA/CIA Multiple-Choice Questions

1. (AICPA) The following information was taken from Kay Company's accounting records for the year ended December 1, 19X1:

Increase in raw materials inventory	$ 15,000
Decrease in finished goods inventory	35,000
Raw materials purchased	430,000
Direct labor payroll	200,000
Factory overhead	300,000
Freight cut	45,000

   There was no work in process inventory at the beginning or end of the year. Kay's 19X1 cost of goods sold is

   a. $950,000.
   b. $965,000.
   c. $975,000.
   d. $995,000.

2–4. (AICPA) Items 2 through 4 are based on the following information pertaining to Arp Company's manufacturing operations:

Inventories	3/1/X9	3/31/X9
Direct materials	$36,000	$30,000
Work in process	18,000	12,000
Finished goods	54,000	72,000

Additional information for the month of March 19X9:

Direct materials purchased	$84,000
Direct labor payroll	60,000
Direct labor rate per hour	7.50
Factory overhead rate per direct labor-hour . . .	10.00

2. For the month of March 19X9, prime cost was

 a. $ 90,000.
 b. $120,000.
 c. $144,000.
 d. $150,000.

3. For the month of March 19X9, conversion cost was

 a. $ 90,000.
 b. $140,000.
 c. $144,000.
 d. $170,000.

4. For the month of March 19X9, cost of goods manufactured was

 a. $218,000.
 b. $224,000.
 c. $230,000.
 d. $236,000.

5. (AICPA) The cost of rent for a manufacturing plant is a

	Prime Cost	Product Cost
a.	No	Yes
b.	No	No
c.	Yes	No
d.	Yes	Yes

6. (CIA) The following cost data were taken from the records of a manufacturing company:

Depreciation on factory equipment	$ 1,000
Depreciation on sales office	500
Advertising	7,000
Freight out (shipping)	3,000
Wages of production workers	28,000
Raw materials used	47,000
Sales salaries and commissions	10,000
Factory rent	2,000
Factory insurance	500
Material handling	1,500
Administrative salaries	2,000

Based upon the above information, the manufacturing cost incurred during the year was

 a. $78,500.
 b. $80,000.
 c. $80,500.
 d. $83,000.

7. (CIA) Certain workers are assigned the task of unpacking production materials received from suppliers. These workers place the material in a storage area pending subsequent use in the production process. The labor cost of such workers is normally classified as:

 a. Direct labor.
 b. Direct materials.
 c. Indirect labor.
 d. Indirect materials.

8. (AICPA) Property taxes on a manufacturing plant are an element of

	Conversion Cost	Period Cost
a.	Yes	No
b.	Yes	Yes
c.	No	Yes
d.	No	No

9. (AICPA) The fixed portion of the semivariable cost of electricity for a manufacturing plant is a

	Period Cost	Product Cost
a.	Yes	No
b.	Yes	Yes
c.	No	Yes
d.	No	No

10. (CIA) The following information is available from the records of a manufacturing company that applies factory overhead based on direct labor hours:

Estimated overhead cost	$500,000
Estimated labor hours	200,000 hours
Actual overhead cost	$515,000
Actual labor hours	210,000 hours

Based on this information, overhead would be:

a. Underapplied by $9,524.
b. Overapplied by $10,000.
c. Overapplied by $15,000.
d. Overapplied by $40,750.

Exercises

E2–1 Significant Underapplied OH (L.O. 1)

Assume that a company has a large underapplied factory overhead balance and top management encourages the accountant to treat the balance as a period cost. If this policy is followed, what is the effect on the financial statements?

E2–2 Cost of Goods Manufactured Statement and Income Statement (L.O. 2)

The following data are extracted from the records of the Paula Company:

Direct material used	$400,000
Gross margin	51,000
Factory overhead	180,000
Sales	660,000
Work in process, January 1, 19X1	16,000
Work in process, December 31, 19X1	15,800
Administrative expenses	24,000
Marketing expenses	15,100
Finished goods inventory, January 1, 19X1	8,000
Finished goods inventory, December 31, 19X1	20,000

Required:

a. Prepare a cost of goods manufactured statement and an income statement for Paula Company.
b. Explain whether this is a capital- or labor-intensive industry.

E2–3 Cost of Goods Manufactured Statement (L.O. 2)

Bank Machine Company applies factory overhead on the basis of a rate per machine-hour. They provide the following data for May 19X1:

Selected inventories have the following balances:

	May 1	May 31
Work in process	$81,000	$ 60,000
Finished goods	90,000	105,000

Prime costs for the month were as follows:

Direct material used	$ 80,000
Direct labor	192,000

Sales have increased 20 percent over April's net sales of $500,000; as a result, gross margin for May is $280,000. Actual machine-hours were 12,000 hours.

Required:

a. Prepare a cost of goods manufactured statement; only show applied factory overhead.

b. Determine the factory overhead application rate.

E2–4 Cost of Goods Manufactured and Partial Income Statement (L.O. 2)

Sweeney, Inc., records reveal the following balances which are arranged in alphabetical order:

	(000)
Direct materials used	$ 100
Finished goods inventory, beginning balance	400
Finished goods inventory, ending balance	100
Gross margin	200
Net sales	1,000
Work in process, beginning balance	300
Work in process, ending balance	800

Factory overhead is applied at one third of direct labor.

Required:

Prepare a cost of goods manufacturing statement and income statement complete through gross margin.

E2–5 Computing Factory Overhead Rate and Cost of Inventories (L.O. 1)

The following information is available for the Ristie Manufacturing Company at December 31, 19X1, for its first year of operation.

Direct materials used (150,000 pounds)	$900,000
Direct labor (39,000 hours)	$390,000
Factory overhead	$292,500
Ending inventories (determined by physical count):	
Work in process	6,000 units
Finished goods	1,000 units
Number of units sold	8,000 units

In processing the company's single product, all direct materials are issued at the start of the production process. Each unit of product contains 10 pounds of direct material. Each completed product contains three hours of labor while the semifinished units contain two hours of labor and all their material. Factory overhead is applied on the basis of direct labor.

Required:

a. Give the cost per finished unit for
    (1) Direct material.
    (2) Direct labor.
    (3) Factory overhead.

b. Compute the cost for the units in work in process and finished goods.

c. Determine the cost of goods sold.

E2–6 Determining Costs Put into Process, Goods Manufactured and Sold (L.O. 2)

The following account balances were on the books of McNutt Company:

	May 1	May 31
Direct materials inventory	$42,000	$52,000
Work in process inventory	68,000	80,000
Finished goods inventory	86,000	90,000

Direct material of $45,000 was purchased during the month, while 30,000 hours of direct labor were incurred in the Preparation Department and 50,000 direct labor-hours were incurred in the Fabricating Department. Machine hours were 40,000 in Preparation and 52,000 in Fabricating. The labor rate for the Preparation Department was $12.75 and $13.50 for the Fabricating Department. Factory overhead is applied at 60 percent of the direct labor cost in the Preparation Department and $2 per machine-hour in the Fabricating Department.

Required:

Without preparing a formal income statement, determine:

a. Total manufacturing costs for the period.
b. Cost of goods manufactured.
c. Cost of goods sold.

E2–7 Budgeted Cost of Goods Manufactured Statement and Income Statement (L.O. 2)

Management of Sparks Company expects to sell 50,000 units of its only product next year at a $100 unit sales price. At the end of the current year on May 31, 19X1, there are 6,000 units of finished goods inventory at a cost of $250,000. and management wishes to have 8,500 units in this inventory on May 31, 19X2. No change is expected in work in process inventory; FIFO costing is used.

Each unit of finished products contains 2 pounds of direct material and material costs $3 per pound. Each unit requires three hours of direct labor before completion; the cost of direct labor is $8 per hour. Factory overhead is applied on the basis of $1 per direct labor-hour. Marketing costs at this budgeted level are $600,000; administrative costs are expected to be $800,000.

Required:

Prepare a budgeted cost of goods manufactured statement and statement of income.

E2–8 Cost of Goods Manufactured (AICPA adapted) (L.O. 2)

Mat Company's cost of goods sold for the month ended March 31, 19X1, was $345,000. Ending work in process inventory was 90 percent of beginning work in process inventory. Factory overhead applied was 50 percent of direct labor cost. Other information pertaining to Mat Company's inventories and production for the month of March is as follows:

Beginning inventories—March 1:	
Direct materials	$ 20,000
Work in process	40,000
Finished goods	102,000
Purchases of direct materials	
during March	110,000
Ending inventories—March 31:	
Direct materials	26,000
Work in process	?
Finished goods	105,000

Required:

a. Prepare a schedule of cost of goods manufactured for the month of March.
b. Prepare a schedule to compute the prime cost incurred during March.
c. Prepare a schedule to compute the conversion cost charged to work in process during March.

Problems

P2–9 Cost of Goods Manufactured and Income Statement (L.O. 2)

Heglund Manufacturing Company provides you with selected account balances for its year ended December 31, 19X2:

Accounts receivable	$ 132,000
Accumulated depreciation	300,500
Advertising expense	50,250
Distribution expense	60,000
Executive staff salaries	80,300
Factory overhead	504,000
Finished goods inventory, January 1, 19X2	113,140
Finished goods inventory, December 31, 19X2	213,400
General office salaries and expense	75,350
Gross margin	472,000
Sales	1,500,000
Salespersons' salaries and expense	40,800
Work in process inventory, December 31, 19X2	81,750
Work in process inventory, January 1, 19X2	55,000

Factory overhead is applied at the rate of 140 percent of direct labor costs.

Required:

Prepare a statement of cost of goods manufactured and an income statement.

P2–10 Preparing Cost of Goods Manufactured Statement and Partial Income Statement from Missing Data (L.O. 2)

Data from the records of Snow Manufacturing Company show the following:

Accounts receivable	$ 7,500
Depreciation of sales equipment	3,000
Direct labor	90,000
Direct materials inventory, October 31, 19X2	15,000
Direct materials inventory, November 1, 19X1	10,000
Factory overhead	120,000
Gross margin	40,000
Marketing materials used	250
Purchase discount on direct materials	800
Purchases of direct materials	65,800
Sales	241,000
Sales discounts	1,000
Work in process, October 31, 19X2	?

At year-end the finished good inventory of $10,000 remained unchanged from the beginning of the year. Beginning work in process was 30 percent of the cost of goods manufactured.

Required:

Prepare a cost of goods manufactured statement and partial income statement for Snow Company for the year ended October 31, 19X2.

P2–11 Statement of Cost of Goods Manufactured and Partial Income Statement (L.O. 2)

The following data were assembled from records of the Duke Manufacturing Company on May 31, 19X2:

	Debits (000 omitted)	Credits (000 omitted)
Purchases discounts		$ 400
Sales		60,000
Direct materials inventory, June 1, 19X1	$ 5,000	
Work in process inventory, June 1, 19X1	6,100	
Finished goods inventory, June 1, 19X1	3,000	
Purchases—direct materials	12,000	
Direct labor	15,000	
Factory overhead, actual	7,100	
Sales discounts	300	
Direct materials inventory, May 31, 19X2	4,200	
Work in process inventory, May 31, 19X2	6,300	
Finished goods inventory, May 31, 19X2	1,000	

Required:

Prepare a combined statement of cost of goods manufactured and income statement through the calculation of gross margin.

P2–12 Factory Overhead Application Rates Using Various Bases (L.O. 3)

Mell Company provides the following estimated data for the next period for the preparation of factory overhead application rates:

Estimated factory overhead	$400,000
Estimated number of units to be produced: Product A—25,000 units; Product B—50,000 units	
Estimated direct labor dollars for period	$500,000
Estimated direct labor-hours for period	125,000
Estimated machine-hours for period	80,000
Estimated material costs for period	$600,000

Required:

Determine total factory overhead application rates using the following bases:

a. Machine-hours.
b. Direct material cost.
c. Units of production assigning 4 points to Product A and 3 points to Product B.
d. Direct labor dollars.
e. Direct labor-hours.

P2–13 Cost of Goods Manufactured Statement and Income Statement (L.O. 2)

Data from the records of Chris Company show the following:

Accounts receivable	$ 8,100
Administrative expense control	12,800
Cash	1,200
Depreciation on factory building	2,700
Direct labor	3,000
Direct materials inventory, January 1, 19X1	6,000
Direct materials inventory, December 31, 19X1	3,000
Factory insurance	650
Factory miscellaneous expense	460
Indirect labor	410
Indirect materials used	380
Marketing expense control	11,600
Purchases of direct materials	6,900
Sales	41,000
Sales discount	3,500
Work in process, January 1, 19X1	2,500
Work in process, December 31, 19X1	5,000

There were 1,000 units completed and transferred to the finished goods storeroom during the year. Finished goods inventory on January 1 contained 100 units at a value of $1,480. Sales during the year totaled 800 units. Inventory is costed out on a first-in, first-out basis.

Required:

Prepare a cost of goods manufactured statement and an income statement for Chris Company for the year 19X1. Carry all unit costs to two decimal places.

P2–14 Preparing Statement of Goods Manufactured and Income Statement (L.O. 2)

Crystal, Inc., provides the following data for its year ended June 30, 19X2:

Sales	$9,000,000
Gross margin	3,460,000
Administrative expenses	1,650,000
Marketing expenses	1,080,000
Direct labor costs (100,000 hours)	1,500,000

Factory overhead is applied at the rate of $6 per direct labor-hour. Selected inventory accounts have the following beginning and ending balances:

	July 1, 19X1	June 30, 19X2
Work in process	$190,000	$240,000
Finished goods	810,000	750,000

Required:

Prepare a statement of cost of goods manufactured and an income statement.

P2–15 Statement of Cost of Goods Manufactured and Partial Income Statement (L.O. 2)

These data were assembled from records of the Watch Manufacturing Company on December 19X1:

	Debits (000)	Credits (000)
Purchase discounts		$ 500
Sales		150,000
Direct materials inventory, January 1, 19X1	$20,000	
Work in process inventory, January 1, 19X1	14,600	
Finished goods inventory, January 1, 19X1	16,000	
Purchases of direct materials	32,000	
Direct labor	40,600	
Factory overhead, actual	12,500	
Sales discounts	600	
Direct materials inventory, December 31, 19X1	19,000	
Work in process inventory, December 31, 19X1	15,000	
Finished goods inventory, December 31, 19X1	14,000	

Required:

Prepare a combined statement of cost of goods manufactured and income statement through the calculation of gross margin.

P2–16 Cost of Goods Manufactured Statement (L.O. 2)

Borkowski Company accounts for costs incurred in the manufacture of its single product by a computerized cost system. A review of the cost of goods manufactured statement for fiscal year ended June 30, 19X1, discloses the following information and relationships:

1. Total manufacturing costs were $650,000 based on actual direct material used, actual direct labor, and applied factory overhead as a percentage of actual direct labor dollars.

2. Cost of goods manufactured was $605,800, also based on actual direct material, actual direct labor, and applied factory overhead.
3. Factory overhead was applied to work in process at 65 percent of direct labor dollars. Applied factory overhead for the year was 25 percent of the total manufacturing costs.
4. Beginning work in process inventory was 48 percent of ending work in process inventory.

Required:

Reconstruct the cost of goods manufactured statement for the year ended June 30, 19X1, in good form. Show supporting computations.

P2–17 Cost of Goods Manufactured and Factory Overhead Application Rate (L.O. 3)

TON Company applies factory overhead on the basis of a rate per machine-hour. The company provides the following data for April 19X1:

Selected inventories have the following balances:

	April 1	April 30
Work in process	$ 90,000	$110,000
Finished goods	70,000	55,000

Prime costs for the month were

Direct material used	$ 42,500
Direct labor (43,000 actual labor hours)	215,000

Sales have increased 30 percent over March's net sales of $400,000; as a result, gross margin for April is $160,000 before any adjustment for under/overapplied factory overhead. Actual factory overhead was $105,000. Actual machine-hours totaled 43,000.

Required:

a. Prepare a cost of goods manufactured statement; only show applied factory overhead.
b. Determine the factory overhead application rate.
c. Determine the amount of over- or underapplied overhead.
d. Determine the application rate if the application base was direct labor cost instead of machine-hours.

P2–18 Determine Overhead Application Rates on Various Bases (L.O. 3)

The following information is taken from next year's budget of the Schulz Company:

Direct materials	$160,000
Direct labor (25,000 hours)	120,000
Marketing managers' salaries	32,000
Factory supplies	22,000
Office supplies	16,000
Factory inspection	20,000
Administrative wages	45,000
Factory utilities	15,000
Rent—factory machinery	9,000
Rent—office machinery	6,000
Depreciation—factory furniture and fixtures	14,000
Depreciation—office furniture and fixtures	5,000
	$464,000

Machine-hours are budgeted at 20,000.

Required:

a. Rounding rates to two decimal places, determine factory overhead application rates on the following bases:

(1) Machine-hours.
(2) Direct materials cost.
(3) Direct labor-hours.
(4) Direct labor cost.

b. Determine the amount of overhead applied to a job having direct material costing $7,500, direct labor (1,200 hours) costing $4,600, and 1,200 machine-hours using each of the four rates computed in requirement *a*.

P2–19 Factory Overhead Application Rate for Use in Cost of Goods Manufactured Statement (L.O. 3)

Cleopatra Company manufactures special motors for industrial use. A computerized costing system accumulates production costs. At the beginning of June, assembly line operations have been changed due to the installation of a process machine that took over some of the work previously performed by direct labor workers. The following data are available at the beginning of June:

Direct materials inventory, June 1		$15,000
Work in process inventory, June 1		
Direct materials	$1,500	
Direct labor (300 hours)	1,800	
Factory overhead applied	750	
Total	$4,050	

During June the following activities occurred:

1. Direct labor totaled 4,500 hours at $6 per hour.
2. Direct materials costing $18,900 were purchased.

At the end of June, inventories consisted of the following:

Direct materials inventory, June 30		$16,500
Work in process inventory, June 30		
Direct materials	$ 5,500	
Direct labor (600 hours)	3,600	
Factory overhead applied	2,460	
Total	$11,560	

Required:

Prepare a detailed cost of goods manufactured statement for June.

P2–20 Budgeted Cost of Goods Manufactured Statement and Income Statement Using FIFO, LIFO, and Weighted Average Inventory Costing (L.O. 4)

Peasant Company produces and sells only one product. For the next year ending May 31, 19X2, management expects to sell 96,000 units at an $80 sales price per unit. There are 7,000 units remaining in finished goods inventory at the end of the current year at a cost of $315,000. Management wants to have 10,000 units in finished goods inventory at the end of the period. The company wishes to maintain the end of period level of partially completed units.

Eight gallons of direct material are required for each unit. Only one direct material is used; it costs $2 per gallon. Two hours of direct labor are required before completion of each unit; the cost of direct labor is $10 per hour. Factory overhead is applied on the basis of $6 per direct labor-hour. Marketing costs at this level are budgeted to be $1,200,000; administrative costs are expected to be $600,000.

Required:

a. Prepare a budgeted cost of goods manufactured statement and statement of income using FIFO costing.
b. Assume that the company uses LIFO costing instead; determine the ending finished goods inventory.

c. Assume that the company uses weighted-average costing instead; determine the ending finished goods inventory. Round to two decimal points.

Appendix 2–A: Problems

P2–21 Impact on Income of the Inventory Costing Method (L.O. 4)

Information about the inventories of Beaty Company using different valuation methods follows. Operations began on January 1, 19X1.

	FIFO Cost	LIFO Cost	Average Cost
December 31, 19X1	$15,600	$15,100	$15,300
December 31, 19X2	10,100	9,800	9,900
December 31, 19X3	12,200	11,600	12,100

Required:

a. Determine which inventory costing method would give the *highest* income for *each* of the three years. Explain your three answers.

19X1_____

19X2_____

19X3_____

b. Which inventory costing method would give the *lowest* net income for the three years combined?

c. Discuss the apparent movement of cost prices based on the preceding data.

P2–22 Using Various Inventory Costing methods (L.O. 4)

Hinton Company has 200 units, each costing $20, in their inventory on June 1. They make the following purchases:

Date	Units	Total Cost
June 10	600	$13,200
23	950	19,950
26	530	12,720

Issues of material were recorded on these dates:

Date	Units
June 7	150
28	1,920

Required:

Compute the cost of materials issued and the ending inventory under the following costing methods:

a. LIFO-perpetual.

b. Moving average.

c. FIFO-perpetual.

Cost Behavior and Cost Estimation

CHAPTER

CHAPTER OBJECTIVES

After studying this chapter, you should be able to:

1. Understand cost behavior patterns and the impact of automated manufacturing on these patterns.

2. Identify the important role of cost accountants in advising management about predicted cost behavior.

3. Use cost estimation methods, including regression analysis, to separate costs into their fixed and variable components.

4. Prepare cost estimating functions for determining budgeted costs to compare with actual costs.

5. Calculate the learning rate and account for deferred learning curve costs.

PRACTICAL
APPLICATION BOX
Cost Management at General Motors

Roger B. Smith, chairperson and chief executive officer of General Motors (GM), stresses the importance of a "lean production system" in every facility—one that implements new technology in a context of innovative human resource management and a clear manufacturing strategy. To be effective, GM managers believe in introducing this system in the context of a well-defined and internally consistent manufacturing strategy that addresses the company's weaknesses, bolsters its strengths, and opens up competitive opportunities. GM introduced activity-based costing in 1986 with the objective of improving their product costing techniques.

They are also developing a new Performance Measurement and Feedback System. By taking account of cross-functional linkages and interactions, this system allows them to measure processes as well as results, gives them a better balance between internal and external measurements, and enables them to measure not only cost and quality but also all of the competitiveness factors, including responsiveness and customer satisfaction. Smith argues for a massive attitude change that includes a commitment to teamwork, a sense of urgency, and an acceptance of change as a way of life.

From: Roger B. Smith, "Competitiveness in the '90s," *Management Accounting*, September 1989, pp. 24–27.

Introduction	Cost behavior concerns how *total* and *unit* costs vary with changes in activity or volume. To better estimate and control cost, understanding its behavior is essential. Because of the large investment in equipment, the importance of cost behavior analysis increases as factories become more automated. Rather than assuming a single mix of cost behavior, the cost management approach examines how to improve profits by managing cost interrelationships.

Cost Behavior Patterns (L.O. 1)

Fixed and Variable Costs

Analyzing cost behavior patterns is an important function of cost accountants. Total **variable costs** vary in direct proportion to changes in the cost driver. Total **fixed costs** remain the same despite changes in the cost driver; depreciation, insurance, and rent are examples. **Semivariable (mixed) costs** behave as partly variable and partly fixed; that is, they vary, but less than proportionately. Costs of indirect material, indirect labor, and utilities may be semivariable. For instance, there is a fixed monthly electricity cost plus a per kilowatt-hour charge.

Finding a truly fixed or truly variable cost in practice is difficult; many costs fall into a semivariable group that displays both fixed and variable characteristics. There is usually little difficulty in determining whether a direct material or direct labor cost in a labor-paced environment is fixed or variable; generally, these costs are variable. Direct labor in a machine-paced, automated factory tends to be a fixed cost. However, overhead cost behavior is harder to determine because some overhead costs vary erratically with production. Before semivariable costs can be used in cost estimates such as budgets, accountants segregate them into their fixed and variable components. This chapter discusses methods for making this distinction.

Fixed costs can be either committed costs or discretionary costs. **Committed costs** are the result of previous managerial actions. Depreciation and property taxes on the manufacturing facilities are committed costs. After acquiring an asset, committed costs are not changed unless economic circumstances indicate a change in the depreciation method or useful life, or the asset is sold.

Other costs, such as factory supervision, are **discretionary costs** because management uses its professional judgment each period in deciding the amount of such costs. These costs are also called programmed or managed costs. Many marketing and administrative costs are discretionary costs. Changes in economic conditions and technology as well as plant layout and facilities location affect management's decision about the level of discretionary costs. For example, if a competitor's product is more technologically advanced, management may find it urgent to change the product design. This design change may involve an employee training program. Such costs arise from periodic appropriation decisions reflecting top management decisions. If unfavorable conditions develop for the company, managers may drastically reduce these costs for a given year. Even though there is often no clear line between committed and discretionary costs, the distinction is useful for planning and control decisions.

EXHIBIT 3–I   Conceptual Analysis and Practical Analysis of Fixed Costs

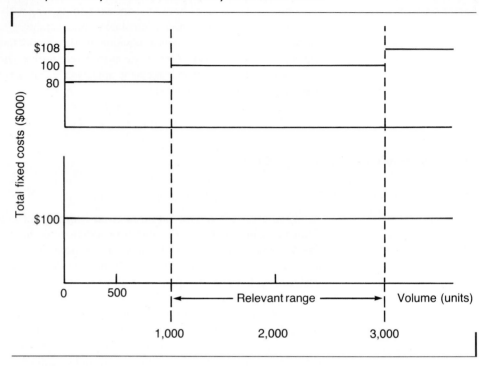

We must distinguish between short- and long-run periods in relation to fixed and variable cost. In the long run, there are no committed costs. Should management decide not to operate plant facilities, they can usually cancel the lease agreement and avoid the rent payment. In the short run, however, management usually cannot inform the lessor that operations have ceased and they wish to terminate the lease immediately. When a cost is fixed, it is fixed for a certain short period—a month or a year. People, machines, and other resources come in lumpy amounts; not all costs are variable in the long run.

Relevant Range

We define fixed and variable costs in relation to a specific period and a designated range or production volume or activity called a **relevant range.** If fixed costs are $100,000 for a year, we assume a certain volume range; for example, 1,000 to 3,000 units. When management finds an expansion of production facilities is necessary, it may either move to a larger plant or use the present facilities with additional shifts. In either case, this change in the production facilities or the number of work shifts can cause a change in the relevant range. This change in the relevant range can affect *total* fixed costs. Although some fixed costs, such as depreciation, do not change unless a company acquires new equipment or a larger plant, other fixed costs may increase. For example, a company may hire more plant supervisors.

Total fixed costs are time-related rather than activity- or volume-related when compared to variable costs. Price changes experienced in a different accounting period affect fixed costs. For example, even if the same number of shifts work next year, or the plant size remains the same, the salary level paid to the plant

EXHIBIT 3–2   Conceptual Analysis and Practical Analysis of Variable Costs

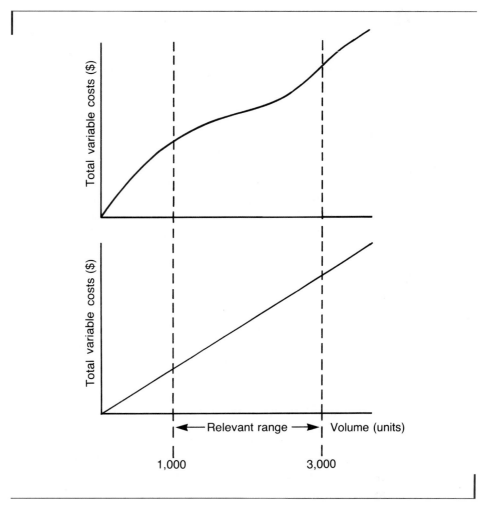

supervisors or rent on present plant facilities may increase. This increase may affect total fixed costs. Thus, total fixed costs remain the same only if we assume the relevant range does not change and prices remain constant.

The top illustration in Exhibit 3–1 shows the fixed costs for activities on either side of the relevant range when companies make major salary adjustments or changes in plant facilities. The fixed cost function depicted is often called a *step function*. Because in practice fixed costs are usually not graphed according to this conceptual analysis, the lower illustration shows the practical analysis of fixed costs. The probability of a company's activity being outside the relevant range is usually small so $100,000 becomes the fixed-costs level.

Nonlinear Relationships

The basic assumption of relevant range applies to variable costs as shown in Exhibit 3–2. Accountants assume variable costs are constant (represented graphically by a straight line), while economists often assume a curve more accurately represents the underlying variable cost relationship as compared to volume. Economists often argue quite convincingly that at higher levels of activity, there might be overcrowding, fatigue, or breakdowns in communications causing variable costs to increase per activity level rather than maintain the constant (linear) relationship that accountants usually assume exists for cost analysis and control purposes. Also, while learning their jobs, workers may waste more raw material or perform at lower activity levels.

Outside the relevant range, raw material, labor, utilities used, and other variable costs may not behave directly with changes in volume. Economists plot variable costs as in the top graph of Exhibit 3–2, showing variable costs are not strictly affected in direct proportion to volume outside the relevant range. Exhibit 3–2 shows costs increase at a decreasing rate for volumes up to 1,000 units; production costs increase faster than the assumed linear rate beyond 3,000 units. However, between 1,000 and 3,000 units, each unit appears to contain the same amount of cost. This range provides linear cost behavior; in practice, we draw total variable costs as shown in the bottom graph in Exhibit 3–2. Economies and diseconomies of scale can cause nonlinear cost behavior. For example, quantity discounts could cause cost per unit to decrease up to 1,000 units in Exhibit 3–2. However, as long as we limit decision making to the relevant range, misleading interpretation does not result.

Unit versus Total Costs

Unit Fixed versus Total Fixed Costs. Accountants express fixed and variable costs either as unit costs or in total. Exhibit 3–3 illustrates these concepts but omits the relevant range; total fixed cost is $100. We divide lump-sum fixed cost by volume to give unit fixed cost. For example, if the company produces one unit, unit fixed cost is $100; if it produces two units, the unit fixed cost is $50 ($100 total fixed cost ÷ 2 units); if it produces 10 units, the unit fixed cost is $10 ($100 total fixed cost ÷ 10 units); and so forth.

Unit Variable versus Total Variable Costs. Exhibit 3–3 also graphs total variable costs and unit variable costs. The relationship between total variable cost and volume is direct; *total variable* costs increase in proportion to volume increases. However, *unit variable* cost remains constant. Assume that a worker uses three yards of material to make each shirt and that total material cost is $20 per shirt. Exhibit 3–3 shows the total variable costs are $20 for one shirt. Total variable costs are $200 when producing 10 shirts; the unit variable cost remains $20 per shirt.

Total Cost per Unit versus Total Cost. We plot total cost by adding the fixed and variable cost curves. Total cost increases with output because of variable costs. We compute total cost per unit, sometimes called *average cost,* by dividing total cost by the units produced. For example, the total cost to produce two units is $140 ($100 fixed cost + $40 variable cost) or $70 total cost per unit ($140/2 units). Average unit cost decreases with output because we spread the $100 fixed cost over more units.

Semivariable (Mixed) Costs

Semivariable or mixed costs vary with volume changes, but the proportional relationship found in variable costs is missing. Part of semivariable costs are costs that a company incurs regardless of the level of work performed, such as

E X H I B I T 3–3   Cost Behavior Patterns Summarized

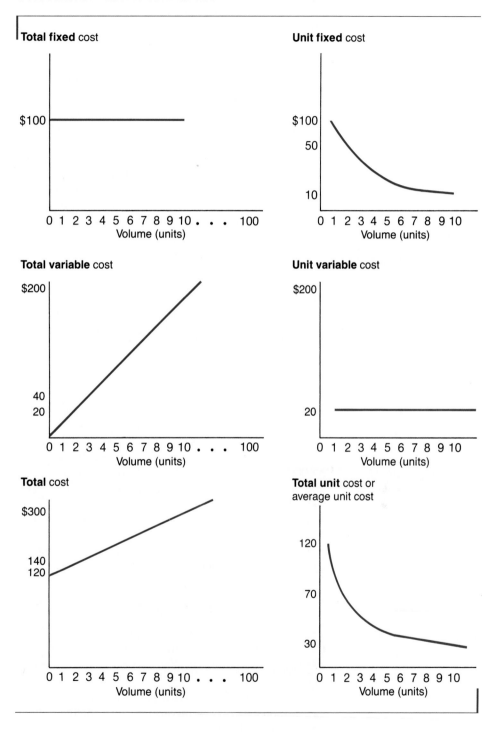

EXHIBIT 3–4   Total Semivariable Costs—Step-Type

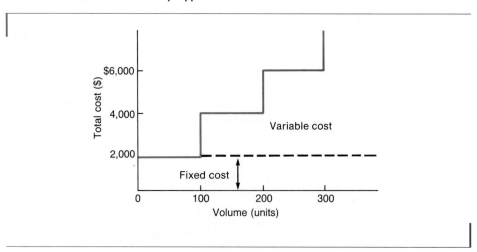

supervision, inspection, or wages of standby repairers. The total cost increases as companies attain higher activity levels because more supervisors, inspectors, and repairers are needed to support a higher production level. In reality, therefore, the costs of processing, monitoring, and expediting are often step functions (e.g., fixed over a certain range of activities). Semivariable costs are also called *semifixed costs.*

Step-Type Semivariable Costs.   Semivariable costs can take several forms: Exhibit 3–4 shows one of these, called a **step cost.** Assume that a person inspects 100 units per month and earns $2,000 monthly. The company hires a second inspector when volume increases beyond 100 units, and total inspection costs are $4,000. The company hires a third inspector when volume reaches 300 units, and so forth. The $2,000 earned by the first inspector represents the fixed portion of the semivariable cost, reflecting the minimum cost of supplying inspection service. The difference between $2,000 and the amount paid is the variable portion related to usage.

Exhibit 3–5 graphs another type of semivariable cost. Maintenance and repair of factory machinery and equipment may follow this semivariable pattern. Management may decide that a good preventive maintenance policy is to always keep one repairer at the plant and pay the person $1,800 per month. As volume increases, the company may need more repairers and additional repair supplies. The $1,800 salary of the first repairer is the fixed component. The remainder of the semivariable costs is the variable portion that may increase at a constant or increasing rate. The variable cost portion in Exhibit 3–5 increases at a constant rate.

In practice, cost behavior patterns vary and many cost structures are not linear. For instance, a semivariable cost such as electricity increases either at a decreasing or increasing rate. Utility companies charge a fixed monthly fee for service—a base charge that is constant for the period—and a demand charge that varies with consumption. With increasing amounts of energy consumed, unit variable cost may decrease. On the other hand, a penalty for increasing consumption may increase the variable cost at an increasing rate.

EXHIBIT 3–5   Total Semivariable Factory Overhead—Increasing at a Constant Rate

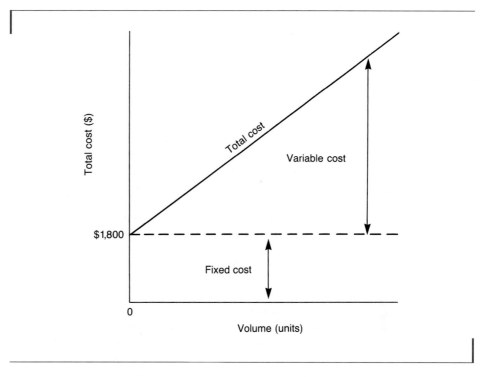

Importance of Cost Behavior to Nonmanufacturing Organizations

Even though our discussion of fixed and variable costs is based on manufacturing companies, analysis of cost behavior is important to all organizations, including not-for-profit and service industries. Effectively managing universities, hospitals, and for-profit service organizations requires an understanding of these concepts. Many of these organizations have a unique cost mix. For example, fixed costs account for 60 to 80 percent of total hospital costs. However, unlike many organizations of this type, labor costs largely comprise hospitals' fixed costs. Labor costs, unlike depreciation, require a cash flow out. This is a characteristic of labor-intensive organizations. Also, hospitals usually allocate 10 to 15 percent of their space for standby emergency events giving them built-in idle capacity. This prevents hospitals from enjoying the advantages of higher profits that a capital-intensive organization realizes at higher volumes beyond the breakeven volume. Thus, the cost structure of healthcare institutions presents challenges to accountants because of their labor-intensive and capital-intensive characteristics.

Impact of Automated Manufacturing (L.O. 2)

Exhibit 3–3 shows unit fixed costs decrease as volume increases. If the plant produces only one unit, the *unit* fixed cost is $100. The cost impact of idle capacity concerns managers because at this low volume total product costs may not be recoverable at competitive prices. As companies produce more units, unit fixed costs decrease. Thus, today's managers have gained experience under a strict discipline based on economies of scale.

Economies of Scale and Scope

Economies of scale assume that because changeover costs are high, companies should avoid changing from manufacturing one product line to another. Thus, longer production runs of standard products lower unit cost. In a traditional production setting, frequent setups and changeovers result in more machine downtime and spoilage, more indirect labor-hours, and less efficient use of direct labor. Because these developments reflect poorly on a supervisor's performance, supervisors learn to run only large batches regardless of the need for the goods being processed or the priority of the batch. Long runs result in a better ratio of direct to indirect labor. This reasoning argues for big batches and long production runs—bigger is better in virtually any circumstance.

Plant managers reason that when a troublesome operation is running well, why not produce many parts so there is no need to run the line again for a long time. For example, producing 50,000 units of the same product is easier than producing five 10,000-piece batches of different models or products—even though the same physical volume of products is manufactured. Producing five different batches requires more scheduling and setups; more placing, receiving, inspecting, and storing of product orders; and more shipping of orders. Even more critical, the assumptions of economies of scale have guided the development of technology, encouraging profitable rigidity and discouraging expensive change.

With computer-integrated manufacturing (CIM) systems becoming more widespread, however, cost accountants are questioning the assumption that increased production volume always leads to increases in profits. More managers now realize that it is better not to produce than to manufacture an unnecessary part to be stored in inventory. Large inventories stored for future use may become obsolete before their sale. Thus, companies are recognizing that sales, not production, generate profits—producing for inventory is not necessarily a value-added activity. Cost accountants are considering market demand when applying variable-fixed cost relationships.

Using **economies-of-scope** logic, companies vary rather than standardize products. They manufacture many custom products that reflect consumer demands. An operating system reflecting economies-of-scope logic is responsive to consumer demands. The economies-of-scope concept assumes that flexibility and variety create profits rather than expenses as under economies-of-scale logic. Shorter product life cycles, shorter setup times, more flexibility in multipurpose automated manufacturing equipment, and emphasis on quality partly explain less emphasis on economies-of-scale thinking and recognition of economies of scope. Manufacturing facilities using an economies-of-scope philosophy are flexible to quickly capture changing customer demands.

In selecting plant size, it may be more economical to acquire a plant capacity greater than the requirements of most months. Thus, current production can satisfy peak demands. Stockpiling inventories to meet peak demand would be necessary if plant capacity were lower. When a company acquires manufacturing facilities to handle its expected needs, management may lease excess space to outside parties until it needs more space. It may also be profitable to operate an additional shift rather than expand plant facilities because the increased usage reduces the building's idle capacity. Actually, the decision to increase the number of shifts depends on many other factors. Even with a pay differential, the company may not be able to hire enough employees for a midnight shift. In addition, it may be necessary to have the plant idle for certain periods for cleaning and maintenance.

Cost Behavior

Direct material and direct labor are usually variable costs in a labor-paced environment. For example, if production of a unit requires one pound of plastic costing $40 and two direct labor-hours costing $10 per hour, we assume these per unit figures do not change when production changes. By contrast, the per unit factory overhead cost includes both fixed and variable costs. Production of another unit does not increase total fixed costs such as rent and insurance. However, variable factory costs such as indirect material may increase directly with volume changes. Semivariable factory overhead costs such as inspection, repairs, and maintenance vary but not in direct proportion to volume changes.

Currently, automation is having an impact on the traditional view of cost behavior. In the new automated factory, direct labor has essentially become a fixed cost, not a variable cost. The labor cost that remains in a CIM system represents wages for the initial machine and material loading, but only for a single shift during a three-shift operation. Process engineers and industrial engineers are assembling equipment, setting up runs, and monitoring the processes. Some factory workers operate sophisticated equipment, while other workers monitor quality at various stations throughout the plant.

These trained factory workers are likely paid on a fixed salary basis, rather than on an hourly basis. Thus, materials, operating supplies, and energy are often the only significant components of variable manufacturing costs in the new environment. Accountants are adapting traditional cost accounting techniques to fit management's needs in environments where direct labor is a fixed cost and overhead is neither traceable to nor associated with labor.

Variable Costs in the Short Run. Even though accountants usually consider direct material and direct labor as variable costs, their behavior is often semivariable. However, direct material is variable more often than direct labor. Managers can acquire materials when needed or place materials in inventory until their use. A company does not use direct material if management decides not to produce on a particular day. However, direct labor is variable with capacity only if labor hours can be accurately and rapidly adjusted to the activity level. As a result, most labor costs—even direct labor, which is generally considered a variable cost—behave in some semivariable fashion in practice. Usually, though, in a labor-paced environment, the fixed portion of direct labor is so small in relation to total labor costs that accountants call the total a variable cost. By ignoring these complexities, we assume we can stop direct labor costs quickly and easily in the short run if management decides not to produce. As a result, direct labor costs tend to be variable when measured over a longer period, say, a month or year, and within a relevant range. The high rate of unemployment during recessionary times is additional support for classifying direct labor as largely a variable cost. The fixed cost inherent in supervisory wages, however, may be significant enough that accountants separate the fixed and variable elements. Also, the trend toward automation significantly affects the behavior pattern of labor costs.

Fixed Costs in the Short Run. Management cannot eliminate fixed costs easily in the short tun. If company managers plan to manufacture, for example, they have to buy or rent a building and incur either depreciation or rent expense on the building. The company also incurs such fixed costs as insurance on plant facilities and wages for a plant superintendent. Then, even if management decides to stop production, the plant superintendent must receive due notice and probably termination pay. Also, the company must sublease or sell the plant, machinery, and equipment. Therefore, it takes some time before management eliminates all fixed costs.

Cost Estimation (L.O. 3)

In estimating cost behavior, **cost estimation studies** attempt to predict relationships based on an activity level or **cost driver** affecting costs. In practice, managers frequently encounter such cost drivers as machine-hours, transactions, units of sales, work cells, order size, direct labor-hours, value of materials, and quality requirements. The **cost estimating function** is

$$y = a + bx$$

where y represents total cost, a equals the fixed component that does not change with activity levels, b refers to variable costs, and x represents the activity volume. The costs predicted (the dependent variable) is y in the preceding formula; x in the formula represents the independent variable. We call the independent variable the *explanatory variable,* or cost driver. It is usually a measure of activity controllable by a decision maker. In cost estimation, we identify some independent variable (the activity) and the functional relationships that permit computation of the corresponding value of the dependent variable (the costs). Cost behavior models are correlational rather than causal; in a **causal model,** x results in y, while in a **correlational model,** occurrences or movements in y are associated with occurrences or movements in x.

Cost Functions and Linearity

Accountants frequently use linear cost functions to estimate the relationships of total costs to a specific range of output or input. When relating total costs to output, several assumptions provide adequate conditions for linearity to exist. One of these assumptions is that the cost of securing each input must be a linear function of the quantity acquired. For example, there are no quantity discounts on the direct material purchased—the unit cost is identical regardless of the quantity bought. As shown in Exhibit 3–2, even if the cost is not linear over the entire range of volume, there may be a range that permits a linearity assumption within specified output limits. Another assumption is that each finished product contains the same amount of direct labor or direct material. We also assume that all input acquired is fully utilized. In estimating cost behavior, we further assume that variations in a single variable, such as machine hours, can explain variations in the total cost level. After making these assumptions, we find the underlying cost behavior pattern of each cost, more frequently called a **cost function.** We can then estimate costs based on projections of the behavior of the independent variable.

Cost Estimation Methods

Accountants use several methods to measure the variability of costs when volume changes. Some methods rely on historical data in determining the fixed and variable elements. Some approaches emphasize statistical analysis, while others stress engineering studies. Each of the methods also differs in cost; thus, cost-benefit analysis often dictates which methods are applied. Because each method has its advantages and disadvantages, we never use one method to the exclusion of others.

We commonly use the following five cost estimation methods in practice to separate mixed costs into their variable and fixed components:

1. Industrial engineering estimates.
2. Account analysis.
3. Scattergraph (visual fit).
4. High-low method.
5. Regression analysis.

Many companies combine several of these methods to estimate the relation between cost behavior and cost drivers or activity levels simultaneously so they can compare results. In fact, accountants may have to go through the cycle several times using different independent variables (cost drivers) before finally finding an acceptable cost function.

Industrial Engineering Approach

With an industrial engineering approach, the focus is on what the cost should be to produce a finished product using the company's production facilities most efficiently. The engineering approach uses time-and-motion studies and production specifications in determining which cost components are needed. Companies with standard cost systems widely use the engineering approach. **Cost standards** are scientifically predetermined costs of production used as a basis for measurement and comparison.

An engineering approach analyzes the relationships between inputs and outputs by carefully studying each phase of the manufacturing process together with the kinds of work performed and the costs involved. Completion times for each manufacturing step are added and serve as a basis for estimating direct labor costs. Cost estimates for material are obtained from engineering drawings and specification sheets.

Engineering estimates often help reveal areas where slack and inefficiencies exist. A benefit to the engineering approach is that it details each step required in operations to compare with similar operations in other settings. However, the engineering method is costly and fails to plan and control some overhead costs.

Account Analysis

Using account analysis, the accountant examines and classifies each ledger account as variable, fixed, or mixed. Mixed accounts are broken down into their variable and fixed components. They base these classifications on experience, on inspection of cost behavior for several past periods, or on managers' intuitive feelings. Assume, for instance, that management has estimated $1,090 variable costs and $1,430 fixed costs to make 100 units using 500 machine-hours. Since machine-hours drives variable costs in our example, they are stated as $1,090/ 500 machine-hours = $2.18. Using our cost equation, we have:

$$\text{Factory overhead costs} = \$1,430 + \$2.18 \text{ per machine-hour}$$

For 550 machine-hours,

$$\text{Factory overhead} = \$1,430 + \$2.18 (550) = \$1,430 + \$1,199 = \underline{\$2,629}$$

The degree to which accountants analyze ledger accounts to obtain historical cost data varies from a superficial inspection of the cost accounts to a detailed analysis of cost behavior over time. In any case, this analysis should determine whether any factors other than output are influencing costs. Such factors might include seasonal changes, the introduction of robots, new products or manufacturing processes, and other conditions that make historical cost data inappropriate for predicting cost activity relationships. For example, assume the company establishes an austerity program during a recession. In this situation, managers control costs so tightly that cost behavior differs considerably from what it would be under more relaxed conditions.

A danger in this approach is that many managers may assume a cost's behavior without further analysis. For example, managers may classify direct labor as variable because traditionally in a labor-paced environment this has been true. In an automated factory, however, any remaining direct labor cost is likely to be fixed.

Scattergraph

The **scattergraph** (also known as a **scattergram**) is a simple analysis method employing only two variables, such as cost and machine-hours. Exhibit 3–6 shows the data for 12 observations of electricity, a semivariable cost. After gathering such data, the first step is to plot the costs on the vertical, or *Y,* axis of a graph. We plot the variable measuring activity level, perhaps machine-hours or work cells, on the horizontal, or *X,* axis. Exhibit 3–7 illustrates the statistical scattergraph for these figures. Each point on the graph represents 1 of the 12 cost observations. For example, we plot the data for June on the horizontal axis (30,000 machine-hours) and on the vertical axis ($61,300 cost). The activity base used for applying electricity cost is machine-hours because there is usually a correlation between electricity costs and machine-hours. However, some other basis may be more appropriate.

Number of Observations. For simplicity, we are using cost data for only 12 months; this may be adequate if production activity levels (machine-hours in our case) and costs are highly stable. A rule of thumb is to use monthly data for three years if the production process has not changed significantly. If, however, a flexible manufacturing system using robots and other computer-controlled production processes has replaced a labor-oriented production process, we should use cost data representing only the automated systems in cost estimating methods.

Trend Line. We may fit the **trend line (line of best fit)** mathematically or visually; it was plotted by visual inspection in Exhibit 3–7. It should be fitted so there is an equal distance between the plotted points above and below the trend line. The fixed component of $40,000 in Exhibit 3–7 is determined where the trend line intersects the vertical axis. From these figures, a quick estimate of

EXHIBIT 3–6   Observations of Semivariable Costs

Month	Volume (Machine-Hours)	Electricity Cost
January	35,000	$ 65,000
February	28,000	59,800
March	34,000	64,100
April	42,000	67,800
May	37,000	70,000
June	30,000	61,300
July	25,000	57,800
August	22,000	55,600
September	20,000	54,200
October	37,000	71,000
November	45,000	72,000
December	41,000	65,000
	396,000	$763,600

EXHIBIT 3–7   Statistical Scattergraph

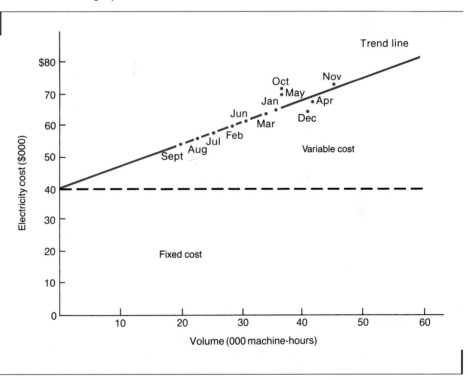

variable costs per hour can be made for the electricity cost in Exhibit 3–6 assuming fixed costs of $40,000 per month:

$763,600 total annual costs
Less 480,000 total annual fixed costs ($40,000 monthly fixed costs × 12)
$283,600 total annual variable costs

$$\frac{\$283,600 \text{ total annual variable costs}}{396,000 \text{ machine-hours}} = \$.7161 \text{ variable cost per machine-hour}$$

Merely plotting points on a graph and visually fitting a trend line may not be adequate to give a clear indication of cost behavior. For example, distortion may result due to the scale of axes. Although the scattergraph is simple to apply and understand, it is not objective. Two accountants might easily fit two very different lines to the same set of data, each believing he or she has the better fit. In addition, there may, in fact, be no correlation between the variables. This should be apparent when the points are plotted on the scattergraph. Sometimes when we fit the trend line by visual inspection (thus the name *visual fit*), personal bias may distort the true picture. Because misleading generalizations about cost behavior can result, we would undertake a more accurate study of cost behavior than the scattergraph.

High-Low Method

If we can describe the cost-activity relationship by a straight line, we may use any two points on a scattergraph in the estimating procedures. Usually, we select the lowest and the highest activity levels; thus, the name, **high-low method.** The **two-point method** is another name for the high-low method. However, these levels should be within the relevant range because we define fixed and variable costs in relation to a specific period of time and a designated range of volume or activity. The costs chosen should represent the normal cost incurred at these levels; all excessive costs resulting from abnormal conditions should be removed.

Exhibit 3–8 shows how the high-low technique separates the fixed and variable elements of electricity cost using the data from Exhibit 3–6. We calculate the variable rate by dividing the change in costs by the change in activity base, which is machine-hours for electricity.

Cost Estimating Function. After determining whether costs are fixed or variable, accountants enter them into the cost estimating function for predicting future costs. The function for electricity is $39,960 per month, plus $0.712 per machine-hour. We divide the change in the semivariable cost of $17,800 by the change of 25,000 hours to give a variable cost rate of $0.712 per machine-hour. The increase in costs when the volume changed from 20,000 machine-hours to

EXHIBIT 3–8   High-Low Method of Separating Fixed and Variable Costs

	Machine-Hours	Cost of Electricity
High capacity—November	45,000	$72,000
Low capacity—September	20,000	54,200
Change in hours and semivariable costs	25,000	$17,800

$$\text{Variable rate} = \frac{\text{Change in semivariable costs}}{\text{Change in machine-hours}} = \frac{\$17,800}{25,000} = \$0.712 \text{ per machine-hour}$$

	Low	High
Total costs	$54,200	$72,000
Variable costs $0.712 per machine-hour	14,240	32,040
Fixed costs	$39,960	$39,960

EXHIBIT 3–9   Diagram of High-Low Cost Estimates

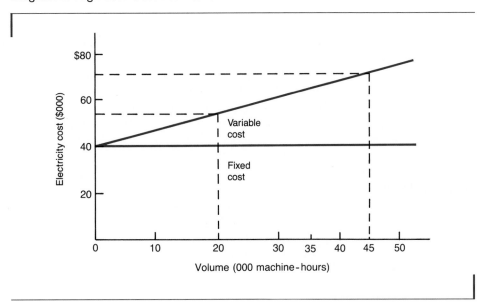

45,000 hours results from variable costs only. The variable cost per hour remains the same while the total variable cost increases. Total fixed costs remain the same at the high and low capacity levels.

Diagram of High-Low Estimates. Exhibit 3–9 shows the construction of the high-low line. We plot the high and low points of 20,000 and 45,000 machine-hours with their respective total costs. The fixed element is the intersection of the cost line with the vertical axis. The high-low technique assumes that the costs for all volumes between these two points fall along a straight line. Thus, we can draw a cost line between these two activity levels. For example, electricity costs at 35,000 machine-hours total nearly $65,000 of which $39,960 is fixed and the remainder, variable. The high-low method uses less information about cost behavior than does the scattergraph because we plot only two data points. We plotted 12 points in our scattergraph in Exhibit 3–7, recognizing then that we were simplifying our illustration by using only 12 points.

Regression Analysis

The use of statistical techniques to analyze cost behavior provides a more scientific analysis. Some of the statistical methods for separating fixed and variable cost elements are beyond the scope of this book. However, the least squares method, sometimes called *simple regression analysis,* is a relatively simple, effective approach. We use **regression analysis** to measure the average amount of change in a dependent variable, such as electricity, that is associated with unit increases in the amounts of one or more independent variables, such as machine-hours. Regression analysis has a major advantage over the high-low technique: it includes all data points—rather than just the high and low—in specifying the relationship.

E X H I B I T 3–10   Manual Calculation of Least Squares Method

Month	(1) Machine-Hours (x)	(2) Difference from Average of 33,000 hours (X)	(3) Total Electricity Costs (y) (00s)	(4) Difference from Average of $636.33 (Y) (0s)	(5) Column (2) Squared (X²)	(6) Column (2) x Column (4) (XY) (00s)
January	35,000	2,000	$ 650	13.67	4,000,000	$ 27,340
February ...	28,000	− 5,000	598	−38.33	25,000,000	191,650
March	34,000	1,000	641	4.67	1,000,000	4,670
April	42,000	9,000	678	41.67	81,000,000	375,030
May	37,000	4,000	700	63.66	16,000,000	254,640
June	30,000	− 3,000	613	−23.33	9,000,000	69,990
July	25,000	− 8,000	578	−58.33	64,000,000	466,640
August	22,000	−11,000	556	−80.33	121,000,000	883,630
September ..	20,000	−13,000	542	−94.33	169,000,000	1,226,290
October	37,000	4,000	710	73.66	16,000,000	294,640
November ..	45,000	12,000	720	83.66	144,000,000	1,003,920
December ..	41,000	8,000	650	13.66	64,000,000	109,280
Total ...	396,000	-0-	$ 7,636	-0-	714,000,000	$4,907,720
Average	33,000		$636.33			

a = Fixed component
b = Variable component
x = Volume
X = Deviations from average of x
y = Costs
Y = Deviations from average of y

Using the straight-line equation, the computation is
$$y = a + bx$$
$$\text{where } b = \frac{\Sigma XY}{\Sigma X^2} \quad \frac{\$490,772,000}{714,000,000} = \$0.687$$

$$y = a + bx$$
$$\$63,633 = a + (0.687 \times 33,000)$$
$$\$63,633 = a + \$22,671$$
$$\$63,633 - \$22,671 = a$$
$$a = \$40,962 \text{ (the fixed cost)}$$

Cost estimating function: $40,962 + $0.687 per machine-hour

Least Squares Method. The **least squares method** is the most widely used regression analysis based on the straight-line equation ($y = a + bx$) with y representing the costs; a, the fixed component; b, the variable element; and x, the volume. This method is most appropriate when data have a uniform variance of deviations along the trend line. If the cost is fixed, b is zero; if the cost is variable, a equals zero in the cost function. For semivariable or mixed costs, both a and b have positive values.

Exhibit 3–10 shows the computations for the least squares method using the cost data from Exhibit 3–6. We divide the total of 396,000 for Column 1, representing machine-hours for each observation, by the 12 observations to give an average of 33,000 hours. We divide the annual total cost of $763,600 in Column 3 by 12 observations to give an average of $63,633. We enter the differences from the average in Columns 2 and 4. The differences in Column 2 are squared, and the square is entered in Column 5 and totaled. Column 6 represents the extension of the data in Columns 2 and 4 with the results added.

Exhibit 3–10 shows cost behavior as dependent on a single measure of machine-hours. However, more than one factor may cause a cost to vary. This book illustrates only simple regression analysis that considers only one independent variable. Multiple regression analysis is a further expansion of the least squares method allowing the consideration of more than one independent variable. We can expand the straight-line equation $(y = a + bx)$ used in simple regression to include more than one independent variable. By including two independent variables, the equation becomes $y = a + bx + cz$ with c the rate of cost variability for z, an additional independent variable. The least squares method is time-consuming to apply manually, especially when we consider more than one independent variable, but a computer can make the computations quickly. Even though this chapter gives the mathematical details of the manual process, you may be as well served by devoting your time and effort only to the pre-programmed microcomputer applications that have been written for this book. Accountants' primary concerns are knowing what data to seek, the criteria the data must meet, and interpretation of the results.

Establishing Correlation. The scattergraph in Exhibit 3–7 was verified visually with a reasonable degree of correlation. If perfect correlation existed, all plotted points would fall on the regression line. We can use several statistics to measure the relationship between x (machine-hours) and y (electricity cost). The **correlation coefficient** (r) is the most commonly used statistic, as the square of this coefficient expresses the extent to which the changes in x explain the variation in y. The closer the r value is to either $+1$ or -1, the stronger the statistical relationship between the two variables. As r approaches -1, a negative, or inverse, relationship is implied, meaning the dependent variable (y) decreases as the independent variable (x) increases. On the other hand, as r approaches $+1$, a positive relationship is implied, meaning the dependent variable (y) increases as the independent variable (x) increases.

We find the **coefficient of determination** (r^2) by squaring the correlation coefficient. Exhibit 3–11 uses the data in Exhibit 3–6 to provide the figures needed in the correlation analysis formula.

In Column 3, each independent variable (x) is multiplied by its corresponding dependent variable (y). Each x value and each y value are squared and entered in Columns 4 and 5, respectively. After totaling all columns, we enter the figures in the following formula. We designate the number of observations (the 12 months in Exhibit 3–11) as n and also use it. (Note that we omitted the computation and show the formula and result.)

$$r = \frac{n\Sigma xy - (\Sigma x)(\Sigma y)}{\sqrt{[n\Sigma x^2 - (\Sigma x)^2][n\Sigma y^2 - (\Sigma y)^2]}}$$

$$= \frac{(12)(256,896,000) - (396,000)(7,636)}{\sqrt{[(12)(13,782,000,000) - (396,000)(396,000)][(12)(4,898,422) - (7,636)(7,636)]}}$$

$$r^2 = 0.8567$$

Application of the correlation analysis technique to these data reveals a coefficient of determination of 0.8567. From this we interpret that more than 85 percent of the change in electricity cost can be explained by the change in machine-hours. Accountants can use this relationship to calculate the electricity overhead rate. However, we are not saying that machine-hours is the best measure of

EXHIBIT 3–11   Correlation Analysis Data

Month	(1) Machine-Hours (x)	(2) Electricity Cost (y) (00s)	(3) xy (00s)	(4) x² (00s)	(5) y² (00s)
January ..	35,000	$ 650	22,750,000	1,225,000,000	422,500
February ..	28,000	598	16,744,000	784,000,000	357,604
March	34,000	641	21,794,000	1,156,000,000	410,881
April	42,000	678	28,476,000	1,764,000,000	459,684
May	37,000	700	25,900,000	1,369,000,000	490,000
June	30,000	613	18,390,000	900,000,000	375,769
July	25,000	578	14,450,000	625,000,000	334,084
August ...	22,000	556	12,232,000	484,000,000	309,136
September	20,000	542	10,840,000	400,000,000	293,764
October ..	37,000	710	26,270,000	1,369,000,000	504,100
November .	45,000	720	32,400,000	2,025,000,000	518,400
December .	41,000	650	26,650,000	1,681,000,000	422,500
Total .	396,000	$7,636	256,896,000	13,782,000,000	4,898,422

activity as there may be a better measure that we have not considered. We need caution in interpreting this relationship. Coefficients of correlation and determination are most meaningful in a model comparison context and high coefficients are often unacceptable while, on other data sets, even relatively low coefficients are all that can be hoped for.

Criteria for Regression Analysis

The results computed using the least squares method differ slightly from those determined by the scattergraph. The least squares method is more objective because personal bias does not enter into fitting the trend line. However, to be of benefit, regression analysis must meet certain criteria:

1. Reasonableness of relationship—A reasonable degree of correlation must exist that meets economic and professional judgment. For example, a high correlation between hemlines and stock prices may only indicate that these two variables move together. This is a **spurious correlation,** a high correlation between two variables that do not seem related at all. We need knowledge of cost behavior and the production function to give plausibility to a relationship. The independent variables under consideration should have some reasonable economic relationship. It is advisable to plot the data first on a scattergraph to be certain there is a reasonable degree of correlation.

2. Examination of r^2 or other tests of goodness of fit help in interpreting the extent to which the independent variable accounts for the variability in the dependent variable. In arriving at the best fit for a pair of variables, regression fits a line to a set of data points such that the sum of the squares of the vertical deviations of the data points is minimized. In selecting the variable with the best fit, we should choose the variable having the smaller sum of square deviations. The coefficient of determination, r^2, embodies this same information, and most computer programs generate this ratio.

3. The following conditions must hold for appropriate regression analysis:
    a. Representative observations.
    b. Linearity in the relevant range.
    c. Constant variance.
    d. Independence.
    e. Normality.
    f. Absence of multicolinearity, which applies only to multiple regression.

Representative Observations. In applying regression analysis, we assume that observations come from a uniform population. For example, in Exhibit 3–10 we obtained machine-hours and electricity costs for the same current period. The scattergraph in Exhibit 3–12 indicates that one unusual observation can have a pronounced effect on the regression line. An accountant might decide to throw out the unusual observation called the **outlier.** Using cheaper skills of labor or grades of material than are normally available could cause this unusual event with its low cost in relation to volume. Expense adjustments that are clearly abnormal also cause outliers. We can justify omitting observations that are not representative of normal operating conditions from the regression analysis.

Linearity in the Relevant Range. Linearity must exist between x and y using the equation $(y = a + bx)$. We can check the presence of linearity by plotting the data on a scattergram if there is one independent variable. The role of the relevant range is very important in interpreting the scattergraph. As discussed earlier in this chapter and illustrated in Exhibit 3–2, the linearity assumption must hold for the relevant range that is under consideration. It is dangerous to extrapolate beyond the relevant range.

Constant Variance. In applying regression analysis, the spread of observations around the regression line must be constant throughout the entire range of observations. Exhibit 3–13 indicates constant variance or **homoscedasticity,** while Exhibit 3–14 indicates that nonconstant variance or **heteroscedasticity** exists, and the constant variance criterion is not met. We often find heteroscedasticity in cost data because it is reasonable to expect a higher degree of variability of costs at high levels of volume than at low levels.

Independence. According to the independence condition, the sequence of observations makes no difference in the level of costs. For example, costs follow one pattern when volume increases, but a different pattern when volume decreases. We frequently see this "stickiness of costs" with direct labor costs because companies hire workers when production volume increases, but do not lay off these same workers as quickly when volume decreases. **Autocorrelation** exists when this assumption of observations is not met. We use statistical tests, such as the Durbin-Watson, to detect autocorrelation. Plotting and numbering the points as shown in Exhibit 3–15 can also detect autocorrelation. An autocorrelation problem exists if there is a pattern in the plotted residuals.

Normality. We use normality criteria—that the points around the regression line are normally distributed—to make probability statements using the **standard error of the estimate.** This is a measure of how far the actual cost figures deviate from an estimate of cost. We know that the level of cost at each activity level cannot be perfectly estimated. Yet, the standard error of the estimate gives

EXHIBIT 3–12   Effect of Outlier Observation

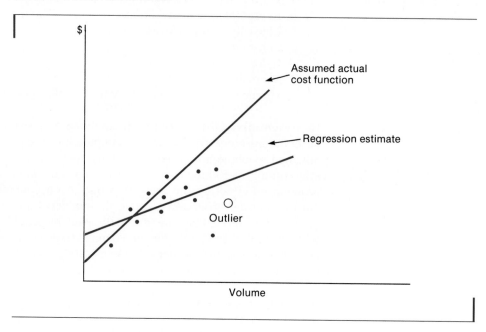

EXHIBIT 3–13   Observations Having Constant Variance

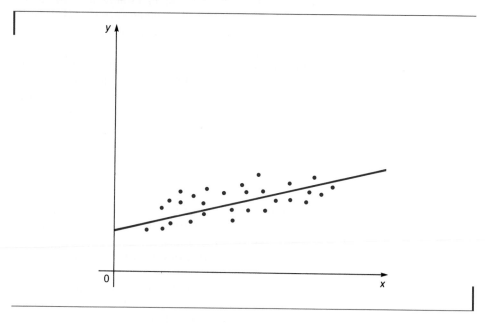

a means for estimating the amount of error that can reasonably be expected around the best estimate of the dependent variable.

Absence of Multicolinearity. The absence of **multicolinearity** is applicable only to multiple regression with two or more independent variables. Multicolinearity exists when the independent variables are highly correlated with each other.

E X H I B I T   3–14   Observations Lacking Constant Variance

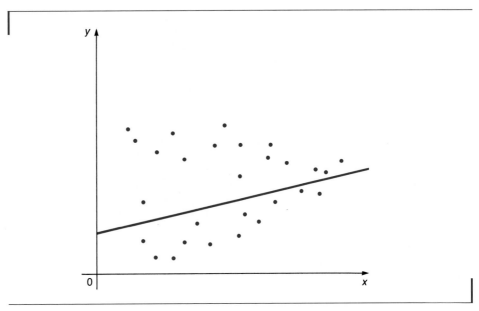

E X H I B I T   3–15   Autocorrelation

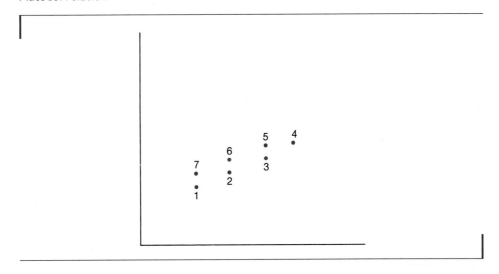

    The results of cost behavior studies like those discussed earlier may differ significantly from prestudy predictions. Cost accountants, therefore, should not presume to estimate the relationship of cost changes to volume variations without conducting such studies of cost behavior patterns.

Budgeted Allowances Using Cost Estimating Function (L.O. 4)

    Accountants separate costs into their fixed and variable components using one of the cost estimating methods presented earlier, such as high-low or least squares. This allows them to better budget costs. The following is a simple illustration of

EXHIBIT 3–16

Factory Overhead Budget at 30,000 Budgeted Hours			
Variable	**Fixed**	**Total**	
Factory supplies $18,420 ($6.14 × 30,000)		$ 18,420	
Electricity 20,610 ($.687 × 30,000)	$40,962	61,572	
Rent	25,000	25,000	
$39,030	$65,962	$104,992	

		Application rate	$3.50	($104,992 ÷ 30,000 hours)

Factory Overhead Budget at 28,000 Actual Hours			**Actual**	**Variance**
Variable	**Fixed**	**Total**		
Factory supplies $17,192 ($6.14 × 28,000)		$ 17,192	$ 18,300	$1,108 Unfavorable
Electricity 19,236 ($.687 × 28,000)	$40,962	60,198	58,800	1,398 Favorable
Rent	25,000	25,000	25,500	500 Unfavorable
$36,428	$65,962	$102,390	$102,600	$ 210 Unfavorable

Factory overhead applied ($3.50 × 28,000)	98,000
Underapplied overhead	$ 4,600

the use of the cost function in budgeting. (Chapter 9 gives an extensive description of this budgeting approach.) Assume we estimate factory supplies as strictly variable at $6.14 per machine-hour and monthly factory rent, a fixed cost, at $25,000. Exhibit 3–10 separates electricity, a semivariable cost, into $40,962 fixed and $0.687 variable per machine-hour using the least squares method. Assuming only these three overhead costs, the cost estimating function for total overhead is $6.827 + $65,962. If monthly capacity is budgeted at 30,000 hours, this yields an applied overhead rate of $3.50 as shown in Exhibit 3–16. Assume further that the company works 28,000 machine-hours during the month, resulting in $3.50 × 28,000 = $98,000 applied factory overhead. At the end of the month, we determine budgeted amounts for the actual capacity worked using the cost estimating function as shown in Exhibit 3–16. Monthly variances result assuming actual costs of $18,300 for supplies, $58,800 for electricity, and $25,500 for rent. A comparison of $102,600 total actual overhead with $98,000 applied yields $4,600 underapplied overhead.

Summary

With CIM facilitating flexible manufacturing systems, cost accountants are now rethinking the assumption of economies of scale and further studying the behavior of costs when volume changes. In practice, few costs are truly variable or truly fixed because countless factors affect cost behavior. Direct labor is truly a variable cost only if the company pays workers on a piecework basis and maintains a tight control over labor costs. Indirect labor costs often fall into the semivariable category because companies need some indirect labor employees for standby services. Companies acquire direct material as needed, thus making materials a variable cost.

While we have demonstrated several techniques such as the high-low, scattergraph, and least squares methods to segregate costs into fixed and variable components, the task in practice is more involved. Costs may vary due to several factors besides volume changes. The methods available to cost accountants may sometimes be inadequate to obtain more than a hint of the causal factors. With some data sets, even relatively low coefficients are all that can be obtained. However, this is much better than carelessly lumping costs into variable and fixed categories without any analysis.

Important Terms and Concepts

Appendix 3–A Learning Curve Theory (L.O. 5)

One assumption we made earlier in estimating cost behavior was that the cost of securing each input is a linear function of the quantity acquired. However, the relationship between costs and independent variables is not always linear. When employees gain experience performing a specific task, a systematic, nonlinear relationship has been found. The **learning curve theory,** also called the **improvement curve theory,** is based on the proposition that as workers gain experience in a task, they need less time to complete the job and productivity increases.

The learning curve theory not only affects direct labor costs but also impacts direct labor-related costs, such as supervision. In addition, this learning affects direct material costs. As workers gain experience, they may have less waste and spoilage.

The time to perform many operations begins slowly and speeds up as employees become more skilled. Much fumbling is likely to occur at the start of a new process. Gradually the time needed to complete an operation becomes *progressively* smaller at a constant percentage as workers find rhythmic work patterns. Because this rate of improvement often has a regular pattern, we can draw **learning curves** to estimate the labor-hours required as workers become more familiar with the process. Learning curves are also called **progress functions** and **experience curves.**

The learning curve model is based on a constant percentage reduction in required inputs. We typically express these reductions in terms of the effect of doubling the output quantity. We state this pattern as follows: As cumulative quantities double, average time per unit falls by a certain percent of the previous time. For example, assuming this reduction is 20 percent and it took two hours to produce the first unit, the accumulated average rate to double the present output from one to two units is two hours $\times$ 0.80 = 1.6 hours. Because the cumulative hours are an average for the units completed, the total time to produce two units is 1.6 $\times$ 2 = 3.2 hours. To double production again from two to four units, the average per unit time decreases to 80 percent of the previous average, 1.6 hours

× 0.80 = 1.3. This makes the total time to produce four units equal to 5.2 hours. We use this progression to obtain the values in the following table:

Cumulative Quantity	Cumulative Average Worker-Hours per Unit	Predicted Total Hours to Perform Task
1	2.0	2.0
2	1.6 (2.0 hours × 80%)	3.2 (2 × 1.6 hours)
4	1.3 (1.6 hours × 80%)	5.2 (4 × 1.3 hours)
8	1.0 (1.3 hours × 80%)	8.0 (8 × 1.0 hours)
16	0.8 (1.0 hours × 80%)	12.8 (16 × 0.8 hours)
32	0.6 (0.8 hours × 80%)	19.2 (32 × 0.6 hours)
64	0.5 (0.6 hours × 80%)	32.0 (64 × 0.5 hours)

The table shows the computations for an 80 percent learning curve, shown in Exhibit 3A–1. In practice, managers plot these curves on log-log graph paper. The slope of the curve for operations that are complex and require much technical skill are steeper than that for routine, repetitive operations. We determine points on the graph by dividing the cumulative quantity at each point by the predicted total hours to perform the task. For example: 1 unit ÷ 2 hours = 0.50, 2 units ÷ 3.2 hours = 0.63, 4 units ÷ 5.2 hours = 0.76, 8 units ÷ 8 hours = 1.0, and so forth. The table shows that the reduction rate of 20 percent is constant at each doubling of the number of tasks performed. Eventually, workers learn the skill and further reductions in time become negligible. As shown in Exhibit 3A–1, a constant productivity state is established.

Learning Rate. The reduction in time varies between 10 and 40 percent depending on the repetitiveness of labor operations, with 20 percent being a common reduction. In calculating the learning rate that applies to the specific situation, data on manufacturing the first two lots of a product can be used. We usually define the **learning rate** as:

$$\frac{\text{Average input quantity (cost) for the first } 2X \text{ units}}{\text{Average input quantity (cost) for the first } X \text{ units}}$$

EXHIBIT 3A–1

Learning Curve

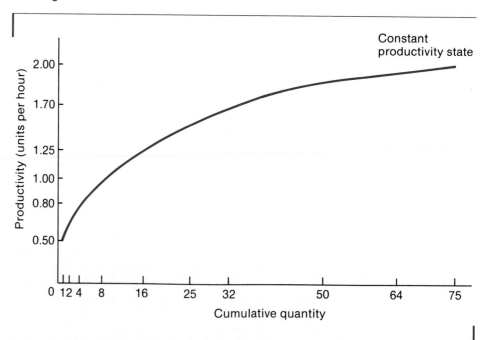

Assume that for another project the first lot of four units required a total of 4,000 direct labor-hours. The second lot of four more units requires an additional 2,800 direct labor-hours. We calculate the learning rate as follows for this operation:

$$\frac{(4,000 + 2,800)/8}{4,000/4} = \frac{850 \text{ average direct labor-hours}}{1,000 \text{ average direct labor-hours}} = 85\%$$

Deferred Learning Curve Costs. Managers can use learning curves to estimate labor requirements and prepare cost estimates. In competitive bidding, we can estimate the effect of learning on costs if we expect repeat orders. For example, assume that a company has recently succeeded in winning a federal contract to build and assemble eight special TV sets. The prototype constructed to win the contract cost $2,000 in materials and $10,000 in labor. Materials are not subject to a learning effect. However, management estimates the labor costs are subject to a 90 percent learning rate. Using the doubling approach, average labor costs for the eight units are $7,290 as shown in the following table. (Note this analysis uses costs rather than hours.) Subtracting the $10,000 labor cost used on the first unit gives a total budgeted labor cost of $48,320 for the seven units needed later. Budgeted material costs for these seven units is $14,000 (7 × $2,000).

Total Units	Average Cost to Produce All Units to Date	Total Cost to Produce All Units to Date
1	$10,000	$10,000
2	9,000 ($10,000 × 90%)	18,000 (2 × $9,000)
4	8,100 ($9,000 × 90%)	32,400 (4 × $8,100)
8	7,290 ($8,100 × 90%)	58,320 (8 × $7,290)

For financial accounting purposes, we usually do not report an increasing trend of profits for each subsequent unit as the actual labor cost decreases. Instead, we charge units to cost of goods sold at the average cost expected to be incurred for all units in the production run. This is $7,290 average costs for the federal contract just described. The actual labor cost to produce the first unit is $10,000. However, we transfer the labor cost to finished goods as $7,290 resulting in a deferred cost of $2,710. We place the deferred cost of $2,710 in a suspense account titled **Deferred Learning Curve Costs.** Even though such costs have a possible relationship to future economic benefits, the disclosure of deferred learning curve costs on a company's balance sheet disagrees with generally accepted accounting principles.

In the early part of the production run, actual labor costs for the units manufactured exceed average production cost. The reverse occurs later in the run with actual cost being less than average cost. Exhibit 3A–2 illustrates the pattern of learning curve costs. By the time the learning effect becomes negligible and a constant productivity state sets in or the production run is complete, the balance in the Deferred Learning Curve Costs account is zero.

The following journal entry reflects *labor cost only* for the transfer of the first and eighth unit from work in process to finished goods inventory. An alternative treatment recognizes deferred learning curve costs at the time the finished product is sold and recorded as a cost of goods sold.

For Unit 1:

Deferred Learning Curve Costs	2,710	
Finished Goods Inventory	7,290	
Work in Process Inventory		10,000

EXHIBIT 3A-2   Pattern of Learning Curve Costs

Unit	Actual Unit Cost		Average Cost	Adjustments to the Deferred Learning Curve Costs Account		Balance in Deferred Learning Curve Costs Account
1	$10,000		$7,290	+$2,710		$2,710
2	8000	($18,000) −10,000	7,290	+ 710		3,420
4	7,200	($32,400 −18,000 $14,400/2 units)	7,290	− 180	($90 × 2)	3,240
8	6,480	($58,320 −32,400 $25,920/4 units)	7,290	− 3,240	($810 × 4)	0

For Unit 8:

Finished Goods Inventory 7,290		
Deferred Learning Curve Costs	810	
Work in Process Inventory	6,480	

Even though the use of the Deferred Learning Curve Costs account causes a smoothing effect on reported company earnings, it does result in a deferred charge account which the company's balance sheet shows as an asset. The company recovers this asset in future cost of goods sold if it completes the production run.

However, if the company fails to produce and sell all the units in the production run for which the learning effect applies, accountants must write the deferred cost balance off as a loss. For example, assume that even though the initial contract was for a total of eight units, after delivering the first four sets (including the prototype), the buyer cancels the contract. Deferred learning curve costs must be written off at the time the buyer cancels the contract if the company valued the four units at the expected average cost for all eight units in the contract. Thus, with the manufacture of each unit, the labor cost portion of that unit for inventory valuation would have been $7,290, or a total for four units of $29,160 (4 × $7,290). This is lower than the actual unit cost for these early units. Actual labor cost for the first four units total $32,400. The difference is $3,240, calculated as follows:

$32,400	Total actual labor cost for four units
29,160	Total average cost for four units assuming eight units were made
$ 3,240	Deferred cost

A Deferred Learning Curve Costs account accumulates this $3,240 difference. Accountants must write the difference off as an additional cost of the job or as a loss at the time the buyer cancels the contract.

Advantages of Learning Curves. Since learning curve theory describes the phenomenon of improving efficiency as a function of time or increasing output, it provides an insight into the ability of workers to learn new skills. Managers use progress reports comparing actual results with estimated accomplishments as depicted by the learning curve to evaluate performance. Learning models bring the behavioral and the quantitative aspects of labor management together. This information assists management in establishing an incentive wage system. Companies should avoid giving bonus pay while workers are in a learning stage. After learning the skill, companies establish standards so employees may earn bonus pay for performing operations in less than standard time. Certainly if companies need standards before the constant productivity state becomes apparent, they should consider the learning curve effect.

Impact of Automation on Learning Curves. Learning curve theory has limited usefulness at the machine level in a flexible manufacturing system. These new technologies alter the whole concept of learning curve costs. After the system learns the operation method, it repeats the task identically each time. Also, direct labor comprises a small percent of total production costs in a machine-paced environment.

Problem for Self-Study

Cost Behavior and Cost Estimating Formula

CMB Company has budgeted factory overhead for four volumes of operations as follows:

	Machine-Hours			
	5,000	**6,000**	**7,000**	**8,000**
Indirect labor	$2,100	$2,400	$2,700	$3,000
Insurance	600	600	600	600
Depreciation	1,000	1,200	1,400	1,600
Utilities	2,000	2,300	2,400	2,900
	$5,700	$6,500	$7,100	$8,100

The year-end factory overhead costs for 6,500 machine-hours were

	Actual Costs
Indirect labor	$2,750
Insurance	500
Depreciation	1,200
Utilities	2,380
	$6,830

Required:

a. Indicate whether each of the four overhead costs budgeted is fixed, variable, or semivariable.
b. Using the high-low method, determine the cost estimating formula for each of the four factory overhead costs.
c. Determine the variance for each of the four costs using a budget based on the cost functions determined in requirement *b*. Indicate whether they are favorable or unfavorable.

Solution to Problem for Self-Study

CMB Company

a. Indirect labor—semivariable
   Insurance—fixed
   Depreciation—variable
   Utilities—semivariable

b.

		Variable Cost		Fixed Cost	
Indirect labor	. . .	$.30 (see below)		$ 600	
Insurance	. . . . .	-0-		600	
Depreciation	. . .	.20 ($1,200/6,000 hours)		-0-	
Utilities	. . . .	.30 (see below)		500	(see below)
		$.80 per machine-hour		+$1,700	

High-Low Method:	Hours	Cost
Indirect labor	8,000	$3,000
	5,000	2,100
Difference	3,000	$ 900

Variable rate $.30 ($900/3,000 hours)
Fixed costs $600 [$3,000 − (8,000 × $.30)]

	Hours	Cost
Utilities	8,000	$2,900
	5,000	2,000
Difference	3,000	$ 900

Variable rate = $.30 ($900/3,000)
Fixed costs = $500 [$2,900 − (8,000 × $.30)]

c.

	Actual Costs	Budget at 6,500 Hours	Variance	
Indirect labor	$2,750	$2,550 [($.30 × 6,500) + $600]	$200	U
Insurance . . .	500	600	100	F
Depreciation .	1,200	1,300 ($.20 × 6,500 hours)	100	F
Utilities	2,380	2,450 [($.30 × 6,500 hours) + $500]	70	F
	$6,830	$6,900	$ 70	F

U = Unfavorable; F = Favorable

Review Questions

1. Compare and distinguish between economies-of-scale logic and economies-of-scope logic.

2. Understanding cost behavior is vital to all organizations, but it is crucial to hospitals because their patterns of cost differ from most manufacturing firms. Discuss why you think the cost structure of healthcare institutions presents additional challenges.

3. A company wants to realize a profit of $150,000. Its salespeople plan to sell 100,000 units of a product for $15 each; fixed costs are $250,000. To realize this desired profit, what would variable costs be?

4. Is depreciation cost a fixed or variable cost? Indicate the factor determining whether the cost is fixed or variable.

5. Even though direct labor has been traditionally classified as a variable cost, discuss why it could now also be a semivariable or fixed cost.

6. Reply to this comment, "There will still be people working in the automated factories of the future, but they sure will be different from the traditional factory labor worker of the past." Do you agree or disagree?

7. Briefly explain three assumptions of regression analysis.

8. When is the least squares method most appropriate?

9. If r^2 = .90 for a relationship, what is the correct interpretation?

10. Contrast the results obtained using the least squares method with those obtained using a statistical scattergraph.

11. How is the trend line fitted on a statistical scattergraph?

12. Discuss the limitations of a statistical scattergraph.

13. Do you agree or disagree with this statement: The basic concept in cost estimation is to estimate the relation between costs and the variables affecting costs. What is likely to be determined by a cost estimation study?

14. Discuss the criteria that should be used in selecting the two activity periods for the high-low method.

15. Which of the three main cost components are more likely to fall into the variable cost behavior pattern? Why?

16. In analyzing cost behavior, why must accountants guard against feeding large amounts of data to the computer and letting a regression program find a relationship among the variables?

17. If total costs for Ban Company are $280,000 for 600,000 machine-hours and $310,000 for 700,000 machine-hours, what are the budgeted fixed costs for the year?

CPA/CMA/CIA Multiple-Choice Questions

1–4. (CMA) These items are based on the following data: The estimated unit costs for a company using full absorption costing and operating at a production level of 12,000 units per month are as follows:

Cost Item	Estimated Unit Cost
Direct material	$32
Direct labor	20
Variable manufacturing overhead	15
Fixed manufacturing overhead	6
Variable selling	3
Fixed selling	4

1. Estimated conversion costs per unit are

   a. $35
   b. $41
   c. $44.
   d. $48.
   e. Some amount other than those given above.

2. Estimated prime costs per unit are

   a. $73.
   b. $32.
   c. $67.
   d. $52.
   e. Some amount other than those given above.

3. Estimated total variable costs per unit are

   a. $67.
   b. $38.
   c. $70.
   d. $52.
   e. Some amount other than those given above.

4. Estimated total costs that would be incurred during a month with a production level of 12,000 units and a sales level of 8,000 units are

   a. $692,000.
   b. $664,000.
   c. $960,000.

  d. $948,000.
  e. Some other amount than those given above.

5. (AICPA) Box Co. has developed the following regression equation to analyze the behavior of its maintenance cost (Y) as a function of machine-hours (X):

$$Y = \$12,000 + \$10.50X$$

Thirty monthly observations were used to develop the foregoing equation. The related coefficient of determination was .90. If 1,000 machine-hours are worked in one month, the related point estimate of total variable maintenance costs would be

  a. $ 9,450.
  b. $10,500.
  c. $11,500.
  d. $22,500.

6. (AICPA) Meg Co. has developed a regression equation to analyze the behavior of its maintenance costs (Q) as a function of machine-hours (Z). The following equation was developed by using 30 monthly observations with a related coefficient of determination of .90:

$$Q = \$6,000 + \$5.25Z$$

If 1,000 machine-hours are worked in one month, the related point estimate of total maintenance costs would be

  a. $11,250.
  b. $10,125.
  c. $ 5,250.
  d. $ 4,725.

7. (AICPA) Simple regression analysis involves the use of

	Dependent Variables	Independent Variables
a.	One	None
b.	One	One
c.	One	Two
d.	None	Two

8. (CIA) In regression analysis, the coefficient of correlation is a measure of
  a. The amount of variation in the dependent variable explained by the independent variables.
  b. The amount of variation in the dependent variable unexplained by the independent variables.
  c. The slope of the regression line.
  d. The predicted value of the dependent variable.

9. (CIA) If regression was applied to the data shown below, the coefficients of correlation and determination would indicate the existence of a:

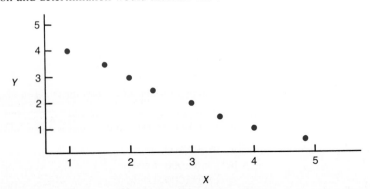

a. Low linear relationship, high explained variation ratio.
b. High inverse linear relationship, high explained variation ratio.
c. High direct linear relationship, high explained variation ratio.
d. High inverse linear relationship, low explained variation ratio.

10. (CMA) As cumulative production increases in an application that is subject to the learning curve, the

a. Average costs per unit of output decrease systematically.
b. Average costs per unit of output increase systematically.
c. Fixed costs per unit of output increase systematically.
d. Total fixed production costs decrease systematically.
e. Cumulative production costs decrease systematically.

11. (CIA) A corporation is considering the addition of new automated manufacturing equipment in one of its production departments. Currently the department produces 50,000 units a year with average unit costs as follows:

Direct material	$50
Direct labor (2 hours at $15 per hour)	30
Fixed overhead	20

Both direct material and direct labor are variable costs. The ratio of unit fixed costs to unit variable costs (direct material plus direct labor) in the current labor-intensive operation is 25 percent (i.e., $20/$80).

The new machinery will increase total fixed overhead costs in the department by $500,000 per year and make production more capital-intensive. Production will double to 100,000 units a year using the same total number of direct labor hours per year as the old labor-intensive operation. Direct material cost will be unchanged at $50 per unit.

Which of the following is the predicted ratio of unit fixed costs to unit variable costs in the new capital-intensive operation?

a. 18.75 percent.
b. 23.07 percent.
c. 31.25 percent.
d. 38.46 percent.

Exercises

E3–1 Budget Variances Based on Cost Estimating Formula (L.O. 4)

JKL Company has the total overhead budget for the following hours within their relevant range:

3,000 hours	. . . .	$12,000
8,000 hours	. . . .	$24,500

They realize that they need a cost accountant to analyze the overhead variances. Actual hours totaled 6,000, and the actual overhead was $14,900 variable and $4,800 fixed.

Required:

a. Analyze the fixed and variable behavior of the budgets and determine the cost estimating formula.
b. Prepare a simplified budget and compute the variances for variable and fixed actual costs.

E3–2 Budgeted Production Cost Estimated for Last Year's Unit Cost (L.O. 1)

In producing 10 units last period, Mustang, Inc., incurred the following unit costs:

Direct material	$ 100
Direct labor	200
Fixed factory overhead	300
Variable factory overhead	400
	$1,000

Required:

Determine the budgeted unit and total cost to produce 12 units if no change in relevant range or price level is planned for next year when these 12 units are produced.

E3–3 Cost Behavior (L.O. 2)

Follett Company provides this summary of its total budgeted production costs at three production levels:

	Volume in Units		
	1,500	**1,800**	**2,100**
Cost A	$1,625	$1,850	$2,075
Cost B	2,400	2,880	3,360
Cost C	1,000	1,000	1,000
Cost D	1,200	1,200	1,800

Required:

a. Indicate the cost behavior for Costs A through D.
b. Determine the total budgeted cost for Costs A through D if the company produces 1,880 units.
c. Give an example of a production cost that could have the same type of behavior as each of Costs A through D.

E3–4 Regression Diagram (L.O. 3)

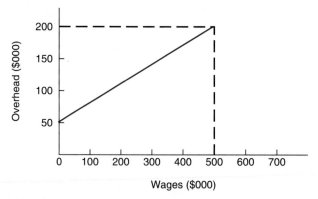

The controller for Stern, Inc., prepared the regression diagram shown, drawing the line of best fit (trend line) for factory overhead and wages. The line of best fit in this diagram is described by the formula $y = a + bx$.

Required:

a. Determine the slope of the line of best fit in numerical terms.
b. Give the estimated overhead if wages amount to $750,000.

E3–5 High-Low Approach (L.O. 3)

Janis Company has the following monthly overhead budget for two volume levels:

4,000	machine-hours	$ 9,000
10,000	machine-hours	12,000

Required:

a. Give an approximate fundamental measure of fixed and variable cost behavior using the high-low method as follows:
   (1) Prepare the mathematical analysis.
   (2) Diagram the high-low estimates.

b. At month-end, you learn that 6,200 hours were actually worked and total overhead costs were $12,500. Prepare a simple budget and indicate whether the total overhead variance is favorable or unfavorable.

E3–6 High-Low Method (L.O. 3)

Joseph, Inc., provides the following for the second quarter of the year for use in determining the fixed portion of its utility expense, a semivariable expense.

	Machine-Hours	Utility Expense
May	200	$ 9,000
June	360	11,100
July	500	13,500
August	480	12,800

Required:

Determine the company's fixed portion of utility expense.

E3–7 Data Observation (L.O. 1)

You have plotted the data points and are now ready to begin a regression analysis.

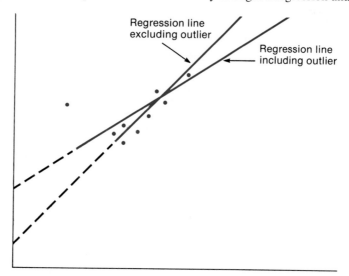

Required:

a. Do you see anything that should be done before running the regression?
b. What could have caused any unusual observations that you detect in the graph?

E3–8 Unit Cost under Seasonal Conditions (L.O. 2)

Fairleigh, Inc., makes children's toys. Retail distribution is achieved through a chain of merchandisers. Even though sales and production increase dramatically near the end of the year, management strives to maintain enough manufacturing activity to keep a labor force employed. Data for the first quarter's production when 60,000 toys were sold at $5 each are

Direct material	$120,000
Commissions on sales	3,000
Wages and salaries	38,000

Administrative expenses	$25,000
Distribution expenses	24,000

Required:

a. Give the total cost per unit sold.

b. Assume that direct material and commissions vary in relation to sales volume while other costs remain fixed; what profit would the company make the last quarter if it sells 100,000 toys?

c. Determine the total cost per unit sold in the last quarter.

d. List additional problems companies operating like Fairleigh would encounter.

E3–9 High-Low Method (L.O. 3)

Smile, Inc., has provided the following actual cost data for your use in determining variable factory overhead costs and fixed factory overhead costs for budgeting purposes.

	Quarters		
	Spring	Summer	Fall
Machine hours	70,000	80,000	90,000
Direct material	$147,000	$168,000	$ 189,000
Direct labor	350,000	400,000	450,000
Factory overhead	50,400	56,700	63,000
Salespersons' salaries .	182,000	208,000	234,000
Warehousing	56,000	64,000	72,000
Executive salaries	90,000	90,000	90,000
	$875,400	$986,700	$1,098,000

Required:

a. Determine an overall variable factory overhead rate per machine-hour and total fixed factory overhead using the high-low method, assuming management believes no other major factors affect cost behavior.

b. Determine the cost estimating function for factory overhead.

c. Give the budgeted amount in each of the six accounts if the management of Smile, Inc., budgets 83,600 machine-hours for the winter quarter.

E3–10 Effectiveness of Regression Model (CIA adapted) (L.O. 3)

An accountant has been asked to review the reasonableness of the budgeted direct costs of a particular product. A study of past direct costs for that product yielded these data:

Units Produced	Direct Costs
1,000	$25,000
2,000	38,863
3,000	46,972
4,000	52,726
5,000	57,189
6,000	60,835
7,000	63,918
8,000	66,589
9,000	68,944
10,000	71,052

The accountant decided to apply regression analysis in the review. The following model was established:

$$Y = 29,864 + 4.608X$$
$$X = \text{units produced}$$
$$Y = \text{direct costs (\$)}$$
$$R^2 = 0.91$$

Required:

a. Comment on the probable effectiveness of the regression model in evaluating the budget and list the underlying assumptions of the methodology.

b. Using the model, estimate the total direct cost of producing 5,000 units.

Problems

P3–11 Using Cost Function to Determine Budget (L.O. 4)

The Martha Sue Ryan Company uses budgets for planning and control in its producing departments. Capacity is based on machine-hours for the Finishing Department.

In May, the Finishing Department operated 22,250 hours. The following budgets had been established previously for the Finishing Department:

	Machine-Hours	
	19,500	**23,000**
Factory supplies	$30,350	$34,900
Indirect labor	31,350	35,550
Maintenance supplies	18,720	22,080
Depreciation	2,200	2,200
Property taxes	1,950	1,950
Insurance	2,340	2,760
	$86,910	$99,440

Required:

a. Indicate the cost behavior of each cost element.

b. Prepare budgeted amounts for each expense element based on the actual volume level.

c. Express the cost estimating formula for total overhead.

d. Indicate the amount of the variance for each expense item and whether favorable or unfavorable if the actual costs were factory supplies, $34,600; indirect labor, $34,900; maintenance supplies, $22,100; depreciation, $2,400; property taxes, $1,890; and insurance, $2,800.

e. Explain why actual depreciation and property taxes could differ from budgeted expenses.

P3–12 Statistical Scattergraph and Least Squares Method (L.O. 3)

The following data are for six bimonthly cost observations of the Morgan Company:

	Direct Labor-Hours	Cost
January–February	22,000	$11,000
March–April	17,000	6,980
May–June	28,000	12,100
July–August	11,000	6,000
September–October	14,000	9,000
November–December	16,000	11,800
	108,000	$56,880

Required:

a. Plot a statistical scattergraph from the data to obtain the fixed and variable cost elements.

b. Use the least squares method to determine the fixed and variable cost elements.

P3–13 Cost Estimating Formula, Application Rates, Variances (L.O. 4)

At the beginning of the year, Burton Company prepared the following monthly factory overhead budgets:

	Machine-Hours	
	50,000	60,000
Supplies	$120,000	$144,000
Indirect labor	67,500	81,000
Utilities	162,500	195,000
Supervision salaries	10,000	10,000
Depreciation	9,000	9,000
Insurance	8,000	8,000
Property taxes	15,000	15,000
	$392,000	$462,000

At the end of the month, analysis of the cost records reveals the following factory overhead incurred in operating at 58,000 machine-hours:

Supplies	$136,000
Indirect labor	80,000
Utilities	190,000
Supervision salaries	10,200
Depreciation	8,880
Insurance	7,600
Property taxes	14,700
	$447,380

Required:

a. Compute the cost estimating formula.
b. Determine the factory overhead application rate using estimated capacity of 60,000 hours.
c. Determine variances for each of the factory overhead items, indicating whether they are favorable or unfavorable.

P3–14 High-Low and Manual Determination of Least Squares Analysis (L.O. 3)

The manager of the Shelby Motel asks your assistance in analyzing housekeeping costs so that cost estimating functions can be developed. You obtain the following cost data for the first four months for a representative section of the motel:

Month	Rooms Occupied	Cost of Housekeeping
January	460	$2,864
February	540	3,144
March	720	4,034
April	640	3,734

Required:

a. Give management an approximate measure of their cost behavior using the high-low mathematical approach.
b. Use the least squares method to determine the fixed and variable cost elements.
c. Determine the coefficient of correlation (r) and the coefficient of determination (r^2).
d. Explain what the coefficient of determination that you computed reveals.

P3–15 Cost-Volume Relationships Illustrated in Graphs: Unit Cost (L.O. 2)

In the graphs shown, assume that *unit* costs for Butcher Company are measured on the vertical axis while the horizontal axis measures production volume.

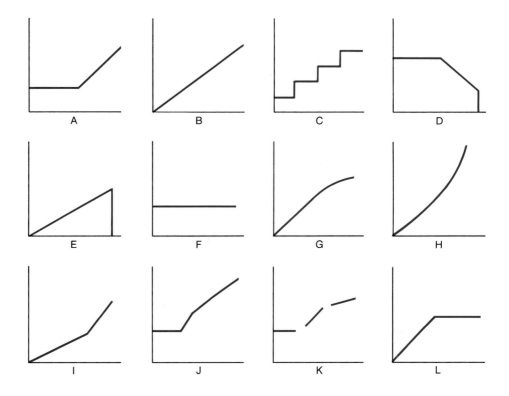

Required:

Indicate the graph that best describes the cost-volume relationship in the following situations (a graph may be used more than once). *(Hint:* The emphasis is placed on *unit* cost, not *total* cost.)

a. Depreciation is calculated on a units-of-production basis.
b. For a fixed fee, a service maintenance company provides a specific number of hours of repair work. When more hours of repair work are needed, Butcher has agreed to pay a stated fee per hour.
c. One component of each finished unit requires two hours of direct labor costing $10 per hour.
d. Depreciation is calculated on a straight-line basis.
e. Salaries of inspection personnel: each earning $1,000 per period, and the span of control is 100 units per inspector.
f. Discounts are not available on material purchased unless the company purchases 1,000 gallons or more per period; increasing discounts are available for each additional 500 gallons purchased.
g. Butcher has a limited number of Department B workers so that when production exceeds a specified number of units per period, these laborers must work in excess of 40 hours per week and be paid time and one half.
h. In its effort to stimulate employment in the region, the Chamber of Commerce has leased the building to Butcher Company under the following conditions: a $12,000 minimum rent covering production up to 2,000 labor-hours; if production exceeds that level per period, there is no rent charge.
i. The present supplier of disposable molds has limited capacity such that when production capacity exceeds a specified number of units, a more expensive mold supplier must be used.
j. Butcher has agreed to pay a certain fee for each plastic container used for each finished product. After a specified number of products are manufactured each period,

there will be no charge for any container used since the supplier believes that advertising for the containers will be sufficient to warrant this arrangement.

k. Containers in which the product is packaged can be purchased according to the following price schedule:

Packages	Per Unit Cost
1–100	$3.00
101–200	2.75
201–300	2.50
301–400	2.25
401–500	2.50
501–600	2.75
601–700	3.00

P3–16 Least Squares, Coefficients of Correlation and Determination (L.O. 3)

During your examination of the financial statements of Arizona Company, you wish to analyze selected aspects of the company's operations. For the first four months of 19X1, machine hours and maintenance costs that are representative for the year were as follows:

Month	Machine-Hours	Total Maintenance Costs
January	3,000	$ 6,580
February	3,500	7,610
March	4,000	8,590
April	4,500	7,820
	15,000	$30,600

Required:

a. Use the least squares method to determine the fixed and variable cost elements.
b. Determine the coefficient of correlation (r) and the coefficient of determination (r^2).
c. Interpret this relationship.
d. Explain your next step in view of this interpretation.

P3–17 Cost-Volume Relationships Illustrated in Graphs: Total Cost (L.O. 2)

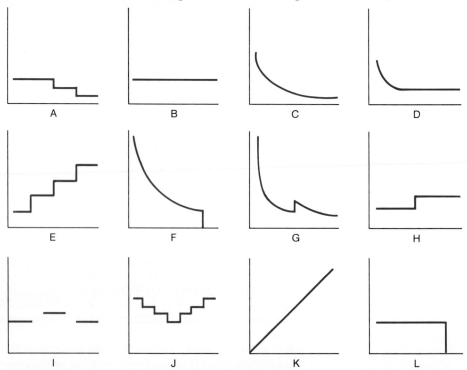

In the graphs shown, assume that *total* costs for the Greer Company are measured on the vertical axis while the horizontal axis measures the volume or activity level.

Required:

Indicate the graph that best describes the cost-volume relationship in the following situations (a graph may be used more than once): *(Hint:* The emphasis is placed on *total* cost, not *unit* cost.)

a. The purchasing department is unable to obtain a discount on the direct material used until production increases to the point where they can buy in large quantities.

b. Depreciation on the building is calculated using a straight-line method.

c. The company has an agreement with an outside repair organization. They have agreed to provide a certain number of hours of repair work for a fixed fee. Greer has agreed to pay a fee per hour of repair work when more hours are required.

d. Depreciation on the factory equipment is calculated on a machine-hours basis.

e. The salaries of manufacturing supervisors when the span of control of each supervisor is overseeing the production of 1,000 units.

f. The company has agreed to pay a certain fee for each mold used in making Product A. After they manufacture and sell a specified quantity of Product A, the company will not be required to pay the fee at that volume and any past fees paid will be refunded. The supplier paying for the use of the mold believes that if enough Product A is introduced into the market, it will stimulate other customers.

g. A supplier of a direct material item has agreed to furnish the material at $1.10 per pound. However, since this supplier has limited capacity, another supplier, whose price is $1.50 per pound, must be used when demand exceeds the first supplier's ability to furnish materials.

h. The electricity bill is determined as follows:

0–500 kilowatt-hours	$1.00 per kilowatt-hour used
501–600 kilowatt-hours	1.15 per kilowatt-hour used
601–700 kilowatt-hours	1.30 per kilowatt-hour used
701–800 kilowatt-hours	1.45 per kilowatt-hour used
And so forth	

i. The Chamber of Commerce in its effort to attract industry furnished the organization with a building on which there is a rent of $500,000 less $1 for each direct labor-hour worked in excess of 100,000 hours. The agreement also specifies that after the organization works 300,000 hours, there will be no rent.

j. The lease agreement on the equipment is as follows:

Minimum $600 per month (this covers up to 500 machine-hours)	
Next 200 machine-hours	$3 per hour
Next 200 machine-hours	2 per hour
Above 900 machine-hours	1 per hour

k. An agreement with an advertising agency specifies that $0.15 per unit sold will be charged with a maximum payment of $10,000 for their work in developing an advertising campaign.

l. The cost of material and direct labor used in production.

P3–18 High-Low Method, Least Squares, and Coefficient of Correlation (L.O. 3)

In manufacturing high-precision medical instruments, Dunn Company employs extensive technology as well as elaborate inspection tests. Each instrument requires five hours of machine time. Production volume is not steady because orders are received in irregular patterns. As a result, several inspectors must be available at all times, while others are transferred over as needed. The cost accounting department has prepared the following data for the first six months for use in analyzing inspection costs:

	Machine-Hours (000)	Inspection Cost (000)
January	200	$500
February	250	618
March	300	670
April	360	840
May	315	790
June	225	560

Required:

a. Use the high-low approach to determine the fixed and variable cost elements included in the inspection cost.

b. Use the least squares method to determine the fixed and variable cost elements.

c. Determine the coefficient of correlation (r) and the coefficient of determination (r^2).

P3–19 Cost Behavior and Cost Estimating Function (L.O. 2)

Sloan Company provided a summary of the total budgeted factory overhead at four different volumes of operation:

	Machine-Hours			
	1,000	1,500	2,000	2,500
Indirect material	$ 3,600	$ 5,400	$ 7,200	$ 9,000
Depreciation	1,300	1,300	1,300	1,300
Utilities	3,100	3,400	3,700	4,000
Inspection	3,000	4,050	5,100	6,150
Budgeted factory overhead	$11,000	$14,150	$17,300	$20,450

At the end of the year, you determine that the following factory overhead was incurred for production at 1,800 machine-hours:

	Actual Costs
Indirect material	$ 7,050
Depreciation	1,250
Utilities	4,100
Inspection	4,450
	$16,850

Required:

a. Indicate the cost behavior for each of the four overhead costs budgeted (i.e., whether fixed, variable, or semivariable).

b. Determine the cost estimating function for each of the four factory overhead costs using the high-low method.

c. Determine the variance for each of the four costs using the cost estimating function. Indicate if favorable (F) or unfavorable (U).

P3–20 High-Low and Least Squares Methods (L.O. 3)

Ewing Company provides the following overhead costs for the past year:

Month	Volume of Production (Direct Labor-Hours)	Overhead Costs
January	13,875	$24,052
February	12,075	23,925
March	10,417	22,387
April	8,085	20,625
May	7,500	19,500
June	9,525	21,450
July	10,425	21,975
August	11,250	22,425
September	12,825	23,250
October	14,250	24,750
November	16,125	25,875
December	16,500	26,250

Required:

a. Compute the budget formula for the fixed and variable amounts using the high-low method of determining the fixed and variable costs.
b. Prepare monthly budgets of fixed and variable overhead for the first quarter using the following capacity volumes:

	Estimated Direct Labor-Hours
January	14,775
February	12,667
March	11,025

c. Use the least squares method to determine the fixed and variable cost elements.
d. Account for any difference between the answers determined in requirement *a* and those determined in requirement *c*.

P3–21 Regression Analysis Theory (CMA) (L.O. 3)

The controller of the Connecticut Electronics Company believes that identification of the variable and fixed components of the firm's costs will enable the firm to make better planning and control decisions. Among the costs the controller is concerned about is the behavior of indirect supplies expense. He believes there is some correlation between the machine-hours worked and the amount of indirect supplies used.

A member of the controller's staff has suggested that a simple linear regression model be used to determine the cost behavior of the indirect supplies. The regression equation shown below was developed from 40 pairs of observations using the least squares method of regression. The regression equation and related measures are as follows:

$$S = \$200 + \$4H$$

where

S = Total monthly costs of indirect supplies
H = Machine-hours per month

Standard error of estimate: $S_e = 100$
Coefficient of correlation: $r = .87$

Required:

a. When a simple linear regression model is used to make inferences about a population relationship from sample data, what assumptions must be made before the inferences can be accepted as valid?
b. Assume the assumptions identified in Requirement *a* are satisfied for the indirect supplies expense of Connecticut Electronics Company.
   (1) Explain the meaning of "200" and "4" in the regression equation $S = \$200 + \$4H$.
   (2) Calculate the estimated cost of indirect supplies if 900 machine-hours are to be used during a month.
c. Explain briefly what the
   (1) Coefficient of correlation measures.
   (2) Value of the coefficient of correlation ($r = .87$) indicates in this case if Connecticut Electronics Company wishes to predict the total cost of indirect supplies on the basis of estimated machine-hours.

P3–22 Concepts and Considerations in Using Regression (CIA) (L.O. 2 and 3)

A Canadian bank has many branch offices. To help prepare budgets for its branch offices, the bank hired the services of a consulting firm. The consulting firm studied the past behavior of different types of costs at several of the branches and, using regression analysis, developed mathematical models to predict costs at the branch offices. One of the regression models developed was:

$$CPC = 200 + 5H + 0.01P$$

where

CPC = Check processing cost per month
   H = Labor-hours per month in the check processing department
   P = Number of checks processed per month

The consulting company reported that the coefficient of determination (R^2) of the regression equation was 0.96. The standard error of the regression was reported to be $50. In the report, they explained that a standard error of $50 implied that, with the probability of 0.95, the actual check processing cost would lie within ± $98 of that estimated by the model. The report also included the following information gathered about the 35 branch banks from which the data was gathered to develop the model:

	Labor-Hours per Month	Number of Checks Processed per Month
Minimum value	120	50,000
Maximum value	600	300,000

Required:

a. Interpret the terms $5H$ and $0.01P$ in the regression model.
b. During a particular month, one of the branch offices used 250 labor-hours to process 120,000 checks and incurred a check processing cost of $2,870. Explain clearly how the regression model can be used to determine whether the operations of the check processing department at this branch office should be examined in more detail. (*Please note.* You are not asked to evaluate this branch's operations but only to explain how the regression model and associated analysis could be used in determining the need for further examination.)
c. The bank is planning to open a new branch office. Management estimates that the labor-hours per month will average 1,200 and that the checks processed per month will average 650,000. Management plans to use the model above for estimating the check processing cost at this new branch. Identify relevant considerations in using the model developed for the 35 branch banks to estimate the costs for the new branch.

Appendix Problems

P3–23 Learning Curve Application (L.O. 5)

Shell, Inc., manufactures complex units for submarines. Fabricating these units requires a high degree of technical skill. However, employees have an opportunity to learn how to produce the units more effectively. In estimating direct labor-hours, a 70 percent learning curve can be used. Completing one prototype unit required 1,200 direct labor-hours at a cost of $18,000.

Required:

a. Determine the cumulative average worker-hours per unit for a total of two units, four units, and eight units.
b. Estimate the direct labor cost for an order of seven additional units, after completing one unit.

P3–24 Estimating Learning Curves (L.O. 5)

The Paul Jensen Company found it takes 600 hours to produce the first unit of a complex motor for a computer system at a labor cost of $7,200. Since much reference was made to the blueprint in making the first unit, management believes there is great opportunity to learn. In estimating direct labor-hours, an 80 percent learning curve can be used.

Required:

a. Determine the cumulative average work-hours per unit for a total of 2 units, 4 units, 8 units, 16 units, 32 units, and 64 units. (Carry hours to two decimal places.)

b. Estimate the direct labor cost of an order for 63 additional units, after completing one unit.

c. Assuming an order for a total of 64 units was received, record the journal entry showing at what unit labor cost the second unit would be entered into finished goods inventory and what would be the deferred learning curve cost.

d. Assuming the firm had erroneously used an 80 percent learning curve when in fact the labor cost followed a 70 percent learning curve, by how much would the:
(1) budget over- or understate the hours? (Carry hours to two decimal places.)
(2) order cost for the 63 units been over/under actual?

P3–25 Using Learning Curves in Standard Setting (L.O. 5)

Based on experience in similar production processes, James Hood, Inc., believes that learning curves can be used in setting the standard for production of a new product called LTT. This new product requires an extensive amount of labor in relation to materials.

Analysis of the first two lots of four units each of LTT is as follows:

4,800 total direct labor-hours for first lot of four units.
2,880 additional direct labor-hours for second lot of four units.

Management believes that the "bugs" and fumbling that occurred in the first two lots will soon be corrected so that there will be no significant improvement in production time after the first 16 units of LTT. Thus, the standard for direct labor-hours will be established based on the average hours per unit for Units 9–16.

Company policy requires that all bids submitted include a markup of 20 percent on total variable manufacturing cost. The direct labor workers employed on LTT production earn $18 per direct labor-hour; variable manufacturing overhead is assigned to products at 125 percent of direct labor costs. Each unit of LTT requires 20 square feet of direct material at a cost of $60 per square foot.

Required:

a. Calculate the learning rate that is applicable to LTT production based on the data for the first eight units.

b. Determine the standard for direct labor-hours that is appropriate for each unit of LTT.

c. Assume that after the first 16 units were manufactured, the company was asked to submit a bid for an additional 30 units. Using appropriate calculations, explain what price the company should bid on this order of 30 units.

P3–26 Learning Rate and Deferred Costs (L.O. 5)

On the first unit produced by A. Arsenault, Inc., workers consulted a blueprint for almost all parts installed; the work required 2,500 direct labor-hours. On the second unit, workers were more familiar with the blueprint for the missile and could go rapidly to the part of the blueprint to review when installing the parts; this required an additional 1,700 direct labor-hours. This pattern is expected to continue until workers make 16 units, at which time they will remember how to install the parts without reference to the blueprint so that further learning is negligible. Workers are paid $10 an hour.

Required:

a. Calculate the learning rate for the company based on the data for the first 16 units.

b. Determine the average labor cost based on the learning pattern expected and the expected labor cost for Units 3–16. Round to whole dollars.

c. Show in a schedule the pattern of learning curve cost with adjustments to the deferred learning curve cost account and the resulting balance in this account. Round to whole dollars.

d. Prepare the journal entry to transfer the labor cost for the 2nd unit and the 16th unit from work in process to finished goods.

e. Assume that even though the initial contract was for a total of 16 units, after the first 8 units were delivered (including the prototype), the contract was canceled. If the eight units had been valued at the expected average cost for all units in the contract, what is the amount that must be written off at the time the contract is canceled?

P3–27 Implications of Learning Curve Effect (CMA adapted) (L.O. 5)

Catonic, Inc., recently developed a new product that includes a rather complex printed circuit board as a component (Catonic's part number PCB-31). Although Catonic has the ability to manufacture the PCB-31 internally, the circuit board is purchased from an independent supplier because the company's printed circuit line has been operating at capacity for some time.

The first contract for 50 units of the PCB-31 was awarded to Rex Engineering Company in September 19X1 on the basis of a competitive bid. Rex was significantly lower than other bidders. Additional orders for 50 units each were placed with Rex as shown in the purchase history schedule below. Rex has proved to be a reliable supplier of other component parts over a period of several years.

Date Ordered	Quantity	Unit Price	Total Price
September 15, 19X1	50	$374	$18,700
November 15, 19X1	50	374	18,700
January 1, 19X2	50	374	18,700
February 1, 19X2	50	374	18,700

Mark Polmik, a buyer for Catonic, has determined that the next order for PCB-31 should be for 600 units. He has contacted Kathy Wentz, a Rex salesperson. Polmik indicated that the next PCB-31 order would be for 600 units and that he believed that Catonic should receive a lower unit price because of the increased quantity. Wentz provided a proposal of $355 per unit for the 600-unit contract a few days later. Polmik has scheduled a meeting with Wentz for next week for the purpose of negotiating the 600-unit contract. He has asked Catonic's cost accounting department for assistance in evaluating the $355 unit price for the PCB-31 circuit board.

The price bid on the original contract for 50 units was estimated to be a "full cost"-based price since, at that time, Catonic was not sure if there would be future contracts for the PCB-31 board. The cost of materials included in the PCB-31 is estimated to be $180 per unit. Cost accounting is fairly sure that Rex applies overhead at 100 percent of direct labor and employee benefit cost. Because Rex Engineering recently received a good deal of coverage by the local media when a strike was narrowly averted, the labor and fringe benefit costs at Rex are known to be approximately $20 per hour. The printed circuit line at Rex is very similar to the one at Catonic, and Rex's overhead is believed to be approximately 50 percent variable and 50 percent fixed. Similar work at Catonic evidences a 90 percent learning curve effect.

Using the foregoing data, the price of a 50-unit order is estimated to comprise the following cost components:

Materials	$ 180
Labor and employee benefits	
(4 labor hours × $20)	80
Overhead (100% of labor and employee benefits)	80
Full cost of PCB-31 component	340
Profit contribution (10% of full cost)	34
Unit price	$ 374
Units purchased	×50
Total contract price	$18,700

Required:

a. Prepare a schedule that may be used by Mark Polmik during his meeting with Kathy Wentz next week. This schedule should incorporate the learning curve effect that Rex would have experienced on the first 200 units produced and should be of use to Polmik in negotiating a contract with Rex Engineering.

b. The learning curve (also known as a progress function or an experience curve) was first formally recognized in the 1920s. Since that time the learning effect has been observed in a number of different industries.

   (1) What are the implications of an 80 percent learning curve as opposed to a 90 percent learning curve?

   (2) Identify factors that would tend to reduce the degree of learning that takes place in an industrial operation.

Activity-Based Costing and Volume-Based Cost Assignments

CHAPTER OBJECTIVES

After studying this chapter, you should be able to:

1. Understand the concepts of traceability that distinguish direct costs from indirect costs.

2. Allocate service department overhead to producing departments to determine overhead application rates.

3. Prepare overhead variances for a normal costing system, recognizing they represent over- or underapplied overhead.

4. Assign costs using activity-based costing with volume- and nonvolume-related cost drivers.

5. Apply materials acquisition and handling costs.

PRACTICAL
APPLICATION BOX

Activity-Based Costing at Cal Electronics Circuits, Inc.

Cal Electronics Circuits, Inc., manufactures printed circuit boards; these mechanical devices are used in many electronics fields. Located in southern California, Cal's manufacturing process is partially automated and capital-intensive. Its manufacturing costs are comprised of 13 percent materials, 8 percent direct labor, and 79 percent overhead. Because direct labor was such a small percentage of total cost, there was no convincing argument for continuing to allocate overhead on the basis of direct labor. Managers discontinued labor vouchering and included direct labor in overhead. In converting to an ABC system, the company first identified the manufacturing processes through which products flow. Their next step was listing potential cost drivers, and then correlating the processes and potential drivers. Managers agreed that cost drivers should be meaningful parameters of operating controls; measurable in reasonable, quantitative terms; and convenient bases of calculating overhead allocations for product costing purposes. Management feels confident that ABC yields improved product costing.

From: John Y. Lee, "Activity-Based Costing at Cal Electronic Circuits," *Management Accounting*, October 1990, pp. 36–38.

Introduction

There is no one "true cost" of a good or service unless a company manufactures only one product or provides one service. In that case, this one good or service receives all costs. Otherwise, accountants must allocate costs incurred for all products or services among the products and services. Methods of allocating costs from departments and activities to products are known as **cost allocations, cost assignments, cost distributions,** or **cost apportionments.** For example, in manufacturing, accountants must allocate the cost of service departments such as factory office, maintenance, and materials storeroom to production departments. Production departments then apply total factory overhead costs to units they manufacture. Similarly, for cost reimbursement purposes, hospitals allocate personnel and equipment costs to patient care centers, while colleges and universities allocate administrative costs to graduate and undergraduate programs to determine a cost per enrolled student.

The overhead allocation system should motivate employees to work in harmony with the company's long-term goals. Precision is sometimes lacking in cost allocations. It is difficult to find a completely valid cause-and-effect relationship between the allocation base and overhead costs incurred. Currently, the traditional methods of allocating overhead on a volume-related basis are in question. Activity-based costing (ABC) is an attempt to improve the accuracy of product costs. This allows accountants to recognize that some costs are more appropriately assigned on nonvolume bases.

Plant Capacity Concepts (L.O. 1)

Chapter 2 illustrated overhead application rates calculated on various volume-related or unit-related bases. However, we postponed the question of which capacity to use in estimating factory overhead rates until this chapter. We budget costs in relation to one specific sales or production volume used for estimating the predetermined factory overhead application rate. Because of the impact of volume changes on fixed and variable costs, the capacity level chosen affects the factory overhead costs applied to the product. In determining factory overhead application rates, accountants distinguish between idle capacity and excess capacity. **Idle capacity** is the temporary nonuse of facilities resulting from a decrease in demand for the company's products or services. **Excess capacity** refers to facilities that are simply not necessary.

The capacity selected depends on whether management uses a short-range or long-range viewpoint and how much allowance management wants to make for possible volume interruptions. Also, experience with the respective industry or company within the industry provides information in selecting the activity level. Next, we discuss these four capacity approaches: theoretical, practical, normal, and expected actual capacity.

Theoretical Capacity. Theoretical capacity (also called the **maximum** or **ideal capacity**) assumes all personnel and equipment operate at peak efficiency using 100 percent of plant capacity. Theoretical capacity is unrealistic; it fails to include normal interruptions for machine breakdowns or maintenance. Thus, accountants usually do not consider theoretical capacity a feasible basis for determining cost allocation rates. However, managers use theoretical capacity to help measure efficiency of operations by providing ideal figures for comparison.

Practical Capacity. Practical capacity does not consider idle time due to inadequate sales demand. This production volume is achieved when demand for the company's products causes the plant to operate continuously. Practical capacity represents the maximum output at which departments or divisions can operate efficiently; thus unused capacity costs are not assigned to products. While this level varies from company to company, managers usually consider practical capacity approximately 80 to 90 percent of theoretical capacity. Practical capacity is more realistic than theoretical capacity. It allows for unavoidable delays due to holidays, vacations, time off for weekends, and machine breakdowns.

Normal Capacity. Normal capacity includes consideration of both idle time due to limited sales orders and human and equipment inefficiencies. It represents an average sales demand expected to exist over a long enough period that includes seasonal and cyclical fluctuations. Managers should review sales figures for a sufficient number of years to observe cyclical changes. Because normal capacity evens out the cyclical changes, it is a more appropriate basis for applying overhead under most circumstances.

Expected Actual Capacity. Expected actual capacity is the production volume necessary to meet sales demand for the next year. This short-range concept does not attempt to even out the cyclical changes in sales demand. If product costs strongly influence the pricing policies or if a company uses cost-plus contracts extensively as in government contracting, there is a danger to using the expected actual activity level in a seasonal or cyclical business. Fixed unit costs would decrease in peak production periods when using the expected actual activity level as the basis for applying factory overhead. Under these conditions, the sales price for these units would be lower in a cost-plus contract than when manufacturing the units in a slack period.

Comparison of Capacity Levels

After a company decides on a specific capacity level, it estimates its variable and fixed costs for the period. For simplicity, Chapter 2 did not divide the overhead application rate into its fixed and variable components as is necessary. Exhibit 4–1 presents several activity levels to illustrate the effect of the capacity level adopted on the estimated fixed factory overhead rate. One level, called the **denominator capacity,** is chosen for recording purposes. Exhibit 4–1 uses a volume-related basis (machine-hours), but the effect on fixed unit cost would be the same if we used a nonvolume-related basis, such as number of setup hours or other transactions. (Later in this chapter, you will learn more about volume- and nonvolume-related bases.)

Effect on Unit Fixed Costs. In Exhibit 4–1, total fixed costs remain at $87,750 within the relevant range of the various capacity volumes listed. When using higher capacity levels, the fixed factory overhead rate is lower than when using the normal or expected actual capacity. This results because we spread fixed overhead over a greater number of machine-hours. For example, if we use 3,600 machine hours, the fixed factory overhead rate is $24.38 per machine-hour ($87,750/3,600 hours). If we use 6,000 machine-hours, the rate is $14.63 per machine-hour ($87,750/6,000 hours). The variable factory overhead rate remains a constant $16.50 per machine-hour at all capacity levels. Although Exhibit 4–1 illustrates overhead rates for different activity levels, we must select one activity level to use for product costing.

EXHIBIT 4–1   Capacity Level Effect on Estimated Fixed Factory Overhead

	Capacity			
	Theoretical	**Practical**	**Normal**	**Expected Actual**
Capacity level	100%	85%	75%	60%
Machine-hours	6,000	5,100	4,500	3,600
Estimated factory overhead:				
Variable overhead				
@ $16.50 per machine-hour .	$ 99,000	$ 84,150	$ 74,250	$ 59,400
Fixed overhead	87,750	87,750	87,750	87,750
Total overhead	$186,750	$171,900	$162,000	$147,150
Factory overhead rate				
per machine-hour:				
Variable overhead	$16.50	$16.50	$16.50	$16.50
Fixed overhead	14.63	17.20	19.50	24.38
Total overhead	$31.13	$33.70	$36.00	$40.88

Allocating Service Department Costs to Production (Operating) Departments (L.O. 2)

After choosing to use theoretical, practical, normal, or expected actual capacity, accountants accumulate costs for production and service departments. **Production** or **operating departments,** such as Fabricating, Assembly, and Finishing, directly process materials into finished goods or produce service revenue. **Service departments** provide support to other manufacturing departments and perform no production work. Service departments, such as Materials Handling and Repairs, do not actively engage in manufacturing the company's products. They help other departments' operations and contribute to their efficiency. Companies allocate service department costs to production departments so goods and services produced reflect the total full cost of production. Also, the allocation of service department costs makes user department managers aware of the cost of services they are using.

Service Organizations. While this discussion has centered around manufacturing activities, the production and service department concept is also applicable to nonmanufacturing service organizations, such as hospitals. For instance, the units that provide direct patient care, such as surgery, are a hospital's production departments. Service or ancillary departments are the administrative support departments, such as patient accounting and materials management.

Direct and Indirect Costs

When calculating overhead application rates, accountants must distinguish between direct and indirect costs. This distinction depends on the *attachability* or *traceability* of the cost element. Accountants do not allocate **direct costs** to the costing center because they arise within the department or job and are clearly traced to this cost center. (Chapter 2 contrasts direct materials and direct labor costs to indirect materials and indirect labor costs, respectively.) **Indirect costs** (also called **common costs**) serve two or more costing centers. For example, rent and depreciation specifically used within the Assembly Department and wages paid to that department's workers are direct costs of the Assembly Department and require no allocations. However, rent and depreciation on the overall plant building is an indirect cost of the Assembly Department. Accountants must allocate indirect cost on some basis, such as square footage, before determining the total cost of that department. Electric power and other utilities are also indirect costs if each department is not individually metered. The term *indirect costs* thus refers to cost elements that accountants cannot trace to one costing center.

Because traceability is the key distinction between direct and indirect costs, we must define the object of costing (such as a product line, a department, or unit of inventory) before we can say whether a cost is direct or indirect. For example, the plant superintendent's salary is an indirect cost for all service and production departments because we cannot trace this cost to only one department. However, when the object of costing is the overall company, the plant superintendent's salary is a direct cost of production.

Exhibit 4–2 diagrams the flow of cost from one service department to two producing departments, Assembly and Treating, that manufacture the company's two products. We trace $34,654 direct costs, but allocate $77,600 indirect costs to the Assembly Department. In distributing indirect costs to production and service departments, we allocate utilities on square footage. Of the $43,500 direct and indirect service department cost, we allocate 44 percent, or $19,140, to Assembly and 56 percent, or $24,360, to Treating. These allocations represent another indirect cost. Dividing Assembly's $131,394 total costs by the 10,000 units produced yields approximately $13.14 per unit cost. Adding Treating's direct, indirect, and allocated service department costs and dividing by the 4,300 units produced yields approximately $30 unit cost for inventory valuation and cost of goods sold.

Although no allocations are necessary for direct costs, indirect costs require a basis for allocations. A plant survey provides the information on which to allocate the indirect costs. We use the information in Exhibit 4–3 to allocate indirect costs *and* service department costs to production departments and then to determine overhead rates for production departments.

EXHIBIT 4–2   Allocating Service Department Costs to Production (Operating) Departments

Service Department—Materials Handling $43,500			
Production Department—Assembly 44%		56% **Production Department—Treating**	
Direct costs	$ 34,654	Direct costs	$ 25,846
Indirect costs	77,600	Indirect costs	78,900
Allocated service department costs. .	19,140 ◄ ──►	Allocated service department costs. .	24,360
Total costs	$131,394	Total costs	$129,106
Divided by units produced	10,000	Units produced.	4,300
Unit cost	$13.14	Unit cost	$30

EXHIBIT 4–3   Heagy Company Plant Survey

	KWHR	Employees	Estimated Cost of Materials Requested	Estimated Labor-Hours of Repair Service Used	Square Footage	Direct Labor	Machine-Hours
Materials Handling	65,550	5			15,140		
Repairs and Maintenance .	70,730	3	$ 30,000		9,460		
Building and Grounds	73,620	2	25,500	5,000			
Production department:							
Assembly	427,300	10	33,000	1,100	40,000	$157,500	2,140
Treating	362,800	15	42,000	2,300	30,000	22,500	4,500
	1,000,000	35	$130,500	8,400	94,600	$180,000	6,640

Cost Allocation Basis. The basis used to allocate indirect costs must bear a relationship to the kind of services a department gives. For example, the number of purchase orders processed or costs of materials used by each department is an appropriate base for allocating purchasing department costs. An appropriate allocation base for a personnel department is the number of employees or labor-hours in each department. Similarly, the number of requisitions is appropriate for allocating materials handling costs. Service hours rendered is a typical allocation base for repairs and maintenance costs. We often allocate building occupancy costs on occupied floor space, although this allocation base is somewhat controversial. Using plant square footage presents some conflict because this assumes all space is equally desirable, regardless of the number of windows or location of space.

Cost accountants recognize they sometimes must resort to a somewhat arbitrary basis because there is no clear cause-and-effect relationship between the basis and the cost. However, there is a danger in relying on a basis such as sales dollars, gross margin, or some other ability-to-bear basis. In such cases, an inaccurate cost allocation will likely result. Instead, the cost accountant determines the basis that most accurately reflects services or benefits received. Accountants may use this data later for allocating service department costs to the other service departments and/or production departments.

Allocating Indirect Costs to Service and Producing Departments. Exhibits 4–4 and 4–5 indicate the bases for allocating indirect costs. The plant survey data in Exhibit 4–3 supplies the bases. For example, we allocate the indirect cost of electricity to both service and producing departments based on the kilowatt-hours (KWHR) used within each department. The Materials Handling Department receives

$$\frac{65,550 \text{ KWHR}}{1,000,000 \text{ total KWHR}} \times \$134,800 \text{ electricity cost} = \$8,840 \text{ (rounded)}$$

Likewise, the Materials Handling Department receives $10,000 superintendence cost:

$$\frac{5 \text{ Materials Handling employees}}{35 \text{ total employees}} \times \$70,000 \text{ total superintendence cost} = \$10,000$$

EXHIBIT 4-4   Direct Method of Allocating Budgeted Service Department Costs

HEAGY COMPANY
Allocation of Service Department Costs to Production Departments—Direct Method
For Year 19X1

	Service Departments			Production Departments		
	Materials Handling	Repairs and Maintenance	Building and Grounds	Assembly	Treating	Total
Direct costs:						
Indirect labor	$ 8,400	$ 6,780	$ 3,810	$ 10,064	$ 1,746	$ 30,800
Depreciation of equipment	16,260	13,935	17,615	24,590	24,100	96,500
Total departmental direct costs .	24,660	20,715	21,425	34,654	25,846	127,300
Indirect costs and allocation base:						
Electricity (KWHR)	8,840	9,535	9,925	57,600	48,900	134,800
Superintendence (no. of employees)	10,000	6,000	4,000	20,000	30,000	70,000
Total departmental indirect costs	18,840	15,535	13,925	77,600	78,900	204,800
Total departmental costs	$43,500	$36,250	$35,350	$112,254	$104,746	$332,100
Allocation of service department costs:						
Materials Handling (estimated cost of materials requisitioned: Assembly, $33,000; Treating, $42,000)	(43,500)			19,140	24,360	
Repairs and Maintenance (estimated labor-hours of service used: Assembly, 1,100; Treating, 2,300)		(36,250)		11,728	24,522	
Building and Grounds (square footage: Assembly, 40,000; Treating, 30,000)				20,200	15,150	
Total overhead			(35,350)	$163,322	$168,778	$332,100
Allocation bases to apply to production:						
Direct labor cost				$157,500		
Machine-hours					4,500	
Total factory overhead rates				104% of direct labor cost	$37.50 per machine-hour	

Note for simplicity that Exhibits 4–4 and 4–5 illustrate few direct and indirect costs.

Allocating Indirect Costs versus Allocating Service Department Costs

Even though service departments, such as Janitorial Service and Materials Store-room, do not directly manufacture products, production departments receive their costs. There are several methods for allocating these costs:

1. *Direct method.* We allocate service department costs to production departments only.

2. *Step, sequential, or step-down method.* We allocate service department costs to other service departments and to production departments that have received their services.

EXHIBIT 4–5   Step Method of Allocating Budgeted Service Department Costs

HEAGY COMPANY
Allocation of Service Department Costs to Production
Departments—Step Method
For Year 19X1

	Service Departments			Production Departments		
	Materials Handling	Repairs and Maintenance	Building and Grounds	Assembly	Treating	Total
Direct costs:						
Indirect labor	$ 8,400	$ 6,780	$ 3,810	$ 10,064	$ 1,746	$ 30,800
Depreciation of equipment	16,260	13,935	17,615	24,590	24,100	96,500
Total departmental direct costs .	24,660	20,715	21,425	34,654	25,846	127,300
Indirect costs and allocation base:						
Electricity (KWHR)	8,840	9,535	9,925	57,600	48,900	134,800
Superintendence (no. of employees)	10,000	6,000	4,000	20,000	30,000	70,000
Total departmental indirect costs	18,840	15,535	13,925	77,600	78,900	204,800
Total departmental costs	$43,500	$36,250	$35,350	$112,254	$104,746	$332,100
Allocation of service department costs:						
Materials Handling (estimated cost of materials requisitioned: Repairs, $30,000; Building, $25,500; Assembly, $33,000; Treating, $42,000)	(43,500)	10,000	8,500	11,001	13,999	
Total Repairs and Maintenance . . .		46,250				
Repairs and Maintenance (estimated labor-hours of service used: Building, 5,000; Assembly, 1,100; Treating, 2,300)		(46,250)	27,530	6,056	12,664	
Total Building and Grounds			71,380			
Building and Grounds (square footage; Assembly, 40,000; Treating, 30,000)			(71,380)	40,789	30,591	
Total overhead				$170,100	$162,000	$332,100
Allocation bases to apply overhead to production:						
Direct labor cost				$157,500		
Machine-hours					4,500	
Total factory overhead rates				108% of direct labor cost	$36.00 per machine-hour	

3. *Linear algebra.* (Also called reciprocal, or matrix method.) The linear algebra method uses simultaneous equations to recognize that service departments render reciprocal services.

Whatever method of service department cost allocation we use, the first step in the procedure is to estimate the overhead costs for the entire plant.

Because producing departments, such as Assembly and Treating, are the only departments that physically work on the product, we assign all factory overhead costs to products through rates developed only for production departments. This means that we must allocate the costs of service departments, such as Repairs and Personnel, to producing departments before establishing a factory overhead application rate for the production departments. However, we allocate to production departments only the portion of service department costs that relate to the production/operating departments. For example, Personnel is a service department that serves both administration and production. We allocate administration's pro rata share of the cost to administrative centers and treat this portion as a period cost. We allocate production's pro rata share of Personnel cost to manufacturing centers and treat it as overhead (product) cost.

Before allocating service department costs to producing departments, however, we must estimate a service department's direct costs as well as its share of indirect costs. Accountants allocate indirect costs, such as superintendent's salary, to both producing and service departments on some logical basis. Allocated service department costs are indirect for the production department.

Note that tracing each department's direct costs and allocating indirect costs to each department are independent of the method of allocating service department costs. (We illustrate the direct, step, and linear algebra methods next.) For example, in Exhibits 4–4, 4–5, and 4–6, each service and production department has the same direct and indirect costs (e.g., Materials Handling has a total cost of $43,500). The exhibits differ, however, in the method of allocating each service department's direct and indirect costs.

Direct Method

Exhibit 4–4 illustrates the direct method in which production departments directly receive service department costs. It shows the allocation of the Materials Handling Department (service department) to Assembly and Treating (production departments). Materials Handling Department costs are $43,500 as shown in the second column in Exhibit 4–4. We allocate the Materials Handling Department costs based on the estimated cost of materials requisitioned, which is $33,000 for the Assembly Department and $42,000 for Treating Department, totaling $75,000, as shown in Exhibit 4–3.

This calculation allocates the Materials Handling Department's $43,500 costs to the Assembly Department:

$$\frac{\$33,000}{\$75,000} \times \$43,500 = \$19,140$$

And this calculation allocates the Materials Handling Department's $43,500 costs to the Treating Department:

$$\frac{\$42,000}{\$75,000} \times \$43,500 = \$24,360$$

We allocate the other service department costs to Assembly and Treating in the same fashion. This method ignores allocating the costs of any Materials Handling services provided to other service departments. Thus, we add only Assembly's $33,000 materials to Treating's $42,000 materials for a total of $75,000 materials requisitions. The direct method is simple because the order of allocating each service department's costs does not matter.

Regardless of the allocation method used (direct, step, or linear algebra), after distributing all service department costs to production departments, we calculate the overhead rates for each production department. Exhibit 4–4 uses direct labor costs as the allocation base for the Assembly Department and machine-hours for the Treating Department. In deciding whether to use different bases for different departments, accountants study the cause-and-effect relationship between the cost and the cost allocation basis. After determining the departmental rate, accountants use the estimated overhead rate to apply overhead to the units produced.

Step Method

When using the step method of service cost allocation, accountants detail the sequence in which to distribute the costs of all service departments to other departments. Generally, the costs of the service department that serves the most other departments should be allocated first, the department servicing the next greatest number should be allocated next, and so forth. The last service department allocated is normally the one serving the fewest other departments. The step method illustrated in Exhibit 4–5 allocates Materials Handling Department costs to all other service and producing departments; Repairs and Maintenance receives $10,000 ($30,000/$130,500 × $43,500) costs. Then we allocate Repairs and Maintenance Department costs, including its share of the Materials Handling cost allocation, to all other departments. We do not allocate any of the $46,250 cost to the Materials Handling Department nor to the Repairs and Maintenance Department because these two departments are closed or are being closed out.

We determine the Building and Grounds' portion of the $46,250 as follows: 5,000/8,400 × $46,250 = $27,530. The distribution base is 5,000 + 1,100 + 2,300 = 8,400 service hours as shown in Exhibit 4–3. Finally, we distribute the Building and Grounds costs, which include the department's share of Materials Handling and Repairs and Maintenance cost allocations.

Normally, the step method is preferable to the direct method because it considers the benefits given by one service department to other service departments. However, the step method fails to recognize that, for example, the Building and Grounds Department may have given some reciprocal service to the Materials Handling and Repairs and Maintenance departments. Since we previously allocated the costs of these departments, we allocate no Building and Grounds costs to these departments. Accountants prefer the linear algebra method because it takes into account these reciprocal services.

Linear Algebra or Reciprocal Method

Exhibit 4–6 illustrates the reciprocal method using linear algebra or simultaneous equations. This method achieves greater exactness than the step method because it recognizes reciprocity between service departments. However, we achieve this greater exactness only if the estimated level of service that departments give to each other is valid. For complex decisions about product pricing, or making or buying products, accountants use the linear algebra method to obtain a more precise allocation of costs.

Computer software packages now make it easy to apply the linear algebra method. However, we introduce this allocation procedure manually even though the figures become detailed. Because Exhibit 4–6 illustrates three service departments, three simultaneous equations are necessary. More simultaneous equations may be required when you have additional service departments. In this case, accountants use matrix algebra to handle the series of equations.

EXHIBIT 4–6 Linear Algebra Method of Allocating Budgeted Service Department Costs

HEAGY COMPANY
Allocation of Service Department Costs to Production Departments—Linear Algebra Method
For Year 19X1

	Service Departments			Production Departments		
	Materials Handling	Repairs and Maintenance	Building and Grounds	Assembly	Treating	Total
Department rendering service:						
Materials Handling	—	23%	20%	25%	32%	100%
Repairs and Maintenance	—	—	60	13	27	100
Building and Grounds	16%	10	—	42	32	100
Departmental costs before allocation of service department costs	$43,500	$36,250	$35,350	$112,254	$104,746	$332,100
Materials Handling Department allocation	(56,468)	12,988	11,293	14,117	18,070	
Repairs and Maintenance Department allocation	—	(57,343)	34,406	7,455	15,482	
Building and Grounds Department allocation	12,968	8,105	(81,049)	34,040	25,936	
Total overhead	-0-	-0-	-0-	$167,866	$164,234	$332,100
Allocation bases to apply overhead to production:						
Direct labor cost				$157,500		
Machine-hours					4,500	
Total overhead rates				107% of direct labor cost	$36.50 per machine-hour	

The three simultaneous equations to solve for the three unknowns are

Let M = Total costs of Materials Handling Department
R = Total costs of Repairs and Maintenance Department
B = Total costs of Building and Grounds Department

(1) $M = \$43,500 + .16B$
(2) $R = \$36,250 + .23M + .10B$
(3) $B = \$35,350 + .20M + .60R$

Substituting in (1)

$M = \$43,500 + .16 (\$35,350 + .20M + .60R)$
$M = \$43,500 + \$5,656 + .032M + .096R$
$.968 M = \$49,156 + .096R$
$M = \$50,780.99 + .0991736R$

Substituting in (2)

$R = \$36,250 + .23(\$50,780.99 + .0991736R) + .10 [\$35,350 + .20 (\$50,780.99 + .0991736R) + .60R]$
$R = \$36,250 + \$11,679.63 + .02281R + .10 (\$35,350 + \$10,156.20 + .019835R + .60R)$
$R = \$36,250 + \$11,679.63 + .02281R + .10 (\$45,506.20 + .619835R)$
$R = \$36,250 + \$11,679.63 + .02281R + \$4,550.62 + .0619835R$
$R = \$52,480.25 + .0847935R$
$.9152065 R = \$52,480.25$
$R = \$57,342.52$ or rounded to $57,343

Substituting in (3)

$B = \$35,350 + .20[\$50,780.99 + .0991736(\$57,342.52)] + .60(\$57,342.52)$
$B = \$35,350 + .20(\$50,780.99 + \$5,686.86) + \$34,405.51$
$B = \$35,350 + .20(\$56,467.85) + \$34,405.51$
$B = \$35,350 + \$11,293.57 + \$34,405.51$
$B = \$81,049$

Substituting in (1)

$M = \$43,500 + .16(\$81,049)$
$M = \$43,500 + \$12,968$
$M = \$56,468$

We base the amount of service department cost assigned on the percentage of usage for each department. For example, Exhibit 4–6 indicates that the Treating Department uses 32 percent of the Materials Handling services. To determine this, we compare the Treating Department's $42,000 estimated materials requested to the $130,500 total, as shown in Exhibit 4–3 ($42,000/$130,500 = 32%). Assembly Department's share is $33,000/$130,500 = 25%. We compute the other departments' shares of Materials Handling in a similar manner. (Note we use some rounding of percents to keep the digits to two places and still equal 100 percent distribution of service department cost.) Likewise, we calculate Building and Grounds' 60 percent usage of Repairs and Maintenance as: 5,000/8,400 labor-hours = 60%. Assembly receives 42 percent of Building and Grounds' total cost because its 40,000 square footage is 42 percent of the 94,600 total square footage.

After inserting these usage percentages in the simultaneous equations, we obtain the estimated total cost for each service department as shown in Exhibit 4–6. After solving all simultaneous equations, we distribute total estimated cost based on the usage percentages. For example, Assembly receives 25% × $56,468 total Materials Handling costs = $14,117, 13% × $57,343 Repairs and Maintenance = $7,455, and 42% × $81,049 Building and Grounds = $34,040. After distributing all service department costs to the producing departments, we divide the total estimated overhead by the allocation base to arrive at the application rate. For example, $167,866 Assembly cost/$157,500 direct labor = 107% rate.

Comparison of Direct, Step, and Linear Algebra Methods. The overhead rates determined in Exhibit 4–4 using the direct method, Exhibit 4–5 using the step method, and Exhibit 4–6 using the linear algebra method vary slightly. For the Assembly Department, the basis is 104 percent of direct labor cost using the direct method, 108 percent using the step method, and 107 percent using the linear algebra method. For the Treating Department, the basis is $37.50 per machine-hour using the direct method, $36.00 using the step method, and $36.50 using the linear algebra method. Even though these results are close, do not conclude that the allocation method chosen makes little difference in other situations. We purposely kept the three exhibits simple, using few departments with small expenses. As stated earlier, the linear algebra method is the preferred method because it considers reciprocal services between departments.

Behavioral Aspects of Allocating Service Department Cost

By knowing service department rates in advance and allocating the cost of one department to others, department heads are more likely to question whether they really need the service before requesting it. When department managers realize they are not charged for services requested, they may request an excessive amount of service because they have little incentive to control costs.

Conversely, allocating service department costs may cause cost center managers to refrain from using needed services. For example, assume department managers realize that they will be charged for asking the systems designers to evaluate and improve their information flows. By avoiding this expense, these managers may retain outdated and inefficient systems. When management wants to encourage producing departments to use specific services, accountants do not allocate these service department costs to users.

Another problem is that sometimes managers of service departments forget what their purpose really is—to provide support. They develop unrealistic charge rates to show a favorable financial picture for their service department. When superiors monitor charge rates of both production and service departments, they can develop fairer rates for services.

Multiple Rates versus a Single Plantwide Rate

The exhibits thus far have calculated departmental overhead rates. The procedure for applying factory overhead is the same whether using a single plantwide rate or multiple departmental rates. A consideration in selecting a plantwide rate or departmental rate is whether all departments use similar operating processes, direct labor, and machines. A single plantwide rate may be appropriate in a small plant with production moving through all departments. However, it is difficult to find such a manufacturing situation in the real world.

Accountants consider multiple overhead rates desirable when plants manufacture various products that do not go through the same departments or use the same technology. Products are subject to different cost drivers, such as worker-hours, machine-hours, throughput, order size, value of materials, or quality requirements, under these manufacturing circumstances.

A factory should be broken down into various production centers to develop different overhead rates on the basis of the level of technology and the types of machines, services, and support each process uses. For example, a high technology company essentially organized by product line can divide its plant into cost pools for various standard and special order products. Based on this division, accountants develop overhead allocation rates that better reflect the cause of the cost incurrence.

Avoid Plantwide Rate. Using a single plantwide rate means using only one activity base. Organizations that use, for example, direct labor as the measure of activity in the overhead application rate assign the same average overhead rate to all direct labor. This often leads to miscosting and mispricing of products. Under this method, we allocate significant portions of overhead costs to the wrong product units just because they use more labor-hours. Also, labor-hours have very little impact on how a technological environment drives overhead costs. A dangerous assumption made in single cost allocations is that a single variable drives costs. This is unlikely for most manufacturing processes.

Exhibit 4–7 uses the departmental cost data from the step method illustrated in Exhibit 4–5, but bases departmental rates on machine-hours for both Assembly and Treating. The plant survey in Exhibit 4–3 gives the machine-hours. If an order receives more services from one department than from another, the use of a plantwide rate results in an inaccurate allocation of costs to the jobs. Order No. 1 in Exhibit 4–7 required eight hours of machine work from the Assembly Department, whose overhead application rate is larger, while it was a light user of the Treating Department machines. Use of the departmental rates results in $708 applied overhead. If, instead, we use the plantwide rate, applied overhead is $500. Use of the departmental rates reflects the difference in time spent in each department. As illustrated in Exhibit 4–7, companies usually need department rates so different jobs bear their share of factory overhead. Otherwise, the application of overhead using a plantwide rate may be incorrect.

EXHIBIT 4–7

HEAGY COMPANY
Departmental Overhead Rates Contrasted to a Single Plantwide Overhead Rate
For Year 19X1

	Departmental Rates		Plantwide Rate
	Assembly	**Treating**	
Budgeted overhead	$170,100	$162,000	$332,100
Machine-hours	2,140	4,500	6,640
Rate per machine-hour	$79.50	$36.00	$50
Overhead application to Order No. 1 using machine-hours:			
Assembly (8 machine-hours @ $79.50)			$636
Treating (2 machine-hours @ $36.00)			72
Total overhead applied using departmental rates . .			$708
Plantwide (10 hours @ $50)			$500

Applied and Actual Factory Overhead

After a company decides whether it is using departmental or plantwide overhead application rates determined by either the direct (Exhibit 4–4), step (Exhibit 4–5), or linear algebra (Exhibit 4–6) method, it applies overhead to units produced. A **normal costing system** applies overhead on actual cost drivers. For example, for every machine-hour used in the Treating Department to finish a product, accountants apply factory overhead costs at $36.00 per machine-hour if using the step method. To have proper matching of actual overhead with applied overhead, we must apply factory overhead to all jobs (both completed and incomplete) worked on during the period. Note we do not enter budgeted factory overhead for a producing department (i.e., $162,000 for the Treating Department using the step method) in the journal or ledger because we use it for determining the application rate. A predetermined overhead rate usually stays the same throughout the year.

Allocating Actual Overhead to Producing Departments

During the time we apply overhead using estimated rates, we debit actual overhead to each service and producing department's Factory Overhead Control account. We also distribute actual indirect cost to each service and producing department on an appropriate basis such as square footage or kilowatt-hours.

After determining each department's actual overhead, accountants allocate service department costs to producing departments using either the direct, step, or linear algebra method. Exhibit 4–8 illustrates the step method of allocating actual factory overhead to producing departments in a manner similar to that used for the estimated overhead in Exhibit 4–5. For example, assume actual cost of materials requisitioned totals $19,200 for Repairs and Maintenance + $25,600 for Buildings and Grounds + $38,400 for Assembly + $44,800 for Treating = $128,000. The Treating Department receives $44,800/$128,000 × $44,000 total Materials Handling Costs = $15,400 Materials Handling allocation. Other actual service department costs are allocated on the basis shown in Exhibit 4–8. After

EXHIBIT 4–8   Step Method of Allocating Actual Service Department Costs

HEAGY COMPANY
Allocation of Actual Service Department Costs—Step Method
For Year 19X1

	Service Departments			Production Departments		
	Materials Handling	**Repairs & Maintenance**	**Buildings & Ground**	**Assembly**	**Treating**	**Total**
Direct costs	$32,000	$24,000	$17,000	$ 28,897	$ 30,103	$132,000
Indirect costs	12,000	12,000	20,000	81,100	77,900	203,000
Total factory overhead costs	$44,000	$36,000	$37,000	$109,997	$108,003	$335,000
Distribution of service department costs: Materials Handling (cost of materials requisitioned: Repairs and Maintenance, $19,200; Building and Grounds, $25,600; Assembly, $38,400; Treating, $44,800)	(44,000)	6,600	8,800	13,200	15,400	
Total Repairs and Maintenance		42,600				
Repairs and Maintenance (actual labor-hours of service used: Building and Grounds, 5,270; Assembly, 1,275; Treating, 1,955)		(42,600)	26,412	6,390	9,798	
Total Building and Grounds			72,212			
Building and Grounds (square footage: Assembly, 40,000; Treating, 30,000)			(72,212)	41,264	30,948	
Total actual overhead				$170,851	$164,149	$335,000

distributing indirect costs and service department costs, the Treating Department's actual overhead totals $164,149.

Assume accountants have journalized and posted the allocations of indirect and service department overhead shown in Exhibit 4–8. Treating Department incurred 4,400 machine-hours during the year. Factory Overhead Control–Treating Department reflects the following totals at year-end:

Factory Overhead Control—Treating Department

Actual direct costs	30,103	Applied ($36 × 4,400 actual machine-hours)	158,400
Actual indirect costs	77,900		
Allocated Materials Handling Department	15,400		
Allocated Repairs and Maintenance Department	9,798		
Allocated Building and Grounds Department	30,948		
Total actual overhead	164,149		

The difference of $5,749 represents an underapplication of overhead. Remember from Chapter 2, a debit balance in the Factory Overhead Control account indicates underapplied overhead and a credit balance indicates overapplied overhead.

Spending and Volume Variances

Two variances—spending and volume—represent the over- or underapplied amount. Exhibit 4–9 contains the computation of the spending and volume variances for the Treating Department. The total of the spending variance and the

EXHIBIT 4–9   Spending and Volume Variances

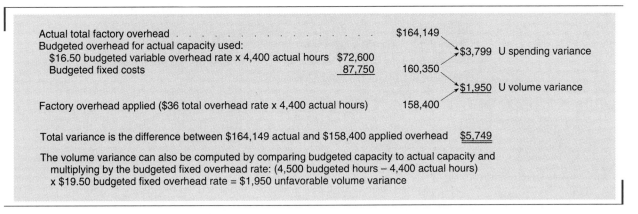

Actual total factory overhead $164,149
Budgeted overhead for actual capacity used:
  $16.50 budgeted variable overhead rate x 4,400 actual hours $72,600
  Budgeted fixed costs   87,750   160,350 $3,799 U spending variance

Factory overhead applied ($36 total overhead rate x 4,400 actual hours)   158,400 $1,950 U volume variance

Total variance is the difference between $164,149 actual and $158,400 applied overhead $5,749

The volume variance can also be computed by comparing budgeted capacity to actual capacity and
  multiplying by the budgeted fixed overhead rate: (4,500 budgeted hours – 4,400 actual hours)
  x $19.50 budgeted fixed overhead rate = $1,950 unfavorable volume variance

volume variance equals the over- or underapplied overhead. We use the **cost estimating formula** introduced in Chapter 3 to determine a budget adjusted to actual capacity.

A **spending variance** (also called a **budget variance**) is due to incurring higher or lower costs on overhead items than originally estimated. Any time actual overhead exceeds budgeted overhead adjusted to actual capacity, the spending variance is unfavorable. Conversely, a favorable spending variance results when the actual overhead is less than the budgeted overhead for the actual capacity attained.

A **volume variance** (also called the *idle capacity variance*) is due to activity or volume factors. If actual production-hours exceed the planned or budgeted hours, the volume variance is favorable. On the other hand, idle capacity hours indicate the company used less volume than planned, and the volume variance is unfavorable. After computing the variances, accountants should determine the cause of any significant variance.

For simplicity, Exhibits 4–4 through 4–6 did not distinguish between variable and fixed overhead. To calculate spending and volume variances, we must compute variable and fixed overhead application rates using the same approach as presented for total overhead. To illustrate the computation of these variances, assume the following for the Treating Department:

Treating Department:
Variable overhead application rate (see Exhibit 4–1) $16.50
Total overhead application rate (see Exhibits 4–1 and 4–5) $36
Budgeted machine hours (see Exhibits 4–1 and 4–5)   4,500
Budgeted total fixed overhead (see Exhibit 4–1) $87,750
Actual machine-hours   4,400
Actual factory overhead (see Exhibit 4–8) $164,149

Spending and volume variances may be set up in ledger accounts as follows:

Total Overhead Spending Variance   3,799
Overhead Volume Variance   1,950
    Factory Overhead Control—Treating Department   5,749

An alternative treatment is to not establish ledger accounts for the variances and still receive the same benefit from the analysis as to their cause. This analysis is the important factor—not whether accountants journalize variances. We close out the Factory Overhead Control account balance which must be done at the end of the accounting period.

Disposition of Over- or Underapplied Overhead

Accountants may have transferred any over- or underapplied overhead amount into spending and volume variances (in a journal entry similar to the preceding one). The variances are then (1) treated as a period cost and charged to Cost of Goods Sold or directly to Income Summary or (2) prorated to Work in Process Inventory, Finished Goods Inventory, and Cost of Goods Sold. Chapter 12 illustrates the proration.

If spending and volume variances recorded in ledger accounts are not material, accountants record the following entry using the data previously illustrated:

Cost of Goods Sold	5,749	
Total Overhead Spending Variance		3,799
Overhead Volume Variance		1,950

If, instead, the variances are not recorded in separate accounts, the entry becomes:

Cost of Goods Sold	5,749	
Factory Overhead Control—Treating Department		5,749

The Factory Overhead Control—Treating Department ledger account is now closed out.

Activity-Based Costing (L.O. 4)

Traditionally, accountants considered volume-related cost drivers as the only factors that caused activities and costs to occur. They used volume-related cost drivers to apply overhead from cost pools to products. **Volume-based** or **unit-based drivers** are allocation measures based on product attributes, such as labor-hours, machine-hours, and materials cost. For example, assume the product generates a demand for machine-hours. In this situation, machine-hours is the cost driver that causes a certain pool of costs to increase. Machine-hours would then be appropriate to use in allocating the costs in that pool.

However, some allocations require nonunit-related bases because volume does not drive all overhead costs. Instead, the complexity and diversity of the manufacturing process is the driver. Accountants should use bases that reflect cost drivers when allocating cost pools to products. **Cost drivers** are the factors that cause activities to occur; they capture the demand placed on an activity by a product.

Volume-Related and Nonvolume-Related Cost Drivers

If some product-related activities are unrelated to the number of units manufactured, using only volume-based (unit-based) allocations distorts product costs. For example, applying overhead on labor-hours incorrectly implies that a reduction in direct labor results in corresponding reductions in receiving, production control, and purchasing. Automating a process or shortening a production run does not reduce the number of purchase orders placed, shipments received, or batches scheduled. Nonunit-level activities, such as setting up the machines, ordering parts, transporting parts to and from the machines, machining the parts, and controlling the part numbers are unrelated to the size of a production run. For example, doubling the size of the batch may not require doubling the number of setups. Thus, a unit-level cost driver, such as direct labor costs or machine-hours illustrated in Exhibits 4–4 to 4–7, fails to capture the complexity of the relationships between volume, batch size, and order size.

Traditionally in labor-paced environments, the error from using only volume-related allocation bases in reported product costs was not significant. We could ignore this problem because the percentage of nonvolume-related costs was much smaller than it is today in high-technology environments. However, in manufacturing processes with high percentages of nonvolume-related costs, cost systems using only volume-related allocation bases produce inaccurate product costs as we see later. Also, the error in reported product costs increases significantly if companies manufacture products in highly varied lot sizes.

Activities/Transactions as Cost Drivers

The assumption that costs vary only with changes in production volume is correct for such unit-related activities as production supplies and parts. However, many costs in plants do not vary with the volume of production but with transactions. Every time we perform an activity, we generate a **transaction**. Every movement of materials from inventory to the shop floor requires a materials requisition (a transaction). Transactions generate overhead costs in such activities as inspection, setup, or scheduling. For example, purchasing department cost is driven by the number of purchase orders processed. The information systems department cost is driven by the amount of bills, parts, and materials to track and handle. The engineering department cost is driven by the number of engineering change orders, and setup cost by the number of setups and hours required. Rather than using the actual duration of the activity such as setup machine-hours, we can use the number of transactions generated by an activity. Additional examples of transaction-based cost drivers include the number of orders processed, the number of shipments processed, and the number of inspections performed. Allocating a nonunit-related cost requires the selection of an allocation base that is itself nonunit-related.

Rather than apply factory overhead costs to products based on departmental overhead rates as illustrated in Exhibits 4–4 through 4–6, **activity-based costing** (ABC) recognizes that performance of activities triggers the consumption of resources that are recorded as costs. **Transaction-based costing** is another name for ABC. The purpose of ABC is to assign costs to the transactions and activities performed in an organization, and then allocate them appropriately to products according to each product's use of the activities.

As defined in Chapter 1, an **activity** is a process or procedure that causes work. Examples are moving parts, performing engineering change orders, setting up machines for a production run, and establishing vendor relations through contacting vendors and setting requirements for purchases. Also included are receiving, disbursing, reorganizing the production flow, redesigning a product, and taking a customer order. ABC traces costs to the activities identified. Then ABC assigns costs of activities to products using both volume- and nonvolume-based drivers.

There are **batch-level activities** and **product-level activities.** An example of a batch-level activity is the manufacture of circuit boards for which customers have specified the number and sizes of holes in the boards. Engineers make specifications for a tooling machine to process the correct number and sizes of holes.

Personnel do not perform this activity for each product unit, but, instead, the setup activity benefits the entire batch. Correcting a defect in product design is an example of a product-level activity. Workers do not perform this engineering change activity on each unit; instead, the activity benefits the entire product line.

ABC recognizes that these different activities cause costs to vary with the diversity and complexity of products. Such costs do not vary with the number of units produced. For example, if total work cell costs add value to the product, we should accumulate these costs at the work cell level. As defined in Chapter 2, a **work cell** is a product-oriented work center that includes the machines and tools necessary to efficiently produce a family of parts. Accountants distribute the costs of the cell to products according to the cell time a product takes within each cell. How fast the inventory moves through the cell is called **inventory velocity.** Accountants use inventory velocity as the basis for assigning overhead to products in this situation. Other cost drivers in ABC systems include: number of setup hours, number of engineering change notices, number of purchase orders, materials-handling hours, number of times handled, ordering hours, number of times ordered, and number of part numbers maintained.

Product Diversity and Volume Diversity

Ignoring batch-level and product-level activities is serious if there is product diversity or volume diversity. **Product diversity** occurs when products consume activities and inputs in different proportions. Thus, there is a difference in the size, complexity, material components, or other characteristics and demands made on a firm's resources by product lines. Complex products may consume more nonunit-level inputs, such as machine setups, but not necessarily more machine-hours or other unit-level inputs than less complex products. **Volume diversity** or **batch-size diversity** occurs when there is a difference in the number of units manufactured by product lines (i.e., companies manufacture products in different-sized batches). Products having materials that take longer to machine may consume a disproportionate share of unit-level inputs; this is called **material diversity.**

Product Diversity Illustrated. ABC does not include materials handling costs as a part of factory overhead and allocate it to producing departments, as illustrated earlier in Exhibits 4–4 through 4–6. Instead, ABC arrives at an application rate per material move or some other transaction basis. The following illustration compares the conventional costing approach with the ABC method. Miscosting results if products are as diverse in their characteristics as are Products A and B:

	Product A	Product B
Units produced	10	10
Material moves per product line	3	7
Direct labor-hours per unit	435	435
Budgeted materials handling costs—$43,500		

Conventional costing yields the following application rate:

$$\frac{\$43,500 \text{ budgeted materials handling costs}}{(435 \times 10 \text{ Product A units}) + (435 \times 10 \text{ Product B units}) = 8,700 \text{ budgeted direct labor-hours}} =$$

$$\frac{\$43,500}{8,700} = \$5 \text{ application rate per direct labor-hour}$$

As shown in the following table, each unit of Products A and B absorbs the same amount of material handling cost even though Product B is a heavier user of this activity. Conventional costing fails to trace the large number of material moves for Product B.

	Product A	Product B
Total material handling cost applied to each product line	$21,750	$21,750
	($5 × 4,350 hrs.)	($5 × 4,350 hrs.)
Materials handling cost per product unit	$2,175	$2,175
	($21,750 ÷ 10 units)	($21,750 ÷ 10 units)

Instead, ABC more accurately traces the cost drivers, as follows:

$$\frac{\$43{,}500 \text{ budgeted materials handling costs}}{10 \text{ budgeted material moves}} = \$4{,}350 \text{ application rate per material move}$$

	Product A	Product B
Total material handling cost applied to each product line	$13,050	$30,450
	($4,350 × 3 moves)	($4,350 × 7 moves)
Materials handling cost per product unit	$1,305	$3,045
	($13,050 ÷ 10 units)	($30,450 ÷ 10 units)

Product B that requires more material moves correctly receives more material handling cost.

Product diversity is also illustrated for Product C and Product D. Product C is a new undeveloped product with production and quality problems requiring many engineering changes. Product D is a more mature product and does not require as much engineering attention, which is a product-level activity.

	Product C	Product D
Units produced	400	400
Engineering change notices per product line . .	10	3
Unit cost per engineering change notice	$500	$500
Machine-hours per unit	2	3

A volume-based allocation yields the following application rate:

$$\frac{13 \text{ total change notices} \times \$500 \text{ unit cost} = \$6{,}500 \text{ budgeted engineering change cost}}{(2 \times 400 \text{ Product C units}) + (3 \times 400 \text{ Product D units}) = 2{,}000 \text{ budgeted machine-hours}} =$$

$$\frac{\$6{,}500}{2{,}000} = \$3.25 \text{ application rate per machine-hour}$$

	Product C	Product D
Total engineering change cost applied to each product line	$2,600	$3,900
	($3.25 × 800 hrs.)	($3.25 × 1,200 hrs.)
Engineering change cost per product unit	$6.50	$9.75
	($2,600 ÷ 400 units)	($3,900 ÷ 400 units)

Conventional costing indicates that Product C has a much lower cost per unit even though it consumes more than three times as much engineering change activity as Product D. A volume-based cost assignment fails to trace the high number of engineering changes for Product C. Because Product D accounts for more of the machine-hours, this product incorrectly absorbs more of the engineering costs. The result is a **cross-subsidy** in which one product absorbs costs that correctly belong to another product. Product C appears to cost less because we averaged indirect costs.

If we use ABC, we trace the following costs according to engineering change notices that drive engineering cost.

	Product C	Product D
Total engineering change cost applied to each product line	$5,000	$1,500
	($500 × 10 eng. changes)	($500 × 3 eng. changes)
Engineering change cost per product unit	$12.50	$3.75
	($5,000 ÷ 400 units)	($1,500 ÷ 400 units)

Volume Diversity Illustrated. The complexity of the product line and the special handling required for special low-volume products cause large amounts of overhead in modern multiproduct factories. Often the high-volume products, such as Product E, are subsidizing the low-volume specialty products, such as Product F.

	Product E	Product F
Units produced	1,000	100
Machine setup hours per product line	5	5
Machine-hours per unit	2	2
Total budgeted machine setup-related cost—$8,800		

The machine setup-related cost is allocated to Products E and F using a traditional costing system with the following application rate:

$$\frac{\$8,800 \text{ budgeted machine setup cost}}{(2 \times 1,000 \text{ Product E units}) + (2 \times 100 \text{ Product F units}) = 2,200 \text{ budgeted machine-hours}} =$$

$$\frac{\$8,800}{2,200} = \$4 \text{ application rate per machine-hour}$$

	Product E	Product F
Total machine setup-related cost applied to each product line	$8,000 ($4 × 2,000 hrs.)	$800 ($4 × 200 hrs.)
Machine setup-related cost per unit	$8 ($8,000 ÷ 1,000 units)	$8 ($800 ÷ 100 units)

As a high-volume product, Product E consumes 10 times the machine-hours and subsequently receives 10 times the machine setup-related cost, even though it requires only five machine setups, as does Product F. Conventional costing overcosts Product E, the high-volume product, and undercosts Product F, the low-volume product. This results because the cost system averages out product costs rather than reflecting volume-based differentials.

Specialty products, such as Product F, appear as high-profit items, even though they often are large losers. When we allocate overhead across all products, inaccurate product costs result, hindering cost reduction and pricing strategies because management receives the wrong signals. For example, marketing managers may believe product proliferation is inexpensive and that low-volume, nonstandard products are no more costly than high-volume, standard products. Further, product engineers may believe that product design component proliferation is free. Engineers may incorrectly assume there is no cost penalty for using a variety of nonstandard parts and that standard and nonstandard parts cost the same.

If, instead, ABC is used, the cost driver is the number of setups:

$$\frac{\$8,800 \text{ budgeted machine setup cost}}{10 \text{ budgeted machine setup-hours}} = \$880 \text{ application rate per machine setup-hour}$$

	Product E	Product F
Total machine setup-related cost applied to each product line	$4,400	$4,400
Machine setup-related cost per unit	$4.40 ($4,400 ÷ 1,000 units)	$44 ($4,400 ÷ 100 units)

Each product line receives $4,400 machine setup-related cost because each line requires the same amount of engineering attention. However, more units of Product E share this total cost. Using ABC, accountants report the increased overhead that specialty products regularly incur rather than distort the cost picture through the traditional averaging effect.

Two-Stage Allocation Process Compared

Both traditional and activity-based costing use a two-stage allocation process. We express the volume for the capacity level selected (i.e., theoretical, practical, normal, or expected actual capacity) in either volume-related (i.e., machine-hours, direct labor costs) or nonvolume-related cost drivers (i.e., setups or work cells). In the first stage, we assign costs to cost centers either through direct charges or some appropriate allocation basis such as floor space for rent. In the second stage of the following traditional volume-based system, we allocate costs to products using machine-hours or other bases that vary directly with the volume of products manufactured. In the second stage of an ABC system, we trace costs from activities to products based on the product's demand for these activities. This simplified example assumes only one production department with 84,000 budgeted machine-hours with these budgeted overhead costs and resulting application rate.

Machine depreciation and maintenance	$ 840,000
Receiving costs	418,600
Engineering costs	360,000
Machine setup costs	37,400
Inspection costs	192,000
	$1,848,000

Assume further that the company manufactures and sells three products with the following attributes:

	Product X	Product Y	Product Z	Total
Units produced and sold	28,000	18,000	6,000	
Unit direct material cost	$20	$15	$13	
Unit direct labor cost	12	14	10	
Machine-hours required per unit	1.5	2	1	84,000
Number per product line:				
Receiving orders	16	40	200	256
Production orders	14	12	19	45
Production runs	4	8	22	34
Inspections	8	4	20	32

Using traditional costing:

$$\frac{\$1,848,000 \text{ budgeted overhead cost}}{84,000 \text{ budgeted machine-hours}} = \$22 \text{ application rate per machine-hour}$$

	Material	Labor	Overhead	
Product X costs:	$20 +	$12 +	(1.5 hr. × $22 = $33) =	$65
Product Y costs:	$15 +	$14 +	(2 hrs. × $22 = $44) =	$73
Product Z costs:	$13 +	$10 +	(1 hr. × $22 = $22) =	$45

If, instead, we use activity-based costing, $840,000 equipment depreciation and maintenance is allocated on machine-hours, a volume-related cost driver, because these costs are volume driven. Costs of the other activities are transaction driven. We assign them on the following nonvolume-related cost drivers. The unit costs for the three products using ABC are

	Product X	Product Y	Product Z
Unit direct material cost	$20.00	$15.00	$ 13.00
Unit direct labor cost	12.00	14.00	10.00
Machine-related overhead[a]	15.00	20.00	10.00
Receiving costs[b]	.93	3.63	54.50
Engineering costs[c]	4.00	5.33	25.33
Machine setup costs[d]	.16	.49	4.03
Inspection costs[e]	1.71	1.33	20.00
Total	$53.80	$59.78	$136.86

[a] $\dfrac{\$840{,}000 \text{ machine depreciation and maintenance}}{84{,}000 \text{ machine-hours}}$ = $10 rate per machine-hour

[b] $\dfrac{\$418{,}600 \text{ receiving cost}}{256 \text{ number of receiving orders}}$ = $1,635 rate per receiving order

Product X: ($1,635 × 16) ÷ 28,000 = $.93
Product Y: ($1,635 × 40) ÷ 18,000 = $3.63
Product Z: ($1,635 × 200) ÷ 6,000 = $54.50

[c] $\dfrac{\$360{,}000 \text{ engineering cost}}{45 \text{ number of production orders}}$ = $8,000 rate per production order

Product X: ($8,000 × 14) ÷ 28,000 = $4.00
Product Y: ($8,000 × 12) ÷ 18,000 = $5.33
Product Z: ($8,000 × 19) ÷ 6,000 = $25.33

[d] $\dfrac{\$37{,}400 \text{ machine setup cost}}{34 \text{ number of production runs}}$ = $1,100 rate per production run

Product X: ($1,100 × 4) ÷ 28,000 = $.16
Product Y: ($1,100 × 8) ÷ 18,000 = $.49
Product Z: ($1,100 × 22) ÷ 6,000 = $4.03

[e] $\dfrac{\$192{,}000 \text{ inspection cost}}{32 \text{ inspections}}$ = $6,000 rate per inspection

Product X: ($6,000 × 8) ÷ 28,000 = $1.71
Product Y: ($6,000 × 4) ÷ 18,000 = $1.33
Product Z: ($6,000 × 20) ÷ 6,000 = $20.00

The following summary shows product costs for X, Y, and Z according to the two methods. It illustrates the distorted product costs that result under conventional costing by overcosting Products X and Y and undercosting Product Z, the low-volume product. This results because Product Z creates more transactions per unit of output than Products X and Y. This further illustrates that conventional costing systems are simplistic because they only consider volume- or unit-based allocations.

	Product X	Product Y	Product Z
Conventional approach	$65.00	$73.00	$ 45.00
Activity-based costing	53.80	59.78	136.86
Difference	$11.20	$13.22	$ 91.86

Activity-Based Management

Activity-based costing yields much information about activities and the resources required to perform these activities. Thus, ABC is much more than a cost assignment process. ABC supplies the information and **activity-based management** (ABM) uses this information in various analyses designed to result in ongoing improvement. ABC helps focus on high-cost activities by identifying resources being consumed by each activity. This helps find the link between the costs and the activities that cause those costs. This process encourages managers to identify and eliminate nonvalue activities. Merely identifying nonvalue activities does not lower costs; managers must reduce excess resources or direct them into more productive areas.

As discussed in Chapter 19, activity-based accounting is not limited to product costing but is used to study and improve marketing activities. ABC contributes to cost reduction in marketing and administrative activities as well as improves product costing. The concepts underlying ABC—that activities consume resources and products require activities—apply as readily in service organizations as they do in manufacturing organizations.

Limitations. As with traditional means of allocating overhead on volume-based cost drivers, an ABC system provides relevant data only if the cost in every activity is strictly proportional to its cost driver. Also, ABC requires much operating data. However, current computer technology and use of bar codes ease this information gathering. Accountants should find the expense of installing an ABC system outweighed by the benefits of having improved product costing data.

ABC for Materials Acquisition and Handling (L.O. 5)

Exhibits 4–4 through 4–6 included materials handling costs in overhead. However, we can use activity-based costing to assign any extra materials handling costs incurred because of the nature of an order. This approach can represent a phased strategy for introducing ABC into the cost accounting system. A strong argument exists for **applying materials acquisition and handling costs** to direct materials cost or increasing the factory overhead application rate on orders requiring extra handling. For instance, if we estimate purchasing department costs at $70,000 and the dollar value of direct materials purchased at $1,000,000 for the next accounting period, the application rate is 7 percent, computed as follows. Alternatively, we can use the number of purchase orders as the cost driver.

$$\frac{\$70,000 \text{ estimated purchasing department cost}}{\$1,000,000 \text{ estimated purchases}} = 7 \text{ percent}$$

Assume estimated receiving department cost is $45,000 and we expect receipt of $900,000 goods. Using these estimates, we develop a 5 percent application rate for applying receiving costs. An alternative cost driver is the estimated items to be received.

$$\frac{\$45,000 \text{ estimated receiving department cost}}{\$900,000 \text{ estimated dollar value received}} = 5 \text{ percent}$$

If we estimate warehousing department costs at $150,000 and the square footage to be 100,000, a $1.50 rate per square foot results. Number of items, dollar value of items warehoused, or warehousing days represent alternative cost drivers.

$$\frac{\$150,000 \text{ estimated warehousing costs}}{100,000 \text{ square feet estimated per period}} = \$1.50 \text{ per square foot}$$

We could use the same approach for freight-in using the following estimate:

$$\frac{\$90,000 \text{ estimated freight-in}}{\$1,000,000 \text{ estimated material purchases}} = 9 \text{ percent}$$

Application of Materials Acquisition and Handling Costs Illustrated

Assume that during the accounting period, we purchased direct materials costing $60,000, received $58,000 of these materials ($2,000 are in transit), and used 3,000 square footage. The following journal entries would then be made to record the application of materials acquisition costs:

Direct Materials Inventory	17,000	
Purchasing Department Expense Control ($60,000 × 7%)		4,200
Receiving Department Expense Control ($58,000 × 5%)		2,900
Materials—Warehousing Department Expense Control		
(3,000 square feet × $1.50)		4,500
Freight-in ($60,000 × 9%)		5,400

We debit actual costs in the applicable expense control account. The applied amount is a credit. For example, if actual Purchasing Department costs total $4,500, there is a $300 underapplied balance in the Purchasing Department Expense Control account, as follows:

Purchasing Department Expense Control		
Actual expenses	4,500	*Applied* expense based on rate per purchase dollar 4,200

We close the balance of the over- or underapplied materials acquisition expenses either to Cost of Goods Sold or directly to the temporary ledger account used for closing revenues and expenses, the Income Summary. Note the similarity between the treatment for applying materials acquisition costs and that for applying factory overhead to units being manufactured. In both cases, actual costs are debits while the applied costs are credits to the ledger account.

Summary

Accountants are questioning conventional costing systems because they hide the true causes of nonvolume-related activities, which in turn hinders cost reduction efforts. The traditional allocation of overhead on a labor-hours basis implies reducing direct labor results in a corresponding decrease in such costs as engineering, receiving, and purchasing. However, automating a production process does not reduce the number of engineering change notices, shipments received, or number of purchase orders placed. Traditional cost systems fail to recognize that nonvolume-related costs vary with such transactions as the number of inspections performed, the number of setups, and the quantity of scheduling. By eliminating distorted cost allocations through ABC, we improve the quality of information. Management can make better profitability assessments. These data also emphasize improvements. Companies with high overhead costs, a diversity of products, and wide variations in the batch size of production runs are most likely to benefit from ABC as described in the chapter.

Important Terms and Concepts

cost allocations, assignments, distributions, and apportionments, 101
idle capacity, 101
excess capacity, 101
theoretical (maximum or ideal) capacity, 101
practical capacity, 101
normal capacity, 102
expected actual capacity, 102
denominator capacity, 102
production (operating) departments, 103
service departments, 103
direct costs, 103
indirect or common costs, 104
direct method of allocation, 108
step (sequential, or step-down) method of allocation, 109

linear algebra (reciprocal) allocation method, 109
normal costing system, 113
cost estimating formula, 115
spending (budget) variance, 115
volume variance, 115
volume-based (unit-based) drivers, 116
cost drivers, 116
transaction, 117
activity-based costing or transaction-based costing, 117
activity, 117
batch-level activities, 117
product-level activities, 117
work cell, 118
inventory velocity, 118
product diversity, 118

Problem for Self-Study 4–1

Comparison of Allocations Using Traditional and ABC Costing Methods

Cappettini Company provides the following information concerning its two product lines:

	Product A	Product B
Units produced	10	20
Machine-hours per unit	3	4
Inspections per product line	5	1
Total budgeted inspection cost—$3,300		

Required:

a. Assume Cappettini Company used activity-based costing; calculate how much inspection cost is allocated to each line. What is the cost per unit for Products A and B?

b. Determine how much inspection cost is allocated to each line if Cappettini Company uses a traditional cost allocation system based on machine-hours. What is the cost per unit for Products A and B?

c. Decide if overhead allocation to Product A and B lines is evidence of product diversity or volume diversity.

Solution to Problem for Self-Study 4–1

Cappettini Company

a.   If ABC is used, the cost driver is the number of inspections:

$$\frac{\$3,300 \text{ budgeted inspection cost}}{6 \text{ budgeted inspections}} = \$550 \text{ application rate per inspection}$$

	Product A	Product B
Total inspection cost applied to each product line .	$2,750	$550
Inspection cost per product unit	$275	$27.50
	($2,750 ÷ 10 units)	($550 ÷ 20 units)

There are more units of Product B to share inspection cost and Product B requires less attention, probably indicating it is a seasoned product.

b.   For a traditional volume-based cost allocation, inspection costs are allocated on machine-hours. Total machine-hours are budgeted as follows: (3 × 10 Product A units) + (4 × 20 Product B units) = 110 machine-hours. This yields the following application rate:

$$\frac{\$3,300 \text{ budgeted inspection cost}}{110 \text{ budgeted machine-hours}} = \$30 \text{ application rate per machine-hour}$$

	Product A	Product B
Total inspection cost applied to each product line .	$900	$2,400
Inspection cost per product unit	$90	$120
	($900 ÷ 10 units)	($2,400 ÷ 20 units)

This gives inaccurate product costs and hinders cost reduction because it gives the wrong signal to management. Conventional costing overcosts Product B, the higher-volume, seasoned product and undercosts Product A, the newer, lower-volume product.

c.   Both product and volume diversity for Products A and B

Problem for Self-Study 4–2

Journal Entries Recording Applied and Actual Material Costs

Bird Company uses the following estimates for applying material acquisition costs:

Annual estimated Purchasing Department costs	$ 55,863,000
Annual estimated Inspection Department costs	$ 31,035,000
Annual estimated Receiving Department costs	$ 1,727,000
Annual estimated direct materials purchases	$620,700,000
Estimated items to be received	550,000

Required:

a. Develop application rates for the material handling costs applying Purchasing and Inspection Department costs on the basis of the dollar value of materials purchased and Receiving Department costs on the basis of items received. Freight on incoming material is available for each invoice.

b. Prepare the journal entries to record the actual cost of a purchase including the application of material acquisition costs if 900 items are bought on account at a cost of $85,250 with freight cost of $1,430.

c. Using the following actual data for the period, which have been recorded, prepare journal entries to close the balances of the material acquisition ledger accounts to Cost of Goods Sold.

Direct materials purchased	
(includes $85,250 purchased in Requirement *b*)	$625,000,000
Purchasing Department cost	$ 56,274,000
Inspection Department cost	$ 31,236,000
Receiving Department cost	$ 1,640,000
Items received	545,500

Solution to Problem for Self-Study 4–2

BIRD COMPANY

a. $\dfrac{\text{Purchasing Department } \$ 55,863,000}{\$620,700,000} = $ 9 percent rate per purchase dollar for Purchasing Department

$\dfrac{\text{Inspection Department } \$ 31,035,000}{\$620,700,000} = $ 5 percent rate per purchase dollar for Inspection Department

$\dfrac{\text{Receiving Department } \$1,727,000}{550,000 \text{ items}} = $ $3.14 per item in Receiving Department

b.
Direct Materials Inventory	85,250.00	
Freight-In	1,430.00	
Accounts Payable		86,680.00
Direct Materials Inventory	14,761.00	
Purchasing Department Expense Control		
(9% × $85,250)		7,672.50
Inspection Department Expense Control		
(5% × $85,250)		4,262.50
Receiving Department Expense Control		
($3.14 × 900)		2,826.00

c.   Receiving Dept. Expense Control
       ($1,712,870* − $1,640,000) 72,870.00

       Inspection Dept. Expense Control ($31,250,000†
       − $31,236,000) 14,000.00
         Purchasing Dept. Exp. Control
         ($56,274,000 − $56,250,000‡) 24,000.00
         Cost of Goods Sold 62,870.00

*Applied Receiving Department cost = $3.14 × 545,500 = $1,712,870
†Applied Inspection Department cost = 5% × $625,000,000 = $31,250,000
‡Applied Purchasing Department cost = 9% × $625,000,000 = $56,250,000

Review Questions

1.   Is there any difference in allocating indirect costs to departments and allocating service department costs to producing departments?

2.   What is the normal criteria for selecting a fair basis of allocating service department costs to operating/production departments? If the criteria or relationship you indicate cannot be identified, how should cost elements be allocated?

3.   What will likely be the result in variances if an unrealistically high capacity level is chosen?

4.   Distinguish between direct and indirect costs. Give examples of each.

5.   Give three methods for allocating service department costs to operating/production departments.

6.   What factors would you consider in determining whether to adopt departmental rates for applying factory overhead costs to products rather than using a single plantwide rate?

7.   In interviewing several manufacturing firms operating in the same industry, you find that Company A's factory overhead application rate is $2 per machine-hour while Company B's rate is $2.50 per machine-hour. Can you conclude that Company A is more efficient? Why or why not?

8.   Assume a company's records are correct and its spending variance is $10,000 favorable while its volume variance is $2,000 unfavorable. What is the amount of over/underapplied factory overhead?

9.   Which factors could cause a company to have both unfavorable spending and volume variances?

10.   If a company uses cost-plus contracts extensively in a business that is seasonal or cyclical, which capacity level would be most appropriate? Why is it necessary to specify the activity level at which managers budget operations?

11.   What is the theoretical justification for applied rates for material acquisition and warehousing costs? Why aren't material acquisition and warehousing costs commonly applied in practice?

12.   Under which conditions would there be a material misstatement of inventory costs if material acquisition and warehousing costs are not allocated?

CPA/CMA/CIA Multiple-Choice Questions

1.   (CIA) An automotive company has three divisions. One division manufactures new replacement parts for automobiles; another rebuilds engines; and the third does repair and overhaul work on a line of trucks. All three divisions use the

services of a central payroll department. The best method of allocating the cost of the payroll department to the various operating divisions is

   a. Total labor-hours incurred in the divisions.
   b. Value of production in the divisions.
   c. Direct labor costs incurred in the divisions.
   d. Machine-hours used in the divisions.

2. (CMA) Woodman Company applies factory overhead on the basis of direct labor-hours. Budget and actual data for direct labor and overhead for 19X3 are as follows:

	Budget	Actual
Direct labor-hours	600,000	550,000
Factory overhead costs	$720,000	$680,000

The factory overhead for Woodman Company in 19X3 is

   a. Overapplied by $20,000.
   b. Overapplied by $40,000.
   c. Underapplied by $20,000.
   d. Underapplied by $40,000.
   e. Neither underapplied nor overapplied.

3. (CIA adapted) A company manufactures plastic products for the home and restaurant market. The company also does contract work for other customers and uses a job order costing system. Budgets covering next year's expected range of activity are

Direct labor-hours	50,000	80,000	110,000
Machine-hours	40,000	64,000	88,000
Variable overhead costs	$100,000	$160,000	$220,000
Fixed overhead costs	150,000	150,000	150,000
Total overhead costs	$250,000	$310,000	$370,000

A predetermined overhead rate based on direct labor-hours is used to apply total overhead. Management has estimated that 100,000 direct labor-hours will be used next year. The predetermined overhead rate per direct labor-hour to be used to apply total overhead to the individual jobs next year is

   a. $3.36.
   b. $3.50.
   c. $3.70.
   d. $3.88.

4.–8. (CMA adapted) These items are based on the following data: Cain Company has an automated production process, and consequently, machine-hours are used to describe production activity. A full absorption costing system is employed by the company.

   The annual profit plan for the coming fiscal year is finalized in April of each year. The profit plan for the fiscal year ending May 31, 19X2, called for 6,000 units to be produced requiring 30,000 machine-hours. The full absorption costing rate for the 19X1–X2 fiscal year was determined using 6,000 units of planned production.

   Cain develops budgets for different levels of activity for use in evaluating performance. A total of 6,200 units were actually produced during the 19X1–19X2 fiscal year requiring 32,000 machine-hours. The schedule presented below compares Cain Company's actual costs for the 19X1–X2 fiscal year with the profit plan and the budgeted costs for two different activity levels.

CAIN COMPANY
Manufacturing Cost Report
For the Fiscal Year Ended May 31, 19X2
(in thousands of dollars)

Item	Profit Plan (6,000 units)	Budgets for 31,000 Machine-Hours	32,000 Machine-Hours	Actual Costs
Direct material:				
G27 aluminum	$ 252.0	$ 260.4	$ 268.8	$ 270.0
M14 steel alloy	78.0	80.6	83.2	83.0
Direct labor:				
Assembler	273.0	282.1	291.2	287.0
Grinder	234.0	241.8	249.6	250.0
Manufacturing overhead:				
Maintenance	24.0	24.8	25.6	25.0
Supplies	129.0	133.3	137.6	130.0
Supervision	80.0	82.0	84.0	81.0
Inspector	144.0	147.0	150.0	147.0
Insurance	50.0	50.0	50.0	50.0
Depreciation	200.0	200.0	200.0	200.0
Total cost	$1,464.0	$1,502.0	$1,540.0	$1,523.0

Use the preceding data in answering items 4 through 8. All answers have been rounded to the second decimal place when necessary.

4. The budgeted number of machine-hours needed to produce one unit of product is

    a. 5.16 machine-hours.
    b. 5.33 machine-hours.
    c. 5.00 machine-hours.
    d. 4.84 machine-hours.
    e. Some amount other than those shown above.

5. The variable manufacturing overhead rate per machine-hour in a cost estimating formula would be

    a. $12.41/machine-hour.
    b. $10.10/machine-hour.
    c. $48.13/machine-hour.
    d. $48.80/machine-hour.
    e. Some amount other than those shown above.

6. Cain Company calculates spending, efficiency, and volume variances when analyzing manufacturing overhead costs. The manufacturing overhead spending variance for 19X1 is

    a. $4,100 favorable.
    b. $14,200 favorable.
    c. $6,000 unfavorable.
    d. $10,100 unfavorable.
    e. Some amount other than those shown above.

7. The manufacturing overhead volume variance for the current year is

    a. $14,900 unfavorable.
    b. $21,600 favorable.
    c. $10,800 favorable.
    d. Zero.
    e. Some amount other than those shown above.

8. Actual production was 6,200 units while the original profit plan was to produce 6,000 units. This change in volume

   a. Increases the variable cost per unit because more machine-hours were required to manufacture the units.
   b. Increases the variable cost per unit because more costs were incurred to manufacture the additional units.
   c. Decreases the variable cost per unit because total variable cost is spread over the greater number of units manufactured.
   d. Has no effect on variable cost per unit because the variable cost per unit is not determined until after actual production has been completed.
   e. Has no effect on variable cost per unit because the variable cost per unit is assumed to be constant.

9. (AICPA) A job order cost system uses a predetermined factory overhead rate based on expected volume and expected fixed cost. At the end of the year, underapplied overhead might be explained by which of the following situations?

	Actual Volume	Actual Fixed Costs
a.	Greater than expected.	Greater than expected.
b.	Greater than expected.	Less than expected.
c.	Less than expected.	Greater than expected.
d.	Less than expected.	Less than expected.

10. and 11.   (CIA) Use the following data for questions 10 and 11. A manufacturing company has the following information for its service departments, S1 and S2, and its production departments, P1 and P2.

	S1	S2	P1	P2
Overhead Cost	$4,000	$7,200	$8,000	$10,000
Service provided by S1	—	30%	30%	40%
Service provided by S2	25%	—	30%	45%

10. Using the direct method of service department cost allocation, how much is to be allocated from S2 to P2? Round calculations to the nearest dollar.

   a. $3,240.
   b. $4,000.
   c. $4,320.
   d. $5,040.

11. Using the reciprocal method of service department allocation, how much is the total overhead cost for P1 for the period? Round calculations to the nearest dollar.

   a. $12,560.
   b. $12,594.
   c. $16,594.
   d. $12,605.

Exercises

E4–1 Motivational Considerations (L.O. 1)

Suggest ways that selection of an allocation base provides an opportunity to formally structure motivational considerations into the organization's control system. (*Hint:* For example, do you see any dangers in allocating a research laboratory's costs to departments within an organization based on usage records kept by the laboratory or repair department expense allocated on maintenance-hours used by each production department?)

E4–2 Comparing Capacity Concepts and Their Application (L.O. 2)

Accountants use various bases, such as direct labor-hours, direct labor dollars, and machine-hours, to apply factory overhead to product costs. They can express each of these bases using four different capacity concepts in a company's budgeting activity.

Required:

a. Define and discuss these four measures of capacity.
b. Describe the differences that can be expected to result when the different capacity concepts are used. Include in your discussion an explanation of the effect of each basis on the differences between actual and applied overhead.

E4–3 Effect of Capacity on Application Rate (L.O. 1)

Northwest Company uses a flexible budgeting system; accountants prepared the following information for 19X1:

	75%	90%
Percent of capacity	75%	90%
Machine-hours	37,500	45,000
Variable factory overhead	$116,250	$139,500
Fixed factory overhead	$165,000	$165,000
Total factory overhead rate per machine-hour	$7.50	$6.77

Factory overhead was applied based on the 90 percent capacity level; however, 37,500 machine-hours were used for the period.

Required:

a. Account for the difference in factory overhead rates between the two capacity levels.
b. Determine the total overhead variance for the year and what kind of variance it is if actual factory overhead was equal to the budgeted amount for the attained capacity.

E4–4 Spending and Volume Variances (L.O. 3)

Appleton, Inc., estimates overhead for the year as follows:

	Unit Cost per Machine-Hour	Total Cost
Variable factory overhead	$7	$560,000
Fixed factory overhead	$5	$400,000

While production for the period reached 90 percent of the budget, actual factory overhead totaled $890,000.

Required:

a. Determine over- or underapplied factory overhead.
b. Calculate spending and volume variances indicating whether favorable or unfavorable.

E4–5 Effect of Volume on Unit Cost (L.O. 1)

Blunt Company's vice president is quite upset regarding the significant increase in per unit cost in the Fabricating Department. The vice president has called a conference that the fabricating supervisor as well as the controller will attend. The vice president believes that this increase is so large that there is justification for firing the supervisor. The cost per unit has increased from $12 budgeted to $13.40 actual. Normal capacity for the company is 30,000 units per period. At this capacity, fixed costs are $240,000 in the Fabricating Department. During the most recent period 25,000 units were manufactured.

Required:

Prepare a report showing the factors causing a change in cost per unit.

E4–6 Volume and Spending Variances (L.O. 3)

A cost accountant estimates that next year's normal capacity for the Dover Company will be 65,000 machine-hours. At this level, she estimates fixed costs at $312,000 with variable costs of $110,500. There were 63,500 actual machine-hours for the year ended May 31, 19X1, and total costs were $435,750.

Required:

a. Give the fixed overhead rate at normal capacity.
b. Determine the total overhead rate used to apply factory overhead during the year.
c. Give the amount of over- or underapplied factory overhead.
d. Compute the volume variance and the spending variance for the year. Are they favorable or unfavorable? Prove your answer.

E4–7 Developing Application Rates using Linear Algebra (Reciprocal) Method (L.O. 2)

Overhead budgets for the production and service departments of Lynn Company are as follows:

Maintenance	$ 75,000
General factory administration	92,000
Tooling	325,000
Processing	380,000
	$872,000

Accountants use the following factory statistics in determining the percentage of service received from each service department. The company uses the number of repair-hours to allocate the Maintenance Department cost, and the number of employees for allocating General Factory Administration.

Departments	Repair Hours	Employees	Machine-Hours
Maintenance	10	6,480	
General factory administration	75	1,000	
Tooling	225	24,840	20,640
Processing	200	22,680	19,965
	510	55,000	40,605

Required:

Determine the overhead application rate per machine-hour using linear algebra method.

E4–8 Application Rates for Material Handling (L.O. 5)

Zeet Manufacturing Company provides you with the following estimates for the coming period:

Estimated freight-in	$ 10,000
Estimated Purchasing Department cost	30,000
Estimated Receiving Department cost	10,500
Estimated Materials Warehousing cost	18,000
Dollar value of purchases (for application of freight-in and Purchasing Department cost)	$500,000
Estimated items to be received (for application of receiving and materials warehousing costs)	600,000

Required:

a. Develop application rates for the material handling costs.
b. Prepare the journal entry to record the actual cost of the purchase including the application of material acquisition cost if 12,000 items are bought on account at a total cost of $10,000.

E4–9 Service Department Cost Allocation and OH Application Theory (L.O. 1)

Regarding the allocation of overhead,

a. Discuss the theoretical merit of three different methods of allocating service department costs to production departments.
b. Distinguish between direct and indirect costs and their relationship in determining overhead application rates for production departments.
c. Discuss three different capacity approaches to use in estimating factory overhead and when (if ever) each would be appropriate.
d. Give three different bases that are appropriate for use with a predetermined, annual factory overhead rate and the objectives and criteria a company should use in selecting each of these bases.

Problems

P4–10 Applying Overhead Using Departmental versus Plantwide Rates (L.O. 1)

The management of Penny Company cannot decide whether to adopt departmental factory overhead application rates for its Mixing and Finishing Departments or a plantwide rate. They ask your advice. You obtain the following budgeted overhead for each department and data for one order so both approaches can be evaluated.

	Department	
	Mixing	**Finishing**
Supplies	$ 800	$1,100
Superintendents' salaries	1,200	1,400
Indirect labor	1,300	2,100
Depreciation	400	1,000
Repairs	800	890
Insurance	180	260
	$4,680	$6,750
Total direct labor-hours	600	250
Direct labor-hours on Order No. 5	20	3

Required:

a. Prepare departmental and plantwide overhead rates. Then apply overhead to Order No. 5 using both approaches.
b. Evaluate the approaches indicating which you prefer.

P4–11 Comparison of Allocations Using Traditional and ABC Costing Methods (L.O. 4)

Lays Company provides the following information concerning its two product lines:

	Product A	Product B
Units produced	10	200
Machine setups per product line	1	1
Machine-hours per unit	4	4
Total budgeted machine setup-related cost— $42,000		

Brown Company provides the following information concerning its two product lines:

	Product C	Product D
Units produced	500	500
Engineering change notices per product line	4	12
Unit cost per engineering change notice	$800	$800
Direct labor-hours per unit	2	1.2

Required:

a. Determine how much machine setup-related cost is allocated to each product line if Lays Company uses a traditional cost allocation system based on machine hours. What is the cost per unit for Products A and B?

b. Assume instead Lays Company uses activity-based costing and compute how much machine setup-related cost is allocated to Product A and B lines. What is the cost per unit for Products A and B?

c. Criticize the allocation methods used by conventional costing systems.

d. Define product diversity and volume diversity.

e. Indicate if overhead allocation to Product A and B lines is evidence of product diversity or volume diversity.

f. Calculate how much engineering change cost is allocated to Product C and D lines if Brown Company uses a traditional costing system based on machine-hours. What is the cost per unit for Products C and D?

g. Assume instead Brown Company uses activity-based costing and compute how much engineering change cost is allocated to Product C and D lines. What is the cost per unit for Products C and D?

h. Indicate if overhead allocation to Product C and D lines is evidence of product diversity or volume diversity.

P4–12 Writing Assignment Concerning Overhead (L.O. 1)

As a CPA with an excellent reputation in the city, Hammermill Company asks your advice concerning the assignment of overhead in its production process. The company manufactures a line of bathroom fixtures that includes pedestal sinks and drop-in sinks of vitreous china. Hammermill also produces solid brass bath fixtures. Business operations are subject to wide cyclical fluctuations because the sales volume follows new housing construction. Production personnel normally complete about 50 percent of their manufacturing in the last quarter of the calendar year to be ready to meet the heavy spring construction demand.

In addition to those fluctuations, material costs vary widely as a percentage of total factory cost because the company uses various combinations of brass, marble powder, and polyester resin. For example, the material cost of a specific item ranges from 20 percent to 65 percent of total inventoriable cost.

Hammermill's labor-intensive processing uses five departments. Even though all products use each of the departments, they are not used proportionately. Each department uses different labor skills. The plant wage rate ranges from $6 to $10.50 an hour. However, within each of the five individual departments, the spread between the high and low wage rate is less than 4 percent. Factory overhead ranges from 35 percent to 80 percent of conversion cost within each department.

Management specifically asks that you study their cost system with reference to these issues concerning overhead:

1. Using department overhead rate or plantwide rate.
2. Basing overhead rates on normal capacity or expected actual capacity.
3. Distributing factory overhead on direct labor-hour, direct labor cost, or material cost.

Required:

Write a memorandum to top management of Hammermill Company stating your position regarding the three different issues in question. Include reasons supporting your recommendations.

P4–13 Journal Entries to Record Spending and Volume Variances (L.O. 3)

Danden Manufacturing Company provides the following data concerning its operations for the year ended December 31, 19X1:

Estimated variable overhead rate per machine-hour	$2.50
Estimated total overhead rate per machine-hour	$6.00
Budgeted capacity	15,000 machine-hours
Actual capacity during year	15,200 machine-hours
Actual factory overhead costs	$96,000

Required:

a. Compute the amount of overhead applied during the year and prepare the summary journal entry required to record this on the books.
b. Determine the amount of the over- or underapplied overhead.
c. Compute the factory overhead spending and volume variances.
d. Prepare the journal entries required to journalize the variances and to close the Factory Overhead Control account; close variances to the Cost of Goods Sold account.

P4–14 Just-In-Time and Profitability of Special Orders (L.O. 4)

Barc Inc. experiences intense price competition in manufacturing a special model of calculators. Barc Inc. has produced an average of 600,000 calculators per year over the past three years. They pride themselves on the product's high quality and find the introduction of new technology is the most promising marketing strategy. Management realizes their marketing program is very important since they presently operate at 75 percent of plant capacity. The product is sold at $300 in the market.

Estimated production costs of one calculator are as follows:

Direct material	$ 50
Direct labor	30
Variable overhead	55
Allocated overhead	47
Total production costs	$182

In an attempt to improve their product costing, management is considering adopting an activity-based costing (ABC) system and introducing just-in-time into the production system. Barc's accountants recognize that many indirect common product costs using a traditional accounting system are changed to direct traceable product costs using an ABC system that incorporates the JIT philosophy.

Barc recently received a special order from one of its dealers for 150,000 calculators at a unit bid sales price of $180. Because Barc has idle capacity, no increase in fixed costs would occur to meet the special order. To better compare their conventional costing system with an ABC system, they determined the following production costs using a JIT system and the allocation of production overhead based on an ABC system:

Direct material	$ 50
Direct labor	35
Variable overhead	60
Fixed overhead	30
Total production costs	$175

Rather than use the traditional departmental overhead rates, an ABC system applies factory overhead costs to products based on cost drivers. Production personnel recognize that this may require a change in layout of factory equipment and the development of decentralized work cells. A JIT production system requires a zero-defect program in which no scrap or waste is allowed. Barc management plans to adopt the philosophy of total quality control. Management plans to maintain minimum inventory levels because JIT is a demand-pull approach.

Because workers in each cell are trained to perform various tasks within the cell, idle time is not permissible. This arrangement facilitates the traceability of costs to the final product. Direct labor costs are usually considered variable costs under traditional accounting systems. However, direct labor costs become fixed costs using an ABC system because workers perform a variety of tasks within a specific work cell.

Required:

a. Prepare computations using a traditional accounting system which indicates whether the special order should be accepted or rejected.
b. Prepare computations using ABC and JIT accounting systems to indicate whether the special order should be accepted or rejected.
c. Determine which cost accounting system is preferable for pricing this special order if the cost activities described in the case will result in different cost estimates and different contribution margins.

P4–15 Step and Direct Methods for Developing Overhead Rates (L.O. 2)

Mixing and Fabricating are the producing departments at Cohry Company. Factory Office, Personnel, and Inspection are the three service departments. Factory Office is responsible for keeping the plant production records, while Personnel maintains employee records for those working as direct and indirect laborers. Inspection insures that products meet the quality demanded by management. The annual budgets of direct and indirect departmental charges and the budgeted operating data for all the departments follow:

	Factory Office	Personnel	Inspection	Mixing	Fabrication	Total
Factory supplies	$ 780	$ 800	$ 615	$3,100	$1,800	$ 7,095
Supervisors' salaries	210	700	180	950	600	2,640
Property taxes	320	80	75	425	410	1,310
Rent	625	130	410	273	301	1,739
Totals	$1,935	$1,710	$1,280	$4,748	$3,111	$12,784
Floor space (square feet) .	100	90	60	120	180	550
Employees	25	26	99	200	400	750
Machine-hours	10	15	52	160	207	444

Required:

(Round to nearest whole dollar.)

a. Allocate the service departments using the step method. Calculate factory overhead application rates using 680 estimated machine-hours for Mixing and 1,224 estimated machine-hours for the Fabrication Department. First, allocate Factory Office based on floor space; next, Personnel based on number of employees; and finally, Inspection based on machine-hours.
b. Compute an overhead allocation rate per service unit using the direct method. Calculate factory overhead application rates using the same machine-hours as in Requirement a.
c. Explain why it is not necessary to break the application rates into their fixed and variable components to answer the requirements of this problem.

P4–16 Developing Application Rates Using the Linear Algebra (Reciprocal) Method (L.O. 2)

Princeton Company has prepared overhead budgets for the production and service departments (before allocation) as follows:

Employee Fitness	$ 20,000
Repair	60,000
Mixing	241,733
Finishing	220,892
	$542,625

Accountants use the following data to determine the percentage of service received from each service department. The company uses the number of employees for allocating Employee Fitness Department costs and square footage for the Repair Department.

Departments	Employees	Square Footage	Direct Labor Dollars
Employee Fitness	18	5,000	
Repair	175	2,000	
Mixing	280	15,000	$ 824,000
Finishing	245	30,000	600,500
	718	52,000	$1,424,500

Required:

(Round to whole dollars.)

Using linear algebra, determine the overhead application rates for the production departments per direct labor dollar.

P4–17 Step and Direct Methods for Developing Overhead Rates (L.O. 2)

The producing departments at Ralph Company are Packaging and Fabrication. The two service departments are Planning and Engineering. Planning is responsible for scheduling, control, and accounting functions, while Engineering plans and designs parts and procedures. The departmental costs budgeted during January were

	Planning	Engineering	Packaging	Fabrication	Total
Indirect labor	$ 949	$ 602	$2,500	$1,600	$5,651
Indirect materials	600	150	900	500	2,150
Insurance	200	450	700	450	1,800
	$1,749	$1,202	$4,100	$2,550	$9,601
Employees	50	100	120	80	350
Engineering-hours	50	50	200	300	600

Required:

(Round to nearest whole dollar except in determining final application rates.)

a. Allocate the Service Department's costs using the direct method. Calculate factory overhead allocation rates using 919 estimated machine-hours for Packaging and 800 estimated machine-hours for the Fabrication Department. First, allocate Planning based on the number of employees, and next, Engineering based on engineering-hours.

b. Compute an overhead allocation rate per service unit using the step method. Calculate factory overhead allocation rates using the same machine-hours as in Requirement *a*.

c. Determine the overhead spending and volume variances of Fabrication using the step method. In January, Fabrication actually worked 850 machine-hours and incurred $4,108.50 overhead cost, which includes its share of service department costs. Of the department's application rate, $3 is fixed.

P4–18 Transaction Costing (L.O. 4)

Lakeview Desk Company budgets factory overhead for next year as:

Utilities	$ 600,000
Materials handling	800,000
Quality control inspections	300,000
Machine setups	800,000
Work cells	2,800,000
Total budgeted costs	$5,300,000

Overhead has been applied on the basis of machine-hours; 500,000 machine-hours are budgeted for next year. The company is considering adopting an activity-based or transaction-based cost system that allocates overhead costs based on nonvolume-based cost drivers. The activity-based cost drivers for next year's budgeted overhead costs are

Utilities	120,000 kilowatt-hours
Materials handling	200,000 material moves
Quality control inspections	25,000 inspections
Machine setups	80,000 production runs
Work cells	400,000 square feet

Lakeview provides the following data concerning the production of 1,000 desks:

Direct material costs	$300,000
Direct labor costs	100,000
Machine-hours	5,000
Direct labor-hours	10,000
Kilowatt-hours	4,000
Work cells—square feet	2,000
Materials handling moves	600
Quality control inspections	80
Setups (production runs)	20

Required:

a. Explain why service department costs are allocated to production/operating departments for product costing.

b. Distinguish between a service and production department.

c. Explain why direct labor is no longer considered the most appropriate measure of throughput for many organizations.

d. Describe briefly activity-based costing.

e. List three typical costs that are not volume dependent.

f. Determine the production costs per desk under a volume-based cost allocation system that applies overhead on machine-hours.

g. Determine the production costs per desk if an activity-based costing (transaction-based costing system) is implemented.

h. Compare the two costing systems, indicating the amount of cost savings between the two methods. Explain the source of any cost savings.

i. Calculate the selling price of desks under both methods if the Lakeview Company policy is to add 50 percent to product costs as gross profit to cover other costs such as administrative expenses, marketing expenses, financial expenses, and research and development expenses, and yield a profit.

P4–19 Comparing Overhead Applied Using Various Basis; Spending and Volume Variances (L.O. 3)

Management of Margery Crawford, Inc., plans to begin applying factory overhead because they have found their present system of using only actual overhead to be inadequate. The following data for an average month are the basis for this study:

	Data for Average Month
Estimated variable factory overhead	$3,060
Estimated fixed factory overhead	2,340
Estimated total factory overhead	$5,400
Estimated material costs	$6,000
Estimated units to be produced	900
Estimated direct labor dollars	$3,000
Estimated direct labor-hours	500
Estimated machine-hours	1,800

At the end of the first month, the job order sheets show the following:

	Job 1	Job 2	Job 3
Beginning inventory:			
Material	$ 400	Begun	Begun
Labor	$ 700	in	in
Overhead	$1,330	current	current
		month	month
January cost:			
Material	-0-	$2,100	$3,800
Labor	$1,000	$ 800	$1,600
Overhead	?	?	?
Units	600	650	480
Stage of completion	100%	30%	100%
Machine-hours	550	490	750
Direct labor-hours	170	140	250

Job No. 1 was 40 percent complete at the beginning of the month. Actual total factory overhead for the current month was $5,900.

Required:

Using the following five bases available for adoption, answer Requirements *a*, *b*, and *c* for each of these bases:

1. Material cost.

2. Units produced.

3. Direct labor dollars.

4. Direct labor-hours.

5. Machine-hours.

   a. The factory overhead applied to each job during the current month.
   b. Amount of over- or underapplied factory overhead.
   c. Spending and volume variances.

P4–20 Revision of Cost Allocations (L.O. 1)

Self Company produces motors for customers' orders. The following income statement was prepared by the company's bookkeeper for the fiscal year ended March 31, 19X2.

	Product Line A	Product Line B	Total
Product line revenue	$200,000	$290,000	$490,000
Product line costs:			
Direct materials	20,000	35,000	55,000
Direct labor	45,000	126,000	171,000
Manufacturing overhead	72,500	137,000	209,500
Total costs	137,500	298,000	435,500
Gross margin	$ 62,500	$ (8,000)	$ 54,500
Marketing and administrative expenses			20,000
Income before income taxes			$ 34,500

From an analysis of the accounts and records of the company, you have determined that:

1. The company has two production departments—Cutting and Molding. In the Molding Department, employees are paid on a piecework basis.

2. The total manufacturing overhead cost ($209,500) consisted of the following:

	Cutting Department	Molding Department	Building Operation Costs	Repair Costs	Total
Indirect labor					
and supervision	$20,000	$ 17,500	$13,000	$4,000	$ 54,500
Indirect material	7,000	5,000	2,000		14,000
Building depreciation			3,500		3,500
Machinery depreciation ...	52,000	80,000	2,000	2,000	136,000
Property taxes			1,500		1,500
	$79,000	$102,500	$22,000	$6,000	$209,500

3. The time required to complete each product line was

	Product Line A	Product Line B	Total
Direct labor-hours:			
Cutting department	3,000	2,500	5,500
Molding department	10,000	27,000	37,000
	13,000	29,500	42,500
Machine-hours:			
Cutting department	11,000	3,000	14,000
Molding department	9,000	21,000	30,000
	20,000	24,000	44,000

4. There was no work in process at either April 1, 19X1, or March 31, 19X2.
5. Of the total repairs, 10 percent were made to the building, 60 percent to machinery in the Cutting Department, and 30 percent to machinery in the Molding Department.
6. Building space is used 70 percent by the Cutting Department and 30 percent by the Molding Department.
7. Product line A required 50 percent more supervision and indirect labor than Product line B.

Required:

Prepare a revised income statement showing the results of each contract, together with supporting schedules showing the appropriate allocation of overhead.

P4–21 Evaluating Various Methods of Applying Material Acquisition Cost (L.O. 5)

As a cost accountant recently hired by Crawford Company, you believe that a better procedure for treating materials handling costs should be utilized. At present, material handling costs are treated as a part of factory overhead, which is allocated on a direct labor-hour basis. You contend that these costs should be an addition to material costs.

Your initial study indicated that some of the material used in manufacturing jewelry, such as diamonds and other rare stones, requires extensive handling and warehousing cost, while materials such as mountings and glue require less handling cost.

Rather than attempt to establish an applied rate for each category of material handling costs, you believe that applied rates for each of the following three material types should be used:

Type I   Material such as glue that is relatively inexpensive to handle.
Type II   Material such as mountings that is three times as expensive to handle per unit as Type I.
Type III Material such as rare stones that is twice as expensive to handle per unit as Type II.

When you present your suggestions, the controller agrees that these handling costs should be treated as additional material costs, but does not believe it is necessary to divide the material into three types. To prove your point, you extract the following data from company records:

Direct Material		Total Costs
Type I	(10,000 units)	$10,000
Type II	(12,000 units)	12,000
Type III	(9,000 units)	43,200
Total direct material costs		$65,200
Direct labor	(4,000 hours)	$20,000
Factory overhead	(including $4,000 of material handling costs)	$18,000

Material and labor costs for two of the five orders completed during the period were the following:

Material	Order No. 101	Order No. 102
Type I	$ 2,000	$ 1,500
Type II	6,000	3,000
Type III	6,000	16,000
Total material	$14,000	$20,500
Direct labor	$ 4,000	$ 4,500
Labor-hours	800	900

Required:

a. Determine the following application rates:
   (1) Factory overhead rate presently used.
   (2) Factory overhead rate if material handling costs are excluded and direct labor-hours are continued as the basis. Material handling costs are applied using the method you, the cost accountant, proposed in which there are separate rates for each type of material using weighted units as the basis for allocating a pro rata share of handling costs to each material as a percentage of its purchase cost.
   (3) Factory overhead rate is computed as in Requirement a(2) and material handling costs are applied using the method preferred by the controller using a blanket rate for all materials. The controller contends that the rate should be based on the total dollar value of material purchased.
b. Determine the total cost of each of the two orders using each of the three approaches in Requirement a.
c. Determine the total cost using each of the three approaches in Requirement a if, instead, the following orders are representative of all jobs processed (round to whole dollars):

Material	Order No. 103	Order No. 104
Type I	$ -0-	$13,000
Type II	11,000	-0-
Type III	11,500	9,500
Total material	$22,500	$22,500
Direct labor	$ 4,000	$ 4,000
Labor-hours	800	900

d. Indicate which factors you would consider in choosing the method to adopt.

P4–22 Developing Application Rates Using Linear Algebra (Reciprocal) Method, Direct Method, and Step Method (L.O. 2)

Overhead budgets for the production and service departments of Pineno Company are as follows:

Employee Relations	$ 150,000
General Factory Administration	100,000
Maintenance	90,000
Tooling	500,000
Processing	600,000
Total	$1,440,000

Accountants use the following factory statistics in determining the percentage of service received from each service department. They use the number of employees to allocate Employee Relations Department cost; square footage for allocating General Factory Administration; and number of repair-hours to allocate the Maintenance Department cost.

Departments	Employees	Square Footage	Repair-Hours	Machine-Hours
Employee Relations	20	10,800	—	
General Factory Administration	66	1,000	—	
Maintenance	64	6,480	50	
Tooling	40	14,040	330	30,000
Processing	30	22,680	270	20,000
Total	220	55,000	650	50,000

Required:

Determine the application rate per machine-hour using:

a. Linear algebra method.
b. Direct method.
c. Step method.

PRODUCT COST ALLOCATION AND ACCUMULATION PROCEDURES

Job Order Costing

CHAPTER OBJECTIVES

After studying this chapter, you should be able to:

1. Identify the manufacturing characteristics that help determine whether a job order, process, or operation costing assignment is most appropriate.

2. Understand the source documents for the job order cost sheet which accountants use to determine product costs.

3. Prepare basic journal entries associated with job order cost accounting systems.

4. Use reciprocal factory and home office ledger accounts.

Introduction

Determining the cost of products and services is an important cost accounting function because it affects the success of contract bidding and product pricing. With increasing national and global competition, small costing disparities can have a large impact on whether a company survives. Also, rapid technological changes have increased the need for accurate cost information. These changes encourage managers to adopt strategies and product designs that improve the production process. Armed with accurate product costs, managers can assess each job's profitability. Product-costing data not only guide continuous improvement but also are required for external reporting.

Job Order, Process, and Operation Costing (L.O. 1)

After accumulating costs by departments or responsibility centers as presented in Chapter 4, accountants assign costs to products or orders through either job order costing, process costing, or operation costing. Job order and process costing are the two polar extremes while operation costing represents a hybrid-costing system. The nature of manufacturing activities determines which cost application system to use. Service organizations use costing systems similar to manufacturers except there are usually no inventories. In providing services, they incur labor and overhead like manufacturing operations. Activity-based management, which was presented in Chapter 4, may be combined with either job order or process costing or a combination of these product costing systems.

Job Order Costing

With a **job order cost** system, costs are assigned to each job. A job may be an order, a contract, a unit of production, or a batch performed to meet customers' specifications. For example, when repairing an automobile, a mechanic uses job order costing to accumulate the costs of the repair job. The mechanic collects the cost of repair parts and the direct labor-hours spent in repairing the car. Overhead costs are applied using an overhead rate. Accountants also use job order costing in the construction of commercial and residential buildings, ships, and machines. For example, a printing company uses job order costing because printers usually produce each printing order to customers' specifications. Job order costing is appropriate for companies making different components for inventory.

Process Costing

Using a **process costing** system, accountants accumulate costs for each department for a time period and allocate them among all the products manufactured during the period. They use process costing in chemical processing, petroleum refining, and other industries where there is a continuous production process. Direct material, direct labor, and applied factory overhead are accumulated for each department for a period, usually a month. At the end of the period, departmental cost is divided by the number of units produced to obtain a cost per unit. Process costing is discussed in detail in Chapters 6 and 7.

Operation costing

Each company develops its own product costing system that meets its specific needs. Many companies employ an **operation costing** system in the manufacture of goods that have some common characteristics plus some individual characteristics. An operation is a routine production method, technique, or step that is repetitively performed. Distinctions are made between batches of product, such as Style A men's suits and Style B men's suits. For example, various styles of men's suits require different fabrics and different hand sewing operations.

As in job order costing, accountants specifically allocate direct materials to the batches using operation costing. However, direct labor and overhead are absorbed in the same manner as under process costing. They apply conversion costs to all physical units passing through the operation by using a single average unit conversion cost for that operation. Operation costing best meets the needs of a batch manufacturer whose products have variations of a single design and require a varying sequence of standardized operations.

Accounting for Materials in Job Order Systems (L.O. 2)

Once a company receives materials, clerks classify them as direct materials if they become a part of the finished product, or indirect material if they are used in the manufacturing process. A material requisition records the material flow. The **material (stores) requisition** form is a basic source document informing the cost accounting department that material has been issued. No material should be issued from the storeroom unless a material requisition is processed. This is a basic internal control procedure.

EXHIBIT 5–1

MATERIAL REQUISITION				
Requisition no: __911__				
Department to be charged __Sewing Department__		Job no.: __101__ Date: __1/12/19X1__		
Deliver to __Sewing Department__		Date wanted __1/15/19X1__		
Quantity	Unit of measure	Description of item	Unit price	Extension
5	Pound	Cotton-polyester thread	$2/lb.	$10
15,000	Yard	72" 14 oz. cloth	$0.43/yd.	$6,450
Bill Cox			_Mary Miller_	
Requested by			Issued by	

Material Requisitions and Issues

Exhibit 5–1 illustrates a typical manufacturing material requisition form indicating that five pounds of thread and 15,000 yards of cloth are needed for Job No. 101 in the Sewing Department. The material requisition not only fixes responsibility for the requisition of goods but also provides information for future reference. Requests for unusual material not normally carried in stock go to the Purchasing Department.

Issuance of Direct Material. Material requisitions facilitate assigning material cost to a job or department. Companies use issue slips that serve the same purpose. Because the material requisition indicates the department requesting the material, it becomes the source document for recording the transfer of costs from Direct Materials Inventory to Work in Process Inventory or Factory Overhead. Accountants charge materials purchased for a specific contract directly to that contract.

Most companies accumulate material requisitions for a week or month and make one entry to record the raw material used; otherwise, a company would have many entries per month. However, for illustrative purposes, the following journal entry charges Job No. 101 for direct materials listed on the material requisition in Exhibit 5–1. Note that Job No. 101 is a subsidiary work in process account to the general ledger account.

Work in Process Inventory—Job No. 101	6,460	
Direct Materials Inventory		6,460

Issues of Indirect Material. When the material requisition requests $1,000 of factory supplies, which are indirect material, accountants charge Factory Overhead Control. And they debit the indirect materials subsidiary ledger for Factory Overhead Control as follows:

Factory Overhead Control—Indirect Materials	1,000	
Factory Supplies Inventory		1,000

Material Credit Slips. Clerks issue **material credit slips** when a department returns material to the storeroom. They also use these slips to correct errors in material issuance. The credit slip transfers the material accountability from the production department back to the storekeeper. Material credit slips transfer only reusable material. Changed or damaged materials become scrap. Material credit slips are the source document used by the accounting department to give credit to the department returning the material. In effect, they offset material requisitions. Normally an entry is made recording a batch of material credit slips. However, for illustrative purposes, the following entry records the issuance of a material credit slip:

Direct Materials Inventory	XXX	
Work in Process Inventory—Job No. 101		XXX

Labor Accounting (L.O. 2)

Accurate, understandable methods for calculating payroll are necessary. Probably no other area in accounting has more impact on the morale of employees than do employee wage and benefit policies. If only a few employees are unsure about how their gross and net wages are calculated or believe errors are involved, they can create discontent in their peer group. For this reason, companies carefully explain wage payment and employee benefit plans to all employees.

Variety of Labor Systems. Wages designate hourly or piece-rate payment which represents a variable cost. **Salaries** describe a fixed periodic payment, such as a weekly or monthly payment. Companies make salary payments at constant periodic intervals to employees. A variety of methods exist to record wages and salaries. The method used depends on such factors as the skills of accounting personnel, size of the company, and frequency of payment. Rather than classify payroll costs at each pay period, some companies wait until the end of the month and then assign the payroll to direct labor, indirect labor, marketing, or administrative costs in a summary entry. Other companies record the expense distribution and payment at the same time. However, after you understand the basic concepts of labor accounting presented in this chapter, you will have little difficulty in adapting them to a company's particular payroll system.

Various laws require employers to withhold from the pay of employees certain taxes and to remit these amounts periodically to the proper authorities. These tax withholdings include federal, state, and city income taxes and social security taxes (FICA). Assume that payroll deductions are $103 for FICA taxes, $263 for federal income taxes, and $104 for state income taxes. The following journal entry charges both the general ledger account (Work in Process Inventory) and its subsidiary ledger account (Job No. 101) for $1,300 direct labor incurred in the Sewing Department:

Work in Process Inventory—Job No. 101	1,300	
FICA Taxes Withheld or Payable		103
Federal income Tax Withheld		263
State Income Tax Withheld		104
Payroll Payable		830

Payroll Taxes. Payroll taxes are also levied directly on the employer for the benefit of employees. The primary payroll taxes include social security (FICA), unemployment taxes, and state workers' compensation insurance. These are not withholdings from the individual employee's payroll check, but are additional labor costs to the employer. The following entry records $103 FICA, $35 state unemployment, and $10 federal unemployment payroll tax on direct labor as indirect cost by charging them to Factory Overhead Control. Chapter 22 illustrates an alternative method of recording payroll taxes by recording them as direct cost to Work in Process Inventory.

Factory Overhead Control	....	148
FICA Taxes Payable	....	103
State Unemployment Taxes Payable	....	35
Federal Unemployment Taxes Payable	....	10

Labor-Related Costs. Labor costs include more than the basic earnings computed for each employee on an hourly or piecework basis, and thus represent a significant amount of money. There are many labor-related costs, such as payroll taxes, as just illustrated. Bonuses, holiday and vacation pay, free uniforms, hospitalization insurance, and retirement pensions are other labor-related costs. Studies have shown that employee benefits add at least an additional 35 percent to the basic labor cost of the average employee. Costs of fringes vary considerably by industry and somewhat by the size of the company and the geographical region.

To account for these labor costs, payroll and cost accountants must work closely together. The cost accountant's prime concern is maintaining records of labor cost by job or department. Payroll accountants are concerned that payroll records conform with government regulations, and also provide the supporting data necessary to calculate each employee's gross pay, withholdings, and net pay.

To effectively control labor costs, management needs accurate, timely information. Accountants should prepare performance reports for each department reflecting the level of workers' efficiency. Departments other than cost accounting also have an impact on labor accounting; these include the Personnel Department, Timekeeping Department, and Payroll Department. A Personnel Department's function is keeping a trained labor force in adequate numbers for the company's operations; the Timekeeping Department is responsible for recording and verifying the total time worked on each job or product, or in each department. The Payroll Department determines and records the employees' gross and net earnings and maintains earnings records for each employee.

Timekeeping Records

Well-documented time records are necessary to protect against overpayments. For hourly employees, some form of timecard ensures that each employee was on the job for the specified hours. In addition, hourly employees receive premiums when working night shifts, working overtime (usually work over 8 hours a day or 40 hours a week is paid at one and one half times the normal earnings), and working on holidays (usually paid at twice the normal rate). Because of these premiums, timekeeping systems record the time of day, the particular days worked, and total hours per day and week. In addition, vacation days, sick days, and other absences must be reported and recorded for correct calculation of pay.

Timecard. Exhibit 5–2 illustrates a **clock card** or **timecard** that provides evidence of when the employee was on the work site. Clock or timecards are filled out manually or by a clock punch. Each employee's timecard or sheet shows the dates worked as well as arrival and departure times.

Job Time Tickets. Because employees' timecards only indicate the total time worked, companies need a **job time ticket** to show the time each employee spent on individual jobs during the day. Exhibit 5–3 illustrates an individual job time

EXHIBIT 5–2   Individual Timecard

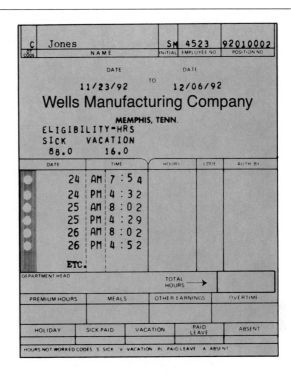

C	Jones		SM	4523	92010002

EXHIBIT 5–3   Individual Job Time Ticket

Date _____   Employee name (or no.) _____
Time started _____   Job No. _____
Time stopped _____   Department _____
Hours worked _____   Pieces completed _____
Rate _____   Amount _____
                                        Approved _____

ticket reflecting where the employee worked during the day, the name of the employee working on a particular job, the time the employee started and stopped, and the rate of pay. Employees can prepare their own forms if the forms are readily available and if a minimum of time is required to complete them. In other instances, supervisors or dispatch clerks complete the forms when employees report to them for a new assignment.

Daily Time Ticket. Instead of having an employee prepare a new ticket for each job worked during the day, a **daily job time ticket** summarizes all jobs the worker performed. The daily job time ticket, as illustrated in Exhibit 5–4, eliminates having more than one ticket per employee each day. The ticket has a space for the starting and stopping time for each job worked on. A tabulation at the bottom of the daily time ticket allows for the accumulation of hours worked on

EXHIBIT 5–4   Daily Job Time Ticket

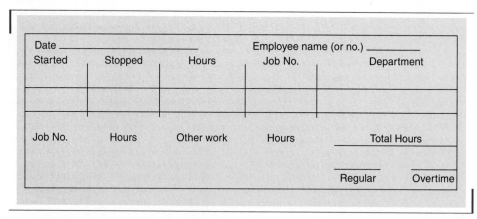

each assignment before the hours are posted to a job order cost sheet. Exhibit 5–4 also shows total regular and overtime hours. Supervisors review and approve timecards and job tickets.

Each day, the timekeeper collects the previous day's job time tickets and timecards. After comparing the time reported on these, any differences are investigated. If the difference is small, it is idle time and charged to Factory Overhead. This often represents the time required for the worker to transfer from one job to another. When the job time ticket shows more hours than the timecard, the timekeeper determines the cause by consulting the employee and supervisor. After receiving the completed timecards and job time tickets, the payroll department uses them in calculating employees' pay.

Factory Overhead Application (L.O. 3)

Factory overhead is an important concern of cost center managers, whatever their responsibilities. Factory overhead costs are all factory costs, except direct material and direct labor, and include many different costs from a variety of sources. Accountants record different factory overhead costs in various ways. For example, certain costs such as electricity, fuel, and water are paid for each month, while other manufacturing costs, such as insurance, vacations, and holidays, are accrued and arise from adjusting journal entries made at the end of the relevant period. The source documents for some factory overhead costs, such as indirect material (material requisitions) and indirect labor (job time tickets), originate internally. Other overhead costs arise from source documents prepared outside the company. The source documents for fire insurance, property taxes, and utility expenses are vendor invoices. The coding of the source documents to the proper factory overhead account and cost center is vital to the success of the budgetary system.

As discussed in Chapter 2, distributing actual factory overhead is usually not practical so we use estimated factory overhead application rates. Wells Manufacturing Company's $50 estimated factory overhead rate is applied to the 300 machine-hours incurred in the Sewing Department and to the 220 machine-hours incurred in the Treating Department to arrive at the charge to Work in Process. We debit both the general ledger account and Job No. 101, the subsidiary work in process ledger account. The entry to record the overhead applied to Job No. 101 is

```
Work in Process Inventory—Job No. 101   . . . . . . . . . . . . . . . . .   26,000
      Factory Overhead Control   . . . . . . . . . . . . . . . . . . . . . . . . . . .          26,000
```

As the entry shows, we apply overhead before transferring a job to finished goods inventory. However, a job does not have to be finished for overhead to be applied. Factory overhead must be applied (1) when a job is completed and (2) at the end of the period to all unfinished jobs. Thus, to have proper matching of actual factory overhead and absorbed or applied overhead, factory overhead must be applied to both complete and incomplete jobs worked on during the period.

Job Order Sheet (L.O. 2)

A **job order cost sheet** is the basic document in job order costing that accumulates costs for each job. Since costs are accumulated for each batch or lot in a job order accounting system, job order sheets indicate the direct material and direct labor incurred on a job, as well as the amount of overhead applied. The file of incomplete job order sheets can serve as the subsidiary ledger for Work in Process Inventory. There are different forms of job order sheets. For example, a patient's medical record listing the cost of all medical services rendered for that patient is a hospital's job order sheet.

In Exhibit 5–5, the heading on the job order cost sheet contains such information as the job order, customer, and date required. Accountants enter the material costs of $6,460 used in the Sewing Department and $1,540 used in the Treating Department on the job sheet. After computing job charges from the job time ticket, accountants also enter the labor cost on the job order sheet. In addition, they enter the overhead applied on the job cost sheet so the total cost of the job is known when the job is completed.

After the company finishes and sells Job No. 101, the accountant completes the summary at the bottom of the job order cost sheet. This entry records the transfer of Job No. 101 to Finished Goods Inventory:

```
Finished Goods Inventory   . . . . . . . . . . . . . . . . . . . . . . . . . . . . .   76,000
      Work in Process—Job No. 101   . . . . . . . . . . . . . . . . . . . . . . .          76,000
```

Basic Journal Entries in Job Order Costing Summarized (L.O. 3)

The following journal entries summarize the basic transactions in a job order cost system used by the Wells Manufacturing Company, including the entries for Job No. 101 previously illustrated. We posted each journal entry to the general ledger accounts illustrated in Exhibit 5–6. In practice, special journals are normally used (i.e., sales entries are recorded in a sales journal, and cash payments in a cash disbursements journal); here we illustrate only a general journal.

Subsidiary Factory Ledgers

Exhibit 5–6 also illustrates the use of the Factory Overhead Control account in the general ledger and the need for using subsidiary ledger accounts to detail actual factory overhead costs. For most companies, the number of factory overhead costs is too great to set up individual accounts in the general ledger, so

EXHIBIT 5–5

JOB ORDER COST SHEET
WELLS MANUFACTURING COMPANY

Customer:

   Douglass Warehouse, Inc.

   309 North 12th Street

   Murray, Kentucky 42071

For stock _____

Job No. __101__

Product __144″ # 8 cloth (144 rolls)__

Date required __1/23/19X1__

Date started __11/16/19X0__

Date completed __1/20/19X1__

SEWING DEPARTMENT

Direct Materials			Direct Labor		Factory Overhead		
Date	Requisition Number	Amount	Date	Amount	Date	Basis	Amount
1/16/19X1	911	$6,460	1/18/19X1	$1,300	1/20/19X1	machine-hours	$15,000

TREATING DEPARTMENT

Direct Materials			Direct Labor		Factory Overhead		
Date	Requisition Number	Amount	Date	Amount	Date	Basis	Amount
1/18/19X1	914	$1,540	1/19/19X1	$ 700	1/20/19X1	machine-hours	$11,000

SUMMARY

	Sewing Department	Treating Department	Total	
Selling price				$100,000
Incurred in prior period ...	$20,000	$20,000	$40,000	
Direct materials costs	6,460	1,540	8,000	
Direct labor costs	1,300	700	2,000	
Factory overhead applied .	15,000	11,000	26,000	76,000
Gross margin				$24,000

accountants establish individual overhead accounts in a subsidiary ledger. The total balance of all accounts in the factory overhead subsidiary ledger should equal the balance in the Factory Overhead Control account in the general ledger. The association between the Factory Overhead Control account and its subsidiary ledger is similar to that for accounts receivable and accounts payable general ledger accounts and their respective subsidiary ledgers. Accountants set up individual subsidiary ledger accounts for each expense item by department or by cost center. Codes in the chart of accounts facilitate the distribution of actual factory overhead to specific expense accounts and also to departments and other cost centers. For example, Account No. 5141 can indicate that indirect material (code 514) is charged to Cost Center No. 1. Instead of using account code numbers, detail for departments can be calculated in other ways. For example, accountants prepare analysis sheets for each department to accumulate the actual factory overhead items incurred. Chapter 4 emphasizes the need for detailing actual factory overhead by department so that departmental factory overhead applied rates can be developed.

EXHIBIT 5–6

Cash

Beginning balance	15,000	(i) Miscellaneous factory costs	1,000
Receipts	191,000	Disbursements	185,000
	206,000		186,000
Balance 20,000			

Accounts Receivable

Beginning balance	90,000	Received on account	314,500
(l) Sales	100,000		
Other sales	199,500		
	389,500		
Balance 75,000			

Direct Materials Inventory

Beginning balance	16,000	(b) Issues	39,000
(a) Purchases	55,000		
	71,000		
Balance 32,000			

Factory Supplies Inventory

Beginning balance	4,000	(b) Issues	5,000
(a) Purchases	7,000		
	11,000		
Balance 6,000			

Work in Process Inventory

Beginning balance	40,000	(k) Transfer to finished goods	130,000
(b) Direct material	39,000		
(c) Direct labor	10,000		
(j) Applied overhead	72,000		
	161,000		
Balance 31,000			

Finished Goods Inventory

Beginning balance	180,000	(l) Transfers to cost of goods sold	76,000
(k) Transfers from work in process	130,000	Transferred to cost of goods sold for other jobs sold	120,000
	310,000		
Balance 114,000			

Prepaid Insurance

Beginning balance	5,000	(g) Expired insurance	3,000
Balance 2,000			

Accumulated Depreciation—Building

		Beginning balance	40,000
		(e) Depreciation expense	10,000
		Balance	50,000

Accumulated Depreciation—Machinery and Equipment

		Beginning balance	15,000
		(e) Depreciation expense	8,000
		(f) Depreciation expense	7,000
		Balance	30,000

(continues)

EXHIBIT 5–6   *(continued)*

Sales

	(*l*) Sale on account	100,000
	Other sales	199,500
		299,500

Cost of Goods Sold

(*l*) Sale	76,000	
Other sales	120,000	
(*m*) Underapplied		
overhead	500	
Balance	196,500	

Factory Overhead Control

(*b*) Indirect material	5,000	(*j*) Applied		72,000
(*c*) Indirect labor	33,000	(*m*) To close underapplied		500
(*e*) Depreciation	28,000			72,500
(*g*) Insurance	3,000			
(*h*) Taxes	2,500			
(*i*) Miscellaneous	1,000			
	72,500			

Marketing Expense Control

(*d*) Payroll	6,000	
(*f*) Depreciation	2,000	
Cash disbursements		
for other expenses	30,000	
Balance	38,000	

Administrative Expense Control

(*d*) Payroll	5,000	
(*f*) Depreciation	5,000	
Cash disbursements		
for other expenses	25,000	
Balance	35,000	

Work in Process Subsidiary Ledger Accounts
Job No. 101

Beginning balance	40,000	(*k*) Transferred to finished		
(*b*) Direct material	8,000	goods		76,000
(*c*) Direct labor	2,000			
(*j*) Applied overhead	26,000			
	76,000			

Job No. 102

(*b*) Direct material	12,000	(*k*) Transferred to finished		
(*c*) Direct labor	3,000	goods		54,000
(*j*) Applied overhead	39,000			
	54,000			

Job No. 103

(*b*) Direct material	19,000	
(*c*) Direct labor	5,000	
(*j*) Applied overhead	7,000	
Balance	31,000	

Factory Overhead Subsidiary Ledger
Indirect Material

(*b*)	5,000

EXHIBIT 5–6   *(concluded)*

Indirect Labor	
(c)	33,000

Depreciation	
(e)	28,000

Insurance	
(g)	3,000

Taxes	
(h)	2,500

Miscellaneous Factory Costs	
(i)	1,000

Exhibit 5–6 also shows a job order subsidiary ledger. Subsidiary ledgers for direct material inventory and finished goods inventory are also normally used, but these ledgers are not illustrated. The total of the three jobs in the work in process subsidiary ledger equal the balance of the Work in Process general ledger account: $76,000 (Job No. 101) + $54,000 (Job No. 102) + $31,000 (Job No. 103) $161,000.

Because subsidiary ledgers for work in process inventory and factory overhead control are usually more difficult to understand, Exhibit 5–6 illustrates these subsidiary ledgers. We omitted the subsidiary ledger account titles from the journal entries illustrated to emphasize the general ledger accounts. To simplify the illustrations, Wells Manufacturing Company is working on only three jobs, including Job No. 101 whose costs were journalized earlier.

Direct and Indirect Materials Purchased.   This entry records the purchase of direct or indirect raw material on account:

a.	Direct Materials Inventory	55,000	
	Accounts Payable		55,000
	Factory Supplies Inventory	7,000	
	Accounts Payable		7,000

Direct and Indirect Materials Issued.   Assume the issuance of $8,000 direct materials for Job No. 101, $12,000 for Job No. 102, and $19,000 for Job No. 103. Work in Process Inventory receives $39,000 total direct materials issued. The job subsidiary ledger records the detailed costs of each job. The following entry also illustrates the issuance of $5,000 of factory supplies charged to Factory Overhead Control and the indirect materials subsidiary ledger account.

b.	Work in Process Inventory	39,000	
	Job No. 101—8,000		
	Job No. 102—12,000		
	Job No. 103—19,000		
	Factory Overhead Control—Indirect Materials	5,000	
	Direct Materials Inventory		39,000
	Factory Supplies Inventory		5,000

Factory Labor Incurred. The following entry to Work in Process Inventory records the direct labor cost for the three jobs. Assume Job No. 101 incurred direct labor costs of $2,000; Job No. 102, $3,000; and Job No. 103, $5,000. Each amount is posted to the respective account in the subsidiary job ledger. The following entry also records $33,000 indirect labor in the Factory Overhead Control account and the factory overhead subsidiary ledger. The credit of $43,000 to Payroll Payable represents the gross amount of wages payable. Additional entries record taxes and other amounts withheld from the employees' wages and the employer's payroll taxes, which are ignored in this illustration for simplicity.

c.   Work in Process Inventory 10,000
        Job No. 101—2,000
        Job No. 102—3,000
        Job No. 103—5,000
      Factory Overhead Control—Indirect Labor 33,000
        Payroll Payable   43,000

Marketing and Administrative Salaries. The following entry records the marketing and administrative salaries of $6,000 and $5,000. Although this entry can be combined with entry c, we separated it here to emphasize that only factory payroll is charged to Work in Process Inventory and Factory Overhead Control. Subsidiary ledgers detail both the Marketing Expense Control and the Administrative Expense Control, but Exhibit 5–6 does not show these.

d.   Marketing Expense Control 6,000
      Administrative Expense Control 5,000
        Payroll Payable   11,000

Factory Depreciation. Assume that depreciation for the period is $15,000 on the factory building and $13,000 on the factory machinery and equipment. We charge the Factory Overhead Control account in the general ledger and the depreciation account in the factory overhead control subsidiary ledger for this period's depreciation. The credits are entered in the accumulated depreciation contra asset accounts.

e.   Factory Overhead Control—Depreciation Expense 28,000
        Accumulated Depreciation—Building   15,000
        Accumulated Depreciation—Machinery
          and Equipment   13,000

Marketing and Administrative Depreciation. A separate entry records depreciation on the office equipment used by sales and administrative personnel. We can also make this entry at the time we record factory depreciation. We charge all other marketing and administrative costs to these control accounts and illustrate only payroll and depreciation here:

f.   Marketing Expense Control 2,000
      Administrative Expense Control 5,000
        Accumulated Depreciation—Machinery and Equipment   7,000

Factory Insurance. The following entry records the expiration of $3,000 of prepaid insurance on the factory building and equipment. Previously, we debited the Prepaid Insurance asset account at payment of the policy premium. An entry to the Factory Overhead Control account in the general ledger and to insurance expense in the factory overhead subsidiary ledger records this cost.

g.   Factory Overhead Control—Insurance Expense 3,000
        Prepaid Insurance   3,000

Property and Payroll Taxes. Estimates for both the tax rate and tax base may be needed for factory property taxes even though the exact amount to be paid may not be known. Normally an accrual for the tax liability occurs when using an estimate based on the rates and bases applicable in the preceding period adjusted for possible changes in the tax rates or assessed values. To record estimated property taxes on the factory, we debit Factory Overhead Control and credit Taxes Payable. A similar entry records the employer's payroll tax as illustrated earlier for Job No. 101. An additional entry debits the taxes account in the factory overhead subsidiary ledger.

h. Factory Overhead Control—Tax Expense 2,500
     Taxes Payable   2,500

When the taxes are paid, we debit Taxes Payable for the amount accrued and debit Prepaid Taxes for the amount applicable to future periods; cash is credited. To simplify the illustration, no adjustment for over- or underaccrual of taxes occurs at payment.

Factory Miscellaneous Costs. A debit to Factory Overhead Control in the general ledger and to the Miscellaneous Factory Cost account in the factory overhead subsidiary ledger records a $1,000 cash payment for miscellaneous factory costs. We credit the cash account in the general ledger. Exhibit 5–6 omits all other individual entries to the Cash account. Other cash receipts totaled $191,000 and other cash disbursements totaled $185,000, including $73,000 for marketing and administrative expense and $30,000 for mortgage payments. The following entry records the payment for miscellaneous factory costs:

i. Factory Overhead Control—Miscellaneous Factory Costs 1,000
     Cash   1,000

Factory Overhead Applied. Using the $50 per machine-hour application rate for Wells Manufacturing Company from Chapter 2, each job receives the following applied overhead based on the machine-hours incurred:

        Job No. 101 . . . . $26,000 ($50 $\times$ 520 machine-hours)
        Job No. 102 . . . . 39,000 ($50 $\times$ 780 machine-hours)
        Job No. 103 . . . . 7,000 ($50 $\times$ 140 machine-hours)

This entry is a summary entry recording the total overhead applied for this period. It transfers $72,000 total overhead applied to Work in Process Inventory. The Factory Overhead Control account is credited as follows:

j. Work in Process Inventory 72,000
     Job No. 101—26,000
     Job No. 102—39,000
     Job No. 103—7,000
       Factory Overhead Control   72,000

Transfer to Finished Goods. Assume that during the period, Wells employees complete Job No. 101 and Job No. 102 and transfer them to Finished Goods Inventory. Job No. 101 had a beginning balance of $40,000; additions this period were direct material of $8,000, direct labor of $2,000, and factory overhead of $26,000. We transfer the $76,000, total cost of Job No. 101, from both the job ledger and Work in Process Inventory by credits to these accounts. Job No. 102 was started and finished this period; the total cost is $54,000. Job No. 103, with costs of $31,000, remains unfinished in Work in Process Inventory at the end of the period.

k.   Finished Goods Inventory 130,000
   Work in Process Inventory   130,000
    Job No. 101—76,000
    Job No. 102—54,000

Sale Is Made. To record the sale on account of Job No. 101 for $100,000, we debit Accounts Receivable and credit Sales. We charge Cost of Goods Sold for the $76,000 cost of Job No. 101. The credit of $76,000 to Finished Goods Inventory removes the cost of Job No. 101 from this asset account.

l.   Accounts Receivable 100,000
   Sales   100,000
  Cost of Goods Sold 76,000
   Finished Goods Inventory   76,000

This journal entry does not illustrate additional sales on account totaling $199,500. A debit to Cost of Goods Sold and a credit to Finished Goods Inventory records the $120,000 cost of these sales. Assume $314,500 is received on account and credited to the accounts receivable ledger.

Underapplied Factory Overhead. The balance in the Factory Overhead Control account at the end of the period arises because actual factory overhead amounted to $72,500, while the overhead applied was only $72,000. The difference of $500 represents an underapplication of overhead. Because this balance reflects inefficiencies of the current month, it is closed as a debit to Cost of Goods Sold. The credit of $500 closes Factory Overhead Control.

m.   Cost of Goods Sold 500
   Factory Overhead Control 500

For the resulting Cost of Goods Manufactured Statement and Statement of Income for Wells Manufacturing Company for the year ended December 31, 19X1, see Exhibits 2–4, 2–5, and 2–7 in Chapter 2.

Summary

Companies use either job order, process costing, or operation costing systems to assign costs to products. Activity-based management may be combined with either of these product costing systems. A batch, a contract, or an order receives costs using a job order system. Direct material and direct labor associated with each job are identified and accumulated on a job order cost sheet. Because factory overhead resources usually cannot be traced to specific jobs, overhead is applied on a causal basis. This chapter illustrates the source documents and journal entries used in job order systems.

Process costing accumulates costs by departments for a time period and allocates costs among the products processed during the period. Process costing requires less record-keeping; however, the benefits of knowing the cost of each job may outweigh the added costs of a job costing system. A company may find that a hybrid of the process costing and job order costing systems best meets its needs; such systems are operation costing systems. Both service and manufacturing organizations should select the system that best meets their individual needs. By omitting direct materials, service organizations can adapt costing methods for manufacturers.

Important Terms and Concepts

job order costing, 145   salaries, 147
process costing, 145   clock card (timecard), 148
operation costing, 145   job time ticket, 148
material (stores) requisition, 145   daily job time ticket, 149
material credit slips, 146   job order cost sheet, 151
wages, 147

Appendix 5–A Reciprocal Accounts (L.O. 4)

Some companies have branch production plants in various locations. Rather than establish a complete set of books at each branch factory, branches may keep only the ledger accounts that apply directly to their production. This system is appropriate if the company wishes to give each of its factories some managerial control, yet to still have summarized managerial control data recorded at the general office. While the records kept at the branch factories may not be uniform, at a minimum each should maintain a factory journal and factory ledger with subsidiary ledgers for materials inventory, work in process, and factory overhead control.

The two reciprocal accounts most often used are a **home office ledger** (known as *general office ledger*) account on the branch books and a **factory ledger** (known as *factory office*) on the home office books. Because these are reciprocal accounts, a debit to the home office ledger account by the factory requires a credit to the factory ledger account by the general office and vice versa. Exhibit 5A–1 illustrates the use of this system.

The number of accounts designated to the branch varies depending on the skill of the accounting personnel employed at the factory and on the size of the production plant. For example, the sole payroll duty of a bookkeeper hired at a branch office may be to total and forward the timecards and time sheets to a central location where the calculation of gross pay, withholdings, and net pay occurs. Other branch offices, however, may prepare their own payroll checks, record payroll deductions, and prepare employees' checks drawn on the branch office's payroll bank account. In this case, the branch office periodically remits the payroll deductions made. Entry *c* in Exhibit 5A–1 assumes the general office makes all payments for payroll.

Entry *i* in Exhibit 5A–1 records the shipment of finished goods to the warehouse under the assumption that the general office maintains the Finished Goods Inventory account. In other companies, when the factory office keeps the finished goods account, the factory office records the entire entry. Similarly, some branch factories may keep their own plant assets and related accumulated depreciation accounts, while other companies centralize all asset accounts at the general office.

Problem for Self-Study

Journal Entries and Supporting Inventory Schedules

The following data for Sardis Company summarize the operations related to production for November, the first month of operations. Sardis uses a job order cost system.

1. Direct materials costing $22,000 and indirect materials of $2,300 were purchased on account.

EXHIBIT 5A–1   Use of Factory Ledger and Home Office Ledger Accounts

	Transaction	Combined Entry on One Set of Books		
(a)	Factory purchases direct materials and factory supplies	Direct Materials Inventory	12,000	
		Factory Supplies Inventory	4,000	
		Accounts Payable		16,000
(b)	Direct materials requisitions	Work in Process Inventory	8,000	
		Direct Materials Inventory		8,000
(c)	Factory payroll	Work in Process Inventory	20,000	
		Factory Overhead Control	8,000	
		FICA Taxes Payable		2,103
		Income Taxes Withheld		9,000
		Salaries Payable		16,897
(d)	Employer's payroll taxes treated as indirect costs	Factory Overhead Control	3,083	
		FICA Taxes Payable		2,103
		State Unemployment Taxes Payable		756
		Federal Unemployment Taxes Payable		224
(e)	Factory supplies used	Factory Overhead Control	2,180	
		Factory Supplies Inventory		2,180
(f)	Cash paid for factory overhead	Factory Overhead Control	500	
		Cash		500
(g)	Factory depreciation and expiration of factory insurance	Factory Overhead Control	2,000	
		Accumulated Depreciation		1,500
		Prepaid Insurance		500
(h)	Factory overhead applied	Work in Process Inventory	15,000	
		Factory Overhead Control		15,000
(i)	Finished goods shipped to warehouse	Finished Goods Inventory	40,000	
		Work in Process Inventory		40,000
(j)	Goods shipped to customers	Accounts Receivable	30,000	
		Sales		30,000
		Cost of Goods sold	20,000	
		Finished Goods Inventory		20,000
(k)	Collections on accounts	Cash	30,000	
		Accounts Receivable		30,000

(continues)

2. Materials requisitioned and factory labor used:

	Materials	Factory Labor
Job No. 1	$2,340	$1,090
Job No. 2	3,390	1,990
Job No. 3	2,980	1,440
Job No. 4	4,765	2,890
Job No. 5	2,240	940
Job No. 6	1,940	1,090
For general factory use	515	690

EXHIBIT 5A-I   *(concluded)*

Home Office Journal			Factory Office Journal		
Factory Ledger	16,000		Direct Materials Inventory	12,000	
Accounts Payable		16,000	Factory Supplies Inventory	4,000	
			Home Office Ledger		16,000
No entry			Work in Process Inventory	8,000	
			Direct Materials Inventory		8,000
Factory Ledger	28,000		Work in Process Inventory	20,000	
FICA Taxes Payable		2,103	Factory Overhead Control	8,000	
Income Taxes Withheld		9,000	Home Office Ledger		28,000
Salaries Payable		16,897			
Factory Ledger	3,083		Factory Overhead Control	3,083	
FICA Taxes Payable		2,103	Home Office Ledger		3,083
State Unemployment Taxes					
Payable		756			
Federal Unemployment Taxes					
Payable		224			
No entry			Factory Overhead Control	2,180	
			Factory Supplies Inventory		2,180
Factory Ledger	500		Factory Overhead Control	500	
Cash		500	Home Office Ledger		500
Factory Ledger	2,000		Factory Overhead Control	2,000	
Accumulated Depreciation		1,500	Home Office Ledger		2,000
Prepaid Insurance		500			
No entry			Work in Process Inventory	15,000	
			Factory Overhead Control		15,000
Finished Goods Inventory	40,000		Home Office Ledger	40,000	
Factory Ledger		40,000	Work in Process Inventory		40,000
Accounts Receivable	30,000		No entry		
Sales		30,000			
Cost of Goods Sold	20,000		No entry		
Finished Goods Inventory		20,000			
Cash	30,000		No entry		
Accounts Receivable		30,000			

Factory Ledger					Home Office Ledger				
(a)	16,000	(i)	40,000		(i)	40,000	(a)	16,000
(c)	28,000						(c)	28,000
(d)	3,083						(d)	3,083
(f)	500						(f)	500
(g)	2,000						(g)	2,000
		To Balance	9,583		To Balance	9,583		
Balance	9,583						Balance	9,583

3. Factory overhead costs incurred on account, $3,265.

4. Factory machinery and equipment depreciation totaled $1,340.

5. Factory overhead is applied at 60 percent of direct labor cost.

6. Jobs completed: Nos. 1, 2, 4, and 5.

7. Jobs No. 1, 2, and 4 were shipped and customers were billed for $5,690, $9,490, and $13,290, respectively.

Required:

a. Prepare entries in general journal form to record the summarized operations.

b. Open T accounts for the Work in Process Inventory and Finished Goods Inventory and post the appropriate entries using the identifying numbers as dates. Insert memorandum account balances as of the end of the month.

c. Support the balance in the Work in Process account with a schedule of unfinished jobs.

d. Support the balance in the Finished Goods account with a schedule of completed jobs on hand.

Solution to Problem for Self-Study

a. **SARDIS COMPANY**

1.	Direct Materials Inventory	22,000	
	Indirect Materials Inventory	2,300	
	Accounts Payable		24,300
2.	Work in Process Inventory	27,095	
	Factory Overhead Control	1,205	
	Direct Materials Inventory		17,655
	Indirect Materials Inventory		515
	Payroll Payable		10,130
3.	Factory Overhead Control	3,265	
	Accounts Payable		3,265
4.	Factory Overhead Control	1,340	
	Accumulated Depreciation—Machinery		
	and Equipment		1,340
5.	Work in Process Inventory	5,664	
	Factory Overhead Control (60% of $9,440)		5,664
6.	Finished Goods Inventory	23,791	
	Work in Process Inventory		23,791

Computation of cost of jobs finished:

Job	Direct Materials	Direct Labor	Overhead	Total
No. 1 ...	$2,340	$1,090	$ 654	$ 4,084
No. 2 ...	3,390	1,990	1,194	6,574
No. 4 ...	4,765	2,890	1,734	9,389
No. 5 ...	2,240	940	564	3,744
				$23,791

7.	Accounts Receivable	28,470	
	Sales		28,470
	Cost of Goods Sold	20,047	
	Finished Goods Inventory		20,047

Computation of cost of jobs sold:

Job No. 1	$ 4,084
Job No. 2	6,574
Job No. 4	9,389
	$20,047

b.

Work in Process Inventory			
2.	27,095	6.	23,791
5.	5,664		
8,968			

Finished Goods Inventory			
6.	23,791	7.	20,047
3,744 Bal.			

c.

Schedule of Unfinished Jobs

	Direct Materials	Direct Labor	Factory Overhead	Total
Job No. 3 . . .	$2,980	$1,440	$864	$5,284
Job No. 6 . . .	1,940	1,090	654	3,684
Balance of work in process, November 30				$8,968

d.

Schedule of Finished Jobs

Job No. 5:	Direct materials	$2,240
	Direct labor	940
	Factory overhead	564
Balance of finished goods, November 30		$3,744

Review Questions

1. Discuss the relationship of the payroll accountant to the cost accountant.

2. Explain how you could use job order costing in a nonmanufacturing firm or industry.

3. Contrast job order and process costing systems. What factors dictate whether a job order or process cost system is more appropriate?

4. How does a dentist or veterinarian use job order cost sheets that you as their patient (or patient's owner) personally see?

5. What is the source document for the distribution of direct labor costs to Work in Process Inventory and indirect labor costs to Factory Overhead Control?

6. What form does the subsidiary ledger for a Work in Process Control account in a job order costing system take?

7. What methods and documents are used to control materials inventories?

8. If the total material cost of 100 units is $200 and a 10 percent increase in material cost is expected at the same time that an increase of 50 percent in volume of production is planned, what is next year's total budgeted cost for materials?

9. What could cause a difference between the time reported on a timecard and that shown on a job time ticket? How should this difference be reported?

CPA/CIA Multiple-Choice Questions

1. (AICPA) In a job order cost system, the use of indirect materials would usually be reflected in the general ledger as an increase in

   a. Stores Control.
   b. Work in Process Control.
   c. Factory Overhead Control.
   d. Factory Overhead Applied.

2. (AICPA) Marc Corp. has a job order cost system. The following debits (credits) appeared in the Work in Process account for the month of May 19X1:

May	Description	Amount
1	Balance	$ 10,000
31	Direct materials	60,000
31	Direct labor	40,000
31	Factory overhead	32,000
31	To finished goods	(120,000)

Marc applies overhead to production at a predetermined rate of 80 percent based on direct labor cost. Job No. 23, the only job still in process at the end of May 19X1, has been charged with direct labor of $5,000. The amount of direct materials charged to Job No. 23 was

a. $ 6,250.
b. $ 7,500.
c. $13,000.
d. $17,000.

3.–4. (AICPA) These items are based on the following data: Blum Corp. manufactures plastic coated metal clips. The following were among Blum's manufacturing costs:

Wages

Machine operators	$200,000
Maintenance workers	30,000
Factory foremen	90,000

Materials used

Metal wire	$500,000
Lubricant for oiling machinery	10,000
Plastic coating	380,000

3. Blum's direct labor amounted to

a. $200,000.
b. $230,000.
c. $290,000.
d. $320,000.

4. Blum's direct materials amounted to

a. $890,000.
b. $880,000.
c. $510,000.
d. $500,000.

5. (AICPA) In a job order cost system, direct labor costs usually are recorded initially as an increase in

a. Factory Overhead Applied.
b. Factory Overhead Control.
c. Finished Goods Control.
d. Work in Process Control.

6. Blackwood uses a job order cost system and applies factory overhead to production orders on the basis of direct labor cost. The overhead rates for 19X2 are 200 percent for Department A and 50 percent for Department B. Job 123, started and completed during 19X2, was charged with the following costs:

	Department	
	A	**B**
Direct materials	$25,000	$ 5,000
Direct labor	?	30,000
Factory overhead	40,000	?

The total manufacturing costs associated with Job 123 should be

a. $135,000.
b. $180,000.
c. $195,000.
d. $240,000.

7. Axe Company has a job order cost system. The following debits (credits) appeared in the Work in Process account for the month of March 19X9:

March	Description	Amount
1	Balance	$ 2,000
31	Direct materials	12,000
31	Direct labor	8,000
31	Factory overhead	6,400
31	To finished goods	(24,000)

Axe applies overhead to production at a predetermined rate of 80 percent based on direct labor cost. Job No. 9, the only job still in process at the end of March 19X9, has been charged with direct labor of $1,000. The amount of direct materials charged to Job No. 9 was

a. $12,000.
b. $ 4,400.
c. $ 2,600.
d. $ 1,500.

8. The completion of goods is recorded as a decrease in work in process control when using

	Job Order Costing	Process Costing
a.	Yes.	No.
b.	Yes.	Yes.
c.	No.	Yes.
d.	No.	No.

9. In a job order cost system, the use of indirect materials previously purchased usually is recorded as a decrease in

a. Stores Control.
b. Work in Process Control.
c. Factory Overhead Control.
d. Factory Overhead Applied.

10. In a job order cost system using predetermined factory overhead rates, indirect materials usually are recorded initially as an increase in

a. Work in Process Control.
b. Factory Overhead Applied.
c. Factory Overhead Control.
d. Stores Control.

Exercises

E5–1 Applying Overhead to Job (L.O. 2)

In 19X1, Jett Company began work on Job No. 218, incurring a direct material cost of $1,200 and a direct labor cost of $4,209 representing an actual labor rate of $6.10. The factory overhead application rate was $4.75 per direct labor-hour for 19X1. After evaluating 19X1 variances and undertaking further study, management revised the factory overhead application rate in 19X2 to $4.90 per direct labor-hour. After additional material costing $500 and 100 hours of direct labor at a $6.15 labor rate were incurred in January 19X2, Job No. 218 was finished and sold to a customer for $14,000 on account.

Required:

a. Compute the balance in Job No. 218 subsidiary ledger account on December 31, 19X1, when the year ends.
b. Give all journal entries relating to Job No. 218 for 19X2.

E5–2 Balances in Inventory Accounts, Over-/Underapplied OH (L.O. 2)

For Box, Inc.'s first month of operations, material and labor costs charged to three jobs worked on in May were:

	Job No.		
	101	**102**	**103**
Direct material	$3,000	$4,500	$1,800
Direct labor at $8 per hour	3,200	2,400	2,000

Overhead is applied at the rate of $6 per direct labor-hour. Jobs No. 101 and No. 102 were completed; Job No. 101 was sold; Job 103 remained incomplete at the end of the month.

The costs incurred during the month:

Direct material purchases	$25,000
Direct and indirect factory labor costs	8,500
Factory overhead excluding indirect labor	5,000

Required:

a. Determine the May 31 balances in each of the three inventory accounts.
b. Compute the amount of over- or underapplied overhead.
c. Prepare the entry to dispose of the over- or underapplied overhead, treating the entire amount as a period cost.

E5–3 Manufacturing Statement; Factory Overhead Schedule (L.O. 2)

Lee Company's records provide the following data:

Janitorial supplies, January 1, 19X1	$ 2,000
Janitorial supplies, December 31, 19X1	1,600
Janitorial supplies purchased	14,000
Direct labor (25,000 hours)	115,000
Depreciation	8,500
Property taxes	1,700
Direct material, January 1, 19X1	65,000
Direct material, December 31, 19X1	70,000
Direct material purchased	80,000
Indirect labor	42,000
Work in process, January 1, 19X1	105,700
Work in process, December 31, 19X1	95,800
Utilities	30,000
Finished goods inventory, January 1, 19X1	120,600
Finished goods inventory, December 31, 19X1	115,000
Rent	22,000

Factory overhead is applied at 105 percent of direct labor cost.

Required:

Prepare a Cost of Goods Manufactured and Sold Statement for the year ended December 31, 19X1, using actual factory overhead. Also prepare a separate schedule for factory overhead showing a calculation of over- or underapplied factory overhead.

E5–4 Journal Entries and Cost of Goods Manufactured Statement (L.O. 3)

O'Neill Company completed the following selected transactions during April 19X1:

1. Direct materials costing $43,000 were purchased on account.
2. Direct materials costing $31,000 were issued into production.
3. Miscellaneous manufacturing costs of $2,700 were paid in cash.
4. The factory payroll was accrued and distributed as follows:

Direct Labor	$29,000
Indirect Labor	3,500

5.   The following adjusting entries were made on April 30:

Depreciation on Factory Machinery and Equipment $5,700
Insurance Expired on Factory Machinery and Equipment . . .   950

6.   Factory overhead is applied at 35 percent of direct labor cost.

7.   The balance in Work in Process Inventory on April 1, 19X1, was $15,000; the balance on April 30, 19X1, was $13,000. Transfer the costs of goods finished to the finished goods storeroom.

8.   Goods costing $61,900 were sold on account for $85,300.

9.   Close the Factory Overhead Control by transferring any over- or underapplied overhead to cost of goods sold.

Required:

a. Prepare journal entries for these transactions using subsidiary ledger accounts for factory overhead.

b. Prepare a Cost of Goods Manufactured Statement for the month showing applied factory overhead instead of actual factory overhead.

E5–5 Journal Entries for Cost Transactions (L.O. 3)

Apple Corporation has asked you to record the following data relating to factory labor and overhead for one period during the year. Before operations began, management estimated direct labor costs for the year at $120,000 and factory overhead costs at $72,000.

1.   An analysis of store requisitions showed indirect material amounted to $15,000.

2.   The labor time tickets showed that actual labor cost was $72,000 including indirect labor of $9,000. Ignore salary deductions.

3.   Cash of $2,100 was paid for miscellaneous factory overhead expenses.

4.   Depreciation was $3,000 for the building and $1,000 for machinery and equipment.

5.   Insurance of $500 on the building and machinery and equipment expired.

6.   Accrued taxes on the factory building and factory machinery and equipment were estimated to be $5,600.

7.   Apply factory overhead and close the under- or overapplied amount to Cost of Goods Sold.

Required:

Prepare journal entries for the transactions.

E5–6 Determination of Job Cost (L.O. 1)

Cavitt Company uses a job order system for its two departments. Budgeted production costs for the year are as follows:

	Department	
	A	**B**
Budgeted costs for year:		
Direct material	$ 60,000	$ 80,000
Direct labor	150,000	200,000
Factory overhead	450,000	80,000
Actual cost charged to Job No. 86 during year:		
Direct material	1,000	800
Direct labor	3,000	2,200

Cavitt applies manufacturing overhead to production orders on the basis of direct labor cost using departmental rates determined at the beginning of the year based on the annual budget.

Required:

Determine the total manufacturing cost associated with Job No. 86 for the year.

E5–7 Income Statement Based on Projections Given (L.O. 2)

James Manufacturing Company engages in the production of one model of a copy machine. The company has experimented with broadening its product line, but has found that it can maintain higher profits by concentrating its resources on one particular model that sells for $2,000 each. James Company's per unit costs are as follows:

Direct materials	$600	
Direct labor	450	
Variable factory overhead	150	
Fixed factory overhead	200	
Marketing expense	150	(20% variable)
Administrative expense	100	(5% variable)

The company sold 8,000 units last year, but wants a 25 percent increase in sales volume this year. It has decided to reduce the sales price 15 percent to achieve the increased sales. The additional units can be produced with no alterations to or expansions of the existing plant facilities. Management estimates that direct material will decrease by $50 per unit by taking advantage of quantity discounts, and that direct labor will increase by $20 per unit.

Required:

a. Prepare a Statement of Income for this year taking into account the company's projections. Instead of preparing a separate Cost of Goods Manufactured Statement, detail the cost of sales on the Statement of Income.

b. Prepare a Statement of Income for last year so you can compare income before taxes on this statement to that prepared in Requirement *a* and advise the company regarding its decision to reduce the price.

E5–8 Journal Entries and Cost of Goods Manufactured Statement (L.O. 3)

Constance Company completed these selected transactions during May 19X1.

1. Purchased $50,000 direct materials and $5,000 factory supplies on account.

2. Issued direct materials costing $40,000 into production and $3,000 factory supplies.

3. Cash was paid for miscellaneous manufacturing expense costing $4,000.

4. The following adjusting entries were made on May 31:

Depreciation on factory machinery and equipment	$11,400
Insurance expired on factory machinery and equipment	$ 2,500

5. The factory payroll was accrued and distributed as follows:

Indirect labor	$13,000
Direct labor (9,000 hours)	$45,000

6. Factory overhead is applied at $4.00 per direct labor-hour.

7. The balance in Work in Process Inventory on May 1, 19X1, was $12,000; the balance on May 31, 19X1, was $16,000. Transfer the costs of goods completed to the finished goods storeroom.

8. The May 1, 19X1, balance in Finished Goods Inventory was $26,000 while the May 31, 19X1, balance was $20,000. Record the entry for the goods sold on account which were priced at 120 percent of cost.

9. Close the Factory Overhead Control and transfer any over- or underapplied overhead to Cost of Goods Sold.

Required:

a. Prepare journal entries for these transactions using a Factory Overhead subsidiary ledger.

b. Prepare a Cost of Goods Manufactured Statement for the month using actual factory overhead.

E5–9 Job Order Costing (L.O. 1)

Ban Enterprises, Inc., began work on four jobs during its first month of operation. Jobs No. 1 and No. 3 were completed during the month. The cost sheets that follow indicate that all costs applicable to them have been recorded. Jobs No. 2 and No. 4 are still in process at the end of the month; accountants have recorded all applicable costs except factory overhead on the related cost sheets. These jobs required a total of $389 of indirect materials and $936 of indirect labor during the month in addition to the materials and labor charged directly to the jobs.

Job No. 1

Direct material	$ 5,145
Direct labor	3,800
Factory overhead	1,786
Total	$10,731

Job No. 2

Direct material	$ 9,500
Direct labor	12,800
Factory overhead	

Job No. 3

Direct material	$ 4,080
Direct labor	7,300
Factory overhead	3,431
Total	$14,811

Job No. 4

Direct material	$ 1,750
Direct labor	2,360
Factory overhead	

Required:

Prepare an entry, in general journal form, to record each of the following operations for the month. Use one entry for each operation and a job order subsidiary ledger.

a. Direct and indirect materials used.
b. Direct and indirect labor used.
c. Apply factory overhead on the basis of direct labor cost using a single overhead rate.
d. Jobs No. 1 and No. 3 completed and transferred out awaiting sale to customers.

Problems

P5–10 Preparing Journal Entries and a Cost of Goods Manufactured Statement (L.O. 3)

A partial list of the account balances on November 1, 19X1, for the Don Manufacturing Company were Direct Materials, $65,000; Indirect Materials, $8,000; Work in Process, $70,000; and Finished Goods, $88,000. Transactions for the month include the following:

1. Purchased direct materials costing $30,000 and indirect materials costing $10,000 on account.
2. Paid cash for the factory rent, $1,500.
3. Issued material costing $28,160 to three jobs for the processing of units.
4. Janitorial supplies costing $1,080 and repair supplies costing $5,780 were issued from the storeroom.

5. Analysis of the payroll records revealed that direct labor of $43,000, indirect labor of $26,000, marketing salaries of $5,000, and administrative salaries of $6,000 were to be recorded. Ignore payroll deductions.
6. Depreciation on the factory machinery amounted to $2,770, and on the factory building to $2,850.
7. Insurance of $500 expired on the factory building and machinery.
8. The cost accountant has budgeted factory overhead for the year to be $450,000 and machine-hours to be 90,000. Machine-hours for November were 8,000. Record the application of overhead.
9. Paid cash for miscellaneous factory overhead of $330.
10. There were 3,000 finished units costing $150,000 transferred into the warehouse.
11. During the month, 4,000 units costing $200,000 were sold on account for $300,000.
12. It was determined that the reason for the difference in actual and applied factory overhead was due to inefficiencies in the operating conditions. Close the Factory Overhead account.
13. Other marketing expenses of $3,000 and administrative expenses of $4,600 were paid.

Required:

a. Prepare journal entries to record the transactions for the month, using subsidiary ledger accounts for factory overhead.
b. Prepare a cost of goods manufactured statement using applied factory overhead costs and also prepare a statement of income for the month.

P5–11 Missing Amounts, Over-/Underapplied Overhead (L.O. 2)

Ron Regis Company presents the following selected general ledger accounts showing balances on May 1 of the current calendar year:

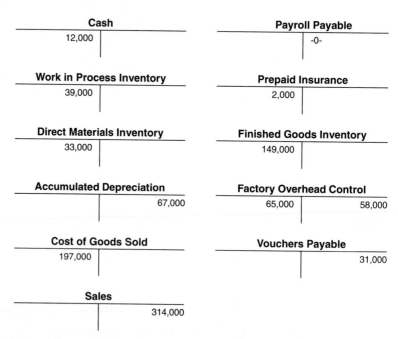

Cash		Payroll Payable	
12,000			-0-

Work in Process Inventory		Prepaid Insurance	
39,000		2,000	

Direct Materials Inventory		Finished Goods Inventory	
33,000		149,000	

Accumulated Depreciation		Factory Overhead Control	
	67,000	65,000	58,000

Cost of Goods Sold		Vouchers Payable	
197,000			31,000

Sales	
	314,000

Correct balances on May 31 of the current year include:

Payroll payable	$ 4,000	(Cr.)
Direct materials inventory	31,000	(Dr.)
Work in process inventory	45,000	(Dr.)
Finished goods inventory	153,000	(Dr.)

Selected May transactions of Ron Regis Company are summarized as follows:

(a)	Cash sales	$107,000
(b)	Materials purchased on account	38,000
(c)	Cash disbursements to creditors	35,100
(d)	Direct materials used	
(e)	Factory payroll paid	24,000
(f)	Direct factory labor incurred	18,000
(g)	Indirect factory labor incurred	
(h)	Factory overhead applied: 125% of direct labor cost	
(i)	Factory insurance expired	400
(j)	Factory depreciation	1,400
(k)	Factory repair services purchased on account	4,000
(l)	Vouchers payable paid	33,000
(m)	Cost of goods manufactured (using applied factory overhead)	
(n)	Cost of goods sold (before over-/underapplied factory overhead)	

Required:

a. Calculate the dollar amounts to fill the five blanks in transactions *d, g, h, m, n.*

b. Post the amounts for all May transactions to the general ledger accounts given, using each transaction letter to cross-reference your posted debits and credits.

c. Prepare the entry to close the over-/underapplied factory overhead to cost of goods sold.

P5–12 Using T-Account Analysis for Cost Flow Determination (L.O. 2)

A mudslide destroyed many of the records of California Company on November 11, 19X7. For insurance reimbursement purposes, you have been asked to determine the cost of inventory destroyed. The company used a job order costing system. You have verified the following information:

1. At the beginning of the fiscal year on July 1, 19X7, the balances in these accounts were Direct Materials Inventory, $10,000; Factory Supplies Inventory, $4,000; Work in Process Inventory, $8,000; and Finished Goods Inventory, $14,000. The balance sheet also showed a $3,000 balance reflecting the liability for accrued payroll.

2. Direct materials costing $18,000 were purchased on account between July 1 and November 11.

3. A total of $17,000 direct materials and $2,000 factory supplies were issued to the factory.

4. A total of $35,000 was paid in factory wages between July 1 and November 11. Ignore all payroll deductions. On November 11 there were $2,000 accrued factory wages payable.

5. Of the factory wages, direct labor totaled $30,000.

6. The debits to the Factory Overhead account during the period before the mudslide totaled $20,000 excluding the indirect materials and indirect labor.

7. Overhead is applied using a rate of 85 percent of direct labor costs.

8. Goods costing $50,000 were finished and transferred to Finished Goods Inventory between July and November.

9. Goods costing $55,000 were sold this period.

10. The company follows the policy that if the balance in Factory Overhead is small, it is distributed to Cost of Goods Sold; otherwise it is apportioned among Work in Process, Finished Goods, and Cost of Goods Sold based on their balances before the apportionment.

Required:

Use T-account analysis in determining the November 11 balance of Direct Materials, Factory Supplies Inventory, Work in Process Inventory, and Finished Goods Inventory.

P5–13 Forecasted Income Statement Based on Projections Given (L.O. 2)

The following information regarding one unit of product has been abstracted from the records for the year ending March 31, 19X2, of Kohn Manufacturing Company.

	Per Unit	
Sales price	$100	
Direct material	22	
Direct labor	15	
Variable factory overhead	10	
Fixed factory overhead	18	
Marketing expense	6	(35% is variable)
Administrative expense	4	(10% is variable)

Management is formulating a strategy to increase company sales; they want to sell more than the 4,200 units sold last year. The alternative being considered is a sales price reduction to stimulate sales. A 10 percent reduction in unit sales price will result in a 20 percent increase in units sold. The existing plant facilities are adequate for producing the increased volume. Because the company will be able to take advantage of quantity discounts, direct material cost will decrease by $2.00 per unit. There will be, however, an 8 percent increase in the labor cost per unit. No other changes are projected. Provide for no change in the level of inventories maintained.

Required:

a. Prepare a pro forma statement of income for the next year using the projections presented. No cost of goods manufactured statement is required; instead, detail the cost of sales on the statement of income.

b. Prepare a statement of income for 19X2. Compare the income before taxes on this statement to that on the pro forma and advise management regarding the proposed price reduction and sales increase. Support your conclusions.

P5–14 Journal Entries (L.O. 3)

The following transactions occurred during March 19X1 for the Lyerly Manufacturing Company:

1. Purchased direct materials of $60,000 and factory supplies of $30,000 on account.
2. Paid miscellaneous factory costs totaling $4,500.
3. Incurred the following wages. Ignore deductions from gross wages and the payment.

Direct labor:	
Job No. 201	$15,000
Job No. 202	24,000
Job No. 203	36,000
	$75,000
Indirect labor	$23,000

4. An analysis of material requisitions showed that the following material was used during the month:

Direct material:	
Job No. 201	$20,000
Job No. 202	12,000
Job No. 203	18,000
	$50,000
Indirect labor	$28,000

5. Job No. 201 was completed and transferred to finished goods. Overhead is applied at 134 percent of direct labor cost to each job on its completion.
6. Use the following data to record an adjusting entry:

Accrued factory taxes payable	$ 2,100
Expired factory insurance	9,010
Depreciation of factory building	21,200
Depreciation of factory machinery	10,500

7. Job No. 201 was sold on account for $63,000.
8. At the end of the cost period, charged overhead to the uncompleted jobs at the rate of 134 percent of direct labor cost.
9. Closed the over- or underapplied overhead to the Cost of Goods Sold.

Required:

a. Prepare general journal entries to record the preceding information. Use a subsidiary job cost ledger.
b. Present statistics to prove the balances of the Work in Process account.

P5–15 Preparing Journal Entries and Using a Subsidiary Ledger for Work in Process (L.O. 3)

Before operations begin for the year 19X2, the management of the Cent Company predicts factory overhead to be $51,200 while estimated machine-hours will be 6,400.

At the beginning of 19X2, the Work in Process account and the job order ledger appear as follows:

Work in Process Inventory			**Job No. 1**		
Balance	8,050		Direct material	2,200	
			Direct labor	1,500	
			Applied factory overhead	1,050	
			Balance	4,750	

Job No. 2			**Job No. 3**		
Direct material	360		Direct material	570	
Direct labor	475		Direct labor	280	
Applied factory overhead	1,015		Applied factory overhead	600	
Balance	1,850		Balance	1,450	

Required:

a. Record the following journal entries using general ledger accounts; in addition use subsidiary ledger accounts for work in process assuming the company employs a perpetual inventory system.

Jan. 2 Purchased direct material of $3,000, repair supplies of $1,800, and factory supplies of $200 for cash.

 4 Issued materials as follows:

Job No. 1	$ 200
Job No. 2	300
Job No. 3	1,000
Repair supplies	1,500

 10 Job No. 1 was finished and transferred to the storeroom. It was determined that during the month of January, direct labor cost on this job was $450 while machine-hours totaled 230.

 16 The following factory items were paid for in cash:

Rent	$700
Insurance	500
Miscellaneous expense	200

 19 Additional material was issued from the materials storeroom:

To Job No. 2	$307
To Job No. 3	116
Factory supplies	80

 20 Job No. 1 was sold for $7,500 on account.

Jan. 24 Job No. 2 was finished and transferred to the storeroom. It was determined that during the month of January, direct labor cost on this job was $345 while machine-hours totaled 202.

31 Analysis of the time sheets showed the following unrecorded factory labor: Job No. 3, $225; factory supervision $150; and maintenance employees, $100.

31 Overhead was applied to the remaining jobs in process. Machine-hours on Job No. 3 during January amounted to 70 hours.

31 Depreciation of $775 on the factory building was recorded.

31 Close the over- or underapplied overhead to Cost of Goods Sold.

b. Prove your balance in Work in Process Inventory.

P5–16 Impact on Gross Margin with Volume and Cost Changes (L.O. 2)

Roof Company produces one product line and expects sales for 19X1 to be $500,000. The following data indicate the cost of goods sold:

Direct materials used	$ 70,000
Direct labor	100,000
Fixed factory overhead	20,000
Variable factory overhead	110,000
	$300,000

Company management expects costs to rise and at year-end predicts the following will occur in 19X2 unless the product is redesigned:

1. Material prices will average 8 percent higher while direct labor rates will average 15 percent higher. Variable factory overhead will vary in proportion to direct labor costs.

2. There will be a 10 percent decrease in the number of units sold in 19X2 if the sales price is increased to produce the same rate of gross margin as the 19X1 rate; gross margin is expressed as a percentage of sales.

If the product is redesigned according to the suggestions of the marketing department, an 18 percent increase can be obtained in the units sold with a 15 percent increase in the unit sales price. Changing the product will affect costs as follows:

1. A lower grade of material will be used that has averaged 6 percent below the price of the material now being used, but 4 percent more of it would be required for each unit. The 6 percent difference in price is expected to continue for the year 19X2.

2. The company can use less-skilled workers whose average pay rate for 19X2 would be 4 percent below the average for 19X1 due to the planned change in processing methods. However, 12 percent more labor per unit would be required than was needed in 19X1.

3. Variable overhead is incurred directly in relation to production, and it is expected to increase 8 percent because of price changes and to increase an additional amount in proportion to the change in labor hours.

Required:

Rounding to whole dollars, determine prospective gross margin if:

a. The same product is continued for 19X2.
b. The product is redesigned for 19X2.

P5–17 Transaction Analysis for Cost Accounting System (L.O. 3)

Lee Wilson Company commenced operations on July 1, 19X1. The following are gross debits and credits in each account of the ledger as of December 31, 19X1, except for Work in Process and Finished Goods Inventory accounts. The company distributes actual factory overhead to the Work in Process account and uses a voucher-based accounting system.

LEE WILSON COMPANY
Adjusted Trial Balance
December 31, 19X1

	Transactions		Balance	
	Dr.	Cr.	Dr.	Cr.
Cash	$498,700	$418,700	$ 80,000	
Notes receivable	13,700	8,700	5,000	
Accounts receivable	310,000	290,000	20,000	
Direct materials inventory	105,000	100,000	5,000	
Finished goods inventory	compute	compute	22,000	
Work in process inventory	compute	compute	16,000	
Factory supplies inventory	18,000	14,000	4,000	
Prepaid insurance	2,000	1,500	500	
Plant and equipment	173,700	-0-	173,700	
Mortgage payable	-0-	65,000		65,000
Accrued mortgage interest	-0-	800		800
Accrued direct labor wages	151,000	153,000		2,000
Common stock	-0-	200,000		200,000
Vouchers payable	418,700	527,400		108,700
Sales	-0-	323,700		323,700
Cost of goods sold	310,000	-0-	310,000	
Marketing expense	28,000	-0-	28,000	
Administrative expense	36,000		36,000	
			$700,200	$700,200

Additional information:

1. The ending work in process inventory consists of materials, $400; direct labor, $3,600; and factory expense, $12,000
2. Insurance premiums: apply two thirds to the plant and one third to the office.
3. The cost of the finished product is made up of materials, 30 percent; labor, 45 percent; and factory overhead, 25 percent.
4. No cash sales are made.
5. Treat all interest expense as administrative expense.

Required:

Show in ledger T accounts the entries making up the transactions included in the figures shown on the adjusted trial balance. Key each entry (debit and offsetting credit) by use of a number. (Begin with the cash account and clear out that account before continuing with the other asset accounts.)

P5–18 Forecasted Income Statement; Percentage Changes (L.O. 2)

The controller of American, Inc., presented the following summarized income statement for the year ended May 31, 19X1, to the board of directors:

AMERICAN, INC.
Income Statement
For the Year Ended May 31, 19X1
($000)

Sales		$550,000
Less: Cost of goods sold:		
Direct material	$210,000	
Direct labor	140,000	
Factory overhead ($80,000 fixed)	120,000	
Cost of goods sold		470,000
Gross margin		80,000
Less: Marketing and administrative expenses:		
Marketing expense ($22,000 variable*) . . .	55,000	
Administrative expense (fixed)	70,000	125,000
Operating loss		($ 45,000)
*Variable with sales dollars.		

After reviewing operations, the board decides that action must be taken immediately before future financial losses occur. They hire additional accounting and marketing personnel who jointly present the following plan for 19X2: increase sales price by 40 percent; increase sales volume by 15 percent by engaging in an additional advertising campaign costing $50,000; all other fixed costs will remain the same. Inflation is expected to cause a 10 percent increase in direct material costs, a 20 percent increase in direct labor costs, and a 6 percent increase for variable factory overhead. Variable marketing expenses will continue to be the same percentage of sales dollars.

Required:

a. Prepare a forecasted income statement for the next year, incorporating all expected changes.
b. Compare the percentage of production, marketing, and administrative costs with sales for 19X1 and 19X2.

P5–19 Budgeted Income Statement and Cost of Goods Manufactured under Certain Assumptions (L.O. 2)

Barton Company's cost of goods manufactured and income statement for the year ended December 31, 19X1, follow. Beside the cost figures is an indication of variable (V) or/ and fixed (F) costs. The company produced 50,000 units in 19X1. Assume that finished goods inventory is carried at the average unit cost of production and material prices have been stable during 19X1.

BARTON COMPANY
Cost of Goods Manufactured
For the Year Ended December 31, 19X1

Direct materials:				
Inventory, January 1, 19X1				-0-
Purchases of direct material				$ 50,250
Direct materials available				$ 50,250
Inventory, December 31, 19X1				250
Direct materials used				$ 50,000 V
Direct labor				35,000 V
Factory overhead:				
Utilities	$ 2,500	V		
Supervision	19,000	($ 5,000 V		
		$14,000 F)		
Miscellaneous overhead	44,000	($ 4,000 V		
		$40,000 F)	65,500	
Cost of goods manufactured			$150,500	

BARTON COMPANY
Income Statement
For the Year Ended December 31, 19X1

Sales			$409,500
Less: Cost of goods sold:			
Finished goods, January 1, 19X1	-0-		
Cost of goods manufactured	$150,500		
Cost of goods available	$150,500		
Finished goods, December 31, 19X1	13,545		
Cost of goods sold			136,955
Gross margin			$272,545
Less marketing and administrative expenses:			
Marketing expenses	$ 25,000	($16,380 V*	
		$ 8,620 F)	
Administration expenses	25,000	F	50,000
Income before income taxes			$222,545
*Variable with sales dollars.			

Required:

Show and label all calculations and supporting computations. Using the preceding information, prepare a budgeted income statement, including a schedule of cost of goods manufactured, for Barton Company for 19X2 under the following assumptions:

1. Unit sales prices will remain the same.
2. Variable cost per unit will remain the same.
3. Fixed costs will remain the same.
4. Sales will increase to 63,000 units.
5. Ending finished goods inventory, December 31, 19X2, will be 3,000 units and will be carried at the average unit cost of production for 19X2.

P5–20 Journal Entry Preparation Using Factory Overhead Subsidiary Ledger (L.O. 3)

Before operations began, Bergen, Inc., decided to apply factory overhead on direct labor-hours. The manager estimated annual factory overhead to be $524,400 based on 114,000 budgeted direct labor-hours. The accountant uses a subsidiary ledger to record the details of factory overhead. At the beginning of the year, the balances in the following accounts were

Direct materials inventory	$ 3,600
Repair supplies inventory	9,000
Work in process inventory	12,000
Finished goods inventory	19,900

Transactions for January follow:

1. Direct material of $13,450 was purchased on account.
2. Direct material of $9,800 was issued out of the storeroom for use in production; $1,600 in materials was also issued for repair work.
3. Analysis of the bimonthly payroll records reveals the following (payroll deductions are ignored):

	Hours	Payroll Costs
Direct laborers	4,500	$36,000
Production superintendents	410	6,000
Factory repairers	300	2,800
Factory janitorial staff	700	3,200

4. Four jobs incurring 2,000 hours of direct labor were finished. (The transfer of total costs to the Finished Goods Inventory will be recorded at the end of the month in a summary entry. Only apply factory overhead; the 2,000 direct labor-hours were included in the 4,500 hours recorded in Transaction 3.)
5. Miscellaneous factory expenses of $800 were paid in cash.
6. Analysis of the monthly depreciation schedules reveals the following:

Factory building	$2,800
Production equipment	3,000
Office building (one quarter of the building is occupied by the marketing manager and marketing salespersons)	1,200
Office equipment (one third of the equipment is used by the marketing staff)	1,500

7. Repair supplies totaling $3,100 were issued from the storeroom.
8. Analysis of the insurance register reveals that the following prepaid insurance expired this month:

Coverage	
Factory building	$700
Factory equipment	150
Office building	600
Office equipment	300

9. End-of-the-month payroll records follow (ignore payroll deductions).

	Hours	Payroll Costs
Direct laborers	3,000	$25,000
Production superintendents	400	5,400
Factory repairers	210	1,900
Factory janitorial staff	650	2,900
Marketing staff (monthly salary)		4,000
Administrative staff (monthly salary)		5,000

10. Factory overhead is applied to the six jobs remaining in process at the end of the month; direct labor costs on these six jobs total $49,500 for 5,500 hours. Assume that the entry to record direct labor has already been made.

11. A physical count was made of the inventories on hand at January 31. The balances were as follows: Direct Material, $7,250; Work in Process, $61,500; and Finished Goods, $23,600. The difference reflects the costs transferred. The difference in the Finished Goods Inventory reflects goods that were sold on account at a markup on costs of 40 percent. This markup was calculated before over- or underapplied overhead is closed.

12. Close all revenue and expense accounts.

Required:

Prepare the general journal entries to record the monthly operations; use a factory overhead subsidiary ledger.

P5–21 Projected Financial Statements (L.O. 2)

Anderson, Inc., manufactures a single product. The basic characteristics of the company's operations and accounting are as follows:

1. Production is assumed to occur evenly throughout the year.
2. Production is scheduled to maintain finished goods inventory at a constant ratio (10 percent) to current sales.
3. Inventories of work in process and raw materials are small and may be ignored.
4. Finished goods inventory at the end of the period is valued at the cost of manufacture for the period.
5. FIFO costing is used; the 4,000 units in 19X1 beginning inventory are valued at the 19X1 unit production cost.
6. Sales in 19X3 are expected to be 28,000 units at $25 per unit.
7. The product is made by mixing Materials A and B. The *relative quantity* of each of the two materials entering production and in finished units can be varied, but was kept constant during 19X1 and 19X2. In 19X3, the quantity of Material A used in a unit of product will be increased 11 percent, and the quantity of Material B used in a unit or product will be decreased 6 percent. The price of Material A is expected to continue the trend of the past two periods, and the price of Material B is expected to increase 8 percent in 19X3.
8. Direct labor-hours per unit have been approximately constant during 19X1 and 19X2 and are expected to remain at the same figure in 19X3. Effective in the middle of 19X1 and 19X2, wage increases of 10 percent per labor-hour have been granted. A similar increase is expected at the middle of 19X3.
9. The amount of fixed factory overhead was $25,800 during 19X1 and 19X2 and is expected to continue at the same amount during 19X3. The variable portion of factory overhead is expected to remain the same amount per unit of production as in 19X1 and 19X2.

Production and sales data for 19X1 and 19X2 are as follows:

	Units	
	19X1	**19X2**
Beginning inventory	4,000	5,000
Production	20,000	30,000
	24,000	35,000
Sales	19,000	32,000
Ending inventory	5,000	3,000

	19X1			19X2		
		Amount	**Per Unit**		**Amount**	**Per Unit**
Sales		$437,000			$768,000	
Cost of sales:						
Direct materials:						
A	$40,000			$70,500		
B	20,000	$ 60,000	$ 3.00	32,100	$102,600	$ 3.42
Direct labor		$160,000	8.00		264,000	8.80
Factory overhead		53,800	2.69		67,800	2.26
Inventory variation		− 13,690			+ 25,010	
Cost of sales		$260,110	$13.69		$459,410	$14.48
Gross margin		$176,890			$308,590	

Required:

Prepare the following projected 19X3 statements based on the preceding data. (Round off all total costs to the nearest dollar and all unit costs to two decimal places.)

a. Production requirements.

b. Cost of goods manufactured statement supported by computations for costs of materials, labor, and fixed and variable overhead.

c. Income statement through gross margin showing inventory variation (increase or decrease).

Appendix 5–A Problems

P5–22 Home Office and Factory Journal Entries (L.O. 4)

Barry Company's factory home office maintains separate sets of records. The factory maintains ledger accounts for direct materials, factory supplies, and work in process as well as for all factory expenses. The company keeps all liabilities and cash at the home office. A partial list of the transactions for July follows:

1. Direct materials of $12,000 and factory supplies of $6,300 were purchased on account.
2. Direct materials costing $7,150 and factory supplies of $4,270 were issued into production.
3. Invoices for material and supplies costing $9,000 on account were paid.
4. The home office paid $5,000 for factory rent in July.
5. The home office paid for direct labor costing $6,825 and indirect labor costing $4,000. Income tax of $3,300 and $763 FICA taxes were withheld. Barry Company also accrued $763 FICA taxes, $292 state unemployment taxes, and $87 federal unemployment taxes. Payroll taxes are treated as indirect cost. The home office maintains the liability for the payroll taxes and taxes withheld. All wages are subject to these taxes.
6. Factory overhead was applied at 80 percent of direct labor costs.

7. Goods costing $19,300 were completed.
8. Goods costing $9,000 were sold on account for $13,000.

Required:

Prepare journal entries on the factory and home office books.

P5–23 Home Office—Factory Journal Entries (L.O. 4)

The home office of John Nixon Company is in Michigan, but its major plant is in San Antonio, Texas. The San Antonio office keeps a set of records separate from those of the home office. The factory trial balance on January 1 shows the following:

Accounts	Debit	Credit
Direct materials inventory	$18,900	
Factory supplies inventory	3,000	
Repair supplies inventory	4,000	
Work in process inventory	9,500	
Finished goods inventory	16,200	
Home office ledger		$51,600
	$51,600	$51,600

The following transactions occurred during January:

1. Direct materials purchased on account, $40,000.
2. Plant supervisor requisitioned direct materials of $22,000 along with repair materials of $2,500 and supplies of $900.
3. Cash in the amount of $26,700 was paid to vendors on account.
4. San Antonio payroll for the month consisted of: $56,000, direct labor; $20,100, indirect labor; $6,500, marketing salaries; $7,000, office salaries. In preparing the checks, the home office deducted $6,729 for FICA tax and $15,800 for federal income tax. Nixon Company also accrued $6,729 FICA taxes, $2,419 state unemployment taxes, and $717 federal unemployment taxes as its payroll taxes. Payroll taxes are treated as indirect cost. The home office maintains the liability for the payroll taxes and taxes withheld. Only expense controls for direct and indirect labor are maintained at the factory. Of the payroll taxes, $8,379 represented taxes on direct and indirect labor, $716 on marketing salaries, and $770 on administrative salaries.
5. The home office paid $10,000 cash for factory overhead and recorded $5,000 factory depreciation and $3,900 depreciation on office furniture and fixtures.
6. Direct materials costing $2,600 were defective and were returned to the vendor for credit.
7. Factory overhead is applied at a rate of 80 percent of direct labor cost.
8. Analysis of the inventory showed goods costing $15,700 remained partially complete at the end of the month. The remainder represented goods completed and transferred.
9. Goods were sold for $150,000, which represented a 40 percent markup on sales.
10. Close the factory overhead control account; any over- or underapplied balance is closed to the cost of goods sold account.

Required:

Prepare journal entries on the books of the home office and the factory to record the preceding transactions.

Process Costing: Weighted-Average and FIFO

CHAPTER OBJECTIVES

After studying this chapter, you should be able to:

1. Explain the difference between process, job order, and operation costing in assigning costs to products.

2. Discuss which characteristics of manufacturing procedures make process costing appropriate.

3. Prepare departmental cost of production reports using weighted-average and FIFO costing.

4. Understand the change an automated manufacturing environment has on process costing and equivalent unit calculations.

Introduction

Organizations assign costs to products through either job order costing, process costing, or operation costing. As you learned in Chapter 5, job order and process costing are the two polar extremes while operation costing represents a hybrid-costing system. The nature of manufacturing activities (i.e., whether automated or manual, making customized products or standard products) determines which of the cost application systems is most appropriate.

Contrast between Job Order, Process, and Operation Costing (L.O. 1)

Process costing is an effective costing system for firms that employ assembly-line production with a continuous flow of goods. After completing manufacturing, workers transfer units to the finished goods warehouse; these goods are not produced for a specific customer. All units in the specific product line are identical. In contrast, **job order** manufacturing normally begins only when a customer places an order. Each job receives varying amounts of skill and attention depending on the customer's specifications; thus, the unit cost per order differs. Firms determine total cost at the time that each job order is finished. Exhibit 6–1 illustrates this, using the three jobs presented in Chapter 5. With process costing, accountants accumulate costs by operating centers for a given period. They determine total cost at the end of the costing period.

An **operation costing** system represents a hybrid method, having some of the characteristics of both process and job order costing. For example, in operation costing, accountants allocate direct materials specifically to the batches. This is like job order costing. They apply direct labor and overhead to all physical units passing through the operation by using a single average unit conversion cost for the operation. This is like process costing.

Companies use operation costing when manufacturing goods that have some common characteristics plus some individual characteristics. Operation costing meets the needs of a batch manufacturer whose products have variations of a single design and require a varying sequence of standardized operations. Job costing continues to be the best alternative for accumulating the cost of contracts and customized manufacturing. However, the trend is toward process costing systems and cost systems that are custom designed, such as operation costing.

Departmentalization of Work in Process Inventory

Process costing assumes a sequential flow from one department to other departments as units travel through the production process. The costs of processing increase the unit's cost as it moves from department to department while each performs its specific task. An easy way to visualize this flow is to think of a snowball gathering snow (costs) as it travels from one department to another. Process costing assumes that units do not skip departments. That is, all units leave the first department and take their costs with them to the second department, and so on to all departments. For example, Exhibit 6–1 illustrates the movement of units and costs through Departments A, B, and C. If this pattern varies, a flowchart outlining the movement of units is helpful. Individual departments maintain a Work in Process Inventory subsidiary ledger and costs are summarized by departments. In job order costing, a Work in Process Inventory subsidiary ledger is maintained for individual job orders, such as for Job 101, 102, and 103 as Exhibit 6–1 illustrates.

Equivalent Units

In a typical manufacturing operation, accountants assign some costs to unfinished units at the end of the period. Thus, a department's total cost is distributed to both the units finished in a period and the partially completed units in ending work in process inventory. Because partially completed units have used fewer resources than complete units, however, division of a department's total costs by physical units is inappropriate. Instead, accountants convert units in work in process inventory into **equivalent finished units** (also called **equivalent production** or **equivalent full units**) and distribute costs on that basis. For example, 320 equivalent units equal 800 units that are 40 percent complete in Exhibit 6–2's beginning inventory. Thus, 40 percent of the processing on these 800 units was done *last* period. The 60 percent processing to complete these 800 units will be done *this* period. Likewise, the cost incurred to process the 200 units in ending inventory to a 20 percent stage is expressed as the cost to complete 40 units. If unit cost is $4, we distribute $160 to these 200 units.

As illustrated for Exhibit 6–2, the stage of completion for each batch of work in process determines the equivalent units. In some industries, figuring the percentage of completion may be easy because the amount of material and hours of labor required before finishing a product are available. Other industries estimate because calculating the additional material, labor, and overhead needed is difficult. To better illustrate the costing procedure, the stages of completion in the exhibits and problems in Chapters 6 and 7 are more exact than is usually practical in actual manufacturing operations.

EXHIBIT 6–1   Process and Job Order Costing Compared

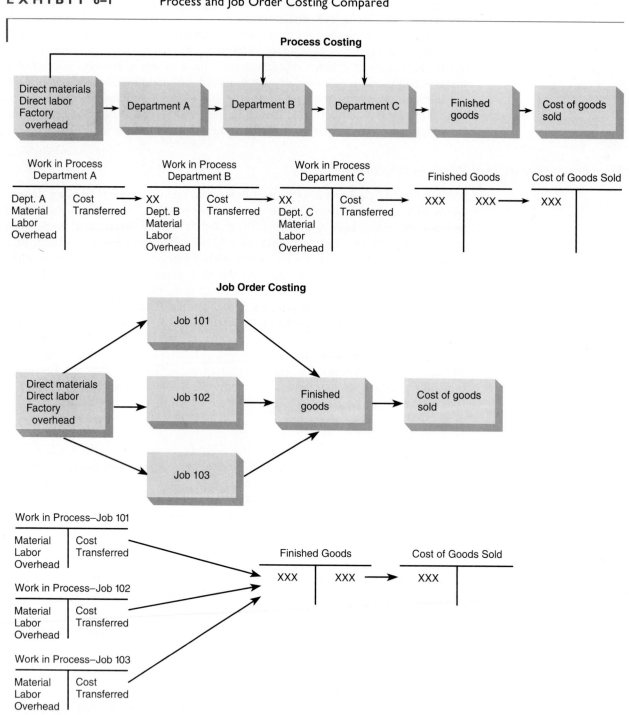

EXHIBIT 6–2   Flow of Units

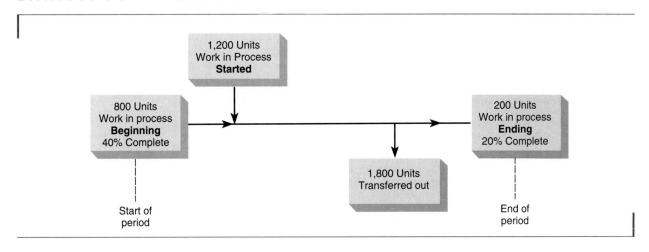

Before moving to the next department, a unit must have completed the entire operating cycle of the department. Once finished in that department, the unit may still not be in a finished state ready for shipping to a customer. Only when it is leaving the company's final department is the product ready for a user.

Weighted-Average and FIFO Costing (L.O. 3)

Two methods account for the opening inventory costs in process costing:

1.   Weighted-average costing: We average the previous period costs of completing the beginning inventory to a semifinished state with the current period's costs to arrive at a unit cost. Units in beginning inventory receive the same unit cost as the units started and finished during the period; thus, all units transferred have an identical unit cost.

2.   First-in, first-out (FIFO) costing: The FIFO method separates the cost of the units finished from beginning inventory from the cost of the units started and finished during the period. We assume the beginning inventory cost flows out of work in process first. The cost of the goods transferred contains the cost of the goods finished that were in beginning inventory and the cost of the goods started and finished during the current period. We value ending work in process inventory at the unit cost of current production for the period. Dividing equivalent units into the production costs incurred in the current period only determines the unit cost of current production.

Difference in Equivalent Units. FIFO equivalent units differ from units based on weighted-average costing because of the difference in the assumption concerning the cost flow of beginning inventory. Units are lost through spoilage, evaporation, and shrinkage during processing. The following weighted-average and FIFO equivalent units (EU) formulas exclude lost units, which we introduce in Chapter 7:

$$\text{EU, weighted-average costing} = \text{Units completed and transferred} \times 100\% + \text{Partially completed ending inventory} \times \text{stage of completion}$$

$$\text{EU, FIFO costing} = \text{Units completed and transferred} \times 100\% + \text{Partially completed ending inventory} \times \text{stage of completion} - \text{Beginning inventory} \times \text{stage of completion}$$

To illustrate the calculation of EU, assume the following data for a department:

Units in beginning inventory (40% complete for all cost elements, $1,556 costs incurred to date)	800	
Units started in process during the current period	1,200	2,000
Units completed and transferred out	1,800	
Units in ending inventory (20% complete for all cost elements)	200	2,000

Using weighted average, EU are as follows:

EU, weighted average = 1,800 units transferred + 40 ending inventory = 1,840
(200 units × 20%)

EU calculated using FIFO costing differ as follows:

EU, FIFO = 1,800 units tranferred + 40 ending inventory − 320 beginning inventory = 1,520
(200 units × 20%)   (800 units × 40%)

Next, we illustrate the difference in distributing the beginning inventory costs under weighted average and FIFO, assuming $1,556 beginning inventory costs and $6,080 current costs.

Weighted-Average Costing

$$\frac{\$1,556 \text{ cost of beginning inventory} + \$6,080 \text{ current costs}}{1,840 \text{ weighted-average EU}} = \frac{\$7,636}{1,840} = \$4.15 \text{ average unit cost}$$

FIFO Costing

$$\frac{\$6,080 \text{ current costs}}{1,520 \text{ FIFO EU}} = \$4 \text{ current unit cost}$$

Sources of Units Transferred

Whether a firm uses FIFO or average costing, the total units transferred to the next department come from these two sources:

1. Beginning inventory
2. Current production, also called **units started and finished** during the period. Note that units started and finished are not the same as units started in process or units transferred. **Units started in process** merely indicate that units were introduced into the production process; they may not have been finished at the end of the period. **Units transferred** come from both current production of units started and finished and from beginning inventory. The classification of *unit transferred* does not indicate the unit's source but merely that the unit left the department.

We always assume that a company finishes beginning inventory before starting units during the period. In weighted-average costing, the source of the units transferred does not matter because we cost out all units transferred during the period at an average. Using FIFO, we keep the costs of the units from these two sources separate. In the earlier example illustrating equivalent unit computations of the 1,800 units transferred, 800 come from beginning inventory and 1,000 from current production.

Cost of Production Report

In process costing, a **cost of production report** summarizes total and unit costs. Either each cost center or department makes such a report, or accountants combine individual reports of several departments. Regardless of the format chosen from the many available, an orderly approach to preparing the cost of production report is important. The following four steps provide a uniform approach; note these steps in parentheses in the chapter's exhibits:

Step 1.   Prepare quantity schedule.
Step 2.   Calculate equivalent units and unit costs.
Step 3.   Determine the costs to account for.
Step 4.   Distribute all costs and prove that all costs are accounted for.

Steps Illustrated Using Weighted-Average Costing

Exhibit 6–3 illustrates a cost of production report using the weighted-average method with only one department, simply called Department 1. The following discusses each section of the cost of production report.

Step 1—Department 1's Quantity Schedule. A quantity schedule lists the units for which the department is responsible. This schedule accounts for all units started in the department. A quantity schedule shows the disposition of these units—whether transferred to finished goods or the next department, lost, or remaining in ending inventory. This part of the cost of production report is often called the physical flow section; it concerns only whole units, regardless of their stage of completion.

The quantity schedule expresses units of the department's finished products in any appropriate measurement, such as feet, gallons, or pounds. We express all units in the same measure. Assume, for example, that a department produces shirts and each shirt requires two yards of fabric. If the department begins cutting and sewing 2,000 yards of fabric, the quantity schedule shows the starting of 1,000 units (2,000 yards/2 yards per shirt) in process because the units transferred out are expressed in finished shirts.

The quantity section shows that Department 1 placed 7,600 units into the production process. It had 600 units in beginning inventory, having all their material and two thirds of their labor and overhead, with a total cost of $7,720. For ease in computing the equivalent units in Step 2, the quantity schedule shows the stage of completion next to the units.

At this introductory stage, you may wonder if the quantity schedule is worth your time and effort. In more complicated process costing operations, where units are added or lost, preparation of the quantity schedule provides assurance that you are accounting for all units.

Step 2—Department 1's Equivalent Units and Unit Costs. The bottom of the cost of production report shows the computations for equivalent units and unit costs. Cost of production reports distributed to nonaccountants often omit the

EXHIBIT 6–3

CASPARI COMPANY
Cost of Production Report—Weighted Average
For Month Ending January 31, 19X1

	Department 1	
Quantity schedule (Step 1):		
Beginning inventory (all material, ⅔ labor and overhead)	600	
Units started in process	7,600	8,200
Units transferred out	7,200	
Ending inventory (all material, ⅕ labor and overhead)	1,000	8,200

	Total Costs	Unit Costs
Costs to account for (Step 3):		
Work in process—beginning inventory:		
Material	$ 2,720	
Labor and overhead	5,000	
Total beginning inventory	$ 7,720	
Current costs in department:		
Material	$13,680	$ 2.00
Labor and overhead	30,520	4.80
Total costs to account for	$51,920	$ 6.80
Costs accounted for as follows (Step 4):		
Costs transferred out (7,200 × $6.80)		$48,960
Work in process—ending inventory:		
Material (1,000 × $2.00)	$ 2,000	
Labor and overhead (1,000 × ⅕ × $4.80)	960	2,960
Total costs accounted for		$51,920

Additional computations (Step 2):

	Transferred		Ending Inventory	
EU, Department 1, material	7,200	+	1,000	= 8,200
$\dfrac{\$2,720 + \$13,680}{8,200} = \dfrac{\$16,400}{8,200} = \$2.00$			(1,000 × 100%)	
EU, Department 1, labor and overhead ..	7,200	+	200	= 7,400
$\dfrac{\$5,000 + \$30,520}{7,400} = \dfrac{\$35,520}{7,400} = \$4.80$			(1,000 × ⅕)	

additional computation section. This explains why the steps are not shown in sequence in the body of the cost of production report. Regardless of whether units transferred came from beginning inventory or from current production, we add them to the equivalent units in ending inventory to determine total equivalent units of production. Department 1 introduces material at the beginning of the operations. This is why we multiply the units in ending inventory by 100 percent in computing equivalent units for materials. They have all the material they need for completion. Because Department 1 adds labor and overhead evenly throughout the process, they are combined. Often the cost of production report labels labor and overhead costs as conversion costs. In computing the equivalent units for labor and factory overhead, we multiply the ending inventory by its one-fifth stage of completion. Before transferring these units out, an additional four fifths is added in subsequent periods. To determine the labor and overhead unit costs, we convert these 1,000 partially completed units into 200 equivalent finished units. This is computed strictly for unit costing purposes; of course, there are still 1,000 unfinished units.

To determine the unit cost for materials, labor, and factory overhead, we consider equivalent units rather than total physical units. While the exhibits and problems in Chapters 6 and 7 carry unit cost out to four or five decimal places, accountants usually round total cost to whole dollars.

Using weighted-average costing, we add the individual cost in the beginning inventory to the current cost. Dividing the equivalent units into this total cost gives the unit cost. For example, units receive all their Department 1 material when they enter the production process. Even though the units in ending inventory are not complete, they have all their Department 1 material. Adding the $2,720 material cost of the semifinished goods in beginning inventory to the $13,680 current material costs gives a total of $16,400 material cost; dividing that total by 8,200 equivalent units gives a $2 unit cost. Department 1 labor and factory overhead require similar computations, yielding a $4.80 unit cost.

We insert each unit cost in the "Costs to account for" section of the cost of production report to arrive at a total departmental unit cost of $6.80 (the total of the calculated equivalent unit costs). The total cost to account for of $51,920 cannot be divided by any one equivalent unit figure to arrive at the unit cost of $6.80 because material and conversion costs involve a different stage of completion.

Step 3—Department 1's Costs to Account for. The costs that a department is responsible for may come from several sources. Costs of material, labor, and factory overhead assigned to partially completed units in last period's ending inventory become the cost of the current period's beginning inventory and are accounted for. Also, if a department is not the first processing center, units received into operations from previous departments have costs attached. In addition, each department incurs materials and/or labor and factory overhead in its own processing. For example, Department 1 incurred a direct material cost of $13,680 and direct labor cost and factory overhead totaling $30,520 during January. We add the $7,720 beginning inventory to these current costs to give $51,920 total costs to account for.

Conversion Costs. Determining only the total costs for each processing department is inadequate for control purposes. Instead, the cost of production report summarizes by department three cost components—direct material, direct labor, and factory overhead. The report also determines unit costs for each of the three elements. When factory overhead is applied on the basis of direct labor or if direct labor is such a small percent of the total production cost as may be found in automated factories, the cost of production report may combine factory overhead and labor. These costs are simply itemized as conversion costs. The cost of production report can detail each item of factory overhead and calculate a unit cost for individual cost elements. For the sake of brevity, the cost of production reports in this book do not calculate unit costs for each item of factory overhead; instead, they show unit costs for total material, labor, and factory overhead or for total material and conversion costs.

Step 4—Distributing Department 1's Costs and Proving All Costs Are Accounted for. Companies distribute costs to cost centers that receive units transferred out of a department. Units remaining in the department and any lost units receive the remaining costs. Chapter 7 discusses the assignment of lost unit costs.

By multiplying the 7,200 units transferred out by the $6.80 unit cost, we get a total cost of $48,960 transferred. There is no need to itemize transferred costs by the three components of material, labor, and factory overhead; we use only the total unit cost of $6.80. Because the 1,000 units in ending inventory have all their material and are 100 percent complete, we multiply all units by the $2 unit cost. The ending inventory is only partially completed for labor and overhead; therefore, the units are multiplied by their one-fifth stage of completion before being multiplied by the $4.80 labor and overhead unit cost. The $2,960 value of the ending inventory becomes the beginning inventory for the next period in Department 1.

Two parts comprise the cost section of the cost of production report. One part determines the total costs that we must account for, while the other section shows the disposition of these costs. There must be agreement between these two sections; otherwise, there is an error. Determining that the total costs accounted for ($51,920) equal the total costs that the department is responsible for completes the cost of production report.

FIFO Costing Illustrated

To demonstrate the difference between FIFO and weighted-average costing, Exhibit 6–4 uses the cost data from Exhibit 6–3 with the assumption that Caspari Company uses FIFO costing. The quantity schedules are identical. Using FIFO, the accountant need not detail the cost of each of the components found in beginning inventory, since only the total inventory valuation is used. However, to compare with Exhibit 6–3, Exhibit 6–4 itemizes material and conversion costs, rather than only show $7,720 total beginning inventory cost. As you recall, weighted-average costing requires this detail to average the beginning inventory costs with current costs.

The difference between FIFO and weighted-average costing becomes clearer with the calculation of equivalent units in Exhibit 6–4. Calculated under FIFO, these represent current production only. Because we include the units completed and transferred from beginning inventory at 100 percent with the units started and finished to give total units transferred, the stage of completion of the beginning inventory is deducted in computing FIFO equivalent units.

Different Formula for EU, FIFO. The following formula for computing FIFO equivalent units differs slightly from that in Exhibit 6–4:

EU, FIFO = Units started + Ending inventory + Beginning inventory
              and completed   × stage of   × stage of
              × 100%   completion   completion to be added

Using this formula, the computation for labor and overhead in Department 1 in Exhibit 6–4 is as follows:

EU, FIFO = 6,600   + 200 ending inventory + 200 beginning inventory = 7,000
              started   (1,000 × ⅕)   (600 × ⅓)
           and finished

Units Started and Finished. As illustrated in the formula, there is a difference between units transferred and units started and finished. The total units transferred come from the units started and finished in current production as well as

EXHIBIT 6–4

CASPARI COMPANY
Cost of Production Report—FIFO
For Month Ending January 31, 19X1

	Department 1	

Quantity schedule (Step 1):

Beginning inventory (all material, ⅔ labor and overhead)	600	
Units started in process	7,600	8,200
Units transferred out	7,200	
Ending inventory (all material, ⅕ labor and overhead)	1,000	8,200

	Total Costs	Unit Costs

Costs to account for (Step 3):

Work in process—beginning inventory:		
Material	$ 2,720	
Labor and overhead	5,000	
Total beginning inventory	$ 7,720	
Current costs in department:		
Material	$13,680	$ 1.80
Labor and overhead	30,520	4.36
Total costs to account for	$51,920	$ 6.16

Costs accounted for as follows (Step 4):

Costs transferred out		
From beginning inventory:		
Value of beginning inventory	$ 7,720	
Labor and overhead added		
(600 × ⅓ × $4.36)	872	$ 8,592
From current production		
(6,600 × $6.16)		40,656
Total cost transferred out		49,248
Work in process—ending inventory:		
Material (1,000 × $1.80)	$ 1,800	
Labor and overhead (1,000 × ⅕ × $4.36)	872	2,672
Total costs accounted for		$51,920

Additional computations (Step 2):

	Transferred		Ending Inventory		Beginning Inventory		
EU, Department 1, material	7,200	+	1,000	−	600	=	7,600
$\frac{\$13,689}{7,600} = \$1.80$			(1,000 × 100%)		(600 × 100%)		
EU, Department 1, labor and overhead	7,200	+	200	−	400	=	7,000
$\frac{\$30,520}{7,000} = \$4.36$			(1,000 × ⅕)		(600 × ⅔)		

---

from beginning inventory. For example, workers started 7,600 units in process but because 1,000 units remained in ending inventory, only 6,600 of the units were finished. This is an important point to remember in choosing the formula that appears easier. The correct use of either formula gives the same results.

Additional differences between FIFO and weighted average appear in determining the cost of the units transferred. Department 1 has 600 units in beginning inventory that need additional labor and overhead. The 600 units that reached a two-third stage of conversion cost completion last period receive an additional one-third equivalent units of conversion cost before being transferred out. For this reason, the 600 units are multiplied by one third before being finally multiplied by $4.36 unit conversion cost. A transfer of 7,200 total units occurs; 600 of these units come from beginning inventory. This leaves 6,600 units started and finished in current production; we assign each a $6.16 total departmental unit cost. The ending inventory in Department 1 is multiplied by its stage of completion and the unit costs.

Subsequent Month Using Weighted Average

January's ending work in process inventory valuation for Caspari Company becomes the beginning inventory for February. Exhibit 6–5 illustrates weighted-average costing for February using the ending inventory valuation for Department 1 from Exhibit 6–3. For example, to get Department 1's 1,000 units in beginning inventory into a semifinished state required costs of $2,960. Exhibit 6–5 adds data for a subsequent department to illustrate the transfer of costs. Department 2's quantity schedule indicates that 200 units were in beginning inventory when operations began. (Note that Department 2's January cost of production report was not illustrated.) Department 1 transferred 8,500 units to Department 2 for further processing. Unless stated otherwise, assume that units from the preceding department are introduced in subsequent departments at the beginning of operations. Department 2 adds materials, labor, and factory overhead before the units become finished products ready for sale to a consumer. Of these 8,500 units, workers finished 8,100 units and transferred them to finished goods. Because Department 2 treats material differently, the ending inventory has only one sixth of its materials needed for completion.

Department 2's Costs to Account for. By adding currently incurred costs of material, labor, and factory overhead and the beginning inventory costs, we get the total costs to account for. Department 2 received 8,500 units from Department 1 and must account for the preceding department costs of these units, totaling $56,100. These costs from the preceding department include material, labor, and overhead. The arrows in Exhibit 6–5 denote both the transfer of units and the transfer of costs.

Because Department 2 adds material uniformly, neither the beginning nor ending inventory has all its material. Assume in February that Department 1 incurred $9,540 labor and $30,000 overhead, and Department 2 incurred $14,200 labor and $60,000 overhead. Because we add labor and factory overhead at the same pace, they are combined.

EU and Unit Costs. We calculate equivalent units for the preceding department costs for departments subsequent to the first because units take on costs as they transfer from one department to another. (Think of the snowball gathering snow, or costs, as it travels through the production process.) Units in Department 2 are 100 percent complete for prior department costs. This is the reason for including 8,100 units transferred and 600 units in ending inventory in their entirety rather than multiplying them by some fraction to determine equivalent units for the preceding department cost.

Using the weighted-average method, we average the costs assigned last month for beginning inventory to reach a semifinished stage with current costs. Breaking down the beginning inventory by individual cost elements, we add the cost

EXHIBIT 6–5

CASPARI COMPANY
Cost of Production Report—Weighted Average
For Month Ending February 28, 19X1

	Department 1			Department 2	
Quantity schedule (Step 1):					
Beginning inventory (all material, ⅕ labor and overhead)	1,000		(¹⁄₁₀ M, ⅖ L and OH)	200	
Units started in process	9,000	10,000		8,500	8,700
Units transferred to next department.	8,500			8,100	
Ending inventory (all material, ⅓ labor and overhead	1,500	10,000	(⅙ M, ¼ L and OH)	600	8,700

	Total Costs	Unit Costs		Total Costs	Unit Costs
Costs to account for (Step 3):					
Work in process—beginning inventory:					
Costs from preceding department	–0–			$ 1,300	
Material	$2,000			10	
Labor and overhead	960			875	
Total beginning inventory	$2,960			$ 2,185	
Costs received from preceding department .				56,100	$ 6.5977
Current costs in department:					
Material	19,000	$ 2.10		3,680	0.4500
Labor and overhead	39,540	4.50		74,200	9.1000
Total costs to account for	$61,500	$ 6.60		$136,165	$16.1477
Costs accounted for as follows (Step 4):					
Costs transferred to next department (8,500 x $6.60)		$56,100	(8,100 x $16.1477)		$130,796
Work in process—ending inventory:					
Costs from preceding department			(600 x $6.5977)	$ 3,959	
Material (1,500 x $2.10)	$3,150		(600 x ⅙ x $0.45)	45	
Labor and overhead (1,500 x ⅓ x $4.50)	2,250	5,400	(600 x ¼ x $9.10)	1,365	5,369
Total costs accounted for		$61,500			$136,165

Additional computations (Step 2):

	Transferred		Ending inventory		
EU, Department 1, material	8,500	+	1,500	=	10,000
$\frac{\$2,000 + \$19,000}{10,000} = \frac{\$21,000}{10,000} = \$2.10$			(1,500 x 100%)		
EU, Department 1, labor.	8,500	+	500	=	9,000
$\frac{\$960 + \$39,540}{9,000} = \frac{\$40,500}{9,000} = \$4.50$			(1,500 x ⅓)		
EU, preceding department costs	8,100	+	600	=	8,700
$\frac{\$1,300 + \$56,100}{8,700} = \frac{\$57,400}{8,700} = \$6.5977$			(600 x 100%)		
EU, Department 2, material	8,100	+	100	=	8,200
$\frac{\$10 + \$3,680}{8,200} = \frac{\$3,690}{8,200} = \$0.45$			(600 x ⅙)		
EU, Department 2, labor and overhead	8,100	+	150	=	8,250
$\frac{\$875 + \$74,200}{8,250} = \frac{\$75,075}{8,250} = \$9.10$			(600 x ¼)		

of material, labor, and overhead to current costs element by element. For example in Exhibit 6–5, we average the $1,300 preceding department cost that the 200 units in Department 2's beginning inventory incurred in a prior period with the current cost of $56,100 transferred from Department 1. The resulting $6.5977 unit cost differs from the $6.60 Department 1 cost in Exhibit 6–5 because we average costs from a prior period with current costs. Avoid the temptation to carry the previous departmental unit cost, which is $6.60 in Exhibit 6–5, over to the next department; usually, the unit cost differs. (Note that if we were using more realistic numbers, the difference would likely be much more.)

Unit costs come out even to two decimal places in Department 1 but not in Department 2. As a result, we express unit costs in four decimal places in Department 2; this numerical precision helps to account for all costs. The cost of production report does not always balance if we round unit costs to two decimal places.

Disposition of Department 2's Costs. After determining the unit costs for Department 2 for material, labor, and overhead, we add them to the previous department costs to arrive at a total unit cost of $16.1477. Each of the 8,100 units leaving Department 2 carries a cost of $16.1477, giving a total of $130,796 transferred to finished goods. Because all of the 600 units in ending inventory have been through a previous department, they each receive the averaged preceding department cost of $6.5977. Current costs assigned to ending inventory reflect the stage of completion. The final step is proving that the $136,165 cost is accounted for.

Subsequent Month Using FIFO

Exhibit 6–6 illustrates FIFO costing for February using the Department 1 ending inventory valuation from Exhibit 6–4. The total costs of $55,799 transferred from Department 1 to Department 2 represent two batches—1,000 units finished during the period and 7,500 units started and finished in current production. Even though $55,799 transferred-in costs represent two batches, the cost is averaged after the batches are received in Department 2. In Exhibit 6–6, dividing the $55,799 total cost received by 8,500 equivalent units gives a single averaged preceding departmental cost of $6.5646, which differs slightly from the $6.6043 computed in Department 1.

Averaging within FIFO. Accountants often call the FIFO method the modified or departmental FIFO method. FIFO costing is strictly applied within each department, but when transferring costs out, we use an averaging technique in the next department. Thus, all units received from a preceding department bear the same average unit cost. Accountants justify this slight modification because of the clerical cost involved in keeping costs strictly attached to each batch. Otherwise, the FIFO method would not be feasible in process costing because of the burdensome task of accounting for the mass of figures. If preferred, a company can use strict FIFO when the goods are transferred out of the last department into finished goods.

Materials Issued at Various Stages

When preparing cost of production reports, it becomes clear that because production processes differ, material enters the process at various stages. Rather than assume the introduction stage for material, you should obtain accurate

EXHIBIT 6–6

CASPARI COMPANY
Cost of Production Report—FIFO
For Month Ending February 28, 19X1

	Department 1			Department 2	
Quantity schedule (Step 1):					
Beginning inventory (all material, ⅕ labor and overhead)	1,000		(¹⁄₁₀ M, ⅖ L & OH)	200	
Units started in process	9,000	10,000	➤ 8,500	8,700	
Units transferred to next department	8,500		8,100		
Ending inventory (all material, ⅓ labor and overhead	1,500	10,000	(⅙ M, ¼ L & OH)	600	8,700

	Total Costs	Unit Costs		Total Costs	Unit Costs
Costs to account for (Step 3):					
Work in process—beginning inventory:					
Costs from preceding department	–0–			$ 1,300	
Material	$1,800			10	
Labor and overhead	872			875	
Total beginning inventory	$2,672			$ 2,185	
Costs received from preceding department .			➤	55,799	$ 6.5646
Current costs in department:					
Material	19,000	$2.1111		3,680	0.4499
Labor and overhead	39,540	4.4932		74,200	9.0820
Total costs to account for	$61,212	$6.6043		$135,864	$16.0965
Costs accounted for as follows (Step 4):					
Costs transferred to next department:					
From beginning inventory:					
Value of beginning inventory	$ 2,672			$ 2,185	
Material added	—		(200 x ⁹⁄₁₀ x $0.4499)	81	
Labor and overhead added					
(1,000 x ⅘ x $4.4932)	3,595	$ 6,267	(200 x ⅗ x $9.082)	1,090	$ 3,356
From current production					
(7,500 x $6.6043)		49,532	(7,900 x $16.0965)		127,162
Total cost transferred		$55,799			$130,518
Work in process—ending inventory:					
Costs from preceding department . . .	—		(600 x $6.5646)	$ 3,939	
Material (1,500 x $2.1111)	$ 3,167		(600 x ⅙ x $0.4499)	45	
Labor and overhead					
(1,500 x ⅓ x $4.4932)	2,246	5,413	(600 x ¼ x $9.0820)	1,362	5,346
Total costs accounted for		$61,212			$135,864

Additional computations (Step 2):

	Transferred		Ending Inventory		Beginning Inventory		
EU, Department 1, material	8,500	+	1,500 (1,500 x 100%)	–	1,000 (1,000 x 100%)	=	9,000
$\dfrac{\$19,000}{9,000} = \$2.1111$							
EU, Department 1, labor and overhead . .	8,500	+	500 (1,500 x ⅓)	–	200 (1,000 x ⅕)	=	8,800
$\dfrac{\$39,540}{8,800} = \$4.4932$							
EU, preceding department costs	8,100	+	600 (600 x 100%)	–	200 (200 x 100%)	=	8,500
$\dfrac{\$55,799}{8,500} = \$6.5646$							
EU, Department 2, material	8,100	+	100 (600 x ⅙)	–	20 (200 x ¹⁄₁₀)	=	8,180
$\dfrac{\$3,680}{8,180} = \$0.4499$							
EU, Department 2, labor and overhead . .	8,100	+	150 (600 x ¼)	–	80 (200 x ⅖)	=	8,170
$\dfrac{\$74,200}{8,170} = \$9.0820$							

information regarding the material issue point in the processing operation. For example, a shirt manufacturing process introduces fabric at the beginning of operations so cutting and sewing operations may begin. In other operations, such as the chemical industry, workers may add material in a continuous flow or at specific points in the manufacturing process. Other companies add some of the direct material at the end of a process in a department.

Journal Entries Using Process Costing

Similar to those for job order costing, entries accumulate direct material, direct labor, and factory overhead in process costing. However, instead of tracing costs to specific jobs or batches, we accumulate costs for departments or cost centers. Next, we explain journal entries for each cost component using data from Exhibit 6–6.

Material Journal Entries Using Process Costing. Chapter 5 describes material requisitions used in job order costing. In process costing, the material requisition indicates the department charged rather than the job order number. The entry charging Departments 1 and 2 for the material used during February is

Work in Process—Department 1—Direct Material	19,000	
Work in Process—Department 2—Direct Material	3,680	
Direct Materials Inventory		22,680

Labor Journal Entries Using Process Costing. Process costing eliminates the detailed work of accumulating labor by jobs on job time tickets. Instead, daily or weekly time tickets or clock cards become the basis of distributing payroll charges. The following entry uses only a payroll summary account to distribute the payroll because we do not discuss payroll deductions until Chapter 22. A typical entry to allocate the direct labor charges for Exhibits 6–5 or 6–6 is as follows. (Remember that during February Department 1 incurred $9,540 labor and $30,000 overhead and Department 2 incurred $14,200 labor and $60,000 overhead; they are combined on Exhibits 6–5 and 6–6.)

Work in Process—Department 1—Direct Labor	9,540	
Work in Process—Department 2—Direct Labor	14,200	
Payroll		23,740

Factory Overhead Using Process Costing. In a job order costing system, factory overhead application rates ease the costing of products. Rather than wait until the end of operations to distribute actual factory overhead, accountants use estimated factory overhead rates in job order costing. In certain process cost systems, on the other hand, accountants use actual factory overhead rather than applied factory overhead costs because they do not accumulate costs until the end of operations. If production is stable from one period to another and total fixed cost does not vary considerably, estimated factory overhead rates are unnecessary. Instead, the fixed cost per unit charged to the product represents that calculated under normal conditions. There is support for using only the actual cost if the processing department's fixed costs are a small percentage of the total departmental costs.

However, accountants use applied factory overhead rates if production is not stable and if the actual fixed costs per unit fluctuate considerably. For example, for seasonal work, production varies so much between peak and slack periods that costs would fluctuate considerably without the use of estimated factory overhead rates. The procedure for determining the factory overhead application rate is similar to that shown under job order costing. Accountants estimate total variable and fixed overhead for the period and select a base, such as estimated direct labor-hours or machine-hours, to compute the factory overhead application rate. Even though accountants may eventually charge actual factory overhead to the departments, they first accumulate actual costs in the Factory Overhead Control account. Subsidiary ledger accounts detail factory overhead. The following is a typical entry for Departments 1 and 2 assuming actual overhead totaled $90,000:

Even if accountants use applied factory overhead rates to cost products, they also allocate actual factory overhead costs to departments. This allows a comparison of actual and applied factory overhead and determination of spending and volume variances as illustrated in Chapter 4. When accountants do not use estimated factory overhead application rates, they allocate actual factory overhead to calculate overhead cost for each product.

To allocate overhead to departments, we use factory overhead subsidiary ledger accounts or a separate departmental expense analysis to summarize actual costs by departments. If we use actual factory overhead rather than an estimated overhead rate to cost the products, we make the following entry to distribute actual factory overhead:

Work in Process—Department 1—Factory Overhead	30,000	
Work in Process—Department 2—Factory Overhead	60,000	
Factory Overhead Control		90,000

This becomes the source for the overhead charged to the departments, as shown on the cost of production report.

When using estimated factory overhead rates, we debit departmental Work in Process accounts and credit Factory Overhead Control for applied overhead based on estimated rates. The difference between actual and applied overhead remains in the Factory Overhead Control account.

Transfer of Costs between Departments. In addition to assigning factory overhead, the process costing accountant records the transfer of costs between departments. When transmitting units from Department 1 to Department 2, the following journal entry records the transfer:

Work in Process—Department 2	55,799	
Work in Process—Department 1		55,799

The following entry transfers the finished units from Department 2 to the Finished Goods Inventory.

Finished Goods Inventory	130,518	
Work in Process—Department 2		130,518

Comparison of Weighted-Average and FIFO Costing. As the chapter's exhibits illustrate, the difference using weighted-average and FIFO costing may be insignificant. This occurs if the raw material price does not fluctuate considerably between periods. In addition, because the production and inventory levels of most industries using process costing usually do not fluctuate, labor and overhead costs per unit stay approximately the same. While FIFO is strictly applied within each department, we would average the costs received from previous departments when the units enter a new department. Although we recognize that FIFO would be burdensome if we did not use this averaging procedure, it does cause the FIFO method to lose some of its value because we average the costs assigned to the different batches.

Impact of Flexible Manufacturing and JIT on Process Costing (L.O. 4)

Traditional manufacturing environments use job orders as the primary scheduling and cost tracking tool. However, in a flexible manufacturing environment, the transfer of workers and even materials among job orders to ensure a smooth flow of process is frequent. Transfers of this type among jobs disrupt the accounting department's attempt to trace the costs of material, labor, and overhead to different job orders.

Also, job orders become less useful in an automated setting because companies are less likely to be producing inventory for stock. Using flexible manufacturing, in which manufacturing of products begins only with the receipt of a sales order, lot sizes become too small to have a unique job order attached to each lot. Increasingly, accountants base their reports on periods rather than the closing of work orders.

Less Costing of Inventory Flow

Using traditional cost accounting, each inventory center separately records the movement of all inventory items from one center to another. However, the prevalence of JIT inventory policies has reduced the need for a detailed tracking of work in process inventory. Work in process inventory does not stay in one place long enough for the maintenance of accurate records as it flows through a manufacturing operation. Detailed inventory tracking is unnecessary in a JIT environment with a kanban pull system in which production is closely tied with sales. In companies using JIT, this inventory detail often creates vast amounts of paperwork and many reporting errors.

After implementing JIT, companies find they do not need to accumulate costs by individual job or workstation. Lot sizes become too small to have a unique job order attached to each lot. Also, data accumulation points are no longer at a department level because JIT does not departmentalize production.

Ignore EU Calculations in JIT

Automated manufacturing impacts the calculation of equivalent units used in process costing to arrive at a unit cost. Companies that manufacture products only after receiving sales orders have insignificant inventory levels. In a successful JIT setting, the composition of inventory changes. There is little or no work in process inventory as a result of reduced lead time. Reduction of finished goods inventory levels occurs because the system is more responsive to customer needs. Elimination of obsolete and slow-moving categories results. Companies keep little raw material because of their ability to plan and coordinate vendor deliveries.

The insignificant inventory levels make the total units transferred and the units in current production (units started and finished) almost identical using JIT. As a result, accountants can forgo the calculation of equivalent units entirely and assign all current costs to the units transferred and none to unfinished inventory. As the levels of work in process and finished goods diminish, the need to separately allocate costs to ending inventories decreases because failing to assign costs to the small amounts of inventory may not be material. This saves much time and cost in the areas of data collection, analysis, and reporting. Ignoring equivalent units calculations does not materially affect reporting accuracy in a successful JIT operation.

Summary

In deciding whether to adopt process, job order, or operation costing, accountants first study the nature of the company's manufacturing operations. Process costing accumulates costs for a given period in each department. This approach differs from job order costing in which the job becomes the focal point for assigning costs. Process costing is adaptable for a company with assembly-line operations, where there is a continuous flow of products. When the products differ considerably because they are manufactured according to customer specifications, process costing is not appropriate. Process costing is effective if the company is manufacturing to meet future sales needs because all units within the product line are alike. Operation costing is more appropriate if direct materials can be specifically allocated to the batches and conversion costs can be applied to all physical units passing through the operation.

The weighted-average and FIFO methods are two approaches for handling opening inventory cost in process costing. FIFO costing keeps the costs of the units in beginning inventory separate from the costs assigned to the units started and finished during the period. The computation of equivalent units differs with these two methods because of the treatment of beginning inventory. Both methods have their advantages, but because the FIFO method of treating opening inventory is more complex, FIFO is less desirable, especially if several different batches of beginning inventory are semifinished.

Using JIT manufacturing, accountants can forgo the calculation of equivalent units entirely. The composition of inventory changes because there is little or no work in process as a result of reduced lead time. With a substantial reduction in the levels of work in process and finished goods inventories, the need to separately allocate costs to ending inventories decreases. These systems charge direct labor and factory overhead costs to cost of goods sold directly rather than to work in process and finished goods. The substantial reduction in accounting costs overrides the marginal decrease in the accuracy of product costs for these companies.

Job order costing may become less useful in an automated setting because lot sizes become too small to have a unique job order attached to each lot. Also, companies are less likely to be mass producing inventory for stock. Job and lot costing systems give way to process and operation costing approaches in flexible manufacturing.

Important Terms and Concepts

process costing, 182
job order costing, 182
operation costing, 182
equivalent units or equivalent production or equivalent full units, 183
units started and finished, 186

units started in process, 186
units transferred, 186
cost of production report, 187
weighted-average costing, 187
FIFO costing, 190

Appendix 6–A Completed and Not Transferred Inventory (L.O. 3)

In practice, transfer of all products finished during a period to the next department may not occur by the time accountants complete costing for that period. Thus, accountants add completed and not transferred units in the following equivalent unit formulas:

$$
\begin{aligned}
\text{EU, Weighted-} \atop \text{Average} \atop \text{Costing}
= \; &\text{Units} \atop \text{completed and} \atop \text{transferred} \atop \times\;100\%
\; + \; \text{Units} \atop \text{completed} \atop \text{and not} \atop \text{transferred} \atop \times\;100\%
\; + \; \text{Partially} \atop \text{completed} \atop \text{ending} \atop \text{inventory} \atop \times\;\text{stage of} \atop \text{completion}
\end{aligned}
$$

$$
\begin{aligned}
\text{EU, FIFO} \atop \text{Costing}
= \; &\text{Units} \atop \text{completed} \atop \text{and} \atop \text{transferred} \atop \times\;100\%
\; + \; \text{Units} \atop \text{completed} \atop \text{and not} \atop \text{transferred} \atop \times\;100\%
\; + \; \text{Partially} \atop \text{completed} \atop \text{ending} \atop \text{inventory} \atop \times\;\text{stage of} \atop \text{completion}
\; - \; \text{Beginning} \atop \text{inventory} \atop \times\;\text{stage of} \atop \text{completion}
\end{aligned}
$$

Using Weighted-Average Costing. Exhibit 6A–1 illustrates the weighted-average process costing approach when a department completes units in inventory but does not transfer them to the next department during the period in which they were finished. The Mixing Department in Exhibit 6A–1 has 500 completed units and 2,400 semifinished units in beginning inventory. Assume the Mixing Department completes the units on the last day of the previous month and did not have time to transfer them to the next department. The ending inventory for the previous month of November includes the completed units.

   In this case, we include the cost allocated to both the completed and semifinished units with the current cost to arrive at the unit cost. In computing the Mixing Department material unit cost, we add the $1,000 material assigned to the completed units to the $1,600 assigned to the 2,400 units to reach a one-third stage of material processing along with the $23,845 current material cost. We divide $26,445 total material cost by the 12,900 material equivalent units to arrive at a $2.05 unit material cost in the Mixing Department. A similar computation for conversion costs arrives at $11.95 unit cost. We assign a total unit cost of $14 to all 11,000 units transferred (500 completed and not transferred last month + 2,400 semifinished units in beginning inventory finished this period + 8,100 units started and completed this period).

Using FIFO Costing. Exhibit 6A–2 illustrates the procedure if Mark Manufacturing Company uses FIFO costing. In arriving at the unit cost, we divide only current cost by the equivalent units. We treat completed units as a separate batch of inventory that is transferred to the next department. The cost transferred comes from three sources: completed units on hand in beginning inventory, semifinished units from beginning inventory that are finished during the month, and units that are started and finished during the month.

EXHIBIT 6A–1

MARK MANUFACTURING COMPANY
Cost of Production Report—Weighted Average
For Month Ending December 31, 19X1

	Mixing Department	
Quantity schedule (Step 1):		
Completed and on hand	500	
Semifinished inventory (⅓ material, ¼ conversion costs)	2,400	
Units started in process	10,000	12,900
Units transferred to next department	11,000	
Ending inventory		
(all materials, ⅖ conversion costs)	1,900	12,900

	Total Costs	Unit Costs
Costs to account for (Step 3):		
Work in process—completed inventory:		
Material	$ 1,000	
Conversion costs	5,750	
	$ 6,750	
Work in process—semifinished inventory:		
Material	1,600	
Conversion costs	6,300	
Total semifinished inventory	$ 7,900	
Current costs in department:		
Material	23,845	$ 2.05
Conversion costs	128,482	11.95
Total costs to account for	$166,977	$ 14.00

Costs accounted for as follows (Step 4):		
Costs transferred to next department (11,000 × $14)		$154,000
Work in process—ending inventory:		
Material (1,900 × $2.05)	$ 3,895	
Conversion costs (1,900 × ⅖ × $11.95)	9,082	12,977
Total costs accounted for		$166,977

Additional computations (Step 2):	Transferred +	Ending Inventory	
EU, Mixing Department, material	11,000 +	1,900	= 12,900
$1,000 + $1,600 + $23,845		(1,900 × 100%)	

$$= \frac{\$26,445}{12,900} = \$2.05$$

EU, Mixing Department, conversion costs . .	11,000 +	760	= 11,760
$5,750 + $6,300 + $128,482		(1,900 × ⅖)	

$$= \frac{\$140,532}{11,760} = \$11.95$$

EXHIBIT 6A–2

MARK MANUFACTURING COMPANY
Cost of Production Report—FIFO
For Month Ending December 31, 19X1

	Mixing Department	
Quantity schedule (Step 1):		
Completed and on hand	500	
Semifinished inventory (⅓ material, ¼ conversion costs)	2,400	
Units started in process	10,000	12,900
Units transferred to next department	11,000	
Ending inventory (all materials, ⅖ conversion costs)	1,900	12,900

	Total Costs	Unit Costs
Costs to account for (Step 3):		
Work in process—completed inventory:		
Material	$ 1,000	
Conversion costs	5,750	
	$ 6,750	
Work in process—semifinished inventory:		
Material	$ 1,600	
Conversion costs	6,300	
Total semifinished inventory	$ 7,900	
Current cost in department:		
Material	23,845	$ 2.0556
Conversion costs	128,482	12.0527
Total costs to account for	$166,977	$14.1083
Costs accounted for as follows (Step 4):		
Costs transferred to next department:		
From completed inventory		$ 6,750
From semifinished inventory:		
Value of semifinished inventory	$ 7,900	
Material added (2,400 × ⅔ × $2.0556)	3,289	
Conversion costs (2,400 × ¾ × $12.0527)	21,695	32,884
From current production (8,100 × $14.1083)		114,277
Total cost transferred		$153,911
Work in process—ending inventory:		
Material (1,900 × 100% × $2.0556)	$ 3,906	
Conversion costs (1,900 × ⅖ × $12.0527)	9,160	13,066
Total costs accounted for		$166,977

Additional computations (Step 2):

	Transferred	+	Ending Inventory	–	Completed Inventory	–	Semifinished Inventory		
EU, Mixing Department, material .... $\frac{\$23,845}{11,600} = \$2.0556$	11,000	+	1,900 (1,900 × 100%)	–	500 (500 × 100%)	–	800 (2,400 × ⅓)	=	11,600
EU, Mixing Department, conversion costs ..... $\frac{\$128,482}{10,660} = \$12.0527$	11,000	+	760 (1,900 × ⅖)	–	500 (500 × 100%)	–	600 (2,400 × ¼)	=	10,660

Review Questions

1. What is the purpose of the quantity schedule on the cost of production report?
2. Why is it necessary to express the units in the quantity schedule on the cost of production report in terms of the department's finished product which may not be the companywide finished product?
3. Discuss the characteristics of the production process that determine whether job order costing or process costing is used.
4. Define equivalent units.
5. Why is it necessary to compute equivalent units and how are they used?
6. On what basis are costs accumulated using process costing?
7. Why is the product unit under process costing similar to a snowball as it travels from one department to another?
8. Why is it necessary to summarize material, labor, and factory overhead by departments rather than merely to determine total cost for the finished product?
9. Why should the accountant be concerned about determining when material is issued into the production process?
10. Why is it not imperative that predetermined factory overhead rates be used in some process costing systems?
11. How does the cost of production report provide proof as to the correctness of the disposition of costs?
12. What cost components does the preceding department cost represent?
13. What is the difference between units transferred and units started and finished during current production?
14. Indicate the journal entry to transfer costs *(a)* from one processing department to another department; and *(b)* on completion from the last processing department.
15. Which changes in job order and process costing systems do you expect to see become more prevalent because of increased use of flexible manufacturing and automation?

CPA/CMA/CIA Multiple Choice Questions

1.–4. (CMA) Questions 1 through 4 concern Levittown Company, which employs a process cost system for its manufacturing operations. All direct materials are added at the beginning of the process and conversion costs are added proportionately. Levittown's production quantity schedule for November is reproduced below.

	Units
Work in process on November 1 (60% complete as to conversion costs)	1,000
Units started during November	5,000
Total units to account for	6,000
Units completed and transferred out from beginning inventory	1,000
Units started and completed during November	3,000
Work in process on November 30 (20% complete as to conversion costs)	2,000
Total units accounted for	6,000

1. Using the FIFO method, the equivalent units for direct materials for November are

   a. 5,000 units.
   b. 6,000 units.
   c. 4,400 units.
   d. 3,800 units.
   e. Some amount other than those given above.

2. Using the FIFO method, the equivalent units for conversion costs for November are

   a. 3,400 units.
   b. 3,800 units.
   c. 4,000 units.
   d. 4,400 units.
   e. Some amount other than those given above.

3. Using the weighted-average method, the equivalent units for conversion costs for November are

   a. 3,400 units.
   b. 3,800 units.
   c. 4,000 units.
   d. 4,400 units.
   e. Some amount other than those given above.

4. Using the weighted-average method, the equivalent units for direct materials for November are

   a. 3,400 units.
   b. 4,400 units.
   c. 5,000 units.
   d. 6,000 units.
   e. Some amount other than those given above.

5. (CIA) The following data refer to the units processed by the Grinding Department for a recent month:

Beginning work in process	12,000
Units started	200,000
Units completed	192,000
Ending work in process	20,000

   The beginning work in process was 60 percent complete, and the ending work in process is 70 percent complete. What are the equivalent units of production for the month using the FIFO method?

   a. 210,800.
   b. 198,800.
   c. 185,200.
   d. 184,000.

6. (CIA) From the industries listed below, choose the one most likely to use process costing in accounting for production costs:

   a. Road builder.
   b. Electrical contractor.
   c. Newspaper publisher.
   d. Automobile repair shop.

7. In process 2, Material G is added when a batch is 60 percent complete. Ending work in process units, which are 50 percent complete, would be included in the computation of equivalent units for

	Conversion Costs	Material G
a.	Yes	No
b.	No	Yes
c.	No	No
d.	Yes	Yes

8. In a process cost system, the application of factory overhead usually would be recorded as an increase in

   a. Cost of goods sold.
   b. Work in process control.
   c. Factory overhead control.
   d. Finished goods control.

9. Walden Company has a process cost system using the FIFO cost flow method. All materials are introduced at the beginning of the process in Department One. The following information is available for the month of January 19X3:

	Units
Work in process, 1/1/X3	
(40% complete as to conversion costs)	500
Started in January	2,000
Transferred to Department Two during January	2,100
Work in process, 1/31/X3	
(25% complete as to conversion costs)	400

   What are the equivalent units of production for the month of January 19X3?

	Materials	Conversion
a.	2,500	2,200
b.	2,500	1,900
c.	2,000	2,200
d.	2,000	2,000

10. (AICPA) Information for the month of January 19X2 concerning Department A, the first stage of Ogden Corporation's production cycle, is as follows:

	Materials	Conversion
Work in process, beginning	$ 8,000	$ 6,000
Current costs	40,000	32,000
Total costs	$48,000	$38,000
Equivalent units using weighted-average method	100,000	95,000
Average unit costs	$ 0.48	$ 0.40
Goods completed	90,000 units	
Work in process, end	10,000 units	

   Materials are added at the beginning of the process. The ending work in process is 50 percent complete as to conversion costs. How would the total costs accounted for be distributed, using the weighted-average method?

	Goods Completed	Work in Process, End
a.	$79,200	$6,800
b.	$79,200	$8,800
c.	$86,000	$0
d.	$88,000	$6,800

11. (AICPA) The Cutting Department is the first stage of Mark Company's production cycle. Conversion costs for this department were 80 percent complete as to the beginning work in process and 50 percent complete as to the ending work in

process. Information as to conversion costs in the Cutting Department for January 19X0 is as follows:

	Units	Conversion Costs
Work in process at January 1, 19X0	25,000	$ 22,000
Units started and costs incurred during January	135,000	$143,000
Units completed and transferred to next department during January	100,000	

Using the FIFO method, what was the conversion cost of the work in process in the Cutting Department at January 31, 19X0?

12. (AICPA) Glo Co., a manufacturer of combs, budgeted sales of 125,000 units for the month of April 19X1. The following additional information is provided:

	Units
Actual inventory at April 1	
Work in process	None
Finished goods	37,500
Budgeted inventory at April 30	
Work in process (75% processed)	8,000
Finished goods	30,000

How many equivalent units of production did Glo budget for April 19X1?

a. 126,500.
b. 125,500.
c. 123,500.
d. 117,500.

13. (AICPA) A process costing system was used for a department that began operations in January 19X1. Approximately the same number of physical units, at the same degree of completion, were in work in process at the end of both January and February. Monthly conversion costs are allocated between ending work in process and units completed. Compared to the FIFO method, would the weighted-average method use the same or a greater number of equivalent units to calculate the monthly allocations?

	Equivalent Units for Weighted Average Compared to FIFO	
	January	February
a.	Same	Same
b.	Greater number	Greater number
c.	Greater number	Same
d.	Same	Greater number

Exercises

E6–1 Equivalent Units: FIFO and Average Costing (L.O. 1)

Production cost records for the Price Company indicate 20,000 units started into production. When production began, the 2,000 units in beginning inventory were one-fourth complete for material and one-fifth complete for labor and overhead. Ending inventory consisted of 5,000 units which had one fifth of their material and one tenth of their labor and overhead.

Required:

a. Calculate the equivalent production units for each cost component using FIFO costing.
b. Calculate the equivalent production units for each cost component using weighted-average costing.

E6–2 Equivalent Units (L.O. 1)

Heam Company used the FIFO method of costing in a process-costing system. Workers add material at the beginning of the process in Department One, and conversion costs are incurred uniformly throughout the process. Beginning work in process inventory on June 1 in Department One consisted of 40,000 units estimated to be 20 percent complete. During June, 140,000 units were started in Department One, and 150,000 units were completed and transferred to Department Two. Estimates indicate that ending work in process inventory on June 30 in Department One was 10 percent complete.

Required:

Determine the equivalent units in Department One for material and conversion costs.

E6–3 EU Calculations Using Average and FIFO Costing (L.O. 2)

Determine finished equivalents for the following process of Watch Company:

	Mixing Department
Units in process—beginning	2,400
stage of completion except material	80%
Units received from prior department	30,000
Units transferred	28,000
Units in process—ending	4,400
stage of completion except material	60%

Workers issued materials at the beginning of the process in this second department of operations.

Required:

a. Determine the equivalent units using average costing for:
   (1) Preceding departmental cost.
   (2) Materials.
   (3) Conversion costs.

b. Repeat Requirement *a* using FIFO costing.

E6–4 FIFO and Weighted-Average Costing EU (L.O. 2)

Moore Company has the following production cost data:

	Units
Beginning inventory (⅓ of inventory is ¼ finished, ½ of inventory is ⅓ finished, and ⅙ of inventory is ½ finished)	6,000
Started into process	12,000
Transferred	16,000
Ending inventory (⅕ of inventory is ⅛ finished, ½ of inventory is ¼ finished, and ³⁄₁₀ of inventory is ⅙ finished)	2,000

Required:

a. Determine the equivalent production units using FIFO costing.
b. Determine the equivalent production units using weighted-average costing.

E6–5 FIFO Process Costing (L.O. 3)

Courtney Company places material in production at the beginning of operations. In April, material costs totaled $16,660; direct labor, $20,560; and factory overhead, $7,139. On April 1, there were 750 units in process, one fifth completed as to direct labor and one third completed as to factory overhead; these had a total cost of $2,788. There were 6,200 units completed and transferred during the month. Ending inventory consisted of 500 units, three-fourths completed as to direct labor and one fifth completed as to factory overhead. The company uses the FIFO method of costing.

Required:

a. Calculate the cost to be assigned to the units transferred.
b. Calculate the cost to be assigned to the units in ending inventory.

E6–6 EU and EU Cost Calculations (L.O. 2)

The departmental Work in Process account for Watters Company follows. Watters places all direct materials in process at the beginning of production.

Work in Process Department A

700 units, 40% completed	4,500	To Department B,	
Direct materials (1,850 @ $9)	16,650	2,550 units	34,185
Direct labor	7,900		
Factory overhead	5,135		
	34,185		34,185

Required:

a. Determine the following, presenting your computations using FIFO costing:
    (1) Equivalent units of production for conversion costs.
    (2) Conversion costs per equivalent unit of production.
    (3) Total and unit cost of products started in previous period and completed in the current period.
    (4) Total and unit cost of current production. Round computations to three decimals.
b. Indicate factors that could cause the unit costs computed in Requirement *a*, items 3 and 4, to vary.
c. Explain if any units are left in work in process ending inventory.

E6–7 Contrasting Average Costing with FIFO (AICPA adapted) (L.O. 1)

Noble Manufacturing Company uses the weighted-average method of process costing when computing manufacturing cost per equivalent unit. The work in process inventory at the beginning of the period was complete as to materials, and one-third complete as to conversion costs. The work in process inventory at the end of the period was complete as to materials, and one-quarter complete as to conversion costs.

Required:

a. Describe how the cost of the beginning work in process inventory is handled using the weighted-average method of process costing when computing manufacturing cost per equivalent unit. Do not describe determination of equivalent units.
b. Identify the conditions under which the weighted-average method of process costing would be inappropriate.
c. Specify the advantages of the weighted-average method of process costing in contrast to the first-in, first-out method.
d. Compute the conversion cost portion of Noble's ending work in process inventory using the weighted-average method.

E6–8 Average and FIFO Costing Items (L.O. 3)

The production and cost data of Touch Company for June are as follows:

Production:	Units
In process, June 1 (material fully issued; ¼ complete for labor and overhead)	16,400
Started in process during June	120,000
Completed and transferred to next department	130,900
In process June 30 (material fully issued; ⅖ complete for labor and overhead)	5,500

Costs:
Work in process inventory, June 1:

Materials	$9,512	
Labor and overhead	1,844	$ 11,356
Materials issued during month		73,692
Labor and overhead		62,044
Total		$147,092

Required:

a. Determine the following using average costing:
   (1) The equivalent units for material.
   (2) The material cost per unit.
   (3) The equivalent units for labor and overhead.
   (4) The labor and overhead cost per unit.
   (5) The total cost transferred to the next department.
   (6) The value of work in process, June 30.
b. Repeat the requirements in *a* using FIFO costing.

E6–9 Sections of Weighted-Average Costing Report (L.O. 3)

By mistake, the cost of production report that you have been working on for the Hazel branch was thrown in the paper shredder. From your notes, you can determine that material unit cost was $4.20 and that conversion cost was $5.05 for this month. Reference to your records reveals that equivalent units were 2,100 for material and 1,950 for conversion cost. A total of 600 units having all of their material and three fourths of their labor was in ending inventory. Last month's ending inventory showed that $560 of material and $380 of conversion cost had been added to these units.

Required:

Prepare the cost to account for and costs accounted for sections of a production report using weighted-average costing.

E6–10 FIFO Costing (L.O. 3)

Department One of Sear Company completed 55,000 units of product and transferred them to finished goods during a cost period. Of these 55,000 units, 15,000 were in process and were one-third completed as to labor and overhead at the beginning of the period and 40,000 units were begun and completed during the period. In addition to the foregoing units, 13,000 more units were in process in the department, three-fifths processed as to labor and overhead at the period end. FIFO costing is used.

Required:

Calculate the equivalent units of material added to the product processed in the first department during the period under each of the following unrelated assumptions:

a. All the material introduced to the product are added when the department's process is first begun.
b. The materials introduced to the product are added evenly throughout the department's process.
c. One half of the materials introduced are added when the department's process is first begun and the other half is added when the process is three-fourths completed.

E6–11 Theory of Process Costing (L.O. 1)

The following computations are for Creite Inc.'s cost of production report. The 200 units in beginning inventory have a total cost of $500.

$$EU, \text{ preceding department cost} = 1{,}000 + 100 - 200 = 900$$

$$\frac{\$450}{900} = \$.50$$

$$EU, \text{ materials} = 1{,}000 + 100 - 200 = 900$$

$$\frac{\$990}{900} = \$1.10$$

$$EU, \text{ conversion costs} = 1{,}000 + 25 - 80 = 945$$
$$(100 \times 25\%) - (200 \times 40\%)$$

$$\frac{\$1{,}890}{945} = \$2$$

Required:

a. Explain why you know that this is not the first processing department.
b. (1) Identify the costing method (FIFO or weighted average) being used.
   (2) Give two reasons why you know this costing method is being used.
c. Explain why 200 units were deducted in computing the equivalent units for the preceding department cost.
d. Explain before what stage of operations material enters this department.
e. Explain why you could not work this problem on the data given using average costing.

E6–12 FIFO Costing; Calculating Current Cost (L.O. 3)

Department One of Bacon, Inc., provides the following limited data for May:

Beginning inventory (1,500 units):	
Material (10% stage of completion)	$ 450
Conversion cost (80% stage of completion)	$1,800
Units transferred	9,000

The ending inventory contains 600 units having 30 percent of material and 40 percent conversion cost. Due to a change in suppliers, material unit cost decreased $0.20 but the cheaper grade of material caused unit conversion cost to increase $0.40 from April.

Required:

Prepare a cost of production report for May using FIFO costing.

Problems

P6–13 Weighted Average Cost of Production Report—Second Department (L.O. 3)

Banks Company uses the weighted-average method of costing. The following data relate to Department 2 for November. No units were lost during November.

Beginning inventory:	
Cost from preceding department	$660
Department 2 material	300
Department 2 labor	500
Department 2 overhead	480
(600 units, stage of completion: ¼ material, ⅙ labor, ⅕ factory overhead)	
Current costs:	
Cost received from preceding department (1,200 units)	$1,467.60
Material	3,277.16
Labor	6,913.85
Overhead	5,623.50
Ending inventory (400 units, ⅕ material, ⅛ labor, ¼ overhead)	

Required:

Prepare a cost of production report for Department 2 for November.

P6–14 Segments of Cost of Production Report (L.O. 3)

Tractor Manufacturing Company provides the following data for Department One. Each unit receives 2 gallons of material at the beginning of operations.

Beginning inventory (500 units)	
Direct materials (1,000 gallons)	$1,000
Conversion cost (30% complete)	400
Current costs:	
Direct material (6,400 gallons)	6,770
Conversion cost	9,980
Ending inventory (400 units)	
Direct materials (800 gallons)	
Conversion cost (40% complete)	

Required:

a. Determine the units transferred to the next department.
b. Using the weighted-average costing method, calculate unit cost per equivalent unit for material and conversion cost.
c. Calculate the cost transferred to the next department.
d. Determine the value of ending inventory.
e. Prove the correctness of your answers to *c* and *d*.
f. Using instead the FIFO costing method, calculate unit cost per equivalent unit for material and conversion cost.
g. Calculate the cost transferred to the next department using FIFO.
h. Determine the value of ending inventory using FIFO.

P6–15 Cost of Production Report (L.O. 2)

COLLINGE COMPANY
Department 2
Cost of Production Report
For the Month Ending February 19X1

Quantity schedule:			
Beginning inventory	100	(¼ M, ⅕ L, ⅒ OH)	
Received from prior department	900		1,000
Transferred	800		
Ending inventory	200	(⅕ M, ½ L, ¼ OH)	1,000
Value of beginning inventory:			
Prior department costs	$100		
Material	55		
Labor	48		
Overhead	34		
Total value of beginning inventory		$ 237	
Current costs:			
Costs received from prior department		990	
Material		2,119	
Labor		1,728	
Overhead		2,520	
Total costs to account for		$7,594	

Required:

Using the preceding partial cost of production report, do the following:

a. Indicate in terms of cost elements what the prior department costs represent.
b. Determine in which department the $100 prior department cost was incurred. To how many units was the $100 applied?
c. Indicate which figure represents the costs of the 900 units received.
d. Indicate which figure represents the cost incurred for the beginning inventory to reach a one-fourth stage of material content. In which department was it incurred? When was the cost incurred?

e. Determine when the $48 labor cost was incurred and in which department.

f. Calculate the equivalent units and unit cost using FIFO costing for material.

g. Calculate the equivalent units and unit cost using FIFO costing for labor.

h. Calculate the equivalent units and unit cost using FIFO costing for overhead.

i. Calculate the equivalent units and unit cost using FIFO costing for prior department cost.

j. Calculate the equivalent units and unit cost using weighted-average costing for material.

k. Calculate the equivalent units and unit cost using weighted-average costing for labor.

l. Calculate the equivalent units and unit cost using weighted-average costing for overhead.

m. Calculate the equivalent units and unit cost using weighted-average costing for prior department cost.

P6–16 FIFO Process Costing; Cost Accounted for Section (L.O. 3)

As another member of the Trident Company's cost accounting department leaves for a committee meeting, she hands you a cost of production report to complete. You notice that she has already determined that equivalent units for material are 2,860 and 2,885 for conversion cost.

Workers transferred a total of 2,785 units to the next department. Ending inventory consisted of 300 units, two-thirds complete as of material and three-fourths complete as of conversion cost. The following data are available for your use:

Beginning inventory (500 units, ¼ complete):	
Material	$ 375
Conversion cost	350
Current cost:	
Material	9,009
Conversion cost	8,078
Cost to account for	$17,812

Required:

Using FIFO costing, determine the cost transferred and the value of ending inventory.

P6–17 Calculating Equivalent Units (CIA adapted) (L.O. 3)

The Brown Company manufactures hair spray in a three-department process. The Molding Department produces the plastic bottles and caps in which the product is placed. The Mixing Department combines the raw materials for the hair spray and puts the mixture into bottles. In the Packaging Department, the product is boxed and sealed in cellophane. A description of the departmental activities as well as the units associated with the work in process at the beginning of March were as follows:

Molding Department. In the Molding Department, the plastic is added at the beginning of the process, overhead is uniformly incurred, and the only direct labor occurs at the end of the process. A worker trims the bottle and cap and places them on a conveyer for transport to the Mixing Department. The work in process at March 1 was 1,000 units estimated to be 50 percent complete.

Mixing Department. All the materials for the hair spray are combined in a large vat, thoroughly mixed, and pumped into the plastic bottles conveyed from the Molding Department. The overhead costs for the Mixing Department are uniformly incurred during the mixing process. Materials and direct labor are added at the beginning of the process. At the beginning of March, no work in process existed in the Mixing Department.

Packaging Department. The capped bottles are conveyed to the Packaging Department where they are automatically boxed. At the end of the process, the boxes are sealed in cellophane and a worker packs them in cases of 24 bottles each. The individual box is added at the beginning of the process and the cellophane, direct labor, and casing are added at the end of the process. Overhead is incurred uniformly. On March 1, 960 units were considered to be 40 percent complete.

Plastic for 100,000 bottles and caps was added into production in the month of March in the Molding Department. The work in process inventories at the end of March included: 2,000 units 80 percent complete in the Molding Department; 1,000 units 50 percent complete in the Mixing Department; and 640 units 25 percent complete in the Packaging Department.

The Molding and Mixing Departments use weighted-average process costing, while the Packaging Department uses first-in, first-out process costing.

Required:

Complete the equivalent unit schedule for March for the three departments. Assume that Brown Company calculates equivalent units for each identifiable input in each department, and that no spoilage occurs in any of the processes.

P6–18 Error in OH Application Rate for Process Costing System (L.O. 1)

You have been asked to review the cost records of Saber, Inc., and to make any changes needed to correct errors in the financial statements of March 31, 19X1. Saber, Inc., started operations on March 1, 19X1, with no beginning inventories. Factory overhead costs are applied at 95 percent of direct labor cost. The determination was

$$\frac{\$1,472,500 \text{ factory overhead costs budgeted}}{\$1,550,000 \text{ direct labor cost budgeted}} = 95 \text{ percent}$$

Work in process inventory of March 31 was fully complete for materials and one-third complete for conversion costs. Costs recorded for March were

Direct material	$84,000
Direct labor	93,500

In the departmental budgets prepared for the year 19X1, the following are administrative expenses:

Factory accountants' salaries	$ 72,500
Payroll taxes applicable to factory	135,000
Depreciation on building and equipment	300,000

Factory operations utilize 60 percent of the building and its equipment. Financial statements prepared on March 31 showed the following:

Work in process inventory, March 31 (15,000 units)	$ 45,450
Finished goods inventory, March 31 (7,500 units)	44,175
Cost of sales for March (30,000 units)	176,700

Required:

a. Determine the corrected balances on March 31 for:
   (1) Work in process inventory.
   (2) Finished goods inventory.
   (3) Cost of goods sold.
b. Explain the impact on the financial statements of using the incorrect factory overhead application rate.

P6–19 Process Costing; FIFO; Average Costing; Second Department (L.O. 3)

The following information is for Department 2 of the Tennis Arts Company which uses a process costing system for May 19X2:

```
Beginning inventory  .................        1,200 units (⅓ material, ⅙ conversion costs)
   Prior department costs  .............     $   800
   Material  .......................       $   500
   Conversion cost  ................      $ 1,600
Started in process  .................        8,000 units
Current material costs  .............       $ 9,500
Current conversion costs  ...........       $62,552
Costs received from prior department  .....  $ 5,640
Transferred  ......................          7,600 units
Ending inventory  .................          1,600 units (¼ material, ⅕ conversion costs)
```

Required:

a. Prepare a production cost report using FIFO costing.

b. Prepare a production cost report using weighted-average costing.

P6–20 FIFO and Average Process Costing: Third Department (L.O. 3)

Data for Department 3 of Key, Inc., for the month of May follow; they use a process cost system.

```
Started in process  ....................       5,000 units
Current material cost  ..................     $ 4,675
Current conversion costs  ...............     $16,926
Costs from prior departments  ...........     $35,000
Transferred  ........................          4,500 units
Beginning inventory  ...................         900 units
                                                    (⅔ material,
                                                     ⅚ conversion costs)

Value of beginning inventory:
   Costs from prior departments  ..........    $ 6,100
   Material  .........................       $   600
   Conversion costs  ...................      $ 3,075
   Ending inventory  ...................        1,400 units
                                                    (¼ material,
                                                     ⅕ conversion costs)
```

Required:

a. Prepare a production cost report using the FIFO method.

b. Prepare a production cost report using the weighted-average method.

P6–21 Average Costing, FIFO for Two Months (L.O. 3)

Rosser Production Company employs a process cost system in the manufacture of industrial chemicals. Three departments are involved in the process: Mixing, Refining, and Finishing. No units are lost in the Refining Department. Data for January and February operations in the Refining Department are as follows:

	January	February
Beginning inventory	600	?
Stage of completion	¾ material	?
	⅖ conversion costs	?
Received from preceding department	1,500	2,000
Ending inventory	330	500
Stage of completion	⅔ material	⅘ material
	⅙ conversion costs	¹⁄₁₀ conversion costs
Value of beginning inventory:		
Costs from preceding department	$1,170	?
Material cost	308	?
Conversion costs	132	?
Costs received from preceding department	3,000	$3,900
Current material cost	3,234	4,422
Current conversion costs	951	1,168

Required:

a. Prepare a cost of production report using FIFO costing.

b. Prepare a cost of production report using weighted-average costing.

P6–22 Weighted-Average and FIFO Production Reports (L.O. 3)

Dawee Company uses a process costing system in the manufacture of industrial chemicals. According to the following data for Departments One and Two, there were several batches of units on hand when operations began for January.

	Department One	Department Two
Started in process	2,900 units	?
Beginning inventory	100 units	500 units
Value of beginning inventory and stage of completion:		
Costs from preceding department		$5,640
Material	$ 40 (1/4)	300 (1/5)
Labor	327 (3/5)	60 (1/10)
Overhead	75 (1/5)	100 (1/5)
Current costs:		
Material	4,429	7,095
Labor	14,933	3,025
Overhead	9,804	1,978
Ending inventory	500 units	800 units
Stage of completion	1/5 material	3/5 material
	3/5 labor	3/4 labor
	1/5 overhead	1/4 overhead

There were no units completed and on hand at the end of the month.

Required:

a. Prepare a cost of production report using weighted-average costing.

b. Prepare a cost of production report using FIFO costing.

P6–23 Process Costing, Two Departments: Weighted-Average Costing and FIFO (L.O. 3)

William Manufacturing Company utilizes a process cost system for its two factory departments. After leaving the Fabricating Department, one third of the goods finished are transferred to finished goods and sold immediately. The remainder are transferred to the Finishing Department.

The following data are from their records for the month ending January 31, 19X1:

	Fabricating Department	Finishing Department
Beginning inventory	100 units	500 units
Stage of completion	1/4 material	1/5 material
	3/5 conversion costs	1/10 conversion costs
Started in process	7,560 units	?
Ending inventory	700	1,140
Stage of completion	1/5 material	3/5 material
	2/7 conversion costs	3/4 conversion costs
Value of beginning inventory:		
Costs from preceding department		$4,157
Material	$ 65	30
Conversion costs	330	43
Current material cost	14,135	2,312
Current conversion costs	41,198	2,870

Required:

a. Prepare a cost of production report using weighted-average costing.

b. Prepare a cost of production report using FIFO costing. Assume the 100 units in beginning inventory are included in the units transferred to the Finishing Department.

P6–24 Average Costing, FIFO: Two Months (L.O. 3)

Amy Wells Production Company employs a process cost system in the manufacture of industrial chemicals. Three departments are involved in the process: Blending, Fabricating, and Finishing. No units are lost in the Fabricating Department. Data for January and February operations in the Fabricating Department are as follows:

	January	February
Beginning inventory	1,200	?
Stage of completion	⅗ material,	?
	⅓ conversion costs	
Received from preceding department	3,000	2,500
Ending inventory	800	900
Stage of completion	½ material,	⅓ material,
	¼ conversion costs	⅙ conversion costs
Value of beginning inventory:		
Costs from preceding department	$4,110	?
Material	1,350	?
Conversion costs	720	?
Cost received from preceding department ..	2,820	$3,225
Current material cost	4,928	3,910
Current conversion costs	864	1,128

Required:

a. Prepare a cost of production report using FIFO costing.

b. Prepare a cost of production report using weighted-average costing.

P6–25 FIFO and Weighted-Average Costing of Production Reports (L.O. 3)

Monthly data for two departments of Albert Manufacturing Company follow:

	Department A	Department B
Beginning inventory	100 units (all material,	300 units (all material,
	¼ labor-overhead)	⅖ labor-overhead)
Prior department cost	-0-	$2,175
Material	$ 337	864
Labor	42	299
Overhead	47	709
Current costs:		
Material	1,925	1,400
Labor	690	1,891
Overhead	1,495	3,233
Units transferred	500	520
Ending inventory	150 units (all material,	280 units (all material,
	⅔ labor-overhead)	¾ labor-overhead)

Required:

a. Prepare a production cost report using FIFO and give the following:

(1) Equivalent units for conversion costs in Department A.

(2) Costs transferred from Department A to Department B.

(3) Equivalent units for prior department cost in Department B.

(4) Equivalent unit cost for material in Department B.

(5) Value of ending inventory in Department B.

(6) Costs transferred from Department B.

b. Prepare a production cost report using the weighted-average method and give the following:

(1) Equivalent units for conversion costs in Department A.

(2) Costs transferred from Department A to Department B.

(3) Equivalent units for prior department cost in Department B.
(4) Equivalent unit cost for material in Department B.
(5) Value of ending inventory in Department B.
(6) Costs transferred from Department B.

P6–26 Two Departments, Two Batches in Inventory, FIFO and Weighted-Average Costing (L.O. 3)

C. Renshaw Manufacturing Company produces units in two departments, Mixing and Finishing. The company introduces material in both departments. It placed a total of 2,000 units in process in the Mixing Department during the month. There were two batches of beginning inventory in the Finishing Department. Data for the month of May follow:

	Mixing Department	Finishing Department	
	Batch Number 1	Batch Number 1	Batch Number 2
Units	100	400	250
Stage of completion	1/5	1/8 material	1/5 material
		3/5 labor	1/10 labor
		1/4 overhead	3/5 overhead
Cost from preceding department:		$1,200	$750
Material	$ 6	55	74
Labor	37	700	80
Overhead	55	260	380
Current costs:			
Material	2,350	$3,680	
Labor	1,692	5,369	
Overhead	1,598	5,450	

Each department had one batch of ending inventory. A total of 300 units were one-third complete as to all cost elements; they were in the Mixing Department ending inventory. The 200 units in the Finishing Department's ending inventory were three-fourths complete as to material; two fifths, labor; and nine-tenths, overhead.

Required:

a. Prepare a cost of production report using FIFO costing.
b. Prepare a cost of production report using weighted-average costing.

Appendix Problems

P6–27 Second Department, Completed and Not Transferred Inventory (L.O. 3)

Refer to the Mark Manufacturing Company in Appendix 6A–1 for data concerning the Mixing Department, the first department. There are both finished and semifinished units in beginning inventory in the Assembly Department, the second and final processing department. Assembly Department provides the following data for December:

Beginning completed inventory	400 units	
Prior department costs	$5,264	
Material	$ 405	
Conversion costs	$3,400	$9,069
Beginning semifinished inventory	300 units (1/6 material, 2/5 conversion costs)	
Prior department costs	$3,951	
Material	$ 53	
Conversion costs	$1,044	$5,048
Current costs:		
Material	$11,752	
Conversion costs	$95,700	
Costs and units received from prior department	(refer to Mixing Department data)	
Transferred	10,900 units	
Ending inventory	800 units (1/4 material, 3/5 conversion costs)	

Required:

a. Prepare a production cost report using the weighted-average method.

b. Prepare a production cost report using FIFO.

c. Record the cost transfer entries using weighted average for both Mixing and Assembly Departments.

P6–28 Process Costing: Completed and Semifinished Units in Beginning Inventory (Weighted-Average and FIFO Costing) (L.O. 3)

Reeves Company uses a process costing system in the Grinding Department and the Assembly Department. There were several batches of units finished and on hand when operations began for February. Data from the records are as follows:

	Grinding Department		Assembly Department	
Started in process	3,900	units	?	
Completed and on hand	200	units	500	units
Value of completed units:				
Costs from preceding department			$ 2,365	
Material	$ 460		400	
Labor	240		825	
Overhead	100		1,650	
Semifinished units on hand	1,800	units	600	units
Value of semifinished units and stage of completion:				
Costs from preceding department			$ 2,300	
Material	$1,125	(1/6)	450	(1/3)
Labor	531	(1/4)	192	(1/5)
Overhead	336	(1/3)	495	(1/4)
Current costs:				
Material	10,588		2,975	
Labor	5,695		7,728	
Overhead	2,420		15,119	
Ending inventory	900	units	1,200	units
Stage of completion:	(1/5 M, 1/3 L, 1/9 OH)		(1/6 M, 1/3 L, 1/4 OH)	

There were no units completed and on hand at the end of the month.

Required:

a. Prepare a cost of production report using weighted-average costing.

b. Prepare a cost of production report using FIFO costing.

Process Costing—Addition of Materials and Lost Units

After studying this chapter, you should be able to:

1. Show the effect on product costs of additional materials.

2. Illustrate the costing procedure when the addition of material results in an increase in units to account for.

3. Prepare cost of production reports using FIFO and weighted-average costing when normal and abnormal losses occur.

4. Understand the impact of quality control concepts and zero defects programs on abnormal and normal losses.

Introduction

The preceding chapter introduces both FIFO and weighted-average methods of process costing. However, Chapter 6 does not discuss many of the complexities that accountants encounter in process costing. For example, the computation of product costs becomes more difficult if the material added to production increases the units to account for or if the manufacturing operations lose units. This chapter illustrates the costing procedures for these complexities.

Addition of Materials (L.O. 1)

The **addition of materials** may either **increase the unit cost** of the product or **increase the number of units** for which managers must account. For example, shirt manufacturers issue fabric at the beginning of production operations. They later add material in the Finishing Department when workers sew buttons on. This material in the form of buttons does not increase the number of shirts. The only effect is an increase in the unit cost. A similar situation occurs when workers add parts to the assembly of microwaves. There is no increase in the units to account for because workers are only changing the nature or character of the product. Chapter 6 introduces the costing procedure used when workers in departments subsequent to the first add materials that do not increase the number of units of product. Chapter 7 addresses the situation where materials added in departments subsequent to the first do increase the number of units of product.

Effect of Addition of Materials on Total Units to Account for Using Weighted Average

Exhibit 7–1 illustrates the weighted-average costing procedure when the introduction of material increases the number of units. Department 2 adds 1,000 gallons of oil to dilute the 6,500-gallon paint mixture received from Department 1. This increases the units to account for to 7,500 gallons plus 500 gallons in beginning inventory. Because workers combine the oil and paint mixture so neither can be distinguished, we spread the preceding department cost over the entire 7,500 gallons.

Department 1 is purposely simple so we can emphasize Department 2. In addition, Exhibit 7–1 combines labor and factory overhead costs in the one category of conversion costs. Department 1 workers introduce material throughout the process; the only effect is that each product completed must absorb a $2 unit material cost. Because there is no beginning inventory in Department 1, all 6,500 units transferred to the next department come from current production. Each of the 6,500 units carries a $5 preceding departmental cost when transferred to Department 2. The ending inventory in Department 1 has only received one fifth of its material and two sevenths of its conversion costs. We multiply the units in ending inventory by their stage of completion and finally by the unit cost to arrive at a valuation.

Effect of Addition of Materials on Unit Costs Using Weighted Average (L.O. 2)

Immediately on arrival, Department 2 workers mix oils costing $6,380 with the 6,500 gallons of paint mixture. This results in an additional 1,000 units to account for. Accountants spread the cost from the preceding department over the combined oil and paint mixture using the following weighted average equivalent unit computation Chapter 6 introduced:

EU, preceding department costs = 7,400 transferred + 600 ending inventory = 8,000
(600 × 100%)

$$\frac{\$2,000 \text{ Beg. Inv. Preced. Dept.} + \$32,500 \text{ Current Preced. Dept.}}{8,000 \text{ units}} = \frac{\$34,500}{8,000 \text{ units}} = \$4.313$$

The 7,400 units transferred come from a mixture of the units in beginning inventory, the units received from the preceding department, and the units added in Department 2.

Change in per Unit Cost. The additional units added in Department 2 cause a decrease in cost per unit. Materials added last month affected the $2,000 cost from preceding department in beginning inventory. We average this $2,000 with the $32,500 current costs received to arrive at a unit cost of $4.313. This is in contrast to the $5 per unit cost from Department 1. This difference partially arises because we spread the costs received from the preceding department over 1,000 additional units. For instance, if Department 2 workers did not dilute the paint mixture with 1,000 gallons of oil, unit cost would be $4.928 instead of $4.313, as follows:

$$\frac{\$2,000 \text{ Beg. Inv. Preced. Dept.} + \$32,500 \text{ Current Preced. Dept.}}{7,000 \text{ units}} = \frac{\$34,500}{7,000 \text{ units}} = \$4.928$$

EXHIBIT 7–1

WELLS MANUFACTURING COMPANY
Cost of Production Report—Weighted-Average Costing—Addition of Material
For the Month Ending January 31, 19X1

	Department 1			Department 2	
Quantity schedule (Step 1):					
Beginning inventory	–0–		(1/5 M, 1/10 CC)	500	
Received from preceding department	–0–			6,500	
Additional units put in process	–0–			1,000	
Started in process	7,200				
Total units to account for		7,200			8,000
Transferred to next department	6,500			7,400	
Ending inventory (1/5 material, 2/7 conversion costs)	700		(1/3 M, 3/4 CC)	600	
Total units accounted for		7,200			8,000
	Total Costs	**Unit Costs**		**Total Costs**	**Unit Costs**
Costs to account for (Step 3):					
Work in process—beginning inventory:					
Costs from preceding department				$ 2,000	
Material				80	
Conversion costs				43	
Total value of beginning inventory				$ 2,123	
Cost from preceding department				32,500	$ 4.313
Current costs:					
Material	$13,280	$ 2.00		6,380	0.850
Conversion costs	20,100	3.00		6,865	0.880
Total costs to account for	$33,380	$ 5.00		$47,868	$ 6.043
Costs accounted for as follows (Step 4):					
Costs transferred to next department (6,500 x $5)		$32,500	(7,400 x $6.043)		$44,714*
Work in process—ending inventory:					
Costs from preceding department			(600 x $4.313)	$ 2,588	
Material (700 x 1/5 x $2)	$ 280		(600 x 1/3 x $0.85)	170	
Conversion costs (700 x 2/7 x $3)	600	880	(600 x 3/4 x $0.88)	396	3,154
Total costs accounted for		$33,380			$47,868

Additional computations (Step 2):

	Transferred	+	Ending inventory		
EU, Department 1, material	6,500	+	140 (700 x 1/5)	=	6,640
$\frac{\$13,280}{6,640} = \$2$					
EU, Department 1, conversion costs	6,500	+	200 (700 x 2/7)	=	6,700
$\frac{\$20,100}{6,700} = \$3$					
EU, preceding department costs	7,400	+	600 (600 x 100%)	=	8,000
$\frac{\$2,000 + \$32,500}{8,000} = \frac{\$34,500}{8,000} = \$4.313$					
EU, Department 2, material	7,400	+	200 (600 x 1/3)	=	7,600
$\frac{\$80 + \$6,380}{7,600} = \frac{\$6,460}{7,600} = \$0.850$					
EU, Department 2, conversion costs	7,400	+	450 (600 x 3/4)	=	7,850
$\frac{\$43 + \$6,865}{7,850} = \frac{\$6,908}{7,850} = \$0.880$					

*7,400 units × $6.043 = $44,718.20. To avoid decimal discrepancy, the cost transferred is computed as follows: $47,868 − $3,154 = $44,714.

This lower cost per unit illustrates unit cost changes from one department to another.

In addition, the 500 units in beginning inventory have a preceding department unit cost of $4 ($2,000 costs from the preceding department ÷ 500 units) which reduces the averaged preceding department per unit cost. (Remember these 500 units went through Department 2's diluting process last month.) Other factors can cause the per unit preceding department cost to differ from the cost calculated in the previous department. This chapter discusses normal loss of units and averaging with FIFO, which can also account for the change in unit cost for a department when units enter the subsequent department. Exhibit 7–4 illustrates these two factors.

The bottom of Exhibit 7–1 illustrates the computation for material and conversion costs. No difference exists between these computations and the ones presented for weighted-average costing in Chapter 6. Because the 600 units in ending inventory have been through the preceding department, we assign the adjusted unit cost of $4.313 to all 600 units. We determine a $3,154 inventory valuation by multiplying the units in ending inventory by their stage of completion and the cost per unit. A decimal discrepancy results because we carry the unit costs out to only three decimal places and use only whole dollars. When we multiply the 7,400 units transferred by the $6.043 unit cost in Department 2, the result is $44,718.20. However, if we add this figure to the $3,154 ending inventory valuation, the total does not equal the costs to account for. Because the difference is so small and we know it is caused by the use of whole dollars and three-digit unit costs, we transfer the costs out at a total of $44,714 ($47,868 costs to account for − $3,154 ending inventory).

We must arrive at a unit cost for each of the following: preceding department costs, Department 2 material, and Department 2 conversion costs. We should not average the $6,380 material cost with the $2,000 and $32,500 preceding department costs, even though this material did result in 1,000 more units to account for. Instead, we compute a separate unit cost for material. In this example, Department 2 workers add material throughout the process, causing the material equivalent units to differ from the equivalent units for the preceding department.

Effect of Addition of Materials on Total Units to Account for Using FIFO

Exhibit 7–2 uses Exhibit 7–1 data to illustrate the FIFO costing procedure for handling the increase in units. The basic costing procedures under weighted-average costing and FIFO remain the same as presented in the previous chapter. However, the increase in units from the diluting effect require additional accounting. Because there is no beginning inventory in Department 1, the equivalent units and unit costs are identical to those shown for the first department in Exhibit 7–1. However, differences arise in Department 2 because of the 500 units in beginning inventory. Using FIFO costing, we subtract the 500 units in beginning inventory in the equivalent units calculation for preceding department costs. We divide only the $32,500 cost transferred from Department 1 by the FIFO equivalent units to arrive at the following unit cost:

$$\frac{\$32,500 \text{ Current Preceding Department Cost}}{7,500 \text{ units}} = \$4.333$$

As in the weighted-average method illustrated in Exhibit 7–1, the preceding department unit cost has decreased because the base unit count has increased by

EXHIBIT 7–2

WELLS MANUFACTURING COMPANY
Cost of Production Report—FIFO—Addition of Material
For the Month Ending January 31, 19X1

	Department 1			Department 2	
Quantity schedule (Step 1):					
Beginning inventory	–0–		($\frac{1}{5}$ M, $\frac{1}{10}$ CC)	500	
Received from preceding department	–0–			6,500	
Additional units put in process	–0–			1,000	
Started in process	7,200				
Total units to account for		7,200			8,000
Transferred to next department	6,500			7,400	
Ending inventory ($\frac{1}{5}$ material, $\frac{2}{7}$ conversion costs)	700		($\frac{1}{3}$ M, $\frac{3}{4}$ CC)	600	
Total units accounted for		7,200			8,000
	Total Costs	**Unit Costs**		**Total Costs**	**Unit Costs**
Costs to account for (Step 3):					
Work in process—beginning inventory:					
Costs from preceding department				$ 2,000	
Material				80	
Conversion costs				43	
Total value of beginning inventory				$ 2,123	
Costs from preceding department				32,500	$ 4.333
Current costs in department:					
Material	$13,280	$ 2.00		6,380	0.851
Conversion costs	20,100	3.00		6,865	0.880
Total costs to account for	$33,380	$ 5.00		$47,868	$ 6.064
Costs accounted for as follows (Step 4):					
Costs transferred to next department:					
From beginning inventory:					
Value of beginning inventory				$ 2,123	
Material added			(500 x $\frac{4}{5}$ x $0.851)	341*	
Conversion costs added			(500 x $\frac{9}{10}$ x $0.880)	396	$ 2,860
From current production (6,500 x $5)		$32,500	(6,900 x $6.064)		41,842
Total cost transferred		$32,500			$44,702
Work in process—ending inventory:					
Costs from preceding department			(600 x $4.333)	$ 2,600	
Material (700 x $\frac{1}{5}$ x $2)	$ 280		(600 x $\frac{1}{3}$ x $0.851)	170	
Conversion costs (700 x $\frac{2}{7}$ x $3)	600	880	(600 x $\frac{3}{4}$ x $0.880)	396	3,166*
Total costs accounted for		$33,380			$47,868

Additional computations (Step 2):

*Rounded up $1 due to decimal discrepancy.

	Transferred	+	Ending Inventory	–	Beginning Inventory	=	
EU, Department 1, material	6,500	+	140 (700 x $\frac{1}{5}$)			=	6,640
$\frac{\$13,280}{6,640} = \$2$							
EU, Department 1, conversion costs	6,500	+	200 (700 x $\frac{2}{7}$)			=	6,700
$\frac{\$20,100}{6,700} = \$3$							
EU, preceding department costs	7,400	+	600 (600 x 100%)	–	500 (500 x 100%)	=	7,500
$\frac{\$32,500}{7,500} = \$4.333$							
EU, Department 2, material	7,400	+	200 (600 x $\frac{1}{3}$)	–	100 (500 x $\frac{1}{5}$)	=	7,500
$\frac{\$6,380}{7,500} = \$0.851$							
EU, Department 2, conversion costs	7,400	+	450 (600 x $\frac{3}{4}$)	–	50 (500 x $\frac{1}{10}$)	=	7,800
$\frac{\$6,865}{7,800} = \$0.880$							

1,000 units. Since the increase in units comes from workers adding 1,000 gallons of oil before Department 2 processes the paint mixture, in Exhibit 7–2 we assume that the larger base unit count relates only to new production. However, if the increase in units develops because workers add materials continuously throughout the production process, the larger base unit count would relate to both new production and beginning inventory.

Effect of Addition of Materials on Unit Costs Using FIFO (L.O. 2)

Because we are using FIFO costing, we subtract the equivalent units in beginning inventory from units transferred and ending inventory to arrive at the unit material and conversion costs for Department 2. Rather than averaging the $2,123 value of beginning inventory in with current cost, we divide equivalent units into current costs only, as shown here:

$$\frac{\$6,380 \text{ current material}}{7,500 \text{ units}} = \$0.851 \qquad \frac{\$6,865 \text{ current conversion cost}}{7,800 \text{ units}} = \$0.880$$

We apply material cost of $341 and conversion costs of $396 to the 500 units in beginning inventory before transferring them out of Department 2. Of the 7,400 total units transferred, workers started and finished 6,900 units during January. The $44,702 cost transferred represents two batches of production—500 units from beginning inventory and 6,900 units from current production. The 600 units in ending inventory each receive the adjusted preceding department unit cost of $4.333. We then compute the cost of completing ending inventory to a one-third material stage and three-fourths conversion costs stage. We complete the cost of production report by accounting for costs of $47,868.

Loss of Units (L.O. 3)

Manufacturing processes sometimes lose, as well as add, units. Units are lost because of spoilage, evaporation, and shrinkage. Even though the company wishes to avoid all possible losses, management may have to accept some spoilage and/or evaporation as an inherent part of the production process. For example, workers may spill or burn some ingredients used in candy manufacturing. In making furniture, workers may ruin lumber to the point that it cannot be sold as scrap, defective units, or spoiled goods. **Scrap** materials cannot be reused in the manufacturing process without additional refining. Scrap may or may not have any market value. **Defective units** require extra work before they can be sold as first-quality products. On the other hand, **spoiled goods** contain such significant imperfections that no amount of additional material, labor, and overhead could turn them into perfect finished products.

Normal versus Abnormal Loss

Even though some industries recognize the loss of units is an unavoidable aspect of their specific manufacturing operations, each company should set normal tolerance limits for such losses. A loss within these limits is a **normal loss.** Loss of units outside these limits is an avoidable or **abnormal loss.** Managers usually set limits so they can estimate the units that will be lost. The nature of the loss and the point in the processing operations at which the loss takes place also help determine whether management classifies it as normal or abnormal. For example, suppose during the cooking stage two vats containing semiprocessed ketchup suffer evaporation, a normal loss. However, an abnormal loss occurs if an errant forklift truck operator punctures one of the vats.

Normal Tolerance Limits

To arrive at this distinction between normal and abnormal loss of units, accountants assist production and engineering personnel in establishing tolerance limits. They can express **tolerance limits for normal loss** as a percentage of the good units that pass the inspection point of the operations. For example, if past inspection made at the end of processing yielded an average of 48 bad units for 1,000 units introduced into operations, the normal loss percentage would be 48/952 or 5 percent of good production. Managers would accept this percentage as the limit if their analysis verified that this loss was uncontrollable and an inherent part of operations. Suppose these managers discover that operations of a given period lose 100 units through spoilage. Assume further that workers completed 1,500 units, which passed inspection at the end of the operations. The normal loss associated with the good units finished would be 75 (5 percent × 1,500 good units). The remaining 25 units would be classified as abnormal loss.

Accountants alternately express normal loss as a percent of total units processed. In this situation the normal loss is 48/100 or 4.8 percent of total units processed. Using either of these approaches, accountants then determine the cost of the normal and abnormal loss separately. This enables management to more easily recognize the investment lost through unavoidable and avoidable circumstances.

Quality Control Concepts and Zero Defects Programs (L.O. 4)

As more companies successfully adopt quality control concepts and zero defects programs, accounting for normal and abnormal losses may change. The **zero defects** performance standard emphasizes doing work right the first time. The zero defects philosophy is not limited to production efforts. Both service and manufacturing companies realize a reduction in waste by eliminating poor practices and lackadaisical employee attitudes.

Produce-and-Rework-if-Defective Program

Traditionally, managers established an acceptable level of defects because they assumed that errors are inevitable. Such a policy encourages employees to operate at an established tolerance level. For example, if management allows a 2 percent defect level, most employees are satisfied if they attain this level. Employees typically do not strive to make further improvements—they operate to the tolerance level of authority. On the other hand, when managers set the defect level at zero, employees work harder to eliminate all defects.

On-the-Spot Correction

When a company adopts a quality control philosophy, employees pledge to make a constant conscious effort to do their jobs correctly the first time. Also, each worker takes personal responsibility for eliminating mistakes. Employees recognize that their individual contributions are a vital part of the organization-wide effort.

A zero defects program controls quality in the early manufacturing stages. Laborers inspect their work at each process to prevent defective parts from reaching the final process. When a mistake does occur, employees try to determine what caused the error. Then, they consider what might be done to prevent similar mistakes in the future. Management relies on workers' self-inspection to reduce the number of full-time inspectors.

Regardless of how many inspectors are in a plant, errors are still likely to occur under conventional inspection systems. Traditionally, each inspector depends on the others to find the error. Or inspection workers may fail to note defects because they are confident the other inspectors will not see errors. Thus, they do not wish to discredit their colleagues.

Changing from the conventional produce-and-rework-if-defective routine to a zero defects concept involves a total commitment from top management down to factory employees. Companies need to retrain their employees before largely reducing spoilage and defective rates. And managers must seriously encourage defect prevention.

Doing it right the first time sounds effective. But how can employees make products right the first time when the incoming material is off-color or their machines are not in good working condition? Managers must coordinate group efforts toward eliminating defects. For example, close association of an organization with its suppliers helps ensure a consistent quality of incoming materials.

Future Spoilage Minimized

Under the traditional produce-and-rework-if-defective routine, employees study any defect detected at the end of the line. They then use this information as feedback. However, the preferred approach is on-the-spot correction because it sharply reduces the time lag between the detection and correction of the defect. On-the-spot correction generally produces fewer defective units because of the immediate feedback workers receive.

Successful practice of quality control concepts emphasizes controlling and reducing all spoilage. Also, quality control recognizes that some waste can be minimized but never completely avoided. Examples include evaporation during processing, adherence of substances to containers during transfers of materials from one container to another, and cutting irregular shapes from a sheet of material.

Timing of Inspections (L.O. 3)

Whether a company operates under a traditional or modern inspection approach incurring abnormal or normal spoilage, the loss of units may occur at the beginning, midpoint, or end of operations within a department. Employees discover lost units at inspection. Traditionally, companies assumed losses occurred at the end of the department's process because they usually inspected operations then and recognized the loss. However, frequent on-the-spot inspection and correction is often less costly than applying cost to a unit that has already been spoiled. A trade-off usually occurs between the expense of additional inspections and the risk of unknowingly incurring material and conversion costs for a unit that has become spoiled.

Inspection at End of Operations

Exhibit 7–3 illustrates a cost of production report for a department that inspects units at the end of operations. Because inspection occurs at the end of processing, units in ending inventory are not inspected. Thus, because none of the units lost come from the current ending work in process inventory, the cost of loss units is charged only to the completed units. With these inspection arrangements, spoiled units complete the department's processing and receive the full departmental cost.

EXHIBIT 7–3

KNIGHT COMPANY—ASSEMBLY DEPARTMENT
Cost of Production Report
Weighted-Average Costing, Lost Units
Inspection at End of Processing
For the Month of January 19X1

Quantity schedule (Step 1):

Units in beginning inventory (¼ M, ⅕ CC)	100
Units started in process	4,900
Total units to account for	5,000
Units transferred	4,500
Units in ending inventory (½ M, ¹⁄₁₀ CC)	350
Normal loss of units	100
Abnormal loss of units	50
Total units accounted for	5,000

	Total Costs	Unit Costs
Costs to account for (Step 3):		
Value of beginning inventory:		
Material	$ 47	
Conversion costs	109	
Total value of beginning inventory	$ 156	
Current costs:		
Material	9,353	$ 2
Conversion costs	13,946	3
Total costs to account for	$23,455	$ 5
Cost accounted for as follows (Step 4):		
Costs of abnormal loss (50 × $5)		$ 250
Costs transferred before normal loss (4,500 × $5)	$22,500	
Costs of normal loss (100 × $5)	500	23,000
Ending inventory:		
Material (½ × 350 × $2)	$ 100	
Conversion costs (¹⁄₁₀ × 350 × $3)	105	205
Total costs accounted for		$23,455

Additional computations (Step 2):

	Transferred +	Ending Inventory +	Normal Loss +	Abnormal Loss	
EU, material	4,500 +	50 (350 × ½) +	100 +	50	= 4,700
$\dfrac{\$47 + \$9,353}{4,700} = \dfrac{\$9,400}{4,700} = \$2$					
EU, conversion costs	4,500 +	35 (350 × ¹⁄₁₀) +	100 +	50	= 4,685
$\dfrac{\$109 + \$13,946}{4,685} = \dfrac{\$14,055}{4,685} = \$3$					

The department in Exhibit 7–3 loses 100 units through normal causes and 50 units to abnormal conditions. Because inspection occurs at the end of processing, all spoiled units have been through the Assembly Department's entire operations. For this reason, the lost units are added in the following equivalent unit (EU) computations. Unit cost calculations are also given:

$$\text{EU, material} = 4{,}500 \text{ transferred} + 50 \text{ ending inventory } (350 \times \tfrac{1}{7}) + 100 \text{ normal loss} + 50 \text{ abnormal loss} = 4{,}700$$

$$\frac{\$47 \text{ beginning inventory materials} + \$9{,}353 \text{ current materials}}{4{,}700} = \frac{\$9{,}400}{4{,}700} = \$2$$

$$\text{EU, conversion cost} = 4{,}500 \text{ transferred} + 35 \text{ ending inventory } (350 \times \tfrac{1}{10}) + 100 \text{ normal loss} + 50 \text{ abnormal loss} = 4{,}685$$

$$\frac{\$109 \text{ beginning inventory conversion costs} + \$13{,}946 \text{ current conversion costs}}{4{,}685} = \frac{\$14{,}055}{4{,}685} = \$3$$

Note that this is the same EU formula introduced in Chapter 6 except we added lost units at the stage of completion when they were discovered lost.

Cost of Abnormal and Normal Loss. After calculating equivalent units for material and conversion costs, we assign the $5 total unit cost to the 4,500 units transferred out of the department to arrive at a total of $22,500 (4,500 units × $5). We also use the $5 unit cost to arrive at the cost of the abnormal loss and the normal loss. The cost of the abnormal loss of units is 50 units × $5 = $250. The cost of the normal loss of units is 100 units × $5 = $500.

We then add the $500 cost charged to the units lost due to normal conditions to the $22,500 cost of the good units completed and transferred to arrive at a total cost transferred of $23,000. Thus, good units must absorb the cost of any normal loss. The 4,500 units leave with a total cost of $23,000 or at a higher unit cost than $5. Note that the effect of the units lost through normal causes has been an increase in the cost of the good units. This higher cost reduces income when the company sells these units. Exhibit 7–3 illustrates only one department, and we assume the next department is Finished Goods. A separate journal entry is not needed to record the normal loss of units; the $500 cost is added to the $22,500 cost of the good units to arrive at the following:

Finished Goods Inventory	23,000	
Work in Process—Assembly Department		23,000

This journal entry assumes that the 100 units lost because of normal conditions have no sales value. This is obviously the case if the normal loss were due to evaporation. If, instead, we assume that the company can sell the spoiled units as irregulars or scrap material for $100, we assign net sales value to the spoilage. Spoilage is set up in an inventory account at this amount. We credit the Work in Process—Assembly Department account for the sales value of the spoilage. The good units completed now bear only a $400 cost ($500 cost of normal loss − $100 sales value of normal loss) due to the normal loss of units. The journal entry is as follows:

Spoiled Goods or Scrap Material Inventory	100	
Work in Process—Assembly Department		100
Finished Goods Inventory ($22,500 + $500 − $100)	22,900	
Work in Process—Assembly Department		22,900

This is the approach Chapter 21 suggests for accounting for scrap and spoiled goods.

When the units lost through normal conditions are sold, the entry is as follows:

Cash or Accounts Receivable   100
    Spoiled Goods or Scrap Material Inventory   100

Journal Entry to Record Abnormal Loss. A separate entry records the abnormal loss of units. We treat normal loss as a product cost by assigning the loss to the good units completed. We treat abnormal loss as a period expense. For example, if we assume that the units lost through abnormal conditions have no salable value, the entry for the Assembly Department in Exhibit 7–3 is

Cost of Lost Units   250
    Work in Process—Assembly Department   250

Now assume that the company can sell the 50 spoiled units for $1 each. This entry sets up the inventory value of the units and removes the cost of the abnormal loss from the department:

Spoiled Goods or Scrap Material Inventory   50
Cost of Lost Units   200
    Work in Process—Assembly Department   250

The same type of entry as illustrated earlier records the sale of these spoiled goods or scrap material:

Cash or Accounts Receivable   50
    Spoiled Goods or Scrap Material Inventory   50

Inspection at the Intermediate Point of Operations

Exhibit 7–4 illustrates FIFO costing where the Mixing Department inspects at the 40 percent stage of operations and the Finishing Department at the 75 percent stage of processing. However, note that inspections can occur, for example, at a 30 percent or a 50 percent stage of operation. We arbitrarily chose these points of inspection for illustration. There is no rule to inspect at the midpoint, at the beginning, or at the end of operations. Exhibit 7–4 rounds costs to whole dollars in both departments. Because workers add material at the beginning of operations in both departments, we include lost units in the equivalent unit calculation for material in both departments as follows:

EU, mixing material	=	5,500 transferred	+	800 ending inventory	+	500 normal loss	+	200 abnormal loss	−	600 beginning inventory	=	6,400
EU, finishing material	=	4,500 transferred	+	1,000 ending inventory	+	400 normal loss	+	100 abnormal loss	−	500 beginning inventory	=	5,500

Next, we must calculate the stage of completion of lost units at inspection. Since the Mixing Department detects the units lost at the 40 percent stage of operations, we assume they receive only 40 percent of their labor and overhead in this department. For example, we compute the equivalent units for labor in the Mixing Department as follows:

EU, mixing labor	=	5,500 transferred	+	160 ending inventory (800 × 20%)	+	200 normal loss (500 × 40%)	+	80 abnormal loss (200 × 40%)	−	90 beginning inventory (600 × 15%)	=	5,850

To determine the cost of abnormal and normal loss, we multiply all units by the unit material cost. The lost units only receive 40 percent of the mixing and 75 percent of the finishing conversion costs. The cost applied to the lost units in

EXHIBIT 7–4

CRAWFORD PRODUCTION COMPANY
Cost of Production Report, FIFO—Inspection at Various Processing Points
For the Month Ending January 31, 19X1

	Mixing Department			Finishing Department		
Quantity schedule (Step 1):						
Beginning inventory (all material, 15% labor, 10% overhead)	600		(all M, 30% L, 65% OH)	500		
Units started in process	6,400	7,000		5,500	6,000	
Units transferred to next department	5,500			4,500		
Ending inventory (all material, 20% labor, 25% overhead)	800		(all M, 40% L, 70% OH)	1,000		
Normal loss of units	500			400		
Abnormal loss of units	200	7,000		100	6,000	

	Total Costs	Unit Costs			Total Costs	Unit Costs
Costs to account for (Step 3):						
Work in process—beginning inventory:						
Cost from preceding department	-0-				$ 5,200	
Material	$ 1,800				290	
Labor	260				600	
Overhead	230				910	
Total value of beginning inventory	$ 2,290				$ 7,000	
Costs received from preceding department					57,298	$ 10.418
Current cost in department:						
Material	$19,840	$ 3.10			3,201	.582
Labor	16,380	2.80			21,525	4.200
Overhead	23,680	4.00			14,700	2.800
Total costs to account for	$62,190	$ 9.90			$103,724	$ 18.000

Cost accounted for as follows (Step 4):						
Costs transferred to next department:						
From beginning inventory:						
Value of beginning inventory	$ 2,290				$ 7,000	
Labor added (600 × 85% × $2.80)	1,428		(500 × 70% × $4.20)		1,470	
Overhead added (600 × 90% × $4)	2,160	$ 5,878	(500 × 35% × $2.80)		490	$ 8,960
From current production (4,900 × $9.90)		48,510	(4,000 × $18)			72,000
Total cost transferred before spoilage		$54,388				$ 80,960
Cost of normal loss:						
Costs from preceding department			(400 × $10.418)		$ 4,167	
Material (500 × $3.10)	$ 1,550		(400 × $.582)		232	
Labor (500 × 40% × $2.80)	560		(400 × 75% × $4.20)		1,260	
Overhead (500 × 40% × $4)	800	2,910	(400 × 75% × $2.80)		840	6,499
Total cost transferred		$57,298				$ 87,459
Work in process—ending inventory:						
Cost from preceding department			(1,000 × $10.418)		$ 10,418	
Material (800 × $3.10)	$ 2,480		(1,000 × $.582)		582	
Labor (800 × 20% × $2.80)	448		(1,000 × 40% × $4.20)		1,680	
Overhead (800 × 25% × $4)	800	3,728	(1,000 × 70% × $2.80)		1,960	14,640
Cost of abnormal loss:						
Costs from preceding department			(100 × $10.418)		$ 1,042	
Material (200 × $3.10)	$ 620		(100 × $.582)		58	
Labor (200 × 40% × $2.80)	224		(100 × 75% × $4.20)		315	
Overhead (200 × 40% × $4)	320	1,164	(100 × 75% × $2.80)		210	1,625
Total costs accounted for		$62,190				$103,724

(continued)

EXHIBIT 7–4   (concluded)

Additional computations (Step 2):	Transferred +	Ending Inventory +	Normal Loss +	Abnormal Loss −	Beginning Inventory	
EU, Mixing, material . . . $\frac{\$19,840}{6,400} = \$3.10$	5,500 +	800 +	500 +	200 −	600	= 6,400
EU, Mixing, labor . . . . . $\frac{\$16,380}{5,850} = \$2.80$	5,500 +	160 (800 × 20%) +	200 (500 × 40%) +	80 (200 × 40%) −	90 (600 × 15%)	= 5,850
EU, Mixing, overhead . . $\frac{\$23,680}{5,920} = \$4.00$	5,500 +	200 (800 × 25%)	200 (500 × 40%) +	80 (200 × 40%) −	60 (600 × 10%)	= 5,920
EU, Preceding department costs . . . . $\frac{\$57,298}{5,500} = \$10.418$	4,500 +	1,000 +	400 +	100 −	500	= 5,500
EU, Finishing, material . $\frac{\$3,201}{5,500} = \$.582$	4,500 +	1,000 +	400 +	100 −	500	= 5,500
EU, Finishing, labor . . . $\frac{\$21,525}{5,125} = \$4.20$	4,500 +	400 (1,000 × 40%) +	300 (400 × 75%) +	75 (100 × 75%) −	150 (500 × 30%)	= 5,125
EU, Finishing, overhead $\frac{\$14,700}{5,250} = \$2.80$	4,500 +	700 (1,000 × 70%) +	300 (400 × 75%) +	75 (100 × 75%) −	325 (500 × 65%)	= 5,250

the Finishing Department represents work performed in the Mixing Department as well as in the Finishing Department. For example, to determine the cost of normal loss in the Finishing Department, Exhibit 7–4 shows the following computations on the cost of production report. The computation considers that the 400 units lost because of normal causes have all been through the Mixing Department and have received an adjusted cost of $10.418.

Costs of normal loss:
Cost from preceding department (400 × $10.418) $4,167
Materials (400 × $.582) 232
Labor (400 × 75% × $4.20) 1,260
Overhead (400 × 75% × $2.80) 840
Total cost of normal loss $6,499

Assigning Current Costs to Units Spoiled. An issue with FIFO costing is whether accountants should cost lost units at the current period's cost (as shown in all examples in this book) or at costs partly influenced by the cost of beginning work in process. Conceptually, if the units in beginning work in process have not passed the inspection stage, some will likely be lost in processing. However, for beginning work in process costs to influence the cost assigned to lost units, we must estimate the number of units spoiled from beginning inventory and the number of units started in the period and spoiled. Thus, the expedient procedure is to assume all losses are from current production and assign current costs to lost units as illustrated.

Change in per Unit Cost. Units lost under normal conditions affect the unit cost of all units transferred. Note that the current unit cost in the Mixing Department shown in Exhibit 7–4 is $9.90. However, the cost increases to $10.418 in the Finishing Department because of the 500 lost units and averaging with FIFO. Averaging with FIFO occurs when the various batches of units transferred are received in the next department. In Exhibit 7–4, the Mixing Department transfers a 600-unit batch and a 4,900-unit batch to the Finishing Department. Combining the cost of the two batches affects the per unit cost in the subsequent department. The ending inventory and the lost units of the Finishing Department receive this higher $10.418 preceding department cost.

Assuming that none of the units lost has any salable value, the following journal entries are necessary to recognize the abnormal loss and to transfer the units from one department to another.

Cost of Lost Units ($1,164 + $1,625)	2,789	
Work in Process—Mixing Department		1,164
Work in Process—Finishing Department		1,625
Work in Process—Finishing Department	57,298	
Work in Process—Mixing Department		57,298
Finished Goods Inventory	87,459	
Work in Process—Finishing Department		87,459

Allocation of Normal Loss (L.O. 3)

In Exhibit 7–4 we do not show **allocation of normal loss.** We do not allocate the cost of the normal loss of units to the units in ending inventory because they have not yet reached the inspection point in the production cycle. Instead, we assign the loss only to the units that have passed inspection. If, however, the ending inventory was more than 40 percent complete in the mixing operations or more than 75 percent complete in the finishing processing, we would assign the normal loss cost to both completed units and ending inventory. *Note we compare the stage in operations at which inspection occurs to the stage of completion of the ending inventory in deciding whether to assign normal loss cost to the units on hand that are partially complete at the end of the period.*

Exhibit 7–5 illustrates the allocation of normal loss cost to units completed and still in process. Assume inspection is at the three-tenths stage of completion; thus, the 1,800 units in ending inventory have passed inspection. We add the $43,200 costs before loss allocation of the 2,400 units transferred to the $18,720 cost of the 1,800 semifinished units in ending inventory, yielding a total of $61,920. Exhibit 7–5 shows the allocation of the normal loss to the cost of the units transferred as:

$$\frac{\$43,200}{\$61,920} \times \$13,500 \text{ normal loss} = \$9,419$$

Exhibit 7–5 shows the allocation of normal loss to the ending inventory as:

$$\frac{\$18,720}{\$61,920} \times \$13,500 \text{ normal loss} = \$4,081$$

EXHIBIT 7–5

REXFORD MANUFACTURING COMPANY
Cost of Production Report—Weighted Average
For the Month Ending June 19XX

Quantity schedule (Step 1):

Beginning inventory (¼ M, ½ CC)	500	
Started in production	7,200	7,700
Transferred	2,400	
Abnormal loss	1,000	
Normal loss	2,500	
Ending inventory (⅖ M, ⅔ CC)	1,800	7,700

	Total Costs	Unit Costs
Costs to account for (Step 3):		
Beginning inventory:		
Material	$ 750	
Conversion costs	2,880	
Costs of beginning inventory	$ 3,630	
Current costs:		
Material	$24,270	$ 6.00
Conversion costs	52,920	12.00
Total costs to account for	$80,820	$ 18.00

Costs accounted for as follows (Step 4):

Costs transferred before loss		
allocation (2,400 × $18)	$43,200	
Loss allocation ($43,200/$61,920) × $13,500	9,419	
Total costs transferred		$52,619
Ending inventory:		
Materials (1,800 × ⅖ × $6)	$ 4,320	
Conversion costs (1,800 × ⅔ × $12)	14,400	
Costs of ending inventory before		
loss allocation	$18,720	
Loss allocation ($18,720/$61,920) × $13,500	4,081	
Total costs of ending inventory		22,801
Abnormal loss:		
Material (1,000 × ³⁄₁₀ × $6)	$ 1,800	
Conversion costs (1,000 × ³⁄₁₀ × $12)	3,600	
Total costs of abnormal loss		5,400
Total costs accounted for		$80,820
Loss allocation:		
Costs of normal loss:		
Material (2,500 × ³⁄₁₀ × $6)	$ 4,500	
Conversion costs (2,500 × ³⁄₁₀ × $12)	9,000	
Total cost of normal loss (2,500 × ³⁄₁₀)	$13,500	

Additional computations (Step 2):

	Transferred	+	Ending Inventory	+	Abnormal Spoilage	+	Normal Spoilage		
EU, material =	2,400	+	720	+	300	+	750	=	4,170
$\dfrac{\$750 + \$24,270}{4,170} = \$6$			(1,800 × ⅖)		(1,000 × ³⁄₁₀)		(2,500 × ³⁄₁₀)		
EU, conversion costs =	2,400	+	1,200	+	300	+	750	=	4,650
$\dfrac{\$2,880 + \$52,920}{4,650} = \$12$			(1,800 × ⅔)						

We add $9,419 to the cost of the good units transferred to give transferred costs totaling $52,619. Also, we add $4,081 to the ending inventory to yield a total valuation of $22,801. Rather than spread normal loss costs over the units completed and still in process on the basis of costs incurred, equivalent units (or less preferably, physical units) can be used as a basis. The Problem for Self-Study 7–1 illustrates FIFO costing allocating normal loss costs on the basis of physical units.

We assign a total cost of $5,400 to the 1,000 units lost through inefficiencies and other abnormalities and show this cost separately on the cost of production report. The remaining steps in completing the cost of production report illustrated in Exhibit 7–5 are identical to those for other reports prepared using the weighted-average approach.

Summary

As goods pass through manufacturing operations, accountants compute product unit costs to determine inventory valuations. Different variables complicate the determination of product cost in this process. The addition of material, for example, can cause an increase in unit cost or in units to account for. It is much simpler if the material added does not increase the units involved as Chapter 6 illustrated. The increase in the units to be accounted for resulting from the addition of material requires that we calculate the preceding department unit cost again to spread the cost over the increased units.

Companies lose units in processing because of uncontrollable factors, for example, shrinkage or evaporation. Management should determine normal tolerance limits for the loss expected. Any loss exceeding these limits is an abnormal loss of units. Equivalent unit calculations include lost units so the units lost receive a cost. The cost of abnormal loss of units is a period cost. The point at which inspection occurs and lost units are detected determines whether both ending inventory and units transferred or only units transferred receive the cost of the normal loss of units. This method of indicating the cost of lost units provides an incentive for management to become more conscious of ways to prevent losses. Increased use of the zero defects concept reduces losses.

Important Terms and Concepts

Problem for Self-Study 7–1

FIFO, Normal Loss Allocated on Physical Units

Joseph Martin, Inc., uses process costing to account for its product. Operations take place in the Mixing Department. Since loss is inherent in the production process, management allocates this to its finished goods transferred and ending inventory. Inspection is made when the units are one third complete in the department. Assume that at the inspection point, material and conversion costs are at the same stage of completion. A summary of the costs incurred is as follows:

Work in process beginning inventory, 400 units:
Material (¼ complete) . . . . $ 85
Conversion costs (⅖ complete) . . . .   315 $ 400

Current period cost:
Material   11,360
Conversion costs   29,064

There were 15,000 units started in production in the Mixing Department, while 12,500 units were transferred to the Finishing Department; 2,000 units were incomplete at the end of the month having three fourths of their material and three fifths conversion costs.

Required:

Prepare a cost of production report using FIFO costing and allocate normal loss costs on physical units.

Solution to Problem for Self-Study 7–1

JOSEPH MARTIN, INC.
Cost of Production Report—FIFO
For Period Ending 19X1

Quantity schedule (Step 1):

Beginning inventory	400	(¼ M, ⅖ L & OH)
Started in production	15,000	15,400
Transferred	12,500	
Still in process	2,000	(¾ M, ⅗ L & OH)
Lost in process	900	15,400

Costs to account for (Step 3):	Total Costs	Unit Costs
Work in process—beginning	$ 400	
Current costs:		
Material	11,360	$ .80
Conversion costs	29,064	2.10
Total costs to account for	$40,824	$ 2.90

Costs accounted for as follows (Step 4):

Transferred from beginning inventory:			
Value of beginning inventory	$ 400		
Material added (400 × ¾ × $.80)	240		
Conversion costs (400 × ⅗ × $2.10)	504		
Total value of beginning inventory finished before loss allocation	$ 1,144		
Transferred from current production (12,100 × $2.90) .	35,090		
Costs transferred before loss allocation		$36,234	
Loss allocation (12,500/14,500 × $870*)		750	
Total costs transferred			$36,984
Work in process—ending:			
Materials (2,000 × ¾ × $.80)	$ 1,200		
Conversion costs (2,000 × ⅗ × $2.10)	2,520		
Value of ending inventory before loss allocation		$ 3,720	
Loss allocation (2,000/14,500 × $870*)		120	3,840
Total costs accounted for			$40,824

Additional computations (Step 2):

EU, material = 12,500 + 1,500 + 300 − 100 = 14,200 $\dfrac{\$11,360}{14,200} = \$ \ .80$

EU, conversion costs = 12,500 + 1,200 + 300 − 160 = 13,840 $\dfrac{\$29,064}{13,840} = \$2.10$

*Loss allocation:
Loss = 900 × ⅓ × $2.90 = $870.

Problem for Self-Study 7–2

Addition of Material Increasing Base Unit Count; Unit Loss

Swann, Inc., manufactures a product known as CXI. For March 19X1, they have incurred the following costs:

	Department A	Department B
Current costs:		
Materials	$35,451.00	$15,620.00
Labor	25,680.00	30,091.28
Overhead	21,838.00	12,744.00
Beginning inventory:		
Prior department costs		$1,170.00
Materials	$3,600.00	198.00
Labor	810.00	72.00
Overhead	540.00 4,950.00	55.00 1,495.00

The material introduced in Department B increases the number of units produced. The beginning inventory in Department A was composed of 1,200 units having one third labor and one fourth overhead. There were 11,700 units started in process in Department A. There were 12,000 units transferred; 600 units were in ending inventory involving one sixth of their labor and one third of their overhead. Of the remaining units, one sixth were lost because a new worker failed to close a valve at the end of the process in Department A; the others represent a loss inherent in the production process. Inspection is made at the end of the process in Department A.

In Department B, 2,200 units of water were added to dilute the mixture received at the beginning of processing from Department A. There were 180 units in beginning inventory that were one fifth complete for labor and one third for overhead. There were 14,000 units transferred; 200 units were in ending inventory at a one fourth stage of completion for labor and one fifth for overhead. Of the remaining units, one third were lost due to abnormal conditions, and two thirds were lost due to normal production conditions.

Required:

a. Prepare a cost of production report using the FIFO method.
b. Prepare a cost of production report using the weighted-average costing method.

Solution to Problem for Self-Study 7–2

a.   FIFO

SWANN, INC.
Cost of Production Report—FIFO
For the Month Ending March 30, 19X1

	Department A		Department B	
Quantity schedule (Step 1):				
Beginning inventory	1,200	(all M, ⅓ L, ¼ OH)	180	(all M, ⅕ L, ⅓ OH)
Started in process	11,700			
Received from Department A			12,000	
Increase in units			2,200	
Total units to account for		12,900		14,380
Transferred	12,000		14,000	
Ending inventory	600	(all M, ⅙ L, ⅓ OH)	200	(all M, ¼ L, ⅕ OH)
Normal loss of units	250		120	
Abnormal loss of units	50		60	
Total units to account for		12,900		14,380

(continued)

Solution to Problem for Self-Study 7–2 (continued)

	Total Costs	Unit Costs		Total Costs	Unit Costs
Costs to account for (Step 3):					
Beginning inventory	$ 4,950.00			$ 1,495.00	
Transferred in during month				85,181.00	$ 6.00
Added by department:					
Material	35,451.00	$ 3.03		15,620.00	1.10
Labor	25,680.00	2.14		30,091.28	2.12
Factory overhead	21,838.00	1.79		12,744.00	0.90
Total costs to be accounted for	$87,919.00	$ 6.96		$145,131.28	$ 10.12
Costs accounted for as follows (Step 4):					
Transferred:					
From beginning inventory	$ 4,950.00			$ 1,495.00	
Labor added (⅔ × 1,200 × $2.14)	1,712.00		(⅘ × 180 × $2.12)	305.28	
OH added (¾ × 1,200 × $1.79)	1,611.00		(⅔ × 180 × $0.90)	108.00	
Transferred from beginning inventory	$ 8,273.00			$ 1,908.28	
Transferred from current production					
(10,800 × $6.96)	75,168.00		(13,820 × $10.12)	139,858.40	
Total cost transferred before loss	$83,441.00			$141,766.68	
Normal loss (250 × $6.96)	1,740.00		(120 × $10.12)	1,214.40	
Total costs transferred		$85,181.00			$142,981.08
Abnormal loss (50 × $6.96) . . .		348.00			588.20*
Work in process—ending:					
Costs in Department A			(200 × $6.00)	$ 1,200.00	
Material (600 × $3.03)	$ 1,818.00		(200 × $1.10)	220.00	
Labor (100 × $2.14)	214.00		(50 × $2.12)	106.00	
Factory overhead (200 × $1.79) . .	358.00	2,390.00	(40 × $0.90)	36.00	1,562.00
Total costs accounted for		$87,919.00			$145,131.28

Additional computations (Step 2):

Department A:

$$\text{EU, material} = 12,000 + 600 + 250 + 50 - 1,200 = 11,700; \frac{\$35,451}{11,700} = \$3.03$$

$$\text{EU, labor} = 12,000 + 100 + 250 + 50 - 400 = 12,000; \frac{\$25,680}{12,000} = \$2.14$$

$$\text{EU, OH} = 12,000 + 200 + 250 + 50 - 300 = 12,200; \frac{\$21,838}{12,200} = \$1.79$$

Department B:
Prior department costs:

Units transferred in 12,000

Additional units put into process . .   2,200

14,200

$$\frac{\$85,181}{14,200} = \$6.00 \text{ adjusted unit cost for prior department}$$

or EU, prior department costs = 14,000 + 200 + 120 + 60 − 180 = 14,200

$$\text{EU, material} = 14,000 + 200 + 120 + 60 - 180 = 14,200; \frac{\$15,620}{14,200} = \$1.10$$

$$\text{EU, labor} = 14,000 + 50 + 120 + 60 - 36 = 14,194; \frac{\$30,091.28}{14,194} = \$2.12$$

$$\text{EU, OH} = 14,000 + 40 + 120 + 60 - 60 = 14,160; \frac{\$12,744.00}{14,160} = \$0.90$$

*To avoid decimal discrepancy, abnormal loss is computed as follows: $145,131.28 − ($142,981.08 + $1,562.00) = $588.20.

(continued)

Solution to Problem for Self-Study 7–2 (continued)

b.   Weighted average

SWANN, INC.
Cost of Production Report—Weighted Average
For the Month Ending March 30, 19X1

	Department A			Department B		
Quantity schedule (Step 1):						
Beginning inventory	1,200	(all M, ⅓ L, ¼ OH)		180	(all M, ⅕ L, ⅓ OH)	
Started in process	11,700					
Received from Department A				12,000		
Increase in units				2,200		
Total units to account for		12,900			14,380	
Transferred	12,000			14,000		
Ending inventory	600	(all M, ⅙ L, ⅓ OH)		200	(all M, ¼ L, ⅕ OH)	
Normal loss of units	250			120		
Abnormal loss of units	50			60		
Total units to account for		12,900			14,380	

	Total Costs	Unit Costs		Total Costs	Unit Costs	
Costs to account for (Step 3):						
Beginning inventory:						
Prior department costs				$ 1,170.00		
Material	$ 3,600.00			198.00		
Labor	810.00			72.00		
Overhead	540.00			55.00		
Value of beginning inventory	$ 4,950.00			$ 1,495.00		
Costs received from preceding department:						
Transferred in during month				85,183.00	$ 6.00507	
Added by department:						
Material	35,451.00	$ 3.02721		15,620.00	1.10000	
Labor	25,680.00	2.13629		30,091.28	2.11970	
Factory overhead	21,838.00	1.79024		12,744.00	.90007	
Total costs to be accounted for	$87,919.00	$ 6.95374		$145,133.28	$ 10.12484	
Costs accounted for as follows (Step 4):						
Transferred before loss (12,000 × $6.95374)		$83,445.00	(14,000 × $10.12484)		$141,747.76	
Normal loss (250 × $6.95374) . . .		1,738.00	(120 × $10.12484)		1,214.98	
Total costs transferred		$85,183.00			$142,962.74	
Abnormal loss (50 × $6.95374) .		348.00			607.55*	
Work in process:						
Prior department costs			(200 × $6.00507)	$ 1,201.01		
Material (600 × $3.02721)	$ 1,816.00		(200 × $1.10)	220.00		
Labor (100 × $2.13629)	214.00		(50 × $2.1197)	105.98		
Factory overhead (200 × $1.79024)	358.00	2,388.00	(40 × $0.90007)	36.00	1,562.99	
Total costs accounted for		$87,919.00			$145,133.28	

(continued)

Solution to Problem for Self-Study 7–2 (concluded)

Additional computations (Step 2):

Department A:

EU, material = 12,000 + 600 + 250 + 50 = 12,900; $\dfrac{\$35,451 + \$3,600}{12,900}$ = $3.02721

EU, labor = 12,000 + 100 + 250 + 50 = 12,400; $\dfrac{\$25,680 + \$810}{12,400}$ = $2.13629

EU, OH = 12,000 + 200 + 250 + 50 = 12,500; $\dfrac{\$21,838 + \$540}{12,500}$ = $1.79024

Department B:

EU, prior department costs = 14,000 + 200 + 120 + 60 = 14,380; $\dfrac{\$1,170.00 + \$85,183.00}{14,380}$ = $6.00507

EU, material = 14,000 + 200 + 120 + 60 = 14,380; $\dfrac{\$15,620.00 + \$198.00}{14,380}$ = $1.10000

EU, labor = 14,000 + 50 + 120 + 60 = 14,230; $\dfrac{\$30,091.28 + \$72.00}{14,230}$ = $2.11970

EU, OH = 14,000 + 40 + 120 + 60 = 14,220; $\dfrac{\$12,744.00 + \$55.00}{14,220}$ = $0.90007

*To avoid decimal discrepancy, abnormal loss is computed as follows: $145,133.28 − ($142,962.74 + $1,562.99) = $607.55.

Note: Costs accounted for in Department A are rounded to whole dollars while the costs in Department B are not. This is illustrated to show variations in practice employed by companies.

Review Questions

1. What two different effects can the addition of material have in a production process?

2. What factors would you consider in deciding at what points in the manufacturing operations to make inspections? Why is there a trade-off in selecting more frequent inspection points?

3. Why are the units lost through either normal or abnormal causes included in the composition of equivalent units?

4. Contrast the treatment for normal and abnormal loss in a process costing system. When would you allocate abnormal loss to cost of units produced under a process costing system?

5. Assume a company's beginning inventory consisted of 2,600 units, one fourth complete for labor and overhead, and ending inventory consisted of 1,500 units, three fourths complete for labor and overhead. Inspection is at the two-thirds stage of production, and 600 units were found to be lost. What is the FIFO equivalent unit calculation for material, labor, and overhead if material is added in processing at the beginning of operations and 12,800 units were started in production?

6. Assume the company has units in beginning and ending inventory. Further, the company dilutes units received from the preceding department with additional material such that there is an increase in units to account for. Indicate the equivalent unit formula for the preceding department cost using (a) weighted-average costing, and (b) FIFO costing.

7. What effect on preceding department unit cost does the condition described in Question 6 have?

8. Is a 2 percent level of losses acceptable? Discuss your answer.

9. Under an actual cost system, indicate reasons why the total unit cost determined in the first department under process costing could differ from the preceding department unit cost computed in the second department.

10. Assuming that inspections are made at the midpoint of the department's processing and that ending inventory is two-thirds complete, how would you allocate the cost of the normal loss of units?

11. What is the entry if Department A:

    a. Transfers 1,000 units costing $2,200 including a cost of $200 resulting from the normal loss of 42 units to Department B?
    b. Sells the 42 units for $1 each as spoiled units?

12. Assume inspection is made at the midpoint of operations in a department subsequent to the first department and material is introduced at the beginning of operations. What cost is assigned to any lost units?

13. Assume a process introduces one half of the material needed at the beginning of operations with the remaining one half material entering at the 60 percent stage of operation. If inspection is at the 30 percent stage of operations and 100 units are discovered to be defective at the inspection stage and are removed from operations, how many equivalent units of material should be included for the lost units?

CPA/CIA Multiple Choice Questions

1. (AICPA) A department adds material at the beginning of a process and identifies defective units when the process is 40 percent complete. At the beginning of the period, there was no work in process. At the end of the period, the number of work in process units equaled the number of units transferred to finished goods. If all units in ending work in process were 66⅔ percent complete, then ending work in process should be allocated

    a. 50 percent of all normal defective unit costs.
    b. 40 percent of all normal defective unit costs.
    c. 50 percent of the material costs and 40 percent of the conversion cost of all normal defective unit costs.
    d. None of the normal defective unit costs.

2. (AICPA) In developing a predetermined factory overhead application rate for use in a process costing system, which of the following could be used in the numerator and denominator?

	Numerator	Denominator
a.	Actual factory overhead.	Actual machine hours.
b.	Actual factory overhead.	Estimated machine hours.
c.	Estimated factory overhead.	Actual machine hours.
d.	Estimated factory overhead.	Estimated machine hours.

3.–4. (CIA) Questions 3 and 4 are based on the following information. On September 30, work in process totaled 9,000 units, which were 60 percent complete (based on conversion costs which are added uniformly throughout the department and material added at the start of the process). A total of 100,000 units were transferred to the next department during October. On October 31, a total of 8,000 units, 40 percent complete (based on conversion costs), were still in process.

3. Using the weighted-average cost flow method, which of the following equivalent units should be used in the calculation of costs for October?

	Equivalent Units		
	Transfer Costs	Materials	Conversion
a.	108,000	100,000	103,200
b.	108,000	100,000	100,000
c.	108,000	108,000	103,200
d.	109,000	101,000	104,200

4. Assume transfers to the next department were 5,000 fewer because of normal spoilage. Total transfer costs for the new equivalent units, relative to those costs calculated in Question 3, would be

   a. The same.
   b. Greater.
   c. Less.
   d. Cannot be determined from information given.

5. (AICPA) Dex Co. had the following production for the month of June:

	Units
Work in process at June 1	10,000
Started during June	40,000
Completed and transferred to finished goods	33,000
Abnormal spoilage incurred	2,000
Work in process at June 30	15,000

   Materials are added at the beginning of the process. As to conversion cost, the beginning work in process was 70 percent completed and the ending work in process was 60 percent completed. Spoilage is detected at the end of the process. Using the weighted-average method, the equivalent units for June, with respect to conversion cost, were

   a. 42,000.
   b. 44,000.
   c. 45,000.
   d. 46,000.

6. (CIA) A company that manufactures baseballs begins operations on January 1. Each baseball requires three elements: a hard plastic core, several yards of twine that are wrapped around the plastic core, and a piece of leather to cover the baseball. The plastic core is started down a conveyor belt and is automatically wrapped with twine to the approximate size of a baseball at which time the leather cover is sewn to the wrapped twine. Finished baseballs are inspected and defective ones are pulled out. Defective baseballs cannot be economically salvaged and are destroyed. Normal spoilage is 3 percent of the number of baseballs that pass inspection. Cost and production reports for the first week of operations are

Raw materials	$ 840
Conversion cost	315
	$1,155

   During the week, 2,100 baseballs were completed and 2,000 passed inspection. There was no ending work in process. Calculate abnormal spoilage.

   a. $33.
   b. $22.
   c. $1,100.
   d. $55.

7. (AICPA) In manufacturing its products for the month of March 19X1, Kane Co. incurred normal spoilage of $10,000 and abnormal spoilage of $12,000. How much spoilage cost should Kane charge as a period cost for the month of March 19X1?

   a. $22,000.
   b. $12,000.
   c. $10,000.
   d. $0.

8. (AICPA) Bart Co. adds materials at the beginning of the process in Department M. The following information pertains to Department M's work in process during April:

	Units
Work in process, April 1	
(60% complete as to conversion cost)	3,000
Started in April	25,000
Completed	20,000
Work in process, April 30	
(75% complete as to conversion cost)	8,000

Under the weighted-average method, the equivalent units for conversion cost are

a. 26,000.
b. 25,000.
c. 24,200.
d. 21,800.

9. (AICPA) In its July 19X1 production, Gage Corp., which does not use a standard cost system, incurred total production costs of $800,000, of which Gage attributed $30,000 to normal spoilage and $20,000 to abnormal spoilage. Gage should account for this spoilage as

a. Inventoriable cost of $30,000 and period cost of $20,000.
b. Period cost of $30,000 and inventoriable cost of $20,000.
c. Inventoriable cost of $50,000.
d. Period cost of $50,000.

10. (CIA) A company manufactures a product which passes through two production departments, Molding and Assembly. Direct materials are added in the Assembly Department when conversion is 50 percent complete. Conversion costs are incurred uniformly. The activity in units for the Assembly Department during April is as follows:

	Units
Work in process inventory, April 1	
(60% complete as to conversion costs)	5,000
Transferred in from Molding Department	32,000
Defective at final inspection	
(within normal limits)	2,500
Transferred out to finished goods inventory	28,500
Work in process inventory, April 30	
(40% complete as to conversion costs)	6,000

The equivalent units for direct materials in the Assembly Department for April calculated on the weighted-average basis would be

a. 31,000 units.
b. 25,000 units.
c. 37,000 units.
d. 34,000 units.

11. (CIA) With a beginning inventory of 20,000 units in work in process that were 30 percent complete, a hard goods manufacturer completed 190,000 units in 19X9 and finished the year with 15,000 units in work in process that were only 20 percent complete. Using the first-in, first-out (FIFO) method, what is the number of equivalent units of production?

a. 187,000.
b. 193,000.
c. 196,000.
d. 205,000.

Exercises

E7–1 Equivalent Units for Lost Units (L.O. 3)

In the third department of Spiceland Inc., inspection occurs at the 80 percent stage of processing. Workers introduce Material A at the beginning of operations and Material B at the end of processing within the third department. During the current month, 500 units were lost due to normal causes.

Required:

Determine the equivalent units for the lost units for each of the following cost components:

a. Prior department cost.
b. Conversion cost.
c. Material A.
d. Material B.

E7–2 Equivalent Units When Units Are Added and Loss Is Incurred (L.O. 2, 3)

Department 2 of Security, Inc., received 1,200 units of product from the preceding department. Immediately on receipt, workers diluted the mixture with 200 units of water. Department 2 workers also added material to the product at the end of processing, which did not increase the units to account for. Department 2's beginning inventory was 75 percent complete.

Inspection occurred at the one-fourth stage of processing in Department 2. Of those entering inspection, 95 percent of the units met the quality control standards. While workers transferred 1,500 units to the next department, 400 units remained in ending inventory at a 40 percent stage of processing. Of those lost, one fifth were due to abnormal causes, while the remainder were due to conditions inherent in the production process.

Required:

a. Prepare a quantity schedule.
b. Calculate equivalent units for preceding department cost, Department 2 material, and Department 2 conversion costs using
   (1) Weighted-average costing.
   (2) FIFO costing.

E7–3 Equivalent Units—Increase in Units, Preceding Department: Material and Conversion Costs (L.O. 2)

Department 2 of the Bartil Company has 630 gallons (one-third complete) in beginning inventory and 400 gallons (two-fifths complete) in ending inventory. Immediately before processing, the 7,800 gallons of paint pigment received from the previous department are mixed with 900 gallons of oil.

Required:

a. Indicate the equivalent unit calculation for the preceding department's costs using
   (1) Weighted-average costing.
   (2) FIFO costing.
b. Indicate the equivalent unit calculation for Department 2's material and conversion costs using
   (1) Weighted-average costing.
   (2) FIFO costing.

E7–4 Material EU Using Various Processing Assumptions (L.O. 1, 2)

Vince Company provides the following data for the month of May:

Units received from preceding department   45,000
Units transferred   38,000
Units in process, May 31 (85% complete except for material) . . .   6,500
Units lost when processing was at $\frac{1}{5}$ stage of completion   500

Required:

Calculate the equivalent units for material under each of the following independent assumptions:

a. Materials are issued at the end of processing.
b. Materials are issued at the beginning of processing.
c. Materials are issued as follows: one fifth when production is started; one fifth when production is 40 percent complete; one fifth when production is 80 percent complete; and two fifths at the end of processing.

E7–5 Equivalent Units and Unit Cost—Loss of Units (L.O. 3)

Judi Company experiences loss in the manufacture of its product. Inspection is at the 60 percent stage of production. Labor and overhead costs are added evenly up to the inspection point. Material is added at the beginning of operations. Beginning inventory consisted of 5,000 gallons, complete for 30 percent processing. Ending inventory consisted of 4,500 gallons, 80 percent complete for processing; 800 gallons were found to be lost. There were 20,000 gallons of materials started in the department.

Required:

a. Prepare a quantity schedule.
b. Determine equivalent units for material, labor, and overhead using FIFO costing.
c. Determine equivalent units for material, labor, and overhead using weighted-average costing.
d. Assume current costs were as follows:
Material, $40,000
Labor and overhead, $17,824
Beginning inventory was comprised of $10,250 material, and $2,389 labor and overhead.
  (1) What is the unit cost using FIFO costing for material and labor and overhead?
  (2) What is the unit cost using weighted-average costing for labor and overhead?

E7–6 Journal Entries for Spoiled Units (L.O. 1, 2)

After passing inspection, 6,000 units are transferred by the Milling Department of James Company to the Finishing Department. The cost per unit is $7.20 before any adjustment is made for the 300 units found to be spoiled.

Required:

a. Record the entry for the transfer, assuming the 300 units were spoiled under normal conditions.
b. Assuming the same conditions as in Requirement *a* except that the 300 units can be sold for $4 each, give the journal entries to record the inventory valuation of the spoiled goods and the transfer of cost to the Finishing Department.
c. Assume, instead, that the loss of 300 units was due to abnormal operating conditions and that the spoiled units could be sold for $4 each. Give the journal entries as in Requirement *b.*

E7–7 Weighted Average and FIFO when Units Are Lost (L.O. 3)

Data relating to operations of Department 2 of the McPatton Company are as follows:

Beginning work in process, 40% completed	600 units
Received from preceding department	3,200 units
Good units transferred out	2,500 units
Ending work in process, 20% completed	100 units
Cost in beginning inventory:	
Preceding department cost	$ 694
Conversion cost	354
	$1,048
Current cost:	
Preceding department cost	3,296
Material	5,000
Conversion cost	2,400

Thirty percent of the lost units were due to abnormal conditions. Inspection is at the 60 percent point of operations. Material in Department 2 is added at the end of operations.

Required:

a. Units lost due to normal conditions.
b. Determine equivalent units and unit cost for:
  (1) Preceding departmental cost under weighted-average costing.
  (2) Conversion costs under weighted-average costing.
  (3) Material cost under weighted-average costing.
  (4) Preceding department cost under FIFO.
  (5) Conversion costs under FIFO.
  (6) Material cost under FIFO.
c. Using weighted-average costing, determine:
  (1) Total costs transferred out to the next department.
  (2) Total costs of ending inventory.
  (3) Total costs of abnormal spoilage.
d. Repeat the requirements for c using FIFO costing.

E7–8 Allocation of Normal Loss (L.O. 4)

Analysis of Ronald, Inc., records reveals the following limited data. The equivalent units for material are 7,600 and unit cost $6.20, while conversion costs' equivalent units were 7,300 with a unit cost of $2.40. Workers transferred 5,800 units, 800 equivalent units of material remained in ending inventory, and 1,000 units were lost due to normal causes. There were 500 equivalent units of labor in ending inventory. Normal loss cost is allocated on costs incurred to date.

Required:

Prepare the "cost to account for" and "costs accounted for" sections of a production report.

E7–9 Determining Equivalent Units with Missing Data (L.O. 2)

Department Two of Type Manufacturers received 100 gallons of semifinished units from Department One during the current month at $2 per gallon. Beginning inventory in Department Two included 10 gallons having 100 percent of their material and 40 percent of conversion cost with a preceding department cost of $16. Workers diluted the mixture from Department One with 50 gallons of water on entering Department Two. Immediately afterwards, they introduce all materials in Department Two. Ending inventory for Department Two consisted of 15 gallons, 100 percent complete for material and 60 percent complete for conversion cost. Workers transferred 115 gallons to the next department. The remaining units unaccounted for were discovered to be lost at the inspection point which occurs at the 30 percent stage of operations. Of the units lost, two thirds were due to normal causes.

Required:

a. Prepare a quantity schedule.
b. Determine equivalent units for preceding department cost, materials, and conversion cost using
   (1) FIFO.
   (2) Weighted-average costing.
c. Determine equivalent unit cost for preceding department cost using
   (1) FIFO.
   (2) Weighted-average costing.

E7–10 Quantity Schedule and Equivalent Units under FIFO and Average (L.O. 3)

Blackmon Company introduces material at the beginning of operations in its process while adding conversion costs evenly throughout production. The following data are available for one period:

Received from preceding department	9,000 units
Units transferred to next department	7,500 units
Beginning inventory (20% processed)	660 units
Ending inventory (40% processed)	700 units
Current material cost	$18,132
Current conversion costs	$12,567
Material cost in beginning inventory	$ 1,188
Conversion costs in beginning inventory	$ 183

A total of 30 percent of the lost units were due to abnormal conditions. Inspection is at the 50 percent stage of operation.

Required:

a. Quantity schedule reflecting units lost.
b. Equivalent units and unit cost for material using
   (1) FIFO costing.
   (2) Weighted-average costing.
c. Equivalent units and unit cost for conversion costs using
   (1) FIFO costing.
   (2) Weighted-average costing.

E7–11 Cost to Account for and Costs Accounted for Sections and Normal Loss Treatment (L.O. 3)

Myrtle Douglass, Inc.'s records reveal the following limited data. The equivalent units for material are 6,000 and unit cost is $4 while conversion costs' equivalent units are 5,500 with a unit cost of $3.10. A total of 4,700 units were transferred, 700 equivalent units of material remained in ending inventory, and 600 equivalent units were lost due to normal causes. There were 200 equivalent units of conversion costs in ending inventory. Normal loss cost is allocated on the basis of costs.

Required:

a. Prepare the "costs to account for" and "costs accounted for" sections of a production report.
b. Explain why even if you had not been told to allocate the normal loss, you would have known the correct manner of handling normal loss.
c. Determine the total cost transferred and the value of ending inventory if the alternative method of handling normal loss is used.

Problems

P7–12 Cost of Production Report—FIFO, Lost Units (L.O. 3)

Tiff Company records the following data for March. Consider any units that are not accounted for to be lost through the normal process. Inspection occurs at the end of the process.

		Department 1
Beginning inventory—units	8,000	(100% material, 40% labor and overhead)
Units entered into process this month	34,000	
Units transferred	32,000	
Ending inventory—units	9,000	(100% material, 30% labor and overhead)
Beginning inventory cost:		
Prior department cost	–0–	
Materials	$ 4,000	
Labor and overhead	7,000	
Current costs:		
Material	21,200	
Labor and overhead	67,970	

Required:

Prepare a production cost report using the FIFO method.

P7–13 Normal Loss of Units; Weighted-Average Costing and FIFO (L.O. 3)

Morgan Company reports the following data for March. Consider any units that are not accounted for to be lost through the normal process. Inspection occurs at the end of the process.

		Department 1
Beginning inventory—units	2,000	(100% material, 60% labor and overhead)
Units entered into process this month ..	18,000	
Units transferred	16,000	
Ending inventory—units	2,500	(100% material, 20% labor and overhead)
Beginning inventory cost:		
Prior department cost	–0–	
Materials	$ 1,700	
Labor and overhead	3,200	
Current costs:		
Material	15,480	
Labor and overhead	43,680	

Required:

a. Prepare a cost of production report using FIFO costing.
b. Prepare a production cost report using the weighted-average method.

P7–14 Weighted-Average Costing, Normal Loss of Units (L.O. 3)

BAX Company has the following data for May. Consider any units that are not accounted for to be lost through the normal process. Inspection occurs at the end of the process.

		Department 1
Beginning inventory—units	600	(80% material, 20% labor and overhead)
Units entered into process this month ..	9,600	
Units transferred	9,100	
Ending inventory—units	900	(100% material, 70% labor and overhead)
Beginning inventory cost:		
Prior department cost	–0–	
Material	$ 400	
Labor and overhead	120	
Current costs:		
Material	8,270	
Labor and overhead	10,803	

Required:

Prepare a production cost report using the weighted-average method.

P7–15 Weighted-Average Costing, Normal Loss Allocated on Physical Units (L.O. 3)

Use the Joseph Martin Company data in Problem for Self-Study 7–1; assume the company is using the weighted-average method. Allocate normal loss costs on physical units.

P7–16 Specific FIFO and Weighted-Average Cost Questions (L.O. 4)

Walker Company has three processing departments, A, B, C. Department B reveals the following information:

Work in process, January 1: 800 pounds	
Department A cost (100%)	$ 3,400
Department B material (80%)	2,500
Department B conversion costs (70%)	900
	$6,800
During January, 2,400 pounds from Department A plus 1,000 pounds in Department B were put into process:	
Department A cost added in January	$10,200
Department B material cost added in January	7,800
Department B conversion costs added in January	3,000
Total costs to account for	$27,800

Completed in January and transferred to Department C: 3,000 pounds. Lost in January (150 pounds is considered a normal loss): 200 pounds. Work in process, January 31: 1,000 pounds.

Department A cost (100%)
Department B material (60%)
Department B conversion costs (40%)

Losses are discovered when the process reaches the 80 percent stage of completion for Department B material and Department B conversion costs. This period, Department B finished and transferred all goods that reached the 80 percent stage.

Required:

a. Assume that Walker Company uses the first-in, first-out method of determining cost. Calculate each of the following:
  (1) The total cost of the 3,000 good pounds completed and transferred to Department C.
  (2) The total cost of the 50 pounds of abnormal loss.
  (3) The total cost of the 1,000 pounds in the ending inventory.
b. Assume Walker Company uses the weighted-average method of determining cost. Calculate the following:
  (1) The total cost of the 3,000 good pounds completed and transferred to Department C.
  (2) The total cost of the 50 pounds of abnormal loss.
  (3) The total cost of the 1,000 pounds in the ending inventory.

P7–17 FIFO—Normal Loss Allocated (L.O. 3)

Texas, Inc., uses the FIFO method to account for its product. Operations take place in the preparation department. Since loss is inherent in the production process, management allocates the loss to its finished goods transferred and ending inventory on the basis of costs before the loss is allocated.

Inspection is at the point where the units reach a stage of one-fifth completion of operations in the department. Assume that at the inspection point material and conversion costs are at the same stage of completion.

A summary of the costs incurred for the month ending December 31, 19X1, is as follows:

Work in process beginning inventory (330 units—⅕ material, ⅓ conversion costs stages of completion) . . .	$ 118.00
Material	5,455.38
Conversion costs	8,779.68

There were 12,100 units started in production in the Preparation Department. There were 6,800 units transferred to the Finishing Department; 3,130 units were incomplete at the end of the month—these had one-half material and two-fifth conversion costs.

Required:

a. Prepare a cost of production report using FIFO costing. Allocate normal loss cost on costs incurred to date.

b. Explain if, with the data given in the problem, you could prepare a cost of production report for this department using weighted-average costing.

P7–18 Process Costing for Two Departments (L.O. 3)

Colby Production Company manufactures a single product in two departments, Machining and Finishing. Production workers add materials to the product in a continuous operation without increasing the number of units produced. For June 19X1, company records indicated the following production statistics for each department:

	Machining Department	Finishing Department
Units in process, June 1, 19X1	–0–	–0–
Units transferred from preceding department . .	–0–	40,000
Units started in production	64,000	–0–
Units completed and transferred out	40,000	32,000
Units in process, June 30, 19X1*	24,000	6,600
Units spoiled in production	–0–	1,400

*Percent of completion of units in process at June 30, 19X1:

Materials	100%	100%
Labor	50%	60%
Overhead	25%	50%

The units lost in production had no scrap value and were 50 percent complete as to material, labor, and overhead. Cost records showed the following charges for June:

	Machining Department	Finishing Department
Materials	$128,000	$49,125
Labor	78,000	54,990
Overhead	46,000	14,400

Required:

Prepare a cost of production report for both departments for June.

P7–19 Quantity Schedule Using FIFO Costing (L.O. 2)

Drake, Inc., uses two departments, A and B, for processing a chemical compound. Workers mix one pound of Chemical X with one pound of Chemical Y for the finished chemical compound. In Department A, they process and transfer one pound of Chemical X to Department B for further processing. There employees add one pound of Chemical Y when the process is 80 percent completed. After processing in Department B, the chemical compound is transferred to finished goods.

Spoilage occurs in Department A as 2 percent of Chemical X is lost within the first few seconds of processing. However, no spoilage occurs in Department B. Conversion costs are incurred uniformly throughout both departments. Drake uses FIFO costing.

The following data are available for July:

	Department A	Department B
Work in process, July 1	10,000 pounds	12,000 pounds
Stage of completion for conversion costs (one batch per department)	25%	75%
Started or transferred in	55,000 pounds	?
Transferred out	50,000 good pounds	?
Work in process, July 31	?	?
Stage of completion for conversion costs (one batch per department)	20%	40%
Total equivalent pounds of material added in Department B	—	48,000 pounds

Required:

a. Prepare quantity schedules for each department.

b. Indicate the pounds started and completed for each department.

P7–20 Weighted Average—Addition of Material Increasing Base Unit Count (L.O. 2)

Hampton Manufacturing Company produces a chemical in Departments A1 and A2. For the month ending January 31, 19X1, they had 500 gallons having one fourth of material and three fifths of conversion cost in beginning inventory in Department A1 and 160 gallons in Department A2 having three fourths of material and one tenth of conversion cost. They entered a total of 6,200 gallons of unprocessed chemicals into production in Department A1 and transferred 6,500 gallons of chemical mixture to Department A2. Upon arrival in Department A2, workers added 840 gallons of alcohol to the chemical mixture; 6,700 gallons of processed chemicals were transferred to finished goods from Department A2. The ending inventory in Department A1 had one fifth of material and one half of its conversion cost; the ending inventory in Department A2 had one eighth of material and three fifths of conversion cost. There were no units lost in either department.

Cost data for the month are as follows:

	Department A1	Department A2
Work in process, January 1, 19X1:		
Costs from preceding department		$ 350
Material	$ 95	20
Conversion costs	310	55
Current costs:		
Material	5,137	1,000
Conversion costs	7,610	2,099

Required:

Prepare a cost of production report for both departments using the weighted-average method of process costing.

P7–21 FIFO Costing; Abnormal and Normal Loss (L.O. 3)

Inspection at the Cunningham Company occurs at the midpoint of processing. The company uses the FIFO method of processing. Both departments introduce material at the beginning of operations. Assume that at the inspection point, conversion costs are one-half complete. The following data from company records are for January 19X1:

	Department A	Department B
Beginning inventory	500 units	600 units
Stage of completion	¾ labor,	⅔ labor,
	⅕ overhead	¾ overhead
Units started in process	9,100	8,200
Normal loss of units	300	260
Abnormal loss of units	200	50
Ending inventory	900	350
Stage of completion	⅓ labor,	½ labor,
	⅙ overhead	⅖ overhead
Value of work in process, January 1, 19X1:		
Costs from preceding department	–0–	$3,240
Material	$ 645	660
Labor	1,035	470
Overhead	120	360
Current costs in department:		
Material	12,103	9,430
Labor	24,290	9,534
Overhead	10,030	6,444

Required:

Prepare a cost of production report for both departments.

P7–22 FIFO, Addition of Material which Increases Base Unit Count, Journal Entries (L.O. 2)

Heagy, Inc., uses the FIFO method of process costing in accounting for its product, which is manufactured in Departments 1 and 2. On June 1, the inventory in Department 1 consisted of 500 units having one fourth material and three fifths labor and overhead added. Costs incurred last month for these units were $200. There were 12,500 units started in process, while 12,000 units were transferred to Department 2. There was no loss in either department. Ending inventory had three fourths material and three fifths labor and overhead added.

In Department 2, workers add material that increases the number of units manufactured. In June, Heagy purchased a total of 3,600 units and added to the units in process at the beginning of operations in the department. There were 800 units in beginning inventory having three fifths of their labor and overhead. The total value of beginning inventory was $2,080. There were 200 units in ending inventory having one fourth of their labor and overhead. All Department 2 material is added at the beginning of operations.

Costs incurred in each department this month are as follows:

	Department 1	Department 2
Material	$5,050	$10,140
Labor	4,182	7,885
Factory overhead	2,706	9,462

Required:

a. Prepare a cost of production report using the FIFO method.
b. Record all the journal entries required for Department 1 for the month.

P7–23 Spoilage Costs (CIA) (L.O. 4)

A manufacturer uses a weighted-average process cost system for its only product. For each unit of finished product, workers add two pounds of Material A at the start of the process and one pound of Material B when the process is 60 percent complete. Labor and overhead costs are incurred uniformly throughout the process.

Inspection occurs at the 50 percent stage of completion and any spoiled units are scrapped with no recovery. Normal spoilage at that stage is expected to be 3 percent of the units processed up to that point. Normal spoilage costs are added to the cost of the good units completed, and abnormal spoilage costs are treated as an expense of the period.

The following information applies to operations for November:

	Units	Percent Complete	Costs
Work in process, November 1	2,000	80%	—
Work in process, November 30	1,000	20	—
Total units spoiled, including			
abnormal spoilage	800	—	—
Good units completed	21,200	—	—
Unit costs incurred:			
Material A, per pound	—	—	$4.00
Material B, per pound	—	—	$2.00
Conversion costs per equivalent unit	—	—	$5.00

Required:

a. Calculate how many pounds of Material A and of Material B were put into production in November.
b. Determine how much should be charged to November expense for abnormal spoilage costs.
c. Compute the total cost of the good units completed during November.
d. Assume management has become aware of a material which, if added at the 75 percent stage of completion, would extend the life of the product. If this material had been added during November's production run, what would be the direct effect on (1) work in process at November 1, (2) work in process at November 30, and (3) spoilage costs for the month? State your reasoning.

P7–24 FIFO Costing: Abnormal and Normal Loss (L.O. 3)

Inspection at the Miller Production Company occurs at the midpoint of processing. The firm uses the FIFO method of processing. Both departments introduce material at the beginning of operations. Assume that at the inspection point conversion costs are at the one-half stage of completion. The following data are from company records for January 19X1:

	Mixing Department	Finishing Department
Beginning inventory—units	1,000	120
Stage of completion	¼ labor, ³⁄₁₀ overhead	⅓ labor, ¼ overhead
Units started in process	6,600	5,300
Normal loss of units	400	320
Abnormal loss of units	100	100
Ending inventory—units	1,800	400
Stage of completion	⅓ labor, ⅕ overhead	¼ labor, ⅕ overhead
Value of work in process, January 1, 19X1:		
Costs from preceding department	–0–	$ 680
Material	$1,500	160
Labor	450	70
Overhead	890	48
Current costs in department:		
Material	$10,890	7,420
Labor	10,797	8,766
Overhead	16,830	8,262

Required:

Prepare a cost of production report for both departments.

P7–25 Inspection at Midpoint of Operations and FIFO (L.O. 3)

Higg Company manufactures Product B in two departments, Mixing and Finishing. Inspection is at the midpoint of operations in both departments; if a spoiled unit is discovered, it is removed from the production process at that time. Both departments introduce all material at the beginning of the operation. Assume that at the inspection point conversion costs are at the same stage of completion.

The following information for January is from the company's books and production reports:

Production Data in Units	Mixing Department	Finishing Department
Opening inventory	1,000 units	600 units
Stage of completion	⅗ labor, ¾ overhead	⅓ labor, ¼ overhead
Started in process	7,000	(?)
Normal loss of units	350	300
Abnormal loss of units	150	100
Ending inventory	1,500	1,200
Stage of completion	⅕ labor, ⅓ overhead	¼ labor, ⅓ overhead
Costs Data		
Work in process—beginning:		
Preceding department costs	—	$ 2,810
Material	$ 1,200	750
Labor	1,140	330
Overhead	1,800	346
Current costs:		
Material	$10,500	$ 7,800
Labor	11,900	10,915
Factory overhead	18,000	9,945

Required:

Prepare a cost of production report for January using the FIFO method of accounting for opening work in process inventories.

P7–26 Addition of Material Using Weighted-Average and FIFO Costing (L.O. 2)

In refining chemicals, David Johnson, Inc., uses two departments, No. 83 and No. 84. Management presently uses the weighted-average method of process costing but wants to investigate the impact of using FIFO costing. The following information is available for use in comparing the two costing approaches:

Chemicals originate in Department No. 83 where materials are added evenly throughout the process. Products leaving Department No. 83 are transferred to Department No. 84 where materials are added only at the 25 percent stage of operation. One gallon of diluting material is added to two gallons of concentrated material from Department No. 83 at the 25 percent stage of the conversion process in Department No. 84. After mixing and further refinement in Department No. 84, the materials are transferred to the next department. No gallons are lost in or between the departments due to tight controls. On November 1, Department No. 83 had a beginning inventory of 600 gallons, 40 percent complete as to material and 10 percent as to conversion costs and 9,400 gallons were started in process. The ending inventory was 70 percent complete as to materials and 25 percent as to conversion costs; 9,500 gallons were transferred to Department No. 84.

Department No. 84 entered into production its beginning inventory of 100 gallons which were 15 percent complete as to conversion costs, along with all the gallons received from the previous department. The 800 gallons in ending inventory were 80 percent complete as to conversion costs.

Cost data are as follows:

	Department No. 83	Department No. 84
Work in process, November 1		
Cost from preceding department		$ 104
Material	$ 90	–0–
Conversion costs	67	23
Current costs:		
Material	3,850	28,800
Conversion costs	10,713	21,337

Required:

a. Prepare a production report for November using the weighted-average method.

b. Using FIFO costing instead, prepare a cost of production report for Department No. 83 only. Carry unit costs to six decimal places.

P7–27 FIFO, Addition of Material Which Increases Base Unit Count, and Journal Entries (L.O. 2)

Fatchett, Inc., produces a secret mixture called LEM in Departments 1 and 2. Fatchett uses the FIFO method of process costing.

In Department 1, the beginning inventory consisted of 250 units having one fifth material and one tenth labor and overhead added; the costs incurred are $60. There were 12,600 units started in process, while workers transferred 12,180 units to Department 2. There was no loss in either department. Ending inventory had two fifths material and one fifth labor and one fifth overhead added.

Department 2 added a total of 5,000 units of purchased material to the units in process at the beginning of operations in the department. This material added in Department 2 increases the number of units manufactured.

There were 300 units in beginning inventory having one third of their labor and one third overhead. The total value of beginning inventory is $670. There were 364 units in ending inventory having one fourth of their labor and one fourth overhead. Department 2 adds all material at the beginning of operations.

Costs incurred in each department for June 19X1 are as follows:

	Department 1	Department 2
Material	$5,703.08	$11,338.80
Labor	3,809.59	13,856.67
Factory overhead	4,792.71	3,592.47

Required:

a. Prepare a cost of production report using the FIFO method.

b. Record all the journal entries required for Department 1 for the month.

P7–28 Normal and Abnormal Units (CMA) (L.O. 3)

APCO Company manufactures various lines of bicycles. Because of the high volume of each type of product, the company employs a process cost system using the weighted-average method to determine unit costs. Bicycle parts are manufactured in the Molding Department. The parts are consolidated into a single bike unit in the Molding Department and transferred to the Assembly Department where they are partially assembled. After assembly, the bicycle is sent to the Packing Department.

Accountants have completed cost per unit data for the 20-inch dirt bike through the Molding Department. Annual cost and production figures for the Assembly Department are presented in the following schedules:

Assembly Department cost data:

	Transferred in from Molding Department	Assembly Material	Assembly Conversion Costs	Total Cost of Dirt Bike through Assembly
Prior period costs	$ 82,200	$ 6,660	$ 11,930	$ 100,790
Current period costs ..	1,237,800	96,840	236,590	1,571,230
Total costs	$1,320,000	$103,500	$248,520	$1,672,020

Assembly Department production data:

	Bicycles	Percent Complete		
		Transferred in	Assembly Material	Assembly Conversion
Beginning inventory	3,000	100%	100%	80%
Transferred in from				
Molding during year	45,000	100	—	—
Transferred out to				
Packing during year	40,000	100	100	100
Ending inventory	4,000	100	50	20

Inspectors identify defective bicycles at an inspection point when the assembly labor process is 70 percent complete; all assembly material has been added at this point of the process. The normal rejection percentage for defective bicycles is 5 percent of the bicycles reaching the inspection point. Any defective bicycles over and above the 5 percent quota are considered as abnormal. All defective bikes are removed from the production process and destroyed.

Required:

a. Compute the number of defective bikes that are considered to be
   (1) A normal amount of defective bikes.
   (2) An abnormal amount of defective bikes.
b. Compute the equivalent units of production for the year for
   (1) Bicycles transferred in from the Molding Department.
   (2) Bicycles produced with regard to Assembly material.
   (3) Bicycles produced with regard to Assembly conversion.
c. Compute the cost per equivalent unit for the fully assembled dirt bike.
d. Compute the amount of the total production cost of $1,672,020 that will be associated with
   (1) Normal defective units.
   (2) Abnormal defective units.
   (3) Good units completed in the Assembly Department.
   (4) Ending work in process inventory in the Assembly Department.
e. Describe how the applicable dollar amounts for the following items would be presented in the financial statements
   (1) Normal defective units.
   (2) Abnormal defective units.
   (3) Completed units transferred into the Packing Department.
   (4) Ending work in process inventory in the Assembly Department.

CHAPTER

8

Joint Product and By-Product Costing

CHAPTER OBJECTIVES

After studying this chapter, you should be able to:

1. Distinguish between joint products, by-products, and scrap.
2. Determine what value, if any, companies should assign to by-products before selling them.
3. Identify the uses of allocating joint costs.
4. Recognize the limitation of joint cost allocations for future planning and control.

5. Choose the most appropriate method of distributing joint costs to by-products and joint products for inventory valuation.
6. Apply differential analysis in deciding whether to further process products.

Introduction

In many manufacturing operations, management has no choice but to produce several products simultaneously. Even though companies manufacture products in different proportions or quantities, they cannot produce one product without the other. For example, in the petroleum industry, the production of gasoline leads to the concurrent production of methane, ethane, raw kerosene, lube distillate, and waxes. A refinery cannot process just gasoline! Likewise, coal distillation gives us gas, coke, and other products; cotton ginning yields cotton fiber and cotton seed; and sugar refining results in sugar, molasses, and bagasse or plant residue.

Whether we call such products joint products or by-products depends on their relative importance. For example, gasoline, kerosene, lube distillate, and important gases are classified as joint products, while such a relatively insignificant product as wax is a by-product. Many other processing operations, such as those handling raw milk, chemicals, and lumber, produce by-products and joint products.

Joint Products, By-Products, and Scrap (L.O. 1)

Joint products, also called **main products,** result from those manufacturing operations in which companies simultaneously produce two or more products of significant sales value. **By-products** are merely incidental products resulting from the processing of another product. The distinction between joint products and by-products is largely dependent on the market value of the products. Companies produce joint products in larger quantities. Joint products have larger market values and make a more meaningful contribution to revenue than by-products. Thus, by-products are a minor result of processing. Although a single by-product may make only a small contribution to revenue, a company's total by-products may make a significant contribution.

Because the dividing line between joint products and by-products is not rigid and is subject to change, managers need professional judgment to make the distinction. Management should be constantly alert for developments that could change a by-product into a more profitable product. For example, a product previously classified as a by-product may suddenly command a higher sales price and become a joint product. Likewise, the market for a joint product may diminish to the point that managers more accurately classify the product as a by-product.

As with by-products and joint products, often the distinction between by-products and scrap is not clear. **Scrap** is salable material resulting from the manufacturing process and having limited dollar value. For example, in manufacturing shirts when employees lay and cut the pattern, any excess fabric between the pattern pieces is scrap. The excess fabric may have a minimal market value or workers may throw it in the waste bin. Because shirt manufacturers produce this scrap while producing shirts, they could call it a joint product or a by-product. However, it has so little value that it is questionable whether manufacturers should refer to this scrap as a product at all. The various methods illustrated in Chapter 21 for the treatment of scrap do not differ significantly from the accounting methods shown in this chapter for by-products. The correct way to treat the market value of both scrap and by-products is as a deduction from the cost of the main products.

Joint Costs and Common Costs

To analyze production costs for joint products and by-products, we distinguish between joint costs and common costs. While the objective of assigning production costs to a costing center is the same for common costs and joint costs, this text does not use these terms interchangeably. The term **joint costs** is more restrictive; we limit it to those costs incurred to simultaneously process two or more products of significant market value. On the other hand, we associate **common costs** with the sharing of facilities by two or more users.

Common costs differ from joint costs because we can obtain common costs separately. Conversely, joint costs are indivisible and must be assigned to products. Joint costs are the production costs incurred up to the point where products are separately identified. Common costs include such service department costs as building repair and maintenance, cafeteria, and utilities. While each production department can have its own service department, companies usually incur common costs to effect cost savings. It is normally less expensive for production departments to share such facilities.

Accountants allocate service departments' costs on the basis of usage; for example, they allocate building occupancy costs on a square footage basis. As you recall, Chapter 4 discusses some of the problems of allocating common costs to departments. The theoretical and practical problems encountered in the treatment of common and joint costs are similar. However, most accountants (and this book) confine joint costs to the narrower meaning of the costs of manufacturing joint products before these products are separately identified.

Why Allocate Joint Costs?

Accountants allocate joint production costs to properly cost products and by-products. Each product's share of material, labor, and overhead costs is inseparable from that of every other product. When produced simultaneously, joint products and by-products do not have traceable, individual costs. Therefore, the allocation of joint production costs to products is necessary. This chapter later discusses various methods of joint cost allocation.

The reasons for allocating joint costs to arrive at product costs include the following:

1. To value Work in Process and Finished Goods inventories and to compute Cost of Goods Sold for both external financial and tax reporting. If we fail to assign joint costs to individual products, Cost of Goods Sold in the Income Statement includes all the costs, and the joint products in ending Work in Process and Finished Goods inventories on the Statement of Financial Position have zero cost. The effect on the Income Statement is an overstatement of Cost of Goods Sold and understatement of income. The effect on the Statement of Financial Position is an understatement of Work in Process and Finished Goods inventories.

2. To value inventory for insurance purposes. If a casualty loss occurs, the insured and the insurance company must agree on the value of the goods lost. One consideration in the settlement is the cost of goods lost. If joint products are destroyed, accountants must divide production costs between the products lost and those not lost.

3. To value inventory and compute a cost of goods sold for internal financial reporting. Many companies calculate executive compensation, at least partly, on the basis of each executive's segment or division earnings. If two or more segments sell a joint product, we must allocate the cost of material and processing to the products involved.

4. To determine cost reimbursement under contracts where a company sells only a portion of the jointly manufactured products or services or delivers to a single customer.

5. To determine the regulated rate where only a subset of the jointly manufactured products or services is subject to price regulation. For example, a common well contains both crude oil and natural gas, but only natural gas is subject to price regulations in the United States. Recent gas utility rates and energy price policies are based in part on joint cost allocations.

Split-Off Point and Separable Costs

To make reasonable cost allocations for joint products and by-products, accountants first determine the **split-off point.** At this point, they can identify joint products separately from by-products. Because it can occur at different stages in operations, the split-off point, also called the **point of separation,** may not be the same for all products. Accountants accumulate the costs incurred for the entire batch of products up to the split-off point and then distribute these costs among the units produced.

After the split-off point where we can identify products, production costs are more easily traceable. **Separable production costs** are material, labor, and overhead used in this later processing of the distinguishable products. Therefore, the cost of each joint product is its allocation of joint cost, plus the separable production costs necessary to put it in a salable condition.

Accounting for By-Products (L.O. 2)

All of the numerous approaches to costing by-products are variations of the following two methods:

1. When we produce by-products, we assign an estimated cost equal to their net market value, or net realizable value. We deduct this amount from the main or joint products' total production costs. Thus, we separate by-products from main products by transferring the amount of the by-products' net market value from Work in Process Inventory to By-Products Inventory. We compute **net market (realizable) value of the by-products produced** as their market value less the separable (a) production costs, (b) marketing costs, and (c) administrative costs. The only transaction when we sell by-products is an increase in Cash or Accounts Receivable and a decrease in By-Products Inventory.

2. We do not assign an inventory value to by-products at their production. Instead, any amount that can be attributable to by-products remains with the main products. We make a memo entry to record only the physical amount of by-products manufactured. When we sell by-products, we record their entire net market value as other income by increasing Cash or Accounts Receivable and Other Income.

Net Market Value Assigned to By-Products Inventory. The distinction between the two methods is the assignment or nonassignment of an estimated cost to by-products at their production. If the value of by-products is large enough to affect inventory or profits, assigning net market value to the by-products inventory when it is produced is preferable. Assigning net market value to by-products resembles the method employed in costing joint products. Also, this method identifies by-products at their production rather than waiting until their sale. Another advantage is that it provides a mechanism for management to make a desired percentage profit on by-products. To do this, we reduce the net market value by the amount of the desired profit, and main products bear more of the production costs.

Net Market Value of By-Products as Other Income. If their value is so small that it does not affect inventory or profits, recording the net market value of by-products as other income is appropriate. The justification for this short-cut method is that the firm's intention is to produce main products, not by-products. Therefore, no part of the joint production costs is attributable to by-products. However, we must trace any separable costs to the by-products using the same approach when we assign inventory value to by-products manufactured. When we sell the by-products, we deduct traceable by-product expenses from the sales proceeds.

Costing By-Products Illustrated

Exhibits 8–1 and 8–2 use the following data to illustrate the two basic methods of accounting for by-products:

	Joint (or Main) Products (Pounds)	By-Products (Pounds)
Production	50,000	20,000
Sales	48,000	19,000
Ending finished goods inventory	2,000	1,000
Sales value	$10 per pound	$1.10 per pound
No beginning finished goods inventory		

	Per Pound
Separable costs of by-products:	
Materials	$0.03
Labor	0.02
Factory overhead applied	0.01
Marketing costs applied	0.015
Administrative costs applied	0.025
	$0.10

Joint production costs for joint (main) products and by-products:	
Material	$ 50,000
Labor	150,000
Factory overhead	100,000
	$300,000

$20,000 marketing + $20,000 administrative costs of joint (main) products = $40,000
Income from by-products: 19,000 pounds sold × $1.00* = $19,000
Net market value, by-products: 20,000 pounds produced × $1.00* = $20,000
*($1.10 sales value − $0.10 separable cost of by-products)

Value of ending inventory of joint (main) product:
Method 1: Net market value of by-products produced assigned to inventory:

$$\frac{2{,}000 \text{ pounds}}{50{,}000 \text{ pounds}} \times \$280{,}000^\dagger = \$11{,}200$$

†($300,000 production cost − $20,000 by-products' net market value)

Method 2: Net market value of by-products as other income:

$$\frac{2{,}000 \text{ pounds}}{50{,}000 \text{ pounds}} \times \$300{,}000 = \$12{,}000$$

For aid in understanding the cost assignment, see the diagram in Exhibit 8–1.

The Income Statement on the left in Exhibit 8–2 illustrates the assignment of net market value to by-product inventory. We deduct the $0.10 per pound of separable cost from $1.10 by-product sales value to give a net market value of $1.00 for the by-products. We then subtract the $20,000 total net market value for the by-products from the $300,000 total production cost yielding a net production cost for the joint product of $280,000. We assign the 2,000 pounds of joint product left in ending inventory a value equal to their net production cost (2,000 pounds/50,000 pounds × $280,000 = $11,200).

Exhibit 8–2 also illustrates the second basic method of accounting for by-products. We assign no value to the 20,000 pounds of by-products at the time of production. Instead, we report the $1.00 net market value per pound ($1.10 sales value less $0.10 cost of further processing and marketing and administrative

EXHIBIT 8–1

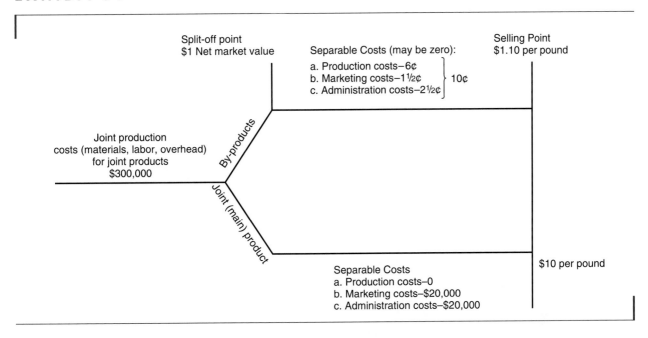

EXHIBIT 8–2   Two Basic Methods of Accounting for By-Products

	Income Statement	
	Method 1 **Net Market Value Assigned** **to By-Products Inventory**	**Method 2** **No Value Assigned to By-Products** **Inventory; Net Market Value** **Treated as Other Income**
Sales, joint (main) products	$480,000	$480,000
Cost of sales:		
Joint production costs	$300,000	$300,000
Less net market value of all by-products produced	20,000	
Net production costs	$280,000	$300,000
Ending inventory	11,200	12,000
Cost of sales	$268,800	$288,000
Gross margin	$211,200	$192,000
Marketing and administrative expense	40,000	40,000
Operating income	$171,200	$152,000
Other income:		
Revenue from by-products sold ...		19,000
Income before taxes	$171,200	$171,000

costs) for the 19,000 pounds of by-products as other income. Because we do not reduce the main product's Finished Goods Inventory for the net market value of by-products, the ending inventory value is 2,000 pounds/50,000 pounds × $300,000 = $12,000.

Difference between Actual and Estimated Values. If we deduct the net market (realizable) value of the by-products from the cost of production (method one illustrated in Exhibit 8–2), we assign the value credited to the cost of production to the By-Products Inventory account. Because we estimated the $1 net market value in Exhibit 8–2, a difference between the actual and estimated value of the by-products can arise. If the market value of the by-products is fairly stable, this difference should be small. It does not warrant restating the By-Products Inventory account and/or adjusting income from prior periods. We can show the difference as income or loss from by-product sales. If the difference is material, we may more properly classify the product involved as a joint or main product, not a by-product.

Journal Entries for By-Products

Using the data given in Exhibit 8–2, these journal entries record transactions using the first method in which we assign the net market value to By-Products Inventory.

We charge the estimated net market value of $1 per pound to the account as follows:

```
By-Products Inventory ...................................  20,000
    Work in Process Inventory  ...........................          20,000
```

As additional processing is completed, we charge separable production costs to the By-Products Inventory account:

```
By-Products Inventory (20,000 lbs. × $0.06) ...............  1,200
    Materials ..........................................          600
    Payroll  ...........................................          400
    Factory Overhead Costs .............................          200
```

The application of marketing and administrative costs is

```
By-Products Inventory (20,000 lbs. × $0.04) ...............  800
    Marketing Expense Control ..........................          300
    Administrative Expense Control .....................          500
```

For simplicity, this assumes we apply all administrative and marketing costs to the 20,000 pounds produced, even though 1,000 pounds remain unsold. Assuming the 19,000 pounds of by-products are sold for cash at $1.10 per pound, the entry is as follows:

```
Cash (19,000 lbs. × $1.10) ...............................  20,900
    By-Products Inventory ..............................          20,900
```

If the By-Products are sold for $1.25 instead of the $1.10 used for product costing, the entry would be as follows:

```
Cash (19,000 lbs. × $1.25) ...............................  23,750
    By-Products Inventory ..............................          20,900
    Gain on Sale of By-Products Inventory (19,000 lbs. × $.15)  ...    2,850
```

The By-Products Inventory account appears as follows:

	By-Products Inventory	
20,000		20,900
1,200		
800		
22,000		
Balance 1,100		

We show the $1,100 balance in the By-Products Inventory ledger account as an asset on the Statement of Financial Position, along with the other inventory accounts.

Selecting a Method of Accounting for By-Products.   Practical, as well as theoretical, factors help determine which method of accounting for by-products is most appropriate. The importance of the by-products involved is an influencing factor. Deducting the net market value of the by-products manufactured from production costs has theoretical merit. However, this approach may not be practical. A company may have no assurance that it can sell the by-products or that the market value for selling will remain stable. The stability of the market and the reliability of the market value for the by-products help determine whether we assign a value before the sale is actually made. The practical response to market instability is to only recognize the sale of by-products as income and assign no value to the by-products inventory. Even though this approach fails to properly match cost with revenue, the by-product's value may not merit assigning a value to the ending inventory of by-products and setting them up in a separate ledger account. If a company produces approximately the same amount of by-products every period, there is no material difference between the methods chosen. In addition, since by-products by definition have a small market value, the choice of the method may not significantly affect operating results.

Assignment of Costs to Joint Products (L.O. 5)

After selecting the method of by-product costing, we can allocate production costs to the joint (main) products. The physical measure and the market or sales value methods are the two basic costing procedures for doing this. We discuss the following variations of these two methods:

1. Physical measures: Quantity method. Average unit cost. Weighted factor.
2. Market or sales value: Gross market value. Net market (realizable) value (also known as relative sales value at the split-off).

Because physical measures require no estimates of a product's sales value, we may assign costs in a manner not proportionate to revenue producing capacity. Thus, we may allocate more cost to a product than the revenue it generates. Consequently, we may use market-based allocations so the assignment of costs results in a better matching of revenue and expense. Regardless of the method chosen to distribute joint costs, we may make arbitrary decisions merely because no alternatives appear preferable. For this reason, this chapter emphasizes that accountants use these methods for inventory valuation only and that the allocation method may have limited usefulness for control and planning.

Diagram Processing Operations.   Exhibit 8–3 portrays the manufacturing operations that we use to illustrate various joint cost allocations. The importance of diagramming the production process will become clearer later when we discuss multiple split-off points. Assume that the net market value of by-products a company manufactures is $10,000. We deduct the $10,000 from the joint cost of $150,000 to arrive at $140,000 net production cost that we assign to joint (main) products. This is the by-product costing approach illustrated in the left column

EXHIBIT 8–3   Diagram of Manufacturing Operations

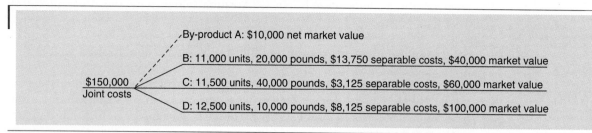

By-product A: $10,000 net market value

B: 11,000 units, 20,000 pounds, $13,750 separable costs, $40,000 market value

$150,000 Joint costs

C: 11,500 units, 40,000 pounds, $3,125 separable costs, $60,000 market value

D: 12,500 units, 10,000 pounds, $8,125 separable costs, $100,000 market value

in Exhibit 8–2. Assume also that each joint product has separable costs as indicated in Exhibit 8–3.

Physical Measures

Exhibits 8–4 through 8–6 illustrate the **physical measures of allocating joint costs.**

Quantity Method. Proponents of the **quantity method of joint cost allocations** argue that since all the joint products come from the original joint material, labor, and factory overhead, all products should receive a share of the joint costs based on a physical measure. This requires that all products be converted to the same physical measure, whether that is tons, gallons, or pounds. Exhibit 8–4 illustrates the assignment of net production cost to the three joint products on the basis of pounds. For example, since there were 20,000 pounds of Product B manufactured out of a total of 70,000 pounds of joint products for this batch, Joint Product B receives $40,000 of the joint costs (20,000/70,000 × $140,000 = $40,000). This procedure simply assumes it costs the same ($2 per pound in Exhibit 8–4) to produce a pound of output regardless of whether it is B, C, or D. For example, if this were a meat-packing operation, each pound of steak would be assumed to cost as much to process as a pound of hamburger. This method ignores the market value of the products involved.

After allocating the net costs of production to the joint products under the quantity method, we add the actual costs incurred after the split-off point (separable costs) to arrive at the inventory valuation. We show this at the bottom of Exhibit 8–4.

Average Unit Cost Approach. Exhibit 8–5 illustrates the **average unit cost method of joint cost allocations.** It is a variation of the physical measure approach to joint product costing that assigns production costs on the basis of units, ignoring the weight or sales value of the products involved. We divide the total units into the net production costs to arrive at a joint cost per unit. As long as the units do not differ greatly, the weaknesses of this simple method are not too severe.

Weighted Factors. Rather than use the number of units, pounds, or other physical measure processed as the basis for allocation, accountants may assign factors to each product. These weighted factors can reflect the varying amounts of time

EXHIBIT 8–4   Use of Quantity Method in Allocating Joint Cost

Joint Products	Pounds	Distribution of Net Cost of Production
B	20,000	$\frac{20,000}{70,000} \times \$140,000 = \$\ 40,000$
C	40,000	$\frac{40,000}{70,000} \times \$140,000 = \ \ \ 80,000$
D	10,000	$\frac{10,000}{70,000} \times \$140,000 = \ \ \ 20,000$
	70,000	$140,000

A slightly different approach is to first obtain the net cost of production per pound. This cost is multiplied by the number of pounds in each joint product to obtain this cost distribution:

$$\frac{\$140,000 \text{ net production cost}}{70,000 \text{ pounds}} = \$2 \text{ net production cost per pound}$$

Joint Products	Distribution of Net Cost of Production
B	20,000 pounds × $2 = $ 40,000
C	40,000 pounds × $2 = 80,000
D	10,000 pounds × $2 = 20,000
	$140,000

After assigning the net costs of production, the inventory valuations are as follows:

Joint Products	Net Cost of Production	Separable Cost	Inventory Valuation
B	$ 40,000	$13,750	$ 53,750
C	80,000	3,125	83,125
D	20,000	8,125	28,125
	$140,000	$25,000	$165,000

EXHIBIT 8–5   Use of Average Unit Cost Method in Allocating Joint Costs

Joint Products	Units	Distribution of Net Cost of Production
B	11,000	$\frac{11,000}{35,000} \times \$140,000 = \$\ 44,000$
C	11,500	$\frac{11,500}{35,000} \times \$140,000 = \ \ \ 46,000$
D	12,500	$\frac{12,500}{35,000} \times \$140,000 = \ \ \ 50,000$
	35,000	$140,000

EXHIBIT 8–6   Use of Weighted Factor Method in Allocating Joint Costs

Joint Products	Units	Points per Unit	Weighted Unit	Distribution of Net Cost of Production
B	11,000	10	110,000	$\dfrac{110,000}{280,000} \times \$140,000 = \$\ 55,000$
C	11,500	5	57,500	$\dfrac{57,500}{280,000} \times \$140,000 =\ \ 28,750$
D	12,500	9	112,500	$\dfrac{112,500}{280,000} \times \$140,000 =\ \ 56,250$
	35,000		280,000	$140,000

EXHIBIT 8–7   Gross Market Value Method

Joint Products	Number of Units Produced	Market Value per Unit	Total Gross Market Value	Distribution of Net Cost of Production
B	40,000	$1	$\ 40,000	$\dfrac{\$40,000}{\$200,000} \times \$140,000 = \$\ 28,000$
C	30,000	2	60,000	$\dfrac{\$60,000}{\$200,000} \times \$140,000 =\ \ 42,000$
D	25,000	4	100,000	$\dfrac{\$100,000}{\$200,000} \times \$140,000 =\ \ 70,000$
			$200,000	$140,000

required to process the units, the difficulty of the processing procedures, the amount of material or labor used, and other factors that management considers significant. Exhibit 8–6 illustrates the **weighted factor method of joint cost allocations,** with the following assignment of points to joint products: Joint Product B, 10 points; C, 5 points; and D, 9 points.

Market or Sales Value

There are several variations of the **market or sales value method of joint product costing** in which accountants use the joint products' sales prices as the basis for allocation. Accountants base the market value approximation on the belief that if a product has a higher sales price, it costs more to produce. Therefore, we prorate joint costs on the basis of the market value of the products manufactured. We use a weighted market value to reflect the various quantities of each product manufactured.

Gross Market Value. Exhibit 8–7 illustrates the use of the **gross market value method of joint cost allocations.** Gross market value is appropriate only if a company can sell its joint products at the split-off point without further processing. In this case, as there are no separable costs, the inventory valuation of the joint products is the joint costs assigned.

The gross margin percentages (gross margin/sales) are identical for all three products because there are no costs after the split-off point. This identical gross margin demonstrates an important concept of the gross market value method—that revenue dollars from each joint product are assumed to make the same percentage contribution at the split-off point as the revenue dollars from every other joint product. Input costs are matched with revenues generated by each output.

Assuming the sales prices shown in Exhibit 8–7 and no further processing cost, the gross margin of Joint Product B is $12,000 ($40,000 gross market value − $28,000 joint cost assigned). This results in a 30 percent gross margin for Product B: $12,000/$40,000 = 30%.

An identical gross margin percentage is calculated for Product C of

$$\frac{\$60,000 - \$42,000}{\$60,000} = \frac{\$18,000}{\$60,000} = 30\%$$

And for Product D

$$\frac{\$100,000 - \$70,000}{\$100,000} = \frac{\$30,000}{\$100,000} = 30\%$$

The market value approach smooths income, and this smoothing and its simplicity are what makes the gross market approach attractive. However, allocations based on the market value approach have limited usefulness for control and planning.

Net Market (Realizable) Value or Relative Sales Value at the Split-Off. Many products cannot be sold at the split-off point; instead, they must be processed further. Because no market value is available for these products at the split-off point, accountants use the **net market (realizable) method of joint cost allocations.** They estimate the market value by subtracting separable costs from the products' sales value after further processing. For example, each cut of meat requires varying amounts of processing before sale. If these separable costs are significant or vary considerably among products, we should consider these costs in allocating joint costs to the products.

For products with no market value at split-off, we use the **relative sales value at split-off method of joint cost allocations.** We can determine an approximate market value at split-off by deducting the separable costs from the market value at the first possible point of sale. Exhibit 8–8 illustrates the procedures involved. Accountants presume the first sales point after split-off gives the best approximation of sales value at split-off even though several possible sales points are available. If the separable costs for each product vary, and separable costs are not proportional to gross sales value, as in Exhibit 8–8, the joint products are not equally profitable. After allocating the cost of production, we add the separable costs to arrive at the inventory valuation. We illustrate this at the bottom of Exhibit 8–8.

Multiple Split-Offs

The production process used to illustrate the joint cost allocation methods in Exhibits 8–4 through 8–8 involved only one split-off point to simplify the discussion. However, many manufacturing operations contain multiple split-off points with separable costs for each stage. For example, suppose a company manufactures three joint products—E, F, and G—having sales prices per pound

EXHIBIT 8–8   Net Market (Realizable) Method of Allocating Net Costs of Production

Joint Products	Total Gross Market Value	Separable Cost	Net Market Value	Distribution of Net Costs to Production
B	$ 40,000	$13,750	$ 26,250	$\frac{\$26,250}{\$175,000} \times \$140,000 = \$ 21,000$
C	60,000	3,125	56,875	$\frac{\$56,875}{\$175,000} \times \$140,000 =$ 45,500
D	100,000	8,125	91,875	$\frac{\$91,875}{\$175,000} \times \$140,000 =$ 73,500
	$200,000	$25,000	$175,000	$140,000

A different approach is to obtain the percentage of cost to market value. We multiply this percentage by each joint product's market value as follows:

$$\frac{\$140,000 \text{ net cost of production}}{\$175,000 \text{ net market value}} = 80\%$$

Joint Products	Net Market Value	Distribution of Net Cost of Production
B	$ 26,250	80% × $26,250 = $ 21,000
C	56,875	80% × $56,875 = 45,500
D	91,875	80% × $91,875 = 73,500
	$175,000	$140,000

Based on the net market method of allocating the net cost of production, the following inventory valuations result:

Joint Products	Net Cost of Production	Separable Cost	Inventory Valuation
B	$ 21,000	$13,750	$ 34,750
C	45,500	3,125	48,625
D	73,500	8,125	81,625
	$140,000	$25,000	$165,000

of $9, $12, and $11 respectively. Department 1 processes 100,000 pounds of raw material at a total cost of $250,000. Department 1 transfers 65 percent of the units to Department 2, where the material is further processed at a total additional cost of $80,000. Department 3 processes the other 35 percent of the units leaving Department 1 at a total additional cost of $11,000. Since evaporation occurs in Department 3, only 21,000 pounds emerge as Product G.

We transfer 80 percent of the units processed in Department 2 to Department 4. The units emerge as Product E after further processing which costs $201,500. Department 5 processes the other 20 percent leaving Department 2 at a cost of $12,500. They emerge as Product F. Exhibit 8–9 illustrates the joint cost allocation for this multiple split-off example.

Are Allocation Methods Arbitrary?

Financial accounting is designed to provide general purpose reports. The purposes for reading financial statements vary widely. We may defend a particular allocation method for a certain single-purpose report because we know the purpose of this report. However, there is no such defense for general purpose

EXHIBIT 8–9   120 Multiple Split-Off Points

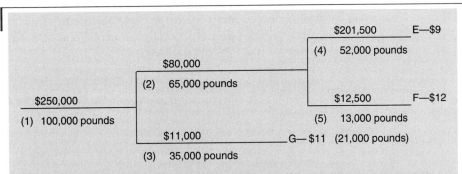

To determine the approximate net market (realizable) value at the split-off point for use in allocating joint cost:

Products E and F:
Market value—E (52,000 pounds × $9) $468,000
Less: Processing—Department 4 . . . .   201,500 $266,500

Market value—F (13,000 pounds × $12) . . . $156,000
Less: Processing—Department 5   12,500   143,500

Total market value $410,000
Less: Processing—Department 2   80,000

Net market value—E and F $330,000

Product G:
Market value—G (21,000 pounds × $11) . . . $231,000
Less: Processing—Department 3   11,000   220,000

Total approximate market value at
split-off point $550,000

To allocate the joint costs of Department 1 on the basis of approximate market value at the split-off point:

Allocated Joint Costs

Products E and F . . . . $\dfrac{\$330,000}{\$550,000}$ × $250,000 = $150,000

Product G . . . . $\dfrac{\$220,000}{\$550,000}$ × $250,000 =   100,000

$250,000

To distribute cost to Products E and F, add the $150,000 allocated joint cost from Department 1 to the $80,000 Department 2 joint costs:

Allocated Joint Costs

Product E . . . . $\dfrac{\$266,500}{\$410,000}$ × $230,000 = $149,500

Product F . . . . $\dfrac{\$143,500}{\$410,000}$ × $230,000 =   80,500

$230,000

To find the inventory valuation:

Products	Allocated Joint Costs	+	Separable Costs	=	Inventory Valuation
E	$149,500		$201,500		$351,000
F	80,500		12,500		93,000
G	100,000		11,000		111,000
					$555,000

financial accounting allocations. There are many different allocation methods and financial accounting has not arrived at a conclusive way to support one approach over other methods. Some of financial accounting's allocations are arbitrary; some are not. An allocation method that we can justify in one instance may be indefensible in others.

Inventories at Sales Price. Because of the difficulty in finding an approach that satisfies all of management's needs, some companies avoid the joint costing issue completely by assigning sales value or sales value net of separable costs to products resulting from joint production. They ignore joint costs completely because they assign only the realizable value or net market value to inventory. However, carrying inventories at sales value or sales value net of separable cost recognizes profits before sales are made. Either approach is contrary to generally accepted inventory costing methods as variations in inventory can affect profit. For example, an increase in inventory can cause an increase in a company's income because less cost is assigned to the goods sold.

If, on the other hand, the joint costs are for perishable items with a rapid turnover, the use of sales prices as a basis for inventory valuation is less subject to criticism. In addition, if the normal profit percentage is small so there is little difference between cost and selling price, the approach is more defensible. Perhaps, the most sensible variation of this method is to deduct a normal profit percentage from the sales price net of separable cost. This procedure avoids the criticism that accountants recognize a profit before making a sale.

To summarize, in certain cases, cost accountants can employ arbitrary allocations without obvious harm. Although we may not be able to defend precisely the allocation method used, allocations are preferred to the extreme alternatives of assigning no value to ending inventory of joint products or assigning them market value. Valuing inventory at market value recognizes a profit for the products in inventory and overstates income.

Process Further Decision Making

Even though inventory valuation requires joint cost allocations, they are irrelevant for decision making. Managers frequently must decide what is the most profitable stage at which to sell products. In these situations, joint costs are sunk costs. As is the case with all decision making, we should consider only future costs and revenues.

Irrelevance of Joint Costs

Chapter 16 discusses in detail that a sell or process-further decision should rest on differential revenue/cost analysis. We mention it briefly here to emphasize the limitation of joint product cost allocation procedures in decision making.

Differential costs, not joint product costs, are the only relevant costs which we should consider in selecting the most profitable stage at which to sell a product. **Differential cost** is the extra cost incurred for different alternatives. When a company is considering further processing, incremental or differential cost is the additional cost for extending operations. **Differential revenue** is the additional revenue. We reserve this classification solely for those costs or revenues that change depending on the decision made. We compare differential revenue and differential cost to arrive at the extra earnings or differential earnings that result.

The following example briefly explains the analysis necessary to determine differential earnings. We assumed in Exhibit 8–8 that Product B has no market value at the split-off point but after incurring costs of $13,750 in processing, we can sell Product B for $40,000. Gross differential revenue in this case is $40,000; differential cost is $13,750; and the **net differential revenue** is $26,250. In effect, the company loses $26,250 if it fails to further process Product B and merely disposes of the waste in an environmentally safe manner.

Erroneous Results Using Joint Costs

Erroneous decisions about when to sell a product can result if we use joint costs. For example, suppose an opportunity arises for the company to further process Product B at an additional cost of $15,000 to become Super Product B. Assume we can sell Super Product B for $52,000. If managers base their decision on joint cost allocations using either the net market value or quantity methods, the resulting margins would be those in Exhibit 8–10.

Product B now has separable costs totaling $28,750 ($13,750 to become Product B and $15,000 to become Super B). Because we normally determine the net market (realizable) value by the first sales possible after split-off, further processing to become Super B does not change the joint cost allocation as determined in Exhibit 8–8. The possibility of further processing Product B also does not change the $40,000 joint cost allocation under the quantity method presented in Exhibit 8–4. We simply add the separable cost to the joint cost allocation determined under each of the methods. The use of the net market value method indicates that further processing Product B would be profitable. Further processing is profitable even though it results in a margin smaller than the $5,250 [$40,000 sales − ($21,000 joint cost allocation + $13,750 separable cost)] determined without the additional processing. However, the quantity method indicates a loss of $16,750.

Exhibit 8–10 shows inconsistent results are obtained if we use either of these approaches. In addition, neither method is relevant to the decision. In deciding whether the additional processing would be profitable, the company should instead compare the additional separable cost with the additional revenue that would be generated:

Additional revenue ($52,000 Super B − $40,000 Product B)	$12,000
Additional separable cost	15,000
Net differential cost	$ 3,000

If we consider no factors other than costs, the decision to sell the product as B rather than to process it further is appropriate.

EXHIBIT 8–10   Comparison of Joint Cost Allocation for Decision Making

	By Net Market (Realizable) Method			By Quantity Method	
Sales of Super Product B		$52,000			$ 52,000
Joint cost (from Exhibit 8–8)	$21,000		(from Exhibit 8–4)	$40,000	
Added cost	28,750	49,750		28,750	68,750
Margin		$ 2,250			$(16,750)

Summary

Accountants face two important problems involving by-products and joint products: (1) the difficulty of allocating joint costs for inventory valuation or product costing purposes and (2) the use of differential analysis in identifying the most profitable point in the manufacturing cycle at which to sell products. We prefer basing further-processing decisions on differential revenue/cost analysis, not allocated joint costs. Joint cost allocations have limited use in internal decision making because many managers think of only full costs. Thus, they are reluctant to continue manufacturing products that report book losses.

The chapter presented two basic methods of accounting for by-products. Accountants can assign a value to the by-products at their production or they can wait until their sale and record the income at that time. Accountants use two basic procedures to assign production costs to joint products—the physical measure and the market or sales value method. There are varying approaches to these two costing procedures. We can base the physical measure solely on the quantity of joint products manufactured. Alternatively, we can use a weighted factor to reflect the amount of time needed to process the unit, the difficulty of processing, and other factors management considers significant. We can use gross market value as the basis for allocating joint cost, but it is appropriate only if we can sell the joint products in their state at the split-off point without further processing. If a joint product requires additional processing before its sale, we should subtract the separable costs incurred from the market value. We then use this as a basis for joint cost allocations.

There is difficulty in deciding which is the most appropriate method of assigning joint cost because each of the allocation methods presented depends on different conditions and assumptions. However, accountants should understand the by-product and joint costing allocation methods available because they need them for financial reporting.

Important Terms and Concepts

joint products, 258
main products, 258
by-products, 258
scrap, 259
joint costs, 259
common costs, 259
split-off point or point of separation, 260
separable production costs, 261
net market (realizable) value of by-products produced, 261
physical measures of joint cost allocations, 266
quantity method of joint cost allocations, 266

average unit cost method of joint cost allocations, 266
weighted factor method of joint cost allocations, 268
market or sales value methods of joint cost allocations, 268
gross market method of joint cost allocations, 268
net market (realizable) method of joint cost allocations, 269
relative sales value at the split-off method of joint cost allocations, 269
differential cost and revenue, 272
net differential revenue, 273

Problem for Self-Study

Joint Cost Allocation and Sell or Process-Further Decision

Shell Company manufactures three products, A, B, and C, from a particular joint process. Each product may be sold at split-off or may be processed further. Joint production costs for the period were $264,000. All production costs of additional processing are of a variable nature and are directly traceable to the products involved.

The following data are from company records:

Joint Product	Units Produced	Total Sales Value at Split-Off	Separable Costs	Sales Value after Further Processing
A	18,000	$330,000	$36,000	$350,000
B	8,000	198,000	6,000	225,000
C	6,000	132,000	9,000	148,000

Required:

a. Using the quantity method, determine the joint costs to allocate to each group of joint products.

b. Assume management assigns weights of 2:3:1 to products A, B, and C, respectively, based on the engineering skills required. What is the joint cost allocation and the joint cost per actual unit produced?

c. Using the gross market value method, distribute joint cost to the joint products.

d. Determine the unit cost that is most relevant to a sell or process-further decision for each product group.

e. Recommend which products should be additionally processed to maximize net contribution to profits. Support your recommendation with a cost analysis.

Solution to Problem for Self-Study

SHELL COMPANY

a.

Joint Product	Joint Cost Allocation	
A	$148,500*	(18,000/32,000 × $264,000)
B	66,000	(8,000/32,000 × $264,000)
C	49,500	(6,000/32,000 × $264,000)
	$264,000	

*Or $264,000/32,000 = $8.25 per unit × 18,000 units = $148,500

b.

Joint Product	Weighted Units	Joint Cost Allocation	Cost Per Actual Unit
A	36,000	$144,000†	$8
B	24,000	96,000	12
C	6,000	24,000	4
	66,000		

$$\frac{\$264,000}{66,000} = \$4 \text{ cost per weighted unit}$$

†$4 × 36,000 = $144,000

c.

Joint Product	Joint Cost Allocation	
A	$132,000	($330,000/$660,000 × $264,000)
B	79,200	($198,000/$660,000 × $264,000)
C	52,800	($132,000/$660,000 × $264,000)
	$264,000	

d. The separable cost per unit is the relevant cost factor in sell or process-further decisions. Unit separable cost is as follows for each joint product:

Joint Product	Unit Separable Cost	
A	$2.00	($36,000/18,000 units)
B	$ .75	($ 6,000/ 8,000 units)
C	$1.50	($ 9,000/ 6,000 units)

e.

	Products		
	A	B	C
Sales value after additional processing	$350,000	$225,000	$148,000
Sales value at split-off	330,000	198,000	132,000
Differential revenue	$ 20,000	$ 27,000	$ 16,000
Differential costs	36,000	6,000	9,000
Increase (decrease) in profits	$ (16,000)	$ 21,000	$ 7,000

Joint Products B and C should be further processed; however, Product A should be sold at the split-off point.

Review Questions

1. Discuss the two basic methods available for accounting for by-products and describe the advantages and weaknesses of each method.

2. Discuss the methods available for accounting for joint products and describe the advantages and weaknesses of each method.

3. Distinguish between a joint product and a by-product.

4. Compare common costs with joint costs.

5. Since by-products by definition have limited market value, why is it important to account for by-product costs?

6. Why is the assignment of joint costs often a result of approximations?

7. Define the relationship between the split-off point and separable costs.

8. Defend the practice of setting up joint product inventories at sale prices and ignoring joint costs completely. What variation of this method overcomes some of the criticisms?

9. Why do the joint cost allocation methods illustrated in the chapter have limited usefulness in cost control and planning?

10. In reference to Question 9, what type of cost analysis would yield results that management can use in deciding on the most profitable stage at which the joint products can be sold?

11. If weight factors are used as the basis for allocation, what can these weight factors reflect?

12. Define differential cost and differential revenue and indicate in what type of decisions they would be useful.

CPA/CIA Multiple-Choice Questions

1. (AICPA) The diagram below represents the production and sales relationships of Joint Products P and Q. Joint costs are incurred until split-off, then separable costs are incurred in refining each product. Market values of P and Q at split-off are used to allocate joint costs.

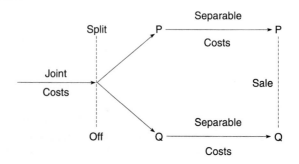

If the market value of P at split-off increases and all other costs and selling prices remain unchanged, then the gross margin of

	P	**Q**
a.	Increases	Decreases
b.	Increases	Increases
c.	Decreases	Decreases
d.	Decreases	Increases

2. (AICPA) Actual sales values at the split-off point for Joint Products Y and Z are not known. For purposes of allocating joint costs to Products Y and Z, the relative sales value at split-off method is used. An increase in the costs beyond split-off occurs for Product Z, while those of Product Y remain constant. If the selling prices of finished Products Y and Z remain constant, the percentage of the total joint costs allocated to Product Y and Product Z would

    a. Decrease for Product Y and increase for Product Z.
    b. Decrease for Product Y and Product Z.
    c. Increase for Product Y and decrease for Product Z.
    d. Increase for Product Y and Product Z.

3. (CIA) A refinery produces gasoline as its main product, with kerosene, naphtha, and fuel oil also produced and sold as secondary products. If changes in technology should result in demand for kerosene becoming as great as for gasoline, which of the following statements best describes the most likely result?

    a. A by-product would become a joint product.
    b. Scrap would become a by-product.
    c. A joint product would become a by-product.
    d. Scrap would become a joint product.

4. (AICPA) Lane Company produces main products Kul and Wu. The process also yields by-product Zef. Net realizable value of by-product Zef is subtracted from joint production cost of Kul and Wu. The following information pertains to production in July 19X5 at a joint cost of $54,000:

Product	Units Produced	Market Value	Additional Cost after Split-Off
Kul	1,000	$40,000	$ 0
Wu	1,500	35,000	0
Zef	500	7,000	3,000

If Lane uses the net realizable value method for allocating joint cost, how much of the joint cost should be allocated to product Kul?

    a. $18,800.
    b. $20,000.
    c. $26,667.
    d. $27,342.

5. (AICPA) Pendall Company manufactures products Dee and Eff from a joint process. Product Dee has been allocated $2,500 of total joint costs of $20,000 for the 1,000 units produced. Dee can be sold at the split-off point for $3 per unit, or it can be processed further with additional costs of $1,000 and sold for $5 per unit. If Dee is processed further and sold, the result would be

    a. A break-even situation.
    b. An additional gain of $1,000 from further processing.
    c. An overall loss of $1,000.
    d. An additional gain of $2,000 from further processing.

6. (CIA) In contrast to joint products, by-products:

   a. Have relatively significant sales value.
   b. Are separately identifiable prior to the split-off point.
   c. Have relatively minor sales value.
   d. Require processing beyond the split-off point.

7. (AICPA) Lee Company produces two joint products, BEX and ROM. Joint production costs for June 19X6 were $30,000. During June 19X6 further processing costs beyond the split-off point, needed to convert the products into salable form, were $25,000 and $35,000 for 1,600 units of BEX and 800 units of ROM, respectively. BEX sells for $50 per unit, and ROM sells for $100 per unit. Lee uses the net realizable value method for allocating joint product costs. For June 19X6, the joint costs allocated to product BEX were

   a. $20,000.
   b. $16,500.
   c. $13,500.
   d. $10,000.

8. (AICPA) Lite Company manufactures Products X and Y from a joint process that also yields a by-product, Z. Revenue from sales of Z is treated as a reduction of joint costs. Additional information is as follows:

   | | Products | | | |
	X	Y	Z	Total
Units produced	20,000	20,000	10,000	50,000
Joint costs	?	?	?	$262,000
Sales value at split-off	$300,000	$150,000	$10,000	$460,000

   Joint costs were allocated using the sales value at split-off approach. The joint costs allocated to Product X were

   a. $ 75,000.
   b. $100,800.
   c. $150,000.
   d. $168,000.

9. (AICPA) Axe Company produces Joint Products J and K from a process that yields By-Product B. The cost assigned to By-Product B is its market value less additional costs incurred after split-off. Information concerning a batch produced in April at a joint cost of $60,000 is as follows:

   | | | After Split-Off | |
Product	Units Produced	Additional Costs	Market Values
J	1,000	$15,000	$50,000
K	2,000	10,000	40,000
B	4,000	2,000	5,000

   How much of the joint cost should be allocated to the joint products?

   a. $53,000.
   b. $55,000.
   c. $57,000.
   d. $58,000.

Exercises

E8–1 Joint Cost per Weighted Pound (L.O. 5)

Macdonald Company produces three different products, C, D, and E, in a common mixture in the following fixed proportions: C—4; D—1; and E—3. One pound of C has a volume of 200 ccs; one pound of D, 150 ccs; one pound of E, 1,000 ccs. Weighted factors are C—1; D—.75; E—.5. A total of 1,600 pounds are processed in a batch costing $25,000. The sales value per pound of C is $14; of D, $55.25; and of E, $15.

Required:

a. Determine the cost per actual pound processed using the weighted factors.
b. Determine the cost per actual pound processed using the market value method.
c. Give explanations for any differences in your assignment of joint costs between the method using weighted factors and the market value method.

E8–2 Classification of Products (L.O. 1)

The McJay Chemical Company mixes chemicals in 5,000-gallon batches. The yield of one batch of raw material and the market price are as follows:

Chemical	Market Price per Gallon	Yield per Batch
A	$30	40%
B	40	25
C	15	20
Waste	0	15

Direct material costs $48,000 per batch; conversion cost per batch is $35,000 at normal capacity.

Required:

Determine the cost per gallon for each product assuming McJay:

a. Classifies chemicals A, B, and C as joint products, and uses the gross market value method to allocate joint costs.
b. Treats Chemical C as a by-product and deducts the net market value of the by-product processed from the production cost. Separable costs per gallon of Chemical C is $8.

E8–3 Net and Gross Sales Method (L.O. 5)

Rogow, Inc., processes five products referred to simply as Products 1, 2, 3, 4, and 5. From a common batch costing $4,000, 100 pounds of Product 1 result, 50 pounds of Product 2, 45 pounds of Product 3, 30 pounds of Product 4, and 20 pounds of Product 5. The sales value per pound of each product is Product 1—$30; Product 2—$50; Product 3—$40; Product 4—$70, and Product 5—$130. Each product receives further processing which costs $400 per batch for Product 1, $300 for Product 2, $700 for Product 3, $100 for Product 4, and $500 for Product 5.

Required:

Determine the cost per pound for inventory purposes using

a. The net market (realizable) value method.
b. The gross market value method.

E8–4 Split-Off Value and Joint Cost Allocation (L.O. 5)

Regency, Inc., manufactures Products A, B, and C from a joint process. Additional information is as follows:

| | Product | | | |
	A	B	C	Total
Market value at split-off	?	?	$110,000	$500,000
Joint cost	$ 54,000	?	?	300,000
Market value if processed further	130,000	380,000	120,000	630,000
Additional costs if processed further	18,000	100,000	6,000	124,000
Units produced	8,000	4,000	2,000	14,000

Required:

a. Determine the market value at split-off for Products A and B.
b. Determine the joint costs allocated to Product B assuming that joint product costs are allocated using the market value at split-off approach.

E8–5 Sell or Process-Further Decision (L.O. 6)

Hand Company manufactures three products, A1, B2, and C3, from a particular joint process. Each product may be sold at split-off or may be processed further. All production costs of additional processing are of a variable nature and are directly traceable to the products involved. Joint production costs for the period were $150,000.

The following data are from company records:

Joint Product	Units Produced	Total Sales Value at Split-off	Separable Costs	Sales Value after Further Processing
A1	25,000	$80,000	$ 5,000	$90,000
B2	15,000	50,000	30,000	75,000
C3	35,000	70,000	17,500	95,000

Required:

a. Using the gross market value approach, determine the joint costs to allocate to each group of joint products.
b. Determine the unit production cost that is most relevant to a sell or process-further decision for each product group.
c. Make a recommendation to management concerning which products should be subjected to additional processing to maximize the net contribution to profits. Support your recommendation with a cost analysis.

E8–6 Market and Physical Basis for Allocation (L.O. 5)

Jo-By Company produces three principal products called Ap, Be, and Ca. In addition, one more product called Dp results. The total processing costs up to the point of split-off were $15,780 for each batch. Data for the four products are

| | Products | | | |
	Ap	Be	Ca	Dp
Sales price per unit	$ 15	$ 26	$ 19	$ 5
Units produced	300	350	500	105
Processing cost after split-off .	$1,355	$1,145	$2,100	—
Cost of disposal	—	—	—	$45
Pounds per units	20	17	14.35	—

The company deducts the net market value of the by-products manufactured from production costs.

Required:

a. Calculate the production costs allocated to the four products assuming Jo-By uses the net market value method of allocating joint costs.

b. Calculate the production costs allocated to the four products assuming that joint costs are assigned on a physical volume basis of total poundage used.

c. Assume a potential customer has approached the company wanting to buy Ap at the point of separation for $12 per unit. If a sale is made to this customer, it will not affect the other products. Also, this customer will buy all the available Ap. What is your advice?

Problems

P8–7 Net Market (Realizable) Value of Allocation (L.O. 5)

Cattermole Company manufactures two products, H1 and H2. Initially, Cattermole processes them from the same raw material; after split-off, they are further processed separately. Additional information is as follows:

	H1	H2	Total
Final sales price	$27,900	$18,600	$46,500
Joint costs prior to split-off . . .	?	?	11,240
Costs beyond split-off	9,660	3,120	12,780

Required:

a. Using the net market (realizable) value approach, what are the assigned joint costs of H1 and H2 respectively?

b. (1) Using the gross market value approach instead, what would be the assigned joint costs of H1 and H2 respectively?

(2) Discuss the weaknesses you see in using the gross market value approach.

(3) Explain when the gross market value approach would be acceptable to use.

P8–8 Physical and Net Market Realizable Value Allocation Methods (L.O. 3)

Freedman Corporation uses a joint process to manufacture Products A, B, and C. Each product may be sold at its split-off point or processed further. Additional processing costs are entirely variable and traceable to the respective products manufactured. Joint production costs for 19X1 were $580,000. The following data are available:

Product	Units Produced	Sales Value after Additional Processing	Separable Costs
A	28,000	$200,000	$24,500
B	32,000	$250,000	$20,500
C	40,000	$280,000	$10,000

Required:

a. Determine the joint cost allocation and inventory value for each product, assuming all products are processed beyond the split-off point:

(1) Using the physical method of allocation.

(2) Using the net market (realizable) value method of allocation.

b. Assume Product A can be sold at the split-off point for $185,000. What would you advise management to do?

c. Assume Product C can be sold at the split-off point for $265,000. What would you advise management to do?

P8–9 Joint Products and By-Products (L.O. 5)

Allen Manufacturing Company produces one by-product, Cy-O, and three joint products—Di-O, Ey-O, and Fe-O. Joint costs of production totaled $508,000 for May. Because the skills needed to process each product vary, the engineering staff has provided points per pound. Data for each product follow:

	Pounds Produced	Points per Pound	Gross Total Market Value of Production	Separable Costs
Cy-O	500	—	$ 7,250	$ 1,050
Di-O	2,000	2	415,000	60,000
Ey-O	4,000	4	289,000	15,000
Fe-O	6,000	3	188,000	45,000

The company uses the approach of deducting the net market value of the by-products manufactured from production costs.

Required:

a. Using the weighted factor method in allocating joint costs, determine the distribution of production costs, total inventory valuation of each of the four products, and their unit costs. Would this method be acceptable for this set of circumstances?

b. Using the net market value method in allocating joint costs, determine the distribution of production costs and total inventory valuation of each of the four products.

P8–10 Allocating Joint Costs to Give Inventory Valuations; Maximum Cost for Additional Refining (L.O. 5, 6)

Klinesmith Company produces chemical products from a joint mixture. At the split-off point, the chemicals are refined and become Dsol, Esol, and Fsol. June's production data are as follows:

	Production (Gallons)	Sales price per Gallon
Dsol	2,000	$100.40
Esol	1,000	134.20
Fsol	100	10.80

Costs during the month were

Joint costs of materials and processing	$161,140
Packaging and labeling, Dsol	1,600
Refining and labeling, Esol	1,400

Chemical wastes were sold for $60. The company treats Fsol as a by-product. Klinesmith deducts the net market value of the by-products from production costs.

Required:

a. Use the net market (realizable) value method of allocation in determining the joint costs allocated to Dsol, Esol, and Fsol.

b. Assuming 200 gallons each of Dsol and Esol are the only products remaining in inventory at the end of the month, determine the cost of ending inventory and the cost of goods sold for June.

c. Using June as a representative month, determine whether it would be profitable to hire laborers to purify Dsol so it can be sold as Esol. The purifying would occur before Esol is refined and labeled. Determine the maximum amount that can be paid monthly for the workers and supplies to perform the purifying before there is a change in income.

P8–11 Joint Cost Allocation (CIA) (L.O. 5)

A company uses a single process to produce three joint products, E, M, and H. Raw materials in the amount of 100,000 gallons are processed in each batch to yield 40,000 gallons of E, 30,000 gallons of M, and 20,000 gallons of H. The joint costs of processing a batch of raw materials are

Materials (100,000 gallons)	$60,000
Conversion costs	75,000

After split-off, Product E can be sold for $1.50 per gallon. Products M and H must be processed further before they can be sold. The separate processing costs are $1.50 per gallon for Product M and $2.00 per gallon for Product H. Product M can then be sold for $3 per gallon and Product H for $4.25 per gallon.

During March, the company processed 100,000 gallons of raw materials. There were no inventories of finished product on hand on March 1. March sales were 30,000 gallons of E, 28,000 gallons of M, and 16,000 gallons of H.

The company uses the net realizable value method for allocating joint costs.

Required:

a. Prepare a schedule showing the allocation of the $135,000 joint cost between Products E, M, and H. Clearly label your answer.

b. Prepare a statement of gross margin for Products E, M, and H for March.

c. Suppose Product E can be processed further into Product Super E by additional processing which costs $14,000; 35,000 gallons of Super E can be produced per batch of 100,000 gallons of raw materials. Super E can be sold for $2 per gallon. Will the company be better off by producing and selling Super E rather than Product E? Show computations to support your answer.

P8–12 Methods of Accounting for By-Products (L.O. 2)

Cates Chemical Company provides the following data regarding its processing operations:

	By-Products	Joint Products
Sales	35,000 gallons	80,000 gallons
Production	40,000 gallons	100,000 gallons
Estimated market value	$7.50 per gallon	$50 per gallon
Costs of further processing:		
Materials	1.25 per gallon	
Labor	0.40 per gallon	
Factory overhead applied	0.35 per gallon	
Marketing costs applied	0.30 per gallon	
Administrative costs applied	0.20 per gallon	
Total production costs		$1,500,000
Total marketing and administrative costs		120,000

Required:

a. Prepare income statements using the two basic methods of accounting for by-products.

b. Using the net market value method, prepare the journal entries to record the costs assigned to the by-products.

c. Assume that the market improves for the by-products and the 35,000 gallons are sold for cash at $8 per gallon. Record the entry.

P8–13 Process Costing and By-Product Costing (L.O. 2)

Ohio Tech manufactures a product known as CLAM in two departments, Mixing and Finishing. In addition to the manufacture of this product, it produces a by-product known as Cx.

The Mixing Department introduces raw materials; however, due to their nature, costs of materials, labor, and overhead are not separately identified in the Mixing Department. On completion of processing in the Mixing Department, by-product Cx is produced; it accounts for 15 percent of the material output. Cx needs no additional processing and is transferred to finished goods.

The current sales price for Cx is $2.65 per pound and the estimated marketing costs total $0.15 per pound. The net market value of the by-product Cx is accounted for as a reduction of the costs of materials and conversion costs in the Mixing Department.

The remaining output is transferred to the Finishing Department for the final processing. Water is added at the beginning of the Finishing Department process which results in a 30 percent gain in weight of the goods in production.

Beginning and ending inventory for the month of April 19X1 are

Mixing Department (no beginning or ending inventory)
Finishing Department—beginning inventory: 400 pounds at an accumulated cost of $7,100, 40% complete as to conversion costs
Finishing Department—ending inventory: 600 pounds, 40% complete as to conversion costs

April costs of production are

Mixing Department—$29,990 total of material and conversion costs (2,000 pounds of materials were used in the Mixing Department)
Finishing Department—$25,080 conversion costs

Required:

Prepare a cost of production report for both departments using FIFO costing. Carry unit costs to five decimal places.

P8–14 Further Processing of Products (L.O. 6)

Flood Corporation uses a joint process in manufacturing Products A, B, and C. Because of the nature of the products, each can be sold at the split-off point or processed further. None of the separable costs are fixed, and all are traceable to the respective product manufactured. Joint production costs total $600,000 and are allocated on the basis of the sales value at split-off point.

		Sales Value and Separable Costs if Processed Further	
Product	**Sales Value at Split-Off**	**Separable Costs**	**Sales Value**
A	$200,000	$40,000	$232,000
B	350,000	25,000	390,000
C	250,000	15,000	285,000
	$800,000		

Required:

a. Determine the joint cost allocated to each product and the inventory valuation assuming the products are further processed.
b. Using the information from Requirement *a*, assume 95,000 gallons were in the batch of Product A. Further assume that 60,000 gallons of Product A were sold and that there was no beginning inventory. Under these conditions, what is the valuation of cost of goods sold and ending inventory for Product A?
c. Determine which products Flood Corporation should further process to maximize profits.

P8–15 Net Market (Realizable) Value Method with Multiple Split-Offs (L.O. 5)

Aune, Inc., manufactures three products, R, S, and T, in a joint process. Aune makes Product T in two phases; in the first phase, raw materials are processed to produce two intermediates in fixed proportions. Workers process one of these intermediates to yield Product R. They convert the other intermediate into Product T in a separate finishing operation, which yields both finished Product T and Product S. Product S must be further processed before yielding a salable product. Product quantity and market price per gallon are as follows for a normal period:

	Gallons	Market Price per Gallon
Product R	60,000	$5
Product S	40,000	3
Product T	80,000	4

The cost of processing is as follows:

	Basic Process	Product R Process	Products S-T Process	Product S Process
Material	$40,000	$ 86,500	$ 60,000	$ 4,000
Direct labor	10,000	20,000	28,000	9,000
Variable factory overhead	16,000	5,000	12,000	2,000
Fixed factory overhead	14,000	10,000	53,500	25,000
	$80,000	$121,500	$153,500	$40,000

Required:

Using the net market (realizable) value method in allocating joint costs, determine the distribution of production costs and the inventoriable cost per gallon for each product.

P8–16 Journal Entries (AICPA adapted) (L.O. 2)

Lares Confectioners, Inc., makes a candy bar called Rey, which sells for $0.50 per pound. The manufacturing process also yields a product known as Nagu. Without further processing, Nagu sells for $0.10 per pound. With further processing, Nagu sells for $0.30 per pound. During the month of April, total joint manufacturing costs up to the split-off point consisted of the following charges to work in process:

Raw materials	$150,000
Direct labor	120,000
Factory overhead	30,000

Production for the month was 394,000 pounds of Rey and 30,000 pounds of Nagu. To complete Nagu during the month of April and obtain a selling price of $0.30 per pound, further processing during April would entail the following additional costs:

Raw materials	$2,000
Direct labor	1,500
Factory overhead	500

Required:

Prepare the April journal entries for Nagu, if Nagu is

a. Transferred as a by-product at sales value to the warehouse without further processing, with a corresponding reduction of Rey's manufacturing costs.
b. Further processed as a by-product and transferred to the warehouse at net realizable value, with a corresponding reduction of Rey's manufacturing costs.
c. Further processed and transferred to finished goods, with joint costs being allocated to Rey and Nagu based on relative sales value at the split-off point.

P8–17 Multiple Split-off Points (L.O. 5)

Alton Corporation produces Products A, B, C, and D. Products A, B, and C are treated as joint products, while D is a by-product. The production processes for a given year are as follows:

In the Mixing Department, 500,000 pounds of raw material are processed at a total cost of $283,000. After processing in the Mixing Department, 40 percent of the units are transferred to the Fabricating Department and 55 percent of the units (now C) are transferred to the Finishing Department. The remaining pounds emerge as D, the by-product, to be sold at $1 per pound. Selling expenses related to disposing of D amount to $2,000. The company accounts for by-product production by deducting the net market value of by-products manufactured from the production costs of the main products.

In the Fabricating Department, the material is further processed at a total cost of $180,000. Sixty percent of the units (now A) are transferred to the Cleaning Department, where they are further processed at a total additional cost of $89,625. After this processing, A is ready to be sold at $3 per pound. The remaining units (now B) are transferred to the Polishing Department, where costs of $69,875 are applied before Product B is ready to be sold at $2 per pound.

In the Finishing Department, C is processed at a total additional cost of $29,250. A normal loss of units of C, which equals 10 percent of the good output of C, occurs in this department. The remaining good output of C is then sold for $1.20 per pound.

Required:

a. Diagram the production process, indicating the quantities, separable costs, and gross market values associated with each product.

b. Using the net market method in allocating joint costs, determine the distribution of production costs and total inventory valuation of each of the four products.

P8–18 Multiple Split-Off Points (L.O. 5)

CSC, Inc., manufactures Products B, C, and D in a joint process. CSC manufactures Product B in two phases; in the first phase, raw materials are processed to produce two intermediates in fixed proportions. One of these intermediates is processed to yield Product C. The other intermediate product is converted into B in a separate finishing operation which yields both finished Product B and another product, D. Product D must be further processed before yielding a salable product. Production quantity and market price per gallon are as follows for a normal period:

	Gallons	Market Price per Gallon
C	70,000	$4
D	38,000	$5
B	46,400	$5

At these normal volumes, material and processing costs are expected to total as follows:

	Basic Process	Product C Process	Products B-D Process	Product D Process
Material	$ 15,000	$12,000	$ 6,000	$ 4,140
Direct labor	5,000	20,000	1,800	6,000
Variable factory overhead	26,000	18,000	14,000	3,600
Fixed factory overhead	84,000	2,000	6,200	8,260
	$130,000	$52,000	$28,000	$22,000

Output can be increased by as much as 15 percent of normal volume without any increase in fixed costs. Marketing and administrative costs are fixed and are not traced to any products.

Required:

Using the net market (realizable) method in allocating joint costs, determine the distribution of production costs and the inventoriable cost per gallon for each product.

P8–19 Multiple Split-Off; Inventory Valuation (L.O. 6)

Forman, Inc., processes salmon meat and eggs into Products A, B, C, and D. The first three products, A, B, and C, are joint products; Product D is a by-product. The production processes for a given accounting period are as follows:

In the Cleaning Department, 3,000,000 pounds of raw fish are processed at a cost of $600,000. After processing in the Cleaning Department, 2 percent of the fish processed is fish eggs, which are then transferred to the Egg Packing Department (Product A). An additional cost of $100,000 is incurred, and Product A is then sold for $25 per pound.

Ninety-six percent of the processed fish is transferred to the Fish Processing Department. The remainder (2 percent) is considered a by-product (Product D) and is sold at $0.50 per pound as animal food with no additional processing. Selling expense to dispose of Product D is $5,000. The company accounts for this by crediting the net market value of by-products manufactured to the production costs of the main products.

In the Fish Processing Department, the meat is processed further at a cost of $800,000. In this department, the fish that is to become Product B is canned, and the fish that is to become Product C is bagged.

Seventy-five percent of the fish (Product B) is transferred to the Cooking Department. After processing at an additional cost of $700,000, B is sold at $2 per pound. The remaining fish (Product C) is transferred to the Freezing Department where additional costs of $300,000 are incurred. Product C is sold for $3 per pound.

Required:

a. Diagram the production process indicating the appropriate data associated with each product (i.e., quantities, separable cost, and gross market values).
b. Using the net market valuation method of allocating joint costs, determine the distribution of production costs and the total inventory valuations for each of the four products. Round to the nearest dollar.

P8–20 Unit Cost Determination (L.O. 3)

Winter Fertilizer Company operates three departments. As a result of the unique process in each department, the company markets a variety of products.

All products originate in Department A. Raw materials are converted at this phase into three products: Z1, Z2, and Z3. Z1 is sold at this stage, but Z2 must be processed further before it can be marketed. Z3 could be sold at this stage, but Winter has chosen to subject it to additional processing.

Z2 is transferred to Department B. Here it is converted into Z2B and is sold at this stage.

Z3 is transferred to Department C. Here another raw material is added and Z3 is converted into Z3C, which is sold at this stage. In processing Z3 into Z3C, an incidental product, Z4, results. Winter has a customer for all the Z4 it produces; there are no additional processing costs beyond this point, neither are there any marketing or administrative costs allocable to Z4.

Since inventory costs are determined on a FIFO basis, the unit cost of the most recently produced items must be determined. Winter accounts for the by-product Z4 by deducting its net market value from the cost of production.

An inspection of company records reveals the following information for March:

Department A:	
Raw materials	$ 4,500
Conversion costs	45,000
Department B:	
Conversion costs	6,120
Department C:	
Raw materials	1,260
Conversion costs	30,000

Inventories:

	Pounds Produced	Ending Inventory Feb. 28	Ending Inventory March 31	Sales Price per Pound
Z1	4,000			$4.32
Z2	3,200	320	120	
Z3	6,000	400	580	4.80
Z2B	3,060			6.00
Z3C	7,000			9.00
Z4	2,000			1.00

Required:

a. Compute Department A's cost per pound of Z1, Z2, and Z3 produced using the average unit cost method based on physical units for March.
b. Compute the costs as in Requirement *a* using the gross market value method.

c. Compute the cost per pound of Z3C produced in March. Assume for this computation that the cost per pound of Z3 produced is $3.90 in February and $4 in March.

P8–21 Inventory Values for Joint Products and By-Products (L.O. 5)

Young Corporation processes, cans, and sells two main orange products: orange sections and orange juice. The orange's skin is treated as a by-product which is sold to a candy-making company for further processing as candied orange peel. Young's production process begins in the Cutting Department where oranges are first processed. The oranges are first sterilized and the outside skin is cut away. The two main products and the by-product (orange skin for candy peel) are recognizable after processing in the Cutting Department. Each product is then transferred to a separate department for final processing.

Some of the peeled oranges are forwarded to the Sectioning Department where the oranges are sectioned and canned. Any juice generated during the sectioning operation is packed in the cans with the orange sections.

The remaining peeled oranges are forwarded to the Juicing Department where they are pulverized into a liquid. An evaporation loss equal to 10 percent of the weight of the good output occurs as the juices are heated. The outside skin is cut and frozen in the Candy Peel Department.

Young Corporation uses the net market value method to assign costs of the joint process to its main products. The by-product is inventoried at its net market value.

The Cutting Department received a total of 50,000 pounds during September. The costs incurred in each department, the proportion by weight transferred to the two final processing departments, and the selling price of each end product follow:

Processing Data and Costs
September 19X1

	Costs Incurred	Product by Weight Transferred to Department (Percent)	Selling Price per Pound of the Final Product
Cutting	$14,000	—	—
Sectioning	3,500	50%	$1.00
Juicing	2,000	40	.50
Skin for candy peel . . .	500	10	.20
	$20,000	100%	

Required:

Using the net market value method to determine inventory values for its main products and by-product, calculate:

a. (1) The pounds of oranges that result as output for orange sections, orange juice, and candy peel.
  (2) The net market value at the split-off point of the two main products.
  (3) The amount of the cost of the Cutting Department assigned to each main product and to the by-product.
  (4) The gross margins for each of the two main products.
b. (1) Why would management need to know gross margin information by main product?
  (2) Would this information be helpful in deciding whether to process the main products further?

P8–22 Numerous Split-Offs of Joint Products (L.O. 5)

Crawford Corporation produces two joint products: DX and EX. Additionally, FX is a by-product of DX. No joint cost is to be allocated to the by-product. The production processes for a given year are as follows:

The first department—Cutting—processes 117,000 pounds of direct material at a total cost of $150,000. After processing in the Cutting Department, workers transfer 62,000 pounds to the Mixing Department and 55,000 pounds (now EX) to the Fabricating Department.

The Mixing Department further processes the material at a total additional cost of $18,000. Of the pounds available, 50,000 pounds (now DX) go to the Finishing Department, and the remaining pounds emerge as FX, the by-product, to be sold at $2 per pound. Marketing expenses related to disposing of FX are $4,000.

The Finishing Department processes DX at a total additional cost of $8,400. After this processing, DX is ready for sale at $5 per pound.

The Fabricating Department processes EX at a total additional cost of $123,600. In this department, a normal loss of units of EX occurs which equals 10 percent of the good output of EX. The remaining good output of EX is then sold for $6 per pound.

Required:

a. Draw a diagram depicting the flow of pounds through the production cycle.
b. Prepare a schedule showing the allocation of the $150,000 joint cost between DX and EX using the net market value approach. The net market value of FX should be treated as an addition to the sales value of DX.
c. Disregard your answer to Requirement b, and assume that $100,000 of total joint costs were appropriately allocated to DX. Assume also that there were 52,000 pounds of DX and 11,000 pounds of FX available to sell. Prepare a statement of gross margin for DX using the following facts:
   (1) During the year, sales of DX were 70 percent of the pounds available for sale. There was no beginning inventory.
   (2) The net market value of FX available for sale is to be deducted from the cost of producing DX. The ending inventory of DX is to be based on the net cost of production.
   (3) Data relating to marketing cost are identical to those presented earlier.

P8–23 By-Product and Joint Costing under Process Costing System (L.O. 5)

Ann Wilson Company produces two principal products known as AX and BX. Incidental to the production of these products, it manufactures a by-product known as Bypo. The company has three producing departments, which it identifies as Departments 1, 2, and 3. Raw materials are started in process in Department 1. On completion of processing in that department, 20 percent of the material is by-product and is transferred directly to stock. Twenty-five percent of the remaining output of Department 1 goes to Department 2 where it is made into AX, and the other 75 percent goes to Department 3 where it becomes BX. The processing of AX in Department 2 results in a gain in weight of material transferred into the department of 25 percent due to the addition of water at the start of the processing. There is no gain or loss of weight in the other processes.

The company considers the income from Bypo, after allowing $0.10 per pound for estimated marketing delivery costs, to be a reduction of the cost of the two principal products. The company assigns Department 1 costs to the two principal products in proportion to their net sales value at point of separation computed by deducting costs to be incurred in subsequent processes from the sales value of the products.

Sales price and additional costs for each product are as follows:

Per Pound
AX—$24 sales price; $4 subsequent processing cost
BX—$18 sales price; $6 subsequent processing cost
Bypo—$.60 sales price; $.10 marketing cost

The following information concerns the operations during May:

	Inventories		
	April 30 Quantity (Pounds)	Value	May 31 Quantity (Pounds)
Department 1	None		None
Department 2	400	$3,360	600
Department 3	200	1,560	800
Finished goods—AX	450	4,500	500
Finished goods—BX	1,000		600
Finished goods—Bypo	None		None

Inventories in process are estimated to be one-half complete in Departments 2 and 3, both at the first and last of the month.

	Costs	
	Material Used	Labor and OH
Department 1	$44,180	$52,000
Department 2	–0–	20,600
Department 3	–0–	73,800

The material used in Department 1 weighed 21,000 pounds. Prices as of May 31 are unchanged from those in effect during the month.

Required:

a. Prepare a statement showing costs and production by departments for May. The company uses the first-in, first-out method to cost production.
b. Prepare a schedule of inventory values for finished goods as of April 30.

Cases

C8–24 Comparing Profitability of Subsequent Processing (L.O. 6)

Vickry, Inc., manufactures a product called FIN in the following four departments: Department 1, mixing; Department 2, cooking; Department 3, cooling; and Department 4, packing.

The first department weighs and mixes materials A and B. Department 2 cooks the mixture; 20 percent of the mixture is lost in evaporation at the end of the departmental process. The remaining 80 percent of the mixture is then sent to Department 3, where it is cooled. At the end of the cooling process, the top 90 percent of the mixture is transferred to Department 4, where it is bottled for shipment. The remaining 10 percent of the mixture represents sediments from the cooling process and is sold in bulk as a product called PRO for $3 a pound.

However, variations occur in the cooling process because of temperature changes, so that the percentage of PRO can be increased to as high as 30 percent of the Department 3 mixture. At a minimum, PRO will always be 10 percent of Department 3 mixture. FIN sells for $10 a bottle.

A prospective use for PRO has been found, but it would require the establishment of a fifth department. This new product, NEW-PRO, would sell for $6 a pound. Producing this product requires adding two pounds of a new material to each pound of sediment obtained from Department 3. The additional processing would require 30 percent shrinkage of the resulting mixture. The following additional costs would result from processing NEW-PRO:

Materials	$ 0.60 per pound
Variable processing costs	$ 1.00 per pound of input
Fixed processing costs	$4,000 per month

Required:

a. Outline briefly the processing flow by departments describing the steps involved with their specific characteristics as to percentage lost and transferred.

b. Prepare statements based on the following cost data and production figures for a month. Show total production cost and gross profit for each of the following three situations assuming that all production is sold:

Material issues to Department 1:   Material A—6,000 pounds @ $1.50 per pound
Material B—4,000 pounds @ $1.10 per pound

Conversion costs:
Department 1—$.50 per pound of departmental output
Department 2—$.40 per pound of departmental output
Department 3—$.90 per pound of departmental output
Department 4—$.20 per pound of departmental output (all is considered variable)

(1) PRO is produced at a rate of 10 percent of the Department 3 mixture with Department 3 cost allocated to both products on a per-pound basis.

(2) NEW-PRO is produced at 10 percent of Department 3 mixture.

(3) PRO is produced at 30 percent of the Department 3 mixture and NEW-PRO is then manufactured.

c. Explain which of the three alternatives you would advise adopting and list factors to consider in making this decision.

C8–25 Bases for Allocating (L.O. 3)

Sellar Cheese Company manufactures a high-quality cheddar cheese using fresh, sweet milk which it pasteurizes. The milk flows from the pasteurizer into stainless steel vats that hold 10,000 pounds of milk each. Seller Company has found it takes about 11 pounds of milk to make 1 pound of cheddar cheese.

In making cheese, the curd, or solid parts, of milk must be separated from the whey, or liquid part. Sellar uses a starter culture of lactic acid bacteria, which is added to each vat to accomplish this separation. When the bacteria are distributed throughout the vat, the milk begins to ripen or ferment. Rennet extract, a substance from the lining of a calf's fourth stomach, is added to make the milk curdle. The milk then coagulates into a curd, or soft, semisolid mass.

Using paddles, workers stir the curd and whey before the mixture is heated to about 102°F to remove any remaining whey and to develop the proper firmness and acidity. Cheese workers drain the whey from the vat and push the curd to the sides.

Curd processing. After the whey is drained off, workers place the curd in a machine that cuts it into pieces about 10 cm long and 13 ml thick. They salt the cut curd and press it into molds. The molds are stacked in a press and kept under great pressure overnight. The next morning, the cheese is removed and placed in a curing room where it remains for 90 days.

Whey processing. Whey is drained off into vats where a preservative agent is added, which allows a two-month storage. After a short mixing and cooking process, the whey is refrigerated for sale to cattle-feed producers. Within the last few years, a new process has been developed in which soybeans are mixed with whey for livestock food. If whey is not further processed, it has no value and is poured down the drain.

Because Seller's cheddar cheese has such a fine reputation, the cheese is easy to sell at $4 per pound and is shipped as fast as it is cured. More effort is required to sell the whey, even though both are sold to the same food-producing companies by the same marketing force. Often, when the accumulation of whey becomes especially heavy and the date of spoilage is coming close, buyers are required to purchase some amount of whey to be able to buy the cheddar cheese. Sellar Company justifies this by arguing that they want to stimulate the use of whey in livestock food processing.

This is the reason why Sellar's marketing manager was excited when Beyer Foods, Inc., offers to buy 100,000 pounds of whey for $0.50 per pound. However, Sellar's production manager argues that the $0.50 per pound offer should not be accepted because the cost of production is at least $0.80 per pound and probably more. The marketing manager points out that the production manager's insistence on $0.80 has led to a heavy accumulation of whey in refrigeration.

The production manager counters this argument by saying, "Your salespeople are so incompetent and so lacking in incentive that they would pour out the whey unless we had inventory controls."

Cost data. Both managers realize they need assistance from the cost accountant and request the preparation of financial data for their use. After analysis of past results, the cost accountant indicates that Sellar Company processes 50,000 pounds of milk into cheese in the one eight-hour shift that operates daily.

Out of 10,000 pounds of milk processed, 1,400 pounds of output are saved—910 pounds of cheese and 490 pounds of whey that can be preserved. Raw milk costs $1,000 per 10,000 pounds, while lactic acid bacteria and rennet extract together average $150 per 10,000 pounds of milk. Labor and overhead costs average $800 per 10,000 pounds of milk processed through the stage where whey is drained off. Labor and overhead in curd processing average $500 per 910 pounds of cheese; salt averages $29 for a 910-pound batch.

In whey processing, the preservatives average $16 for a 490-pound batch. Labor and overhead per 490-pound batch average $25. Selling costs average $0.10 per finished pound each for the cheese and the whey.

Production manager's basis. After studying the cost data, the production manager presents the following support for refusing the offer of $0.50 sales price per pound of whey:

$$\frac{\$1,000 \text{ milk} + \$150 \text{ bacteria and rennet extract}}{1,400 \text{ pounds of output}} = \$0.82$$

The production manager emphasizes that an $0.80 price per pound does not even cover the materials much less the labor and overhead.

Marketing manager's basis. The marketing manager contends that the production manager's basis has no merit because it assumes that the company had just as soon make whey as cheese, and everyone knows that is a fallacy. Instead, the marketing manager presents the argument that the material for the cheese initially is worth more per pound than the material for the whey. Based on this contention, he presents the following analysis:

	Output of 10,000 Pounds of Milk	Market Price per Pound	Total Market Value	Percent of Total	Costs Applicable to Each	Cost per Pound
Cheese	910	$4.00	$3,640	93.7	$1,827*	$2.00
Whey	490	.50	245	6.3	123	.25
			$3,885	100.0	$1,950	

*93.7% × ($1,000 + $150 + $800).

The production manager disagrees with the approach, arguing that the cost allocation should not be a function of their relative market prices. The marketing manager then asks, "Why not treat the whey as a by-product, because you'll agree that we prefer to process cheese all the time rather than whey if we could." Under this approach, the market value of the whey ($.50) is deducted from the cost of operations and all income or loss is carried by the cheese.

The production manager does not completely agree with this approach because the cost allocated is still a function of the market value of the whey. The belief that an accurate cost is needed to establish sales policy is still strong.

Because of their inability to solve the issue, they consulted the controller and president to determine whether a $0.50 per pound sales offer for the whey should be accepted.

Required:

a. Evaluate the following bases proposed:
   (1) The production manager's allocation of material resulting in an $0.82 cost per pound of total output.
   (2) The marketing manager's allocation resulting in a $0.25 cost per pound of whey.
   (3) The marketing manager's by-product allocation.
b. Suggest other bases that you believe appropriate and determine the cost per pound of cheese and whey using these bases.
c. Determine if the offer of $0.50 per pound of whey should be accepted.

COST DATA
FOR
PERFORMANCE
EVALUATION

Flexible Budgeting and the Budgeting Process

After studying this chapter, you should be able to:

1. Explain the advantages of budgets as a management tool for performance evaluation.

2. Understand the important role of top management in the budgeting process.

3. Distinguish between variances obtained using fixed budgets and variances obtained using flexible budgets.

4. Prepare budgets in the master budget plan.

Introduction

Budgeting is a means of coordinating the combined intelligence of an entire organization into a plan of action. This plan is based on past performance and governed by rational judgments about factors influencing the course of business in the future. Without the coordination provided by budgeting, department heads may follow courses beneficial for their own departments, but not for the overall company. Budgeting control is a companywide operation with a complete plan of execution—a program that encompasses much more than monetary aspects. Many behavioral factors are inherent in the budgeting process. For example, as we discuss in this chapter, employees are more willing to accept departmental budgets if managers make honest attempts to explain the budgeting procedure and to involve them in the process.

Master budgets include both operating and financing budgets. This chapter discusses **operating budgets,** whose focus is the acquisition and use of scarce resources. As discussed in the next chapter, **financial budgets,** such as cash budgets, direct attention to acquiring funds to obtain resources. Chapters 17 and 18 discuss capital budgeting and provide definite procedures and methods for evaluating each proposed project's merit.

Accountants prepare effective operating budgets using a flexible budgeting approach. Flexible budgets are useful for determining the efficiency of operations because we compare the actual costs at any output level to a budget adjusted to the actual activity level. A flexible budgeting approach eliminates distortions due to volume variations.

Advantages of Budgets (L.O. 1)

We can prepare budgets in numerous ways depending on the desired complexity. Even simple budgets offer many external and internal advantages. Budgets make the decision-making process more effective by helping managers meet uncertainties. The objective of budgeting is to substitute deliberate, well-conceived business judgment for accidental success in enterprise management. Budgets should not be expressions of wishful thinking but rather descriptions of attainable objectives. Certainly, budgets reflect plans—managers must plan before preparing budgets.

Communication, Coordination, and Performance Evaluation

The general operating budget or annual profit plan is not only an important operating tool but also represents a formal communication channel within a company. In the initial phase of the budgetary process, managers are forced to communicate with each other. This process encourages necessary coordination among segment activities as managers consider the organization structure and interrelationship between segments. Because budgets force managers to plan, they exchange views about where they want the company to be in the next 5 or 10 years. In this process, different views of future company objectives usually arise; budgets help managers to compromise. When this compromise is not made, each company segment may follow a course of action that benefits only itself, not the entire company. If the budgeting process does not facilitate long-range planning, management is likely to be concerned with meeting only daily operational goals. Coordination is best achieved using a participative budgeting approach in which all managers provide input into the goal setting process.

Budgets represent management's formal commitment to take positive actions to make actual events correspond to the formal plan. Profit plans also contain explicit statements concerning implementation of management objectives for a period of time; managers communicate these to all parties with control responsibility. Comparison of actual results with the profit plan forms the basis for management control, motivation, and performance evaluation.

Cost accounting provides the total and detailed costs of the products manufactured or the services provided by a company. To measure the efficiency of these costs, they must be compared with a yardstick that was prepared in advance of production and that reflects a good level of performance. The most common method of evaluating actual performance is through budget analysis. Combining a standard cost system with budgets also leads to better performance of assigned tasks and goals.

Budgets and Standards

As discussed in Chapters 11 and 12, standard costs serve as the building blocks with which budgets are constructed. Budgets are statements of expected costs and forecasts of production requirements. Budgets attempt to set up a predetermined standard of operations for a period or project taken as a whole, while standards are concerned with cost per unit. Thus, when standard costs are employed, the budget is largely a summary of standards for all items of revenue and expense.

The following list summarizes a few of the advantages a formalized system of budgeting or profit planning offers:

1. It obligates management to specify objectives for the short and long run.
2. It forces management to analyze future problems so that alternative plans are recognized.
3. It directs effort and funds toward the most profitable of possible alternatives.
4. It emphasizes the need for coordination of all elements of a company since budgeting reveals lack of control in an organization.
5. It serves as a means of communication.
6. It provides performance standards that serve as incentives to perform more effectively.
7. It indicates those areas lacking control by providing data used to analyze variances between actual and budgeted operations. These variances should provide the springboard for study of the source of the problem.

Principles of Budgeting (L.O. 1)

General principles apply to the budgeting process. Top management's support is crucial to the success of the budgetary program. Top management's philosophy toward budgeting soon filters down in the company even though these executives may not realize their importance in the process. If they view the budget as some mechanical process to complete as quickly as possible, employees are less likely to give budget preparation much attention. The budgeting process also fails if management views budgets as a scapegoat on which to blame company problems. On the other hand, if management considers the budget an excellent means of planning and takes an active role in the budgeting process, a company is more likely to gain many benefits.

Relation to Organizational Structure and Environment

Accountants should design budgetary control systems around each organization's formal structure because of the necessary differentiation and integration between areas of the organization. Integration is especially important when the output of one area is the input of another area. **Decentralization** or **differentiation** is the degree to which managers have freedom to use their own management techniques and make their own decisions. Generally, the larger the organizational size and more complex the technology, the greater the degree of decentralization. The compilation of a comprehensive budget requires integration among segments.

The size and technology of an organization also determine the degree of individual participation in the budgeting process. In a small firm, many employees can participate, while participation in a large firm may be limited to managers. In high-technology firms, changes often occur so rapidly there is no time available for full participation. In low-technology firms, there can be a more definite period for preparation, allowing the additional time that participation requires.

Budgetary control systems cannot function properly in isolation from the operational context of the organization—the separation from reality makes them ineffective. The efficiency of a department depends on factors internal to a cost center, external to a cost center, and external to the company. The internal factors are more important for a production department. External factors are vital for a research and development department, and both external and exogenous factors play an essential role for a marketing department. To increase effectiveness, turbulence of the environment is a consideration in selecting control mechanisms.

Budget Revisions

Changes in conditions both inside and outside the company may justify making budget revisions, rather than using unattainable budgets. If companies fail to adjust budgets for external unforeseen situations, frustration can result. For example, additional competitors may enter the market and make meeting budgeted market share and sales unlikely, despite increased promotional expenditures. However, companies should not revise budgets every time they fail to meet a budgeted goal because this type of revising defeats the control functions of budgets. Top managers usually approve or make budget revisions.

Budget Committee

Line management has the responsibility for the preparation of individual budgets. There is also a need for someone to provide technical, unbiased assistance. The president or chief executive officer normally establishes budgeting guidelines and policies. The budget committee generally directs and executes all budget procedures. The budget committee serves as a consulting body to the budget officer; members include the budget director and top executives representing all company financial segments.

Because the budget committee's functions include coordination of all planning, the committee should review and evaluate all reports prepared at the initiation of the budgetary system. A company can more easily eliminate duplication if the budget committee prepares a list of the reports to supply the information needed. The budget committee then asks other managers within the company whether these reports are sufficient. Otherwise, given the normal resistance to change, most managers continue to request reports, even if they are redundant. After preparing budgets, the budget committee continues in an advisory capacity, periodically reviewing the budget and approving budget changes as conditions warrant.

Budget Manual. The budget committee's functions also include reviewing and approving budget estimates and suggesting revisions. It should review segment budgets to determine whether they are excessively optimistic, conservative, or make provision for slack. The committee also has the responsibility of recommending action to improve efficiency where necessary. In addition, it is helpful for the budget committee to prepare a policy manual as a reference for implementation of a budget program. This manual has long-range usefulness because it documents procedures.

Budget Director. The budget director, who serves in a staff capacity, is usually the controller or someone reporting to the controller. The budget director requests estimates of the cost of running each cost center from department heads and supervisors. Similarly, sales executives submit sales estimates. The budget director should also supply executives with information about past operations to guide in the preparation of new budgets. Many accountants fail as budget directors, not because they lack accounting knowledge, but because they fail to recognize the administrative problems inherent in the budgeting process. The success of budget directors in generating goodwill toward themselves and the budget department is crucial to the success of the budget program.

Length of Budget Period

Generally, a company's budget corresponds to the fiscal period used in the accounting system. Budgets can be short or long range. While the long-range budget lacks the detail supplied by a short-range operational budget, it does provide broad guidelines. For example, a long-range budget covering as many as 5 or 10 years anticipates long-term needs and opportunities that may require the company to take definite steps in the short run. Because long-range budgets are subject to many changes, they may not be circulated among middle and lower management. Because we prepare short-term budgets for shorter periods, they have the advantage of being more accurate.

Some companies prepare detailed **rolling,** also known as **continuous,** budgets. For example, using a rolling budget, at the end of May of each year, the company adds a budget for May of the next year. As each month ends, companies add a new 12th month. With this method, companies always have a 12-month detailed budget in advance. Rolling budgets incorporate changing economic conditions into the plans each time companies add a new month. Budgeting thus becomes a continual process rather than a once-a-year task. Other companies prepare their annual budgets in two phases. They detail the first half of the year and summarize the remaining six months by quarters in less detail. They prepare a new, short-range, detailed budget every six months, partly on the basis of earlier summarized data and partly on the results of the previous six months.

Bottom-Up Budgeting Approach

Budgets should follow the lines of responsibility and authority of organization charts. Clear lines of authority and responsibility should be indicated so there is no question which individual to hold accountable for each expenditure. An organization chart should identify employees whose operations justify a budget.

There is little purpose to setting goals if the individuals who must meet these goals are unaware of their existence. Holding a person responsible for a level of achievement that he or she does not know about is an unfair management practice. Failure to communicate results to involved parties is also unfair. The more rapidly a company communicates results, the greater the chance that employees will make needed corrections and achieve more efficient performance.

The development of an annual profit plan employing a bottom-up approach uses the following steps. A **bottom-up approach** combines budgets at successively higher levels of management. The approach also indicates the level of management involved and the nature and direction of the communication process.

1. Identification of planning guidelines by top management. All levels of management are involved and communication is downward.

2. Preparation of the general operating budget or profit plan beginning with a sales budget. Lower levels of management receive sales targets, providing a basis for the preparation of production budgets and other components. Consultation with a higher (middle) management level may be needed to arrive at certain aspects of the specific manager's budget. The communication process is primarily lateral with some upward communication possible.

3. Negotiation may be necessary to arrive at final plans; communication is upward.

4. Coordination and review of the profit plan; top-level management makes recommendations and returns the various plans to middle-level management. After middle management makes these changes, the plan is resubmitted for approval. Communication is generally downward; however, there may be some lateral communication during the adjustment phase.

5. Final approval and distribution of the formal plan; top management gives final approval and communicates its decision downward.

If the company is of any size, accomplishing these steps in implementing a budget takes time. Employees may resent the time and effort devoted to budgeting especially if managers present budgets as abstract listings of numerical data. Rather, managers should translate the quantitative data into individual human endeavor. This translation shows how the company's objectives will be reached and what equipment, material, and personnel are required. By involving employees, budgets are more likely to reflect changing conditions. Most companies experience drastically changeable market conditions and few completely predictable situations.

Fixed (Static) and Flexible (Variable) Budgeting (L.O. 3)

To reflect the changing environment and obtain the full advantages of budgeting, companies should use a flexible, not a fixed, budget. A **fixed** or **static budget** approach estimates costs for a single activity volume and does not adjust the budget when actual volume differs. Actual results are later compared with this one budget. Fixed budgeting is appropriate only if a company can estimate its operating volume within close limits and if the costs are behaving predictably. Few companies are fortunate enough to fall into this group. As a result of these factors, a fixed budget is generally not adequate.

A flexible budget is an alternative to the fixed budget. While accountants establish fixed, or static, budgets for one activity level, they prepare **flexible,** or **variable budgets** for more than one level of activity. A flexible budget adjusts revenues, costs, and expenses to the actual volume experienced, and compares

EXHIBIT 9–1   Performance Report Using a Fixed Budget

COST CENTER A
Performance Report Using a Fixed Budget
January 19X1

	Budget	Actual	Variance
Units	1,000	900	100 units
Machine-hours	2,000	1,800	200 hours
Variable costs:			
Direct material	$ 1,000	$ 980	$ 20 favorable
Direct labor	4,000	3,820	180 favorable
Factory overhead:			
Indirect materials	3,000	2,600	400 favorable
Indirect labor	8,500	8,400	100 favorable
Factory utilities	2,000	1,800	200 favorable
Total variable costs ...	$18,500	$17,600	$900 favorable
Fixed costs:			
Factory overhead:			
Depreciation—production equipment	$ 900	$ 960	$ 60 unfavorable
Rent—manufacturing building ..	600	570	30 favorable
Total fixed costs	$ 1,500	$ 1,530	$ 30 unfavorable
Total costs	$20,000	$19,130	$870 favorable

---

these amounts to actual results. Flexible budgets incorporate changes in volume to provide a valid basis of comparison with actual costs.

Fixed and Flexible Budget Variances Compared

Exhibits 9–1 through 9–3 illustrate the problems that can arise from using a fixed or static budget and why flexible budgets are more appropriate. Flexible budgets also include revenue and variable and fixed marketing and administrative expenses. To simplify the example, the budgets illustrated in Exhibits 9–1 through 9–3 include only production costs.

Exhibit 9–1 shows the fixed budget for one cost center for January. Managers expect Cost Center A to produce 1,000 units, each requiring two hours of machine time, and they estimated costs at that level. However, monthly production was only 900 units. Exhibit 9–1 compares the costs incurred to produce 900 units with the fixed budget for 1,000 units. In this case, management may incorrectly believe that costs are under control because all variable costs have favorable variances. However, the variable costs to produce 900 units should be less than that to produce 1,000 units. Even though fixed costs are generally easier to estimate in the short run, actual fixed costs may vary from budgeted fixed costs. As shown in Exhibit 9–1, the two fixed costs vary from their budgeted amounts.

Cost of Acquired Resources Not Utilized

Fixed budget variances mislead managers regarding the impact of not using all acquired resources. Fixed cost must now be shared by only 1,800 machine-hours rather than the estimated 2,000 hours. Cost Center A incurred idle capac-

EXHIBIT 9–2   Flexible Budgets Illustrated for Various Volume Levels

COST CENTER A
Flexible Budgets for Various Projected Activity Levels
January 19X1

	Various Levels of Activity (Budgeted)			Budget Formula
Units	800	1,000	1,400	
Machine-hours	1,600	2,000	2,800	
Variable costs:				
Direct material	$ 800	$ 1,000	$ 1,400	$ 1.00 per unit
Direct labor	3,200	4,000	5,600	4.00 per unit
Indirect materials	2,400	3,000	4,200	3.00 per unit
Indirect labor	6,800	8,500	11,900	8.50 per unit
Factory utilities	1,600	2,000	2,800	2.00 per unit
Total variable costs	$14,800	$18,500	$25,900	$18.50 per unit
Fixed costs:				
Depreciation—production equipment	$ 900	$ 900	$ 900	$ 900 per month
Rent—manufacturing building	600	600	600	$ 600 per month
Total fixed costs	$ 1,500	$ 1,500	$ 1,500	$1,500 per month
Total costs	$16,300	$20,000	$27,400	$18.50 per unit and $1,500 per month
Cost per unit	$20.375	$20.00	$19.572	

ity costs because it did not fully use its budgeted capacity. Managers cannot ignore market demand; if the consumer demand is only 900 units, a cost center should not produce 1,000 units. Instead, management needs to expand into other product lines or reduce its resource spending for capacity. Exhibits 9–2 and 9–3 depict a flexible (variable) budget, which more accurately describes the cost situation.

With flexible budgets, costs can be different in each month or in selected months according to seasonal variation and the activity of the cost center. Accountants, on the other hand, do not adjust fixed budgets to the actual volume attained. Instead, they base the fixed budget on certain definite assumed conditions and compare actual results with this point fixed in advance. A fixed budget is satisfactory only when a company can estimate its activities within close limits.

Exhibit 9–2 gives the **flexible budget formula** for fixed and variable cost behavior used to compute budgeted costs at any capacity level. In Chapter 3 we refer to this formula as the **cost estimating function** used to estimate cost behavior. The flexible budget formula for *production cost* is $18.50 per unit and $1,500 per month.

Expressing factory overhead on an hourly basis is often more appropriate than on a unit basis. Thus, we generally restate output in the quantity of labor or machine-hours it takes to produce budgeted units. In this case, factory overhead is $6.75 per machine-hour ($3,000 + $8,500 + $2,000 = $13,500/2,000 budgeted hours = $6.75) and $1,500 per month. Should Cost Center A select 1,600 machine-hours, rather than 2,000 machine-hours, as normal capacity, the budgeted production cost is $10.1875 per machine-hour ($16,300/1,600 budgeted hours = $10.1875).

Choice of Activity Level. For simplicity, we expressed the flexible budget formula on a single basis, machine-hours. As Chapter 4 discusses, the type of activity determines which volume-related or nonvolume-related cost driver is most appropriate. For example, if accountants establish flexible budgets on direct labor-hours in a machine-paced environment, misleading conclusions may arise from the variances computed. Many variable overhead costs in an automated manufacturing setting do not vary with direct labor as assumed by a flexible budget formula expressed on a direct labor basis. Instead, variable overhead in an automated manufacturing setting varies with other measures of activity such as machine-hours, kilwatt-hours, setups, and materials.

Also, the use of only one activity measure reduces the ability of the cost system to predict the variation in cost with changes in the volume and mix of actual production. Instead, use of multiple bases for different cost centers better reflects cost behavior. By breaking the factory down into various production centers, companies can use different overhead rates on the basis of the level of technology, types of machines, and services in each center.

Exhibit 9–2 shows a series of three possible volumes—800, 1,000, and 1,400 units—all within the relevant range of this cost center. Accountants prepare these different flexible budgets for various levels of projected volume before operations begin on January 1, 19X1. Just because we illustrate more than one budget, do not assume that accountants must prepare many budgets under a flexible budgeting approach. This is not correct. As shown in Exhibits 9–1 and 9–2, Cost Center A's preestablished budgets did not reflect in advance the actual volume obtained of 900 units or 1,800 machine-hours. Indeed, the chances of preparing a budget

EXHIBIT 9–3   Performance Report Using Flexible Budget

COST CENTER A
Performance Report Using Flexible Budget
Assuming 900 Units Produced
For the Month Ended January 19X1

	Budget Adjusted to Actual Volume	Actual	Variance
Units	900	900	–0–
Machine-hours	1,800	1,800	
Variable costs:			
Direct materials	$ 900	$ 980	$ 80 unfavorable
Direct labor	3,600	3,820	220 unfavorable
Indirect materials	2,700	2,600	100 favorable
Indirect labor	7,650	8,400	750 unfavorable
Factory utilities	1,800	1,800	–0–
Total variable costs ...	$16,650	$17,600	$950 unfavorable
Fixed costs:			
Depreciation—production equipment	$ 900	$ 960	$ 60 unfavorable
Rent—manufacturing building ..	600	570	30 favorable
Total fixed costs	$ 1,500	$ 1,530	$ 30 unfavorable
Total costs	$18,150	$19,130	$980 unfavorable

in advance with a volume that coincides exactly with actual volume are very small. A flexible budgeting approach only requires a forecast of total costs at the estimated volume level. If actual volume differs from expected volume, we adjust the budget to actual volume at the end of the period. By having a flexible budget formula, a budget adjusted to or allowed for actual volume is easy to compute at the end of the accounting period.

Using the data in Exhibit 9–1, an actual performance report using a flexible budget yields the variances for actual production shown in Exhibit 9–3. For example, we compare $8,400 actual indirect labor costs to $7,650 ($8.50 × 900 units = $7,650) budgeted costs, yielding a $750 unfavorable variance. Instead of a $900 favorable net variance for variable costs shown in a fixed budget in Exhibit 9–1, the variance is $950 unfavorable. Comparing the costs of operations for 900 units against a budget prepared for the same volume judges the efficiency of the cost center more accurately.

Assume instead, we produce 1,000 units in January 19X1, incurring the actual costs shown in Exhibit 9–4. We compare actual costs with budgeted costs for the same volume (from the 1,000-unit flexible budget).

As stated earlier, in addition to incorporating all manufacturing costs, a flexible (variable) budget may also include revenue and marketing and administrative expenses. In any case, adjusting all budgeted amounts to the actual volume is appropriate whether they result from factory-related transactions or from other phases of the company's operations. Flexible budgeting has many advantages, especially when the production requirements reflect standard costs.

EXHIBIT 9–4   Performance Report Using a Flexible Budget

COST CENTER A
Performance Report Using Flexible Budget
Assuming 1,000 Units Produced
For the Month Ended January 19X1

	Budget Adjusted to Actual Volume	Actual	Variance
Units	1,000	1,000	–0–
Machine-hours	2,000	2,000	
Variable costs:			
Direct materials	$ 1,000	$ 1,100	$100 unfavorable
Direct labor	4,000	4,270	270 unfavorable
Indirect materials	3,000	2,920	80 favorable
Indirect labor	8,500	9,000	500 unfavorable
Factory utilities	2,000	1,910	90 favorable
Total variable costs	$18,500	$19,200	$700 unfavorable
Fixed costs:			
Depreciation—production equipment	$ 900	$ 960	$ 60 unfavorable
Rent—manufacturing building	600	570	30 favorable
Total fixed costs	$ 1,500	$ 1,530	$ 30 unfavorable
Total costs	$20,000	$20,730	$730 unfavorable

Master Budget (L.O. 2)

The master budget for a manufacturing company covers various types of budgets; additional budget schedules support many of these. The following budgets are illustrated in this book:

1. Sales budget broken down by
   a. Territory and product.
   b. Territory, product, and customer grouping.
2. Production budget in units.
3. Direct materials purchases budget.
4. Direct labor budget.*
5. Factory overhead budget.*
6. Cost of goods sold budget.
7. Marketing and administrative budgets.
8. Research and development budget.
9. Budgeted income statement.
10. Budgeted statement of cash receipts and disbursements.
11. Capital expenditure budget.
12. Budgeted statement of financial position.

*Can be combined with direct material in a manufacturing budget estimate.

Chapter 10 discusses and illustrates the marketing and administrative budget, the research and development budget, the budgeted income statement, the budgeted statement of cash receipts and disbursements, and the budgeted statement of financial position. Chapters 17 and 18 discuss the capital expenditure budget. We discuss and illustrate all other budgets in this chapter.

Master Budget Interrelationships

The budget preparation process flows from the sales budget supported by sales forecasts to the projected financial statements as shown in Exhibit 9–5. The resulting budgeted income statement and statement of financial position incorporate elements from all budgets and schedules prepared. The budgeting process begins with management's plans and objectives for the next period. These plans result in various policy decisions concerning selling price, distribution network, advertising expenditures, and environmental influences. Managers prepare sales forecasts for the period (in units by product or product line) from this information. Multiplying units by selling price gives the sales budget in dollars.

Volume and inventory policies influence the preparation of the direct materials purchases budget and the production budget. Accountants base the cost of goods sold budget on expected production, sales volume, and inventory policy. They make detailed budgets for each major type of manufacturing, marketing, and administrative expense on both a cost center (responsibility) basis and in the aggregate. Accountants prepare a budgeted statement of financial position using information contained in the budgeted income statement. It is also influenced by policy decisions about dividends, inventory, credit, capital expenditures, and financial plans.

EXHIBIT 9–5   Budget Interrelationships

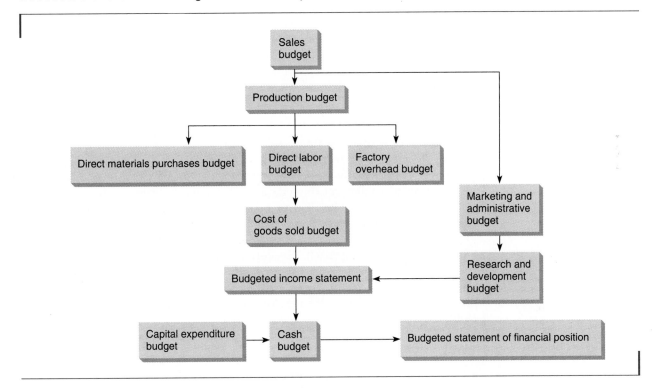

Sales Forecasts (L.O. 2)

Before preparing the master budget, companies prepare a forecast of sales for the budget period. Although the vice president of marketing is responsible for preparing sales forecasts, other individuals and factors are involved. Sales forecasts usually determine the activity level on which a company establishes all budgets. However, if a company can sell more than it can produce, it must first consider its production constraint. For example, if a company can sell 1,000 units but its manufacturing facilities produce only 750 units, it bases all budgets on a 750-unit activity level unless it acquires additional production facilities.

The vice president of marketing also considers internal factors, such as the historical sales pattern, desired profit, product characteristics (whether it is a new product or a seasonal one), and sales force estimates. Among other things, managers analyze previous period sales and other information for possible fluctuations caused by seasonal variations, economic cycles, and labor strikes. However, historical sales may not fully reflect previous period demand because most companies have no record of unfilled orders. A figure closer to past demand is unfilled orders added to past sales; unfortunately, this is usually unavailable.

Many external economic and social conditions—such as government monetary and fiscal policies for taxation and international trade—and the technological, social, and legal environment affect future sales. Industry prospects, purchasing power of the population, population shifts, and changes in buying habits are important considerations. If a causal relationship can be established, more accurate sales estimates result. For example, historical data may reveal a relationship between a company's sales and personal discretionary income or gross national product. A company may also study the relationships of its products with each other. A company should make allowances for varying conditions that affect products, territories, or the strength of competitors. For example, changes in sales promotion of the company and its competitors affect sales.

Employees' Experienced Judgment

The methods of estimating future sales vary widely depending on the products sold and channels of distribution used. A company's sales force can supply supervisors with sales estimates for their territories. Not only is information gained from a firsthand source but this can also stimulate the salespersons' interest in the budgeting process. The district marketing manager should review each of these individual estimates because they are often biased.

Executives can also refine sales estimates determined through other sources, as in the bottom-up approach. Executive experience provides subjective estimates of factors that are difficult to quantify, such as general economic and industry conditions, competition, and the quality of the sales force. At other times, companies begin their sales forecasting process with estimates from key executives.

Trend and Correlation Analysis

Past experience alone is not sufficient to forecast sales; therefore, most companies use a market research department or outside market research firm that develops and analyzes the sales forecast data centrally. Using correlation analysis, cycle projection, and trend analysis, market researchers arrive at projected sales. The market research department may also use motivation research to measure the factors influencing consumers' decisions. They study the subconscious motives of buyers using word association, in-depth interviews, and other behavioral science techniques. Such techniques may be of more use in making industry forecasts than in a sales forecast for a single company. Statistical forecasting techniques are most effective for products having stable market patterns. For products with markets that fluctuate considerably and require extensive sales promotion, subjective estimates are appropriate.

Market researchers may study actual sales for several years in the past as well as for the corresponding period in the previous year to project a **trend.** Using only historical sales data in forecasting has some weaknesses because some of the company's policies may have changed, which, in turn, affects future sales. For example, improved quality may have created a higher demand for the product. The company may have adopted more liberal credit terms. Managers should give the most recent historical data more significance than older data when using moving averages of past sales data, rather than an average of all available data for specific past periods. Plotting sales for previous periods on a moving-average basis may forecast secular or long-term trends.

Correlation analysis attempts to establish the relationship between the values of two attributes—that is, the relationship between an economic indicator (independent variable) and sales (dependent variable). Companies frequently use an economic indicator such as the gross national product (GNP) or a forecast of personal income. To use this method, the indicator must be predictable. A rela-

E X H I B I T 9–6   Using Regression Analysis in Predicting Sales

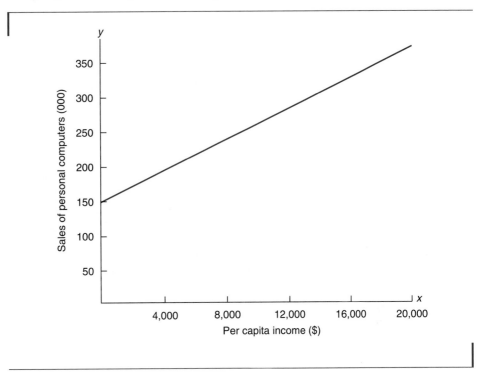

tionship must also exist between the indicator and the product for which sales are being forecasted. For example, in predicting sales for baby bottles, the projected birth rate is the independent variable. This relationship can predict sales for the entire industry or for one firm.

To illustrate this sales forecasting method, assume a relationship between personal computers and per capita income. We plot this relationship in Exhibit 9–6. We can use regression analysis, introduced in Chapter 3, to fit a straight line to the points. Assume that the line crosses the vertical axis at 150,000 personal computers. The slope of the line would be about 12 personal computers per dollar of per capita income. We can describe the relationship by this equation: $Y = 150,000 + 12x$. If per capita income is predicted to be $20,000, the sales forecast would be 390,000 personal computers.

Documentation. Forecasters should document their underlying assumptions for each forecast, major sources of information, and the techniques used to arrive at the final forecast. Documentation of the data provides a good source for reviewing the accuracy of the forecast. Documentation also enables forecasters to refine their assumptions. We must not overlook the importance of the sales forecast because if this forecast is weak, all budgets, in turn, become poor planning tools.

Territorial Sales Budget

The sales budget in Exhibit 9–7 is classified by monthly sales of products. A sales budget can also indicate whether purchasers are wholesalers, retailers, government agencies, or foreign buyers. With this customer breakdown, management can better determine the percentage of sales generated by each group. To

EXHIBIT 9–7 Sales Budget

	Product A		Product B		Product C		
	Quantity	Sales	Quantity	Sales	Quantity	Sales	Total
January	100	$ 10,000	1,150	$ 138,000	800	$ 144,000	$ 292,000
February ...	120	12,000	980	117,600	770	138,600	268,200
March	110	11,000	1,000	120,000	650	117,000	248,000
April	115	11,500	1,080	129,600	600	108,000	249,100
May	140	14,000	1,200	144,000	680	122,400	280,400
June	150	15,000	1,250	150,000	725	130,500	295,500
July	145	14,500	1,375	165,000	780	140,400	319,900
August	155	15,500	1,400	168,000	820	147,600	331,100
September ..	160	16,000	1,500	180,000	850	153,000	349,000
October	150	15,000	1,600	192,000	900	162,000	369,000
November ..	145	14,500	1,770	212,400	925	166,500	393,400
December ..	130	13,000	1,800	216,000	975	175,500	404,500
Total ...	1,620	$162,000	16,105	$1,932,600	9,475	$1,705,500	$3,800,100

HART COMPANY
Sales Budget
For Year Ending December 31, 19X2

simplify, the budgets illustrated in Exhibits 9–7 through 9–14 do not indicate customer groups or individual territories. They use only combined data.

Production-Related Budgets (L.O. 4)

After completing the sales budget, we prepare a production budget stating the physical units to manufacture. The production budget is the sales budget adjusted for any changes in inventory, as follows:

Units to produce = Budgeted sales
+ Desired ending finished goods inventory
+ Desired equivalent units in ending work in process inventory
− Beginning finished goods inventory
− Equivalent units in beginning work in process inventory

Note that we can apply the budgeting formula, Sources = Uses, for many budgeting decisions. For example, Beginning inventory (a source) + Units to produce (a source) = Desired ending inventory (a use) + Budgeted withdrawals for sales (a use). By solving for units to produce, we mathematically derive the production budget from its necessary antecedent, the sales budget.

Although their sales may be of a seasonal nature, many companies tend to stabilize their production through inventory. That is, inventory is the buffer absorbing extra production when demand is slack and from which they draw units during heavy demand periods. If work in process inventory does not constitute a significant portion of the inventory, we can ignore partially completed goods. We can also ignore them if a company does not extend the production cycle as in the case of pull systems using a just-in-time approach. Assume we obtain data about finished goods inventory and beginning work in process and its stage of comple-

EXHIBIT 9–8

HART COMPANY
Total Production Budget
For Year Ending December 31, 19X2

	Products		
	A	**B**	**C**
Units required for sales (from Exhibit 9–7)	1,620	16,105	9,475
Add ending inventory of finished units	80	350	130
Total finished units required	1,700	16,455	9,605
Less beginning inventory of finished units	65	395	495
Units to be transferred to finished goods	1,635	16,060	9,110
Add ending work in process inventory (in equivalent units)	20	150	320
	1,655	16,210	9,430
Less beginning work in process inventory (in equivalent units)	5	80	30
Equivalent units to be produced	1,650	16,130	9,400

tion from Hart Company's records. Management supplies desired ending inventory information. The inventory data are as follows:

	Work in Process Inventory				Finished Goods Inventory	
Product	**Beginning Units**	**Percent Processed**	**Ending Units**	**Percent Processed**	**Beginning Units**	**Ending Units**
A	50	10%	100	20%	65	80
B	200	40	300	50	395	350
C	100	30	400	80	495	130

Production Budget

Exhibit 9–8 illustrates a production budget using work in process and finished goods inventory. The production budget in Exhibit 9–9 reflects production each quarter for one product. (Note we cannot add horizontally the equivalent units in inventory to yield the total for 19X2. Instead, we use 70 beginning and 100 ending equivalent units for the year.)

The two production budgets in Exhibits 9–8 and 9–9 are readily adaptable for a company manufacturing a standard product. However, for a company that manufactures only after receipt of a customer order, plans have to be less detailed. Preferably, a company uses standardized direct material parts in production, thus allowing it to budget in a similar manner. The important factor in job order costing, performing manufacturing to customer specification, is to avoid delays and costly overtime by properly routing and scheduling work through the factory.

To provide as smooth a flow of production as possible, management should coordinate the marketing and production budgets. Often marketing personnel are not fully aware of the plant capacity available. They may fail to consider what the company's manufacturing facilities can produce. They may have to shift marketing efforts to avoid idle capacity and to fully utilize production facilities. Because the production budget determines the volume of manufacturing operations, it becomes the basis for the direct materials purchases budget, labor budget, and factory overhead budget.

EXHIBIT 9–9   Production Budget for One Product

HART COMPANY
Product A Production Budget
By Quarters for Year Ending December 31, 19X2

	First Quarter	Second Quarter	Third Quarter	Fourth Quarter	Total
Planned sales	330	405	460	425	1,620
Desired ending equivalent units in inventory	60	65	85	100	100
Total units to provide for	390	470	545	525	1,720
Less beginning equivalent units in inventory	70	60	65	85	70
Units to be produced	320	410	480	440	1,650

EXHIBIT 9–10   Direct Materials Purchases Budget

HART COMPANY
Direct Materials Purchases Budget
For Year Ending December 31, 19X2

	Material AA2	Material BB3	Total
Units needed for production (from below)	48,260	88,270	
Desired ending direct materials inventory	2,500	4,500	
Total material units to provide for	50,760	92,770	
Less: Beginning direct materials inventory	1,900	5,000	
Units to be purchased	48,860	87,770	
Unit purchase price	$ 1.10	$ 2.50	
Total purchase cost	$53,746	$219,425	$273,171

Direct material usage

	Production					
	Product A (1,650 units)	Product B (16,130 units)	Product C (9,400 units)	Total Direct Material Usage	Material Unit Cost	Cost of Material Used
AA2 (4 units per finished product for A, 2 for B, 1 for C)	6,600	32,260	9,400	48,260	$1.10	$ 53,086
BB3 (3 units per finished product for A, 4 for B, 2 for C)	4,950	64,520	18,800	88,270	$2.50	220,675
						$273,761

Direct Materials Purchases Budget

After determining the number of units of each product we plan to manufacture, we calculate the materials each operation requires. We then combine these requirements in a direct materials purchases budget, as shown in Exhibit 9–10. We prepare the budget in the unit of measure (pounds, gallons, etc.) used for the material. Exhibit 9–10 shows only two different material items to keep the illus-

EXHIBIT 9–11   Purchases Budget for One Material

HART COMPANY
Material AA2 Purchase Budget
By Quarters for Year Ending December 31, 19X2

Direct Material AA2	First Quarter	Second Quarter	Third Quarter	Fourth Quarter	Total
Units needed for production	8,990	11,000	12,420	15,850	48,260
Desired ending direct materials inventory	1,000	1,200	1,600	2,500	2,500
Total material units to provide for	9,990	12,200	14,020	18,350	50,760
Less: beginning direct materials inventory	1,900	1,000	1,200	1,600	1,900
Units to be purchased	8,090	11,200	12,820	16,750	48,860
Unit purchase price	$ 1.10	$ 1.10	$ 1.10	$ 1.10	$ 1.10
Total purchase cost	$8,899	$12,320	$14,102	$18,425	$53,746

tration simple. Managers indicate the desired level of ending direct materials inventory they wish to maintain. If they use a **just-in-time system,** inventory represents only the amount needed in production until the next order arrives. They do not need to stockpile inventory. For the just-in-time system to operate efficiently, suppliers must be reliable and provide parts of high quality. We obtain the beginning direct materials inventory balance from the inventory records.

Exhibit 9–10 summarizes the annual direct material needs, with data obtained from the monthly budgets for each direct material. Exhibit 9–11 illustrates the production and inventory requirements for Direct Material AA2 broken down on a quarterly basis. We can prepare a similar budget for each item of direct material, especially for the significant material items. Exhibits 9–10 and 9–11 show only direct material, since the factory overhead budget usually shows indirect material and supplies.

Note again that in determining units to purchase, we apply the formula, Sources = Uses, as follows: Beginning inventory (a source) + Purchases (a source) = Desired ending inventory (a use) + Units needed for production (a use). By solving for Purchases, we derive mathematically the direct materials purchases budget from its necessary antecedent, the production budget.

Direct Labor Budget

The direct labor budget reflects the number of units to be produced according to the production budget. Generally, this budget includes only direct labor as indirect labor is part of the factory overhead budget. The information provided in the direct labor budget guides a personnel department in filling positions so the required employee skills are available. By referring to the annual direct labor budget, the personnel department has time to make arrangements to either hire or lay off workers. After determining the number of direct labor-hours needed per period, we translate the hours into dollars by applying appropriate labor rates. Exhibit 9–12 illustrates a summarized annual direct labor budget because we assume Hart Company pays only one wage rate. We should prepare more detailed budgets for each department by month.

EXHIBIT 9–12   Direct Labor Budget

HART COMPANY
Direct Labor Budget
For the Year Ending December 31, 19X2

	Units Produced	Direct Labor-Hours per Unit	Total Hours	Total Budget @ $12 per Hour
Product A	1,650	3	4,950	$ 59,400
Product B	16,130	5	80,650	967,800
Product C	9,400	10	94,000	1,128,000
			179,600	$2,155,200

EXHIBIT 9–13   Factory Overhead Budget

HART COMPANY
Factory Overhead Budget
For the Year Ending December 31, 19X2
(at budgeted capacity of 11,225 machine-hours)

Indirect material	$ 94,000	
Indirect labor	75,000	
Depreciation—Variable portion	25,000	
Total variable overhead		$194,000
Insurance	$ 50,000	
Depreciation—Fixed portion	125,000	
Supervision	80,000	
Total fixed overhead		255,000
Total factory overhead		$449,000

($449,000 ÷ 11,225 hours = $40 per machine-hour)
Relevant range is 11,000 to 12,000 machine-hours

Factory Overhead Budget

Even though we can group factory overhead expenses in several ways, such as by function, cost behavior, or department, usually we use the natural expense classification. However, the natural expense classification, which involves such categories as utilities, indirect labor, and indirect material, has limited usefulness for budgeting purposes. Instead, we should prepare factory overhead budgets for each cost center so the cost centers' supervisors are held accountable and responsible for the costs incurred. We should make a distinction between controllable and noncontrollable costs so supervisors are held accountable for only those expenses over which they have control. An annual factory overhead budget similar to the one in Exhibit 9–13 summarizes each departmental factory overhead budget. Exhibit 9–13 shows a limited number of costs.

EXHIBIT 9–14   Cost of Goods Sold Budget

HART COMPANY
Cost of Goods Sold Budget
For the Year Ending December 31, 19X2

Direct materials used (from Exhibit 9–10)	$ 273,761
Direct labor (from Exhibit 9–12)	2,155,200
Factory overhead (from Exhibit 9–13)	449,000
Total current manufacturing costs	$2,877,961
Add: Work in process January 1, 19X2 (per accounting records)	11,563
Total costs to account for	$2,889,524
Less: Work in process, December 31, 19X2	61,156
Cost of goods manufactured	$2,828,368
Add: finished goods January 1, 19X2 (per accounting records)	111,344
Cost of goods available for sale	$2,939,712
Less: finished goods, December 31, 19X2 (see below)	55,559
Cost of goods sold	$2,884,153

	Unit Cost	Product A Units	Product A Amount	Product B Units	Product B Amount	Product C Units	Product C Amount
Direct Material AA2 ...	$ 1.10	4	$ 4.40	2	$ 2.20	1	$ 1.10
Direct Material BB3 ...	2.50	3	7.50	4	10.00	2	5.00
Direct labor	12.00	3	36.00	5	60.00	10	120.00
Factory overhead	4.00	10.2	40.80	3	12.00	5	20.00
			$88.70		$84.20		$146.10

	Unit Cost	Work in Process Equivalent Units	Work in Process Total Amount	Finished Goods Units	Finished Goods Total Amount
Ending balance:					
Product A	$ 88.70	20	$ 1,774	80	$ 7,096
Product B	84.20	150	12,630	350	29,470
Product C	146.10	320	46,752	130	18,993
			$61,156		$55,559

Cost of Goods Sold Budget

After determining the budgets for direct material, direct labor, and factory overhead, we summarize the data in a cost of goods sold budget, as illustrated in Exhibit 9–14. We show the unit cost for each of the three products so we can place a valuation on the ending balance of finished goods inventory. We obtain the beginning balance of finished goods inventory from the accounting records.

Summary

Budgets can be extremely useful internal control tools, but there is a problem if budget estimates and bases are not as accurate as possible. However, accuracy should not be interpreted as complexity; budgets should not be too complex for common usage. In addition, the budget should neither take the place of management nor be used to hide the inefficiencies of a company. Budgets can serve as excellent planning and control tools when managers devote attention to properly establishing them. Further, managers must explain to employees how they function.

Companies need to make a careful study of the behavior of costs before preparing flexible budgets. Flexible budgeting procedures are useful for determining the efficiency of operations because they compare actual costs at any output level against a budget adjusted to the actual activity level. A flexible budgeting approach eliminates distortions due to volume variations. The flexible budget formula, also known as the cost estimating function, is prepared in advance of operations for each department or cost center, indicating both fixed costs and the variable cost rates per unit. These budgeted costs can then be applied to various levels of activity. Flexible budgets are valuable tools for judging the efficiency of operations by comparing actual revenues and costs to the flexible budget adjusted for the actual level of activity.

To be effective, those individuals responsible for the operations that the budget is measuring should participate in the budget-setting process. They should know the criteria used in evaluation so they have a guide when incurring expenditures. The budgeting process allows for thorough review of operations. However, there is little value in merely determining that a difference between actual and budgeted performance exists. Instead, the true value of a budgetary program comes from identifying the causes of the variances. When used properly, budgets pave the way to higher morale and a better working relationship among employees and management.

Important Terms and Concepts

operating budgets, 296
financial budgets, 296
decentralization or differentiation, 298
rolling (continuous) budget, 300
bottom-up budgeting approach, 301
fixed (static) budgets, 301

flexible (variable) budgets, 301
flexible budget formula, 303
cost estimating function, 303
trend analysis, 308
correlation analysis, 308
just-in-time system, 313

Problem for Self-Study

Materials Purchases Budget

Alexander, Inc., manufactures Products X, Y, and Z. Each product requires different quantities of material input. Planned unit production of each product in 19X1 is 10,000 for X, 40,000 for Y, and 30,000 for Z. The direct material requirements for one unit of each product are

Product	Unit Material Requirements			
	A	B	C	D
X	3	—	2	—
Y	1	1	—	4
Z	2	2	1	3

Beginning and desired ending inventory as well as unit costs are as follows for each direct material:

Inventory in units:	A	B	C	D
January 1, 19X1	20,000	5,000	3,000	10,000
December 31, 19X1	8,000	1,000	6,000	30,000
19X1 unit cost	$4.00	$7.00	$8.00	$2.00

Direct material unit prices as budgeted are the delivered unit costs experienced.

Required:

Prepare a direct materials purchases budget for 19X1.

Solution to Problem for Self-Study

ALEXANDER, INC.
Direct Materials Purchases Budget
19X1

	Units
Direct Material A:	
Product X, 10,000 units @ 3	30,000
Product Y, 40,000 units @ 1	40,000
Product Z, 30,000 units @ 2	60,000
Production needs	130,000
Scheduled inventory decrease	(12,000)
Required to be purchased	118,000
Direct Material B:	
Product Y, 40,000 units @ 1	40,000
Product Z, 30,000 units @ 2	60,000
Production needs	100,000
Scheduled inventory decrease	(4,000)
Required to be purchased	96,000
Direct Material C:	
Product X, 10,000 @ 2	20,000
Product Z, 30,000 @ 1	30,000
Production needs	50,000
Scheduled inventory increase	3,000
Required to be purchased	53,000
Direct Material D:	
Product Y, 40,000 @ 4	160,000
Product Z, 30,000 @ 3	90,000
Production needs	250,000
Scheduled inventory increase	20,000
Required to be purchased	270,000

Direct Material	Quantity	Price	Total Purchase Price
A	118,000	$4	$ 472,000
B	96,000	7	672,000
C	53,000	8	424,000
D	270,000	2	540,000
			$2,108,000

Review Questions

1. Discuss the membership of the budget committee and the committee's functions.

2. What information is needed to prepare a direct materials purchases budget and a direct labor budget?

3. Why is preparing the sales budget a critical step in the budgeting process?

4. Why can't budgetary control systems be designed and operated in isolation of their organizational context?

5. Under which conditions do you think a fixed budget would be appropriate? What advantages does a flexible budget offer that a fixed budget does not?

6. Which factors should be evaluated in deciding to purchase enough materials to maintain a large ending inventory?

7. If a company's policy is that each month's units of ending inventory should be equal to 130 percent of the next month's units of sale, what may this suggest?

8. Discuss the rolling (continuous) budget approach and indicate any advantages that you see.

9. How is the number of units to produce determined? How is this shown on the production budget?

10. Why do some managers believe that the purpose of budgetary control has already been accomplished after a new budget for the next period has been prepared?

11. Compute the number of units of finished goods that management expects to have on March 1 if 75,000 units are to be manufactured in March, finished goods ending inventory of 16,000 units is desired, and sales are forecast to be 69,000 units in March.

CPA/CMA/CIA Multiple Choice Questions

1. (AICPA) A flexible budget is appropriate for a(an)

	Administrative Budget	Marketing Budget
a.	Yes	Yes
b.	Yes	No
c.	No	No
d.	No	Yes

2. (CIA) A company has estimated its production-expense budget to be $500,000 at 10,000 units of output. However, owing to a strike at a major competitor's plant, the company has determined that output should be increased to 20,000 units of output, although that means a substantial amount of overtime by employees at one-and-a-half normal pay. The total production budget was estimated based on last year's output of 12,000 units, using the flexible budgeting formula of $100,000 + $40 (units produced). This budget should be revised to

a. $580,000.
b. A number between $580,000 and $900,000
c. $900,000.
d. A number greater than $900,000.

3. (CMA) In developing a comprehensive budget for a manufacturing company, which one of the following items should be done first?

a. Development of a sales plan.
b. Determination of manufacturing capacity.
c. Development of the capital budget.
d. Determination of the advertising budget.
e. Preparation of a pro forma income statement.

4. (AICPA) Dean Company is preparing a flexible budget for 19X2 and the following maximum capacity estimates for Department M are available:

	At Maximum Capacity
Direct labor-hours	60,000
Variable factory overhead	$150,000
Fixed factory overhead	$240,000

Assume that Dean's normal capacity is 80 percent of maximum capacity. What would be the total factory overhead rate, based on direct labor-hours, in a flexible budget at normal capacity?

    a. $6.00.

    b. $6.50.

    c. $7.50

    d. $8.13.

5. (CMA) Which one of the following schedules would be the last item to be prepared in the normal budget preparation process?

    a. Direct labor budget.

    b. Cash budget.

    c. Cost of goods sold budget.

    d. Manufacturing overhead budget.

    e. Selling expense budget.

6. (CMA) When budgeting, the items to be considered by a manufacturing firm in going from a sales quantity budget to a production budget would be the

    a. Expected change in the quantity of work in process inventories.

    b. Expected change in the quantity of finished goods and work in process inventories.

    c. Expected change in the quantity of finished goods and raw material inventories.

    d. Expected change in the availability of raw material without regard to inventory levels.

    e. Sales value of the various products of the company.

7. (CMA) Flexible budgets

    a. Accommodate changes in the inflation rate.

    b. Are used to evaluate capacity utilization.

    c. Are static budgets that have been revised for changes in prices.

    d. Provide for all factors affecting company profitability.

    e. Accommodate changes in activity levels.

8. (AICPA) When a flexible budget is used, a decrease in production levels within a relevant range would

    a. Increase total fixed costs.

    b. Increase variable cost per unit.

    c. Decrease variable cost per unit.

    d. Decrease total costs.

9. (CMA) Wilson Company uses a comprehensive planning and budgeting system. The proper order for Wilson to prepare certain budget schedules would be

    a. Cost of Goods Sold, Balance Sheet, Income Statement, and Statement of Cash Flows.

    b. Income Statement, Balance Sheet, Statement of Cash Flows, and Cost of Goods Sold.

    c. Statement of Cash Flows, Cost of Goods Sold, Income Statement, and Balance Sheet.

    d. Statement of Cash Flows, Balance Sheet, Income Statement, and Cost of Goods Sold.

    e. Cost of Goods Sold, Income Statement, Statement of Cash Flows, and Balance Sheet.

10. (CMA) Adams Manufacturing Inc. produces farm tractors. The details of its budgeted Cost of Goods Manufactured Schedule should come from which of the following schedules?

    a. Cost of Goods Sold plus or minus the change planned in Finished Goods.

    b. Direct Material Used, Direct Labor, Manufacturing Overhead, and Work In Process.

    c. Purchases, Direct Labor, Manufacturing Overhead, Finished Goods, and Work In Process.

    d. Purchases, Raw Material, Work In Process, and Finished Goods.

    e. Production Quantity schedule and the Standard Bill of Materials.

Exercises

E9–1 Flexible Budgeting (L.O. 3)

Key Company operated its producing departments using a flexible budgeting approach. The company bases capacity on machine-hours with 18,000 machine-hours representing 90 percent normal capacity.

In May, the Mixing Department operated at an 82 percent volume level. The following budgets had previously been established for the Mixing Department:

	Percentage of Capacity	
	75%	**90%**
Machine-hours	15,000	18,000
Indirect material	$33,750	$40,500
Indirect labor	16,500	19,800
Repair supplies	12,900	15,480
Depreciation	1,800	1,800
Taxes	1,500	1,500
Insurance	2,000	2,000
	$68,450	$81,080

Required:

Prepare a flexible budget for the 82 percent volume level.

E9–2 Production Requirements (L.O. 4)

Budgeted data for the McHood Company indicate that 25,000 pounds should remain in direct materials ending inventory on January 31, 19X1. Beginning direct materials inventory on January 1, 19X1 contains 31,000 pounds. The expected cost per unit of direct materials is $0.75 per pound. The expected total cost of direct materials purchases is $150,000.

Required:

From the information, compute the production requirements in terms of pounds of direct materials.

E9–3 Production Budget (L.O. 4)

Salabor Company produces three soft drinks. The following tentative sales budget for the winter season of the company year is

Soft Drink	Units
Cola	500,000
Grape Soda	250,000
Ginger Ale	425,000

The inventory levels follow:

	Work in Process Inventory				Finished Goods Inventory	
	Beginning Units	**Percent Processed**	**Ending Units**	**Percent Processed**	**Beginning Units**	**Ending Units**
Cola	3,000	45%	3,500	50%	15,000	16,500
Grape Soda	5,000	33	4,215	40	13,000	11,350
Ginger Ale	4,175	40	4,050	22	12,175	16,775

Required:

Prepare a production budget by product lines.

E9–4 Factory Labor Budget (L.O. 4)

Elder Company manufactures Products A, B, and C in the Mixing, Fabricating, Finishing, and Wrapping Departments. Accountants developed standard costs for each product as follows for the budget year 19X1:

Product	19X1 Budgeted Unit Production	Standard Hours per Unit				Total Standard Direct Labor-Hours per Unit
		Mixing	Fabricating	Finishing	Wrapping	
A	200,000	.6	1.0	.4	.2	2.2
B	400,000	1.0	—	2.8	.6	4.4
C	300,000	1.6	3.0	—	.4	5
Hourly labor rate		$6.00	$5.50	$7.50	$6.50	
Annual capacity in direct labor-hours		900,000	1,200,000	1,250,000	350,000	

Elder bases annual capacity on a normal two-shift operation; any hours required in excess of budgeted capacity are provided by overtime labor at 150 percent of normal hourly rates.

Required:

Prepare a direct labor-hour requirements schedule for 19X1 and related direct labor cost budget.

E9–5 Flexible Budget Formula at Different Relevant Ranges (L.O. 3)

Edgar Manufacturing Company supplies you with the following factory overhead budgets for four plant volumes, all within different relevant ranges. Fixed costs (F) and variable costs (V) are indicated.

	Machine-Hours			
	500	800	1,000	1,200
Indirect materials (V)	$1,200	$1,700	$ 2,000	$ 2,350
Indirect labor (V)	950	2,000	3,000	3,500
Expired insurance (F)	1,000	1,850	2,200	2,400
Utilities (V)	600	1,000	1,200	1,350
Depreciation (F)	750	950	1,200	1,200
Miscellaneous (V)	500	900	1,100	1,200
	$5,000	$8,400	$10,700	$12,000

Required:

a. Determine the flexible budget formula for factory overhead for each of the four volumes. Budget formulas for the four volumes:

     500 machine-hours = _____

     800 machine-hours = _____

   1,000 machine-hours = _____

   1,200 machine-hours = _____

b. Assuming that each finished unit requires two hours of machine time, indicate the total estimated factory overhead cost per finished unit at each output.

     500 machine-hours = _____

     800 machine-hours = _____

   1,000 machine-hours = _____

   1,200 machine-hours = _____

E9–6 Production and Sales Budgets (L.O. 4)

Democrat, Inc., a producer of fine linen tablecloths, provides the following production records for the past four years. Provided in three different dimensions, tablecloths are simply referred to as Products A, B, and C.

| | Unit Sales in 000s | | | |
Product Line	Year 1	Year 2	Year 3	Year 4
A	50	75	100	125
B	200	220	242	266
C	500	450	405	365

The trends over the past four years are expected to extend to Year 5. Inventory estimates for Year 5 are

Product Line	000s Beginning Inventory	000s Ending Inventory
A	10	20
B	15	12
C	25	25

Required:

Prepare sales and production forecasts for Year 5, in units by each product line. (Round up to the next whole unit.)

E9–7 Direct Materials Purchases Requirements (L.O. 4)

Whitten Company will begin operations in January 19X1 to produce a finished product requiring the following materials:

Materials	Quantity	Price per Gallon
A	2 gallons	$2
B	6 gallons	$3
C	3 gallons	$1
D	1 gallon	$4

Sales for the first four months of the year have been scheduled as follows:

	Budgeted Unit Sales
January	4,000
February	4,250
March	4,600
April	4,800
May	5,000

At the end of each month, management desires an ending finished goods inventory that represents 20 percent of the next month's sales requirements. Also required is a direct materials ending inventory equal to 10 percent of the next month's production requirements.

Required:

Determine the direct materials purchases requirements for January, February, and March for each material.

E9–8 Flexible Budget Formula and Variances (L.O. 3)

Harold Company presents you with the following monthly budgets that were prepared at the beginning of the year. Budgeted capacity was set at 15,000 units:

| | Units Produced and Sold | |
	15,000	20,000
Direct material	$ 24,000	$ 32,000
Direct labor	18,000	24,000
Factory utilities	37,500	50,000
Production supervision salaries	7,500	7,500
Sales promotion	6,000	8,000
Marketing manager's salary	6,000	6,000
Administrative salaries	24,000	24,000
	$123,000	$151,500

At the end of the month, analysis of the cost records reveals that the following costs/expenses were incurred in producing and selling 17,000 units:

Direct material	$ 27,000
Direct labor	21,400
Factory utilities	42,000
Production supervision salaries	9,000
Sales promotion	6,300
Marketing manager's salary	6,100
Administrative salaries	24,500
	$136,300

Required:

a. Determine the flexible budget formula for all costs and expenses, expressing variable costs on a per unit basis.
b. Compute the factory overhead application rate.
c. Determine variances for each line item using a flexible budget, indicating whether the variances are favorable or unfavorable.

E9–9 Budgets Using Standards (L.O. 4)

Scott, Inc.'s standard cost of each unit in finished goods is

Finished Goods—Material A	$ 8
Material B	12
Direct labor	45
Factory overhead	18
	$83

The standard cost of Material A is $1.60 per pound and $2 for Material B. Scott pays direct labor workers $15 per hour.

Management expects to sell 10,000 units of the finished products in 19X1. Beginning inventory consists of Finished Goods—800 units, Material A—1,800 pounds, and Material B—2,500 pounds. Desired ending inventory is Finished Goods—1,600 units; Material A—2,200 pounds, and Material B—3,600 pounds.

Required:

a. Prepare a production budget.
b. Prepare a direct materials purchases budget.
c. Prepare a direct labor budget.

Problems

P9–10 Quantity to Order and Factors in Inventory Levels (L.O. 1)

Home Products Company management asks that you determine the number of gallons of Material X2R to order for March delivery. According to the production schedule, 2,800 gallons of Material X2R will be used in January; 4,600 gallons in February; 4,000 gallons in March; and 10,000 gallons in April.

The material ledger card showed 3,700 gallons in inventory on January 1, 4,200 gallons on order for January delivery, and 4,100 gallons on order for February delivery. Management wants to have an April 1 inventory equal to 20 percent of the April production needs.

Required:

a. Determine the number of gallons to order for March delivery.
b. Determine the estimated number of gallons on hand on March 1.
c. Assume a member of top management believes that too much storage space and company funds and expenses are being incurred by maintaining an inventory level of 20

percent. Suggest ways that the company can reduce the inventory and safety stock maintained.

d. Name important characteristics of the company and its environment that influence the amount of inventory needed to maintain the production flow.

P9–11 Budget Preparation (L.O. 4)

Bristol, Inc., budgets sales for 1,000 units to be sold for $50 each. Direct materials required are ½ pound of B2 and 2 pounds of G8. The estimated cost of direct material of B2 is $2 per pound, while G8 is expected to be $0.70 per pound. Direct labor of 2.5 hours is required per unit; the direct labor rate is expected to be $5. The factory overhead application rate is 80 percent of direct labor dollars. Management indicates that inventories are to be as follows:

	January 1, 19X1	January 31, 19X1
Finished goods	170 units ($4,250)	200 units
Direct material—B2	100 pounds ($200)	185 pounds
Direct material—G8	185 pounds ($129.50)	165 pounds

Bristol uses LIFO inventory costing.

Required:

a. Prepare the following for January 19X1:
   (1) Direct materials purchases budget.
   (2) Direct labor budget.
   (3) Cost of goods sold budget.
b. Assuming FIFO costing, calculate the cost of goods sold.

P9–12 Quantity to Order, Factors in Inventory Levels, and Just-in-Time System (L.O. 1)

Management of the Mattie Crawford Company asks that you determine the number of gallons of Material ABC to order for March delivery. According to the production schedule, workers will use 4,900 gallons of Material ABC in January; 5,500 gallons in February; 7,000 in March; and 9,000 in April.

The material ledger card showed 5,600 gallons in inventory on January 1; 6,900 gallons on order for January delivery; and 6,800 on order for February delivery. Management wants to have an April 1 inventory equal to 15 percent of the April production needs.

Required:

a. Determine the number of gallons to order for March delivery.
b. Determine the estimated number of gallons on hand on March 1.
c. Assume management desires to have an April 1 inventory that reflects 90 percent of the production for April. Would this be excessive? Explain your answer.
d. Discuss how the ordering pattern of this company would differ if they adopted a just-in-time system.
e. Explain the impact the just-in-time system should have on communication and cooperation with suppliers and the suppliers' reliability and quality control.
f. List some factors to consider in deciding on the inventory level to maintain.

P9–13 Preparation of Five Production Budgets (L.O. 4)

The budget committee of Econo Company provides the following information. The budget period is the year ending December 31, 19X4. The company manufactures only one chemical product selling for $100 per gallon.

They expect a total of 10,000 gallons of finished goods to be sold during 19X4. Finished goods expected to be on hand on January 1, 19X4, total 2,500 gallons with 2,800 gallons on hand on December 31, 19X4.

Direct materials expected to be on hand on January 1, 19X4, total 1,000 gallons; direct materials expected to be on hand on December 31, 19X4, total 1,200 gallons. Econo uses only one kind of direct material to produce the product; 1.5 gallons of direct material are needed to produce each gallon of finished goods, due to evaporation. Direct materials are expected to continue to cost $20 per gallon during 19X4.

Manufacturing each product requires five hours of direct labor and direct labor workers receive $5.10 per hour.

Accountants apply factory overhead to work in process on the basis of direct labor-hours. Variable factory overhead at the expected level of operations is expected to amount to $150,075. Fixed overhead is expected to be $110,000.

The finished goods inventory on January 12, 19X4, amounts to $199,800.

Required:

Prepare the following budgets:

a. Sales budget.
b. Production budget.
c. Direct materials purchases budget.
d. Direct labor budget.
e. Cost of goods sold budget using FIFO inventory costing.
f. Cost of goods sold budget using LIFO inventory costing.

P9–14 Variances under a Fixed Budget (L.O. 3)

Fleet Company has requested that you help them calculate their monthly variances. They supply you with the following budget, which has been broken down on a monthly basis:

FLEET COMPANY—COST CENTER A
Fixed Budget
Factory Overhead
For the Month Beginning January 19X2

Direct labor-hours		5,000
Indirect materials	$ 5,000	
Indirect labor	10,000	
Repair supplies	2,500	
Utilities	3,000	
Miscellaneous	2,050	
Total variable costs	$22,550	
Insurance	$ 400	
Depreciation—equipment	600	
Utilities	1,000	
Superintendent	1,500	
Total fixed cost	$ 3,500	
Total factory overhead	$26,050	

The actual data is as follows:

Actual direct labor-hours		4,500
Indirect material	$ 4,600	
Indirect labor	9,000	
Repair supplies	3,000	
Utilities—variable	2,600	
Miscellaneous	1,900	
Insurance	390	
Depreciation—equipment	650	
Utilities—fixed	980	
Superintendent	1,250	
	$24,370	

Required:

a. Compute the variances under a fixed budget.
b. If you do not believe the variances you computed in Requirement *a* properly reflect the true conditions, calculate another set of variances and indicate why you think this set is better.

P9–15 Flexible Budget Preparation with Price Increases (L.O. 3)

Each unit produced by Paige, Inc., requires 0.4 hours of direct labor. Last year, when the company operated at 80 percent of capacity, 120,000 units were produced. The following percentages indicate the makeup of fixed and variable costs:

Fixed Costs	Percent	Variable Costs	Percent
Depreciation	35	Factory supplies	20
Rent	20	Utilities	40
Factory supervisor's salary ...	15	Indirect material	30
Insurance	30	Indirect labor	8
	100	Miscellaneous	2
			100

Management expects to increase next year's volume to 95 percent of capacity. Total factory overhead is expected to be $360,000 at this level, using a ratio of variable cost to fixed cost of 2:1, with variable costs based on direct labor-hours. Not included in the $360,000 is a recent notice of a 20 percent price increase from the utility company. This utilities price rise is expected regardless of any capacity changes. (Note that 2:1 variable to fixed cost ratio will not be in effect after the utilities price increase.)

Required:

a. Prepare a flexible budget for next year using 80, 95, 100, and 120 percent capacity levels; for each capacity level, determine the factory overhead rate per hour of production. Round to whole dollars for total costs, but carry variable cost per hour to five decimal places. Determine the budget formula for each line expense item.
b. Explain why the total factory overhead rate per hour has an inverse relationship to capacity.

P9–16 Conflict of Policy on Production Budget Preparation (L.O. 1)

Gloria, Inc., produces shirts. When the plant is operating at 90 percent of capacity, it can produce 80,000 shirts in one month. This level, which is considered full capacity, requires a 45-hour workweek. The company tries to follow a policy of no personnel layoffs by adjusting the hours in the workweek to maintain a constant work force. When the workweek is reduced to 40 hours, 72,000 shirts are produced monthly; at 35 hours, only 64,000 shirts are produced.

Maximum storage capacity for Finished Goods Inventory is 40,000 shirts. The firm's policy is to have a minimum of 10,000 shirts on hand for special orders.

The sales forecast for next year is as follows:

January	....	72,000	July	88,000
February	....	46,000	August	80,000
March	....	62,000	September	72,000
April	....	66,000	October	90,000
May	....	72,000	November	92,000
June	....	76,000	December	62,000

Beginning finished goods inventory for next year consists of 10,000 shirts. Management desires a supply of 20,000 shirts on hand at year-end.

Required:

a. Complete a monthly unit production budget for next year indicating monthly beginning and ending inventory balances assuming that:
(1) 72,000 shirts are produced monthly.
(2) 80,000 shirts are produced monthly.
b. Using each of the production budgets prepared in Requirement a, indicate the months in which (1) management policy, (2) storage capacity, and (3) availability of product to meet sales demand are violated.
c. Prepare monthly production and sales budgets that do not violate any of the three factors mentioned in Requirement b. The workweek can be increased only in even increments of five hours from one month to the next because of layoff policies.

P9–17 Preparation of Various Budgets (L.O. 4)

McBrayer Corporation manufactures and sells Products A and B. In July 19X1, McBrayer's budget department gathered the following data to project sales and budget requirements for 19X2.

19X2 Projected Sales

Product	Units	Price
A	50,000	$100
B	75,000	$ 50

Inventories—in units

Product	Expected January 1, 19X2	Desired December 31, 19X2
A	30,000	25,000
B	10,000	12,000

Producing one unit of A and B requires the following direct materials:

		Amount per Unit	
Direct material	Unit	A	B
R	lbs.	3	6
S	lbs.	4	3
T	each		1

Projected direct material data for 19X2 are as follows:

Direct Materials	Anticipated Purchase Price	Expected Inventories January 1, 19X2	Desired Inventories December 31, 19X2
R	$10 per lb.	40,000 lbs.	35,000 lbs.
S	$ 5 per lb.	30,000 lbs.	32,000 lbs.
T	$ 3 per unit	6,000 each	10,000 each

Projected direct labor requirements for 19X2 and rates are as follows:

Product	Hours per Unit	Rate per Hour
A	4	$6
B	5	$8

Accountants apply overhead at the rate of $5 per direct labor-hour.

Required:

Based on these projections and budget requirements for 19X2 for A and B, prepare the following budgets for 19X2:

a. Sales budget (in dollars).
b. Production budget (in units).
c. Raw materials purchase budget (in quantities).
d. Raw materials purchase budget (in dollars).
e. Direct labor budget (in dollars).
f. Budgeted finished goods inventory at December 31, 19X2 (in dollars).

P9–18 Territorial Sales and Production Budgets (L.O. 4)

Earth Products, Inc., plans expansion into the eastern territory after experiencing success in the western territory. The company forecasts eastern territory sales based on western territory forecasted sales data.

Forecasted sales data for the western territory for the quarter ending March 31, 19X2:

	Product 1		Product 2		Product 3	
	Quantity	Unit Sales Price	Quantity	Unit Sales Price	Quantity	Unit Sales Price
January	100	$56.00	1,150	$11.00	800	$8.00
February	120	57.00	980	10.00	770	7.00
March	110	53.00	1,000	10.00	650	7.50

Management plans to introduce only Product 1 and Product 2 in the eastern territory. They base forecasts of the sales quantities on a percentage of the western market for each product.

	Product 1		Product 2	
	Percentage of Western Market	Unit Sales Price	Percentage of Western Market	Unit Sales Price
January	70%	$56	18%	$8
February	60	58	20	8
March	60	58	22	9

On January 1, 19X2, an inventory count of Product 1 revealed 42 finished units; 525 units of Product 2; and 140 units of Product 3. Management desires an ending inventory on January 31, 19X2, of 50 units of Product 1, 325 units of Product 2, and 160 units of Product 3.

Material and labor requirements for each of the products are as follows:

	Product 1	Product 2	Product 3
Material 229	3 pounds	5 pounds	7 pounds
Material 415	4 gallons	3 gallons	5 gallons
Direct labor	3 hours	5 hours	4 hours

Material 229 costs $1.80 per pound, while Material 415 is expected to cost $2.20 per gallon. Direct labor workers are under a union contract which specifies that they receive $9.80 per hour. On January 1, 19X2, an inventory count showed 1,110 pounds of Material 229 and 1,600 gallons of Material 415. Management desires an ending inventory for each of these materials that is 30 percent of the material needed for the next month's sales.

Required:

a. Prepare monthly sales budgets for the first quarter for each territory broken down for each of the three products. Round to the nearest dollar.
b. Prepare a production budget for January only for both territories combined.
c. Prepare a direct materials purchases budget for January only for both territories including any needed direct materials usage budgets. Round to the nearest dollar.
d. Prepare a direct labor budget for January only for both territories combined. Round to the nearest dollar.

P9–19 Variances Using a Fixed and a Flexible Budgeting Approach (L.O. 3)

The 1,000-bed ARD Hospital is in a large metropolitan area. Because the hospital has a number of highly specialized physicians, it draws patients from a 300-mile radius. The hospital experiences greater capacity in the winter months, up to 95 percent occupancy; in the summer months capacity often declines to 75 percent occupancy. The administrator believes that 85 percent capacity represents normal capacity, and this is the basis used for budgeting.

The January 19X3 budget for the laundry department is as follows:

1,000-BED ARD HOSPITAL LAUNDRY DEPARTMENT
Fixed Budget
For the Month Beginning January 1, 19X3

	Budget 850 Beds 85 Percent Capacity
Variable costs:	
Linen replacement	$ 12,801
Detergent and other cleaning supplies	6,290
Utilities	6,000
Total variable costs	$ 25,091

Fixed costs:

Laundry supervisors' salaries	$ 10,180
Laundry washers' salaries	26,260
Laundry flatwork ironers	61,170
Laundry travel expense	190
Total fixed costs	$ 97,800
Total costs	$122,891

Due to an emphasis in the community on obtaining flu shots, the hospital had only an 80 percent occupancy in January. At the end of January, the controller determines that the hospital incurred the folllowing actual costs:

Variable costs:

Linen replacement	$ 12,640
Detergent and other cleaning supplies	6,000
Utilities	5,800
Total variable costs	$ 24,440

Fixed costs:

Laundry supervisors' salaries	$ 11,010
Laundry washers' salaries	25,900
Laundry flatwork ironers	62,000
Laundry travel expense	200
Total fixed costs	$ 99,110
Total costs	$123,550

Required:

a. Compute the variances by line items for the laundry department for January using the fixed budget given; indicate if they are favorable (F) or unfavorable (U).

b. Comment on the budgeting approach used.

c. Assuming you convince the hospital administrators that they should adopt a flexible budgeting approach, construct a budget for 80 percent (800-bed), 85 percent (850-bed), and 90 percent (900-bed) occupancy and give the budget formula by line item.

d. Using the information you computed in Requirement *c*, perform variance analyses for each expense item using the appropriate flexible budget; indicate if variances are favorable (F) or unfavorable (U).

P9–20 Production and Labor Budgets (CMA) (L.O. 4)

Roletter Company makes and sells artistic frames for pictures of weddings, graduations, christenings, and other special events. Bob Anderson, controller, is responsible for preparing Roletter's master budget and has accumulated this information for 19X2.

	19X2				
	January	**February**	**March**	**April**	**May**
Estimated unit sales	10,000	12,000	8,000	9,000	9,000
Sales price per unit	$50.00	$47.50	$47.50	$47.50	$47.50
Direct labor-hours per unit	2.0	2.0	1.5	1.5	1.5
Wage per direct labor-hour	$8.00	$8.00	$8.00	$9.00	$9.00

Labor related costs include pension contributions of $0.25 per hour, workers' compensation insurance of $0.10 per hour, employee medical insurance of $0.40 per hour, and social security taxes. Assume that as of January 1, 19X2, the base figure for computing social security taxes is $37,800 and that the rates are 7 percent for employers and 6.7 percent for employees. The cost of employee benefits paid by Roletter on its employees is treated as a direct labor cost.

Roletter has a labor contract that calls for a wage increase to $9 per hour on April 1, 19X2. The firm has installed new, labor-saving machinery that will be fully operational by March 1, 19X2.

Roletter expects to have 16,000 frames on hand at December 31, 19X1, and has a policy of carrying an end-of-month inventory of 100 percent of the following month's sales plus 50 percent of the second following month's sales.

Required:

a. Prepare a production budget and a direct labor budget for Roletter Company by month and for the first quarter of 19X2. Both budgets may be combined in one schedule. The direct labor budget should include direct labor-hours and show the detail for each direct labor cost category.

b. Determine for each item in Roletter's production budget and its direct labor budget the other component(s) of the master budget (budget package) that would also use these data.

Cases

C9–21 Evaluating Budget Cuts (L.O. 2)

Thelma Ezell, Inc., is a small, dynamic, and very successful electronics company. In its first year of operations, management decided the accounting system must keep pace with the rapid changes taking place in the firm. Thus, the system has become complex. The original purpose of accounting was to provide profitability data for use by top management, since the major concerns of the company were survival and preparation for the future. If the company proved successful, the original members of the management team would receive sizable rewards in promotions and increases in stock ownership. As the company began to grow, however, the reporting system changed since there were fewer and fewer direct personal benefits from increases in corporate profits.

In the last few years, the focus has been on greater accomplishment. As a result, the accounting system has developed another set of reports that emphasize budget aspects rather than departmental profitability. These reports include the standard, or goal, to be used as a measuring stick of performance and the actual results of operation. Management has found that standards are more acceptable when operating personnel participate in their establishment; therefore, the division manager being evaluated is allowed sufficient voice in setting the standards. Budgets are determined at the division manager level and are discussed and revised until each division manager is satisfied with the budget for his or her division. Then each division manager subdivides this budget among the various departments.

Division managers are concerned primarily with their overall performance because they are judged on whether they meet the aggregate goals. Determining how these goals are achieved is the division manager's job. Generally, division managers believe that it is as bad to be under target as to be over target. If the division is under target, either the manager was too optimistic in the projection or the projection had slack in it; if over target, the project was either incorrect or new, unplanned costs have appeared.

An insight into this budgeting process can be gained by examining a specific division. Jay Hugg's report at midyear shows his departments' goals and expenditures have been:

Department	Goal	Expenditures	Variance
A	$100,000	$110,000	$10,000 unfavorable
B	100,000	90,000	10,000 favorable
C	100,000	100,000	—
	$300,000	$300,000	$ —

The original division budget was $600,000, equally divided among three departments. Jay is concerned that Department A has exceeded its goal, but Department B has offset this variance, and the division as a whole is on target. Jay is considering taking $10,000 out of B's budget and transferring it to A's.

Required:

a. Give your reactions to this budgeting system.

b. Explain if you would advise the division manager to make this trade-off of $10,000 between departments.

    c. Assume that at midyear the entire division's budget must be cut.
       (1) How would you advise Jay to pass the cut along to subordinate departments?
       (2) To what extent should human factors be considered in this decision?
       (3) Discuss the order in which specific budget items should be cut.
       (4) What do you think of a deep-cut approach that dictates an arbitrary cut of X percent across the board?

C9–22 Appropriation Budgets and Implications of Budgetary Systems (L.O. 1)

Five years ago Randy Mart, president of Leisure Products, announced plans to enter the computer market and began appointing senior executives to a microcomputer division. However, the company soon realized that competition was stiffer than anticipated and that they had failed to prepare adequate plans for this venture. As a result, the company suffered alarming financial reversals in this division, but Mart insisted that the fault was due to the executives' lack of expertise in this area as well as inadequate dedication to company goals. The president was correct in forecasting increased demand for company products other than microcomputers. Production activity was expanded in these divisions to meet the larger market.

Before leaving on a recent trip to visit plants in Japan that were developing unique software applications for microcomputers, Mart announced the reassignment of key senior executives. In his absence, four of the senior executives, who had formerly been in the microcomputer division, convinced the board of directors that Mart's reorganization was inappropriate and that he should be replaced. They were so successful that when Mart returned, he was handed a letter of resignation for his signature.

Guy Cunningham was brought in to assume presidency. Cunningham had worked his way up through factory operations and was an expert on matters dealing with production. However, his experience with administrative work was limited. He soon let it be known indirectly that he considered administrative departments as necessary evils because they represented expenses that had to be allocated to revenue-producing departments.

Cunningham's former employment was as president of a manufacturing concern about the same size as Leisure Products, except that his former company manufactured few product lines in large lots and sold them to relatively few customers. Leisure Products, on the other hand, makes a wide variety of products in small lots and sells them in small orders to many customers. Cunningham was amazed at the size of the office force of Leisure Products and believed they were overstaffed.

Cunningham obtained past data showing the number of employees by administrative department. He was told by a number of the department heads that past top management had given them freedom to add to their staffs as they saw fit, except that new supervisors and assistants to department heads were to be cleared with the president. Budgets had been established for all factory departments, but no budgetary control procedures had been developed for the administrative departments. The administrative departments included Personnel, Purchasing, Credit and Collections, Order Filling, and Accounting. A monthly report of expenses was furnished to all department heads.

After studying the situation, Cunningham called a conference with the vice presidents and showed them his plan for adopting an appropriation budget for the administrative departments and for later expanding its adoption to all departments. Under this approach, fixed amounts were to be established for each department which could be applied to achieve the objectives of the organizational unit for the next period. The vice president of finance had previously worked in a governmental unit and did not believe this budgeting system would be appropriate for Leisure Products. He convinced Cunningham to postpone adoption of this budgeting plan.

Word leaked to the administrative department heads that the new president had been heard to remark, "I must turn this company around quickly; otherwise, I will also be asked to sign a letter of resignation. Therefore, I should be an autocratic boss and impose a budget even if it isn't an appropriation budget." These department heads began meeting informally to discuss possible future events. They knew that some of their departments had, in fact, overexpanded their staffs. Some of these department heads had been employed by Leisure for 15 years and commented, "I wish we could go back to the good ole days."

However, the personnel and purchasing department heads knew that their own departments could not handle additional work without more help and that, with announced plans for expansion, more work was expected. These two department heads realized that they would have to do their best to convince the new president that their departments should have increased budgets, reflecting the additional employees needed in the near future.

Required:

a. Discuss the behavioral impact you would expect Randy Mart's replacement as president to have on implementing the budgetary system.
b. If Leisure Products should adopt an appropriation basis for its budgeting process
   (1) Describe the expected effect on the department heads' behavior.
   (2) Explain why these department heads would likely behave in this manner.
c. Contrast the behavioral implications on the budgetary control system if Leisure Products employs a participative versus an imposed budgetary approach.
d. Suggest how Leisure's top management can effectively apply the expectancy theory of motivation in implementing their budgetary system.
e. Compare the administrative department heads' behavior before Cunningham assumed the presidency with their expected behavior after implementation of a new budget system by Cunningham. Explain the changes in behavior.
f. Describe the accounting data the purchasing and personnel department heads could use to support their conviction that they are performing efficiently and need additional funding.
g. Describe the role the accounting department head should play in light of the new management style. How will the administrative department heads react to the accountant's monthly reports of departmental activity?

C9–23 Impact of Automation on Budgeting and Strategic Planning (L.O. 1, 2)

Annual sales for automobiles produced by Meador, Inc., are in the range of $40-$50 million; annual sales increases for the past four years have averaged 6 percent. Over 800 persons are employed including national account salespersons and traveling sales representatives. The home office and production plant are located in Grand Rapids, Michigan, and all products are distributed in the western United States.

Marketing personnel pride themselves on their ability to convince management that additional varieties and features of their automobiles should be made available to the public. Thus, now consumers have an extensive range of options available.

Management has contacted consultants to evaluate their plant to determine if newer technology would be cost beneficial. The consultants find a snake-type process production organization that fails to follow straight-line flows. They also point out several areas where robotics would be appropriate; however, management believes that it should approach this environment very slowly and has tentatively decided to install robotics in a simple welding process, rather than utilize these in the more complex painting and testing arenas.

The consultants also are amazed at the vast amount of inventory Meador carries. In fact, the consultants summarize their feelings to top management in the following remark: "Inventory is evidence of all management's problems." The consultants suggest management adopt a just-in-time (JIT) inventory system. However, Meador's conservative management ignores this suggestion on the basis that their suppliers are entirely too unreliable and they don't want to miss a sale.

Meador uses a plantwide overhead rate applied on the basis of direct labor. Overhead is allocated to cost centers and then manufacturing departments assign material, direct labor, and overhead costs to products.

Required:

a. What major topics should be addressed in the company's strategic planning issues, ignoring whether the new technology is installed or not?

b. Why did you select the topics indicated in Requirement *a*?

c. What initial specific procedure will be followed each year in developing the master budget? Indicate the factors that will impact upon this beginning budgeting step.

d. What is the impact on the budget procedures of having so many options available for consumers?

e. What will be the effect on the following if the expensive new technology is correctly installed and implemented?

(1) Labor and factory overhead budgets.

(2) Product quality.

f. What is the meaning of the consultant's statement regarding inventory being evidence of management's problems?

g. What is your reaction to management's decision regarding JIT? What do you see as a solution to their real problem?

CHAPTER

10

Nonmanufacturing Budgets, Forecasted Statements, and Behavioral Issues

CHAPTER OBJECTIVES

After studying this chapter, you should be able to:

1. Prepare budgets for marketing, administrative, and research activities.
2. Estimate cash collections from credit sales and cash disbursements needed in preparing a cash budget.
3. Prepare a budgeted statement of income and statement of financial position, including gross profit analysis.
4. Compare appropriation, incremental, and zero-base budgeting.
5. Understand inherent behavioral implications of budgeting and how the misuse of budgets leads to long-run problems.

Introduction

As introduced in Chapter 9, budgets are important in internal control. If properly developed and followed, the budgetary process can be a springboard for many control techniques. Companies implement control by measuring and comparing actual results with budgeted plans at designated intervals. This chapter discusses marketing and administrative budgets, cash budgets, and forecasted statements. Also, we emphasize the importance of companywide participation and recognition of the human factors involved in the budgeting process.

Today many companies sell their products through a multitude of channels. To prevent excessive inventories, accurate forecasts from marketing personnel are essential. When budgets are unreliable, company resources are unavailable to produce needed goods or services. Thus, budgets provide a means for communications among accounting, production, and marketing personnel.

Marketing and Administrative Budgets (L.O. 1)

It is usually more difficult to control and budget marketing and administrative expenses than production costs because marketing and administrative functions lack standardization. Because these expenses are often large, management should also apply budgeting techniques to this area. Exhibit 10–1 illustrates an annual marketing and administrative expense budget classified as to fixed and variable expenses. Accountants break down the annual budget on a monthly basis and then by individual expense budgets for each marketing function. This

EXHIBIT 10-1   Marketing and Administrative Expense Budget

HART COMPANY
Marketing and Administrative Expense Budget
For Year Ending December 31, 19X2

Variable marketing expenses:		
Salaries and wages	$ 19,800	
Sales commissions	20,000	
Advertising	20,000	
Traveling	28,000	
Total variable marketing expenses		$ 87,800
Fixed marketing expenses:		
Warehousing	$ 60,000	
Advertising	30,000	
Marketing manager's salary	66,000	
Total fixed marketing expenses		156,000
Total marketing expenses		$243,800
Variable administrative expenses:		
Clerical wages	$ 40,000	
Supplies	20,213	
Total variable administrative expenses		$ 60,213
Fixed administrative expenses:		
Depreciation	$ 90,000	
Salaries	100,000	
Total fixed administrative expenses		190,000
Total administrative expenses		$250,213
Total marketing and administrative expenses		$494,013

encourages a consideration of the factors affecting expenses. For example, the promotional budget should consider the projects and dollars involved and the timing of the projects.

Promotional Budgets

Promotional budgets are difficult to establish because so many factors influence the success of promotional campaigns. Promotional activities include advertising, personal selling, publicity, sales promotion, and public relations. Availability of money or credit, the salesperson's technique, and economic conditions are influences. The time lag between advertising expenditures and sales also increases the difficulty of setting the promotional budget. Often companies use one of the following bases for establishing the promotional budget: a percentage of sales, an amount per unit of product in budgeted sales, competitors' actions, an all we can afford amount, market research, or the task method.

Fixed Percentage of Sales. Even though setting the promotional budget as a fixed percentage of sales is a popular approach because it makes additional funds available for following a favorable market, this method lacks flexibility. Also, we assume sales result from promotional activities rather than vice versa. It is more logical to use this approach to correlate advertising appropriations with forecasted sales.

Amount per Unit. Instead of setting the promotional budget as a percentage of sales, managers may base the promotional budget on a unit cost per product grouping, per customer, or other segment. This approach is easily adapted with flexible budgeting using standard costs. For example, managers may set the promotional budget based on the cost per promotion item mailed, cost per newspaper inch, or cost per minute of radio or television time.

Competitors' Actions. Companies may gauge their promotional expenditures by competitors' actions to prevent spending more than competitors. However, merely reacting to competitors causes a company to ignore its own competitive strengths. Instead, many factors including demographics should affect the specific type and kind of media used for advertising in each territory.

All We Can Afford. This method disregards the relationship between promotional costs and promotional effects; it funds promotional activities only after budgeting all other expenses. One form of this approach is to specify a fixed sum to spend for advertising without regard to other factors.

Market Research. Market research can determine the probable relationship between demographic and psychographic characteristics and the promotional medium chosen. In determining promotional expenditures, marketing managers should consider the density of the population, whether the area is urban or rural, types of industry found in the market territory, the characteristics of the target market, and climate. To observe the returns from incremental increases in these costs, management can vary the amount spent on promotional activities in limited market areas.

Task Method or Sales Objective. The task method establishes a definite promotional objective for each product, such as a desired level of customer awareness. The promotional budget is the total amount of money considered necessary to meet each product's objective.

Because advertising is a **discretionary cost** arising from periodic appropriation decisions that reflect top management policies, the size of the advertising budget may merely be the amount of funds available. If there are excess funds, companies increase their advertising budgets. While there is no logic in this approach, the appropriation may reflect the business climate in which a company is operating. Because of the significance of advertising expenditures, however, companies should use a more valid approach. Most companies, in practice, use a combination of the approaches presented. Chapter 19 illustrates standards for advertising and personal selling activities.

Research and Development Budgets

A budget is the most useful tool for both planning and controlling research and development expenses. In the short run, a company must direct research and development efforts toward projects expected to earn a satisfactory rate of return on the funds invested. The long-run objective is assurance that research programs are in line with forecasted future market trends.

Budgets for research and development activities should be broken down by projects. Each project should then be broken down into departments or phases, and the completion date for each phase forecasted. Exhibit 10–2 illustrates a

EXHIBIT 10–2   New Product Budget

BUDGET FOR NEW PRODUCT ZERXX
Project director: Harold Douglas
Project number: 2118

| Expenses | Department or Phase | | | Total Budget |
	Planning	Production	Promotion	
Direct materials	$ 4,000	$ 26,300	$ 2,700	$ 33,000
Labor cost	1,000	29,000	6,000	36,000
Consulting fees	10,000	3,000	5,000	18,000
Indirect labor	1,500	2,800	300	4,600
Supplies and other indirect material	1,500	6,800	2,900	11,200
Equipment	–0–	40,000	–0–	40,000
Overhead allocation	1,500	9,000	3,000	13,500
	$19,500	$116,900	$19,900	$156,300
Estimated machine-hours	50	300	100	450
Completion date	May 31, 19X1	January 31, 19X2	April 30, 19X2	

EXHIBIT 10–3   Status Report for New Product

STATUS REPORT FOR NEW PRODUCT ZERXX—PROJECT NUMBER 2118
Production Department
December 31, 19X1

Expense	Budget	Expenditures to Date	Commitments	Encumbered	Unexpended
Direct materials	$ 26,300	$ 25,100	$ 100	$ 25,200	$ 1,100
Labor cost	29,000	20,000	1,000	21,000	8,000
Consulting fees	3,000	2,700	200	2,900	100
Indirect labor	2,800	2,300	700	3,000	(200)
Supplies and other indirect material	6,800	4,200	1,800	6,000	800
Equipment	40,000	40,000	–0–	40,000	–0–
Overhead allocation	9,000	6,800	1,800	8,600	400
	$116,900	$101,100	$5,600	$106,700	$10,200

detailed budget for the development of the new product Zerxx, broken down by expense items for the three phases of the project. Overhead is applied on the basis of $30 per machine-hour to complete the different phases.

Status Reports. Periodically, companies prepare a status report, as illustrated in Exhibit 10–3, for all phases or departments involved in each project. The expenditures incurred to date and the commitments made represent the **encumbered amount.** Accountants match encumberances against the budget to determine the unexpended amount. If the unexpended amount is insufficient to complete the phase, a company should take corrective action and/or make budget revisions.

EXHIBIT 10–4 Research and Development Cost Summary

RESEARCH AND DEVELOPMENT COST SUMMARY
December 31, 19X1

Project	Project Description	Costs to January 1, 19X1	Year 19X1 Costs	Future Costs	Expected Total Costs	Annual Forecasted Income
2118	Product ZERXX	–0–	$101,100	$5,600	$106,700	$16,000
2119	Product YERXX	$5,000	4,000	3,000	12,000	4,000
2120	Improve Product AAX	1,000	15,000	2,000	18,000	5,000

EXHIBIT 10–5 Time Budget Analysis

TIME BUDGET ANALYSIS—PRODUCT ZERXX
May 31, 19X2

Phase	Hours Budgeted	Actual Hours	Variance
Planning:			
Product specification	20	24	4 unfavorable
Personnel involved	5	3	2 favorable
Research	6	8	2 unfavorable
Market analysis	10	7	3 favorable
Finance	9	14	5 unfavorable
	50	56	6 unfavorable
Production:			
Personnel training	25	26	1 unfavorable
Purchasing	15	20	5 unfavorable
Control functions	10	8	2 favorable
Test runs	200	225	25 unfavorable
Product revisions	50	40	10 favorable
	300	319	19 unfavorable
Promotion:			
Field testing	15	20	5 unfavorable
Advertising	85	82	3 favorable
	100	102	2 unfavorable
Total hours	450	477	27 unfavorable

Exhibit 10–4 reviews three research projects in process. The cost summary shows costs incurred in previous periods and the current year's expenses. Adding future costs to these two expenses gives the expected total cost of the project. The inclusion of annual forecasted income assists in evaluating the project's success.

Time Budget Analysis. Exhibit 10–5 compares actual hours spent on a project with the hours budgeted. Managers need this evaluation in addition to analyzing expenses. Product Zerxx used 27 more hours in development than forecasted.

Often the competition for market share makes time more important than dollars. Managers should compare the differential or extra revenue gained by introducing a product several months early and beating competition to market with the differential or extra cost of increasing production and market tests. They should then compare this differential income with the income estimated by following the original time schedule. These efforts to complete the project ahead of schedule are called **crashing** and are part of **Program Evaluation and Review Technique (PERT)** analysis. Chapter 26 discusses PERT-time and PERT-cost analysis involving networks that show paths to completion. A detailed timetable is essential to any new product introduction, whether it involves a simple method of preparing calendars or a more sophisticated computerized PERT network.

Cash Management (L.O. 2)

Effective management of cash plays an essential role in capital budgets and in the survival of a company. Failure to provide cash resources to meet liabilities as they come due is one of the most common causes of business failure. Collecting accounts receivable and making cash disbursements have always been functions of cash management. Today cash utilization also involves evaluating the cost of money or its ability to earn a return. Improvements in communication and transportation have facilitated the movement and clearing of funds. The expansion of business firms with subsidiaries in foreign countries has increased the problems of controlling and funding corporate operations.

Many companies have reserves of cash and near-cash securities totaling more than immediate or expected future requirements because they make no analysis of how much cash they need to support expected activity levels. Companies generally have three objectives in managing their cash; in descending order they are security of principal, liquidity of principal, and yield. Companies are often willing to accept low **yields,** or rates of return, to achieve security and liquidity of principal. **Liquidity,** or the ability to meet debts as they come due, is also of concern. **Security of principal** refers to the protection, or assurance, that the obligation will be paid. Companies can justify a conservative policy if the cash balance is low and necessary to meet operating needs and emergencies. However, when these cash funds have grown to the point where they exceed projected or probable expected uses, this policy has less importance.

Centralization of Cash

High interest rates cause companies to reduce their cash balances and examine the age of their receivables. Rather than a piecemeal analysis by individual departments, a multidepartmental review of cash functions is critical to better cash management. Generally, there are advantages to having cash-handling functions centralized. With consolidated management of cash, receipts are deposited in centrally controlled bank accounts and branch disbursements are made from imprest funds or payroll accounts. The appendix to Chapter 5 illustrates reciprocal accounts for these transactions. Usually companies limit decentralized functions to the payment of local operating expenses and receipt of payment from local customers. Authority over major capital expenditures and functions, such as capital stock sales and income tax and dividend payments, are centralized. Centralization of cash also prevents the unauthorized payment of funds and helps control all bank borrowing. In addition, it is often more economical to have accounting and other paperwork related to cash centralized at a single location.

Concentrating its accounts in a few banks enables a company to increase its importance as a customer of a particular bank. A company obtains credit more easily and quickly. Cash balances in many local banks are also released for investment. For public relations, some companies have a policy of maintaining deposit accounts in every bank in communities where they have a business office. However, cost-benefit analysis often fails to justify this policy.

Earlier Availability of Receipts. Cash management also requires improving cash collections. A review of credit, billing, discount, and collection procedures discloses opportunities to obtain prompt payments from customers. A review of credit policies determines whether the granting of credit is too strict and is cutting down the inflow of cash by rejecting sound sales. Conversely, the credit terms may be too liberal, increasing the number of slow-paying customers and bad-debt losses. Any delay in billing obviously results in delayed receipt of cash. Errors in bills mailed to customers also slow down cash receipts.

Cash Budgets (L.O. 2)

Forecasts of future cash receipts and disbursements, as shown in Exhibit 10–6, may reveal a company is holding unnecessary cash in bank accounts. Management needs both short- and long-range forecasts of cash positions. Long-range cash projections do not detail estimates of revenues and expenses because their purpose is to show long-term trends indicating whether working capital growth will generate funds when needed.

A budget showing expected cash receipts and disbursements indicates the months having cash shortages and excesses so managers can take corrective action in advance. Accountants usually prepare cash budgets for a year in the future, broken down by months, to ease the comparison of actual cash receipts and disbursements with budgeted amounts. For simplicity, Exhibit 10–6 illustrates a cash budget for only January, February, and December. The procedure used for Exhibit 10–6 is to estimate each expected source and disbursement of cash for the given period. Budgeted 19X2 sales come from Exhibit 9–7, the sales budget. The only source of cash assumed in Exhibit 10–6 is from charge sales, with 97 percent of the charge sales collected. The following collection pattern and sales are assumed in Exhibit 10–6:

> 40% in the month of sale
> 30% in the month following sale
> 27% in the second month following sale
>   3% uncollectible
> —————
> 100%
>
> Actual sales:
>   November $250,000
>   December   270,000

Hart Company pays for 80 percent of each month's purchase by the 10th of the following month to take advantage of the 2 percent purchase discount. They pay gross for the remaining 20 percent in the month following purchase. Following are the purchases by month:

> December 19X1 . . . . $20,000
> January 19X2   22,000
> November 19X2   30,000

EXHIBIT 10–6   Budgeted Cash Receipts and Disbursements

HART COMPANY
Budgeted Statement of Cash Receipts and Disbursements
For Year Ending December 31, 19X2

	January	February	December	Total
Cash receipts from sales:				
From November 19X1 sales:				
27% x $250,000	$ 67,500			
From December 19X1 sales:				
30% x $270,000	81,000			
27% x $270,000		$ 72,900		
From January 19X2 sales:				
40% x $292,000	116,800			
30% x $292,000		87,600		
From February 19X2 sales:				
40% x $268,200		107,280		
From October 19X2 sales:				
27% x $369,000			$ 99,630	
From November 19X2 sales:				
30% x $393,400			118,020	
From December 19X2 sales:				
40% x $404,500			161,800	
Total receipts	$265,300	$267,780	$379,450	$3,720,000
Disbursements:				
Purchases:				
From December 19X1 purchases:				
80% x $20,000 x 98%	$ 15,680			
20% x $20,000	4,000			
From January 19X2 purchases:				
80% x $22,000 x 98%		$ 17,248		
20% x $22,000		4,400		
From November 19X2 purchases:				
80% x $30,000 x 98%			$ 23,520	
20% x $30,000			6,000	
Fixed costs	100,000	100,000	150,000	
Variable costs:				
January sales:				
25% x $292,000 = $73,000				
30% x $73,000	21,900			
70% x $73,000		51,100		
February sales:				
25% x $268,200 = $67,050				
30% x $67,050		20,115		
November sales:				
25% x $393,400 = $98,350				
70% x $98,350			68,845	
December sales:				
25% x $404,500 = $101,125				
30% x $101,125			30,338	
Property taxes		75,000		
Dividends			80,000	
Equipment purchases.	110,000			
Total disbursements	$251,580	$267,863	$358,703	$3,687,983
Excess of receipts over disbursements .	$ 13,720	$ (83)	$ 20,747	$ 32,017
Beginning cash balance.	20,100	33,820	31,370	20,100
Ending cash balance	$ 33,820	$ 33,737	$ 52,117	$ 52,117

Hart Company expects cash disbursements for fixed costs to be $100,000 per month for the first half of the year and $150,000 for the remainder of the year. They expect cash disbursements for variable costs to be 25 percent of monthly sales; they pay 30 percent in the month incurred and 70 percent in the following month.

Hart Company plans to pay $75,000 for property taxes in February and $80,000 in dividends in December. The cash balance on January 1 is $20,100 and $31,370 on December 1. They expect to pay equipment purchases totaling $110,000 in January. The total budget column in Exhibit 10–6 shows only total receipts and disbursements since we omitted nine months from the cash budget for simplicity.

Determining Collections Based on Accounts Receivable Balances

The collection pattern and balances in the accounts receivable account identified by specific periods are bases for estimating the collections of accounts receivable. For example, assume Clevenger Company's collection pattern is 30 percent in the month of sale, 48 percent in the month after sale, and 20 percent in the second month after the sale. Clevenger Company expects 2 percent of all credit sales to be uncollectible. Assume accounts receivable balances as of March 1 are $70,000 from February sales and $44,000 from January sales; no bad debts have been written off. Also assume expected March sales are $180,000. Based on these data, expected collections to be included in the cash budget are as follows:

From March sales (30% × $180,000)	$ 54,000
From February sales $\left(\dfrac{\$70,000}{.70} \times 48\%\right)$	48,000
From January sales $\left(\dfrac{\$44,000}{.22} \times 20\%\right)$	40,000
	$142,000

Note that the $70,000 accounts receivable remaining uncollected from February sales represent 70 percent of sales made in February (100% − 30% collected in February). Also, note that the $44,000 accounts receivable from January sales represents 22 percent of January sales [100% − (30% + 48%) = 22%].

Budgeted Statement of Income and Statement of Financial Position (L.O. 3)

After completing the sales budget and all expense budgets, we prepare a budgeted Statement of Income similar to that in Exhibit 10–7. We make no new estimates; instead, we take figures from budgets previously prepared as indicated. In practice, companies should prepare more detailed budgeted statements of income on a monthly basis. With monthly forecasted statements of income, management can frequently analyze actual performance and investigate causes for variances. In addition, most companies round these figures to hundreds of dollars or thousands of dollars. However, we rounded Exhibit 10–7 figures to the nearest dollar to ease the carryover from one budget to another.

We can study percentage changes by comparing the 19X2 budgeted statement of income to the 19X1 actual statement of income. For instance, even though Hart Company expects 19X2 sales to increase $600,100 or 18.8 percent ($600,100/$3,200,000), managers also expect the cost of goods sold as a

EXHIBIT 10-7   Income Statement Analysis

HART COMPANY
Budgeted and Actual Income Statement
For Year Ending December 31

	19X2 (Budgeted)		19X1 (Actual)	
	Amount	**Percent**	**Amount**	**Percent**
Sales (from Exhibit 9–7)	$3,800,100	100.0%	$3,200,000	100.0%
Cost of goods sold (from Exhibit 9–14)	2,884,153	75.9	2,240,000	70.0
Gross margin	$ 915,947	24.1	$ 960,000	30.0
Marketing and administrative expenses (from Exhibit 10–1)	494,013	13.0	320,000	10.0
Income before income taxes	$ 421,934	11.1	$ 640,000	20.0
Income taxes assumed	304,008	8.0	256,000	8.0
Net income after income taxes	$ 117,926	3.1%	$ 384,000	12.0%

percentage of sales to increase. This results in lower percentages for gross margin and net income after taxes.

Analysis of Gross Margin

A detailed analysis of the causes for the change in gross margin for Hart Company follows:

$960,000	Gross margin 19X1
915,947	Gross margin 19X2
$ 44,053	Decrease in gross margin

If the same conditions exist in 19X2 with no change in unit sales price:

Sales for 19X2	$3,800,100	
Cost of goods sold for 19X2	$2,884,153	
Cost based on 19X1 rate (70% × $3,800,100) .	2,660,070	
Net increase in cost of goods sold		$224,083
Gross margin earned on increased sales (30% × $600,100)		180,030
Decrease in gross margin		$ 44,053

Exhibit 10–8 illustrates a budgeted statement of financial position representing all expected changes in assets, liabilities, and owners' equity. Companies can prepare similar budgets on a monthly basis. We could make a comparative analysis similar to that in Exhibit 10–7 for the statement of financial position. Exhibit 10–8 shows the means of calculating ending balance. We take most of these data from other budgets. As a result, we use a budgeted statement of financial position to prove the accuracy of all other budgets. For example, the ending cash balance reported on Exhibit 10–6 also appears on the budgeted statement of financial position along with all other changes in assets, liabilities, and owners' equity. We can apply ratio analysis to the budgeted statement of financial position to discover expected unfavorable ratios in time to take corrective action. We can also prepare a return on investment ratio by relating expected net income to the capital employed. A lower return than desired by management may provide the stimulus to adjust management plans and budgets.

EXHIBIT 10–8 Budgeted Statement of Financial Position

HART COMPANY
Budgeted Statement of Financial Position
December 31

		Amount	Percent
Current Assets			
Cash (from Exhibit 10–6)		$ 52,117	6.3%
Accounts receivable (beginning balance $30,250 + $3,800,100 sales − $3,720,000 receipts)		110,350	13.2
Direct materials inventory (from Exhibit 9–10)		14,000	1.7
Work in process inventory (from Exhibit 9–14) . . .		61,156	7.3
Finished goods inventory (from Exhibit 9–14)		55,559	6.7
Total current assets		$293,182	35.2
Plant Assets			
Land (from beginning balance)		$ 80,000	9.6
Building and equipment ($650,000 beginning balance + $110,000 purchases)	$ 760,000		
Less accumulated depreciation ($60,000 beginning balance + $150,000 from Exhibit 9–13 + $90,000 from Exhibit 10–1)	(300,000)	460,000	55.2
Total plant assets		$540,000	
Total assets		$833,182	100.0%
Current Liabilities			
Accounts payable (beginning balance + purchases of material, labor, overhead − disbursements of material, labor, and overhead)		$ 40,933	4.9%
Income taxes payable (from Exhibit 10–7)		304,008	36.5
Total current liabilities		$344,941	41.4
Stockholders' Equity			
Common stock (from beginning balance sheet) . . .		$200,500	24.1
Retained earnings (from beginning balance sheet + $117,926 net income − $80,000 dividends from Exhibit 10–6)		287,741	34.5
Total stockholders' equity		$488,241	58.6
Total liabilities and stockholders' equity		$833,182	100.0%

Government Budgeting (L.O. 4)

Budgeting differs depending on the profit status of the organization involved. For example, nonprofit budgets, such as government budgets, are appropriation budgets and differ from business budgets. An **appropriation budget** establishes fixed dollar amounts to achieve the objectives of the organizational unit for the period specified. Several factors in government cause the use of appropriation budgets. The stewardship function with its spending limits is very strong as the government unit is spending taxpayers' funds. The revenue sources of governments are limited and fixed for selected periods. Thus, we cannot base many expenditures on changing demands for services because revenues do not vary with demand. In addition, taxpayers' votes or legislative actions earmark specific revenues, such as taxes, for certain activities. Available revenues limit expenditures on such activities.

Due to the appropriation budget concept, managers often focus more on spending resources than on obtaining results. At year-end, government managers are tempted to spend the appropriated amounts, even if not needed. Unfortunately, this budgeting concept encourages managers to think of incremental increases in budget amounts rather than to consider the services offered. A cost/benefit relationship is usually not the basis of performance evaluation. Further, failure to spend to the allowable limit implies the amount is not needed, leading to reduced budgets for future periods.

A Step Toward Improvement. One modification in government budgeting results in more effective management control by relating cost to outputs or results. **Performance budgeting** achieves this by focusing on the government entity's results, such as the services performed and number of people served, rather than on dollars spent. In formulating a performance budget, we make a precise definition of the work to be done and a careful estimate of what that work will cost. Work units and unit cost then become the basis for evaluating service levels. The functions and objectives of government agencies and departments become the basis for preparing performance budgets. An extreme form of **program budgeting,** performance budgeting involves attempts to describe program objectives and alternative methods of meeting them. Objectives are then matched with the costs of achieving them.

Another budget modification, **zero-base budgeting** calls for a reevaluation of all activities and their costs on a regular basis. The focus in zero-base budgeting, similar to program budgeting, is on the objectives of the organization. When using the zero-base procedure, all programs are reviewed on a line item basis. This requires managers to justify their entire budgets, not just the changes proposed for the budget year. That is, we assume that zero money will be spent on each activity until we can justify a greater expenditure—thus, the term *zero base*. The beginning point in the budgeting procedure is zero, rather than the amount already being spent as is often the approach used in incremental budgeting. Even though zero-base budgeting often generates much paperwork, companies can adapt certain of its aspects and acquire a valuable control process. A review of each department's purpose, costs, and methods of operations may reveal areas needing improvements.

Incremental Budgeting (L.O. 4)

Traditional budgeting directs attention to changes or differences between existing budget appropriations and proposed expenditures. Because such a budgeting procedure accepts the existing base and examines only the increments involved, it is called **incremental budgeting.** A decision maker focuses attention on a small number of the total relevant factors involved and analyzes only areas containing different alternatives. Incremental budgeting proponents argue that managers should move toward new projects slowly because of their limited ability to forecast the future. However, incremental budgeting has the weakness of often encouraging companies to maintain functions and duties that have lost their usefulness. It is often difficult to allocate resources away from outdated functions to new tasks. Companies need to periodically review all functions to obtain optimum utilization of resources.

Behavioral Aspects of Budgeting (L.O. 5)

A budgetary program needs the cooperation and participation of all members of management to yield its greatest benefits. Too often, a budgetary plan fails because top management lacks enthusiasm and pays only lip service to its execution. Some companies ignore the human factors and fail to educate personnel about the important benefits of the budgeting process. One cause of friction between budget and production personnel is the difference in outlook and background. Budgets emphasize past and future performance, while production personnel are usually more concerned with daily operations. In addition, management often fails to realize that, because the natural reaction to control and criticism is resistance and self-defense, they must sell the budget.

Narrow Viewpoint. In addition, the administration of budgets often fosters a narrow viewpoint. Management may decide to forward to supervisors only the budgets for their departments. This encourages the philosophy that supervisors need only to concern themselves with their own departments. Further, companies hold supervisors responsible for only their individual cost centers. However, a company is more than the sum of its individual parts. The various segments of a company operate in a certain relationship to each other. Companies should not overlook these important relationships.

Budgets for Performance Evaluation

Top management may adopt a budget-constrained or a profit-conscious style for evaluating the performance of managers. A budget-constrained style evaluates performance on the ability to meet short-term budgets. A manager using a budget-constrained style of evaluation establishes well-defined work procedures and uses accounting data for evaluation because this information has the aura of clarity and objectivity. Efficiency of operations and strict role discernment—rather than individual employee needs—is this manager's concern. A manager using this style of evaluation is insensitive to interpersonal relations and directs more attention to task and goal attainment.

Evaluation under a budget-constrained style encourages managers to avoid drastically reducing expenses for fear the company will cut next period's budgets. They may also attempt to have favorable variances by avoiding maintenance expenses and purchasing inferior material. Fear of failure keeps them from starting new projects that are expected to be profitable. Budget-constrained managers are likely to get the job accomplished without cost overruns, regardless of the human cost.

By way of contrast, a manager's ability to increase a unit's long-term effectiveness in relation to the organization's goals is the basis for evaluation under the profit-conscious style. This management style is much more concerned with cost measures within the profit center than with meeting budget considerations. This management style is both efficient and people conscious. Managers being evaluated under the profit-conscious style realize they will not be penalized for expenses in this period that would otherwise reduce later profits. They are more willing to take on new projects as long as such projects are expected to be profitable.

Fear of Failure

A factor causing misunderstandings is the method used by budget personnel to report shortcomings. Budget personnel cannot go directly to the supervisor involved because they have to follow the lines of authority and responsibility. In fact, it may be a violation of policy for staff personnel to go directly to line personnel. Also, budgetary accountants want their immediate supervisors to know they found errors and are performing effectively. Thus, they relate information about shortcomings up the line and down into the factory organization structure. This places factory supervisors in an embarrassing position because they know that their superiors are aware of the errors. They also realize they have placed their superiors in an undesirable position.

The effects of failure on people are usually significant. Some factory supervisors, however, do not feel failure when singled out because of errors. These employees are not extremely concerned about doing a good job. Other supervisors highly interested in their work may suffer unduly when their departments incur deficiencies. These factory supervisors tend to lose interest in their work and confidence in themselves. They may refuse to try new methods if they fear failure. They may also develop a tendency to blame others and to be overcritical of others' work. The method of reporting unfavorable variances is important because of its differing effects on supervisors.

Unfortunately, budgets often become such inhibiting factors that management is afraid to take any risks for fear of not meeting the budget. Certainly, budgets are not a substitute for skilled management. They depict only a series of estimates that appear to represent good measurements at the time the budgets are established. When conditions change, managers should not believe that the budget is a straitjacket that they cannot revise.

Unrealistic Budgets

Despite increased recognition by managers that units should not be produced unless they can be sold, budgets are often a means of demanding higher productivity from employees. Even if managers do not overtly express this assumption to employees, it often filters down to them in very subtle ways. For example, when managers keep the budget purposely tight so it is almost impossible to meet. The unrealistic budget does not motivate; it breeds resentment. Supervisors resent this practice for it places both them and their workers in situations in which they can never succeed. This practice also implies that a company does not believe the supervisor's own desire to do a good job is sufficient to meet a reasonable budget.

Often after meeting a budget, companies set a new higher goal in the next budget. Such constantly increasing pressure for greater production often leads to negative results in the long run. People living under conditions of tension tend to become suspicious of every new move management makes to increase production. To combat such tensions, employees may establish informal groups antagonistic to management. These groups may be difficult to disband even after the tension dissipates.

Many supervisors avoid using the term *budget* with their employees because they believe discussing budgets creates resentful work groups. The word *budget* often represents a penny-pinching, negative brand of managerial pressure. Budgets often arouse fear, resentment, hostility, and aggression among employees—all of which may lead to decreased production. Many supervisors try to combat such resentment and fear by translating budget results into informal shop language.

Supervisors receive budgeting pressure from top management, but they hesitate to discuss budgets freely with people reporting to them. They may release this pressure by blaming unfavorable variances on the budget. They may spend more time finding excuses for exceeding the budget than they do trying to keep within it. Under such circumstances, budgets and budgetary accountants are likely to be unpopular with all employees. On the other hand, employees may bottle up the pressure and make it a part of themselves. Constant tension leads to frustration; frustrated persons cannot operate as effectively as they would normally.

Management needs to guard against demanding immediate increases in efficiency that hinder long-range growth in employee relations. Applying too much pressure to increase efficiency generates forces that decrease productivity in the long run. The better approach is to involve employees and thereby weaken the forces that tend to decrease efficiency.

Budget personnel think budgets are extremely important because they provide a goal, a motivating force, for production employees. Budgetary accountants often find it hard to understand why factory executives do not think highly of budgets designed to help individuals improve. Budget personnel constantly look for errors and deficiencies in the plant and single out the responsible parties. Rather than also praising workers for favorable variances, the accounting staff believes it only achieves success by finding fault with production personnel. Constant faultfinding alienates production personnel.

Participative Budgeting Process

Because a crucial problem in budget administration is acceptance of the budgets by employees, a participative budgeting process may offer solutions. **Participative budgeting** is the practice of allowing individuals who are accountable for budgeted activities and performance to participate in establishing budgets. People directly involved in certain functions have more understanding of those particular functions and their needs. Research in motivational theory has shown that it is in an organization's best interest to attempt to meet the esteem and self-actualization needs of participants. Making tasks more challenging and giving individuals a greater sense of responsibility can help meet these needs. Encouraging employees to participate in preparing budgets and comparing actual results often leads to increased goal acceptance. Participation in the budgetary control system gets the participants' egos involved and committed to the budget; they are not just task involved.

Participative budgeting increases the probability that involved individuals will accept budget goals as their own and become personally committed to the control system. When employees participate in the budget-setting process, they tend to believe that the budget is theirs and not just management's. Employees better understand how costs are assembled in a budget, as well as for which items they are responsible. Participative budget systems have a greater probability of achieving goal congruence than other models. Improved morale and greater initiative are often the result of a high degree of participation.

Often management wants employees to believe that it solicits their suggestions when, in fact, it desires only false participation. Management may go through the motions of participative budgeting techniques without encouraging real participation. This may prove to be even more damaging because such insincere attitudes soon filter down the line to the employees. Employees strongly resent managers leading them to believe they are assisting in the budgetary process when they really are not. False participation is no better than imposing the budget—halfhearted acceptance is risky. When management requests the signatures of the acceptors so they cannot later deny that they accepted the budget, this is usually resented.

Limitations of Participation. Participative budgeting does offer strong improvement over more traditional and authoritarian practices; however, letting employees participate in the budgeting process may not be the best solution for all companies. Participation introduces several psychological variables that can lead to decreased performance. The freedom managers have in establishing their own budgets can have negative results for the organization. Often in budget development and other decisions, employees use their influence to arrive at goals that are less demanding or in conflict with companywide objectives.

Managers can use participation to build organizational slack into their budgets by overestimating costs and underestimating revenues. **Slack** is the difference between the total resources available to the firm and the total resources necessary to maintain organizational activities. Behavioral scientists recognize some slack is desirable since it allows the blending of personal and organizational goals. However, excessive slack is clearly detrimental to the best interests of an organization. In-depth reviews during budget development often overcome this problem.

Participative budgeting's influence on aspiration levels is another possible limitation. By participating, individuals accept budgeted objectives as their own aspiration levels or personal goals. The interaction between aspiration levels and actual performance can result in behavior that is either desirable or undesirable. This depends on the difficulty of achieving budgeted performance, the nature of the task, and the personality of the individual. Companies should create an atmosphere in which individuals are encouraged to continually set and meet high personal performance standards. Repeatedly achieving easy goals or continually failing to attain goals that are too high can adversely influence aspiration levels and performance.

Expectancy theory suggests that individuals alter their behavior based on the expected outcome of an event. The utility derived from an expected outcome can be either intrinsic (such as praise or self-respect) or extrinsic (such as pay, praise, or promotion). Companies influence behavior and enhance performance by designing their budgeting systems to provide either intrinsic or extrinsic rewards in sufficient degrees.

A company's budgeting system provides the opportunity for much interaction between various management levels. Before beginning participative budgeting, top management should decide if they can be flexible and accept refined decisions jointly made by employees and low- and middle-level managers. Management should determine whether the personality and history of its work force are conducive to participation. Participative budgeting is not an all-or-nothing proposition. In practice, companies differ dramatically in both the amount and form of participation and influence they afford their operating managers in the budget- or target-setting process. Because the budgeting process differs from manufacturing tasks, line personnel often prefer to relinquish budget responsibilities to the budget staff, rather than bother with budgets.

Basic Constraints. By taking part in developing budgets, individuals become aware of the reasons for budget constraints. Budget staffs may increase line participation in developing budgets by giving employees a framework of basic constraints in advance. Budget staffs should explain management goals and future events expected to significantly affect operations. Managers should never discredit the intelligence and human dignity of employees at lower organizational levels. Employees who do not understand and accept their company's objectives are less willing to attempt to meet its goals.

Summary

The true success of any budgetary system depends on its acceptance by all company members affected by the budget. Properly conducted participation should build acceptance of the budget by those responsible for meeting the budget. Accountants should not view their function as primarily one of criticizing the actions of others; instead, they should show they are willing to recommend needed budget revisions. Despite their advantages, budgets do have limitations because they can lead to faultfinding and pressure. The accountant should try to separate the budget from the person involved and look for the cause of, or reason for, unfavorable performance. Certainly the administration of the budget should not be rigid; changed conditions may require budget revisions.

Companies simply cannot operate or grow without adequate working capital or cash resources. This makes it imperative that more timely, more detailed, and more reliable information about cash flows be available. Reliable forecasts of future cash receipts and disbursements are essential for more effective management of cash and receivables. Companies should adapt the cash budgets presented in the chapter to fit their needs to better understand their cash flows. Proper use of cash by management can bring additional savings to the company.

This chapter also discusses the preparation of marketing and administrative budgets, including budgets for promotion and research expenditures. Since the nature of these activities may be less standardized and repetitive than production activities, the construction of these budgets may challenge the accountant. Even though it is impossible to budget marketing and administrative activities as factually as production expenses, careful planning of expenditures and comparison of actual expenses with the budgeted amounts avoids wasteful spending without impairing effectiveness.

Important Terms and Concepts

discretionary cost, 336
encumbered amount, 337
crashing, 339
program evaluation and review
   technique (PERT), 339
yield, 339
liquidity, 339
security of principal, 339

appropriation budget, 344
performance budgeting, 345
program budgeting, 345
zero-base budgeting, 345
incremental budgeting, 345
participative budgeting, 348
slack, 349
expectancy theory, 349

Problem for Self-Study

Additional Financing Necessary

Osborne, Inc., is a manufacturer of electrical motors. Actual sales for the first quarter of 19X2 and projected sales for April and May are as follows:

January (actual)	$300,000
February (actual)	308,000
March (actual)	312,000
April (projected)	316,000
May (projected)	322,000

The average markup on cost for the company's merchandise is 40 percent. The company collects 60 percent of its sales during the month in which the sale is made, 25 percent during the month following the sale, and 15 percent in the second month following the sale.

Osborne pays for purchases of merchandise as follows: 40 percent are paid during the month of purchase and 60 percent during the month following the purchase. Merchandise is purchased in the month preceding the sale. The company plans to maintain the current level of inventory.

To meet loan obligations, there must be a cash balance of $25,000 on hand at the end of the coming month of April. Other cash payments anticipated during the month of April are salaries and wages, $58,000; other expenses, $12,000; and equipment purchases, $15,000. The cash balance on April 1, 19X2, is $1,800.

Required:

Prepare a cash budget for April 19X2. Round to nearest whole dollar. Will additional financing be necessary to have the required ending cash balance?

Solution to Problem for Self-Study

OSBORNE, INC.

Beginning cash, April 1, 19X2		$ 1,800
Cash receipts:		
From February sales (.15 × $308,000)	$46,200	
From March sales (.25 × $312,000)	78,000	
From April sales (.60 × $316,000)	189,600	313,800
Total of beginning cash and receipts		$315,600
Cash disbursements:		
From April purchases [($322,000 ÷ 140%) × 40%]	$ 92,000	
From March purchases [($316,000 ÷ 140%) × 60%]	135,429	
Salaries and wages	58,000	
Other expenses	12,000	
Equipment purchases	15,000	
Total cash disbursements		312,429
Ending cash balance		$ 3,171

Osborne needs additional financing of $21,829 to meet the desired $25,000 cash balance.

Review Questions

1. Why may it be more important to allow for a margin of safety in advertising budgets than in other budgets?

2. Discuss four different approaches to establishing an advertising budget.

3. Of what significance is a status report for research and development projects?

4. Discuss the characteristics in the government sector encouraging the use of appropriation budgeting.

5. List several modifications of government budgeting that would allow more effective managerial control.

6. Discuss how the design of the budgeting system influences managerial behavior and performance.

7. Why is it important that top management become involved in the budgeting process? How can budgets be viewed as a means of coordination?

8. What dangers are inherent in unrealistic budgets?

9. How can the reporting of variances cause further breakdowns in the working relationship of employees and supervisors? Suggest a better approach for reporting variances.

10. Discuss the strengths and the weaknesses of participative budgeting.

CPA/CMA/CIA Multiple Choice Questions

1. (CMA) DeBerg Company has developed the following sales projections for calendar year 19X2:

May	$100,000	August	$160,000
June	120,000	September	150,000
July	140,000	October	130,000

Normal cash collection experience has been that 50 percent of sales are collected during the month of sale and 45 percent in the month following sale. The remaining 5 percent of sales is never collected. DeBerg's budgeted cash collections for the third calendar quarter are:

a. $360,000.
b. $427,500.
c. $414,000.
d. $440,000.
e. $450,000.

2. (AICPA) In preparing its cash budget for May 19X1, Ben Company made the following projections:

Sales	$3,000,000
Gross margin (based on sales)	25%
Decrease in inventories	140,000
Decrease in accounts payable for inventories	240,000

For May 19X1, the estimated cash disbursements for inventories were:

a. $2,350,000.
b. $2,110,000.
c. $2,100,000.
d. $1,870,000.

3. (CMA) Each organization plans and budgets its operations for slightly different reasons. Which one of the following is not a significant reason for planning?

a. Providing a basis for controlling operations.
b. Forcing managers to consider expected future trends and conditions.
c. Ensuring profitable operations.
d. Checking progress toward the objectives of the organization.
e. Promoting coordination among operating units.

4. (CIA) Actual and projected sales of a company for September and October are as follows:

	Cash Sales	Credit Sales
September (actual)	$20,000	$50,000
October (projected)	30,000	55,000

All credit sales are collected in the month following the month in which the sale is made. The September 30 cash balance is $23,000. Cash disbursements in October are projected to be $94,000.

To maintain a minimum cash balance of $15,000 on October 31, the company will need to borrow:

a. $0.
b. $6,000.
c. $11,000.
d. $16,000.

5. (CMA) The most direct way to prepare a cash budget for a manufacturing firm is to include

a. Projected sales, credit terms, and net income.
b. Projected net income, depreciation, and goodwill amortization.
c. Projected purchases, percentages of purchases paid, and net income.
d. Revenues, expenditures, and depreciation.
e. Projected sales and purchases, percentages of collections, and terms of payments.

6. (AICPA) Reid Company is developing a forecast of March 19X0 cash receipts from credit sales. Credit sales for March 19X0 are estimated to be $320,000. The accounts receivable balance at February 29, 19X0, is $300,000; one quarter of the balance represents January credit sales and the remainder is from February sales. All accounts receivable from months prior to January of 19X0 have been collected or written off. Reid's history of accounts receivable collections is as follows:

In the month of sale	20%
In the first month after month of sale	50%
In the second month after month of sale	25%
Written off as uncollectible at the end of the second month after month of sale	5%

Based on the above information, Reid is forecasting March 19X0 cash receipts from credit sales of:

a. $176,500.
b. $195,250.
c. $253,769.
d. $267,125.

7. (AICPA) In preparing its cash budget for July 19X1, Reed Company made the following projections:

Sales	$1,500,000
Gross profit (based on sales)	25%
Decrease in inventories	$ 70,000
Decrease in accounts payable for inventories . .	$ 120,000

For July 19X1, what were the estimated cash disbursements for inventories?

a. $ 935,000.
b. $1,050,000.
c. $1,055,000.
d. $1,175,000.

8.–9.   (CMA) Use the following data for these items:

Esplanade Company has the following historical pattern on its credit sales:

70 percent collected in month of sale
15 percent collected in the first month after sale
10 percent collected in the second month after sale
4 percent collected in the third month after sale
1 percent uncollectible

The sales on open account have been budgeted for the last six months of 19X1 as shown below.

July	$ 60,000
August	70,000
September	80,000
October	90,000
November	100,000
December	85,000

8.   The estimated total cash collections during October 19X1 from accounts receivable would be

   a. $63,000.
   b. $84,400.
   c. $89,100.
   d. $21,400.
   e. Some amount other than those given above.

9.   The estimated total cash collections during the fourth calendar quarter from sales made on open account during the fourth calendar quarter would be

   a. $172,500.
   b. $275,000.
   c. $230,000.
   d. $251,400.
   e. Some amount other than those given above.

Exercises

E10–1 Impact on Budgeted Income (L.O. 1)

The tentative budget for a product manufactured by Jacob Company is as follows:

Sales	$425,000
Variable production cost	135,500
Fixed costs:	
Production	42,750
Marketing and administrative	48,000

Management is studying a sales campaign that costs an additional $35,000 and is expected to result in a 20 percent unit sales increase for the product. Assume the 20 percent increase in production does not remove the company from the present relevant range.

Required:

a. Calculate the increase in budgeted operating income for next year if the sales campaign is included in the budget.
b. Assuming the sales campaign allows only a 20 percent increase in sales price with the same cost behavior, what would be the increase in budgeted operating income for next year?
c. Determine if management would choose a 20 percent unit sales increase or a 20 percent increase in sales price. Explain why.

E10–2 Gross Profit Analysis (L.O. 4)

You have acquired the following data for the calendar years 19X1 and 19X2 for Missouri, Inc.:

	19X1		19X2		Dollar Increase
Sales	$400,000	100%	$720,000	100%	$320,000
Cost of goods sold	200,000	50	432,000	60	232,000
Gross margin	$200,000	50%	$288,000	40%	$ 88,000
Unit selling price	$40		$60		

Required:

Prepare a statement in good form that analyzes the variations in sales and cost of goods sold between 19X1 and 19X2.

E10–3 Cash Sales Collections with Discounts (L.O. 3)

You have been asked to forecast the cash receipts from credit sales for June for Akron Company. The company is engaged in computer production, and June credit sales are estimated to be $240,000. Discount terms of 2/10, n/30 are offered customers as an incentive to pay their bills early. The collection pattern is assumed to be 40 percent during the discount period and month of sale; 30 percent after the discount period has expired, but within the month of sale; 20 percent in the first month after sale; 5 percent in the second month after sale. April sales were $100,000 and May sales, $150,000.

Required:

a. Determine the June cash receipts from credit sales.
b. Discuss your reaction if Akron Company management tells you that their collection pattern is instead 45 percent during the discount period and month of sale; 30 percent after the discount period has expired, but within the month of the sale; 20 percent in the first month after sale; 5 percent in the second month after sale.

E10–4 Forecasting Cash Disbursements and Collections (L.O. 3)

Dorette Corporation management makes the following data available:

	Sales	Purchases
February	$75,000	$50,000
March	85,000	58,000
April	50,000	31,000
May	60,000	45,000
June (budgeted)	80,000	62,000

The company takes full advantage of the 3 percent discount allowed on purchases paid for by the 10th of the following month. Dorette expects $13,560 June operating expenses, including $3,000 depreciation. The company's cash balance at June 1 is $8,500.

Collections from customers are normally 50 percent in the month of sale, 30 percent in the month following the sale, and 12 percent in the second month following the sale. The balance is expected to be uncollectible.

Required:

a. Calculate the cash disbursement expected during June.
b. Compute the cash collections expected during June.
c. Give the cash balance at June 30 which is forecasted.

E10–5 Gross Profit Analysis (L.O. 4)

You have acquired the following data for the calendar years 19X1 and 19X2 for Century, Inc.

	19X1		19X2		Dollar Increase
Sales	$4,140,000	100%	$5,000,000	100%	$860,000
Cost of goods sold	2,691,000	65	3,500,000	70	809,000
Gross margin	$1,449,000	35%	$1,500,000	30%	$ 51,000
Unit selling price	$90		$100		

Required:

Prepare a statement in good form that analyzes the variations in sales and cost of goods sold between 19X1 and 19X2.

E10–6 Monthly Detailed Cash Budget (L.O. 3)

The management of Bosco Company requests that you prepare a cash budget for December. The cash balance is $51,068 on December 1. December sales are forecasted to be $150,000.

Analysis of their collection pattern in the past shows that accounts receivable are paid as follows: 50 percent during the month of sale, 35 percent in the first month after the sale, 10 percent in the second month after the sale, 2 percent in the third month after the sale.

On December 1, accounts receivable are $114,000. Of this balance, $80,000 came from November sales; $21,000 from October sales; $8,500 from September sales; and $4,500 from August sales. No accounts receivable have been written off.

A 6 percent $50,000 loan is due at the end of the month. Only interest has been paid at the end of each previous month. A final monthly interest payment is due at the end of December. Additional expenses for the month will be:

Payroll	$35,000
Materials and supplies	40,000
Depreciation	15,000
Insurance	4,000*

*This has not been prepaid in a previous month.

Required:

Prepare a detailed cash budget for December.

E10–7 Monthly Cash Budget (L.O. 3)

Salmon Corporation asks you to prepare its cash budget for November. Management expects sales for November to be $120,000, with a beginning cash balance of $80,000. Their collection pattern in the past, which you believe will continue in the future, has been 30 percent in the month of sale, 60 percent in the next month after sale, and 4 percent in the second month after sale.

The Accounts Receivable as of November 1 are $49,000 from October sales and $4,000 from September sales. No bad debts have been written off from the sales of these months.

The company has experienced a 20 percent gross profit on sales before considering the purchase discount. They have enough stock in inventory for lead time and safety stock and have been following the purchase pattern in the last three months of ordering only enough for current sales. Their payment pattern is 45 percent in the month in which the sale is made because their suppliers allow a cash discount then of 2 percent. The remaining 55 percent is paid in the month after the sale is made.

Payroll disbursements for November will be $15,700. Other disbursements will be as follows:

Rent	$ 1,000
Loan repayment and interest	15,000
Miscellaneous cash expenses	5,400

Required:

Prepare a cash budget for November.

E10–8 Cash Receipts Forecasted Using Credit Cards (L.O. 1)

William Griffin Manufacturers has decided not to accept personal business checks on credit sales but only to accept VISA, MasterCard, and American Express. VISA and MasterCard deduct 6 percent of accepted transactions before remitting payment; American Express discounts 7 percent. Estimated data for two months are as follows:

	January	February
Cash sales	$40,000	$ 48,000
Accepted credit sales by VISA and MasterCard	90,000	100,000
Accepted credit sales by American Express . . .	75,000	80,000

Eighty percent of the cash due from the credit card company on charge sales will be received in the month of sale, the remainder in the following month. The firm expects VISA and MasterCard to each disallow an average of $1,000 each month of charges made on cancelled cards, while American Express will have $800 of disallowed charges.

Required:

a. Determine cash receipts expected for February from total sales transactions.

b. Comment on the advantages of accepting credit cards for purchases and how the manufacturer could have avoided the loss it suffered during February.

E10–9 Credit Sales Collections with Discounts (L.O. 3)

Vaughn, Inc., offers a discount of 2/10, n/30 to its customers as an incentive to pay their bills early. The firm estimates its credit sales for October to be $100,000. The collection pattern is assumed to be 20 percent within the discount period and month of sale; 25 percent after the discount period has expired, but within the month of sale; 15 percent in the first month after sale; 5 percent in the second month after sale; and 30 percent in the third month after sale.

The Accounts Receivable account balance as of September appears as follows:

Accounts Receivable		
From July sales	21,500	
From August sales	24,000	
From September sales	35,200	

No bad debts were written off from August and September sales; however, Sue Smith's account balance of $3,000 resulting from a sale made in July was written off in September at the time Smith declared bankruptcy. The company uses the allowance method for recording the bad debts expense adjustment.

Required:

a. Determine the October cash receipts from credit sales.

b. Explain the difference, if there is any, between October cash receipts from September sales and the $35,200 balance in the Accounts Receivable account from September sales.

E10–10 Additional Financing Necessary (L.O. 3)

Salter, Inc., is a manufacturer of electrical motors. Actual sales for the last month of 19X2 and the first two months of 19X3 and projected sales for March and April are as follows:

December (actual)	$298,000
January (actual)	300,000
February (actual)	350,000
March (projected)	400,000
April (projected)	410,000

The average markup on cost for the company's merchandise is 60 percent. The company collects 58 percent of its sales during the month the sale is made; 20 percent is collected during the month following the sale; and 18 percent is collected in the second month following the sale.

Purchases of merchandise are paid for as follows: 30 percent paid during the month of purchase and 70 percent during the month following the purchase. Merchandise is purchased in the month preceding the sale. The company plans to maintain the current level of inventory.

To meet loan obligations, there must be a cash balance of $45,000 on hand at the end of the coming month of March. Other cash payments anticipated during March are salaries and wages, $42,000; other expenses, $10,000; equipment purchases, $28,000. The cash balance on March 1, 19X3, is $2,500.

Required:

a. Prepare a cash budget for March 19X3.
b. Indicate the financing needed, if additional financing is necessary, to have the required ending cash balance.

Problems

P10–11 Budgeted Cash Receipts and Disbursements (L.O. 3)

Brackton Corporation's trial balance on June 1 included the following accounts receivable:

From March sales	$ 3,000
From April sales	6,600
From May sales	9,000
	$18,600

Analysis of the past revealed that its collection pattern is: 40 percent of sales are collected in the month of sale, 30 percent in the next month after the sale, 15 percent in the second month after the sale, and 10 percent in the third month after the sale.

Sales on account for June are forecasted to be $23,000. The corporation's gross margin on sales averages 8 percent. Desired ending merchandise inventory balance on June 30 is $5,000 at invoice price before the discount. Beginning merchandise inventory on June 1 is $3,000 at invoice price before the discount.

Management has a policy of paying for 70 percent of the month's purchases in the month of sale to take advantage of the available cash discount of 2 percent. The remaining 30 percent of each month's purchases are paid for in the month following the sale. The only purchases made for May were for the monthly sales.

Required:

a. Determine the cash receipts in June from sales on account.
b. Determine the cash disbursement in June for purchases.

P10–12 Cash Budget for Collections and Production Budget (L.O. 3)

Crockett, Inc., budgeted sales at 60,000 units for October 19X1; 75,000 units for November 19X1; and 80,000 units each for December 19X1 and January 19X2. The selling price is $30 per unit. All sales are on credit and are billed on the 15th and last day of each month with terms of 2/15, n/30. Past experience indicates sales are even throughout the month and 20 percent of the collections are received within the discount period. The remaining collections are received by the end of 30 days; bad debts average 4 percent of gross sales. Crockett, Inc., deducts the estimated amounts of cash discounts on sales and the losses from bad debts from sales on its income statement.

The inventory of finished goods on October 1 was 8,000 units; the finished goods inventory at the end of each month is to be maintained at 10 percent of sales anticipated for the following month. There is no work in process inventory. The company uses FIFO inventory costing.

Required:

a. Determine cash collections from Accounts Receivable for November.
b. Assume the collection pattern is a percentage of gross sales as follows and the discount terms are 2/10, n/30:

> 20% within discount period
> 16% received by the end of 11 days—15 days after sale
>
> 60% received by the end of 16 days—30 days after sale
> 4% uncollected

Using this collection pattern, what would the collection from sales be in November?
c. Prepare a production budget for the quarter ending December 31, 19X1.

P10–13 Monthly Cash Forecast for a Quarter (L.O. 3)

As a CPA employed by Barnett, Inc., you must prepare a cash forecast. In relation to last year's performance, you believe that sales beginning in January for each month will increase 10 percent over the previous month. Units sold in December 19X1 were 500, and in November 19X1 were 440 units. The $60 sales price will remain the same. The collection pattern from credit sales expected is

> 70 percent in the month of sale
> 20 percent in the first subsequent month
> 5 percent in the second subsequent month

Beginning with the current year, management's inventory policy is that the ending inventory for each month should represent one half of next month's sales. Gross margin represents 30 percent of sales on the average. All purchases are paid in the following month. On January 1, there is $10,000 of merchandise on hand and accounts payable for purchases from December of $11,000. The cash balance on January 1 is $16,800.

Monthly fixed costs total $8,000, including depreciation of $5,000. Variable costs amount to 10 percent of monthly sales; these are paid for as incurred. An insurance premium of $4,100 is due in March. Dividends of $20,000 are scheduled for payment in February.

Required:

Prepare a cash forecast for the first quarter by months, rounding to whole units.

P10–14 Monthly Cash Budgets (L.O. 3)

Capp Company has these actual and projected monthly sales for 19X1:

July	$75,000
August	72,000
September	78,000
October	80,000
November	79,000

In the past, 47 percent of sales have been collected in the month of sale, 32 percent in the first month following sale, 18 percent in the second month following sale, and 3 percent proving uncollectible.

Capp Company pays for merchandise purchases 15 days after purchase. This means that about half the purchases in each month are paid for the next month. Capp Company's cost per unit of merchandise is $25 and it sells its merchandise for $50 per unit. The company tries to keep a month-end inventory of 150 units plus 50 percent of the units that are planned to be sold next month. The company was able to accomplish this objective for July and August. Operating expenses incurred by Capp Company are $300,000 per year (exclusive of depreciation). These are spread evenly throughout the year. The August 31 cash balance of Capp Company is $15,000.

Required:

Prepare a monthly cash budget for September and October along with supporting schedules showing cash receipts from collections of receivables and cash payments for merchandise purchases. Round to nearest dollar.

P10–15 Cash Collections and Disbursements (L.O. 3)

The following information is from Freeman Corporation's books:

	Sales	Purchases
July	$72,000	$42,000
August	66,000	48,000
September	60,000	36,000
October	78,000	60,000
November (budgeted)	66,000	51,000

Credit terms of 2/10, n/30 are available for customers. Collections from customers are normally 70 percent in the month of sale, 20 percent in the month following the sale, and 9 percent in the second month following the sale. The balance is expected to be uncollectible. Of the November credit customers who pay in November, 30 percent pay within the discount period; of the October credit customers paying in November, 5 percent take the cash discount. Freeman pays for all of each month's purchases by the 10th of the following month so it can take advantage of the 2 percent discount allowed on purchases. Cash disbursements for expenses are expected to be $15,800 for November. The company's cash balance at November 1 was $25,000.

Required:

Prepare the following schedules, rounding to whole numbers:

a. Expected cash disbursement during November.
b. Expected cash collections during November.
c. Expected cash balance at November 30.

P10–16 Quarterly Cash Budget (L.O. 3)

Earl Douglass Wholesalers asks your advice in preparing cash and other budget information for October, November, and December 19X1. The September 30, 19X1, balance sheet showed the following balances:

Cash	$ 20,100
Accounts receivable	995,816
Accounts payable	289,915

Management supplies you with these assumptions to use in budget preparation. All sales are credit sales and are billed on the last day of the month, and customers are allowed a 3 percent discount if they pay within 10 days after the billing date. Receivables are recorded at gross. The estimated collection pattern is 60 percent within the discount period, an additional 25 percent in the month after billing that does not receive a discount, and 9 percent in the second month after billing.

Fifty-four percent of all material purchases and marketing and administrative expenses are expected to be paid for in the month purchased and the remainder in the following month. Each month's units of ending inventory are equal to 120 percent of the next month's units of sale. Each unit of inventory costs $50. Marketing and administrative expenses, of which $3,500 is monthly depreciation, are equal to 10 percent of the current month's sale. Actual and budgeted sales are as follows:

	Units	Dollars
August	10,000	$750,000
September	10,500	787,500
October	11,000	836,000
November	11,200	851,200
December	11,500	874,300
January 19X2	11,800	890,000

Equipment costing $200,000 is paid for in November. Dividends of $40,000 are paid in December.

Required:

a. Prepare a cash budget for the last quarter of 19X1, rounding to whole dollars.
b. Explain what you can logically conclude regarding accuracy and fluctuations in market demand, reliability of suppliers, and lead time in view of management's desired inventory level.

P10–17 Monthly Cash Forecast for Six Months (L.O. 3)

As Harris Company's accountant, you are to prepare a cash receipts and disbursements budget for the coming year, ending December 31, 19X2.

Marketing research and the executive committee provide you with the estimated sales for 19X2. The company manufactures a highly seasonal product.

January	$ 45,000
February	48,000
March	52,500
April	56,000
May	57,000
June	62,000
July	68,000
August	70,000
September	71,500
October	72,000
November	75,000
December	76,000
	$753,000

On December 31, 19X1, the accounts receivable balance reflects $7,400 from November sales and $18,900 from December sales. No bad debts have been written off from the sales of these months. The sales collection pattern follows this pattern:

During month of sales	55%
In first subsequent month	35
In second subsequent month	5
Bad debts	5
	100%

The purchase cost of goods averages 45 percent of selling price. Harris Company wants to maintain the inventory at the end of each month at a level of the next three months' sales as determined by the sales forecast for the next three months. Purchases are paid for in the month following the purchase.

Variable expenses amount to 8 percent of sales, of which 40 percent are paid for during the month incurred. The company pays for the remainder of the variable expenses in the following month. Fixed expenses amount to $9,000 per month, including $1,000 depreciation and $300 patent amortization.

Payments for fixed costs are made in the month incurred.

Management plans to pay $1,000 cash dividends each quarter on the 20th day of the third month of the quarter. Equipment replacements of $5,000 will be made in January.

Harris Company's outstanding $45,000 bank loan requires a monthly payment of $3,000 on the last day of each month plus interest at 1 percent per month on the unpaid balance at the first of the month.

The cash balance at January 1, 19X2, is $19,100. The inventory balance on January 1 is $40,500. Accounts payable for purchases on December 31 total $45,000.

Required:

Prepare a cash forecast statement by months for the first six months of 19X2 showing the amount of cash on hand at the end of each month.

P10–18 Budgeted Collections and Pro Forma Balances (L.O. 3)

The January 31, 19X1, balance sheet of Brown Company for the first month of operations follows:

Cash	$ 22,750
Accounts receivable (net of allowance for	
uncollectible accounts of $2,700)	33,300
Inventory	41,700
Property, plant, and equipment (net of allowance	
for accumulated depreciation of $62,000)	54,600
	$ 152,350
Accounts payable	$ 89,600
Common stock	100,000
Retained earnings (deficit)	(37,250)
	$ 152,350
Budget sales:	
February	$ 140,000
March	$ 179,000

Collections on sales are expected to be 60 percent in the month of sale, 37 percent in the next month, and 3 percent uncollectible. The gross margin is 36 percent of sales. Purchases each month are for the next month's projected sales. The purchases are paid in full in the following month. Other expenses for each month, paid in cash, are expected to be $19,000. Depreciation on marketing and administrative facilities each month is $5,200.

Required:

a. Calculate the budgeted cash collections for February 19X1.
b. Determine the pro forma income (loss) before income taxes for February 19X1.
c. Compute the projected balance in accounts payable on February 28, 19X1.

P10–19 Production Budgets, Projected Income Statements, and Cash Budgets (L.O. 4)

Laurena, Inc., budgeted sales at 599,000 units for October 19X1; 600,000 units for November 19X1; and 610,000 units each for December 19X1 and January 19X2. The selling price is $28 per unit. All sales are on credit and are billed on the 15th and last day of each month with terms 2/10, net 30. Past experience indicates sales are even throughout the month and 30 percent of the collections are received within the discount period. The remaining collections are received by the end of 30 days; bad debts average 1 percent of gross sales. Laurena, Inc., deducts the estimated amounts of cash discounts on sales and the losses from bad debts from sales on its income statement.

Finished Goods Inventory on October 1 was 90,000 units; the Finished Goods Inventory at the end of each month is to be maintained at 25 percent of sales anticipated for the following month. There is no Work in Process Inventory. The firm uses FIFO inventory costing.

Direct materials of one-half gallon of A432 and one and one-half gallons of B287 are required per finished unit. Direct Materials Inventory on October 1 was 20,125 gallons of A432 and 80,375 gallons of B287. A432 costs $2.25 per gallon while B287 costs $0.80 per gallon. At the end of each month, the Direct Materials Inventory is to be maintained at 10 percent of production requirements for the following month. Direct material purchases for each month are paid in the next succeeding month on terms of net 30 days.

Direct labor of one-half hour is required per unit; the direct labor rate is expected to be $8. All salaries are paid in the month earned. A factory overhead application rate of 60 percent of direct labor dollars is used; depreciation of $60,000 per month is included in the rate. Marketing and administrative expenses total $5 million per month, which include depreciation of $4,000 per month. All manufacturing overhead and marketing and administrative expenses are paid on the 10th of the month following the month in which they are incurred.

Accountants expect the cash balance on November 1 to be only $10,000; a loan of $3,550,000 is due on November 10.

Required:

Prepare the following for Laurena, Inc.:

a. Direct materials purchases budget by month for October and November.
b. Direct labor budgets for October and November.
c. Projected income statement for November. Do not consider income taxes and ignore over- and underapplied overhead. Round to the nearest whole dollar.
d. A cash forcast for November, showing the opening balance, receipts itemized by date of collection, disbursements, and balance at the end of month.

P10–20 Quarterly Cash Budget (L.O. 3)

Wells Manufacturers believe that their collection pattern and sales will be as follows for the first quarter:

30%	in the month of sale
40%	in the month following sale
20%	in the second month following sale
7%	in the third month following sale
3%	uncollectible
100%	

Actual sales for October	$600,000
Actual sales for November	650,000
Actual sales for December	680,000
Budgeted sales for January	725,000
Budgeted sales for February	760,000
Budgeted sales for March	810,000

Accounts payable are paid in the month following the purchase, and no purchase discounts are available. The following purchases by months are given:

December	$325,000
January	350,000
February	380,000
March	389,000

Wells expects cash disbursements for fixed costs to be $90,000 per month. Cash disbursements for variable costs should be 10 percent of monthly sales; 40 percent will be paid in the month of incurrence and 60 percent in the following month. Property taxes of $190,000 will be paid in February; dividends of $50,000 are expected to be paid in March. Equipment purchases totaling $300,000 are expected to be paid for in March. The cash balance on January 1 is $18,168.

Required:

Prepare a cash budget for the first quarter.

P10–21 Standard Variances, High-Low, and Cash Budget (L.O. 3, 4)

L. Mosyer Company management is generally pleased with 19X1 operations in which net income of $72,000 is projected. The president is not satisfied, however, with the earnings per share projection and would like to increase this figure from a projected $3.60 for 19X1 to at least $4 for 19X2. She wants this projection to be included in the 19X2 budgets.

For 19X1, Mosyer expects to sell 50,000 units at $120 each and projects an annual increase of 10 percent in unit sales for 19X2 and 19X3. An increase of $8 per unit selling price will begin in 19X2, but the marketing staff is confident that demand is high enough that the sales price increase will not affect the expected increase in unit sales.

Mosyer uses two materials in production, and has developed the following standard costs for all manufacturing costs reflecting 19X2 standard quantities and prices to produce one final unit:

Material A (3 pounds @ $2/pound)	$ 6
Material B (4 gallons @ $3.75/gallon)	15
Direct labor (2 hours @ $15/hour)	30
Factory overhead (to be developed using budgets below)	

The following budgets have been developed for manufacturing overhead with the standard overhead rate based on a normal capacity of 100,000 direct labor-hours.

	Direct Labor-Hours		
	90,000	**100,000**	**115,000**
Indirect material and supplies	$ 630,000	$ 700,000	$ 805,000
Supervisory salaries	810,000	900,000	1,035,000
Plant maintenance	380,000	420,000	480,000
Plant rent	300,000	300,000	300,000
Depreciation on factory facilities	280,000	280,000	280,000
Total overhead	$2,400,000	$2,600,000	$2,900,000

Mosyer management desires to have 20 percent of the expected annual unit sales for the coming year in ending finished goods inventory of the prior year. Finished goods inventory on December 31, 19X1, is forecasted to consist of 11,000 units at a total standard cost of $935,000. The company uses LIFO inventory costing.

Marketing expenses are determined to be variable, while administrative expenses are all fixed. Budgeted marketing expense is expected to average 5 percent of sales revenue in 19X2; however, administrative expenses for 19X2 are expected to be 30 percent higher than the 19X1 estimated amount of $400,000. The price of Material B rose $0.25 a gallon to $4 per gallon near the end of 19X1; however, management believes this is temporary and did not revise its standard for this increase. Also the company has suffered a sharp increase in labor turnover recently which has increased the production time per unit by 12 minutes. Managers expect that as the new workers become more skilled, they will meet standard.

Required:

a. Prepare a budgeted income statement for 19X2 for the company incorporating management's specifications. Use the standards as developed but consider the most unfavorable situation for 19X2 with regard to Material B and direct labor. Identify production variances separately and add or subtract them from budgeted cost of goods sold. Assume Mosyer is subject to a 42 percent income tax rate.

b. Analyze the 19X2 budgeted income statement prepared to determine if the president's objective of $4 earnings per share is feasible.

c. Assume the company uses FIFO inventory costing and compute the budgeted cost of goods sold at standard cost.

P10–22 Interim Income Statements (L.O. 4)

Each subsidiary of the Beatle Corporation submits interim financial statements. These statements are then combined into companywide quarterly statements. One of its subsidiaries, the Dobbs Company, provides the following data regarding sales forecasts for the year:

Quarter	Bug Killer Units	Percent
First	100,000	10
Second	400,000	40
Third	300,000	30
Fourth	200,000	20
	1,000,000	100

Additional data are as follows:

1. The company has achieved first and second quarter sales as forecasted.
2. The president is considering raising the sales price of the bug killer spray from $80 to $100. Other managers are concerned, however, that this increase will reduce sales volume forecasts for the first and fourth quarters, which are already low.
3. Although manufacturing facilities can produce 1,400,000 units per year or 350,000 units per quarter during regular hours, the production schedule calls for only 1,000,000 units this year. This is the quarterly schedule for production:

Quarter	Units of Production Scheduled	Percent
First	375,000	37.5%
Second	400,000	40.0
Third	150,000	15.0
Fourth	75,000	7.5
	1,000,000	100.0%

4. The standard production cost, which does not incorporate any charges for overtime, was established at the beginning of the current year as follows:

Direct material	$35
Labor	10
Variable factory overhead	5
Fixed factory overhead	6
	$56

5. An unfavorable material price variance of $210,000 resulted in the second quarter because of a significant and permanent price increase.
6. As unfavorable direct labor variance also resulted in the second quarter in the amount of $277,500 partially due to overtime pay to meet the heavy production schedule. Whenever production requires work beyond regular hours, an overtime premium equal to 0.5 times the standard labor rate is paid. The remaining portion of the labor variance during the second quarter is due to expected inefficiencies.
7. In addition, a $40,000 unfavorable variable overhead variance resulted in the second quarter which was related to the excess direct labor costs.
8. A total of $6,000,000 fixed overhead expected to be incurred is budgeted for the year; $3,600,000 of fixed overhead has been absorbed into production through the first two quarters. Of this total, $2,400,000 was absorbed in the second quarter. For the first two quarters, a $600,000 total fixed overhead volume variance resulted due to the high manufacturing activity.
9. Marketing expenses are 10 percent of sales and are expected to total $8,000,000 annually.

10. The $6,000,000 annual administrative expenses are incurred uniformly throughout the period.

11. At the end of the second quarter, inventory balances are

Direct material—at actual cost	$ 750,000
Work in process—50% complete—at standard cost	168,000
Finished goods—at standard cost	1,680,000

12. The bug killer product line is expected to earn $10,000,000 before taxes this year with estimated state and federal income taxes of $4,200,000 for the year.

13. The accountant prorates any unplanned variances which are significant and permanent in nature to the applicable accounts during the quarter in which the variances were incurred.

Required:

a. Prepare the second quarter interim income statement for the Dobbs subsidiary of the Beatle Corporation.

b. Evaluate the production scheduling that Dobbs Company is proposing.

P10–23 Cash Budget (AICPA) (L.O. 2)

Mayne Manufacturing Company has incurred substantial losses for several years, and has become insolvent. On March 31, 19X1, Mayne petitioned the court for protection from creditors, and submitted the following statement of financial position:

MAYNE MANUFACTURING COMPANY
Statement of Financial Position
March 31, 19X1

Assets:	Book Value	Liquidation Value
Accounts receivable	$100,000	$ 50,000
Inventories	90,000	40,000
Plant and equipment	150,000	160,000
Totals	$340,000	$250,000

Liabilities and Stockholders' Equity:	
Accounts payable—general creditors	$600,000
Common stock outstanding	60,000
Deficit	(320,000)
Total	$340,000

Mayne's management informed the court that the company has developed a new product, and that a prospective customer is willing to sign a contract for the purchase of 10,000 units of this product during the year ending March 31, 19X2; 12,000 units of this product during the year ending March 31, 19X3; and 15,000 units of this product during the year ending March 31, 19X4, at a price of $90 per unit. This product can be manufactured using Mayne's present facilities. Monthly production with immediate delivery is expected to be uniform within each year. Receivables are expected to be collected during the calendar month following sales.

Unit production costs of the new product are expected to be as follows:

Direct materials	$20
Direct labor	30
Variable overhead	10

Fixed costs (excluding depreciation) will amount to $130,000 per year.

Purchases of direct materials will be paid during the calendar month following purchase. Fixed costs, direct labor, and variable overhead will be paid as incurred. Inventory of direct materials will be equal to 60 days' usage. After the first month of operations, 30 days' usage of direct materials will be ordered each month.

The general creditors have agreed to reduce their total claims to 60 percent of their March 31, 19X1, balances, under the following conditions:

- Existing accounts receivable and inventories are to be liquidated immediately, with the proceeds turned over to the general creditors.
- The balance of reduced accounts payable is to be paid as cash is generated from future operations, but in no event later than March 31, 19X3. No interest will be paid on these obligations.

Under this proposed plan, the general creditors would receive $110,000 more than the current liquidation value of Mayne's assets. The court has engaged you to determine the feasibility of this plan.

Required:

Ignoring any need to borrow and repay short-term funds for working capital purposes, prepare a cash budget for the years ending March 31, 19X2 and 19X3, showing the cash expected to be available to pay the claims of the general creditors, payments to general creditors, and the cash remaining after payment of claims.

Cases

C10–24 Top Management's Influence on Divisional Behavior (L.O. 5)

The six divisions of Beale, Inc., are in different regions of the United States, and all but one are situated a great distance from corporate headquarters. The Western Division is the exception; its offices as well as Beale's corporate headquarters are in San Diego. Two months ago, division managers received a notice from the president requesting their attendance at a meeting in San Diego to hear a presentation on a proposed budgeting system. Division managers were told to plan to be in attendance at the meeting for two days and to be certain that their assistant managers were in their division's office during their absence.

According to the agenda, the first morning of the meeting was to be spent in introducing the budgeting system. After lunch on the first day, the division managers were to vote concerning their acceptance of the system. Then, assuming the vote was positive to accept the system, the remainder of the two days would be spent in learning the system's details and how to implement it.

Under the present budgeting system, division managers submit budgeted revenue and expense figures to corporate headquarters. It is understood that since these were merely ballpark figures the corporate controller and president would refine them. However, before the expense and revenue projections are finalized, a conference call is made to each division to receive their input.

The morning of the first day of the division managers' meeting was spent in presenting the new budget system. Top management explained that they believed the divisions needed more autonomy and in turn, the division managers should have the opportunity to earn a bonus if they performed within the budget. The bonus would be calculated on divisional return on investment using an asset base composed of divisional plant assets employed. Corporate management would establish divisional budgets since they were more aware of the role of each division in achieving the overall company objectives. The previous year's data adjusted for economic and industry changes would be the basis for each division's budget. Since each division differs significantly in operating and marketing techniques used, corporate managers explained that they would consider these variations. In addition, after corporate management established divisional budgets, they cannot be modified by division managers under the new system because of the confusion it would create in developing the total companywide budget. As in the past, corporate managers would have the final decision regarding the commitment of funds to purchase machinery and other capital assets as well as expand existing facilities. Division executives would continue to propose investment projects for their own segments for corporate review.

After the president outlined the proposed procedure, the Western Division manager explained the challenges each individual would have supporting the new system. Further, the opportunity to earn a bonus was presented as a significant advantage. The Western Division manager urged adoption of the system and used data from his segment to reveal what he expected his bonus to be next year if the plan was accepted.

Since he had more immediate access to the corporate managers and knew what was being planned for the meeting, he had previously taken the specifics of the proposal and applied them to his own situation in preparation for this presentation. To further his argument, he stressed how much more aware each division manager would be of the income/asset relationship. He concluded by stating that he was confident of their vote, and that if they had any questions, they could be answered in the implementation session which would begin after the vote was conducted.

As the division managers broke for lunch, several commented, "Where do we go from here?" The Northern Division manager remarked, "Now, you are smarter than that; do we have any choice? Besides if we render a negative vote, what do we do during the one and one-half days remaining?"

Required:

a. Identify the behavioral problems you expect the company to encounter as a result of the meeting.
b. Evaluate the proposed budgeting system, identifying the major disadvantages in implementation.

C10–25 Behavioral Implications of Budgeting: Impact of Volume (L.O. 5)

Rambo Manufacturing Company produces men's formal and informal clothing; its annual sales volume is $6 million. Managers spread production fairly evenly over the 12 months of operation. They hire part-time workers from the nearby university's student body to cover for employees on vacations during the summer months.

Operations are divided into five departments—Cutting, Raw Sewing, Finish Sewing, Design Work, and Pressing. Fixed production cost is assigned using a plantwide rate of square footage; the size of the space occupied varies considerably between departments. Research, marketing, and administrative costs are distributed equally to all departments. Predetermined factory overhead application rates are based on the previous operating cycle.

Recently, the vice president of finance received complete authority to design a new budgetary system. In delegating this authority, the president made the following comment: "A lot of people don't know that much about accounting, and they don't get into it; it is a lot like electricity—the average person won't go and touch a shorted wire. So you as an accountant will win argument after argument in this situation."

The new system divides the annual budget into 12 periods and uses it as a monthly performance report. The vice president of finance prepares the budgets and then forwards them to the divisions at the end of each month.

The following report illustrates the one received by the division manager of the Finish Sewing segment, Gordon Ely.

RAMBO MANUFACTURING COMPANY
Finish Sewing Performance Report
For the Month Ended May 31, 19X1

	Actual	Budget	Variance
Units	2,200	2,000	200 F
Variable production costs:			
Direct material	$ 6,300	$ 6,000	$ 300 U
Direct labor	10,800	10,000	800 U
Variable factory overhead . .	9,500	9,000	500 U
Fixed production costs:			
Indirect labor	8,200	8,000	200 U
Depreciation	9,350	8,500	850 U
Taxes	3,500	3,200	300 U
Insurance	4,780	4,600	180 U
Administration	11,000	10,000	1,000 U
Marketing	8,800	8,000	800 U
Research	4,700	4,500	200 U
Total costs	$76,930	$71,800	$5,130 U

When the production manager distributed the monthly reports at the weekly meeting of all five division managers, he remarked, "Gordon, I am going to have to talk with you about getting that division of yours back in line!"

Ely could not understand what the problem was because he believed the division had operated more efficiently in May than in other months. Also the embarrassment was compounded in the division managers' meeting because Ely and the Cutting Division manager were in the running for the next promotion among the manufacturing hierarchy. Ely couldn't help but notice the twinkle in the Cutting Division manager's eye and the nudge he gave the Pressing Division manager sitting next to him.

Required:

a. (1) Briefly identify the weaknesses of the monthly performance report and the new budget system.
   (2) Explain how the report should be revised to eliminate each weakness cited; use quantitative data where appropriate.

b. Discuss the behavioral implications of using either an imposed or a participatory budget approach.

C10–26 Budget Construction and Behavioral Implications of Management by Exception (L.O. 5)

Resorts Hotel is on the Mississippi gulf shores, a popular summer resort area. During the summer months, the population of the area doubles, and management relies on university students for much of its labor force. There is never a shortage of students to fill the positions. These university students are supervised by regular staff, many of whom have not completed a high-school education, but have learned their management skills through on-the-job training.

The hotel is organized by departments with each department head reporting to a recently hired central manager. She has instituted several new changes in the reporting system. One change she is trying to implement is to install standards in the routine area of operations. For instance, she has used time and motion studies to determine the average time it should take to clean a hotel room. Also, she has installed standards in the Linen Cleaning and Maintenance Department.

With the introduction of standards, she also began a new management-by-exception reporting system. The responsibility reports now show budget variances so that more attention can be given to costs that differ significantly from budget. The central manager explained this as an added advantage to the department heads. However, to be fair, she indicated that she would allow each department head a 3 percent cushion and not get exceedingly upset as long as the variance stayed within a 3 percent range either over or under budget.

In establishing the budget which is expressed on a quarterly basis, the central manager used last year's spring quarter as the basis with a 5 percent inflation factor added. The hotel operates on a calendar year basis. Motel rooms occupied is the primary activity level with additional activities pertinent to each department. For example, a copy of the Linen Cleaning and Maintenance Department's recently distributed report follows:

RESORTS HOTEL
Linen Cleaning and Maintenance
Third Quarter, 19X2

	Budget	Actual	Over (Under) Budget	Percent Over (Under) Budget
Rooms occupied	12,000	15,100		
Pounds of linens processed	60,000	74,800		
Expenses:				
Cleaning and maintenance labor	$160,000	$163,000	$3,000	1.9%
Electricity and water	36,000	37,000	1,000	2.8
Bleach and detergent	25,000	29,700	4,700	18.8
Other laundry supplies	15,000	18,500	3,500	23.3
Leasing of equipment	46,000	52,000	6,000	13.0
Marketing expenses—allocated	10,000	11,000	1,000	10.0
Administrative expenses—allocated	5,000	5,250	250	.5

The central manager commented: "Department heads, please note that equipment leasing, marketing expenses, and administrative expenses exceeded budget by more than the 3 percent margin of error we agreed was acceptable. Also, attention must immediately be directed to bleach, detergent, and supplies expenses."

Required:

a. Enumerate any negative behavioral implications to management by exception as it is normally applied.
b. Describe the net effect of having a three percent cushion.
c. Evaluate the method used to construct the budget.
d. Decide if the information given to the department heads is sufficient for them to improve their performance.
e. Determine if the central manager can effectively appraise departmental performance with the system presently in effect.
f. List the advantages and disadvantages in employing university students during the peak season from a cost standpoint.
g. Assume a management viewpoint and describe the problems likely encountered with employing university students during the peak season on a part-time basis.

C10–27 Behavioral Problems in Divisional Budgets (L.O. 5)

Cleveland, Inc., is a medium-sized company with several manufacturing divisions in various geographical locations. Each division operates as an autonomous profit center responsible for sales, operations, and purchasing. In fact, the corporate headquarters gets involved only in strategic decisions and allows each division to control its own operations and meet market needs by processing the right product.

Even though operations are decentralized, corporate headquarters personnel carefully compare monthly performance figures with the budget. When actual sales or expenses vary from budget by 5 percent, the division people are immediately asked to give explanations. All managers at both the corporate level and division level are eligible for bonuses if actual net income is considerably greater than budget.

All of the divisions have been operating profitably except for the Texas plant. The problems there have been traced to poor control over plant expenses. In an attempt to secure this control, managers have implemented various techniques. Five plant managers have resigned or been terminated within the last four years.

It is this concern and its impact on bonuses that prompted John Douglass to recommend Kimberly Wells as the new manager of the Texas plant. Douglass has been impressed with Wells's managerial ability and enthusiasm. Douglass explained to Wells that she had been approved and appointed effective February 15, 19X2, despite objections from other members of the top management team. Many of the older male managers questioned if a woman could handle the job. However, Wells is a young, aggressive individual who advanced rapidly in the organization. Douglass informed her that he had complete confidence in her ability to turn the division around. Therefore, he expected her to have the division on budget by June 30, 19X2, at the end of the second quarter.

The 19X2 budget was prepared during the last six months of 19X1 before Wells was appointed division manager. Corporate management uses prior year data adjusted for inflation and industry trends in establishing divisional budgets by quarter and by year. Top management attempts to recognize problems unique to each division in this budget-setting process. Division managers cannot modify the yearly divisional budget after it has been established by corporate management. An entire day—the first of December—had been spent presenting and explaining the corporate and divisional budgets to the division managers and their division controllers. A mid-April meeting of all division managers generated much discussion as all of these managers cited reasons why first quarter results in their segments represented effective control and proclaimed that "no one else could have presented more favorable results." Corporate management has remained unconvinced and informed division managers that they must bring results into line with the budget by the end of the second quarter.

Wells listened to these remarks carefully, knowing that she is being excused this time since she had only held the division manager's position for six weeks. The budget report for the Texas division ending March 31, 19X2, showed that expenses were slightly over budget. At a meeting with Douglass a few days later, Wells described the changes she had instituted in March; she further expressed confidence that the expenses would be kept under control and that conditions would not deteriorate for the rest of the year.

However, Douglass is not satisfied; not only did he want control over expenses, but he also wanted the Texas Division to be on budget by June 30, 19X2. Wells tried to reason with Douglass by pointing out that conditions have been poor for the last four years in the Texas Division and that she has been in charge for only a short time. She agreed that she appreciated the opportunity to turn the division around, but she questioned if she is a miracle worker. Douglass again expressed his confidence in her ability and stated, "The only way either of us can receive a bonus is for the division to control its expenses and achieve its budget. I'm expected to see that my subordinates exercise due control."

Required:

a. Explain the major disadvantages in the procedures employed by Cleveland's corporate management in preparing and implementing the divisional budgets.

b. List four budgeting game tactics. Some are mentioned in the case, but you can list others also.

c. Explain why these tactics often go undetected.

d. Describe the behavioral problems expected by having division managers meet quarterly budgeted figures as well as annual budgeted net income figures.

e. Describe the impact on Wells's performance of Douglass's statement that he has complete confidence in her ability.

CHAPTER

11

Standard Costs and Variances for Materials and Labor

CHAPTER OBJECTIVES

After studying this chapter, you should be able to:

1. Understand the benefits of a standard cost system and how automation is affecting traditional variance measures.

2. Analyze material and labor variances in either a job order or process costing system.

3. Recognize the role variances play in evaluating actual performance.

4. Prepare journal entries that incorporate standards in the accounting system.

Introduction

Proper control of costs requires a comparison of actual cost results with some base data. Top management wants to know not only what costs are but also whether they represent an efficient level of productive operations. Comparing actual costs with those incurred in a previous period is one way to evaluate costs. However, the findings can be misleading if the company is operating under conditions different from those of the earlier period or if past costs are not consistent with company objectives. To properly interpret and control costs, we compare actual costs with standard costs so we can study any difference or variance. Thus, standards are yardsticks that measure achievement or lack of achievement.

Standard costs are closely related to budgets because they serve as building blocks for the construction of the budget. Budgets become a summary of standards for revenue and cost items. Budgets and standards are indispensable when they are administered skillfully. They both aim toward the same goal of better managerial control. Both budgets and standard costs make reports available to guide executives in comparing actual costs with predetermined costs.

Managers perform many traditional performance evaluations using a standard cost system. However, conventional monthly variance analysis is becoming obsolete because the information arrives too late and at too aggregate a level to be helpful for operational control. Modern cost management systems compile standard cost variances quickly and frequently. Managers recognize effective control of materials, labor, and overhead occurs daily. If a problem arises in any of these areas, production managers strive to handle it immediately.

Standard Cost Systems (L.O. 1)

Because historical data cannot satisfy the need for determining the acceptability of performance, accountants developed a system of costing on a predetermined basis—standard costing. Cost standards are carefully predetermined costs of production used as a basis for measurement and comparison. **Standard costs** represent what costs should be under attainable, acceptable performance. Standard costs do not necessarily represent what the cost would be if perfection in performance had actually been attained. Standards establish desirable minimum costs; when actual operations exceed standards, we investigate the variances.

Standard costs may differ from **estimated costs** because estimated costs are usually determined less accurately. Standard costs are determined scientifically using time studies and engineering estimates. However, this difference is not conclusive, for estimated costs may also be established on a scientific basis.

Process of Setting Standards. Establishing correct standards for a company's manufacturing expense is important because the accuracy of the standards usually determines the success of the standard cost system. In determining standards, each cost should be carefully analyzed to ensure that all factors have been considered.

In addition, managers in charge of the departments responsible for meeting the standards should approve the bases for the standards. Also, those responsible for meeting standards should have the opportunity to participate in the standard setting process. Supervisors should also have an honest desire to meet the standards. They should believe that the standard is accurate and expressed in terms that the employees under their supervision will understand. While accountants and industrial engineers provide technical information about the tightness of standards, the final decision should reflect input from the production line managers and their immediate supervisors. Standards should be set only after there has been face-to-face communication, bargaining, and interaction between the individuals involved. Finally, the basic plan should win the support of top management.

Advantages of a Standard Cost System

A standard cost system makes managers and employees cost conscious because variances between standard costs and actual costs are reported. They can study variances and determine the causes. Thus, standards provide a measuring device calling attention to cost variations. In turn, these standards serve as a compass that guide managers toward improvements.

The process of setting standards also assists in management's planning for efficient and economical operations. When setting standards, managers thoroughly study all factors affecting costs. They often discover operations that they can improve.

Standard cost systems also integrate managerial, accounting, and engineering functions. This encourages coordination because all elements of the organization are striving for the same goal. Setting standards involves defining goals and reviewing with all concerned their role in the attainment of those goals. For example, workers know what is expected of them when their standard is expressed as so many units per hour and they have helped establish this standard.

Levels of Activity and Efficiency

Managers should make certain decisions before setting standards: First, they must determine the number of units that a company plans to make and sell. Second, managers should decide how demanding they want their standards to be before estimating the hours of operation needed to provide for this production level. We use the theoretical, practical, normal, and expected actual capacity levels introduced in Chapter 4 for setting standards. Standards set on the basis of theoretical capacity are **ideal standards,** because they reflect maximum efficiency. Even though standards set on a theoretical or practical capacity are usually not attainable, they can be useful in motivating employees. Generally, we set standards on a less demanding level. **Normal** and **expected actual standards** make allowance for machine breakdowns, normal material loss, and expected lost time. However, normal standards make no allowance for abnormal loss or waste.

There are varying degrees of tightness in standards based on attainable performance. Many competent managers believe that to encourage high standards of performance, standards should provide a goal. However, this is often detrimental to employee morale. Tight standards may discourage those individuals whose efforts managers are measuring, and they may slow down their results. Cost figures derived from unrealistic standards can give management a false sense of security. Some managers may provide for contingencies in standards by making them fairly loose. However, standard costs based on comparatively low efficiency tend to hide and to perpetuate waste that should be highlighted. Loose standards provide unreliable data for measuring cost because they underwrite inefficiencies that need to be reviewed and corrected.

Rigid adherence to either extreme is usually unsound. Because inclusion of excessive contingencies and abnormal losses defeats the purpose of a standard cost system, we should not include budgetary slack in cost standards. We should set standards on a reasonable basis that considers all known normal factors and use of proper processing methods. Such standards involve expectation of more than a continuation of the past. We usually set standards tightly enough so operating personnel consider achievement possible.

Budgets, Standard Costs, and Target Costs

Standard costs become the unit building block for the company's budget. After establishing standards for each unit produced, we multiply standard costs by the total units we plan to produce to determine budgeted costs. When estimating costs for new products, managers do not completely rely on prevailing engineering standards. Instead, they establish target costs derived from estimates of a competitive market price. **Target costs** are below currently achievable costs, based on standard processes and technologies. Companies calculate backward from a product's sales price to arrive at a target cost the engineers must design to. Serving as "should costs," target costs become goals for designers and production personnel. Standards are benchmarks that measure incremental progress toward meeting the target cost objectives.

Incorporation in the Accounting System

Rather than enter standard costs in journals, managers sometimes use them only for statistical purposes with variances analyzed to determine corrective measures. Generally, managers take standard costs and variances more seriously and are more responsive to cost reduction if accountants enter standards in the ledger accounts. Incorporating cost standards in the accounting system provides an orderly and somewhat compulsory plan for cost analysis. However, the important factor is subjecting actual costs to proper measurement and control.

Setting Material Standards (L.O. 2)

Industrial engineers develop specifications for the kinds and quantities of material used in producing the goods budgeted. A manufacturing supervisor who is familiar with the raw materials composing the finished article is also of valuable assistance in setting standards. Managers can study results by placing a quantity of material in process under controlled conditions. There may, however, be a tendency for workers to produce with less scrap material under these test conditions. Accountants should watch for this artificial element because, if they fail to consider it, the material quantity standard could be understated.

Material Quantity Standards

Operation schedules list the materials and quantities required for the expected volume of production. Traditionally, quantity standards contained an allowance for waste or shrinkage using a formula similar to the following:

$$\frac{\text{Waste expressed in pounds (or tons, etc.)}}{\text{Net pounds (or tons, etc.) in finished unit}} = \text{Percent waste to be added}$$

Zero Defect's Influence on Material Quantity Standards. The popular zero defect philosophy does not include an allowance for waste. Including an allowance for defective items and scrap often prevents improvement because companies accept losses as normal and ignore product waste. Instead, the focus under zero defect is to avoid losses of material and isolate them for study when they do occur. Production standards no longer reflect planned scrap, lost materials, and inefficiencies in the production process. Instead, companies improve control by charging resources lost due to waste directly to the supervisor whose group caused the error.

Also, failing to establish a separate account with a budget for rework leaves the impression that companies do not expect rework. When rework time comes out of regular production hours assigned to a job, workers become more careful in preventing errors. However, we appropriately add a waste allowance when we buy materials in bars or lengths and cut definite sizes of parts from sheet stocks of material. The purchasing department receives the operation schedule and bills of material established jointly by the engineering department, the manufacturing supervisor, and the accountant. This information becomes the basis for the material price standard.

Material Price Standards

Because purchasing agents are responsible for material price variances, they should help set the price standards. Price standards should reflect managers' study of market conditions, vendors' quoted prices, and the optimum size of a purchase order. The just-in-time (JIT) management philosophy minimizes inventories, keeping on hand only the amount needed in production until the next order arrives. The impact on material price standards of more frequent, smaller orders is a consideration. In addition, we should consider the entire operation associated with acquiring goods, including any exhaustive bargaining for the lowest material price. We should also review the adequacy of a company's cash balance for taking advantage of cash discounts. Even where a company fails to take cash discounts, there is support for deducting these discounts from the material cost. We then record discounts not taken in the expense section of the financial statement to reflect standard costs.

Purchasing Responsible for Quality. Some companies hold their purchasing departments accountable for only the price of purchased components, not their quality. Thus, purchasing's motivation is to find inexpensive vendors without concern for meeting the material quality specifications. Because cheaper materials often require substantial manufacturing rework time, unfavorable labor efficiency variances may result at the same time the purchasing department has a favorable material price variance. To prevent this from occurring, the purchasing department should also meet the material quality specified.

Applied Rates for Material Handling. If accountants apply material handling costs to the materials inventory accounts, as illustrated in Chapter 4, the price standard should also reflect this. Accountants can develop applied rates for freight in, purchasing, receiving, and other costs associated with the material handling function. An alternative to using applied rates for freight charges on raw material is to use only FOB destination prices in establishing the standards.

Setting Labor Standards (L.O. 2)

The human factor makes it more difficult to set labor standard costs than material standard costs. There are many elements, such as the state of a person's health and fatigue, that can cause variances in productivity. A person's attitude toward a supervisor, along with other psychological factors, also affects productive efficiency. These factors, as well as skill and seniority, are important considerations in establishing labor standards.

Labor Efficiency Standards

Examination of past payroll and production records can reveal the worker-hours used on various jobs and can help determine standard performance. However, if the layout of the present plant differs from that of the past plant, a special investigation may be necessary to determine the probable effect of these changes. Also, historical records may include unnecessary operations. In industries where no data reflecting past performance are available, it may be necessary to obtain time reports from the workers for a limited period as a basis for the standards.

Time and Motion Study. If possible, time study should be the basis for setting labor efficiency standards. The objective of a time study is to develop time standards and piece rates which the average operator can meet daily without affecting his or her well-being. A time study breaks up the operating cycle into distinct elements. With these smaller work units, we can detect stalling attempts and irregularities earlier. Managers place the rating of the operation and the employee's skill and effort on time-study sheets. Rating calls for expert knowledge and skill, as an incorrect estimate of the operator's skill or speed distorts the standard.

Selection of the worker representative to be studied is very important. It is best for the plant supervisor to observe the employee's work habits before selection. The workers assigned should not be abnormally fast or slow but rather seasoned workers who perform at a steady pace. The character and honesty of the worker are also important, as is the worker's willingness to participate in the study. There should be no evidence of an attempt to confuse the person making the time and motion study. Results may vary substantially between workers. The time-study analyst should exercise judgment in excluding those observations that reflect abnormal conditions. If workers can incorporate improvements in their methods, the time standard analyst should refer the matter to the supervisor. Advance estimates become the basis for setting labor standards if the operation has never been performed before. Estimates also are the basis if the operation is of a special type that is not expected to be repeated.

Test Runs. Test runs are another approach to establishing labor quantity standards. A weakness is that an average situation is difficult to find because plant conditions are never static and no two similar jobs take the same amount of manufacturing time. Past performance, on the other hand, gives an average, while time and motion study gives an objective result. Management should consider using a combination of these methods to obtain more accurate labor standards.

Labor Rate Standards

Referring only to the rates paid previously may result in inaccurate rate standards. Competitive markets in which supply and demand are active and constantly changing often determine labor rates. The labor rate standard should adhere closely to the actual labor rates paid in the next period.

Determining labor rate standards depends on which of two general methods a company uses to pay employees. A company may establish a standard rate for the job; regardless who performs the job, the rate stays the same. Or a company may establish a rate for an individual worker, and the worker receives this rate regardless of the work performed. If labor contracts exist, the wage is relatively fixed and can be used as standard.

The nature of direct labor operations in each cost center determines whether separate rates for each labor operation should be used. If these operations are not uniform and require varying degrees of skill, each operation should have a separate standard hourly labor rate. Using a continuous manufacturing operation employing a conveyor system, a company may base the wage payment on the speed of the conveyor belt with reference to estimated production.

Group Piece Rates. Departments where it is very difficult to apply a straight piecework plan can adapt a group piece rate plan. Departments performing multiple operations use this plan and pay for completed jobs, not for individual units. The total price of the completed job is the sum of the unit rates. This price includes an allowance for repairing defective work, supervision, and training new employees. Group rates also allow for time lost due to the handling of parts.

Incentive Wages. If workers receive the opportunity to increase their earnings by producing more units than standard, the hourly base rate for the standard can be obtained from time studies and job evaluations. The hourly rate on the job evaluation sheet used for pricing the allowed time on the job may also be used. This base rate also often becomes the guaranteed rate that a company pays its workers regardless of their output. Management may believe they should establish a guaranteed wage rate to be fair to new, inexperienced workers who cannot produce at a high level of output because of inadequate training and experience. In determining the guaranteed and incentive wage rates, management should make certain that the spread between the figure used as a base rate and possible earnings is great enough to encourage workers to greater productivity.

Salaried Direct Labor Workers. Labor costs in an automated manufacturing system are largely fixed even though wages are expressed on an hourly basis. When there is a temporary delay in production, companies do not stop paying their workers. The labor cost that remains in a flexible manufacturing system represents the cost of workers performing the initial machine and material loading, but only for a single shift of a three-shift operation. Because direct labor workers are performing a greater variety of tasks and working on multiple products, increasingly they are receiving salaries. Accountants derive an average salary figure from a schedule showing the number of salaried people and their individual salaries. The average plant salary figure should also include payroll taxes and such employee benefits as vacation pay, jury duty allowance, insurance, and pensions.

Variances Illustrated for Job Order Costing (L.O. 2)

After determining quantity and price standards, accountants prepare a **standard specification** for each product unit. Even though Chapter 12 discusses establishing overhead standards, the following standard specification for a unit includes overhead to be complete. Note that overhead is applied on the basis of machine-hours. For instance, at the same time that 1.2 hours of labor occurs in making the product, overhead is being applied. The standard does not specify 3.2 total hours to finish the product, but 1.2 hours of labor and 2 hours of machine time.

Material (3 pounds @ $4 per pound)	$12
Labor (1.2 labor-hours @ $15 per hour)	18
Overhead (2 machine-hours @ $20 per hour) . .	40
Total standard cost per unit	$70

Material Variances

Material variances are as follows:

1. Material price variance: (Actual material price − Standard material price) × Actual material quantity.

2. Material usage or quantity or efficiency variance: (Actual material quantity − Standard material quantity) × Standard material price.

The following data illustrate the calculation of material variances:

Standard cost per unit as shown in the standard specification:
   3 pounds @ $4 per pound = $12
Actual pounds purchased: 2,820 pounds @ $3.90 per pound
Actual pounds used in production: 2,750
Units finished: 900

Material Price Variances. Assume the company purchased 2,820 pounds of material costing $3.90 per pound, but only used 2,750 pounds in production. We can compute the price variance either on the basis of material purchased or material used as follows:

Material purchase price variance

($3.90 actual material price − $4.00 standard material price) × 2,820 pounds purchased = $282 favorable **material purchase price variance**

Material usage price variance

($3.90 actual material price − $4.00 standard material price) × 2,750 pounds used = $275 favorable **material usage price variance**

Regardless of the approach used, the variance is favorable because materials were purchased at a savings of $0.10 per pound ($3.90 − $4). We assume that the same grade of material specified was purchased and that the saving does not result from acquiring a lower and cheaper grade of material.

Standard Quantity Allowed. We apply standards to actual production of finished units. Because there were 900 units produced, the **standard quantity allowed** must be 2,700 pounds (900 units × 3 pounds = 2,700). In computing the material usage variance, we compare 2,750 actual pounds used to produce the 900 units with the 2,700 standard pounds allowed. We multiply the difference in quantity used by the standard material price to arrive at the material usage variance.

Material usage (quantity or efficiency) variance

(2,750 actual material quantity − 2,700 standard material quantity) × $4 standard material price = $200 unfavorable **material quantity variance**

The material usage variance is unfavorable since 50 more pounds were used to make the 900 units than were specified in the standard. Of course, one way to have favorable material quantity variances is to inject only a portion of the material required to make each finished unit. However, an imperfect product will result; quality control established in the factory should prevent this from occurring. We always assume the units produced are perfect units that have passed inspection.

Diagram Approach. Instead of using the equation approach of determining material price and usage variances, you may find the diagram approach easier. The diagram approach has a built-in proof when the quantity purchased exactly equals the quantity used. The built-in proof results because the two variances should equal the difference between actual and standard costs. When we are determining a material purchase price variance, we cannot determine the proof of a net variance because the quantity variance and the price variance are based on different amounts of input. We use the general terms *input* and *output* to make the approach applicable to all measures. Input is typically measured in gallons, pounds, machine-hours, or labor-hours. Output is the product manufactured, such as shirts or desks. Output may not be a finished product ready for use; instead, it is the product completed through the cost center's processing. Note that the variances are the same as we computed using equations.

Diagram Approach for Material Purchase Price Variance and Quantity Variance

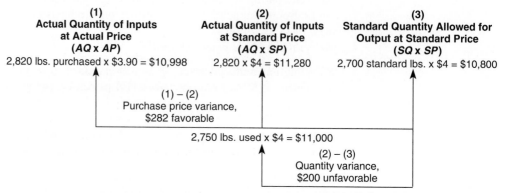

Diagram Approach for Material Usage Price Variance and Quantity Variance

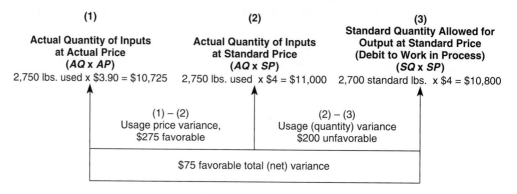

Avoid Rote Memory in Interpreting Variances. We encourage you *not* to memorize the formulas for standard variances; instead, try to analyze the components of each variance. Also, think of comparing actual quantity and price with standard quantity and price. In turn, avoid seeing if their signs are negative or positive when labeling variances as favorable or unfavorable. Instead of using rote memory, think through the situation. If you were to use only 2,700 pounds of material and you used 2,750 pounds, logic tells you that the variance is unfavorable because you used 50 more pounds than the standard said you should. Likewise, if you paid only $3.90 a pound for material and the standard price is $4, you have saved the company 10 cents a pound, resulting in a favorable variance. It is for this reason that we encourage you not to think of a negative or positive sign when comparing actual and standard.

Journal Entries for Material

As illustrated earlier, we can compute the material price variance on the basis of either pounds used or pounds purchased. The approach chosen depends on when we integrate the material standards in the accounting system. There are three different methods of reflecting material price and quantity variances.

1. Isolating the price variance at the time of purchase, and keeping the materials inventory at standard cost is a first method. Recording material purchase price variances is the preferred method; it saves clerical costs because no actual inventory costing method (such as FIFO, LIFO, or average cost) is needed. Also, this approach allows for more timely investigation of the variance.

2. Not recording the price variance until materials are issued from the storeroom into production is a second method. When recording material usage price variances, the Material Inventory ledger account must be kept on some actual costing basis. An appendix to Chapter 2 discusses the FIFO, LIFO, and weighted-average costing methods of inventory costing. All of these are actual cost methods and require much clerical effort to account for inventories. An alternative treatment for recording the usage price variance is to wait until all unused materials are returned to the storeroom and total usage on the job is determined.

3. Recording a material purchase price variance when materials are received from a supplier and allowing the Direct Materials Inventory account to be kept at standard is a third method. Then the price variance on the material used is transferred from the Purchase Price Variance ledger account to the Material Usage Price Variance ledger account. The remaining balance in the purchase price variance is treated as a valuation account. This balance represents the price variance for the material remaining unused in inventory. It is deducted from (if a favorable or credit balance) or is added to (if an unfavorable or debit balance) the standard cost of material to arrive at an adjusted actual cost of material.

The last approach is a combination of the two previous methods; it determines both a material purchase price and a material usage price variance. If there is a large difference between the amount of material purchased and the amount of material used each accounting period, the additional effort required under this method is warranted. With recognition of JIT and inventory carrying costs, however, more companies are closely matching their material purchases with usage.

The following illustrates each of these methods using the data presented earlier for a job order costing system:

> Standard cost per unit: 3 pounds @ $4 per pound = $12
> Pounds purchased: 2,820 pounds @ $3.90 per pound
> Pounds used in production: 2,750
> Units finished: 900
> No beginning inventory in the Direct Materials Inventory account

Note that because managers rarely know the eventual output at the time materials are issued, the practical procedure is to charge the entire quantity to work in process and determine any quantity variance after workers complete the job.

Whenever lost or spoiled units are likely to result from the production process, or whenever managers do not know the eventual yield at the start of a job, they estimate how much material they need to complete the order and requisition accordingly.

Managers monitor progress and estimate costs at key points during production. Often there are inspection points where they can measure the ratio of bad units to good ones. Also, if the performance of certain machines or operators is typical of the entire process, these points can serve as reliable indicators of the job. These indicators serve as frequent performance appraisals without awaiting variance analyses. The journal entries are as follows under each of the three methods showing material variances:

Material price variance recognized at time of purchase (material inventory at standard)

```
Direct Materials Inventory (2,820 pounds × $4) ..............  11,280
  Material Purchase Price Variance (2,820 pounds ×
    $0.10 @ pound) .....................................              282
  Accounts Payable (2,820 pounds × $3.90) ..............           10,998

Work in Process Inventory (2,750 pounds × $4) ..............  11,000
  Direct Materials Inventory (2,750 pounds × $4) ............          11,000
```

We make the following entry when the output of 900 units is known:

```
Material Quantity Variance (50 pounds × $4) ................    200
  Work in Process Inventory ...........................               200
```

Material price variance recognized at time of usage (material inventory at actual)

```
Direct Materials Inventory (2,820 pounds × $3.90) ...........  10,998
  Accounts Payable ....................................           10,998

Work in Process Inventory (2,750 pounds × $4) ..............  11,000
  Direct Materials Inventory (2,750 pounds × $3.90) ..........          10,725
  Material Usage Price Variance (2,750 pounds × $0.10) .......             275
```

We make the following entry when output is known:

```
Material Quantity Variance (50 pounds × $4) ................    200
  Work in Process Inventory ...........................               200
```

Material purchase price and usage price variance

```
Direct Materials Inventory (2,820 pounds × $4) ..............  11,280
  Material Purchase Price Variance (2,820 pounds ×
    $0.10 per pound) ...................................              282
  Accounts Payable (2,820 pounds × $3.90) ..............           10,998

Work in Process Inventory (2,750 pounds × $4) ..............  11,000
  Direct Materials Inventory (2,750 pounds × $4) ............          11,000

Material Purchase Price Variance .......................    275
  Material Usage Price Variance (2,750 pounds × $0.10) .......             275

Material Quantity Variance (50 pounds × $4) ................    200
  Work in Process Inventory ...........................               200
```

This leaves a balance of $7 in the Material Purchase Price Variance account which reflects the $0.10 variance per pound for the 70 pounds left in inventory.

Material Purchase Price Variance

| (2,750 pounds used × $0.10 variance) | 275 | (2,820 pounds purchased × $0.10 variance) (this equals 70 pounds in inventory × $0.10 variance) | 282 |
| | | | Balance 7 |

This method leaves a balance sheet like this:

Direct materials inventory (70 pounds at $4 standard cost) $280
Less material purchase price variance   7
Direct materials inventory (adjusted to actual) $273

Other combinations of journal entries record the material price and quantity variances, depending on the sequence of events occurring. Remember that the net amount debited to Work in Process as the cost of the job should reflect standard quantity allowed × standard price. You do not have to determine the standard cost of a job to compute the material variances. However, when you enter standards in the journal, you compute the standard cost of the job. Thus, Finished Goods Inventory is always at standard cost.

Labor Variances

We can compute labor variances identical to those illustrated for material after determining labor standards. The labor variances are

1. **Labor rate variance:** (Actual labor rate − Standard labor rate) × Actual labor-hours.
2. **Labor efficiency (quantity or time) variance:** (Actual labor-hours − Standard labor-hours) × Standard labor rate per hour.

Unlike materials, companies cannot purchase labor services in one period, store them, and then use these services in the next period. Thus, both labor variances relate to the same period.

To illustrate the computation of these variances, assume the following for a job order company:

Standard cost per unit as shown in the standard specification:
   1.2 hours @ $15 per hour = $18
Total direct wages paid: 1,280 hours @ $15.20 per hour = $19,456
Units: 900 units finished

Labor rate variance

($15.20 actual labor rate − $15 standard labor rate) × 1,280 actual labor-hours = $256 unfavorable labor rate variance

The labor rate variance is unfavorable because workers received $0.20 more per actual hour worked than was indicated in the standard specifications.

Standard Hours Allowed. The standard hours allowed for actual production amount to 1,080 (1.2 hour × 900 units produced). We compute standard hours in a similar manner as standard pounds. The labor efficiency variance is

Labor efficiency (quantity or time) variance

(1,280 actual labor-hours − 1,080 standard labor-hours) × $15 standard labor rate per hour = $3,000 unfavorable labor efficiency variance

The labor efficiency variance is unfavorable because workers used 200 more hours to manufacture the 900 units than specified in the standard. We multiply the 200 excess hours by the standard labor rate to isolate the effects of quantity only. Alternatively, using the diagram approach, the variances are the same as follows:

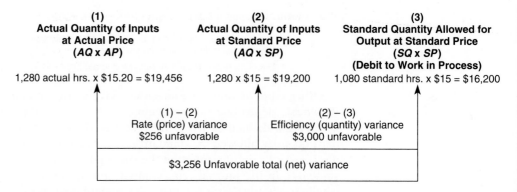

Labor Efficiency under JIT

Because productivity measures based on direct labor efficiency can be manipulated on the plant floor in dysfunctional ways, interpreting labor variances requires care. Standards for different products are not identical. Thus, managers may increase efficiency by running simple products and avoiding more complex, harder-to-run jobs. Also, managers can improve direct labor efficiency by increasing the lot size because setups and changeovers are often included in overhead rather than in direct labor. However, long production runs may not be profitable because there may be insufficient demand for the product manufactured.

Under traditional manufacturing systems, long runs lead to better use of direct labor for a given amount of indirect labor. Today, supervisors realize that keeping machines working to produce inventory not yet needed is contradictory to the JIT philosophy. Instead, they schedule short production runs coupled with frequent changeovers. Using a JIT system, if a worker's output during a day is lower than expected, bottlenecks either before or after the worker are the likely cause. Regardless of where bottlenecks occur, they force workers to stop producing through no fault of their own.

Also, when a company bases incentive pay on the total output produced—not the output that passes inspection—workers focus on the amount of goods produced, regardless of how much of the product is unusable. Therefore, companies should consider the quality of the products manufactured in measuring worker efficiency.

Conversion to an automated, JIT system makes the performance of production managers look unfavorable unless the company changes its evaluation measures to reflect this. Thus, JIT production policies make the traditional evaluation of labor and machine time invalid. Companies that maintain their previous efficiency measures after adopting the JIT production philosophy confuse both workers and managers. Using multiple performance measures—including the effect of a manager's operations on productivity and quality—is a better indicator than sole reliance on labor efficiency variances. Managers should ensure that labor efficiency does not reward production while demand is ignored. Otherwise, the Finished Goods storeroom may be overstocked with products no one wishes to buy.

Journal Entries for Labor

Several combinations of journal entries record the labor variances. The following illustrates one combination that records only the rate variance while the job is in process. We do not know the amount or the direction (whether favorable or unfavorable) until workers complete the job. We adjust Work in Process at that time, not while the job is in process.

```
Work in Process Inventory (1,280 hours × $15 per hour) . . . . . . . .   19,200
Labor Rate Variance ($0.20 × 1,280 hours) . . . . . . . . . . . . . . . . .      256
     Wages Payable (1,280 hours × $15.20 per hour) . . . . . . . . . .              19,456
```

When the output of 900 units is determined, the Labor Efficiency Variance is recorded as follows:

```
Labor Efficiency Variance (200 hours × $15) . . . . . . . . . . . . . . .    3,000
     Work in Process Inventory . . . . . . . . . . . . . . . . . . . . . . . . . .            3,000
```

We do not transfer the job into Finished Goods Inventory until we have applied its factory overhead. Chapter 12 discusses the standards for factory overhead costs.

Combined Net Variances. Rather than determine separate price and quantity variances for material and labor, some companies merely determine total variances for these factors. We do not recommend this approach, as it provides no way to identify factors that cause the variance. Instead of combining all contributing factors, an approach should pinpoint each.

Material and Labor Variances Using Process Costing (L.O. 2)

The previous examples illustrated standards in a job order costing system. Standards in process costing effectively eliminate the conflicts and complexities of the FIFO and weighted-average methods that Chapters 6 and 7 introduced. In a process costing system, as in a job order cost system, we know in advance the standard cost specifications for all three cost components: material, labor, and overhead. However, we cannot determine the standard hours, gallons, pounds, or other measures allowed for process costing operations until the accounting period ends. Then we multiply the standard quantity per unit by the equivalent units for each cost element.

Assume another company employing a process costing system uses the same material standards illustrated for job order costing. There was no beginning inventory, and the following goods were transferred to or remain in ending inventory:

```
Units transferred . . . . . . . . . . . . . . . . . . . .   1,000 units
Ending Inventory (⅕ material, ¾ labor) . . . . . .     100 units
```

The equivalent units (EU) for material and labor are

```
EU, material = 1,000 + 20 (100 units × ⅕) = 1,020
EU, labor = 1,000 + 75 (100 units × ¾) = 1,075
```

Material Variances. The standard pounds allowed are 3,060 (1,020 EU × 3 pounds). If this process costing company used 3,000 pounds, the material quantity variance would be favorable, as follows:

(3,000 actual material quantity − 3,060 standard material quantity) × $4 standard material price = $240 favorable material quantity variance

Assume further that this processing company purchased 3,150 pounds of material costing $4.15 per pound. As in a job order costing system, we can compute the price variance in either of the following ways:

Material purchase price variance

($4.15 actual material price − $4.00 standard material price) × 3,150 pounds purchased = $472.50 unfavorable material purchase price variance

Material usage price variance

($4.15 actual material price − $4.00 standard material price) × 3,000 pounds used = $450 unfavorable material usage price variance

Labor Variances. Assuming the process costing company used 1,040 hours of labor this period at a $14.75 hourly rate, the labor variances are

Labor efficiency variance
Standard hours allowed: 1,290 hours (1,075 EU × 1.2)

(1,040 actual labor-hours − 1,290 standard labor-hours) × $15 standard labor rate per hour = $3,750 favorable labor efficiency variance

Labor rate variance

($14.75 actual labor rate − $15.00 standard labor rate) × 1,040 actual labor-hours = $260 favorable labor rate variance

   Self-study problems at the end of Chapters 11 and 12 illustrate the use of standards in a process cost system.

Standard Costs in Future Factories (L.O. 1)

Companies are changing their traditional standard cost models to meet the needs of their flexible manufacturing systems. New cost accounting procedures are replacing the standard cost model to make standards current and relevant when: *(a)* short production runs are tailored for each customer, *(b)* product characteristics are changing, and *(c)* the production method changes for each batch depending on which machines are available when the order is processed. Because automation provides opportunities for more predictable yields, variances are being determined much more rapidly in time for corrections. To summarize the impact of flexible manufacturing systems on standard costs is as follows:

1. Standard cost models based on large-scale production of an item with unchanging specifications are less common.
2. Standard cost systems are less oriented toward standard direct labor-hours and direct material costs with more measurement of all significant resource costs. While an orientation directed to labor and material may be adequate for accounting purposes, it is insufficient for decision making and performance improvement/reporting purposes.
3. Emphasis solely on price variances is shifting to include the costs for rejected materials or late deliveries. By focusing on the lowest price, a system de-emphasizes material quality and delivery. This lack of attention creates downstream quality problems and forces the company to maintain inventory buffers to compensate for poor delivery performance.
4. Price fixation is shifting to consolidate vendors and to develop long-term partnership arrangements with them. Former systems measuring price variances forced buyers to judge vendors strictly on price. Thus, buyers

showed no loyalty to suppliers and adversarial relationships with vendors resulted. Vendors were unwilling to raise quality, improve schedule performance, or work to solve supply problems because they knew the company buys strictly on price.

5. Costs of larger size orders are being traced to purchases and matched with their price variances. A system concentrating only on price variances encourages buyers to increase their order quantities for higher discounts. Larger orders create the potential risk of excess inventory, tie up cash, and extend lead times. Also, large purchase quantities increase inventory buffers and require more warehousing space.

6. Material standard specifications do not include costs of rework and spoiled units. A company is more likely to accept a specified amount of defective items with no improvement if the standard includes spoiled unit costs. Instead, rework and spoiled unit costs are isolated so attention is directed to reducing these costs.

7. Timely variance analysis is replacing monthly aggregate material usage variances.

8. Less attention is given to direct labor efficiency because direct labor costs usually are such a small percent of product costs in machine-paced factories.

9. Incentive systems and traditional variance measures are changing because workers are performing a variety of tasks on multiple products.

10. By focusing less on direct labor variances, managers direct more attention to crucial manufacturing strategies.

11. Product costing is improved because standard cost models are less commonly based on the assumption that overhead cost is proportionate to the amount of direct labor consumed by the product.

Interactions Among Factors of Input and Variances (L.O. 1)

Earlier in the chapter we assumed that when we purchased material at a savings of $0.10 per pound we were buying the same grade of material specified. Instead, suppose a company buys a grade of material lower than standard because its price is lower. What is the likely impact on the resulting variances? The favorable material price variance may cause high material usage and poor labor efficiency. An unfavorable material quantity variance and unfavorable labor efficiency variance normally results. Under these circumstances, we cannot blame an unfavorable labor efficiency variance on the workers who require more time to handle lower-grade materials. This illustrates that most variances are due to interactions among the factors of input. There is usually not a single, independent cause of each variance.

In deciding whether a company made a correct decision in purchasing the cheaper-priced, lower-grade material, we compare the resulting variances. If the favorable material price variance more than offsets the unfavorable material usage and unfavorable labor efficiency variances, the trade-off was appropriate. Otherwise, the company should buy standard-grade materials. The following summary pinpoints possible causes of each variance including the impact of the interactions between factors of production.

Summary of Material and Labor Variances

Material Price Variances

(Actual material price − Standard material price) × Actual material quantity

Companies compute price variances at different times by recording a material *purchase* price and/or *usage* price variance. However, computing the price variance at the time of purchase provides better control. To compute a purchase price variance, we multiply the difference between actual and standard material price by the material quantity *purchased*. In computing a material *usage* price variance, we multiply this difference by the material quantity *used*. To delay the computation until the issuance of material usually destroys the usefulness of the information for control. Then corrective action is seldom possible. Since this treatment charges material inventory at standard, we simplify detailed record-keeping, for we keep records in quantities only. An objection to this procedure is that if buying is not closely allied to production and sales volume, variations in the volume of purchasing can cause a distortion in operating results.

Possible causes of unfavorable variances:

1. Fluctuations in material market prices.
2. Purchasing from distant suppliers, which results in additional transportation costs.
3. Failure to take cash discounts available.
4. Purchasing in nonstandard or uneconomical lots.
5. Purchasing from suppliers other than those offering the most favorable terms.

Responsibility. The Purchasing Department is usually responsible for material price variances. However, supervisory factory personnel are responsible when they specify certain brand-name materials or materials of certain grade or quality. If a price variance occurs because a request was made for a rush order, the Production Planning Department could be responsible, as this may be the result of poor scheduling.

Material Usage (Quantity or Efficiency) Variances

(Actual material quantity − Standard material quantity)
× Standard material price

For control purposes, this variance should be isolated as quickly as possible; however, it may be impossible to calculate until the work is completed.

Possible causes of unfavorable variances:

1. Waste and loss of material in handling and processing.
2. Spoilage or production of excess scrap.
3. Changes in product specifications that have not been incorporated in standards.
4. Substitution of nonstandard materials.
5. Variation in yields from material.

Responsibility. Line supervisors should be held responsible for material under their control.

Labor Rate Variances

(Actual labor rate − Standard labor rate) × Actual labor-hours

Possible causes of unfavorable variances:

1. Change in labor rate that has not been incorporated in standard rate.
2. Use of an employee having a wage classification other than that assumed when the standard for a job was set.
3. Use of a greater number of higher-paid employees in the group than anticipated. (This applies when the standard rate is an average.)

Responsibility. If line supervisors have the authority to match workers and machines to tasks by using the proper grade of labor, line supervisors should be responsible. Line supervisors should also be responsible if they control the wage rate of their labor force. If they do not, the Personnel Department may be responsible.

Labor Time (Quantity or Efficiency) Variances

(Actual labor-hours − Standard labor-hours) × Standard labor rate per hour

Possible causes of unfavorable variances:

1. Inefficient labor.
2. Poorly trained labor.
3. Rerouted work.
4. Inefficient equipment.
5. Machine breakdowns.
6. Nonstandard material being used.

Responsibility. Line supervisors should be held responsible for labor under their control. The Production Planning Department or the Purchasing Department should be held responsible for any labor efficiency variance that results from the use of nonstandard material.

Summary

Under an actual cost system, accountants determine production costs too late to be of much benefit in planning and control. Actual costs become meaningful when compared with standard costs. Standard costs separate historical costs into the portion representing the standard allowance and the portion representing the deviation from the standard.

Equitable cost standards require much time and effort in their development. A standard should consider past prices, anticipated prices, and all foreseeable factors such as strikes, wide fluctuations in prices, weather conditions, and union agreements. The process of setting standards also requires a review of the company's plant layout and workflow. This review provides management with a better understanding of possible cost savings.

Standard cost systems are changing as companies place less focus on direct labor in automated environments. Instead, they direct more attention to quantifying resources that affect costs and vary proportionally with production volume. Rather than make an allowance in the standard for spoilage, they consider product waste as abnormal and controllable. Analysis of variances between actual and standard costs remains a very useful means of evaluating operations and finding areas that need correction.

Important Terms and Concepts

standard costs, 373
estimated costs, 373
ideal standards, 374
normal standards, 374
expected actual standards, 374
target costs, 374
standard specifications, 378
material purchase price variance, 379

material usage price variance, 379
standard quantity allowed, 379
material usage (quantity or efficiency) variance, 379
labor rate variance, 383
labor efficiency (quantity or time) variance, 383

Problem for Self-Study

Journalizing Material and Labor Variances in a Process Costing System

Anderson, Inc., produces a chemical product on an assembly line. Standard costs per unit are as follows:

	Total
Direct materials (10 pounds) . .	$50
Direct labor (8 hours)	$96

Workers completed a total of 2,000 units and transferred them this period; ending inventory consists of 500 units, 40 percent complete for all components.
The beginning inventory of 800 units had the following costs:

110 pounds of material costing $572, 15% completion stage.
1,200 hours of labor costing $15,000, 20% completion stage.

Anderson incurred the following costs in the current period:

| Direct materials used . . . . | 19,700 pounds costing $102,440 |
| Direct labor used . . . . | 15,000 hours costing $187,500 |

Required:

a. Prepare a variance analysis for material and labor using FIFO costing.
b. Prepare a variance analysis for material and labor using average costing.
c. Prove your variances using weighted-average costing.
d. Record the purchase of material and the variances using FIFO costing; assume the recognition of the material price variance at the time of usage.

Solution to Problem for Self-Study

ANDERSON, INC.

a. FIFO Costing

$$\text{EU, material} = 2,000 + \underset{(500 \times 40\%)}{200} - \underset{(800 \times 15\%)}{120} = 2,080$$

$$\text{EU, labor} = 2,000 + \underset{(500 \times 40\%)}{200} - \underset{(800 \times 20\%)}{160} = 2,040$$

Material quantity variance
2,080 × 10 pounds = 20,800 standard pounds
(19,700 actual pounds − 20,800 standard pounds)
× $5 standard rate = $5,500 favorable.

Material price variance
$$\frac{\$102,440 \text{ actual material cost}}{19,700 \text{ actual pounds}} = \$5.20 \text{ actual rate}$$
($5.20 actual rate − $5 standard rate) × 19,700 = $3,940 unfavorable

Using the diagram approach, we outline the following variances:

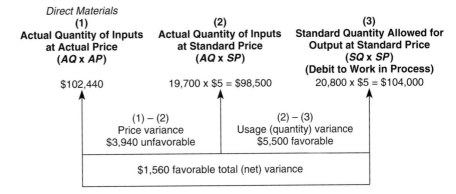

Labor quantity variance
  2,040 × 8 hours = 16,320 standard hours
    (15,000 actual hours − 16,320 standard hours) × $12 standard rate = $15,840 favorable

Labor rate variance
$$\frac{\$187,500}{15,000 \text{ hours}} = \$12.50 \text{ actual rate}$$
    ($12.50 actual rate − $12 standard rate) × 15,000 actual hours
    = $7,500 unfavorable

Using the diagram approach, we outline the following variances:

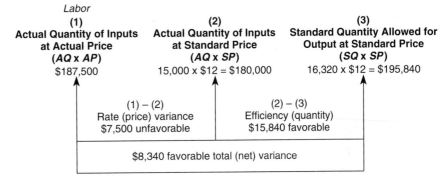

b. *Average Costing*
  EU = 2,000 + 200 = 2,200 units
    (500 × 40%)

Material quantity variance
  2,200 units × 10 pounds = 22,000 standard pounds
    (110 + 19,700 = 19,810 actual pounds − 22,000 standard pounds)
    × $5 standard rate = $10,950 favorable.

Material price variance
$$\frac{\$102,440 + \$572 = \$103,012 \text{ actual material cost}}{19,810 \text{ actual pounds}} = \$5.20 \text{ actual rate}$$
    ($5.20 actual rate − $5.00 standard rate) × 19,810 actual pounds
        = $3,962 Unfavorable

Using the diagram approach, we outline the following variances:

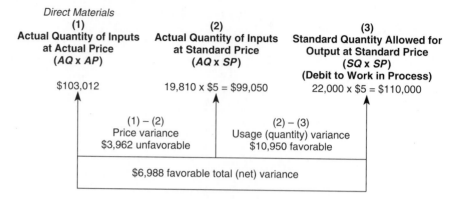

Direct Materials

(1) Actual Quantity of Inputs at Actual Price (AQ x AP)	(2) Actual Quantity of Inputs at Standard Price (AQ x SP)	(3) Standard Quantity Allowed for Output at Standard Price (SQ x SP) (Debit to Work in Process)
$103,012	19,810 x $5 = $99,050	22,000 x $5 = $110,000

(1) – (2)
Price variance
$3,962 unfavorable

(2) – (3)
Usage (quantity) variance
$10,950 favorable

$6,988 favorable total (net) variance

Labor quantity variance
2,200 units × 8 hours = 17,600 standard hours
(15,000 + 1,200 = 16,200 actual hours − 17,600 standard hours)
× $12 standard rate = $16,800 favorable

Labor rate variance
$$\frac{\$15,000 + \$187,500 = \$202,500}{16,200 \text{ hours}} = \$12.50 \text{ actual rate}$$
($12.50 actual rate − $12 standard rate) × 16,200 actual hours
= $8,100 unfavorable

Using the diagram approach, we outline the following variances:

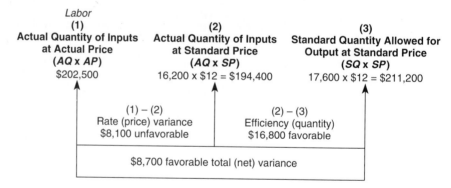

Labor

(1) Actual Quantity of Inputs at Actual Price (AQ x AP)	(2) Actual Quantity of Inputs at Standard Price (AQ x SP)	(3) Standard Quantity Allowed for Output at Standard Price (SQ x SP)
$202,500	16,200 x $12 = $194,400	17,600 x $12 = $211,200

(1) – (2)
Rate (price) variance
$8,100 unfavorable

(2) – (3)
Efficiency (quantity)
$16,800 favorable

$8,700 favorable total (net) variance

c. The diagram approach has the proof built in; otherwise, the following proofs apply:

Proof of material variances

Standard material costs (22,000 standard pounds × $5)	$110,000
Actual material costs	103,012
Net favorable variance	$ 6,988
Material price variance	$ 3,962 (U)
Material quantity variance	10,950 (F)
	$ 6,988

Proof of labor variances

Standard labor cost (17,600 standard hours × $12 standard rate) ..	$211,200
Actual labor costs	202,500
Net favorable variance	$ 8,700
Labor quantity variance	$ 16,800 (F)
Labor rate variance	8,100 (U)
Net variance	$ 8,700

F = favorable; U = unfavorable.

d.

Direct Materials Inventory	102,440	
Accounts Payable		102,440
Work in Process Inventory	104,000	
Material Usage Price Variance . . .	3,940	
Material Quantity Variance		5,500
Direct Materials Inventory		102,440
Work in Process Inventory	195,840	
Labor Rate Variance	7,500	
Labor Efficiency Variance		15,840
Wages Payable		187,500

Review Questions

1. Name four objectives of a standard cost system.

2. Who should assist the cost accountant in setting material price standards?

3. What is the relationship between budgets and standard costs?

4. Discuss the advantages of a standard cost system.

5. Why is it imperative that the standard cost system have the support of top management before initiation of the system?

6. Which factors should a company consider in deciding how tight standards should be?

7. Why are yardsticks for performance measurement needed? What limitations are inherent in any approach in which actual current costs are compared with historical cost data?

8. Discuss the methods available for developing labor rate standards.

9. When can the total standard quantity allowed be determined? How is it determined?

10. What are the advantages of integrating standards in the accounting system as opposed to only using them for statistical analysis?

11. Discuss the procedures to establish material quantity standards.

12. *a.* Discuss why you agree or disagree with the following: "A primary focus on direct labor standards and variances leads to long production runs."
    b. Discuss whether long production runs are profitable.

13. Discuss whether you think an allowance for waste and shrinkage should be made in material quantity standards. Which factors should a company consider in making this decision?

14. Why is it incorrect in a labor efficiency variance to compare actual hours and budgeted hours?

15. Which departments should be held responsible for an
    a. Unfavorable materials usage variance?
    b. Unfavorable materials price variance?

CPA/CMA/CIA Multiple Choice Questions

1. (CIA) The total budgeted direct labor cost of a company for the month was set at $75,000 when 5,000 units were planned to be produced. The following cost standard, stated in terms of direct labor-hours (DLH), was used to develop the budget for direct labor cost:

   1.25 DLH @ $12.00/DLH = $15.00/unit produced

The actual operating results for the month were as follows:

Actual units produced	5,200
Actual direct labor-hours worked	6,600
Actual direct labor cost	$77,220

The direct labor efficiency variance for the month would be:

a. $4,200 unfavorable.
b. $3,000 unfavorable.
c. $2,220 unfavorable.
d. $1,200 unfavorable.

2. (AICPA) On the diagram below, the line *OW* represents the standard labor cost at any output volume expressed in direct labor-hours. Point *S* indicates the actual output at standard cost, and point *A* indicates the actual hours and actual cost required to produce *S*.

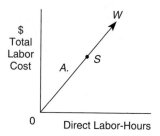

Which of the following variances are favorable or unfavorable?

	Rate Variance	Efficiency Variance
a.	Favorable	Unfavorable
b.	Favorable	Favorable
c.	Unfavorable	Unfavorable
d.	Unfavorable	Favorable

3. (AICPA) Tub Company uses a standard cost system. The following information pertains to direct labor for Product B for the month of October:

Actual rate paid	$8.40 per hour
Standard rate	$8.00 per hour
Standard hours allowed for actual production ..	2,000 hours
Labor efficiency variance	$1,600 unfavorable

What were the actual hours worked?

a. 1,800.
b. 1,810.
c. 2,190.
d. 2,200.

4. (AICPA) For the month of April, Thorp Company's records disclosed the following data relating to direct labor:

Actual costs	$10,000	
Rate variance	1,000	favorable
Efficiency variance	1,500	unfavorable
Standard cost	$ 9,500	

For the month of April, actual direct labor hours amounted to 2,000. In April, Thorp's standard direct labor rate per hour was

a. $5.50.
b. $5.00.
c. $4.75.
d. $4.50.

5. (CIA) A company producing a single product employs the following direct material cost standard for each unit of output:

    3 pounds of material @ $4.00/pound = $12.00/output unit

    Data regarding the operations for the current month are as follows:

Planned production	26,000 units
Actual production	23,000 units
Actual purchases of direct materials	
(75,000 pounds)	$297,000
Direct materials used in production	70,000 pounds

    What would be the amount of the direct material purchase price variance and direct material quantity variance that the company would recognize for the month?

	Purchase Price Variance	**Quantity Variance**
a.	$3,120 favorable	$32,000 favorable
b.	$3,000 favorable	$24,000 unfavorable
c.	$3,000 favorable	$4,000 unfavorable
d.	$2,800 favorable	$4,000 unfavorable

6. (AICPA) Dahl Company uses a standard costing system in connection with the manufacture of a one-size-fits-all article of clothing. Each unit of finished product contains 2 yards of direct material. However, a 20 percent direct material spoilage calculated on input quantities occurs during the manufacturing process. The cost of the direct material is $3 per yard. The standard direct material cost per unit of finished product is

    a. $4.80.
    b. $6.00.
    c. $7.20.
    d. $7.50.

7. (CIA) Abnormal spoilage is

    a. Not expected to occur when perfection standards are used.
    b. Not usually controllable by the production supervisor.
    c. The result of unrealistic production standards.
    d. Not expected to occur under efficient operating conditions.

8. (AICPA) Information on Rex Company's direct material costs for May 19X5 is as follows:

Actual quantity of direct materials purchased and	
used	30,000 pounds
Actual cost of direct materials	$84,000
Unfavorable direct materials usage variance . .	$ 3,000
Standard quantity of direct materials allowed for	
May production	29,000 pounds

    For the month of May, what was Rex's direct materials price variance?

    a. $2,800 favorable.
    b. $2,800 unfavorable.
    c. $6,000 unfavorable.
    d. $6,000 favorable.

9. (AICPA) Palo Corporation manufactures one product with a standard direct labor cost of two hours at $6.00 per hour. During March, 500 units were produced using 1,050 hours at $6.10 per hour. The unfavorable direct labor efficiency variance is

    a. $100.
    b. $105.
    c. $300.
    d. $305.

10.–13.   (CMA) These items use the following data:

Arrow Industries employs a standard cost system in which direct materials inventory is carried at standard cost. Arrow has established the following standards for the prime costs of one unit of product:

	Standard Quantity	Standard Price	Standard Cost
Direct materials	8 pounds	$1.80 per pound	$14.40
Direct labor	0.25 hour	$8.00 per hour	2.00
			$16.40

During May, Arrow purchased 160,000 pounds of direct material at a total cost of $304,000. The total factory wages for May were $42,000, 90 percent of which were for direct labor. Arrow manufactured 19,000 units of product during May using 142,500 pounds of direct material and 5,000 direct labor-hours.

10.   The direct material purchase price variance for May is

   a. $16,000 favorable.
   b. $16,000 unfavorable.
   c. $14,250 favorable.
   d. $14,250 unfavorable.
   e.   Some amount other than those given above.

11.   The direct material usage (quantity) variance for May is

   a. $14,400 unfavorable.
   b. $1,100 favorable.
   c. $17,100 unfavorable.
   d. $17,100 favorable.
   e.   Some amount other than those given above.

12.   The direct labor price (rate) variance for May is

   a. $2,200 favorable.
   b. $1,900 unfavorable.
   c. $2,000 unfavorable.
   d. $2,090 favorable.
   e.   Some amount other than those given above.

13.   The direct labor usage (efficiency) variance for May is

   a. $2,200 favorable.
   b. $2,000 favorable.
   c. $2,000 unfavorable.
   d. $1,800 unfavorable.
   e.   Some amount other than those given above.

Exercises

E11–1 Direct-Labor Variance (L.O. 2)

Data regarding William Company's direct labor costs for June are as follows:

Total direct labor payroll	$244,500
Actual direct labor-hours	28,200
Standard direct labor-hours	29,000
Direct labor efficiency variance—favorable	6,480

Required:

Determine the direct labor rate variance for the William Company. Indicate whether it is favorable or unfavorable.

E11–2 Material Variances (L.O. 2)

Bowman Company's direct material costs for the manufacture of a product are as follows for a month:

Actual unit purchase price	$ 3.30
Standard quantity allowed for actual production	5,100
Quantity purchased and used for actual production	5,500
Standard unit price	$ 3.00

Required:

a. Determine the material price variance.
b. Determine the material usage variance.
c. Prove your answers.

E11–3 Direct Labor Entries Using Standard Costs (L.O. 4)

The standard rate is $24 per direct labor-hour for Ace Company. In the current month, actual hours were 12,800 at an actual price of $23.50 per hour. For the output achieved, the standard direct labor-hours allowed were 12,000.

Required:

Prepare general journal entries isolating labor and efficiency variances under the following two systems assuming:
a. Work in Process Inventory is carried at standard hours allowed times standard prices.
b. Price variances are isolated when labor costs are originally journalized and efficiency variances are isolated when units are transferred to Finished Goods from Work in Process Inventory.

E11–4 Unit Standard and Actual Material Cost (L.O. 3)

Jeanne, Inc.'s records show the following data relating to direct materials cost for November:

Units of finished product manufactured	$ 8,500
Standard direct materials per unit of production	8 lbs.
Quantity of direct materials used	68,750 lbs.
Direct materials quantity variance (unfavorable)	$ 2,850
Direct materials price variance (favorable)	$13,750

There is no work in process either at the beginning or the end of the month.

Required:

a. Calculate the standard direct material cost per unit of finished product.
b. Derive the actual direct material cost per unit of finished product.

E11–5 Quantity Variances for Material and Labor (L.O. 2)

NB Company uses standard costing as one of the controlling techniques to manage its manufacturing cost. For June, the following data apply to its two products:

	Standard Material per Unit	Standard Labor per Unit	Units Produced in June
Product 01	4 pounds	1 hour	1,250
Product 22	3 pounds	2 hours	1,000

Actual usage in June was 7,600 pounds of materials and 3,550 labor-hours.

Required:

a. Calculate the material usage variance in pounds and the labor efficiency variance in hours.
b. Restate the variances in monetary terms if the standard materials price is $5 per pound and the standard labor rate is $8 per hour.

E11–6 Material and Labor Variances (L.O. 2)

Bolton Corporation engaged its engineers to analyze factory conditions and to determine material and labor standards. Their analysis generated the following standards:

	Per Finished Unit
Material (20 pounds @ $4)	$80
Labor (4 hours @ $5)	20

Management had planned to produce 1,500 units, but due to favorable conditions, produced 1,550 units. There were 30,400 pounds of material used at a cost of $118,560. There were 6,380 hours of labor employed at a cost of $32,410.40.

Required:

Calculate material and labor variances, indicating whether they are favorable or unfavorable.

E11–7 Material and Labor Variances in a Process Costing System (L.O. 2)

Mary Miller, Inc., produces batches of a petroleum product on an assembly line. The standard costs per batch are as follows:

	Total
Direct materials (80 gallons)	$ 40
Direct labor (60 hours)	216

Workers completed 480 batches this period; ending inventory consists of 69 batches, one-third complete. There was no beginning inventory. The following costs were incurred:

Direct materials used (40,743 gallons)	$ 17,519.49
Direct labor (29,677 hours)	108,321.05

Required:

a. Prepare a variance analysis for material and labor.
b. Prove your material variances.
c. Prove your labor variances.

E11–8 Material and Labor Variances (L.O. 2)

Dexter Company's management and production personnel analyzed factory conditions and determined the following material and labor standards:

	Per Finished Unit
Material (12 pounds @ $4)	$48
Labor (2 hours @ $5)	$10

Management had planned to produce 2,000 units, but due to machine breakdowns produced only 1,500 units. There were 15,000 pounds of material used at a cost of $75,000. There were 3,080 hours of labor employed at a cost of $13,860.

Required:

a. Calculate material and labor variances, indicating whether favorable or unfavorable.
b. Provide possible explanations for these variances.

Problems

P11–9 Different Systems for Recording Material (L.O. 4)

Byrd Company has 35 pounds of direct material R4 in its beginning inventory, the actual unit cost of which was $5.15. The company uses a LIFO perpetual inventory system. During May, Byrd made the following purchases of direct material R4 on account:

May 4:	60 pounds @ $4.90 per pound
May 6:	40 pounds @ $5.05 per pound

The engineering staff has determined that for each finished unit, the standard should be four pounds at a standard price of $5 per pound.

On May 7, workers requisitioned 106 pounds of raw material to make 28 units. They returned three pounds to the material storeroom at the end of the month.

Required:

a. Prepare the journal entries necessary to record the material transactions under each of the following accounting systems:
   (1) Standard cost system with direct material inventory kept at standard cost. (Record only one type of price variance.)
   (2) Actual cost system.
   (3) Standard cost system with direct materials inventory kept at actual cost.
b. Account for the difference in the material price variance computed using Requirement *a* (1) and (3). Show the details of your computation.

P11–10 Impact of Bonuses on Material Variances (L.O. 3)

Vinson, Inc., has installed a bonus system in which the purchasing agent receives 8 percent of any favorable purchase price variance. The production supervisor, in turn, receives an 8 percent bonus on favorable material usage variances. Vinson established the following standards per finished unit:

Material (2 gallons of Grade A @ $6 a gallon)	$12 per unit
Labor (4 hour @ $8 per hour)	$32 per unit

The purchasing agent bought 1,450 gallons of Grade C material at $5.50 a gallon. The production supervisor was disappointed that actual units produced were 100 fewer than the 600 units budgeted for the period. Using a total of 1,200 gallons of material, direct labor workers reported 2,300 hours of labor for a total pay of $18,860.

Required:

a. Prepare journal entries for all materials transactions needed to record direct materials inventory at actual cost assuming a standard cost system is used.
b. Make journal entries for all materials transactions needed to record direct materials inventory at standard cost. (Record only one price variance.)
c. Prepare journal entries for all direct labor transactions.
d. Point out the oversight the company has made in establishing the bonus.

P11–11 Different Systems for Recording Material (L.O. 4)

Hilton, Inc., has 10 pounds of Direct Material BX in its beginning inventory, which has an actual unit cost of $45. The company uses a LIFO perpetual inventory system. During June, Hilton made the following purchases of Direct Material BX on account:

June 5	70 pounds @ $48.00 per pound
20	40 pounds @ $52.00 per pound

The engineering staff has determined that for each finished unit, the standard should be 4 pounds at a standard price of $50 per pound.

On June 25, workers requisitioned 66 pounds of direct material for a 14-unit order. After producing 14 units, they returned 6 unused pounds to the material storeroom at the end of the month.

Required:

a. Prepare the journal entries necessary to record the materials transactions under each of the following accounting systems. (Record a separate entry for each date and do not combine entries; also record in a separate entry the return of the unused material.)
   (1) Standard cost system with direct materials inventory kept at actual cost.
   (2) Standard cost system with direct materials inventory kept at standard cost. (Record only one price variance.)
   (3) Actual cost system.

b. Account for the difference in the materials price variance computed using (1) and (2) from Requirement *a*. Show details of computation.

c. Explain which approach you would advise using under these circumstances. Why?

P11–12 Impact of Planned and Sales Activity on Prime Cost Variance (L.O. 3)

Trueblood Company is a toy manufacturing company. Two major products of Trueblood, AJI and XTF, are the two fastest-selling toys in the market. Each toy uses Materials X and Y. The following unit standard costs apply:

	Material X	Material Y	Direct Labor
AJI	3 pounds @ $5	2 pounds @ $7	1 hour @ $8
XTF	2 pounds @ $5	3 pounds @ $7	2 hours @ $8

During May, workers completed 4,900 units of AJI and 2,950 units of XTF and transferred them to the Package Department. Ending inventory in May consisted of 200 units of AJI and 100 units of XTF; both products were at the 50 percent stage of completion.

Beginning inventory comprised 100 units of AJI and 100 units of XTF with the following cost:

> AJI and XTF were at the 50 percent stage of completion.
> 560 pounds of Material X costing $3,080.
> 520 pounds of Material Y costing $3,536.
> 160 hours of labor costing $1,360.

The following costs were incurred in May:

> Material X used = 20,940 pounds costing $103,345
> Material Y used = 18,360 pounds costing $131,456
> Direct labor used = 10,990 hours costing $83,380.

Required:

a. Calculate the material price and usage variances for the month using weighted-average costing.

b. Calculate the labor rate and efficiency variances for the month using weighted-average costing.

c. Explain how your answers to Requirements *a* and *b* would change if Trueblood Company wants to add a new shift in its production schedule starting in June.

d. Determine if you would change your answers to Requirements *a* and *b* if you had been told that the fire insurance premium of Trueblood Company had been raised to $5,000 per month starting in May.

P11–13 Recording Material and Labor (L.O. 4)

Sharon Perfume Company had planned to produce 1,000 units of Vrago, a secret mixture, each month. Sharon's budget included engineering standards of 6,000 pounds of direct material at a total cost of $12,000. The labor budget was for 4,000 hours at a total cost of $48,000.

At the end of the month, the accountant determined that 1,200 units of Vrago were produced and that 7,600 pounds of direct material were purchased at a cost of $18,000. The storekeeper reported 600 pounds were not used and were still in the raw material inventory. The labor cost summary revealed 5,400 actual hours at a total cost of $70,200 were incurred.

Required:

a. Prepare all journal entries for material transactions in a system in which the only type of price variance used is a material purchase price variance.

b. Prepare all journal entries for material transactions in a system in which the only type of price variance used is a material usage price variance.

c. Make the labor journal entries needed to record price and quantity variances regardless of the system of recording material price variances used.

P11–14 Journal Entries for Material and Labor (L.O. 4)

Robertson, Inc., has established the following standards per finished batch:

Material (6 pounds @ $4)	$24 per batch
Labor (2 hours @ $15)	$30 per batch

The Purchasing Department reported buying 80 pounds at a total cost of $332. The supervisor of the Production Department reported using 62 pounds to make 10 batches even though production plans were to manufacture 12 batches. Actual labor cost was $370 for a total of 25 hours.

Required:

a. Prepare all journal entries for material transactions assuming that the price variance reflects usage; record only one price variance.
b. Prepare all journal entries for the material transactions assuming that material price variances are isolated on purchase; record only one price variance.
c. Prepare all journal entries for labor transactions.

P11–15 Impact of Bonuses on Material Variances (L.O. 3)

Hill Corporation has installed a bonus system in which the purchasing agent receives 10 percent of any favorable purchase price variances. The production supervisor receives 10 percent of any favorable material usage variances.

The Engineering Department established the following standards per finished unit:

Material (5 pounds of Grade A @ $4 a pound)	$ 20 per unit
Labor (8 hours @ $20 an hour)	$160 per unit

The purchasing agent purchased 200 pounds of Grade C material at $3 per pound.

The production supervisor reported that even though 40 units were budgeted to be produced, only 30 units were finished. The supervisor used 180 pounds of material. Direct labor workers reported 260 hours of labor at a total pay of $7,800.

Required:

a. Make journal entries for all material transactions needed to record direct material inventory at actual cost assuming a standard cost system is used.
b. Make journal entries for all material transactions needed to record direct material inventory at standard cost; record only one price variance.
c. Make journal entries for all labor transactions.
d. Explain the oversight the company made in establishing the bonus.

P11–16 Methods of Recording Materials Using a Standard Cost System (L.O. 4)

Murray, Inc., has asked their CPA to provide them with three different approaches for recording material price variations. In their first month of operation, they decided to adopt a standard cost system and have purchased enough raw materials for several months of operations using the following data:

Standard cost per unit	4 gallons @ $3.00 per gallon
Gallons purchased	40,000 for $90,000
Gallons used in production	13,200
Units finished	3,000

Required:

a. Using the three different methods illustrated in this chapter for recording materials in a standard cost system, prepare the journal entries. Label your different methods.
b. Evaluate these methods using the data given.

P11–17 Analysis of Material and Labor (L.O. 3)

ABC Company uses standard costing to control its manufacturing cost. Its single product passes through two production operations. Under normal conditions, 2.5 pounds of direct material are required to make one unit of product; the standard price of direct material is $3 per pound. All of the materials for a unit are issued to and used in operation 1. In operation 1, standard labor time is 10 molded units per direct labor-hour at a standard wage rate of $8.25. In operation 2, where the molded units are painted, standard output is eight units per direct labor-hour, with a standard wage rate of $9.15 per hour. Normal volume is 256,000 units per month. In October, output was 204,800 units and 563,200 pounds of direct material were consumed. In addition, ABC purchased 800,000 pounds of direct material for $2,240,000. No spoilage occurred in operation 2. There was no beginning or ending work in process inventory. October direct labor-hours and costs were as follows:

	Direct Labor	
	Hours	Costs
Operation 1	20,500	$164,000
Operation 2	25,800	239,940

Required:

a. Prepare an analysis of direct labor in October for ABC's two operations.

b. Compute the material usage price and quantity variances.

c. Assume that in operation 1, standard labor performance was expressed as 25 pounds of direct material processed per direct labor-hour (rather than 10 molded units per direct labor-hour). It has come to your attention that the unfavorable material quantity variance in October was caused by the purchasing agent's buying direct materials of an off-standard quality.

   (1) With this knowledge, how would you—if at all—change your analysis of direct labor costs for October?

   (2) Who should be charged with the material quantity variance?

d. Explain if the purchasing agent made a wise decision in purchasing the off-standard direct material.

P11–18 Material and Labor Variances (L.O. 2)

Spokane Company established these standards for its only product:

Direct material A	4 gallons @ $3 per gallon
Direct material B	3 gallons @ $4 per gallon
Direct labor	2 hours @ $8 per hour
Factory overhead	Applied at $15 per machine hour

A summary of the first year's costs and related data for the manufacturing process follows:

1. Purchases of material were 2,500 gallons of Material A for a total of $7,375; 1,000 gallons of Material B for a total of $4,050. (Direct Materials Inventory is recorded at standard.)

2. Five hundred units were finished and 60 units were at the one-third stage of completion. This required 2,100 gallons of Material A, 1,600 gallons of Material B, and 1,100 hours of direct labor costing $9,350.

Required:

a. Indicate the total credits to the direct materials account for the issuance of Material A for the year.

b. Determine:

   (1) The material quantity variance for Materials A and B.

   (2) The material purchase price variance for Materials A and B.

   (3) The labor quantity variance.

   (4) The labor rate variance.

c. Explain how your answers to Requirement *b* would change if you were told that management planned to make 600 units during their first year of operations.

d. Explain how your answers to Requirement *b* would change if you were told that sales were 480 units during their first year of operations.

P11–19 Developing Standard Costs (CMA) (L.O. 2, 3)

Ogwood Company is a small manufacturer of wooden household items. Al Rivkin, corporate controller, plans to implement a standard cost system for Ogwood. Rivkin has information from several co-workers that will assist him in developing standards for Ogwood's products.

One of Ogwood's products is a wooden cutting board. Each cutting board requires 1.25 board feet of lumber and 12 minutes of direct labor time to prepare and cut the lumber. The cutting boards are inspected after they are cut. Because the cutting boards are made of a natural material that has imperfections, one board is normally rejected for each five that are accepted. Workers attach four rubber foot pads to each good cutting board. It takes a total of fifteen minutes of direct labor time to attach all four foot pads and finish each cutting board. The lumber for the cutting boards costs $3 per board foot, and each foot pad costs $0.05. Direct labor is paid at the rate of $8 per hour.

Required:

a. Develop the standard cost for the direct cost components of the cutting board. For each direct cost component of the cutting board, the standard cost should identify the
   (1) Standard quantity.
   (2) Standard rate.
   (3) Standard cost per unit.
b. Identify the advantages of implementing a standard cost system.
c. Explain the role of each of the following persons in developing standards:
   (1) Purchasing manager.
   (2) Industrial engineer.
   (3) Cost accountant.

Cases

C11–20 Tight and Current Standards (L.O. 3)

BMD Corporation has recently installed a standard cost system. Management adopted fairly tight standards that can be achieved if the workers perform at an efficient level. The monthly labor budget established for 1,600 units called for 5,600 hours at a total cost of $79,800. The monthly direct material budget for 3,600 gallons was set as $10,800.

The vice president in charge of manufacturing believes that the quantity standards established are too tight and that an additional set of "expected standards" should be established. He believes that an extra hour of labor and three-fourths gallon of materials per unit should be added to the standards. He also believes, however, that the standard labor rate and the standard material prices correctly reflect current conditions. His reasoning is that top management is not going to get upset if the employees take an extra hour to complete the units or use more material because they recognize that the standards are tight.

The cost clerk determines that 1,550 units were completed during the month. The summary of labor time tickets reveals that 5,813 direct labor-hours were used at a cost of $81,382. There were 4,650 gallons used at an actual cost of $14,415.

Required:

a. Explain what you would advise the company to do in regard to establishing another set of standards.
b. Compute the direct material variances and labor variances using the tight standards. Label each variance indicating whether it is favorable or unfavorable.

c. Determine what the direct material variances and labor variances would be using the vice president's "expected standards." Label each variance indicating whether it is favorable or unfavorable.

C11–21 The Use of Standards as a Motivational Device (L.O. 1)

The management of Pinkerton Manufacturing Company has become alarmed over a consistent increase in production costs. Most of the increase is attributed to direct labor. Accountants advised the company that a standard cost system would help control labor as well as other costs.

Since detailed production records have not been maintained, the company has hired Comer Consulting Engineers to establish labor standards. On conclusion of a thorough study of the manufacturing process, Comer recommended a labor standard of one unit of production every 15 minutes, or 32 units per day per worker. As a part of their report to management, the engineers informed Pinkerton that their wage rates were below the industry average of $24.50 per hour.

The production manager was somewhat concerned about Comer's labor standard. It was her position that the employees could not attain it because it is too tight. Based on firsthand experience, she considered one unit of production every 20 minutes, or 24 units per day, more reasonable.

Management recognized that the standard should be at a high level to motivate workers, but not so high that it fails to provide adequate information for control and cost comparison purposes. After giving the matter much thought, management agreed on a dual standard. The engineers' labor standard of one unit every 15 minutes was adopted by the plant as a motivational device, but a labor standard of one unit every 20 minutes was adopted for reporting purposes. The workers were not to be informed of the different labor reporting standard.

The production manager held a meeting with the workers to inform them that a standard cost system was being implemented and to educate them about how the system works.

The new cost system was put into effect on March 1 along with a wage increase to $24.50 per hour. Six months later, the following data, based on the standards recommended by Comer, were reviewed by management:

	March	April	May	June	July	August
Production in units	10,000	9,800	9,200	9,000	8,600	8,800
Direct labor-hours	2,800	2,650	2,700	2,750	2,850	2,800
Variance from labor standard	$ 1,350(U)	$ 900(U)	$1,800(U)	$2,250(U)	$3,150(U)	$2,700(U)

U = Unfavorable.

Other factors of production had not changed materially during this six-month period.

Required:

a. Discuss the different standards and their influence on motivation. Include the effect on plant workers of Pinkerton's acceptance of the engineering firm's labor standard.
b. Discuss your reaction to the adoption of dual standards.

C11–22 Dysfunctional Behavior and Standards (CMA) (L.O. 3)

Seaburg Corporation is a manufacturer of personal computers. Because of rapidly changing technology in the computer industry, Seaburg has developed a strategy of rapid implementation of new products in order to survive in this highly competitive market.

Because of this rapid implementation of new products, Seaburg must react quickly to develop standard manufacturing costs for new products. The standards for the newest product, a portable computer, were developed almost overnight in the Accounting and Engineering Departments by referring to the standards of a closely related nonportable computer which had been in production for more than two years.

Frank Ceci, Assembly Department manager, was pleased with his department's morale and performance over the last two years when the nonportable model was being produced. During that period, he had repeatedly earned bonuses based on performance reports that compared actual and standard manufacturing costs.

However, implementation of the new portable computer and its related standards have led to unfavorable performance reports for the Assembly Department. In an attempt to improve departmental performance, Ceci made a number of changes in the production process. These changes were not popular with the assembly workers and resulted in some harsh exchanges between Ceci and two of the more influential and outspoken employees in the department. All that Ceci and the departmental employees agreed on during the exchanges was that the standards for the new portable computer were not realistic. Departmental employees reacted to Ceci's most recent changes to the production process with a deliberate slowdown until he restored operations to the former procedures.

In spite of Ceci's efforts to improve departmental performance, unfavorable reports have continued. Consequently, Ceci is considering resigning from his position to accept employment with a competitor.

Required:

a. Explain if Seaburg Corporation's strategy of rapid implementation of new products should be changed because of:
   (1) Unfavorable performance reports for the Assembly Department.
   (2) Dysfunctional behavior by Assembly Department employees.
b. With reference to the development of standard manufacturing costs for the new portable computer:
   (1) Describe the errors made by Seaburg Corporation in establishing and implementing the standards.
   (2) Recommend how Seaburg Corporation should have established standards in order that they would more likely be accepted by the Assembly Department employees.
c. Describe procedures that could be used by Frank Ceci in making production process changes that would be more acceptable to the Assembly Department employees.

Standard Costs and Variances for Factory Overhead

After studying this chapter, you should be able to:

1. Prepare factory overhead variance analyses using a standard cost system.

2. Journalize and prorate overhead variances.

3. Understand the purpose of a standard cost system and that its value begins when the causes of variances are analyzed.

4. Explain why the overall objective of making money is achieved by reducing inventory and operating expenses, and by increasing throughput and product quality rather than by making sure one cost center has a favorable variance.

PRACTICAL
APPLICATION BOX
Performance Measurement for World-Class Manufacturers

J. I. Case Company, a division of Tenneco, Inc., is in the process of implementing JIT procedures and controls for running plant operations. This program includes an in-depth look at these five general categories of performance measurements: quality, delivery, production process time, flexibility, and finance costs. Managers find better control of inventory occurs with JIT because there is less inventory. Inventory levels in world-class manufacturing facilities are measured by dollar amount comparisons of pres-

ently held raw material, work in process, and finished goods to the prior period. Dollar amounts are at standard cost. The percent of scheduled orders delivered on time is another performance measure. The goal of minimizing manufacturing process time increases quality and flexibility and reduces delivery time and costs. Flexibility addresses how well an operation can adapt to changes. A final performance measure is ensuring that financial reports provide useful management information on a timely basis.

From: Michael R. Sellenheim, "J. I. Case Company: Performance Measurement," *Management Accounting*, September 1991, pp. 50–53.

Introduction

Factory overhead cost standards provide a means of allocating factory overhead to cost inventories for pricing decisions and controlling expenses. However, cost accountants are recognizing that accounting measures such as standard cost variances require monitoring. Reporting variances for individual departments encourages cost center managers to focus only on improving their performance. When individual segments of an organization attempt to enhance their individual efficiencies with favorable standard cost variances without regard to subsequent effects, throughput decreases and the goal of making money is sacrificed.

Further, accountants recognize that it is a waste of their time to simply compute variances and place them neatly on a page for distribution to management. Computing variances is not as important as knowing what to do if a significant variance occurs. The benefit of a standard cost system comes from determining the cause of the variance and correcting the situation. Accountants do not investigate every variance. By studying only significant variances, they emphasize the management by exception principle.

Setting Overhead Standards (L.O. 1)

There is a close similarity between setting overhead standards and applying factory overhead in a **normal costing system** and in a standard cost system. An actual costing system uses actual overhead rates to apply indirect costs while a normal costing system uses budgeted rates to apply indirect costs based on actual hours or other cost drivers. A standard cost system uses budgeted rates based on standard hours or other cost drivers allowed for actual production. In a cost system not employing standards, there are no standard hours—actual hours or another cost driver is the only means available for applying overhead. A standard cost system has both actual and standard hours, but we use standard hours to apply overhead to Work in Process Inventory. Our definition of applied overhead in a standard cost system differs from applied overhead in a system not employing standards.

Selecting Budgeted Capacity

As discussed in Chapter 4, one of these four capacity levels—theoretical, practical, normal, and expected actual—is selected as the volume basis or **denominator capacity. Theoretical capacity** is rarely chosen because it does not represent an attainable level of performance. Standards set on **practical capacity** are more likely to be attainable and are more realistic than theoretical standards. Either **normal capacity** or **expected actual capacity** is the basis for current standards. A disadvantage of using expected actual capacity is that frequent, costly revisions of the standards may be necessary.

After selecting the capacity level, we allocate costs on a volume-related or nonvolume-related base. Commonly used volume-related bases include machine-hours, direct labor-hours, direct labor costs, direct material costs, and units of production. The evaluation of these bases given in Chapter 2 also applies to a standard cost system. An activity-based costing system uses such nonvolume-related activities as number of scheduled production runs or inspections. After expressing volume based on machine-hours, the number of inspections, or another basis, we estimate the factory overhead incurred at this level.

Plantwide or Departmental Rates

Some companies use a single plantwide rate for standard factory overhead while others set a standard overhead rate for each cost center or department. Each cost center should have its own rate if the amount of overhead varies significantly between departments. Departmental overhead rates are also appropriate if all products do not pass through the same departments.

We determine standard factory overhead rates to cost inventory for producing departments only. Chapter 4 illustrated a normal costing system of allocating budgeted indirect costs to production and service departments and then distributing the service department budgeted costs to production departments. Standard costing also uses this procedure. However, normal costing may give less attention to estimating factory overhead costs by referring only to historical cost.

Assume an automated factory selects a normal capacity level of 1,000 units or 2,000 machine-hours as its budgeted volume. The company uses machine-hours as its basis because it has found a causal relationship between machine hours and the incurrence of factory depreciation, supplies, indirect labor, and other overhead costs. To determine the standard factory overhead rates, accountants then estimate the following standard variable and fixed factory overhead for this volume.

Normal capacity or budgeted volume (1,000 units × 2 hours each)	2,000 machine-hours
Standard variable factory overhead	$ 8,000
Standard fixed factory overhead	32,000
Standard total factory overhead	$40,000

Standard variable factory overhead rate per machine-hour: $\dfrac{\$8,000}{2,000 \text{ machine-hours}} = \$4$

Standard (budgeted) fixed factory overhead rate per machine-hour: $\dfrac{\$32,000}{2,000 \text{ machine-hours}} = \$16$

Standard (budgeted) total factory overhead rate per machine-hour: $\dfrac{\$40,000}{2,000 \text{ machine-hours}} = \$20$

Because this $20 overhead rate is known throughout the accounting period, the company applies overhead to each job as it is finished. Overhead is also applied to unfinished jobs remaining in work in process at the end of the period. A process costing system applies the standard overhead rate to the equivalent units calculated for overhead, as illustrated in the Problem for Self-Study at the end of the chapter.

Overhead Variance Methods (L.O. 1)

Accountants do not agree on which of the following three sets of factory overhead variances is most appropriate. All sets analyze the **net overhead variance,** which is the difference between the actual overhead incurred and the overhead applied to the products using the total standard factory overhead rate. Note that the three- and four-variance methods are detailed variations of the two-variance method.

1. Two-variance method:

    a. Controllable variance.
    b. Production volume variance.

2. Three-variance method:

    a. Total overhead spending variance.
    b. Variable overhead efficiency variance.
    c. Production volume variance.

3.   Four-variance method:

   a.   Variable overhead spending variance.
   b.   Fixed overhead spending variance.
   c.   Variable overhead efficiency variance.
   d.   Production volume variance.

All three methods compute the production volume variance in the same manner.

Data for Overhead Variance. Exhibits 12–1, 12–2, and 12–4 present the three methods of computing factory overhead variances based on the following data:

Standard variable overhead (2 machine-hours @ $4 per hour)	$ 8 per unit
Standard fixed overhead (2 machine-hours @ $16 per hour)	$32 per unit
Budgeted fixed factory overhead at standard	$32,000
Budgeted volume: 1,000 units × 2 hours = 2,000 machine-hours	
900 units of finished product were completed.	
Actual machine-hours	1,890 hours
Actual variable factory overhead	$ 9,000
Actual fixed factory overhead	31,000
Actual total factory overhead	$40,000

Three Volume Levels Used

Overhead variance analysis uses these three volume levels that become available at different times.

1.   Known before operations begin: Budgeted, normal, denominator, predetermined capacity—2,000 machine-hours.
2.   Known after operations end: Standard volume allowed—900 units × 2 hours = 1,800 machine-hours.
3.   Known after operations end: Actual volume—1,890 machine-hours.

Accountants cannot correctly compute standard volume allowed when using units of production as the basis for standards. This explains why units of production is usually not an appropriate basis for a standard cost system.

Two-Variance Method

These variances comprise the two-variance method for factory overhead:

1.   *Controllable variance*
     Actual total factory overhead
     Compared with: Budget based on *standard* capacity used [(Standard variable factory overhead rate × Standard hours) + Total budgeted fixed factory overhead costs].

2.   *Production volume variance (noncontrollable variance)*
     (Budgeted hours, such as normal capacity hours, used for determining standard overhead rates − Standard hours allowed for the output achieved) × Standard fixed factory overhead rate at budgeted capacity.

Exhibit 12–1 illustrates both the diagram and equation approaches for the two-variance method. You may select whichever approach you find easier. The diagram approach offers the advantage of containing a built-in proof.

Production Volume Variance. A **production volume variance** arises whenever the volume level achieved for actual factory output differs from the

EXHIBIT 12–1   Two-Variance Method Illustrated

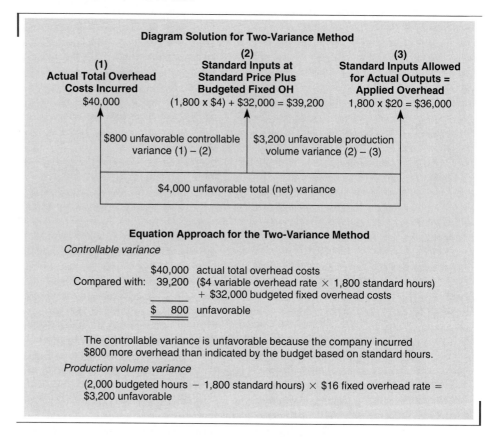

Diagram Solution for Two-Variance Method

| (1) Actual Total Overhead Costs Incurred $40,000 | (2) Standard Inputs at Standard Price Plus Budgeted Fixed OH (1,800 x $4) + $32,000 = $39,200 | (3) Standard Inputs Allowed for Actual Outputs = Applied Overhead 1,800 x $20 = $36,000 |

$800 unfavorable controllable variance (1) – (2)

$3,200 unfavorable production volume variance (2) – (3)

$4,000 unfavorable total (net) variance

Equation Approach for the Two-Variance Method

Controllable variance

$40,000   actual total overhead costs
Compared with: 39,200   ($4 variable overhead rate × 1,800 standard hours) + $32,000 budgeted fixed overhead costs
$ 800   unfavorable

The controllable variance is unfavorable because the company incurred $800 more overhead than indicated by the budget based on standard hours.

Production volume variance

(2,000 budgeted hours − 1,800 standard hours) × $16 fixed overhead rate = $3,200 unfavorable

denominator volume level used for determining the fixed overhead application rate. We refer to this as a production volume variance to distinguish it from the sales volume variance presented in Chapter 24. For simplicity, however, we often simply call it a volume variance. The production volume variance measures the costs or savings from not operating at the volume level planned. Exhibit 12–2 contains a graph illustrating the $3,200 production volume variance. If the volume variance is unfavorable, as shown in Exhibits 12–1 and 12–2, the company did not use its facilities to the extent planned. The company applied $28,800 (1,800 standard hours × $16) fixed overhead, but budgeted to have 2,000 hours on which to apply overhead. The volume variance is unfavorable because there were 200 idle hours to which the lump-sum budgeted fixed factory overhead could not be applied. Instead, if the company produced more than 1,000 units, the volume variance represents the advantage of a higher use of production facilities than expected.

Volume variances distinguish between resource spending and resource usage. **Resource spending** refers to acquiring the facilities to perform activities, such as manufacturing 1,000 units. The company has created a capacity of 1,000 units on which to spend money. **Resource usage** refers to actual performance (i.e., 900 units). Volume variances measure how many available resources are used and the cost of excess capacity or the savings from a better use of facilities than expected. As discussed later in this chapter, management must monitor production to ensure excess inventory is not manufactured merely to ensure a favorable production volume variance.

EXHIBIT 12–2   Production Volume Variance

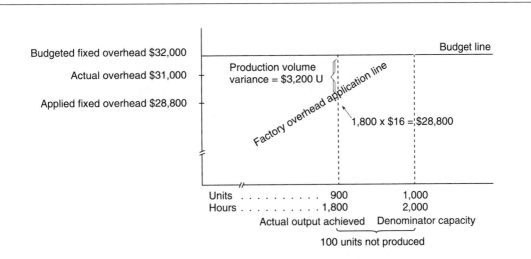

Budgeted fixed overhead $32,000

Actual overhead $31,000

Applied fixed overhead $28,800

Production volume variance = $3,200 U

Factory overhead application line

Budget line

1,800 x $16 = $28,800

Units	900	1,000
Hours	1,800	2,000
	Actual output achieved	Denominator capacity

100 units not produced

Three-Variance Method

In comparing the three-variance method with the two-variance method, note that further division occurs. The controllable variance for the two-variance method divides into the total overhead spending variance and the variable overhead efficiency variance for the three-variance method. The **total overhead spending variance** compares actual total factory overhead to a budget adjusted to actual capacity using the flexible budget formula presented in Chapter 9. These variances comprise the three-variance method:

Controllable variances

1. Total overhead spending variance:
    Actual total factory overhead
    Compared with: Flexible budget allowance adjusted to actual capacity used (Standard variable factory overhead rate × Actual hours) + Total budgeted fixed factory overhead costs.
    Note that this is the same spending variance that is computed under a normal costing system using applied factory overhead rates introduced in Chapter 4.
2. Variable factory overhead efficiency variance:
    (Actual hours − Standard hours) × Standard variable factory overhead rate.

Noncontrollable variance

3. Production volume variance:
    (Budgeted hours − Standard hours) × Standard fixed factory overhead rate at budgeted capacity.

Using the same data as for the two-variance method, Exhibit 12–3 illustrates the three-variance method using the diagram and equation solution.

Variable Overhead Efficiency Variance. The **variable overhead efficiency variance** reflects the efficient or inefficient use of the base on which a company

EXHIBIT 12–3 Three-Variance Method Illustrated

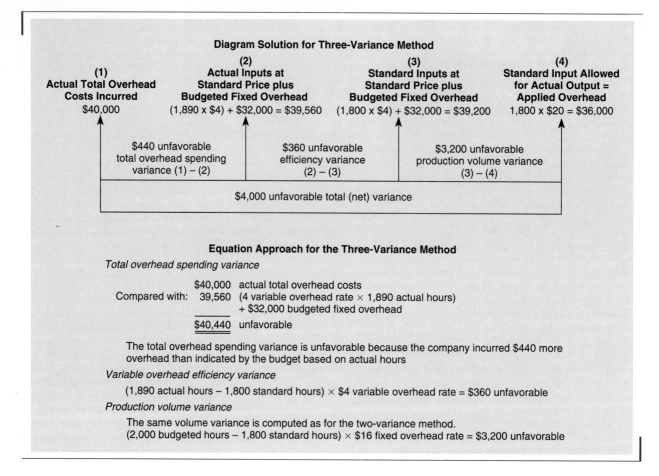

Diagram Solution for Three-Variance Method

| (1) Actual Total Overhead Costs Incurred $40,000 | (2) Actual Inputs at Standard Price plus Budgeted Fixed Overhead (1,890 x $4) + $32,000 = $39,560 | (3) Standard Inputs at Standard Price plus Budgeted Fixed Overhead (1,800 x $4) + $32,000 = $39,200 | (4) Standard Input Allowed for Actual Output = Applied Overhead 1,800 x $20 = $36,000 |

$440 unfavorable total overhead spending variance (1) – (2) $360 unfavorable efficiency variance (2) – (3) $3,200 unfavorable production volume variance (3) – (4)

$4,000 unfavorable total (net) variance

Equation Approach for the Three-Variance Method

Total overhead spending variance

$40,000   actual total overhead costs
Compared with: 39,560   (4 variable overhead rate × 1,890 actual hours)
                          + $32,000 budgeted fixed overhead
$40,440   unfavorable

The total overhead spending variance is unfavorable because the company incurred $440 more overhead than indicated by the budget based on actual hours

Variable overhead efficiency variance

(1,890 actual hours – 1,800 standard hours) × $4 variable overhead rate = $360 unfavorable

Production volume variance

The same volume variance is computed as for the two-variance method.
(2,000 budgeted hours – 1,800 standard hours) × $16 fixed overhead rate = $3,200 unfavorable

applies variable overhead. Note the similarity between this variance and the labor efficiency variance computed in Chapter 11. We assume that inefficiencies in using the base (i.e., machine-hours or production runs scheduled) causes an increase in variable overhead. However, the assumption that variable overhead fluctuates in direct proportion to a specific production volume, such as machine-hours, is fairly weak. Whether this clear-cut relationship exists depends on the specific circumstances.

Machine-hours is the base used in Exhibit 12–3. Because actual machine-hours are greater than the standard allowed, the variance is unfavorable, reflecting an inefficient use of machines. If, instead, a labor-intensive process uses direct labor-hours or direct labor costs, the variable overhead efficiency variance reflects the effect of labor efficiency on overhead. Managers who are responsible for the cost driver are usually held accountable for variable overhead efficiency.

Four-Variance Method

The total overhead spending variance in the three-variance method divides into the variable overhead spending variance and the fixed overhead spending variance for the four-variance method. The variable factory overhead efficiency variance and the production volume variance are the same as for the three-variance method. These four variances make up this method.

Controllable variances

1. Variable overhead spending variance: Actual variable factory overhead
    Compared with: Budget allowance for variable costs adjusted to actual capacity used (Standard variable factory overhead rate × Actual hours).

    Alternatively, (Actual variable overhead rate − Standard variable overhead rate) × actual hours.
    (Note the similarity of this alternative computation and the material price and labor rate variances.)
2. Variable overhead efficiency variance: (Actual hours − Standard hours) × Standard variable factory overhead rate.
3. Fixed overhead spending variance: Budgeted fixed factory overhead
    Compared with: Actual fixed factory overhead.

Noncontrollable variance

4. Production volume variance: (Budgeted hours − Standard hours) × Standard fixed factory overhead rate at budgeted capacity.

Exhibit 12–4 illustrates the diagram and equation solution approach for the four-variance method.

Variable Overhead Spending Variance. A **variable overhead spending variance** occurs because actual costs (such as utilities, supplies, and indirect labor) differ from those budgeted for the actual hours incurred. The spending variance in Exhibit 12–4 is unfavorable because the company incurred $1,440 more factory overhead than indicated by the budget based on actual hours. Also, the spending variance could have occurred because the relationship between machine-hours and variable factory overhead is not perfect. The variable overhead spending variance contains some price items; hence it is also called a **variable overhead price variance.** For example, if supplies cost more than expected, the spending variance will be unfavorable.

The spending variance also contains some efficiency (usage) items. For example, employees may waste some supplies causing cost to be higher than expected. Some companies compute a separate spending variance for certain key components of variable overhead; for example, energy costs in an automated factory. This breakdown analyzes waste and efficiency by cost component. When a spending variance is computed for each cost center or department, the variance becomes the responsibility of the supervisor of the center involved.

Fixed Overhead Spending Variance. The **fixed overhead spending or price variance** reflects the impact of the actual price level on fixed factory overhead. The variance measures changes in fixed overhead costs from the amounts budgeted. The fixed overhead spending variance in Exhibit 12–4 is favorable because actual fixed factory overhead is less than budgeted fixed factory overhead. However, if factory supervisors' salaries, machinery depreciation, or other fixed overhead costs are higher than expected, an unfavorable fixed overhead spending variance results. Even though lacking universal acceptance, we classify the fixed overhead spending variance as controllable. Although low and possibly

EXHIBIT 12–4 Four-Variance Method Illustrated

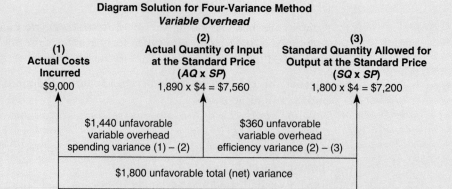

Diagram Solution for Four-Variance Method
Variable Overhead

| (1)
Actual Costs
Incurred
$9,000 | (2)
Actual Quantity of Input
at the Standard Price
(*AQ* x *SP*)
1,890 x $4 = $7,560 | (3)
Standard Quantity Allowed for
Output at the Standard Price
(*SQ* x *SP*)
1,800 x $4 = $7,200 |

$1,440 unfavorable
variable overhead
spending variance (1) – (2)

$360 unfavorable
variable overhead
efficiency variance (2) – (3)

$1,800 unfavorable total (net) variance

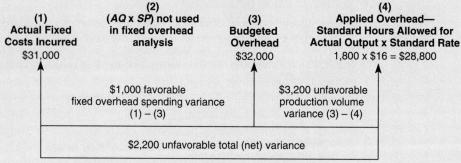

Fixed Overhead

| (1)
Actual Fixed
Costs Incurred
$31,000 | (2)
(*AQ* x *SP*) not used
in fixed overhead
analysis | (3)
Budgeted
Overhead
$32,000 | (4)
Applied Overhead—
Standard Hours Allowed for
Actual Output x Standard Rate
1,800 x $16 = $28,800 |

$1,000 favorable
fixed overhead spending variance
(1) – (3)

$3,200 unfavorable
production volume
variance (3) – (4)

$2,200 unfavorable total (net) variance

AQ = Actual quantity; *SQ* = Standard quantity; *SP* = Standard price;
AP = Actual price

Equation Approach for the Four-Variance Method

Variable overhead spending variance

	$9,000	actual variable overhead costs
Compared with:	7,560	budget allowance for variable overhead ($4 variable overhead rate × 1,890 actual hours)
	$1,400	unfavorable

Alternatively: $9,000/1,890 actual hours = $4.762; ($4.762 – $4) × 1,890 = $1,440 unfavorable

Variable overhead efficiency variance
The variable factory overhead efficiency variance is as computed using the three-variance method.
(1,890 actual hours – 1,800 standard hours) × $4 variable overhead rate = $360 unfavorable

Fixed overhead spending variance

$31,000	actual fixed overhead
32,000	budgeted fixed overhead
$ 1,000	favorable

Production volume variance
The volume variance is the same for the three methods presented:
(2,000 budgeted hours – 1,800 standard hours) x $16 fixed overhead rate = $3,200 unfavorable

middle managers may be unable to control fixed costs, top-level managers can. Despite being unable to control committed costs, line supervisors can often control discretionary fixed factory overhead.

Outline of Interrelationship. Exhibit 12–5 contains an outline of the methods discussed showing their interrelationship. The four-variance method involves a more detailed breakdown of factors not directly related to volume than does the two-variance method. Thus, the four-variance method is more costly and time-consuming to prepare. Also, it is often difficult to separate actual overhead into fixed and variable components.

However, accountants usually prefer the four-variance method because it distinguishes between cost behavior better than the two- or three-variance methods. The additional variances computed give better insight into the reasons why actual overhead differed from that budgeted. Control and responsibility for fixed and variable overhead usually rests with different members of the management team. For example, it would be unfair to hold line supervisors responsible for the difference between actual fixed and budgeted fixed overhead because they usually lack the authority to select plant facilities or insurance policies to cover these facilities. As a result, top managers are accountable for fixed overhead variances.

Proof of Method Used. Regardless of the method used, the variances computed represent a breakdown of the total difference between actual and standard costs. We use this difference called the total or *net factory overhead variance* to prove the variances computed regardless of the method used, as shown in Exhibit 12–5. Using the different methods, the total or net variance equals $4,000:

$40,000 actual total overhead
 36,000 (1,800 standard hours × $20 total standard overhead rate per hour)
$ 4,000 unfavorable net factory overhead variance

Journal Entries Illustrated

The following summary entry records actual fixed and variable factory overhead incurred.

Factory Overhead Control ($9,000 + $31,000) 40,000
    Various Credits 40,000

Accountants can use separate ledger accounts for fixed and variable overhead. Such accounts as supplies, inventory, payroll, accumulated depreciation, and prepaid insurance are credited during the accounting period to record actual factory overhead.

The following entry records the application of total overhead to the products included in the Work in Process Inventory based on the standard hours allowed. Note again that in a normal costing system not employing standards, we would use 1,890 actual hours to apply overhead of $37,800 ($20 × 1,890 actual hours).

Work in Process Inventory (1,800 standard hours × $20
    total standard overhead rate) 36,000
        Factory Overhead Control 36,000

The Factory Overhead Control account now appears as follows:

Factory Overhead Control			
Actual	40,000	Applied at standard	36,000
Balance 4,000			

EXHIBIT 12–5   Overhead Variance Analysis

Two-variance method

Controllable variance

Actual total overhead − [(standard variable
overhead rate x standard hours) + total
budgeted fixed overhead costs] =
$40,000 − [($4 x 1,800) + $32,000] =
$40,000 − ($7,200 + $32,000) =
$40,000 − $39,200   = $ 800(U)

Volume variance

(Budgeted hours − standard hours) x standard
fixed overhead rate =
(2,000 − 1,800) x $16
200   x $16   =   3,200(U)
Total (net) variance   = $4,000(U)

Proof:
(Actual total overhead − applied overhead (standard direct labor-hours x standard overhead rate) =
   $40,000   −   (1,800 x $20)
   $40,000   − $36,000

Three-variance method

Total overhead spending variance

Actual total overhead − [(standard variable
overhead rate x actual hours) + total
budgeted fixed overhead costs] =
$40,000 − [($4 x 1,890) + $32,000] =
$40,000 − ($7,560 + $32,000) =
$40,000 − $39,560   = $ 440(U)

Variable overhead efficiency variance

(Actual hours − standard hours) x standard
variable overhead rate =
(1,890 − 1,800) x $4
90 x $4   =   360(U)

Volume variance

(Same computation as for two-variance
method)
                               =   3,200(U)
                               = $4,000(U)

Four-variance method

Variable overhead spending variance

Actual variable overhead − (standard variable
overhead rate x actual hours) =
$9,000 − ($4 x 1,890) =
$9,000 − $7,560   = $1,440(U)

Fixed overhead spending variance

Actual fixed overhead − total budgeted fixed
overhead costs
$31,000 − $32,000   =   1,000(F)

Variable overhead efficiency variance

(Same computation as that for three-variance
method)
                          360(U)

Volume variance

(Same computation as for two-variance
method)
                      =   3,200(U)
                      = $4,000(U)

                      = $4,000(U)

U = unfavorable; F = favorable

The underapplied factory overhead balance of $4,000 reflects the four over-head variances computed. The Factory Overhead Control account is closed by recording these overhead variances under the four-variance method:

Variable Overhead Spending Variance	1,440	
Variable Overhead Efficiency Variance	360	
Volume Variance	3,200	
Fixed Overhead Spending Variance		1,000
Factory Overhead Control		4,000

We record the three unfavorable variances as debits, while the favorable fixed overhead spending variance is recorded as a credit. Avoid the impression there will always be a special combination of unfavorable and favorable variances. Only the actual operating facts, in addition to the standards established, deter-mine whether variances are favorable or not.

Disposition of Variances (L.O. 2)

To dispose of standard cost variances, we use two basic procedures: (1) close them entirely to Cost of Goods Sold or Income Summary; or (2) allocate them to inventories and Cost of Goods Sold. Chapter 4 introduced the disposition of over- or underapplied overhead as a period cost.

Variances Treated as Period Costs

If a company charges or credits its variances against the revenues of the period, it considers them as a cost of inefficiency rather than as a cost of the product. Variances are closed entirely to either Cost of Goods Sold or Income Summary. We use the $70 unit standard cost given in Chapter 11 and the related variances for material, labor, and overhead calculated in Chapters 11 and 12 for a job order system. The disposition of variances to Income Summary at the end of the pe-riod is

Material Purchase Price Variance	282	
Fixed Overhead Spending Variance	1,000	
Income Summary	7,174	
Material Quantity Variance		200
Labor Efficiency Variance		3,000
Labor Rate Variance		256
Variable Overhead Spending Variance		1,440
Variable Overhead Efficiency Variance		360
Volume Variance		3,200

If, instead, we consider the variances as the responsibility of production, we close them to Cost of Goods Sold. Later we close the balance in Cost of Goods Sold to Income Summary.

Assuming we close the variances to Income Summary and the company sells 600 units at $160 each, Exhibit 12–6 illustrates a partial income statement stating Cost of Goods Sold at standard. We deduct favorable production cost variances from unfavorable production cost variances to yield a $7,174 deduction from the gross margin at standard. Since we closed these variances to Income Summary, they appear in the income statement. If, instead, we had closed the variances to the Cost of Goods Sold account, they would appear as adjustments to Cost of Goods Sold at standard.

EXHIBIT 12–6   Gross Margin Adjusted for Variances

Partial Income Statement
for Month Ended 19X1

Sales (600 units @ $160)		$96,000
Cost of goods sold at standard (600 units @ $70)		42,000
Gross margin at standard		$54,000
Adjustments for standard cost variances:		
Material quantity variance	$ 200	
Labor efficiency variance	3,000	
Labor rate variance	256	
Variable overhead spending variance	1,440	
Variable overhead efficiency variance	360	
Volume variance	3,200	
Total unfavorable variances		$8,456
Material purchase price variance	$ 282	
Fixed overhead spending variance	1,000	
Total favorable variances	1,282	7,174
Gross margin adjusted		$46,826

Proration of Variances

The other procedure is to consider variances as a cost of the product and allocate them to Work in Process, Finished Goods, and Cost of Goods Sold. Significant material purchase price variances are allocated not only to these but also to Direct Materials Inventory and the Material Quantity Variance accounts. However, Direct Materials Inventory would not receive any of the material quantity variance or the labor and overhead variance allocation. Chapter 1 briefly discussed the Cost Accounting Standards Board; its regulations require significant standard cost variances to be included in inventories. Internal Revenue Service regulations also require the inclusion of a portion of significant variances in inventories. However, if the variances are not significant, they need not be inventoried for tax purposes unless an allocation is made for financial reporting purposes. Internal Revenue Service regulations do require the consistent treatment for both favorable and unfavorable variances. However, the volume variance can be expensed irrespective of the treatment of other variances.

Exhibit 12–7 illustrates the allocation of variances. Assume that of the 900 units mentioned in earlier exhibits, the company sells 600 units, 200 units remain in finished goods, and 200 units were in process at a 50 percent stage of completion for all three cost elements. This yields 100 equivalent units in Work in Process Inventory. Exhibit 12–7 uses the unit standard cost of $12 for materials, $18 for labor, and $40 for overhead. As you recall from Chapter 11, there were 2,820 pounds of material purchased while production used 2,750 pounds. The 70 pounds remaining in Direct Materials Inventory are valued at a standard price of $4 for a total of $280. (Note in advance that for simplicity we use very few digits to illustrate variance calculations. Do not be misled; prorating variances is not a waste of effort just because we allocate such small amounts in Exhibit 12–7.)

For distributing the material price variance, we use direct materials at standard prices within each of the inventories, cost of goods sold, and material quantity variance for a basis of $11,280 ($280 in Direct Materials + $1,200 in Work in Process + $2,400 in Finished Goods + $7,200 in Cost of Goods Sold + $200 Material Quantity Variance = $11,280). For example, we credit Direct Materials Inventory for $7 ($280/$11,280 × $282 = $7) and Work in Process Inventory for $30 ($1,200/$11,280 × $282 = $30).

The journal entry is as follows:

Material Purchase Price Variance	282	
Direct Materials Inventory		7
Work in Process Inventory		30
Finished Goods Inventory		60
Cost of Goods Sold		180
Material Quantity Variance		5

If the material quantity variance is favorable, we divide the quantity used in production less the quantity in the material quantity variance by the equivalent units of production to arrive at the pounds per equivalent unit worked on. Then we apply the price variance per pound or gallon to each of the pounds or other measurement per equivalent unit worked on.

The materials quantity variance is now $195 ($200 − $5 prorated from materials price variance). We prorate the materials quantity variance to Work in Process, Finished Goods, and Cost of Goods Sold. We use the $10,800 original materials balance before prorating the material price variance as a basis ($1,200 in Work in Process + $2,400 in Finished Goods, and $7,200 in Cost of Goods Sold = $10,800). For example, we debit Work in Process Inventory for $22 ($1,200/$10,800 × $195 = $22). The same allocation results if we use the materials balances after the material price variance is prorated. The journal entry to prorate the material quantity variance is

Work in Process Inventory	22	
Finished Goods Inventory	43	
Cost of Goods Sold	130	
Material Quantity Variance		195

We allocate the remaining labor and overhead variances to Work in Process, Finished Goods Inventory, and Cost of Goods Sold on the basis of their ending balance of standard labor and overhead costs. We allocate the $3,256 total labor variance on the basis of $16,200 ($1,800 Work in Process + $3,600 Finished Goods + $10,800 Cost of Goods Sold). For example, Cost of Goods Sold receives $10,800/$16,200 × $3,256 = $2,171 proration as shown in this journal entry:

Work in Process Inventory	361	
Finished Goods Inventory	724	
Cost of Goods Sold	2,171	
Labor Rate Variance		256
Labor Efficiency Variance		3,000

We allocate the overhead variances on the basis of $36,000 ($4,000 Work in Process + $8,000 Finished Goods + $24,000 Cost of Goods Sold). For example, Finished Goods receives $8,000/$36,000 × $4,000 = $888 proration as shown in this journal entry:

Work in Process Inventory	444	
Finished Goods Inventory	888	
Cost of Goods Sold	2,668	
Fixed Overhead Spending Variance	1,000	
Variable Overhead Spending Variance		1,440
Variable Overhead Efficiency Variance		360
Volume Variance		3,200

EXHIBIT 12–7 Variance Allocation

Accounts	Direct Materials (70 lbs. × $4)	Work in Process (100 EU × $70)	Finished Goods (200 units × $70)	Cost of Goods Sold (600 units × $70)	Total
Standard cost balances .	$280	$7,000	$14,000	$42,000	$63,280
Allocations:					
Material price	$(7)	(30)	(60)	(180)	(277)*
Material quantity	–0–	22	43	130	195†
Labor	–0–	361	724	2,171	3,256
Overhead	–0–	444	888	2,668	4,000
Ending balances	$273	$7,797	$15,595	$46,789	$70,454

*$282 − $5 allocation to material quantity variance
†$200 material quantity variance − $5 material purchase price variance allocated

When we post this entry, the inventories and Cost of Goods Sold have the ending balances as indicated in Exhibit 12–7. We could have used equivalent units for the proration instead of costs, and approximately the same amounts would have resulted depending on what rounding of figures was used.

Most Appropriate Alternative. The method chosen for allocating variances should depend on the significance of the amounts involved. If the variances are not material, we can close them to Cost of Goods Sold and Income Summary. However, when the variances arise because of some unforeseen condition, allocation is the more appropriate procedure.

Analysis of Material, Labor, and Overhead Variances (L.O. 3 and 4)

Netting out the separate variances aggregates the data so the need for corrective action is hard to detect. On the other hand, it is counterproductive to provide so many variances that managers ignore them. It is erroneous thinking that because a manual system calculated few variances, a computerized system should calculate several variances. The first step in system redesign is to establish minimum information requirements for legal and management purposes within the context of the manufacturing process. Accountants should eliminate unnecessary detail and irrelevant information.

Role of Probabilities and Timing. Chapter 16 discusses the use of probabilities in deciding when to investigate variances. Timing is very important in a standard cost system. The person responsible for a cost should know the standard in advance, and receive variance information promptly. The more quickly a variance is isolated, the greater the chance that the cause of the variance is detected and corrected before the firm incurs excessive cost. One of operating management's most common problems is that cost information often arrives too late for effective decision making.

The effectiveness of the control is often in direct proportion to the speed with which a change is recommended after discovering an unsatisfactory operating condition. The quality and price of materials are best controlled prior to or at the time of purchase. Overhead costs should be analyzed as the decisions creating such cost elements are made. Many times the accounting system fails by compiling lengthy reports that arrive long after the cost is incurred. Such reports are of little value for cost control.

As a first step in interpreting variances, managers must identify who has primary responsibility for each of the variances. The individual who has authority to incur a cost should be held responsible for that cost. Thus, we must separate cost factors directly controllable by operating supervisors from those for which executive management is responsible.

Monitor Efficiency and Production Volume Variances to Prevent Excess Inventory

JIT production dictates that every process produces parts only when needed, and only in the quantity needed. JIT recognizes profits when goods are sold, not when they are produced. Using a volume variance to measure segment performance encourages long production runs that may not meet market demand. Today product life cycles are shorter, and products change more frequently than in the past. A large inventory stored for future use may become obsolete before it can be sold. In addition, the expense of holding inventory increases.

Local Efficiencies. Even though managers set standards to increase efficiency and encourage total utilization of the resource, the result may be decreased throughput of the organization as a whole. The local efficiency does increase, but only at the expense of the entire entity. Use of **local efficiencies,** such as the incentive to incur a favorable efficiency or volume variance, may be in direct contradiction with the company's goal of making money. When an entire plant is not efficient, the productivity of any one department does not increase the profitability of the entire plant. The primary reason for this counterproductivity is evaluating managers on their efficiency and volume variances while ignoring market needs.

Computing labor efficiency and volume variances often encourages managers to keep workers busy in production activities without regard to market demand. Because of the influence of variance analysis, managers may act to achieve a high level of segment efficiency, while overall performance of the plant is declining. With uneven production capacity, accounting performance measures, such as standard cost variances that emphasize only local efficiencies, may place a company in a position of carrying excess inventory and increasing operating expenses while reducing throughput.

For example, assume a company has an older blending machine that performs operations equally well—but not as fast—as a blending machine purchased last year. The older machine produces a unit in 18 minutes while the newer machine takes only 13 minutes. The cost standard is set on the faster machine's operation. Even though ingredients blended with the older machine take 18 minutes, managers receive credit for only 13 minutes of earned standard minutes allowed based on output. All product managers strive to route their units through the faster machine rather than the older machine. The older machine is not used unless absolutely necessary because managers are motivated to run as many products as possible through the faster machine and have no incentive to run any products through the older machine. Thus, product managers are not willing to damage their performance by incurring unfavorable variances on all products processed through the older machine. Unless companywide performance affects their evaluations, it is doubtful that managers are concerned about the performance of the entire system.

As a result, managers delay throughput by waiting to use the newer machine to incur favorable variances. The end result is that often the newer blending machine becomes a temporary bottleneck. The company increases the time that its final product is shipped. Consequently, production costs increase instead of decrease because the new machine is the basis for the standard. Thus, the production standard appears to be disguising any benefits associated with using the older machine. Because the older machine cannot operate as quickly as the new one, any production on this machine appears inefficient. However, management has not considered the effect of the new machine's insufficient capacity on the system's throughput.

The cost accountant set the standard with a view to increasing efficiency. However, the result is excess inventory before the bottleneck resource that increases operating expenses (through increased inventory carrying cost) and decreases throughput. While segment managers maximize their own efficiencies, the organization as a whole suffers. The primary reason for this counterproductivity is basing the rating of managers on the faster machine.

Causes of and Responsibility for Variances

The following outline provides a basic understanding of possible causes of unfavorable controllable and noncontrollable variances. With this general knowledge, management gains insight into which operations they should investigate to determine more exact causes of the variances reported. In addition, the outline identifies the individual responsible for any deviation.

Possible causes of unfavorable controllable variances

1. Unfavorable terms in buying supplies and services.
2. Waste of indirect material.
3. Avoidable machine breakdowns.
4. Using wrong grade of indirect material or indirect labor.
5. Poor indirect labor scheduling.
6. Lack of operators or tools.

Responsibility for controllable (spending) variances

Supervisors of cost centers are responsible because they have some degree of control over these budget or expense factors.

Responsibility for variable factory overhead efficiency variances

Line supervisors are responsible because this variance reflects the effects of labor efficiency on factory overhead when labor dollars or labor-hours are the basis for applying factory overhead. This variance shows how much of the factory's capacity has been consumed or released by off-standard labor performance. If machine-hours are the basis for applying factory overhead, the variance measures the efficiency of machine usage.

Possible causes for unfavorable noncontrollable variances

1. Poor production scheduling.
2. Unusual machine breakdowns.
3. Storms or strikes.
4. Fluctuations over time.

5. Shortage of skilled workers.

6. Excess plant capacity.

7. Decrease in customer demand.

Responsibility for noncontrollable variances

Line supervisors can control fixed overhead when the costs are discretionary rather than committed.

Top sales executives may be held responsible if budgeted volume (i.e., theoretical, practice, or normal capacity) is matched with anticipated long-run sales.

Responsibility usually rests with top management, for the volume variance represents under- or overutilization of plant and equipment.

Revision of Standards

To be effective measures of performance, standards should be accurate. This requires that management continuously review standards and make any necessary revisions. However, managers should not adjust standards too frequently in an attempt to keep them in line with actual results. This destroys the control aspect of standards and adds clerical costs. Managers should adjust standards only when events such as labor rate changes, material price changes, changes in production flow, or technological advances warrant. If managers fail to revise standards when plant operations are automated, standard costs are based on the assumption that overhead cost is proportionate to the direct labor consumed by each product. The result is inaccurate product costs.

Summary

Recognizing that companies earn profits through selling, not by producing inventory for stock, affects variance analysis. Stressing lower production costs through long production runs no longer meets market needs. Performance measurements, such as efficiency and volume variances, may result in several types of conflict. In particular, segment managers may be torn between the performance that is most efficient for the overall company versus what appears efficient according to the accountant's performance measurements. While standard cost systems offer many advantages in quickly pointing out matters needing control, they require monitoring. This better ensures the discovery of opportunities for cost reduction and control and prevents misguided decisions on product pricing, product sourcing, product mix, and responses to rival products.

Important Terms and Concepts

normal costing system, 407
denominator capacity, 407
theoretical capacity, 407
practical capacity, 407
normal capacity, 407
expected actual capacity, 407
net overhead variance, 408
controllable variance, 409
production volume variance, 409
resource spending, 410

resource usage, 410
total overhead spending variance, 411
variable overhead efficiency
   variance, 411
variable overhead spending
   variance, 413
variable overhead price variance, 413
fixed overhead spending variance, 413
fixed overhead price variance, 413
local efficiencies, 421

Problem for Self-Study

Material, Labor, and Overhead Variances in a Process Costing System

The Glen Jones Company manufactures products in batches using a standard cost system. Management budgets 750 of these batches per period. Fixed factory overhead at this level is $90,000. The standard costs per batch are as follows:

	Total
Direct material (80 gallons)	$ 32
Direct labor (60 hours)	324
Total factory overhead (30 machine-hours)	378
	$734

The following costs were incurred in finishing 700 batches during the period. In addition, 109 batches were one-half complete as to all cost elements in ending inventory; there was no beginning inventory.

Direct material used (61,114.5 gallons)	$ 23,223.51
Direct labor (44,515.5 hours)	244,835.25
Actual variable factory overhead	195,687.00
Actual fixed factory overhead	90,750.00
Actual machine-hours	21,900

Required:

Prepare a variance analysis and proof of variances for:

a. Material.
b. Labor.
c. Factory overhead: Four-variance method.
d. Factory overhead: Three-variance method.
e. Factory overhead: Two-variance method.

Solution to Problem for Self-Study

$$EU = 700 + 54.5 = 754.5 \text{ batches}$$
$$(109 \times 0.5)$$

a. Material quantity variance

$$754.5 \text{ batches} \times 80 \text{ gallons} = 60,360 \text{ standard gallons}$$
$$[(61,114.5 \text{ actual gallons} - 60,360 \text{ standard gallons}) \times \$0.40 \text{ standard rate}]$$
$$= \$301.80 \text{ unfavorable}$$

Material price variance

$$\frac{\$23,223.51 \text{ actual material cost}}{61,114.5 \text{ actual gallons}} = \$0.38 \text{ actual rate}$$

$$[(\$0.38 \text{ actual rate} - \$0.40 \text{ standard rate}) \times 61,114.5 \text{ gallons}] = \$1,222.29 \text{ favorable}$$

Proof:

Actual material cost	$23,223.51
Standard material cost (60,360 × $0.40)	24,144.00
Favorable	$ 920.49
Material price variance—favorable	$ 1,222.29
Material quantity variance—unfavorable	301.80
Total (net) variance	$ 920.49

Using the diagram approach, the following variances are outlined:

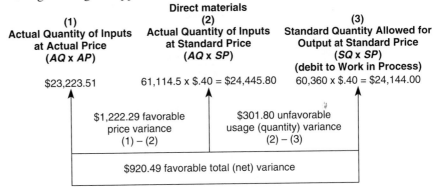

Direct materials

(1) Actual Quantity of Inputs at Actual Price (*AQ* x *AP*)	(2) Actual Quantity of Inputs at Standard Price (*AQ* x *SP*)	(3) Standard Quantity Allowed for Output at Standard Price (*SQ* x *SP*) (debit to Work in Process)
$23,223.51	61,114.5 x $.40 = $24,445.80	60,360 x $.40 = $24,144.00

$1,222.29 favorable price variance (1) – (2)

$301.80 unfavorable usage (quantity) variance (2) – (3)

$920.49 favorable total (net) variance

b. Labor quantity variance

$$754.5 \text{ batches} \times 60 \text{ hours} = 45,270 \text{ standard hours}$$
$$[(44,515.5 \text{ actual hours} - 45,270 \text{ standard hours}) \times \$5.40 \text{ standard rate}]$$
$$= \$4,074.30 \text{ favorable}$$

Labor rate variance

$$\frac{\$244,835.25}{44,515.5 \text{ hours}} = \$5.50 \text{ actual rate}$$

$[(\$5.50 \text{ actual rate} - \$5.40 \text{ standard rate}) \times 44,515.5 \text{ actual hours}] = \$4,451.55$ unfavorable

Proof:

Actual labor cost	$244,835.25
Standard labor cost (45,270 × $5.40)	244,458.00
Unfavorable	$ 377.25
Labor rate variance—unfavorable	$ 4,451.55
Labor quantity variance—favorable	4,074.30
Total (net) variance	$ 377.25

Using the diagram approach, the following variances are outlined:

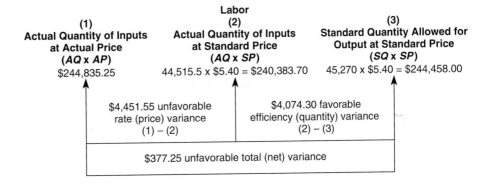

Labor

(1) Actual Quantity of Inputs at Actual Price (*AQ* x *AP*) $244,835.25	(2) Actual Quantity of Inputs at Standard Price (*AQ* x *SP*) 44,515.5 x $5.40 = $240,383.70	(3) Standard Quantity Allowed for Output at Standard Price (*SQ* x *SP*) 45,270 x $5.40 = $244,458.00

$4,451.55 unfavorable rate (price) variance (1) – (2)

$4,074.30 favorable efficiency (quantity) variance (2) – (3)

$377.25 unfavorable total (net) variance

c. Four-variance method for factory overhead

750 batches × 30 hours =	<u>22,500</u> budgeted hours
Total overhead rate	$12.60 per hour ($378/30 hours)
Less:	
$90,000 fixed overhead / 22,500 budgeted hours =	$4.00 fixed factory overhead rate
Variable overhead rate	<u>$8.60</u>

754.5 batches × 30 machine-hours = 22,635 standard machine-hours

Controllable

1. Variable overhead efficiency variance

(21,900 actual hours − 22,635 standard hours) × $8.60 = $6,321 favorable

2. Variable overhead spending variance

Actual variable overhead	$195,687
Budget for actual hours (21,900 actual hours × $8.60)	<u>188,340</u>
	<u>$ 7,347</u> unfavorable

3. Fixed overhead spending variance

Actual fixed overhead	$90,750
Budgeted fixed overhead	<u>90,000</u>
	<u>$ 750</u> unfavorable

4. Volume variance

(22,500 budgeted hours − 22,635 standard hours) × $4 = $540 favorable

Proof:

Actual overhead	$286,437
Standard overhead	<u>285,201</u>
Unfavorable	<u>$ 1,236</u>

Variable overhead spending variance— unfavorable	$7,347	
Fixed overhead spending variance—unfavorable	<u>750</u>	$8,097
Variable overhead efficiency variance—favorable	$6,321	
Volume variance favorable	<u>540</u>	<u>6,861</u>
Total (net) variance		<u>$1,236</u>

If the following diagram approach is used, the proof is built in.

Variable Overhead

(1) **Actual Quantity of Inputs at Actual Price (AQ x AP)** $195,687	(2) **Actual Quantity of Inputs at Standard Price (AQ x SP)** 21,900 x $8.60 = $188,340	(3) **Standard Quantity Allowed for Output at the Standard Price (SQ x SP)** 22,635 x $8.60 = $194,661

$7,347 unfavorable
variable overhead
spending variance (1) – (2)

$6,321 favorable
efficiency variance (2) – (3)

$1,026 unfavorable total (net) variance

Fixed Overhead

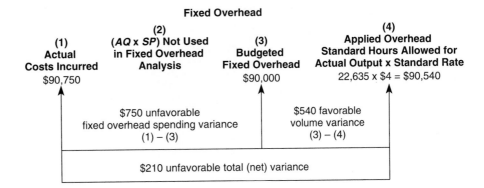

d. Three-variance method for factory overhead

Controllable

1. Total overhead spending variance

Total actual overhead costs	$286,437
Flexible budget for actual hours	
$90,000 budgeted fixed overhead +	
($8.60 variable factory overhead × 21,900 actual hours)	278,340
	$ 8,097 unfavorable

2. Variable overhead efficiency variance
(21,900 actual hours − 22,635 standard hours) × $8.60 = $6,321 favorable

Noncontrollable

3. Volume variance
(22,500 budgeted hours − 22,635 standard hours) × $4 = $540 favorable

Proof:

Actual overhead		$286,437
Standard overhead		285,201
Unfavorable		$ 1,236
Total overhead spending variance—unfavorable ..		$ 8,097
Variable overhead efficiency variance—		
favorable	$6,321	
Volume variance—favorable	540	6,861
Total (net) variance		$ 1,236

Alternatively, a diagram solution may also be used for the three-variance method as follows:

Diagram Solution for Three-Variance Method

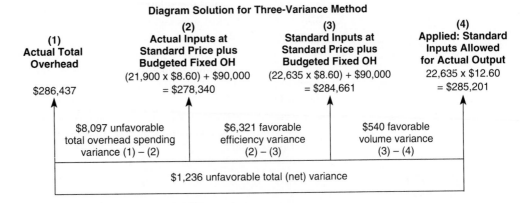

e. Two-variance method for factory overhead

   1. Controllable variance

Actual overhead	$286,437
Flexible budget (22,635 standard hours × $8.60 variable overhead rate = $194,661 variable overhead + $90,000 budgeted fixed)	284,661
Unfavorable controllable variance	$ 1,776

   2. Volume variance

(22,500 budgeted hours − 22,635 standard hours) × $4 fixed factory overhead	$540 favorable

Proof:

Actual overhead ($195,687 + $90,750)	$286,437
Standard overhead (22,635 × $12.60)	285,201
Unfavorable	$ 1,236
Controllable variance—unfavorable	$ 1,776
Volume variance—favorable	540
Total (net) variance	$ 1,236

Alternatively, a diagram solution may also be used for the two-variance method as follows:

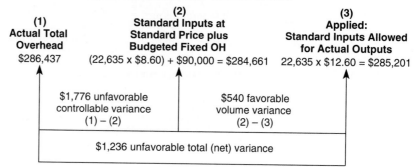

Diagram Solution for Two-Variance Method

Review Questions

1. What are the objectives of establishing factory overhead standards?

2. Why is the determination of factory overhead standards often more difficult than determination of material and labor standards?

3. Why is it more critical to compare standard hours with budgeted hours in measuring volume utilization than to compare actual hours with budgeted hours?

4. What similarities are there between factory overhead application rates in a normal costing system and standard factory overhead rates? Discuss the difference between applying factory overhead in a normal costing system and applying it in a standard cost system.

5. *a.* Discuss two reasons that could cause factory overhead to be overapplied.
   b. How should an accountant dispose of an overapplied factory overhead balance if it is material?

6. What is the danger involved if a company automatically loosens a standard every time an unfavorable variance occurs? Why is there a danger in frequently revising standards?

7. What is the difference between the controllable variance in the two-variance method and the total overhead spending variance in the three-variance method? What features do they share?

8. When would total standard hours for operations equal budgeted (normal capacity) hours?

9. What effect does an overabsorption of factory overhead have on the cost of goods manufactured and in process during the period?

10. What does the volume variance measure? What conditions are necessary for it to be favorable?

11. With what conditions would it be appropriate to determine plantwide standard overhead rates?

CPA/CMA/CIA Multiple-Choice Questions

1. (AICPA) Universal Company uses a standard cost system and prepared the following budget at normal capacity for the month of January 19X1:

Direct labor-hours	24,000
Variable factory overhead	$ 48,000
Fixed factory overhead	$108,000
Total factory overhead per direct-labor hour . . .	$ 6.50

Actual data for January 19X1 were as follows:

Direct labor-hours worked	22,000
Total factory overhead	$147,000
Standard direct labor-hours allowed for capacity attained	21,000

Using the two-way analysis of overhead variances, what is the budget (controllable) variance for January 19X1?

   a. $3,000 favorable.
   b. $5,000 favorable.
   c. $9,000 favorable.
   d. $10,500 unfavorable.

2. (AICPA) Under the two-variance method for analyzing factory overhead, which of the following is used in the computation of the controllable (budget) variance?

	Budget Allowance Based on Actual hours	Budget Allowance Based on Standard hours
a.	Yes	Yes
b.	Yes	No
c.	No	No
d.	No	Yes

3.–4. (AICPA) Items 3 and 4 are based on the following diagram that depicts a factory overhead flexible budget line *DB* and standard overhead application line *OA*. Activity is expressed in machine-hours with Point *V* indicating the standard hours required for the actual output in September 19X1. Point *S* indicates the actual machine-hours (inputs) and actual costs in September 19X1.

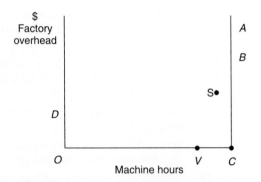

3. Are the following overhead variances favorable or unfavorable?

	Volume (Capacity) Variance	Efficiency Variance
a.	Favorable	Favorable
b.	Favorable	Unfavorable
c.	Unfavorable	Favorable
d.	Unfavorable	Unfavorable

4. The budgeted total variable overhead cost for *C* machine-hours is

    a. *AB*.
    b. *BC*.
    c. *AC* minus *DO*.
    d. *BC* minus *DO*.

5.–6. (AICPA) Items 5 and 6 are based on the following information that relates to a given department of Herman Company for the fourth quarter of 19X1:

Actual total overhead (fixed plus variable)	$178,500
Budget formula	$110,000 plus $0.50 per hour
Total overhead application rate	$1.50 per hour
Spending variance	$ 8,000 unfavorable
Volume variance	$ 5,000 favorable

The total overhead variance is divided into three variances—spending, efficiency, and volume.

5. What were the actual hours worked in this department during the quarter?

    a. 110,000.
    b. 121,000.
    c. 137,000.
    d. 153,000.

6. What were the standard hours allowed for good output in this department during the quarter?

    a. 105,000.
    b. 106,667.
    c. 110,000.
    d. 115,000.

7.–10. (CMA) The following data pertain to King Company's manufacturing operations:

King Company estimates that it will operate its manufacturing facilities at 800,000 direct labor-hours for the year. The estimate for total budgeted overhead is $2,000,000. The standard variable overhead rate is estimated to be $2 per direct labor-hour or $6 per unit. The actual data for the year are

Actual finished units	250,000
Actual direct labor-hours	764,000
Actual variable overhead	$1,610,000
Actual fixed overhead	$ 392,000

7. The variable overhead spending variance for the year is

    a. $2,000 favorable.
    b. $10,000 unfavorable.
    c. $82,000 unfavorable.
    d. $110,000 unfavorable.
    e. Some amount other than those shown above.

8. The variable overhead efficiency variance for the year is

    a. $28,000 unfavorable.
    b. $100,000 unfavorable.
    c. $110,000 unfavorable.
    d. Determined from information other than that given above.
    e. Some response other than those shown above.

9. The fixed overhead spending variance for the year is

    a. $8,000 favorable.
    b. $10,000 unfavorable.
    c. $17,000 unfavorable.
    d. $74,000 unfavorable.
    e. Some amount other than those shown above.

10. The fixed overhead volume variance for the year is

    a. $7,000 unfavorable.
    b. $25,000 unfavorable.
    c. $41,667 unfavorable.
    d. $18,000 favorable.
    e. Some amount other than those shown above.

11. (CIA) A company uses an absorption-costing system with standard costs. For the year just ended, it showed a $24,875 unfavorable production volume variance. The unfavorable production volume variance occurred because the

    a. Estimated fixed overhead used in determining the fixed overhead rate was less than actual fixed overhead.
    b. Estimated fixed overhead used in determining the fixed overhead rate was more than actual fixed overhead.
    c. Actual activity level for output was greater than the denominator volume (pre-chosen activity level).
    d. Actual activity level for output was less than the denominator volume (pre-chosen activity level).

12. (AICPA) During 1990, a department's three-variance overhead standard costing system reported unfavorable spending and volume variances. The activity level selected for allocating overhead to the product was based on 80 percent of practical capacity. If 100 percent of practical capacity had been selected instead, how would the reported unfavorable spending and volume variances be affected?

	Spending Variance	**Volume Variance**
a.	Increased	Unchanged
b.	Increased	Increased
c.	Unchanged	Increased
d.	Unchanged	Unchanged

432

PART THREE Cost Data for Performance Evaluation

Exercises

E12–1 Two-Variance Overhead Analysis (L.O. 1)

Oiler Company's standard fixed overhead cost is $8,000 per month and the standard variable overhead cost is $2 per machine-hour. Management plans to operate 4,000 machine-hours a month so that it can produce 2,500 units. Actual overhead costs for January were $16,250, output was 2,550 units, and actual machine-hours were 4,335.

Required:

a. Calculate the budgeted overhead at normal volume.
b. Give the overhead absorption rate per machine-hour.
c. Compute the overhead costs absorbed in January.
d. Calculate January's overhead production volume variance.
e. Give January's overhead controllable variance.
f. Compute January's net overhead variance.

E12–2 Flexible Budget Formula and Two-Variance OH Analysis (L.O. 1)

KTRK Company's expected monthly volume for the year was 1,000 units. At this volume, planned monthly overhead costs were $6,000 variable overhead and $3,000 fixed overhead. In May, output was 1,050 units and actual overhead expense was $9,825.

Required:

Determine for May the following:

a. The overhead flexible budget formula.
b. Standard overhead per unit of output.
c. Two-way overhead variances.

E12–3 Specifics of Standard Cost (L.O. 3)

Engineers have determined that it should take four direct labor-hours to make one of the products manufactured by Black, Inc. Total budgeted fixed overhead for the year is $120,000 and the standard fixed overhead per hour is $30. At the end of operations, the time clock cards were added and labor-hours totaled 5,800.

Required:

a. Determine the budgeted hours for the company.
b. Compute how many units the company planned to make.
c. Calculate the actual hours.
d. Give the standard hours allowed.
e. Explain the purpose of having the standard fixed overhead hourly rate during operations.

E12–4 Journalizing the Four-Variance Method of Overhead Analysis (L.O. 2)

West, Inc.'s budget for next year includes plans to operate its production facilities a total of 20,000 machine-hours. Total budgeted overhead is estimated to be $400,000. The standard variable overhead rate is four hours at $5 per hour. At the end of the accounting period, the following actual data were accumulated:

Actual fixed factory overhead	$296,800
Actual variable factory overhead	108,100
Actual machine-hours	21,300
Actual finished units	5,250

Required:

a. Calculate the overhead variances for a standard cost system, using the four-variance method of analysis.

b. Prepare journal entries to summarize actual factory overhead incurred and to apply overhead. Dispose of the variances as period costs.

E12–5 Determining Ingredients for Variance Analysis (L.O. 1)

Before operations began, Nap, Inc., management used time and motion studies in determining that it should take two hours to complete a shirt. They plan to make 100 shirts for the next period. At this capacity, managers expect $6,000 variable overhead and $4,000 fixed overhead.

Required:

Determine the following if you have the information:

a. Total standard hours allowed.
b. Actual hours.
c. Budgeted hours.
d. Variable overhead rate per hour. In which variance(s) is this used? Consider all variance methods for overhead.
e. Fixed overhead rate per hour. In which variance(s) is this used?
f. Total overhead rate per hour. In which variance(s) is this used?

E12–6 Quality Control and Efficiency Variances (L.O. 4)

Butts, Inc., uses a standard cost system for the manufacture of mechanical pencils. This system allows for some spoilage in the Assembly Department. However, the Assembly Department supervisor has been complaining about the extra work his employees have been performing for the year-end rush shipments. In many cases, the holes where the lead drops through are too large so assemblers must heat the holes and dry them for shrinkage.

Quality control efforts have been made. All mechanical pencil parts are examined and measured before being forwarded to the Assembly Department. However, slight variations in size are difficult to detect. The Molding Department supervisor believes that the tubing supplied by the outside vendor is inferior because it is not consistent in size. The Assembly Department supervisor claims that he should not be held accountable for any unfavorable labor efficiency variance.

Required:

Suggest ways that this matter should be settled. Make recommendations for any needed changes in the reporting system.

E12–7 Determining Specific Standard Cost Data (L.O. 3)

On April 1, 19X1, Lake Company began the manufacture of a new device known as Whiz. The company installed a standard cost system in accounting for manufacturing costs. The standard costs for a unit of Whiz are as follows:

Direct materials (6 pounds at $1 per pound) . . .	$ 6
Direct labor (1 hour at $4 per hour)	4
Overhead (75 percent of direct labor cost)	3
	$13

Lake's records included the following data for April:

Actual production of Whiz	2,000
Units sold of Whiz	1,250

	Debit	Credit
Sales		$25,000
Purchases	$13,650	
Material price variance	650	
Material quantity variance	500	
Direct labor rate variance	380	
Direct labor efficiency variance		400
Manufacturing overhead total variance	250	

The amount shown for the material price variance is applicable to direct material purchased during April.

Required:

Compute each of the following items for April:

a. Standard quantity of direct materials allowed (in pounds).
b. Actual quantity of direct materials allowed (in pounds).
c. Standard hours allowed.
d. Actual hours worked.
e. Actual direct labor rate.
f. Actual total overhead.

Problems

P12–8 Material, Labor, and Overhead Variances Using Different Bases for Standards (L.O. 1)

The Regional Company established the following standards:

	Per Unit
Material (3 lbs. at $6 per lb.)	$18
Labor (2 labor-hours at $8 per hr.)	16
Variable overhead (5 machine-hours at $2 per hr.)	10
Fixed overhead (5 machine-hours at $3 per hr.)	15

Management has budgeted to make 1,000 units monthly.

Regional's records revealed the following monthly data:

Actual variable factory overhead	$ 8,670
Actual fixed factory overhead	$13,000
Actual units produced	850 units
Actual machine-hours	4,100 hours
Actual material	2,610 lbs. at a total cost of $15,399
Actual labor	1,890 hours at a total cost of $19,013.40

Required:

Calculate these variances:

a. Material.
b. Labor.
c. Two-variance method for overhead.
d. Three-variance method for overhead.
e. Four-variance method for overhead.

P12–9 Flexible Budget and Standard Costs (L.O. 3)

CD Company manufactured compact disc players. The company uses a standard cost system plus a flexible budget for overhead expense. The accountant determined standard unit overhead cost by dividing budgeted costs at the normal volume by the number of compact disc players which that volume level represented.

Certain cost information is shown in the following table. When filling in the blank spaces, closely analyze the relationships among the figures given for allocated service and general overhead to determine normal volume.

	Actual Cost, June	Standard Charge per CD Player	Total Standard Cost, June	Flexible Overhead Budget, June	Overhead Budget Formula
Direct labor	$ 9,650	$10	$ ___	Not used	
Direct material	14,200	15	14,250	Not used	
Department direct overhead expense ..	6,700	___	___	$ 6,900	$5,000 per month plus $2 per CD player
Allocated service and general overhead ...	11,000	10	9,500	10,000	$10,000
Total	$41,550	$ ___	$ ___	$16,900	per month

Required:

a. Determine how many disk players the company produced in June.
b. Calculate the normal volume of disk player output at which the standard unit overhead charge was determined.
c. Fill in the blanks.
d. Explain as much of the difference between total actual costs and total standard costs as you can on the basis of the information given by calculating all the variances you can for material, labor, and overhead.

P12–10 Labor and Variance Analysis Methods (L.O. 1)

Nichols Company provided the following information from their cost system:

Standard hours allowed	2,880
Actual hours	3,200
Budgeted total overhead	$33,000
Actual labor cost	$16,800
Actual variable overhead	$12,000
Actual fixed overhead	$21,700

Standard specification per unit of finished product:

Direct labor (6 hours)	$30
Variable overhead	24
Fixed overhead	42

Required:

Compute the following variances:

a. Labor.
b. Four-variance method for overhead.
c. Three-variance method for overhead.
d. Two-variance method for overhead.
e. Prove your figures for the four-variance overhead method.

P12–11 Variances for Material, Labor, and Overhead (L.O. 1)

Barry Corporation manufactures a product with the following standard costs:

Direct materials (20 yards @ $1.25 per yard)	$25
Direct labor (5 hours @ $8 per hour)	40
Factory overhead (applied at ¾ of direct labor) Ratio of variable costs to fixed costs: 2 to 1	30
Total standard cost per unit of output	$95

Standards are based on normal monthly production involving 3,500 direct labor-hours (700 units of output). The following information pertains to March:

Direct materials purchases (19,000 yards @ $1.29 per yard) ...	$24,510
Direct materials used (11,800 yards)	
Direct labor (3,050 hours @ $8.20 per hour)	25,010
Actual variable factory overhead	12,250
Actual fixed factory overhead	7,200
600 units of the product were actually produced in March.	

Required:

a. Prepare the following schedules computing:
   (1) Variable factory overhead rate per direct labor-hour.
   (2) Total fixed factory overhead based on normal activity.
b. Prepare the following schedules for March, labeling each variance and indicating whether each variance is favorable or unfavorable:
   (1) Two material variances (price variance based on purchases).
   (2) Two labor variances.
   (3) Two-way analysis for factory overhead.
   (4) Three-way analysis for factory overhead.
   (5) Four-way analysis for factory overhead.

P12–12 Material, Labor, and Two-Variance Overhead Method, Journalizing Variances (L.O. 1)

Bell Company uses a standard cost system. Engineers have determined that there are two standard pounds of material in one of Bell's finished products. The standard direct material cost is $2 per pound. Each unit requires one direct labor-hour and one machine-hour. Standard direct labor cost is $8 per hour. The overhead budget formula is $1,500 per month plus $4 per machine-hour for a normal volume of 4,000 units.

Bell purchased and received a total of 9,000 pounds of material costing $19,800; workers used 8,050 pounds of materials. Direct labor cost incurred for 4,000 hours was $36,000. Actual overhead of $17,700 was incurred in making 4,000 units.

Required:

a. Compute the:
   (1) Material usage variance.
   (2) Material purchase price variance.
   (3) Material usage price variance.
b. Compute the labor efficiency and rate variances.
c. Calculate the absorption rate for overhead.
d. Compute the overhead variances using the two-variance method.
e. Prepare summary journal entries to record actual and applied factory overhead; also record overhead variances.

P12–13 Two-Way Overhead Variance Analysis for Three Months (L.O. 1)

In January, Whipple Company's overhead volume variance was $0 and its controllable variance was $200 favorable; actual overhead expense was $7,800 for an output of 1,250 units. In February, overhead expense was $7,250 and output was 1,000 units; controllable variance was $0. In March, output was 1,100 units and actual overhead expense was $7,500.

Required:

Fill in the following blanks. (Note that some of the figures for the blanks are given in the problem.)

	January		February	March
Flexible budgeted costs	$_____		$_____	$_____
Absorbed costs	$_____		$_____	$_____
Normal volume	_____	units		
Overhead application rate	$_____	/unit		
Volume variance	$_____		$_____	$_____
Controllable variance	$_____		$_____	$_____
Actual expense	$_____		$_____	$_____
Volume	_____	units	_____ units	_____ units

P12–14 Impact of Quality Control Program on Behavior (L.O. 4)

McSparrin Company is a manufacturer of costume jewelry and employs a standard cost system. The ingredients for the fake stones are combined in the Mixing Department. From there, the mixture is sent in 500-gallon batches to the Molding Department, where various sizes of stones are molded. After the stones are removed from the molds and cleaned, they are forwarded to the Assembly Department, where the stones are mounted in rings, bracelets, and necklaces. The frames for these are purchased from an outside vendor.

McSparrin operates a modified job order process system. For example, all operations use a mass-production, assembly-line approach; however, they do produce according to job order. A job order calling for 1,000 rings of a specified type may be received for inventory stock. After this order is completed, another job order is issued for the production of other types of jewelry. No jewelry is manufactured according to customer specification.

A standard cost system allows for some spoilage in the Assembly Department. However, the supervisor of the department has been complaining recently about the extra work her employees do when they cut stones to fit the bracelets they are assembling. If the stones are even ¹⁄₆₄ of an inch too large, the assembler must cut and polish the stone so that it can be inserted in the bracelet frame and clasped down.

The plant supervisor has had conferences with the Molding Department supervisor, and together they have inspected the quality control program. All stones are examined and measured before being forwarded to the Assembly Department. However, slight variations in size are difficult to detect. The Molding Department supervisor believes that the bracelet frames supplied by the outside vendor are at fault; he claims that many of these are not consistent in size.

The Assembly Department supervisor claims that she should not be held accountable for any unfavorable labor quantity variance. She admits that the quantity standard was explained to her before operations began and that an allowance for some stone cutting was made in the standard.

Required:

Suggest ways that this matter should be settled. Make recommendations for any needed changes in the reporting system.

P12–15 Material, Labor, and Two-Variance Analysis for Factory Overhead (L.O. 1)

The Tucker Company manufactures products using a standard cost system. Management budgets to make 200 of these units per period. Fixed factory overhead at this level is $72,000. The standard costs per unit are as follows:

Direct material (40 gallons)	$240
Direct labor (20 hours)	220
Total factory overhead (20 hours)	500
Total	$960

In producing 205 units during the period, the following costs were incurred:

Direct material used (7,900 gallons)	$48,980
Direct labor (4,350 hours)	52,200
Actual variable factory overhead	30,000
Actual fixed factory overhead	72,260

Required:

Develop a variance analysis for material, labor, and factory overhead using the two-variance method for overhead.

P12–16 Comparison of Various Variance Analysis Methods (L.O. 1)

Taylor Company records revealed the following monthly data:

Actual variable factory overhead	$ 8,707
Actual fixed factory overhead	$13,353
Actual units produced	1,200 units
Actual machine-hours	4,010 hours
Standard machine-hours per unit	3 hours

Management has budgeted 1,300 units monthly. Budgeted variable cost at this level is $8,385, while fixed cost was budgeted to be $14,040.

Required:

Calculate overhead variances using the:

a. Two-variance method.
b. Three-variance method.
c. Four-variance method.

P12–17 Comparison of Various Variance Analysis Methods (L.O. 1)

Pitts Company records contained the following monthly data:

Actual variable factory overhead	$10,100
Actual fixed factory overhead	8,000
Actual units produced	500 units
Actual machine-hours	1,420 hours

Standard per unit:

Variable factory overhead	(3 hours at $6 per hour)
Fixed factory overhead	(3 hours at $5 per hour)

Management has budgeted to make 575 units monthly.

Required:

a. Calculate overhead variances indicating whether controllable or noncontrollable using the:
   (1) Two-variance method.
   (2) Three-variance method.
   (3) Four-variance method.
b. Prepare journal entries to summarize actual factory overhead incurred and to apply overhead. Record overhead variances using the four-variance method. Dispose of the variances as period costs.

P12–18 Two Variance Factory Overhead, Material, and Labor Variances (L.O. 2)

Rose Manufacturing Inc. maintains perpetual inventory accounts for direct materials, work in process, and finished goods in their standard cost system. Their Engineering Department has established the following standard costs per unit:

Direct material: 2½ pounds @ $2 per pound . .	$ 5
Direct labor: 2 hours @ $6 per hour	12
Factory overhead: 2 machine-hours @ $2.50*	
per hour	5
Total	$22

*Total budgeted fixed costs amounted to $30,000 of this total factory overhead with variable costs representing the remainder.

For the first month of the current year, there were no beginning or ending balances in the work in process account. The following transactions occurred during the month which related to production:

1. Direct materials purchased on account, $48,000.
2. Direct materials used, $45,100. This represented 22,000 pounds at $2.05 per pound. (For simplicity now, enter actual material and labor costs to work in process inventory rather than standard costs for material and labor.)
3. Direct labor paid, $103,250. This represented 17,500 hours at $5.90 per hour. There were no accruals at either the beginning or the end of the period. (Ignore payroll withholdings; no payroll summary is used.)
4. Monthly factory overhead of $15,000 depreciation on plant and equipment, $18,000 indirect labor, $7,000 insurance, and $8,750 miscellaneous factory costs were paid in cash. The insurance represents an expiration of prepaid insurance. Record the indirect labor in a liability account.
5. There were 8,500 units finished during the period. First apply standard overhead for these units before sending them to the warehouse at standard cost.

Required:

a. Journalize the transactions in general journal form.
b. Prepare schedules of variances for direct materials cost, direct labor cost, and factory overhead cost. Use two-variance method for overhead. Normal productive capacity for the plant is 20,000 machine-hours. Prove your variances for all three cost elements.
c. Prepare a T account for Work in Process Inventory and for Factory Overhead Control and post the journal entries made in Requirement *a* to these two accounts. Use identifying letters as dates. What does the balance represent in each of these two accounts?
d. Now close the balances determined in Requirement *c* in the Work in Process Inventory account and Factory Overhead Control by recording unfavorable variances as debits and favorable variances as credits.

P12–19 (AICPA) Standard Costs for a Process Operation (L.O. 1)

Webb & Company is engaged in the preparation of income tax returns for individuals. Webb uses the weighted-average method and actual costs for financial reporting purposes. However, for internal reporting, Webb uses a standard cost system. The standards, based on equivalent performance, have been established as follows:

Labor per return	5 hours @ $20 per hour
Overhead per return	5 hours @ $10 per hour

For March 19X7 performance, budgeted overhead is $49,000 for the standard labor-hours allowed. The following additional information pertains to the month of March 19X7:

Inventory Data

Returns in process, March 1 (25% complete) . .	200
Returns started in March	825
Returns in process, March 31 (80% complete) .	125

Actual cost data

Returns in process March 1:

Labor	$ 6,000
Overhead	2,500

Labor, March 1 to 31,

4,000 hours	89,000
Overhead, March 1 to 31	45,000

Required:

a. Using the weighted-average method, compute the following for each cost element:
   (1) Equivalent units of performance.
   (2) Actual cost per equivalent unit.
b. Compute the actual cost of returns in process at March 31.
c. Compute the standard cost per return.
d. Prepare a schedule for internal reporting analyzing March performance, using the following variances, and indicating whether these variances are favorable or unfavorable:
   (1) Total labor.
   (2) Labor rate.
   (3) Labor efficiency.
   (4) Total overhead.
   (5) Overhead volume.
   (6) Overhead controllable.

P12–20 Variances for Material, Labor, and Overhead (Two-Way) (L.O. 1)

Brown Company has established the following standard costs per unit:

Material (6 pounds @ $.50 per pound)	$ 3.00
Direct labor (1 hour @ $8 per hour)	8.00
Factory overhead (1 hour @ $5.50 per hour) ..	5.50
Total standard cost	$16.50

The $5.50 per direct labor-hour overhead rate is based on a normal capacity budgeted at 95 percent operating level. The following flexible budget information reveals:

	Operating Levels		
	85%	**95%**	**100%**
Units of production	4,250	4,750	5,000
Standard direct labor-hours ..	4,250	4,750	5,000
Variable factory overhead ...	8,500	9,500	10,000
Fixed factory overhead	16,625	16,625	16,625

During March, the company operated at 85 percent of capacity, producing 4,250 units of product which they charged with the following standard costs:

Material (25,500 pounds @ $.50 per pound)	$12,750
Direct labor (4,250 hours @ $8 per hour)	34,000
Factory overhead costs (4,250 hours @ $5.50 per hour)	23,375
Total standard cost	$70,125

Actual costs incurred during March were

Material (26,100 pounds)	$11,745
Direct labor (4,150 hours)	34,445
Fixed factory overhead costs	16,625
Variable factory overhead costs	7,650
Total actual costs	$70,465

Required:

Isolate the material and labor variances into price and quantity variances and isolate the overhead variance into the volume variance and controllable variance.

P12–21 Proration of Variances (L.O. 2)

Farris Company established a standard cost system several years ago. All material variances are prorated at year-end on the basis of direct material balances in the appropriate accounts. Variances associated with direct labor and manufacturing overhead are prorated based on the direct labor balances in the appropriate accounts.

Farris made the following information available for the year ended December 31, 19X1:

Cost of goods sold for the year ended December 31, 19X1:	
Direct material	$ 400,000
Direct labor	600,000
Factory overhead applied	450,000
Direct materials inventory at December 31, 19X1:	80,000
Finished goods inventory at December 31, 19X1:	
Direct material	60,000
Direct labor	100,000
Factory overhead applied	75,000
Direct material price variance (favorable)	(81,000)
Direct material usage variance (unfavorable)	32,200
Direct labor rate variance (unfavorable)	55,200
Direct labor efficiency variance (favorable)	(36,800)
Manufacturing overhead incurred	539,000

There were no beginning inventories and no ending work in process inventory. Manufacturing overhead is applied at 75 percent of standard direct labor.

Required:

a. Allocate all variances.
b. Give the balances in Direct Materials Inventory, Finished Goods Inventory, and Cost of Goods Sold at year-end after all variances have been prorated.

P12–22 (AICPA) Material, Labor, and Overhead Variances (L.O. 1)

Tredco Company is engaged in seasonal tree-spraying and uses chemicals to prevent disease and bug-infestation. Employees are guaranteed 165 hours of work per month at $8 per hour and receive a bonus equal to 75 percent of their net favorable direct labor efficiency variance. The efficiency variance represents the difference between actual time consumed in spraying a tree and the standard time allowed for the height of the tree (specified in feet), multiplied by the $8 standard hourly wage rate. For budgeting purposes, there is a standard allowance of one hour per customer for travel, setup, and clearup time. However, since several factors are uncontrollable by the employee, this one-hour budget allowance is excluded from the bonus calculation. Employees are responsible for keeping their own daily timecards.

Chemical usage should vary directly with the tree-footage sprayed. Variable overhead includes costs that vary directly with the number of customers, as well as costs that vary according to tree-footage sprayed. Customers pay a service charge of $10 per visit and $1 per tree-foot sprayed. The standard static budget and actual results for June are as follows:

		Static Budget			Actual Results
Service calls	(200 customers)	$ 2,000	(210 customers)		$ 2,100
Footage sprayed	(18,000 feet)	18,000	(21,000 feet)		21,000
Total revenues		$20,000			$23,100
Chemicals	(1,800 gallons)	$ 4,500	(2,400 gallons)		$ 5,880
Direct labor:					
Travel, setup, and clearup	(200 hours)	$1,600	(300 hours)	$2,400	
Tree-spraying	(900 hours)	7,200	(910 hours)	7,280	
Total direct labor		8,800			9,680

(continued)

	Static Budget	Actual Results
Overhead:		
Variable based on number of customers	1,200	
Variable based on tree footage	1,800	
Fixed	2,000	
Total overhead	5,000	5,400
Total costs	$18,300	$20,960
Gross profit before bonus	$ 1,700	$ 2,140

July's demand is expected to be in excess of June's and may be met by either paying a 25 percent overtime premium to current employees or by hiring an additional employee. A new employee will cause fixed costs to increase by $100 per month. The potential increased demand may be estimated by considering the impact of increases of 20 and 30 customers, with probabilities of 70 percent and 30 percent, respectively.

Required:

a. Compute the following for June:
   (1) Direct materials price variance.
   (2) Direct materials usage (efficiency) variance.
   (3) Direct labor travel, setup, and clearup variance.
   (4) Direct labor bonus.
   (5) Overhead spending (flexible budget) variance.
   Indicate whether each variance is favorable or unfavorable.
b. Assume that Tredoc accepts all orders for services in July. Should Tredoc hire an additional employee? Provide supporting computations based on standard cost.

Cases

C12–23 Analysis of Standard Cost System and Variance Computation (L.O. 3)

Florida Company is a medium-sized manufacturer located in a relatively small community to take advantage of a cheap labor force. Florida Company established standards four years ago based on a sequence of three job operations—A, B, and C—requiring a total elapsed time of four hours. Direct labor workers are paid $15 an hour. According to standard specifications, three pounds of Raw Material R at a cost of $6 per pound are mixed with two pounds of Material S costing $1 per pound. This results in a weighted-average cost per pound of $4 which is used as the standard. Material R costs more because it is a durable, high-quality material needed to give strength and long life to the product which the company's marketing department promotes. Material S is a filler that adds bulk to the product.

Standard specifications per unit are as follows:

		Per Unit
Material: 5 pounds @ $4 per pound		$ 20
Labor: 4 labor-hours @ $15 per hour		60
Overhead—Variable: 8 machine-hours @ $3 per hour . . .	$24	
Overhead—Fixed: 8 machine-hours @ $7 per hour	56	80
Total per unit		$160

Two years ago the company hired engineering consultants who evaluated the production work flow and revised the sequence of operations to B, C, A which reduced the required time to three hours. Because management believed this was a production method change only, the cost accountant was not aware of this event.

The production manager has been experimenting with different combinations of Materials R and S and has found that with a slight altering of the raw material ingredient ratios, the product can still pass initial inspection.

The company budgeted a total of 120 units but actually produced only 100 units during the current period. According to company records, the following are actual results for the period:

Material R—100 pounds for a total cost of	$ 800
Material S—400 pounds for a total cost of	1,000
500 pounds	$1,800
Labor—325 hours for a total cost of	$5,980
Overhead—860 machine-hours: Variable	$2,700
Fixed	6,900
Total overhead	$9,600

The following standard cost variances appeared on the cost production report for the period. The company uses the two-way variance analysis for overhead.

Material price variance

Standard cost (100 units × $20)	$2,000
Actual cost	1,800
Favorable price variance	$ 200

Material quantity variance

(100 units × 5 pounds each @ standard = 500 pounds used) . . . . –0–

Labor variance

(100 units × $60 @ standard = $6,000 – $5,980 actual cost) = $20 favorable

Volume variance

(860 machine-hours – 960 machine-hours) × $10 = $1,000 unfavorable

Controllable variance

Actual overhead	$9,600
Standard overhead (100 units × $80)	8,000
	$1,600 unfavorable

Required:

a. Evaluate the standard cost system employed by the company and list any weaknesses.
b. Suggest needed improvement; where appropriate, recalculate any variances you believe are incorrect.
c. List the objectives of a standard cost system.
d. Indicate specific ways that these objectives are not being met with Florida Company's present system.
e. Discuss briefly the critical information needs that an effective standard cost system can provide for the following:
   (1) Production manager.
   (2) Marketing manager.
   (3) President.

C12–24 Evaluating Standard Cost Systems Indicating Weaknesses (L.O. 3, 4)

Standard cost data help managers keep cost centers under control and running efficiently according to predetermined plans. If appropriately applied, they can evaluate performance through variance analysis. While standard cost systems offer many opportunities for improving cost control, these systems often include features that destroy much of their usefulness. After studying the standard cost systems employed by the following companies, you may detect areas in which managers are being hindered in performing their functions. When this occurs, the company's profitability is endangered.

Company A management boasts of their performance by emphasizing that they have consistently had favorable variances for the last three reporting periods. Initially, standards were scientifically determined using time and motion studies and material sampling. However, management found over the years since, that these initial standards were not realistic because unfavorable variances were being reported. Thus, the standards were relaxed so that achievable standards were used. For example, after the Purchasing Department ordered materials costing $.10 over standard one year, the price standard was raised $.50 just to make certain that the extra $.40 would be available to cover unforeseen possibilities. Likewise, industrial engineers estimated that the standard quantity per unit should be 5 pounds including normal waste; however, plant management convinced them to add another pound to the standard to give them some flexibility. Labor and overhead standards are handled in a similar manner. Standard markups for pricing are added to the full standard cost.

Company B is a relatively small manufacturer; in fact, they do not have an industrial engineering department. However, they did employ engineers as consultants when the standards were first set up four years ago. They have since revised standard unit prices for material and labor but the quantities for material or the time allotments for labor have remained fixed. Two years ago, Company B increased production capacity by more than 100 percent by adding a second labor shift. Existing standards are applied to this second shift. As a result, the company's income statement reported large unfavorable labor efficiency variances.

Company C prides itself on its strict schedule of events. For example, on the fifth working day after the end of a month, income statements are scheduled to be on the controller's desk for review. Managers also established official dates for revising standard cost cards that are the basis for preparing variance reports. Top management believes this policy is most appropriate even though the company's cost accountant has some reservations. For example, at mid-year last year, the company changed its production techniques; the effect on standard costs was then incorporated six months later according to the official schedule for revising standards. The cost accountant recalls this also happening during the 1970s as a result of the Arab oil embargo when prices were accelerating.

Company D uses the following two-way analysis for factory overhead:

Controllable variance

Actual fixed overhead of $9,500 + $10,000 budgeted fixed overhead . .	$19,500
Compared with: [($4 fixed overhead rate + $3 variable overhead rate)	
× 2,000 standard hours] + $5,000 actual variable overhead	19,000
	$ 500 unfavorable

Volume variance

(2,500 budgeted hours − 2,300 actual hours) × $3 variable overhead rate = $600 favorable

Company E uses two sets of standards; they revise one set once a year and use it for interim financial statements. The other set is changed continually to keep price and quantity standards current for all three cost components.

Company F manufactures and sells a line of fabrics in three different manufacturing plants. There are significant differences among the various production lines; also some grades of fabric can only be produced on certain lines. Equipment capacities vary between plants so that the most efficient run size in each line differs. Production personnel constantly monitor sales orders with the equipment capacities to achieve the most economic production cost. They use a standard cost system in which standards are based on the one most efficient compatible production line with each order size.

Company G manufactures a plastic product in five strengths; to obtain the varying strengths, workers alter the ratios of the ingredients. However, the only standard product cost card represents an average of the strengths that are to be made. Accountants calculate mix variances based on this average standard. They compute the mix variance by comparing the standard formula to the standard cost of material or labor actually used. A mix variance results if the actual product strength does not match the strength on the cost card. Because management must take time in explaining these resulting mix variances, they are considering a proposal to base the standard on one of the five strengths.

Required:

a. Evaluate the standard cost systems employed by the seven companies: for each, indicate any impact on the company's financial statements and any behavioral effect of the system.

b. Suggest needed improvements, giving specific examples if appropriate. Set up your answers so that Requirements *a* and *b* follow each other for each company.

Capstone Case

C12–25 Evaluating a Manufacturer's Cost Accounting System

You have just received a call from an engineering associate requesting your assistance in a consulting project at Murrell Wax Company. Even though the pay is minimal, you agree to work on the project because the project topic appears relevant to your current interest. Your engineering associate tells you that Murrell managers have many pet projects that should not be discussed. Also, you will not have access to any company financial data. Management informs you that keeping their financial data confidential should not pose a problem since Murrell is audited annually by a reputable CPA firm. Because you do not foresee a need for examining financial data, protecting the confidentiality of the accounting records does not appear to be a problem. You decide to confront pet projects at the appropriate time.

It does not take long before you discover these pet projects. You expected them to be a favorite product line that top management refuses to admit is unprofitable. However, it is a new information system. Referred to generically as XXSY, management believes this system holds the answer to all their problems. Management committed themselves to this project at a considerable expense four years ago; presently, the company is in the second of five phases. They thought phase three would be ready for their adaptation two years ago, but the debugging process has taken much longer than expected. Management, however, has complete faith that the wait will be worthwhile if they can make do with their present information system a few more months. Currently, they manually gather needed data that is not readily available from their computer.

During your initial conference, you are somewhat surprised when the vice president of production leaves in the middle of the engineer's presentation. Both you and the engineer learn for the first time that the company is for sale. They will receive private bids the next day.

Later you tactfully ask the engineer why the vice president of production left your conference. The engineer explains that this vice president may not be totally committed to your consulting project. The vice president of production began his career with the company 16 years ago as a line foreman and has risen through the management ranks. He has taken additional education courses and prides himself on keeping up with new ideas. He vividly remembers the days when the company used baling wire to keep the outdated machinery running. Thus, when the current president was promoted from production supervisor to president, he and this vice president began updating equipment. Even though they purchased more capacity than they needed at the time, both currently believe it was the correct decision and refuse to admit any possible mistakes. Both indicated they would do it over again if given the chance because the intermediate steps in machinery purchases were almost as expensive. The initial purchase cost of larger-scale machinery was only a few thousand dollars more; however, both now admit they failed to consider the additional cost of storing and maintaining unused equipment. Because they paid cash for the equipment, management believes their only equipment expense is depreciation.

The engineer explains that company owners heard about the the revolution occurring in cost management due to new technology and engineering. The owners decided this was exactly what they needed to give Murrell a shot in the arm. Gradually, you realize that the owners failed to inform many of the company managers of their decision to seek your help. This is apparent when you try to make appointments with sales managers and have to spend much time explaining your objectives and assuring them that you are not spying for a competitor. In fact, when you arrived for several appointments, the managers conveniently had problems arise that needed immediate attention. They were unable to meet with you.

Murrell managers admit they need your advice in solving their problem of allocating overhead. Further, they are having trouble fixing responsibility. They do not know if the allocation issue is a production or accounting problem. The plant is currently operating at 36 percent of capacity. Because current operations are such a low percentage of capacity, top management has decided to accept $200,000 overhead as a given loss and not assign all the overhead to production. Instead, $200,000 is to be reported as a period expense on their financial statements. Otherwise, management believes their costs per product line would not be competitive.

When you approach the vice president of production asking if he isn't concerned that a less informed person might hold him completely responsible for the $200,000 cost of idle capacity, he says, "No," and quickly changes the subject. Management appears content to accept the idle capacity cost because the owners continue to enjoy an above-market return on their investments. Management feels comfortable with this arrangement of charging off idle capacity cost as long as there is a companywide net income.

After examining the present production schedule, the production manager explains the flexibility for which he must provide. For example, he may receive a call in the afternoon from a clerk in the front office demanding that he run an order for a customer by the end of the day. Or top management may pull direct labor workers off production lines in process to move furniture in the front office, plant tulips, or mow the yard. This often causes an entire product line to be shut down. Because the production manager has received these calls in the past, he has adjusted the work force to protect himself by scheduling production so that if operations progress as planned or slightly close to plans, his production for the day is finished by 2:00 in the afternoon. This allows him to have extra workers available to fill any emergency orders, move furniture, or perform yard work.

When you ask the production manager if he realizes how much this scheduling approach costs Murrell, he replies that the cost is zero. He reasons that since they have more workers than production orders, this approach saves the company the expense of employing outside lawn or moving services.

Next, you discover that some scarce product ingredients are distributed based on allocations. Often, Murrell customers are able to secure these scarce ingredients easier than Murrell can. Customers then furnish Murrell with these specialty ingredients for processing into their finished products. Because a large chain store distributor commands such a large share of their sales, Murrell accedes to requests to store the chain store distributor's raw, scarce chemical ingredients several months in advance of processing. Whenever chain store managers are able to obtain allocations of these ingredients, the distributor often has its suppliers ship these raw chemicals directly to Murrell for storage. Murrell management claims a favorable tradeoff for storing the products because when current sales orders are slack, Murrell workers can process the chain store's finished products before actually receiving an order.

Murrell management indicates they realize the risks and costs involved, but they believe filling these requests helps them in bargaining for any future sales prices. Murrell managers emphasize that these favors to the chain store distributor put them in a good bargaining position. For example, they can remind the chain store management that earlier in the year they helped them out when the chain store needed Murrell to store and process chemicals used to make that customer's blend of wax.

After several conferences with the president, the vice president of production, and other managers, as well as plant tours, you obtain additional details:

- Even though labor costs have become an increasingly minor portion of the overall manufacturing costs, Murrell continues to assign overhead on the basis of direct labor. The plantwide overhead application rate is 600 percent of direct labor costs based on estimated overhead that excludes $200,000. Currently management estimates that there is one direct labor worker to two indirect labor workers. Also, there is a wide range of labor devoted to each product line depending on the thickness of the product blended. Rational managers focus their attention on reducing labor costs which in turn reduces their allocated overhead. Direct material accounts for a large portion of each product's direct costs, and this cost varies widely depending on the product line.
- Certain product lines require much more equipment than other lines. Overhead is assigned based on direct labor costs.
- To gain a large market share for a chain store distributor, Murrell promises delivery within 48 hours after an order is received. This causes the company to have a skeleton second shift to finish any orders not filled during the regular shift.
- Management is proud of the fact that they never have back orders.
- There is a four-hour production cycle between requesting the raw ingredients from the tanks stored on site and the completed filled containers being transferred to the finished goods warehouse. However, cleaning the waxes and detergents blended out of the tanks and machines requires additional time. Because of this, management always tries to run extra products when it receives an order of any product line. The company stores these extra units in inventory. Thus, inventory fluctuates widely and always represents several months of sales.
- Observation of inventory levels determines the production schedules for the current week.
- The vice president of production explains that the addition of modern, automated machinery four years ago has caused the company breakeven point to be so high that he is having difficulty operating at a breakeven capacity because of the lack of sales. Despite the purchase of this automated machinery, none of the eight product lines are completely automated. The speed of the line in filling orders depends not only on the number of employees assigned to the line but also on the temperature because some of the ingredients stored outdoors are thick and more difficult to pour in cold weather. Normally the five or six employees per product line include one machine operator who has the responsibility of determining the speed of the line.
- The plant is not unionized. Workers receive a $6.50 hourly rate during their first year of employment with annual increases of $1 per year up to a maximum of $9.50 per hour.
- Murrell established standards for material, labor, and overhead three years ago and is currently revising them. Presently, the standard wage rate is based on an average plantwide wage rate that lumps together line workers and machine operators for all product lines. One line may have three line operators and one machine operator and another line may have five line operators and one machine operator. Machine operators earn a higher hourly rate than line operators. Workers transfer between lines.
- Accountants compute a net labor variance for each department.
- Managers spend much time and effort to record labor time in detail before converting it to labor cost. Managers focus their attention on reducing labor costs; this in turn reduces their allocated overhead.

- Workers spend much time waiting until materials are on the floor or machines are operating properly before they perform productive work. Accountants calculate direct labor time per product line based on machine time. However, machine time calculations are not valid because machines do not always operate properly.

- After workers complete their production schedule for the day, they frequently engage in extensive busy work. Management explains this behavior as risk aversion because workers hesitate to begin producing a job scheduled for the next day for fear the overall lack of sales demand will not warrant a full production operation tomorrow.

- Murrell Wax shuts down its production line only if errors exceed predetermined limits. Inspectors are added at the end of the line to test whether goods produced meet specifications. Any defect detected at the end of the line is studied and used as feedback information. In the meantime, the process produces more defective units because of the time lag between the detection and correction of the defect.

- Each of the three manufacturing plants located close by produces similar product lines. Workers are not allowed to transfer between plants on a flexible basis, however, since plant supervisors are held responsible for their own operations.

- Murrell does not have its own sales force; instead, it uses agents who represent several products and companies; each agent earns a commission.

- Since Murrell performs contract packaging and contract product development, there are many varieties of products. The final product is packaged in a wide variety of container sizes ranging from gallon drums for industrial use to quart sizes for household use.

- In the finished goods warehouse, you see forklift operators handpicking certain orders. Other orders are for full pallets.

- Middle and top managers attend monthly continuing education dinner meetings that focus on new management techniques and the behavioral aspects of management. Management claims it has tried to make its line employees feel a part of the management team by including them in Dale Carnegie-type motivational seminars. However, the company's attempt to make direct labor workers responsible for machine maintenance was a failure. Now the firm has assigned engineers to each line; these engineers have acquired their skills primarily on the job and can rotate between lines. When not involved in maintenance, they set up the lines.

When you suggest to managers that current thinking within management accounting suggests workers are more profitable performing maintenance tasks or drinking coffee around their machines rather than producing stock whose sale is uncertain, they quickly refute the argument as being totally off the wall. Murrell management states that they would not sell any of their warehouses even if they were vacant. Further, they discard your idea of leasing excess space as not being practical. Managers reason there is no opportunity cost of the warehouse because these warehouses are fully paid for; thus, there is no cause for concern over having excess inventory.

Five months later as you complete the project, you note that no action has yet occurred regarding the sale of the company. Also, you remember management's defensiveness with every initial suggestion you made. They had ready reasons why your suggestions would not work. Management appears confident that this idle capacity is temporary and justified. They repeatedly inform you that the company is making lots of money. In fact, as you walk away from the project, the vice president's words that Murrell really has no problems keep ringing in your ears.

Required:

a. What are the critical issues Murrell is facing? Do these issues result from accounting, production, or other factors?

b. Explain some of top management's defensiveness to your initial suggestions.

c. Evaluate Murrell's standard cost system, making any recommendations you think are needed.

     d. Discuss the danger of using direct labor to allocate overhead costs when the burden rate is 600 percent of direct labor costs.

     e. Justify the managers' present behavior of focusing so much attention on direct labor time and trying to avoid idle nonmanufacturing time recorded by their workers.

     f. Evaluate the approach used of holding excess inventory. Would you advise immediate adoption of JIT?

     g. Explain if management is correct in believing that because the equipment purchase involved no financing, there is really no expense of having excess facilities.

     h. Discuss why even though never having back orders may be considered an effective selling technique, this may indicate signs of other problems. Evaluate their 48-hour turnaround time policy and wide variety of container sizes.

     i. Explain whether you think a skeleton second shift is needed.

     j. Evaluate Murrell's produce-and-rework-if-defective routine.

     k. Cite evidence supporting whether you agree or disagree that the present wage system provides incentives for employees. Does it encourage working harder or working smarter?

     l. Discuss the advantages of Murrell having its own sales force instead of using commission agents.

     m. Describe the dangers of a company such as Murrell depending on one large customer for most of its sales and providing extra services for some customers.

     n. Criticize the current production scheduling. Explain why you can understand the tendency of the vice president of production to employ more workers than are needed in view of his environment.

     o. Give evidence of lack of control in the company.

     p. Cite four specific instances that indicate management does not understand what the company's critical problems really are.

COST ACCOUNTING/ COST MANAGEMENT FOR DECISION MAKING

13

Cost-Volume-Profit Analysis

CHAPTER OBJECTIVES

After studying this chapter, you should be able to:

1. Explain the cost-volume-profit relationships that exist in a company.
2. Compute and use breakeven analysis.
3. Recognize that even though rigid assumptions underlie breakeven analysis, it can result in effective answers without costly analysis.

4. Examine through sensitivity analysis the effect on profit and the breakeven point of changing an input value.

Introduction

This chapter focuses on cost-volume-profit relationships and the impact of cost behavior patterns on decision making. An understanding of a company's cost behavior patterns is helpful in making management decisions on such matters as product pricing, accepting or rejecting sales orders, and promotion of more profitable product lines. Cost-volume-profit analysis determines the target volume, which is the volume necessary to achieve target or desired operating income. One of the more popular forms of cost-volume-profit analysis is the computation of a company's breakeven point.

Computing Breakeven Point (L.O. 2)

The **breakeven point** is the volume of sales at which there is no profit or loss. Even though breakeven analysis is a static concept, its application to a dynamic situation aids management in planning and controlling operations. The focus of breakeven analysis is the impact of volume on costs and profits within a **relevant range,** as introduced in Chapter 3. Because operating at the breakeven point is not the goal of managers, they may question the benefit of breakeven analysis. However, breakeven analysis forces a study of a company's fixed and variable cost behavior. The actual breakeven point is of less importance than the effect of decisions on costs and sales. Cost-volume-profit analysis is valuable because it determines the sales volume to earn target operating income.

Impact of Automation on Breakeven

As machines replace laborers and factories become more automated, many formerly variable costs—such as payroll—become fixed. Plants with increased fixed costs resulting from automation have higher breakeven points and require higher levels of utilization to be profitable. Thus, understanding cost behavior becomes even more important in making management decisions on product pricing, accepting or rejecting sales orders, cost reduction analysis, and promotion of more profitable product lines. Cost accountants assign greater importance to the variable-fixed cost relationships in an automated environment.

Contribution Margin Approach

Accountants can use either an equation or a graph to determine a company's breakeven point. They express breakeven in units or in sales dollars. For example, assume a $10 unit sales price, $4 unit variable expenses, and fixed expenses of $36,000. The contribution margin is

$10 unit sales price − $4 variable expense = $6 unit contribution margin

Contribution margin represents the sales dollars left after deducting variable expenses that cover fixed costs plus produce a profit. Contribution margin may be expressed as a total, as an amount per unit, or as a percentage. The following equation indicates sales equal expenses because there is no income at the breakeven point:

$$X = \text{Units to be sold at breakeven point}$$
$$S = \text{Variable expenses} + \text{Fixed expenses}$$
$$\$10X = \$4X + \$36,000$$
$$\$6X = \$36,000$$
$$X = \frac{\$36,000 \text{ Fixed expense}}{\$6 \text{ Unit contribution margin}} = 6,000 \text{ Units to break even}$$

Remember that Chapter 3 defined **variable costs** as those costs varying directly with changes in the volume of output. For example, direct materials used is a variable cost. **Fixed costs,** on the other hand, remain the same in total for a given period and production level. Insurance and rent are examples of fixed costs. Note that we are substituting *expense* for *cost* as there is a widespread tendency to use these terms interchangeably. In this context, *costs* refer to costs expiring and thus will become expenses in the period studied.

Breakeven Units. The preceding equation indicates that if a company sold in the range of 6,000 units, it would break even. We should not assume, however, that when the company's volume is exactly 6,000 units, breakeven conditions automatically occur. Breakeven may not occur because actual costs may vary from those forecasted. For example, the actual unit variable expenses may not be $4, and actual total fixed expenses may vary from $36,000.

Breakeven Sales Dollars. After arriving at the 6,000 units needed to sell to break even, we can determine breakeven sales. Breakeven sales result from multiplying breakeven units by the unit sales price to yield $60,000 (6,000 units × $10 sales price).

Variable Cost Ratio

Rather than multiplying breakeven units by unit sales price, we can use the variable cost ratio or contribution margin ratio to determine breakeven sales dollars. The **variable cost ratio** results from dividing variable costs by sales. Using the previous illustration, the variable cost ratio is 40 percent ($4 unit variable cost/ $10 unit sales price). We can also determine the variable cost ratio by subtracting the contribution margin ratio from 100 percent. The **contribution margin ratio** is the ratio of contribution margin to sales price. With a 60 percent contribution margin ratio, the result is a 40 percent variable cost ratio. Dividing total fixed costs by the 60 percent contribution margin ratio, breakeven sales dollars are

$$100\% \text{ Sales price} = \$4/\$10 \text{ Variable cost percentage} + \$36,000 \text{ Fixed expenses}$$
$$100\% = 40\% + \$36,000$$
$$60\% = \$36,000$$

$$\frac{\$36,000 \text{ Fixed expense}}{60\% \text{ Contribution margin ratio}} = \$60,000 \text{ Breakeven sales}$$

Breakeven Chart

Breakeven charts graphically display the relationship of cost to volume and profits and show profit or loss at any sales volume within a relevant range. A breakeven chart may better indicate cost-volume-profit relationships to line managers and nonaccountants than a numerical exhibit. A breakeven chart vividly shows the impact of volume on costs and profits.

A breakeven chart expresses dollars of revenue, costs, and expenses on the vertical scale. Its horizontal scale indicates volume that may represent units of sales, direct labor-hours, machine-hours, percent of capacity, or other suitable volume drivers. The relationships depicted in breakeven graphs are valid only within the relevant range that underlies the construction of the graph. We assume that 0 to $100,000 sales fall within Exhibit 13–1's relevant range, representing up to 75 percent capacity.

The three lines in Exhibit 13–1 represent fixed expenses, total expenses, and sales revenue. A horizontal line at $36,000 represents fixed expenses. Even if there are no sales, fixed expenses for this relative range remain at $36,000. Adding variable expenses to fixed expenses gives a total expense line. Variable expenses are zero if there are no sales because of the direct relationship between sales and variable expenses. As sales increase, the total expense line increases, reflecting the $4 per unit variable charge. We draw the sales revenue line from the zero intersection of the horizontal and vertical scales to $100,000 maximum sales for this relevant range.

We can construct breakeven charts in an alternate manner that readily shows the contribution margin at any sales volume. Exhibit 13–2 illustrates capacity percentages, rather than units sold, on the horizontal axis using the facts given in the previous example.

Because breakeven charts are best used as a simple means of illustrating various cost-volume-profit alternatives, we did not include a complex breakeven chart. However, occasions may arise in which the probable effects of complex alternative proposals are best communicated through more elaborate breakeven charts. We can construct a curved sales line to indicate that the sales line does not have to be constant at all capacity levels. We can also divide fixed and

EXHIBIT 13–1   Breakeven Chart

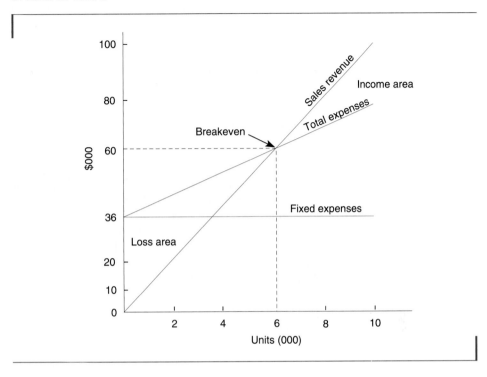

EXHIBIT 13–2   Breakeven Chart Showing Contribution Margin

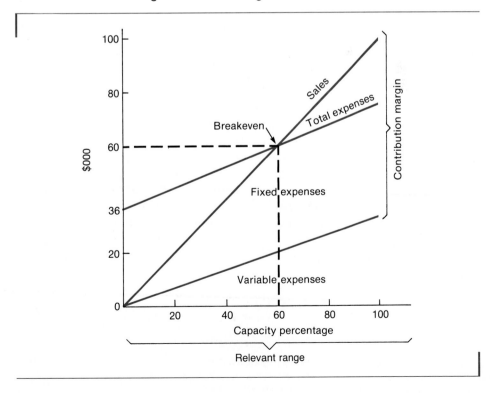

variable expenses into production, administrative, and marketing expenses. And we can draw fixed expenses in a step fashion to indicate the increase expected at various capacity levels. Even though all of the breakeven charts illustrated in this chapter depict a constant unit variable cost, we can alter the slope of the variable cost line at different capacity levels. Increases in variable costs and declines in sales are among other conditions shown on breakeven charts.

Extensions of Breakeven Analysis (L.O. 3)

Marginal Income

Some people use the term *contribution margin* interchangeably with **marginal income.** However, *marginal* often refers to only one product unit. Thus, when accountants refer to marginal income, they generally mean the contribution margin generated by the sale of one additional unit. The contribution margin ratio is the **profit-volume (P/V) ratio** or the **marginal income ratio.** Exhibit 13–3 illustrates the calculation of the P/V ratio. The contribution margin is $48,000; the profit-volume ratio is 60 percent.

Margin of Safety

Margin of safety, another key concept of breakeven analysis, is the excess of actual or budgeted sales over the breakeven sales volume. This provides the buffer by which sales may decrease before a loss occurs. The margin of safety concept is a mechanical way of saying a company is (or is not) close to the breakeven point. With breakeven sales of $60,000 ($36,000 fixed cost ÷ 60 percent P/V ratio) and actual sales of $80,000, the margin of safety becomes:

Margin of safety = $80,000 actual sales − $60,000 breakeven sales = $20,000
Margin of safety ratio (M/S ratio) = $20,000/$80,000 actual sales = 25 percent

Used with the contribution margin ratio (or P/V ratio), the margin of safety determines the percentage of sales that income represents. Using the 25 percent margin of safety ratio and the 60 percent contribution margin ratio from Exhibit 13–1, income is 15 percent (25 percent × 60 percent) of sales. When applied against $80,000 sales, this income percentage yields $12,000 (15 percent × $80,000) income before taxes.

Margin of safety draws management's attention to the importance of maintaining efficient operating conditions. Because not all administrators have financial backgrounds, the margin of safety concept may impress on them how close to breakeven the company's operations really are and how critical certain cost controls are. Examining its contribution margin and total fixed costs is an effective strategy when management finds its margin of safety is low. With high

EXHIBIT 13–3

Sales (8,000 × $10)	$80,000	100%
Variable expenses (8,000 × $4)	32,000	40
Contribution margin	$48,000	60%
Fixed costs	36,000	45
Income before taxes	$12,000	15%

contribution margins and high fixed costs, management should concentrate on reducing the fixed costs or increasing sales. A low margin of safety accompanied by a low contribution margin ratio requires effort to increase the contribution margin ratio by either reducing variable costs or increasing sales price. While the preceding statements represent oversimplifications of uncertain real situations, management should act in those directions.

Cash Flow Breakeven Point

In addition to calculating the breakeven point at which net taxable income equals zero, we can determine the breakeven point at which cash flow equals zero. In calculating the breakeven point where sales equal expenses, we use the same expenses as we used for determining net income. For example, with $4 unit variable expenses and $36,000 fixed expenses, the contribution margin approach yields a breakeven point of $36,000 ÷ $6 = 6,000 units.

Assume the fixed costs are comprised of the following:

Superintendent's salary	$17,000
Rent—building	11,000
Insurance	2,000
Depreciation—equipment	6,000
	$36,000

Because depreciation does not represent a cash outflow, the **cash flow breakeven point** is

Cash flow fixed costs:

Superintendent's salary	$17,000
Rent	11,000
Insurance	2,000
	$30,000

$$\frac{\$30,000}{\$6} = 5,000 \text{ units for cash flow breakeven}$$

To simplify, this cash flow breakeven ignores the tax shield that depreciation provides. Although most expenses involve cash payments, such charges as depreciation and amortization are noncash reductions in income. We deduct depreciation expense along with other expenses in arriving at net taxable income. Because depreciation does not require a cash expenditure, the tax rate multiplied by the depreciation charge yields a tax shield. We call it a **tax shield** because it protects that amount of income from taxation. Chapter 17 introduces this concept in capital expenditure analysis. Even though the company project or segment being examined has no income at breakeven point, companywide income may be taxed at the income tax rate. Because depreciation from this project may be a tax shield against any companywide income, the following improved cash flow breakeven point results. Note we are using a 48 percent income tax rate and $6 unit contribution margin, and considering the tax effect.

Cash flow fixed costs:

Superintendent's salary	$17,000
Rent	11,000
Insurance	2,000
	$30,000
Less tax shield on noncash expense:	
Fixed costs of depreciation (48% × $6,000)	2,880
	$27,120

$$\frac{\$27,120}{\$6} = 4,520 \text{ units for cash flow breakeven}$$

Regardless of whether we consider the tax shield, the cash flow breakeven computation assumes that all sales are collected in cash and all variable and fixed costs represent cash flows out. (Remember that by dividing by the $6 contribution margin, we have deducted cash variable expenses from cash sales.) In reality, few companies operate on a cash only basis. Accruals of assets and liabilities and a change in inventories affect the computation. Cash flow breakeven also ignores the different timing of cash flows; that is, cash outflows may occur faster than cash inflows. Despite its limitations and assumptions, cash flow breakeven gives management a different perspective because it reveals the volume needed for cash inflow to equal cash outflow.

Assumptions and Limitations of Breakeven Analysis

Breakeven analysis is easy to use and inexpensive to apply. However, several **assumptions of breakeven analysis** limit using cost-volume-profit analysis in managerial decision making. The following are among these limitations:

1. The breakeven chart is fundamentally a static analysis; normally, changes can only be shown by drawing a new chart or a series of charts.

2. Relevant range is specified to define fixed and variable costs in relation to a specific period and designated range of production level. The relevant range is usually a range of activities in which the company has operated. This volume of activity is expressed in common terms for sales and expenses; direct labor or machine-hours, units produced, and sales value of production are often used. We must then redefine the amount of fixed and variable cost for any activity outside the relevant range.

3. All costs fall into either a fixed or variable cost classification.

4. Unit variable costs remain the same and there is a direct relationship between costs and volume. For example, no quantity discounts on materials, increases in labor productivity, or other possible savings in cost are assumed.

5. Volume is assumed to be the only important factor affecting cost behavior. Other influencing factors such as unit prices, sales mix, labor strikes, and production method are ignored. A change in expected cost behavior causes a modification in the breakeven point.

6. Unit sales price and other market conditions are assumed to remain unchanged. No quantity discounts are assumed to be available.

7. Total fixed costs remain constant over the relevant range considered.

8. Inventory changes are so insignificant that they have no impact on the analysis.

9. No increase in efficiency occurs in the period of activity studied, and managerial policies and techniques have no effect on costs.

10. Product technology is assumed to remain unchanged.

11. If breakeven analysis covers more than one product line, there is a specific sales mix assumed. **Sales mix** is the combination of quantities of products that a company sells. For example, in a tennis sporting shop, it may be six cans of tennis balls to one tennis dress to one tennis racket. Some accountants argue that the constant sales mix assumption is not such a limiting assumption because the sales mix is relatively stable for most product lines. Many individual products have similar gross margins because

companies price them to yield a targeted gross margin. Also, if there are many products, a change in the mix will not be significant.

Even though breakeven analysis assumes total fixed costs are constant over a relevant range, we, of course, know that fixed costs may change between periods. Management may decide, for example, to purchase machinery to replace direct labor workers, which, in turn, may lower unit variable costs but increase total fixed costs through increased depreciation costs. Increases in the sales force or advertising also alter fixed costs. When one of these events occurs, we construct a new breakeven point and a new breakeven chart.

Although the limitations of breakeven analysis do not invalidate the concept, the assumptions are so restrictive that a breakeven calculation should be interpreted cautiously. The value of breakeven analysis is the insight it gives into cost behavior patterns and the cost-volume-profit relationship. Effective managers recognize that breakeven analysis is not always a cut-and-dried decision tool. There are other opportunity and relevant cost considerations. For example, maintaining good relations with current, large customers whose supplies are critical may override the decision that breakeven analysis suggests.

Sales Mix Effect on Breakeven

Breakeven analysis assumes sales of only one product or a specified sales mix for a company selling more than one product. An assumption regarding sales mix is needed to compute average revenues and average costs. In the following example, the two-product company used to calculate a breakeven point for the overall company may not be realistic because many companies sell a number of product lines. However, to simplify, assume that Product A sells for $16 and its unit variable cost is $12 while Product B sells for $20 with unit variable cost of $12. This gives a $4 per unit or 25 percent ($4/$16 sales price) contribution margin for Product A and an $8 per unit or 40 percent ($8/$20) contribution margin for Product B. Total fixed costs are $196,000. If the company only sells Product A, the breakeven point is

$$\frac{\$196,000}{\$4} = 49,000 \text{ units of Product A to break even}$$

If the company only sells Product B, the breakeven point is

$$\frac{\$196,000}{\$8} = 24,500 \text{ units of Product B to break even}$$

Assume management plans to sell a total of 5,000 units with a planned mix of 2 units of Product A (or 2,000) to 3 units of Product B (or 3,000), resulting in this contribution margin for the combined products:

A   B
2($4) + 3($8) = $8 + $24 = $32/5 = $6.40 weighted-average budgeted
                                        contribution margin

With a $6.40 weighted-average budgeted contribution margin, the breakeven point for the two products becomes:

$$\frac{\$196,000}{\$6.40} = 30,625 \text{ units resulting in } 12,250 \text{ of Product A}$$
$$\text{and } 18,375 \text{ of Product B}$$

This calculation indicates the company must sell 30,625 units to break even. When we apply the planned mix of 2:3 (2 units of Product A to 3 units of Product B), there are 12,250 units of Product A (i.e., $\frac{2}{5} \times 30,625 = 12,250$) and 18,375 (i.e., $\frac{3}{5} \times 30,625 = 18,375$) units of Product B at the planned breakeven point.

Market Bundle. Rather than compute the average budgeted contribution margin, it may be easier to think of this combination as a **market bundle of goods** containing two units of Product A and three units of Product B resulting in a total contribution margin for the bundle of $32. This results in a breakeven volume of 6,125 market bundles as follows:

$$\frac{\$196,000}{\$32} = 6,125 \text{ market bundles}$$

$$6,125 \text{ bundles} \times 2 \text{ units of A} = 12,250 \text{ units of Product A}$$
$$6,125 \text{ bundles} \times 3 \text{ units of B} = 18,375 \text{ units of Product B}$$

Suppose, instead, that the company sells 4,000 units composed of 3,000 units of Product A and 1,000 units of Product B, resulting in an actual sales mix of 3 units of Product A to 1 unit of Product B for a total of 4. Now the breakeven point for the two products is higher, as follows:

A   B
$$3(\$4) + 1(\$8) = \$12 + \$8 = \$20/4 = \$5 \text{ average actual contribution margin}$$

$$\frac{\$196,000}{\$5} = 39,200 \text{ units resulting in } 29,400^* \text{ units of Product A}$$
$$\text{and } 9,800^\dagger \text{ units of Product B}$$

*$\frac{3}{4} \times 39,200$ units = 29,400 units of Product A
$^\dagger\frac{1}{4} \times 39,200$ units = 9,800 units of Product B

Using the market bundle approach with a total contribution margin of $20, the computation is

$$\frac{\$196,000}{\$20} = 9,800 \text{ market bundles}$$

$$9,800 \text{ bundles} \times 3 \text{ units of A} = 29,400 \text{ units of Product A}$$
$$9,800 \text{ bundles} \times 1 \text{ unit of B} = 9,800 \text{ units of Product B}$$

The actual mix of 3:1 (three units of Product A to one unit of Product B) results in a higher breakeven point because the company sold fewer units of the higher contribution margin Product B than planned. Breakeven analysis becomes less valid when involving more than one segment or division of a company because we must allocate companywide indirect fixed costs to each segment. Thus, we should determine the breakeven point for as small a segment as possible.

The company expressed its sales mix for Products A and B in a ratio of units. Alternatively, sales mix can be stated in sales dollars. The following breakeven sales computation expresses sales mix as a percentage of sales dollars. Assume for 19X1 the following unit sales price and variable costs for three different products with $185,000 fixed costs:

	Products		
	X	Y	Z
Sales	$40	$30	$20
Variable costs	20	18	16

Assuming the sales mix in dollars is 30 percent X, 40 percent Y, and 30 percent Z, the 19X2 breakeven sales dollars would be:

	Products		
	X	**Y**	**Z**
Sales price	$40	$30	$20
Variable costs	20	18	16
Contribution margin	$20	$12	$ 4
Contribution margin ratio	50%	40%	20%
Percentage of sales dollars	30%	40%	30%
Weighted contribution margin	15% +	16% +	6% = 37%

$185,000/37% = $500,000 breakeven sales dollars resulting in $150,000*
Product A sales; $200,000† Product B sales; and $150,000* Product C sales

*30% × $500,000 = $150,000
†40% × $500,000 = $200,000

Now, assume the company expresses its sales mix in units as 30 percent X, 40 percent Y, and 30 percent Z. This sales mix expression indicates that 30 percent of total units sold result from Product X unit sales, 40 percent from Product Y unit sales, and 30 percent from Product Z unit sales. Converting the percentages into ratios, the mix becomes 3:4:3 resulting in this contribution margin for the combined products:

$$3(\$20) + 4(\$12) + 3(\$4) = \$120/10 = \$12 \text{ average budgeted}$$
$$\text{contribution margin}$$

With a $12 average budgeted contribution margin, the breakeven point for the three products becomes:

$$\frac{\$185,000}{\$12} = 15,417 \text{ units resulting in 4,625 of Product X,}$$
$$6,167 \text{ of Product Y, and 4,625 of Product Z.}$$

Target Beforetax and Aftertax Income

We can adapt the breakeven equation to reveal more useful information indicating the sales necessary to yield a specified target income. For example, assuming a $10 unit sales price, $4 unit variable cost, $36,000 fixed costs, and a target income before taxes of $6,000, this number of units must be sold:

Let X = Number of units to be sold to yield a target operating income
Sales = Variable expenses + Fixed expenses + Target income
$10X = $4X + $36,000 + $6,000
$6X = $42,000
X = 7,000 units

This calculation reveals that the company must sell 7,000 units to earn a $6,000 beforetax target income.

We use the same basic approach to compute the number of units a company must sell if management expresses income as a percent of sales. Assume that with a $10 unit sales price, $4 unit variable cost (or $4/$10 = 40% variable cost to sales), and $36,000 fixed costs, management wishes to earn a 15 percent return on sales before taxes. The calculation to determine the sales level to earn this return is as follows:

Sales	=	Variable expense	+	Fixed expense	+	Target beforetax income
100%X =		40%X	+	$36,000	+	15%X
45%X =		$36,000				
X =		$80,000 sales to earn 15 percent return on sales before tax.				

EXHIBIT 13–4

$$\text{Sales} = \frac{\text{Variable}}{\text{Expense}} + \frac{\text{Fixed}}{\text{Expense}} + \frac{\text{Desired Aftertax}}{\text{Income}}$$

$$100\%X = 40\%X + \$36{,}000 + \frac{10\%X}{100\% - 48\%}$$

$$100\%X = 40\%X + \$36{,}000 + 19.23\%X$$
$$100\%X - 59.23\%X = \$36{,}000$$
$$40.77\%X = \$36{,}000$$
$$X = \$88{,}300 \text{ sales to earn 10 percent}$$
$$\text{aftertax income}$$

The following simplified statement of income proves that the sales figure determined is correct:

Statement of Income

Sales		$80,000
Expenses:		
Variable expenses (40% × $80,000)	$32,000	
Fixed expenses	36,000	68,000
Income before taxes (15% × $80,000)		$12,000

Aftertax Target Income. Management may desire a target return after taxes. Exhibit 13–4 indicates $88,300 target sales based on 40 percent variable cost ratio, $36,000 fixed expenses, a 10 percent target aftertax return on sales, and a 48 percent tax rate.

With a 10 percent target aftertax return, the sales needed to fulfill this objective must not only support variable and fixed expenses but also cover income taxes before yielding an aftertax income. With a 48 percent income tax rate, the desired aftertax income represents 19.23 percent ($10\%X \div 52\%X$) of sales. The following statement of income proves this sales figure:

Statement of Income

Sales		$88,300
Expenses:		
Variable expenses (40% × $88,300)	$35,320	
Fixed expenses	36,000	71,320
Income before taxes		$16,980
Income taxes (48% × $16,980)		8,150
Net income after taxes (10% × $88,300) . . .		$ 8,830

If a company is manufacturing a product with not only a declining market but also a decreasing volume, income, and profit margin, it may not be feasible to establish an $88,300 sales objective. After using market research to determine which sales range is realistic, management may be forced to reassess its objectives or change the promotional expenditures planned. Sensitivity analysis is a helpful tool for making such decisions.

Sensitivity Analysis (L.O. 4)

Sensitivity analysis examines the effect on the outcome for changes in one or more input values and asks what if an input value changed. For example, when the unit variable cost, sales mix, sales price, total fixed cost, or other inputs for cost-volume-profit analysis change, the breakeven point changes, as well as the amount of profit or loss. Sensitivity analysis allows management to determine the impact on the breakeven point and profit if an input value changes.

To illustrate, assume management believes that the $88,300 sales calculated in Exhibit 13–4 is unrealistic. However, it wishes to earn an aftertax income of $8,600. It investigates several alternatives, one of which involves the reduction of fixed costs by $6,000. We can use the following formula to determine the target sales dollars needed to earn an aftertax net income of $8,600 if this alternative is chosen assuming a 48 percent tax rate. We deduct variable costs of 40 percent and $30,000 fixed costs from sales. The resulting profit is subject to a 48 percent tax. We project this alternative to yield the target profit in the sales range of $77,564.

$$X = \text{Sales to earn \$8,600 aftertax net income}$$
$$100\%X = \text{Sales to earn \$8,600 aftertax net income}$$
$$\$8,600 = [(100\%X - 40\%X) - \$30,000] \times (1.00 - .48)$$
$$\$8,600 = 31.2\%X - \$15,600$$
$$31.2\%X = \$24,200$$
$$X = \$77,564$$

To prove this sales range, managers could prepare the following income statement:

Sales		$77,564
Variable cost (40% × $77,564)	$31,026	
Fixed cost	30,000	61,026
Income before taxes		$16,538
Tax (48% × $16,538)		7,938
Aftertax income		$ 8,600

Effect of Volume Change

We can also use sensitivity analysis to estimate the effect on earnings if the company expands facilities, resulting in an increase in sales volume. In the example displayed in Exhibit 13–1, the company must achieve 60 percent of theoretical capacity to break even. If we estimate operations to reach 80 percent of capacity, sensitivity analysis estimates income to be $80,000 − [$36,000 + (40% × $80,000)] = $12,000. Managers can use this information in estimating the most profitable alternative for expansion of plant facilities and product lines, as well as financing and dividend policies.

Assume that in the previous illustration, management has the opportunity to purchase an adjacent building and expand operations to a maximum sales volume of $125,000. However, this expansion would increase fixed costs to $42,000. With variable costs remaining at 40 percent of sales, we can make the following calculation:

	With Present Facilities	With Expanded Facilities
Sales at breakeven	$100\%X = 0.40X + \$36,000$ $= \$60,000$	$100\%X = 0.40X + \$42,000$ $= \$70,000$
Income at $80,000 sales	$80,000 − [(40\% × \$80,000)$ $+ \$36,000]$ $= \$12,000$	$80,000 − [(40\% × \$80,000)$ $+ \$42,000]$ $= \$6,000$
Sales necessary to earn $20,000 income before taxes	$X = \$36,000 + 0.40X$ $+ \$20,000$ $= \$93,333$	$X = \$42,000 + 0.40X$ $+ 20,000$ $= \$103,333$
Income at 90% capacity	$90,000 − [(40\% × \$90,000)$ $+ \$36,000]$ $= \$18,000$	$112,500 − [(40\% × \$112,500)$ $+ \$42,000]$ $= \$25,500$

EXHIBIT 13–5   Breakeven Chart with an Increase in Fixed Costs

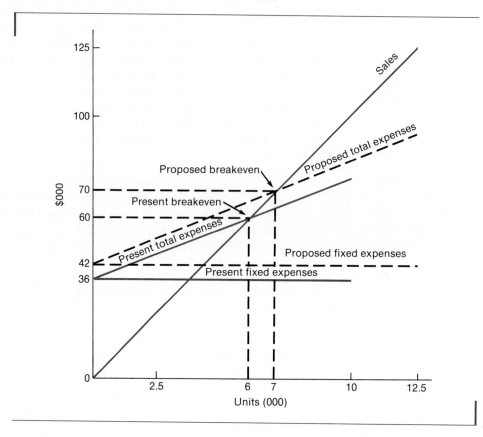

A breakeven chart, as shown in Exhibit 13–5, illustrates the effect of increasing fixed expenses on the breakeven point. Broken dotted lines indicate the proposed total expense and fixed expense lines. On the chart, the proposed increase in fixed expenses has caused the breakeven point to be higher. Remember, however, assuming that cost behavior is linear over the relevant range may limit the reliability of breakeven analysis. Users of cost-volume-profit analysis must constantly reexamine the assumptions of breakeven analysis. Otherwise, they may mistakenly assume that volume is the only cost driver and that uncertainty does not exist.

In deciding whether the company should expand, management should determine potential sales possibilities. The plant expansion requires a higher sales volume to break even. In addition, a higher sales volume is necessary to earn $20,000 in income using the expanded facilities. However, if a significant market for the product exists, the company has the chance of earning a higher level of income using expanded facilities operating at 90 percent capacity. (As previous chapters have emphasized, it is not realistic to assume a company can obtain maximum capacity.)

Price and Volume Alternatives

Cost-volume-profit analysis is helpful in predicting the change in income that occurs when altering sales price or sales volume. Using spreadsheet software and a personal computer, an accountant can generate an analysis similar to that in

EXHIBIT 13–6   Effect of Sales Price and Volume Changes on Income and Breakeven

	(1) Budgeted 7,000 Units @ $10	(2) 10% Increase in Sales Price 5% Decrease in Volume	(3) 15% Decrease in Sales Price 20% Increase in Volume	(4) 5% Increase in Sales Price No Change in Volume
Sales:				
7,000 units @ $10	$70,000			
6,650 units @ $11		$73,150		
8,400 units @ $8.50			$71,400	
7,000 units @ $10.50				$73,500
Variable expense:				
7,000 units @ $4	28,000			
6,650 units @ $4		26,600		
8,400 units @ $4			33,600	
7,000 units @ $4				28,000
Contribution margin	$42,000	$46,550	$37,800	$45,500
Fixed costs	36,000	36,000	36,000	36,000
Income before taxes	$ 6,000	$10,550	$ 1,800	$ 9,500
P/V ratio (contribution margin ÷ sales)	60%	63.6%	52.9%	61.9%
Breakeven sales (fixed expenses ÷ P/V ratio) .	$60,000	$56,604	$68,053	$58,158

Exhibit 13–6. This analysis measures the effects of various sales prices and volumes. We expect no change in unit variable cost or total fixed costs. This analysis assumes that management's budget is based on selling 7,000 units at a $10 per unit sales price, yielding $6,000 net income before taxes, as shown in Column 1. Because of the influence of supply and demand, Column 2 assumes that an increase in sales price would result in a lower volume sold. Column 3 illustrates the results obtained if there is a decrease in sales price and an increase in volume. Marketing research should assist in arriving at such probable sales price and volume combinations. Column 4 indicates the effect on the breakeven point and income when a 5 percent increase in sales price occurs with no decrease in volume. Management may believe demand for their product is high enough because of brand loyalty or product quality that a sales price increase would have no effect on volume.

Exhibit 13–6 shows projected income is highest when there is a 10 percent increase in sales price with a 5 percent decrease in volume. Breakeven sales with these conditions are also lower than at budgeted volume. The least favorable alternative is to lower the sales price 15 percent with a resulting 20 percent increase in volume. Not only is income lowest with this alternative but breakeven sales are also highest. A 5 percent increase in sales price, with no corresponding decrease in volume, causes a marked increase over budgeted income.

P/V Charts (L.O. 1)

A **profit-volume graph,** also called a **P/V chart,** illustrates the impact of sale price and volume changes on income and breakeven. Even though the P/V chart appears quite different from the breakeven chart, it really is a reformatting of information already portrayed in the breakeven chart. The first graph in Exhibit 13–7 illustrates such a chart using data from Exhibit 13–1 in which fixed

EXHIBIT 13–7   P/V Chart

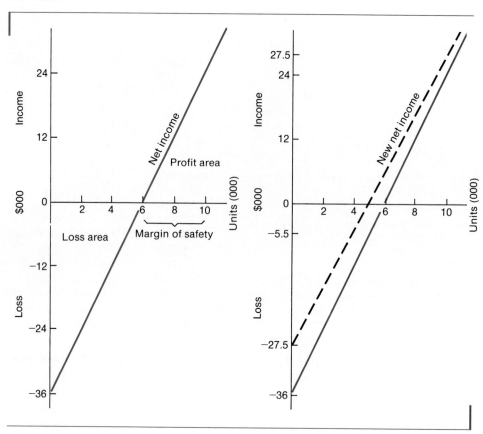

expenses are $36,000, unit variable expenses are $4, and unit sales price is $10. The vertical axis represents net income in dollars, while the horizontal axis is volume, expressed in units or sales dollars. If the company produces no units, the net loss will be $36,000, the amount of the fixed expense. The net income line intersects the volume axis at the breakeven point of 6,000 units, indicating zero net income at this breakeven volume. Net income at 10,000 units becomes $24,000.

The second graph in Exhibit 13–7 shows the impact on net income and the breakeven point if the unit variable expense increases to $4.50 while total fixed expense decreases to $27,500. The breakeven point falls from 6,000 units to 5,000 units, as follows:

$$\frac{\$27,500}{\$5.50 \text{ unit contribution margin}} = 5,000 \text{ units}$$

The new net income, the dashed line in the second graph, is steeper because the net income would increase at a faster rate as volume increases.

Data presented in any cost-volume-profit analysis such as those illustrated in Exhibits 13–6 and 13–7 are of great importance in analyzing which available alternative is most profitable. However, accountants usually have to spend time studying the information because cost-volume-profit analysis requires the segregation of fixed and variable costs. They cannot directly use data that appear on conventional absorption statements of income. Instead, semivariable expense must be broken down into variable and fixed components. Accountants use the cost estimation methods presented in Chapter 3 and establish separate ledger accounts for fixed and variable costs. In addition, the data used in any cost-volume-profit analysis should reflect current conditions, since the behavior of variable and fixed costs tends to change over time.

Computer Spreadsheets and Cost-Volume-Profit Analysis (L.O. 3)

The wide-spread availability of personal computers encourages more managers to apply cost-volume-profit analysis. Even though this chapter gives the mathematical details of the manual process, the preprogrammed microcomputer applications written for this book introduce the ease of using sensitivity analysis. Computers can quickly make the computations for changes in the assumptions underlying proposed projects. For example, computer spreadsheets allow managers to determine the most profitable combination of selling price, variable and fixed costs, and volume. A manager enters into the computer various numbers for price and cost in an equation based on cost-volume-profit relationships to yield target income for each combination. Because of a computer's speed and accuracy in providing this information, the manager can select the most profitable actions.

Summary

Cost-volume-profit analysis provides useful information about pricing, short-term bidding, and deleting or adding product lines. Management must know the contribution margin ratios for each product so they can promote high contribution margin products and reduce emphasis on less profitable products. Contribution margin analysis allows managers to decide whether to accept an extra order when capacity is below normal.

While breakeven point analysis portrays only static cost-volume-profit relationships under limiting assumptions, it offers insight into the effect on profits when a change occurs in any of these components. A breakeven chart may also more vividly illustrate these relationships for line management than would detailed numerical statements. However, rigid limitations designed to simplify real-world situations underlie breakeven analysis. Nevertheless, rather than apply more complex decision-making tools requiring costly analysis, accountants often use computer spreadsheet programs to find cost-volume-profit answers quickly. Also, accountants make many decisions within the relevant volume range where the linearity assumption is more accurate.

Important Terms and Concepts

breakeven point, 452

relevant range, 452

contribution margin, 453

variable costs, 453

fixed costs, 453

variable cost ratio, 454

contribution margin ratio, 454

breakeven chart, 454

Problem for Self-Study

Breakeven Units and Units to Earn Target Profit Percentage

Covington Company has conducted cost studies and projected the following annual cost based on 50,000 units of production and sales:

	Total Annual Cost	Percent of Variable Portion of Total Annual Cost
Direct material	$150,000	100%
Direct labor	90,000	65
Factory overhead	140,000	40
Marketing and administrative	250,000	40

Required:

a. Determine the number of units that must be sold for the company to break even if the unit sales price is $17.91.

b. Compute the company's unit sales price that will yield a return on sales of 15 percent before taxes if sales are 50,000 units.

Solution to Problem for Self-Study

a.

COVINGTON COMPANY

Variable costs:
Direct material	$150,000
Direct labor (65% × $90,000)	58,500
Factory overhead (40% × $140,000)	56,000
Marketing and administrative (40% × $250,000)	100,000
	$364,500

Fixed costs:
Direct labor (35% × $90,000)	$ 31,500
Factory overhead (60% × $140,000)	84,000
Marketing and administrative (60% × $250,000)	150,000
	$265,500

$$\frac{\$364,500}{50,000 \text{ units}} = \$7.29 \text{ unit variable cost}$$

$$\frac{\$265,500}{\$17.91 - \$7.29} = 25,000 \text{ units to break even}$$

b.
$$50,000X = (\$7.29)(50,000) + 15\%(50,000X) + \$265,500$$
$$50,000X = \$364,500 + 15\%(50,000X) + \$265,500$$
$$50,000X - 7,500X = \$630,000$$
$$42,500X = \$630,000$$
$$X = \$14.824$$

Review Questions

1. Explain how increased automation affects:

    a. A company's breakeven point.
    b. The importance of cost accountants fully understanding a company's cost behavior.

2. The budget formula for the Brown Company is $200,000 plus $0.75 per machine-hour. It takes four hours to manufacture a unit before it can be sold for $7. Based on the overhead budget formula, how many units must be sold for the company to generate $60,000 more than total budgeted overhead costs?

3. Assume the president of a company wishes to earn a 10 percent profit on sales. How can breakeven analysis be used to determine the unit sales to earn this desired profit percentage?

4. Assume that unit variable cost is expressed as a percentage of sales price and this percentage increases from a previous period. What impact would this increase have on breakeven units?

5. Assume the market saturation point for a product is almost met and management does not feel it can increase present sales volume; in fact, they would not be surprised if there is a decrease in volume. With these conditions, the company has the opportunity of replacing some of its equipment and machinery, which is being depreciated on a straight-line basis, with direct labor workers. Assume at present volume there is an equal exchange of total fixed costs for total variable costs. Ignoring other factors, what recommendations would you make?

6. List five limitations of breakeven analysis in managerial decision making.

7. What is the relationship between a company's product mix and its breakeven point? Does a change in the assumed product mix affect the breakeven point previously determined?

8. What should management do when a low margin of safety is accompanied by:

    a. A high contribution margin and high fixed costs?
    b. A low contribution margin ratio?

9. At a breakeven point of 1,000 units sold, variable costs were $1,500 and fixed costs were $750. What will the 1,001th unit sold contribute to profit before income tax?

10. Explain the meaning of each of the following terms that are implicit in cost-volume-profit analysis:

    a. Breakeven point.
    b. Fixed costs.
    c. Variable costs.
    d. Sales mix.
    e. Relevant range.
    f. Margin of safety.

CPA/CMA/CIA Multiple Choice Questions

1. (AICPA) In the proft-volume chart below, *EF* and *GH* represent the profit-volume graphs of a single-product company for 19X1 and 19X2, respectively.

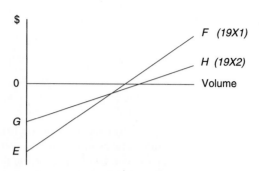

If 19X1 and 19X2 unit sales prices are identical, how did total fixed costs and unit variable costs of 19X2 change compared to 19X1?

	19X2 Total Fixed Costs	19X2 Unit Variable Costs
a.	Decreased	Increased
b.	Decreased	Decreased
c.	Increased	Increased
d.	Increased	Decreased

2.–3. (CIA) Use the following data for questions 2 and 3:
A company makes a product which has variable costs estimated at $4.00 per unit and which sells for $6.00 per unit. Fixed costs for the coming year are estimated to be $130,000.

2. How many units must the company sell in order to generate pretax income of $30,000?

   a. 26,667.
   b. 50,000.
   c. 65,000.
   d. 80,000.

3. Assume that the actual unit sales were 30 percent below the level required to earn $50,000 pretax income. Under those conditions, the pretax income or (loss) would be:

   a. $39,000.
   b. $35,000.
   c. $(4,000).
   d. $126,000.

4. (AICPA) Breakeven analysis assumes that over the relevant range

   a. Total costs are unchanged.
   b. Unit variable costs are unchanged.
   c. Variable costs are nonlinear.
   d. Unit fixed costs are unchanged.

5. (AICPA) The following information pertains to Mete Company:

Sales	$400,000
Variable costs	80,000
Fixed costs	20,000

Mete's breakeven point in sales dollars is

   a. $ 20,000.
   b. $ 25,000.
   c. $ 80,000.
   d. $100,000.

6. (AICPA) The following information pertains to Sisk Company:

Sales (25,000 units)	$500,000
Direct materials and direct labor	150,000
Factory overhead:	
Variable	20,000
Fixed	35,000
Selling and general expenses:	
Variable	5,000
Fixed	30,000

Sisk's breakeven point in number of units is

a. 4,924
b. 5,000
c. 6,250
d. 9,286

7.–8. (CIA) Use the following information for questions 7 and 8:
A company has the following data regarding one of its products which currently sells 10,000 units annually:

	Per Unit
Price	$10
Direct materials	$ 4
Direct labor	$ 2
Variable overhead	$ 1

7. If per unit direct materials cost increases by 25 percent, what will the new total contribution margin be?

a. ($30,000).
b. $20,000.
c. $30,000.
d. $40,000.

8. If instead, volume of sales was reduced by 10 percent, what would be the new total contribution margin?

a. $20,000.
b. $27,000.
c. $30,000.
d. $33,000.

9.–11. (CMA) These questions concern the following budget data for the Bidwell Company:

	Fixed	Variable	
Sales (100,000 units)			$1,000,000
Costs:			
Raw material	$ –0–	$300,000	
Direct labor	–0–	200,000	
Factory costs	100,000	150,000	
Selling and administrative costs	110,000	50,000	
Total costs	$210,000	$700,000	910,000
Budgeted operating income			$ 90,000

9. (CMA) Based on this data, the breakeven sales in units would be

a. 30,000 units.
b. 91,000 units.
c. 60,000 units.
d. 70,000 units.
e. Some amount other than those given above.

10. (CMA) If Bidwell Company is subject to an effective income tax rate of 40 percent, the number of units Bidwell would have to sell to earn an aftertax profit of $90,000 is

   a. 100,000 units.
   b. 120,000 units.
   c. 112,000 units.
   d. 145,000 units.
   e. Some amount other than those given above.

11. (CMA) If fixed costs increased $31,500 with no other cost or revenue factors changing, the breakeven sales in units would be

   a. 34,500 units.
   b. 80,500 units.
   c. 69,000 units.
   d. 94,500 units.
   e. Some amount other than those given above.

Exercises

E13–1 Calculating Income with Contribution Margin and Margin of Safety Ratios Given (L.O. 1)

Analysis of the budget for the Capri Company reveals that variable manufacturing costs are $25 per unit and variable marketing and administrative costs are $10 per unit. Budgeted fixed factory overhead is $500,000, while budgeted fixed marketing and administrative cost is $250,000. Normal capacity for the plant is 160,000 units per year. The unit sales price is $50.

Required:

a. Calculate:
   (1) The breakeven point expressed in dollars.
   (2) The units that must be sold to earn a beforetax income of 20 percent on sales.
b. Determine the actual income before taxes if actual operations for the year resulted in a margin of safety ratio of 30 percent and a contribution margin ratio of 25 percent. Assume actual fixed costs were 5 percent more than those budgeted.

E13–2 Volume of Sales Needed (L.O. 3)

Rebecca's Fashions is considering whether to stay open on Saturday evenings. Salary expense for another four hours is approximately $80 while other extra costs should be about $40. Contribution margin on sales averages 40 percent.

Required:

Determine the volume of sales that would warrant staying open on Saturday evenings. Show your calculations.

E13–3 Target Beforetax Profit (L.O. 1)

The cost estimating function for the SK Company is $200,000 plus $0.75 per machine-hour. It takes four hours to manufacture each unit sold for $7. Based on the flexible (variable) budget formula, how many units must be sold for the company to generate a $60,000 beforetax profit?

E13–4 High-Low and Breakeven Point (L.O. 2)

Jones Company sells each unit produced for $20. Analysis of the cost records reveals the following various capacity levels:

	Volume in Units	Costs
July	20,000	$125,000
August	22,000	135,000
September	18,000	115,000
October	23,000	140,000
November	20,000	125,000
December	21,500	132,500

Required:

Calculate the breakeven point in sales dollars.

E13–5 Units to Sell to Earn Target Profit (L.O. 1)

A department of Terry Company provides the following information relating to the fourth quarter 19X1:

Budget formula	$50,000 plus $1.00/hour variable
Volume variance	1,000 favorable
Actual total overhead (fixed plus variable)	77,500
Spending variance	2,000 unfavorable

Required:

Assume each unit takes two hours to manufacture, and the selling price is $6.00 per unit. Use the overhead budget formula to determine how many units must be sold to generate $50,000 beforetax profit.

E13–6 Determining Breakeven Point and Breakeven Chart (L.O. 2)

Management of the Brown Company wants to earn a 25 percent return on sales. The sales price is $50 per unit and variable cost is $20 per unit. Fixed expenses amount to $35,000.

Required:

a. Calculate how many units must be sold to earn the income desired.
b. Determine the breakeven point for the company in units.
c. Assume the maximum capacity is 4,000 units and construct a breakeven chart.

E13–7 Computing Sales with Target Income and Breakeven Sales (L.O. 3)

Annual costs for Winkler Company based on a 48,000-unit volume of production and sales are as follows:

	Percent of Fixed Portion of Total Annual Costs	Total Annual Costs
Direct material	0	$514,360
Direct labor	20	280,000
Factory overhead	65	360,000
Marketing	40	185,000
Administrative	100	195,680

Required:

a. Determine the unit sales price that will yield a projected 18 percent profit if sales are 48,000 units.
b. Using the variable-fixed costs relationships and a $40 unit sales price:
   (1) Determine breakeven units.
   (2) Determine how many units must be sold to yield a projected 18 percent profit on sales.

E13–8 Breakeven Units under Forecasted Conditions (L.O. 4)

Wyoming Company produced and sold 3,000 units for the year ended July 31, 19X1. Their income statement appears as follows:

Sales		$45,000
Direct material	$10,000	
Direct labor	14,000	
Variable overhead	6,000	
Fixed overhead	6,050	36,050
Income before taxes		$ 8,950

Required:

a. Compute the units the company must sell to break even.
b. Compute the sales in dollars necessary to earn $12,950 beforetax income.
c. Compute breakeven units under these forecasted conditions: Management expects direct material costs to increase 12 percent next year; in addition, analysis of the component parts of variable overhead reveal that a 5 percent decline is expected. Additional fixed costs of $577 will be incurred.

Problems

P13–9 Breakeven and Capacity Relationships (L.O. 1)

The unit sales price for a product sold by Berr, Inc., is $15 and unit variable cost is $12. The company presently operates at 25 percent capacity.

Fixed costs total $140,000 when operations are completely idle; for capacity up to 30 percent, the total fixed cost is $161,000; for 31 to 70 percent capacity, $167,000; and for more than 70 percent capacity, $190,000. Full capacity is 20,000 units.

Required:

a. Determine at which sales level in units it would be more economical to close the factory rather than operate.
b. Prove your answer to Requirement *a*.
c. Compute the present breakeven point in dollars and units.
d. Evaluate the situation and advise management as to the future.
e. Determine at which percentage of capacity the company must operate to break even if it uses a cheaper grade of direct material to save $5 a unit in direct material cost with a corresponding sales price increase of $2.

P13–10 Sales to Break Even (L.O. 2)

LAT Company is considering establishing a branch plant in Peru. Predicting sales of 50,000 units, they provide the following estimated expense:

	Total Annual Expenses	Percent of Total Annual Cost That is Variable
Material	$ 30,000	70%
Labor	28,000	60
Factory overhead	36,000	55
Marketing and administrative	20,000	42
	$114,000	

For each unit it sells, a marketing firm in Peru will receive a commission of 20 percent of the sales price. None of the home office expense will be allocated to the plant in Peru.

Required:

a. Compute the sales price per unit that would cover all total annual expenses for the plant in Peru.
b. Compute the breakeven point in sales dollars for the plant in Peru if the unit sales price is $3.

P13–11 Sales Mix and BE (L.O. 4)

Burn Company produces product lines A, B, and C. Its budget for the next period is based on the following:

	Product Lines		
	A	**B**	**C**
Sales price	$ 8.00	$12.00	$10.00
Variable expenses	4.00	9.00	4.00
Budgeted volume	3,000	7,500	4,500
Total fixed expenses			$26,650

Required:

a. Compute a companywide breakeven point for this multiproduct firm, indicating the breakeven point in units per product line.

b. Assume that at the end of the period you determine 12,000 units were sold consisting of 2,000 units of Product A, 4,000 units of Product B, and 6,000 units of Product C.

A style change in Product C costs an additional $1 in direct material per unit. However, the sales price did not vary from the budgeted figure. Compute the new actual breakeven point in units per product line for the overall company.

P13–12 Sales Mix Expressed in Units and in Dollars (L.O. 4)

Desert Company incurs fixed costs of $150,000 in its sales of Products A, B, and C. For 19X1, the unit sales price and variable costs of these products were

	Products		
	A	**B**	**C**
Sales	$37.50	$100.00	$30.00
Variable costs	22.50	65.00	25.50

Required:

a. Assuming the sales mix in *dollars* is 40 percent A, 25 percent B, and 35 percent C, compute the 19X2 breakeven sales dollars broken down by sales dollars for each of the three products.

b. Assume the sales mix in *units* is 40 percent A, 25 percent B, and 35 percent C.
   (1) Give the weighted-average contribution margin ratio, rounding to four decimal places.
   (2) Give the weighted-average unit contribution margin in dollars.
   (3) Compute the companywide breakeven point broken down in dollars and units for each of the three products.

c. Assume that you, as management, have a choice; explain which product you would rather sell and which you least prefer to sell.

P13–13 Factors Affecting Profitability and Cost-Volume-Profit Analysis (L.O. 1)

Recently you agreed to act as a consultant to a company manufacturing high-tech audio equipment. The company produces remote control AM/FM stereo/CD players and receivers with 8- and 16-program memory modules, 5- and 10-band graphic equalizers, and various speaker systems. The company markets the audio equipment as both systems and component parts. Company headquarters are in Detroit, Michigan, with distribution centers scattered across the United States. The company employs 1,000 workers in production.

Required:

To assist in your consulting activities, provide probable answers to the following:

a. List the company's objectives.

b. Suggest ways the company can make a profit.

c. Determine which major external factors affect the audio company's profitability.

d. Determine which major internal factors affect the audio company's profitability.

e. Explain what impact each of the following would have on profitability:

(1) Increase in labor rate.

(2) Increase in prices of foreign audio equipment.

(3) Increase in sales price of company products.

(4) Increased quality control.

(5) Increased automation.

(6) Increased advertising.

P13–14 Cash Flow Breakeven Point (L.O. 2)

Four years ago George Austin started a company that manufactures motors. The motors sell for $56 and are produced in a building Austin rents for $300 per month. He purchased the necessary equipment with cash four years ago. Austin hired two plant supervisors to oversee the direct labor workers. Since business has increased over the last four years, Austin has increased the number of direct labor workers employed. An outside accountant, who is paid $150 per month, is hired for tax and bookkeeping purposes. Profits are subject to a 48 percent income tax rate. Over the last four years, profits before taxes have increased more than six times without the same increase in sales. Austin cannot understand why profits have increased faster than sales. All sales are on a cash only basis.

Income Statements
For the Years Ended June 30

	19X1	19X4
Sales	$56,000	$112,000
Cost of materials sold	$12,000	$ 24,000
Cost of direct labor sold	13,600	27,200
Utilities	3,400	6,800
Plant supervisors' salaries	14,000	14,000
Rent	3,600	3,600
Accounting services	1,800	1,800
Depreciation	2,600	2,600
Total	$51,000	$ 80,000
Income before taxes	$ 5,000	$ 32,000

Required:

a. Determine the breakeven point in the number of motors that must be sold.

b. Determine the cash flow breakeven point in the number of motors that must be sold.

c. Assume Austin wants the cash balance to show an increase of $10,000 between June 30, 19X3, and June 30, 19X4. How much cash can he use during the year 19X4 for expansion?

d. Indicate how much the cash flow for 19X4 will exceed profits. Explain why.

e. Explain briefly to Austin why his profits have increased at a faster rate than his sales.

P13–15 Calculating Aftertax Income (L.O. 3)

Wallis Company produces quality bicycles. Its income statement for the year ended June 30, 19X1, is as follows:

Income Statement

Sales (300 units)		$63,000
Less variable expenses:		
Direct material	$15,300	
Direct labor	13,500	
Variable overhead	9,000	
Total variable expenses		37,800
Contribution margin		$25,200

Fixed expenses:		
Manufacturing	$5,000	
Marketing	2,000	
Administrative	4,100	
Total fixed expenses		11,100
Income before taxes		$14,100

Harold Wallis, the company's president, believes that 375 units can be sold in 19X2. The tax rate is 38 percent, including state income tax.

Required:

a. Give the forecasted aftertax income for 19X2.
b. Calculate the breakeven point for 19X2 in units.
c. Calculate the breakeven volume in dollars if additional advertising is undertaken. Wallis believes that $5,700 additional advertising will be necessary to maintain the forecasted sales in 19X2.
d. Assume the $5,700 additional advertising cost is incurred. How many sales dollars are required to maintain the aftertax net income in dollars for 19X2 determined in Requirement *a*?
e. Assume Wallis wishes to earn $10,000 aftertax net income and management believes that the forecast of 375 units is accurate. What is the maximum additional amount Wallis can spend on advertising to achieve these objectives?

P13–16 Sales Mix and Breakeven (L.O. 4)

The next year's budget for Max Company, a multiproduct firm, is

	Product Lines			
	A	**B**	**C**	**Total**
Sales	$1,500,000	$1,100,000	$800,000	$3,400,000
Less: Variable costs	900,000	500,000	500,000	1,900,000
Fixed costs allocated on direct labor dollars . . .	300,000	300,000	200,000	800,000
Income before taxes	$ 300,000	$ 300,000	$100,000	$ 700,000
Units	300,000	200,000	50,000	550,000

Required:

a. Compute the budgeted breakeven point in units per product line for the overall company.
b. Assume that at year-end, the sales price, total fixed costs, and unit variable costs were exactly as budgeted and the following units per product line were sold. Determine the company's breakeven point in units using the actual sales mix.

Product Line	**Units**
A	280,000
B	220,000
C	60,000
	560,000

P13–17 Constructing Breakeven Charts under Varying Conditions (L.O. 1)

A product line of the Gunn Company produced the following results during 19X1:

Sales (9,000 units)	$135,000
Total fixed expenses	24,000
Total variable expenses	108,000

During 19X2, company management plans to slightly modify the product by reducing the direct material cost per unit by $0.80. In addition, the sales price will be reduced by $1.80 per unit. An extensive advertising campaign will be started that will increase total fixed expenses by $1,000. Maximum capacity for the company is 15,000 units.

Required:

a. Give the breakeven point for the company in dollars and units before taking account of the changes.

b. Determine the margin of safety before allowing for the changes.

c. Give the breakeven point for the company in dollars and units after accounting for the changes.

d. Draw a breakeven chart using the original data, *not* involving the expected changes.

e. Draw the following on the breakeven graph that you prepared for Requirement *d*: (1) the 19X2 sales line, with the changes; (2) the 19X2 fixed expenses line; and (3) the 19X2 total cost line.

P13–18 Sensitivity Analysis (L.O. 4)

Nik Company produces quality cameras. The statement of income for the year ended December 31, 19X1, is as follows:

NIK COMPANY
Income Statement
For the Year Ended December 31, 19X1

Sales (5,000 units)		$1,500,000
Less variable expenses:		
Direct material	$375,000	
Direct labor	250,000	
Variable overhead	225,000	
Total variable expenses		850,000
Contribution margin		$ 650,000
Fixed expenses:		
Manufacturing	$240,000	
Marketing	200,000	
Administrative	100,000	540,000
Income before taxes		$ 110,000

Company management believes the firm can sell 4,500 units in 19X2. Assume a tax rate of 35 percent.

Required:

a. Compute the forecasted aftertax income for 19X2, assuming the same cost behavior as in 19X1.

b. Calculate the breakeven point for 19X2 in units.

c. Assume management believes that forecasted 19X2 sales can be maintained even if a sales promotion costing $40,000 included in 19X1 expenses is eliminated. What will the breakeven volume in dollars be if this sales promotion is canceled?

d. Assume management believes that if the selling price of cameras decreases to $250, a total of 10,000 units can be sold in 19X2. Assume the fixed cost remains the same; what is the breakeven point for 19X2 in dollars?

P13–19 Cost-Volume-Profit Relationships (L.O. 3)

Tennessee Instrument produces sophisticated pocket calculators. The president of the company asks you, his chief management accountant, to perform a price analysis for the company. Based on the information from all internal reports and sales forecasts, you have collected this information:

Current selling price per unit		$80
Variable cost per unit:		
Material		$20
Labor		10
Overhead		5
Total		$35
Annual volume of sales		10,000 units
Fixed costs		$100,000

Management expects a 10 percent increase in direct labor costs because it has just approved a pay increase for production workers. Due to inflation, the price of direct materials will increase 5 percent next year. However, the overhead cost and both the beginning and ending inventories are not expected to have any significant changes.

Required:

Provide the following for the president using cost-volume-profit analysis:

a. Give the new selling price for a calculator if the president wants to maintain the same profit-volume ratio as this year.

b. Compute how many additional calculators need to be sold so that the net income next year will equal this year's if the selling price is still $80 but the production costs change.

c. Assume the president of the company believes a new piece of equipment costing $250,000 could boost production volume by 20 percent. To sell the additional calculators, Tennessee Instruments needs to lower the selling price per unit from $80 to $75. Based on your analysis of net income of the company before and after expansion, should the equipment be purchased? The new machine would be depreciated 10 percent per year. Use the next year's expected production cost in your calculations.

d. Determine the new breakeven point of the company if the machine is purchased.

P13–20 Breakeven Charts (L.O. 2)

Elaine Company's income statement for the year ended December 31, 19X1, was as follows:

Sales ($8 per unit)		$100,000
Variable costs	$42,000	
Fixed costs	24,000	66,000
Income		$ 34,000

Required:

a. Calculate the present breakeven point in dollars and units.

b. Assume the company is considering adopting a new production procedure that would increase the contribution margin by 15 percent and increase fixed cost by $4,300.
  (1) Calculate the breakeven point in dollars and units under these conditions.
  (2) Graph present and forecasted total and unit fixed costs and total and unit variable costs. Label the forecasted costs TFC (total fixed costs), UFC (unit fixed costs), TVC (total variable costs), and UVC (unit variable costs). Graph paper is not necessary as you are showing only the change in cost behavior.

c. Assume the company is also considering an alternative marketing plan that would increase sales volume by 15 percent and decrease fixed costs by 10 percent.
  (1) Calculate the breakeven point in dollars and units under these conditions.
  (2) Graph present and forecasted total and unit fixed costs and total and unit variable costs. Label the forecasted costs TFC, UFC, TVC, and UVC. Graph paper is not necessary, as you are showing only the change in the cost behavior.

P13–21 Sensitivity Analysis in an Automated Production Process (L.O. 4)

Towery Company presently has a highly automated production process. Management is concerned because annual budgeted fixed costs are $1.4 million for next year. The current sales price is $12 per unit, and unit variable cost is $5.

An outsider has approached the company wanting to buy some of its machinery, which Towery could sell at book value. Management has been considering replacing its machines with direct labor workers since the product could be produced as skillfully in this manner. This proposed change would lower fixed cost by $200,000, with a resulting increase of $2 per unit in variable costs.

Required:

a. Compute the budgeted breakeven point in units and sales dollars under present conditions.
b. Compute the breakeven point in units and sales dollars if the machines are replaced by direct labor workers.
c. Assume that market research indicates 300,000 units could be sold; prepare income statements and margin of safety ratios for each alternative using this sales volume. Indicate which alternative you recommend.
d. Prepare the same analysis as in Requirement *c* assuming that 420,000 units can be sold.
e. Prepare only income statements for the two alternatives assuming a depressed market in the future when 180,000 units will be sold. Indicate which alternative you recommend.
f. Based on your analyses in Requirements *c* through *e*, prepare a general recommendation statement.

P13–22 (AICPA) Breakeven, Target Profit (L.O. 3)

Seco Corporation, a wholesale supply company, engages independent sales agents to market the company's lines. These agents currently receive a commission of 20 percent of sales, but they are demanding an increase to 25 percent of sales made during the year ending December 31, 19X9. Seco had already prepared its 19X9 budget before learning of the agents' demand for an increase in commissions. The following pro forma income statement is based on this budget:

SECO CORPORATION
Pro Forma Income Statement
For the Year Ending December 31, 19X9

Sales		$10,000,000
Cost of sales		6,000,000
Gross margin		4,000,000
Selling and administrative costs:		
Commissions	$2,000,000	
All other costs (fixed)	100,000	2,100,000
Income before income tax		1,900,000
Income tax (30%)		570,000
Net income		$ 1,330,000

Seco is considering the possibility of employing its own salespersons. Three individuals would be required, at an estimated annual salary of $30,000 each, plus commissions of 5 percent of sales. In addition, a sales manager would be employed at a fixed annual salary of $160,000. All other fixed costs, as well as the variable cost percentages, would remain the same as the estimates in the 19X9 pro forma income statement.

Required:

a. Compute Seco's estimated breakeven point in sales dollars for the year ending December 31, 19X9, based on the pro forma income statement prepared by the company.
b. Compute Seco's estimated breakeven point in sales dollars for the year ending December 31, 19X9, if the company employs its own salespersons.
c. Compute the estimated volume in sales dollars that would be required for the year ending December 31, 19X9, to yield the same net income as projected in the pro forma income statement, if Seco continues to use the independent sales agents and agrees to their demand for a 25 percent sales commission.
d. Compute the estimated volume in sales dollars that would generate an identical net income for the year ending December 31, 19X9, regardless of whether Seco employs its own salespersons or continues to use the independent sales agents and pays them a 25 percent commission.

P13–23 Breakeven Analysis: Changing Costs (L.O. 4)

Operating results for the fiscal year just ended for Daniel Humphreys, Inc., follow:

Sales (3,500 units)		$70,000
Variable costs:		
Production	$31,500	
Marketing and administrative	10,500	
Total variable costs		42,000
Contribution margin		$28,000
Fixed costs:		
Production	$10,600	
Marketing and administrative	7,000	
Total fixed costs		17,600
Income before income taxes		$10,400
Income taxes (40%)		4,160
Net income after income taxes		$ 6,240

The manufacturing capacity of the company's facilities is 5,000 units of product.

Required:

Consider each of the following items independently of the other items:

a. Compute the breakeven volume in units of product.

b. Assume a potential foreign customer has offered to buy 1,700 units at $15 per unit. If all of Humphreys's costs and rates were to stay at last year's levels, what net income after taxes will Humphreys make if it takes this order and rejects some business from regular customers to prevent exceeding capacity?

c. Suppose the sales price is reduced by 20 percent, and management expects to sell 4,100 units. What is the aftertax net income or loss that Humphreys can expect next year if costs and rates stay at the same levels?

d. Assume Humphreys is considering replacing a highly labor intensive process with an automatic machine; this should result in an annual increase of $16,000 in production fixed costs. However, variable production costs will decrease $4 per unit. Compute the:

(1) New breakeven volume in units.

(2) Sales volume in dollars that would be required to earn an aftertax net income of $8,340 next year if the automatic machine is purchased.

e. Suppose Humphreys has an opportunity to market the product in a new area. Using this strategy, an advertising and promotion program costing $8,400 annually must be undertaken for the next two or three years. A $2 per unit sales commission in addition to the current commission will be required for the sales force in the new territory. How many units will have to be sold in the new territory to maintain Humphreys's current aftertax income of $6,240? Show proof of your answer.

f. Assume management estimates that the per unit sales price should decline 15 percent next year. Production materials should increase $1 due to the scarcity of petroleum products, but fixed costs should not change. What sales volume in units will be required to earn an aftertax net income of $7,500 next year? Is this feasible?

Cases

C13–24 Breakeven and Cash Flow Breakeven for Professional Services (L.O. 1)

Dr. Douglass Edwards asks your financial advice regarding the establishment of an emergency center designed and staffed to care for minor emergencies and general medical visits. Market analysis reveals that an individual with unexpected illness or minor injury can presently receive medical treatment from two sources: a physician's office between prescheduled appointments or a hospital emergency room. Both sources are regarded as inconvenient and generally require waits of two to four hours. Emergency room visits cost three to four times more than an office visit and costs of most minor complaints are not reimbursed; physicians' offices are not often accessible to new patients. Edwards' emergency center would provide medical care at any time, for any reason, on a freely accessible basis and at a reasonable cost. He believes consumers will appreciate the quick purchase of medical care under pleasant circumstances they voluntarily selected.

The center would utilize a sophisticated marketing campaign to attract patients who routinely use hospital emergency rooms for their medical needs. Patients who do not have a physician or who have a physician but are unable to obtain unscheduled visits would find the clinic designed to meet their needs. The medical resource would be highly visible and provide excellent, convenient (no appointments) care. Expediency is another factor since the mean total visit time would be less than 60 minutes. The medical care would be relatively inexpensive with a mean visit charge of $40, which is less than the $65 charge for an emergency room visit.

The center would be designed to treat a maximum of 100 patients per day. It will be housed in a 4,500 square-foot ground-floor space in an existing building remodeled to specifications at no cost to Edwards. The site is near a major retail center in a city of approximately 1 million. Parking space for 10 cars will be immediately adjacent, with a lighted sign visible from the street. The facility will be open 365 days a year, 16 hours each day from 7:00 A.M. to 11:00 P.M. using two 8-hour shifts. Minimum staff on duty per shift includes one physician, one licensed practical nurse, one clerk, one receptionist, and one off-duty fire department paramedic assisting in routine nursing and orderly duties.

Charges. All charges will be payable at the time of service by cash, personal check, or major credit card. No personal credit will be extended, and no Medicare or Medicaid assignments will be accepted. Insurance assignments will be accepted only on a very limited basis for known policies and on known reimbursable charges, with the deductible payable at the time of treatment. Since Edwards is operating the center as a private physician's office, there is no legal or ethical requirement to accept indigent or nonpaying patients.

Marketing. The community in general and the private medical practitioners' patients will constitute the two markets served. Advertising will be directed toward the middle-income, suburban population. A concentrated media effort will launch the project, and subsequent advertising will be limited to Yellow Pages listings and Welcome Wagon literature. Word of mouth will be the most important long-term advertising.

Expenses. Edwards supplies you with the following hourly salary expense per person: physician—$45; nurse—$10.50; clerk—$5; receptionist—$5; paramedic—$8. Fringe benefits and payroll taxes are expected to average 36 percent of the hourly salary expense. Since the facilities will be open daily, some workers will be required to work more than 40 hours a week. Included in the total hours of operation for the entire year are 160 hours of overtime for each class of worker. Assume personnel are paid time and one half for overtime hours, and base the overtime premium on an amount that includes the wage rate per hour as well as the fringe benefit and payroll tax rate per hour.

Desired space can be leased for $11 per square foot annually. Property insurance of $6,000 and malpractice insurance of $11,000 are expected per year. An average annual expenditure of $3,000 is planned for advertising. The fixed portion of utilities for the facilities is estimated to total $18,000. Each patient visit is expected to cause an increase of $4.50 in medical/office supplies and $0.50 in utilities because of the additional usage of the facilities.

Edwards is concerned about the large outlay of funds required for necessary equipment. His analysis indicates $10,000 of office equipment, $70,000 of minor medical equipment, and $38,000 of X-ray equipment will be needed initially. All equipment is assumed to have a five-year life.

Required:

a. Determine the number of patient visits on an annual, daily, and hourly basis:
   (1) To break even.
   (2) For cash flow breakeven for the first year (ignore the tax shield on noncash fixed expenses).
b. Suggest other factors that should be studied before plans are implemented.

C13–25 (CMA) Using Cost-Volume-Profit Analysis to Select Alternatives (L.O. 3)

Almo Company manufactures and sells adjustable canopies that attach to motor homes and trailers. The market covers new unit purchases as well as replacement canopies. Almo developed its 19X1 business plan based on the assumption that canopies would sell at a price of $400 each. The variable costs for each canopy were projected at $200, and the annual fixed costs were budgeted at $100,000. Almo's aftertax profit objective was $240,000; the company's effective tax rate is 40 percent.

While Almo's sales usually rise during the second quarter, the May financial statements reported that sales were not meeting expectations. For the first five months of the year, only 350 units had been sold at the established price, with variable costs as planned, and it was clear that the 19X1 aftertax profit projection would not be reached unless some actions were taken. Almo's president assigned a management committee to analyze the situation and develop several alternative courses of action. The following mutually exclusive alternatives were presented to the president.

- Reduce the sales price by $40. The sales organization forecasts that with the significantly reduced sales price, 2,700 units can be sold during the remainder of the year. Total fixed and variable unit costs will stay as budgeted.
- Lower variable costs per unit by $25 through the use of less expensive raw materials and slightly modified manufacturing techniques. The sales price will also be reduced by $30, and sales of 2,200 units for the remainder of the year are forecast.
- Cut fixed costs by $10,000 and lower the sales price by 5 percent. Variable costs per unit will be unchanged. Sales of 2,000 units are expected for the remainder of the year.

Required:

a. If no changes are made to the selling price or cost structure, determine the number of units that Almo Company must sell
   (1) To break even.
   (2) To achieve its aftertax profit objective.
b. Determine which one of the alternatives Almo Company should select to achieve its annual aftertax profit objective. Be sure to support your selection with appropriate calculations.
c. The precision and reliability of cost-volume-profit analysis are limited by several underlying assumptions. Identity at least four of these assumptions.

C13–26 Cost-Volume-Profit Analysis in a Service Organization (L.O. 3)

To decentralize operations, Barnes Hospitals rents some of its facilities to for-profit entities for such specialized areas as psychiatry, pediatrics, and cardiac care. Barnes charges each separate entity for such common patient services as meals, laundry, and administrative services, including billings and collections. All uncollectible accounts are charged directly to each entity. Space and bed rentals are fixed for the year.

The Psychiatry Department's $70 average daily patient charge for 19X3 resulted in total revenue of $1,278,200. The Psychiatry Department had a capacity of 70 beds and operated 24 hours per day. Expenses charged by the hospital to the Psychiatry Department for the year ended June 30, 19X3, were as follows:

	Basis of Allocation	
	Patient Days	Bed Capacity
Dietary	$ 63,255	
Laboratory, other than direct charges to patients	29,785	
Repairs and maintenance	10,150	$ 8,280
Uncollectible accounts expense	9,500	
Billings and collections	12,000	
Janitorial		16,420
Laundry	22,690	
Pharmacy	34,200	
General administrative services		145,760
Rent		261,470
Other	1,020	65,270
	$182,600	$497,200

The only personnel directly employed by the Psychiatry Department are supervising nurses, nurses, and aides. The hospital has minimum personnel requirements based on total annual patient days. Hospital requirements beginning at the minimum expected level of operation are

Annual Patient Days	Aides	Nurses	Supervising Nurses
10,000–14,000	10	8	5
14,001–17,000	11	10	5
17,001–23,725	11	11	5
23,726–25,550	12	12	5
25,551–27,375	13	12	6
27,376–29,200	14	13	7

These staffing levels represent full-time equivalents. Assume that the Psychiatry Department always employs only the minimum number of required full-time equivalent personnel.

Annual salaries for each class of employee are supervising nurses, $25,000; nurses, $21,000; and aides, $12,000. Salary expense for the year ended June 30, 19X3, for supervising nurses, nurses, and aides was $125,000, $252,000, and $144,000, respectively.

The Psychiatry Department operated at 100 percent capacity during 111 days for the past year. It is estimated that during 90 of these capacity days, the demand averaged 15 patients more than capacity. The hospital has an additional 20 beds available for rent for the year ending June 30, 19X4.

Required:

a. Determine the minimum number of patient days required for the Psychiatry Department to breakeven for the year ending June 30, 19X4, if the additional 20 beds are not rented. Patient demand is unknown, but assume that revenue per patient day, cost per patient day, cost per bed, and employee salary rates will remain the same as for the year ended June 30, 19X3. Present calculations in good form.

b. Decide if the Psychiatry Department should rent the additional beds assuming that patient demand, revenue and cost per patient day, and employee salary rates remain the same for 19X4 as in 19X3. Show the annual gain or loss from the additional beds.

Performance Evaluation and Segment Analysis

CHAPTER OBJECTIVES

After studying this chapter, you should be able to:

1. Explain the conceptual framework for measuring and evaluating segment performance.

2. Discuss the advantages and disadvantages of the various degrees of decentralization.

3. Analyze segment performance using contribution margin, segment margin, ROI, and residual income.

4. Explain how short-term performance measures have many weaknesses, such as rewarding undesirable behavior.

5. Discuss the advantages of using multiple performance measures that include nonfinancial evaluations.

PRACTICAL
APPLICATION BOX   **Financial and Nonfinancial Performance Measures**

When there is lack of agreement between nonfinancial and financial measures, tension and polarization of organizational factions often result. Many companies, such as Caterpillar, Wang Laboratories, and Analog Devices, are creating new performance measurement systems. These systems measure customer satisfaction, flexibility, and productivity requirements. Management accountants should be participating in the information revolution by providing the right information at the right time and by translating financial goals into terms that operating management can understand. One of the accountant's most important roles is focusing management attention on the few vital things that need to be done, rather than the trivial many. When permanent changes occur in capacity, methods, or costs, synchronization of financial and nonfinancial systems is needed. When the differences reflect volume-based effects or changes that will smooth out over the long run, however, there is little value in forcing them to balance.

From: C. J. McNair, Richard L. Lynch, and Kelvin F. Cross, "Do Financial and Nonfinancial Performance Measures Have to Agree?" *Management Accounting*, November 1990, pp. 28–36.

Introduction

Recently, many companies have expanded their activities into different markets, foreign countries, and various industries. The resulting size and complexity of these companies make it urgent that their operations be decentralized. This creation of various company segments, in turn, requires that accountants provide some measure of each segment's level of efficiency. Accountants recognize they should design manufacturing cost and control systems for the needs of production and line management. Cost accountants are developing new performance measures causing executives to emphasize long-range rather than short-range results. Further, these measures recognize that profits are earned when the sale of goods occurs, not when they are produced.

Accountants expect their measurements to change in the future due to extensive automation that has created the need for measurement and control points. New performance measures will focus on optimizing an organization's performance globally, not locally. As labor cost and productivity become less relevant, measurement systems that help product line managers monitor raw materials will be implemented. Managers need these systems because raw material will be one of the major variable costs in the factory of the future. Future accounting measures will also motivate managers to look beyond segmental interest to organizational cost reduction and profit improvement.

Responsibility Accounting (L.O. 1)

Responsibility accounting involves using accounting to evaluate performance. Variance analysis and budgeting, as discussed in Chapters 9 through 12, comprise part of the responsibility accounting process. Chapter 25 also discusses the behavioral impact of responsibility accounting on improving the measurement of performance. These systems accumulate costs by **responsibility centers** to evaluate their effectiveness.

Responsibility Centers

Cost centers are the smallest areas of responsibility for which accountants accumulate costs. A cost center may be a department or a grouping within a department. At a somewhat higher level, the branch or territory manager's cost center is the entire segment for which he or she is responsible. The chief operating executive's cost center is the entire company, because he or she performs certain duties of the overall company. Thus, every operating cost is traceable to a responsibility center, whether that center makes a product or not. Accountants measure the performance of a cost center by comparing actual controllable costs with budgeted controllable costs for a specified period. Controllable costs result from decisions made by the manager of the cost center.

The classification of costs by cost centers should follow a company's responsibility accounting system. Costs should be accumulated following lines of responsibility and authority within an organization. Thus, accountants consider the organization chart and chart of accounts as the basic framework of the responsibility accounting system. The organization chart defines functional responsibility for each manager. Accountants should design a chart of accounts around cost centers to establish proper accountability for costs. After assigning costs to cost centers, managers set the budget for each output level.

Some companies find that merely setting up cost centers does not provide their managers with enough incentive to perform effectively. They have found that changing cost centers to profit centers is effective. This change makes managers more concerned with finding ways to increase the center's revenue by expanding production or improving distribution methods. A **cost center** is a segment responsible only for costs. A **profit center** is accountable for both revenues and costs. Accountants should base the performance measure for a profit center on controllable revenues and expenses that are matched to determine the segment's income. A profit center, however, must have the authority to earn revenue and incur costs.

Some companies go one step further and establish **investment centers.** Investment center managers are responsible for the expenses, profits, and assets of their centers. In evaluating performance, accountants relate investment center income to the invested capital in each segment to determine the return on investment.

Principal-Agent Relationships

Many companies fail to distinguish between controllable and noncontrollable costs in performance evaluation. They base managers' bonuses and other rewards on income figures that contain some uncontrollable elements. According to **agency theory, principal-agent relationships** are found when authority is decentralized. A principal delegates duties to a subordinate, called an *agent.* Corporate managers represent principals; segment managers represent agents. Principals use accounting information to evaluate agents' performances and as a basis for employee bonuses and commissions. As discussed in the next chapter, agents sometimes act only in their own best interests, to the detriment of their companies.

Degree of Decentralization (L.O. 2)

As companies grow larger and more diverse, they generally divide into several segments or divisions. Each segment becomes a separately identifiable center of operating activity and managerial responsibility. The degree of autonomy enjoyed by these segments varies because some companies establish tightly defined policies for segment managers. Other companies give their segment managers flexibility and hold them responsible only for the broad task of operating efficiently and profitably. This degree of autonomy reflects the extent of a company's decentralization. The more autonomous each segment, the more decentralized the company is as a whole.

A company's human relations philosophy also influences its degree of decentralization. If a company adopts a behavioral science approach, it is likely to decentralize operations. As discussed in Chapter 25, companies using a behavioral science approach eliminate autocratic leadership and give individuals the opportunity to prove their ability.

At one extreme is **total decentralization,** in which managers operate under minimum constraints and have maximum freedom because there is a lack of central authority. At the other extreme is **total centralization,** in which division managers have limited authority because top management maintains tight constraints. Few companies use either of these extremes. Absolute centralization is rarely effective because large volumes of decisions are difficult to administer at the top management level. On the other hand, absolute decentralization is rarely practical because each division may focus only on its own operations, disregarding companywide goals.

Not All Profit Centers Are Decentralized. Accounting and management literature often spreads the misconception that the profit center concept is synonymous with a decentralized subunit. However, not all profit centers have the freedom to make most of their decisions. A highly centralized organization could have many segments called profit centers, but the segment managers may have little autonomy in decision making. These segment managers may need corporate approval before buying or selling to outsiders or purchasing capital assets over a set amount, say, $5,000. Corporate staff closely monitor segment managers in highly centralized organizations. Conversely, in other companies, managers of cost centers have more latitude in making decisions affecting their divisions. Thus, the terms *profit center* and *cost center* may provide no accurate gauge about the degree of decentralization.

Advantages of Decentralization

Because decentralization has various degrees, management should determine at what point the benefits exceed the costs. Decentralization offers the following advantages:

1. Frees top management from daily operating problems so they can direct attention to strategic planning.
2. Allows decision making as near as possible to the scene of action. This permits true teamwork among all executives, each skilled in his or her own area.
3. Results in more accurate, timely decisions because segment managers are more familiar with local conditions than is top management.
4. Provides training in decision making for segment managers so they are better prepared to advance in the organizational hierarchy.
5. Offers stimulus for more efficient performance because decentralization gives managers authority to match their responsibility.
6. Eliminates unprofitable activities more rapidly since, for example, decentralization may give managers authority to purchase direct materials from outside parties rather than force them to buy from one of the company's segments.
7. Encourages each segment manager to look for outside markets for the division's products.

Disadvantages of Decentralization

Although the preceding advantages should lead to profits greater than those in a more heavily centralized organization, we cannot ignore the costs associated with decentralization. One of decentralization's greatest threats comes from the barriers it presents to goal congruence. The goals of the individual segments of a decentralized company may not be in harmony with overall company goals. Decentralization encourages segment managers to focus attention on local operating conditions. Decentralization fails to fully emphasize the contribution that each segment should make to the profitability of the overall company. In addition, because decision making is decentralized, there may be little communication among segment managers. As a result, decentralization may require a more elaborate and effective information system, which can be expensive.

Traditional Methods for Evaluating Segment Performance (L.O. 3)

Regardless of the degree of decentralization, top management needs a dependable method of measuring segment performance. We define the term **segment** in various ways. Generally a segment refers to any logical subcomponent of a company, identified with the responsibility of supplying a product or service at a profit. Some companies formally designate distinct organization subcomponents, such as divisions, as their segments. An example is the Truck and Coach Division of General Motors Corporation. Other companies designate territories, departments, service centers, or branch offices as segments. In analyzing marketing operations, we also find other types of segments, such as a product line, class of customer, or channel of distribution. However, these are not separate organizational entities. The important characteristic of a segment is that its operating performance is separately identifiable and measurable.

Management should study several factors in determining whether to group products or services into one segment. Products or services may be related based on similar characteristics such as rates of profitability, degrees of risk, or opportunities for growth. Or products may be related based on their production process; for example, products may require similar materials, labor, and manufacturing facilities. Products or services may also be related based on similar labor skills or marketing methods.

Even if a company is earning an acceptable profit, management should still ensure that every segment is making a profit. Previous chapters discussed several means of evaluating performance. Chapters 9 and 10 illustrated comparisons of actual and budgeted revenue and expenses. Chapters 11 and 12 presented variance analysis; breakeven analysis (Chapter 13) and variable costing analysis (Chapter 20) are additional performance measures. Chapter 17 discusses the use of cash payback, return on investment, and present value for capital expenditures. Chapter 19 discusses establishing standards for marketing activities. Some of these methods have inherent weaknesses for segment evaluation because of either the dissimilarity of segments involved or the difficulty of establishing objective measurements. However, despite these weaknesses, they are helpful in pinpointing areas needing additional investigation.

Contribution Reporting

Determining cost behavior patterns provides a helpful starting point in evaluating segment performance. Exhibit 14–1 uses **contribution reporting** to present a condensed profitability analysis of two territories. (In practice, companies detail the expenses more thoroughly.) Exhibit 14–1 illustrates two kinds of segments: territories and salespersons. Each territory has two salespersons. As you read across Exhibit 14–1, the focus becomes narrower, going from the overall company, to the Northeast and Northwest Territories, and then to the salespersons in each territory.

EXHIBIT 14–1

		Territory		Northeast Territory		Northwest Territory	
DOUGLASS COMPANY **Contribution Analysis for Territories and Salespeople** **For Period Ending 19X1** **($ thousands)**	Company Totals	Northeast	Northwest	Mr. A	Ms. B	Mr. C	Ms. D
Sales	$500	$300	$200	$175.0	$125.0	$70	$130
Less: Variable production expense	200	140	60	80.0	60.0	25	35
Variable marketing and administrative expenses	80	25	55	14.5	10.5	23	32
Total variable expenses	280	165	115	94.5	70.5	48	67
Contribution margin	$220	$135	$ 85	$ 80.5	$ 54.5	$22	$ 63
Contribution margin as a percent of sales ..	44%	45%	42.5%	46%	43.6%	31.4%	48.5%
Less: Fixed costs traceable to segments	130	69	61	33.5	35.5	18	43
Segment margin	$ 90	$ 66	$ 24	$ 47.0	$ 19.0	$ 4	$ 20
Segment margin as a percent of sales	18%	22%	12%	26.9%	15.2%	5.7%	15.4%
Nontraceable costs	20						
Income before taxes	$ 70						
Beforetax income as a percent of sales ...	14%						

Contribution Margin. Deducting only segment variable costs from segment revenue yields a **contribution margin** that companies use to evaluate segments. We can usually determine each segment's revenue and variable costs directly because they are identifiable with a specific segment. (This chapter assumes no intersegment sales; Chapter 15 discusses pricing of intersegment sales.) Contribution margin is useful in understanding the impact on income of short-run volume changes. We calculate changes in income by multiplying any sales increase by the contribution margin ratio. For example, the increase in pretax income resulting from a $10,000 increase in Mr. A's sales volume is 46% × $10,000, or $4,600. If Ms. D earns a similar $10,000 sales volume increase, pretax income increases 48.5% × $10,000, or $4,850. These calculations of contribution margin assume no change in sales price, operating efficiency, or fixed costs.

Segment Margin

The best contribution reporting method for evaluating segments is segment margin. **Segment margin** reflects each segment's contribution to indirect expenses and to the income of the company as a whole. Segment margin represents what remains after subtracting both the direct, or traceable, variable and fixed costs from each segment's revenue. Traceable expenses include both fixed and variable expenses, with the larger part composed of variable expenses. Examples of traceable variable costs include salaries earned by employees who devote efforts strictly to the segment and material and supplies used for the segment. If a company discontinues a segment, it would eliminate these traceable, or direct, expenses. Nonvariable costs traceable to the segment include depreciation, rent, and insurance on plant assets used by the individual territories and salespeople. Accountants do not allocate **nontraceable costs** that benefit more than one segment.

As shown in Exhibit 14–1, the Northeast Territory has a much more favorable operating performance, because of its larger segment margin. The segment margins generated by Mr. A and Ms. D also are greater than the performances of the other two salespersons.

Adding Segments. Segment margin is useful when making decisions about long-run capacity and the allocation of resources to each segment. For example, suppose Douglass Company is considering adding another salesperson to the Northwest Territory. Estimates reveal that the fifth salesperson would generate the following revenue and costs:

Sales		$90,000
Less: Variable production expense	$40,000	
Variable marketing and administrative expenses	10,000	50,000
Contribution margin		$40,000
Less: Fixed costs traceable to segment		45,000
Segment margin		$ (5,000)

The fifth salesperson incurs $45,000 fixed costs because the company must rent additional office space and equipment, which results in a negative segment margin. Even though this segment projects a $40,000 contribution margin, segment margin should form the basis for the decision because long-run capacity is involved. Contribution margin is most useful for short-run decisions such as the pricing of special orders; however, segment margin is the best gauge of the long-run profitability of a segment.

Nontraceable Costs. Arbitrary allocations of indirect or nontraceable costs distort the costs over which a segment manager has control. As a result, internal performance appraisal does not include nontraceable costs. Arbitrary allocations of nontraceable costs may imply that a specific segment is unprofitable when, in fact, there is a positive segment margin. This segment margin is contributing to overall indirect costs and any income. Generally, a company should retain a segment as long as its segment margin is positive, unless a more profitable investment alternative is available.

Breakeven Analysis

Another means of evaluating segments is to apply the breakeven analysis presented in Chapter 13. The breakeven point is the level of sales at which the segment recovers all expenses and shows neither income nor loss. However, breakeven analysis has limitations when applied to segments, because we must consider fixed costs in determining the breakeven point. Allocating fixed costs may be difficult and involve some arbitrary allocations. Chapter 13 discusses additional limitations of breakeven analysis.

Return on Investment

The relationship of profit margin to invested capital or assets is a better measure of profitability than income or sales dollars alone, particularly if the amount of resources committed to segments differs. The following formula outlines this relationship called **return on investment (ROI):**

Segment ROI =

$$\frac{\text{Segment revenues}}{\text{Investment center assets}} \times \frac{\text{Operating profits}}{\text{Revenues}} = \frac{\text{Operating profits}}{\text{Investment center assets}}$$

The ROI formula can also be expressed as follows:

Return on investment = Asset turnover × Profit margin percentage on revenue

Asset turnover ratio measures the investment center's ability to generate revenue for each dollar of assets invested in the segment. **Profit margin** measures the investment center's ability to control costs for a specific level of revenue. The lower the cost required to generate a dollar of revenue, the higher the profit margin.

ROI focuses attention on the optimum asset investment. ROI enables management to determine whether the activity is profitable enough to support the amount of resources devoted to it. In addition, ROI analyses can identify segments that need top management's attention. For example, if a segment's ROI is lower than planned or than that earned by other segments, corrective action may be taken to improve performance. On the other hand, management may also be able to capitalize on a situation in which the ROI is higher than expected. ROI analysis emphasizes that long-run profits are maximized if the optimum level of investment in each asset is achieved.

Companies use return on investment (ROI), **rate of return, return on assets (ROA),** and **return on assets committed (ROAC)** to refer to the same performance measurement. Even though ROAC and ROA are more descriptive because they emphasize that the return is calculated on the assets committed, ROI is more popularly used.

Segment Assets. The important factor is that only those assets used exclusively by the segment should be included. Assets that the overall company controls and uses for the general benefit of all segments should not be included. Some companies calculate a return on the assets employed by excluding standby equipment and other assets available but not used. This has the obvious result of increasing the rate of return, because we assume idle assets generate no income. However, it fails to measure how efficiently assets are used. The presence of idle assets suggests inefficient utilization of resources, and the rate of return should reflect this.

Determining the appropriate measurement of a segment's assets to compute the ROI is difficult. Although the most readily available measure is usually the book value of the assets, as reported in the company's accounts, this measure may be least useful. When a significant portion of a segment's assets are depreciable, using the book value of assets committed causes the rate of return to increase as the assets become older and increasingly depreciated. The rate of return rises as long as the segment's margin does not decline as rapidly as the book value of the assets identifiable with the segment. Using the gross value of depreciable assets without a deduction for depreciation eliminates such a meaningless increase in the rate of return. However, this basis still does not reflect the current economic value of the assets. Use of the current replacement costs of the assets committed is generally a more appropriate basis on which to measure the segment's performance. Even though ledger accounts do not reflect replacement cost, it can be obtained fairly readily. Quoted market prices can be used for inventories and equipment for which an actual market exists, and appraisals can be made of building, land, and other assets. Reliable replacement costs for intangible assets and special equipment are more difficult to obtain. However, if no other current value estimate is possible, the original cost of the asset can be adjusted for a change in the general price level.

Measuring segment profit also poses many difficulties. Just as companies use different terms in referring to the rate of return calculated, they also use various profit figures. For example, if assets are based on replacement cost, depreciation expense should be calculated on this basis in determining segment margin. To calculate ROI for an entire company, accountants use operating profit after income taxes, but they prefer segment margin for computing a segment's ROI.

Computing Segment ROI. Since capital investments are scarce resources, relating profits to capital investment provides an intuitively appealing performance measure. For example, Exhibit 14–1 indicates that the Northeast Territory is more profitable than the Northwest Territory and that Mr. A is most profitable. However, a danger exists in the use of segment margin expressed as a percentage of sales. The Northeast Territory and Mr. A are not the most profitable if they require more resources. If a large difference in the resources committed to each segment exists, segment margin should be expressed as a return on the assets employed.

Assets employed can include working capital and the current value of long-term assets or, less desirably, their gross value. For example, assume the assets of the Northwest Territory are as follows, resulting in a 15 percent ROI:

Assets Employed by Northwest Territory
For Period Ending 19X1

Working capital	$ 40,000
Current replacement cost of long-term assets	120,000
Net assets	$160,000
Segment margin (from Exhibit 14–1)	$ 24,000
Return on assets committed ($24,000/$160,000)	15%

Certainly, if the assets employed vary as significantly as they do in Exhibit 14–2, ROI evaluation is necessary. The segment margin for each division as calculated in Exhibit 14–1 is divided by the assets employed to determine how profitably the resources are being used. In Exhibit 14–2, the return generated by

EXHIBIT 14–2

DOUGLASS COMPANY
Segment Margin as a Percentage of Assets Employed
For Period Ending 19X1

	Territory		Northeast Territory		Northwest Territory	
	Northeast	Northwest	Mr. A	Ms. B	Mr. C	Ms. D
Segment margin	$ 66,000	$ 24,000	$ 47,000	$ 19,000	$ 4,000	$ 20,000
Assets employed	660,000	160,000	335,714	324,286	20,000	140,000
Return on investment	10.0%	15.0%	14.0%	5.9%	20.0%	14.3%

Mr. C is highest although his segment contribution margin is lowest. A similar situation arises when product lines are being evaluated if the hours to complete a unit vary considerably. In this case, the segment margin per hour required to complete the product is a better means of evaluating the segments than is the total segment contribution. As you can see, ROI analysis provides different results from segment margin analysis.

By evaluating the segments through ROI, managers focus attention on the factors that increase ROI by either increasing sales or reducing invested capital or expenses. Likewise, an improvement in capital turnover or the gross margin percentage without a change in the other factors increases ROI.

Residual Income

Instead of using ROI or segment margin to evaluate a segment, a company may use residual income. **Residual income** is the segment margin of the investment center after deducting the imputed interest on the assets used by the center. Residual income eliminates some of the problems associated with expressing a rate of return because it is not expressed as a ratio. Accountants normally use a company's average cost of capital, which Chapter 18 discusses, to compute imputed interest.

Rather than compute imputed interest on the segment's *invested capital* or assets, analysts may consider only interest on the segment's *controllable investment* (assets). This approach recognizes that segment managers cannot currently control much of the segment's plant and equipment because plant assets remain unchanged for long periods. Instead, firms evaluate their segment managers on the investment in working capital, especially receivables and inventories. Segment managers can control the receivable investment through their credit and collection policies. Likewise, the reordering levels chosen affect inventory investment. Usually, accountants subtract a segment's accounts payable and accrual balances from its receivables and inventories to arrive at the controllable investment.

To calculate residual income, assume a segment earns a $50,000 segment margin while employing $200,000 of assets, with a 12 percent cost of capital:

Segment margin	$50,000
Less imputed interest on investment center assets	
(12% × $200,000)	24,000
Residual income	$26,000

ROI and Residual Income Compared. If the company focuses attention on residual income, the preceding segment manager would be encouraged to purchase a new asset for $50,000. This purchase would generate a segment margin of $10,000, even though the rate on the asset is not as high as the 25 percent ($50,000/$200,000) ROI currently earned. Assume the overall company's cost of capital is 12 percent and it has excess cash of $50,000 that the company may otherwise invest in marketable securities yielding 10 percent. The new asset earns only a 20 percent ($10,000/$50,000) ROI, which is higher than the cost of capital, with an increased residual income as follows:

Segment margin	$60,000
Less imputed interest on investment center assets	
(12% × $250,000)	30,000
Residual income	$30,000

If the company evaluates the segment manager strictly on the basis of the rate of return rather than also giving some attention to the dollar amount of segment margin generated, the segment manager may not make the purchase. If evaluated on ROI, the segment manager may be tempted to dispose of any asset that is not earning a 25 percent ROI. For example, if the manager holds an asset valued at $100,000 that can be disposed of with a resulting reduction in segment margin of less than $25,000, the manager's ROI increases in the short run when he or she disposes of the asset. However, this decision may weaken the company in the long run.

Also, by using controllable assets rather than invested assets, the evaluation does not hold the segment manager responsible for plant and equipment decisions that top managers usually make. By using residual income as a performance measure, a company encourages segment managers to concentrate on maximizing dollars of residual income rather than maximizing a percentage return. Thus, the residual income concept overcomes one of the dysfunctional aspects of the ROI measure in which managers can increase their reported ROI by rejecting investments that yield returns greater than their company's or segment's cost of capital, but that are below their current average ROI. However, since no external reporting authority requires an explicit charge for the use of invested capital, companies lack an incentive to use residual income in their profit center income analysis.

Ratios

Accountants can compute a limitless number of ratios for each segment operation. These ratios range from the current ratio, which compares current assets to current liabilities, to ratios of various expenses to sales. Many trade associations collect and make available to their members information in ratio form for comparative purposes. However, because of the wide variation in classifying items such as marketing and distribution expenses, these comparisons may have little meaning. For example, one company may employ account titles identical to those used by the rest of the industry, but charge different cost items to the titles. In addition, different management concepts within the same industry militate against valid intercompany cost comparisons. Industry figures are representative of an average firm with characteristics that may differ significantly from those of any given company making the comparison. Thus, the value of this analysis depends on the analysts' ability to interpret differences between a given company and the industry average.

Full Costing

Even though full costing is necessary for external segment reporting, it has limited usefulness in segment evaluation. As we discuss in Chapter 16, accountants should not use **full costing** to test alternatives because the alternative does not affect some of the costs allocated. For example, if a territory reports a net loss, the company cannot avoid the entire loss reported by eliminating the territory because the indirect costs allocated to the territory are nonescapable.

Instead of using contribution reporting, if the accountant applied full costing to the data in Exhibit 14–1, the performance picture would be quite different. In arriving at a full-costing income, the accountants would allocate $20,000 nontraceable cost to the territories and salespersons. Using full-cost reporting is likely to cause the performance of Mr. C in the Northwest Territory to reflect a net loss. An evaluation of profitability is especially important when managers must decide whether to eliminate a segment. A segment is considered profitable if its revenue exceeds its traceable costs, regardless of whether it covers what someone has determined is its fair share of the nontraceable costs. A company should retain a segment as long as it yields a positive contribution and management cannot put the segment resources to better use.

Controllable and Noncontrollable Costs

Regardless whether analysts use full costing or contribution reporting, controllable costs should be separated from noncontrollable costs. Advocates of contribution reporting argue that noncontrollable costs should not be shown in segment reports at all. Instead, full-costing proponents believe that segment managers should be aware of the costs of the services they receive from other parts of the company so they are supportive of cost control. However, the company should assure its segment managers that even though their controllable costs are small in relation to noncontrollable costs, it is urgent that they direct full attention to those areas over which they have authority and responsibility.

Because it is unfair to hold segment managers responsible for costs over which they have no control, segment reporting may use the full-costing approach, but *segment evaluation* should not. However, this does not imply that a company should not expect each segment to contribute toward these indirect costs. Only the overall company can earn income; all that each segment can do is to contribute to that income. Segment managers should understand that they maximize companywide income only when they maximize the marginal contribution of each segment. Thus, managers should receive contribution margin analyses for each segment when evaluating the individual divisions of a company.

Limitations of Traditional Methods for Evaluating Segment Performance (L.O. 4)

As companies decentralize their operations, accountants use quantifiable short-term financial measurements, such as ROI and segment margin, for evaluating profit center performance. However, these evaluation methods give too much weight to short-term benefits and costs. Further, they assign no cost to lost opportunities and no benefit to potential strategic advantages. In most companies, bonuses for short-term performance are larger than payments from long-term incentive programs. Thus, managers are motivated to pursue their own interests and ignore the long-term financial advantages of effective manufacturing performance.

ROI in Automated Manufactured Environments

Although quality and inventory control are of increasing importance today, most segment evaluation methods, including ROI, neglect them. ROI is inadequate for estimating the advantages of robots and automated equipment (which are added in as segment assets), particularly where the company narrowly defined the analysis as a comparison of the return on the investment in one segment with the return on the investment in another. Also, the development of customer loyalty, recruiting costs, and research expenditures have a value beyond the current accounting period. Accountants do not usually capitalize such costs as assets. Accountants also rarely estimate the earnings effect of intangible assets such as employee talent and morale, an efficient distribution network, and knowledge of high-quality, flexible manufacturing processes.

Often analysts make monthly estimates for income and expense adjustments, such as depreciation, interest, and amortization. They then wait until year-end to determine more exact figures. Because ROI uses both revenues and profit, they may determine an inaccurate ratio by using estimated monthly revenues and expenses. On the other hand, waiting until year-end to calculate ROI is limiting, since management needs current information concerning operations.

In addition, historical cost and current economic value may have no direct relationship because some assets depreciate in value while others appreciate. Historical cost is the result of decisions made several years ago. Its current economic usefulness depends on the current market, technology, and other facts. Both the numerator and the denominator in ROI are the result of and/or subject to wide ranges of arbitrary decisions that make them somewhat unreliable.

Therefore, ROI is a useful index of performance only if reasonable criteria for comparison are available. Such criteria include the ROI for the same segment in previous periods, the ratio in other segments, the rate in another company, or some desired rate of return. However, considerable danger exists in comparing the ROI of one company with that earned by another company, even if they are approximately the same size and are in the same industry. This is because a segment can rely on overall company management for many services that a separate company must provide for itself. In addition, analysts consider a segment to be more profitable per sales dollar volume than a separate company. Otherwise, there would be little advantage to having a large company with many operating segments. ROI can most effectively evaluate segment operations that are somewhat independent of each other and produce output that can be objectively valued.

Local versus Overall Performance Measurements

A performance measure is fundamentally wrong when the actions that benefit a company hurt the segment manager and vice versa. For example, emphasizing only local or segment performance fails to encourage the use of standard parts. Using standard parts lowers material costs because of aggressive volume buying for the whole company. Segment managers may not recognize these economies on a product-by-product basis. For example, assume a company produces several different products. The products all use one or two parts bought in approximately equal amounts. Part X costs $15 per unit and Y, $8. Because Part X can be used in place of Part Y, a supplier has offered to sell Part X at $10 per unit, if the company doubles its present purchase volume. For products that incorporate both parts, substituting X for Y makes sense to qualify for the discount because the total parts cost is $23 using X and Y, but only $20 using Xs only. Part X should become a standard part for the factory. Segments building products that only require Part Y, however, would hesitate to substitute the higher-priced Part X. Even discounted, the cost of X exceeds that of Y.

Additional conflicts in local versus overall performance measurements result because many companies suffer from the end-of-reporting period "hockey stick phenomenon." These plants issue shipments at a steady rate for a period, then shipments rise sharply and drop even more rapidly to the original rate. As the end of the reporting period approaches, corporate management focuses on the overall performance of the company, instead of segment performance. Corporate managers want to know how much product will be shipped and how much money the company will make. Top management pushes shipments aggressively by using small runs to finish orders, emphasizing productivity over efficiency.

As a result, companies ship most of the month's production in the last week of the month, disrupting any semblance of uniform flow. Manufacturing departments are pushed to make their numbers, regardless of cost. Shops schedule overtime, expedite vendors, and "cherry pick" orders. Segment managers engage in such inefficient practices as running jobs on less-efficient machines, authorizing additional overtime, and splitting and overlapping batches to get the shipments out.

Such a system appears to work as each company ships more product and makes more money than it would have by following efficient practices. This phenomenon creates a management mindset that focuses on shipping targets and not cost control. To meet its targets, management believes it must ship a certain number of units. After the reporting period ends, however, managers reinstitute the old measurement systems. Thus, the conflict between local and overall performance measurements continues.

Performance Measures for World-Class Companies (L.O. 5)

As previously discussed, traditional performance measures focus on achieving short-run financial success and encourage **suboptimization;** this occurs when each segment benefits to the detriment of the overall company. Segment managers attempt to make their own segments look good in the short run. This especially occurs in companies with bonus systems from which they can personally gain by profitable performance. They learn how to manipulate ROI targets, not by selling more products or services, but by reducing discretionary expenditures, exploiting accounting conventions, and other nonproductive procedures. With only a short-term view, managers fail to perceive the need for automation and improved technology because the company gears its measurement and reward systems to achieving short-term results. To overcome this, companies are using additional performance measures that focus on longer-term objectives and plans.

Segregate Discretionary Expenses

Exhibit 14–3 illustrates the sacrificing of a company's long-term financial health by postponing discretionary costs, such as advertising, research, and repairs. **Discretionary costs** arise from periodic appropriation decisions and include expenditures for advertising, research, repairs, customer relations, human resources, and quality improvements. All of these criteria are vital to a company's long-term competitive position. Discretionary costs reflect management judgment in deciding the amount to incur each accounting period.

The segment income statement in Exhibit 14–3 segregates discretionary expenses to clarify which segments are achieving their profit goals by risking their future competitive positions. Variable production expenses include factory repairs and maintenance. Advertising and public relations are variable marketing expenses. It appears that the Northeast Territory manager is reducing or deferring such discretionary expenditures as preventive maintenance, advertising, and research solely to increase short-run segment margin. A format such as Exhibit

EXHIBIT 14-3   Highlighting Discretionary Expenses

DOUGLASS COMPANY
Segment Analysis
For the Year Ending May 31, 19X1
($ thousands)

	Companywide	Northeast Territory	Northwest Territory
Sales	$500,000	$300,000	$200,000
Less: Variable production expense	200,000	140,000	60,000
Manufacturing contribution margin	$300,000	$160,000	$140,000
Less traceable variable expenses:			
Discretionary variable marketing expenses ..	$ 30,000	—	$ 30,000
Other variable marketing expenses	12,000	10,000	2,000
Discretionary variable administrative expenses	20,000	—	20,000
Other variable administrative expenses	18,000	15,000	3,000
Total traceable variable expenses	$ 80,000	$ 25,000	$ 55,000
Net contribution margin	$220,000	$135,000	$ 85,000
Less traceable fixed expenses:			
Discretionary fixed marketing expenses	$ 19,000	—	$ 19,000
Other fixed marketing expenses	32,000	$ 30,000	2,000
Discretionary fixed administrative expenses .	10,000	—	10,000
Other fixed administrative expenses	69,000	39,000	30,000
Total traceable fixed expenses	$130,000	$ 69,000	$ 61,000
Segment margin	$ 90,000	$ 66,000	$ 24,000

14–3 encourages this detection. Otherwise, the evaluation would unduly penalize the Northwest Territory manager in the short run.

The allocation base selected for discretionary expenses often leads to dysfunctional consequences. For example, accountants often allocate repair and maintenance departmental cost on the basis of usage. As a result, accountants assign a larger share of the repair cost to the department that is properly maintaining its equipment than to the department neglecting its equipment. Segment managers rationalize that incurring regular maintenance and servicing, engaging in research, or purchasing depreciable safety equipment unfavorably affects their profits (and, in turn, their bonuses). Such evaluation encourages segment managers to postpone regular repairs, sell off equipment, and stifle research to develop short-term advantages. It takes several months before costly breakdowns and repairs occur to offset the apparent savings from deferring such maintenance. Obviously, such behavior may be dysfunctional in the long run. The organization may more rapidly replace the equipment in the segment that was not under a preventive maintenance program and in turn received less short-run repair expense.

Dysfunctional Consequences of Accounting Measurements

Corporate managers assume that segment managers engage in long-run research programs that will be profitable later. However, usually the basis of the reward system is short-run earnings. Thus, segment managers lack the needed incentive to engage in costly research projects whose outcome is questionable. Even if the probability of success appears high, it will likely be years before profits occur.

Managers often apply this same reasoning to pollution control. For instance, the staff at corporate headquarters may discover one of its divisional plants dumping chromates directly into a nearby river and ask the division manager to solve the problem. The division manager rationalizes that installing the necessary equipment to solve the problem may exceed the budget and increase divisional depreciation expense. The division manager also knows a decreased segment margin decreases his or her salary raise or bonus because the company bases raises and bonuses on segment margin.

Further, despite the chance that a government agency will detect the pollution, it would take years before the case would come to trial and the company would be convicted. Then even if the company is convicted, the fine would be small in relation to the initial capital outlay for the pollution equipment. Also, the present value of money would weigh in favor of postponing action.

Admittedly, at the time of the fine, the company must buy the pollution equipment. However, the division manager's logic is that someone else may be segment manager at that time. To maximize short-run profits, managers ignore the law. Not only does this action reward the division manager but creditors and stockholders also reward corporate management for profitability. Profitability is a criteria totally unrelated to the number of fish poisoned or amount of water contaminated. The company's compensation system rewards disobedience while hoping that the division manager obeys orders despite the dysfunctional effect of the reward system.

Historical cost accounting procedures and generally accepted accounting principles provide other opportunities to time revenues and expenses to achieve a targeted ROI. Such one-shot opportunities as changing from accelerated to straight-line depreciation, lengthening depreciable lives, and amortizing pension costs over a longer period are examples. Selling assets whose market values exceed their book values also creates one-shot profits. A segment that needs these assets can lease them back. Leasing and pension costs offer opportunities for clever financial accounting maneuvers, too. Creative rearrangement of ownership claims through mergers and acquisitions, divestitures and spin-offs, and leveraged buy-outs create earnings. Because of the opportunity for misapplication of financial accounting, companies need performance measures highlighting such tactics.

Throughput

Throughput is a nontraditional performance measure that recognizes inventory profits are not real profits. **Throughput** is the rate at which the system generates money through sales. Production is not throughput if the product isn't sold. By adopting throughput as a performance measure, managers try to reduce inventories and increase the throughput rate by attacking the causes of high inventory levels. **Throughput speeds,** defined as how long it takes the product to get through the manufacturing process, are shrinking along with product life cycles.

Productivity Measurements. Local performance measurements, such as efficiencies, variances, and direct and indirect labor ratios, are attempts to measure the effective use of current capacity. These productivity measures generally increase when output expands because the firm's capital resources receive greater use. This productivity gain is due to external market forces, however, not to improved efficiency within the factory. Productivity measurements estimate the effects of substitution among labor, capital, materials, energy, and other key inputs.

Nonfinancial Evaluations

Some useful measures of performance do not involve financial data. For example, companies emphasizing quality could measure such internal failure indicators as scrap, rework, and unscheduled machine downtime. The quality measure includes external failure indicators, such as customer complaints, warranty expenses, and service calls. Companies wishing to become lower-cost producers develop productivity measures to show trends in their ability to produce more with less. When the focus is on just-in-time production and delivery systems, average setup times, throughput times, and lead times would support this objective. Companies wanting to improve their design and process flexibility can measure the total parts per product, the percentage of common versus unique parts in products, and the number of subassembly levels.

Analysts also evaluate a segment on the basis of employee attitudes, delivery schedules, customer relations, and plant asset maintenance. While corporate management may hope for employee effort in the area of interpersonal relations, creativity, and team building, often these are not formally rewarded. Companies may not reward this behavior simply because it is hard to observe. However, use of nonfinancial indicators such as safety programs, decreased absenteeism, improved morale, reduced turnover, recruiting success, and improved promotability rates convince employees that management is giving more than mere lip service to these measures. Although all these factors affect the financial performance of a segment, the direct measurement itself involves nonfinancial data.

Multiple Performance Measures

Performance evaluations with a short-range time frame often reward behavior the company is trying to discourage while desired behavior goes unrewarded. Measures of performance covering three to five years more appropriately evaluate managers. Multiple criteria, rather than a single performance measure, provide flexible evaluations because they study short-range as well as long-range objectives. Additionally, companies are more likely to achieve goal congruence by evaluating segment managers on their contributions to the overall organizations, rather than their segments' performance only.

Application of Segment Analysis. The approach to profitability analysis suggested in this chapter has a wide range of applicability regardless of whether the company is profit oriented. For example, in hospitals the segments could be patient floors, therapy services, X-ray, and pharmacy. In a university, the segments could be various graduate and undergraduate programs in the different colleges. A continuing education division can consider each course offering as a separate segment, such as CPA review, CMA review, or art appreciation. Managers can compare the tuition generated by each course with the instructor's salary and other traceable costs to determine whether the course can pay for itself. Both of these institutions, however, have other objectives that may assume priority over profitability.

Summary

Multiple performance measures, which include a variety of short-range and long-range financial and nonfinancial indicators, provide better targets and predictors for the firm's long-term profitability goals. Recognizing that any single financial measure is inadequate is important. Each company should select the measures most appropriate for their individual circumstances.

A danger exists in managers maximizing the segment's short-run performance to the detriment of the overall company. Companies should not reject projects profitable to the overall company but not as favorable to a specific segment as alternative projects. To be meaningful, an understanding of the consequences of the costs being incurred must accompany short-term market evaluations. Also, measurement needs change as companies become more automated.

Important Terms and Concepts

Problem for Self-Study

Segment Margin and ROI

NNA Company manufactures two products, RR and TT, and employs Ms. A and Mr. B to sell Product RR and Mr. C and Ms. D to sell Product TT. Data for the year ending December 31, 19X1, follow:

	Product RR		**Product TT**	
	Ms. A	**Mr. B**	**Mr. C**	**Ms. D**
Sales	$250,000	$180,000	$300,000	$225,000
Variable production expense	40%	45%	60%	50%
Variable marketing and administration expense	10%	8%	6%	12%
Traceable fixed costs	$ 80,000	$ 48,600	$ 40,500	$ 31,500
Nontraceable costs totaled $33,750.				

Required:

a. Prepare segment analysis for each product line and for each of the salespersons by determining contribution margin and segment margin. Express each of these and income for the overall company as a percentage of sales.

b. Prepare any additional analysis necessary if the assets employed are as follows: Product RR—Ms. A, $281,250; Mr. B, $180,000; Product TT—Mr. C, $768,750; and Ms. D, $450,000.

Solution to Problem for Self-Study

a.

NNA COMPANY
Contribution Analysis for Product Groups and Salespeople
For Year Ending December 31, 19X1

	Company Totals	Product		Product RR		Product TT	
		RR	TT	Ms. A	Mr. B	Mr. C	Ms. D
Sales	$955,000	$430,000	$525,000	$250,000	$180,000	$300,000	$225,000
Less variable production expense	$473,500	$181,000	$292,500	$100,000	$ 81,000	$180,000	$112,500
Variable marketing and administration expenses	84,400	39,400	45,000	25,000	14,400	18,000	27,000
Total variable expenses	$557,900	$220,400	$337,500	$125,000	$ 95,400	$198,000	$139,500
Contribution margin	$397,100	$209,600	$187,500	$125,000	$ 84,600	$102,000	$ 85,500
Percent of sales	42%	49%	36%	50%	47%	34%	38%
Less fixed costs traceable to segments	200,600	128,600	72,000	80,000	48,600	40,500	31,500
Segment margin	$196,500	$ 81,000	$115,500	$ 45,000	$ 36,000	$ 61,500	$ 54,000
Percent of sales	21%	19%	22%	18%	20%	21%	24%
Nontraceable costs	33,750						
Income before taxes	$162,750						
Percent of sales	17%						

b.

NNA COMPANY
Segmental Margin as a Percentage of Assets Employed
For Year Ending December 31, 19X1

	Product		Product RR		Product TT	
	RR	TT	Ms. A	Mr. B	Mr. C	Ms. D
Segment margin	$ 81,000	$ 115,500	$ 45,000	$ 36,000	$ 61,500	$ 54,000
Assets employed	$461,250	$1,218,750	$281,250	$180,000	$768,750	$450,000
Segment margin as percent of assets employed	17.6%	9.5%	16%	20%	8%	12%

Review Questions

1. Explain why you agree or disagree that short-term profits are no index of the ability of top management. Regardless of whether you agree or disagree, indicate other indicators of productivity or profitability that reflect good management.

2. Discuss some limitations of traditional evaluation methods. Which criteria should be adopted in using these ratios in comparison analysis?

3. Do you believe that idle assets should be included in the asset base when calculating ROI? Why or why not?

4. Why is there often a difference between divisional action and overall company profitability?

5. Contrast total decentralization with total centralization. Are examples of these two extremes often found in practice? Why or why not?

6. Discuss your views of the trend toward more extensive use of nonfinancial indicators. Include in your discussion some examples of nonfinancial measures.

7. Discuss several ways that a segment's assets may be measured. Which of these do you consider most appropriate?

8. What complexities arise in measuring segment income for use in ROI analysis?

9. If you were evaluating the performance of a segment, would you consider non-traceable costs in your analysis? Why or why not?

10. In choosing which segment performance measurements to use, why should management be concerned about suboptimization?

11. Explain why, when using ROI as the single performance measure, projects that result in an increase in segment margin may be rejected.

12. What is the difference between a cost center, a profit center, and an investment center?

CPA/CMA/CIA Multiple Choice Questions

1. (CMA) If a manufacturing company uses responsibility accounting, which one of the following items is least likely to appear in a performance report for a manager of an assembly line?

   a. Supervisory salaries.
   b. Materials.
   c. Repairs and maintenance.
   d. Direct labor.
   e. Depreciation on equipment.

2. (CMA) In a highly decentralized organization, the best option for measuring the performance of subunits is the establishment of

   a. Marketing centers.
   b. Product centers.
   c. Revenue centers.
   d. Cost centers.
   e. Investment centers.

3. (CMA) Most firms use return on investment (ROI) to evaluate the performance of investment center managers. If top management wishes division managers to utilize all assets without regard to financing, the denominator in the ROI calculation will be

   a. Total assets available.
   b. Total assets employed.
   c. Working capital.
   d. Working capital plus other assets.
   e. Shareholders' equity.

4. (CMA) Residual income is a better measure for performance evaluation of an investment center manager than return on investment because

   a. The problems associated with measuring the asset base are eliminated.
   b. Desirable investment decisions will not be neglected by high return divisions.
   c. Only the gross book value of assets needs to be calculated.
   d. Returns do not increase as assets are depreciated.
   e. The arguments over the implicit cost of interest are eliminated.

5. (AICPA) Controllable revenues would be included in the performance reports of which of the following types of responsibility centers?

	Cost Centers	Investment Centers
a.	Yes	No
b.	Yes	Yes
c.	No	No
d.	No	Yes

6. (CIA) The receipt of raw materials used in the manufacture of products and the shipping of finished goods to customers is under the control of the warehouse supervisor. The warehouse supervisor's time is spent approximately 60 percent on receiving activities and 40 percent on shipping activities. Separate staffs for the receiving and shipping operations are employed. The labor-related costs for the warehousing function are as follows:

Warehouse supervisor's salary	$ 40,000
Receiving clerks' wages	75,000
Shipping clerks' wages	55,000
Employee benefit costs (30% of wage and salary costs)	51,000
	$221,000

   The company employs a responsibility accounting system for performance reporting purposes. The costs are classified on the report as period or product costs.

   The total labor-related costs that would be listed on the responsibility accounting performance report as product costs under the control of the warehouse supervisor for the warehousing function would be:

   a. $97,500.
   b. $128,700.
   c. $130,000.
   d. $221,000.

7. (CIA) A company plans to implement a bonus plan based on segment performance. In addition, the company plans to convert to a responsibility accounting system for segment reporting. The following costs, which have been included in the segment performance reports that have been prepared under the current system, are being reviewed to determine if they should be included in the responsibility accounting segment reports:
   I.   Corporate administrative costs allocated on the basis of net segment sales.
   II. Personnel costs assigned on the basis of the number of employees in each segment.
   III. Fixed computer facility costs divided equally among each segment.
   IV. Variable computer operational costs charged to each segment based on actual hours used times a predetermined standard rate; any variable cost efficiency or inefficiency remains in the Computer Department.

Of these four cost items, the only item which could logically be included in the segment performance reports prepared on a responsibility accounting basis would be the:

    a. Corporate administrative costs.
    b. Personnel costs.
    c. Fixed computer facility costs.
    d. Variable computer operational costs.

8. (AICPA) Which combination of changes in asset turnover and income as a percentage of sales will maximize the return on investment?

	Asset Turnover	Income as a Percentage of Sales
a.	Increase	Decrease
b.	Increase	Increase
c.	Decrease	Increase
d.	Decrease	Decrease

9. (AICPA) Division A is considering a project that will earn a rate of return which is greater than the imputed interest charge for invested capital, but less than the division's historical return on invested capital. Division B is considering a project that will earn a rate of return which is greater than the division's historical return on invested capital, but less than the imputed interest charge for invested capital. If the objective is to maximize residual income, should these divisions accept or reject their projects?

	A	B
a.	Accept	Accept
b.	Reject	Accept
c.	Reject	Reject
d.	Accept	Reject

10. (AICPA) A company's return on investment (ROI) would generally increase when

    a. Assets increase.
    b. Selling prices decrease.
    c. Costs decrease.
    d. Costs increase.

Exercises

E14–1 Disclosure of Segment Information (L.O. 1)

Luther, Inc.'s controller advocates segment reporting and argues the merits of management identifying and reporting significant aspects of the organization's operations. Other members of the management team are not convinced that the effort involved is worth it.

Required:

a. Present arguments against the disclosure of segment information.
b. Present arguments for the disclosure of segment information.

E14–2 Emphasis on Short-Run Goals (L.O. 4)

Last year, the president of Page Company believed his department managers were not working as efficiently as they could. As a result, he decided to give each of his department managers a bonus equal to 5 percent of their department's favorable variations from the budget. He hoped this would provide a stimulus to perform at top efficiency.

This year, the president hired you to evaluate the success of his incentive system. You find that the supervisor of Department A is very unhappy about his bonus. He feels that the company chose an unfair method of allocating general and administrative expenses to his department. While he realized that such allocations must be made, he feels that he was mistreated.

After examining the financial statements for Department B, you notice that many expenses have been cut drastically. The supervisor explains that repair and maintenance expenditures have been reduced because many service contracts have been canceled. In addition, she postponed the purchase of some advanced technology equipment because she did not want to incur the additional depreciation expense.

The supervisor of Department D can temporarily buy material in a semiprocessed stage from an outside supplier rather than using the material produced by Department C. Since outside buying is cheaper, the supervisor of Department D chose to buy from the outside supplier. Department C must temporarily cut back production if Department D does not accept its semiprocessed material and buys from the outside supplier.

Required:

Comment on the effectiveness of the incentive plan. (For example, how would it affect morale? Should the company be concerned with short-run efficiency or long-run survival?)

E14–3 Profitability of Product Lines (L.O. 3)

Douglass, Inc., makes three different products and wishes to evaluate the profitability of each product line. The following data are for the year ended September 30, 19X2:

Sales—Product A (2,000 units)	$200,000
Sales—Product B (4,000 units)	500,000
Sales—Product C (6,000 units)	180,000
Direct cost—Product A	80,000
Direct cost—Product B	360,000
Direct cost—Product C	90,000
Indirect costs—allocated on per unit basis	240,000

Each unit of Product A requires six hours to produce; Product B, four hours; and Product C, five hours.

Required:

Evaluate the profitability of each product line.

E14–4 Divisional Breakeven and Rate of Return (L.O. 3)

The management of Walter, Inc., wishes to earn a 20 percent return on assets employed by all segments. Assets employed by the Ace product line amount to $400,000, while fixed costs directly attributable to this product line amount to $50,000. The accountant for this territory informs you that the variable cost per unit is $8.

Required:

a. Calculate how many units must be sold if the sales price is $12 per unit to earn the desired rate of return.
b. Determine breakeven sales in units for this division.
c. Compute the rate of return earned if 25,000 units were sold at an $11.50 sales price.
d. Calculate the segment's residual income assuming an interest rate of 10 percent if 30,000 units were sold at a $12 unit sales price.

E14–5 Residual Income (L.O. 3)

Data from the Hutchison Company's records are as follows:

	Products		
	A	**B**	**C**
Units sold	2,000	6,000	3,000
Unit sales price	$70.00	$30.00	$70.00
Unit cost of goods sold:			
Direct material	17.50	12.50	20.00
Direct labor	10.00	2.50	10.00
Variable factory overhead	17.00	3.00	8.00
Fixed factory overhead	7.50	1.00	9.50
Unit variable marketing and administrative			
expense	5.00	3.00	9.00
Other traceable fixed costs	6,000	2,500	1,500

Hutchison requires various types of machinery to manufacture each product depending on the features involved. In addition, the plant facilities housing each production process differ. As a result, the invested capital for each product line is as follows: (A) $100,000; (B) $400,000; (C) $150,000. A recent study indicates the company's cost of capital is 12 percent.

Required:

Prepare a profit report for use in appraising product line performance. Use the residual income approach.

Problems

P14–6 Segment Analysis (L.O. 5)

Jennings, Inc., manufactures two products, A and B, and employs Ms. Brown and Mr. Smith to sell Product A and Mr. Jones and Ms. Black to sell Product B. The following data are for the year ending December 31, 19X1:

	Product A		Product B	
	Ms. Brown	**Mr. Smith**	**Mr. Jones**	**Ms. Black**
Revenue	$400,000	$180,000	$500,000	$300,000
Variable production expense	60%	38%	55%	42%
Variable marketing and administrative				
expense	12%	10%	7%	8%
Traceable fixed costs	$ 75,000	$ 48,400	$ 39,800	$ 40,500

Required:

(Round all percentages to two decimal places.)

a. Prepare a segment analysis for each product line and for each of the salespersons by determining contribution margin and segment margin. Express each of these and income for the overall company as a percentage of sales.

b. Prepare any additional analysis necessary if the assets employed are as follows: Product A—Ms. Brown, $281,250; Mr. Smith, $180,000; Product B—Mr. Jones, $768,750; and Ms. Black, $450,000.

P14–7 Decentralization Issues (L.O. 2)

Within a company, decentralization exists in various degrees, often reflecting the scope of the decision-making authority given to a particular segment manager. Under this classification scheme, the decentralized units are often referred to as investment centers, profit centers, or cost centers.

Required:

a. Describe the characteristics that distinguish an investment center, a profit center, and a cost center from each other.

b. Discuss how the performance of a manager of each type of center should be evaluated.

c. Define return on investment and residual income and discuss whether or not these measures are appropriate for measuring the performance of managers responsible for each type of center.

d. Explain the ramifications of using residual income as compared to the more traditional return on investment approach for internal decisions for those centers where appropriate.

e. Discuss if residual income, or a variation of it, could be usable in the future for financial reports for external users.

f. Discuss the limitations of return on investment and residual income as performance measures and indicate some additional measures that could be used for performance evaluation. For each measure you list, give reasons why it would be appropriate for evaluating performance.

P14–8 Overemphasis on Short-Term Profitability (L.O. 4)

D. Yates, president of Yates Enterprises, recently attended a seminar introducing the advantages of flexible manufacturing systems utilizing robots. On returning to the plant site, he immediately called his production management team together to present statistics obtained from the seminar. One statistic impressed Yates—every time labor costs increase $1 an hour, more robots become economical. Also, in industries that are heavily unionized and hourly wage rates are very high, robots are especially appealing. Yates Enterprises operates in this type of environment. Yates is convinced that robots are the answer to rising costs in the factory and that this equipment will help return the company to a more profitable financial picture.

Yates asked the managers to devote all their attention in the next few days to determining where robots would be appropriate in their areas of responsibility.

A week later, Yates called a meeting asking the top managers to summarize their findings. One of the production managers suggested installing robots in settings where dust and fumes endangered workers. However, the application she was considering did not show the initial direct labor savings that Yates desired.

Another production manager had contacted equipment dealers with the objective of purchasing automated equipment designed to improve the quality of Product AR, which has a bad reputation for breaking and failing to meet other claims made by Yates Enterprises. The financial information obtained showed that instead of achieving a cost savings, costs would actually increase due to the large initial outlay for the robot.

At that point, Yates threw up his hands and said, "Wow, I have been deceived by the seminar—robots are just fancy, costly equipment that cannot be cost-justified."

Required:

a. Discuss how an overemphasis on short-term profitability from a robot can jeopardize the success of a robotics project from the beginning.

b. Explain how an overemphasis on short-term profitability can cause managers to overlook workers' interests.

P14–9 Segment Analysis for Product Lines (L.O. 3)

The following Ostendorf Company data are available for segment analysis:

	Northern Territory		Southern Territory	
	Product A	**Product B**	**Product A**	**Product C**
Sales	$40,000	$12,000	$80,000	$100,000
Contribution margin	30%	60%	30%	40%
Traceable fixed expenses	$ 4,000	$ 1,000	$ 9,000	$ 15,000

Nondirect fixed costs total $12,000 for the company.

Required:

a. Prepare segment analyses by product line and determine income before taxes for the overall company.

b. Assume the company's Research and Development Department has found ways that improvements can be made in Products B and C. However, company funds are limited so that only $5,000 can be spent to complete the improvements to either Product B or Product C. These improvements would increase the sale of Product B by 40 percent and Product C by 25 percent. On which product line should the company spend the funds?

c. Assume a proposed advertising campaign for Product A costing $6,000 in the Northern Territory is expected to increase sales by $27,500. Would you advise management to go through with the campaign?

d. Assume that after you present your segment statements computed in Requirement *a* to the president, she asked you to explain why segment statements prepared by another accountant on a territorial basis showed traceable costs of $7,000 for the Northern Territory and $28,000 for the Southern Territory. What would you tell her?

P14–10 Divisional Profitability (L.O. 5)

The California and Arizona divisions of a company produce and sell equipment designed for oil drilling in Arctic conditions. California's manager prefers to use machines for labor-intensive tasks, while Arizona's manager prefers to maintain a large work force and avoid the expenditure of capital funds for expensive equipment. These are the respective costs of the two companies:

	Cost Per Equipment	
	California	Arizona
Materials	$2.50	$7.00
Labor	1.60	2.00
Variable factory overhead	1.90	4.00
Fixed factory overhead	4.00	2.00

Fixed costs for California are $400,000 per year, and for Arizona, $200,000 per year.

A total of 100,000 units is expected to continue to be used as the normal volume for each division's sales and production. Each unit of drilling equipment is expected to sell for $18.

Required:

a. Calculate the manufacturing volume level at which both divisions would have the same operating results.

b. Prove your answer to Requirement *a*.

c. Compute the expected operating results for both divisions at the normal level of output.

d. Explain why one division outperformed the other in your answer to Requirement *c*.

e. 1. Assume that the sales outlook for next year is bleak and each division will produce and sell only 80,000 units. Compute their respective profits or losses.

   2. Explain why one division would outperform the other.

f. Discuss which division manager would most likely be willing to reduce the sales price to obtain a larger volume of sales. Why?

P14–11 Counterproductive Strategies (L.O. 4)

Los Angeles Company manufactures a variety of products. In making one of its products, workers can use two machines in the tooling process. Machine A is a newer, faster machine, requiring only five minutes for the operations. Machine B uses a slightly outdated technology and the same operation requires nine minutes. Both machines perform the same operation and produce a product of equal quality. When the engineers and cost accountants established the standard time for the tooling operation, they reasoned that standards should reflect efficient operating conditions, so they used five minutes as the standard. This shorter time was also the basis used for determining the overhead costs per minute of tooling machine time. For example, the accountant and engineer estimated that 1,000 units would be processed in a normal month and that $60,000 were the budgeted overhead costs for the tooling department. Allowing five minutes per processing time for each unit gives a normal capacity of 5,000 minutes. The overhead applied per minute of processing time becomes $12 as follows: $60,000/5,000 minutes = $12.

After the first reporting period in which the standards were in effect, the tooling supervisor was heard to remark, "Never again will I run units on Machine B unless it is absolutely necessary. I would rather hold the units needing tooling in a backlog and run all units on Machine A. The cost accounting report showed that I had large unfavorable variances and production managers have trouble understanding why identical products processed on Machine A and Machine B have different production costs. Production managers have informed me that they will strive to route their products through Machine A rather than Machine B to minimize production costs."

The tooling supervisor's remarks filtered up through the organization to the production vice president who immediately addressed the issue. The vice president believes that the tooling supervisor's plans to use only Machine A will be counterproductive to the overall company since there is sufficient market demand to sell all products manufactured by both machines in the tooling process.

Required:

a. Explain why the tooling supervisor's performance suffered.
b. Explain why identical products processed on Machines A and B have different product costs.
c. Discuss if the tooling supervisor's actions are indeed counterproductive to company profits. Explain your answer.
d. Decide if, from the tooling supervisor's viewpoint, the supervisor is making a wise decision to avoid running products through Machine B even though Machine A becomes a temporary bottleneck. Explain your answer.

P14–12 Evaluating Monthly Performance, Breakeven, and Variance Analysis (L.O. 3)

In preparing its annual budget, the management of Austin Company, Inc., expected that for the year as a whole the profit before taxes would total $495,000. Austin makes only one product; it has a selling price of $1 per unit.

	Annual Budget	
	Amount	Percent of Sales
Sales	$3,300,000	100%
Standard cost of sales:		
Prime costs	$1,485,000	45%
Production overhead	825,000	25
Gross margin	$ 990,000	30
Marketing and administrative expenses	495,000	15
Income before taxes	$ 495,000	15%

Management defined prime costs as the direct materials and direct labor in a product. The production overhead included both fixed and variable costs; variable production overhead would be equal to 25 percent of prime costs. Thus, the total production overhead budgeted for the year consisted of $371,250 of variable costs (25 percent of $1,485,000) and $453,750 of fixed costs. All of the marketing and administrative expenses were fixed, except for commissions on sales equal to 5 percent of the sales price.

Sal Cotter, the president of the company, approved the budget, stating that, "A profit of $41,250 a month isn't bad for a medium-sized company in this business." During January, however, sales suffered the normal seasonal dips, and production was also cut back. The result, which came as some surprise to the president, was that January showed a loss of $5,000 as follows:

January Operating Statement

Sales		$170,000
Standard cost of sales		119,000
Standard gross margin		$ 51,000
Manufacturing variances:		
Prime cost variances (Unfavorable)	$ (5,000)	
Production overhead:		
Spending variance (Favorable)	1,500	
Volume variance (Unfavorable)	(15,000)	(18,500)
Actual gross margin		$ 32,500
Marketing and administrative expenses		37,500
Loss before taxes		$ (5,000)

Required:

a. Explain, as best you can with the data available, why the January profit was $46,250 less than the average monthly profit expected by the president.
b. Calculate the level of monthly volume at which Austin can expect to earn exactly zero profit.
c. Give Austin's January production volume.
d. Compute how much the units in finished goods inventory changed in January.
e. Give the actual production overhead costs in January.

P14–13 Contributions Margins by Markets and Products (L.O. 3)

R. Reynolds, Inc., manufactures two types of computer chips, RAM and ROM. Both chips are sold in a local market and an overseas market. The following is the latest quarterly income statement:

	Local	Overseas	Total
Sales	$150,000	$200,000	$350,000
Cost of goods sold	50,000	165,000	215,000
Gross margin	$100,000	$ 35,000	$135,000
Marketing expenses	$ 20,000	$ 15,000	$ 35,000
Administrative expenses	10,000	10,000	20,000
Total expenses	$ 30,000	$ 25,000	$ 55,000
Operating income	$ 70,000	$ 10,000	$ 80,000

The management is very concerned with its overseas market because of the low return on sales. Many computer chip manufacturers are retreating from their overseas markets and the demand for computer chips does not seem like it will increase in the near future. Thus, management desires a final analysis of its overseas market so it can decide whether to leave this market. The cost structure is as follows for the individual products:

	RAM	ROM
Sales	$200,000	$150,000
Variable production cost as a percentage		
of its sales	24%	28%
Variable marketing expense as a percentage		
of its sales	4%	8%
Sales by markets:		
Local	$100,000	$50,000
Overseas	$100,000	$100,000

All fixed production expenses and all administrative expenses are indirect to the two products and the two markets and are fixed for the period. The remaining marketing expenses are fixed for the period and traceable to the markets. Reynolds's management bases fixed expenses on a prorated yearly amount.

Required:

a. Prepare the quarterly income statement showing contribution margin and segment margin by markets.

b. Assume R. Reynolds, Inc., decides to abandon its overseas market under the assumption there are no alternative uses for their capacity. Prepare the new income statement based on the preceding information. Should R. Reynolds, Inc., keep the overseas market?

c. Prepare the quarterly income statement showing contribution margin by products.

d. Assume that according to its production department, R. Reynolds, Inc., can begin producing a new version of the ROM chip next year. Then, the company will no longer produce the current ROM chip. However, to manufacture the new version, R. Reynolds, Inc., needs to buy a new machine that costs $200,000, has $0 salvage value, and has a useful life of 10 years. Reynolds uses straight-line depreciation. Besides the purchase of the new machine, Reynolds will not incur any additional cost if the new ROM is produced. What must be the minimum contribution margin per quarter for the new product to make the changeover financially feasible?

P14–14 Awarding Bonus on ROI (L.O. 4)

Sadhwani Company is the leading food distributor in the nation. The company is organized by geographical regions: North, East, South, and West, and each region has its own sales department. At the beginning of each year, corporate officers of Sadhwani Company determine the desired minimum return on investment (ROI) of the regional branches. Bonuses are awarded to the sales personnel in the region with the highest return on investment, provided that return exceeds the established goal. The current year company goal is 10 percent ROI, and the regional results follow:

	North	East	South	West	Total
Estimated market	$ 250,000	$ 350,000	$500,000	$ 400,000	$1,500,000
Regional sales	$ 175,000	$ 210,000	$150,000	$ 120,000	$ 655,000
Variable costs	$ 52,500	$ 63,000	$ 45,000	$ 36,000	$ 196,500
Discretionary costs* ...	22,500	32,000	55,000	44,000	153,500
Common fixed costs† ..	13,500	16,000	11,500	9,000	50,000
Total costs	$ 88,500	$ 111,000	$111,500	$ 89,000	$ 400,000
Net income	$ 86,500	$ 99,000	$ 38,500	$ 31,000	$ 255,000
Assets committed	$1,000,000	$1,500,000	$800,000	$1,250,000	$4,550,000
Liabilities	135,000	600,000	433,000	850,000	2,018,000
Net investment	$ 865,000	$ 900,000	$367,000	$ 400,000	$2,532,000

*Discretionary costs include costs for research, advertising, and other avoidable activities.
†The allocation of the common fixed cost is based on the percentage of each region's sales to the total sales.

The South region recently purchased several personal computers; the cost was treated as an office expense.

Although the company policy requires each regional branch to purchase a company car for every salesperson, the North region decided not to follow the policy. Instead, the North region reimburses their sales personnel for gasoline only.

Required:

a. Decide which region deserves the bonuses based on the preceding information. Show all supporting calculations.

b. Compute the effect on their ROI if the South region debited the capital asset account for the personal computer and North region purchased company cars for its sales personnel.

c. Explain which factor makes the company's established minimum return on investment criterion inappropriate for measuring the performance of each region.

d. Recommend which methods Sadhwani corporate officers should use to evaluate the performance of each region.

P14–15 (AICPA) Criteria for Performance Measures (L.O. 1)

The Star Paper Division of Royal Industries is located outside of Los Angeles. A major expansion of the division's only plant was completed in April of 19X0. The expansion consisted of an addition to the existing building, additions to the production-line machinery, and the replacement of obsolete and fully depreciated equipment that was no longer efficient or cost effective.

On May 1, 19X0, George Harris became manager of Star. Harris had a meeting with Marie Fortner, vice president of operations for Royal, who explained to Harris that the company measured the performance of divisions and division managers on the basis of return on gross assets (ROA). When Harris asked if other measures were used in conjunction with ROA, Fortner replied, "Royal's top management prefers to use a single performance measure. There is no conflict when there is only one measure. Star should do well this year now that it has expanded and replaced all of that old equipment. You should have no problem exceeding the division's historical rate. I'll check with you at the end of each quarter to see how you are doing."

Fortner called Harris after the first quarter results were completed because Star's ROA was considerably below the historical rate for the division. Harris told Fortner that he did not believe that ROA was a valid performance measure for Star. Fortner indicated that she would discuss this with others at headquarters and get back to Harris. However, there was no further discussion of the use of ROA, only reports on divisional performance at the end of the second and third quarters. Now that the fiscal year has ended, Harris has received the memorandum shown here.

To: George Harris, Star Paper Division
From: Marie Fortner, Royal Industries
Subject: Divisional Performance

The operating results for the fourth quarter and for our fiscal year ended on April 30 are now complete. Your fourth quarter return on gross assets was only 9 percent, resulting in a return for the year of slightly under 11 percent. I recall discussing your low return after the first quarter and reminding you after the second and third quarters that this level of return is not considered adequate for the Star Paper Division.

The return on gross assets at Star has ranged from 15 to 18 percent for the past five years. An 11 percent return may be acceptable at some of Royal's other divisions, but not at a proven winner like Star, especially in light of your recently improved facility. Please arrange to meet with me in the near future to discuss ways to restore Star's return on gross assets to its former level.

Harris is looking forward to meeting with Fortner as he plans to pursue the discussion about the appropriateness of ROA as a performance measure for Star. While the ROA for Star is below historical levels, the division's profits for the year are higher than at any previous time. Harris is going to recommend that ROA be replaced with multiple criteria for evaluating performance, namely, dollar profit, receivable turnover, and inventory turnover.

Required:

a. Identify general criteria that should be used in selecting performance measures to evaluate operating managers.
b. Describe the probable cause of the decline in the Star Paper Division's return on gross assets during the fiscal year ended April 30, 19X1.
c. On the basis of the relationship between Marie Fortner and George Harris, as well as the memorandum from Fortner, discuss apparent weaknesses in the performance evaluation process at Royal Industries.
d. Discuss whether the multiple performance evaluation criteria suggested by George Harris would be appropriate for the evaluation of the Star Paper Division.

Cases

C14–16 Increasing the Divisional Manager's Bonus (L.O. 5)

As a management accountant employed by Sanks, Inc., you were involved with the decentralization plan of organization. Three years ago top management made each division a profit center and began giving bonuses to each division head based on the gross margin percentage. This plan of organization has worked rather smoothly.

Recently, the company has suffered sharp financial setbacks and lost a major customer. This change of events has caused a freeze on all salaries. However, marketing management has convinced top management that sales promotion should not be curtailed since the objective is to generate additional sales. Also the company is planning the introduction of a new product line and the salespersons strongly argued for extensive advertising campaigns to support this new product line.

Yesterday, Joe Brown, the production manager, called for a confidential appointment. When he arrived at your office, he closed the door and asked for your help in one of his difficult management problems. He stated that Sara Jones, a division manager, has sharply felt the financial crunch from not receiving a salary raise because she had just begun construction on a new family residence when the freeze was announced. In addition, since that time, she has had to help her elderly parents with some medical bills. Jones is threatening to leave the company unless some help can be found for her.

Brown explains that since he is not an accountant, he wants your advice on what kinds of entries can be made to increase the gross margin percentage for Jones's division. This would increase Jones's bonus which is based in part on gross margin. Brown reemphasizes that Jones is a key person and if she does not receive a monetary increase, he is certain that she will leave.

Before you can interrupt Brown, he pulls out his clipboard and begins asking if the division ignores the recording of some of their sales, would this have a favorable impact on gross margin? He continues by asking what could be done with ending inventory to effect the desired result—should ending inventory be overstated or understated? He further states that he believes one of the best policies to achieve a higher gross margin for Jones's division is to charge Advertising Expense and credit Purchases Discount for various amounts throughout the period. His logic is that since top management has not frozen sales promotion, this practice is less likely to be detected.

Your telephone rings and since it is a long-distance call, Brown leaves and says, "I'll be in touch."

Required:

a. Discuss what you, as Sanks' management accountant, would do with Brown's request to manipulate the gross margin percentage. List the alternatives available and the reasons for choosing one of these.

b. Describe what role, if any, you should assume in suggesting alternative evaluation techniques or changes in the salary freeze policy.

c. Discuss the impact on gross margin of:
   (1) Ignoring the recording of Jones's division sales.
   (2) Understating ending inventory.
   (3) Overstating ending inventory.
   (4) Charging Advertising Expense with fictitious purchase discounts.

d. Evaluate the behavioral impact Brown's actions or encouragement could have on the future actions of subordinates like Jones.

C14–17 Divisional ROI as Performance Measure (L.O. 3)

John Thompson Corporation has divided its organization into autonomous divisions. Each division is an investment center with responsibility and authority for purchases of assets as well as marketing, product development, and manufacturing. Senior corporate managers evaluate the performance of division managers on divisional return on investment (ROI) solely. This policy is justified by top management because quantitative data from both the division's income statement and balance sheet are used. In addition, both divisions produce and sell the same type of product.

For example, data for Division A and Division B follow:

	(in $ millions)	
	Division A	**Division B**
Sales	$80	$50
Less: Variable cost of goods sold	60	20
Fixed cost of goods sold	4	15
Gross margin	$16	$15
Operating expenses:		
Repairs	–0–	$ 8
Allocated corporate expense	$ 4	6
Total operating expense	$ 4	$14
Net income	$12	$ 1
÷ Invested capital	$30	$50
ROI	40%	2%

Division A's manager is evaluated much more favorably than Division B's manager because of the higher ROI. However, Division B's manager argues that this is unfair since Division B occupies a large, old plant space and corporate expense is allocated on the basis of square footage. Division B's manager contends that the difference in bonus received is not justified.

Required:

a. Evaluate the Division B manager's complaint that using ROI as the sole criterion to evaluate division managers is unfair.

b. Discuss which other criteria would be appropriate for use in evaluating division managers.

c. Describe the advantages in using multiple criteria for this evaluation rather than one single criterion.

d. List any problems you anticipate in implementing multiple criteria in performance evaluation.

C14–18 Decentralized versus Centralized Organization Structure (L.O. 2)

In the 1940s John Lewis, an energetic and talented engineer, invented an item that revolutionized the assembly of motors. He formed a closely held company to manufacture and market this product. As the company grew, more stock was issued, but only to family members. Lewis also maintained a majority interest in the company, which has now been given to his only daughter, Jean.

At his encouragement, Jean attended engineering school and also received a masters in business administration. Now that John has retired, Jean is the president, overseeing each of the four territories. Ms. Lewis travels to each of the divisions regularly. She says, "I just do not have time for tennis and bridge because I have to fly weekly from one territory to another to put out fires. My boys in the four territories just do not have the historical background to understand the overall company as I do. Why, Daddy let me work in his office beginning when I was a teenager." She continues, "But I want my territory managers to be able to express themselves and have the freedom to experiment with various ideas and styles of management. They do not have to get my approval first. Now that I am approaching middle age, I want to relieve myself of some duties. That is what a decentralized organization with managers who have complete autonomy is supposed to be about."

Each of the four territories is headed by a division manager who reports to Lewis. In recruiting and hiring these division managers, extensive procedures were used in an attempt to secure the best person. Since the territories are established as profit centers, performance evaluation is based on segment margin. In addition to using segment margin as the basis for bonus calculation, Lewis then adds her own evaluation based on the difficulty of the tasks involved. Two of the territories are producing intricate items requiring much supervision.

Lewis believes that the company recently has experienced more tension than ever before. The Eastern Territory has expanded its facilities to a maximum due to what is considered a temporary demand for its products. The territory manager, Bill Oury, wanted to buy a new building, but Lewis would not agree to review his proposal. Instead she made the decision to remain in the present building and operate three labor shifts. This has placed an increased burden on Oury as there is a lack of trained supervisors willing to work at night. The result has been an increase in waste and defective products.

When Oury called to ask for four days off work, Lewis reminded him of the troubles he was having at his plant. Oury insisted that he really needed to have these days off and counted on his accumulated vacation days even though he could understand the possible inconvenience to the plant. Finally, Oury informed Lewis that he was interviewing elsewhere because he needed more opportunity to test his abilities. To this, Ms. Lewis exploded, "You have all the responsibility and opportunity that you can adequately handle now."

Lewis is somewhat surprised at her outburst but attributes this loss of composure to several other management problems which have arisen lately. Don Brown, a sales supervisor in the Western Territory, has requested a demotion to a sales position; his request was accompanied by a letter from his physician. Brown indicates that he cannot handle the pressure of work and fears that he will have a heart attack if he continues under the present conditions. Lewis did not expect to receive such a request because four months ago Brown was assigned an experienced assistant to relieve him of some marketing, clerical, and management duties. The purpose was to allow Brown to concentrate his efforts on creative ventures in promotion. The Southern Territory is also experiencing a high turnover of middle management personnel. She has felt that this could be explained by the opening of increased job opportunities for all workers as more companies make a move to more favorable geographical and economic surroundings. However, Lewis admits that she is surprised at what is happening to "Daddy's Company," and she wonders what needs to be corrected.

Required:

a. Choose examples and descriptions of company activities that characterize centralized and those that characterize decentralized management.

b. Evaluate Ms. Lewis's recommendation not to expand facilities in the Eastern Territory.

c. Explain how recent events at Lewis Company could have been expected.

C14–19 Merits of Decentralization and Centralization (L.O. 2)

A. Potts Processing Company is a manufacturer of a wide variety of industrial cleaning products. The company has total sales of $200 million and comprises eight processing divisions in six northern states. Top management has always believed that division managers should have authority to run their plants as they thought best. The degree of decentralization enjoyed has been rather extreme as it allows each division manager to set prices and decide on the optimal product mix.

Purchasing of raw materials is performed by each division. Division managers are able to approve capital expenditures. In addition, each division establishes its own objectives and budgets. Top management at the home office performs a cursory review of these objectives and budgets.

Top management receives quarterly performance reports for each division showing income before taxes for each segment. Recently, the New York division has been reporting a loss; however, the manager of the New York division believes that the loss results from unfair allocation of home office fixed expenses. This issue is coupled with a proposal from Kimberly Wells, a former management consultant with the company's auditor, and presently assistant controller for Potts Company, concerning the purchase of larger computer facilities and greater centralization of decision-making responsibility. Wells strongly believes that management should be receiving more current performance reports in a different format. In addition, she thinks that the increased capabilities of the new computer will provide corporate management with enough relevant information to enable them to effectively make major decisions for each division. In fact, she argues that to justify the cost of such a large computer, all accounting functions including billing, budgeting, performance reporting, cost accounting, purchasing of raw materials, and credit extension should be performed at the home office rather than at each divisional level.

A strong supporter of centralization, Wells further argues that many of the functions presently performed by the division managers should be centralized including recruitment of personnel, production scheduling, and pricing. She supports her proposal by emphasizing the lack of coordination between the divisions as evidenced by a recent case where the Boston division and the Albany division were marketing competing products. She feels that much of the poor performance of the New York division is due to lack of strong top-management leadership.

Top management is undecided if their policy of decentralization should be abandoned. However, they all agree that this issue should be decided before a larger computer is acquired.

Required:

a. Give some additional advantages and disadvantages of decentralization.

b. Explain which of the functions cited by Wells could be more effectively performed if centralized.

c. Explain which functions should remain decentralized.

d. Describe the information now available to division managers that would not probably be available to top management through a formal centralized information system.

e. Suggest any improvements to the present division performance reports received by top management.

f. Decide which action the company should take in regard to Wells's proposal. State your reasons for this action.

C14–20 Behavioral Impact of Short/Long Trade-Offs (L.O. 4)

Three years ago, Klammer, Inc., suffered a recession along with other firms in the industry. As a result of the poor economic condition, the firm reduced administrative staff by 30 percent. Top management issued a policy stating that they were trying to create an atmosphere that stimulated creative thinking and some risk taking. This staff reduction eliminated three layers of management leaving division managers responsible for implementing corporate strategic goals. Decisions regarding capital outlays, personnel, product mix, and promotion, which formerly were jointly decided by division managers and top management, are now under the authority of division managers. Along with this change, which leaves division managers responsible for the success or failure of their operations, the company instituted a bonus based on these three items for each division manager:

1. Division net income.
2. Return on investment for each division.
3. Achievement of budgeted profit.

Klammer, Inc., uses a fixed or static budgeting system assembled during the prior year; in order for the budget to be printed and distributed, it is prepared five months before the operating year begins. Because there are now few top managers and their time is valuable, the budget for each division is not changed after its preparation. As a result of the recent financial downturn, division managers are encouraged to think optimistically when submitting raw financial data for the budget which is translated into the final budget by top management. Rather than express future division performance in realistic terms, many division managers overstate revenues or understate expenses in the hope that conditions will improve. In fact, word has leaked out that the division managers who failed to follow this optimistic approach were called into corporate offices to explain why they thought conditions would be so unfavorable for their divisions.

Evaluation is made quarterly for each division for all revenue and expense items used to arrive at divisional net income. Since the budget is not adjusted for competitors' actions or the state of the economy, division managers who failed to live within their budgets received unfavorable performance evaluations. Several division managers have been heard to remark that there is no way to win with this system because they are criticized for presenting realistic data, but if they fail to meet the optimistic budgets, they receive no bonuses.

Required:

a. Describe the expected behavior of division managers as a result of the present system of performance evaluation regarding:
   (1) Operating expenses.
   (2) Product mix.
   (3) Capital outlays.
b. Evaluate whether these behavioral patterns are normal for division managers under the current evaluation system. Why or why not?
c. Discuss some disastrous long-term effects resulting from performance evaluation plans such as that used by Klammer, Inc.
d. Outline five features of an evaluation system that would overcome some of the problems inherent in the present system used by Klammer.

C14–21 Segment Performance Evaluation (L.O. 5)

Vanderbilt, Inc., produces many products in the metal works industry. Because the company is separated geographically, it uses a decentralized management structure. Each territory manager receives a bonus whenever actual residual income exceeds budgeted residual income. This company computes residual income by determining each segment's contribution to company profits before taxes less an investment charge of 20 percent on each segment's investment base. The investment base is the total of the segment's year-end balances of accounts receivable, inventories, and the book value of plant assets for each segment. Top management has informed each manager that each segment's investment in receivables and inventories is to be minimized because of its unfavorable impact on cash flow.

Each segment manager is responsible for production and marketing of company products in the geographical area surrounding the territory served. Also, requests for each territory's plant asset purchases are initiated by the segment manager. They are then evaluated based on need for the asset, feasibility studies, and available company funds.

Bob Weatherly, manager of the Northern Territory, is very proud of his segment's performance for the current year. In fact, he is so confident that he will receive a significant bonus that he has already purchased airline tickets for his family to spend Christmas in Hawaii. The current year's income statement in comparison with the annual budget is as follows for the Northern Territory with $000 omitted:

	Annual Budget	Annual Actual
Sales	$2,300	$2,500
Territory costs and expenses:		
Direct materials	460	540
Direct labor	115	140
Repairs and maintenance	120	70
Depreciation on production facilities	40	30
Other traceable costs	100	100
Segment margin	$1,465	$1,620
Allocated company fixed costs	250	200
Segment contribution to company profits	$1,215	$1,420
Imputed interest on segment investment (20%)	300	276
Residual income for segment	$ 915	$1,144

	Budgeted End-of-Year Account Balance	Actual End-of-Year Account Balances
Segment investment:		
Accounts receivable	$ 150	$ 200
Inventories	350	380
Plant and equipment (net)	1,000	800
Total	$1,500	$1,380
Imputed interest (20%)	$ 300	$ 276

Beginning of the year territorial assets were accounts receivable, $120,000; inventories, $280,000; and plant and equipment, $800,000.

Required:

a. Evaluate Weatherly's performance and decide if he should receive a bonus. Support your decision with relevant facts from the data given.

b. Identify any weaknesses in the company's performance evaluation, and indicate how they should be corrected.

Capstone Case

Determining Information Needed from an Accounting System

Plywood Plastics Manufacturing Company was formed as a partnership 25 years ago by Buell Edmonds and Harold Douglass after Edmonds, a successful business executive in the floor-covering business, acquired a plastics franchise. His new product was to be bonded with plywood and used for sink tops, paneling, and tabletops. Edmonds and Douglass were long-time friends, and Edmonds considered Douglass to have the technical expertise necessary to successfully produce a product. For years, Douglass had been an industrial arts teacher in a large metropolitan school district.

Each partner placed $5,000 in the business, and the partnership leased space behind a garage. Edmonds worked for the business in an administrative capacity, while Douglass worked part-time, mainly at night and on Saturdays. After approximately two years, the business was prospering, and the company moved to a larger location at which time each partner invested additional money.

Originally, the company's business consisted of custom-made products for new and remodeled homes; however, it gradually expanded operations so that emphasis shifted from single custom orders to larger commercial orders. Eventually, the bulk of its business came from several large national motel chains and one large, national mail-order house. Operations expanded to the extent that Plywood Plastics was producing custom countertops for mail-order catalog sales for the entire United States and Canada. In addition, it was engaged in shipping vanity tops and bathroom sink tops all over the world for the motel chains. After the purchase of new equipment, Plywood Plastics began producing rough-slab products for sale to several large makers of kitchen tables; these firms further processed the products.

By this time, Douglass had resigned from his teaching position and was working full time with the company. Eventually, Plywood Plastics became a corporation with each partner receiving 50 percent of the stock and Douglass was named the general manager. Ten years ago, when Edmonds retired, Douglass purchased his holdings and became the sole owner. Five years later, Douglass sold all his holdings to a group of six investors; however, he remained on the board of directors because the investors owed him a portion of the sales price which was secured by collateral in the company.

Immediately after the sale, the assistant manager, who was also one of the six investors, became president and general manager. Within one year a very profitable business began to lose money, at which time the board fired the manager and rehired Douglass on a daily consulting-fee basis. Within six months, Plywood Plastics was once again experiencing sizable profits; however, since Douglass did not want to remain active, the board hired another full-time manager and president. Profits have decreased to the point where the company is breaking even.

At present, the company has a work force of 40 employees, a reduction from the 100 workers employed during peak production. Although the production work force has been cut, the administrative staff remains the same—a general manager, two bookkeepers, and two salespersons. The company remains approximately one month behind in filling orders, presenting some problems since its competitors are able to fill orders much more quickly. Often the company is unable to begin processing an order after it is received because the material necessary must be ordered first. The only finished goods inventory produced for stock are vanity tops processed for the mail-order company; all other items are manufactured only after an order is received.

Plywood and plastic constitute the two main raw material inputs. The manufacturing process operates on an assembly line with the following four main steps involved:

1. A section where the plywood and plastic are glued together.
2. A section where any necessary bending takes place.
3. A section where the slab is cut to specifications.
4. The final section where any molding or other refinements take place.

When Douglass was general manager, he would call the three factory supervisors into his office and give them their work orders for the day. When the regular assembly line employees reported each day, material necessary for production had already been obtained from the storeroom. Because of his long experience, Douglass was able to correctly estimate the labor-hours needed for each batch of products, and profits per square foot of production could be forecast with a high degree of accuracy. During each workday, Douglass would check with the supervisors on the progress of each job.

The company does not have any type of cost accounting system nor does it maintain a perpetual inventory system. Even though the company is closing its books each month, a physical inventory is taken only once per quarter; management estimates inventory values for other months. Earnings are usually determined only for months in which management has estimated the inventory values. Finished goods are valued at 80 percent of sales price, and work in process at 70 percent of sales price. A local CPA firm prepares the year-end statements and tax returns.

Required:

Recommend steps the company could take to improve profitability. In your recommendations, specify the type of information the company needs from its accounting system.

CHAPTER

15

Transfer Pricing in Multidivisional Companies

CHAPTER OBJECTIVES

After studying this chapter, you should be able to:

1. Explain the relationship between the degrees of interdependence and the need for establishing transfer prices.
2. Apply appropriate criteria for choosing transfer prices.
3. Use variations of the two transfer pricing methods that impact a segment's profitability.

4. Recognize that transfer prices should reflect the factors surrounding each specified situation.
5. Monitor the behavioral implications inherent in decentralized segments and the potential for suboptimization and other dysfunctional behavior.

Introduction

In the days when all companies were small and management was centralized, accountants tranferred goods and services from one cost center to another at the cost of production. Today, many companies are giant conglomerates having multiple divisions. Simply transferring goods and services at cost no longer serves the needs of these decentralized organizations.

Transfer pricing becomes complex because of the need to evaluate an organization's segments. To the department selling goods and services, the transfer price is its revenue. To the department buying the goods and services, the transfer price is its cost. Therefore, transfer prices have a direct bearing on segment margin. Corporate managers should set transfer pricing policies ensuring that divisions do not purchase outside when high-fixed-cost internal facilities can provide the product. Allowing these facilities to be idle is detrimental to the overall company.

Transfer Pricing Bases (L.O. 2 and 3)

Transfer pricing refers to the unit price assigned to goods or services that one segment transfers to another segment. Accountants use transfer prices for purposes other than inventory costing. Regardless of the transfer price in effect, consolidated financial statements still show the unit production cost computed according to generally accepted accounting principles. On consolidated financial statements, accountants eliminate transactions between segments to reduce inventories on hand to cost. Usually, the greater the degree of interdependence among segments, the greater the transfer pricing problem. For instance, large volumes of intracompany transfers occur in a vertically integrated firm such as a paper supply company that owns timberland and manufactures paper cut to customer specification.

The transfer price accountants derive internally replaces the independent market transaction for directing the allocation of economic resources. The appropriate price used for transferring goods and services from one organizational segment to another is important because it affects the reported income of both the selling segment and the buying segment. A particular transfer pricing basis may also be an excellent management tool for motivating division managers, for establishing and maintaining cost control systems, and for measuring internal performance.

There are two basic methods for establishing transfer prices. The first involves some form of cost derived from the company accounting records or from financial analysis. Included are differential or variable cost, opportunity cost, marginal cost, full cost, and full cost plus a markup for a reasonable profit. The second method includes market price, negotiated price, or some variation of the two. After discussing these methods, we illustrate the applicability of different transfer prices. Remember that any solution is situation specific and depends on the individual circumstances of the divisions involved.

General Formula for Transfer Prices

The following general formula provides a beginning point for computing minimum transfer pricing:

$$\text{Differential costs per unit} + \text{lost contribution margin on outside sales}$$

The formula indicates that the transfer price should equal the unit differential cost of the product being transferred, plus the contribution margin per unit that the selling division loses as a result of giving up outside sales. If the selling division is not operating at full capacity, it does not lose contribution margin unless it has to give up some of its present outside customers. **Differential cost** is the increase in total company cost if a company adds the contemplated alternative to its present volume of activities. For transfer pricing purposes, we define **opportunity cost** as the maximum contribution to profit lost if the company does not sell the goods outside, but transfers them internally. Although the accounting records show differential costs, they do not show opportunity costs.

If the intermediate product has a perfectly competitive market in which the maximum available output may be sold at unchanging prices, the opportunity cost to the selling segment is the market price less the differential costs incurred for the product. The reason is that in refusing to accept outside business and instead making an internal transfer, the selling segment has forgone income that it could have earned on this business. If there is no intermediate market, the opportunity costs are zero, and the most appropriate transfer price is the differential cost. The buying segment's opportunity cost is the lower of either its net marginal revenue or the price at which it could obtain the intermediate product in the open market.

Differential/Variable Cost Transfer Prices

Rather than add lost opportunity cost to differential costs, we may use only variable or differential cost as a transfer price. Variable costs approximate differential costs in many situations. However, when fixed costs increase because of a transfer of goods between segments, they are differential costs and we should include these fixed costs in the transfer price. Variable cost transfer pricing has the advantage of ensuring, in the short run, the best use of total corporate facilities. Because total fixed costs do not change in the short run, variable cost pricing focuses attention on the contribution margin a transfer generates and on how it increases short-run profitability.

One limitation of variable cost transfer pricing is that a company must cover all costs before earning a profit. A company cannot ignore fixed costs. As a result, a variable cost transfer price may be profitable in the short run, but not in the long run. Another weakness of a variable or differential cost transfer price is that it allows one segment manager to make a profit at the expense of another segment manager, because the receiving segment receives all the profit. In addition, if a segment must forgo outside sales to make products for other internal segments, the use of variable or differential cost transfer prices can lead to dysfunctional decisions. Also, transfer prices based on differential costs diminish the decision-making autonomy of the profit center. If differential cost increases with volume, the segment is dependent on the total demands of the buying division and the supplying division's external customers. This means that neither segment can make its output decisions independently.

Full Cost Transfer Prices

Using full cost as a transfer price is probably the oldest transfer pricing method. **Full cost** includes actual manufacturing cost plus portions of marketing and administrative costs. Full cost is firmly established in centralized companies because almost all companies use full cost to value inventory for external reporting.

Companies primarily use full cost because it is convenient to apply. Probably the greatest single advantage of any cost-based pricing method is its simplicity. Full-costing data are already available and can be obtained at very low expense and a tremendous savings of time. Another prime advantage of the full-cost transfer price is that it leaves no intracompany profits in inventory to eliminate when preparing consolidated statements. When accountants record intracompany transfers below cost, they must increase inventories to cost before consolidating the inventory accounts. When accountants record intracompany transfers at prices above cost, they must eliminate all profits in ending inventories before consolidating inventory accounts. Managers may compare transferred costs with budgeted costs to measure production efficiency. This method allows simple and adequate end-product costing for profit analysis by product lines.

Despite these advantages, full cost is not suitable for companies with decentralized structures that measure the profitability of autonomous units. Full-cost transfer pricing has little worth for evaluating performance because it shows no income on interdivisional sales. A criticism of full cost as well as all cost pricing methods is that they do not create incentives for segment managers to control or reduce costs. All cost-based transfer prices reflect the accumulated efficiency level of the supplying division. As a result, accumulated inefficiencies from divisions that previously handled the product affect the reported income of the division in question.

Adding an arbitrary markup results in meaningless data that could even mislead management into believing that a division is profitable when it is not. Full cost does not provide management with a divisional profit figure for the selling division. Therefore, decentralized companies that must measure the profitability of autonomous units do not find cost-based transfer prices appropriate. In addition, segments tend to become complacent and less concerned about controlling costs when they know their costs are merely passed along to the next segment.

Another justifiable criticism of the full-cost method is that it departs from goal congruence. The use of full-cost transfer prices can lead to decisions that are not goal congruent when the supplying division is not operating at capacity. For example, a division may decide to purchase outside the company at an apparent savings. However, a reduction of the full-cost transfer price to the market price would recover all variable costs and a portion of fixed costs. The company fails to cover these fixed costs because of the decision to purchase outside. To avoid such suboptimization, top management must order the lowering of transfer prices or require internal purchasing. Yet, both of these solutions dilute the authority of individual divisions.

Standard Full Cost. The use of standard full cost rather than historical average cost eliminates the negative effect of fluctuations in production efficiency in one division on the reported income of another division. Standard full cost also permits division managers to know in advance what price they will receive or what price they will pay for transferred goods. This eliminates one source of delay in processing transfers. The supplying division should absorb spending variances from standard costs, which are primarily due to variable costs. Both the supplying and receiving divisions should receive allocations of volume or capacity variances from standard costs that reflect the effect of fixed costs.

Using either actual or standard full cost weakens the statement of income as a performance measure because the firm's long-range profitability is not emphasized. The local unit lacks the incentive to control or reduce cost when cost recovery is assured. A full-cost transfer price also does not provide an accurate guide for decision making because it offers no sound basis on which management can delegate decision-making authority to segment managers. For this reason, companies should restrict full-cost transfer prices to situations where segment managers lack decision-making authority.

Market-Based Transfer Prices

Using **market price** as a transfer price is essentially an opportunity cost approach. Company segments and outside customers pay the same price. However, some companies have a discount for any economies resulting from intracompany transfers or for large purchases. Since each segment is a completely separate company, internal transfers of intermediate products are priced at market price. Thus, others establish market prices objectively rather than the parties who have an interest in the results. A division might transfer products at a price lower than market price to reflect trade discounts and economies obtained by intracompany transfers.

The principal argument for use of market price is that it represents the opportunity cost of the intermediate product. The price the buying unit is paying is the same as if it bought from an outside source. The use of the market price creates a fair and equal chance for both the buying and selling departments to make the most profit they can. Market-based pricing also places segment operations on a competitive basis. Market-based pricing results in charging all internal and external customers the same price and reflects product profitability at various stages of production.

Also, if a segment cannot improve on the market sufficiently to recover both the acquisition cost of the product on the open market and the production cost of the department, the segment should not be in operation. For example, if a segment cannot afford to pay market prices, the company should not allow it to buy internally at less than market. Conversely, if a segment can sell outside at market, the company should not require it to sell internally for less. However, this argument is weak in the short run since this is a customer service. Through this customer service, the company can acquire a larger piece of the market and the segment becomes profitable.

The use of market prices as transfer prices is especially appropriate when evaluating the performance of segments. We determine segment income by how well the division functions in a competitive market because intermediate products are transferred from one segment to another at market price. The income determined in this way also shows how effectively the segment can perform in an outside independent market. In appraising efficiency, this type of income measurement has stronger appeal than the arbitrary income that results when using variable cost or full-cost transfer pricing.

A serious disadvantage to market-based transfer pricing, however, is that it requires the existence of a well-developed outside competitive market. Transfers based on market prices work well in a decentralized organization if there is a perfectly competitive intermediate market and the supply and demand of segments are practically independent of one another. However, the product may not be actively traded on the open market and have no market price. This is most likely to occur when all companies in the industry are fully integrated and each division produces only for internal consumption. For example, a department may produce a unit that is not sold to outsiders, as when parts are secretly designed. Also, if the transfer is nonrepetitive, there may not be a large enough market for the product to give a valid market price.

Negotiated Transfer Prices

To overcome these difficulties, very often we use a compromise transfer price that takes into consideration the competition and a fair return to the supplying division. The supplying and receiving departments can negotiate a price, with top management serving as arbitrator to avoid time-consuming and inflammatory negotiations.

A **negotiated price** is an attempt to simulate an arm's-length transaction between supplying and buying segments. Generally, we use it if there is no competitive outside market price. In theory, we can make a strong case for market-based negotiated prices, because all market prices are based on negotiation between buyer and seller. It follows then that if companies give segment managers autonomous authority to buy and sell as they think necessary and if they bargain in good faith, the result of this bargaining is the equivalent of a market price.

An additional advantage of pricing through negotiation is that usually sales of intracompany products are in such large volume that the use of any market price is meaningless because the quoted market price is based on smaller, normal order sizes. For example, assume that the selling division has excess capacity and the buying division can use more of the product. In this case, a negotiated price somewhere between the market price and the seller's differential cost increases the profits of both segments and is advantageous to the company as a whole.

However, negotiation may be very time-consuming and require frequent re-examination and revision of prices. For this method to work, the company must allow subunits to go to the outside markets if negotiation fails. In addition, negotiated prices eliminate the objectivity necessary to ensure maximization of companywide profits. As a result, the negotiated price may distort segment financial statements and mislead top management in its attempts to evaluate performance and make decisions.

The primary problem with negotiated transfer pricing arises when there is no established market price and the segment managers cannot reach agreement. Top management must then intervene to establish an arbitrary transfer price. This central control should exist to prevent suboptimization of company profits by division managers when the purchasing division can buy more cheaply outside than it can within the company. If the segment managers cannot agree on the transfer price and the purchasing manager has the option of purchasing in the outside market without the approval of top management, overall profit may be reduced.

When arbitration between subunits becomes necessary, divisional authority is breached and the purpose of decentralization and profit centers is subverted. In fact, frequent arbitration completely nullifies the purpose of decentralization. Certainly, such arbitrary pricing severely hampers the profit incentive of segment managers. However, management cannot carry decentralization to the point where they ignore all profits to allow local managers full control of purchasing when the product is available within the company.

Transfer Prices for Services

Divisions of many large organizations sell products and perform services for customers and for each other internally. One department's transfer of services to a second department is part of its sales yielding income. That same transfer is the second department's purchase of services. Companies typically bill administrative services, such as accounting, computer processing, personnel, and payroll, to the divisions they support. In each of the cases, they must establish equitable transfer prices to appraise division performance for its own return on invested capital. We can adopt many of the principles applied to the transfer of products for the transfer of services.

A first step in setting transfer pricing for services is to identify the different departments contributing various services and to estimate the corresponding skill and experience of personnel involved in delivering services. The second step is estimating each department's contribution to the value of the service generated. Because services are intangible, the service unit is often difficult to define.

Impact of Product/Service Life Cycles on Transfer Prices

Managers should recognize the stage in the life cycle of the product or service function and incorporate it in transfer pricing issues. A different set of environmental and technological factors characterizes each stage in the life cycle. The transfer pricing mechanism should vary according to these stages. Chapter 1 discusses life-cycle costing and includes planning and product design in addition to the generally accepted four stages of the product life cycle: introduction, growth, maturity, and decline. Because planning and product design do not need transfer prices, the following list excludes these two stages when describing the characteristics of the stages and the appropriate transfer prices.

1. *Introduction* Low sales volume and high introduction costs result in a loss situation; near monopoly exists for service; intensive marketing activity generates awareness of product or service. Because the division has a monopoly for the product/service and there are no close substitutes available in the market, a market price is ambiguous. Thus, a company should use a transfer price based on the outlay cost plus a fixed fee or the outlay cost plus a profit share depending on whether the buying or selling division should bear the risk.

2. *Growth* Unit cost is the lowest as a result of large sales increases and production and distribution economies; profits reach their highest level. The degree and extent of competition in the market, strength of the marketing department in the entity, and the speed of improvements in the service function affect the transfer price. Generally, the most appropriate transfer price is market price less any savings in transaction costs because of the internal transfer. The more unique the product or service, the less the competition, and the more difficult it is to determine a market reference price.

3. *Maturity* Costs increase as a result of product/service modifications, increased marketing mix expenditures and other efforts to maintain market position; profits decline causing weak firms to withdraw from the market; price competition intensifies as the factors responsible for the monopoly disappear. Gradually, identical products or services become available from many sources; marketing conditions become highly competitive, and rate of sales growth declines. At the maturity stage, the degree of elasticity of buyers switching to other suppliers, the extent and degree of standardization, degree of differentiation and price competition, relative intensity of price competition, and the relative strength of the marketing department should affect the transfer pricing chosen.

4. *Decline* The market for the product or service decreases causing sales and profits to decline; divisions usually leave the market. The extent of cost control possible by the transferor, the degree of sophistication among customers, the relative degree of a firm's overcapacity vis-à-vis industry's capacity, and the extent of product differentiation influence the transfer price.

Transfer Pricing Illustrated

The following example considers the application of several transfer prices. Assume the Transistor Division of a company supplies transistors to outside customers at a price of $3.50 each. The company has just acquired a radio assembly company. The president believes this newly acquired Radio Division should purchase transistors from the company's own Transistor Division because this division has excess capacity. Until the acquisition, the radio assembly company had purchased transistors for $3.50 less a 10 percent discount.

Assume no additional machines or supervisors will be acquired for the internal transfers and the Transistor Division's unit cost is

Direct material	$1.00
Direct labor	1.15
Variable overhead	0.50
Fixed overhead (now operating at 1,000,000 units activity level)	0.30
Total cost	$2.95

Various members of management have proposed the following transfer prices:

1. *Prime cost*—$2.15. This price would not be appropriate because it does not cover all the differential costs of the Transistor Division.

2. *Differential cost*—$2.65. This is an appropriate transfer price for guiding top management in deciding whether there should be transfers between the two divisions as long as the total differential costs are less than the outside purchase price of the buying division. This transfer price would be appropriate only when the selling division has excess capacity as it does in this example. This transfer price also would be appropriate in situations where there is no outside market. All benefits of using differential costs as the basis for the transfer price accrue to the buying division.

3. *Full cost*—$2.95. This transfer price would be appropriate if the company treats both divisions as cost centers rather than as independent, autonomous profit centers. Transistor Division profits are reflected in the profits of the Radio Division when using this transfer price.

4. *Market price*—$3.15 ($3.50 − $0.35 discount = $3.15). This transfer price represents the price that the Radio Division pays an independent, outside supplier and is appropriate if the company treats both divisions as independent units.

5. *Negotiated price*—$2.90. A negotiated price of $2.90 would be appropriate if the company treats both divisions as profit centers and both divisions share in the benefits. The $0.50 ($3.15 − $2.65) difference between the Transistor Division's differential cost and the net outside purchase price is divided between the two divisions.

6. *Full cost plus markup*—$3.50. This price is not appropriate because it exceeds the price that the Radio Division pays an outside supplier. In addition, the Transistor Division has excess capacity, and its opportunity costs are zero because it loses no contribution margin if the internal transfer occurs. However, if the Transistor Division receives more outside orders than it can fill and has no excess capacity, $0.85 represents the Transistor Division's opportunity cost ($3.50 − $2.65 = $0.85). Using the general formula of adding opportunity cost to differential costs results in a $3.50 transfer price as follows: $2.65 differential costs per unit + $0.85 lost contribution margin on outside sales = $3.50.

As just illustrated, the transfer price selected should depend on the capacity level at which the selling division is operating, as well as on other factors unique to the situation.

Recording Internal Transfers

Regardless of the basis used for transfer prices, the accounting system should provide a means of adjusting internal company data to a cost basis for external financial reporting. If the transfer price is less than inventory cost as when using variable costing as a basis, accountants should apply a portion of the fixed cost to goods remaining in inventory. Conversely, if the transfer price is above inventory cost, as with market or negotiated prices, accountants must subtract the excess from inventory and profit accounts in consolidation.

Consolidated income statements eliminate intradivisional sales including transfers made at standard full cost. Managers must distinguish between external and internal purchases to consolidate financial data and to provide information about the relative importance of intracompany transactions.

With this approach, an accountant uses the following entries to record a shipment from one segment to another at a 20 percent markup on sales.

On the supplying division's books:

Accounts Receivable—Purchasing Division	1,000	
Intracompany Sales		1,000
Cost of Goods Sold—Intracompany	800	
Inventory		800

On the purchasing division's books:

Inventory—from Supplying Division	1,000	
Accounts Payable—Supplying Division		1,000

Assume the Purchasing Division sells one fourth of these goods to an external customer for $500. The entries on the Purchasing Division's books are as follows:

Accounts Receivable—External Customer	500	
Sales		500
Cost of Goods Sold—External Customer (¼ × $1,000)	250	
Inventory—from Supplying Division		250

Assuming intracompany sales are handled in this manner, the accountant makes the following adjusting entry at the end of the period:

Intracompany Sales	1,000	
Cost of Goods Sold—Intracompany		800
Cost of Goods Sold—External Customer (20% × $250)		50
Inventory Adjustment Allowance (20% × $750)		150

The **Inventory Adjustment Allowance account** credited in the preceding journal entry is a contra account to inventory for external financial reporting. This allows for the elimination of intracompany inventory sales at prices above cost from both the overall company statement of financial position and the statement of income. Segment income is computed from the segment books, unadjusted.

Multinational Transfer Pricing (L.O. 4)

Many companies transfer goods and services between segments located in different countries. The transfer prices for these goods and services should reflect that countries have different tax rates and tax regulations. Because of these varying tax rates, a corporate group has an incentive to transfer most of its income to the subsidiary that has a tax advantage over other members of the corporate group. In addition, some countries restrict the payment of income or dividends to parties outside their national borders. Under these circumstances, the company often increases the transfer price so they pay more funds out of these countries while appearing to follow regulations. Transfers from foreign countries, where the wage level and/or tax rate is low, may also be made at a domestic market price rather than on a cost basis because foreign economic conditions are so different from domestic conditions. Foreign currency exchange rates, tariffs, and custom duties are additional factors influencing the multinational transfer price chosen.

Dual Transfer Pricing (L.O. 1)

In discussing transfer pricing, this chapter has emphasized the advantage of each base and the effect of specific circumstances. Having only one transfer pricing method may not be appropriate for a company because it is unlikely that any one method fulfills all management's needs. **Dual pricing** allows each segment to use the transfer price that provides the optimum decision for the segment and still meet the goals of the overall company. Accountants apply dual pricing primarily to evaluate performance, while still allowing goal congruence and autonomy. Dual pricing does not fit into the neat balancing act of accounting. Company profit does not equal the sum of division profits. Therefore, accountants must eliminate some of the segment profits.

For example, suppose that Segment A can sell its product in the market for $20 but its differential cost is only $14, and Segment B can further refine this product. However, the Segment B manager is unwilling to pay the same price as an outsider, especially because top management is forcing a purchase from Segment A. If management wishes to evaluate the performance of Segment A, it should consider using the market price as the transfer price. There is no reason for Segment A to transfer at a lower price. This gives Segment A credit for the opportunity it loses in the market by making the sale to another segment of the company. If this market price is, in turn, imposed on the buying division which does not have the complete authority to choose whether to buy from Segment A or not, a conflict can arise. Segment B manager probably resents Segment A's making a profit at Segment B's expense when the manager does not have the authority to buy elsewhere. The better procedure in this circumstance is to charge the buying division with differential cost. This recognizes the interdependence of the subunits. This solution does not allow one segment manager to make a profit at the expense of another segment manager.

Missing Incentive to Control Cost

In practice, companies have not widely adopted dual pricing because of a major inherent weakness—all segment managers may win, but the overall company may lose. This results because the buying segment purchases at a low price while the supplying segment sells at a high price. As a result, the incentive to control cost is missing and inefficiencies may develop.

Do not assume, however, that dual pricing always uses market price as the selling segment's transfer price and a cost-based transfer price for the buying division. For example, suppose the full cost or differential cost of a product from Segment X is $10 and Segment Y further refines this product. Also assume that Segment Y could purchase this elsewhere for $9. The solution using dual pricing should involve Segment X's selling the product to the home office for $10 and, in turn, Segment Y's buying it for $9 from the home office. In this case, the home office has created a fictitious loss that is eliminated when determining the overall company profit.

If a company fails to take this approach, the manager of Segment Y will try to buy from the outside resulting in a $1 savings. However, this lower external price could be the result of temporary excess capacity in a competitor's plant. If management fails to investigate the situation and eliminates Segment X because it believes it can buy all the products it needs on the outside for $9, the company may be hurt financially when the outside party sells its excess supply and raises prices above $10. A company should guard against such suboptimization. Sub-optimization can occur if the external purchase price is lower than a related segment's differential cost.

Behavioral Implications of Transfer Pricing (L.O. 5)

As we have just discussed, when decentralization leads to **suboptimization,** the goals of the whole organization become secondary. Transfer prices do, however, offer a behavioral advantage by providing for units to operate autonomously in a decentralized organization even when there is no externally determined market price for the products and services exchanged internally. When managers deter-mine transfer prices logically, segments can maintain their autonomy while also making decisions that benefit the entire organization. Because segment managers are closer to the market place, they provide more relevant information concern-ing the price of inputs and outputs.

Suboptimization

The use of opportunity cost and differential cost gives an immediate indication of the proper decision about selling the product inside or outside the company if a perfectly competitive market for the intermediate product exists. However, where there is imperfect competition in the intermediate market, the manager of either the buying or selling division can decrease the overall income of the com-pany by attempting to maximize his or her own income. This might result in improved performance for the segment, but it does not result in goal congruence because the income of the company as a whole is less than optimum.

For example, suppose the selling division is operating at capacity and can sell all of its products at $5 each. However, the buying division must operate at 70 percent capacity because it cannot secure enough products. Should manage-ment force the selling division to transfer products at $4 if the selling division's unit differential cost is $3? For the selling segment to maximize income, it should continue to sell outside the company, yet this strategy hurts overall com-pany income. Assume the buying division's cost of the finished product is as follows:

Part (being manufactured by selling division)	$ 4
Other variable cost	6
Allocated expenses	7
	$17

Assuming the allocated expenses represent expenses that the company incurs re-gardless, the company gains $6 ($7 allocated expenses minus $1 difference in outside sales price and inside transfer price) to contribute to unavoidable fixed expenses by transferring internally rather than selling outside. This assumes the buying division sells its product for at least $17. In the short run, there is an advantage to the internal transfer even though this action is counter to the purposes of decentralized decision making. This results because it requires top management to overrule the selling management's decision. If this action occurs on a regular basis, this situation would not be viable in a divisional organizational structure.

Suboptimization also often occurs when the total full cost at the transfer point is greater than the outside purchase price available to the purchasing division. To maximize division income, a manager will buy from the outside source. Assuming the supplying division has excess capacity, the outside purchase decreases the total profit of the company. This decrease occurs if the difference between the full-cost transfer price and the outside purchase price is less than the difference between the differential cost in the selling division and the full-cost transfer price. Stated differently, suboptimization can arise if the outside purchase price is greater than the differential cost in the supplying division, but less than the full cost of the supplying division.

The following example illustrates suboptimization; assume Selling Division A is not operating at full capacity:

	Unit Cost
Material	$ 20
Labor	30
Overhead, 40% fixed	100
Full-cost transfer price of product in Division A	$150
Outside purchase price available to Division B for product identical in quality, delivered	$130

Given these conditions, Division B's manager has an incentive to purchase the product outside, which results in a $20 savings to the division. Yet, Division A's manager may argue for coverage of its full cost. The differential costs in this division amount to $110 (material, $20; labor, $30; and variable overhead, $60). If Division B accepts the competitor's bid, the loss in company total income is $20 per unit, as shown here:

Addition to total company cost to purchase externally	$130
Addition to total company cost if produced by Division A	110
Decrease in total company income	$ 20

The company should not adhere to completely decentralized decision making in this situation. Management should also be cautious in establishing policies requiring that divisions always purchase internally.

Divisional Performance Evaluation

The ideal transfer pricing system should motivate segment managers to most effectively fulfill overall company objectives. Often, this is difficult because of the division performance evaluation used by many companies. Such companies evaluate division managers on the basis of the profit the segment earns; but if one segment charges another segment too much, overall company performance decreases. When setting transfer prices, accountants must consider the interests of both the buyer and the seller. An advantage given to one of these parties is a disadvantage to the other. The problem becomes even more crucial if the company gives each segment manager a bonus based on the segment's performance. This may cause managers to try all the harder to get maximum beneficial prices from the other segments. Under these circumstances, segment managers have good reason to argue for a high transfer price for the goods they sell to other segments. In turn, they argue for a low price for goods bought from other segments. The transfer price thus chosen is likely to lead to a lack of goal congruence for the overall company.

A bonus system actually encourages segment managers to make decisions that may be good for their segments but detrimental to the entire company. For instance, using the previous example illustrating suboptimization, if segment managers receive bonuses based on their division's income, the Division B manager will be more eager to accept the outside offer resulting in a $20 savings per unit. Buying outside increases the segment's income which, in turn, increases the manager's bonus.

The company can solve this problem with complete goal congruence by reducing the transfer price to $130 at which both the individual segments and the overall company benefit because the selling division has excess capacity. Another solution is a transfer price that divides the difference between Division A's differential cost and the outside purchase price. For example, the $20 ($130 − $110) difference can be divided equally, resulting in a transfer price of $120 [$110 differential cost + $10 difference ($20/2)]. Even though transfer pricing should be a tool for motivating segment managers, it should also lead to segment actions benefiting the entire company.

Reward Team Players. A company's reward system should encourage segment managers to be team players. Companies should carefully establish transfer pricing so segments do not purchase outside when there are high-fixed-cost internal facilities that would remain idle. Often, as in the case when idle facilities exist, the company must make decisions for its overall benefit. By having a thorough knowledge of their segments' cost behavior, segment managers understand their profits are not decreased when they sell internally at differential cost.

Internal Competition

Internal competition between segments of a company is often very healthy. Division managers may feel assured of a market for their production if the company does not allow buying segments the freedom to purchase externally. A supply division with a captive source of sales is less likely to be aggressive in developing more efficient methods that lower costs than if it must meet competition on each sale. **Internal competition** is, therefore, one means of preventing division managers from becoming complacent and failing to incorporate current technological developments.

Division performance should also be compared to that of outside companies. A company may overlook how outdated and unprofitable a division really is by failing to compare its performance with like companies outside the organization. In determining transfer prices, a company should focus attention on uneconomical activities that otherwise might go undetected. Further, they should force managers to check outside markets and supplies carefully.

External Procurement

Management should establish a policy concerning outside purchases of products and services. When the company's own product is superior to or equal in quality and performance to that from outside sources, segments should buy the product internally. This assumes meeting an acceptable delivery schedule. If the internal source of supply is not competitive, however, management may agree to outside procurement as long as the receiving division can justify its action. It is reasonable to allow division managers the freedom to purchase externally if the external price is lower and the quality comparable. In justifying outside purchasing, the division should supply evidence of a reasonable effort to bring the internal supplier's terms into competition with those of the outside source.

Some companies have a policy of splitting purchases between external and internal supplying divisions. This policy is appropriate only when management considers it important to have alternative sources available or when internal facilities are not adequate.

Not imposing the strict requirement that segments can purchase only from other segments allows segment managers some flexibility in purchasing from outsiders. This arrangement may motivate segment managers to determine whether to sell intermediate products in their present form or process them further. When segment managers see that a competitor's price is cheaper, they become stimulated to find the reasons. Flexible purchasing encourages them to seek each other's advice about the best plant layout and work flow. This approach emphasizes each segment manager's contribution to the overall company.

Although some conflict of interest is usually unavoidable no matter how well developed the transfer pricing system, management can design a workable system that resolves much of this conflict by monitoring certain issues. Management should avoid holding division managers responsible for their segments' performance while restricting their purchasing function. If managers have income responsibility, they need the authority to purchase material that best meets their requirements. It is, therefore, important that the system provide objective measures of division income as free from administrative bias as possible. The objective should be to prevent the transfer price from becoming an alibi for poor income performance.

Summary

The shift from centralized to decentralized organizations has increased the role of transfer pricing as portions of the revenue from one income center become portions of the costs of another. Transfer pricing and divisional income measurement serve several purposes: to guide division managers in decision making; to help evaluate divisional performance; and to aid top management in allocating resources and in long-range planning. A supplying decision that is always assured of a market for its products may lapse into inefficiencies difficult and expensive to discover and correct. There is no single best pricing method from an absolute point of view, but there may be a best method for a particular set of circumstances. Product type, degree of decentralization, stage in the life cycle, and managerial skills are considerations in selecting a transfer price. In establishing transfer prices, management should encourage segment managers not only to communicate with each other but also to study and eliminate uneconomical activities within their divisions.

Companies guard against suboptimization, which can arise if the outside purchase price is greater than the supplying division's differential cost, but less than its full cost. Companies should establish transfer pricing policies so divisions do not purchase outside when there are high-fixed-cost internal facilities that remain idle, thus hurting the overall company. Extreme decentralization granting complete freedom to decide in the best interests of the segment alone, and not of the overall company, is not advisable. To help prevent dysfunctional behavior, a company's reward system should encourage segment managers to become team players.

Important Terms and Concepts

transfer pricing, 524
differential cost, 525
opportunity cost, 525
full cost, 526
market price, 527
negotiated price, 528

Inventory Adjustment Allowance
    account, 532
dual pricing, 533
suboptimization, 534
internal competition, 536

Problem for Self-Study

Segment Margin Using Various Transfer Prices

The Motor Division of Haggs-Scranton manufactures three-horsepower gasoline motors for both go-carts and lawn mowers. Sales are made to the Go-Cart Division of Haggs-Scranton as well as to outsiders. Motors are sold for $75 to outsiders. Go-carts are sold for $275 to wholesale distributors. Operating results of the divisions for 19X1 are

	Motor Division	Go-Cart Division
Intracompany sales	6,000 units	–0–
Sales—outsiders	8,000 units	6,000 units
Direct material	$280,000	$100,000
Direct labor	420,000	180,000
Variable factory overhead	40,000	30,000
Fixed factory overhead	127,000	145,000
Traceable fixed home office expense	14,000	132,000
Marketing and administrative—variable	30,000	86,000
Marketing and administrative—fixed	13,000	128,000

If either of the divisions were discounted, two thirds of the traceable home office expense could be eliminated.

Required:

Prepare statements of segment margin for each division under each of the following conditions:

a. Intracompany sales are made at average segment cost.
b. Intracompany sales are made at market price.
c. Intracompany sales are made at variable cost.

Solution to Problem for Self-Study

HAGGS-SCRANTON
Segment Margin for Motor and Go-Cart Divisions
For Year 19X1

a.	Motor Division	Go-Cart Division
Revenue:		
Sales—outsiders	$ 600,000 (8,000 × $75)	$1,650,000 (6,000 × $275)
Sales—Go-Cart Division	396,000 (6,000 × $66)*	–0–
	$ 996,000	$1,650,000

	Motor Division	**Go-Cart Division**
Less variable costs:		
Cost from Motor Division		$ 396,000
Direct material	$ 280,000	100,000
Direct labor	420,000	180,000
Variable factory overhead	40,000	30,000
Marketing and administrative—		
variable	30,000	86,000
Total variable expenses	$ 770,000	$ 792,000
Contribution margin	$ 226,000	$ 858,000
Less traceable fixed expenses:		
Fixed factory overhead	$ 127,000	$ 145,000
Home office expenses	14,000	132,000
Marketing and administrative . . .	13,000	128,000
Total traceable fixed		
expenses	$ 154,000	$ 405,000
Segment margin	$ 72,000	$ 453,000

*$770,000 total variable expenses + $154,000 traceable fixed = $924,000 ÷ 14,000 units = $66.

b.

	Motor Division	**Go-Cart Division**
Sales—outsiders	$ 600,000	$1,650,000
Sales—Go-Cart Division	450,000 (6,000 × $75)	–0–
	$1,050,000	$1,650,000
Less variable costs:		
Cost from Motor Division		$ 450,000
Direct material	$ 280,000	100,000
Direct labor	420,000	180,000
Variable factory overhead	40,000	30,000
Marketing and administrative—		
variable	30,000	86,000
Total variable expenses	$ 770,000	$ 846,000
Contribution margin	$ 280,000	$ 804,000
Total traceable fixed		
expenses (as		
shown above)	154,000	405,000
Segment margin	$ 126,000	$ 399,000

c.

	Motor Division	**Go-Cart Division**
Sales—outsiders	$ 600,000	$1,650,000
Sales—Go-Cart Division	330,000 (6,000 × $55)[†]	–0–
	$ 930,000	$1,650,000
Less variable costs:		
Cost from Motor Division		$ 330,000
Direct material	$ 280,000	100,000
Direct labor	420,000	180,000
Variable factory overhead	40,000	30,000
Marketing and administrative—		
variable	30,000	86,000
Total variable expenses	$ 770,000	$ 726,000
Contribution margin	$ 160,000	$ 924,000
Traceable fixed expenses	154,000	405,000
Segment margin	$ 6,000	$ 519,000

[†]$\dfrac{\$770,000}{14,000} = \$55.$

Review Questions

1. What is the impact of product life cycles on transfer prices?

2. Give two advantages of establishing independent and autonomous profit centers and three behavioral problems that are likely to develop.

3. State two advantages and disadvantages of negotiated transfer prices.

4. Why may dual pricing be the optimum solution for establishing transfer prices?

5. Discuss how a service company uses transfer prices.

6. Why is some conflict of interest inherent in almost any transfer pricing system?

7. In preparing consolidated financial statements, how are intradivisional sales treated?

8. Discuss the dangers of establishing a bonus system for segment managers based on segment profit.

9. What advantages do you see to allowing internal competition to exist among segment managers?

10. When would you allow segment managers to purchase outside the company?

11. In determining a transfer price for divisions, what factors are relevant?

12. What advantages does standard full cost have over historical average cost as a transfer price?

CPA/CIA Multiple Choice Questions

1. (AICPA) An internal report for a decentralized organization reports transfers between segments. For this internal report, transfer prices charged for a product with a determinable market price would usually be based on

    a. Cost or market, whichever is lower.
    b. Market price.
    c. Historical cost.
    d. Variable cost.

2.–3. (AICPA) These items are based on the following data:
    Ajax Division of Carlyle Corporation produces electric motors, 20 percent of which are sold to Bradley Division of Carlyle and the remainder to outside customers. Carlyle treats its divisions as profit centers and allows division managers to choose their sources of sale and supply. Corporate policy requires that all interdivisional sales and purchases be recorded at variable cost as a transfer price. Ajax Division's estimated sales and standard cost data for the year ending December 31, 19X2, based on the full capacity of 100,000 units, are as follows:

	Bradley	Outsiders
Sales	$ 900,000	$ 8,000,000
Variable costs	(900,000)	(3,600,000)
Fixed costs	(300,000)	(1,200,000)
Gross margin	$(300,000)	$ 3,200,000
Unit sales	20,000	80,000

Ajax has an opportunity to sell the 20,000 units to an outside customer at a price of $75 per unit during 19X2 on a continuing basis. Bradley can purchase its requirements from an outside supplier at a price of $85 per unit.

2. Assuming that Ajax Division desires to maximize its gross margin, should Ajax take on the new customer and drop its sales to Bradley for 19X2? Why?

    a. No, because the gross margin of the corporation as a whole would decrease by $200,000.

    b. Yes, because Ajax Division's gross margin would increase by $300,000.

    c. Yes, because Ajax Division's gross margin would increase by $600,000.

    d. No, because Bradley Division's gross margin would decrease by $800,000.

3. Assume, instead, that Carlyle permits the division managers to negotiate the transfer price for 19X2. The managers agreed on a tentative transfer price of $75 per unit, to be reduced based on an equal sharing of the additional gross margin to Ajax resulting from the sale to Bradley of 20,000 motors at $75 per unit. The actual transfer price for 19X2 would be

    a. $52.50.

    b. $55.00.

    c. $60.00.

    d. $67.50.

4. (CIA) Given a competitive outside market for identical intermediate goods, what is the best transfer price, assuming all relevant information is readily available?

    a. Average cost of production.

    b. Average cost of production, plus average production department allocated profit.

    c. Market price of the intermediate goods.

    d. Market price of the intermediate goods, less average production department allocated profit.

5. (AICPA) The Blade Division of Dana Company produces hardened steel blades. One third of the Blade Division's output is sold to the Lawn Products Division of Dana; the remainder is sold to outside customers. The Blade Division's estimated sales and standard cost data for the fiscal year ending June 30, 19X1, are as follows:

	Lawn Products	Outsiders
Sales	$ 15,000	$ 40,000
Variable costs	(10,000)	(20,000)
Fixed costs	(3,000)	(6,000)
Gross margin	$ 2,000	$14,000
Unit sales	10,000	20,000

The Lawn Products Division has an opportunity to purchase 10,000 identical quality blades from an outside supplier at a cost of $1.25 per unit on a continuing basis. Assume that the Blade Division cannot sell any additional products to outside customers. Should Dana allow its Lawn Products Division to purchase the blades from the outside supplier, and why?

    a. Yes, because buying the blades would save Dana Company $500.

    b. No, because making the blades would save Dana Company $1,500.

    c. Yes, because buying the blades would save Dana Company $2,500.

    d. No, because making the blades would save Dana Company $2,500.

6. (CIA) A company recently established a branch to sell its most popular fan. The company purchases these fans and stores them in a warehouse. The fans are then shipped from the warehouse to both the home office and the new branch FOB destination. Home office management is responsible for setting the transfer price of the fans charged to the branch in a manner that will measure the long-run incremental cost of supplying the fans to the branch on a continuing basis. Per unit costs for the fans are as follows:

$50.00	purchase price
2.50	shipping cost to warehouse
3.00	handling cost including $1.00 of allocated administrative overhead
3.50	shipping cost to branch paid by home office
1.25	shipping cost to home office

The minimum transfer price that the home office should charge the branch to meet its measurement objective is

   a. $53.50.
   b. $54.50.
   c. $58.00.
   d. $59.00.

7. (CIA) A company's independent manufacturing division sells 50,000 units to outsiders and transfers 3,000 units to another division. The product has a perfectly competitive market price of $7.00. Variable unit cost is $4.00, fixed costs are $110,000, and manufacturing capacity is 55,000 units. The optimal transfer price for the company is

   a. $4.00.
   b. $6.00.
   c. $6.08.
   d. $7.00.

Exercises

E15–1 Behavioral Problems Associated with Segmentation and Transfer Prices (L.O. 5)

Multidivisional corporations benefit by establishing independent and autonomous profit centers. Each division manager's nearness to the marketplace provides relevant information regarding the price of inputs and outputs. Also, more effective coordination of production factors is possible at the division level. However, dividing an organization into independent segments has strong behavioral implications.

Required:

Discuss the behavioral problems often encountered in establishing segments and the related transfer pricing situations that normally arise.

E15–2 Impact of Transfer Pricing on Segment Margin (L.O. 3)

Costley, Inc., adopted the policy several years ago that all intracompany sales must be made at current market price. The Massachusetts Division asked the Texas Division to quote a price for 500 motors. The Texas Division plant manager submitted a unit price of $40 that would yield a contribution margin of $6,000 for the 500 motors; $1,000 traceable fixed costs are estimated for the order. An outside company, facing depressed financial conditions with an oversupply of these motors, quoted a unit price of $32 forcing Texas Division to meet this price.

Required:

a. Compute the segment margin the Texas Division will earn on the order at unit transfer prices of $32 and at $40.
b. Assume that after Costley management realizes it would be more profitable for the overall company if the Texas Division supplied the order, the outside company submitted another price of $26 for the motors. Should Costley management force Texas Division to meet this price? Why or why not?

E15–3 Conditions Conducive to Transfers (L.O. 4)

The Motor Division of French Company produces components that the Fabricating Division incorporates into a final product. Components from the Motor Division can also be sold to outsiders. Each division is a separate profit center. Data gathered from records of both segments reveal the following:

```
Market price—final product ......................  $600
Market price—components ......................   300
Motor Division—variable cost ...................   170
Fabricating Division—variable completion cost .......   375
```

Required:

a. Describe the conditions under which transfers should be made to the Fabricating Division. Support your answer with a quantitative analysis.

b. Assume the conditions that you suggested in Requirement *a* exist. At which price should transfers be made?

E15–4 Rejection of Outside Order (L.O. 4)

At practical capacity, the Fabricating Division of Crossville Company has facilities to produce 8,000 units per month. Each unit requires five direct labor-hours. The Assembly Division of the company has forwarded a requisition for 8,000 units to the Fabricating Division. Since Crossville Company uses a market-based transfer pricing system, contribution margin using a $50 market price would be $168,000. The receipt of this requisition from the Assembly Division upset the Fabricating Division manager as he had just been approached by an outside buyer with a rush order for 5,000 units at a $56 unit sale price. Top management's initial reaction to the conflict is that the outside order should be rejected so that the Assembly Division's order can be filled.

Required:

a. Determine how the income of the Fabricating Division and Crossville Company would be affected if the outside order is rejected.

b. List four additional factors that should be known before a final decision is made.

E15–5 Evaluation of Various Transfer Prices (L.O. 4)

The Bobbin Division of the Henry Company supplies bobbin units to outside customers at a price of $15.00 per bobbin. The company has just acquired a sewing machine company, and the president believes that this Sewing Machine Division should purchase bobbins from the company's own Bobbin Division even though the Bobbin Division presently receives more orders than it can fill.

   Until their acquisition by the Henry Company, the sewing machine company had purchased bobbins for $15.00 less a 10 percent discount. The Bobbin Division's cost per unit is

```
Direct material .......................................  $ 9.30
Direct labor ........................................    2.80
Variable overhead ....................................    0.90
Fixed overhead (now operating at 500,000 units activity level) ......     .60
    Total cost ......................................  $13.60
```

Henry Company management is undecided about which transfer price to use for the sales between the two divisions.

Required:

a. Explain why each of the following transfer prices would or would not be appropriate to charge the Sewing Machine Division on the intracompany sales.
   (1) $15.00
   (2) $13.60
   (3) $13.50
   (4) $13.25
   (5) $13.00
   (6) $12.10

b. Assume that the Bobbin Division does not receive more outside orders than it can fill. In view of the fact that the Bobbin Division has excess capacity, explain why each of the transfer prices in Requirement *a* would or would not be appropriate to charge the Sewing Machine Division.

E15–6 Sales to Company Division (L.O. 2)

Owens Company is a producer of various pumps. After recently acquiring a home appliance assembly company, management is trying to decide whether to establish two autonomous divisions. Presently, the Appliance Division is purchasing 1,500 pumps a month at $40 per pump from an outside supplier that gives the division a 10 percent quantity discount.

The Pump Division supplies you with the following costs per pump:

Direct materials	$16
Direct labor	10
Variable factory overhead	2
Fixed factory overhead, based on 3,600	
pumps (normal capacity) per month	4
	$32

The Pump Division presently sells 2,100 units of this pump with a 25 percent markup on cost. The Pump Division gives no quantity discount.

Required:

a. Advise the Pump Division about selling to the Appliance Division. If they should sell, suggest a transfer price.

b. Assume that the Pump Division presently sells 3,600 pumps to outsiders. Under these conditions, should the Pump Division sell to the Appliance Division? If so, at what transfer price?

c. Disregard your answers to Requirements *a* and *b* and assume that presently the Pump Division sells 2,100 pumps to outsiders and the Appliance Division manager offers to purchase 1,500 pumps a month for $30 each. What decision should each make? Why?

Problems

P15–7 Recommendations Regarding Transfer Prices (L.O. 1)

Newberg Division's budget for next year for producing 60,000 units of a storage container is as follows:

Direct material	$162,000
Direct labor	156,000
Factory overhead—variable	66,000
Factory overhead—fixed	170,000
Marketing expense	42,000
Administrative expense	49,000
	$645,000

Of the fixed factory overhead, $50,000 represents allocated joint costs. Management's analysis shows that shipping and handling expense, which is included in the marketing expense, amounts to $0.50 per unit; the remainder is divisional fixed expense. The division manager's salary of $30,000 is included in administrative expenses. This represents the only administrative expense that could be eliminated because the other components are allocated home office expense.

Required:

a. Give the segment cost per unit.

b. Assume Newberg Division has no market for its containers except for inside sales to other divisions and is not operating at normal capacity. What should the transfer price be?

c. Assume buying divisions within the company are able to purchase containers at a price of $14, less 8 percent discount from outside suppliers. What should the transfer price be?

d. Assume that Newberg Division can sell all its production to outsiders for $15. Which transfer price would you recommend?

P15–8 Comparison of Gross Margin Using Different Transfer Prices (L.O. 3)

The Pump Division of Grogan Company sells various styles of pumps to outsiders. Recently, an engineer for Grogan Company's newly acquired dishwasher company developed a unique idea for employing a pump in one of their models.

The Pump Division produced and sold 132,000 pumps of this style for $154 each. The plant has an annual capacity to produce 165,000 pumps, whose unit variable cost is $88. Fixed cost related to this style amounts to $3,960,000 per year.

The Dishwasher Division plans to sell 33,000 dishwashers for $385 each and has received offers from outside companies to supply the pumps needed for $137.50 each. Total variable cost per dishwasher amounts to $170.50 including the pumps supplied externally. Fixed cost for 33,000 dishwashers assembled per year amounts to $3,300,000.

The Pump Division offers to supply the Dishwasher Division with the style of pump needed for $154; however, the Dishwasher Division manager wants to refuse the offer.

Required:

a. Determine the gross margin for each division and the total company if the Dishwasher Division's pumps are
   (1) Purchased from outside companies.
   (2) Obtained from Grogan's Pump Division with a pricing system based on cost and assuming a production level of 165,000 pumps.
b. Choose the alternative you advise adopting.
c. Discuss if the Pump Division manager has any valid basis for strongly arguing for a $154 transfer price. Defend your answer.

P15–9 Choice of Transfer Price (L.O. 2)

Minnesota, Inc., a large, diversified corporation, operates its divisions on a decentralized basis. The New York Division makes Product A that is sold either to the Illinois Division or to outside customers. The Illinois Division processes Product A into Product B. The additional variable cost of producing Product B is $4 per unit with a sales price of $20. At current levels of production, the variable costs of making Product A is $2 per unit, the fixed cost is $0.50, and the market price is $3 per unit.

Top management is reviewing the following bases for setting transfer prices to establish a corporate transfer policy: full cost, variable cost, and market price.

Required:

a. Assume that the New York Division is currently operating at full capacity when the Illinois Division offers to pay $2.40 for Product A. Should top management require the New York Division to sell to the Illinois Division? Why or why not?
b. Assume that the New York Division is only operating at 60 percent capacity when the Illinois Division offers to buy at:
   (1) $1.85. Explain why it should or should not sell.
   (2) $2.25. Explain why it should or should not sell.
c. List two possible advantages the Illinois Division might enjoy by purchasing internally at the current market price.
d. Discuss the disadvantage the New York Division might experience if it sold all its Product A to the Illinois Division at market price.
e. Determine which of the transfer prices being reviewed would:
   (1) Encourage the best short-run utilization of the company's production capacity. Why would this not be true for long-run utilization?
   (2) Encourage maximum efficiency and waste avoidance up to the transfer point.

P15–10 Economic Advantage of Interdivisional Sales (L.O. 3)

Management of MacDonald, Inc., has recently incorporated a companywide policy for their divisions stating that a selling division must always sell to a buying division at current market price. The South Division submitted bids to the North Division on 3,600 standard parts, which represented 12 percent of its normal capacity for the year. South Division quoted a price of $50 but was forced by company policy to fill the order at $45, the price an outside supplier quoted. At a price of $48, South Division could have earned a contribution margin of $28,800.

Required:

a. Determine how much the total contribution margin of South Division decreased due to its selling price of $45.
b. Discuss the impact on total income of MacDonald, Inc., caused by requiring North Division to buy internally.
c. Assume that by selling to North Division, South Division must forgo an order to an outside company for making 3,000 units of special design. These specially designed parts could be sold for $54 each; the variable cost per unit is $38. The company is unable to process both North Division's parts and the outside order because of volume limitations. By requiring North Division to buy inside, how will the income of South Division and overall income be affected? What would you suggest as a solution?

P15–11 Profitable Volume for Decentralized Organization (L.O. 3)

Emma's Deodorant Company organized several years ago to manufacture both men's and women's deodorant. When first organized, the company sold the deodorant as a paste in a plain jar. Then, one of the supervisors developed a roll-on bottle and sales skyrocketed. It was so successful that Emma's management decided to set up two divisions: a Manufacturing Division and a Bottle Division. Competition between the two divisions has become quite intense because each division manager receives a bonus based on the center's contribution margin.

The president is quite concerned that the transfer price used is not fair and has called you in as a consultant to evaluate the circumstances. Your first project is to determine the costs of each division; then your second project is to discover the prices charged by competitive bottle companies. Your findings are as follows:

Quantity	Bottle Division's Cost per Case	Average Competitor's Sales Price per Case
1,000,000 cases	$10.00	$12.00
4,000,000 cases	9.50	11.00
8,000,000 cases	9.10	10.50

The Manufacturing Division's costs of ingredients and sales prices are as follows:

Quantity	Cost per Case	Sales Price per Case for Packaged Product
1,000,000 cases	$25.00	$45.00
4,000,000 cases	23.40	43.60
8,000,000 cases	22.60	41.80

Required:

a. Evaluate the success of decentralizing the divisions.
b. Assume the market price is used as the transfer price and calculate the income for each division and for the overall organization using a volume of 1 million cases, 4 million cases, and 8 million cases.
c. Recommend the most profitable volume for each of the divisions and for the overall company.

P15–12 Evaluating the Merits of Transfer Pricing Positions (L.O. 1)

The Kentucky Division of the Kenneth Company manufactures and distributes a wide range of industrial pumps. This division sells pumps at $10 to the Texas Division of the company, which uses the pumps in the manufacture of washing machines. The Kentucky Division also sells these pumps for $12 to outside customers.

The Texas Division manager complained that pumps similar to the ones purchased from the Kentucky Division can be bought from an outside supplier for $9. As a result, the Texas Division manager argues that the maximum he should pay is $9.

When the Kentucky Division manager is confronted, she refuses to meet this price on the basis that it is less than costs. She provides the Texas Division with the following previous year's actual product line income statement in support of the position that a $9 transfer price would be lower than her cost of $10.50.

Sales—outside (50,000 × $12)	$600,000
Sales—Texas Division (10,000 × $10)	100,000
Total sales	700,000
Direct materials	180,000
Direct labor	90,000
Variable factory overhead	120,000
Fixed factory overhead	180,000
	570,000
Segment margin	130,000
Allocated indirect fixed costs	60,000
Net profit before taxes	$ 70,000

Cost per pump: $\dfrac{\$630{,}000}{60{,}000} = \$10.50$

Required:

a. Draft a letter as controller of the Texas Division to the top management of Kenneth Company explaining your position in support of the proposed $9 price.

b. Describe how you, as top management, would evaluate the merits of the arguments supplied by the controller.

P15–13 Segment Margin for Divisions (L.O. 3)

Gray Cosmetics Company manufactures pressed powder in compacts. The manufacturing process is a series of mixing operations with various coloring ingredients added to obtain specified shades. Workers then press the powder into company-produced compacts and pack them in cases containing 24 compacts. Gray Cosmetics management believes that the sale of its product is heavily influenced by the highly decorated compact. Much advertising has stressed the uniqueness of the compact's decorative style.

The company has organized its process into two divisions: the powder process and compact production. Each division is supervised by a plant superintendent, with supervisors of the various cost centers reporting to the plant superintendent. All compact production has been used by the powder division. Little interchange of management ideas or personnel takes place between the two divisions; unfortunately, this has caused intense rivalry to develop between the divisions. Top management believes that their decision several years ago to establish each division as a profit center may have also contributed to the rivalry. Each plant superintendent receives a commission based on the net income generated by the division.

You are to determine a proper transfer price for the compact division to use in charging the powder profit center. The compact plant superintendent informs you that cost studies have determined variable costs are $11 per case, while total annual fixed costs are $1 million. An outside compact production company has contacted the company president and supplied the following price quotations:

Cases	Price per Case
250,000	$18
500,000	16
750,000	13

Top management has reviewed the reliability of the outside supplier and is confident that a compact identical in quality to that of the Compact Division can be supplied.

In addition to the compact costs, the Powder Division has the following costs. The sales price for the finished product reflects the price-demand relationship.

Cases	Powder Cost per Case	Sales Price per Case
250,000	$19	$60
500,000	18	54
750,000	16	48

The current market value is presently used as the transfer price.

Required:

a. Determine the segment margin for each division and income for the overall company at a volume of 500,000 cases.
b. Determine the volume that would be most profitable for each division and the overall company.
c. Explain the conditions that should exist for a division to be established as a profit center.
d. Discuss if the Compact and Powder Divisions should be organized as profit centers.
e. Indicate two other transfer pricing methods that Gray could use, and show the prices at various volume levels.

P15–14 Cost Plus Markup Transfer Price and Variance Analysis (L.O. 3)

Warship Company has two decentralized divisions known simply as the Buying and Selling Divisions. The company treats each division as a profit center, even though products of the Selling Division are presently only sold internally. Management is considering a change in the transfer pricing method involving determining the price by adding a 15 percent markup to the standard cost per unit. Budgeted volume is 85,000 hours. Budgets for various outputs of the Selling Division are as follows:

	Budgeted			
Hours	80,000	85,000	90,000	95,000
Units	40,000	42,500	45,000	47,500
Direct material	$224,000	$238,000	$252,000	$266,000
Direct labor	448,000	476,000	504,000	532,000
Overhead:				
Indirect labor	150,000	152,100	153,600	154,800
Utilities	153,250	158,000	160,800	163,000
Supplies	16,000	17,000	18,000	19,000
Rent	110,100	110,100	110,100	110,100
	$1,101,350	$1,151,200	$1,198,500	$1,244,900

Required:

a. Calculate the transfer price per unit under the proposed plan using the high-low method to separate into fixed and variable costs.
b. Determine overhead variances using the four-variance method assuming actual variable overhead is $105,720 and fixed overhead is $332,000 at an output of 42,400 units and 86,000 hours. Indicate who should be held responsible for each of these variances.
c. With actual direct material of $230,000 and actual direct labor of $475,000, compute the Selling Division's income using the information given in Requirement *b*. Should the Selling Division's performance be evaluated on this income?

P15–15 Negotiating a Transfer Price (L.O. 1 and 2)

Formerly independently owned, Abbott and Bennett Companies merged to form AB, Inc., several years ago. Since each of the two companies had spent large sums of money in promotions recently, they each retained their own names, but insiders simply refer to them as Division A and Division B. Each division also maintained its own production and marketing staff and facilities. Division management is responsible for acquiring and financing current and plant divisional assets, revenue, and cost of operations. They evaluate division managers on return on investment generated. Corporate management has no restrictions regarding where each division must purchase parts and supplies as long as corporate profits are not adversely affected.

Division B recently received a contract for a product that uses a component Division A manufactures and sells to outsiders for $5. In submitting its bid, Division B used a cost figure of $2.70 for the component Division A produces. Division A would still incur variable marketing expenses on sales to Division B. Division B management had obtained an outside purchase price for the component of $5.10 but reasoned that it should only be charged $2.70 by Division A which represented total variable cost of the part to Division A. Before preparing the bid, Division B secured the following unit cost data for the component from Division A:

Standard variable production cost	$2.20
Standard variable marketing expenses	0.50
Standard fixed production cost	0.80
Selling price to outsiders	5.00

Division A's salespeople are actively securing new customers but do not believe the demand will be so great that they would lose any regular customers if Division A produced the component for Division B.

Since this transfer pricing issue has never arisen before in the company, there is no policy regarding the price. Division A and B management have been meeting trying to decide on a fair price while still protecting their own segments because whatever price is chosen will affect their performance evaluation.

Required:

a. Assume management believes that controversy between its divisions can lead to disharmony affecting long-range profits. It proposes to settle the transfer pricing issue by choosing a price. Explain why you do or do not advise such a procedure.

b. Assume Division A and B managers agree that they should be allowed to work out a satisfactory solution to this transfer pricing issue.
   (1) Would you advise such a procedure?
   (2) List three surrounding circumstances needed for a negotiated transfer pricing method to work satisfactorily.

c. Discuss the impact of the following proposed transfer prices and indicate if they should be accepted:
   (1) Standard variable production cost.
   (2) Standard variable production cost plus 10 percent of that cost.
   (3) Standard variable production plus variable marketing expenses.
   (4) Division A's sales price to outsiders.
   (5) Standard full production cost.

d. Assume the division managers cannot agree on a transfer price and Division B begins making arrangements to buy externally for $5.10. Explain why Division B should or should not be allowed to do this.

e. Determine the upper and lower limits within which a fair transfer price should fall in this situation.

P15–16 Interest of Company and Division in Transfer Pricing (L.O. 1 and 3)

As a distinct segment of the highly diversified Water Sports, Inc., the Boat Division produces small fishing and ski boats. Next year's income statement follows. The Boat Division manager is pleased that the budgeted income on this statement is higher than the current year because division performance is evaluated using segment net income before taxes.

BOAT DIVISION
Budgeted Income Statement for the Next Fiscal Year

		Total (000)
Sales (20,000 units)		$50,000
Production costs:		
Motors	$16,000	
Other direct materials	3,600	
Direct labor	4,000	
Variable overhead	2,400	
Fixed overhead	8,000	34,000
Gross margin		$16,000
Operating expenses:		
Variable marketing	$ 200	
Fixed marketing and administrative	4,000	4,200
Net income before taxes		$11,800

Currently, the Boat Division purchases the motors in its boats from an outside supplier for $800 per unit. The Boat Division manager has asked the manager of the Motor Division if they would be interested in supplying this motor component. Presently the Motor Division is producing and selling a motor component similar to that used by the Boat Division. The only difference in the motor components is that less detail work is required for the motor used by the Boat Division; this saving in labor time reduces the direct labor cost per unit to $10. No variable marketing costs would be incurred by the Motor Division in any sales to the Boat Division.

The Boat Division manager requires that all motors it uses be purchased from the same supplier so that quality control can be better maintained. The Boat Division manager has offered to pay $550 for each motor purchased.

The Motor Division expects to sell 35,000 units next year without considering the Boat Division proposal; however, it has the capacity to produce 50,000 units. The Motor Division's income statement for next year is as follows:

MOTOR DIVISION
Budgeted Income Statement for the Next Fiscal Year

		Total (000)
Sales		$35,000
Production costs:		
Direct materials	$8,750	
Direct labor	2,100	
Variable overhead	1,400	
Fixed overhead	2,800	15,050
Gross margin		$19,950
Operating expenses:		
Variable marketing	$ 350	
Fixed marketing and administrative	1,750	2,100
Net income before taxes		$17,850

Before joining Water Sports, Inc., the Boat Division manager spent five years in sales promotion of another product that used consumers' discretionary income in forecasting sales. Based on experience with this firm, the manager believes that more consumers would demand boats if the sales price were reduced. An initial marketing study shows that sales would increase 10 percent if the sales price were reduced to $2,100. Also, this price reduction would allow the division to reduce advertising to a level in which variable marketing unit cost was $4. Other costs would not be affected because the Boat Division has sufficient capacity to handle the increased volume.

Required:

a. Assume the Boat Division needs 20,000 motors. Should the Motor Division be willing to supply the units for $550 each? Support your conclusions with appropriate calculations.

b. (1) Assume the Boat Division is only willing to pay $450 for the motors. Use calculations to support whether you believe the Motor Division should be willing to supply 20,000 units internally.

(2) Assume the Boat Division needs 20,000 motors. Would it be to the company's overall best interest if the Motor Division supplied these at $450 each to the Boat Division? Use calculations to support your decision.

c. Show the calculations to support your advice concerning whether the Boat Division should revise its sales price to $2,100 as proposed. Account for the change in financial conditions resulting from any volume and/or price difference.

CASES

C15–17 Transfer Pricing Using Opportunity Cost (L.O. 3)

With the current emphasis on health awareness and physical fitness, the Chicago Division of Illinois, Inc., designed an incline bench with leg flexion for serious weight lifters. Illinois, Inc., is a highly diversified manufacturer of couches, padded chairs, and other furniture. Each division has been acquired by Illinois, Inc., within the last few years. Since they were already in existence, there has been no attempt to change the buying and selling patterns of each division. As a result, top management has made no attempt to encourage transfers between divisions.

However, with the design of the incline bench, the Chicago Division manager has contacted the Carbondale Division manager whose unit specializes in the production of padded office chairs in a streamlined, modern design. The incline bench will include extra-wide two-inch polyurethane foam-padded boards fairly similar in construction to some of the chair and bench cushions presently produced by Carbondale. These incline boards are expected to take the same amount of labor time as the contemporary chair cushions presently do. The Carbondale Division has been asked to submit a price for the padded boards needed for the incline benches; there would be no wood or metal strips on the incline boards, thus saving the labor of this assembly.

After studying the design for the incline bench, the Carbondale Division manager believes that the cushion presently used on its contemporary chair style could be modified. However, by producing the incline benches for Chicago, production will be cut on Carbondale's two present chair lines, contemporary and traditional. The proposed order from Chicago arrived at a time when Carbondale presently is enjoying excess demand for its two chair lines. In the past, the Carbondale plant tried working its labor force on an overtime basis but received so much bad public relations in the community for working its employees long hours and on Sunday that this is not feasible. The fabric for the incline bench boards is expected to cost about 15 percent more than the cushion material presently used on the contemporary chair style. Based on the cost studies conducted, Carbondale offers to supply the incline boards for full cost plus 20 percent markup, which is the regular sales price. Carbondale management recognizes that it will be able to switch some workers from assembling contemporary office chairs to producing more traditional style chairs.

This high transfer price surprised the Chicago Division management because they expected to pay only variable production cost under the philosophy that Carbondale's capacity cost would be incurred regardless of whether they accepted the incline bench job or not. Chicago Division managers have also heard that a transfer price based on variable production cost plus opportunity cost is an appropriate price for certain situations.

Rather than cause ill feelings, the Carbondale manager provides the following unit standard costs for its two chair lines along with its budgeted overhead costs.

	Contemporary Chairs	Traditional Chairs
Direct material:		
Wood and metal strips	$40.00	$ 50.00
Fabric	13.00	14.00
Direct labor:		
Wood assembly (0.8 × $8/DLH) . .	6.40	10.40 (1.3 × $8/DLH)
Cushion assembly (0.4 × $8/DLH)	3.20	5.60 (0.7 × $8/DLH)
Production overhead		
(1.2 DLH × $15/DLH)	18.00	30.00 (2 DLH × $15/DLH)
Total standard cost	$80.60	$110.00
Regular sales price (20% markup) . .	$96.72	$132.00

Carbondale Division—Production Overhead Budget

Utilities:	
Variable	$ 480,000
Fixed	300,000
Indirect labor—variable	310,000
Plant supervision—fixed	500,000
Repairs—variable	80,000
Property insurance and taxes—fixed	100,000
Depreciation on plant facilities—fixed	700,000
Direct and indirect labor benefits—variable	330,000
Plant supervision benefits–fixed	200,000
Total overhead	$3,000,000
Overhead rate per DLH	$ 15

Required:

a. Evaluate the several transfer pricing policies mentioned by division management of Illinois, Inc., including full cost plus a markup, variable production cost, and variable production cost plus opportunity cost. Which would be a better underlying concept for this company to use for the transfer price of the bench boards?

b. Calculate a transfer price per unit for the bench boards on the basis of variable production cost plus opportunity cost.

c. Assume that instead of contemporary chair workers making the incline bench cushions, the traditional chair cushions could be modified:

(1) Use cost analysis to explain whether it would be more profitable for contemporary chair workers or traditional chair workers to make the incline bench cushions.

(2) Determine which additional factors are needed before deciding whether contemporary chair workers or traditional chair workers should make the incline bench cushions.

C15–18 Transfer Pricing for Auto Dealers (L.O. 5)

The New York Automobile Dealership serves as a leader in its field because it has undertaken innovative techniques that have received the recognition of its peers. Sales are expected to exceed 1,500 units or $10 million next year.

The dealership maintains separate Parts and Service Departments in addition to the Sales Department. The Sales Department is treated as a customer of both Service and Parts Departments.

Management of New York Automobile Dealership is basically uninformed about the merits of transfer pricing theory. Transfer prices are arbitrarily set to ensure profitability of all company segments. The dealer-owner set the following prices in conjunction with the service manager and parts manager. The implied intention is to give both the Service and Parts Departments a share of the Sales Department's profit. The following prices are not retail or wholesale prices; they simply are arbitrary transfer prices. This is the practice that the dealer-owner has found commonly used by the company's competitors also.

All the items purchased by Sales from Parts and Services are products the Sales Department can readily obtain as there is an excess in the market of these products.

Products, Services	Invoice Price to Parts Department	Cost to Service Department	Hours to Install*	Cost to Sales Department
Vinyl seatcovers	$150	NA	1	$200.00
Material for paint protection . .	$ 10	$ 10	1.3	86.40
AM-FM stereo cassette	$200	$210	1.2	302.40
Air conditioning	$400	$450	5.0	800.00

*The cost to install per hour averages $20.

The sales manager believed that he was being charged excessive prices for these four products and services and began soliciting bids from outsiders. The sales manager was especially frustrated because all three department managers are paid a bonus on their departments' net income. After a short time, he found a subcontractor willing to supply comparable products at considerable savings. The outside price for seatcovers was $190; for stereo cassettes installed, $282.40; and for air conditioners, $660 installed.

This practice continued for three years; during this period the sales manager was excited about his increased bonuses, while the parts and service managers were upset over their departments' declining profits and idle capacity. The Sales Department sold and had installed 400 seat covers, 300 stereo cassettes, and 800 air conditioners. Of these, 150 seat covers, 100 stereo cassettes, and 200 air conditioners were purchased internally.

Finally, in the third year, the dealer-owner called in all three department managers to analyze and solve the problems that were developing. After agreeing that a problem did exist and that long-run survival of the company should be the chief concern, the three department managers and the dealer-owner reluctantly agreed on the following transfer prices:

Products and Services

Vinyl seatcovers	$170
Material for paint protection	40
AM-FM stereo cassette	220
Air conditioning	690

The dealer-owner, however, decided to call in a management accountant to analyze departmental costs and operations before any changes were implemented. The accountant was also asked to investigate the revised transfer prices that the four individuals agreed on and determine if further revisions were needed. The management accountant began her investigation by calling together the three managers in a conference to discuss the problem. All managers argued their respective points to support their position and practice. The sales manager was unwilling to pay more for a product than the outside competitors' prices. The sales manager further argued that he and his family had become accustomed to a higher standard of living because of the bonus and he did not believe it was fair for the company to ask him to take a cut in pay just because he had to assume some of the costs of the Parts and Service Departments' inefficiencies. The parts and service managers argued that they could not afford to sell their products and services to the Sales Department without earning a reasonable profit, and they also wanted to provide a higher standard of living for their families.

After several days of negotiation, the three department managers agreed to leave the responsibility for establishing the transfer prices with the management accountant. These three individuals recognized that an outsider would not be biased and would use cost accounting theory in arriving at a decision. Further, they all admitted that close interaction and harmony was essential for long-run survival and that one individual should not be allowed to benefit at the expense of the other two managers.

Required:

a. Use the present transfer prices and determine the markup on cost for each of the four products or services sold to the Sales Department.

b. Compute how much the Sales Department saved on air conditioners, cassette radios, and seat covers by purchasing externally.

c. Calculate how much the company as a whole lost by the Sales Department making the outside purchases.

d. Identify the person who should bear the blame for the amount the company as a whole lost from the Sales Department buying externally.

e. Calculate the opportunity cost of the four products and services being transferred between departments.

f. Determine if the transfer prices suggested by the four individuals within the company were fair and acceptable. Provide support for your answer.

g. Indicate what transfer prices you would suggest as the management accountant given responsibility for solving the problem.

C15–19 Interference by Top Management in Transfer Pricing (L.O. 1)

Ten years ago, Subbett Company, a mid-sized subsidiary of Paulett Corporation, began research on developing a chemical, similar in nature to CHEMX, for mixture in a commercial detergent. Within Paulett Corporation, CHEMX is presently being purchased by Stoney Company, another subsidiary. Stoney began purchasing CHEMX eight years ago from Outter Company.

While Stoney has been pleased with the quality of CHEMX, its relationships with Outter have been somewhat disagreeable at times. For instance, Stoney recognizes that even though it is not the only Outter buyer, its demand is significant in relation to Outter's capacity. Further, in making suggestions to Outter for product improvement, Stoney realizes that its competitors buying from Outter are also going to reap the benefit from these suggestions. However, of even more concern is the fear of monopolistic pricing practices as Stoney does not have a second source for CHEMX.

Five years ago Subbett was successful in developing a chemical substitute for CHEMX. Subbett required $40 million of capital equipment to enter the market. One of Subbett's objectives is to supply chemicals that support Paulett Corporation's worldwide consumer markets. However, Paulett has a policy of decentralized operations. Given these policies, only Subbett resources funded the project. Subbett knew that Stoney Company was free to select the chemical it thought best met its needs.

Upon entry of Subbett into the market, Outter Company immediately lowered its price of CHEMX to Stoney. Outter explained this move by stating that after several years of manufacturing, it has been able to maximize production efficiencies and could achieve lower costs. Subbett realized that it was at a cost disadvantage and might meet resistance if it tried to price on a full cost basis with an additional percent return on invested capital. Subbett also recognized that it must beat Outter's prices and minimize production costs. Otherwise, it would never be more than Stoney's second source of supply even though Subbett had the capacity to produce all the chemicals required by Stoney.

Subbett's president requested a meeting with Paulett's chief executive officer in hopes of getting the CEO to force Stoney to buy internally at full cost plus a return on invested capital. However, a letter received by both Stoney and Subbett's presidents from Paulett's CEO indicated that this matter should first be presented to the executive committee of the parent company. After meeting with the executive committee, there was no consensus as to the transfer price. Then the presidents of Stoney and Subbett brought the problem to the CEO.

In a short meeting, the CEO made it clear that this was the two subsidiary presidents' problem. Based on their extensive prior experience, if they could not work out a solution, new presidents could. Thus, the division presidents were sent back to their companies.

In reflecting on his action, the CEO questioned if he had done the right thing. In his earlier days as the new top manager, subordinates were constantly asking for his suggestions. Finally, when asked for a solution, he began asking subordinates, "What do you recommend?" Subordinates thus realized that they would be asked for suggestions and began thinking through their problems before approaching him. Oftentimes, subordinates found they could arrive at the solutions themselves and did not need the CEO's advice. However, the CEO found that because he keeps space between those he manages and himself, he is sometimes lonely; he misses workers dropping in and taking up his time just chatting. He questions whether he adopted the correct management style after all.

Required:

a. Explain the problem from each of the following points of view:
  (1) Subbett Company, the selling division.
  (2) Stoney Company, the buying division.
  (3) Paulett, the parent company.
b. Forecast the result if Subbett establishes a full cost plus markup price for its product.
c. Suggest a more appropriate price rather than a full cost plus markup price for the product.
d. Evaluate if Paulett's CEO took the correct stance from:
  (1) An accounting-financial (income statement) regard.
  (2) A behavioral view.
e. Discuss if there are good reasons for the cliche about it being lonely at the top.

C15–20 Conflict in Pricing Quotes (L.O. 5)

Robert Bingham, Inc., manufactures force pumps for water wells and fire engines. Force pumps resemble lift pumps, the simplest type of reciprocating pump used to pump water from wells. However, force pumps discharge water at high pressure instead of merely lifting the water out. Force pumps are generally run by mechanical power rather than by hand power.

Bingham has three divisions, each specializing in various components of the pump. Sales of these components are also made to outsiders. The Southern Division produces the piston and valve; the Northern Division, the pump handles that attach to the piston; and the Western Division, the cylinder and outside container.

Bingham, Inc., is highly decentralized, with each division being judged independently as a profit center. Management uses profit and return on investment to evaluate each division manager. Top management believes that in the past five years, while this decentralized policy has been in force, profits have improved. Each division manager is normally free to buy from whichever supplier he or she desires. For sales within the company, divisions are expected to meet the current market price.

Juan Weston, the Western Division manager, has completed the design of a special water well for leisure-home owners. Such wells are smaller than those for residential homes and less expensive. After requesting bids for 1,000 completed pistons and valves, the following bids per completed unit were received: Southern Division—$500; Outboard Company—$400; Exxel Company—$425. The Southern Division had received an agreement from the Northern Division to supply pump handles at the present market price of $112.50 per unit. The Northern Division presently is operating at full capacity and does not have excess inventory; however, the Northern Division has agreed to sell the needed handles to Southern by adding more workers to avoid losing any sales to outside customers. The differential cost of pump handles is $65.

Scarlett Smith, the division manager of the Southern Division, indicates that she cannot quote a unit price lower than $500 because she must cover full cost as well as give her division some profit for their efforts. She provides further support for her position by arguing that her salespeople have been told they must cover full costs in all price quotes. An analysis of the accounting records reveals that the differential cost of each completed piston and valve is $375. Of this amount, 30 percent represents the cost of the pump handles to Southern.

In the Exxel Company bid, there was an agreement to buy certain unassembled parts from both the Southern and Northern Divisions. The price agreed to with Southern for a portion of the valve is $50 for each part. Exxel agreed to purchase 1,000 handles from the Northern Division for $70 each. The unit differential cost of Southern's valve is $20, and it is $30 for Northern's handles.

Weston is quite annoyed that Southern's price quote is so much higher than the competitors' quotes. He calls the controller at corporate headquarters for advice. Weston indicates that unless told otherwise, he plans to accept the lowest bid.

The controller is concerned that Smith has submitted such a high bid in view of the recent slack in work experienced by her division. However, the controller also knows that intervention by top management must be carefully handled because a precedent may be established that could raise similar problems later.

Required:

You may find it useful to diagram the alternatives with the respective prices and differential costs.

a. Provide support indicating the most profitable action for:
   (1) The Western Division.
   (2) Bingham, Inc.
b. Decide if the controller should instruct Western to buy from Southern. If so, at what price?
c. Assume the controller intervenes in this situation. What will the effect be on:
   (1) The division profit measurement system?
   (2) Outside firms?
d. Determine if the controller should ask Northern to lower its bid of $112.50 to Southern. Why or why not?
e. Assume Southern had idle capacity for several months. How would your answer be affected?
f. Discuss the impact on the situation if division managers receive a bonus based on division profits.

C15–21 Internal Competition and Transfer Pricing (L.O. 3)

Determining a transfer price to charge the Production Department for packaging is a recurring problem at Bonner Paper Supplies. Bonner is a leading producer of paper products packaged in varying numbers of sheets. Some of the products require the insertion of holes for use in notebooks. The Packaging Department is required to perform this hole cutting.

Being firmly convinced of the advantages of a standard cost system, the company had established, through the Engineering Department, detailed standards for each of its manufacturing operations. Management introduced a standard cost system and gave department heads authority as cost centers. Top management indicated each cost center constituted a separate business within the company. Department heads were also responsible for earning income for their own departments.

To pique the department managers' interest and stimulate internal competition, the company adopted an income sharing plan in which department managers receive a percent of their segments' net income. The Production Department could place orders with competing firms should the company's own Packaging Department fail to meet competitive costs. Due to the company's location, there are a number of local competitors which have facilities to do the required packaging.

Management believes that internal competition is healthy because department managers will be too certain of a market for their production if the company does not allow external purchases. This certainty is not conducive to effective cost control.

Management mandated internal procurement only when the company's product is superior or equal in quality and performance to the competition's, assuming an acceptable delivery schedule can be met. If the internal source of supply is not competitive, management stated that outside purchases may be made as long as the receiving department can justify its action. In justifying purchasing outside, the department should supply evidence that a reasonable effort was made to bring the internal supplier's terms into competition with those of the outside source.

The company is filling a special order. When the first roll of paper was produced, the company's own Packaging Department was requested to cut the paper to a customer's specification and insert the required holes. The sheets were then bundled 5,000 sheets to a package. The cost of packaging by the company's own department is $160, as shown here:

Packaging Department—Cost Estimates

	Standard Cost per Package
Packaging material	$ 20.00
Packaging labor (4 hours)	30.00
Overhead—40% fixed ($25 burden rate per direct labor-hour)	100.00
Income to packaging department	10.00
	$160.00

The supervisor of the Production Department felt that this cost was excessive and began contacting competitors for bids when the customer forwarded a second order for 100 packages. One competitor, Brown Paper Products, offered to package the paper and perform the necessary hole cutting and paper cutting at $130 per package, delivered. Given these conditions, the production manager has an incentive to have the packaging performed outside, resulting in what the manager believes will be a $30 savings.

Required:

a. Evaluate the desirability of an income sharing bonus to encourage internal competition.

b. Describe any advantages to keeping the work within the company.

c. Decide if the company's own Packaging Department should receive any departmental income.

d. Estimate the price the Packaging Department should quote for the packaging job.

e. Give the minimum amount the company's own Packaging Department should be paid.

f. Assume you were the supervisor of the Production Department. What action would you take?

After investigating the correct transfer pricing method to use, accountants determine the following:

The selling price per package, cut to customer's specifications with the required holes punched	$170
The selling price of the paper, not cut, but processed in rolls	$100
The cost of the paper processing:	
Material	$ 20
Labor	10
Overhead (40% fixed)	10
	$ 40

g. Explain why the Packaging Department supervisor would suggest that the paper be packaged by the company. What contribution to income does the manager see if the transfer price is based on variable cost.

h. Recommend what the company should do.

16

Decision Models and Cost Analysis under Uncertainty

CHAPTER OBJECTIVES

After studying this chapter, you should be able to:

1. Discuss the factors affecting decision making and the constraints placed on the decision maker.

2. Employ different costs in various decision models used in uncertain situations.

3. Illustrate the various applications of differential costs in decision making, such as making or buying, accepting or declining sales orders, and eliminating segments.

4. Understand the advantages of calculating the payoff and expected values of the alternatives being considered as opposed to a subjective evaluation of opportunity cost.

5. Explain the role of probabilities in optimizing correction and inspection costs in deciding which variances to investigate.

6. Discuss the relevance of replacement cost data to decision making.

Introduction

This chapter presents various decision models and cost analyses. When making decisions that affect the future, managers ask accountants to prepare special cost analyses. Because costs collected for inventory valuation often are inadequate for these analyses, accountants use different costs. Decision making requires costs such as opportunity costs and replacement costs that accountants do not enter in formal accounting records. When providing cost analyses to management, accountants use initiative, professional knowledge, and personal judgment in assessing which data are most beneficial. Although accountants would like to be able to prepare financial data that produces flawless predictions of events, they recognize the uncertainty and, in turn, errors in forecasts.

Framework for Decision Making (L.O. 1)

Decision making is the process of studying and evaluating two or more available alternatives leading to a final choice. This selection process is not automatic; rather, it is a conscious procedure. Intimately involved with planning for the future, decision making is directed toward a specific objective or goal.

The environment of a firm affects the decision-making process by defining and limiting the discretion of the decision maker. Company and departmental goals provide the framework for making decisions. Company policy may encourage or discourage changes to established procedures. Managers and employees may be reluctant to change their behavior patterns. For example, if the company has a tradition of operating flamboyantly, employees may resist cost control programs. The adequacy of cost accounting data as well as personal factors, such as ethical standards, family background, and stress, affect decision making.

Constraints on Decision Making

Decision makers face both environmental and resource constraints, including governmental tariffs and the economic climate. Trade associations, government agencies, and other external groups have regulations that influence decisions. For example, the existence of a strong labor union may restrict freedom in business planning. Decision makers are concerned not only about the welfare of subordinates, superiors, and others but also about their opinions. As managers strive to make decisions to meet the organization's objectives, they must have the necessary authority to make and implement their decisions.

The shorter the time planned for, the more accurate and detailed the analysis. Thus, a company should guard against planning for longer periods than is economically justifiable. Conversely, planning can be misleading when the planning period is too short. In addition, the more time devoted to planning, the better the plans. However, beyond a certain point, additional time devoted to a decision becomes too costly to be justified. As always, managers should balance the benefit of the data accumulated and analyzed against the cost of obtaining information. Managers must also consider the time necessary to implement the alternatives available. For example, in make-or-buy decisions discussed later in the chapter, management may have to reject manufacturing a machine or component parts simply because the company does not have time to design, test, and begin production while the market is favorable.

After considering relevant factors, a decision maker may choose a solution only to find that it is not economically feasible. Cost trade-offs occur in most decisions, and management may find that the first decision is too expensive. Similarly, technology may not be advanced enough to implement the decision. Even though technological changes may be rapid, at any given time, the available technology is relatively inflexible.

Relevant-Irrelevant Costs

Accountants should emphasize only relevant costs in reports prepared for managerial decisions. **Relevant costs** are those that are pertinent and bear on the decision to be made. All others become **irrelevant costs** and do not apply to that particular selection process. The ability to distinguish between costs that are critical to the decision and costs that have no significance is important in arriving at correct conclusions. Emphasizing the relevant costs avoids management's investment of time (also a scarce resource) in irrelevant details.

Out-of-pocket costs involve either an immediate or near-future cash outlay; they are usually relevant to decisions. Frequently, variable costs fall into this classification. For example, the direct materials needed to fill additional orders are both relevant and out-of-pocket costs while depreciation on the existing manufacturing facilities is not. Out-of-pocket costs are important in decision making because management should determine whether a proposed project would, at the minimum, return its initial cash outlay.

Sunk costs are historical expenditures for equipment or other productive resources having no economic relevance to the present decision-making process.

Managers decided in the past to incur these costs, and no present or future decision can change it. Thus, the costs are irrevocable in a given situation. Book value of plant assets are common examples of sunk costs. When exchanging an old asset for a new one, a company cannot change the old asset's undepreciated book value. The book value is irrelevant to the decision except in determining income tax liability. In deciding whether to continue or abandon operations, the book value of any equipment that will be discarded at no scrap value is ignored. If operations are continued, depreciation of the equipment is a production cost. However, the book value of the equipment is irrelevant in deciding to abandon operations.

Differential Cost Analysis (L.O. 3)

Differential costs are very useful in planning and decision making. **Differential costs,** or **incremental costs,** are the differences in the cost of two alternatives. Chapter 8 introduced differential costs as being useful when managers try to find the most profitable stage of production at which to sell a product. Differential cost analysis also involves such choices as accepting or rejecting orders, deciding to make or buy, and increasing or abandoning operations.

Differential and marginal costs are closely related because **marginal costs** refer to the change in total cost resulting from increasing the volume of activity by one unit per period. If fixed and semivariable costs do not increase due to the enlarged production, we measure marginal cost by the change in total variable cost.

Cost Behavior for Volume and Transaction Changes

Understanding cost behavior is helpful for many short-term decisions such as accepting or rejecting special orders or bidding on small jobs to cover differential costs. The cost-volume-profit relationship presented in Chapter 13 uses variable direct costs, such as material, and variable indirect or overhead costs, such as utilities, in short-term decisions. These short-term costs should reflect the physical demands on a company's scarce or capacity resources made by the product or project under consideration. Even though a differential cost is more likely to be variable or semivariable, differential costs include fixed costs when management anticipates a change in capacity or production scheduling. For example, assume present plant facilities can manufacture between 7,000 and 8,500 units without adding plant space or machinery. The differential cost of these two capacity levels is strictly variable costs, as shown in Exhibit 16–1. However, if the company increases production to 12,500 units, it requires additional factory space, equipment, and factory supervisors costing a total of $15,000. The variable costs of $29 per unit remains the same, yielding a total of $362,500 variable cost for manufacturing 12,500 units. The differential costs for the extra 4,000 units manufactured to yield a total production of 12,500 units is $131,000 [$116,000 variable costs ($29 variable costs × 4,000 units) + $15,000 additional fixed costs = $131,000].

As shown in Exhibit 16–1, the company can lower average unit cost from $41.14 ($288,000/7,000) to $39 ($331,500/8,500) by expanding production within the present facilities. The company reduces average unit costs by distributing the $85,000 total fixed cost over 1,500 more units. This results in a

EXHIBIT 16–1   Differential Cost Analysis

	Normal Capacity		
Volume	70%	85%	125%
Units of output	7,000	8,500	12,500
Variable costs: $29 per unit	$203,000	$246,500	$362,500
Fixed costs	85,000	85,000	100,000
	$288,000	$331,500	$462,500
Unit variable costs	$ 29.00	$ 29.00	$ 29.00
Unit fixed costs	$ 12.14	$ 10.00	$ 8.00
Average unit costs	$ 41.14	$ 39.00	$ 37.00
Total differential costs		$43,500	$131,000
Unit differential costs ($43,500/1,500 units = $29; $131,000/4,000 units = $32.75)		$29.00	$32.75

decrease in unit costs from $12.14 to $10. Fixed costs do not increase because the company uses the idle capacity to produce the additional 1,500 units. Despite the increase in total fixed costs when acquiring additional plant facilities to produce 12,500 units, average unit costs have decreased from $39 to $37 due to the $2 decrease in unit fixed costs.

Transaction Changes. Costs change with production volume in Exhibit 16–1. As discussed in Chapter 4, transactions, such as engineering work orders, machine setups, and purchase orders, also consume resources. A change in manufacturing volume is not the only activity that consumes overhead resources. Thus, differential cost analysis is also appropriate for analyzing cost changes based on managerial decisions using alternative transactions.

Accept-or-Decline Decisions

Exhibit 16–1 is useful for decision making and profit planning if a company faces an accept-or-decline decision. Managers should compare the differential costs of the additional 4,000 units with the revenue they expect to receive in deciding whether manufacturing additional units is profitable. For example, assume the company is producing 8,500 units when it receives an offer to sell 4,000 units at a unit sales price of $36. The average unit cost, as shown in Exhibit 16–1, indicates that this $36 sales price is below the $37 average unit full cost at the 125 percent capacity level.

Management may not take advantage of the sales offer if it relies on the unit average costs. Instead, managers should use differential costs in evaluating short-term projects when the objective is to make better use of existing facilities.

The company should compare the revenue received from this extra production with the differential cost as follows to determine whether the increased production is profitable:

Differential revenue (4,000 units × $36)	$144,000
Differential cost (4,000 × $32.75)	131,000
Differential income	$ 13,000

EXHIBIT 16–2   Net Differential Income Analysis

Differential revenue from 5,000-unit order			$130,000
The differential cost of the 5,000-unit order:			
Costs incurred to fill the order:			
Direct materials (5,000 units × $6)	$30,000		
Direct labor (5,000 units × $8)	40,000		
Variable factory overhead (5,000 units × $4) ...	20,000		
Tools	2,000		
Differential cost of 5,000-unit order		92,000	
Differential income from 5,000-unit order			$38,000
Less: Differential income from regular production:			
Regular production sales		$ 92,750	
Costs reduced for regular production:			
Direct material (⅓ × $68,000)	$22,667		
Direct labor (⅓ × $127,500)	42,500		
Variable factory overhead (⅓ × $51,000)	17,000	82,167	10,583
Net differential income—advantage of accepting			
5,000-unit order			$27,417

If it accepts the sales offer, the company receives a $13,000 contribution to the recovery of fixed costs and, after full recovery, to income. The company should accept the sales price even though it is lower than average unit costs. Companies should accept new short-term business as long as they recover differential costs—differential costs represent the minimum sales price under these conditions. If a factory has excess capacity everywhere, it can produce additional products for essentially raw material costs in an automated environment, with direct labor and factory overhead displaying a fixed cost pattern. Likewise, for an existing plant to assign overhead rates on activity-based cost drivers at the product design stage provides appropriate signals only if the overhead rates represent differential costs.

Reducing Regular Sales. For accept-or-reject decisions involving changes in present sales, companies must compare differential revenues to differential costs. Assume that when the company is operating at 85 percent capacity, it receives an order for 5,000 units that are slightly different from their regular products. Believing that this is a one-time order, management does not wish to expand plant facilities. After evaluating the requirements of the new order, management finds that it must temporarily cut regular production by one third. Under these conditions, the company must calculate its net change in income, or **net differential income.** Assume simply that each of the 5,000 units in the order requires $6 direct material, $8 direct labor, and $4 variable factory overhead. The company must purchase new tools costing $2,000 to make the 5,000 units. These tools will have no use after the order is completed. Exhibit 16–2 illustrates the analysis needed to determine whether they should accept the order. We assume that the company can sell one third of the regular production for $92,570 and that the sales price of the order is $130,000. As seen in Exhibit 16–2, the company will receive net differential income of $27,417 after comparing the $38,000 differential income from the 5,000-unit order with the $10,583 income from regular production that the company will not earn. The company can prepare an analysis similar to that in Exhibit 16–2 comparing the $92,000

EXHIBIT 16–3   Make-or-Buy Analysis

	Part X2	Part Y4
Outside purchase price	$9.50	$12.50
Relevant unit production cost	6.00	7.00
Potential cost savings per unit	$3.50	$ 5.50
Machine-hours per unit	÷ 7	÷ 5
Potential cost savings per machine-hour	$0.50	$ 1.10

differential cost of the 5,000-unit order with the $82,167 differential cost of one third regular production. Managers then compare this difference, called **net differential cost,** to the $37,250 difference in revenue to yield a $27,417 advantage of accepting the order. Before accepting the order, they should consider many qualitative factors, such as (1) the impact on future earnings of temporarily cutting regular production by one third, (2) the possibility of selling additional units beyond the 5,000-unit initial order, and (3) the reliability of the cost estimates associated with the order.

Make-or-Buy Decisions

Differential cost analysis is also appropriate for short-run make-or-buy decisions involving the construction of plant assets or component parts of the finished product on the company premises rather than acquiring them outside. As in accept-or-decline decisions, the company's objective is to profitably use the various levels of productive capacity available with the existing facilities. Differential cost analysis is especially valid if the company can use idle capacity and personnel to realize a cost saving.

For example, suppose a company has determined these standard costs for two component parts it uses in processing:

	Part X2	Part Y4
Variable materials, labor, and overhead	$ 6	$ 7
Fixed factory overhead	3	4
Total	$ 9	$11
Machine-hours per unit	7	5

The company has been producing the 10,000 units of X2 and the 9,000 of Y4 needed annually. However, a recent fire destroyed part of the building where manufacturing of the parts occurred. As a result, the company can devote only 87,000 hours of otherwise idle machine-hours to the production of these two parts. An outside company has offered to supply a comparable quality of parts at $9.50 for X2 and $12.50 for Y4. Management wants to schedule the 87,000 available machine-hours to maximize potential cost savings. Since machine hours is the constraint, management wishes to maximize this constraint. Exhibit 16–3 illustrates the allocation of machine time based on potential cost savings per machine-hour. Note that only variable production costs are relevant in this make-or-buy decision. The company should include any additional overhead incurred in the buying process, such as purchasing agents' salaries, as a differential cost.

Because the potential cost saving is greater for Y4, the company should give priority to using as much capacity as possible to produce Y4. After using the remaining capacity to manufacture Part X2, the company would make the following purchases from the outside supplier:

Available machine-hours	87,000
Part Y4 annual usage (9,000 × 5 hours)	45,000
Remaining machine-hours	42,000
Part X2 annual usage in units	10,000
Units to be manufactured: $\left(\dfrac{42,000 \text{ remaining machine-hours}}{7 \text{ machine-hours per unit}}\right)$	6,000
Part X2 units to be purchased from outside suppliers	4,000

It is difficult to make clear-cut rules for make-or-buy decisions because each individual circumstance warrants additional considerations. On-site construction may be necessary because the company cannot purchase the asset from an outside supplier due to required specifications or the allotted time period. The company may also base the decision to make the parts or plant assets on the desire to control their quality. In comparing the cost to make with the purchase price, management should use identical quantities and product quality levels, and consider quantity discounts. The price quoted by an outside supplier to make the products should be competitive. The first quoted price may be high, so bargaining may be necessary.

The make-or-buy decision is often complex, involving not only present costs but also projections of future costs resulting from such factors as capacity, trade secrets, technological innovation, product quality, seasonal sales, and production fluctuations. For example, many alternatives may be available in designing the product, including various types of material. Top management should, therefore, provide basic policies identifying the factors to be taken into account in make-or-buy decisions. They should also specify the division of responsibility among the management team. Make-or-buy decisions are not the exclusive problem of top management. In making these decisions, management must keep prevailing market forces in mind. The Purchasing Department and the Production and Industrial Engineering Departments often have more responsibility in such cost studies than does the Cost Accounting Department. Before undertaking make-or-buy cost studies, management should analyze the capacity available. It may not be feasible to operate the number of shifts required both for normal production and for manufacture of the asset in question.

The technical ability of the labor force making the product is an important factor in make-or-buy decisions. Managers should evaluate workers' ability against any special training or skills required. A company needs assurance that workers' knowledge is adequate to manufacture a product of the quality desired. Likewise, a company may need to acquire specialized plant facilities and equipment to manufacture the new asset. In addition, they may require new material sources.

It is difficult to find a comparative cost figure for making an asset rather than buying it from an outside supplier. Likewise, accountants encounter special cost measurement problems when companies contemplate buying a component part or service that they have been producing. While the experience of the past may prove helpful, historical cost data have serious limitations for planning and decision making because conditions may have changed. Companies should use the current and prospective level of costs, rather than historical costs, in the estimation process. By using the costs the company incurs by continuing to perform the work rather than employing an outside supplier, the management makes a more valid decision.

Escapable Costs

Costs that a company eliminates by discontinuing an activity are **escapable costs. Nonescapable costs** are costs that a company does not eliminate by discontinuing the activity. Instead, accountants reassign nonescapable costs to other segments. When management is considering dropping a product line or customer group, the only relevant costs are those that a company would avoid by dropping the product or customer. For example, if the company stops manufacturing component parts and purchases parts instead, the material costs for making the parts are an escapable cost. On the other hand, factory rent and insurance may remain unchanged. The remaining product lines must absorb these nonescapable costs, as shown in the following example. Suppose a company furnishes the following recent operating statement for its three product lines, A, B, and C:

	Product Lines			
	A	**B**	**C**	**Total**
Sales	$200,000	$180,000	$150,000	$530,000
Variable expenses	$140,000	$108,000	$120,000	$368,000
Fixed expenses:				
Salaries of product line supervisors	15,000	16,000	20,000	51,000
Marketing costs allocated to product lines on basis of sales	4,000	3,600	3,000	10,600
Administrative costs allocated equally	11,000	11,000	11,000	33,000
Total expenses	$170,000	$138,600	$154,000	$462,600
Operating income (loss)	$ 30,000	$ 41,400	$ (4,000)	$ 67,400

Management is considering discontinuing Product C operations and expects Product A sales to increase 10 percent. They expect Product B sales to increase 15 percent if this happens. They project no increase in fixed costs as a result of the increased sales of Product A. However, the salaries of Product B's product line supervisors would increase 10 percent due to the increased sales. Managers expect no increase in total assets required. The company can sell assets used in Product C operations at book value. They would lay off the Product C supervisor with no termination pay.

Exhibit 16–4 illustrates the projected operating statement assuming the company discontinues Product C operations. Notice that variable expenses for Products A and B remain the same percentage of sales, and Product C's variable expenses are escapable. However, fixed marketing and administrative expenses are nonescapable, and Products A and B must now cover Product C's share. As shown in Exhibit 16–4, net income increases slightly from $67,400 to $72,600 with no increase in total assets required. However, management should consider other factors such as the future sales of Product C and whether the increased sales of Products A and B will continue or would occur without eliminating Product C operations.

Management also considers escapable and nonescapable costs in make-or-buy decisions, as shown in Exhibit 16–5. Assume a company has the costs indicated in Exhibit 16–5 when it receives an offer from an outside company to supply the parts at $7 per unit. On first observation, this offer appears lower than the manufacturing cost of $9 per unit. However, accountants must determine which costs are relevant in the future. If the company can avoid all $3,000 direct fixed costs

EXHIBIT 16–4   Projected Income Statement if Product C Is Discontinued

	Product Lines		
	A	**B**	**Total**
Sales	$220,000	$207,000	$427,000
Variable costs and expenses	$154,000 (70%)	$124,200 (60%)	$278,200
Fixed expenses:			
Salaries of product line supervisors ..	15,000	17,600 (110%)	32,600
Marketing costs $\left(\dfrac{\$10,600}{\$427,000} = 2.4824\% \text{ of sales} \right)$	5,461	5,139	10,600
Administrative costs	16,500	16,500	33,000
Total expenses	$190,961	$163,439	$354,400
Operating income (loss) before taxes ...	$ 29,039	$ 43,561	$ 72,600

EXHIBIT 16–5   Make-or-Buy Decisions

	Per Unit	**Per 1,000 Units**
Full costs:		
Direct material, direct labor, variable overhead ...	$2	$2,000
Fixed overhead, direct	3	3,000
Fixed overhead, indirect but allocated	4	4,000
	$9	$9,000
Escapable costs:		
Direct material, direct labor, variable overhead ...	$2	
Fixed overhead, direct	3	
	$5	
Outside purchase price	$7 which is higher	

in the future by buying units, these costs are escapable costs and relevant. However, if the $4,000 indirect fixed cost continues regardless of the decision, it is a nonescapable cost and irrelevant.

Assume for the data given in Exhibit 16–5 that by buying the units, the company avoids $3,000 direct fixed overhead, but $4,000 indirect fixed overhead is nonescapable. Thus, the escapable costs total $2,000 + $3,000 = $5,000, or $5 per unit, which is lower than the outside price of $7 per unit. This indicates that the company should continue manufacturing the unit. Exhibit 16–3 illustrates a make-or-buy decision in which variable costs are the only relevant costs. However, as we see in Exhibit 16–5, fixed costs may also be relevant.

Dangers of Differential Cost Analysis

There is a danger in using short-term variable costs for many decisions about product pricing and order acceptance. Often short-term decisions involve the commitment of the company's capacity resources. Thus, managers should consider the long-term, not the short-term, variability of costs in such decisions.

Wise managers use variable and differential cost analysis cautiously because companies must cover all costs, both fixed and variable, in the long run before earning profits. Even though contribution margin and differential cost analysis are useful for accept-or-decline decisions, they are not valid for use in long-term planning and pricing.

Basing the accept-or-decline decision on the differential profit generated is defensive planning and pricing. The objective is to best use existing plant facilities given the circumstances. By using differential cost analysis, management accepts that if the company cannot obtain profits, a contribution to overhead is acceptable. However, this approach ignores long-run survival because no company can continue without covering all costs and earning a normal rate of return on capital.

Rather than merely accept any short-run project that generates a contribution to overhead, therefore, wise managers investigate the possibility of using idle capacity for more profitable alternatives. Even though the company experiences idle capacity, management should guard against placing no cost on these facilities. The accountant should help management search for profitable ways to eliminate idle existing facilities.

Another danger inherent in short-term pricing is that price reductions may be carried over to sales of repeat orders and into future periods. Differential cost analysis can lead to effective decision making only if managers apply it to non-repeat orders that will not compete with the regular sale of products at the normal sales price. To protect the future sales price of recurring orders, short-term pricing strategy is best limited to orders that are nonrepetitive or are subject to competitive bidding. An additional safeguard is to avoid such pricing techniques unless the orders are different in design or brand name from current product lines.

Robinson-Patman Amendment. As we discuss in Chapter 19, the Robinson-Patman Amendment may be a legal deterrent to accepting or rejecting orders based on differential profit analysis. According to this amendment, a company cannot quote different prices to different competing customers unless such price differentials represent cost savings passed on to the customer or unless the pricing strategy is used to meet competitors' price quotations. Generally, courts have not accepted costs established with the exclusion of fixed costs as a defense for price differentials. Thus, managers should consult legal counsel before engaging in a short-term pricing strategy.

Opportunity Cost Analysis (L.O. 4)

When a company is considering eliminating one activity and using plant facilities advantageously in another activity, opportunity costs are relevant. **Opportunity costs** are the profits lost by the diversion of an input factor from one use to another. Usually, formal accounting systems do not record opportunity costs, because such costs do not involve cash receipts or outlays. Accountants usually record only data concerning the alternative selected rather than alternatives rejected. However, these rejected alternatives do have significance in decision making. The merits of any particular course of action are relative merits because they involve the difference between this action and some alternative.

Even though most managers are continually weighing alternatives, they may not actually use opportunity cost to their advantage. Some managers may resort to rough, subjective evaluations of opportunity cost. These rough evaluations are risky because opportunity costs are significant for many decisions. For example, a single proprietor or partner has forgone the opportunity to earn a salary elsewhere by owning a company. In deciding to own a business, the proprietor weighs the salary that would have been earned if he or she worked elsewhere. Likewise, the opportunity cost of using a machine or laborer to manufacture a product is the sacrifice of the earnings from using that machine or laborer to make other products. In deciding which product to manufacture, the earnings received from other products should be a major influencing factor. Wholly owned company assets also involve opportunity costs, because the company could invest the funds used to purchase company assets elsewhere and earn a return.

Opportunity costs are called **alternative costs.** When a firm uses resources in the manufacture of a product, certain quantities of other products, which those resources aid in producing, must be forgone by society. This is true because the economy has limited supplies of economic resources in relation to human wants.

In Exhibit 16–5 illustrating escapable and nonescapable costs, the $5,000 escapable cost is lower than the outside offer to supply parts for $7,000. In addition, there is the opportunity cost of continuing to make the part; this is the earnings the company could have made if it had applied the capacity to some alternative use. Suppose forecasts show that another company wants to rent the plant capacity for $500. Because this opportunity cost becomes relevant to the decision, we should consider the following factors:

	Make	Buy
Cost of obtaining parts	$5,000	$7,000
Opportunity cost, rental income lost	500	
	$5,500	$7,000

Even with opportunity cost included, the company should continue to manufacture the parts.

Payoffs of Alternative Actions

The preceding examples illustrate that opportunity costs are important factors in decision making even though the statement of income does not include them. For example, when a company has a large sum of money to invest, management should identify the alternative actions and determine the respective payoffs of each. A payoff table displays the results expected for each alternative under consideration using possible states of the environment. The net benefit expressed in cash flow or income is the **payoff.** The first step in preparing a payoff table is to identify the alternative actions management will analyze. As seen in Exhibit 16–6, management has established payoffs for four alternatives considered feasible in view of the company's funds and objectives. Two of these alternatives involve the introduction of new products, while the other two involve strategy changes for Product A which the company presently manufactures. Exhibit 16–6 lists only four of many alternatives. For instance, the company could invest funds in stocks or bonds of other companies. Exhibit 16–6 omits other alternatives for simplification. Speed in gathering data is important, for management should not take so much time in analyzing alternatives that they delay action.

EXHIBIT 16–6   Payoffs of Alternative Actions

Alternative Actions	Payoffs under Various Environmental Conditions		
	Excellent	Average	Poor
Physical improvements to present Product A ..	$200,000	$ 80,000	$ −15,000
Advertising campaign for present Product A ...	100,000	75,000	−10,000
Manufacture new Product B	500,000	100,000	−100,000
Manufacture new Product C	300,000	200,000	−80,000

EXHIBIT 16–7   Opportunity Costs of Alternative Actions

Alternative Actions	Opportunity Costs under Various Environmental Conditions		
	Excellent	Average	Poor
Physical improvements to present Product A ..	$300,000	$120,000	$ 5,000
Advertising campaign for present Product A ...	400,000	125,000	—
Manufacture new Product B	—	100,000	90,000
Manufacture new Product C	200,000	—	70,000

The second step involves adding the environmental conditions influencing the payoff. The payoff table lists these environmental conditions across the top. Each cell on the payoff table contains a unique combination of an alternative action and an environmental condition. The third step involves estimating the payoff for each alternative and environmental condition since conditions prevailing in the future affect the income generated. Each cell indicates the estimated payoff for the alternative actions studied if the environmental condition at the head of the column prevails. For example, management forecasts that physical improvements to Product A would result in $200,000 in income in an excellent environment, $80,000 in income in an average environment, and a $15,000 loss if a poor market exists. Exhibit 16–6 indicates that manufacturing Product B is most profitable in an excellent market, while producing Product C is the most profitable alternative in an average market. However, the strategy of an advertising campaign for Product A involves less loss in a poor environment.

If managers base their decisions solely on the information in Exhibit 16–6, they assume one environmental condition to exist. An improvement to this analysis considers the likelihood of the various environmental conditions. A decision problem exists because the payoff table in Exhibit 16–6 does not contain a clearly dominant alternative.

Quantified Regrets Table

One way of choosing the most desirable alternative is to choose the alternative whose maximum opportunity cost is the minimum. The **quantified regrets table** in Exhibit 16–7 shows that the maximum opportunity cost for physical improvements to Product A is $300,000; $400,000 for an advertising campaign for Product A; $100,000 to manufacture Product B; and $200,000 to manufacture Product C. Of these maximum opportunity costs, the $100,000 associated with manufacturing Product B is lowest; this is why management should manufacture Product B. As with the payoff table in Exhibit 16–6, this analysis fails to consider the probabilities of the various environmental conditions.

Decision Making under Uncertainty (L.O. 5)

Management may know enough about the likelihood of each environment to attach probabilities of occurrence to each alternative. If so, management certainly wants to select the alternative that appears to produce the largest income, as long as that alternative does not expose the company to a high probability of a large loss. We can reduce the payoffs using each alternative to one figure. One way to do this is to weigh the possible payoffs according to the relative probabilities that the various conditions will occur.

Assigning Probabilities

Because decision makers normally deal with uncertainty, rather than certainty, they must estimate the probability of various outcomes. It is useful to assign probabilities that represent the likelihood of various events occurring. A **probability distribution** describes the chance or likelihood of each of the collectively exhaustive and mutually exclusive set of events. Decision makers have much information to guide the assignment of probabilities in some cases. Managers can base the probability distribution on past data if they believe that the same forces will continue to operate in the future. For instance, if certain machines have turned out 1 percent defective units for the last several operating periods, management could reasonably expect this same defective percentage to continue. In other cases, such as the introduction of a new product line or service, decision makers have little information on which to base the probability assignments. In these circumstances, they assign probabilities that they believe appropriate to the possible states of nature. The probabilities for the states of nature (market conditions) usually vary among the alternatives according to management's evaluation of market forecasts. The state of the economy also causes the probabilities to vary. When possible, the decision maker should use relevant and reliable evidence to improve the assignment of probabilities.

Assume the probabilities assigned are 30 percent each for an excellent or average environment and 40 percent for a poor environment. We find the resultant weighted payoff, called the **expected monetary value** (or simply *expected value*), by multiplying each possible payoff by its probability and adding the products, as shown in Exhibit 16–8. The higher the expected value, the more favorable the investment. The difference between the highest expected value and that of other alternatives represents an **opportunity gain** from investing in the most desirable alternative rather than the other alternatives. The expected values indicate manufacturing Product B maximizes profits. If managers chose this approach, $118,000 is lost from the manufacture of Product C; $78,000 from the physical improvements to Product A; and $48,500 from the advertising campaign.

Like all models, the expected monetary value criterion is logically oversimplified even though it is mathematically distinctive. Since the payoffs and the

EXHIBIT 16–8   Probability of the Payoffs of Alternative Actions

Alternatives	Excellent Environmental Conditions (Probability × Payoff)	Average Environmental Conditions (Probability × Payoff)	Poor Environmental Conditions (Probability × Payoff)	Expected Value
Physical improvements to Product A	.3 × $200,000 = $ 60,000	.3 × $ 80,000 = $24,000	.4 × −$ 15,000 = −$ 6,000	$ 78,000
Advertising campaign for Product A	.3 × $100,000 = $ 30,000	.3 × $ 75,000 = $22,500	.4 × −$ 10,000 = −$ 4,000	$ 48,500
Manufacture Product B	.3 × $500,000 = $150,000	.3 × $100,000 = $30,000	.4 × −$100,000 = −$40,000	$140,000
Manufacture Product C	.3 × $300,000 = $ 90,000	.3 × $200,000 = $60,000	.4 × −$ 80,000 = −$32,000	$118,000

probabilities of success for various strategies are forecasts, they can be inaccurate. The probabilities of success are subject to management's bias and preference for one alternative over another. In addition, the expected value criterion does not consider risk. The model omits other important considerations or assumptions. For example, the model excludes psychological factors, including aversion to risky alternatives, that may require an adjustment. The degree of risk that a company is willing to assume influences the alternative chosen. Management's preference for or aversion to risky alternatives may depend on how much they subjectively value dollar amounts in Exhibit 16–8. For example, if a $100,000 loss in manufacturing Product B would throw the company into bankruptcy or, less seriously, cut working capital considerably, management should be cautious and weigh the possible loss by a factor much larger than its relative probability. Under these circumstances, management may want to use a criterion other than expected value.

On the other hand, if the company needs income of at least $300,000 to satisfy a certain goal—such as paying off a pressing debt—the decision maker may consider the production of only Products B and C with the hope of operating in excellent environmental conditions. In this way, factors that affect the subjective worth of income or loss do influence the decision process.

Expected Value of Perfect Information

Even though the $140,000 expected value of manufacturing Product B is highest in Exhibit 16–8, management and/or owners may resist exposure to the percentages involved in making a decision under risk. The probabilities associated with which environmntal conditions will actually occur (for instance, a 30 percent probability of an excellent environment) are based on existing information. The company may hire a marketing consultant to obtain additional information on the environmental situation. The **expected value of perfect information** is the amount that the company is willing to pay for the marketing research team's errorless advice. If we assume the research team could indicate with certainty which condition would occur, a manager would decide with complete certainty. For example, if the research team tells management that an excellent environment will prevail, the company would manufacture Product B and obtain a $500,000 payoff.

Of course, "perfect" information isn't perfect in the sense of absolute predictions. Thus, we identify the probabilities of each event or environmental condition. Assume that these probabilities are 30 percent each for an excellent or average environment and 40 percent for a poor environment. This allows the computation of the expected value with perfect information using the highest payoff for each given environment. The expected value of the decision with perfect information is the sum of the optimum outcome for each event multiplied by its probability as follows:

$$(.3 \times \$500,000) + (.3 \times \$200,000) + (.4 \times -\$10,000) = \$206,000$$

We then compare the expected value with perfect information with the expected value with existing information to arrive at the following expected value of perfect information:

Expected value with perfect information	$206,000
Expected value with existing information	140,000
Expected value of perfect information	$ 66,000

In this example, $66,000 represents the upper limit that a decision maker would be willing to spend to reduce uncertainty. This amount is the maximum amount to spend for perfect information because in a real world, perfect forecasters are difficult to find.

Probabilities in Investigating Variances

Other types of decision making use probabilities. For example, Chapter 21 introduces the role of probability in determining the optimum level of safety stock. Managers can estimate the probability of running out of safety stock for various inventory levels and use this information to arrive at the expected stockout cost. As the units of safety stock and the resulting carrying cost increase, stockout cost decreases to a level at which total cost is at its lowest point.

Managers can use probabilities in deciding when to investigate variances from standards and budgets. As Chapter 12 emphasized, accountants use the management-by-exception principle and investigate both significant favorable and unfavorable variances. The size of the variance may be a crucial factor in assessing the probabilities of deciding whether to investigate.

Expected Value of Investigation

When we use the payoff table format introduced earlier with the two possible conditions or states—being in control or being out of control—we have two alternatives available, investigating or not investigating. Assume management believes there is a 20 percent probability of a process being out of control; thus, there is an 80 percent chance of that process being in control. Managers estimate a $4,000 cost of investigation and an additional $5,000 cost of correction if, in fact, the process is out of control. However, if the process is out of control but the company takes no action, managers assume $18,000 is the present value of the extra costs over the relevant planning period. This planning period may be the time until the company schedules a routine periodic inspection or the time until managers expect the process to go out of control again. This present value depends on expected future action.

As shown in Exhibit 16–9, the cost of investigation and correction is $9,000 ($4,000 inspection cost + $5,000 correction cost) if managers investigate the variance and find the process out of control. Thus, the company should not undertake the investigation because the expected value or costs are $1,400 more than not investigating the variances. Note that we assume all correction and inspection costs to be incremental to doing nothing with the process in control.

EXHIBIT 16–9   Probability of the Payoffs of Alternative Actions of Investigating Variances

Alternatives	In Control	Out of Control	Expected Cost
Investigate variances	.8 × $4,000	.2 × $ 9,000	$5,000
Do not investigate variances	–0–	.2 × $18,000	3,600

EXHIBIT 16–10   Effect of Probabilities Assigned to Investigation

Alternatives	In Control	Out of Control	Expected Cost
Investigate variances	.6 × $4,000	.4 × $ 9,000	$6,000
Do not investigate variances	–0–	.4 × $18,000	7,200

Changing Probabilities. When the probability of the process being out of control is higher, the expected costs and benefits are affected, resulting in possibly a different optimal action. Assume, for instance, that the probability of being out of control is 40 percent; as shown in Exhibit 16–10, this results in the expected cost of investigation being less.

Point of Indifference. As shown in Exhibits 16–9 and 16–10, the optimal action depends on the probability of an out-of-control occurrence and the costs and benefits related to each alternative. Using the following formula, a **point of indifference** can be determined at which the expected cost of each alternative is the same.

Let:

p = Level of probability where alternatives are the same
I = Inspection cost
C = Correction cost
E = Extra cost of later actions

$$I(1 - p) + (I + C)p = Ep$$
$$I - Ip + Ip + Cp = Ep$$
$$I + Cp = Ep$$
$$I = Ep - Cp$$
$$p = \frac{I}{E - C}$$

Using the cost data from Exhibits 16–9 and 16–10 and substituting I = $4,000, C = $5,000, and E = $18,000:

$$p = \frac{I}{E - C} = \frac{\$4,000}{\$18,000 - \$5,000} = .307$$

Thus, investigation is desirable only if the probability of being out of control exceeds 30 percent.

Replacement Cost Analysis (L.O. 6)

Replacement cost is another cost that, while not entered in the company's accounting records, is useful for decision making. **Replacement cost** is what would be paid if an asset were acquired at present price levels. By valuing assets at current replacement cost, the accountant determines the cost that is currently required to purchase assets with the same service potential as those now used. The replacement costs chosen may be based on prices in the current or anticipated future market. Decision makers should use the lowest replacement cost found in the market in which the company trades. An added advantage of using replacement cost is that it assumes survival is a basic need of the company, and the net income reported should be positive only if there has been provision made for the survival of the company as a going concern. In other words, the company must have the capacity to replace the productive services used, which are expressed in current replacement cost terms.

Replacement Cost of Plant and Equipment

Because replacement cost data are probably of greatest significance when making decisions about depreciable assets, accountants should restate the value of plant and equipment in current replacement cost at periodic intervals. This restatement reveals which assets are most expensive to replace and assists in capital investment and capacity planning. Accountants may mislead managers if they do not restate assets to replacement cost because asset turnover ratios based on historical costs are usually higher in the long run than those based on replacement costs.

Accountants must also compute replacement value for depreciation charges. Because this computation of depreciation reflects inflation, they should use a realistic useful life. This restatement is helpful for internal decisions despite the recognition that the purpose of depreciation is to record operating costs, not to provide funds.

Even though restating plant and equipment to replacement cost is useful for decision making, these assets are difficult to measure because of the distinction between the physical object and the services it renders. Namely, the market for the services the plant asset gives is in the future while the market for the physical asset itself is in the present. Another problem with restatement is that current technology may differ from what it was when acquiring the assets.

Usually, current technology assets require higher capital investment for each unit of productive capacity than do existing assets. However, a company may neither be able to nor want to replace its existing assets with current technology because of the cost and availability of capital, risks associated with higher fixed costs, and consideraton for the present labor force. Developing replacement cost data as if current technology has been adopted would be interpreted as an intention to make drastic reductions in the labor force. On the other hand, developing replacement cost data on existing assets would be interpreted as an intention to reproduce assets as they are now. Obviously, there is no easy solution to restating plant and equipment at replacement cost.

Replacement Cost of Land

The measurement and replacement cost of land, as opposed to plant and equipment, depends in part on what use the company makes of the land. Urban land, on the one hand, may not be subject to erosion, yet its value may increase or decrease due to the environment or other factors. For example, management expects the value of urban land in a deteriorated downtown section of a city to decrease in value. Conversely, land in the suburbs could increase in value as the city expands.

Restatement of Inventories

Management may find it helpful to restate assets other than plant, equipment, and land on a replacement cost basis for internal purposes. For example, regardless of the actual inventory valuation method used, a manufacturer should use replacement cost in estimating the cost of filling an order, even though the material may come from the stock on hand. Assume the cost of a manufacturer's material inventory is $20 using the LIFO valuation, but it costs $23 to replace the material. The relevant cost is the $23 replacement cost, not historical cost. Accountants should measure inventories at net realizable value on a replacement cost basis. They obtain this value by subtracting the costs of completion and disposal from the sales proceeds. Accountants measure by-product inventories on the same basis. The use of replacement cost as the basis for inventory valuation eliminates some assumptions, such as LIFO and FIFO, and does not consider the flow of actual goods.

Accountants should give serious thought to a substitute for historical cost-revenue realization. Even though replacement costs are not acceptable substitutes for historical costs in financial reporting, they may be more appropriate for certain decisions. A wise policy about the internal use of replacement costs is to examine each particular situation on its own merit.

Summary

Accounting records and financial statements do not provide all of the costs that decision makers need. This is true because accounting records normally show only costs that have or will require an outlay of cash or its equivalent at a future date. Some decision-making costs, such as opportunity costs, do not involve cash outlays. Costs prepared for financial statement purposes may thus be of limited use when management is choosing between alternative courses of action. To be effective, accountants tailor costs to fit the specific problem and consider only relevant costs.

Relevant costs are generally those that respond to managerial decision making, but they vary with individual projects and the length of the project planning period. Differential costs should form the base for defensive decision making, with the objective of better utilizing existing facilities to increase profits or reduce loss. A cost study prepared for a make-or-buy decision merely indicates the direction of a decision. Other factors such as trade secrets, seasonal sales, production fluctuations, and the quality and design of the product are considerations.

Certainly, most managers are continually weighing alternatives. Managers must make decisions not only when problems exist, but also when opportunities arise. In decision making, many managers try to incorporate a subjective evaluation of opportunity cost into the final decision. Many, however, fail to fully understand its significance and do not focus enough attention on the sacrifice of the profit that might have been made if an alternative decision were chosen.

The opportunity cost approach is primarily an economic concept that should be included only in internal cost analysis. Managers can apply opportunity cost when evaluating the relative economies of different methods of production, make-or-buy decisions, or proposals for investment of assets. As a rule, managers should not accept a potential investment unless the rate of return will at least equal what they can earn from other investment alternatives in the same risk category. Assembling the outcomes of each alternative on a payoff table directs attention to the profit lost from rejected alternatives.

Replacement costs and opportunity costs are highly subjective. For example, it is often difficult to determine a rate of return on an investment involving risk comparable to those of the alternatives in question. However, this risk is part of the decision-making process, because managers make decisions on the basis of possibilities, not facts. Determining the replacement cost of productive facilities also presents challenges in deciding whether to assume the replacement of existing facilities as they are or with new technology. Certainly, cost accountants face the challenge of fulfilling management's needs for varied cost studies designed for various problems that may arise.

Important Terms and Concepts

relevant costs, 559
irrelevant costs, 559
out-of-pocket costs, 559
sunk costs, 559
differential costs, 560
incremental costs, 560
marginal costs, 560
net differential income, 562
net differential costs, 563
escapable costs, 565
nonescapable costs, 565

opportunity costs, 567
alternative costs, 568
payoff, 568
quantified regrets table, 569
probability distribution, 570
expected monetary value, 570
opportunity gain, 570
expected value of perfect
   information, 571
point of indifference, 573
replacement costs, 574

Problem for Self-Study

Escapable-Nonescapable Costs

Norris Manufacturing Corporation furnished the following operating statement broken down by its product lines, A, B, and C:

| | Product Lines | | | |
	A	B	C	Total
Sales	$120,000	$300,000	$180,000	$600,000
Variable costs and expenses	$ 80,000	$180,000	$126,000	$386,000
Fixed expenses:				
Salaries of product line supervisors	30,000	20,000	18,000	68,000
Marketing expenses allocated to product				
lines on basis of sales	5,460	13,650	8,190	27,300
Administrative costs allocated 2:3:1	10,000	15,000	5,000	30,000
Total costs and expenses	$125,460	$228,650	$157,190	$511,300
Operating income (loss) before tax	$ (5,460)	$ 71,350	$ 22,810	$ 88,700

Required:

a. Assume that management discontinues Product A operations, and that this causes Product B sales to increase 10 percent and Product C sales to increase 20 percent. The only increase in fixed costs is an increase of 12 percent in Product C's product-line supervisors' salaries. Assets used in Product A operations can be sold at book value, and no other assets are required for continuing operations. Product A supervisors will be laid off with no termination pay. Prepare a projected operating statement based on this forecast.

b. Determine if, on the basis of the statement you have prepared, you would advise the elimination of Product A operations. Defend your answer.

Solution to Problem for Self-Study

a.

NORRIS MANUFACTURING COMPANY

	Product Lines		
	B	**C**	**Total**
Sales	$330,000	$216,000	$546,000
Variable costs and expenses	$198,000 (60%)	$151,200 (70%)	$349,200
Fixed expenses:			
Salaries of product line supervisors	20,000	20,160 (112%)	40,160
Marketing expenses			
$\dfrac{\$27,300}{\$546,000} = 5\%$ of sales	16,500	10,800	27,300
Administrative costs	22,500	7,500	30,000
Total costs and expenses	$257,000	$189,660	$446,660
Operating income (loss) before tax	$ 73,000	$ 26,340	$ 99,340

b. Income would be increased slightly from $88,700 to $99,340 with no increase in total assets required. The total impact on all product lines from eliminating Product A should be evaluated because Product A may serve as an inducement or have other direct influences on sales of other product lines. Product lines rarely operate independently because often there is an interrelationship between them.

Review Questions

1. Support your agreement or disagreement with the following statement: "If a plant has excess capacity everywhere, it can produce additional products for essentially raw material costs."

2. Why are sunk costs generally considered irrelevant for current decision-making purposes? Give an example of a sunk cost.

3. Does management have full discretion in making decisions? If not, why not?

4. Comment on this statement: "All accounting information is relevant for some purpose."

5. What are relevant costs, and why is the ability to determine relevant costs necessary in decision making?

6. Define out-of-pocket costs and indicate their significance in decision making.

7. Why are opportunity costs not incorporated in accounting records?

8. Generally, would you advise choosing an alternative if unit differential cost exceeded present average unit cost for a given choice? Why or why not?

9. Define the term *marginal costs.*

10. What is the importance of establishing payoff tables for all alternatives?

11. Indicate the type of decisions in which differential cost analysis may be helpful. When would net differential income be calculated and used in decision making?

12. If, to fill a sales order, a company purchases a machine or other asset that has no use beyond the order, how much of the asset cost should be included in determining the differential cost of the sales order?

AICPA/CMA/CIA Multiple Choice Questions

1. (AICPA) Gata Co. plans to discontinue a department with a $48,000 contribution to overhead, and allocated overhead of $96,000, of which $42,000 cannot be eliminated. What would be the effect of this discontinuance on Gata's pretax profit?

a. Increase of $48,000.
b. Decrease of $48,000.
c. Increase of $6,000.
d. Decrease of $6,000.

2.–3. (CMA) Use the following data to answer questions 2 and 3:

Atway Company has met all production requirements for the current month and has an opportunity to produce additional units of product with its excess capacity. Unit selling prices and unit costs for three models of one of its product lines are as follows:

	Plain Model	Regular Model	Super Model
Selling price	$60	$65	$80
Direct material	18	20	19
Direct labor	10	15	20
Variable overhead	8	12	16
Fixed overhead	16	5	15

Variable overhead is applied on the basis of direct labor-dollars while fixed overhead is applied on the basis of machine-hours. There is sufficient demand for the additional production of any model of the product line.

2. If Atway Company has excess machine capacity and can add more labor as needed (i.e., neither machine capacity nor labor is a constraint), the excess production capacity should be devoted to producing.

a. The plain model.
b. The regular model.
c. The super model.
d. An equal number of regular and super models.
e. An equal number of plain and regular models.

3. If Atway has excess machine capacity but a limited amount of labor time available, the excess production capacity should be devoted to producing

a. The plain model.
b. The regular model.
c. The super model.
d. An equal number of regular and super models.
e. An equal number of each model.

4. (CMA) Dixon Company manufactures Part 347 for use in one of its main products. Normal annual production for Part 347 is 100,000 units. The cost per 100-unit lot of the part is as follows:

Direct material	$260
Direct labor	100
Manufacturing overhead:	
Variable	120
Fixed	160
Total cost per 100 units	$640

Cext Company has offered to sell Dixon all 100,000 units it will need during the coming year for $600 per 100 units. If Dixon accepts the offer from Cext, the facilities used to manufacture Part 347 could be used in the production of Part 483. This change would save Dixon $90,000 in relevant costs. In addition, a $100,000 cost item included in the fixed overhead is specifically related to Part 347 and would be eliminated.

Should Dixon Company accept the offer from Cext Company?

a. No, Dixon should continue to make Part 347 because a savings of $20,000 can be realized.

    b. No, Dixon should continue to make Part 347 because a savings of $30,000 can be realized.

    c. Yes, Dixon should buy Part 347 because a savings of $150,000 can be realized.

    d. Yes, Dixon should buy Part 347 because a savings of $70,000 can be realized.

    e. Some response other than those given above is correct.

5.–7. (CIA) Use the following information to answer questions 5 through 7:

A company has had the following production experience over the last 10 quarters for product P1:

Quarterly Production	Frequency
1,000 units	2
1,500 "	3
2,000 "	4
2,500 "	1
	10

Additional information for P1:

Unit variable costs	$7
Quarterly unavoidable allocated fixed costs	$4,000

A unit of P1 can be purchased from an outside supplier for $8.75. If P1 is purchased, the plant facilities now used for its manufacture can be used to produce another product that will generate a quarterly contribution margin of $5,500.

    5. Assuming that P1 is to be produced internally, what is the expected quarterly production?

        a. 700.

        b. 1,000.

        c. 1,700.

        d. 2,000.

    6. Assume future sales can be predicted with complete accuracy. Up to what amount should the company be willing to pay for this information?

        a. The difference between the profit that would be expected to be lost if too few are produced and the additional carrying costs that would be expected if too many are produced.

        b. The sum of the profit that would be expected to be lost if too few are produced and the additional carrying costs that would be expected if too many are produced.

        c. The expected profit from the sales of P1 less the expected additional carrying costs if too many of P1 were manufactured.

        d. The difference between the expected profit with perfect information and the highest expected profit with existing information.

    7. Assume that 2,500 units of P1 will be sold next quarter. Should P1 be purchased next quarter from the outside supplier?

        a. Yes. Outside purchase would reduce total costs by $1,125.

        b. Yes. Outside purchase would reduce total costs by $5,125.

        c. No. Outside purchase would increase total costs by $4,375.

        d. No. Outside purchase would increase total costs by $9,875.

    8. (AICPA) Plainfield Company manufactures Part G for use in its production cycle. The costs per unit for 10,000 units of Part G are as follows:

Direct materials	$ 3
Direct labor	15
Variable overhead	6
Fixed overhead	8
	$32

Verona Company has offered to sell Plainfield 10,000 units of Part G for $30 per unit. If Plainfield accepts Verona's offer, the released facilities could be used to save $45,000 in relevant costs in the manufacture of Part H. In addition, $5 per unit of the fixed overhead applied to Part G would be totally eliminated. What alternative is more desirable and by what amount is it more desirable?

	Alternative	**Amount**
a.	Manufacture	$10,000
b.	Manufacture	$15,000
c.	Buy	$35,000
d.	Buy	$65,000

9. (AICPA) The following standard costs pertain to a component part manufactured by Bor Company:

Direct materials	$ 4
Direct labor	10
Factory overhead	40
Standard cost per unit	$54

Factory overhead is applied at $1 per standard machine-hour. Fixed capacity cost is 60 percent of applied factory overhead, and is not affected by any make-or-buy decision. It would cost $49 per unit to buy the part from an outside supplier. In the decision to make or buy, what is the total relevant unit manufacturing cost?

a. $54.
b. $38.
c. $30.
d. $ 5.

10. (AICPA) Mili Company plans to discontinue a division with a $20,000 contribution to overhead. Overhead allocated to the division is $50,000, of which $5,000 cannot be eliminated. The effect of this discontinuance on Mili's pretax income would be an increase of

a. $ 5,000.
b. $20,000.
c. $25,000.
d. $30,000.

Exercises

E16–1 Make-or-Buy Decision (L.O. 3)

The following standard cost is for a part Jones Company uses in processing:

	Part A
Direct material	$ 6.00
Direct labor	3.20
Factory overhead:	
Variable	1.25
Fixed	2.50
Total	$12.95

Jones makes 2,000 units each year. If it purchases Component Part X2 of the unit from an outside supplier, the company can reduce direct material cost by $3 per unit and direct labor cost by $1.20 per unit. The purchase price of the component part is $5 per unit. Placing the outside order will allow Jones to rent one of its buildings to a local firm for $10,000 per year.

Required:

Recommend if Jones should make or buy Component X2. Indicate the amount of advantage of your decision over the other alternative.

E16–2 Using Probability in Investigation (L.O. 5)

Novella Clevenger Inc.'s labor efficiency and price variances for a job containing 100 motors was $10,000 and $12,000 unfavorable, respectively. The standard labor cost for the job is $140,000. The owner asks you, as the newly employed cost analyst, whether investigation is necessary.

The owner indicates that the cost to investigate is expected to be $600 and the cost to correct if the process is out of control is $800. Management believes there is a 70 percent chance that the process is in control and that, if nothing is done and the process is *out of control,* the present value of the extra costs over the planning period is $5,000.

Required:

a. Decide whether to investigate the process based on supporting computations.
b. Give the level of probability at the point of indifference with regard to investigating the variances.

E16–3 Costs for Decision Making (L.O. 1)

Decision makers often need a new set of cost data that is not provided by financial accounting.

Required:

a. Discuss the following terms as they relate to decision making:
   (1) *Relevant cost*
   (2) *Sunk cost*
   (3) *Incremental cost or differential cost*
   (4) *Marginal cost*
   (5) *Escapable cost*
   (6) *Opportunity cost*
   (7) *Imputed cost*
   (8) *Out-of-pocket cost*
b. Suggest at least one type of decision in which the terms used in (2) through (8) would be appropriate.

E16–4 Determining Unit and Differential Cost for Various Capacity Levels (L.O. 3)

The variable costs of Gerr Company, including direct material and direct labor, amount to $20 per unit. The fixed costs of operating Gerr's present facilities—whose normal capacity is 60,000 units—amount to $640,000. Management is considering renting an additional building for $160,000 per period where workers can process 15,000 units per period above normal capacity. Other fixed costs associated with the rented building total $32,500.

Required:

a. Determine unit variable cost, unit fixed cost, average unit cost, total differential cost, and unit differential cost at these three capacity levels: 50,000 units, 60,000 units, and 75,000 units. (Compare with preceding lower volume.)
b. Advise management about the alternative to select and explain the factors involved in your decision.

E16–5 Relevant Costs for Make-or-Buy Decision (L.O. 3)

Carter Company has established the following standard cost for two component parts it uses in processing:

	Machine Part A	Machine Part B
Direct material	$3.00	$ 3.50
Direct labor	2.60	2.90
Factory overhead:		
Variable	1.80	1.50
Fixed	2.50	3.50
Total	$9.90	$11.40

The company has been producing the 5,000 units of A and the 8,000 units of B needed annually. However, a recent hurricane destroyed part of the building in which the parts were manufactured. As a result, only 34,000 hours of otherwise idle machine-hours can be devoted to the production of these two parts. An outside company has offered to supply comparable-quality units at $13 for A and $12 for B. Management wants to schedule the 34,000 available machine-hours so that the company realizes maximum potential cost savings. Each unit of A requires 5 machine-hours, while B requires 4½ machine-hours.

Required:

a. Determine which costs are relevant to the make-or-buy decision.
b. Determine the number of units of A and B to be produced to meet the company's needs, assuming the allocation of machine time is based on potential cost savings per machine-hour.

E16–6 Accepting Single Order (L.O. 3)

Schmidt Production Company signs a five-year lease on a building in which to manufacture large decorated flower pots. At the beginning of the lease, management purchases a machine costing $9,000 that mixes the clay and other ingredients. The machine has a life of 10 years and can be economically removed from the building. Salvage value is expected to be $1,000 at the end of 10 years. Double-declining-balance depreciation is used.

Schmidt also purchased a molding machine costing $37,500. Engineers estimate that the machine can mold 7,500 pots per year for eight years. The molding machine cannot be removed from the manufacturing facilities without incurring more expense than the machine is worth. The productive-output method of depreciation is used.

During the first year of operations, Schmidt produced 5,000 pots. Costs per flower pot exclusive of depreciation were as follows:

Direct material	$1.40
Direct labor	0.80
Variable factory overhead	0.15
Fixed factory overhead	0.24

Schmidt sold 4,800 pots for a total sales revenue of $24,000.

Required:

a. Calculate the total cost per flower pot for the first year of operations.
b. Assume that early in the second year of operations, a European buyer approaches the company wanting to buy a single order of 2,000 flower pots for a unit sales price of $3.85. The company estimates that it will cost $0.10 per flower pot to ship the order. The company believes that the annual domestic market for flower pots will become saturated above a 5,000-unit level. Management does not believe accepting this order will affect the domestic sales price, nor will the company face difficulty in securing the material and labor necessary to fill the foreign order. What would you advise management to do?

E16–7 Deciding When to Investigate Variances (L.O. 5)

As manager of Dufour, Inc., you receive a report indicating a $20,000 unfavorable labor efficiency variance for the past week's operations. You estimate the probability of the process being out of control at .40 and the cost to investigate at $1,000. If the process is out of control, the cost to correct the error is estimated to be $2,000 in addition to the $1,000 cost of investigating. Further, if you do not investigate and the process is out of control, the present value of future unfavorable variances that would be saved by making the necessary changes if the process is operating improperly is $7,600.

Required:

a. Use the expected cost of investigation and no investigation as the basis for your decision. Should the process be investigated?
b. Determine the level of probability that the process is out of control where the expected costs of each action would be the same.
c. Explain why the present value of the cost savings over the planning period ($7,600 in this case) is not equal to the unfavorable variance ($20,000 in this case).

Problems

P16–8 Differential Cost and Cash Flow Analysis in Make-or-Buy Decision (L.O. 2)

Jeffrey, Inc., a manufacturer of mopeds, is trying to decide whether to continue manufacturing its own engine units or to purchase them from an outside supplier. Bids have been taken, and a unit that meets all specifications can be purchased for $35 each. Jeffrey needs 12,000 units a year.

The Fabricating Department makes all of the engine parts. The unit is completed by direct labor in the Finishing Department and is then installed in the moped by the Assembly Department.

The Fabricating Department is used 25 percent for the production of the engine parts; however, phasing out this segment will reduce the labor, utilities, and supplies allocated to the engine units. Last year's records show the following information for the Fabricating Department for 12,000 units:

	Total Costs	Allocation to Engine Units
Direct materials	$1,200,000	$125,000
Direct labor	700,000	160,000
Indirect labor	90,000	30,000
Utilities	24,000	6,000
Depreciation	25,000	6,250
Property taxes and insurance	32,000	8,000
Miscellaneous supplies	18,000	2,000

The Finishing Department incurred $60,000 of direct labor costs on the engine units. The basis for overhead allocation in the Finishing Department is 25 percent of direct labor cost. If the engine units are not manufactured, the direct labor cost in the Finishing Department will be eliminated.

Machinery can be sold at its book value of $50,000 and the proceeds invested to yield 10 percent. The machinery has a remaining useful life of eight years with no estimated salvage value. Sale of the machinery will reduce property taxes and insurance by $2,000 a year. Purchasing the units will result in shipping costs of $2 a unit, and receiving, handling, and inspection costs of $6,000 annually.

Required:

a. Compare the total annual differential cost of engine units, if they are manufactured, to their annual cost if purchased. Ignore income taxes.
b. Assume that the annual cost of engine units if manufactured or purchased was $425,000 each, without regard to your answer in Requirement *a*. Compute the annual net cash outflow (ignoring income taxes) if:
   (1) Engine units are manufactured.
   (2) Engine units are purchased.

c. Explain the working capital requirements that should be considered in deciding whether to make or buy.

P16–9 Calculating Unit and Total Differential Costs (L.O. 3)

Case Manufacturing Company has established the following standard specification based on a normal capacity of 10,000 units:

	Standard Specification per Unit
Direct material (variable)	$ 3.50
Direct labor (variable)	2.60
Variable factory overhead	1.50
Fixed factory overhead	3.00
	$10.60

Management believes the present manufacturing facilities are adequate to produce a maximum of 11,000 units. If additional units are produced, additional plant space and equipment must be acquired at an annual cost of $6,000 and additional supervisors employed at a cost of $5,000.

If it produces in a volume larger than 10,000 units, the company will be able to take a 5 percent quantity discount on direct materials because of the increased purchases. Management has hesitated to produce more than 10,000 units in the present factory because the additional direct labor workers required would be eligible for a 5 percent night-shift differential pay. Management plans to employ only one day shift in the new factory producing 1,000 units.

Required:

a. Prepare flexible budgets for volume levels of 9,000, 10,000, 11,000, and 12,000 units.
b. Calculate average unit cost, broken down into unit variable and unit fixed costs. (Carry to three decimal places.)
c. Calculate total differential cost, comparing with the preceding lower volume.
d. Calculate unit differential cost.
e. Advise management about which alternative to choose.

P16–10 Payoff Table, Expected Value of Alternatives, and Perfect Information (L.O. 4)

Recently, Curbo Company has received a large sum of money from the estate of a former stockholder. Management is undecided about the most profitable means of investing this money. The Accounting Department has worked with the Engineering and Production Departments, and the Market Research Department is evaluating the alternatives available. After eliminating a few alternatives that would not fully meet company objectives, they believe the following actions are feasible:

1. Hire sales training personnel to upgrade the selling techniques of the marketing force. Management believes that income will increase $100,000 if an excellent market prevails and $90,000 in an average market, and there would be a $20,000 loss in a poor market.
2. Upgrade their present product by employing skilled engineers to improve the quality of the motors contained in the product. With these operations, a sales price increase will be warranted that is expected to result in a $200,000 income increase in an excellent market, a $125,000 income increase in an average market, and a $140,000 loss in a poor market.
3. Manufacture a complementary product that would also increase sales for the present product. Forecasts indicate a $160,000 increase in total income in an excellent market, a $120,000 total income increase in an average market, and a $50,000 loss in a poor market.

An assessment of the probabilities for each environmental condition is excellent, 40 percent; average, 15 percent; and poor, 45 percent.

Required:

a. Prepare a payoff table for each of the alternatives available.
b. Determine the opportunity cost of the alternatives available.
c. Determine the expected value of the alternative actions being considered.
d. Evaluate the alternatives, including the course of action you would advise the company to take.
e. Assume perfect advance information can be obtained. How much should the company be willing to pay for it?

P16–11 Differential and Opportunity Cost of Taking Additional Order (L.O. 3)

Jean Company builds regular and deluxe truck oil filters. A customer has asked whether the company could produce 2,000 super filters. Because management believes that this may be a one-time order, they do not wish to expand plant facilities. Instead, they have evaluated the requirements of the super filter and find that if they cut regular filter production by one fourth and deluxe filters by one third, the super filter order can be completed in one year.

The customer has agreed to pay $12 for each super filter at the end of the year when the entire order is completed. The engineering staff of Jean estimates that the direct material cost will be $5 per unit and the direct labor cost will be $3 per unit. In addition to using the machines presently located in the regular and deluxe facilities, super filter production will require a special machine costing $5,000. Management expects to be able to sell the machine after one year for $2,400. Cash will be required initially for the purchase. Jean management expects to sell an investment currently earning 10 percent interest to provide these funds. The special machine purchased for super filter production will require $515 annual power expense in addition to the power required for the regular and deluxe filter machines that will be devoted to super filter production.

Rent and other utilities, heating and lighting, are allocated on the basis of floor space. The accountant furnishes you with this portion of last year's financial statements:

	Regular	Deluxe
Sales	$8,000	$6,000
Direct material	$2,400	$1,500
Direct labor	1,600	900
Factory overhead:		
Indirect labor	300	150
Depreciation	500	450
Power	400	600
Rent	200	60
Other utilities	552	90
Total expenses	$5,952	$3,750
Operating income	$2,048	$2,250

Required:

a. Calculate the net differential cost of the order for 2,000 super filters.
b. Determine the opportunity cost of taking the order.
c. Compute the full cost of the super filter order.
d. Decide if Jean Company should accept the order. Support your decision with quantitative as well as qualitative findings.

P16–12 Evaluating Alternatives (L.O. 2)

The Freeman Company produces three different products, U–1, U–2, and U–3. All fixed costs are allocated as follows: fixed cost of units sold according to various allocation bases, such as square footage for factory rent and machine-hours for repairs; fixed general and administrative expenses based on a percentage of revenues.

These pro forma income statements by product line are for next year:

	U–1	U–2	U–3	Total
Sales (units)	20,000	400,000	200,000	620,000
Revenue	$1,000,000	$800,000	$650,000	$2,450,000
Variable cost of units sold . . .	$ 200,000	$250,000	$175,000	$ 625,000
Fixed cost of units sold	350,000	325,000	200,000	875,000
Gross margin	$ 450,000	$225,000	$275,000	$ 950,000
Variable general and administrative expenses . . .	175,000	200,000	52,500	427,500
Fixed general and administrative expenses . . .	120,000	96,000	78,000	294,000
Income (loss) before taxes . . .	$ 155,000	$ (71,000)	$144,500	$ 228,500

Because management is concerned about the loss for U–2, it has taken under advisement two alternative courses of action, either of which should remedy the situation.

First alternative—discontinue producing U–2. This will have several effects. Some of the machinery used in the production of U–2 can be sold at scrap value. The proceeds will just cover the removal costs. Without this machinery, however, fixed costs allocated to U–2 will be reduced by $55,000 a year. The remaining fixed costs allocated to U–2 include $130,000 annual rent expense. The space used for production of U–2 can be rented to another firm for $135,000 annually. The selling prices of U–1 and U–3 will remain constant. U–3 production and revenues should increase by 30 percent.

Second alternative—purchase some new machinery for the production of U–2. This will require an initial cash outlay of $500,000. The new machinery will reduce total variable costs (cost of units sold and general and administrative expenses) for U–2 to 50 percent of revenues. Total fixed costs allocated to U–2 will increase to $450,000. No additional fixed costs will be allocated to U–1 and U–3.

Required:

Analyze the effects of each alternative on total projected income before taxes.

P16–13 Unit and Total Differential Cost (L.O. 3)

The president of the King Company has asked you, the company's accountant, to advise him concerning several alternatives. King Company presently rents a building to house its processing plant. The landlord has indicated that he does not plan to raise rent from $1,000 per month. These facilities are presently being used with one work shift to manufacture 5,000 units monthly. The following sales price and unit cost have been determined based on a 5,000-unit normal capacity:

	Per unit
Sales price	$35.00
Direct material	$10.00
Direct labor	8.00
Variable factory overhead	5.00
Fixed factory overhead (including rent)	4.20
	$27.20

The president is considering the following alternatives and wants you to provide cost studies for each:

1. Renew the lease on the present building but increase to two work shifts. Management would produce 5,000 units on the day shift and 3,000 units on the night shift.

Night-shift workers would get a shift differential causing a $0.10 per unit cost increase for units produced on the night shift. Because a larger quantity of raw material would be purchased, the company can take an 8 percent quantity discount. However, to sell this larger volume, sales price must be lowered to $33. No additional machinery would be required.

2. A smaller building nearby is available for a monthly rent of $850. However, King Company must purchase additional machinery costing $960 that would be depreciated over four years with no salvage value. Other fixed factory overhead would amount to $17,000 monthly. Unit variable factory overhead would be $5.20. Two shifts would produce 4,000 units each. The night-shift differential presented in Alternative 1 would be used. The material quantity discount would also be available; a $33 sales price would be in effect.

Required:

Determine the following on a monthly basis for present conditions and for each of the two alternatives presented:

a. Income before taxes.
b. Average unit cost, broken down into variable and fixed components.
c. Total differential cost compared to present operations.
d. Unit differential cost compared to present operations.

P16–14 Accept-Reject Bid (L.O. 2)

Management of the May Company was quite upset when they received the following income statement for the first six months of the year:

MAY COMPANY
Income Statement
For the Six-Month Period Ended June 30, 19X1

Sales (15,000 units @ $70)		$1,050,000
Cost of sales:		
Material (15,000 units @ $25.10)	$376,500	
Labor (15,000 units @ $10.15)	152,250	
Factory overhead—variable (15,000 units @ $16)	240,000	
Factory overhead—fixed ($600,000 × ½)	300,000	
Marketing expense—fixed (at $12,000 per month)	72,000	1,140,750
Loss		$ (90,750)

The production cost for the company's single product, which normally sells for $70, is as follows:

Direct material	$25.10 per unit
Direct labor	10.15 per unit
Factory overhead—variable	16.00 per unit
Factory overhead—fixed ($600,000 for the year applied to production on the basis of 50,000 units of production for the year)	12.00 per unit
	$63.25 per unit

Management is not optimistic that sales for the last half of the year will improve; in fact, they expect sales to be significantly below the initial forecast of 50,000 units which the production plant can handle.

In July the president received a letter from a governmental agency inviting the company to bid on a contract for 10,000 units of Material 1R–15, which is similar to the product May now produces. The agency will entertain a bid not to exceed $53 per unit to be completed within six months. The letter assures the company that the submission of such a bid in no way obligates or binds the company in bidding for similar government contracts in the future.

In studying the requirements of Material 1R–15, the engineering department believes that $4,000 of outside designing and drafting time will be required. However, since the same type of material and labor will be needed as for the present product, no additional machinery need be purchased. Material 1R–15 is expected to take slightly less material than the present product; on the other hand, it will require a higher quality material, which will result in more spoilage than experienced on the present product. These factors will offset each other. No change in the amount of labor required for the present product is expected. Because of the existing idle capacity, management expects to complete the contract without overtime work.

Required:

a. Prepare an analysis management can use to decide if the bid should be entered.
b. Assuming sales stay at the same level for the remainder of the year, prepare statements of income for the entire year comparing the results if the government contract is not processed with those if it is processed.

P16–15 Eliminating a Product Line (L.O. 3)

Wallace Company furnished the following recent operating statement for its three product lines, A, B, and C:

	A	B	C	Total
Sales	$300,000	$260,000	$190,000	$750,000
Variable costs and expenses	$180,000	$160,000	$133,000	$473,000
Fixed expenses:				
Salaries of product line supervisors	25,000	80,000	20,000	125,000
Marketing costs allocated to product lines on basis of sales	9,000	8,000	3,000	20,000
Administrative costs allocated equally	20,000	20,000	20,000	60,000
Total costs and expenses	$234,000	$268,000	$176,000	$678,000
Operating income (loss)	$ 66,000	($ 8,000)	$ 14,000	$ 72,000

Management is considering discontinuing Product B operations and expects Product A sales to increase 20 percent, while Product C sales will increase 25 percent if this happens. No increase in fixed costs is projected as a result of the increased sales of Product A. However, the salaries of Product C's product line supervisors will increase 10 percent due to the increased sales. No increase in total assets required is expected. Assets used in Product B operations can be sold at book value. Product B supervisors will be laid off with no termination pay.

Required:

a. Prepare a projected operating statement based on the assumption that Product B operations are discontinued.
b. List other factors to consider before making the decision to eliminate Product B.

P16–16 Escapable-Nonescapable Costs (L.O. 3)

McLain Company maintains its home office in Chicago and leases a plant and office facilities in each of its three territories. All plants manufacture the company's single product, EGOO. There is some variation in the production process at each plant, however. Management supplied the following data concerning last year's operations. Home office expense is allocated on the basis of sales dollars. Company management cannot decide whether certain territory operations should be expanded or reduced.

	(000)		
	Southeastern Territory	**Northwestern Territory**	**Northeastern Territory**
Sales ($15 per unit)	$3,000	$4,500	$2,400
Variable costs:			
Material	$ 800	$ 900	$ 800
Labor	1,000	1,200	880
Factory overhead	500	600	1,040
Direct fixed costs:			
Factory overhead	100	200	70
Marketing	50	80	90
Administrative	75	100	87
Allocated home office expense	150	225	120
Total	$2,675	$3,305	$3,087
Income from operations	$ 325	$1,195	$ (687)

Because of the unprofitable operations in the Northeastern Territory, management is considering closing the plant facilities there. Two alternatives are available to continue serving the Northeastern Territory customers: One is to expand the Northwestern plant to absorb the units presently produced by the Northeastern facilities. The only increase in fixed costs from this alternative will be a 10 percent increase in factory overhead; there will be additional shipping and selling costs of $3 per unit on the increased production.

The other alternative is to enter into a contract with an outside producer that will pay McLain Company a commission of 10 percent of sales price. The outside company plans to reduce the sales price to $14 because its marketing research department believes that the lower price will enable the company to sell 25 percent more units. All Northeastern Territory fixed costs and allocated home office expense will be eliminated under this arrangement.

Required:

a. Prepare a schedule showing the company's total income if:
   (1) The Northwestern plant is expanded.
   (2) The company enters into the commission agreement.
b. Discuss other implications that management should study before acting on either of the alternatives.

P16–17 Make-or-Buy Decision (L.O. 1)

The Marketing Research Department of the Chester Company has developed a unique idea that will appeal to children. They are presently packaging their chewing gum in a simple paper wrapper in a stick form. They are considering processing the gum in individual balls and placing them in a decorated plastic bank. A child desiring a gum ball must deposit a nickel in the bank.

The company will be able to make the plastic banks in the present facilities by converting a machine to process the banks. The machine cost $100,000 and is being depreciated on a straight-line basis over a five-year period. The only other fixed costs to be allocated to the production of chewing gum and banks will be $10,000, which represents a portion of the company's present fixed costs.

The cost accounting department estimates the company can sell 100,000 banks if they are placed on the market before the Christmas season begins. Accountants developed estimates of the costs, including chewing gum and the banks, as follows:

Direct material	$1.25	per bank with gum inside
Direct labor	0.80	per bank with gum inside
Total overhead	0.90	per bank* with gum inside
	$2.95	per bank with gum inside

*The overhead does include the machine's depreciation and allocated fixed costs.

A plastic specialties company has approached the Chester Company and offered to supply the banks for $0.40 per unit. Based on their study, Chester feels that if it buys the banks and merely puts gum balls in them, the firm can cut its direct material cost by 6 percent, variable overhead by 15 percent, and direct labor by 25 percent.

Required:

a. Determine if Chester Company should purchase the plastic banks or manufacture them in the company's own facilities. Support your answer with cost data.

b. Assume that after the marketing department conducts more extensive tests, they believe that since they will be able to sell the banks through a variety of distribution channels, 150,000 banks can be sold. The company's present facilities will not be able to exceed the production of 100,000 banks. The company must rent a nearby empty building for $20,000 and equipment for $6,300 to handle the extra production. How would you advise management to obtain the plastic banks under these conditions?

c. List the qualitative factors you would advise the company to consider before making a decision.

P16–18 Capacity Issues; Acceptance of Order (L.O. 1)

Elizah Corporation manufactures only one product. Its budget for the following year is

ELIZAH CORPORATION
Budgeted Income Statement
For the Year Ended December 31, 19X1

Sales (270,000 units of LX7 @ $67 per unit)		$18,090,000
Variable costs and expenses:		
Direct material (LX material, 6 pounds per unit @ $1.25 per pound)	$2,025,000	
Direct labor (8 hours per unit @ $4.45 per hour)	9,612,000	
Manufacturing overhead (30% of direct labor cost)	2,883,600	
Marketing and administrative expense ($1.22 per unit) .	329,400	14,850,000
Contribution margin		$ 3,240,000
Fixed expenses		1,049,000
Income before tax		$ 2,191,000

Required:

Consider each part independent of the others.

a. Compute the income if actual sales in 19X1 are 10 percent below the budgeted figure.

b. Calculate the income if actual sales in 19X1 are 15 percent above the budgeted figure.

c. Assume that the existing capacity is sufficient to handle the transaction. What cost per unit would the company incur if it made additional sales beyond the budgeted figure?

d. Assume the beginning inventory of LX7 is 45,000 units; the company wants to have an ending inventory of 50,000 units. How many LX7 units must be produced this year according to the budget? Based on this production level, how many pounds of LX material must be acquired, assuming management wants to have 15,000 pounds in ending inventory and beginning inventory of LX material is 12,000 pounds?

e. Assume Elizah Corporation is operating at capacity when it sells 270,000 units of LX7. The company receives an additional order for 25,000 units of LX7 at a sales price of $59 per unit. If the firm accepts the order, it will incur an additional $91,000 of fixed expense. If the only criterion in this decision is the impact on income, should the order be accepted? Support your conclusion by showing the change in income.

P16–19 Cost Data in Closing Segment (L.O. 3)

Data for the Falton Company are as follows:

Expenses	Functions		
	Warehousing	Order Taking	Transportation
Salaries	$36,000	$78,000	$35,000
Telephone and telegraph	1,200	1,800	700
Packing supplies	5,600	–0–	800
Utilities	2,300	4,200	8,500
Taxes and insurance	6,000	750	11,000
Administrative	1,600	1,400	800
Gasoline and oil	–0–	–0–	7,000
Depreciation	5,000	1,500	6,000
	$57,700	$87,650	$69,800

Falton's accountants determined these annual costs for each of the functions. Management is considering closing its private warehouse and using a nearby public warehouse. The public warehouse will rent for $3,000 a month including utilities. It is estimated that this change will cause the following to occur:

1. Salaries of transportation will increase by $2,000. Two warehousing clerks will be retained and transferred to the plant office to record the transfers to the public warehouse. They each earn $5,000. All employees who are released will receive two weeks' salary; this termination pay will not be allocated to any other year.
2. Included in the telephone and telegraph costs are $700 for warehousing and $400 for transportation, which represent long-distance charges. The transfer to the public warehouse will cut this charge in half; the remainder of the expense represents the organization's basic service charge which has been allocated on the number of employees within each department. Warehousing has been employing 5 workers; order taking, 15 workers; and transportation, 3 workers.
3. Transportation and order taking packing supplies will not be affected by the move. Warehousing packing supplies will be cut to one fourth.
4. Each function has its own utility meter. In addition, the overall organization has a basic service charge of $24,000, which it allocates on the following ratios: manufacturing, 5; warehousing, 1; order taking, 2; and transportation, 4. It is forecasted that the transportation direct utility cost will increase $50.
5. Taxes and insurance will not be affected by the move; however, management will be able to sublease its warehouse for $1,000 per month.
6. The move will not cause a reduction in administrative staff. The amount allocated to each function is determined by top management on an arbitrary basis.
7. Due to the increase in miles required to transfer the inventory to the public warehouse, gasoline and oil expense will increase $600 per year.
8. An additional used truck costing $8,000 will be required which will increase transportation's annual depreciation by $1,000. The warehouse equipment can be sold for its book value of $50,000 at no gain or loss. Those funds in excess of the used truck purchase and termination pay can be invested in government bonds and earn 6 percent interest. The building is fully depreciated.

Required:

Prepare cost comparisons showing the net savings before tax or extra cost of transferring to the public warehouse.

Cases

C16–20 Cost of Alternatives (L.O. 1)

Top management of Walley Company is very interested in converting as many of the company's records to microfilm as possible. However, any additional cost or cost saving resulting from the adoption of microfilm must be identified before the project can be approved.

The general accounting supervisor has made a study revealing that the microfilm application will require two independent microfilming systems. The first is a source document microfilming system in which documents such as vendor invoices, billing documents, and other accounting-related documents will be reduced to $\frac{1}{24}$ of the original size and stored on rolls of film in the department using the documents.

The second is a computer output microfilm system in which computer-generated reports would be produced on 4 by 6 inch film, called microfiche, thus eliminating some of the bulky hard copy of the report.

The following equipment must be purchased for the microfilming systems; a life of six years is assumed. (The equipment can also be leased, but these data have not been obtained.)

	Purchase Price	Maintenance Contract per Year
Source document system:		
One camera	$ 3,438	$ 325
Two readers	2,350	230
One reader/printer	2,140	220
Total	$ 7,928	$ 775
Computer output system:		
Seven 75% viewers	$ 1,155	$ 100
Four 100% viewers	960	50
Two 60% viewers	230	24
One viewer/printer	925	70
Total	$ 3,270	$ 244
Total equipment	$11,198	$1,019

Investigation by the accounting supervisor revealed the following comparison of monthly costs.

Computer Subsystem	Reports	Present Cost	Computer Output Microfilm Proposed Cost Hard Copy	Computer Output Microfilm Proposed Cost Microfilm
Master files	9	$ 57.42	$ 0.20	$ 41.84
Sales	15	194.12	77.84	153.63
Inventory	8	27.00	4.31	235.56
Fixed assets	24	73.05	3.94	76.75
Accounts payable	6	42.72	3.87	63.20
General ledger	23	148.60	74.76	193.02
Billing	2	1,596.00	—	1,066.00
Total	87	$2,138.91	$164.92	$1,830.00

In addition, the supplies used in operating this system, including photocopies of the reports, cost $360 per year. The source document system film and processing will require 402 rolls of film for microfilm storage. The film cost per roll will be $8.37.

However, microfilming will result in the annual saving of 275 storage boxes that will not be needed; storage boxes cost $1.15 each. Each box requires 1.95 square feet; annual storage cost is estimated to be $3 per square foot.

Required:

a. Determine the difference in annual costs if the microfilming system is adopted.

b. Discuss other factors that should be considered.

c. List any additional analysis that top management may need to make a decision on the formal request for approval of the project.

d. Recommend a decision to management regarding this project.

C16–21 Differential Margin under Various Volumes in a Nonprofit Organization (L.O. 3)

Harry Moss, administrator of Las Vegas General Hospital, requests your assistance in preparing a cost analysis for a proposed addition to the telemetry unit. The hospital presently has 10 telemetry units in operation on a 40-bed floor. A telemetry unit monitors patients who have heart attacks or cardiac problems. This unit allows a patient to move about freely in that particular hospital wing without being confined to a hospital bed. A radio-controlled device attached to the patient monitors the cardiac system. The present 10-unit telemetry monitoring system is located in the nursing station that can accommodate the proposed 8 additional units without renovation.

Telemetry units represent a step down from cardiac intensive care rooms. Not only do telemetry units offer patients more freedom but there is also a considerable cost saving. Cardiac care rooms average $300 per day, while the telemetry unit charge is the regular room charge of $120 plus an additional $80 to $120 daily.

Expected revenue. Hospital management is undecided whether to charge a $40 or $60 differential a day for the proposed unit. Also, there is lack of consensus among the managers regarding the rate of utilization. The expected range is from 40 to 60 percent. A 10 percent allowance for bad debts and insurance discount is estimated.

Expected cost. Space for the unit will be obtained by converting a wing of the hospital presently being used for medical-surgical patients; the regular room rate is charged for this wing. Equipment total cost is expected to be $44,570; the life is estimated to be only five years due to technological changes. Straight-line depreciation will be used.

The administrator indicates that you are to determine total cost for the five-year period for each cost element and then divide by five years to obtain an average for the five-year period.

Service contract costs for routine maintenance and service call costs for overtime, labor, and parts are expected to be $3,060 and $2,400 respectively in Year 2, with an increase of 10 percent per year thereafter for inflation; no such costs are expected for Year 1 since the equipment will be under warranty during this time. Costs of supplies will be $2,800 for the first year, with a 12 percent annual increase thereafter due to inflation and aging of the equipment. One registered nurse earning $25,000 annually, and two licensed practical nurses, each earning $17,000 annually, are needed for the eight-bed unit. Personnel cost in the hospital industry has increased 8 percent annually in the last few years.

Required:

a. Determine differential margin that will be received and the annual percentage return on equipment using a:
   (1) $ 80 charge per day and a 40 percent use rate.
   (2) $ 80 charge per day and a 50 percent use rate.
   (3) $ 80 charge per day and a 60 percent use rate.
   (4) $120 charge per day and a 40 percent use rate.
   (5) $120 charge per day and a 60 percent use rate.

b. Advise management as to the alternative to choose.

c. List other factors that should be considered before installation of the unit.

Capital Budgeting

After studying this chapter, you should be able to:

1. Explain the present value concept and how it applies to capital expenditure analysis.
2. Apply discounted cash flow methods of evaluating capital assets.

3. Use payback and other alternatives to discounted cash flow methods.
4. Prepare aftertax analyses for equipment replacement using the total-cost and differential-cost approaches.

Introduction

Because capital expenditures involve significant resources that companies commit for a long time in the future, much time and effort should go into the evaluation of proposed capital investments. The length of time for which companies commit resources makes capital expenditures more risky than short-term investments. Capital expenditure analysis is also crucial because after making a commitment for a capital investment, management may have difficulty in recovering the cost other than through using the capital asset. Thus, high initial equipment costs hinder a company's ability to change products and processes to respond to shorter product life cycles and changing consumer demands.

Most companies do not have all the funds necessary to finance all proposed capital expenditure projects. Thus, they can put their available funds to different uses. As a result, before beginning a capital expenditure program involving a large outlay of funds that a company would tie up for several years, management should seek assurance that the company will receive an acceptable return on the investment. When managers evaluate projects on quantitative criteria, they compare predicted cash flows with the investment required. Management then determines whether the return generated by these projects exceeds the minimum acceptable return. Determining which rate is acceptable is a difficult problem involving more financial than accounting concepts. This chapter discusses the discounted cash flow methods and alternative methods for evaluating capital expenditures. The next chapter addresses the impact of automation on capital budgeting techniques, sensitivity analysis, and other related topics.

Top Management Involvement. Top management should evaluate large capital expenditure proposals because individual projects must be consistent with overall company objectives. However, top managers must delegate some authority to middle managers who have the required competence for properly evaluating capital expenditure proposals. Companies vary in decentralization of authority for capital expenditure approval. For example, some companies allow division managers much discretion in selecting the plant and equipment to use in operating their divisions. Other companies specify a small dollar amount as the limit for approval by division managers; only top management can approve capital expenditure proposals greater than this limit.

Managers should establish policies reflecting their objectives in advance so the firm's capital expenditure evaluation can be objective and consistent. Detailed capital expenditure guidelines are especially necessary at lower management levels. Policy manuals usually detail the procedures and document flow for administering capital expenditure proposals. Managers should design these manuals to encourage employees to search for profitable investments within their own technical specialties. Although a thorough review is important, management must guard against having such detailed, time-consuming procedures that employees hesitate to introduce new projects, thus impeding rapid project development. Employees are also more likely to search for capital improvements when they believe that their proposals will be given a fair review.

Sunk Cost in Replacement Decisions. Managers facing replacement of plant assets should consider only future cost savings and revenue changes. This type of analysis is difficult to prepare because managers must estimate the economic life of the new asset in addition to the prospective purchase price less any salvage value they expect. Book value—the original cost less the accumulated depreciation—on the equipment being replaced is a **sunk cost.** Because a company cannot change the cost by any future decision, sunk cost is irrelevant to the decision regarding the replacement of the equipment. However, book values do affect income tax liability related to plant asset transactions because of Internal Revenue Service regulations regarding the recognition of gains and losses on exchanges of plant assets.

Tax Impact on Capital Decisions (L.O. 1)

Income tax laws that apply to capital budgeting situations are often complex. Because the main objective of this book is not to explain current tax law, and tax provisions change frequently, we use only a few pertinent provisions in our illustrations. Even though the illustrations and problems represent an attempt to follow the current tax rulings regarding depreciation and other aspects of capital budgeting, the coverage does not necessarily reflect current tax treatment.

Income Tax Deduction for Depreciation

An allocated share of the purchase cost of capital assets is deductible as yearly depreciation. Sometimes the amount allowable for depreciation is equal to the purchase cost of the asset. In other cases, it is less than or more than the cost of the asset required. In those countries where companies have the option of claiming investment tax credits, they may reduce the amount allowable for depreciation below the cost of the asset acquired. An **investment tax credit** is a direct reduction of income taxes arising from acquiring depreciable assets. Governments use the investment tax credit option to stimulate capital investment in specific industries and in certain assets.

Tax authorities allow these three main methods of depreciation:

1. *Straight-line depreciation.* Each year companies claim an equal amount of depreciation.

2. *Accelerated depreciation.* Companies write off depreciable assets more quickly than by using straight-line depreciation.

3. *Allowable percentage write-offs.* Tax legislation specifies a table of percentages for depreciation. These tables usually allow companies to recover the cost of plant assets for tax purposes over a shorter period than the assets' physical lives. Capital projects are more attractive because this tax incentive makes projects' cash inflows larger in the early years.

Tax Shield

Although depreciation does not involve a cash outflow, it is deductible from taxable income. Thus, depreciation reduces the amount of cash outflow for income taxes. Because depreciation expense protects an equal amount of income from taxation, it creates a tax shield or tax savings. Multiplying the tax rate by the amount of depreciation gives the **tax shield** or savings. The formula is

$$\text{Depreciation deduction} \times \text{Tax rate} = \text{Tax shield}$$

To illustrate the impact of this tax shield, assume Sweeney Company is considering the purchase of a new machine costing $120,000. Managers expect the life of the machine to be eight years with no salvage value. They expect the machine to produce cash inflow of $95,000 and cash outflows of $60,000 per year. Assuming a straight-line depreciation deduction of $15,000 per year for tax purposes and a 40 percent tax rate, the amount of the tax shield is $6,000 (40 percent × $15,000 depreciation). Considering taxes and depreciation, Exhibit 17–1 gives the annual net cash inflow generated from the $120,000 machine investment.

If no tax shield resulted from the depreciation expense, the income tax would have been $14,000 ($35,000 × 40%), and the net aftertax cash inflow from the investment would have been $21,000 [$35,000 − $14,000 or $35,000 × (1 − 40%) = $21,000]. In the same way that additional income causes income taxes to increase, depreciation expense causes income taxes to decrease. The tax shield reduces income tax by $6,000 ($15,000 × 40%) and increases the investment's aftertax net cash inflow by $6,000. Thus, the following formula can also determine the aftertax net cash inflow from an investment:

EXHIBIT 17–1   Aftertax Net Cash Inflow

	Change in Net Income	Change in Cash Flow
Cash inflows generated	$95,000	$95,000
Cash outflows	60,000	60,000
Beforetax net cash inflow	$35,000	$35,000
Depreciation	15,000	
Beforetax net income	$20,000	
Tax at 40%	8,000	8,000
Aftertax net income	$12,000	
Aftertax net cash inflow		$27,000

$$\begin{array}{l} \text{Aftertax net} \\ \text{cash inflow} \end{array} = \left[\begin{array}{l} \text{Beforetax} \\ \text{net cash inflow} \end{array} \times (1 - \text{Tax rate}) \right] + \overset{\begin{array}{c} \text{Tax shield attributable} \\ \text{to depreciation} \end{array}}{\left[\begin{array}{l} \text{Depreciation} \\ \text{deduction} \end{array} \times \begin{array}{l} \text{Tax} \\ \text{rate} \end{array} \right]}$$

Present Value (L.O. 1)

After arriving at the aftertax net cash inflow, we must express these cash flows in dollars at the same time for a useful comparison. This requires discounting future dollars or bringing them back to the present using present value concepts. The value of money today is its **present value.** The present value concept is important because capital budgeting involves long-term projects. Most capital-budgeting decisions involve a comparison of cash flows in and out of the company.

The **time value of money** concept explains why a dollar today is preferred over receiving a dollar at some future date. For example, the present value of one dollar is $1, while the present value of $1 available at some time in the future is less than $1, assuming no deflation. This preference results because (1) there is risk that the company will never receive the future dollar, and (2) the company can invest the dollar on hand at present, resulting in an increase in total dollars possessed at that future date.

Present Value of a Dollar

In present value terms, the rights to future cash receipts are owned now. For example, assume a company expects a machine it is considering buying to generate $10,000 in cash receipts one year from now. The present value is less than $10,000 because the company will not have access to the receipts for one year.

We use a process called **discounting** to convert the cash inflows for each year to their present value by multiplying each year's cash inflow by the appropriate factor from a present value table. The appendix at the end of the book includes present value tables to facilitate applying the discounted cash flow methods. Table A gives the present value for a single amount to be received n years from now. By multiplying the appropriate present value factor from the table by an expected future cash flow, you can determine the present value of the cash flow.

Present Value of an Annuity

An **annuity** is a series of equal cash flows equally spaced in time. We use Table B in the appendix to find the present value of a stream of equal cash inflows received annually for any given numbers of years. Tables A and B are both based on the assumption that cash inflows are received only once annually on the last day of the year.

Present Value of Depreciation Tax Shield

Tax policymakers use the tax allowance for depreciation to stimulate long-term capital investments. The faster we depreciate an asset's cost for tax purposes, the sooner the tax reductions are realized. Thus, the greater the net present value of the tax shield.

Assume a company depreciates an asset having a $1 million depreciation tax basis over five years. Exhibit 17–2 computes the annual depreciation tax shield

EXHIBIT 17–2   Present Value of Depreciation Tax Shield
(35 percent tax rate, $1 million depreciation basis)

Year	(1) Depreciation Deduction on the Tax Return	(2) Tax Shield (35% × Depreciation Deduction)	(3) Present Value Factor	(4) (2) × (3) = Present Value
1	$ 350,000	$122,500	.909	$111,353
2	260,000	91,000	.826	75,166
3	170,000	59,500	.751	44,685
4	110,000	38,500	.683	26,296
5	110,000	38,500	.621	23,909
	$1,000,000	$350,000		$281,409

and the present value of the tax shield, using a 35 percent tax rate and a 10 percent discount rate. We assume no salvage value.

Depreciation deducted for tax purposes is shown in Column 1. The tax shield shown in Column 2 is the tax savings from deducting the depreciation that protects an equal amount of income from taxation. We determine the tax shield by multiplying the tax rate by the depreciation deduction. Column 3 indicates the present value factors using Table A, Present Value of $1, in the appendix. Column 4 shows the present value of each year's tax shield. Note that even though Years 4 and 5 reported the same $110,000 depreciation deduction, the present value of the expense deduction for Year 4 is $26,296. For Year 5, it is only $23,909, illustrating the present value concept.

When applying present value to a capital investment, the future return is in the form of cash inflows generated by the asset acquired. Because a company must make an outflow of cash in the present to purchase the asset, management questions whether the cash inflow generated by this asset warrants making the investment.

Evaluation Techniques for Capital Expenditures (L.O. 2)

Management uses several techniques for evaluating capital expenditure proposals. These range from simple methods such as cash payback to more sophisticated methods using the time value of money in computing an estimated return on investment. We discuss three capital budgeting quantitative methods and their advantages and weaknesses: (1) discounted cash flow, (2) payback or payout, and (3) unadjusted return on investment. Two variations of the discounted cash flow method are net present value (also called excess present value) and internal rate of return (often called time-adjusted rate of return). In evaluating proposals involving large sums of money, the use of more than one approach may be advantageous. However, when comparing several proposals, we should use the same evaluation techniques consistently for each project across all segments of the company. Because the detail and cost of applying each evaluation technique vary, the dollar amount of the prospective investment becomes the criteria in justifying the evaluation technique used.

EXHIBIT 17–3   Aftertax Cash Flow for Equipment A—Krebs Company

Year	(1) Pretax Increase in Cash Inflow	(2) Income Tax Deduction for Depreciation	(3) (1 – 2) Cash Inflow Subject to Tax	(4) Column 3 × Rate for Federal and State Income Tax*	(5) (1 – 4) Net Increase in Aftertax Cash Flow
1	$52,000	$32,000	$20,000	$ 6,000	$ 46,000
2	46,000	17,600	28,400	14,000	32,000
3	50,000	14,000	36,000	15,000	35,000
4	58,000	10,400	47,600	20,000	38,000
5	40,000	6,000	34,000	16,000	24,000
		$80,000			$175,000

*Percentage varies each year.

Net Cash Inflow

In capital budgeting, the net increase in aftertax cash flow (or simply net cash inflow) is the net cash benefit expected from a project in a period. The **net cash inflow** is the difference between the periodic cash inflows and the periodic cash outflows of a proposed project.

To illustrate the calculation of net cash inflow, assume the Krebs Company considers expanding its production facilities by purchasing a five-year asset costing $80,000. Exhibit 17–3 shows the cash flows associated with the proposal. We use these cash flows to illustrate the application of the four evaluation techniques discussed. (Note that this is a slightly different format for computing aftertax cash flow than presented earlier using data in Exhibit 17–1.)

For ease of computation, Exhibit 17–3 expresses the net increase in aftertax cash flow in even thousands of dollars. However, to reach these figures, we use a varying federal and state income tax rate. The pretax cash inflow is the difference between cash revenue and expenditures. For example, assume in Year 1 that the cash revenue generated from use of the capital asset is $92,000 while cash costs were $40,000, yielding a $52,000 pretax cash flow increase. The depreciation percentages are 40 percent, 22 percent, 17.5 percent, 13 percent, and 7.5 percent for Years 1 through 5, respectively. The effect of subtracting federal and state income tax from the pretax increase in cash flow is to add depreciation back in to measure the full amount of cash that flows into the business. One of the most difficult and important stages in the capital budgeting process involves defining and estimating cash flows.

Discounted Cash Flow Methods (L.O. 2)

The net present value method and the internal rate of return are variations of the **discounted cash flow method** that consider the time value of money. We represent cash inflows and outflows of a capital investment at a common point for better comparison. The discounted cash flow model's focus is on cash flows, rather than on net income. Because of this focus and of the weight given to the time value of money, the discounted cash flow model is generally the preferred model for long-range decisions.

Net Present Value Method

The **net present value method** is also called the *excess present value method.* Just as we arrive at a future value by adding interest earned to an investment made today, we can determine present value if we know the future value as well as the interest earned over the respective time period.

The present value method assumes some minimum desired rate of return, called the **required rate of return.** The required rate of return, also called the **hurdle rate, cost of capital, discount rate,** or **cutoff rate,** is the rate at which we discount cash inflows to the present. Chapter 18 discusses issues encountered in estimating this rate.

Managers consider a capital investment proposal acceptable if the present value of its future expected net cash inflows equals or exceeds the amount of the initial investment. When considering more than one investment, managers compare the net present value of each alternative with that of the others to choose the investment with the highest net present value.

Tables A and B indicate the higher the required rate of return, the lower the present value of the cash inflows. As a result, if managers use a higher required rate of return, fewer capital expenditure proposals have cash inflows that exceed the initial outflow of the investment cost. This means that a company may have to adjust its desired rate of return if it rejects too many proposals. Conversely, if the company finds that more proposals are acceptable than management believes are warranted, the firm should consider raising the rate of return.

The rate used is usually greater than the general level of interest rates at which banks and other institutions are lending money because there is greater risk with a capital investment than with a bank loan. We use this approach for investment proposals considered to involve average risk. For projects considered higher risks, we raise the required rate of return for this uncertainty. Also, the discount rate may be raised for future inflation.

After managers estimate a company's required rate of return (cost of capital) using the methods discussed in the next chapter, they apply the present value method. Exhibit 17–4 illustrates the net present value concept using the data from Exhibit 17–3 with a 12 percent estimated cost of capital. The starting point for capital expenditures is assumed to be time 0. Thus, we do not discount cash outlays at the beginning of the project. We enter these cash outlays at their full amount.

EXHIBIT 17–4   Net Present Value Method

Year	Aftertax Cash (Outflow) or Inflow	Present Value of $1 at 12%	Net Present Value of Flow
0	$(80,000)	1.000	$(80,000)
1	46,000	0.893	41,078
2	32,000	0.797	25,504
3	35,000	0.712	24,920
4	38,000	0.636	24,168
5	24,000	0.567	13,608
Net present value			$49,278

Since the project in Exhibit 17–4 has a positive net present value, the effective rate of return earned is greater than the 12 percent cost of capital used. When the annual cash flows vary as they do in this illustration, we must use Table A showing the present value of $1 for each period. However, if the cash flows are uniform, we use Table B, the present value of $1 received annually for N years. We multiply the cumulative factor by the cash flow of one period. For example, if the $175,000 annual net increase in aftertax cash flows in Exhibit 17–3 had been earned uniformly, giving a $35,000 annual cash flow ($175,000/5 years), we could make the following computation using a cumulative factor of 3.605 from Table B for the annual cash flow:

Present value of annual cash flows	$126,175 ($35,000 × 3.605)
Less initial investment	80,000
Net present value	$ 46,175

Weighted Net Present Value or Expected Value

Managers can make an allowance for risk and uncertainty by determining the present value of the net cash flows for each alternative investment according to various assumptions about future conditions. For example, managers should determine the present value of the net cash flows for normal conditions, for pessimistic conditions, and for optimistic conditions. Management determines the probability of each of these conditions occurring and then applies them to the net cash flows so they calculate the **weighted net present value,** or **expected value.** The net present value calculated in Exhibit 17–4 is rounded to $49,000. Managers assume this to represent the normal condition most likely to occur. Managers make similar computations to arrive at a $66,000 net present value for the optimistic conditions and $30,000 for the pessimistic conditions. Exhibit 17–5 shows the weighted net present value, or expected present value, for this investment.

In Exhibit 17–5, we determined the net present values given for the optimistic conditions and pessimistic conditions using the present value method; however, the calculations are not shown. Managers employ this method to estimate the most likely amount of future cash receipts.

Profitability Index

The net present value method does not provide a valid means by which to rank the projects in order of contribution to income or desirability when companies compare investment projects costing different amounts. However, we can relate a

EXHIBIT 17–5   Weighted Net Present Value

	Net Present Value	×	Probability Weights	=	Weighted Net Present Value
Normal conditions	$49,000		0.60		$29,400
Optimistic conditions	66,000		0.25		16,500
Pessimistic conditions	30,000		0.15		4,500
Weighted net present value or expected present value . .					$50,400

proposal's present value of cash inflows to initial outlay to obtain a profitability index. As the following formula shows, the **profitability index** method is simply a further refinement of the net present value method; this is why it is called the **present value index.**

Profitability Index =

$$\frac{\text{Present value of aftertax net cash benefits}}{\text{Initial outlay (or present value of cash outlays if future outlays are required)}}$$

Use of the formula allows managers to evaluate all possible proposals and rank them according to their desirability. Only those proposals with a profitability index greater than or equal to 1.00 are eligible for further consideration. Those with a profitability index of less than 1.00 would not yield the minimum rate of return because the present value of the expected cash inflows is less than the initial cash outlay. The higher the profitability index, the more profitable the project per dollar of investment.

The following formula illustrates the profitability index using the data for the equipment in Exhibit 17–4. Note that in calculating the profitability index we are not using the net present value of $49,278, which is the present value of cash inflows less initial outlays, as shown in Exhibit 17–4.

$$\text{For Equipment A: } \frac{\$129,278 \text{ present value of cash inflows}}{\$80,000 \text{ initial outlay}} = 1.62$$

Internal Rate of Return

A second variation of the discounted cash flow method is the **internal rate of return,** often called the **time-adjusted rate of return.** Similar to the present value method, the internal rate of return approach measures project profitability. However, it differs from the net present value method in that no discount rate is known in advance with this approach. We determine the computation in Exhibit 17–6 by trial and error before finding a discounted rate that yields a zero net present value. To obtain a starting point, we compute an approximate payback period by dividing the average annual cash flow into the plant asset cost. For example, $80,000/$35,000 average cash flow (determined by dividing $175,000 by five years) yields 2.286. Then we look for a factor of 2.286 on the horizontal row of an annuity for five years in Table B in the appendix. This asset

EXHIBIT 17–6   Internal Rate of Return

Year	Cash (Outflow) or Inflow	Present Value of $1 (35 Percent)	Net Present Value of Flow	Present Value of $1 (40 Percent)	Net Present Value of Flow
0	$(80,000)	1.000	$(80,000)	1.000	$(80,000)
1	46,000	0.741	34,086	0.714	32,844
2	32,000	0.549	17,568	0.510	16,320
3	35,000	0.406	14,210	0.364	12,740
4	38,000	0.301	11,438	0.260	9,880
5	24,000	0.223	5,352	0.186	4,464
			$2,654		$ (3,752)

is not yielding a 35 percent return so interpolation is necessary. If the factor had exactly matched the factor of one of the percent returns, the asset would have yielded that exact return.

The discounted rate is greater than 35 percent because a positive net present value results, but it is less than 40 percent because we determine a negative present value at this level. If we do not use the payback period clue to the starting point, the trial-and-error search should continue until we find adjacent rates in the table such that a positive net present value is achieved with the lower rate and a negative net present value with the higher rate. If using present value tables no more detailed than Tables A and B, we can obtain an approximation of the percentage by interpolation, as follows:

$$35\% + \left(5\% \times \frac{\$2,654}{\$6,406^*}\right) = 35\% + (5\% \times 0.414)$$
$$= 35\% + 2.07\% = \underline{37.07\%}$$
$$= \underline{37\%}$$

*$2,654 + $3,752.

Using the internal rate of return, management can choose the proposal with the highest rate of return. This return should be higher than the company's cost of capital. Using either present value or internal rate of return does not normally affect the indicated desirability of investment proposals. However, the rankings of mutually exclusive investments determined using the internal rate of return are often different from those determined using the net present value method. This can occur when the mutually exclusive proposals have unequal lives or when the size of the investment differs even though the lives are identical. The differences in these two variations of discounted cash flow result from the assumptions made regarding the reinvestment rate of return. With the internal rate of return, earnings are assumed to be reinvested at the same rate earned by the shorter-lived project. However, many people argue it is more reasonable to adopt the net present value method assumption that earnings are reinvested at the rate of discount, which is the company's minimum rate of return.

Exhibit 17–7 indicates the different rankings for mutually exclusive capital investment proposals obtained using the net present value and internal rate of return methods. With identical annual aftertax net cash inflows, but with varying investments and years of life, the rankings differ. (Because Exhibit 17–7 omits the computations, check your understanding of the methods by making the calculations using the present value tables.) There is a difference in results because

EXHIBIT 17–7   Comparison of Rankings for Mutually Exclusive Proposals

Capital Investment Proposal	Investment	Life (Years)	Annual Aftertax Net Cash Inflow	Net Present Value Method of Using 12 Percent Discount		Internal Rate of Return	
				Amount of Net Present Value	Rank	Rate of Return	Rank
A	$2,500	4	$1,000	$ 537	3	22%	1
B	5,000	12	1,000	1,194	2	17	2
C	6,000	18	1,000	1,250	1	15	3

the internal rate of return method assumes that Proposal A's amount at the end of the fourth year will be reinvested to earn a 22 percent rate of return. However, the net present value method assumes Proposal A's amount at the end of the fourth year will be reinvested to earn only a 12 percent return, which is presumed to be the minimum desired rate of return.

Thus, as long as the minimum desired rate of return is lower than the internal rate of return, projects with shorter lives will show a higher rank with the internal rate of return. A company that expects reinvestment at the minimum desired rate of return should use the net present value approach because it better reflects the opportunity rate of return.

Opinions differ concerning comparison of the profitability of projects with different lives or significantly different cash inflow patterns. The rate of return earned on the reinvestment of funds recovered by the project with the shorter life span is thus an important factor. One way to reflect different asset lives is to consider the shorter-lived investment's period only and include an estimate of the recoverable value of the longer-lived investment at the end of the shorter period. The analysis would cover only the shorter period, with the recoverable value of the longer-lived investment treated as a cash inflow at the end of the period.

Alternatives to Discounted Cash Flow Methods (L.O. 3)

Other capital expenditure evaluation techniques do not consider the time value of money. Such evaluation may satisfy an immediate pressing need because time or data do not permit a more sophisticated analysis. Although these techniques may be intuitively appealing because they are easy (present value concepts are not used) or quick to apply, they have many limitations. The time value of money is such an important concept to capital budgeting that accountants prefer discounted cash flow methods. Computer programs can ease the complexities of discounted cash flow methods. However, all methods share the weakness of assuming future cash flows are certain.

Payback or Payout Method

The **payback** or **payout method** is a simple approach measuring the length of time required to recover the initial outlay for a project. Despite this model's lack of sophistication, it represents an improvement over merely basing the decision on management's intuition. A company can appropriately use the payback method if managers must screen proposals rapidly and if decisions involve extremely risky proposals. The payback formula is

$$\text{Payback period} = \frac{\text{Investment (cash outflow)}}{\text{Annual aftertax cash inflow}}$$

If the net increase in aftertax cash flow in Exhibit 17–3 were an even $35,000 ($175,000/5 years) each year, we could divide the $80,000 purchase price of the asset by the cash flow to give the payback of 2.29 ($80,000/$35,000). However, because the annual net increase in cash flow in not uniform, a different calculation is required, as shown in Exhibit 17–8. We accumulate each year's net cash inflows until we recover the initial investment. With the net annual cash inflows as a given, we recover the amount of the investment in 2.06 years.

EXHIBIT 17–8   Traditional Payback for Equipment A

	Aftertax Cash Flow	Payback Years
Year 1	$46,000	1.00
Year 2	32,000	1.00
Year 3	2,000	0.06 $\left(\dfrac{\$2,000}{\$35,000}\right)$
Investment	$80,000	2.06 years

Payback Reciprocal. When the annual cash inflows are equal and the useful life of the project is at least twice the payback period, we may use the **payback reciprocal** to estimate the investment's rate of return. The payback reciprocal for Equipment A illustrated in Exhibit 17–8 is

$$\text{Payback reciprocal} = \frac{1}{\text{Payback time}} = \frac{1}{2.06} = .49 \text{ or } 49\%$$

Even though the payback reciprocal approximates the internal rate of return reasonably well, it is better to calculate the internal rate of return rather than depend on an approximation of it.

Companies often hesitate to apply methods more sophisticated than the payback method because many investment decisions are automatic if the company wishes to maintain operations. In these cases, management relies on professional judgment coupled with the payback method. In other cases, management may believe that the proposals are unacceptable when first presented and use the payback method to screen them. The payback method emphasizes liquidity, is easy to understand and apply, and gives a quick evaluation that offers some improvement over strictly intuitive judgment. Serious inherent weaknesses of the payback method are that it ignores the time value of money and the salvage value of the investment. Cash flows generated beyond the payback period are also given consideration. Also, the payback method does not measure profitability. Despite these disadvantages, companies use the payback method as an initial screening for capital expenditure proposals.

Bailout Payback Method. The **bailout payback method** is a variation of the payback method focusing on measuring the risk involved in a capital expenditure. The traditional payback approach attempts to answer the question: "How soon will I recover my investment if operations proceed as planned?" The bailout payback method instead asks: "If conditions go wrong, which alternative offers the best bailout protection?" For example, if the capital item is of a special type, and its disposal value is less than that of standard equipment, the bailout payback reflects these disposal values. Suppose we are comparing Equipment A under consideration in Exhibits 17–3 and 17–8 with Equipment B costing $60,000, which we expect to produce uniform annual cash savings of $15,000. We expect Equipment A's disposal value to be $20,000 at the end of Year 1 and to decline to $1,000 at the end of Year 2 due to the special nature of its technology. We expect Equipment B's disposal value to be $45,000 at the end of Year 1 and

EXHIBIT 17–9   Bailout Payback

	At End of Year	Cumulative Cash	Disposal Value	Cumulative Total
Equipment A	1	$46,000	$20,000	$ 66,000
	2	78,000	1,000	79,000
	3	113,000	–0–	113,000

Bailout payback is between Years 2 and 3, depending on assumptions made regarding cash flow.

Equipment B	1	$15,000	$45,000	$60,000

Bailout payback is at the end of Year 1.
Traditional payback of Equipment B: $60,000/$15,000 = 4 years

EXHIBIT 17–10   Present Value Payback

Year	Net Present Value of Cash Flow	Payback Years
1	$41,078	1.00
2	25,504	1.00
3	13,418	0.54 $\left(\dfrac{\$13,418}{\$24,920}\right)$
	$80,000	2.54 years

decline only $5,000 annually because of its general adaptability. Both are five-year property items. The bailout payback period is reached when the cumulative net increase in aftertax cash flow plus the disposal value equals the original cost. As seen in Exhibit 17–9, there is less risk with purchasing Equipment B because it reaches its bailout period at the end of Year 1. However, as Exhibit 17–9 shows, its traditional payback period is four years, which is longer than Equipment A's traditional payback period of 2.06 years. Exhibit 17–9 also indicates that different analyses of the payback method can yield different results.

Present Value Payback. With the **present value payback method,** management knows the minimum necessary life over which a project will recover its initial investment and still earn the desired rate of return. Exhibit 17–10 shows the present value payback years required using the net present value of the flow from Exhibit 17–4. Based on the calculations in Exhibit 17–10, 2.54 years are required to recover the $80,000 initial investment and earn the desired 12 percent rate of return on the annual unrecovered investment balance.

Unadjusted Return on Investment

The **unadjusted return on investment** is also called the book value rate of return, the **accounting rate of return**, the financial statement method, or the approximate rate of return. We use the following equation to determine the unadjusted return on investment:

$$\frac{\text{Average annual net aftertax income}}{\text{Initial investment}}$$

Using the data from Exhibit 17–3, we deduct depreciation of $80,000 from the $175,000 net increase in aftertax cash and divide the remainder by five years to

$$\frac{\$175,000 - \$80,000}{5 \text{ years}} = \$19,000$$

give a $19,000 average annual income after taxes. We then divide the average annual income by the $80,000 initial investment to give a 23.75 percent return as follows:

$$\frac{\$19,000 \text{ average annual net aftertax income}}{\$80,000 \text{ initial investment}} = 23.75 \text{ percent}$$

Instead of computing the return on initial investment, we can determine a return on average investment. Because this illustration does not use straight-line depreciation, the original book value and the book values at the end of each year must be averaged to determine average investment as follows:

Year	Book Value (End of Year)
1	$ 48,000
2	30,400
3	16,400
4	6,000
5	–0–
Original Investment	80,000
	$180,800

$180,800/6 = $30,133 average investment

Using these data, the return on average investment becomes:

$$\frac{\$19,000 \text{ average annual net aftertax income}}{\$30,133 \text{ average investment}} = 63 \text{ percent}$$

If, instead, we use straight-line depreciation, we divide the original investment by 2 to arrive at the average investment since this $80,000 asset had no salvage value. When an asset has a scrap value at the end of its economic life, we would add the scrap value to determine average investment, regardless of the depreciation method used. Scrap value represents the investment at the end of its economic life.

The unadjusted return on investment does improve on the weaknesses of the payback method by taking into account profitability. However, it fails to consider the time value of money and it does not emphasize cash flows. Also, the unadjusted rate of return compares savings to be received in the future to an investment that requires a current outlay of funds. Thus, we misstate the true return of projects. However, the unadjusted return on investment is familiar because it is based on the accrual method of preparing financial statements and is easy to apply. It facilitates follow-up of expenditures, since the data are available in the accounting records. It also ties in with performance evaluation. Despite its advantages, the unadjusted return on investment is not appropriate if a company makes additional capital expenditures after the project has started.

Aftertax Analysis of Equipment Replacement (L.O. 4)

Computing net cash flow is more complex for a replacement decision than for an acquisition decision because we are considering cash inflows and outflows for the asset being replaced and the new asset. Exhibits 17–11 and 17–12 provide a step-by-step analysis illustrating the expansion of net present value to include the total-cost and differential-cost approaches when considering income taxes. Note that we ignore the cash inflow from revenue generated from the cameras because we assume it to be the same whether the old cameras are replaced or not.

Assume Maddox Theater management is considering replacing its floor cameras with new cameras having a purchase price of $150,000. Annual operating costs for the old floor cameras total $62,000. However, Maddox will realize savings with the new cameras since total annual operating costs would decrease to $50,000. After five years' use, Maddox can sell the new cameras for $18,000, but we ignore this salvage value in computing annual depreciation charges. If Maddox makes the purchase, they cannot sell the old cameras for their book value of $60,000 because the expected present salvage value is only $25,000. If Maddox does not replace the old cameras, the theater can use them for five more years and then scrap them for $3,000 salvage. (For simplicity, assume we originally estimated no salvage value in calculating annual depreciation on the old cameras.) However, in two more years Maddox must make major repair expenses costing $36,000 on the old cameras. Maddox depreciates the new cameras for tax purposes as indicated; they use straight-line depreciation for the old cameras. The theater's tax rate is 45 percent, and its aftertax cost of capital is 12 percent.

In deciding whether to keep the old cameras or replace them, Maddox may use either the total-cost or differential-cost approach. If there are only two alternatives (i.e., keep or replace a capital asset), the differential-cost approach is appropriate. However, when a company is considering more than two alternatives, the total-cost approach is needed to reflect additional computations.

Exhibits 17–11 and 17–12 contain a complete solution for Maddox Theater. They show a sketch of the relevant cash flows by years, which may be helpful. For simplicity, we assume all cash outflows or inflows occur at the beginning or end of a year. Also, we separate cash operating costs from the income tax savings generated by depreciation deductions even though we could have combined them if preferred. The separation of these helps compare alternative depreciation effects and allows the use of annuity tables when either depreciation or cash operating costs are equal each year. We are assuming that any cash receipts or disbursements and their related tax effects occur in the same period. We can refine the analysis to reflect possible lags in tax payments and related pretax operating cash flows. Assume that gains and losses on capital asset disposal are taxed as ordinary gains and losses. However, note that rules on tax rates and other impacts on taxes vary considerably depending on the type of asset and period involved.

Total-Cost Approach

In deciding whether to replace the old cameras, the analysis in Exhibit 17–11 using the **total-cost approach** indicates a net present value advantage in keeping the old cameras. Notice that depreciation charges, which do not require a cash outflow, do provide a tax shield equal to the deduction multiplied by the 45 percent tax rate for Maddox Theater.

EXHIBIT 17–11   Capital Budgeting Using Total-Cost Approach

Items and Computations		Year(s) Having Cash Flows	Amount of Cash Flows	12% Factor	Present Value of Cash Flows	Now	1	2	3	4	5
Buy the new cameras:											
Initial investment		Now	$(150,000)	1.000	$(150,000)	◄—($150,000)					
Annual cash operating expenses. . .	$50,000										
Multiply by 1 − 45%	× 55%										
Aftertax expenses	$27,500	1–5	(27,500)	3.605	(99,138)		◄——($27,500)	($27,500)	($27,500)	($27,500)	($27,500)
Depreciation (see below)		1	27,000	0.893	24,111		◄—— 27,000				
		2	14,850	0.797	11,836			◄—— 14,850			
		3	10,125	0.712	7,209				◄—— 10,125		
		4	8,325	0.636	5,295					◄—— 8,325	
		5	7,200	0.567	4,082						◄— 7,200
Cash from disposal of the old cameras:											
Cash received from sale		Now	25,000	1.000	25,000	◄— 25,000					
Tax shield from loss:											
Book value now	$60,000										
Less sale price	25,000										
Loss from disposal.	35,000										
Income tax savings at 45% .	× 45%										
Income tax savings	$15,750	Now	15,750	1.000	15,750	◄— 15,750					
Salvage value of the new cameras .	$18,000										
Multiply by 1 − 45%	× 55%										
Net cash inflow.	$ 9,900	5	9,900	0.567	5,613						◄— 9,900
Present value of cash flows of buying new cameras					$(150,242)						

Years Having Cash Flows

EXHIBIT 17–11 (concluded)

Depreciation:

Year	Cameras Cost	Income Tax Depreciation Deduction	Tax Shield: Income Tax Savings at 45%
1	$150,000	$60,000	$27,000
2	150,000	33,000	14,850
3	150,000	22,500	10,125
4	150,000	18,500	8,325
5	150,000	16,000	7,200

Items and Computations		Year(s) Having Cash Flows	Amount of Cash Flows	12% Factor	Present Value of Cash Flows
Keep the old cameras:					
Annual cash operating costs	$62,000				
Multiply by 1 – 45%	x 55%				
Aftertax cost	$34,100	1–5	$(34,100)	3.605	$(122,931)
Repairs needed	$36,000				
Multiply by 1 – 45%	x 55%				
Aftertax cost	$19,800	2	(19,800)	0.797	(15,781)
Depreciation deduction	$12,000*				
Multiply by 45%	x 45%				
Income tax savings	$ 5,400	1–5	5,400	3.605	19,467
Salvage value	$ 3,000				
Multiply by 1 – 45%	x 55%				
Net cash inflow	$ 1,650	5	1,650	0.567	935
Present value of cash flows of keeping old cameras					$(118,310)
Net present value in favor of keeping the old cameras					$ (31,932)

	Now	1	2	3	4	5
			Years Having Cash Flows			
		($34,100)	($34,100)	($34,100)	($34,100)	($34,100)
			(19,800)			
		5,400	5,400	5,400	5,400	5,400
						1,650

*$60,000/5 years = $12,000

EXHIBIT 17-12   Capital Budgeting Using Differential-Cost Approach

Items and Computations	Year(s) Having Cash Flows	Amount of Cash Flows	12% Factor	Present Value of Cash Flows	Now	1	2	3	4	5
Initial investment $12,000	Now	$(150,000)	1.000	$(150,000)	($150,000)					
Savings in cash operating expenses . . $12,000										
Multiply by 1 − 45% . . . . x 55%										
Net cash inflow. . . . . $ 6,600	1–5	6,600	3.605	23,793		$6,600	$6,600	$6,600	$6,600	$6,600
Difference in depreciation: (see below)	1	21,600	0.893	19,289		21,600				
	2	9,450	0.797	7,532			9,450			
	3	4,725	0.712	3,364				4,725		
	4	2,925	0.636	1,860					2,925	
	5	1,800	0.567	1,021						1,800
Cash from disposal of the old cameras:										
Cash received from sale	Now	25,000	1.000	25,000	25,000					
Income tax savings from loss	Now	15,750	1.000	15,750	15,750					
(see Exhibit 17–11)										
Repairs avoided $36,000										
Multiply by 1 − 45% . . . . x 55%										
Net cash inflow. $19,800	2	19,800	0.797	15,781			19,800			
Difference in salvage value										
in 5 years $15,000										
Multiply by 1 − 45% . . . . x 55%										
Net cash inflow. . . . . $ 8,250	5	8,250	0.567	4,678						8,250
Net present value in favor of keeping old cameras				$ (31,932)						

Depreciation on Cameras

Year	New	Old	Difference in Depreciation	Income Tax Savings @ 45%
1	$60,000	$12,000	$48,000	$21,600
2	33,000	12,000	21,000	9,450
3	22,500	12,000	10,500	4,725
4	18,500	12,000	6,500	2,925
5	16,000	12,000	4,000	1,800

Years Having Cash Flows

Differential-Cost Approach

If, instead, we use the **differential-cost approach** for deciding whether to keep the cameras, we include only differences in cash operating costs, depreciation tax shield, and salvage value as shown in Exhibit 17–12. We obtain the $31,932 net present value advantage to keeping the old cameras as computed in Exhibit 17–11.

Summary

Capital budgeting decisions are among the most difficult that management must make, primarily because they usually involve large commitments. Also, the returns on these commitments are complex to forecast. This chapter presented three techniques for evaluating capital expenditures: (1) discounted cash flow, (2) payback or payout, and (3) unadjusted return on investment. Chapter illustrations include two variations of the discounted cash flow method—net present value (also called excess present value) and internal rate of return (often called time-adjusted rate of return).

Accountants prefer the present value and internal rate of return because these methods consider the time value of money. We determine the present value of expected future cash inflows by applying appropriate present value factors for the rate of return required. We can base the required rate of return on the cost of capital employed, or it can be a rate greater than the general level of interest rates at which institutions are lending money. The internal rate of return differs from the present value method because no discount rate is known in advance. We find a discounted rate that yields a zero net present value.

The payback method determines the length of time a project requires to recover the initial outlay. However, we ignore the time value of money and the salvage value of the investment. Profitability is considered in the unadjusted return on investment method by determining the relationship of average annual net aftertax income to the initial or average investment. While the adjusted return on investment method is familiar because it is based on the accrual method of financial statement preparation, it fails to take into consideration the time value of money.

Important Terms and Concepts

sunk cost, 595
investment tax credit, 595
tax shield, 596
present value, 597
time value of money, 597
discounting, 597
annuity, 597
net cash inflow, 599
discounted cash flow method, 599
net present value method, 600
required rate of return, 600
hurdle rate, 600
cost of capital, 600
discount rate, 600
cutoff rate, 600

weighted net present value or expected value, 601
profitability index (present value index), 602
internal rate of return or time-adjusted rate of return, 602
payback or payout method, 604
payback reciprocal, 605
bailout payback method, 605
present value payback, 606
unadjusted return on investment (accounting rate of return), 606
total-cost approach, 608
differential-cost approach, 612

Problem for Self-Study

Capital Budgeting Techniques

Keat Company is considering a machine involving an initial outlay of $43,000. Accountants will use straight-line depreciation with no salvage value at the end of the machine's useful life of 10 years. Net annual *aftertax* cash inflow is forecasted to be $9,000 for 10 years.

Required:

Determine the following:

a. Payback period.
b. Unadjusted rate of return on initial investment.
c. Unadjusted rate of return on average investment.
d. Net present value at 10 percent and present value payback period.
e. Internal rate of return.

Solution to Problem for Self-Study

KEAT COMPANY

a. Payback

Year		Net Cash Inflow	Year
1	....	$ 9,000	1
2	....	9,000	1
3	....	9,000	1
4	....	9,000	1
5	....	7,000	0.78 ($7,000/$9,000)
		$43,000	4.78 years payback period

or $43,000/$9,000 = 4.78 years

b. Unadjusted rate of return on initial investment

$$\$9,000 \times 10 = \$90,000$$

$$\frac{\$90,000 - \$43,000}{10 \text{ years}} = \$4,700; \frac{\$4,700}{\$43,000} = 10.93\%$$

c. Unadjusted rate of return on average investment

$$\frac{\$90,000 - \$43,000}{10 \text{ years}} = \$4,700; \$43,000/2 = \$21,500 \text{ average investment}$$

$$\frac{\$4,700}{\$21,500 \text{ average investment}} = 21.86\%$$

d. Net present value at 10%

$$
\begin{array}{ll}
(\$43,000) \times 1.000 = & \$(43,000) \\
\$9,000 \times 6.145 \quad = & \underline{55,305} \\
\text{Net present value} & \underline{\underline{\$ 12,305}}
\end{array}
$$

Present value payback period

Year	Cash Flow	Present Value of $1 at 10%	Net Present Value of Flow Total	Net Present Value of Flow Needed	Present Value Payback Years Required
1	$9,000	0.909	$8,181	$ 8,181	1.0
2	9,000	0.826	7,434	7,434	1.0
3	9,000	0.751	6,759	6,759	1.0
4	9,000	0.683	6,147	6,147	1.0
5	9,000	0.621	5,589	5,589	1.0
6	9,000	0.564	5,076	5,076	1.0
7	9,000	0.513	4,617	3,814	$0.8 \dfrac{\$3,814}{\$4,617}$
Investment				$43,000	
Total present value payback in years					6.8

e. Internal rate of return

Cash Inflow	PV at 16%		PV at 18%	
Investment	$(43,000)		$(43,000)	
$9,000 for 10 years . . .	43,497	($9,000 × 4.833)	40,446	($9,000 × 4.494)
Net present value	$ 497		$ (2,554)	

$$16\% + \left(2\% \times \frac{\$497}{\$3,051}\right) = 16\% + 2\%\,(0.16289)$$

$$= 16.3258\% \text{ discounted rate of return}$$

Review Questions

1. As the cost accountant of a company requesting a loan for the purchase of expensive robots, what is your reaction when the banker says, "I will not lend money for new equipment unless your company can demonstrate by statistical evidence that you are using your present equipment to reasonably full capacity"?

2. How is the tax shield computed and how is it used in capital expenditure analysis?

3. How can the probability of occurrence be given consideration in the net present value approach to evaluating plant asset proposals?

4. Compare the differential-cost approach and total-cost approach, indicating the situations in which each approach would be more appropriate.

5. How is a project's profitability index determined? What does use of the formula achieve?

6. How does use of the profitability index overcome a weakness of the net present value method in ranking projects in order of contribution to income or desirability when comparing investment projects costing different amounts?

7. Assume proposed Project A has a profitability index greater than 1.00, while proposed Project B has a profitability index of less than 1.00. What does this mean and how do these indexes affect their selection of capital assets?

8. *a.* Why should so much time and effort go into the evaluation of plant asset proposals?
    b. To what extent should management be involved in evaluating large capital expenditure proposals?

9. Discuss the strengths and weaknesses of these capital budgeting methods:

    a. Net present value method.
    b. Internal rate of return.

         c.   Unadjusted return on investment.

         d.   Payback.

10.   *a.*   What information is gained from the present value payback method?

       b.   What does the payback or payout method measure?

11.   On what two different bases can the unadjusted return on investment be calculated?

12.   In comparisons of plant asset proposals, what guidelines should be followed regarding the use of the various evaluation techniques?

CPA/CMA/CIA Multiple Choice Questions

1.   (AICPA) Which of the following capital budgeting techniques implicitly assumes that the cash flows are reinvested at the company's minimum required rate of return?

	Net Present Value	Internal Rate of Return
a.	Yes	Yes
b.	Yes	No
c.	No	Yes
d.	No	No

2.   (CIA) At a company's cost of capital (hurdle rate) of 15 percent, a prospective investment has a positive net present value. Based on this information, it can be concluded that:

   a.   The accounting rate of return on the project is greater than 15 percent.

   b.   The internal rate of return on the project is less than 15 percent.

   c.   The payback period is shorter than the life of the asset.

   d.   The internal rate of return on the project is greater than 15 percent.

3.   (AICPA) The discount rate (hurdle rate of return) must be determined in advance for the

   a.   Payback period method.

   b.   Time adjusted rate of return method.

   c.   Net present value method.

   d.   Internal rate of return method.

4.   (CIA) A company is considering a capital budgeting decision involving a risky foreign investment. Risk can best be minimized by selecting the investment alternative with the:

   a.   Shortest payback period.

   b.   Highest internal rate of return (IRR).

   c.   Highest net present value (NPV).

   d.   Highest net present value index.

5.   (CMA) Fitzgerald Company is planning to acquire a $250,000 machine that will provide increased efficiencies, thereby reducing annual operating costs by $80,000. The machine will be depreciated by the straight-line method over a five-year life with no salvage value at the end of five years. Assuming a 40 percent income tax rate, the machine's payback period is

   a.   3.13 years.

   b.   3.21 years.

   c.   3.68 years.

   d.   4.81 years.

   e.   5.21 years.

6. (CMA) Capital budgeting methods are often divided into two classifications: project screening and project ranking. Which one of the following is considered a ranking method rather than a screening method?

   a. Payback method.
   b. Net present value.
   c. Time-adjusted rate of return.
   d. Profitability index.
   e. Accounting rate of return.

7. (CMA) The accounting rate of return

   a. is synonymous with the internal rate of return.
   b. focuses on income as opposed to cash flows.
   c. is inconsistent with the divisional performance measure known as return on investment.
   d. recognizes the time value of money.
   e. should be used only with mutually exclusive projects.

8. (CMA) The internal rate of return on an investment

   a. frequently results in positive net present values on attractive projects.
   b. generally coincides with the company's hurdle rate.
   c. disregards discounted cash flows.
   d. may produce different rankings than the net present value method on mutually exclusive projects.
   e. would tend to be reduced if a company used an accelerated method of depreciation for tax purposes rather than the straight-line method.

9. (AICPA) Garwood Company purchased a machine which will be depreciated on the straight-line basis over an estimated useful life of seven years and no salvage value. The machine is expected to generate cash flow from operations, net of income taxes, of $80,000 in each of the seven years. Garwood's expected rate of return is 12 percent. Information on present value factors is as follows:
   Present value of $1 at 12 percent for seven periods .... .0452
   Present value of an ordinary annuity of $1
     at 12 percent for seven periods 4.564
   Assuming a positive net present value of $12,720, what was the cost of the machine?

   a. $240,400.
   b. $253,120.
   c. $352,400.
   d. $377,840.

10. (AICPA) At December 31, 19X4, Zar Company had a machine with an original cost of $84,000, accumulated depreciation of $60,000, and an estimated salvage value of zero. On December 31, 19X4, Zar was considering the purchase of a new machine having a five-year life, costing $120,000, and having an estimated salvage value of $20,000 at the end of five years. In its decision concerning the possible purchase of the new machine, how much should Zar consider as sunk cost at December 31, 19X4?

    a. $120,000.
    b. $100,000.
    c. $ 24,000.
    d. $ 4,000.

11. (AICPA) Nelson Company is planning to purchase a new machine for $500,000. The new machine is expected to produce cash flow from operations, before income taxes, of $135,000 a year in each of the next five years. Depreciation of

$100,000 a year will be charged to income for each of the next five years. Assume that the income tax rate is 40 percent. The payback period would be approximately

   a. 2.2 years.
   b. 3.4 years.
   c. 3.7 years.
   d. 4.1 years.

12.–13. (AICPA) Items 12 and 13 are based on the following data:

Apex Corporation is planning to buy production machinery costing $100,000. This machinery's expected useful life is five years, with no residual value. Apex requires a rate of return of 20 percent, and has calculated the following data pertaining to the purchase and operation of this machinery:

Year	Estimated Annual Cash Inflow	Present Value of 1 at 20 Percent
1	$ 60,000	.91
2	30,000	.76
3	20,000	.63
4	20,000	.53
5	20,000	.44
Totals	$150,000	3.27

Assume that the cash inflow was received evenly during the year.

12. The payback period is

   a. 2.50 years.
   b. 2.75 years.
   c. 3.00 years.
   d. 5.00 years.

13. The net present value is

   a. $ 9,400.
   b. $ 54,128.
   c. $ 80,000.
   d. $109,400.

Exercises

E17–1 Aftertax Benefits, Present Value, Payback Period (L.O. 2 and 3)

Hodges Company is planning to purchase a machine costing $117,000 to use in their Mixing Department. Management determined that this machine has a 10-year life with an estimated salvage value of $5,000. Depreciation for tax purposes is $9,360 for Year 1. The estimated annual cash savings from using this machine is $22,000. The company's cost of capital is 14 percent and its income tax rate, including state income tax, is 45 percent.

Required:

a. Calculate the annual aftertax net cash benefits of this machine for Year 1.
b. Calculate the net present value of this investment if the annual aftertax cash benefits of this machine were $20,000 each year for the machine's life.
c. Calculate the payback period assuming that the annual aftertax cash benefits of this machine were $20,000 each year for the machine's life.

E17–2 Present Value of Net Cash Flow (L.O. 1)

Woods, Inc., is planning an $800,000 investment that is projected to give three years of operating service. Cash flow, net of income taxes, will be $500,000 for the first year and $300,000 for the second year.

Required:

Assume the rate of return is exactly 12 percent and give the cash flow, net of income taxes, for the third year.

E17–3 Maximum Interest Rate (L.O. 1)

Georgia Company acquired a machine costing $49,650. The machine had an estimated life of five years. Estimated annual aftertax net cash benefits are $14,125 at the end of each year. The following amounts appear in the interest table for the present value of an annuity of $1 at year-end for five years:

12%	3.60
14%	3.43
16%	3.27

Required:

Calculate the maximum interest rate that could be paid for the capital employed over the life of this asset without loss on this project.

E17–4 Present Value Analysis (L.O. 4)

The Raymond Dairy Company manually wraps its sticks of butter for sale. One part-time employee, who is paid minimum wage, performs this operation involving no machines. Direct costs of operations are:

Salaries and payroll taxes	$7,608
Paper wrappers and other supplies ...	2,000

A company has offered to sell Raymond an automatic machine to use in the butter wrapping operations. The machine will cost $30,000 with $2,000 disposal value at the end of a seven-year life. Sales terms are cash on delivery. The machine is expected to become jammed periodically, resulting in the waste of 10 percent more paper wrappers and supplies. Even though the machine is automatic, it will require some supervision. However, management plans to have an employee presently working in the processing plant perform these duties in addition to those duties he now has. He is expected to devote an average of one tenth of his time to loading and supervising the machine; his annual salary including payroll taxes is $20,000.

Annually, the machine will cost a total of $500 for electricity and utilities. All machine repairs are guaranteed by the manufacturer. The new machine will occupy the space presently being used by the manual operations.

Required:

(Ignore the income tax effect.)

a. Assume a 14 percent cost of capital and use present value analysis to show whether the new equipment should be purchased.
b. Determine which additional factors Raymond should consider before making a decision regarding the purchase.

E17–5 Aftertax Cash Benefits and Payback Period (L.O. 3)

Bart Company is planning to purchase a machine costing $108,000 to use in their Mixing Department. Management estimates that the life of the machine will be 12 years, and the salvage value is $3,000.

Bart Company estimates annual cash savings from using this machine will be $15,000. The company's cost of capital was determined to be 6 percent and its income tax rate is 44 percent, including state income tax.

Required:

a. Calculate the annual aftertax net cash benefits of this machine.

b. Assume the annual aftertax cash benefits of this machine were $13,000 and compute the net present value of this investment.

c. Assume the annual aftertax cash benefits of this machine were $13,000 and compute the payback period.

E17–6 Net Present Value and Internal Rate of Return (L.O. 2)

Sylvester Company is considering the purchase of either Machine A or B. Machine A costs $28,000 and has a life of 10 years while Machine B costs $64,000 and has a life of 15 years. The cost of removing either machine at the end of its life is expected to equal any salvage value. Annual aftertax cash inflow for Machine A is expected to be $4,900 and $8,000 for Machine B.

Required:

For both machines, prepare the following analysis:

a. Internal rate of return.
   (1) How do you know where to start in determining the rate?
   (2) Why do you know you will have to interpolate to arrive at the rate?
   (3) Determine the rate for each machine.
b. Net present value at 14 percent.

Problems

P17–7 Net Present Value and Expected Value (L.O. 1)

Crawford Company is considering the purchase of a machine to use in their processing plant. Its cost is $75,000, and the machine salesperson requires a cash payment on delivery. Life of the machine is expected to be five years; there is no salvage value.

The following estimates of aftertax cash flow are based on three different market conditions. The probability of a poor market is 30 percent; of a normal market, 50 percent; and of an excellent market, 20 percent.

Year	Poor Market	Normal Market	Excellent Market
1	$18,000	$20,000	$28,000
2	10,000	15,000	16,000
3	11,000	18,000	19,000
4	18,000	20,000	22,000
5	20,000	25,000	28,000

Required:

a. Use an interest rate of 12 percent and determine the net present value of the cash flow for each of the three market conditions.

b. Assume the net present value was ($15,000) for the poor market, ($3,000) for the normal market, and $8,000 for the excellent market, and calculate the weighted net present value or expected value of the investment.

P17–8 Net Present Value, Profitability Index, Internal Rate of Return, and Bailout Payback (L.O. 2)

Harlen Company management is evaluating the purchase of either a machine built by the Betz Company or a longer-life machine built by the Cullen Company. The Betz machine cost $70,000 and has a useful life of 12 years while the Cullen machine costs $75,000 with a useful life of 18 years. Neither machine is expected to have any salvage value at the end of its life. The annual aftertax net cash inflow for both machines is expected to be $17,000. The Betz machine's disposal value is expected to be $40,000 at the end of the first year and decline at the rate of $6,000 annually. The Cullen machine's disposal value is expected to be $30,000 at the end of the first year and decline $9,000 annually.

Required:

Prepare the following analysis for both machines:

a. Net present value at 8 percent.
b. Profitability index using present value at 8 percent.
c. Internal rate of return.
d. Bailout payback.
e. Which machine would you advise purchasing? Explain why.

P17–9 Ranking Proposals Using Net Present Value, Profitability Index, Internal Rate, and Bailout Payback (L.O. 2 and 3)

Cody, Inc., is considering the purchase of Machines A, B, or C. The president believes the final decision should depend on the ranking determined by the net present value method, while other members of the management team believe the internal rate of return is more appropriate. The predicted annual aftertax cash inflow is $1,000 for each machine, and no machine is expected to have any salvage value at the end of its life. Machine A's purchase price is $2,500 with a 4-year life; Machine B's cost is $5,000 with a 12-year life; Machine C's cost is $6,000 with an 18-year life. The disposal value at the end of the first year is $1,200—Machine A, $3,500—Machine B, and $4,000—Machine C. Analysts expect Machine A to decline in disposal value of $400 annually after the first year and Machines B and C by $500 each annually.

Required:

Prepare the ranking for all three machines according to:

a. Net present value method at 12 percent.
b. Profitability index using present value at 12 percent.
c. Internal rate of return.
d. Bailout payback.
e. Which machine would you advise purchasing? Explain why.

P17–10 Capital Budgeting Techniques (L.O. 2 and 3)

Salespersons have approached Camp Company management with promotional material introducing a machine with innovative technological devices. The machine whose initial cost is $50,000 has an estimated life of six years. The expected salvage value is $2,000 with straight-line depreciation being used; a $14,000 aftertax cash inflow for six years is forecasted.

Required:

Calculate the following:

a. Payback period.
b. Unadjusted rate of return on initial investment.
c. Unadjusted rate of return on average investment.
d. Net present value at 8 percent and present value payback period.
e. Internal rate of return.

P17–11 Net Present Value and Expected Value (L.O. 2)

Sanford Company is considering the purchase of a large molding machine that will enable their bottle production process to be completed more rapidly. The machine will cost $190,000 and has an expected life of eight years. Estimated salvage value is $10,000; straight-line depreciation is to be used. Assume a 46 percent tax rate including state income tax, and an 8 percent cost of capital.

Because the market for the bottles produced by the company is unstable, management is unable to forecast beforetax cash flow with much accuracy. They believe that much of the success will depend on effective advertising to impress the public with the safety features of their medicine bottles.

The following beforetax cash flows depend on the market conditions assumed:

Year	Depressed Market	Normal Market	Optimistic Market
1	$23,000	$24,000	$26,000
2	24,000	26,000	30,000
3	24,000	27,000	35,000
4	28,000	32,000	38,000
5	30,000	35,000	42,000
6	32,000	38,000	46,000
7	35,000	41,000	48,000
8	36,000	45,000	50,000

The probability of a depressed market is 20 percent; of a normal market, 65 percent; and of an optimistic market, 15 percent.

Required:

a. Determine the net present value of the cash flow for each of the three market conditions assumed.
b. Using the information determined in (a), calculate the weighted net present value or expected value of the investment.

P17–12 Capital Budgeting Techniques (L.O. 2 and 3)

McNeely Company is considering the purchase of a large cutting machine costing $300,000. The estimated cash benefit is as follows:

Year	Beforetax Cash Benefit
1	$ 80,000
2	90,000
3	95,000
4	100,000
5	90,000
6	85,000
7	70,000
8	60,000

The machine is to be depreciated over eight years on a straight-line basis. No salvage value is expected. Assume a 48 percent tax rate and a 12 percent cost of capital.

Required:

Calculate the following:

a. Payback period.
b. Unadjusted rate of return on initial investment.
c. Unadjusted rate of return on average investment.
d. Net present value and present value payback period.
e. Profitability index using present value at 12 percent.
f. Internal rate of return method.

P17–13 (AICPA) Capital Budgeting for CAD/CAM Project (L.O. 2)

Spara Corporation is considering the various benefits that may result from the shortening of its product cycle by changing from the company's present manual system to a computer-aided design/computer-aided manufacturing (CAD/CAM) system. The proposed system can provide productive time equivalency close to the 20,000 hours currently available with the manual system. The incremental annual out-of-pocket costs of maintaining the manual system are $20 per hour.

The incremental annual out-of-pocket costs of maintaining the CAD/CAM system are estimated to be $200,000, with an initial investment of $480,000 in the proposed system. The estimated useful life of this system is six years. For tax purposes, assume a level accelerated cost recovery with a full year allowable in each year. The tax rate is expected to remain constant at 30 percent over the life of the project. Spara requires a minimum aftertax return of 20 percent on projects of this type. Full capacity will be utilized.

Required:

a. Compute the relevant annual aftertax cash flows related to the CAD/CAM project.
b. Based on the computation in (*a*), compute the following on an aftertax basis:
    1. Payback period for recovery of investment.
    2. Internal rate of return.
    3. Net present value.
    4. Excess present value index (profitability index).

P17–14 Capital Budgeting Techniques (L.O. 2 and 3)

Whitehead Company is considering a machine involving an initial outlay of $75,000. Straight-line depreciation is to be used, with no estimated salvage value at the end of its useful life of five years. Net annual aftertax cash flow is forecasted to be $18,000 for each of the five years.

Required:

Determine the following:

a. Payback period.
b. Unadjusted rate of return on initial investment.
c. Unadjusted rate of return on average investment.
d. Net present value at 12 percent.
e. Internal rate of return.

P17–15 Net Present Value and Expected Value (L.O. 1)

Kingston Company is considering the purchase of equipment to use in their processing plant. Its cost is $80,000, and the equipment dealer requires a cash payment on delivery. The expected life of the machine is four years with a salvage value at the end of $5,000.

    The following estimates of aftertax cash flow reflect three market conditions. The probability of a poor market is 40 percent; of a normal market, 45 percent; and of an excellent market, 15 percent.

Year	Poor Market	Normal Market	Excellent Market
1	$10,000	$15,000	$18,000
2	18,000	25,000	29,000
3	25,000	32,000	36,000
4	30,000	40,000	45,000

Required:

a. Use an interest rate of 10 percent and determine the net present value of the cash flow for each of the three market conditions.
b. Assume the net present value was $(12,000) for the poor market, $10,000 for the normal market, and $22,000 for the excellent market. Calculate the weighted net present value or expected value of the investment.

P17–16 Total-Cost and Differential-Cost Approaches (L.O. 4)

Management of Cornelius Industries is considering replacing an old machine with a new machine costing $50,000. The annual operating expense of the old machine is $8,000. The old machine can continue to operate for the next five years. It is depreciated under the straight-line method. The current book value is $7,500 and no salvage value was used originally in determining annual depreciation charges. However, management is confident that the old machine can be sold for $1,500 at Year 5 or $6,500 now. If the company purchases the new machine, the operating cost will decrease to $6,750.

Depreciation on the new machine is deducted for tax purposes as follows: Year 1, $20,000; Year 2, $15,000; Year 3, $8,000; Year 4, $5,000; and Year 5, $2,000. Cornelius management plans to use the new machine until the end of Year 5 and then sell it for $5,500. The tax rate of Cornelius Industries is 34 percent and its aftertax cost of capital is 8 percent.

Hint: A sketch of the relevant cash flows by years is not required, but you may find it helpful in preparing your solution.

Required:

(Round to whole dollars.)

a. Prepare an analysis using the total-cost approach incorporating the effects of income tax and present value.
b. Prepare an analysis using the differential-cost approach incorporating the effects of income tax and present value.

P17–17 Numerous Capital Budgeting Techniques (L.O. 2 and 3)

Management of Frank Barton Company is considering expanding its operations through the purchase of a blending machine costing $165,000. The tax and economic life of the asset is five years. The estimated salvage value at the end of its life is $45,000. Depreciation is deducted for tax purposes as follows: Year 1, $60,000; Year 2, $42,000; Year 3, $25,000; Year 4, $20,000; and Year 5, $18,000. Based on engineering and accounting studies, management believes the pretax increase in cash inflow will be as follows: Year 1, $65,000; Year 2, $73,000; Year 3, $85,000; Year 4, $98,000; and Year 5, $96,000. Federal and state income taxes have averaged 52 percent in the past, and no change is expected in this rate.

Required:

Determine the following:

a. Payback period.
b. Unadjusted rate of return on investment based on initial investment and on average investment (ignore salvage).
c. Net present value of the machine assuming the cost of capital is 14 percent.
d. Present value payback.
e. Internal rate of return approach to determine the discount rate.
f. Payback period assuming that the aftertax cash flow was even over the five years.
g. Profitability index using present value of 14 percent.

P17–18 Aftertax Cash Flow Net Present Value (L.O. 1)

Springfield Company is considering replacing its present manufacturing equipment with robots costing $200,000 and having an estimated five-year life. The robotics supplier promises that if the equipment is purchased at the beginning of the project year, the robots will be in operation by the end of the second quarter of the project year. This will result in 50 percent of the estimated annual savings being realized in the project's first year. The estimated savings in direct labor from the use of robots is $100,000 annually. Management expects no change in capacity from the use of the robots.

Springfield will incur a $20,000 one-time expense to transfer manufacturing activities from its present equipment to the automated equipment. Because operations are well arranged, no loss in sales is expected in the transfer to robots.

The current equipment is carried in the accounts at zero book value since it is fully depreciated. However, Springfield engineers believe the equipment can be used an additional five years based on their recent examination. Springfield Company would receive $10,000 net of removal costs if it elected to buy the new equipment and dispose of its current equipment at this time.

Springfield currently leases its manufacturing plant. The annual lease payments are $50,000. The lease, which will have five years remaining when the equipment installation begins, is not renewable. Springfield Company would be required to remove any equipment in the plant at the end of the lease. The cost of equipment removal is expected to equal the salvage value of either the old or new equipment at the time of removal. The company is subject to a 30 percent income tax rate and requires an aftertax return of at least 10 percent on any investment.

Required:

a. Calculate the annual incremental aftertax cash flows for Springfield Company's proposal to acquire the new manufacturing equipment. For ease of calculation, use straight-line depreciation for tax purposes. Take a full year's depreciation in the first year the asset is put into use.
b. Calculate the net present value of Springfield Company's proposal to acquire the new manufacturing equipment using the cash flows calculated in Requirement *a* and indicate what action Springfield's mangement should take. For ease in calculation, assume all recurring flows take place at the end of the year.

P17–19 Capital Budgeting Techniques (L.O. 2 and 3)

Logo Company is considering replacing an obsolete machine with new equipment costing $15,000 and having an estimated useful life of five years. The old machine is fully depreciated, and no salvage value can be realized on its disposal. The new machine would provide annual cash savings of $5,000 before income taxes. No salvage value would be used for depreciation purposes because the equipment is expected to have no value at the end of five years.

Logo uses the straight-line depreciation method on all equipment for both book and tax purposes. The company is subject to a 30 percent tax rate. Logo has an aftertax cost of capital of 12 percent.

Required:

a. Use each of the following methods to evaluate Logo Company's proposed investment. Assume all operating revenues and expenses occur at the end of the year.
   1. Net present value.
   2. Profitability index using present value at 12 percent.
   3. Internal rate of return.
   4. Payback period.
   5. Accounting rate of return on initial investment.
   6. Accounting rate of return on average investment.
b. Assume you are a cost accounting consultant employed by Logo Company. Identify and discuss the issues management should consider in choosing one of the five capital budgeting techniques to compare and evaluate alternative capital investment projects.

P17–20 Total-Cost and Differential-Cost Approaches (L.O. 4)

Baldwin Company is considering buying new equipment having a purchase price of $65,000 to replace a present machine. The old equipment can operate three more years before it will be sold for $2,000. The annual cash operating expense of the old equipment is $36,000. If the old equipment is sold now, Baldwin Company will receive $5,000, which is its book value. The annual depreciation of the old equipment is $1,000 calculated using the straight-line basis. If the new equipment is purchased, the operating expense is $24,000 annually. The new equipment is expected to have a three-year life and its salvage value to be $4,000 at the end of Year 3. Depreciation on the new equipment is deducted for tax purposes as follows: Year 1, $35,000; Year 2, $20,000; and Year 3, $10,000. Baldwin's tax rate is 34 percent and its aftertax cost of capital is 10 percent.

Required:

(Round to whole dollars.)

a. Prepare an analysis using the total-cost approach incorporating the effects of income tax and present value.

b. Prepare an analysis using the differential-cost approach incorporating the effects of income tax and present value.

P17–21 Evaluating Discounted Cash Flow Techniques (L.O. 1)

The Mann Company designs and sews a nationally known brand of men's shirts. On January 2, 19X1, Mann purchased a special fabric cutting machine; this machine has been utilized for three years. A sales representative has been talking with Mann's production manager concerning the purchase of a newer, more efficient machine. If purchased, the new machine would be acquired on January 2, 19X4. Mann expects to sell 50,000 shirts in each of the next four years. The unit selling price of the shirts is expected to average $10.

Mann Company has two options: (1) continue to operate the old machine, or (2) sell the old machine and purchase the new machine. No trade-in was offered by the seller of the new machine. The following information has been assembled to help decide which option is more desirable:

	Old Machine	New Machine
Original cost of machine at acquisition	$90,000	$200,000
Salvage value at the end of useful life for depreciation purposes	$20,000	$ 40,000
Useful life from date of acquisition	7 years	4 years
Estimated cash value of machines:		
January 2, 19X4	$50,000	$200,000
December 31, 19X7	$10,000	$ 40,000
Expected annual cash operating expenses:		
Variable cost per shirt	$ 4	$ 3
Total fixed costs	$20,000	$ 19,500

Mann Company is subject to an overall income tax rate of 30 percent. Assume that all operating revenues and expenses occur at the end of the year. Assume that any gain or loss on the sale of machinery is treated as an ordinary tax item and will affect the taxes paid by Mann Company at the end of the year in which it occurred. Assume for simplicity that straight-line depreciation will be used for tax purposes on both machines.

Required:

a. Identify and discuss the advantages and disadvantages of using discounted cash flow techniques (such as the net present value method and the internal rate of return) for capital investment decisions.

b. Use an aftertax return of 14 percent and determine whether Mann Company should purchase the new machine based on the net present value method.

c. Assume Mann's cost accountant believes that the information assembled to help decide which option is more desirable fails to consider all factors. For example, the cash operating expenses include only product costs, such as labor, materials, and overhead. There is no consideration given to the savings in manufacturing cost that result because the new machine will have a lower incidence of defects. Additionally, the higher quality of the product that can be produced from the new machine is ignored. Do you think such factors should be included to obtain a more realistic and accurate analysis? If so, how would you arrive at the savings a company would have if its defect rate was reduced?

d. List some other important nonquantitative factors that Mann Company should consider in addition to the quantitative analysis using a capital budgeting technique.

Capital Budgeting—
Additional Topics

CHAPTER OBJECTIVES

After studying this chapter, you should be able to:

1. Apply sensitivity analysis to capital budgeting decisions.

2. Incorporate inflation into capital budgeting analysis.

3. Identify and quantify the subjective benefits of new automated plant assets that should be incor-

porated into conventional capital expenditure analysis.

4. Compare the costs of constructing assets for a company's own use versus leasing or purchasing.

PRACTICAL
APPLICATION BOX

Quality Control at Formosa Plastics Group

Management of Formosa Plastics Group, a Taiwan-based international conglomerate, believes that quality does not result from mere recognition of its importance. They developed an analytical program for the evaluation of quality costs that contained these four categories of quality cost: prevention cost, appraisal cost, internal failure cost, and external failure cost. They recognized that prevention and appraisal costs are voluntary or discretionary costs, incurred only when management believes ap-

propriate. In contrast, internal and external failure costs are involuntary and occur when a product fails to comply with expected standards of quality. Managers focused on a reasonable level of quality assurance by analyzing the relationship between dollars spent for voluntary costs and decreases in failure costs. This overcomes the unrealistic expectation that the ideal state of quality control is absolute perfection or 100 percent quality conformance.

From: Thomas P. Edmonds, Bor-Yi Tsay, and Wen-Wei Lin, "Analyzing Quality Costs," *Management Accounting*, November 1989, pp. 25–29.

Introduction

Traditional differential cost studies and capital budgeting techniques often fail when managers propose purchasing automated equipment. Accountants find it difficult to quantify many of the important advantages of automation, such as increased flexibility; improved quality and customer service; and increased opportunities for responding to changes in material availability, product design, or product-mix demand. If companies ignore these gains from improved manufacturing performance, their conventional single-purpose, high-volume machines prevent them from changing products and operations. A narrow interpretation of the discounted cash flow procedures may inhibit desirable investment projects.

Chapter 17 presented several evaluation techniques for capital expenditures. However, the chapter did not discuss the issues encountered in estimating the hurdle rate or cost of capital. This chapter presents methods for estimating this rate and demonstrates the effect of changing prices on capital budgeting. Changes in the purchasing power cause future cash flows to have a different real value than dollars received today.

Capital expenditure proposals involve not only additions of new plant assets but also expansion and improvement of existing investments and the replacement of capital assets. The basis of analyzing the improvement and replacement of capital assets involves comparing the costs of existing facilities with future cost savings.

Cost of Capital (L.O. 1)

The interest rate used in discounted cash flow methods is the minimum rate that must be earned to prevent dilution of shareholders' interests. This rate is called the **cost of capital** or the **hurdle rate.**[1] The cost of capital is a composite of the cost of various sources of funds from debt and equity that make up a firm's capital structure. It is a weighted average found by determining the costs of the individual types of capital and multiplying the cost of each by its proportion in the firm's total capital structure. For example, assume a company uses three types of financing: debt, preferred stock, and common equity (retained earnings and common stock), with aftertax costs of 5 percent, 16 percent, and 12 percent, respectively. Exhibit 18–1 shows a 12 percent cost of capital if debt comprises 20 percent of the capital structure, preferred stock is 35 percent, and common equity is 45 percent. We multiply the cost of capital by the prospective cost of the various capital components, rather than by a company's historical costs.

In computing the cost of each of the various components of the capital structure, we should consider the amortization of premiums or discounts as part of the debt cost. Because the firm deducts interest payments when determining taxable income, the effective cost of debt is lower than the interest rate stated. To equate the tax treatment of debt and equity, we use the interest rate net of the applicable tax rate in determining the weighted cost of capital. In computing the cost of preferred stock, we divide the preferred dividend by the actual proceeds (cost) of the stock or the current price per share. The cost of equity capital is the most difficult component to calculate, and there are several methods available for use in the estimation process.

The historical rate of return, earnings/price ratio, dividend growth model, capital asset pricing model, and bond yield plus risk premium are five methods that we can use to estimate the cost of equity capital.

■ Using the historical rate of return method, we calculate the rate of return earned by an investor, who is assumed to have purchased the stock in the past, held it until the present, and sold it at current market prices.

---

[1] For additional exploration of this subject, see Statement on Management Accounting No. 4A, "Cost of Capital" (Montvale, N.J.: National Association of Accountants, 1984).

EXHIBIT 18–1 Weighted Cost of Capital

	Aftertax Costs	Percent of Capital Structure	Weighted Cost
Debt	5%	20%	1.0%
Preferred stock	16	35	5.6
Common equity	12	45	5.4
		100%	12.0%

- Dividing earnings per share by the average price per share yields an earnings/ price ratio.
- Reflecting a market value approach to determining the cost of equity capital is the dividend growth model. This method assumes the market price of a stock equals the cash flow from such expected future incomes as dividends and market price appreciation, discounted to their present value.
- Using the capital asset pricing model assumes the required rate of return on any security equals the riskless rate of interest plus a premium for risk.
- Using the bond yield plus risk premium method results in adding a risk premium to the interest rate on the firm's long-term debt to arrive at an estimated cost of equity. The risk premium is judgmental and varies depending on market conditions and other factors.

After estimating the costs of its capital structure components, a company must weight the components before calculating its cost of capital. Preferably, a company bases the weight on the proportions that it should maintain in its target capital structure to provide an optimum balance of risk and return. However, a company can use the existing proportions of the capital components on its statement of financial position or the current proportions of the market values of the firm's outstanding securities. The advantage of using the balance sheet book value weight is that consistency is preserved since it corresponds to the amounts shown on the financial statement. However, the market value of the firm's securities may differ from their book value. Using the market value weight is consistent with using market values to determine the cost of the individual components of capital. Finally, we multiply the cost of each source of capital by its proportion in the capital structure to obtain a weighted cost for each element. The sum of these weighted costs is the weighted cost of capital.

Sensitivity Analysis for Capital Budgeting Decisions under Uncertainty (L.O. 1)

All of the capital budgeting methods presented share the weakness of assuming future cash flows are certain. Companies can use **sensitivity analysis** to offset this certainty weakness by measuring the effect on the estimate if the critical data inputs change. Sensitivity analysis attempts to determine the effect on the internal rate of return, net present value, or other calculations if the various predictions, such as cash flow or economic life, change or are in error.

For example, accountants use sensitivity analysis to determine how much net cash inflow can decrease before net present value equals zero or before the internal rate of return equals the required rate of return. Also, we can calculate the net present value and the internal rate of return using pessimistic and optimistic cash flow estimates. Sensitivity analysis also determines how short a proposed capital asset's useful life would have to be before net present value equals zero or before the internal rate of return equals the required rate of return. In addition, sensitivity analysis measures the potential increases in net present value and in the rate of return if cash inflow is larger or if the economic life is longer than expected. We can determine the cost of errors in estimating an asset's cash flow or life assuming there are or are not acceptable alternatives. The financial cost of possible errors as measured by sensitivity analysis helps management focus their attention on more crucial and reactive decisions.

Cash Flow Changes and Present Value

We can use sensitivity analysis to determine how much annual cash savings can decrease before a company breaks even on an investment. Sensitivity analysis also measures the impact on net present value or internal rate of return if actual cash flows differ from estimated cash inflows. For example, assume a company's cost of capital is 12 percent and management estimates $35,000 annual cash inflow for equipment having a cost of $80,000 and a five-year life. Managers wish to know how much these cash savings can decrease before reaching the point of indifference about the investment. Using a cumulative factor of 3.605 from Table B in the appendix, letting X = annual cash inflows and net present value = 0, then

$$3.605(X) - \$80,000 \text{ initial investment} = 0$$
$$3.605(X) = \$80,000$$
$$X = \$80,000 \div 3.605 = \$22,191$$

Sensitivity analysis indicates that the annual cash savings can decrease $12,809 ($35,000 − $22,191) before the net project value equals zero.

Should managers fear the actual cash inflow may be only $20,000 rather than the optimistic estimate of $35,000, the following sensitivity analysis measures the impact on net present value of using the pessimistic cash flow estimate:

Present value of $20,000 × 3.605	$72,100
Less initial investment	80,000
Net present value	$ (7,900)

The original net present value was $46,175, determined by subtracting $80,000 from $126,175 ($35,000 × 3.605). The net present value using the revised cash inflow is $(7,900). This indicates the impact of a $15,000 annual difference in cash flow is a $54,075 difference in net present value (i.e., $7,900 + $46,175 = $54,075).

Cost of Estimation Errors in Cash Flows and Present Value

Before management purchases the $80,000 worth of equipment, accountants should calculate the **cost of estimation error** or the **cost of prediction error.** This is the cost to a company of incorrectly estimating the value of one or more parameters used in evaluating the project. Such costs occur in two situations: (1) a company has no other acceptable projects to choose if they reject the project under study, and (2) a company has other acceptable projects from which to choose if they reject the project in question.

No Acceptable Alternatives. When a company has no other projects that are acceptable, the cost of estimation error analysis involves comparing the cost of selecting the project with the cost of not selecting the project. If the cash flow from the project is only $20,000, sensitivity analysis reveals that the best decision is to reject the project because, if the company purchases $80,000 worth of equipment, a $7,900 cost of estimation error occurs as follows:

Net present value of optimal decision of not investing	$ –0–
Less net present value if project gives $20,000 cash flow	(7,900)
Cost of estimation error	$7,900

If instead of a $15,000 error in annual cash savings, the error is only $5,000 (i.e., cash flows are $30,000 annually instead of the $35,000 originally expected), the net present value is positive as follows:

Present value of cash inflows ($30,000 × 3.605)	$108,150
Less initial investment	80,000
Net present value	$ 28,150

Because the net present value of the equipment is positive with either a $30,000 or $35,000 annual cash flow, the decision in both cases is to invest in the project. Remember that net present value represents the difference between the discounted cash inflow and outflow. Whether the difference is positive or negative only indicates that the actual return on the capital asset is larger or smaller than the cost of capital.

Acceptable Alternatives. If a company has more acceptable projects than it can engage in, management accepts first the project that best meets company goals. When a company accepts one project and turns down another project, the cost of estimation error is a comparison of the net present value of the accepted investment with the net present value of the best project rejected. Using the original net present value of $46,175 calculated on page 601, and assuming the company does not accept a comparable project with a $32,000 net present value, the $32,000 is an opportunity cost representing the best investment forgone. However, if the $35,000 annual cash flow estimated is overly optimistic and $30,000 cash flow results each year, the cost of estimation error in this type of analysis is

Net present value of best alternative forgone	$32,000
Net present value of project accepted with actual cash flow of	
$30,000	28,150
Cost of estimation error	$ 3,850

Cash Flow Changes and Internal Rate of Return

Sensitivity analysis indicates the following impact on internal rate of return if actual cash flow is $20,000 instead of the $35,000 estimate:

Interest rate of return with expected cash flow	
$80,000/$35,000 = 2.286; from Exhibit 17–6 by interpolation .	37.07 percent
Internal rate of return with actual cash flow	
$80,000/$20,000 = 4; by interpolation	7.94 percent
Difference in internal rate of return	29.13 percent

If the cash flow is not as favorable as originally expected, selecting this project would result in approximately 29.13 percent less return than anticipated.

Cost of Estimation Errors in Cash Flows and Internal Rate of Return

No Acceptable Alternatives. The cost of estimating the incorrect internal rate of return when there are no acceptable alternative projects is the difference between the expected and actual annual return. With an expected internal rate of return of 37.07 percent and an actual return of 7.94 percent, if the cash flow is $20,000 rather than $35,000, the cost of estimation error is

Expected annual return ($80,000 × 37.07%)	$29,656
Actual annual return ($80,000 × 7.94%)	6,352
Cost of estimation error	$23,304

A shorter calculation is to multiply the project's cost by the difference between expected and actual internal rate of return as follows: $80,000 × 29.13% = $23,304, yielding the same cost of estimation error.

Acceptable Alternatives. If the internal rate of return of the best alternative forgone is 10 percent and that for the actual annual return is 7.94 percent, the cost of estimation error is

$$\$80,000 \times 2.06\%^* = \$1,648$$
*10.00% − 7.94% = 2.06%

Economic Life Changes and Present Value

Companies also use sensitivity analysis to measure the uncertainty attached to a capital asset's useful life. For example, if the proposed project's life is three years rather than five years, the net present value is $4,070 as shown next, instead of $46,175 as computed on page 601.

Present value using revised life ($35,000 × 2.402, cumulative	
factor for three years, 12% from Table B)	$84,070
Less initial investment	80,000
Net present value	$ 4,070

Even though the net present value still exceeds the original investment cost, this type of analysis does not tell management how much the estimation error costs the company.

Cost of Estimation Errors in Economic Lives

As just illustrated, errors in estimation may also occur in the useful life of a project. If instead of a five-year life, the project's actual life is only two years, its net present value is

Present value using revised life ($35,000 × 1.609 cumulative	
factor for two years, 12% from Table B)	$ 56,315
Less initial investment	80,000
Net present value	$(23,685)

Because the net present value is negative, the optimal decision is not to invest in the project. If the investment is made based on the original five-year estimate and there are no alternative investments, the **cost of the estimation error** or **cost of prediction error** is

Net present value of optimal decision of not investing	$ −0−
Net present value if equipment's life is two years	(23,685)
Cost of prediction error	$23,685

If, however, an alternative with a positive net present value of $5,000 exists, the cost of estimation error is $28,685.

Computer Studies. Various computer models simulating possibilities and probabilities offer management additional means of evaluation that are not feasibly done manually. For example, a computer simulation can combine probabilistic estimates of cash flows into a probabilistic distribution of the internal rate of return. Computer studies yield more reliable information than manual evaluation techniques.

Managers should carefully examine projects with forecasted results very near the cutoff point because there is little room for error. For example, if they expect an investment proposal to yield an 11 percent return when the required rate of return is 10 percent, there is a smaller zone for error than for an investment forecasted to yield a 20 percent return. Companies need higher sophisticated evaluation to better determine the profitability of the proposal. This additional cost is warranted if two alternative proposals yield approximately the same acceptable results, or if the evaluation indicates results that are near the rejection point.

Choice of a Method. Managers often hesitate to apply present value or internal rate of return and rely on nondiscounting criteria, such as professional judgment, the payback method, or the unadjusted rate of return. These managers do not use discounting techniques because they believe that cash flows and economic life represent such rough estimates, in many cases, that they cannot justify the cost of applying such refined methods. Granted, it is difficult to determine the cost of capital used to discount the cash flows. Also, the cash flows used are point estimates rather than more realistic estimates of ranges. Therefore, it is difficult to relate this variability or risk to an appropriate discount factor. However, discounted cash flow techniques consider the time value of money and the cash flows over the entire life of the project. Discounted cash flow techniques have the advantage of using cash flows rather than accounting income. Using the payback method or the unadjusted return is understandable if a company has no choice but to purchase the asset. For example, the Environmental Protection Agency may require a particular pollution device. Similarly, profitability is not the prime consideration when incurring some capital expenditures, such as luxurious offices, because they are status symbols.

Even though management should apply one or more evaluation techniques in making capital investment decisions, they cannot ignore such factors as legal requirements and social responsibilities. The capital investment program must also allow for emergencies. For example, a machine that managers expect to operate efficiently for several more years may break down. If this machine is crucial to production, management may have no choice but to incur major expenditures in repairing or replacing it. Managers must make provisions to handle proposals of this nature more rapidly than less critical projects.

Inflation in the Capital Budgeting Process (L.O. 2)

An important aspect of capital budgeting is the impact of inflation on budgeting techniques, particularly incorporating price level changes into the model. In a taxless economy, inflation would affect cash flows and the applicable discount rate in a comparable manner. Therefore, the effect on present value calculations would be irrelevant. However, we do not live in such an economy, and we must consider the impact of taxes in almost all business decisions. In addition, assuming a constant price level is erroneous because the general price level changes over the life of the project. An increase in the general price level index increases future revenues, wages, materials, and other project costs.

Inflation's Effect.   To illustrate the **impact of inflation on capital budgeting,** assume that in the current year, 19X0, a company is considering the purchase of equipment with an expected life of five years. The controller indicates that the company's cost of capital unadjusted for inflation is 8 percent. Economic advisors determine that the general price level index should rise by 6 percent a year for the next five years. The company anticipates operations from the equipment to yield $55,000 in cash revenues and require $20,000 cash expenses, all in 19X0 prices. The requested 8 percent rate for the cost of capital (the discount rate) is adjusted for inflation and rounded to 15 percent as follows:

$$1.08 \times 1.06 = 1.145 - 1.000 = 15\%$$

Adding the cost of capital to the inflation rate is not appropriate; instead, these values should be multiplied to incorporate the compounding effect of inflation.

Exhibit 18–2 illustrates an adjustment for inflation for both the discount rate and the predicted cash inflows. Each year is adjusted for an inflation increase of 6 percent for the next five years; for example, in Year 2, 106 percent × 106 percent = 112.4 percent. Alternatively, we could have used the estimated specific year-end index value for each of the next five years in Exhibit 18–2. The present value factors obtained from Table A in the appendix reflect the discount rate adjusted for inflation (15 percent in Exhibit 18–2). Note that inflation does not affect depreciation and its tax shield because we must base the income tax deduction on the original cost of the asset in 19X0 dollars. Assume we deduct a 45 percent tax rate and the depreciation shown in Exhibit 18–2 for tax purposes.

EXHIBIT 18–2   The Effects of Inflation on Capital Budgeting Procedures

Revenue	19X1	19X2	19X3	19X4	19X5	Total
Revenue	$55,000	$55,000	$55,000	$55,000	$55,000	
Less: Cash expenses	20,000	20,000	20,000	20,000	20,000	
Pretax cash flow unadjusted for inflation	$35,000	$35,000	$35,000	$35,000	$35,000	
Inflation index	1.06	1.124	1.191	1.262	1.338	
Inflation adjusted pretax cash flow ..	$37,100	$39,340	$41,685	$44,170	$46,830	
Less: Depreciation	35,000	27,000	18,000	12,000	8,000	
Inflation adjusted taxable income ...	$ 2,100	$12,340	$23,685	$32,170	$38,830	
Less: Income tax (45%)	945	5,553	10,658	14,477	17,474	
Inflation adjusted aftertax income ...	$ 1,155	$ 6,787	$13,027	$17,693	$21,356	
Add: Noncash depreciation expense .	35,000	27,000	18,000	12,000	8,000	
Net aftertax cash flow adjusted for inflation	$36,155	$33,787	$31,027	$29,693	$29,356	
Present value factor	.870	.756	.658	.572	.497	
Present value	$31,455	$25,543	$20,416	$16,984	$14,590	$108,988
Less: Investment in equipment (1.00 × $100,000)						100,000
Net present value						$ 8,988

The project appears acceptable because the real cash inflows from the equipment purchase are adequate. To prevent the erroneous acceptance of capital investment projects and provide optimum resource allocation during times of changing prices, the capital budgeting process should incorporate the effects of inflation.

Capital Budgeting in the Automated Environment (L.O. 3)

The difficulty of justifying the large investment required in computerization is a big obstacle to purchasing an automated manufacturing system. Traditional capital expenditure analysis focuses on future cash inflows that come mainly from savings in labor costs. Traditional models often do not provide managers with enough incentive for changing to flexible manufacturing systems because of inadequate means for quantifying the benefits from increased manufacturing flexibility, reduced inventory levels, and the capacity for increased product innovations. As a result, companies may ignore these benefits and delay automation.

Replacement-Trigger Thinking

In studying proposed capital expenditures in the past, most managers used **replacement-trigger thinking,** which assumes they replace only worn-out or unworkable equipment. Important advantages of automated factory equipment include increased flexibility and opportunities for responding to changes in material availability, product design, or product-mix demand. These advantages destroy replacement-trigger thinking. Usually, managers cannot legitimately evaluate advanced automated equipment on a machine-for-machine basis. Even though the advantages derived from replacing a single machine have merit, that is not the final goal. Instead, greater benefits flow from such systematic, overall changes as reductions in design time and errors, and an increase in product quality.

Advantages of Automating

Acquiring equipment capable of manufacturing varieties of quality products leads to increased revenues. This equipment allows companies to better meet changing consumer needs. Computers and robots are consistent because they perform the same tasks. Unfortunately, human beings do not operate in the same manner for every task because they make random errors. Robots and automation make **deterministic errors.** If a computer is programmed that one plus one is three, it produces a three every time it encounters one plus one. Deterministic errors are much easier to correct; this is the reason automation produces higher-quality products.

Robots perform many functions more accurately and at lower cost than human workers. Robots are useful for dirty jobs such as automobile spot welding where welding errors can cause large losses. Robots are also effective for intricate, repetitive jobs such as assembling computer components. Highly automated equipment may not be cost-effective, however, for operations involving nonrepetitive short production runs.

The management of some companies views flexible, automated machines as offering additional capabilities and, in turn, profitable challenges. Robots are investments in overcapacity that keep pressure on the company to grow, to develop new products and services, and to market these products and services effectively and aggressively. Automated equipment forces managers to search for new markets or to increase their market share in present markets. Their incentive is to profitably use the automated machine's competence and volume capabilities.

Automation also provides capability that never existed before. As parts flow through factories, automated reading devices continuously track them. Managers find it valuable knowing where inventories are, what operations are in process, and how long inventories remain at any given operation.

Flexible manufacturing systems facilitate **repetitive manufacturing** that involves assembling components into a product rather than fabricating a product. The characteristics of repetitive manufacturing are small lot sizes, fast setup times, pull material systems, total quality control, significantly reduced inventories and floor space, rate scheduling, fixed routings, short cycle times, and a flexible work force. Repetitive manufacturing implies the elimination of job order production in which costs are assigned to each order or unit of production manufactured according to customers' specifications. Repetitive manufacturing also eliminates cost collection by work orders.

Failure of Traditional Capital Budgeting Techniques (L.O. 3)

Managers first recognized the need for change in capital asset evaluation while studying proposed acquisitions of capital investments in computer-integrated manufacturing (CIM) technology. Investment evaluation and decision criteria must be broader when considering automated equipment because these purchases involve more company segments and activities. Additionally, the criteria include more qualitative than quantitative factors. Thus, traditional capital budgeting models fail to truly evaluate automated manufacturing systems for several reasons.

Benefits of Quality Improvement

Traditional capital budgeting models often overlook various indirect and intangible benefits. Discounted cash flow models focus on future net cash savings in reduced labor costs and energy costs that the proposed equipment generates. The danger is relying solely on the easily quantified savings in labor, energy, and materials from new capital investments and ignoring those subjective gains more difficult to quantify.

When robots and other new equipment cause increases in product quality, capital budgeting analysis should reflect these benefits. Anticipated savings from fewer customer complaints and reduced warranty costs from achieving a lower incidence of defects represent additional benefits of proposed capital assets. Also, the proposed capital expenditure may permit faster, more flexible, or more reliable production scheduling that reduces inventory levels. The purchase decision should include the decrease in total inventory carrying costs from releasing factory space. With increased flexibility available to accommodate product changes, inventory buffers are no longer needed and turnaround time can drop dramatically. Shorter lead times allow companies to respond quickly to customer demands. An increase in the quality of the products may also lead to an increase in demand.

Quantifying the benefits from increased manufacturing flexibility, reduced inventory levels, and the capacity for increased product innovation is subjective. However, this does not justify ignoring such benefits. If ignored, managers assume the value of these benefits is zero. Instead, improving the measurement of these factors should promote more congruence and improved profitability. No longer should managers reject proposed equipment on the basis of its insufficient labor or energy savings without considering the equipment's impact on product or service quality.

Profitable Quality. However, justifying capital expenditures solely on the basis of quality is inadvisable. Even though quality is important, the main objective of a company is to make money in the present and in the future. For public relations purposes, companies advertise that their objective is to provide customers with a better quality product; however, profitability should be their goal. For example, companies manufacturing personal computers should not install expensive keyboards with speed capabilities that exceed the typing ability of users. For improved quality to have real merit, higher revenues and/or lower expenses should result.

Hurdle Rate Set Too High

An additional weakness of traditional capital budgeting occurs when managers use too high a discount, hurdle, and payback rate. The rate should not be higher than what a company could earn on its common stock or other investments. A company can justify a lower hurdle rate if the new investment involves the installation of flexible manufacturing systems. New technologies enable companies to manufacture products of better quality with fewer rejects and recalls, thereby reducing the risk in the product output and the capital expenditure.

Projects Rather than Strategies Justified

Traditional capital budgeting techniques also attempt to justify projects rather than strategies. A long-run opportunity is often missed because of management's orientation toward short-term returns. Standard evaluation criteria like net present value, payback, and return on investment typically assume that change involves replacement of individual machines. This assumption reinforces the short-term focus because it permits consideration of only differential benefits. Also, publicly traded companies are required to issue quarterly financial reports emphasizing a short-term orientation.

Effects of Not Automating Not Evaluated

Traditional capital budgeting techniques that consider the time value of money assume money in hand is worth more than money promised in the future. By implication, a cost deferred is preferable to a cost incurred. Although this is often true—and sometimes useful—managers often extend this concept to a point where they view present activities as bearing little or no risk and see new activities as risky. Thus, conventional capital budgeting analysis fails to quantify the difference between making and not making the investment.

Companies find that not only do they need to carefully analyze the impact of purchasing automated equipment but they also have to closely evaluate the impact of not acquiring new equipment. Companies that spend millions of dollars on single-purpose, high-volume equipment are likely to lock themselves into unchanging products and processes. Because of high machinery cost and the difficulty of replacing equipment, companies are often slow to respond to changing tastes and demands, with serious consequences for market share and cost positions. However, greater flexibility allows companies to use automated equipment for successive generations of products, providing a longer useful life than conventional equipment.

After the purchase, it is very difficult to measure whether an investment in a robot or a numerically controlled machine tool accomplished what managers expected. Much of the investment in new manufacturing technology provides increased quality, reduced lead time, and maximum flexibility for product and volume change. After purchasing and using automated equipment, managers are now evaluating the dollar impact of their greater flexibility. Even after quantifying indirect benefits, the investment may not meet the heightened expectations of production managers.

All Trade-Offs Not Considered

Managers give the substitution of machines for production labor as a justification for factory automation. Many times robots can perform more consistently, accurately, and at lower cost than human workers. However, significant trade-offs are involved in the substitution of machinery for factory labor. In justifying the investment in robots, numerically controlled machine tools, and other techniques of automation, discounted cash flow or ROI calculations make certain assumptions about future operating costs. Management believes costs will decrease while quality increases with automation. Yet, automation affects other indirect costs, such as programming, material handling, setup, inventory levels, and relationships with suppliers. Automated factories require higher-skilled personnel, and a company may find such qualified personnel unavailable. Reductions in direct labor may have already been optimized, so that total out-of-pocket costs may actually increase with automation.

Assets Constructed for Own Use (L.O. 4)

Measurement problems arise in determining the asset cost that companies should capitalize when they construct assets for their own use. The material, labor, and factory overhead costs that accountants can directly identify with the assets present little difficulty. However, determining the normal factory overhead to capitalize is more complex.

In determining the amount of factory overhead to assign, the capacity level at which the plant operates is an influencing factor. For example, if the plant is operating at planned capacity at the time a company constructs the asset, management must postpone manufacturing some products so plant space, machinery, and personnel are available to build the asset. Under these conditions, they should allocate a fair share of general factory overhead to the asset on the same basis as that applied to goods manufactured for sale.

If the plant is operating with idle capacity and management uses part of this capacity in manufacturing the asset rather than purchasing from an outsider, they may not reduce production of units. In this case, the question arises whether they should assign any of the general factory overhead that is normally allocated to the units produced to the constructed asset. No doubt exists about the capitalization of direct material, direct labor, and additional factory overhead caused by the construction. However, accountants have differing views concerning general factory overhead.

Capitalizing General Factory Overhead

Some accountants believe the full cost of constructed assets should include general factory overhead; otherwise, they overstate the cost of idle capacity. They argue for not penalizing normal manufacturing operations by having it bear all general factory overhead when other assets are using some of the facilities. They also argue that future periods will reap the benefit of constructed assets. Further, these accountants believe the costs should be deferred since special status should not be given to these assets.

Other accountants believe they should assign no general factory overhead to constructed assets when utilizing idle plant capacity. They argue that the company did not consider this cost in the differential cost analysis used in deciding to make the asset. They believe that the cost of this idle capacity would occur regardless of whether they undertook construction or not. Thus, they assign no general factory overhead to keep from affecting the cost of producing units. Admittedly, both positions have merit. However, this author argues for assigning a fair portion of general factory overhead to determine the cost of assets constructed for a company's own use. This approach conforms more closely to the cost principle that an allocation is necessary to determine appropriate costs for both the units produced and the asset constructed. This position does not penalize either asset involved.

Excess Construction Cost

If the constructed asset cost materially exceeds its fair market value, accountants should treat the excess cost as a period cost. Under these conditions, full construction cost does not represent a valid charge against future operations through capitalization. The company may have been less efficient than an outside producer, and they should recognize this in the current period.

After approving a project, accountants must apply control techniques to ensure that the company is following planned objectives. Periodically, accountants should compare actual costs incurred on the project with budgeted costs and note variances. If actual costs begin exceeding the original estimate, managers must either approve additional appropriations of funds or revise plans. After the capital expenditure is operating, managers should compare its actual performance with expected performance to determine whether overly optimistic claims were made about its efficiency. Even though the investment now represents a sunk cost, this comparison is helpful for future decisions and evaluation of managers involved in the process. If individuals realize that the company makes postmortem examinations of all capital expenditures, this discourages them from making overly optimistic estimates. They are more likely to support their claims with as much data as are feasible.

Summary

Labor or energy savings are not the only justification for new capital investments. Qualitative factors, such as improvements in product quality, market share, customer service, and competitive posture, are relevant. Managers should include such factory floor benefits as reduced raw materials and work in process inventory and the resulting increases in inventory turnover. The hidden benefits of CIM result from the close integration, improved speed and flexibility, higher quality, and greater product variation these systems can support.

It is no longer a question of whether to replace older technologies. Instead, the question is whether survival is possible if companies fail to acquire new technologies. The price of delay may be disastrous. Reliance strictly on traditional capital budgeting techniques without quantifying the additional benefits automation brings is inadvisable. Although the benefits of automation may be difficult to quantify, they are significant.

Important Terms and Concepts

cost of capital (hurdle rate), 627
sensitivity analysis, 628
cost of estimation error (cost of prediction error), 629

inflation impact on capital budgeting, 633
replacement-trigger thinking, 634
deterministic errors, 634
repetitive manufacturing, 635

Problem for Self-Study

Inflation Impact in Capital Budgeting

Futuristic Industries, Inc.'s Denver Division is considering buying a robot for use in its factory. If the robot is purchased, five positions would be eliminated. Other expenses, such as utilities and repairs, would increase with the use of the robot. These are the expected changes in costs.

Wages and benefits of five positions eliminated	$72,000
Increase in utilities expense	18,000
Estimated repair expense increase	5,000

The robot would cost $125,000 and would be ready for use at the start of the next year. The robot would have a five-year life expectancy. Depreciation is deducted for tax purposes as follows: Year 1, $45,000; Year 2, $27,500; Year 3, $26,250; Year 4, $15,750; and Year 5, $10,500.

According to company policy, no special approval from the home office is needed for the proposed purchase. However, top management wants a 9 percent cost of capital rate used for analysis. The effects of inflation should be considered. Inflation is forecast at an average annual rate of 6 percent over the next five years. Therefore, cash flows should be adjusted by an estimated price level index. Then the appropriate discount rate is used to discount aftertax cash flows. The discount rate is the cost of capital multiplied by the inflation rate.

The estimated year-end index values for the next six years are as follows:

Year	Year-End Price Index
19X0 (current year)	1.00
19X1	1.02
19X2	1.04
19X3	1.06
19X4	1.08
19X5	1.10
19X6	1.12

Required:

Futuristic Industries, Inc., pays taxes at a rate of 46 percent. Assume all computations are made at year-end and round to whole dollars.

a. Using the price indexes provided, prepare a schedule of aftertax annual cash flows adjusted for inflation for the robot.
b. (1) Calculate the net present value for the robot.
   (2) Advise the Denver Division about buying the robot. Why or why not?
c. Assume a management consultant told the Denver Division chief that the division has not been properly reflecting inflation in the capital expenditure analysis. The consultant recommends adding the expected inflation rate to the cost of capital and then using the inflation adjusted cost of capital to discount projected cash flows. Use this approach to analyze the robot ignoring the year-end price indexes.
d. Compare the approach of the management consultant with the one currently being used to compensate for inflation. Which do you advise using?

Solution to Problem for Self-Study

FUTURISTIC INDUSTRIES, INC.

a.

	19X1	19X2	19X3	19X4	19X5
Wages and benefits saved	$72,000	$72,000	$72,000	$72,000	$72,000
Less additional:					
Utilities	(18,000)	(18,000)	(18,000)	(18,000)	(18,000)
Repair expenses	(5,000)	(5,000)	(5,000)	(5,000)	(5,000)
Net cost savings	$49,000	$49,000	$49,000	$49,000	$49,000
Inflation index	1.02	1.04	1.06	1.08	1.10
Inflation adjusted cost savings	$49,980	$50,960	$51,940	$52,920	$53,900
Less depreciation	45,000	27,500	26,250	15,750	10,500
Inflation adjusted taxable income . . .	$ 4,980	$23,460	$25,690	$37,170	$43,400
Income tax (46%)	2,291	10,792	11,817	17,098	19,964
Inflation adjusted aftertax					
income	$ 2,689	$12,668	$13,873	$20,072	$23,436
Add noncash depreciation expense .	45,000	27,500	26,250	15,750	10,500
Net aftertax cash flow adjusted					
for inflation*	$47,689	$40,168	$40,123	$35,822	$33,936

*Alternative approach is to subtract income taxes from inflation adjusted cost savings. For example, in 19X1, $49,980 − $2,291 = $47,689.

b.   1.   Cost of capital adjusted for inflation $= 1.09 \times 1.06 = 1.155 = 16\%$

Year	Net Aftertax Cash Flow Adjusted for Inflation	Discount Rate*	Present Value
19X0 (current)	$(125,000)	1.000	$(125,000)
19X1	47,689	.862	41,108
19X2	40,168	.743	29,845
19X3	40,123	.641	25,719
19X4	35,822	.552	19,774
19X5	33,936	.476	16,154
			$ 7,600

*Using Present Value of $1 Table

2.   Based on the preceding analyses with the 9 percent cost of capital rate, adjusted for inflation, the machine should be purchased because there is a positive net present value.

c.

	19X1	19X2	19X3	19X4	19X5	Total
Net cash cost savings (from Requirement *a*)	$49,000	$49,000	$49,000	$49,000	$49,000	
Less increase in depreciation expense .	45,000	27,500	26,250	15,750	10,500	
Increase in taxable income	$ 4,000	$21,500	$22,750	$33,250	$38,500	
Increase in income taxes (46 percent)	1,840	9,890	10,465	15,295	17,710	
Increase in aftertax income	$ 2,160	$11,610	$12,285	$17,955	$20,790	
Add back noncash expense (depreciation)	45,000	27,500	26,250	15,750	10,500	
Net aftertax annual cash inflow unadjusted for inflation	$47,160	$39,110	$38,535	$33,705	$31,290	
Present value factor at 15%*	.870	.756	.658	.572	.497	
Present value	$41,029	$29,567	$25,356	$19,279	$15,551	$130,782
Investment required						125,000
Net present value						$ 5,782

*Present value of $1 at 15 percent, which is 9 percent cost of capital plus 6 percent inflation rate.

d. The company's present method is preferred. Adding the cost of the capital to the inflation rate is not the most appropriate method as suggested by the management consultant; instead, these values should be multiplied to incorporate the compounding effect of inflation.

Review Questions

1. Discuss the ideal conditions under which to introduce automation.

2. Provide evidence to support or dispute the following statement: The probability of success of a robot installation is directly proportional to the number of affected people involved in the discussions and planning of the robot project.

3. Give three advantages of using robots in the manufacturing process.

4. Contrast traditional production equipment with flexible automation; include advantages that flexible manufacturing systems offer.

5. In justifying the purchase of new capital equipment, explain why reliance on labor or energy savings may not be adequate for management's evaluation process.

6. Discuss the reasons why a manager might make the following comment: "Not only does my company need to evaluate very carefully the impact of purchasing a robot, but we also have to evaluate very carefully the impact of not acquiring the latest automated equipment."

7. Why might a far-sighted manager purchase a second robot soon after successfully installing and using a first robot even though, at present, there is no need for the expensive second robot?

8. Define replacement-trigger thinking and indicate why it is inadequate when evaluating automated capital expenditures.

9. Name some benefits of automated equipment that are difficult to quantify.

10. Briefly discuss three changes a company's traditional cost accounting system must make to fulfill the purpose of the accounting system as automated manufacturing is implemented.

11. Explain why a narrow interpretation of the capital budgeting procedures traditionally used may keep desirable investment projects from being accepted.

CPA/CMA/CIA Multiple Choice Questions

1. (AICPA) The capital budgeting technique known as accounting rate of return uses

	Depreciation Expense	Time Value of Money
a.	No	No
b.	No	Yes
c.	Yes	Yes
d.	Yes	No

2. (AICPA) A company is considering exchanging an old asset for a new asset. Ignoring income tax considerations, which of the following is (are) economically relevant to the decision?

	Carrying Amount of Old Asset	Disposal Value of Old Asset
a.	No	No
b.	No	Yes
c.	Yes	Yes
d.	Yes	No

3. (AICPA) The discount rate (hurdle rate of return) must be determined in advance for the

   a. Payback period method.
   b. Time adjusted rate of return method.
   c. Internal rate of return method.
   d. Net present value method.

4. (AICPA) Which of the following capital budgeting techniques consider(s) cash flow over the entire life of the project?

	Internal Rate of Return	Payback
a.	Yes	Yes
b.	Yes	No
c.	No	Yes
d.	No	No

5. (AICPA) The payback capital budgeting technique considers

	Income over Entire Life of Project	Time Value of Money
a.	No	No
b.	No	Yes
c.	Yes	Yes
d.	Yes	No

6. (CIA) Risk can be controlled in capital budgeting situations by assuming a:

   a. High accounting rate of return.
   b. Large net present value.
   c. High net income.
   d. Short payback period.

7.–10. (CMA) Questions 7 through 10 are based on Plasto Corporation, a manufacturer of plastic products. The company is embarking on a five-year modernization and expansion plan. Thus, management is identifying all of the capital projects that it should consider. Financial analyses will be prepared for each identified project. Plasto will not select and implement all of the projects because some may not be financially attractive and some are mutually exclusive (i.e., choice of one project precludes the selection of any others). In addition, not all projects can be implemented due to a maximum dollar limit for capital projects.

The list of projects being considered follows. All modernization and expansion projects would be completed in three years. The projects have varying lives, but none exceeds seven years. Plasto's criteria for evaluating and selecting projects are maximization of return and quickness of investment recovery.

Project Identification and Description	Investment	Estimated Life (In Years)
• Maintenance: Extensive maintenance of current manufacturing facilities including repairs and some replacement of equipment. This work must be done to keep existing facilities in operation until any retooling and/or expansion projects are completed.	$2,000,000	3
• Retooling: Major retooling of current manufacturing facilities using general purpose equipment.	$6,000,000	5
• Retooling: Major retooling of current manufacturing facilities using special purpose equipment (this project and the prior project are mutually exclusive projects).	$8,500,000	5
• Make versus Buy: Construction of new facilities to manufacture parts and supplies used in making products. Parts and supplies are currently being purchased.	$5,000,000	7
• Expansion: Construction of new facilities to introduce new product NX-42.	$10,000,000	6
• Expansion: Construction of new facilities to introduce new product LV-221.	$12,000,000	7

7. Which one of the following pairs of capital investment evaluation techniques would best satisfy Plasto's criteria for selecting capital projects?

   a. Accounting rate of return and present value payback.
   b. Net present value and payback.
   c. Accounting rate of return and bailout payback.
   d. Internal rate of return and present value payback.
   e. Excess present value index and internal rate of return.

8. If Plasto is faced with capital rationing (i.e., maximum dollar amount allowed for capital projects is less than the outlays required for all projects), the best general method to employ to rank the projects would be the

   a. Present value payback.
   b. Excess present value index.
   c. Net present value.
   d. Internal rate of return.
   e. Payback.

9. If Plasto must decide between the two mutually exclusive retooling projects, the best general method to employ to decide between these projects would be the

   a. Present value payback.
   b. Excess present value index.
   c. Net present value.
   d. Internal rate of return.
   e. Payback.

10. If Plasto employs discounted cash flow techniques in evaluating capital investment projects, this reflects that management recognizes

    a. The importance of the time value of money.
    b. That cash flow is important to maintaining operations and generating future acceptable profits.
    c. The volatility of inflation and its effect on operations.

  d. The importance of recovering the initial investment outlay as soon as possible.

  e. The importance of incorporating risk in the evaluation process.

Exercises

E18–1 Quality in Capital Budgeting Approvals (L.O. 3)

A division manager of Waterhouse Company approaches the budgeting committee with a proposal to purchase a $500,000 cutting machine. When asked to justify this expenditure, the division manager replies, "Forget about all those capital budgeting techniques that cost accounting courses introduce. Instead our company must focus solely on quality. Certainly, I believe this new cutting machine will help us improve quality."

Required:

Assume you are the cost accountant on the budgeting committee. What is your reply?

E18–2 Internal Rate of Return Earned, Cost of Estimation Error (L.O. 2)

NANN, Inc., recently purchased a machine costing $226,000; management expects it to generate a 10-year stream of net cash benefits amounting to $40,000 annually.

Required:

a. Calculate the rate of return NANN expects to earn from this machine.

b. Assume actual net cash benefits are less favorable than anticipated and amount to $30,707.
 (1) What is the difference in the internal rate of return?
 (2) If the internal rate of return on the best alternative forgone is 9 percent, what is the cost of the estimation error?

c. Assume actual net cash benefits are more favorable than expected and should amount to $53,912. What is the difference in the internal rate of return?

E18–3 Selecting Interest Rate (L.O. 3)

Ellen Company purchased an asset costing $18,490 and having a useful life of five years. The cost accountant estimates annual aftertax net cash benefits to be $5,000 at the end of each year. The following portion of a present value table shows an annuity of $1 at year-end for five years:

10%	3.791
12%	3.605
14%	3.433

Required:

Indicate the maximum interest rate that Ellen Company could pay for the capital employed over the life of this asset without loss on this project.

E18–4 Comparing Profits with Machine Acquisition (L.O. 4)

A salesperson has approached Wellington Company concerning the purchase of a new machine to replace one of its present machines. The new machine would cost $120,000, have no estimated salvage value, and a six-year life. Variable operating costs would be $65,000 per year.

  The book value of the present machine is $60,000 and it has a remaining life of six years. The disposal value of the present machine is $10,000, but it would be zero after six years. The variable operating costs presently are $85,000 per year.

Required:

Ignoring present value calculations and income tax, determine the difference in profit before income taxes for the six years in total if the new machine is acquired rather than retaining the present one.

E18–5 Equipment Costs to Capitalize (L.O. 4)

Brodnax, Inc., received bids from several companies for a machine needed in production. Bids range from $100,000 to $125,000. Management decided to construct the machine using its own facilities. Costs incurred are as follows:

Materials	$40,000	(2/10, n/30 discount not taken because of a cash shortage)
Direct labor	30,000	
Variable overhead	34,000	
Fixed overhead	10,000	(allocated on basis of direct labor cost)
Installation	1,000	
Operational test time and test material	600	

The company would bear the installation and the testing costs if the machine were purchased.

Required:

(Ignore interest capitalization.)

a. Determine what costs management should consider in arriving at the decision to make or buy the machine. Indicate the dollar amount.
b. Decide which costs should be entered in the accounting records. Provide support for your answer.
c. Determine if management was correct in deciding to construct the machine rather than to buy it.

E18–6 Aftertax Cash Benefit, Payback Period, and Cost of Estimation Error in Economic Lives (L.O. 2)

Hancock Company is planning to purchase machinery costing $72,000 to use in their operations. Management estimates that the life of the machine will be 12 years, and the depreciation for Year 1 is $6,000. The company estimates the first year's pretax cash savings from using this machine will be $15,000. The company's income tax rate is 35 percent.

Required:

a. Calculate the annual aftertax net cash benefits of this machine for Year 1.
b. Assume the annual aftertax cash benefits of this machine were $12,400. What would the payback period be?
c. Assume the annual aftertax cash benefits of this machine were $12,000 for each of the years of its life. What would the net present value of this investment be, assuming management estimates its cost of capital to be 14 percent?
d. Assume the useful life should be 10 years and annual aftertax net cash benefits are $12,000. What is the cost of estimation error if there are no alternative investments, and the machine is purchased based on the original 12-year estimate?

E18–7 Make or Buy Machine (L.O. 4)

Clark Manufacturing Company secured bids from several outside companies for a machine needed in production. The bids ranged from a high of $60,000 to a low of $53,000.

Management decided to construct the machine using its own facilities by adding a third work shift to perform the construction. Workers used materials with a list price of $20,000 subject to 2/10, n/30 terms. A shortage of cash prevented the company from paying the invoice within the discount period and the discount was lost. Clark's costs included direct labor of $15,000 and variable overhead of $17,000. Fixed overhead allocated on the basis of direct labor-hours amounted to $6,600.

Installation of the new machine cost $700. The machine required 40 hours of an operator's time, costing $200, in testing its performance; materials of $180 were wasted in this testing process. The company would have to bear the same installation and testing cost if the machine were purchased.

Required:

a. Indicate the costs management should consider in arriving at the decision to make or buy the machine.
b. Determine what advice you would give management in arriving at a decision.
c. Compute the cost of a new machine that should be entered in the accounting records.

E18–8 Differential Costs and Cash Flows (L.O. 2)

Management of Freeman Company is considering the purchase of manufacturing facilities needed to process a new product. The new equipment will cost $200,000, with a useful life of five years with no salvage value. Straight-line depreciation will be used. The processing facilities will occupy space in the existing plant that is now being used by the office staff. When the new product occupies the office space, on which the actual depreciation is $15,000 based on a 15-year life, Freeman Company will rent an adjacent building for an annual cost of $18,500. You obtain the following estimates of differential revenue and expense on an average annual basis:

Sales	$800,000
Cost of products sold (excluding depreciation)	600,000
Administrative and marketing expense (excluding rent)	30,000

Freeman Company requires an accounting rate of return of 12 percent after income taxes on average investment proposals. The effective income tax rate is 48 percent. Ignore the time value of money.

Required:

Determine the following:

a. The average annual differential costs for the first five years (including income taxes) which must be considered in evaluating this decision.
b. The minimum annual net income needed to meet the company's requirement for this investment.
c. Estimated differential cash flow during the second year.
d. Estimated annual operating income after allowing for income taxes and the return on investment in the new equipment resulting from introducing the new product.

Problems

P18–9 Automatic versus Manual Operation (L.O. 3)

McBride Corporation has been manually placing the label on its perfume sold in designer bottles. Part-time employees earning minimum wages have put the labels on these perfume bottles. Direct costs of performing this task have been:

Wages and payroll taxes	$10,500
Labels, glue, and other supplies	3,000

The company presently uses a machine to seal labels for its other cosmetic products since these containers are of standard design.

A salesperson for an equipment dealer has recently approached management with an automatic machine that seals labels on unique containers. The machine will cost $40,000 with $2,000 salvage value at the end of an eight-year life. Straight-line depreciation will be used. Sales terms are cash on delivery. Since the machine is expected to become jammed periodically, 15 percent more labels and supplies will be used than were used with manual operations. In addition to labor required placing labels in the machine, some supervision will be required while the machine is in operation. Management proposes to use an employee presently working in the manufacturing plant; she will also perform her present duties. This employee will devote one fifth of her time to the supervision of the new machine; the annual salary of this employee is $15,000, including payroll taxes.

Utilities are expected to increase $1,200 annually due to the operations of the proposed machine; however, all machinery repairs costing more than $800 per year will be covered by the equipment company. The machine will occupy space presently being used for the manual operations.

The company presently has taxable income on its other operations and pays an average 42 percent rate of income tax.

Required:

a. Assume an 18 percent cost of capital and use present value analysis to determine whether the new equipment should be purchased.

b. Determine the payback period.

c. Decide which additional factors McBride should consider before making a decision regarding the purchase.

P18–10 Approaches to Introducing Automation (L.O. 3)

Melody Company management has recently approved the purchase of an expensive automated machine for installation in the factory. Now that formal approval has been received and the funding secured, management must decide the most appropriate way to introduce the machine into the manufacturing process.

Joe Smith, a manager, argues that Melody Company should not use formal announcements or elaborate education programs because there is no reason to exaggerate the importance of robots. Instead, Smith argues, workers should see robots as just a part of ongoing automation. He argues that no managers should be told, not even the supervisor, about the machine. Smith believes that worker unrest will not be serious and no worker will file a grievance.

Smith also believes that a rapid introduction of the automated system is the best approach because the sooner the company can reap the benefits of the robots, the better for all concerned. Also, he points to the number of accidents that have occurred in the hazardous areas in which robots will be placed.

Jan Jones agrees with Smith that the company should not use formal announcements or elaborate education programs because there is no reason to exaggerate the importance of robots. However, she believes that supervisors and managers involved should be informed three to four months in advance of installation. Later, personnel and engineering staff should show slides explaining why the company is automating, stressing that the robot's sole purpose is to eliminate hazardous jobs, which is true for Melody Company. Also, managers should tell employees in advance about safety precautions when working with robots.

Jones also believes she has a unique idea to encourage worker acceptance of the robot. She proposes having a contest, open to employees in the affected departments, to name the robot. Once the name is chosen, a special nameplate will be designed for the robot. Some of the managers agree that this will be good public relations for the automated system, while others voice some concern over the idea. One manager even proposes that Melody Company adopt a corporate policy that robots are not to be named.

Tom Brown disagrees totally with Jones and Smith's approach to introducing robots. He argues that since Melody anticipates future large-scale use of robots, it is in the best interest of management to educate as many employees as possible and sell the idea of robots before they arrive.

Brown obviously disagrees with Smith's approach to introducing robots into operations. Brown believes that a gradual introduction is wiser. In fact, Brown believes that Melody should have on-site debugging of the robots—that the new equipment should be delivered directly to the plant and set up on-site, allowing engineers to work out the bugs before integrating the robot into the production system.

Required:

a. Discuss reasons why you think Brown believes that the introduction of robots should be gradual and debugging should be conducted on-site.
b. Describe any advantage to Smith's rapid introduction approach.
c. Suggest additional considerations management should address in advance of installing robots.
d. Indicate if Melody Company should adopt a corporate policy that robots are not to be named. Or do you agree with Jones concerning the naming the robot? Discuss support for both views.

P18–11 Aftertax Cash Benefit, Payback Period, and Cost of Estimation Error in Economic Lives (L.O. 2)

Black & Root Company is planning to purchase construction equipment that costs $1 million. Management estimates that the life of the machine will be nine years, salvage value is $100,000, and the straight-line depreciation method is to be used. The company estimates the annual cash savings from using this machine will be $150,000. The company income tax rate is 35 percent.

Required:

a. Calculate the annual aftertax net cash benefits of this machine for Year 3.
b. Assume the annual aftertax cash benefits of this equipment were $130,000 for each of the years of its life. What would the net present value of this investment be, assuming the company's cost of capital is determined to be 8 percent?
c. Assume the annual aftertax cash benefits of this machine were $130,000. What would the payback period be?
d. Assume the useful life should be 12 years and annual aftertax net cash benefits are $140,000. What is the cost of estimation error if there are no alternative investments and the equipment is purchased based on the original nine-year estimate?

P18–12 (CIA) Cost of Capital (L.O. 1)

If a company employs the net present value approach to capital budgeting, the appropriate discount rate is the cost of capital.

Required:

a. Define the finance term *cost of capital*. Include in your definition the major components of cost of capital, how the components are weighted, and whether it is based on average costs or marginal costs.
b. Note that one assumption inherent in using the cost of capital approach is that investments will be made in projects with a rate of return greater than the cost of capital. Identify three other underlying assumptions regarding either investments or sources of capital inherent in using the cost of capital figure in capital budgeting decisions.
c. Explain how expectations of future periods of high inflation, such as inflation greater than 10 percent per year, should be utilized or factored into the use of the cost of capital concept in the capital budgeting process.

P18–13 Capital Budgeting Techniques (L.O. 2)

Boatman Company is considering a machine whose initial outlay is $1.2 million. Straight-line depreciation is to be used, with no salvage value at the end of its useful life of 10 years. Net annual aftertax cash receipts are forecasted to be $175,000 for each of the 10 years.

Required:

Determine the:

a. Payback period.
b. Unadjusted rate of return on initial investment.
c. Unadjusted rate of return on average investment.
d. Net present value of the machine; the cost of capital is 10 percent.
e. Internal rate of return approach.

P18–14 Sensitivity Analysis (continuation of P18–13)

Using the data given in Problem 18–13 for Boatman Company, and assuming a 10 percent cost of capital, provide management with the following sensitivity analysis:

Required:

a. Calculate by how much net annual aftertax cash receipts would have to increase before the net project value equals zero.
b. Determine the net present value if the life of the proposed project should be 8 years instead of the originally estimated 10 years using $175,000 annual aftertax cash flow.
c. Assume the demand for Boatman's product increases to a level that is higher than expected and net annual aftertax cash receipts should be $196,000. What is the impact on net present value of this $21,000 annual increase in estimated net annual aftertax cash receipts? (Assume a 10-year life.)
d. Compute the impact of the cash flow difference on internal rate of return, assuming the annual cash flow should be $196,000.
e. Give the cost of the estimation error if the company rejected a project estimated to have a $4,000 net present value to invest in this project yielding a $175,000 annual aftertax cash flow.
f. Assume the annual aftertax cash flow is $175,000, the useful life of the machine is 10 years, and the company has no other acceptable projects. What is the cost of the estimation error, and what is the best decision for the company to make?

P18–15 Present Value and Cash Inflow Related to Purchasing (L.O. 4)

After careful study, top management of Jan Humphreys, Inc., has agreed on a model of equipment for use in manufacturing. However, management is undecided whether a purchase or leasing arrangement should be made. The equipment may be acquired by an outright cash purchase of $50,000 or by a leasing alternative of $13,000 per year for the life of the machine plus $0.25 per hour operated. Salvage value is estimated to be $2,000 with a six-year life; straight-line depreciation will be used. If the equipment is purchased, the annual cost of its maintenance contract will be $650. In addition, the electricity cost per hour operated is expected to cost $5. The lease would cover plant maintenance and all other normal operating costs except the electricity used.

If the equipment is purchased, the full purchase price could be borrowed from the bank at 8 percent annual interest and repaid in one payment at the end of the fifth year. No funds will be borrowed if the leasing arrangement is chosen. For purpose of this analysis, assume all expenditures including the lease rental will be made at the end of the year.

Assume a 48 percent income tax rate and an 8 percent minimum desired rate of return on investment. Management expects to operate the machine 1,800 hours the first year with an additional 200 hours each additional year.

Required:

a. Determine the present value of the purchase price of the equipment and the present value of the estimated salvage value under the purchase alternative.

b. Assume the purchase alternative is chosen and determine the annual cash inflow (tax reduction) related to depreciation.

c. Determine the annual aftertax cash outflow for interest and maintenance if the purchase alternative is chosen.

d. Advise the company if it should lease or buy. Support your answer with cost data.

P18–16 Inflation Impact in Capital Budgeting (L.O. 1)

The New York Division of Sandra Rogers, Inc., is evaluating the purchase of an assembly and finishing machine for use in the production of its appliances. Estimates indicate that if the machine is purchased, three positions could be eliminated. However, additional utilities and indirect material would be required to operate the machine. Analysis shows the following cost savings and additional costs in current 19X0 prices:

Wages and employee benefits of the three positions eliminated . . .	$62,500
Cost of additional utilities	12,000
Cost of additional indirect material	4,000

All equipment dealers contacted have promised delivery at the end of the current year. The machine will be purchased and installed at a cost of $100,000. This machine will be classified as five-year property for tax and economic purposes. Depreciation is deducted for tax purposes as follows: Year 1, $40,000; Year 2, $22,000; Year 3, $21,000; Year 4, $15,000; and Year 5, $2,000.

Management's philosophy is to allow division management much freedom in decision making, believing this is good training for future corporate leaders. As a result, each division has the authority to make capital expenditures up to $250,000 without corporate headquarters' approval.

However, corporate management does insist that a 10 percent rate for cost of capital be used in all analyses. This rate does not include an allowance for inflation, which is expected to occur at an average annual rate of 4 percent over the next five years. The New York Division accounts for inflation in capital expenditures analyses through adjusting the cash flows by an estimated price level index. The adjusted aftertax cash flows are then discounted using the appropriate discount rate. The discount rate used is the cost of capital multiplied by the inflation rate. The estimated year-end index values for each of the next six years are as follows:

Year	Year-End Price Index
19X0 (current year)	1.00
19X1	1.04
19X2	1.08
19X3	1.12
19X4	1.15
19X5	1.20
19X6	1.23

Sandra Rogers, Inc., pays income taxes at a 38 percent rate. Assume all operating revenues and expenditures occur at the end of the year.

Required:

(Round to whole dollars.)

a. Prepare a schedule, using the price indexes provided, showing the aftertax annual cash flows adjusted for inflation for the machine under consideration by the New York Division.

b. (1) Determine the net present value for the New York Division's machine.
   (2) Indicate what advice you would give New York Division management regarding the purchase.

c. Assume an investment analyst informs New York Division management that they are not properly recognizing inflation in the capital expenditure analysis. The analyst's approach compensates for inflation by adding the anticipated inflation rate to the cost of capital and then using the inflation-adjusted cost of capital to discount the projected cash flows. The year-end price indexes are ignored using this method. Use this approach to analyze the machine under consideration.

d. Compare the investment analyst's approach with the one presently used to compensate for inflation.

P18–17 Discounting Differential Cost in a Make-or-Buy Decision (L.O. 4)

Because Lamb Company's old equipment for making motor parts is no longer operable, the company principals are faced with the following alternatives:

1. Replace the old equipment with new equipment.
2. Buy motor parts from an outside supplier who quoted a unit price of $2 per part on an eight-year contract for a minimum of 70,000 units per year.

For the past three years, production has averaged 80,000 units in each year, and forecasts are that this level will remain unchanged for the next eight years. Records for the past three years reveal the following costs of manufacturing the motor parts on the old equipment:

Direct material	$0.38
Direct labor	0.37
Variable factory overhead	0.17
Fixed factory overhead (including $0.30 depreciation and $0.15 for supervision and other direct departmental fixed overhead)	0.45
	$1.37

The new equipment would cost $250,000 and have a disposal value of $10,000 at the end of its eight-year life. Straight-line depreciation is to be used on the new equipment. Assume a tax rate of 40 percent.

The sales representative for the new equipment provides the following information regarding operations. The new machine will allow direct labor and variable overhead to be reduced by $0.16 per unit. Based on cost data supplied by a competitor using identical equipment and similar operating conditions—except that production generally averages 60,000 units per year—the unit costs are

Direct material	$0.45
Direct labor	0.30
Variable factory overhead	0.08
Fixed factory overhead including $0.30 depreciation	0.50
	$1.33

Required:

a. Determine which alternative is more attractive, assuming the company desires a 12 percent return on investment. Support your decision with calculations.

b. List additional factors to consider before a decision is made.

P18–18 Comparison of Return on Investment and Discounted Cash Flow (L.O. 4)

Two years ago when Pershing Corporation purchased new equipment costing $200,000, an internal rate of return analysis showed that the equipment would save $69,832 in operating expenses per year over a five-year period, or a 22 percent return on capital before taxes per year.

Management has generally been pleased with the new equipment's performance and is surprised to read the accountant's report showing only a 16.6 percent return on investment (ROI) for the first year. To support the calculation, the accountant provides the following analysis:

Reduced operating expenses due to new equipment	$ 69,832
Less: Depreciation—20% of cost	40,000
Beforetax contribution	$ 29,832
Investment—beginning of Year 1	$200,000
Investment—ending of Year 1	$160,000
Average investment for Year 1	$180,000

$$\text{ROI} = \left(\frac{\$29,832}{\$180,000} \right) = 16.6\%$$

The accountant used the internal rate of return method for capital expenditure analysis, while using ROI for performance evaluation.

Required:

a. Give some reasons why the 16.6 percent return on investment for the new equipment as calculated by the accountant is not identical to the 22 percent internal rate of return calculated at the time the machine was approved for purchase.

b. Explain how the ROI calculation performed by Pershing's accountant differs from the unadjusted return on investment as illustrated in the chapter.

c. (1) Name the one factor that accounts for the major difference between the accountant's ROI calculation and internal rate of return analysis.

   (2) Discuss if the internal rate of return analysis can be restructured to make it consistent with ROI as calculated by Pershing's accountant.

P18–19 Comparing Methods of Giving Effect to Inflation (L.O. 1)

In analyzing the purchase of finishing equipment, Fonda, Inc., estimates that the annual cash cost savings expected from the machine will be $42,000 in current 19X0 annual prices. The equipment can be purchased and installed at a cost of $90,000. The economic and tax life is three years. Depreciation is deducted for tax purposes as follows: Year 1, $34,200; Year 2, $33,300; and Year 3, $22,500.

Management insists on using a 10 percent rate for cost of capital. This rate does not include an allowance for inflation, which is expected to occur at an average annual rate of 5.2 percent over the next three years. The company adjusts for inflation in capital expenditure analyses by adding the anticipated inflation rate to the cost of capital and then using the inflation-adjusted cost of capital to discount the projected cash flows. The company pays an average income tax rate of 38 percent. Assume all operating revenues and expenditures occur at the end of the year and would be subject to the effects of inflation.

Required:

(Round to the nearest percentage to determine the cost of capital.)

a. Analyze the expenditure under consideration using the company's method.

b. Assume a consulting firm proposes a different adjustment for inflation in capital expenditure analyses by adjusting the cash flows by an estimated price level index. The adjusted aftertax cash flows are then discounted using the appropriate discount rate. The estimated year-end index values for each of the next four years are as follows:

Year	Year-End Price Index
19X0 (current year)	1.00
19X1	1.04
19X2	1.09
19X3	1.15

Prepare a schedule, using the price index values provided, showing the aftertax annual cash flows adjusted for the equipment under consideration.

c. Determine the net present value for the equipment using the method proposed by the consulting firm, assuming the discount rate used is the cost of capital multiplied by a 5.2 percent inflation rate.

d. Advise management regarding the purchase.

e. Compare the consulting firm's approach to the one presently used to compensate for inflation.

P18–20 Discounted Cash Flow Analysis (L.O. 4)

Kent Company manufactures several lines of industrial products. The specialized machinery that Kent uses to make rotary wheels needs to be replaced. These machines were designed especially for this product. Management has decided that the only alternative to replacing these machines is to acquire the rotary wheels from an outside source. A sales price of $25 per rotary wheel has been quoted by a supplier if at least 75,000 units are ordered annually.

Over the past three years Kent's average usage of rotary wheels has been 80,000 units each year. This volume is expected to remain constant over the next five years. According to Kent's cost records, unit manufacturing costs for the last several years have been as follows:

Direct material	$ 5.80
Direct labor	4.20
Variable overhead	1.80
Fixed overhead*	6.00
Total unit cost	$17.80

*Cash expenditures for factory costs account for one third of the fixed overhead; the balance is depreciation.

If purchased, the specialized machines will cost $2.8 million and have a disposal value of $200,000 after their expected economic life of five years. Depreciation for tax and book purposes will be as follows: Year 1, $1,200,000; Year 2, $900,000; and Year 3, $700,000. The company has a 45 percent marginal tax rate, and management requires a 12 percent aftertax return on investment.

In its sales promotion, the machine manufacturer provided evidence that direct labor and variable overhead would be reduced by $1.50 per unit through use of the new machinery. Kent's production managers contacted a customer of the machine manufacturer using identical facilities and confirmed these findings except that this customer had annual production exceeding Kent's of 20,000 to 30,000 units. Also, the customer indicates that it experienced an increase in direct material cost due to the higher quality of material that had to be used with the new machinery. The customer indicated that its costs have been as follows:

Direct material	$ 6.50
Direct labor	3.70
Variable overhead	.80
Fixed overhead	6.50
Total unit cost	$17.50

Required:

a. Present a discounted cash flow analysis covering the economic life of the new specialized machinery to determine whether Kent Company should replace the old machines or purchase the rotary wheels from an outside supplier. Give consideration to all typical tax implications. (Round to nearest dollar.)

b. Discuss additional factors Kent Company should consider before making a decision to replace the machines or purchase the rotary wheels from an outside supplier.

c. Using only the data given in this problem and no other sources, could you prepare an internal rate of return analysis?

Cases

C18–21 Management Decision Process (L.O. 3)

Established in 1948, the Vital Aviations Company produces commercial airplanes. The company employs more than 4,000 employees and has maintained this level of work force fairly consistently since its organization. Subcontractors produce jet engines, radar, radio, and landing gear and ship them to the Oakland, California, plant for assembly. The Oakland plant mass produces the remaining structural parts of the aircraft and installs the subcontracted components.

Because top management is concerned about the lack of space for the large amounts of inventory, over the years the company has built several warehouses to store the components. Presently, additional space is needed. Vital's president is proud of the fact that now all departments adhere to the strict policy that any purchases over $500 must be subject to at least four bids because he believes this policy saves the company a large amount of money.

The Research and Development Division of the plant also prides itself on being on the cutting edge of technology. This division takes credit for the plant's moving from steel riveted planes in the 1950s to aluminum alloy electronic welded jet airplanes in the 1960s. These innovations in manufacturing were acknowledged by the entire aviation industry. The plant still uses this mass production technology. Because additional workstations have been added throughout the years, the work flow weaves around the plant. However, many managers believe no change in the manufacturing layout is warranted. Contracts were awarded during this period on a cost-plus basis. Demand for dependable commercial planes during this period was high, and Vital Aviations earned good profits for its shareholders.

In the late 1980s Vital Aviations developed a radical prototype for a new class of planes. The body of the new prototype is a titanium-aluminum structure body with ceramics trim. The structural shape and back-fire engine are fuel efficient. Private airlines are so impressed with the new class prototype that many want to replace all their fleets over the next 10 years. Private airlines are ready to offer a lump-sum contract for 200 planes at $10 million each per year for the next 10 years. Since this is not a cost-plus contract, Vital Aviations is at risk because its cost might be more than the bid price of the planes.

Vital Aviations also states that as the new planes are put in service, the design will be modified as requested. Thus, the mass production process will not be practical; shorter production runs will be necessary. Also, Vital Aviations believes that customer needs will differ enough that their manufacturing operations must be capable of rapidly adjusting to meet changing demands. For Vital's new plane to be functional and acceptable, consistent quality has to be guaranteed. Management is faced with the decision of hiring and training an additional 3,000 employees or automating their plant.

In numerous meetings, middle and top managers discussed the implications of installing a Just-in-Time (JIT) inventory system and purchasing robots to perform some of the dirty, dangerous assembly tasks. Both the advantages and disadvantages of the innovations are discussed. One manager suggests that the company investigate the feasibility of installing a Materials Requirements Planning (MRP) system as a solution to the anticipated problems they will encounter with the expansion in sales.

One of the older managers strongly argues that the company is not ready for automation because of the difficulty they have had in implementing other new techniques in the past. This manager reminds the other managers of the problems they had in implementing a new budgeting system and the education process involved in relating one budget to another. This manager closes by stating that most employees today still do not understand the company's budgeting procedures and what information serves as the basis for the different budgets in the master plan. Furthermore, the manager asks what budgeting and automation have in common with strategic planning which the company has talked about for years without much success.

Some of the managers believe that the robots are too expensive for the company to consider and that the company should not incur the risk of a JIT system because managers are accustomed to having safety stock on hand to cover longer lead times than planned. At the close of one of these meetings, Mary Jones, a middle manager, summed up her feelings by stating, "I would much rather have a robot working for me than a human being." However, her statement did not convince the managers opposed to automation.

Required:

a. List the benefits of increased automation that Vital management should consider of most importance. How does Vital's company objectives and mission relate to the decision of whether to automate or not?

b. Discuss the preconditions necessary for JIT to be feasible.

c. Describe the relationship of MRP and production schedules.

d. Explain why Mary Jones would rather have a robot working for her than a human being.

e. Discuss the information sources required to prepare the master budget to which the manager referred.

f. Explain what budgeting and automation have in common with strategic planning.

C18–22 (CMA) Impact of Robots on Overhead Application (L.O. 3)

Rose Bach has recently been hired as controller of Empco, Inc., a sheet metal manufacturer. Empco has been in the sheet metal business for many years and is currently investigating ways to modernize its manufacturing process. At the first staff meeting Bach attended, Bob Kelley, chief engineer, presented a proposal for automating the Drilling Department. Kelley recommended that Empco purchase two robots that would have the capability of replacing the eight direct labor workers in the department. The cost savings outlined in Kelley's proposal included the elimination of direct labor cost in the Drilling Department plus a reduction of manufacturing overhead cost in the department to zero because Empco charges manufacturing overhead on the basis of direct labor dollars using a plantwide rate.

The president of Empco was puzzled by Kelley's explanation of cost savings, believing it made no sense. Bach agreed, explaining that as firms become more automated, they should rethink their manufacturing overhead systems. The president then asked Bach to look into the matter and prepare a report for the next staff meeting.

To refresh her knowledge, Bach reviewed articles on manufacturing overhead allocation for an automated factory and discussed the matter with some of her peers. Bach also gathered the following historical data on the manufacturing overhead rates experienced by Empco. Wanting to have some departmental data to present at the meeting, Bach used Empco's accounting records to estimate the annual averages for each manufacturing department in the 1990s.

HISTORICAL DATA

Date	Average Annual Direct Labor Cost	Average Annual Manufacturing Overhead Cost	Average Manufacturing Overhead Application Rate
1940s	$1,000,000	$ 1,000,000	100%
1950s	1,200,000	3,000,000	250
1960s	2,000,000	7,000,000	350
1970s	3,000,000	12,000,000	400
1980s	4,000,000	20,000,000	500

ANNUAL AVERAGES

	Cutting Department	Grinding Department	Drilling Department
Direct labor	$ 2,000,000	$1,750,000	$ 250,000
Manufacturing overhead	11,000,000	7,000,000	2,000,000

Required:

a. Disregard the proposed use of robots in the Drilling Department and describe the shortcomings for applying overhead of the system currently used by Empco, Inc.

b. Explain the misconceptions underlying Bob Kelley's statement that the manufacturing overhead cost in the Drilling Department would be reduced to zero if the automation proposal were implemented.

c. Recommend ways to improve Empco, Inc.'s method for applying overhead by describing how it should revise its overhead accounting system:

(1) In the Cutting and Grinding Departments.

(2) To accommodate the automation of the Drilling Department.

Activity-Based Management for Marketing Cost Standards

CHAPTER OBJECTIVES

After studying this chapter, you should be able to:

1. Describe the responsibility of cost accountants in applying cost control and analysis to marketing activities.

2. Use activity-based management to establish standards based on cost drivers for marketing activities.

3. Perform segment profitability analyses.

4. Compute variances using marketing standards and understand the care needed to interpret them.

PRACTICAL
APPLICATION BOX

Using Activity-Based Costing (ABC) in a Warehouse

ABC provides benefits not only for product costing but also for service functions. When accountants use ABC to cost service, they classify activities by levels. They use cost as a basis for charging clients. Accountants charge clients for unit-level, batch-level, and product-level activities based on their use of the activities. For example, receiving, put-away, order picking, packing, and shipping could be either unit-, batch-, or product-level activities depending on whether the shipments and orders contained more than one unit and/or product. Companies in-cur unit-level activities, such as inserting a bolt, for each unit produced. Companies perform batch-level activities once for a group of units; moving a pallet containing many units from one process to the next is an example. Companies incur product-level activities to support the manufacture of different products; maintaining bills of materials and expediting production are examples. Effective warehousing management requires the proper costing by specific activity and the allocation to products based on their unique storage and handling requirements.

From: Harold M. Roth and Linda T. Sims, "Costing for Warehousing and Distribution," *Management Accounting*, August 1991, pp. 42–45.

Introduction   Changes in marketing strategy require the rapid introduction of new and modified products. An overriding concern is to accomplish all these changes at reduced cost. Increasingly, cost accountants are assisting production and engineering personnel to ensure that companies' products and services meet global standards for quality, cost, product design, and competitive production technology. Traditionally, cost accountants only compared a company's internal performance to its budget and goals. They have ignored detailed comparisons of internal operations with the performance of competitors. Increasingly, however, society measures a company's products and services against those of a competitor half way around the world.

Accountants expense most marketing costs and do not allocate them to products as required for factory overhead costs. Thus, cost analysis and evaluation are easier to ignore. All too often, companies have simply accepted the costs associated with inefficient marketing as inevitable. Failing to include marketing costs when evaluating segment performance or considering the introduction of new products provides inaccurate estimates of relative profitability. Activity-based management, as first presented in Chapter 4, offers opportunities to better understand how companies generate profits at the customer level by using standards for marketing cost activities.

Significance of Marketing Costs (L.O. 1)

The American Marketing Association defines marketing as the process of planning and executing the conception, pricing, promotion, and distribution of ideas, goods, and services to create exchanges that satisfy individual and organizational objectives. Accountants sometimes use the terms **distribution costs** and **selling costs** interchangeably with *marketing costs.*

Chapter 2 introduced three classes of costs: production, marketing, and administrative. Companies incur **production costs,** which include direct material, direct labor, and factory overhead, to process a product. **Marketing costs** arise from exchanges between companies and consumers. These costs include sales promotion and advertising, as well as physical distribution, market research, and product development. Both production and marketing activities incur administrative costs. **Administrative costs** include management salaries, financial accounting, clerical costs, telephone and fax, rent, and legal fees.

Expanded Role of Marketing

Marketing has become more complicated in recent years. Because specialized machinery, labor, and materials improve production efficiency, companies must sell large volumes of goods to offset expensive capital investments. Strong global competitive pressures and deregulation of the transportation industry are other causes of increased demands on the marketing function. Increasingly, managers are studying the relationship between marketing costs and profits. As production costs and taxes become more standardized, the best opportunity for a company to gain a competitive advantage is through better utilization of its marketing resources.

Marketing Management Concept. The growing importance of marketing cost has led to the **marketing management concept.** Now the marketing manager assumes an important role in production/marketing decisions and helps develop a companywide plan that involves all aspects of the operating cycle. Clearly, the expanding role of marketing demands more of accountants in developing tools for analysis. To this end, accountants and marketing managers should work together to develop improved methods of measuring marketing efficiency.

Objectives of Marketing Cost Accounting (L.O. 1)

Generally, there are two purposes of marketing cost accounting. First, companies need more effective means of controlling and analyzing marketing costs. Second, companies must be able to justify courses of action to regulatory bodies concerned with marketing policies.

Cost Control and Cost Analysis

Cost control and cost analysis use different approaches involving divergent techniques. Efficient utilization of company assets is a concern of **cost control.** Marketing cost control employs budgets and standards to compare actual performance with predetermined goals so managers can investigate differences.

Marketing cost accounting tries to ensure the most effective use of marketing expenditures to increase profits. This approach differs from production cost accounting whose objective usually is cost reduction. Production cost accounting emphasizes full utilization of manufacturing capacity so that additional units absorb fixed costs. The result is that unit production cost decreases as manufacturing volume increases. The effect on marketing of increased production volume is that companies must exert more effort to find additional customers and to open new territories. Hence, unit marketing cost normally increases when the company attempts to expand sales volume, especially during periods of strong competition.

Cost or activity analysis searches for better ways to perform tasks. Accountants collect marketing costs in such meaningful classifications as advertising, warehousing, and transportation so they can compare costs with alternative expenditures and with related sales volumes and gross margins. Increased sales volume should not be the sole measure of marketing efficiency, however, because increased sales volume does not necessarily mean increased income.

Government Regulations

Federal legislation concerning marketing practices and price fixing makes knowledge of marketing costs a necessity. The Sherman Antitrust Act, the Federal Trade Commission Act, and the Clayton Act reflect the government's concern with marketing. The Sherman Act declares every contract, combination in the form of a trust, or conspiracy in restraint of trade to be illegal. The Federal Trade Commission has jurisdiction over a wide range of unfair competitive methods and practices. One provision of the Federal Trade Commission Act declares that unfair methods of competition are unlawful. The Clayton Act eliminates certain competitive methods considered to be potential weapons of monopoly. These competitive methods include price discrimination, interlocking directorates, acquisition of stock in competing corporations, and tying contracts that force the buyer to purchase supplementary and possibly undesirable lines. The Clayton Act prohibits discrimination only when it has a serious effect on competition generally.

Robinson-Patman Amendment. In June 1936, Congress passed the Robinson-Patman Act that amended Section 2 of the Clayton Act. With the passage of this amendment, knowledge of marketing costs became a prerequisite for intelligent price determination. The amendment concerns price differentials caused by charging different prices to different customers in a single market. The amendment does not entirely prohibit price differentials or state that price differentials must be granted. The relationship between the prices different customers pay in a single market is the primary concern.

The Robinson-Patman Amendment protects small business organizations from the advantages larger competitors obtain because of their size and buying power. The amendment declares that a price differential may not exceed the difference in costs of serving different customers. For this purpose, the cost of serving customers includes the costs of manufacturing, selling, and delivery. A company may be required to support any discounts granted with a cost justification study. The Robinson-Patman Amendment results in pricing schedules that consider the differences in marketing costs. These pricing schedules give consumers the advantage of buying in quantities and by methods resulting in savings to the seller.

Because companies can avoid discriminatory price setting if complete cost information is available, the Robinson-Patman Amendment continues to be a motivator for improving marketing cost accounting methods. Cost accountants should study the subject continuously to avoid unintentional price discrimination that may be in violation of the law. In addition, successful enforcement of such regulatory measures as the Robinson-Patman Amendment requires the development and improvement of marketing cost accounting techniques. ABC techniques for marketing costs represent one such improvement.

ABC System for Marketing Costs (L.O. 2)

Activity-based costing (ABC) concepts not only improve resource utilization in manufacturing but also readily apply to marketing functions. Marketing activities consume resources; customer groupings, territories, and other segments require activities. ABC more appropriately costs the marketing activities needed to service each customer or order size. The extensive variability in marketing costs across customer types and distribution channels merits attention in the costing system. ABC helps manage the customer mix by encouraging the elimination of low-volume customers for whom prices cannot be raised. Alternatively, ABC provides costing to support the addition of a surcharge on small orders.

As discussed in Chapter 4, an activity-based accounting system is a two-stage allocation process that fully allocates costs to customers, products, or other ultimate cost objects. In the first stage of an ABC system, accountants separate costs into detailed activities or other cost pools. In the second stage, they allocate cost pools to customers, products, or other segments based on activity measures or cost drivers unique to each cost pool.

Steps for Implementing ABC for Marketing Activities

We use the following steps to measure the profitability of marketing costs:

1. Select the segments on which to base profitability analyses. Territories, customer groupings, and product lines are examples.
2. Establish detailed marketing activities for these broad functions: Warehousing and handling, transportation, credit and collection, general marketing activities, personal selling, advertising, and sales promotion. (To simplify, the illustrations in this chapter detail only the warehousing and handling activity.)

3. Accumulate the direct costs for each activity and separate them into variable and fixed cost categories.

4. Determine cost drivers for each activity; this chapter lists a representative sample.

5. Compute unit costs for each activity by dividing the total activity cost by the cost driver selected. Use the unit cost to establish standards and flexible budgets.

6. Allocate costs to segments to analyze segment profitability.

7. Compare budgeted/standard costs with actual costs for each marketing activity and compute the price and efficiency variances.

8. Determine the cause of resulting variances.

Natural Expense Classification. Most companies initially record costs by the nature or object of the expenditure; for example, material, wages, and rent. This **natural expense classification** identifies the kind of service the company secures for its expense. Accountants then determine how to accumulate the costs. Territories, products, salespersons, or customer groupings are typical cost pools or segments that they use. After determining production, marketing, or administrative costs, accountants distribute individual natural expense items to products and activities within each segment.

Segmentation

Many companies currently sell their products through multiple distribution channels. The cost of marketing and delivering the product varies dramatically by distribution channel. The costs associated with these channels can be as high as 25 percent of total cost. For example, in a direct channel, customers simply call and place their orders. Other channels require frequent customer calls by specially trained salespersons to earn sales. Obviously, marketing costs are much higher in the channel requiring specially trained salespersons.

Segmentation is the difficult task of tracing marketing costs to individual segments such as product lines or salespersons. Accurately attributing marketing costs to segments involves interviewing marketing and salespeople to learn how they allocate their time and effort across buyer segments and distribution channels. An estimate is a dramatic improvement over a system that applies cost accounting principles only to production costs and treats marketing costs as single line items. Identifying the specific costs of different segments and channels improves company profitability.

Marketing Activities

After choosing the segments, accountants determine which activities to cost, such as transportation, warehousing, or personal selling. For instance, marketing activities are the separate and distinct marketing functions a company undertakes. Then accountants accumulate costs by these functions. They consider cost responsibility and control because assignment of responsibility to individuals within a company is generally by activity. For example, one individual is responsible for warehousing and handling while another employee is in charge of advertising. Marketing executives and accountants should jointly determine the activities to be costed. The selection depends on the degree of cost control and cost responsibility desired. The size of the company and its method of operation also help determine the number of activities chosen. Representative marketing activities are difficult to establish because companies engage in many marketing procedures and practices. To illustrate the procedures involved, this chapter uses the following broad marketing activities: warehousing and handling, transportaton, credit and collection, personal selling, advertising and sales promotion, and general marketing.

Detailed Activities. Expenses included in each of these marketing activities not only should be closely related but also should vary according to the same activity or cost driver. Accountants use this cause and effect analysis in production cost accounting. For example, advertising and sales promotion may be further broken down into such detail as radio, television, and direct mail. We divide major activities into small classifications of responsibility to ensure that the work performed is homogeneous. The extent of homogeneity within marketing activities varies. For example, pricing and tagging finished products for storage and shipment is so different from soliciting sales orders by telephone that these two marketing activities need different cost drivers.

Cost Assignment to Marketing Activities. Direct marketing costs require no allocation. However, accountants must distribute indirect costs on some basis. This requires the same process used in allocating indirect manufacturing overhead costs to producing and service departments. Accountants allocate wages and salaries on the basis of the duties performed by the individuals involved. They allocate depreciation of assets used solely by marketing personnel to their respective activities. For example, accountants allocate depreciation of automobiles used by salespersons to personal selling. They also allocate depreciation of assets used in common on some reasonable basis. For example, they allocate building depreciation to the administrative and marketing activities within that building on the basis of relative floor space utilized. We can find or develop methods to allocate any expense in this general way, although some of these allocations may represent only a reasonable relationship.

Some companies integrate the cost assignment to activities in their ledger accounts while other companies assign costs independent of the accounting records. Digit codes can facilitate analysis both by function and by segment, with charges coded at the source of the expenditure. For example, the company could use a 1 as the third digit of the account numbers to refer to the Northern Territory, a 2 for the Eastern Territory, and so forth. A 1 as the fourth digit could indicate the activity, such as warehousing or personal selling, being costed. Accountants would assign each segment and activity a different number to facilitate costing. Where possible, accountants designate the accounts so as many costs as possible are charged to the function directly rather than through allocation.

Marketing Standards Based on ABC Drivers (L.O. 2)

Accountants use standards to help control and interpret marketing costs. However, the methods of establishing standards for marketing costs differ somewhat from the approach suggested for production costs in Chapters 11 and 12. In setting standards for marketing costs, accountants identify the factor causing the marketing costs to vary. The **ABC driver, unit of variability,** or **work unit** is the activity measure.

Because accountants base standards on the ABC driver, they should exercise great care in selecting cost drivers. A company should be practical so its cost drivers are measurable and produce reasonably accurate results that are economical in application. It may not be feasible, for instance, for a small company to detail all its activities. Instead, it can establish a standard for the entire marketing activity using the most appropriate ABC driver.

The same marketing standards may not be applicable in different geographical areas. The distance of the territory from the manufacturing plant, for example, is an important factor. Obviously, markets farther from the manufacturing plant have greater transportation expense per unit than markets in the same territory as the plant.

Standard costs for advertising also vary according to the different zones that advertising covers. One explanation for this is that companies use different advertising media in selected territories because they find dissimilar consumers in various territories. For example, an industrial goods manufacturer likely has only a few practical media alternatives, such as advertising in the one trade publication or direct mail. A consumer products manufacturer has more potential customers and several media from which to choose. A salesperson working in a highly populated area also has a lower standard cost per customer than does a salesperson traveling in a sparsely settled area. The nature of the coverage also affects the time and cost required to serve a territory. Salespersons in some locales may visit customers weekly while their counterparts in other territories must see their customers less frequently. The nature of the competition in the different regions also affects the standard costs for advertising and personal selling.

Order-Getting and Order-Filling Costs

Marketing cost can be broken down into two categories: order-getting and order-filling. Personal selling, advertising, and sales promotion activities incur **order-getting costs. Order-filling** activities relate to the other marketing costs necessary to complete a sale. For example, marketing costs to perform warehousing and handling, transportation, and credit and collection functions are necessary to complete a sale even after a customer has made a commitment to buy the product. These are order-filling costs. Standards are easier to establish for order-filling costs because many of these activities are repetitive, such as the physical handling of goods and clerical operations. In contrast, order-getting activities are generally nonrepetitive. The ABC driver for order-getting activities usually measures efforts expended rather than results obtained. For example, we may base the standard for personal selling cost on a unit cost per customer or sales call, while the standard for advertising may be cost per item mailed or per newspaper inch.

Even though most order-filling costs vary with sales volume, the individual cost units respond to different sales activities. For example, managers expect warehousing costs to increase as the number of shipments made increases. However, the receiving function varies with the number of items received, and the cost of handling returns relates more to the number of returns handled. Managers should establish this relationship between the cost component and an appropriate activity measure or cost driver. Companies that sell products on consignment, for example, incur the costs of transporting the product to the consignee in one month, while sales of the product may not occur until several months later.

Warehousing and Handling

Warehousing and handling involve receiving finished goods from the manufacturing process or from another business concern and storing them until they are delivered to customers. Because the nature of such operations is largely repetitive, accountants can apply standardization and cost control like that applied for manufacturing operations. If each territory or other segment has its own warehousing and handling facilities and clerical employees for handling the orders, these costs are direct segment costs requiring no allocation. However, when the segments use central facilities, accountants allocate cost to the segments. To facilitate this allocation, the employees involved may record the time spent for each segment's orders.

JIT Inventory Management Systems. A just-in-time (JIT) inventory management system affects not only accounting and production but also warehousing, purchasing, transportation, and other marketing activities. As introduced in Chapter 1, JIT purchases products and manufactures products only when needed and only in the quantity needed. JIT directs attention to work in process inventory and turnover performance. Managers monitor what they have in their inventory, from raw materials to finished goods, virtually on a real-time basis. Even though shipping and receiving cost may increase because production lot sizes are small, JIT eliminates the double handling of products by moving storage to work areas.

Properly implemented, JIT can drastically reduce inventory and the associated costs of holding inventory. Carrying costs increase when inventory sits in the warehouse waiting for a sale or use in the production process. Costs rise due to increased pilferage, obsolescence, insurance, and other maintenance costs. Strategic planning and profitability require the reduction of funds invested in nonperforming assets, such as materials inventories not needed immediately in production. Thus, JIT offers a potential for improved warehousing and handling by focusing attention on nonvalued activities.

Transportation

The transportation activity consists of the shipping and delivery operations in getting products to customers. To set standard costs for this activity, a company establishes economic traffic routings for the required distribution pattern. If each territory or other segment has its own delivery equipment, the transportation cost is a direct charge. Otherwise, accountants allocate the cost of centralized facilities to the territories. Because most transportation activities involve physical operations, the techniques applied to manufacturing operations are appropriate to develop transportation standards. Accountants conduct time and motion studies for broader operations than those on which production studies are based. For example, rather than conduct time and motion studies for each procedure, as they do for production operations, time studies for marketing functions represent longer periods involving several operations. Because the cost of operating each class of delivery equipment varies, accountants compute separate standard costs for each type of equipment used.

Credit and Collection

The costs of extending credit to customers for the purchase of goods and later processing collections vary considerably among companies. Accountants apply internal engineering methods to study repetitive office operations such as preparing invoices, posting charges and credits to accounts receivable, and preparing customers' statements. For example, the typing of each letter and invoice requires uniform procedures, with length becoming the variable factor.

General Marketing Activities

Additional marketing costs, such as clerical, office, and accounting costs, vary in importance in different companies. In some companies, these activities are not significant enough to be treated as a separate activity. A company generally needs past experience and knowledge of the segment's activities before successfully establishing standards for general marketing activities. Analysis of invoices and charges, for example, provides information for establishing an ABC driver for such factors as supplies, telephone, and stationery. Typically, costs of general marketing activities are indirect costs of the segment and require allocations.

Personal Selling

As opposed to advertising, personal selling involves securing orders through personal contact. Repetitive personal selling activities are easier to standardize than nonrepetitive activities. Despite individual differences among salespersons and sales situations, certain sales techniques—such as product presentation—are standardized enough that managers can determine an allotted time for each sales call. Industry's widespread use of sales training programs is evidence of this trend toward uniformity.

To determine sales call standards, a time-study observer can accompany salespersons on calls to examine how they spend their working time. This approach, however, has some inherent weaknesses because the presence of the observer may embarrass both the salesperson and the customer and cause atypical salesperson behavior. A more practical approach may be to obtain data from the salesperson's daily reports showing the time spent with each customer and the number of sales made. This information yields a standard list of activities that salespersons perform so accountants can develop standards for the number of accounts per salesperson and calls per day. The type of assistance salespersons render each customer and the number of individual products they sell are considerations in establishing standards for sales calls per day. The standard number of calls increases if the salesperson conducts calls by telephone rather than through personal contact.

An analysis of sales salaries provides the basis for setting standard salary rates for each class of employee in each segment. In addition, accountants study each segment before preparing the standards for salespersons' traveling expense. The estimated number of customer calls required to meet the sales quota becomes the basis for determining the expected sales calls per day. Since segment conditions significantly influence personal selling expenses, each segment requires different standards. For example, the variety of products sold and the channel of distribution among company segments cause differences in the cost drivers selected. For expediency, companies express personal selling standards as a percentage of gross margin or gross or net sales. However, other cost drivers achieve better control.

Advertising and Sales Promotion

The advertising and sales promotion function creates a demand for the company's products and services while building and maintaining goodwill toward the organization. Some companies handle all their own advertising campaigns and produce their own advertising and sales promotion material. Other firms contract all their advertising to an outside firm. Because advertising and promotion activities vary so widely among companies, it is difficult to develop cost standards. The cost measure should be general and applied to considerable periods for institutional promotional expenditures in which the objective is to develop favorable customer attitudes toward the company. For example, since the prime objective of institutional advertising is not to increase sales in the short run, we should not express standard costs as a percentage of sales. We can develop more accurate cost standards for a product or service promotion meant to increase consumer awareness or sales of a product or service. Some of these standards may be quantity measurements only and not reflect the quality of the output. We use historical data extensively because most companies must maintain some continuity in their advertising programs.

Some companies design their advertising programs to reach more than one territory or other segment. This requires allocating costs on the basis of cost drivers. For example, we can allocate advertising cost to territories based on the number of families in each segment who watch the television station used for advertising on an average day or night. We can distribute newspaper advertising based on the circulation in each territory. Additional allocations may be necessary for the costs of dealers' promotions including displays, store arrangement services, and demonstrations. The amount of service each segment receives is a general basis.

If companies design sales promotion to stimulate immediate sales of specific products, we express the standard as a cost per dollar of sales. *Share-of-the-market statistics* supplement comparisons of standard and actual costs of advertising per dollar of sales to measure the effect of general changes in market conditions. When industry sales are down, for example, analysis of an individual company's share of the market indicates an increase or decrease in its percentage share.

ABC Drivers for Marketing Activities

The following brief list includes cost drivers used to establish standards for detailed marketing activities. Accountants should choose the most appropriate of these cost drivers to determine standard and actual unit costs. The degree to which they further break down each marketing activity into detailed activity varies.

Detailed Activity	ABC Drivers
Warehousing and Handling—Receiving, pricing, tagging, and marking, assembling stock for shipment, and packing	Dollars of merchandise purchased, shipments, weight or number of shipping units, or purchase invoice lines
Transportation—Loading and unloading, handling claims, gasoline, repairs, and planning and supervision	Deliveries or shipments, truck-miles, truck-hours of operation, units of products shipped, or dollars of shipments
Credit and collection—Preparing invoices, making street or window collections, credit correspondence, records, and files, and credit investigation and approval	Accounts sold, credit sales transactions, invoices, collections, sales orders, or letters

Detailed Activity	ABC Drivers
General marketing activities—Sales analyses and statistics, letters, vouchering, cashiering, and mail handling	Orders, invoice lines, customers' orders, units filed, transactions, sales slips, time spent, or vouchers
Personal selling—telephone solicitation, sales-person subsistence, and customer entertainment	Customer served, sales transaction, sales order, unit of product sold, days, or customers
Advertising and sales promotion—Newspaper advertising, outdoor billboards and sign advertising, radio and television advertising, and product demonstrations	Newspaper inches, sign unit, cost-per-thousand consumers reached, prospects secured, sales transactions, or product units sold

Marketing Profitability Analysis Illustrated (L.O. 3)

Exhibits 19–1 through 19–5 provide information about marketing profitability using standard costs based on ABC cost drivers. Exhibit 19–1 shows sales prices, unit production costs, units sold, and cost drivers. Exhibit 19–2 shows total variable and fixed costs for each marketing activity and develops standard rates. To simplify, warehousing and handling is the only broad marketing activity broken down into detailed activities. In practice, we would detail all marketing activities.

The profitability analysis by territories shown in Exhibit 19–3 shows that the Southern Territory is more profitable than the Northern Territory. Exhibit 19–3 assumes that actual unit sales prices, unit production costs, and units sold were the same as budgeted. For example, the Southern Territory's sales revenue is (350 Product A units $\times$ \$40 = \$14,000) + (400 Product B units $\times$ \$60 = \$24,000) for a total of \$38,000.

However, both territories had some actual cost drivers that differed from those budgeted. Also, Southern Territory's actual rent and depreciation varied from budgeted. We allocate marketing costs in the profitability analysis on these actual cost drivers:

	Northern	Southern
Shipments	80	420
Units handled	477	223
Customers' orders	52	108
Returns	29	71
Warehouse unit	370	1,630
Clerical items	120	780
Accounts sold	70	30
Sales calls	150	50
Newspaper advertising inches	100	400

The profitability statement by product line in Exhibit 19–4 indicates an operating loss of \$3,605 for Product A. Although the overall company is profitable, one of its product lines requires further analysis. Accountants can prepare additional exhibits using data by product line for each separate territory to further isolate the operating loss of Product A.

Flexible Budgets

After establishing standards for marketing costs, we prepare a flexible (variable) budget using the approaches suggested in Chapter 9. Levels of marketing activity appropriate to the levels of production output are most practical. We estimate the

EXHIBIT 19–1   Monthly Budgeted Data for Territory and Product Line Analyses

	A	B	Northern	Southern	Total
Unit sales price	$40	$60			
Unit production cost	$ 8	$12			
Shipments	300	200	100	400	500
Units handled	300	400	500	200	700
Customers' orders	100	60	50	110	160
Returns	20	80	30	70	100
Warehouse units	1,500	500	400	1,600	2,000
Units sold	400	600	50 A	350 A	
			200 B	400 B	
Accounts sold	20	80	70	30	100
Sales calls	60	140	150	50	200
Clerical items	500	400	150	750	900
Newspaper advertising inches	300	200	100	400	500

EXHIBIT 19–2   Budgeted Monthly Unit Costs for ABC Drivers

Marketing Activity	Total ABC Drivers	Variable Total	Variable Unit	Fixed Total	Fixed Unit
Warehousing and handling:					
Variable costs:					
Receiving .... 500 shipments		$10,500	$21.00		
Pricing, tagging, and marking .... 700 units handled		4,200	6.00		
Sorting .... 160 customers' orders		800	5.00		
Handling returns .... 100 returns		1,000	10.00		
Taking physical inventory .... 2,000 warehouse units		1,000	0.50		
Clerical handling of shipping orders ..... 900 clerical items		1,800	2.00		
Fixed costs:					
Rent .... $600 per month per territory					
Depreciation .... 450 per month per territory					
Transportation .... 500 shipments		$2,000	$ 4	$ 500	$1
Credit and collection .... 100 accounts sold		900	9	300	3
General marketing activities .... 160 customers' orders		320	2	800	5
Personal selling .... 200 sales calls		2,000	10	800	4
Advertising and sales promotion .... 500 newspaper inches		1,500	3	1,000	2

marketing requirements needed to achieve the sales goals. We cost these marketing efforts by applying the standards previously established.

Variance Analysis (L.O. 4)

As with production costing, analysis of marketing cost variances is the first step toward identifying the factors that caused any difference between standard and actual costs and eliminating any inefficiencies. Each company selects its own specific variance analyses. Often companies only compute a net variance for

EXHIBIT 19–3   Territory Profitability Analysis

	Northern	Southern	Total
Sales revenue	$14,000	$38,000	$52,000
Less cost of sales	2,800	7,600	10,400
Gross margin	$11,200	$30,400	$41,600
Less: Expenses:			
Warehousing and handling:			
Receiving	$ 1,680 (80 × $21)	$ 8,820 (420 × $21)	$10,500
Pricing, tagging, and marking	2,862 (477 × $6)	1,338 (223 × $6)	4,200
Sorting	260 (52 × $5)	540 (108 × $5)	800
Handling returns	290 (29 × $10)	710 (71 × $10)	1,000
Taking physical inventory	185 (370 × $.50)	815 (1,630 × $.50)	1,000
Clerical handling of shipping orders	240 (120 × $2)	1,560 (780 × $2)	1,800
Rent	600	650	1,250
Depreciation	450	445	895
Transportation	400 (80 × $5)	2,100 (420 × $5)	2,500
Credit and collection	840 (70 × $12)	360 (30 × $12)	1,200
General marketing activities	350 (50 × $7)	770 (110 × $7)	1,120
Personal selling	2,100 (150 × $14)	700 (50 × $14)	2,800
Advertising and sales promotion	500 (100 × $5)	2,000 (400 × $5)	2,500
Total expense	$10,757	$20,808	$31,565
Operating income (loss)	$ 443	$ 9,592	$10,035

EXHIBIT 19–4   Product Line Profitability Analysis

	A	B	Allocation Basis
Sales revenue	$16,000	$36,000	
Less cost of sales	3,200	7,200	
Gross margin	$12,800	$28,800	
Less: Expenses:			
Warehousing and handling:			
Receiving	$6,300	$4,200	$21 per shipment
Pricing, tagging, and marking	1,800	2,400	$6 per unit handled
Sorting	500	300	$5 per order
Handling returns	200	800	$10 per return
Taking physical inventory	750	250	$.50 per warehouse unit
Clerical handling of shipping orders	1,000	800	$2 per unit sold
Rent	625	625	
Depreciation	450	445	
Transportation	1,500	1,000	$5 per shipment
Credit and collection	240	960	$12 per account
General marketing activities	700	420	$7 per customers' order
Personal selling	840	1,960	$14 per sales call
Advertising and sales promotion	1,500	1,000	$5 per newspaper inch
Total expense	$16,405	$15,160	
Operating income (loss)	$ (3,605)	$13,640	

marketing costs and do not attempt to break the variance down into causal factors. We do not encourage this practice, however, since it tends to hide inefficiencies. Instead, to be meaningful, we compute price and efficiency variances. This is the computation for each of these variances:

Price variance
(Standard price − Actual price) × Actual cost drivers

Quantity or efficiency variance
(Budgeted or standard cost drivers − Actual cost drivers) × Standard price

Expense Variance Report

Exhibit 19–5 illustrates a detailed variance report for the warehousing and handling activity analyzed by territories. Exhibit 19–5 shows only the Southern Territory. The standards for the warehousing and handling activities repeated from Exhibit 19–2 are

	Total Standard for Direct and Indirect Costs (in Dollars)
Variable costs:	
Receiving	$ 21.00 per shipment
Pricing, tagging, and marking	6.00 per unit handled
Sorting	5.00 per order
Handling returns	10.00 per return
Taking physical inventory	0.50 per warehouse unit
Clerical handling of shipping orders	2.00 per clerical unit
Fixed costs:	
Rent	$600.00 per month per territory
Depreciation	450.00 per month per territory

Repeating, Southern Territory's budgeted and actual ABC drivers for January relating to warehousing and handling are

	Budgeted	Actual
Shipments	400	420
Units handled	200	223
Customers' orders	110	108
Returns	70	71
Warehouse unit	1,600	1,630
Clerical items	750	780

Southern Territory's actual warehousing and handling direct costs for the month are

Receiving	$6,400
Pricing, tagging, and marking	1,115
Sorting	565
Handling returns	680
Taking physical inventory	880
Clerical handling of shipping orders	500
Rent	650
Depreciation	445

The company allocates the following actual indirect costs to its Southern and Northern Territories:

Receiving (allocated on actual shipments: Southern, 420; Northern, 80)	$2,500
Clerical handling of shipping orders (allocated on actual clerical unit: Southern, 780; Northern, 120)	$1,223

Efficiency Variance

Shipments received is the cost driver chosen for the receiving activity. The firm received a total of 420 shipments, while they budgeted for only 400 shipments. This results in an unfavorable efficiency variance because actual shipments exceeded those budgeted. The efficiency variance in this case is unfavorable because they received 20 more shipments than planned. Hence, the company should encourage orders of larger quantities to save costs in receiving, but only if they need the parts received for production. Larger-size shipments are not cost justified if the increase in inventory carrying costs exceeds the savings in receiving cost.

However, if actual sales exceeded budgeted sales by more than 5 percent (20 extra shipments over budgeted shipments/400 budgeted shipments) it would not be appropriate to classify the receiving efficiency variance as unfavorable. It is reasonable to assume that a larger than budgeted sales volume requires additional shipments. Managers should exercise care in analyzing marketing cost variances because it is easy to misinterpret the results associated with marketing costs. Initially, they should consider each marketing cost variance as favorable or unfavorable in reference to that individual detailed activity, not for its effect on the overall company. Later, they can interpret marketing cost variances in view of other factors, such as sales volume achieved.

Some situations use standard cost drivers rather than budgeted cost drivers in variance analysis for marketing functions, following a treatment similar to that for production activities. If some measure of marketing output, such as sample kits, is available, accountants can set standards for the components of this output. It is more appropriate to compute the standard allowed for this level of marketing activity using a treatment identical to direct material and direct labor efficiency or quantity variances. We then compare the standard cost drivers allowed with actual cost drivers in the efficiency variance.

Price Variance

Exhibit 19–5 shows a favorable receiving price variance because the $21 standard price exceeds $20.238 actual cost per shipment ($8,500 total actual receiving cost divided by 420 actual units). We multiply this difference in price by the actual shipments to give a total favorable variance of $320. We do not have to compute the actual cost per unit using the format illustrated in Exhibit 19–5. We can determine the price variance by comparing total actual cost to the actual cost driver at the standard price shown in Column 2.

We compute efficiency and price variances for variable costs only. Exhibit 19–5 shows only net variances for the two fixed expenses. Net variances measure the difference between budgeted costs (budgeted drivers at standard price) and actual costs (actual drivers at actual price).

Marketing Standards in Accounting Records

After completing preliminary work, we may set up the accounts needed for the system in the general ledger. The ledger accounts may incorporate marketing standards by debiting the accounts for each activity with the actual cost and crediting them with the standard cost for the number of cost drivers performed. Incorporation of standards in the accounting journals and ledgers may make executives take standards more seriously. As in certain aspects of production

EXHIBIT 19–5

HILL COMPANY—SOUTHERN TERRITORY
Expense Variance Report—Warehousing and Handling
January 19X1

Detailed Activity: / ABC Drivers	(1) Actual Cost (Actual Drivers @ Actual Price)	(2) Actual Drivers @ Standard Price	(3) Budgeted Costs (Budgeted Drivers @ Standard Price)	(2 − 1) Price Variance	(3 − 2) Efficiency Variance	(3 − 1) Net Variance
Receiving .... Shipment						
Direct costs	$6,400					
Indirect costs .... $\left(\frac{420}{500} \times \$2,500\right)$	2,100					
Total	$ 8,500	$8,820 (420 × $21)	$ 8,400 (400 × $21)	$320F	$420U	$100U
Pricing, tagging, and marking: ... Unit handled						
Direct costs	1,115	1,338 (223 × $6)	1,200 (200 × $6)	223F	138U	85F
Sorting: Direct costs .... Order	565	540 (108 × $5)	550 (110 × $5)	25U	10F	15U
Handling returns: ... Return						
Direct costs	680	710 (71 × $10)	700 (70 × $10)	30F	10U	20F
Taking physical inventory ..... Warehouse unit	880	815 (1,630 × $0.50)	800 (1,600 × $0.50)	65U	15U	80U
Clerical handling of shipping orders: ... Clerical item						
Direct costs	$ 500					
Indirect costs .... $\left(\frac{780}{900} \times \$1,223\right)$	1,060					
Total	1,560	1,560 (780 × $2)	1,500 (750 × $2)	–0–	60U	60U
Total variable expense	$13,300		$13,150	$483F	$633U	$150U
Fixed expense:						
Rent	650		600			50U
Depreciation	445		450			5F
Total warehousing and handling	$14,395		$14,200			$195U

F = favorable; U = unfavorable.

accounting, however, it is not practical to incorporate marketing standards in the accounting system because marketing costs are constantly fluctuating. Fortunately, incorporation is not as important here as for production cost standards because we do not usually charge marketing costs to inventory.

If we incorporate marketing cost standards within the accounting records, we must dispose of the variances because they usually are period costs. This approach charges or credits variances against the accounting period's revenues using the assumption that the variance represents an inefficiency or saving from standard.

Marginal Contribution versus Full Cost. By using the marginal cost approach for segment reporting, we develop cost drivers only for direct marketing costs. Advocates of the marginal contribution approach believe that an effort to allocate costs is confusing and misleading. Advocates of full costing believe that each segment of the company should bear its share of the company's indirect cost in addition to its own direct costs. They argue for assigning indirect costs to the segment or activity being costed on the basis of demonstrable cost relationship, even if there is only a reasonably strong cost and effect association.

Summary

Global competition has increased the importance of efficient marketing activities. However, accountants allow greater latitude in establishing marketing standards and interpreting variances. In fact, companies may increase marketing costs to attract a greater market share. Because repetitive marketing operations are fully as measurable as manufacturing activities, accountants can adapt the techniques used in setting production standards. They use less scientific approaches for nonrepetitive marketing activities. Although accountants prefer that standards be set only after conducting rigorous engineering studies, less scientific standards can also provide meaningful variance analysis. ABC offers an opportunity for continuous improvement by establishing standards based on cost drivers for each detailed marketing activity. This allows management to examine marketing activities more thoroughly than it could by comparing actual cost only to historical data.

Important Terms and Concepts

distribution costs, 659
selling costs, 659
production costs, 659
marketing costs, 659
administrative costs, 659
marketing management concept, 659
cost control, 660

cost or activity analysis, 660
natural expense classification, 662
segmentation, 662
ABC drivers or units of variability or
 work units, 664
order-getting costs, 664
order-filling costs, 664

Problem for Self-Study

Revising Sales Price on Order Size Cost

E. Milam, Inc., requests that you allocate its marketing costs on order size as a way of determining if its sales price per unit reflects any variation in the nonmanufacturing cost per volume-unit. Their order sizes fall into these three categories: small (1–4 items), medium (5–26 items), and large (over 26 items).

The marketing costs actually incurred last year and the basis for allocation are

Marketing Cost	Amount	Basis for Allocation
1. Transportation	$ 7,920	Units shipped
2. Sales promotion	8,000	Circulation pieces distributed
3. Credit and collection	5,000	Number of orders
4. Marketing salaries	36,000	Direct charge

An analysis of their records produced the following statistics:

	Order Sizes			
	Small	Medium	Large	Total
Units shipped	500	1,800	2,100	4,400
Circulation pieces distributed	50,000	75,000	125,000	250,000
Number of orders	150	70	30	250
Marketing salaries	$2,400	$16,900	$16,700	$36,000

Required:

a. Prepare a detailed schedule showing the marketing cost per order size and per unit within each order size. Carry cost per unit to three decimal places.

b. Assume that presently the company charges a constant price per unit. Management desires an analysis showing the revised sales price per unit based on marketing costs. However, they believe marketing cost per unit decreases with an increase in the size of the order. Prepare a schedule showing the unit sales price revised upward or downward for each order size while also maintaining total sales of $500,000.

Solution to Problem for Self-Study

E. MILAM COMPANY

a.

Marketing Cost	Order Sizes			
	Small	Medium	Large	Total
Transportation $\left(\dfrac{\$7,920}{4,400 \text{ units}} = \$1.80\right)$	$ 900 ($1.80 × 500)	$ 3,240 ($1.80 × 1,800)	$ 3,780 ($1.80 × 2,100)	$ 7,920
Sales promotion $\left(\dfrac{\$8,000}{250,000} = \$.032\right)$	1,600 ($.032 × 50,000)	2,400 ($.032 × 75,000)	4,000 ($.032 × 125,000)	8,000
Credit and collection . . . . . . ($5,000/250 orders = $20)	3,000	1,400	600	5,000
Marketing salaries	2,400	16,900	16,700	36,000
Total marketing costs	$7,900	$23,940	$25,080	$56,920
Marketing cost per unit	$15.80 ($7,900/500)	$ 13.30 ($23,940/1,800)	$11.943 ($25,080/2,100)	

b.   Computation of revised sales price

$$500X + 1,800(X - \$2.50) + 2,100\,(X - \$3.857) = \$500,000$$
$$500X + 1,800X - 4,500 + 2,100X - 8,100 = \$500,000$$
$$4,400X = \$500,000 + 12,600$$
$$X = \$\ 116.50$$

Revised Prices

Small order	$116.50
Medium order ($116.50 − $2.50)	114.00
Large order ($116.50 − $3.857)	112.643

Proof

500 units × $116.50	$ 58,250
1,800 units × $114.00	205,200
2,100 units × $112.643	236,550
	$500,000

Review Questions

1. Why is the selection of the ABC cost drivers for marketing costs so important?
2. Indicate the distinction between production, marketing, and administrative costs.
3. Why is it important for companies to evaluate the effectiveness of their marketing expenditures?
4. Define the marketing management concept.
5. Why have accountants traditionally devoted less attention to the study of marketing costs than to production costs?
6. Which variance analysis can be used for variable and fixed marketing costs?
7. Discuss the objectives of marketing cost accounting.
8. Discuss the impact of the Sherman Act, the Federal Trade Commission Act, the Clayton Act, and the Robinson-Patman Amendment on marketing activities.
9. Discuss the various segments used to analyze marketing costs.
10. Why is the incorporation into the accounting records of marketing cost standards not as important as the incorporation of production cost standards?
11. Should direct selling standards be expressed as a percentage of gross margin or as a percentage of gross sales?
12. Why are cost standards most difficult to develop for advertising and sales promotion?

Exercises

E19–1 Discontinue Product Line (L.O. 1)

Morlock Company's marketing manager is disappointed that the introduction of Product A six months ago has not resulted in a more favorable financial performance. Top management is placing much pressure on the marketing department to drop Product A and requests a cost analysis to support a decision concerning its discontinuance. The following product statement is for the six months just ended:

Sales of Product A		$ 650,000
Cost of goods sold:		
Direct material	$200,000	
Direct labor	300,000	
Variable factory overhead	180,000	
Fixed factory overhead	40,000	720,000
Gross margin		$ (70,000)
Marketing and administrative expense		50,000
Net loss		$(120,000)

Required:

a. Present quantitative analysis to support your position regarding the continuance of this product line.
b. Discuss additional relevant marketing issues that need further investigation before deciding to discontinue the product line.

E19–2 Profitability Analysis for Transportation Activity (L.O. 3)

Kipp Company provides you with information concerning the standards established for their detailed transportation activity. Actual data also include the following:

Activity	Budgeted Cost	Standard Cost per Driver	Actual Cost	Actual Cost per Driver
Clerical work (per shipment)	$1,000	$2.00	$1,350	$2.25
Planning and supervision (per unit shipped)	8,000	0.50 + $4,000 per period	8,880	.60 + $4,020 per period
Loading and unloading (per pound loaded)	975	0.65	1,131	0.78
Drivers' and helpers' wages (per truck-mile)	2,400	0.80	2,646	0.84

Required:

Calculate variances for each of the activities detailed assuming budgeted sales volume was attained.

E19–3 Volume to Justify Advertising (L.O. 1)

Sales of Choco-Nut, a peanut butter, chocolate, and coffee flavored candy bar, have not been as high as expected. To combat this, the marketing manager of Shwayka, Inc., is planning an extensive advertising campaign that will cost $80,000. The president is concerned that the market is so saturated with Choco-Nut and other candy bars that the demand is not sufficient to absorb the extra volume that must be sold to achieve Choco-Nut's budgeted aftertax net income.

Based on a budgeted sales volume of 60,000 cases, the fixed expenses per case are $21.6667, while total variable expenses are $2,700,000. The budgeted aftertax income at this level is $130,000.

Required:

a. Calculate how many total units Shwayka must sell to achieve the budgeted aftertax income of $130,000 if the advertising campaign is undertaken and cost behavior and unit sales price remain the same. Assume the company is in a 35 percent tax bracket.
b. Discuss marketing issues relevant to this decision of whether to incur the advertising expense.

E19–4 Minimum Order Size (L.O. 3)

Louis Wells, salesperson for Ann Martin Manufacturing, was upset about the amount of time he thought he was wasting with customers that ordered only small amounts. He discussed his complaint with Harold Douglass, the sales manager. Douglass informed him that other salespersons had raised the same question.

Together, they approached the controller to prepare a sales order analysis so that top management would be better able to set guidelines for the salespeople.

A cost clerk prepared the following average processing cost per order, based on 2,000 orders per period:

Receiving	$0.40
Warehousing and handling	0.50
Preparing invoice	0.25
Posting charges and credits to Accounts Receivable	0.35
Credit investigation	0.30
Total cost per order	$1.80

A markup of 25 percent over production cost is planned.

Required:

a. Compute the minimum order size in dollars that the company should accept using the $1.80 unit-processing cost per order.
b. Evaluate any weaknesses that you see in this approach for deciding on minimum order sizes.

E19–5 Standards for Order Filling Costs Similarly Established as in Production (L.O. 4)

Flesher, Inc., believes that it can effectively apply its experience in using standards in production to two of its order-filling costs. The company's delicate china statuettes are carefully wrapped and packaged by skilled laborers before shipment. Specially designed materials are used for this packaging process. The following information for budgeted operations also gives actual data for the corresponding period just completed:

	Budgeted Operations	Actual Operations
Packages shipped	1,000	950
Package handling function:		
Total quantity	3,000 hours	3,300 hours
Total cost	$24,000	$26,202
Shipping materials:		
Total quantity	1,500 lbs.	1,400 lbs.
Total cost	$1,125	$1,148

Required:

Using the approach for production, compute price and efficiency variances from standard cost. Use the most appropriate method for computing efficiency variances. Prove your variances for:

a. Packaging and handling function.
b. Shipping materials.

Problems

P19–6 Cost per Order Size (L.O. 3)

Although Outland Company management realizes that they need additional marketing cost studies, they lack the personnel and funds at present to establish marketing cost standards. They suspect that Outland may be accepting orders that are too small. As a result, they analyzed the orders received last year and broke them down into categories: small (1 to 20 items), medium (21 to 100 items), and large (over 100 items). The actual marketing costs incurred last year were as follows:

Marketing Cost	Amount	Basis for Distribution
Marketing personnel salaries	$27,000	Number of personnel
Marketing manager's salary	20,000	Time spent
Salespeople's commissions	3,000	Sales dollars
Advertising and direct selling	37,500	Sales dollars
Packing and shipping	26,250	Weight shipped
Delivery	19,000	Weight shipped
Credit and collection	15,000	Number of orders

An analysis of their records produced the following statistics:

	Order Sizes			
	Small	Medium	Large	Total
Number of personnel	5	3	1	9
Time spent by marketing manager	60%	10%	30%	100%
Amount of sales	$250,000	$300,000	$200,000	$750,000
Weight	6,090	2,940	1,470	10,500
Number of orders	612	170	68	850

Required:

a. Prepare a detailed schedule showing the marketing cost per order size and marketing cost as a percentage of total sales for each order size.

b. Make recommendations to management regarding the size of order they should accept.

P19–7 Analyzing Financial Trends in Inventory (L.O. 1)

John Schmidt is the owner of Big John's, a barbecue restaurant with a separate carryout counter. Schmidt's accountant usually prepares adjustments, financial statements, and tax returns at year-end only. This year, Schmidt has noticed that sales receipts seem to be lower, although business seems to be as good as usual. Schmidt has decided to have his accountant prepare condensed statements for each month, to find out what the problem is before the whole year passes by. Schmidt expects a gross margin of 38 percent. A physical inventory taken by Schmidt and his accountant for each of the four months follows:

	May		June	
	Restaurant	**Carryout Counter**	**Restaurant**	**Carryout Counter**
Sales	$37,200	$54,600	$39,500	$43,200
Cost of goods sold	24,100	32,400	24,850	30,950
Gross margin	$13,100	$22,200	$14,650	$12,250

	July		August	
	Restaurant	**Carryout Counter**	**Restaurant**	**Carryout Counter**
Sales	$38,750	$39,450	$41,550	$35,700
Cost of goods sold	23,050	30,800	25,600	31,200
Gross margin	$15,700	$ 8,650	$15,950	$ 4,500

Required:

Analyze these financial reports and indicate any suspicions you have. To correct this condition, which sales control techniques does Schmidt need?

P19–8 Price and Quantity Variances (L.O. 4)

Management of Woodside Manufacturing, Inc., has broken down its marketing costs by functions to establish and use standards for marketing cost analysis. By having standard costing rates set for various functional costs, they can make an analysis of the difference between budgeted and actual results. The following data were obtained from the controller:

	Units Handled	Truck-Miles	Credit Orders	Sales Orders
Planned Results				
Wholesalers	2,000	24,000	600	1,000
Retailers	2,400	36,000	760	1,200
Warehousing and handling:				
Wholesalers	$ .65 per unit			
Retailers	.85 per unit			
Transportation	1.20 per truck-mile + $5,000 per customer class			
Credit and collection	.50 per credit order + $3,000 per customer class			
Direct selling	1.00 per sales order			
Advertising	.40 per sales order			
Actual Results for the Period				
Wholesalers	1,900	24,980	640	980
Retailers	2,600	35,760	750	1,240

	Actual Expenses for the Period			
	Wholesalers		**Retailers**	
	Fixed	**Variable**	**Fixed**	**Variable**
Warehousing and handling . . .		$ 1,102		$ 2,184
Transportation	$4,984	31,225	$5,112	41,124
Credit and collection	3,143	352	3,020	450
Direct selling		1,078		1,178
Advertising		441		434

Required:

Prepare an analysis of marketing expense showing budgeted expenses contrasted with actual expenses and the resulting variances for each class of customer. (If appropriate, compute two variances; otherwise, only one variance for each expense component.) Assume budgeted sales were achieved.

P19–9 Trade-Off of Excess Inventory Cost versus Improved Customer Service (L.O. 1)

As a management consultant specializing in cost accounting systems, you are in consultation with Ms. Dawn Smith, production manager of Smith Producers, when she receives an important telephone call. Smith insists that you remain in her office when she takes the call. It is a call from one of the company's major customers, and you hear her say, "Why, Bill, you know this request is really going to interrupt our regular production schedule, but since you are such a valuable customer, I will try to honor your order. We are really pushed on an order now, but we will try to work something out with you. I will get back with you shortly."

Smith Producers manufactures custom-designed motors; its technology is so complex that only three other companies in the country have the machinery to produce these motors. Smith Producers has built an excellent reputation for the quality of its motors because it has been willing to engage in extensive research for their improvement.

Two years ago it began a new policy designed to expand its customer service. This policy included manufacturing a larger volume of motors than a customer needed and keeping the motors in inventory so that later if the customer had an emergency need for motors, Smith Producers could fill the request within hours. Smith's customers are unaware of this policy and are highly impressed that their business is so valued that the Smith production department stops all manufacturing in process to honor emergency requests. Smith management believes that this policy, along with the excellent engineering quality of its motors, has created a group of loyal customers even through a specific customer will rarely, if ever, use this service. Word about this service, however, has spread among Smith's customers despite its infrequent use.

Unfortunately, Smith is running out of storage space for the extra motors produced that remain unsold awaiting a customer's emergency. The fact that each order received differs even in some small aspects prevents Smith from easily adapting extra motors produced on one order to fill another customer's order. Smith Producers has followed the practice of expensing the extra cost of production overruns as a component of the cost of the motors sold. However, it is uncertain as to what policy it should follow and also what price it should charge its customers when it sells any of the motors produced as part of the production overruns. In addition, some members of the management team question the profitability of these overruns.

Required:

Write a technical memo to Smith Producers top management outlining the factors that they should study before abandoning or continuing the production overrun policy.

P19–10 (AICPA) Standards for Pricing and Delivery (L.O. 3)

The following information pertains to the pricing and delivery functions of Tapa Wholesale Company:

Number of sales made to customers in 19X1   20,000
Average number of items per sale in 19X1   4
Number of sales projected for 19X2 24,000
Average number of items per sale projected for 19X2   5

Sales invoices are priced by clerks whose wage rate is $6.00 per hour. Labor negotiations have resulted in a 10 percent increase in the hourly rate for 19X2. It is expected that Tapa's pricing function will operate at the same level of productivity in 19X2 as it did in 19X1. Payroll tax rates and workers' compensation insurance rates will be the same in 19X2 as in 19X1. Prices for various items of supplies are expected to be the same in 19X2 as in 19X1.

Pricing function in 19X1:
Variable:

Wages	$40,000
Payroll taxes	4,000
Workers' compensation insurance	2,000
Supplies	1,000
Total variable	$47,000
Fixed	3,400
Total costs	$50,400

Fixed costs are allocated equally to all units. Except for delivery costs, all variable costs vary directly with the number of items priced. Supplies increase in proportion to the increase in the number of items priced. Tapa sells three products: Arcil, Balo, and Cacha. Differences in size and weight among these products affect variable delivery costs. For example, truck capacity is 10 units of Arcil, or 5 units of Balo, or 4 units of Cacha. Units projected to be delivered in 19X2 are as follows:

Arcil	60,000
Balo	40,000
Cacha	20,000
Total	120,000

Projected 19X2 costs for the delivery function are as follows:

Variable	$228,000
Fixed	30,000

Required:

a. Prepare the 19X2 budget of all costs for Tapa's pricing function.

b. Prepare a schedule showing the 19X2 standard delivery cost per unit of each of the three products sold by Tapa.

P19–11 Variance Analysis for Direct Selling (L.O. 4)

The management of Bourne Company has established the following standards for each detailed function of the direct selling activity. The company separates direct selling into customer groups.

	Retailers		Wholesalers	
	Unit Cost	**Estimated ABC Drivers**	**Unit Cost**	**Estimated ABC Drivers**
Salespersons' salaries (per call)	$ 3.20	75	$ 3.50	60
Salespersons' commissions and bonuses (per product unit sold)	.55	1,200	.75	1,000
Entertainment (per customer)	20.00	20	20.00	30
Salespersons' traveling expense (per day traveled)	45.00	35	45.00	25
Telephone solicitation (per call)	1.00	600	1.25	550

The following actual ABC drivers and actual costs were incurred for each customer group:

	Retailers		Wholesalers	
	Cost per ABC Driver	Actual ABC Drivers	Cost per ABC Driver	Actual ABC Drivers
Salespersons' salaries	$ 3.50	70	$ 3.60	65
Salespersons' commissions and bonuses	.50	1,100	.75	1,200
Entertainment	22.00	25	22.00	35
Salespersons' traveling expense	48.00	35	47.00	20
Telephone solicitation	.90	550	1.30	600

Required:

Prepare variance analyses for each customer group; a formal statement is not required. Assume budgeted sales were achieved.

P19–12 Using Expected Monetary Value in Transportation Decisions (L.O. 1)

A supplier of raw manufacturing materials, known simply as the Supply Company, has agreed to furnish materials to a company, known simply as the Buying Company. Because these materials are essential to the Buying Company's process, it is agreed that the Supply Company will pay a penalty of $1,500 for any shipment that does not reach the Buying Company on the day that it is needed.

The Supply Company makes other materials, and often when it receives orders from the Buying Company, it cannot interrupt its other production to produce these raw materials. However, the Buying Company recognizes this and agrees to forward orders two weeks in advance. The Supply Company can produce the materials in five days of operation after initiating processing. This arrangement requires timing in delivery because sometimes the Supply Company may finish production only one or two days before the raw materials are needed by the Buying Company. Fortunately, the contract between the two companies allows the Supply Company to choose its mode of transportation and also specifies the day required by the Buying Company's manufacturing division.

The following table shows the degree of reliability and costs of the three modes of transportation available for the Supply Company. (For example, there is a 60 percent probability that using water transportation the materials will not reach the Buying Company in four days.)

Transportation Mode	Cost per Shipment	Probability that the Shipment Will Take _____ Days					
		1	2	3	4	5	6
Water	$200	*	*	.10	.30	.40	.20
Rail	$300	*	.30	.50	.20	†	†
Air	$500	.80	.20	†	†	†	†

*Cannot reach Buying Company in this length of time.
†100 percent probability will have reached Buying Company by this time.

Required:

Using the expected monetary value decision criteria, prepare a decision table that the Supply Company transportation clerk can use in deciding which mode of transportation to use.

P19–13 Product Line Profitability Analysis (L.O. 3)

The management of the Scenic Toy Company plans to establish marketing standards in the near future. Now all they do in analyzing marketing costs is to allocate actual costs at the end of the period to three major product lines: bicycles, tricycles, and wagons. Scenic Toy incurred the following direct and indirect actual marketing costs last year:

Marketing Costs	Amount	Basis for Distribution
Sales salaries	$90,000	Direct charge
Warehousing and handling	7,500	Item handled
Transportation	6,000	Shipments
Credit and collection	10,500	Amount of sales orders
Direct selling	18,000	Customers served
Advertising and sales promotion	7,500	Amount of sales orders
General accounting	5,400	Customers served

Statistics extracted from the records of the company are as follows:

	Bicycle	Tricycle	Wagon
Sales salaries	$ 32,000	$ 40,000	$ 18,000
Items handled	40,000	25,600	14,400
Shipments	800	500	700
Sales orders	$300,000	$504,000	$396,000
Customers served	50	30	20

Required:

Distribute these actual marketing costs to the three product lines, and then compare marketing costs as a percentage of sales for each product line.

P19–14 Use of High-Low with Marketing Costs (L.O. 3)

Patricia Lyerly, cost accountant for the Dyersburg Manufacturing Company, provides you with data for selected marketing costs determined on the basis of sales. She informs you that management has decided that the relevant range for the company is 70,000 to 100,000 units of sales per period. Budgeted sales are set at 85,000 units. They set the following standards for these two volumes:

	70,000	100,000
Units of sale	70,000	100,000
Sales (@ $10 per unit)	$700,000	$1,000,000
Marketing expenses:		
Transportation	$ 17,000	$ 23,000
Credit and collection	21,300	28,800
General marketing activities	36,000	48,000
Direct selling	28,500	39,000
Advertising and sales promotion	40,500	57,000

During the period, the cost accountant reported these sales and marketing expenses:

Sales (@ $10 per unit) .... 82,000 units

	Variable	Fixed
Marketing expenses:		
Transportation	$16,900	$2,600
Credit and collection	21,000	4,000
General marketing activities	33,100	8,100
Direct selling	28,900	3,700
Advertising and sales promotion	44,800	1,850

Required:

a. Prepare an expense variance report, breaking marketing costs down into their fixed and variable components. Compute two variances for individual marketing expenses where appropriate; otherwise, only one variance for each expense item.

b. Based on the report you prepared in Requirement *a*, do you see any disadvantages of using units of sales as the factor of variability on which to establish the standards?

P19–15 Price and Efficiency Variance: Prices for Different Order Sizes (L.O. 2 and 4)

Actual and standard distribution cost data for March 19X1 for Martin, Inc., were as follows:

	Actual Operations	Budget at Standard Cost
Sales—Net of cash discount	$855,000	$900,000
Warehousing costs:		
Packing and wrapping salaries	23,600	20,000
Shipping salaries	24,080	24,000
Order-filling costs	33,500	32,000

March shipping-hours data follow:

	Shipping Hours
Budgeted	4,000
Standard operating level	3,800
Actual	4,300

All warehousing salaries are allocated on the basis of shipping-hours. Order-filling costs are allocated on the basis of sales and comprise freight, packing, and warehousing costs. An analysis of the amount of these standard costs by unit order size follows:

	Order-Filling Standard Costs Classified by Unit Order Size			
Unit-Volume Classifications	1–10	11–30	30+	Total
Units sold	18,000	32,000	20,000	70,000
Freight	$ 2,700	$ 3,520	$ 1,600	$ 7,820
Packing	7,200	10,240	4,480	21,920
Warehousing	900	960	400	2,260
Total	$10,800	$14,720	$ 6,480	$32,000

Required:

a. Using the most appropriate method, compute price and efficiency variances from standard cost and prove your variances for:
   (1) Packing and wrapping salaries.
   (2) Shipping salaries.
b. Assume that presently, Martin Company is charging a constant price per unit sold. However, management is considering revising its unit sales prices upward or downward on the basis of quantity ordered in proportion to the allocated freight, packing, and warehousing standard cost because they believe that the distribution cost per unit decreases with an increase in the size of the order.
   (1) To help management in this pricing decision, prepare a schedule computing the standard cost per unit for each order-filling cost—freight, packing, and warehousing—for each unit volume classification.
   (2) Prepare a schedule computing the revised unit sales price for each unit-volume classification while at the same time maintaining total sales of $900,000.

P19–16 Cost of Placing Order and Storing Unit; EOQ and High-Low (L.O. 1)

Williford, Inc., an assembler of bicycles, has decided to use the EOQ method to help determine the optimal quantities of wheels to order from the different manufacturers. Annual demand for the wheels totals 48,000. Values for the cost of placing an order and the annual cost of storage can be developed by using cost data from last year. During the lowest activity month of May, 250 orders were placed, while 800 orders were placed during December.

Samples are distributed as part of the company's promotion strategy. The purchasing department places all orders, and the accounts payable division of the Accounting Department processes the purchase order for payment. The shipping clerks process all sales orders to customers, and the receiving clerks inspect all incoming shipment and store items received.

Cost data from last year were as follows:

	Costs for May—250 Orders	Costs for Dec.—800 Orders	Annual Costs
Samples distribution	$ 2,500	$ 8,000	$ 43,200
Purchasing department:			
Salaries	3,000	8,000	49,000
Supplies and other expenses	800	1,200	12,100
Accounting department:			
Accounts payable:			
Clerks	1,500	2,600	21,000
Office supplies	700	1,500	10,000
Salespersons' salaries	3,000	4,800	42,000
Salespersons' travel	1,000	2,600	26,800
Warehousing department:			
Shipping clerks	2,800	7,000	60,000
Receiving clerks	2,100	4,700	29,000
Managers	1,800	1,800	21,600
Packing and wrapping	800	2,000	12,800
	$20,000	$44,200	$327,500

Space is leased in a public warehouse based on a rental fee per square foot occupied. The charge totaled $34,000 last year. Wheels are stored in containers of approximately the same size; consequently, each wheel occupies about the same amount of storage space in the warehouse. Insurance and property taxes on the wheels stored amounted to $1,200. Long-term capital investment is expected to earn 15 percent after taxes. The effective tax rate is 40 percent. The company pays 14 percent annual interest charge on a short-term seasonal bank loan.

Inventory balances tend to fluctuate during the year depending on the demand for wheels. Selected data on inventory balances:

	Units	Amount
May inventory balance	1,000	$ 8,000
December inventory balance	7,000	56,000
Average monthly inventory	4,000	32,000

Required:

a. Use last year's data to determine estimated values for:
   (1) The cost of placing an order.
   (2) The annual cost of storing a unit.
b. Calculate the EOQ and the number of orders that will be made using the EOQ.

Cases

C19–17 Steps in Establishing Marketing Cost Standards (L.O. 1)

Verba Key Yarn Company is being organized to produce various yarns and threads. Key, the president and major stockholder, has spent several months studying the feasibility of entry into the thread industry. Most of the thread sold in the United States is produced by three large companies. Each company is well established and has been in business for many years. Even though Key Yarn Company would be smaller, management feels that it would be able to concentrate on producing a fine quality of thread rather than diversifying operations by also producing needles, buttons, and zippers as done by the three large producers.

The thread produced by all companies in the market has the same basic characteristics. Generally the companies offer either a polyester or a cotton thread, with the polyester thread gaining an increasing market share. The consumer research study conducted by Key Yarn revealed that several shortcomings exist in the polyester thread now being marketed. Consumers expressed a desire for fuzz-free thread and for a heavier spool that would be more stable when turning on a spindle.

The company plans to conduct national advertising on television to introduce its thread. It will emphasize the product's uniqueness including the fuzz-free and heavier spool characteristics. In addition, Key will purchase mailing lists from several needlecraft magazine publishers. Subscribers to these magazines will receive free samples of the smaller spools of thread. Cents-off coupons will also be attached to the packages. In addition, company salespersons will call on wholesalers and vending companies. Management believes that a market exists in grocery stores for a limited variety of thread colors.

Key Yarn Company management has spent much time studying the flow of work they plan to use. After the thread is processed and wound on spools, workers will place them in boxes that they send to the finished goods warehouse. The boxes of thread will remain here until they are assembled to fill a shipment. After an order is assembled for shipment, it is packed and wrapped.

Key Yarn Company plans to have an employee in the credit and collection department investigate all credit sales transactions before shipments are made. Approval will be determined by the financial stability of the buying company. If this approval is made, an invoice is prepared by the credit and collection department. Other employees in this department will be responsible for posting charges and credits to accounts receivable accounts.

The company has its own trucks to deliver the orders to regional warehouses. Each truck driver and helper will be paid an hourly wage. They will be furnished credit cards from major oil companies from which they will purchase gasoline and oil.

Management plans to establish production standards for its manufacturing process and is keenly interested in measuring the efficiency of its marketing operation in this manner also. However, they are at a loss as to how they should proceed.

Required:

Assume that you are employed as a management consultant to help the company establish and use marketing standards. Outline the steps you would take in this process and suggest ways of establishing the standards.

C19–18 Marketing Cost Analysis for Department Stores (L.O. 2)

Fink Department Stores, Inc., operates three department stores. One of the stores is basically a soft goods store specializing in ladies' and men's ready-to-wear clothes and accessories. It is in the downtown section that is suffering decaying economic conditions. Another store carries hard goods merchandise such as furniture, household appliances, radios, and television sets; it is in the city's wealthy suburb. The company also has a branch store in another state which performs some marketing activities independently.

Management has not incorporated standards into the accounting system, but they use statistical standards for planning and control. Fink's managers use the statistics obtained through a publication of the Controllers' Congress, which is a division of the National Retail Merchants Association, in establishing marketing standards. (Members of the association submit their sales and cost figures to this division, which compiles the data. All the standards are expressed as a percentage of net sales and are broken down into different sales volume classifications.) Since Fink Department Stores fall in the $5 to $10 million sales volume, they refer to the percentages for this classification. Even though department stores are not required to report their cost percentages, so many stores participate that management believes the figures are representative. The Controllers' Congress publishes this pamphlet once a year.

Fink management does not establish its standards entirely on these representative figures, however, since it believes the peculiarities of its operations should also be given some consideration. They also refer to past experiences and future plans in establishing the standards.

Accountants prepare monthly income and expense statements for each store; these show dollar amounts and percentages for current operations, budgeted operations, and the prior year's operation for the same month. A statement also shows the actual and budgeted dollar amounts and percentages for the direct expenses of each and profits. The treasurer and controller hold monthly conferences with each supervisor responsible for a cost center's performance to discuss the expense elements which have unfavorable variances.

Required:

Evaluate the store's system for establishing and analyzing standard costs for marketing expense.

C19–19 Standard Cost System for Marketing Costs (L.O. 1)

Paragon Luggage Company has established a reputation for producing attractive, high-quality luggage, handbags, and leather accessories. The leather goods manufactured in three facilities in the southeastern United States are sold through company-owned retail stores in the eastern United States. The home office is in one of the manufacturing facilities and has three departments—production, marketing, and administration. Each department is evaluated independently.

The company recognizes the advantages of a standard cost system and has been using this system in accounting for its manufacturing operations for several years. Attempts are being made to incorporate standards in accounting for marketing costs as well, but adequate effort has not been put into determining the units of variability. As a result too many marketing activities are simply based on a percentage of sales. For example, unsalable (stores) account, which is the account for irregular products, is related to sales, and the standard is expressed as a percentage of this unit.

Managers established standards for packaging material through work sampling. They set standards for boxes, tape, liners, and dividers. The individual boxes are packed in master shipping box cases. Since these box cases are reusable, an estimate was made of the expected life, based on actual experience, to arrive at a standard cost. This estimate has proved to be reliable, so it is unusual for a significant variance to occur.

An outside engineering firm established standards for packaging labor through time and motion studies. Workers keep a daily record of the number of leather goods packaged and the packaging material and labor used. Accountants use a packaging material quantity variance account and a packaging labor efficiency variance account to ascertain any difference between actual and standard usage. They do not study packaging material standards in as great detail as raw material standards, since the company found that packaging materials are easier to control than are leather materials.

The manufacturing facilities package the leather goods and transfer them to the Transportation Department; this department's expenses appear on the operating budgets for the manufacturing plants. The retail stores submit orders of the Transportation Department and are billed at standard cost. The leather goods are transported on company-owned trailer trucks. Most of the expense items are expressed as a standard cost per mile traveled, but some, such as gasoline, are based on historical data and are expressed as a percentage of sales. Time studies were used to establish transportation labor standards.

The standards of repair and maintenance are based on historical data and the age of the vehicles. A report is prepared listing each vehicle by age. The company revises the maintenance standard to increase the cost as the vehicle becomes older. Vehicle depreciation standards are based on what actual depreciation is expected to be.

The company revised its advertising standards three years ago to decrease the standard, which is expressed as a percentage of gross sales. Before that, the company employed an advertising agency to plan sales promotion. Both company management and the agency established standards based on what they thought was needed to accomplish the sales objective. But when Paragon decided to use its own marketing personnel for all advertising activities, advertising expenditures were reduced.

Since management considers percentage analysis important in evaluating performance efficiency, they use percentage analysis extensively for control and planning. A total operations standard is set for the seasonal retail stores that have been in operation for some length of time. This standard is expressed as a percentage of sales. A store is considered unprofitable if its expenses are more than 30 percent of gross sales, because then either sales volume is too low or expenses are too high. Generally, for the seasoned stores, expenses are less than 30 percent of actual gross sales.

At the end of each four-week period, store variances are analyzed. If a variance is significant in the opinion of the regional sales manager, the accountant or the store manager begins an investigation to determine the cause. If an actual expense deviates from standard by a material amount, the standard and actual percentage of sales are evaluated to determine whether a trend can be detected. Management uses the information gained from variance analysis in revising standards for the next budget year.

Required:

Evaluate Paragon's standard cost system for marketing costs.

C19–20 Marketing Standards in a Production Operation (L.O. 2)

Glen Jones Aluminum and Chemical Corporation entered the aluminum industry in 1946; since that time the company has grown and its interests have been diversified. It has used an engineered standard cost system since it began operations. This system is based on an engineered standard cost which is established through sound engineering and accounting studies. An integrated standard cost system is used in which the cost system is an integral part of the plant financial accounting system. Cost centers, general ledger accounts, and cost element codes are established for the purpose of identifying, classifying, and accumulating costs.

Standards are set on a reasonable basis that takes into account all known normal factors. There is no provision for abnormal losses. Standards are set tight enough to encourage high performance, yet they are not set so tight as to be detrimental to employee morale.

Standards are set for one year; at the end of each year a study is made to determine whether standard revision is required. The conditions under which the standards are operating may change during the year; for example, the shipping department may change from rail to barge transportation. In this case, the standard is updated at the time of the change.

After the industrial engineer completes the study and arrives at a standard for each cost center, the person responsible for the cost center's performance is asked to sign the standard. On this expense standard is spelled out in dollars the standard costs necessary to operate this cost center. There is a definite basis for the computation of each cost.

A total is made for all items, and the total is the standard cost for this particular cost center. A supervisor who does not agree with the standard established by the industrial engineer must provide support for the agreement or disagreement. If any adjustments are necessary, they are made and the expense standard is forwarded to the controller for approval. The expense standard is then sent to the cost accounting department, where it is utilized in a computer program.

The shipping department's three major expense items are loadout operators, power, and repair and maintenance. Some loadout operators must be present continuously during the normal working day, even though actual loading may be performed for only four hours on some days. The base unit for this minimum work force is scheduled days, which is a standard work day, Monday through Friday. Scheduled days will vary with each month; the normal monthly quantity is 21.73 scheduled days.

Industrial engineers establish by time study the worker-hour requirements to load 70-ton and 100-ton railcars. Time-study analysis is essential; for example, shipping department employees can load a 100-ton car faster than a 70-ton car, as the 70-ton car has to be moved twice because of hopper locations. This is a variable expense determined by the number of cars loaded. Power expense also varies with the tons shipped.

Some personnel are assigned to the shipping department on a flexible basis. Workers not needed to load cars are used in the production process. The worker-hours in each cost center are determined through the use of time cards. The job ticket shows the expense distribution by hour to each cost center. This source document will report whether a shipping clerk is changed to a production cost center during the day.

The corporation computes two variances for its marketing costs: the price variance and the operations practice variance. The price variance reflects changes in wages or purchased materials. All labor is first isolated to determine whether there is any price variance before it is charged to the cost centers. The negotiation of labor cost changes is the responsibility of the industrial relations department. Material price variances are the responsibility of the purchasing department. These variances are not controllable by the cost center manager.

The operations practice variance indicates the use of alternate production methods, that is, situations in which the product was not manufactured or shipped in the manner planned. An example of this variance is the underloading of railcars. This would not necessarily be under the control of the cost center manager.

Required:

While recognizing that Jones Aluminum and Chemical Corporation has installed a fairly effective system for marketing cost standards, do you see any areas in which additional work is needed?

C19–21 Marketing Cost Standards for Distribution (L.O. 1)

Kim's Cookie Corporation has a sales organization and three production plants manufacturing products in the sweet goods industry. The company sells cookies and cakes in 13 southern and eastern states. The three major departments in the corporate organization are production, marketing, and administration. The marketing department is responsible for marketing the products and is not concerned with where the goods are produced. The performance of each of these major departments is measured independently, as each department has a separate basis of evaluation.

The corporation integrates its standard for production cost into its accounting system; however, marketing cost standards are a percentage of gross sales. For example, Unsalable (Stores) account, which is the account for stale products, is related to sales and the standard is expressed as a percentage of this unit. Route and distribution volume discounts also use a percentage of gross sales as their standard. Many of the delivery expense items are expressed as a standard cost per mile traveled.

Delivery expense standards vary among sales branches because of the influence of geographical conditions. The standards for repair and maintenance are based on historical data and the age of the vehicles in each branch. A branch vehicle report is a listing of each vehicle by age. The company has found that the maintenance standard must be revised to increase the cost as the vehicle becomes older. Vehicle depreciation standards are based on expected actual depreciation.

The company revised its advertising standards three years ago to decrease the standard expressed as a percentage of gross sales. The company had employed an advertising agency for six years to plan their sales promotion. The standards were established by both management and the advertising agency on the basis of what these people thought was needed to accomplish the sales objective. With a change in the marketing department personnel, the company decided to reduce their advertising expenditures.

They used work sampling to establish standards for packaging materials. Standards were established for such packaging materials as tape, liners, and dividers. Master shipping box cases are used to pack bags and boxes. Since these box cases are reusable, an estimate of the expected life is made based on actual experience to arrive at a standard cost. This estimate has been found to be very realistic, and it is unusual for a significant variance to occur.

Management employed industrial engineers from another firm to use time study to determine the packaging labor standards. Packaging standards are based on two types of units. One unit is a box containing 360 bulk cookies. Six of these boxes can be shipped in the reusable master box cases. The other unit has 12 bags containing 24 cookies which can be placed in a box case.

Daily, workers record the number of sweet goods packaged and units of material used in this process. A material quantity variance is used to accumulate any difference between actual and standard usage. Packaging material standards are not studied in as great detail as raw material standards because the company has found packaging materials are easier to control than raw sweet goods material.

The production plant manufactures and packages the goods and transfers these into the Transportation Department. Sales branches submit orders to the Transportation Department and are billed at standard cost. Sales branches are not responsible for Transportation Department performance, and this expense item appears on the operating budget for the plant. The sweet goods are shipped in the company's trailer trucks. Most of the units are 40-foot trailers; each trailer holds approximately one million cookies. Sweet goods are also delivered through direct lines to large chain stores. Time studies established transportation labor standards. Standards for other transportation expenses such as gasoline are established using historical data and are expressed as a percentage of sales.

Percentage analysis is used extensively for control and planning purposes, for management feels that percentage analysis is important in evaluating performance efficiency. A total operations standard is set for the seasoned branches that have been in operation for some length of time. This standard is expressed as a percentage of sales. A branch is considered profitable if its branch expenses are less than 30 percent of actual gross sales within the branch. If branch expenses exceed 30 percent of gross sales, this indicates an unprofitable situation because either sales volume is too low or branch expenses are too high. Generally, the seasoned branches operate with expenses that are less than 30 percent of actual gross sales.

At the end of each four-week period, branch variances are analyzed. If a variance is significant in the opinion of the regional sales manager, the regional accountant or the branch manager begins an investigation to determine the cause. If an actual expense deviates from standard in a material amount, the standard and actual percentages of sales are evaluated to determine if a trend can be detected. Management uses the information gained from variance analysis in revising standards for the next budget year.

Required:

Evaluate the standard cost system for marketing costs.

CHAPTER

20

Variable Costing

CHAPTER OBJECTIVES

After studying this chapter, you should be able to:

1. Contrast the application of variable and absorption costing in product costing and income determination.
2. Convert variable costing income to absorption costing income.
3. Show that changes in inventory affect absorption costing income.

4. Evaluate the impact of automation and changes in the manufacturing environment on variable costing.
5. Understand the advantages variable costing offers in decision making, as well as its dangers.

Introduction

Previous chapters discussed only absorption costing that treats variable and fixed costs as product costs. **Absorption costing** (also called **conventional costing** or **full costing**) is required for external reporting. This chapter discusses a different approach to product costing known as *variable* or *direct costing* that is used only for internal reporting and analysis. Variable and absorption costing are not mutually exclusive. Accountants find that variable costing more effectively meets internal requirements because it provides better insight into cost relationships while the absorption costing method meets external reporting requirements.

Variable Costing (Direct Costing) (L.O. 1)

The **variable** or **direct costing** concept considers only those production costs varying directly with volume as **product costs.** This leaves all other manufacturing costs to be treated as **period costs.** Since direct material and direct labor are usually variable in a labor intensive environment, variable costing treats these costs and variable factory overhead as product costs. Accountants therefore charge off all other costs as expenses in the period incurred. In an automated factory, however, direct labor is usually fixed and a smaller component of product costs. Thus, in a machine-driven environment, direct material and variable factory overhead may be the only product costs using variable costing. Variable costing considers all other costs as the costs of providing for a level of capacity and charges the entire costs against the revenue of the period.

Cost Flows under Variable Costing

Exhibit 20–1 graphically shows the cost flows under variable costing. Accountants assign all variable manufacturing costs to production, and they become part of the unit costs of the products manufactured. Accountants do not assign fixed costs to inventory; they consider them as expenses for the year and charge them to Income Summary.

In referring to variable costing, I prefer not to use the often-heard term *direct costing. Variable costing* is the more accurate term because it treats those costs that vary with production volume (generally direct material, direct labor, and variable overhead) as product costs. Variable costing treats all fixed costs as period costs. On the other hand, recall that direct costs are traceable to a cost center. Because indirect costs are not traceable, they must be allocated to the cost center. Direct and indirect costs may be either product or period costs. Variable costing treats variable overhead costs (indirect costs), as well as other variable manufacturing costs, as product costs. Using the term *direct costing* implies that the method treats only traceable costs as product costs. Traceability is not the emphasis, however, as both variable and fixed costs can be direct costs. For example, in a department that makes only one product, direct product costs are all costs which accountants can trace to the department, including supervision, depreciation, and other fixed costs as well as variable costs.

Variable costing differs from **prime costing** that inventories only direct material and direct labor. The prime cost method is based on a weak theoretical concept and is not acceptable for external reporting.

E X H I B I T   20–1   Cost Flows under Variable Costing

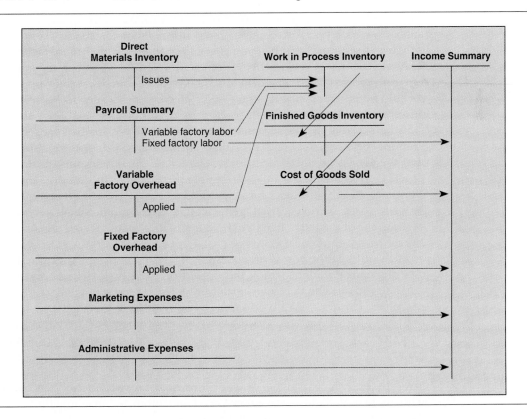

Absorption Costing

Absorption costing, as discussed previously, distinguishes between production and nonproduction costs in determining which costs to capitalize as assets. Absorption costing only inventories production costs and expenses marketing and administrative costs in the period incurred. Absorption costing defers a part of both fixed and variable manufacturing cost until sale of the product. At that time, the cost is matched with revenue. Variable costing distinguishes between fixed and variable costs in addition to making the same distinction as absorption costing among production, marketing, and administrative costs.

Both absorption and variable costing exclude marketing and administrative costs from inventory; thus, these two methods differ only in this: Variable costing excludes fixed production costs from the costs of goods manufactured, while absorption costing does not. This treatment of fixed factory costs—whether it is charged off against income when the cost is incurred, or against income when the goods are sold—is the primary difference between variable and absorption costing.

Impact of Automated Manufacturing Environment

Variable costing was appropriate when variable costs were a high proportion of total production costs. Also, variable costing was appropriate when product diversity was small and there was not a wide variation of product demands made on the firm's production and marketing resources. Changes in the factory environment have decreased the percentage of variable costs in total manufacturing cost. With automation on the increase in industry, fixed costs become an ever larger element. Depreciation and related costs of automated equipment cause a large portion of overhead to be fixed, not variable. The spread of guaranteed annual wage contracts also causes more of the labor costs to be fixed.

Thus, fixed costs are becoming a larger share of total manufacturing costs. The competitive environment is forcing companies to produce an increasing variety of products that make different demands on equipment and support departments. Some accountants argue that in this cost accounting environment, absorption costing becomes the only meaningful costing method. Other accountants believe that as automation increases, variable costing becomes more important for decision making, and that absorption costing is dysfunctional for management accounting decisions. They base their view on the idea that all product costs are based on assumptions, estimates, allocations, and averages. This is especially prevalent for assigning factory overhead cost and other indirect product costs. Variable costing overcomes the dysfunctionality of absorption costing, but it excludes fixed cost elements that many accountants believe they should assign to products.

Such shifts in the cost characteristics of a company emphasize the importance of management understanding the impact of fixed costs. The company has less flexibility in altering decisions because it has invested more dollars in machinery and plant. However, merely grouping fixed overhead items together to charge to the period under variable costing may be insufficient for a company to control rising fixed overhead costs. On the other hand, differentiating between fixed and variable costs as plants become more automated can be a first step in controlling costs. Managers need better information because they have to deliberate more carefully over the expansion of labor force and production facilities. Admittedly, with increased fixed costs experienced in automated manufacturing, omitting fixed costs from products may have less merit.

Comparison of Variable and Absorption Costing (L.O. 2 and 3)

In addition to long-range statements to evaluate factors affecting income, companies need short-period income statements that do not consider the entire production and sales cycle. Variable costing meets this need even in small businesses where there is a limited cost accounting system. Variable costing is an overhead costing approach that consolidates the desirable features of breakeven analysis and profit planning involving the relationship between volume, costs, and profits.

Production and Sales Variations Cause Income Distortion

With an increase in fixed costs, seasonal variations in production and sales cause a distortion in income reported on the income statement. Absorption costing assumes that existing facilities and management were set up to make and sell an average volume of goods over a period of years. Absorption costing supplies a base for cost determination and eliminates great fluctuations in inventory values, but it still distorts income as Exhibit 20–2 illustrates. To simplify, Exhibit 20–2 assumes no partially completed units are in inventory. The top part of the exhibit provides production and sales statistics. Exhibit 20–2 assumes a $10 unit sales price, $6 unit variable production costs (direct material, $2; direct labor, $3; and variable overhead, $1), and $250,000 total production fixed costs at a budgeted capacity of 125,000 units each year. Fixed marketing and administrative expenses total $30,000. Both absorption and variable costing treat marketing and administrative expenses as period costs. However, the variable costing concept separates fixed and variable marketing and administrative expenses to determine the net **contribution margin.**

With absorption costing, when production volume exceeds sales in the first year, fixed costs are built up in inventory and are not charged off until the inventory is sold. Thus, even though there is a lag in sales, absorption costing shows higher profits than does variable costing during this period of heavy production. The opposite is true during the reverse cycle, as can be seen for the second year in Exhibit 20–2. Even though the sales volume has increased from 80,000 units to 140,000 units, absorption costing income does not reflect this increase as dramatically as does variable costing. Management could become confused as income often seems to have no direct relationship to sales volume in absorption costing.

Because production was only 100,000 units in the first year, $50,000 of underapplied fixed production expenses resulted. Under the variable cost approach, units of production receive no application of fixed expenses. Instead, variable costing charges off the entire $250,000 fixed production expense each year.

In studying Exhibit 20–2, which compares absorption and variable costing, observe the following:

1. Statements of income using absorption costing make no distinction between fixed and variable costs. As a result, absorption costing income statements do not show cost-volume-profit relationships as clearly as variable costing statements of income.

2. Inventory values are smaller with variable costing because it only capitalizes $6 variable cost as assets. Inventory values using absorption costing have an additional $2 fixed factory overhead per unit.

3. Variable costing income in the first year is lower than that for absorption costing because production exceeds sales. Variable costing charges total

EXHIBIT 20–2

HICKS COMPANY
Comparison of Absorption and Variable Costing Income Statements
For Years Indicated

	First Year	Second Year	Two Years Combined
Production and sales statistics:			
Finished goods inventory:			
Units in beginning inventory	–0–	20,000	
Units produced	100,000	130,000	230,000
Units sold	80,000	140,000	220,000
Units in ending inventory	20,000	10,000	10,000
Absorption costing:			
Sales @ $10	$800,000	$1,400,000	$2,200,000
Less: Cost of goods sold:			
Cost of goods manufactured	$800,000	$1,040,000	$1,840,000
Add: Beginning inventory @ $8		160,000	
Available for sale	$800,000	$1,200,000	$1,840,000
Less: Ending inventory @ $8	160,000	80,000	80,000
Cost of goods sold	$640,000	$1,120,000	$1,760,000
Volume variance*	(50,000)	10,000	40,000
Adjusted cost of goods sold	$690,000	$1,110,000	$1,800,000
Gross margin	$110,000	$ 290,000	$ 400,000
Marketing and administrative expenses	60,000	80,000	140,000
Absorption costing income before taxes	$ 50,000	$ 210,000	$ 260,000
Variable costing:			
Sales @ $10	$800,000	$1,400,000	$2,200,000
Less: Cost of goods sold:			
Total variable manufacturing cost	$600,000	$ 780,000	$1,380,000
Add: Beginning inventory @ $6		120,000	
Available for sale	$600,000	$ 900,000	$ 1,380,000
Less: Ending inventory @ $6	120,000	60,000	60,000
Cost of goods sold	$480,000	$ 840,000	$1,320,000
Manufacturing contribution margin	$320,000	$ 560,000	$ 880,000
Less: Variable marketing and administrative expenses	30,000	50,000	80,000
Net contribution margin	$290,000	$ 510,000	$ 800,000
Less: Fixed factory overhead	250,000	250,000	500,000
Fixed marketing and administrative expenses	30,000	30,000	60,000
Variable costing income before taxes	$ 10,000	$ 230,000	$ 240,000

*Volume variance based on normal capacity of 125,000 units. $\dfrac{\$250,000 \text{ fixed overhead}}{125,000 \text{ units}} = \$2$

First year: $50,000 underapplied $(125,000 - 100,000) \times \$2$
Second year: $10,000 overapplied $(125,000 - 130,000) \times \$2$

fixed cost incurred against sales revenue, while absorption costing applies part of it to inventory and defers the cost until sale of the product. If there is an increase in inventories, variable costing income will be less than absorption costing income, as seen in the first year.

4. In the second year, variable costing income is higher than absorption costing income because units sold exceed units produced. Variable costing in-

come always moves in the same direction as sales volume. The cost of goods sold using variable costing includes only a $6 per unit variable cost. The unit cost of goods sold is $8 with absorption costing.

5. Conventional absorption costing determines an intermediate income figure called **gross margin,** which reflects the difference between sales and the fixed and variable costs of sales. This figure normally varies significantly from the **manufacturing contribution margin** determined with variable costing, because we subtract only the variable expenses of the goods sold from sales revenue in determining manufacturing contribution margin. We subtract all production, marketing, and administrative variable expenses from sales to determine the **net contribution margin.**

6. The income for the two years combined using the two concepts differs by $20,000 ($260,000 absorption costing income; $240,000 variable costing income). This $20,000 difference in income results from the 10,000 units remaining in ending inventory; they have $2 fixed overhead assigned to each under absorption costing. However, over a complete cycle of inventory buildup and liquidation, total income is identical. Note that we cannot add the costs available for sale horizontally in Exhibit 20–2 because of the inclusion of inventory values more than once.

7. As discussed in Chapters 4 and 12, we should prorate the volume variance computed for absorption costing if it is a significant amount. However, to simplify the illustration, Exhibit 20–2 treats the volume variance as a period cost.

Later in this chapter, Exhibits 20–6 and 20–7 illustrate that changes in inventory do not affect variable costing profits as they do with absorption costing profits.

Volume Variance

Absorption costing determines both fixed and variable factory overhead rates. In Exhibit 20–2, the variable factory overhead rate is $1 and the fixed overhead rate is $2. However, variable costing does not inventory fixed costs. As a result, variable costing does not determine an application rate for fixed factory overhead. With the absorption costing concept, a favorable or unfavorable **volume variance** results when actual production differs from budgeted production used to compute the fixed overhead rate. The bottom of Exhibit 20–2 shows a volume variance for the absorption costing method. For example, in the first year, the company budgeted to produce 125,000 units, but produced only 100,000 units. This results in a $50,000 [(125,000 units − 100,000 units) × $2] underapplication of overhead. Variable costing computes no volume variance, since it closes total fixed factory overhead directly to the temporary account, Income Summary.

Standard Costs for Absorption and Variable Costing

Variable costing can use either strictly actual costs or standard costs. If accountants combine a variable costing system with standard costs, they establish estimates for only variable production costs (i.e., direct material, direct labor in a labor intensive operation, and variable factory overhead). They set no standard for fixed factory costs in a variable costing system.

Both variable and absorption costing determine variable cost variances. If a company uses a three- or four-variance method of analysis for overhead, the

EXHIBIT 20–3   Adjustment of Variable Costing Income to Absorption Costing Basis with Overhead Application Rate Unchanged

	First Year	Second Year	Two Years Combined
Variable costing income per Exhibit 20–2	$10,000	$230,000	$240,000
Variation for fixed cost influence of inventory (Units produced – Units sold) × Fixed factory overhead per unit at normal capacity	40,000	(20,000)	20,000
Absorption costing income per Exhibit 20–2 ...	$50,000	$210,000	$260,000

spending and efficiency variances reflect differences between actual and standard variable costs. If, instead, a company uses a two-variance method of overhead analysis, it determines a controllable variance for both variable and absorption costing since the controllable variance reflects variable cost efficiency. When using a four-variance method, a company computes a fixed overhead spending variance only for absorption costing since this variance reflects the difference between budgeted and actual fixed costs.

Adjustments to Include Fixed Costs

Overhead Application Rate Unchanged.   Because external reporting does not allow variable costing, companies must adjust to an absorption costing basis. Exhibit 20–3 shows this adjustment for periods in which the application rate remains unchanged. We determine the adjustment by multiplying the change in the quantity of all inventory by the $2 fixed factory cost per unit. For example, in the first year, there was an increase of 20,000 units in finished goods inventory (from a zero beginning inventory to 20,000 units). We multiply this change of 20,000 units by the $2 fixed factory overhead rate to arrive at an adjustment of $40,000. We add this adjustment to the variable costing income from Exhibit 20–2 to determine absorption costing income. In the second year, there is a 10,000-unit decrease in inventory. We multiply this decrease by a $2 fixed factory overhead cost per unit to arrive at the $20,000 adjustment. We then deduct the adjustment from the variable costing income in calculating absorption costing income. In a period like the second year, in which the units sold exceed the units produced, we deduct the fixed factory overhead adjustment for the change in inventory from variable costing income to determine absorption costing income.

Overhead Application Rate Changed.   Exhibit 20–3 represents an oversimplification of the reconciliation of absorption and variable costing. Exhibit 20–3 assumes that the $2 fixed overhead application rate did not change over the two-year period. If beginning and ending inventories carry different fixed overhead rates, the reconciliation of absorption costing and variable costing income becomes more complex. Assuming first-in, first-out inventory costing, Exhibit 20–4 uses the data given in Exhibit 20–2, but the fixed overhead application rate increases to $2.20. This increase causes second-year ending inventory under absorption costing to be valued at $8.20 × 10,000 units = $82,000.

EXHIBIT 20–4

HICKS COMPANY
Comparison of Absorption and Variable Costing Income Statements
With Change in Application Rate
For Years Indicated

	First Year	Second Year
Production and sales statistics:		
Finished goods inventory:		
Units in beginning inventory	–0–	20,000
Units produced	100,000	130,000
Units sold	80,000	140,000
Units in ending inventory	20,000	10,000
Absorption costing:		
Sales @ $10	$800,000	$1,400,000
Less: Cost of goods sold:		
Cost of goods manufactured	$800,000	$1,066,000
Add: Beginning inventory @ $8		160,000
Available for sale	$800,000	$1,226,000
Less: Ending inventory	160,000	82,000
Cost of goods sold	$640,000	$1,144,000
Volume variance*	(50,000)	11,000
Adjusted cost of goods sold	$690,000	$1,133,000
Gross margin	$110,000	$ 267,000
Marketing and administrative expenses	60,000	80,000
Absorption costing income before taxes	$ 50,000	$ 187,000
Variable costing:		
Sales @ $10	$800,000	$1,400,000
Less: Cost of goods sold:		
Total variable manufacturing cost	$600,000	$ 780,000
Add: Beginning inventory @ $6		120,000
Available for sale	$600,000	$ 900,000
Less: Ending inventory @ $6	120,000	60,000
Costs of goods sold	$480,000	$ 840,000
Manufacturing contribution margin	$320,000	$ 560,000
Less: Variable marketing and		
administrative expenses	30,000	50,000
Net contribution margin	$290,000	$ 510,000
Less: Fixed factory overhead	250,000	275,000
Fixed marketing and		
administrative expenses	30,000	30,000
Variable costing income before taxes	$ 10,000	$ 205,000

*Volume variance based on normal capacity of 125,000 units.

First Year	**Second Year**
$\dfrac{\$250,000 \text{ fixed overhead}}{125,000 \text{ units}} = \$2$	$\dfrac{\$275,000 \text{ fixed overhead}}{125,000 \text{ units}} = \$2.20$

First year: $50,000 underapplied (125,000 − 100,000) × $2
Second year: $11,000 overapplied (125,000 − 130,000) × $2.20

Rather than use the formula multiplying the change in inventory by the fixed overhead rate, the analysis in Exhibit 20–5 should be used. This analysis is appropriate for periods in which a rate change occurs as well as for periods in which the rate remains unchanged.

EXHIBIT 20-5   Adjustment of Variable Costing Income to Absorption Costing Basis with Overhead Application Rate Changed

	First Year		Second Year	
Variable costing income before taxes	$10,000		$205,000	
Add: Fixed costs of period deferred in ending inventory	40,000	($160,000 −$120,000)	22,000	($82,000 −$60,000)
	$50,000		$227,000	
Less: Fixed costs of prior year absorbed in period through beginning inventory	–0–		40,000	($160,000 −$120,000)
Absorption costing income before taxes	$50,000		$187,000	

Advantages of Variable Costing (L.O. 5)

Once you realize the inadequacies of absorption costing, you can more easily understand the advantages of variable costing. The greatest of these is that management can easily comprehend variable costing data. Accountants want to provide information that is accurate, complete, and timely; but none of this matters if the information cannot be understood. When managers find company reports are too complex, they have no faith in the figures and do not realize their importance. Variable costing overcomes this problem.

Inventory Changes Do Not Affect Profit

Managers can better understand variable costing statements because profits more rapidly move in the same direction as sales. Sales and changes in inventory affect absorption costing profits. For example, if sales exceed production, inventory decreases and absorption costing profits are lower than variable costing profits. This difference results when sales exceed production because we take the cost for the excess of the number of units sold over the number of units produced out of inventory and add it to cost of goods sold. In both variable costing and absorption costing, we take the variable costs of these excess units out of inventory. However, in absorption costing, we take one additional cost, fixed manufacturing overhead, out of inventory and add it to cost of goods sold. Recall that in variable costing, we do not add fixed manufacturing overhead to inventory. Rather, we treat it as a period cost along with all other fixed costs. This additional cost in cost of goods sold using absorption costing causes net income to be lower than the net income using variable costing.

If production exceeds sales, inventory increases and profits using absorption costing are higher than profits using variable costing. Both variable and absorption costing add the variable costs of the excess units produced to inventory. However, absorption costing also adds fixed manufacturing overhead to inventory. Because absorption costing treats fixed manufacturing overhead as a product cost, absorption costing profits are higher than when using variable costing

EXHIBIT 20–6   Income Statement under Absorption Costing

TRAUGH COMPANY
Absorption Costing Income Statement
For the Year Ending May 31
($000s)

	19X1	19X2
Sales (4,000,000 units)	$28,000	$28,000
Cost of goods sold:		
Beginning inventory (1,000,000 units)	$ 6,500	$ 6,500
Cost of goods manufactured ($4 unit		
variable + $10,000,000 fixed overhead) . .	26,000	30,000
Goods available for sale	$32,500	$36,500
Less: Ending inventory	6,500	12,000
Cost of goods sold	26,000	24,500
Gross margin	$ 2,000	$ 3,500
Fixed marketing and administrative expenses .	3,000	3,000
Absorption costing income (loss) before taxes .	$ (1,000)	$ 500

where fixed manufacturing overhead is treated as a period cost along with all other fixed costs. If production and sales are equal, profits are the same under both absorption and variable costing.

For example, assume that Traugh Company operations for 19X1 resulted in a loss as shown in Exhibit 20–6. An individual agreeing to accept only compensation equal to 50 percent of profits generated replaced the president. Within the next year the president had the production facilities operating at full capacity of 5,000,000 units, up from 19X1's production of 4,000,000 units. Despite no growth in sales, the next period's income statement showed a profit with no change in total fixed costs or unit variable cost. The new president was delighted with the bonus, but is it deserved?

In 19X1, absorption costing applied fixed manufacturing overhead costs at $2.50 per unit produced ($10,000,000/4,000,000 units). In 19X2, Traugh Company applied fixed manufacturing overhead costs at $2.00 per unit produced ($10,000,000/5,000,000 units). Therefore, the full cost per unit of inventory in 19X1 is $6.50, the total of the direct materials, direct labor, and variable and fixed manufacturing overhead. Using absorption costing, product cost in 19X2 is $6 resulting in an ending inventory of $12,000,000 ($6 × 2,000,000 units).

If, instead, Traugh Company uses variable costing in 19X2, the income statement would show a loss as Exhibit 20–7 illustrates, and the president would not receive a bonus. Variable costing inventories $4 variable costs of production as product costs. Variable costing considers all $10,000,000 fixed manufacturing overhead costs as period costs, charged to expense in 19X2.

Note that sales volume is constant and variable costing shows a loss of $1,000,000 for 19X2 which equals that reported for 19X1. A change in inventory does not affect variable costing profits or losses. The new president does not deserve a bonus because true profits are not generated by merely increasing production with no increase in sales.

EXHIBIT 20–7   Income Statement under Variable Costing

TRAUGH COMPANY
Variable Costing Income Statement
For the Period Ending May 31, 19X2
($000s)

Sales (4,000,000 units)		$28,000
Cost of goods sold:		
Beginning inventory (1,000,000 units)	$ 4,000	
Cost of goods manufactured ($4 unit		
variable × 5,000,000 units)	20,000	
Goods available for sale	$24,000	
Less: Ending inventory (2,000,000 units)	8,000	
Cost of goods sold		16,000
Manufacturing contribution margin		$12,000
Fixed manufacturing overhead	$10,000	
Fixed marketing and administrative expenses	3,000	13,000
Variable costing loss before taxes		$ (1,000)

Phantom Profits Are Ignored

The president's action resulted in larger inventory, which increases absorption costing income on the financial statement, although the company sold no additional goods. Absorption costing operates using this dysfunctional concept—the larger the volume of operations, the more inventory to absorb overhead, the lower the unit cost, and the more profit generated. Increasing production without a corresponding rise in sales assumes converting raw materials to work in process increases profits. Usually raw materials have a higher resale value than work in process and are easier to sell. Absorption costing profits reflect absorbed labor and overhead costs as assets and ignore expenses associated with carrying additional inventory. These inventory profits or **phantom profits** are a contradiction in terms generated by manufacturing more products, not selling more.

Further, absorption costing ignores expenses associated with carrying additional inventory. Holding inventory is expensive because of increased costs for insurance, property taxes, storage space, inventory handling and transfer, and record maintenance. Larger plants are more vulnerable to accidents, supply disruption, product obsolescence, and technological change. A large factory is also more difficult to coordinate, simply because it covers more floor space. In addition, increased risk of theft, technological obsolescence, and physical deterioration occur. Further, a company does not receive any return on investments in inventory and storage space.

Cost-Volume-Profit Relationships

Another advantage of variable costing is that it facilitates the analysis of cost-volume-profit relationships by separating fixed and variable costs on the statement of income. Management is able to identify the cost-volume-profit ratio therefore without working with two and sometimes several sets of data. In addition, variable costing emphasizes the contribution margin, discussed in Chapter

13. This emphasis aids management in selecting product lines, in determining the optimal sales mix for pricing purposes, and in solving other problems involving choices. The data are especially important to companies that face make-or-buy decisions because variable costing facilitates comparing company costs with the costs of buying from outsiders. The cost-volume-profit relationship also provides a valuable tool for other short-run planning activities.

Marginal Products

Variable costing is also of use in appraising **marginal products** or **marginal volume,** because variable costs correspond closely with current out-of-pocket expenditures for a product. The problem of product line simplification is not always easy. Yet, an important aspect of the appraisal becomes apparent using variable costing because it provides a sharper focus on the profitability of products, customers, and territories. Multiplying the volume of an item by its unit contribution margin discloses the relative importance of a product's contribution. Management can then study the contribution the product has made to fixed overhead and more easily identify the unprofitable items to eliminate. This is true because the allocation of fixed costs does not obscure the data.

Because accountants can present variable costing data in an uncomplicated manner, managers without strong accounting backgrounds can understand and use the information for profit planning. Often, the application of fixed overhead may be difficult for a nonaccountant to understand because budgeted costs and budgeted capacity must be estimated. The nonaccountant can better grasp the relationship of variable costs and profit planning. Forecasting costs and profits is easier if fixed factory overhead applications are not included.

Impact of Fixed Costs

Some managers argue that they can more easily make decisions if fixed expenses are separated and not buried in inventory or cost of sales. Showing the total fixed expense for the period in the variable costing income statement emphasizes the impact of fixed expenses on profits. Variable costing proponents contend that fixed costs represent **committed costs** arising from a basic organization of providing property, plant, equipment, and other facilities to produce. They feel this justifies treating fixed costs as period costs because, they argue, product costs should reflect only those costs that expire when they sell the asset.

Variable costing advocates believe that variable costs are the crucial costs for decision making. Thus, they claim that one of the important purposes of variable costing is in helping management control operating costs. They contend that separating fixed and variable costs automatically focuses a manager's attention on cost reduction. Variable costing advocates also believe that the concept is an accurate means of measuring responsibility for departmental supervisors. Responsibility accounting is easier with variable costing than it is with conventional absorption costing. Variable costing does not allocate fixed costs to products; it simplifies tracing costs by lines of managerial responsibility.

This fixed-variable manufacturing cost breakdown aids in the preparation of budgets. Each account is broken down into variable and fixed costs. Multiplying the unit variable cost by actual monthly sales and adding the fixed costs yields expected costs. Managers can then easily make monthly comparisons of budgeted costs and actual costs.

Pricing Policies

Variable costing advocates also believe variable costing provides more relevant information concerning pricing policies than does absorption costing. Managers often assume they should not keep a product line for an extended time unless its price is higher than average full cost. However, pricing to cover average full costs may not be advantageous for a company in specialized situations because pricing decisions must consider the effect of prices on volume and the effects of volume on cost. With variable costing, management has the data to determine when it is advisable to accept orders if other than normal conditions exist. In this way, management can take advantage of sales that may contribute only partly to fixed expenses. A knowledge of the contribution margin provides guidelines for the most profitable pricing policies.

For example, assume Yunker Company is producing and selling 10,000 units at a $40 unit sales price when it receives an offer from a foreign distributor to buy 2,000 units at a unit sales price of $30. The absorption cost per unit as shown in Exhibit 20–8 indicates that this $30 sales price is less than the $34 average unit full cost to make 12,000 units. Management may not take advantage of the sales offer if it relies on the absorption cost per unit to make the decision. Instead, managers should use variable costs along with any extra costs of the foreign sale in evaluating this sales offer.

With $19 unit variable costs, $40 unit sales price, and $180,000 annual fixed costs, budgeted net income before taxes is $30,000, computed as follows:

Sales (10,000 units at $40)		$400,000
Costs:		
Variable (10,000 units at $19)	$190,000	
Fixed	180,000	370,000
Net income before taxes		$ 30,000

If the order is accepted and can be produced without any plant expansion, net income will be $52,000, computed as follows:

Sales (10,000 units at $40, 2,000 units at $30)		$460,000
Costs:		
Variable (12,000 units at $19)	$228,000	
Fixed	180,000	408,000
Net income before taxes		$ 52,000

Yunker Company should accept the $30 sales price even though it is lower than average unit cost because unit contribution margin of $11 on the new units

---

EXHIBIT 20–8   Use of Variable Costing in Pricing

	10,000	12,000
Volume in units	10,000	12,000
Variable costs:		
Direct materials @ $2	$ 20,000	$ 24,000
Direct labor @ $5	50,000	60,000
Factory overhead @ $12	120,000	144,000
Fixed factory overhead	180,000	180,000
Total cost	$370,000	$408,000
Absorption cost per unit	$37	$34

results. By accepting the sales offer, the company makes a $22,000 contribution to the recovery of fixed costs and, after full recovery, to income. Net income of only $30,000 results from continuing to produce 10,000 units. Because the export of the product at a sharply reduced price is unlikely to affect the regular market, the company should accept the order, assuming it does not violate international trade agreements.

Even though this example gives the price and does not involve setting a minimum sales price, a company should accept new short-term business as long as it recovers its variable cost—variable costs represent the minimum sales price under these conditions. Chapter 23 discusses contribution pricing in more detail. However, opponents of variable costing argue that a company determines sales price by more than reference to contribution margin.

Finally, variable costing highlights the serious results that often accompany price cutting. Cutting prices by a certain percentage and trying to increase volume by the same percentage under the assumption that the volume increase will compensate for the price reduction is a common error. To gain market share from a competitor, however, one should understand just how far a cut in price can go before it becomes unprofitable. After management understands how price cutting to gain market share seriously affects profits, they should be more cautious about cutting prices to undersell a competitor, since they may be cutting themselves out of business.

Dangers of Variable Costing (L.O. 5)

The simplicity of variable costing allows management to easily understand the resulting figures. However, they may misapply the principle of variable costing. Many accountants contend that variable costing does not provide all the answers or the best answers in certain business situations.

Many nonaccountants outside and inside companies use accounting figures. These people have become accustomed to the normal relationship of sales to total costs and to using gross margin and net income data. A change to another accounting method that gives a completely different picture under similar labels may confuse them. Although the purpose of the change in costing methods is to bring about better understanding, it may cause more confusion instead.

Another danger is that managers may assign variable costing income a broader significance than it deserves. When sales substantially exceed current production, for instance, variable costing profits are higher than those under absorption costing, and management may take improper action based on these increased profits. These profits may mislead marketing executives to ask for lower prices. Managers may also demand higher employee benefits or sales bonuses when, in fact, there is no justification for such actions. At the other extreme, variable costing results may mislead management during a business recession because, when sales lag behind production during early recession stages, the variable costing profit will be minimized and the variable costing loss maximized. Management may miss future profit opportunities by thus misreading the severity of the recession.

When management decides to expand or contract activities connected with specific product lines or other specific business units, they may need to adjust income figures determined using variable costing. For example, take most businesses that produce or sell several products differing in ratios of variable costs to sales revenue and contribution rates. They can improve the total profit picture by eliminating the products contributing the smallest amount and by continuing to carry the products making large contributions to profits. On the other hand, this approach, too, can be misleading. If companies drop the items contributing small amounts of profits, the fixed unit cost that other products must cover will increase. As a result, profits will likely decrease if the company fails to add other products to its line. A company must also consider intangible factors because a product with a low contribution margin ratio may be necessary for the convenience of customers. The loss in consumer goodwill that might result from dropping this item could easily offset any gain from products with higher contribution margin ratios.

Long-Range Pricing Policies

Since variable costing income is higher than absorption costing income when sales substantially exceed current production, opponents of variable costing also argue that managers who receive only variable cost data are tempted to cut prices to the degree that company profits suffer. Yet, an adequate pricing system avoids this because companies allocate fixed overhead on some volume base for long-range pricing policies. Admittedly, allocations are somewhat arbitrary; however, more companies are improving their cost allocation techniques as they gain access to computer facilities. Thus, variable costing generates product figures providing little basis for long-range pricing policies.

In addition, opponents of variable costing argue that all costs are variable in the long run. Further, companies should avoid too great an emphasis on the arbitrary classification of costs into variable and fixed categories. Strictly separating costs into two categories is impossible, as many costs have both fixed and variable components. It is not enough merely to define fixed and variable costs according to the rate of output. Classifying a cost as fixed or variable depends on how managers measure output, the period allowed for adjustments, the degree of flexibility, and the extent to which managers calculate certain costs in advance. Even strict fixed costs have some variable characteristics. The behavior of certain costs, especially overhead, is exceedingly complex. Thus, managers occasionally separate costs into fixed and variable categories on the basis of practicality or expediency rather than strict adherence to an established accounting principle. There may be a strong temptation to include as product costs only those obviously variable costs such as direct material and direct labor in a labor-intensive process. In extreme cases, companies use the *prime cost method* that eliminates variable overhead from product cost. This produces misleading profit contribution data. Variable costing advocates, however, argue that while this separation of fixed and variable costs sometimes is arbitrary, accountants can usually arrive at figures that are accurate enough. They believe that cost behavior is usually not so erratic that managers cannot reasonably predict it.

Because variable costing considers fixed expenses as period costs, it minimizes over- or underapplied factory overhead. An additional weakness is variable costing's failure to express the volume variance in monetary terms.

Fixed Costs Must Be Covered. Elimination of fixed overhead costs from inventories is questionable in view of the increased fixed costs automation brings. It is possible to foresee a time when direct material constitutes the only variable manufacturing cost. Thus, the company with the largest fixed expenses would have the smallest unit inventory costs. This appears contrary to management's objective of having expenses covered by sales—regardless of how they value inventory. With automation, the higher ratios of fixed costs to variable costs limit the ability of companies to respond to changes in the economy. While labor-intensive industries can cut costs during a recession by laying off workers, companies with robots lack this flexibility. This is a serious threat to the usefulness of variable costing and its acceptability for inventory valuation. This is one reason that the FASB and the Internal Revenue Service have not recognized variable costing as an acceptable method of inventory costing.

Variable Costing for External Reporting (L.O. 5)

FASB Position. Even though most accountants agree that variable costing provides valid information for internal decision making, there is no agreement concerning its appropriateness for external reporting. The FASB has not recognized variable costing as a generally accepted inventory valuation method because of its belief that fixed production costs are as much a part of manufacturing the product as are variable costs. In addition, variable costing violates the cost attaching and matching principle.

IRS Regulations. Likewise, the IRS does not recognize variable costing as an acceptable inventory valuation method. The Tax Reform Act (TRA) of 1986 changed inventory accounting for income tax purposes by requiring the capitalization of additional costs to inventory. Product costing under pre-TRA regulations followed the absorption costing concepts specified by generally accepted accounting principles. TRA requires capitalizing additional indirect product costs, making product costing more complicated.

Variable Costing Need Not Replace Absorption Costing

While reporting for external purposes must conform to generally accepted accounting principles, financial data prepared for internal uses need not. The unacceptability of variable costing for external reporting does not affect its importance and special usefulness as an analysis tool. The basic objective of costing should be to meet internal requirements. Variable costing can contribute to this objective because it overcomes many of the weaknesses in reporting with conventional absorption costing. Many companies have converted to variable costing to obtain certain advantages and have found many others not thought of initially. Variable costing need not replace absorption costing. A well-informed management needs both contribution margin analysis and full cost data in budgeting and decision making.

Combined Approach. This chapter suggests arranging the income statement to show both an income under variable costing and the net income required for external reporting. We can do this by deducting an increment measuring the effect of the change in the fixed cost components of inventory variation from variable costing income to arrive at conventional profits. We can distinguish income resulting only from sales from that resulting from inventory changes. One advantage of this approach is the income statement separates variable costs from fixed costs.

Having both sets of profit figures enables the executive to form judgments with much greater facility than if only one profit figure were available; it also facilitates responsibility accounting by making it possible to have information by organizational level. This dual approach provides the additional information that management needs for making decisions and still follows generally accepted accounting principles. A system combining variable costing and absorption costing with standard costs and flexible budgets provides more effective cost control.

Summary

With full absorption costing, fixed production costs are product costs that become period costs when the product is sold. Full absorption costing is consistent with external inventory valuation rules. External reports cannot use variable costing because it treats fixed production costs as period costs. However, it is difficult to state with full assurance which costing concept presents the best measure of unit cost. Thus, we recommend a combined approach that adjusts inventories to include fixed costs on all external reports. We can prepare a variable costing income statement by subtracting variable costs from sales to give a net contribution to fixed costs and income. Then we subtract fixed costs to give income before taxes.

Rather than reject variable costing because companies cannot use the concept for external reporting, accountants should be aware of its advantages. For example, in evaluating the effectiveness of individual and departmental performance, variable costing is useful. It readily offers solutions to such problems as determination of the effect on overall profits of a new product. Also, in preparing cost control reports, there is little need to include such cost items as insurance and depreciation if the manager lacks the authority to incur the expense. A departmental income statement prepared on the variable costing basis is more useful.

There is danger in exclusive use of variable costing because a company must cover both fixed and variable costs in the long run to be profitable. Variable costing can jeopardize a company whose managers only add a profit allowance to a product's variable cost to determine the sales price, thus ignoring fixed costs. Although variable costing may be superior to absorption costing in giving the short-range view of profits, its merit is questionable in long-range profit planning. Usually companies commit period costs for relatively long periods; such costs are important in long-term, not day-to-day, decisions. Average full cost is a better measure of the resources required for other than short-run decisions. Yet, when accountants use variable costing with an awareness of its limitations and weaknesses, it is one of their most useful tools in aiding management.

Important Terms and Concepts

absorption (conventional or full) costing, 692
variable (direct) costing, 692
product costs, 692
period costs, 692
prime costing, 693
contribution margin, 695
gross margin, 697

manufacturing contribution margin, 697
net contribution margin, 697
volume variance, 697
phantom profits, 702
marginal products or marginal volume, 703
committed costs, 703

Problem for Self-Study

Adjustment from Variable Costing Income to Absorption Costing Income

Mason Company uses variable costing for internal purposes with income adjustments to an absorption costing basis made at year end. The firm uses FIFO inventory costing. Analysis over the first three years of operation shows the following data:

	1st Year	2nd Year	3rd Year
Units sold	690,000	555,000	580,000
Units produced	700,000	560,000	600,000
Variable costing income	$ 34,500	$ 28,000	$ 30,000
Budgeted capacity in units . . .	500,000	600,000	600,000
Budgeted fixed overhead	$1,500,000	$1,650,000	$1,680,000

Required:

Indicate the absorption costing income for each year by determining the adjustment necessary each year to convert the variable costing income to an absorption costing basis.

Solution to Problem for Self-Study

MASON COMPANY

	First Year	Second Year	Third Year
Beginning inventory	–0–	10,000	15,000
Units produced	700,000	560,000	600,000
Units available	700,000	570,000	615,000
Units sold	690,000	555,000	580,000
Ending inventory	10,000	15,000	35,000
Variable costing income before taxes	$34,500	$28,000	$ 30,000
Add: Fixed costs of period deferred in ending inventory	30,000 (10,000 × $3)	41,250 (15,000 × $2.75)	98,000 (35,000 × $2.80)
	$64,500	$69,250	$128,000
Less: Fixed costs of prior year absorbed in period through beginning inventory	–0–	30,000 (10,000 × $3)	41,250 (15,000 × $2.75)
Absorption costing income before taxes	$64,500	$39,250	$ 86,750

Review Questions

1. Which features associated with variable costing income measurement should a marketing manager find attractive?

2. Assuming you were using a four-variance method of analyzing overhead, what variances would you compute with a standard variable costing approach? How do these differ from those variances computed with a standard absorption costing approach?

3. What distinction in cost behavior is made with variable costing and how does this differ from the distinction made with absorption costing? What is the primary difference between variable costing and absorption costing?

4. What is the future of variable costing with the current emphasis on robots and automated manufacturing?

5. Discuss how the contribution margin and the breakeven point are easily calculated using variable costing.

6. Contrast and explain the difference in income using absorption and variable costing if:

   a. Producton volume exceeds sales volume.
   b. Sales volume exceeds production volume.
   c. Sales volume equals production volume.
   d. Sales volume remains constant, while production volume fluctuates.

7. How is the difference between absorption costing net income and variable costing net income calculated?

8. Compare the difference between the absorption and variable costing incomes as the accounting periods get longer.

9. Indicate several questions or decisions for which the use of variable costing would be more appropriate than the use of absorption costing.

10. Why have many manufacturing companies experienced an increase in fixed costs in recent years?

11. Should sales volume and/or production volume affect income?

12. Why do variable costing advocates believe that it is a better index of profit performance?

CPA/CMA/CIA Multiple Choice Questions

1. (AICPA) A single-product company prepares income statements using both absorption and variable costing methods. Manufacturing overhead cost applied per unit produced in 19X2 was the same as in 19X1. The 19X2 variable costing statement reported a profit whereas the 19X2 absorption costing statement reported a loss. The difference in reported income could be explained by units produced in 19X2 being

   a. Less than units sold in 19X2.
   b. Less than the activity level used for allocating overhead to the product.
   c. In excess of the activity level used for allocating overhead to the product.
   d. In excess of units sold in 19X2.

2. (CMA) In a situation where inventories are expected to change, the type of costing that provides the best information for breakeven analysis is

   a. Job order costing.
   b. Variable (direct) costing.
   c. Joint costing.
   d. Absorption (full) costing.
   e. Operation costing.

3.–4. (CIA) Use the following data for questions 3 and 4.

> Product sales: 1,000 units at $10 each
> Variable manufacturing costs: $5.50 per unit
> Fixed manufacturing overhead: $1,200
> Variable selling and administrative costs: $.50 per unit sold
> Fixed selling and administrative costs: $1,000
> No beginning inventory
> Units produced: 1,200

3. Operating income under variable (direct) costing would be:

    a. $ 600.
    b. $1,800.
    c. $2,000.
    d. $2,300.

4. Operating income under absorption costing would be:

    a. $1,800.
    b. $1,967.
    c. $2,000.
    d. $2,167.

5. (CIA) A company manufactures 50,000 units of a product and sells 40,000 units. Total manufacturing cost per unit is $50 (variable manufacturing cost $10, fixed manufacturing cost $40). Assuming no beginning inventory, what is the effect on net income if absorption costing is used instead of variable costing?

    a. Net income is $400,000 lower.
    b. Net income is $400,000 higher.
    c. Net income is the same.
    d. Net income is $200,000 higher.

6. (CIA) Variable costing techniques would be most appropriate in performing which of the following tasks?

    a. Evaluating pricing and promotional alternatives through use of contribution margins.
    b. Preparing financial statements for shareholders.
    c. Valuing inventories with all manufacturing overhead included to avoid expensing the fixed portion as period cost.
    d. Calculating profit before selling and administrative expenses (i.e., the gross margin) so that all manufacturing costs are taken into account.

7.–8. (AICPA) Questions 7 and 8 are based on the following data:
Bates Co. incurred the following costs:

Direct materials and direct labor	$600,000
Variable factory overhead	80,000
Straight-line depreciation:	
Production machinery	70,000
Factory building	50,000

7. Under absorption costing, the inventoriable costs are

    a. $680,000.
    b. $730,000.
    c. $750,000.
    d. $800,000.

8. The absorption costing method includes in inventory

	Fixed Factory Overhead	Variable Factory Overhead
a.	No	No
b.	No	Yes
c.	Yes	Yes
d.	Yes	No

9.–10. (CMA) These questions are based on Osawa Inc., which planned and actually manufactured 200,000 units of its single product in 19X1, its first year of operations. Variable manufacturing costs were $30 per unit of product. Planned and actual fixed manufacturing costs were $600,000 and selling and administrative costs totaled $400,000 in 19X1. Osawa sold 120,000 units of product in 19X1 at a selling price of $40 per unit.

9. Osawa's 19X1 operating income using absorption (full) costing is

  a. $200,000.
  b. $440,000.
  c. $600,000.
  d. $840,000.
  e. Some amount other than those given above.

10. Osawa's 19X1 operating income using variable (direct) costing is

  a. $200,000.
  b. $440,000.
  c. $800,000.
  d. $840,000.
  e. Some amount other than those given above.

Exercises

E20–1 Absorption Costing and Variable Costing Income (L.O. 1)

The following information pertains to BBC Company's first year of operation in which 25,000 units were produced:

Sales ($50 per unit)	$850,000
Total fixed production cost	200,000
Total variable production cost	250,000
Total variable marketing and administrative costs	150,000
Total fixed marketing and administration costs	82,000

Required:

a. Without preparing a formal income statement, determine income using:
  (1) Absorption costing.
  (2) Variable costing.
b. Explain the differences in absorption costing income and variable costing income.

E20–2 Effect of Variable Costing (L.O. 5)

Jumbo Jet Company manufactures a product that employs expensive automated machinery in its processing. Jumbo Jet uses straight-line depreciation for this automated machinery. Because of a lag in the economy, Jumbo Jet has a large stock of Finished Goods Inventory, which constitutes a material item on the balance sheet at year-end. A departmental cost accounting system assigns production costs to the units processed each period.

The controller of the company informs you that management is considering adopting variable costing as a method of accounting for plant operations and inventory valuation for internal decision making. They understand that conventional or absorption costing must continue to be used for external purposes.

Required:

Explain the effect, if any, such a change would have on:

a. Year-end financial statements.
b. Net income for the year.

E20–3 Comparison of Absorption and Variable Costing (L.O. 1)

The following information is available for Rowe Company's new product line:

Variable production cost per unit	$ 26
Total annual fixed production cost (50,000 units budgeted capacity)	150,000
Total annual fixed marketing and administrative costs	68,000
Variable marketing and administrative cost per unit of sales	10
Selling price per unit	60

There was no inventory at the beginning of the year. During the year 50,000 units were produced and 44,000 units were sold.

Required:

a. Determine the cost of ending inventory assuming Rowe uses absorption costing.
b. Determine the cost of ending inventory assuming Rowe uses variable costing.
c. Determine the total variable cost charged to expenses for the year assuming Rowe uses variable costing.
d. Determine the total fixed costs charged against the current year's operations assuming Rowe uses absorption costing.
e. Without preparing a formal income statement, determine income using variable costing.
f. Without preparing a formal income statement, determine income using absorption costing.
g. Account for the difference in income between the two concepts.

E20–4 Standard Absorption Costing Recast to Variable Costing (L.O. 5)

Marquerite Company uses a standard absorption costing system. The standard variable production cost is $20 per unit. Standard fixed factory overhead is $300,000 for 60,000 units or $5 per unit for normal activity. Variable marketing and administrative costs are $3 per unit sold, and fixed marketing and administrative costs are $85,000. Variances from standard variable production costs during the year totaled $60,000 unfavorable. Sales during 19X1 were 55,000 units. Beginning inventory was 2,000 units; ending inventory was 8,000 units. Sales price per unit is $40.

Required:

a. Prepare an absorption costing income statement for 19X1 assuming all variances are written off directly as an adjustment to the Cost of Goods Sold account at year-end.
b. Recast the income statement as it would appear using variable costing.
c. Explain the differences in income as calculated in Requirements *a* and *b*.

E20–5 Adjustment to Convert from Variable Costing to Absorption Costing (L.O. 2)

Carrell Company's budgeted fixed factory overhead is $3 million at a normal capacity of 600,000 units. The company uses variable costing for internal purposes and adjusts the income to an absorption costing basis at year-end. Analysis over the last three years shows the following:

	1st Year	2nd Year	3rd Year
Units produced	602,000	598,000	595,000
Units sold	596,000	603,000	595,000
Variable costing income	$500,000	$521,000	$497,000

Required:

Determine the adjustment necessary each year to convert the variable costing income to an absorption costing income. Indicate the absorption costing income for each year.

E20–6 Variable Costing Impact on Inventory (L.O. 2)

Baddour, Inc., manufactures a product whose unit variable and fixed production costs are $5 and $3 respectively. There was no beginning inventory of this product, but 80 units remained unsold at the end of the year.

Required:

Assume the variable (direct) costing method is used instead of the absorption costing method. What would be the change in the dollar amount of ending inventory?

E20–7 Absorption Costing and Variable Costing Income (L.O. 3)

For its first year of operations, Casey Company produced 50,000 units. Other information is as follows:

Sales ($60 per unit)	$2,100,000
Total fixed production cost	800,000
Total variable production cost	900,000
Total variable marketing and administrative costs	160,000
Total fixed marketing and administration costs	150,000

Required:

a. Compute the income—without preparing a formal income statement—using:
   (1) Variable costing.
   (2) Absorption costing.
b. Account for the differences in income computed under variable and absorption costing.

Problems

P20–8 Comparative Statements (L.O. 1)

Clark Company began manufacturing lawn mowers on January 1. During January and February, the company produced 12,000 units each month. At this production volume, unit cost was as follows: direct material, $20; direct labor, $25; variable factory overhead, $5; and fixed factory overhead, $10. Variable marketing costs per month were $7,000, while fixed marketing costs per month were $30,000. Variable administration costs per month were $4,000, while fixed administration costs per month were $50,000. There was no over- or underapplied factory overhead in either month. No work in process inventories existed in either month. At $88 per unit, Clark sold 10,000 units in January and 13,000 units in February.

Required:

Prepare comparative income statements for January and February using:

a. The absorption costing method.
b. The variable costing method.

P20–9 Converting from Absorption to Variable Costing (L.O. 2)

The management of Schmidt Company has asked you to compute the income before income taxes for 19X2 under the assumption that the company had used variable costing procedures for several years for internal purposes. You have determined that fixed manufacturing costs amount to $14,000 per year. There are never any goods in process at the end of the year.

Data from Income Statements Based on Absorption Costing

	19X1	19X2
Sales	$112,000	$95,200
Cost of goods sold:		
Beginning inventory—Finished goods	$ 8,400	$ 6,300
Cost of goods manufactured	63,000	56,000
Total	$ 71,400	$62,300
Ending inventory—Finished goods	6,300	6,720
Cost of goods sold	$ 65,100	$55,580
Marketing and administrative expenses ($8,000 of which are fixed)	29,400	26,600
Total deductions	$ 94,500	$82,180
Net income before income taxes	$ 17,500	$13,020

Required:

a. Convert the income statement from an absorption costing basis to a variable costing basis.
b. Using variable costing, what production costs are assigned to the units manufactured for 19X1 and 19X2?

P20–10 Absorption Costing and Variable Costing Income Statements (L.O. 1)

The president of Britten Enterprises projects the following data for November 19X1:

	Units
Beginning inventory	6,000
Production	20,000
Available for sale	26,000
Sales	23,000
Ending inventory	3,000

Management has established the following standard cost per unit for the product the company manufactures:

	Standard Cost per Unit
Direct material (all variable)	$20.00
Direct labor (all variable)	15.00
Factory overhead:	
Variable cost	3.00
Fixed costs (based on 22,000 units per month)	2.00
Marketing and administrative:	
Variable cost (per unit sold)	1.80
Fixed costs (based on 22,000 units per month)	1.20

The sales price per unit is projected to be $50. The fixed costs remain static within the relevant range of 15,000 to 25,000 units of production.

Required:

a. Prepare projected income statements for November 19X1 for management purposes, using the following product costing methods:
   (1) Absorption costing with production variances charged to cost of goods sold each month.
   (2) Variable (direct) costing.
b. Reconcile the difference in the income reported with the two methods.

P20–11 Absorption and Variable Costing's Influence on Bonus

Management of the Sharon Russell Company is concerned because last year's operations resulted in the worst loss in the history of the company, as shown here:

Sales (50,000 units)		$500,000
Cost of goods sold:		
Beginning inventory (10,000 units)	$ 75,000	
Cost of goods manufactured (50,000 units) . . .	375,000*	
Goods available for sale	$450,000	
Less: Ending inventory (10,000 units)	75,000	
Cost of goods sold		375,000
Gross margin		$125,000
Marketing and administrative expenses		140,000
Loss		$ (15,000)

*Includes $125,000 fixed factory overhead; remaining costs are $5 variable per unit.

The board of directors replaced the president and hired an individual who agreed to assume the position if he would receive a bonus of 60 percent of profits generated. The new president agreed to reimburse the company for any losses incurred. Within a short period, the new president had the production facilities operating at full capacity of 75,000 units.

Despite no growth in sales, the next period's income statement showed a profit with no change in the cost behavior patterns or normal volume. Immediately after the income statement was prepared, the new president accepted his bonus and resigned with no explanation. The board of directors cannot understand the president's actions.

Required:

a. Explain why you know that the company's income statement for last year was prepared on a variable costing or an absorption costing basis.
b. Determine normal volume used for overhead application.
c. Prepare an income statement for the next year based on absorption costing assuming there was no change in sales, cost behavior patterns, or normal volume.
d. Using an alternative reporting procedure, prepare an income statement which would have contradicted the new president's stance.
e. Explain why the new president deserved, or did not deserve, the bonus.

P20–12 Use of High-Low Method of Separating Cost Components and Comparative Statements (L.O. 3)

Marlow Company provides you with the following two condensed budgets for standard costs and expenses:

	10,000 Units	12,000 Units
Direct material	$ 21,000	$ 25,200
Direct labor	79,000	94,800
Factory overhead	62,000	65,600
	$162,000	$185,600

Marketing and administrative expenses were budgeted as follows:

Marketing expense:		
Variable	$1.40 per unit sold	
Fixed	$20,000	
Administrative expense:		
Variable	$2.50 per unit sold	
Fixed	$40,000	

Overhead is applied on the basis of a standard capacity of 11,000 units.

Required:

a. Using the high-low method of separating cost components, determine the standard product cost per unit under absorption costing.
b. Assume that 11,500 units are manufactured and 10,800 are sold at a price of $40. Determine the income under: (1) absorption costing and (2) variable costing.
c. Account for the differences in absorption costing income and variable costing income.

P20–13 Variable and Absorption Costing Comparison for Income and Inventory (L.O. 1)

At the end of last year, management of M. Tiller, Inc., planned to produce 1,000 units for the current year. Fixed factory overhead was budgeted for $5,000 and variable factory overhead for $3,000. Based on the standards established, direct material was expected to be $6 per unit and direct labor $2 per unit. There were 300 units in inventory at the beginning of the current year.

Of the 900 units produced during the current year, 700 units sold at a $25 unit sales price. Variable marketing and administration expenses totaled $2,000, and fixed marketing and administration expenses totaled $1,000. There were no price or efficiency variances for factory costs.

Required:

a. Determine cost of goods sold using:
   (1) Variable costing.
   (2) Absorption costing.
b. Determine the value of ending inventory using:
   (1) Variable costing.
   (2) Absorption costing.
c. Compute the volume variance using:
   (1) Variable costing.
   (2) Absorption costing.
d. Calculate income before taxes using:
   (1) Variable costing.
   (2) Absorption costing.
e. Account for the difference in income using the two methods.

P20–14 Variable Costing Where All Costs Are Fixed (L.O. 5)

Several years ago, the city of Oxford approached the management of Mississippi Fertilizer Company concerning the possibility of using garbage obtained from the city's residents in manufacturing fertilizer. After conducting many engineering studies, the company built a completely automated processing plant with its own source of utilities. Under the agreement with the city, garbage is delivered to the plant daily at no cost to the company. Because of the factory's unique features, volume can be easily adjusted. All operating costs are fixed, and employees are paid a fixed salary. Fertilizer is sold in bulk at $2 per pound to farmers who bring their trucks to the factory for filling. The following data relate to the first three years of operation:

	19X1	19X2	19X3
Pounds processed	10,000	6,000	12,000
Pounds sold	6,000	10,000	11,000
Fixed production costs	$15,000	$15,000	$15,000
Fixed marketing and administrative expense	$ 2,000	$ 2,000	$ 2,000

Required:

a. Using 10,000 pounds as normal capacity, prepare income statements using variable costing and absorption costing.

b. Indicate the inventory value shown on the balance sheet at year-end for each of the three years using each method.

c. If the company changes its manufacturing facilities, purchases utilities from the city, and pays its employees on an hourly basis, fixed costs will be reduced to $10,000 per year and variable cost per pound will become $0.60. Using the same data except for the change in cost behavior, prepare income statements using variable costing and absorption costing.

d. Account for the difference in income for 19X2 using conditions in which all costs are fixed as compared to having both fixed and variable costs.

P20–15 Reconciling Difference between Absorption Costing and Variable Costing (L.O. 3)

The June 1, 19X1, balance sheet for Soule Company contained an inventory amounting to $250,000 that included fixed overhead costs of $30,000. The June 30, 19X1, balance sheet revealed an inventory amounting to $120,000 that included fixed overhead amounting to $18,000.

Operations for the month of June 19X1 resulted in the following:

Variable costs:	
Direct materials used in production	$620,000
Direct labor used in production	401,000
Factory overhead	210,000
Marketing expenses	45,000
Administration expenses	90,000
Fixed costs:	
Factory overhead	170,000
Marketing expenses	50,000
Administration expenses	57,000

Net sales for June 19X1 were $1,800,000.

Required:

a. Prepare an income statement for the month using variable costing.

b. Prepare an income statement for the month using absorption costing.

c. Reconcile the difference in the income figures reported using each of these costing methods.

P20–16 (CMA Adapted) Variable Costing Income Statement (L.O. 1)

Portland Optics, Inc., specializes in manufacturing lenses for large telescopes and cameras used in space exploration. As the specifications for the lenses are determined by the customer and vary considerably, the company uses a job order cost system. Factory overhead is applied to jobs on the basis of direct labor hours, utilizing the absorption (full) costing method. Portland's predetermined overhead rates for 19X2 and 19X3 were based on the following estimates.

	19X2	19X3
Direct labor hours	32,500	44,000
Direct labor cost	$325,000	$462,000
Fixed factory overhead	130,000	176,000
Variable factory overhead . . .	162,500	198,000

Jim Bradford, Portland's controller, would like to use variable (direct) costing for internal reporting purposes as he believes statements prepared using variable costing are more appropriate for making product decisions. In order to explain the benefits of variable costing to the other members of Portland's management team, Bradford plans to convert the company's income statement from absorption costing to variable costing and has gathered the following information for this purpose, along with a copy of Portland's 19X2–19X3 comparative income statement.

PORTLAND OPTICS INC.
Comparative Income Statement
For the Years 19X2–X3

	19X2	19X3
Net sales	$1,140,000	$1,520,000
Cost of goods sold:		
Finished goods at January 1	$ 16,000	$ 25,000
Cost of goods manufactured	720,000	976,000
Total available	$ 736,000	$1,001,000
Finished goods at December 31	25,000	14,000
Cost of goods sold before overhead adjustment	$ 711,000	$ 987,000
Overhead adjustment	12,000	7,000
Cost of goods sold	$ 723,000	$ 994,000
Gross profit	$ 417,000	$ 526,000
Selling expense	$ 150,000	$ 190,000
Administrative expense	160,000	187,000
Operating income	$ 107,000	$ 149,000

■ Portland's actual manufacturing data for the two years are

	19X2	19X3
Direct labor hours	30,000	42,000
Direct labor cost	$300,000	$435,000
Raw materials used	140,000	210,000
Fixed factory overhead	132,000	175,000

■ The company's actual inventory balances on December 31 were

	19X1	19X2	19X3
Raw material	$32,000	$36,000	$18,000
Work in process:			
Costs	$44,000	$34,000	$60,000
Direct labor hours	1,800	1,400	2,500
Finished goods:			
Costs	$16,000	$25,000	$14,000
Direct labor hours	700	1,080	550

■ For both years, all administrative costs were fixed, while a portion of the selling expense resulting from an 8 percent commission on net sales was variable. Portland reports any over- or underapplied overhead as an adjustment to the cost of goods sold.

Required:

a. For the year ended December 31, 19X3, prepare the revised income statement for Portland Optics, Inc., utilizing the variable costing method. Be sure to include the contribution margin on the revised income statement.

b. Describe two advantages of using variable costing rather than absorption costing.

P20–17 Absorption Costing and Variable Costing Income Statements (L.O. 1)

L. Tatikonda, president of Tatikonda Enterprises, projects the following data for November 19X1:

	Units
Beginning inventory	5,000
Production	18,000
Available for sale	23,000
Sales	21,800
Ending inventory	1,200

Tatikonda has established the following standard cost per unit for the product her company manufactures:

	Standard Cost per Unit
Direct material (all variable)	$45.00
Direct labor (all variable)	16.00
Factory overhead:	
Variable cost	2.00
Fixed costs (based on 20,000 units per month)	7.50
Marketing and administration:	
Variable cost (based on units sold)	1.25
Fixed costs (based on 20,000 units per month)	2.70

The sales price per unit is projected to be $90 per unit. The fixed costs remain static within the relevant range of 15,000 to 25,000 units of production.

Required:

a. Prepare projected income statements for November 19X1 for management purposes using each of the following product-costing methods:
   (1) Absorption costing with all variances charged to cost of goods sold each month.
   (2) Variable (direct) costing.

b. Reconcile the difference in the income reported with the two methods.

P20–18 Decrease in Earnings with Increased Sales (L.O. 3)

One of the objectives that Hasin Company's top management has established for next year is to produce income before taxes of $75,000. They are confident that this objective can be achieved because sales revenues have been exceeding the budget by 8 percent. But now the accountant in charge of cost functions presents them with the following data:

Hasin Company Operating Forecast

	Budgeted Forecast as of 1/1/19X2	Adjusted Forecast as of 10/31/19X2
Sales	$300,000	$324,000
Cost of sales at standard	180,000	199,400*
Gross margin	$120,000	$124,600
Marketing expenses ($5,000 is fixed cost) ..	$ 20,000	$ 28,000
Administrative expenses (all fixed cost)	25,000	24,000
Total operating expenses	$ 45,000	$ 52,000
Income before taxes	$ 75,000	$ 72,600

*Standard cost of sales includes over- or underabsorbed fixed overhead.

The variable cost of sales remained the same percentage of sales as budgeted. Fixed production overhead was budgeted to be $50,000; there were 20,000 estimated production units. Due to a scarcity of skilled labor, only 18,000 units were produced. There was no change in sales mix or sales price. Top management cannot understand why income before taxes is below budgeted income, even though sales revenue has increased. Hasin's finished goods inventory was large enough to fill all sales orders received.

Required:

a. Prepare a schedule explaining to management why there is a decrease in income before taxes in spite of increased sales.
b. Suggest how the company can improve its performance.
c. Illustrate an alternative internal cost reporting procedure which would better show the financial picture. Explain why you chose the approach you did.
d. Account for any difference in income using the procedures in Requirement c with the $72,600 income before taxes as of 10/31/19X2.

P20–19 Variable Costing and Absorption Costing Income Statements (L.O. 1)

Rainey Company uses absorption costing for external reporting purposes and variable costing for internal management purposes. To satisfy external requirements, at the end of each year financial information is converted from variable (direct) costing to absorption costing.

At the end of 19X1, management anticipated that sales would rise 10 percent the next year. Therefore, production was increased from 18,000 units to 19,600 units to meet this expected demand. However, economic conditions kept the market demand steady and the sales level was at 18,000 units for both years.

	19X1	19X2
Sales price per unit	$ 26	$ 26
Production (units)	18,000	19,600
Sales (units)	18,000	18,000
Beginning inventory (units)	1,800	1,800
Ending inventory (units)	1,800	3,400
Unfavorable materials, labor, and variable overhead variances (total)	$ 4,500	$ 3,600

Annual budgeted and actual fixed costs for 19X1 and 19X2:

Production	$ 72,000
Marketing and administrative	80,000
	$152,000

Unit standard variable costs for 19X1 and 19X2:

Labor	$ 7
Materials	4
Variable overhead	3
	$14

The overhead rate under absorption costing is based on practical plant capacity, which is 24,000 units per year. All variances and under- or overabsorbed overhead are taken to Cost of Goods Sold. Ignore all taxes.

Required:

a. Prepare an income statement based on absorption costing for 19X2.
b. Prepare an income statement based on variable costing for 19X2.
c. Explain the difference, if any, between the net income figures. What entries, if any, are necessary to adjust the book figures to the financial statement figure?
d. Give arguments for and against the use of variable costing in external reporting.
e. List the advantages and disadvantages to using variable costing for internal purposes.

P20–20 Standard Variable Costing Income Statement (L.O. 2)

Cill Company operates a variable costing system employing standard costs. Management expects to operate the plant 24,000 machine-hours per month. The following data are obtained for April 19X1, the first month of operations:

Standard variable product cost per unit:	
Direct material	$1.50
Direct labor	2.75
Variable factory overhead (2 machine-hours × $1)	2.00
Variable marketing expense (per unit sold)	1.25
Variable administration expense (per unit sold)	0.80
Total variable cost per unit	$8.30

Production and sales data:

Units started in operations 10,000
Units completed 7,000
Units in ending work in process (all material, ⅔ labor
　and factory overhead) 3,000
Units sold ($15 sales price per unit) 6,000

Cost data for the month:

	Actual	Budgeted at Normal Capacity
Direct material used	$15,870	
Direct labor cost	24,300	
Variable factory overhead	18,540	
Variable marketing expense	7,425	
Variable administration expense	4,900	
Fixed factory overhead expense	17,100	$16,800
Fixed marketing expense	5,150	5,000
Fixed administration expense	9,000	9,000

Required:

Prepare an income statement using variable costing showing actual and standard cost with a variance for each item. Indicate if each variance is favorable (F) or unfavorable (U). After determining the variable costing income, adjust it to an absorption costing basis.

SELECTED TOPICS FOR FURTHER STUDY

Product Quality and Inventory Management in a JIT Environment

CHAPTER OBJECTIVES

After studying this chapter, you should be able to:

1. Explain the theories underlying the different methods of accounting for scrap material, spoilage, and defective units.

2. Apply selective controls to prevent inventory overages and shortages.

3. Compute economic order quantity and show the effects of quantity discounts and additional costs in selecting the most economical order size.

4. Discuss the impact of lead time and safety stock on inventory management.

5. Consider setup costs by using the EOQ model to compute the optimum size of a production run.

6. Understand the challenge of the JIT and zero defect concepts to EOQ and product waste.

PRACTICAL APPLICATION BOX   **Finding the Right Path to Quality**

Launching quality techniques can produce cultural changes that are potentially disruptive. Alcoa began its program for employees with managers explaining why quality is important, what quality is, and how to apply it. This training was reinforced through field visits to companies with reputations for quality and supplemented with specific problem-solving assignments. The company also exposed middle managers to the same training. Alcoa avoids making people feel defensive about the past, ignorant about the present, or apprehensive about the future. Making people angry causes unnecessary resistance to the quality message. The company believes that quality training is a never-ending process.

From: Anthony R. Tierno, "Teaching Quality: Lessons from Alcoa," *Mangement Accounting*, August 1991, pp. 27–30.

Introduction

Traditionally, managers have found economic order quantity (EOQ) useful in establishing optimal inventory lot sizes that minimize the combined costs of production and inventory. Now the Just-in-time (JIT) concept that advocates zero or minimal, rather than optimal, lot sizes offers a major challenge to EOQ. The cost management view is that inventory is a waste. Properly implemented inventory management procedures can drastically reduce inventory and the associated costs of holding inventory. Using these procedures, manufacturing processes operate on a demand-pull basis. The demand of a subsequent work center activates each work center's activity. The emphasis is on avoiding producing any unnecessary items.

The Effect of Product Waste (L.O. 1)

Managers are increasingly considering quality as a key feature for reducing long-term manufacturing costs. On-the-spot correction is replacing the traditional produce-and-rework-if-defective routine. However, even with increased emphasis on improved quality, defects may occur and accountants must estimate and record their costs. Cost accountants assume leadership roles in product waste prevention and in the adoption of a zero defect program.

Zero Defect Approach

A **zero defect approach** reduces uncertainty in an organization by closer coordination with its suppliers and customers. This approach evaluates management practices, rearranges plants to focus on products and procedures, and installs automated process controls and computers. In applying a zero defect program, organizations find if they permit suppliers a 2 percent defective rate, there may be 5 percent errors in parts received, but if they set the standard at zero, they come closer to obtaining perfect supplies. Thus, people and companies operate to the tolerance level of authority.

Waste control is an important element of inventory planning. Controlling scrap, spoilage, and defective units affects not only costs but also a company's reputation. Rather than risk selling imperfect goods, a company often decides that increased quality control techniques and additional inspection points affect long-run profitability. A company has several means for controlling excessive production costs. For example, some control is accomplished through more effective supervision of the manufacturing facilities. Also, using scrap and spoiled goods reports showing the dollars lost because of imperfect goods makes management more aware of the importance of avoiding unnecessary spoilage costs.

Scrap materials cannot be reused in the manufacturing process without additional refining. Scrap may or may not have a market value. Many companies pay to have unsalable scrap hauled away. Conversely, other scrap, such as silver and gold recovered from making jewelry, is very valuable. Still other types of scrap have limited dollar value.

Even though each unit of scrap has limited dollar value, the total value of scrap for any period may amount to a significant amount of money. For this reason, companies need to control their scrap so they can sell all that is marketable. Otherwise, if workers see that a company is not properly accounting for scrap, they may be tempted to steal it. Workers may believe that the company would never discover the theft.

Scrap Report

When scrap occurs, individual scrap tickets report the details. Periodically, companies prepare a summary of these scrap tickets in triplicate with the original given to the person responsible for maintaining the materials records, the second copy distributed to the accounting department for recording purposes, and the third copy retained in the department responsible for the scrap. Exhibit 21–1

EXHIBIT 21–1

Summary Scrap Report

Job	2509						Supervisor	Kent Miller
Department	Fabricating						Period	April 19X1

Material Part No.	Description	Quantity Scrapped	Unit Cost	Total Cost	Expected Scrap	Variances	Sales Value	Causes of Actual Scrap
20A	Supports	15	$1.25	$ 18.75	13	$ 2.50	$ 6.00	Defective material
39B	Copper pipe	5	4.80	24.00	1	19.20	Not known	Machine malfunction
39C	Plastic	11	8.70	95.70	5	52.20	$21.18	Defective molds
41E	Oak lumber	4	1.08	4.32	2	2.16	Not known	Operator inefficiency
41K	Tubing	12	0.60	7.20	8	2.40	$ 4.10	Machine malfunction
		47		$149.97	29	$78.46		

illustrates a summary scrap report that shows not only the quantity of each item or part scrapped but also the cost and reason for the scrap. In addition, the scrap report can provide space for comparing the actual scrap against the scrap expected on that particular job. Often, companies include an allowance for scrap in the material issued. For example, the material cost may include a 1 percent factor for cutting waste. Because scrap is sometimes inherent in the production process, the concern is whether actual scrap loss is within the norms established. Exhibit 21–1 shows a fairly large unfavorable variance for Material Part 39C. After determining that the cause of the 39C scrap is defective molds, the company should direct attention to correcting the molds. When managers do not expect the cause of the scrap variance to occur again, they may decide not to spend much time and effort in trying to correct the problem. The company should return the defective material causing the scrap in Part 20A to the vendor for credit. Exhibit 21–1 includes a space for inserting the sales value of scrap if it is known in advance. Often companies do not know the value of scrap until a sale to the customer or scrap dealer.

Accounting for the Various Types of Material Waste (L.O. 1)

The methods used in accounting for scrap depend on whether or not the sales value is known when the scrapping of material occurs.

Sales Value of Scrap Is Not Known

Time Scrap Occurs. We make no journal entry but itemize the quantity of scrap material on the material ledger card.

Time of Sale. The accountant debits Cash or Accounts Receivable and may credit one of three possible accounts:

1. Credit the job or department in which the scrap occurs:

Cash or Accounts Receivable	. . . .	XXX
Work in Process Inventory	. . . .	XXX

Accounting theory indicates that this is the most correct approach because it leaves the net cost in the job or department. Yet, it may present some practical problems. If the scrap is not significant for each job, it may not be feasible to associate scrap with a particular job. However, the company may agree to credit customers for any revenues from scrap on their jobs. This occurs more frequently on difficult manufacturing jobs in which significant scrap is expected.

2. Credit the factory overhead control:

        Cash or Accounts Receivable   XXX
              Factory Overhead Control—Recovery of Scrap   XXX

We credit the subsidiary ledger account, Recovery of Scrap, for the sales price of the scrap. This method does not directly subtract the scrap sale from the cost of the job or department. Thus, it does not have as strong a theoretical justification as does the method crediting the sales value to Work in Process Inventory. Crediting Factory Overhead Control is easier but the scrap sales are not traced to individual jobs or departments. All products bear a portion of the scrap loss under this practical approach. Using this approach requires that we estimate scrap revenue and deduct it from budgeted factory overhead costs when establishing factory overhead application rates. Deducting the value of scrap results in a lower factory overhead application rate.

3. Credit another income account:

        Cash or Accounts Receivable   XXX
              Income from Sale of Scrap   XXX

While crediting other income lacks theoretical merit, accountants justify it when more accurate accounting is costly and burdensome, the scrap sales price is uncertain, or the scrap value is relatively small.

Sales Value of Scrap Can Be Reliably Estimated

Time Scrap Occurs. We record both the quantity of scrap and the dollar value when the scrap is sent to the storeroom. We set up an asset account titled Scrap Inventory with a credit to one of these three accounts:

1. Work in Process Inventory.
2. Factory Overhead Control—Recovery of Scrap.
3. Income from Sale of Scrap.

The same advantages and disadvantages apply as those mentioned earlier when we credit one of these accounts at the time of sale. However, Alternative 3 has some inherent problems because in this situation we can estimate the sales value and record the scrap when it occurs. Crediting the Income from Sale of Scrap account recognizes income before making a sale. Variations in inventory cause an increase in income. However, as long as the income from scrap is not significant, we do not materially misstate the product or process cost by crediting income at the time scrap occurs.

Time of Scrap Sale. Regardless of which of the accounts we credit, Scrap Inventory is credited at the time of sale as follows:

        Cash or Accounts Receivable   XXX
              Scrap Inventory   XXX

A company improperly records its assets by assigning no value to scrap inventory if the dollar value of scrap is material. This understatement of assets occurs even though the company does not know the exact sales price of the scrap at the time scrap occurs or expects a time lag before selling the scrap. Thus, the best approach is to estimate and assign the scrap's expected market value to Scrap Inventory.

Accounting for Scrap Illustrated

The following example describes the various methods used to account for scrap. Assume that in processing Job No. 42 managers determine that 10 parts have to be scrapped. We illustrate two different alternatives for scrap accounting.

First, assume that at the time the scrap occurs, managers cannot estimate the sales value of scrap. Later the scrap is sold for $300 cash.

Time Scrap Occurs
Ten parts scrapped on Job No. 42 (memo entry only).
(A material ledger card is set up showing quantity.)

Time of Sale

```
1.  Cash .............................................. 300
        Work in Process Inventory—Job No. 42 ...................    300
Or

2.  Cash .............................................. 300
        Factory Overhead Control—Recovery of Scrap ..............    300
Or

3.  Cash .............................................. 300
        Income from Sale of Scrap ..............................    300
```

A second possibility is that at the time the scrap occurs, managers reliably estimate they can sell the scrap for $300. Later the scrap is, in fact, sold for $300. Using the three methods available, the entry is as follows:

Time Scrap Occurs

```
1.  Scrap Inventory .................................... 300
        Work in Process Inventory—Job No. 42 ...................    300
Or

2.  Scrap Inventory .................................... 300
        Factory Overhead Control—Recovery of Scrap ..............    300
Or

3.  Scrap Inventory .................................... 300
        Income from Sale of Scrap ..............................    300
```

Time of Sale

```
Cash .............................................. 300
    Scrap Inventory ...................................    300
```

Any difference between the amount recognized in the Scrap Inventory account and the sale price actually received is treated as a debit or credit adjustment. We adjust the Work in Process account, Factory Overhead Control account, or Scrap Income account, consistent with the account credited at the time scrap occurred.

Cause of Material Scrap. When scrapping of parts with high unit costs occurs, management should account for the scrap and determine the cause so corrective action can occur. For example, in Exhibit 21–1 workers scrapped eleven 39C plastic parts having a total cost of $95.70. While the company expected some scrap, the actual quantity exceeds the norm. At this point, management should study the reasons for the scrap. Even though it may be possible to eliminate much scrap material, it may not always be economical to do so. Before establishing controls, managers should compare the value of the scrap lost to the cost of controlling this scrap. Cost-benefit analysis enables management to determine which corrective action is economical.

Defective Units

Another form of product waste is **defective units.** As opposed to scrap, defective units require extra work before they can be sold as first-quality products. Two methods are available to account for the added costs incurred to correct defective units:

1. If the defective units result from unusual job requirements, the additional rework costs should be treated as direct costs of that job order. For example, if a customer requests an order on a rush basis, the cost of defective units should be charged to the job when time pressure has caused the defective units.
2. If the defective units occur irregularly and are not the result of specific job requirements, the costs should be treated as departmental overhead costs. The rework costs are charged to Factory Overhead Control and to a subsidiary ledger account called Rework Costs. When determining the factory overhead application rate at the beginning of the year, accountants should include an estimate for rework costs as additional factory overhead costs.

Accounting for Rework Costs. For example, assume that Job No. 50 accumulates $500 direct material costs, $120 direct labor costs, and $150 factory overhead costs. Then, we determine that four units are defective and require additional total direct material costing $65, direct labor of $40, and 2 machine-hours. Because we are applying factory overhead at $25 per machine-hour, we apply an additional $50 factory overhead for reworking. The entries to record the cost of this job follows:

Original accumulation of costs

Work in Process Inventory—Job No. 50	770	
Direct Materials Inventory		500
Wages Payable		120
Factory Overhead Control—Overhead Applied		150

Rework costs assigned to job

When rework cost is assigned to the job, accountants make the following entry:

Work in Process Inventory—Job No. 50	155	
Direct Materials Inventory		65
Wages Payable		40
Factory Overhead Control—Overhead Applied		50

Transferred to finished goods

The following entry transfers the job to the finished goods storeroom:

Finished Goods Inventory	925	
Work in Process Inventory—Job No. 50		925

The costs of all units in the job have increased because of the rework costs. Without the rework costs, the job would have cost $770. If the factory overhead application rate includes an estimate for rework costs, a minor overcharge of factory overhead results when rework costs are charged directly to the job. To remedy this overcharge we can either use an independent factory overhead application rate or accumulate separate costs for this special job.

Rework Costs Assigned to Overhead. If the defective units were not the result of the job specifications, we use the following approach to charge rework costs to factory overhead:

Original accumulation of costs

Work in Process Inventory—Job No. 50	770	
Direct Materials Inventory		500
Wages Payable		120
Factory Overhead Control—Overhead Applied		150

Rework costs assigned to factory overhead

Factory Overhead Control—Rework Costs	155	
Direct Materials Inventory		65
Wages Payable		40
Factory Overhead Control—Overhead Applied		50

Transferred to finished goods

Finished Goods Inventory	770	
Work in Process Inventory—Job No. 50		770

All rework costs are transferred to Factory Overhead Control—Rework Costs. Job No. 50 does not bear any rework costs.

Before reworking defective units, a company must determine that it is economical to perform such work. Sometimes, rather than spend many dollars to correct defective units so they can be sold as first quality, a company may find it more profitable to sell them in their current stage as seconds or spoiled goods. Operating procedures should prescribe when to rework defective units. Defective units should be reworked only after the production manager has authorized the rework or when company operating procedures indicate it is economical.

Spoiled Goods

Although defective goods can be economically reworked so they can be sold as first-quality finished goods, it is usually not profitable to correct spoiled goods enough for sale as first quality. **Spoiled goods** are products containing such significant imperfections that even with additional expenditures for material, labor, and overhead, they cannot be made into perfect finished products. Effective spoilage control requires a distinction between spoilage due to factors in the overall production process versus spoilage that occurs because of the nature of the job being worked on. Some spoilage results from human error which is practically unavoidable. Workers become fatigued and cannot perform at peak efficiency during the entire workday. As a result, they may make errors in cutting fabric or wood or in mixing ingredients.

Treatment of Spoilage Costs. Even though this chapter focuses only on job order costing, the procedures for process costing illustrated in Chapter 7 follow approximately the same treatment of spoilage costs. Basically, we treat spoilage costs in two ways:

1. If spoilage is expected to occur regularly, the difference between the sales price of the spoiled goods and their total production costs should be accumulated in Factory Overhead Control.

2.   If the spoilage is clearly traceable to a job because of its special requirements, the difference between the sales price of the spoilage and its costs is
added to the cost of the good units only in that job.

We reduce the market value of spoiled goods by increasing materials handling
and storage costs. We may reduce the market value further by subtracting the
cost of disrupting the production schedule when defective output is produced.
These methods encourage the elimination of waste in the production process
because the focus is on its cost.

The following example illustrates both methods of accounting for spoilage using a separate work in process account to accumulate each cost element. Assume
a firm manufactures men's suits with the following cost per unit:

Materials	$30
Labor	15
Factory Overhead	20 (using the applied rate)

If Job No. 60 contains 100 suits, the entry to record the costs in production is as
follows. (Note that the Work in Process subsidiary ledger details the cost components for illustration purposes.)

Work in Process—Job No. 60, Materials	3,000	
Work in Process—Job No. 60, Labor	1,500	
Work in Process—Job No. 60, Factory Overhead	2,000	
Direct Materials Inventory		3,000
Wages Payable		1,500
Factory Overhead Control		2,000

Assume spoilage resulting from many unpredictable factors causes 10 suits not
to meet specifications; they will be sold as irregulars for $260. Spoilage cost of
the suits is charged to Factory Overhead Control. This removes the entire cost
of the spoiled units from the three Work in Process accounts. We transfer the 90
good units into finished goods inventory at a cost of $65 per unit (material, $30;
labor, $15; and overhead, $20). The sales value of the spoiled goods enters a
special inventory account labeled Spoiled Goods Inventory. Factory Overhead
Control with its subsidiary ledger account, Loss on Spoiled Goods, absorbs the
difference as illustrated next. Budgeted factory overhead costs should include an
estimate for the loss on spoiled goods when factory overhead application rates
are established.

Spoilage charge to total production

Spoiled Goods Inventory	260	
Factory Overhead Control—Loss on Spoiled Goods	390	
Work in Process—Job No. 60, Materials		300
Work in Process—Job No. 60, Labor		150
Work in Process—Job No. 60, Overhead		200
Finished Goods Inventory	5,850	
Work in Process—Job No. 60, Materials		2,700
Work in Process—Job No. 60, Labor		1,350
Work in Process—Job No. 60, Overhead		1,800

Spoilage Charged to Job. If the spoiled units result because the job requires a
special fabric or difficult pattern details, the 90 good units should bear the cost
of all 100 suits, including the 10 spoiled units. The entry to record the original
costs under these circumstances is the same as shown earlier:

Work in Process—Job No. 60, Materials	3,000	
Work in Process—Job No. 60, Labor	1,500	
Work in Process—Job No. 60, Factory Overhead	2,000	
Direct Materials Inventory		3,000
Wages Payable		1,500
Factory Overhead Control		2,000

Instead of crediting the three work in process accounts for the full cost of the spoiled units, we remove only a portion of the cost. We determine the portion removed as follows:

$$\frac{\$260 \text{ sales recovery of } 10 \text{ units}}{\$650 \text{ total cost of } 10 \text{ units}} = 40 \text{ percent sales recovery}$$

40% × $300 material cost of 10 units	$120
40% × $150 labor cost of 10 units	60
40% × $200 overhead cost of 10 units	80
	$260

Spoiled Goods Inventory 260		
Work in Process—Job No. 60, Material	120	
Work in Process—Job No. 60, Labor	60	
Work in Process—Job No. 60, Overhead	80	

Similar computations can be determined using the following approach, which includes:

$$\frac{\$3,000 \text{ material cost of } 100 \text{ units}}{\$6,500 \text{ total } 100\text{-unit job cost}} \times \$260 \text{ sales value} = \$120$$

$$\frac{\$1,500 \text{ labor cost of } 100 \text{ units}}{\$6,500 \text{ total } 100\text{-unit job cost}} \times \$260 \text{ sales value} = \$\ 60$$

$$\frac{\$2,000 \text{ overhead cost of } 100 \text{ units}}{\$6,500 \text{ total } 100\text{-unit job cost}} \times \$260 \text{ sales value} = \$\ 80$$

The cost of the remaining 90 good units has increased from $65 per unit to $69.33 ($6,500 total job cost − $260 sales recovery value of spoilage = $6,240 ÷ 90 good units = $69.33). We transfer the 90 good units to finished goods at the $69.33 unit cost as follows:

Finished Goods Inventory 6,240	
Work in Process—Job No. 60, Material ($3,000 − $120)	2,880
Work in Process—Job No. 60, Labor ($1,500 − $60)	1,440
Work in Process—Job No. 60, Overhead ($2,000 − $80)	1,920

Defective and Spoilage Report. A report similar to the one illustrated in Exhibit 21–1 for scrap can summarize defective units and spoilage. Alternatively, one summary report may combine all loss from scrap, defective units, and spoilage. These reports should include (1) the number of defective or spoiled units, (2) the cost involved, and (3) the cause of the spoilage. It is often difficult to determine who is responsible for the mistake causing the scrap, defective units, or spoilage. The person responsible for the mistake is not likely to admit it; as a result, such losses often go unreported. Requiring the supervisor to prepare such reports benefits the company when workers use the information to control scrap, defective units, and spoilage. Only if managers are willing to spend time in studying the causes of material waste can they feel they have this aspect of material costs under control.

Inventory Planning (L.O. 2)

Inventory planning and control involve much more than minimizing the loss from scrap, spoilage, and defective units. A company must schedule its purchasing; otherwise its inventory will be overstocked during some periods and out of stock during others. The goal of management is that the investment in inventory represent an optimum balance between the two extremes of having inadequate or excessive inventories. Between these two extremes is a desirable inventory level; the objective is to find this level. The controller wants to maintain the optimum inventory investment for the same reasons the financial manager wants to avoid idle cash on which no return is earned. The cost of carrying unnecessary inventory stock reduces the profitability of the firm.

Stockouts, Temporarily Out of Stock, and Back Orders

Stockouts, temporarily out of stock (TOS), and **back orders (B/O)** refer to a company running out of inventory. If raw material is not quickly available after the receipt of sales orders, there is a possibility that the production cycle must stop or slow down. Such delays cause lost sales. The type of product a company sells influences this risk; for example, when a stockout occurs for a convenience item, customers usually switch brands.

The degree of service reliability that a company wishes to offer its customers is a consideration when determining inventory size. The willingness of its customers to tolerate a delayed delivery influences the size of inventory a company carries. In the past, managers using traditional inventory systems clearly recognized that the higher the degree of service reliability offered, the larger the investment in inventory. Fortunately, JIT, zero defect, flexible manufacturing, and other cost management concepts now make possible large reductions in inventory without sacrificing service reliability. JIT eliminates most safety stock; orders are smaller but more frequent. JIT depends on orders arriving regularly and on time to shorten production lead time.

Carrying a large inventory investment is not advisable for any materials, certainly not those used in the manufacture of products subject to short, intense sales periods, such as novelties or high-fashion products. The company involved in such sales should try to match its purchases with sales and maintain zero or minimum inventory. Often companies fail to meet this goal because their sales forecast is incorrect. Fortunately, carrying stocks of materials used in manufacturing products with longer sales lives and not subject to rapid market changes, technological obsolescence, or physical deterioration is less risky. However, companies should avoid inventory buildups because product life cycles are decreasing due to intense global competition. In addition, carrying costs increase with inventory buildups.

Costs of the Two Extremes. In selecting an inventory level that minimizes costs in the long run, the company should weigh the costs of carrying too much inventory against the cost of not carrying enough. Many of these costs do not actually appear in accounting records because companies use them for planning purposes only. For example, accountants do not record the loss of customer goodwill or contribution margin on missed sales in formal accounting records. These costs are, of course, important in determining the **optimum inventory level.**

Under conventional manufacturing systems, there is a trade-off between carrying too much inventory and not carrying enough. As more companies adopt newer inventory management techniques, this trade-off may disappear.

The costs of not carrying enough inventory are

Raw Material Inventory	**Finished Goods Inventory**
1. Additional costs due to interruptions of production.	1. Loss of customer goodwill.
2. Lost quantity discounts.	2. Contribution margin on lost sales.
3. Additional purchasing costs (due to rush).	3. Additional transportation costs.

The costs of carrying both excessive raw material and excessive finished goods inventories are

1. Increased cost of the storage space.
2. Increased insurance and property taxes.
3. Increased cost of handling and transferring inventory.
4. Increased risk of theft, technological obsolescence, and physical deterioration.
5. Increased clerical costs in maintaining records.
6. Loss of desired return on investments in inventory and storage space.

To minimize costs in the long run, the company should decide when inventory items warrant the highest degree of control. Unless a company has unlimited funds to install all the control features the cost accountant wishes, managers must decide which controls are feasible for the type of inventories carried.

ABC Analysis and Two-Bin System (L.O. 2)

One method of inventory control is ABC analysis, a commonsense approach to deciding which inventories should receive tighter control. This selective approach is called 80/20 (i.e., 80 percent of the dollar cost of material used is in 20 percent of the inventory items). The method operates on the exception principle, because it is neither feasible nor possible to give the same amount of attention to all inventory stock. Those inventories that are important either because they are critical to production or have a large dollar value deserve frequent reviews and tight control. Managers can use a ranking of inventory, comparing the costs of running out of stock with carrying costs, to determine which inventories to closely control.

The inventory items in Exhibit 21–2 illustrate the **ABC inventory system.** In this system, managers first determine the future usage of each material item for a designated period. Then they estimate the unit price of each material to determine the total consumption cost. Some ABC systems are based solely on unit cost, while others use only turnover in identifying the controls necessary. One approach is to base the inventory controls on both usage and unit costs; this is the approach presented here.

EXHIBIT 21–2   ABC Analysis of Inventory

Material Part No.	Budgeted Unit Usage	Unit Price	Total Cost
X1	3,300	$ 4.00	$ 13,200
X2	11,900	0.54	6,426
X3	15,750	0.26	4,095
X4	3,600	13.15	47,340
X5	990	26.70	26,433
X6	9,980	0.90	8,982
	45,520		$106,476

EXHIBIT 21–3

Item	Budgeted Unit Usage	Total Cost
X4	3,600	$ 47,340
X5	990	26,433
X1	3,300	13,200
X6	9,980	8,982
X2	11,900	6,426
X3	15,750	4,095
	45,520	$106,476

EXHIBIT 21–4

Class	Unit Usage	Percent of Total Units	Total Cost	Percent of Total Cost
A	4,590	10	$ 73,773	69%
B	13,280	29	22,182	21
C	27,650	61	10,521	10
	45,520	100	$106,476	100

Exhibit 21–3 lists the items from Exhibit 21–2 in descending order by total consumption cost. Next, we divide the items into classes based on their total cost. Management chooses arbitrary criteria to reflect both the number and the break between classes. Class divisions depend on the storage facilities, personnel, and other resources available.

ABC Classes. In the three classes established, Class A contains Items X4 and X5; Class B, Items X1 and X6; and Class C, Items X2 and X3. As demonstrated here, management usually finds a relatively large percentage of its inventory costs tied up in a small percentage of the material items carried in stock. Exhibit 21–4 shows that only 10 percent of the total units account for 69 percent of the cost. Because Class A contains so much cost, managers should apply the greatest degree of control here. Employees should frequently review the stock in Class A so the company can safely carry small inventory levels. Managers should apply less control to Class B items, and even less control for Class C items. The low-value items in Class C do not require elaborate controls. Because the cost of each item in Class C is proportionately small, carrying more stock in Class C inventory than is needed for the period's production is less cause for concern.

Inexpensive Control Systems

For their low-value, noncritical items, some companies use a simple **two-bin system.** They use two bins, piles, or other measures, with the first bin containing enough material to meet manufacturing needs between the receipt of one order and the placement of another. The reserve bin contains enough stock to satisfy production requirements for the time between placing an order and receiving the goods. When the first bin is empty and the reserve bin tapped, personnel immediately prepare a purchase requisition for additional stock. If they fail to place a purchase order when units are first withdrawn from the reserve stock, the company may use all its inventory stock, causing a stockout. A two-bin system does not require perpetual inventory records for material items because the expense of maintaining these records may outweigh the cost of the material being controlled. Because the two-bin system is an inexpensive means of material control, it is appropriate only for Class C, low-value material items.

Managers may use various other simple methods for indicating a reorder point. They may place a line or some other mark on the storage bins, indicating the point at which personnel should place a purchase order. This mark represents the minimum level the stock can reach before reordering. Because most companies have limited storage space and limited investments for inventory, they should establish quantity and dollar maximums for each inventory. There is less chance of overstocking if companies maintain only the maximum quantity of inventory on hand.

Automatic Reorder System

Inventory systems can have an automatic reorder procedure built in that issues a purchase order whenever the balance on hand drops to a designated level. A computer can indicate the quantity to be ordered when it generates the purchase order. A company can use more elaborate inventory techniques depending on the capabilities of its electronic data processing equipment.

Just-in-Time and Materials Requirements Planning (L.O. 6)

The **Just-in-time (JIT)** concept is a recent inventory concept affecting not only accounting and production but also warehousing and marketing functions. The basic principle of Just-in-time is receiving production parts as needed, rather than building up inventories of these components. Instead of stockpiling inventory, the Just-in-time approach depends on orders arriving regularly and on time. It demands on-time deliveries from suppliers, rather than building in additional safety stocks to compensate for possible delays. Thus, JIT is based on short, rapidly changing production runs operating in a timely and efficient manner, rather than long, inflexible runs. This approach argues for no inventory stock, rather than a regular supply plus safety stock. It operates under the premise of zero defects in parts supplied by other companies as well as products manufactured internally.

Using the JIT approach, managers reduce inventory to a minimum level, keeping on hand only the amount needed in production until the next order arrives. JIT eliminates most safety stock, and orders are smaller but more frequent. This system's use of reduced inventories and increased orders requires accountants to make more frequent journal entries. Because orders are smaller, however, employees can receive and process them more quickly and accurately than under other systems. Also, fewer goods on hand require less warehouse space and storage equipment with a resulting cost saving. While shipping and receiving cost may increase, the JIT concept eliminates the double handling of products by relocating storage to the work area. JIT shortens production lead time and virtually eliminates unnecessary work in process and finished goods inventories by having continuous delivery of items. Employees closely monitor purchases to ensure that the company receives the quantity ordered. Even though some companies may have difficulty adopting JIT in its entirety, often they can make changes in their operations to use some of its aspects to reduce costs.

A **materials requirements planning (MRP) system** does not assume an even or constant demand throughout a production period. MRP is an actual demand driven system rather than a system based on an average demand. Employees place purchase orders for materials only when a *master production schedule (MPS)* has materials actually scheduled for use in production. An MRP system examines the finished goods requirements before determining the demand for raw materials, components, and subassemblies at each of the prior production stages. MRP's purpose is to maintain the lowest possible level of inventory while also making certain materials and parts are available.

Economic Order Quantity (L.O. 3)

Unlike MRP, the **economic order quantity (EOQ)** approach assumes a stable level of demand that is known with certainty. EOQ is the order size that minimizes both the costs of ordering and the costs of carrying inventory in stock over time. The ordering costs include the costs of preparing and processing an order and receiving the materials. Carrying costs include costs that vary with the average number of units held in inventory, such as taxes and insurance on inventory and inventory spoilage costs, as well as the desired return on investment. In determining the desired return, the cost of capital is multiplied by the costs that vary with the number of units purchased, such as the purchase price, freight, and unloading costs. Carrying costs are often expressed as a percent of the unit's purchase cost. Because costs such as depreciation and rent on plant facilities and supervisor's salary often do not vary with the number of units held in inventory or the units purchased, these costs are usually irelevant for this short-range decision even though they may be important for long-range decision making. We can calculate economic order quantity by table, graph, or formula. For this example, assume the following facts for a company:

Annual requirements	1,000 units
Ordering cost per purchase order (includes postage, telephone, clerical costs)	$15 per order
Carrying costs per unit for a year (taxes, insurance, and desired return on inventory investment)	$0.75 per unit

Tabular Determination of EOQ. Exhibit 21–5 includes an approximate value for EOQ using a tabular analysis. We choose varying order sizes arbitrarily to satisfy the annual requirement of 1,000 units. Because we assume that the inventory level is zero when we receive each purchase order and the inventory level increases to the order size on the order's arrival, we compute the average inventory as one half the order size.

Inventory stock decreases with the use of units so just before the receipt of another order, the stock is zero. As the order size increases, the number of orders necessary to meet annual total needs decreases. Conversely, total ordering costs decrease when we make fewer orders, but the carrying costs increase because we require more space to hold the larger orders. Carrying costs and ordering costs move in opposite directions; at some point, an order size minimizes total costs. Because the total annual costs for carrying and ordering are lowest at 200 units, this order size reflects the EOQ, given the indicated order size.

EXHIBIT 21–5   Tabular Determination of Economic Order Quantity

	100	200	400	600	800	1,000
Order size (selected arbitrarily)	100	200	400	600	800	1,000
Average inventory (order size/2)	50	100	200	300	400	500
Number of orders: $\dfrac{\text{Annual requirements}}{\text{Order size}}$	10	5	2.5	1.6	1.25	1
Total order cost (no. of orders @ $15)	$150	$ 75	$ 38	$ 24	$ 19	$ 15
Total carrying cost (average inventory @ $0.75)	38	75	150	225	300	375
Total costs of carrying and ordering inventory	$188	$150	$188	$249	$319	$390

Graphic Determination of EOQ. Rather than calculating the EOQ using a tabular analysis, a company can prepare graphs. Exhibit 21–6 illustrates the graphic method of determining EOQ. The ordering costs curve shows that total ordering costs decrease as the order size increases. Carrying costs move in the opposite direction; they increase as the order size increases because there is more inventory on hand. The curve representing the total costs of carrying and ordering begins to flatten between 200 and 400 units. After finding this range, we choose an order size in this area at the lowest point. In Exhibit 21–6, the low point is 200 units, which is the EOQ.

EOQ Formula. A formula method of determining EOQ is even more accurate and timesaving than either the tabular or graphic approaches. The widely used EOQ formula is expressed in several ways using a variety of symbols. One simple variation of the formula is as follows:

$$EOQ = \sqrt{\frac{2QO}{C}}$$

where

Q = Annual quantity required in units.
O = Cost of placing an order.
C = Annual cost of carrying a unit in stock.

Using the data presented earlier with Q = 1,000, O = $15, and C = $0.75, the EOQ is 200:

$$\sqrt{\frac{2(1,000)(\$15)}{\$0.75}} = 200$$

Not all calculations of EOQ result in such a neat answer as 200 units. Depending on annual requirements, ordering costs, and carrying costs, the answer could have been 218 or some other odd figure.

The EOQ determined by all three methods is the same only because we selected the order sizes in Exhibits 21–5 and 21–6 to correspond to the EOQ using

EXHIBIT 21–6   Economic Order Quantity Graph

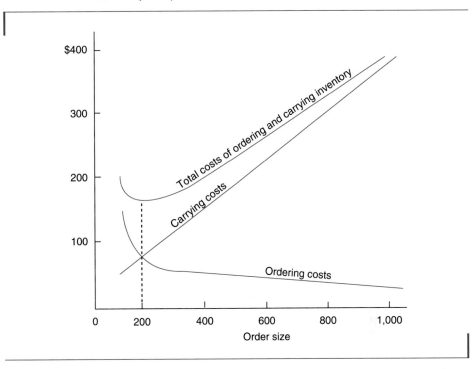

the formula. If we used other data and the formula calculated an EOQ of 415, it would be very unlikely that an order size of 415 was arbitrarily chosen for the tabular analysis or the graphic approach. The tabular or graphic approaches are, after all, not as exact as the EOQ formula. This is why the answer obtained through the tabular or graphic approach is only an approximate value. Accountants usually prefer the formula method because of ease of application. However, even though we use the formula method, the graphical analysis provides a useful visual representation of the relationship between carrying and ordering costs and gives some appreciation of the consequences of ordering some amount greater or less than optimal. In addition, we can use the tabular presentation as a convenient form for communicating such relationships to some party not involved in the analysis.

Regardless of the method used to compute EOQ, we can determine the total cost of buying and carrying the units ordered through the following formula:

$$\frac{EOQ}{2} \text{ (Carrying cost per unit)} + \frac{\text{Annual requirements}}{EOQ} \text{ (Ordering cost per order)}$$

Using an EOQ of 200 units, $0.75 carrying cost per unit, a 1,000-unit annual requirement, and a $15 ordering cost per order, the buying and carrying costs become the following:

$$\frac{200}{2} \, (\$0.75) + \frac{1,000}{200} \, (\$15) = \$150$$

Ignoring Stockouts and Other Costs

In the past, accountants considered EOQ the most competent mechanism for maintaining an efficient level of materials inventories. With today's automated manufacturing environment, the EOQ model loses its practical usefulness. Use of the simple deterministic EOQ model encourages companies to carry inventory. Managers assume the setup cost of starting a new production run or switching from one model to another increases with each change in production run. This generates a preference for production runs longer than needed to fill an immediate demand. Also, companies hold inventory as a buffer at work centers to prevent halting the entire assembly line when a breakdown or stoppage occurs at an individual work center. The excess inventory allows the production line to continue operating even when one or more work centers on the assembly line have halted production to rework defective output.

Although the answer determined using EOQ analysis is mathematically correct, a company may still buy a quantity other than the EOQ. Although economic order quantity does represent a trade-off between carrying and ordering costs that move in opposite directions, the EOQ model may not contain all relevant costs.

The prime objective using MRP and JIT is to minimize inventory levels while eliminating stockouts. However, EOQ balances carrying costs and ordering costs, usually ignoring stockout costs. Carrying costs and ordering costs may not cover all the costs associated with controlling and maintaining inventory. Not all manufacturing processes have a smooth or level production curve; for the majority, demand occurs at intermittent times. This means that they may maintain unneeded inventories, or costly stockouts occur. The EOQ formula in use by most companies today ignores this potentially costly problem. Also, having a few days of safety stock on hand to cover shipments that were not received on time usually does not solve this problem. In addition, safety stock sits in inventory, increasing costs even further.

The simplified EOQ models presented do not contain all the relevant costs affecting the order size decision. For example, a company may buy 50 or 100 units at a time rather than the 200 EOQ determined earlier in the illustrations because it cannot pay for the larger order even though it is more economical. In addition, a company may wish to maintain a larger stock of inventory than indicated by EOQ analysis, to provide a higher level of customer service. Also, because the basic EOQ formula ignores inventory's purchase price, the formula does not consider the reduction in material costs of taking quantity discounts. Therefore, we may have to formally consider additional costs in a more complicated model or informally through some judgmental process external to the model.

Effect of Quantity Discounts

The tabular approach to determining EOQ can include the effect of quantity discounts. Exhibit 21–7 employs the same data presented in Exhibits 21–5 and 21–6 except that the cost of forgoing the largest discount available is included for the smaller order sizes. Assuming that no safety stock is included, we calculate average inventory as one half the order size. The data assumptions are as follows:

Annual quantity required	1,000 units
Costs of ordering per purchase order	$ 15.00
Carrying costs per unit	$ 0.75 per unit
Material cost ($10 per unit at list price)	$10,000

EXHIBIT 21–7   Economic Order Table with Quantity Discount Effect

	100	200	400	600	800	1,000
Order size (arbitrarily selected) . .	100	200	400	600	800	1,000
Average inventory	50	100	200	300	400	500
Number of orders	10	5	2.5	1.6	1.25	1
Quantity discount	1%	2%	4%	5%	5%	5.5%
Total ordering costs	$150	$ 75	$ 38	$ 24	$ 19	$ 15
Total carrying costs	38	75	150	225	300	375
Additional expense of forgoing discount	450	350	150	50	50	—
Total	$638	$500	$338	$299	$369	$390

The following discount is offered by the supplier:

Order Size in Units	Quantity Discount (Percent)	Price per Unit
0–99	0	$10.00
100–199	1 %	9.90
200–399	2	9.80
400–599	4	9.60
600–799	5	9.50
800–999	5	9.50
1,000 and over	5.5	9.45

Each of the five smaller orders loses some quantity discount because these order sizes do not take advantage of the largest discount of 5.5 percent. For example, by ordering in lot sizes of 100, the material costs $9.90 rather than the $9.45 for units purchased in 1,000-unit orders. Thus, the forgone discount for 100-unit orders is $450 [1,000 units × ($9.90 − $9.45)]. The most economical order, as shown in Exhibit 21–7, is 600 units (increased from 200 units in Exhibit 21–5) because of the effect of quantity discounts. Depending on the size of the quantity discount, management may find it cheaper to buy in larger quantities and destroy units not needed. (Note that we determine a neat answer of 600 only because its cost is lower than any of the other five order sizes arbitrarily selected. Also, the company may not purchase 600 units because of an inadequate cash flow.)

Order Size Restrictions

We can use the EOQ formula in combination with the tabular approach when there are restrictions on the order size. Many companies accept only orders in round lot sizes because of packing and assembly-line requirements. The EOQ obtained through the formula may yield a size that is not an acceptable order quantity. In this case, it is necessary to determine the annual ordering and carrying costs through use of a tabular determination.

Assume a company can only order in lot sizes of 1,000 units. However, with costs to place each order of $128, a 360,000-unit annual demand, and $4 unit carrying cost, the EOQ formula yields the following:

$$EOQ = \sqrt{\frac{2(360,000)(\$128)}{\$4}} = \sqrt{\frac{\$92,160,000}{\$4}} = \sqrt{23,040,000} = 4,800 \text{ units}$$

EXHIBIT 21–8   Tabular Determination of Economic Order Quantity

Order size	4,000	5,000
Average inventory (order size/2)	2,000	2,500
Number of orders:		
$\dfrac{\text{Annual requirements}}{\text{Order size}}$	90	72
Total ordering cost (no. of orders @ $128)	$11,520	$ 9,216
Total carrying cost (average inventory @ $4)	8,000	10,000
Total costs of carrying and ordering inventory	$19,520	$19,216

Because the 4,800 units represent an unacceptable order quantity, Exhibit 21–8 shows the total annual costs of ordering and carrying the two acceptable quantities on either side of 4,800 (4,000 and 5,000 in this case).

The difference in the annual cost is relatively small ($304). Generally, when the EOQ determined through the formula is close to an acceptable order quantity, the EOQ formula is relatively insensitive to small changes in order quantity. In this example, the 4,800-unit order is close to the 5,000 acceptable order. However, when these differences are larger, cost changes may be significant and the tabular approach is justified.

Constraints from Storage. Managers need additional analysis if the EOQ determined exceeds the storage available to receive the order. Assume that a company has facilities to store only 3,000 units. If the EOQ model indicates 4,800 units are optimum, the company should compare the cost of additional warehouse space with the cost savings obtained from ordering in a quantity larger than 3,000. In choosing the optimum solution, we must examine the differential costs of the alternative available, such as the extra warehousing cost. Chapters 8 and 16 further discuss differential costs.

Lead Time. EOQ analysis determines the optimal order size; now the question is when to order. One of the factors affecting this decision is **lead time**—the time it takes to receive an order after it is placed. If its supplier is reliable, a company can predict the time needed for delivery, or lead time, with a high degree of certainty. However, for most products, it is not possible to predict lead time because of uncertainties in delivery schedules. In addition, it may be difficult to estimate the amount of material that will be used during the lead time. If material usage is not steady, there is a danger that stockouts will occur or that new customer orders will arrive before receipt of the stock ordered.

Calculating Safety Stock and Reorder Points (L.O. 4)

Because it is difficult to forecast lead time and inventory usage with a high degree of certainty, companies often need an inventory buffer, or **safety stock,** to protect against stockouts. Often management is tempted to be conservative and maintain a large stock. However, this can be costly and may result in excessive inventory carrying cost. If a company maintains inadequate safety stock, interruptions and inconveniences can result and stockouts may become frequent. The ideal safety stock level minimizes the possibility of stockouts and the cost of carrying inventory. The intangible costs of stockouts are difficult to measure because a company cannot easily quantify the loss of a customer's goodwill and possible repeat sales.

Several means are available to estimate safety stock. According to one method, management arbitrarily decides to use a certain number of average days' usage as its safety stock. Another method allows for the fluctuations between maximum daily usage and average daily usage. To illustrate, the following data refer to one material item used by a company:

Maximum daily usage	40 units
Average daily usage	30 units
Minimum daily usage	15 units
Lead time	18 days

The safety stock is computed as follows:

$$10 \text{ units (40 maximum daily usage} - 30 \text{ average daily usage)}$$
$$\underline{\times \ 18 \text{ days}}$$
$$180 \text{ units of safety stock}$$

Another method is to calculate the probability of running out of stock at various levels of safety stock and to determine an annual expected stockout cost. The annual cost of carrying safety stock in inventory is added to this cost. Total annual carrying cost increases with the level of safety stock maintained, but stockout cost decreases as the level of stock increases. The goal is to determine which amount of safety stock results in the lowest annual cost. Assume the following options are available for a product:

Units of Safety Stock	Probability of Running Out of Safety Stock (Percent)
20	50%
40	30
60	25
Stockout cost	$100 per occurrence
Carrying cost of safety stock	$4 per unit per year
Number of purchase orders	8 per year

Exhibit 21–9 contains an analysis of these costs. The lowest cost results with 40 units of safety stock.

EXHIBIT 21–9

	Safety Stock Costs				Stockout Costs				
Units of Safety Stock	×	Unit Carrying Cost per Year	= Total Annual Carrying Cost	Cost per Stockout	×	Probability of Stockout	×	Annual Purchase Orders	= Expected Annual Stockout Cost	Expected Total Cost
20	×	$4	= $ 80	$100	×	.50	×	8	= $400	$480
40	×	4	= 160	100	×	.30	×	8	= 240	400*
60	×	4	= 240	100	×	.25	×	8	= 200	440

*Lowest costs.

Reorder Point. After determining safety stock, it is possible to determine a **reorder point,** the inventory level to place an order. The reorder point is

$$
\begin{array}{l}
180 \text{ safety stock} \\
\underline{+\ 540} \text{ (18 days lead time} \times 30 \text{ average daily usage)} \\
720 \text{ reorder point in units}
\end{array}
$$

We compute the order point by adding the safety stock to the average usage during the lead time. To build safety stock into the computation, we multiply the maximum daily usage by the lead time as follows:

$$
\begin{array}{l}
40 \text{ maximum daily usage} \\
\underline{\times\ 18} \text{ days lead time} \\
720 \text{ reorder points in units}
\end{array}
$$

We may need to expand this computation if lead time is long and/or the order quantity is small. Under these circumstances, there may be one or more orders placed but not received that must be included in the computation determining when to reorder. Using the preceding example, the company would reorder when units on hand plus **orders in transit** equal 720.

Reorder Point with Certainty. We based the previous computation on realistic assumptions because we made an allowance for variations in lead time and in daily usage. Safety stock provides a cushion against stockouts and, in turn, this increases the reorder point. However, if usage is even throughout the year and lead time is always reliable, we can omit safety stock from the reorder point computation. The reorder point then becomes the average usage during the lead time or 540 (18 days' lead time $\times$ 30 average daily usage) for the preceding example.

Economic Production Runs (L.O. 5)

If a company manufactures a product with constant demand that becomes inventory instantaneously, we can use the economic order quantity model to determine **economic production runs.** This model makes the implicit assumption that a company adds units to inventory while production is in process. That is, as a company produces units, it takes them to the storeroom and adds them to inventory stock. We substitute the setup cost for a new production run for the unit ordering cost in the EOQ model. The setup cost includes the labor and other costs involved in rearranging and adjusting machines for a run of a different production item. Setup costs include preparing facilities to perform the job and to dismantle them after the job is finished. The following example solves the problem of deciding when to start and stop production runs and the number of production runs needed per year. We can expand this simplified model to include other factors.

Assume management has determined the following costs are associated with one of its product lines:

$$
\begin{array}{l}
Q = 60{,}000 \text{ units produced each year to meet demand.} \\
S = \$200 \text{ setup cost to change a production run.} \\
C = \$4 \text{ carrying cost per unit.}
\end{array}
$$

A variation of the EOQ formula determines the following optimal production run:

$$\text{Optimal production run} = \sqrt{\frac{2 \times 60{,}000 \times \$200}{\$4}}$$

$$= \sqrt{\frac{\$24{,}000{,}000}{\$4}} = 2{,}450$$

$$\text{Annual runs} = \frac{60{,}000 \text{ annual demand}}{2{,}450 \text{ optimal run size}} = 24.5 \text{ or } 25 \text{ runs}$$

The relatively high setup cost requires large production runs; as a result, using production runs of approximately 2,450 units minimizes overall cost. Based on this, the company needs 25 runs per year to meet demand.

Reducing Setup Cost

As illustrated in determining the optimal production run, the relatively high setup cost causes a preference for production runs longer than needed for immediate demand. A company that can reduce its setup costs to a minimum can match production closely with demand, eliminating the holding of inventory. Savings in holding excess inventory often occur when companies undertake investment projects to reduce setup costs or to schedule deliveries and production so there is less overall uncertainty in the production system.

Cost accountants may find that rather than use the EOQ formula to compute an optimal production run size that balances setup and holding costs, a better use of their time is to help find ways to reduce setup costs. Additionally, they may find that reducing the setup on different machines may involve the same expense, but if one machine is a bottleneck and the other is not, the effect of these actions is very different. Certainly if investigation shows setup costs are already at a minimum, the company can consider the market impact of offering less variety in the units they produce.

Summary

Many plant managers consider some level of product waste normal because of the inherent nature of the material or manufacturing process involved. Also, even though it may be technically possible to eliminate defective units and spoiled goods in some instances, it may not be economical on a cost/benefit basis. This occurs if the costs of lowering product waste exceed the cost of the current spoilage. However, accounting controls should ensure that product waste is minimized.

The ABC system of inventory control recognizes there is always a trade-off between the cost of the control tool used and the cost of the material controlled. By analyzing which inventory accounts for most of the company's cost, management can select its control sensibly. Efficient managers use frequent reviews and tight controls for material parts that are of high value or are critical to the manufacturing process.

Some of the control tools introduced in this chapter, such as safety stock and EOQ, are approximations at best. However, they do allow management to find the range from which to choose the quantity ordered. The simplified EOQ model presented gives accurate answers if usage or demand is stable. Unfortunately, many companies experience erratic patterns. However, managers can gain insight into the relevant range of inventory levels by using the tabular, graphic, or formula methods of determining EOQ. If managers desire a more exact answer that considers variable usage rates and variable lead times as well as costs other than ordering and carrying costs, more complex models are available.

Important Terms and Concepts

zero defect approach, 725
scrap materials, 725
defective units, 729
spoiled goods, 730
stockouts, TOS, B/O, 733
optimum inventory level, 733
ABC inventory system, 734
two-bin inventory system, 735
Just-in-time concept (JIT), 736

materials requirements planning (MRP) system, 737
economic order quantity (EOQ), 737
lead time, 742
safety stock, 742
reorder point, 744
orders in transit, 744
economic production runs, 744

Problem for Self-Study

Trade-Off of Spoilage and Inspection Costs

Richardson Company manufactures children's microscopes selling for $8 each. The machine grinding the glass lenses and eyepieces is very critical to production and must be maintained in proper adjustment. Management has determined that of the 1,200 produced daily, the number of toy microscopes rejected is equal to 64 divided by the number of adjustments made. Each microscope costs $5, and those rejected are of no value. The departmental supervisor adjusts the machine before work begins and then relies on the operator to perform other adjustments. Each adjustment costs $8; however, no microscopes are lost during the adjustment process.

Required:

Determine the optimal number of adjustments that each operator should make on a daily basis.

Solution to Problem for Self-Study

RICHARDSON COMPANY

X = number of adjustments and require $X \geq 1$

$$\$8X = 64/X \,(\$8)$$
$$\$8X^2 = \$512$$
$$X^2 = 64$$
$$X = 8$$

An iterative calculation of profit for each adjustment is another solution approach.

Adjustments	Revenue	Cost	Profit
1	$9,088 (1,136 × $8)	$6,008	$3,080
2	9,344 (1,168 × $8)	6,016	3,328
3	9,424 (1,178 × $8)	6,024	3,400
4	9,472 (1,184 × $8)	6,032	3,440
5	9,496 (1,187 × $8)	6,040	3,456
6	9,512 (1,189 × $8)	6,048	3,464
7	9,520 (1,190 × $8)	6,056	3,464
8	9,536 (1,192 × $8)	6,064	3,472 ←
9	9,536 (1,192 × $8)	6,072	3,464

Review Questions

1. Under what conditions would a company find the ABC method impractical? What alternatives are available in this case? How frequently should material parts in Class A of the ABC method be reviewed?

2. How would you decide whether reworking defective units would be profitable?

3. What effect does the company's degree of service reliability have on the inventory level carried?

4. Discuss the two-bin system of inventory control and how it works. For what type of inventory do you think the two-bin system would be appropriate?

5. Why is EOQ only one factor in determining order quantity? What additional qualitative and quantitative factors should be considered in selecting economic order quantity?

6. Why is quality increasingly being considered by management as a key feature for reducing long-term manufacturing costs?

7. Briefly discuss several relevant factors to a company's decision regarding how much to pay to assure zero defects.

8. Assume a production operation prides itself on having four inspectors; yet, it is surprised when customers' complaints concerning quality continue. What do you suspect is the problem? Are four inspectors evidence of negligence?

9. As the cost accountant, what should you advise managers to do when a defect occurs in manufacturing?

10. What is the trade-off if additional funds are spent in assuring absolute adherence to rigid quality standards?

11. What is your reaction to manager's boastful statement that the company's goal is to have only a two percent level of defectives?

CPA/CMA/CIA Multiple Choice Questions

1.–2.   (AICPA) Items 1 and 2 are based on the following information:
Harper Company's Job 501 for the manufacture of 2,200 coats was completed during August 19X2 at the following unit costs:

Direct materials	$20
Direct labor	18
Factory overhead (includes an allowance of $1 for spoiled work)	18
	$56

Final inspection of Job 501 disclosed 200 spoiled coats which were sold to a jobber for $6,000.

1. Assume that spoilage loss is charged to all production during August 19X2. What would be the unit cost of the good coats produced on Job 501?

    a. $53.00.
    b. $55.00.
    c. $56.00.
    d. $58.60.

2. Assume, instead, that the spoilage loss is attributable to exacting specifications of Job 501 and is charged to this specific job. What would be the unit cost of the good coats produced on Job 501?

   a. $55.00.
   b. $57.50.
   c. $58.60.
   d. $61.60.

3. (AICPA) The sale of scrap from a manufacturing process usually would be recorded as a(an)

   a. Decrease in factory overhead control.
   b. Increase in factory overhead control.
   c. Decrease in finished goods control.
   d. Increase in finished goods control.

4. (CMA) A decrease in inventory order costs will

   a. Decrease the economic order quantity.
   b. Increase the reorder point.
   c. Have no effect on the economic order quantity.
   d. Increase the economic order quantity.
   e. Decrease the holding cost percentage.

5. (CMA) An increase in inventory holding costs will

   a. Decrease the economic order quantity.
   b. Increase the safety stock required.
   c. Have no effect on the economic order quantity.
   d. Increase the economic order quantity.
   e. Decrease the number of orders issued per year.

6. (CMA) Safety stocks are used to compensate for

   a. Variations in inventory usage rates and lead times.
   b. Variations in inventory prices and lead times.
   c. Variations in inventory usage rates and prices.
   d. Inventory obsolescence and sales returns.
   e. Variations in customer needs and inventory pricing.

7. (CIA) A company has the following requirement for a part during production of a finished product:

Daily Requirement for Part	Probability
50	.2
60	.5
70	.2
80	.1
	1.0

   To ensure a 90 percent probability of sufficient stockage, the daily beginning balance of the part should be:

   a. 50.
   b. 60.
   c. 70.
   d. 80.

8. (CMA) The result of the economic order quantity formula indicates the

   a. Annual quantity of inventory to be carried.
   b. Annual usage of materials during the year.
   c. Safety stock plus estimated inventory for the year.

    d. Quantity of each individual order during the year.

    e. Annual quantity ordered for the year.

9. (CIA) Which of the following is an advantage of adopting a just-in-time (JIT) inventory system?

    a. A formal receiving department may be eliminated.

    b. A bill of materials outlines when all materials will be needed on a week-by-week basis.

    c. Greater emphasis on reducing per unit purchase costs.

    d. Late deliveries of materials are less of a problem.

10. (CIA) What are the three factors a manager should consider in controlling stockouts?

    a. Holding costs, quality costs, and physical inventories.

    b. Economic order quantity, annual demand, and quality costs.

    c. Time needed for delivery, rate of inventory usage, and safety stock.

    d. Economic order quantity, production bottlenecks, and safety stock.

Exercises

E21–1 Zero Defect Pledges (L.O. 6)

It has come to your attention as the accountant assigned responsibility for implementing the zero defect program that Jean Brown, a Yares Company employee, refuses to sign her zero defect pledge until the bearings in her machine are replaced. In the initial introduction of the program to all employees, it was agreed that success of the program requires 100 percent commitment by both management and employees. On additional investigation you find that Brown had reported these bearings needed correction earlier but maintenance had failed to replace the bearings when necessary due to lack of time in completing previous jobs. Brown's supervisor is quite distraught; he fears that Brown's refusal reflects poorly on his performance as a manager.

Required:

Discuss whether Brown should be coerced into signing the zero defect pledge immediately so production managers can report 100 percent support for the program to top management.

E21–2 Computing Safety Stock and Reorder Point (L.O. 4)

Herald Company provides the following data concerning two inventory items:

	Metal Disks	Pumps
Maximum daily usage	120 units	750 units
Average daily usage	100 units	690 units
Minimum daily usage	80 units	510 units
Lead time	20 days	15 days

Required:

a. Compute the safety stock allowing for the fluctuations between maximum daily usage and average daily usage.

b. Determine the reorder point in units using the safety stock computed in Requirement *a.*

E21–3 Theory Concerning Accounting for Scrap (L.O. 6)

Susan Smith is confused as to why the company she works for insists on setting up scrap inventory as an asset. Her reaction to the present system is that it is strictly a waste of time and accounting effort since the value of scrap is not large. The company that employs Susan has a continuing agreement with a quilt-making specialty company that purchases all scrap fabrics from the shirt-making process.

Required:

a. Give as many reasons as you can for the company policy.
b. Determine the result if scrap inventory was ignored in this company.

E21–4 Economical Production Runs (L.O. 5)

The management of Hyde Manufacturing has been quite concerned over the optimum production run. The company produces special pumps for a customer who orders 80,000 Type A pumps and 65,000 Type B pumps each year. Rather than manufacture these pumps as the orders are received monthly from the customer, management feels assured enough that the customer will continue these purchases to manufacture in larger lots. The setup cost is $800 for Type A pumps and $650 for Type B pumps. Carrying costs are estimated to be 10 percent of unit production cost per year. The production cost is $20 for the Type A pump and $15 for the Type B pump.

Required:

Compute the most economical production run for each pump. Also indicate the number of production runs per year for each type of pump.

E21–5 Calculating Annual Savings through Use of EOQ (L.O. 5)

Cinnatti Company has been purchasing motors in lot sizes of 500 units, which represents a six months' supply. The cost to place an order is $80, and the annual cost to carry one unit in inventory is $4. The list price of the motors is $30.

Required:

a. Determine the economic order quantity.
b. Compute how many orders will be placed using the economic order quantity.
c. Calculate the savings if the company buys in economical lot quantities.

E21–6 Calculating EOQ and Number of Orders (L.O. 3)

According to its production schedule, Jacksonville Company estimates that 12,000 yards of polyester at a cost of $45 per yard will be needed next year. The estimated carrying cost is 30 percent of purchase price for each yard, and the ordering cost per purchase order is $62.50. Use a 360-day business year.

Required:

a. Determine the most economical number of yards to order.
b. Calculate how many orders must be placed next year.
c. Decide how frequently the orders must be placed.

E21–7 Viewing Zero Defect as a Naive Management Tool (L.O. 6)

When Thoren Company adopted a zero defect program last year, workers greeted the program with skepticism. They believed a quality control and zero defects program was another new management fad—such as background music, suggestion boxes, and psychological counseling. Thoren employees remember trying suggestion boxes and abandoning them because workers feared retribution if they suggested something that management viewed negatively. Workers consider the zero defect concept as another naive attempt by management to increase productivity. Their skepticism toward the zero defect program is somewhat justified because they can cite many recent instances in which parts rejected for not meeting inspection standards were returned to the manufacturing department for correction. However, the manufacturing department did nothing to correct the parts and merely sent them back through inspection, only to find they passed quality control this time.

Required:

Evaluate Thoren Company's zero defect program.

E21–8 Determining EOQ and Annual Savings (L.O. 3)

In the production of pumps Dennis Company uses two valves, 1X and 2X. Valve 1X costs $20 and Valve 2X costs $5. The ordering cost is $18 per order and the carrying cost per annum is 8 percent of the valve cost. Dennis Company has been purchasing Valve 1X in lots of 4,000 units, which represents a three-months' supply, and Valve 2X in lots of 2,000, which represents one month's supply.

Required:

a. Determine the economic order quantity for each valve.
b. Identify the number of orders needed per year using the economic quantity (round up, considering any partial order as a whole order).
c. Determine the total annual saving from buying in economical quantities (it is not necessary to break down by type of pump).

E21–9 Control over Waste (L.O. 6)

Zelcer Company's president was quite concerned on reading the latest quality control report. He found the Finished Tire Department's percent of defects continues to remain high despite additional efforts to control waste. Recently Zelcer purchased new machines to replace the six-year-old ones thinking this would help reduce automobile tire waste. Fred Zelcer was especially concerned because their defective tires have so little recovery value; they have found it cost prohibitive to melt them down for reuse. In fact, employees buy defective tires at very reduced prices. Their children and grandchildren enjoy using them as tire swings in their playgrounds. The president noted that the company incurs little expense in hauling off these tires so he assumed good use of the tires as playground equipment. However, he believes the hefty waste expense can no longer be ignored and begins his own private investigation. On conclusion of this study, for which he has documentation, he walks into the Inspection Department unannounced and begins slashing the so-called defective tires with a knife several times. He plans to continue this approach because he believes such drastic action is justified until Zelcer employees get the message.

Required:

Describe the findings President Fred Zelcer obtained that caused him to take these dramatic actions. Were these actions justified?

E21–10 Economic Production Run (L.O. 5)

Crain Company believes that it can save costs by determining the optimum production run for its chemical products. Annual demand for one of its products is forecasted to be 60,000 units. The setup cost is $5 per run and annual carrying costs are estimated to be 8 percent of gross material cost. The list price of material per finished unit is $40, subject to 5 percent purchase discount.

Required:

a. Determine the most economic production run size.
b. Indicate the number of production runs per year.
c. Decide if Crain Company is using a traditional or flexible manufacturing system based on the financial data given.

Problems

P21–11 Tabular EOQ Considering the Effect of Quantity Discounts (L.O. 5)

Maker, Inc., uses 100 kegs of a special type of screw annually in its furniture manufacturing. It costs the company $10 every time a purchase order is placed and $5 annually to store each keg. Suppliers of the furniture screws provide the following purchase discount schedule:

Order Quantity	Purchase Discount (per Keg)
1–9	none
10–49	$2
50–99	$3
100 and above	$4

Required:

a. Calculate the economic order quantity using the tabular approach for selected order sizes of 5, 10, 20, 40, 50, and 100.
b. Calculate the economic order quantity using the formula approach.
c. Explain any differences in your answers to Requirements *a* and *b*.

P21–12 Economic Purchase Lot Size (L.O. 3)

Tilley Company is trying to decide the most economical size of purchase order for motors. The following estimates have been made for this analysis:

Purchase price: $5 per motor with quantity discounts of 1 percent on orders of 1,000 or more; 3 percent on orders of 10,000 or more.

Purchasing costs:
Fixed costs: $8,000 per year.
Variable costs: 20 cents per motor plus $40 per order

Storage costs:
Fixed costs: $15,000 per year
Variable costs: 60 cents per year per motor in storage

Receiving costs:
Variable costs: 18 cents per motor received and issued

Annual requirements: 100,000 motors purchased in assorted sizes

Safety stock: 1,000 motors regardless of order size

The company can earn 10 percent interest on any funds not needed for operating purposes. For imputing interest, management considers only the variable purchasing costs and purchase price as funds invested in inventory. Assume the safety stock of 1,000 motors is already on hand. Ignore the opportunity cost of lost discounts.

Required:

a. Compare the relative advantages of buying in lots of 2,000 motors and 10,000 motors per year using the whole dollars. Show calculations to support your analysis.
b. Give two examples of the types of costs that should be included in the estimate for:
(1) Fixed storage costs per year per motor in storage.
(2) Variable purchasing costs per order.

P21–13 Implementing a Zero Defect Program (L.O. 6)

Boer Company's top management recently returned from a seminar emphasizing the importance of quality control and zero defects. Immediately, they began taking steps to implement such a program within their production ranks. However, to their disappointment, progress toward zero defects in the goods produced has been slow. For example, they investigated why Bill Smith, a parts manufacturing supervisor, is behind schedule.

According to Smith, production control does not give him adequate parts on time and when he does get parts, they usually are not the correct size or of the specified material. Also, Smith believes that the Inspection Department has no sense of urgency and continually holds up his operation by not being reasonable about items. Smith supports this belief by showing a recent inspection report in which some of his parts were rejected for being a mere ¹⁄₁₆ of an inch off size. Smith's biggest complaint is the feeling that others in the organization ram the production schedule down his throat without fully understanding the constraints under which he has to work. He believes schedules are prepared by those who do not know what the production environment is really like.

When asked to describe the steps he has taken to inform others in the organization of these problems, Smith merely shook his head and replied, "What's the use?"

Required:

Discuss if these are merely excuses commonly given by a manufacturing person behind schedule or if these complaints merit further investigating.

P21–14 Alternative Approaches for Recording Scrap (L.O. 1)

Job No. 42, which is being processed by the Karen Costley Company, is expected to yield some amount of scrap. On November 22, 19X1, 10 items had to be scrapped.

Required:

Record entries for each situation:

a. (1) When the items were scrapped, their sales value could not be determined. Record any necessary entries.
   (2) On December 10, 19X1, the scrap was sold for $1,600. Record the sale using three alternative methods.
b. (1) When the items were scrapped, the sales value was estimated at $1,400. Make appropriate entries using three alternative approaches.
   (2) On December 10, 19X1, the scrap was sold for $1,600. Record the sale using three alternative methods.

P21–15 Summary Scrap Report (L.O. 1)

Harold Douglass, supervisor of the Fabricating Department of Alexander Company, provided this summary of the scrap incurred in April 19X1 on Job No. 2218.

Material	Description	Actual Scrap (Lbs.)	Expected Scrap (Lbs.)	Unit Cost	Sales Value of Actual Quantity
218B	Yellow plastic	56	45	$ 4.00	$ –0–
300A	Cotton fiber	13	14	20.00	140.00
418XR	Burlap	29	38	2.10	25.00
555BX	Cotton duck	40	35	8.10	Not Known

The cause for the Material 418XR and 555BX scrap is a new, inexperienced operator. The scrapping of Material 300A is due to operator inefficiency, while defective molds accounted for the loss of 218B.

Required:

a. Prepare a summary scrap report indicating the variances from expected scrap.
b. Indicate the action you would advise management to take regarding this scrap loss.

P21–16 Alternative Treatment of Rework Cost with Defective Units (L.O. 1)

Reba Manufacturing Company produces various home appliances. On one of its new product lines, mini-microwave ovens, it encountered some difficulty. The ovens are produced in 500-unit lots with total costs as follows:

Material	$3,000
Labor	6,000
Factory overhead (applied on the basis of machine-hours)	2,250

Producing each oven takes an average of three machine-hours. When inspection was made at the end of the processing, 80 units were defective and had to be reworked. The total cost for reworking was as follows:

Materials	$500
Labor	800

The rework operations required one machine-hour per defective oven. The company uses a separate ledger account for each cost component of work in process inventory.

Required:

Assuming no entries have been made in connection with this order, record all journal entries to complete the order and transfer it to the warehouse when:

a. The cost of the rework is to be charged to the job.
b. The cost of the rework is to be charged to the production of the period.
c. Prepare journal entries for the cash sale of 100 ovens at $40 per oven for:
   (1) Requirement *a.*
   (2) Requirement *b.*

P21–17 ABC Analysis of Inventory Control (L.O. 2)

Pat's Manufacturing Company produces four different product lines. Each of the products requires varying amounts of the eight materials (M1 to M8) carried in stock.

The following table indicates the budgeted pounds required of each material. Materials M1 and M2 are subject to credit terms of 1/10, n/30; M4 and M5, 2/10, n/30; and M7 and M8, 3/10, n/30. Assume all discounts are taken.

	Material Part Numbers							
	M1	**M2**	**M3**	**M4**	**M5**	**M6**	**M7**	**M8**
Product A	1	—	—	30	6	5	1	2
Product B	2	4	3	2	8	3	—	7
Product C	3	2	2	6	4	—	5	1
Product D	—	6	—	4	3	—	10	—
Invoice price per pound	$11	$9	$5	$12	$5	$8	$4	$3

Management plans to produce the following units of each product line:

Product A	2,500 units
Product B	3,000 units
Product C	1,500 units
Product D	4,000 units

The storekeeper in a secured warehouse can only oversee the annual issuance of approximately 108,000 material parts.

Required:

Using the ABC analysis of inventory, divide the materials into three different classes for control purposes. Which inventory controls would you advise management to use for each of the three inventory classes? Explain your advice.

P21–18 Trade-off of Costs (L.O. 6)

Householder, Inc., produces fancy glass flower vases selling for $5 each. Demand is so high that Householder is unable to produce all that they could sell. Machine No. 212 in the firing operation is very critical to production and must be maintained in proper adjustment; otherwise, the vases will not pass inspection. Past data reveal that of the 1,000 vases produced daily, the number rejected is equal to 25 divided by the number of additional adjustments made. Each vase costs $3, and the rejected vases are worthless. The supervisor adjusts the machine before operations begin each day. Any additional adjustments are made at the supervisor's discretion. Each adjustment costs $5, but no vases are lost during the adjustment phase.

Required:

Determine the optimal number of adjustments, including the initial adjustment, that should be made daily.

P21–19 Economic Order Table with Quantity Discount Effect (L.O. 3)

Gaff, Inc., can order lubricating material for its fabricating operation in cartons weighing two pounds each. It projects annual usage to be 3,600 cartons and material list price to be $10 per carton. The cost of placing an order is estimated to be $15, while the annual carrying cost per carton is estimated at $25. Management does not believe it is feasible to order more than one month's usage at a time. The supplier offers the following discount:

Order Size (Cartons)	Quantity Discount (Percent)
0–60	3%
61–120	4
121–150	6
151–200	7
over 200	8

Required:

a. Prepare a tabular analysis for determining the most economical order quantity using selected order sizes of 40, 90, 100, 150, 180, 200, and 300 cartons.
b. Explain which size order you would advise based on your analysis in Requirement *a* as well as other factors.

P21–20 Evaluating Treatment for Spoilage (L.O. 1)

The cost per unit for Holder Company's Product A is $10 for materials, $20 for labor, and $30 for overhead costs. During the current month, there were 100 units of Product A spoiled. These units could be sold for $15 each. A member of top management said that the entry to be made for these 100 spoiled units could be one of the following four:

Entry No. 1:

Spoiled Goods Inventory	1,500	
Loss on Spoiled Goods	4,500	
Work in Process—Materials		1,000
Work in Process—Labor		2,000
Work in Process—Overhead		3,000

Entry No. 2:

Spoiled Goods Inventory	1,500	
Work in Process—Materials		250
Work in Process—Labor		500
Work in Process—Overhead		750

Entry No. 3:

Finished Goods Inventory	6,000	
Work in Process—Materials		1,000
Work in Process—Labor		2,000
Work in Process—Overhead		3,000

Entry No. 4:

Spoiled Goods Inventory	1,500	
Factory Overhead Control—Loss on Spoiled Goods	4,500	
Work in Process—Materials		1,000
Work in Process—Labor		2,000
Work in Process—Overhead		3,000

Required:

Indicate the conditions, if any are appropriate, for making each of the four preceding entries.

Cases

C21–21 Cost-Plus Contracts (L.O. 1)

A company is so anxious for Karol, Inc., to make a special order of athletic uniforms that it is willing to let Karol's cost accountant decide the costing procedure to use in submitting a bid. The company agreed to pay Karol $19,750 for the 500 uniforms of special design, or to pay cost plus 15 percent. Even though the cost accountant intends to act ethically and according to good accounting principles, he is looking for the costing procedure most financially favorable to Karol, Inc. If a cost-plus contract is chosen, the cost accountant will be required to provide the supplier with source documents and other records in support of the cost figures.

In evaluating the alternatives, he determined:

	Cost per Uniform
Material	$7
Labor	2 hours @ $10 per hour
Factory overhead	$4 per direct labor-hour

Scrap from cutting out the uniforms will result; its exact sales value is not known at the time scrapping occurs. The production supervisor believes the scrap can be sold for $600, but the production manager doubts that the scrap will be worth anything. Both agree that it depends on the size of the scrap pieces, which cannot be determined at this time. Also, sale of this scrap is partially dependent on Karol's obtaining another order requiring material like that used in the uniforms. If both orders are received, Karol will have enough scrap to attract further scrap sales.

A quick examination of the details of the uniform requested by the potential customer indicates that rework is likely. To sew in the zipper, the sewers must be well trained; otherwise, units will be defective. Several of the workers now employed have completed other jobs requiring such detail, so they can be expected to create little rework. Workers who have less on-the-job training are expected to find the sewing more challenging. The production supervisor expects 25 of the uniforms to require reworking. A new zipper costing $0.20 each, including thread, will be required for each defective uniform. It will require one-half hour of a direct laborer's time to remove the old zipper and correct the uniform.

In addition to the 25 uniforms expected to be defective, the production supervisor expects the zippers in an additional 5 uniforms to be so badly sewn that it will be impossible to rework these and sell them as first-quality uniforms. Some of this error will be due to worker fatigue because careful attention must be paid to sew in these zippers. Management believes that it can remove the supplier's name from these five uniforms and sell them for $15 each. Inspection will occur only at the end of production, at which time spoiled and defective units will be identified.

Required:

a. Indicate which approach you would choose regarding the following if you were Karol's cost accountant:
   (1) Scrap.
   (2) Defective units.
   (3) Spoiled goods.
b. Determine the cost of the order using the approach chosen in Requirement *a*.
c. Indicate the price you would choose: $19,570 or a cost-plus contract.

C21–22 Alternative Spoilage Treatment (L.O. 1)

In talking with a group of managers for Manchos, Inc., regarding the costly spoilage of 100 units on Job No. X20, you discover a variety of suggestions as to the proper accounting treatment for the spoilage.

The president believes that the original cost of the 100 units should be assigned to the Spoilage Inventory account with Work in Process Inventory—Job No. X20 credited. He acknowledges that the company will not recover their original full cost, but plans to record the loss at the time the 100 units are sold because the exact amount of the loss will be known then. That way, he claims, the accountant does not have to confuse the issue with estimates of a future sales price for the spoiled units.

The marketing manager disagrees because she stresses that the company's salespersons will be lucky if they find a buyer for the spoiled units. Even though she plays it safe by emphasizing that the salesperson must exert extra marketing effort in finding a buyer for the spoiled units, she has no real fear that they cannot find a buyer. Instead she proposes the approach of recording only a memorandum entry at the time spoilage occurred indicating the number of units spoiled. At the time of sale, the cash proceeds are to be credited to an Other Income account.

The production manager, instead, argues that this spoilage is due to the nature of Job No. X20 and its related unique specifications. Thus, the approach he suggests is to record the 100 units at their expected market value in a Spoiled Goods Inventory account. The difference in the cost and the market value is assigned to Factory Overhead Control—Loss on Spoiled Goods using this approach.

The vice president of personnel agrees with the approach suggested by the production manager except that she prefers recording the difference between the market value of the spoilage and the original cost as an operating, nonmanufacturing expense rather than as a part of factory overhead.

Required:

a. Evaluate each of the approaches suggested by the four managers.
b. Indicate which of these four methods, if any, is the appropriate one to use in this case. If you do not agree with any of these methods, describe the method you would prefer.

C21–23 Lot Sizes for Bottleneck and Nonbottleneck Operations (L.O. 6)

Middle Company's production supervisor, L. Farmer, doesn't understand the directive he recently received from the production vice president. The directive indicates that changes are being made in the manufacturing operation. Farmer is no longer to have long production runs of big batches of parts. Instead, the company is adopting a pull manufacturing process and he is to run smaller batches.

Farmer begins thinking about the impact this directive will have on his performance. He knows that long runs result in a better ratio of direct to indirect labor. He further reasons that when a troublesome operation is running well, one should produce many parts and avoid having to run them again for a long time. He believes that he should avoid stopping the run because experience has taught him that frequent setups and changeovers result in more scrap and downtime. Frequent setups also result in less efficient use of direct labor and an increased use of indirect labor. He knows his performance will suffer if he adopts the shorter runs. Based on this line of reasoning, Farmer believes his past practice of running only large batches, regardless of the need for the parts processed or the priority of the batch, is justified.

Required:

a. Discuss why the traditional procedure of running large lot sizes is often financially inappropriate especially if a company has both bottleneck and nonbottleneck operations.
b. Advise the production supervisor regarding lot sizes for bottleneck operations and for nonbottleneck operations.

Payroll Accounting and Incentive Plans

CHAPTER OBJECTIVES

After studying this chapter, you should be able to:

1. Record labor distribution, employee withholdings, and payroll taxes.

2. Prepare adjusting and reversing labor entries.

3. Accrue vacation, holiday, and bonus pay.

4. Apply varieties of incentive wage plans and evaluate their impact on total product cost.

5. Evaluate the impact of JIT on incentive programs.

| PRACTICAL APPLICATION BOX | **Activity-Based Accounting Makes It Easy to Identify Cost Savings** |

Weyerhaeuser's Payroll Service Department uses activity-based costing to measure payroll efficiency. After establishing the major services of a payroll department and the related activities, allocating the employee time spent on each activity determines their costs. Weyerhaeuser asks its employees to estimate their time spent on each function over one year. By recommending a one-year time frame, cost profiles include activities that occur annually such as W–2s or budgeting. By providing departmental cost data, employees have the knowledge to develop and implement process efficiencies that result in cost reductions.

From: R. Brian Pederson, "Weyerhaeuser: Sreamlining Payroll," *Management Accounting*, October 1991, pp. 38–41.

Introduction

In many companies, labor as a percentage of total production costs is decreasing due to automation. Nevertheless, all companies need payroll accounting, which is complicated because of the many amounts deducted from employees' wages. These deductions include federal income taxes and social security taxes (FICA) and some voluntary withholdings, such as medical insurance premiums and charitable contributions. Each pay period employers withhold payroll deductions and remit them periodically to the appropriate parties. In addition to deductions from employees' wages, accountants must record the employer's payroll taxes. Because of its complexity, payroll accounting often is the first system that companies automate so they can prepare payroll checks and records in a timely, accurate manner.

Previous examples in this book have assumed that all employees' wages and salaries were payable directly to them. This chapter explains how to correctly account for payroll costs and liabilities. We also examine other aspects of employment such as legislation, fringe benefits, and incentive compensation plans.

Withholdings from Employees' Wages (L.O. 1)

Voluntary Withholdings

Employees voluntarily agree to have various payments deducted from their pay. The employer remits these deductions to the appropriate party on the employee's behalf. Examples of voluntary withholding include:

1. Union dues.
2. Pension funds.
3. Medical and life insurance premiums.
4. Withholding for the purchase of savings bonds or other savings deposits.
5. Charitable contributions.

For any such amount withheld, the company must establish a separate liability account that is reduced when the deduction is remitted to the appropriate party. For example, if the company has agreed to withhold union dues from employees' wages, they establish a liability account called Union Dues Collected at the time they make deductions. At specified intervals, they forward union dues to the union treasurer; then they debit the liability account and credit Cash. Often, companies share the costs of health and life insurance plans with employees. The amounts withheld from employees represent liabilities until payment to the insurer.

Another form of payroll deduction results from the payment of payroll advances. Due to the nature of their jobs and their travel requirements, salespersons and other employees often request payroll advances. Employees may also ask for advances for personal reasons. Prior authorization from the employee's supervisor, from a person in a higher management level, or from the treasurer's department is necessary because control over these advances is very important. After making such advances, accountants debit an asset account called Payroll Advances, Salespersons' Advances, or Employee Advances, and credit Cash. At the time accountants make the advance, they record the repayment terms. When accountants deduct the advance from the employee's payroll check, they credit a Payroll Advance account. Before agreeing to handle optional payroll deductions, the company should recognize the additional accounting costs involved and establish a policy regarding the type of deductions made.

Involuntary Withholdings

Various laws require that the employer withhold from the pay of employees certain taxes and remit these amounts periodically to the proper authorities. These tax withholdings are

1. *Income tax.* Federal, state, and city income tax authorities furnish tables indicating the amount to be withheld.

2. *Social security taxes (FICA).* In January 1991, the social security tax deduction (FICA) split into two parts: the Old Age Survivors and Disability Insurance (FICA:OASDI) and the FICA Medicare tax. The law provided that in 1992 employees would pay 6.2 percent on wages up to $55,500 and the FICA Medicare tax at 1.45 percent on wages up to $130,200. Congress annually reviews the maximum amount of wages subject to FICA and often increases both the rate and maximum amount. Because changes are almost certain and no single rate is likely to be correct for the year you use this text, we assume a total FICA tax rate of 8 percent.

Before starting work, employees must complete an **Employee's Withholding Exemption Certificate (Form W–4)** on which they indicate the income tax exemptions they claim. The federal income tax deduction from an employee's gross wages depends on the amount of the employee's earnings and the exemptions claimed on Form W–4. Employers must furnish each employee with a **Wage and Tax Statement (Form W–2)** on or before January 31 of the year following the one in which wages were earned. If employment ends before December 31, employers must provide a W–2 form within 30 days of the last payday. Form W–2 indicates wages earned and taxes withheld.

Payroll Accounting Entries (L.O. 1)

Despite the variations found in practice, payroll accounting entries are of two basic types: One, recording salary and wage distribution, together with the liabilities from employee withholdings and net earnings. Two, recording the employer's payroll taxes. Understanding these two basic labor entries allows you to adjust to any payroll system found in practice.

1. Salary and Wage Distribution

The payroll distribution requires entries to record the direct labor costs to Work in Process Inventory, indirect labor costs to Factory Overhead Control, and marketing and administrative wages and salaries to their respective control accounts. In this process, accountants record the amount of employee withholdings from gross pay as liabilities and the net earnings in a liability account titled Payroll Payable, Accrued Salaries, or Salaries Payable. Voluntary and involuntary employee withholdings are not additional costs to the employer; an employer's cost is the employees' gross pay. However, accountants must make accounting entries to record these deductions from gross pay to arrive at net pay.

The following general ledger entry records and pays a particular payroll of $3,910 in which direct labor workers earned $2,300; indirect labor workers, $710; marketing personnel, $400; and administrative personnel, $500:

Work in Process Inventory	2,300.00	
Factory Overhead Control	710.00	
Marketing Expense Control	400.00	
Administrative Expense Control	500.00	
FICA Taxes Withheld or Payable (required liability)		312.80
Federal Income Tax Withheld (required liability)		899.50
State Income Tax Withheld (required liability)		203.00
Union Dues Collected (liability)		125.00
Health Insurance Payable (liability)		180.00
Payroll Payable (liability)		2,189.70
Payroll Payable	2,189.70	
Cash		2,189.70

The preceding entry shows the total effect on the general ledger accounts. However, it may not be possible to record the total effect at one time. At the time the company pays wages, the data may not be available to record the wage and salary distribution. In that case, accountants establish a temporary ledger account called Payroll for deferred recording purposes. The following entries use a deferred payroll distribution. At the end of each pay period, the financial accountant records:

Payroll	3,910.00	
FICA Taxes Payable		312.80
Federal Income Tax Withheld		899.50
State Income Tax Withheld		203.00
Union Dues Collected		125.00
Health Insurance Payable		180.00
Payroll Payable		2,189.70
Payroll Payable	2,189.70	
Cash		2,189.70

At the end of each month or some other period, the cost accountant analyzes the balance in the Payroll Summary account. Assume there were several additional pay periods in the month and the Payroll account has a balance of $6,010. The cost accountant determines that direct labor costs account for $2,810 (including $2,300 incurred in the first pay period); indirect labor of $1,270 (including $710 incurred in the first pay period); marketing salaries of $1,015 (including $400 incurred in the first pay period); and $915 of administrative wages and salaries (including $500 incurred in the first pay period). In this case, this is the labor distribution entry:

Work in Process Inventory	2,810.00	
Factory Overhead Control	1,270.00	
Marketing Expense Control	1,015.00	
Administrative Expense Control	915.00	
Payroll		6,010.00

2. Payroll Taxes

The second type of labor entry involves recording the taxes levied directly on the employer for the benefit of employees. The primary payroll taxes include social security (FICA), federal and state unemployment taxes, and state workers' compensation insurance. These are not withholdings from the individual employee's payroll check, but are additional labor costs to the employer.

FICA. Unless they are in excluded classes of employment, all employers must withhold from employees and contribute an equal amount to the FICA taxes withheld from their employees. According to current regulations, the FICA tax applies to earnings up to a maximum per employee, per year. An employee making $70,000 in 1992 would pay FICA:OASDI tax on only the first $55,500, for instance.

Federal and State Unemployment Taxes. Under the Federal Unemployment Tax Act, employers of one or more workers in covered employment must pay an unemployment insurance tax. The law specifies the annual earnings base on which to compute this tax. Employees do not contribute to federal unemployment tax. Various states require employers to contribute to a state unemployment compensation plan. Some states also tax employees, but not at the same rate as they tax employers. Employers with few employees collecting unemployment compensation receive certain credits.

State Workers' Compensation Insurance. Workers' compensation insurance compensates workers or their survivors for losses caused by employment-related accidents or occupational diseases. Only employers pay this tax; the rate they pay varies according to degree of occupational risk. This tax is determined by state law, with the benefits and premiums differing among states.

Recording Payroll Taxes. Accountants can use two approaches to record an employer's payroll taxes on factory salaries and wages. One is to treat the taxes as a direct cost; the second is to treat them as an indirect cost. Treating payroll taxes as a direct cost means including them as an additional cost of direct labor and accumulating them in the Work in Process Inventory account. Even though accountants recognize the theoretical soundness of the direct cost approach, many do not believe the extra refinement is worth the effort. The practical approach to payroll taxes is to treat them as an indirect cost, which means including them in Factory Overhead Control.

Employers pay FICA and federal and state unemployment taxes on employees' first earnings ($55,500 for FICA:OASDI, $130,200 for FICA Medicare tax, $7,000 for federal unemployment, and generally $7,000 for state unemployment in 1992). Therefore, it is more correct to record an amount for payroll taxes based on a predetermined rate assigned to the salaries and wages rather than the actual amount. The predetermined rate smooths costs over the entire year; otherwise, companies would overcharge early-year cost objects and undercharge later-year cost objects. For simplicity, however, we are using actual tax rates for illustrations, rather than predetermined rates.

The timing of the employer's liability for payroll taxes differs. Some companies record the payroll tax as a liability when employees earn the salaries and wages, while other employers wait until paying the salaries and wages because the legal liability is not incurred until then. However, payroll taxes are related to incurring salary and wage costs and not to their payment. Thus, the preferred treatment is to accrue payroll tax liability at the time salary and wage costs are recognized. The practice of waiting to recognize the liability at payroll payment is acceptable if the amounts are not material and if a company follows this practice consistently.

Data from the previous example illustrate the two approaches for recording the employer's payroll taxes. We use only three payroll taxes under the assumption that all wages are subject to these: 8 percent FICA tax, a 2.7 percent state unemployment tax, and 0.8 percent federal unemployment tax.

Employer's payroll tax treated as direct cost

Work in Process Inventory (11.5 percent total tax on $2,300 direct factory labor)	264.50	
Factory Overhead Control (11.5 percent total tax on $710 indirect factory labor)	81.65	
Marketing Expense Control (11.5 percent total tax on $400 marketing labor)	46.00	
Administrative Expense Control (11.5 percent total tax on $500 administrative labor)	57.50	
FICA Taxes Payable (8 percent × $3,910)		312.80
State Unemployment Taxes Payable (2.7 percent × $3,910)		105.57
Federal Unemployment Taxes Payable (0.8 percent × $3,910)		31.28

Employer's payroll tax treated as indirect cost

Factory Overhead Control (11.5 percent total tax on $2,300 direct and $710 indirect factory labor)	346.15	
Marketing Expense Control (tax on marketing labor as above)	46.00	
Administrative Expense Control (tax on administrative labor as above)	57.50	
FICA Taxes Payable		312.80
State Unemployment Taxes Payable		105.57
Federal Unemployment Taxes Payable		31.28

Note that the entries for the employer's payroll taxes on marketing and administrative salaries and labor are identical regardless of the method used for factory salaries and wages.

The preceding illustration follows the typical practice of combining the employees' and employer's contributions to FICA into one account titled FICA Taxes Payable. However, accountants could use an account titled FICA Taxes Withheld to record the employees' deductions and another liability account titled FICA Taxes Payable to record the employer's tax.

This entry records the payment of the $312.80 FICA tax withheld from the employees' gross wages and the $312.80 FICA tax reflecting the employer's contribution:

FICA Taxes Payable ($312.80 employees' withholdings + $312.80 employer's contribution)	625.60	
Cash		625.60

Employers must deposit the federal income tax and FICA withheld together with the employer's FICA tax to either an authorized commercial bank depository or a Federal Reserve Bank by a designated time. In addition, the employer must pay state and federal unemployment taxes. The following summary indicates the journal entry that a company makes when paying these taxes. In all cases, they debit a liability account and credit Cash.

Federal Income Tax Withheld	XX	
State Income Tax Withheld	XX	
FICA Taxes Payable	XX	
State Unemployment Taxes Payable	XX	
Federal Unemployment Taxes Payable	XX	
Cash		XX

Adjusting and Reversing Salary and Wage Entries (L.O. 2)

In addition to the two basic payroll accounting entries just illustrated, the company may use adjusting and reversing labor entries. Adjusting entries record accrued payroll costs that properly match the period in which the employee earns compensation. If a company does not make adjusting entries to record accrued payroll costs, it misstates both its salary and wage costs and liabilities.

Assume that total earnings are $2,000 per day for direct labor workers, $1,000 for indirect labor, $500 for marketing personnel, and $750 for administrative personnel. Assume further that the company pays all employees working a five-day week every Friday for the previous week. If the company's accounting system is on a calendar year and December 31 is a Tuesday, the following adjusting journal entry should be dated as of December 31. (Note that the entry omits FICA tax and income tax liability on these wages.)

```
Work in Process Inventory ($2,000 × 2 days) . . . . . . . . . . . . . . . .  4,000
Factory Overhead Control ($1,000 × 2 days) . . . . . . . . . . . . . . . .  2,000
Marketing Expense Control ($500 × 2 days) . . . . . . . . . . . . . . . .  1,000
Administrative Expense Control ($750 × 2 days) . . . . . . . . . . . .  1,500
     Payroll Payable  . . . . . . . . . . . . . . . . . . . . . . . . . . . . . . . . . . . .            8,500
```

Most companies have a timing problem—they cannot pay payroll up to the day of earnings, so they often pay employees late. Some companies stagger payment throughout the week or month; for example, they pay Departments 1 to 20 on Monday, Departments 21 to 40 on Tuesday, and so forth. Under this plan, they make all payments 3 to 10 days after the end of the payroll period.

Reversing Labor Entry. To reverse the adjusting entry made at the end of the preceding period, companies use reversing entries. They date reversing entries the first day of the next period. Reversing entries for salary and wage costs are optional, as companies can achieve the same result regardless of whether they use reversing entries.

A company can date a reversing entry as of the first working day of the next period, as it closes the balances in the three expense control accounts through a closing entry at year-end. A company can distribute the entire gross wages and payroll tax for the first pay period in the new year to the Work in Process Inventory and the three expense controls. The credits in the expense control accounts resulting from the reversing entry offset the gross wage and payroll tax expenses recorded for the first pay period. The net amount remaining in the expense control accounts represents the total wage costs incurred in the new accounting period. A company could date the following reversing entries on the first working day of the next accounting period:

```
Payroll Payable . . . . . . . . . . . . . . . . . . . . . . . . . . . . . . . . . . . . . . . . . . . .  8,500
     Work in Process Inventory . . . . . . . . . . . . . . . . . . . . . . . . . . . .            4,000
     Factory Overhead Control . . . . . . . . . . . . . . . . . . . . . . . . . . . .            2,000
     Marketing Expense Control . . . . . . . . . . . . . . . . . . . . . . . . . . .            1,000
     Administrative Expense Control . . . . . . . . . . . . . . . . . . . . . . .            1,500
```

Government Legislation Affecting Employment (L.O. 1)

Government regulations cover various aspects of employment such as minimum and overtime wages, discrimination, and job hazards. Complying with these regulations normally falls within the scope of a Personnel Department, and this administration is a definite cost to the firm. For example, the Fair Labor Standards Act of 1938—called the Wages and Hours Law—established a minimum wage per hour with time-and-a-half pay for those working more than 40 hours in one week. However, certain types of workers and organizations are exempt from the act's provisions. In 1964, Congress passed an amendment to the Civil Rights Act. Title VII specifically prohibits discrimination for reasons of race, creed, color, national origin, age, physical disability, political affiliation, and sex. Title VII established the Equal Employment Opportunity Commission (EEOC) to administer the law and to receive, investigate, and reconcile employment discrimination charges under Title VII. The commission's responsibility is to ensure that all Americans are considered for hiring and promotion on the basis of their ability and qualifications, without regard to race, color, religion, sex, or national origin. Another government regulation that affects employment is the

Occupational Safety and Health Act (OSHA). While protecting the worker and the environment, the act has had a costly impact on many companies. OSHA has required them to invest millions of dollars to change production methods to conform to OSHA regulations.

Indirect or Fringe Benefits (L.O. 3)

In addition to wages and salaries, employees receive other types of employment compensation that may not directly or immediately benefit them. Many of these require a year-end labor cost entry. Briefly, some of the major items include:

Holidays. Each year, most firms pay employees for certain days that they do not work.

Vacations. Most firms have a policy of granting vacations with pay to their employees; the length of vacation usually relates to tenure with the company. For example, a company may grant annual two-week vacations for employees with five years or less of service and annual three-week vacations for those with more than five years of service.

Bonus Pay. Firms may reward employees—especially those in managerial positions—with bonuses based on the amount by which a company, division, or plant exceeds a specified income target. The agreement between employer and employee determines the amount; companies often calculate bonuses at year-end. For example, a company may give the manager of Plant A a bonus of 1 percent of all net income (after bonuses and taxes) that exceeds $2 million for the year. In all instances, companies must spell out the specifics so the bonus plan is an incentive to increase income. Otherwise, misunderstandings and hard feelings result. Because bonus payments based on income are not known until after the period ends, accountants estimate and accrue them throughout the accounting period.

Insurance. Many firms pay all or part of their employees' premiums for medical, dental, or life insurance. These are definite benefits to employees.

Pensions. Pensions are an employee benefit that most firms provide; however, employees may not receive them until many years after earning them. The basic concept behind a pension is that employees earn this benefit each year they work, and they defer the receipt of cash payments until leaving the firm. It is not possible to generalize about pension plans; the agreement between the employees and management determines the actual specifics.

Stock and Thrift Plans. Some companies have **thrift plans** that usually allow employees to borrow on a thrift fund or to purchase company stock. Another common compensation plan, primarily for salaried persons, is stock options; basically such plans grant employees options (rights) to purchase a certain number of shares of company stock at a specified price within a certain period. The employees' compensation is the difference between the option price and the price of the stock on the date they exercise the option.

Holidays, Vacations, and Bonus Pay

Even though companies calculate bonuses at specified points, and employees take holidays and vacations at irregular times throughout the year, employees earn these benefits throughout the year. They represent expenses of the entire year, rather than the period in which employees receive the benefits.

Therefore, Work in Process Inventory should accumulate vacation, holiday, and bonus payments earned by direct labor workers as additional labor cost. Companies rarely use this approach in practice, however, because it is difficult to apply. The more common procedure is to classify vacation and bonus payments to direct labor workers as indirect costs chargeable to the Factory Overhead Control account with the payments made to indirect labor workers. Companies should charge vacation, holiday, and bonus payments for the marketing and administrative staff to their respective control accounts.

Most companies do not attempt to classify vacations, holiday pay, and bonus pay as a direct labor cost; instead they use the simpler approach of accumulating these costs in the Factory Overhead Control. However, the problem still exists of charging the costs of these employee benefits to the accounting period in which the benefits are earned. Basically, companies should spread the cost of these employee benefits over the entire year by including an estimate for vacation, holiday, and bonus pay in the predetermined factory overhead rate. There are several ways to develop an estimate of the cost of holidays, vacations, and bonuses to charge to each accounting period. Accountants may estimate the total amount for each employee or for a homogeneous group of employees.

Accruing Vacations, Holiday Pay, and Bonus Pay. To illustrate the accrual of these benefits, assume that an employee earns $80 per day. The union contract, company policy, or employment agreement specifies the employee is to receive 10 working days of vacation and 5 working days of holidays. In addition, at fiscal year-end, the employee is to receive a bonus of 0.1 percent of company income. The company expects total net income to be $1 million. The accountant estimates benefit payments as follows:

Vacations (10 days × $80 per day)	$800	
Holidays (5 days × $80 per day)	400	$1,200
Bonus (0.1% of $1,000,000 expected net income) ...		1,000

The company spreads the cost of these employee benefits over the productive labor time of each employee. Assume the company pays employees weekly and spreads these employee benefit costs over 49 weeks [52 weeks − (2 weeks of vacation + 1 week of holidays)] as follows:

$$\frac{\$1,200}{49 \text{ weeks}} = \$24.49 \text{ per week for vacations and holiday pay}$$

$$\frac{\$1,000}{49 \text{ weeks}} = \$20.41 \text{ per week for bonus pay}$$

The following entries use a Payroll summary account rather than illustrate the withholding for taxes for five days of productive labor for an employee:

Work in Process (5 days × $80 per day)	400.00	
Factory Overhead Control ($24.49 + $20.41)	44.90	
Payroll		400.00
Accrued Vacation and Holiday Pay		24.49
Accrued Bonus Pay		20.41

Payment for Holidays and Vacations. The company records withholdings from the employees' gross pay when paying them for holidays and vacations. The following journal entry records vacation pay received by the employee in the previous example:

Accrued Vacation and Holiday Pay	800.00	
Federal Income Tax Withheld		160.00
State Income Tax Withheld		48.00
FICA Taxes Payable (8% × $800)		64.00
Payroll Payable		528.00
Payroll Payable	528.00	
Cash		528.00

A company makes an entry similar to the preceding one for bonus payments. Rather than calculate the cost of these employee benefits each pay period, a company may use a percentage of cost or time. For example, assume that the previous employee works 1,960 productive hours during the year. Because the company expects vacation and holidays to total 15 days or 120 hours (15 days × 8 hours assuming an 8-hour workday), it accrues a liability equal to 6.122 percent of wages every pay period.

$$\frac{120 \text{ nonproductive hours}}{1,960 \text{ productive hours}} = 6.122 \text{ percent}$$

Administrative and other personnel, who receive fixed salaries regardless of the hours worked, receive holidays, vacations, and bonuses. A company can treat the cost of these employee benefits in the manner illustrated for direct labor workers to achieve proper matching of costs and benefits. However, some companies consider vacation pay and holiday pay as a cost of the period in which employees receive the benefit. Usually, a company does not temporarily employ other persons to assume the duties of administrators. While they are taking holidays or vacations, their workloads accumulate.

Overtime Premium Pay

Another added employee benefit is **overtime premium pay.** The Fair Labor Standards Act established a minimum wage for most nonfarm workers engaged in interstate commerce, prohibited child labor, and required time-and-a-half pay for those working more than 40 hours per week. For example, assume a company pays an individual $12 per hour. If the individual works 44 hours in a week, the payroll clerk computes the weekly earnings as follows:

Regular earnings (40 hours × $12)		$480
Overtime pay:		
At regular rate (4 hours × $12)	$48	
Overtime premium (4 hours × $6)	24	72
Total weekly gross earnings		$552

Accountants debit total hours at the regular pay for direct labor workers to Work in Process, as the following entry shows:

Work in Process Inventory (44 hours × $12)	528.00	
FICA Taxes Payable		39.65
Federal Income Taxes Withheld		105.35
Payroll Payable		383.00

In addition to federally mandated time-and-a-half pay, a union contract may specify additional premium pay. Examples include double pay for Sunday work and time-and-a-half pay for working more than eight hours per day. Companies should segregate such overtime earnings into the base pay component and the premium pay component for planning, control, and reporting purposes. A Work in Process Inventory account should accumulate the overtime premium pay as a cost of the job or department if the demands of the job or process cause the overtime hours. For example, assume a company accepts an order on Monday with a promised delivery date of Wednesday and requires its workers to work overtime to complete the order. Accountants should charge the premium pay to this job in addition to the regular direct labor charge for total hours computed at the regular rate. When employees work overtime because the workload is heavier than normal and the company cannot attribute the overtime to a specific job, the Work in Process Inventory account should accumulate only the total hours at the regular rate as a direct labor cost. Accountants should charge the overtime premium pay to the Factory Overhead Control account. In determining the overhead application rate, management should include an estimate for overtime premium pay when they expect overtime.

Shift Premium

Shift premium pay, similar to overtime pay, affects labor costs. Either a union contract agreement or company policy may require that evening- or night-shift employees receive a higher wage rate to compensate for the less desirable schedule. It is not logical to charge larger direct labor costs for a finished unit simply because it is manufactured on an evening or night shift. The preferred treatment is to accumulate the shift premium amount in the Factory Overhead Control account rather than to charge the entire wage (the regular pay and the shift premium) to Work in Process Inventory. In determining the factory overhead application rate, total indirect expenses should include an estimate of the shift premium. For example, assume that an employee on the night shift receives $12.40 per hour rather than the regular day-shift rate of $12 per hour. This entry distributes the weekly wage for this night-shift employee:

```
Work in Process Inventory (40 hours × $12) . . . . . . . . . . . . . . . . . . . . . . 480
Factory Overhead Control—Shift Premium (40 hours × $0.40) . . . . . . . . .  16
    Payroll . . . . . . . . . . . . . . . . . . . . . . . . . . . . . . . . . . . . . . . . . . . . . .       496
```

This approach facilitates the comparison of payroll costs for different work shifts.

Incentive Compensation Plans (L.O. 4)

In addition to meeting payroll deadlines and government requirements, management is concerned about maximizing the productivity of labor. One of the tools they use to achieve this goal is some form of **incentive compensation plan.** This provides additional compensation to employees whose performance exceeds a predetermined goal or standard. Companies adopt incentive plans for these reasons:

1. To give employees an opportunity to earn additional pay by performing at a more efficient level.

2. To reduce the cost per unit of finished products. Even though wages may increase with an incentive compensation plan, management does not expect

EXHIBIT 22–1   Effect on Unit Conversion Cost after Wage Incentive Plan Is Introduced

	Units Produced	Cost per Time Period		Cost per Unit		
		Direct Labor	Overhead	Direct Labor	Overhead	Total Conversion
Before initiating incentive plan	600	$180	$120	$0.30	$0.20	$0.50
After initiating incentive plan	750	240	120	0.32	0.16	0.48

factory overhead to increase significantly. They expect conversion cost per unit to decrease after spreading the increased direct labor cost and lower per unit factory overhead cost over additional finished units. For example, Exhibit 22–1 assumes workers produced 600 units before and 750 units after introduction of an incentive plan. Although direct labor cost increased from $180 to $240, we assume factory overhead did not change. The labor cost per unit has increased from $0.30 to $0.32, but the decrease in overhead costs per unit has been large enough to produce a lower total conversion cost per unit. The example in Exhibit 22–1 indicates that productivity, measured by units produced, has increased; however, incentive systems cannot guarantee higher production and greater efficiency.

Individual Incentive Plans

Several incentive plans are available, including the straight piecework plan, the 100 Percent Bonus Plan, and versions of Taylor Differential Piece Rate, Gantt Task, and the Emerson Efficiency System. As an example, a straight piecework plan computes the production standard in minutes per piece and then transforms it into money per piece. Assuming time studies showed that one unit required two minutes of time, the standard becomes 30 units per hour. If the worker's base rate is $9 per hour, the piece rate is $0.30. If the worker completes 260 units in an eight-hour day, the pay is $78 (260 units × $.30). Workers are often guaranteed a base pay rate even if they do not meet the standard.

Some incentive plans express standards in units per hour rather than in money. For example, the following computations illustrate an incentive plan in which employees receive a guaranteed rate of $12 per hour and a premium of 70 percent of the time saved on production exceeding the standard of 50 units per hour. Assume an employee has produced 450 units on Monday and 525 units on Tuesday during the eight hours worked each day. The daily earnings would be:

$$\text{Monday: } \frac{50 \text{ units}}{50} = 1 \text{ hour saved} \times \$12 \times 70\% = \qquad \$ \quad 8.40 \text{ premium}$$
$$\underline{\qquad 96.00 \text{ (8 hours} \times \$12)}$$
$$\$104.40$$

$$\text{Tuesday: } \frac{125 \text{ units}}{50} = 2.5 \text{ hours saved} \times \$12 = \$30 \times 70\% = \$ \quad 21.00 \text{ premium}$$
$$\underline{\qquad 96.00}$$
$$\$117.00$$

E X H I B I T 22–2   Daily Earnings Summary—Eight-Hour Day*

	Guaranteed Hourly Minimum Wage	Regular Wage	Bonus	Total
Employee A . . .	$8.00	$64.00	$4.00 (50 units × $0.08)	$68.00
Employee B . . .	6.00	48.00	3.00 (50 units × $0.06)	51.00
Employee C . . .	7.00	56.00	3.50 (50 units × $0.07)	59.50

*Standard production, 400 units; actual production, 450 units.

An incentive plan's effect on reducing the unit cost of finished products while providing the employees an opportunity to earn additional wages is important in evaluating a plan. As with all wage payment plans, managers should explain the mechanics of the system to production employees so they can compute their incentive payments. Unfortunately, in practice some incentive plans are so complex that this is not always possible.

Group Incentive Plans

Determining the individual production of each employee is impossible in some production processes because operations require the joint effort of a group of employees. When a process requires teamwork, one individual cannot increase output without increasing the productivity of the entire crew. Because individual incentive plans are impossible to implement under these conditions, companies use group incentive plans.

Exhibit 22–2 illustrates bonus computations under a group incentive plan. Each worker receives a guaranteed minimum hourly wage; in addition, each receives a bonus equal to 1 percent of the worker's hourly guaranteed minimum for each unit produced over standard. Standard production is 50 units per hour or 400 units per eight-hour day. Actual production for the group is 450 units.

Group incentive plans reduce the amount of clerical effort required to compute a bonus. Another advantage is employees have a stronger incentive to work together as a team and may be more cooperative because each employee's bonus depends on the group's output. Also, the group may apply pressure on slower workers because the bonus calculated depends on the group's efforts.

Group incentive plans have a danger of encouraging too much competition between individual departments and thereby threatening goal congruence. **Suboptimization** occurs when managers ignore what is best for the overall company while improving the profit performance of their own departments. Suboptimization occurs when individual managers disregard major company goals and interrelationships and focus their attention solely on their own divisions' activities. Often, incentive plans force employees to look only at short-run benefits for themselves rather than at long-run benefits for both themselves and the company. In addition, incentive plans can lead to much quarreling within the team because individual members may believe they are doing more than a fair share of the group's tasks.

Controls on Incentive Plans

Regardless of the incentive plan used, companies must establish controls to ensure that their plans work properly. A common incentive plan includes a

EXHIBIT 22–3   Weekly Earnings Summary

Employee A	Actual Production	Turns in	Secret Reserve Balance	Daily Earnings
Monday	18	16	2	$48
Tuesday	22	24	0	52*
Wednesday	20	17	3	48
Thursday	23	26	0	54†

*$48 guaranteed minimum + ($1 × 4 units) = $52.
†$48 guaranteed minimum + ($1 × 6 units) = $54.

guaranteed minimum rate plus a piece rate for work completed. Companies that provide a guaranteed wage regardless of the worker's output need controls to prevent employees from improperly recording direct versus indirect time. Also, some employees may cheat by hiding excess production in their work areas or lockers so they receive only the guaranteed wage that day. Then, the next day the employee may turn in the overproduction with that day's production and receive an excessive bonus. Exhibit 22–3 illustrates one way Employee A has misused the incentive plan. Assume that the guaranteed daily wage is $48. After producing 20 units, each worker receives an additional $1 per unit bonus. As can be seen in Exhibit 22–3, Employee A has increased earnings on Tuesday and Thursday by including excess production from the previous day in the units turned in. Supervisors and timekeepers should be aware of the possibility of this happening and check variations in the production reported by individual employees.

Impact of JIT on Incentive Plans (L.O. 5)

Just-in-time (JIT) production policies often make traditional incentive plans invalid. The objective of JIT is to keep inventory at a minimum and eliminate much of the warehousing and storage costs. Lot sizes are small, and the plant workload is uniform. Keeping employees working to produce inventory not yet needed is contradictory to the JIT philosophy. Whenever a company slows down or stops its machines or production line, workers can use their off time performing a variety of tasks. They will probably take more pride in their work and be more content performing these tasks:

1. Housekeeping to manage stock on hand, put things in order, arrange work sites, discuss how to maintain work flow at the bottlenecks, and prepare notices and manuals.
2. Maintenance of machines, routine equipment, and tools.
3. Machine setups so workers can prepare for the next use of the same machine or another machine.
4. Educational or training activities help workers acquire skills for using other machines or different applications of the same machine.
5. Self-improvement seminars can help employees with any problems associated with drugs, alcohol, and so on.

6. Creativity experimentation programs encourage employees to develop better production techniques or different products.

7. Socialization gives workers an opportunity to meet employees that work with the product after they complete their tasks as this interchange may lead to suggestions for improvements.

8. Versatility programs train employees on other machines, to reduce the chance that absenteeism would antagonize an existing bottleneck.

9. Customer relations programs encourage employees to call customers and ask if they had any problems with products.

10. Team management allows workers to make internal work assignments, make production trade-off decisions, diagnose and solve production problems, and select personnel replacements for their team.

Avoid Creating Busy Work

Not only should managers avoid creating work to keep employees busy but they should also monitor a policy of allowing workers free time once they finish their workloads. In this case, workers may work as fast as possible to enjoy extra time if they do not have to keep working. In that case, there is a greater possibility of increased defects because of careless work. An effective quality control program should prevent this from occurring.

Also, if certain department workers continually finish early and have extra free time, managers should reexamine the workload of the employees' department in relation to bottlenecks. Managers need to reconsider the flow of production process to utilize the extra time of one department to prevent bottlenecks. Above all, managers must control the down time with an adequate maintenance plan. The malfunctioning of certain equipment stops the whole production process. Therefore, managers must prepare a systematic maintenance schedule to minimize down time loss.

Under JIT if a worker's output during a day is lower than expected, bottlenecks either before or after the worker are the likely cause. Either situation compels workers to stop producing through no fault of their own. Thus, the adoption of the JIT production philosophy without a change in previous labor efficiency measures confuses both workers and managers. Also, a company must revise its incentive plans to reflect the impact of this change.

Summary

The importance of maintaining employees' morale through prompt and correct payment of wages, and the size of employers' expenditures for labor services, emphasize the need for timely and proper accounting in personnel services. However, given the various labor-related costs, labor accounting involves many complexities.

Companies often introduce incentive wage systems to lower the unit conversion cost while also giving workers an opportunity to earn additional wages. Companies use group incentive plans when the work flow requires a team effort and it is not possible to determine the number of units each employee produces. Group incentive wage systems may introduce some behavior problems because individual workers may believe they are doing more than a fair share of the group's workload. Regardless of the wage system used, it is imperative that workers understand how to calculate gross and net pay.

In traditional manufacturing systems, direct labor is generally considered to be a variable cost. In practice, however, it is normally a semivariable cost because a temporary decrease in product demand normally does not result in extensive production worker layoffs. Instead, companies may provide employment to workers even though there is not enough work available to keep the full work force busy. After automating a production process, cost behavior changes significantly. Not only is there a sharp decrease in the proportion of product cost attributed to labor, but the remaining labor is also mostly a fixed cost. Additionally, keeping workers busy to produce inventory not yet needed is contradictory to the JIT concept. JIT, in turn, has a significant impact on a company's incentive plans.

Important Terms and Concepts

Form W–4, Employee's Withholding
  Exemption Certificate, 760
Form W–2, Wage and Tax
  Statement, 760
thrift plans, 765

overtime premium pay, 767
shift premium pay, 768
incentive compensation plans, 768
suboptimization, 770
Just-in-time (JIT), 771

Problem for Self-Study

Daily Earnings and Effective Hourly Rate Using Proposed Incentive Plans

Standard production in the Mary Noble Company is 45 units per hour. For the first week in June, a worker's record shows the following:

Monday	370 units	8 hours
Tuesday	390 units	8 hours
Wednesday	350 units	8 hours
Thursday	360 units	8 hours
Friday	380 units	8 hours

Management is considering the adoption of a different incentive plan and wants to use this representative worker's record to study the earnings using two proposed incentive plans.

With incentive Plan A, Noble guarantees workers a rate of $4.05 per hour and a premium of 70 percent of the time saved on production in excess of standard.

With incentive Plan B, the company pays workers $0.07 per unit when daily output is less than standard; $0.09 per unit when daily output is at standard or up to 5 percent more than standard; $0.10 per unit for all production when the daily output exceeds 5 percent more than standard.

Required:

Compute daily earnings and the effective rate per hour for each day using each of the incentive plans proposed.

Solution to Problem for Self-Study

MARY NOBLE COMPANY

Plan A

$$\frac{\$4.05}{45 \text{ units}} = \$0.09 \text{ per unit} \times 70\% = \$0.063 \text{ per unit}$$

$4.05 \times 8 \text{ hours} = \$32.40 \text{ guaranteed wage}$

	Daily Earnings	Effective Rate per Hour	
Monday	$ 33.03 ($32.40) + (10 units × $0.063)	$4.1288	($33.03 8 hours)
Tuesday	34.29 ($32.40) + (30 units × $0.063)	4.2863	($34.29 8 hours)
Wednesday	32.40 ($32.40) + (0 units × $0.063)	4.05	($32.40 8 hours)
Thursday	32.40 ($32.40) + (0 units × $0.063)	4.05	($32.40 8 hours)
Friday	33.66 ($32.40) + (20 units × $0.063)	4.2075	($33.66 8 hours)
Weekly earnings ...	$165.78		

Plan B
Standard production = 360 units
105% standard production = 378 units

	Daily Earnings	Effective Rate per Hour	
Monday	$ 33.30 (370 × $0.09)	$4.1625	($33.30 8 hours)
Tuesday	39.00 (390 × $0.10)	4.8750	($39.00 8 hours)
Wednesday	24.50 (350 × $0.07)	3.0625	($24.50 8 hours)
Thursday	32.40 (360 × $0.09)	4.0500	($32.40 8 hours)
Friday	38.00 (380 × $0.10)	4.7500	($38.00 8 hours)
Weekly earnings	$167.20		

Review Questions

1. How do companies demonstrate concern for their workers by the first assignment of robots?

2. Discuss the relation of a no-layoff policy and workers' acceptance of robots. What is a preferred approach when introducing automation?

3. What is the impact of JIT and newer management philosophies on incentive plans?

4. Suppose as a manufacturing company's cost accountant, you recognize the importance of understanding the production process. Periodically, you walk through the plant to reorient yourself to any changes occurring. On a recent trip, you notice several Finishing Department employees standing around the last 1½ hours each day waiting for the end of their work shift. Explain whether you should or should not report such actions to their supervisors.

5. As far as employee behavior is concerned, why is it important to have accurate, understandable methods for calculating payroll?

6. As a member of the management team, what factor would you consider most important when evaluating an incentive plan?

7. Discuss the advantages and the disadvantages of group incentive payroll plans.

8. Why might you advise companies to stagger payrolls throughout the week or month?

9. Explain the theory behind, and the accounting for, withholdings from employees' checks.

10. Indicate whether the employer or the employee pays the following taxes:
    a. Federal unemployment tax.
    b. Federal income tax.
    c. FICA tax.
    d. State unemployment tax.
    e. State income tax.

11. Discuss several factors that cause complexities in labor accounting.

12. Which account is usually charged for vacation, holiday, and bonus payments made to direct labor workers? Why?

CPA/CMA/CIA Multiple Choice Questions

1. (AICPA) A direct labor overtime premium should be charged to a specific job when the overtime is caused by the

   a. Increased overall level of activity.
   b. Customer's requirement for early completion of job.
   c. Management's failure to include the job in the production schedule.
   d. Management's requirement that the job be completed before the annual factory vacation closure.

2. (CIA) To comply with the matching principle, the cost of labor services of an employee who participates in the manufacturing of a product normally should be charged to the income statement in the period in which the:

   a. Work is performed.
   b. Employee is paid.
   c. Product is completed.
   d. Product is sold.

3. (CIA) The Gray Company has a staff of five clerks in its general accounting department. The three clerks who work during the day perform sundry accounting tasks; the two clerks who work in the evening are responsible for (1) collecting the cost data for the various jobs in process, (2) verifying manufacturing material and labor reports, and (3) supplying the production reports to the supervisors by the next morning. The salaries of these two clerks who work at night should be classified as

   a. Period costs.
   b. Opportunity costs.
   c. Product costs.
   d. Direct costs.

4. (AICPA) Regan Company operates its factory on a two-shift basis and pays a late-shift differential of 15 percent. Regan also pays a premium of 50 percent for overtime work. Since Regan manufactures only for stock, the cost system provides for uniform direct labor hourly charges for production done without regard to shift worked or work done on an overtime basis. Overtime and late-shift differentials are included in Regan's factory overhead application rate. The May 19X1 payroll for production workers is as follows:

Wages at base direct labor rates	$325,000
Shift differentials	25,000
Overtime premiums	10,000

   For the month of May 19X1, what amount of direct labor should Regan charge to work in process?

   a. $325,000.
   b. $335,000.
   c. $350,000.
   d. $360,000.

5. (CMA) Each unit of Product XK-46 requires three direct labor-hours. Employee benefit costs are treated as direct labor costs. Data on direct labor are as follows:

Number of direct employees	25
Weekly productive hours per employee	35
Estimated weekly wages per employee	$245
Employee benefits (related to weekly wages)	25%

The standard direct labor cost per unit of Product XK-46 is

   a. $21.00.
   b. $26.25.
   c. $29.40.
   d. $36.75.
   e. Some amount other than those given above.

Exercises

E22–1 Incentive Wage Plan (L.O. 4)

Flynn Company has installed an incentive wage system. Workers receive their guaranteed wage per hour and a premium of 70 percent of the time saved on production in excess of the standard 50 units per hour.

The production and guaranteed wage for an eight-hour day for two employees is

	Hourly Guaranteed Rate	Production	
		Monday	Tuesday
Abe Appleton	$13.75	380	475
Ben Brown	$13.00	450	525

Required:

Calculate the daily wages for the two employees.

E22–2 Vacation and Holiday Pay (L.O. 3)

Pauley, Inc., uses a payroll account to record its weekly payroll. The labor summary for March shows Pauley incurred $15,800 direct labor and $6,100 indirect labor. Vacation and holiday pay is charged to current production at a rate of 5 percent of total payroll and is treated as factory overhead. All wages are subject to an 8 percent FICA tax rate, 2.7 percent state unemployment tax rate, and 0.8 percent federal unemployment tax rate. Pauley treats payroll taxes as indirect costs.

Required:

Prepare the labor summary entry on March 30, distributing the payroll and recording payroll taxes and costs of vacations and holidays. Record subsidiary ledger accounts for factory overhead.

E22–3 Daily Earnings Using an Incentive Plan (L.O. 3)

Dapple Company pays its employees under an incentive plan. Employees receive a $9 per hour guaranteed rate plus a premium of 65 percent of time saved on production in excess of the standard 90 units per hour, assuming an eight-hour day. Sam Smith has produced 830 units on Thursday and 810 units on Friday.

Required:

Compute Smith's daily earnings for these two days.

E22–4 Treatment of Overtime Premium Pay (L.O. 1)

An employee at the Jay Company receives $13.50 per hour for a regular week of 40 hours. The employee worked 52 hours on Job No. 4168 and earned time-and-a-half for overtime hours for the week ending November 12. Jay Company uses a job order subsidiary ledger for work in process.

Required:

a. Prepare the entry to distribute the labor cost if the overtime premium is charged to factory overhead costs.

b. Prepare the entry to distribute the labor cost if the overtime premium is charged to the production worked on during the overtime hours.

E22–5 Introducing Robots into the Workplace (L.O. 5)

Several months ago to the surprise of all assembly-line workers and their supervisor in Department 24 of Parade Company, three men brought in a large power saw and began moving tools over to clear a space. They then commenced cutting a hole in the plant floor. When asked what they were doing, the three men replied that this was where the new automated system would be placed. No employee volunteered to point out that the robot was being installed directly over a joint in the concrete floor.

Workers resented having to walk around the hole in the floor. Rumors of job loss became widespread. Workers immediately called union management for information. When the robot arrived, employees were curious and expressed concern over potential job loss. However, managers were tight-lipped. Employees openly predicted that the robots "would never be able to complete the tasks as successfully as a human worker." In trying to debug the robot, no employee suggested any way to make it work. Finally, the company removed the robot.

Required:

a. Explain how Parade Company went wrong in introducing the robot.

b. Suggest improved ways to smooth the introduction of robots.

c. Describe what managers can do well in advance of introducing robots into their operations regarding future job requirements.

E22–6 Accounting for Vacation and Bonus Pay (L.O. 3)

Hottum Company has signed a union agreement specifying that all employees receive 20 working days of vacation. In addition to the paid vacation, each employee receives a bonus at year-end of 0.05 percent of net company income. A $500,000 net income is projected for the company.

Required:

a. Prepare the journal entry to record the total weekly cost for one employee who earns $40 for one day of productive labor. Assume a payroll summary account has previously been used and you are to distribute only the labor cost.

b. Prepare the journal entry when the employee in Requirement *a* receives the entire vacation pay. Assume $110 federal income tax, $38 state income tax, and 8 percent FICA tax are withheld.

c. Rather than calculate the cost of vacations each pay period, compute them as a percentage of productive labor cost for this employee, assuming a 40-hour week.

E22–7 Distribution of Payrolls Recording Vacation and Holiday Pay (L.O. 3)

Raleigh Company uses a payroll account to record its weekly payroll. The labor summary for March shows $7,600 indirect labor and $24,800 direct labor were incurred. Vacation and holiday pay is charged to current production at 7 percent of total payroll and is treated as factory overhead. All wages are subject to an 8 percent FICA tax rate, 2.7 percent state unemployment tax rate, and .8 percent federal unemployment tax rate.

Required:

Prepare the labor summary entry on March 30 distributing the payroll and recording payroll taxes and costs of vacations and holidays for factory overhead. Treat payroll taxes and vacation and holiday pay as indirect costs.

Problems

P22–8 Impact of Incentive Plan on Conversion Cost (L.O. 4)

The management of Teacher Company has recently adopted an incentive plan for its employees. Standards for each employee are expressed in time per unit of output. A performance efficiency ratio is computed for each employee by comparing actual output with standard output. This ratio is then applied against each employee's base rate. All employees are guaranteed $15 per hour whether or not they meet standard production. The labor time sheets for the week ended June 15 are as follows:

Employee	Hours Worked	Hourly Wage for Standard Production	Actual Output	Standard Units per Hour
Betty Burns	40	$18	796	20
Jim Carnes	40	20	440	10
Sue Jones	36	15	300	11
Bill York	40	16	1,050	25

Required:

a. Compute the gross wages for each employee.
b. Prior to the enactment of the incentive plan, the weekly output of the four employees was 2,400 units for the same number of hours worked. Total weekly labor costs were $2,560. Total factory overhead averaged $800 per week prior to the incentive plan, but it was $829 after the plan was enacted. Determine the conversion costs per unit prior to and after the enactment of the incentive plan.

P22–9 Control of Piecework (L.O. 4)

Payroll, Inc., has adopted an incentive plan. Employees earn 10 percent of their hourly minimum wage for each unit that they produce above standard. Because the nature of their jobs varies, a standard and hourly minimum are established for each job. Employees receive the guaranteed minimum wage if they fail to meet their daily standard. Employees work eight hours per day.

	Actual Output	Standard per Day	Minimum Hourly Wage
Employee Able:		50	$12.00
Monday	48		
Tuesday	56		
Wednesday	58		
Thursday	52		
Friday	54		
Employee Benton:		60	$13.50
Monday	45		
Tuesday	65		
Wednesday	40		
Thursday	80		
Friday	64		

Required:

a. Calculate each employee's wages.
b. Review these employees' outputs. Does your review lead you to believe that a control feature is needed? Explain your answer.

P22–10 Reversing Labor Entries and Recording Payroll Taxes (L.O. 1)

England Company pays its employees every two weeks on Friday. The last pay period of 19X1 ended on December 21; as a result, the company made the following adjusting entry on December 31:

Work in Process Inventory	1,000	
Factory Overhead Control	3,000	
Marketing Expense Control	1,000	
Administrative Expense Control	800	
Payroll Payable		5,800

Gross regular earnings for the first payroll ending on January 6, 19X2, were direct labor, $3,000; indirect labor, $6,000; sales and distribution personnel, $1,500; and administrative costs, $2,100. Because Job No. 20 required extra attention, the company incurred overtime premium pay totaling $780. Authorizations from employees to withhold contributions to the United Neighbors charitable fund of $700 and union dues of $500 were received. Income taxes of $3,180 were withheld. The following tax rates were in effect: 8 percent FICA tax; 0.8 percent federal unemployment taxes; and 2.7 percent state unemployment taxes. All wages were subject to these taxes.

Required:

a. Record the reversing entry for wages on January 1.
b. Assuming a reversing entry was made, prepare the entries on January 6 to record the labor costs and their subsequent payment.
c. Prepare the entries on January 6 assuming *no* reversing entry was made.
d. Prepare the entry to record payroll taxes, treating them as direct costs.
e. Prepare the entry to record the payment of all taxes that have accrued.

P22–11 Incentive Plan Evaluation (L.O. 4)

Fluid Corporation is considering two different incentive plans for its production employees. Plan A rewards group effort. For each full 200 units produced in excess of the weekly group standard of 6,600 units, each worker receives, in addition to a guaranteed hourly minimum, a bonus of 4 percent of a guaranteed hourly minimum.

Under Plan B, each worker receives a piece rate of $.20 per unit. In addition, for each unit over the standard of 60 units per hour, the worker receives a bonus of 25 percent of the regular piece rate. There is no guaranteed wage.

For the week ending June 30, 19X1, each employee worked 40 hours.

	Weekly Production in Units	Guaranteed Hourly Minimum (for Plan A)
Edward Kirk	2,500	$8.00
Sandra Miller	2,310	9.00
June Yates	2,460	8.25

Required:

a. Compute the gross earnings for each employee under:
   (1) Plan A.
   (2) Plan B.
b. Evaluate the plans and indicate which you believe is more appropriate in these circumstances.

P22–12 Incentive Pay (L.O. 5)

Loeb Company recently began conversion from batch production to a just-in-time, pull production system. Ten years ago, Loeb gave workers the opportunity to earn significant bonuses by working at a faster pace and producing more units. Even though this incentive pay resulted in excessive inventory during Loeb's slack sales period, the president justified continuing the incentive pay system. Workers became accustomed to the extra pay;

in fact, the incentive portion often averaged more than the regular pay of the faster workers.

The consultant hired to help Loeb cut lot sizes and make the conversion to the pull system suggested abandoning individual incentives. However, management believes they will face rebellion if Loeb halts the incentive system.

Required:

a. Provide support for this statement: There is little or no room for incentive pay in companies using a just-in-time, pull production system where the rule is "make only what is used, as it is used"; however, incentive pay may be appropriate in batch production, where the rule is "make as much as you can."
b. Suggest ways Loeb can make the transition in eliminating individual incentives without a corresponding rebellion.

P22–13 Reversing Entries for Labor Costs (L.O. 2)

Richard Company pays its employees every other Friday. Because the last pay period of 19X2 ended on December 24, the company made the following adjusting entry on December 31 so that its financial statements would be correctly stated:

Work in Process Inventory	2,000	
Factory Overhead Control	6,000	
Marketing Expense Control	1,500	
Administrative Expense Control	900	
Payroll Payable		10,400

Gross regular earnings for the first payroll ending on January 7, 19X3, were direct labor, $4,000; indirect labor, $12,000; sales and distribution personnel, $3,000; administrative costs, $1,800. Because Job No. 49 had a time deadline, the company incurred overtime premium pay totaling $820. Authorizations from employees to withhold contributions to the United Neighbors charitable fund of $850 and union dues of $750 were received. Federal income taxes of $5,250 were withheld. The following taxes were imposed on 100 percent of wages at the rates indicated: FICA at 8 percent each for employer and employee; federal unemployment tax at 0.8 percent; and state unemployment tax at 2.7 percent.

Required:

a. Record the reversing entry for wages on January 1.
b. Assuming a reversing entry was made, prepare the entries on January 7 to record the labor cost and its subsequent payment.
c. Prepare the entries on January 7 assuming no reversing entry was made.

P22–14 Evaluating Alternative Incentive Plans (L.O. 4)

Blake Company, a management consulting firm, has designed two different incentive plans for a client. Plan A does not provide a guaranteed wage. Instead, workers are paid at a piece rate of $0.36 a unit. A bonus of 25 percent of the regular piece rate is paid for each unit over standard. The standard is 25 units per hour.

Plan B, a group incentive plan, includes an extra 4 percent on a guaranteed minimum wage for each 100 units over the group's weekly standard. The weekly standard for the group is 3,000 units. Data follow for all the employees in the group for a 40-hour week. The bonus will be calculated for every hour worked.

Employee	Units Produced	Guaranteed Hourly Minimum (for Plan B)
C. Xedus	900	$13.05
F. York	1,100	10.65
R. Zillis	1,200	10.95

Required:

a. Compute the gross earnings for each employee, first under Plan A and then under Plan B.

b. Evaluate the plans and indicate which is more appropriate in these circumstances.

P22–15 Journal Entries for Payroll, Labor Distribution, and Payroll Tax (L.O. 1)

Taylor Motor Corporation has the following payroll for the pay period just ended:

	Gross Wages	Wages Subject to FICA
Direct labor	$7,000	$5,500
Indirect labor	4,500	1,500
Marketing salaries	2,500	2,000
Administrative salaries	4,000	3,500

Income tax withheld totals $3,050. Applicable tax rates are FICA, 8 percent; state unemployment, 2.7 percent; federal unemployment, 0.8 percent. Only $2,000 direct labor wages are subject to unemployment tax.

Required:

a. Using a temporary payroll account, prepare the payroll entry. Then prepare the labor distribution entry and the subsequent wage payment entry.

b. Record the payroll taxes using the direct cost method.

P22–16 (CMA) Comparing Direct and Indirect Labor (L.O. 1)

A portion of the costs incurred by business organizations is designated as direct labor cost. As used in practice, the term *direct labor cost* has a wide variety of meanings. Unless the meaning intended in a given context is clear, misunderstanding and confusion are likely to ensue. If a user does not understand the elements included in direct labor cost, erroneous interpretations of the numbers may occur and could result in poor management decisions.

The National Association of Accountants has issued *Statement on Management Accounting (SMA) Number 4C*, "Definition and Measurement of Direct Labor Cost," to assist management accountants in dealing with problems that may arise in interpreting and understanding direct labor costs. Along with providing a conceptual definition of direct labor cost, this statement describes how direct labor costs should be measured. Measurement of direct labor costs has two aspects: *(a)* the quantity of labor effort that is to be included, that is, the types of hours or other units of time that are to be counted, and *(b)* the unit price by which each of these quantities is multiplied to arrive at a monetary cost.

Required:

a. Distinguish between direct labor and indirect labor.

b. Explain why some nonproductive labor (e.g., coffee breaks, personal time) is treated as direct labor while other nonproductive labor (e.g., downtime, training) is treated as indirect labor.

c. Following are labor cost elements that a company has classified as direct labor, manufacturing overhead, or either direct labor or manufacturing overhead depending upon the situation.

- Direct labor—Included in the company's direct labor are cost production efficiency bonuses and certain benefits for direct labor workers such as FICA (employer's portion), group life insurance, vacation pay, and workers' compensation insurance.
- Manufacturing overhead—The company's calculation of manufacturing overhead includes the cost of the following: wage continuation plans, the company-sponsored cafeteria, the personnel department, and recreational facilities.

- Direct labor or manufacturing overhead—The costs that the company includes in this category are maintenance expense, overtime premiums, and shift premiums.

Explain the rationale used by the company in classifying the cost elements in each of the three categories.

P22–17 Effect of Incentive Plan on Unit Product Cost (L.O. 4)

The management of Vita, Inc., wants to maximize the productivity of its labor. In pursuing this objective, it is investigating the pros and cons of a wage incentive plan. The company has analyzed past results and arrived at the following data representative of an actual average month:

Actual production	20,000 units
Direct material used	$49,000
Direct labor costs	63,000
Variable factory overhead	10,000
Fixed factory overhead	36,000

After conducting tests, management is satisfied that the units produced will increase by 25 percent per month if it adopts the proposed incentive plan. After the incentive plan is initiated, Vita anticipates the total labor costs will be $80,000. Other factory costs behave as they have in the past. Vita, Inc., can sell the increased production without additional expense.

Required:

Advise management about adopting the incentive plan. Base your recommendations solely on the effect that the incentive plan has on unit product cost. What other factors should Vita, Inc. consider before adopting the incentive plan?

P22–18 Journal Entries Treating Payroll Taxes as Indirect Cost (L.O. 1)

The records for the Boat Manufacturing Company show the following for the first payroll period in November:

Direct labor	$36,000
Indirect labor	5,500
Marketing salaries	4,000
Office salaries	2,500

FICA taxes apply to only 70 percent of the payroll; city payroll taxes apply to all payroll and are withheld from employees' wages; unemployment insurance taxes apply to only 25 percent of the payroll. Assume the following tax rates: FICA, employee and employer, 8 percent each; state unemployment, 2.7 percent; federal unemployment, 0.8 percent; and city payroll tax, 3 percent. A total of $4,600 is to be withheld for federal income taxes.

Required:

Prepare journal entries to pay employees and to record payroll taxes; payroll taxes are treated as indirect cost. (Round to whole dollars.)

P22–19 Recording and Paying Payroll and Payroll Taxes (L.O. 1)

The following liability accounts of the FTA Company contained these credit balances on November 30:

Federal income tax withheld	$3,025
Federal unemployment taxes payable	12
FICA taxes payable	145
State unemployment taxes payable	85

For the December payroll, direct labor totaled $6,175; indirect labor, $1,550; marketing expense control, $1,425; and administrative expense control, $475. Income taxes of $2,250 were withheld. Only $1,500 of the payroll was subject to the 8 percent FICA tax rate, while $1,000 of the payroll was subject to the 2.7 percent state unemployment tax rate and the 0.8 percent federal unemployment tax rate. Of the payroll taxes, 60 percent apply to direct labor, 25 percent to indirect labor, 10 percent to marketing personnel, and 5 percent to administration.

Required:

a. Prepare the entry to record, distribute, and pay the payroll for December initially using a Payroll account.
b. Prepare the entry recording the employer's payroll taxes for December. Treat payroll taxes as direct costs.
c. Prepare the entry to pay all taxes due government agencies for the period ending December 31.

P22–20 Accounting for Vacation, Holiday, and Bonus Pay (L.O. 3)

A union agreement was recently entered into by the management of Greg Jones Company granting employees 10 working days of vacation and 5 working days of holidays. In addition, at fiscal year-end, each employee is to receive a bonus of 0.03 percent of net company income. Total net income is expected to be $500,000.

Required:

a. Prepare the journal entry to record the total weekly labor cost for one employee who earns $45 for one day of productive labor. Assume a payroll summary account has previously been used and you are to distribute only the labor cost.
b. Prepare the journal entry when the employee in Requirement *a* receives his entire vacation pay. Assume that amounts withheld are $90 federal income tax, $32 state income tax, and 8 percent FICA tax.
c. Compute the cost of holidays and vacations accruing to each pay period as a percentage of cost for this employee, assuming a 40-hour week.

P22–21 Distributing Labor Costs and Alternative Treatment of Payroll Tax (L.O. 1)

Brock, Inc., is subject to the following tax rates; FICA, 8 percent; state unemployment, 2.7 percent; and federal unemployment, 0.8 percent.

The company pays its employees biweekly and shows the following current pay period information for four employees:

1. Cab, president, has earned $1,900, from which $570 federal income is withheld. None of this salary is subject to FICA or unemployment tax.
2. Ted, sales representative, has earned $1,700, from which $300 federal income tax is withheld; $400 of his salary is subject to FICA tax only.
3. Hal, machine operator, has earned $500 for the current pay period, from which $80 is withheld; all of his salary is subject to FICA tax only.
4. Dan, janitor, has earned $300 from which $30 federal income is withheld; all of his salary is subject to FICA and unemployment tax.

Required:

a. Record the distribution of labor cost for the current pay period and its subsequent payment.
b. Record the payroll taxes, treating them as indirect costs.

P22–22 Journal Entries for Payroll, Labor Distribution, and Payroll Tax (L.O. 1)

Mentor Corporation's payroll is as follows for the week just ended:

	Gross Wages	Wages Subject to FICA
Direct labor	$5,500	$5,500
Indirect labor	1,500	1,500
Marketing salaries	2,000	1,600
Administrative salaries	3,500	–0–

Income tax withheld totals $2,000. Applicable tax rates are FICA, 8 percent; state unemployment, 2.7 percent; and federal unemployment, 0.8 percent.

Only $1,000 of direct labor wages are subject to unemployment taxes.

Required:

a. Using a temporary payroll account, make the payroll entry. Then make the labor distribution entry and the subsequent wage payment entry.
b. Record the payroll taxes using the direct cost method.

P22–23 Bottlenecks (L.O. 5)

A. Swang Company has a more than adequate supply of labor, but only one machine to finish the products after direct labor workers complete their tasks. There is sufficient market demand for their product so that the finishing machine is fully utilized. However, this capacity level uses only 80 percent of direct labor capacity, thus representing a non-bottleneck operation whose capacity exceeds market demand.

One of Swang's cost accountants argues that direct labor workers should be laid off so that there is no excess capacity. She stresses that employing direct labor workers at the current 100 percent level results in excess labor costs and a lower profit for the company. Further, she argues that by fully implementing the labor resource, throughput is not improved because the finishing machine prevents the increase of sales.

Another cost accountant believes that the company has an obligation to all direct labor workers employed and offers another solution. He believes enough raw material should be purchased to keep all workers busy, thus fully utilizing labor.

A third accountant then asks if any consideration is being given to inventory profits or phantom profits in either of the solutions offered. At this point, the production and marketing managers remark that they are totally confused and want an explanation.

Required:

a. Explain why all plants should include at least one bottleneck operation whose capacity is less than or equal to market demand.
b. Explain if the labor resource should be fully implemented.
c. Explain if a company should have excess capacity everywhere so as to prevent bottlenecks.
d. Explain why you would or would not advise Swang Company to have only exact capacity everywhere.
e. Explain why you agree or disagree with the cost accountant's suggestion of purchasing enough raw materials to keep workers fully utilized.
f. Define inventory profits and explain how they are achieved.

P22–24 Daily Earnings and Effective Hourly Rate Using Proposed Incentive Plans (L.O. 4)

Standard production in the Night Hawk Company is 20 units per hour. For the first week in April, a worker's record shows the following:

Monday	170 units	8 hours
Tuesday	190 units	8 hours
Wednesday	146 units	8 hours
Thursday	182 units	8 hours
Friday	160 units	8 hours

Management is considering adopting one of two incentive plans and wants to use this representative worker's record to compare the earnings of each proposed incentive plan.

With Incentive Plan A, workers are guaranteed a rate of $9.80 per hour and a premium of 60 percent of the time saved on production in excess of standard.

With Incentive Plan B, workers are paid $.22 per unit when daily output is below standard, $.24 per unit when daily output is at standard or up to 10 percent above standard, and $.25 per unit for all production when the daily output exceeds 10 percent above standard.

Required:

Compute daily earnings and the effective rate per hour for each day using each of the incentive plans proposed.

Cases

C22–25 Change in Image with Mixture of Duties and Involvement (L.O. 5)

Threathven Company is in the process of installing factory equipment. They first put their robots in painting and welding, which are usually difficult for humans to do the same way over and over. Threathven Company management stressed that they were not installing automated equipment to replace labor; they reminded workers that only humans can think and solve problems, not dumb machines. Workers were encouraged to think of this transition to automation as a personal opportunity to grow and learn new skills.

Threathven Company soon realized that the labor skills presently employed need to be upgraded. Also, they learned that automation demands that operators be versatile, able to move to where the work is. Assembly line workers who formerly turned out parts now are receiving training for their expanded duties. They learn how to record data and investigate variances, which are jobs formerly performed by management and technicians. Assembly line workers now have a mixture of duties. In fact, it is common to see assembly line workers in consultation with engineers and production supervisors, meeting together solving problems as they occur.

With the expanding duties of direct labor workers, the cost accountant begins questioning the direct and indirect labor cost classifications currently in use. The accountant notes that no longer are distinctions as clear-cut as in the past.

After walking through the plant observing operations recently, Threathven's president was heard to remark, "Fortunately, we are maturing in our thinking and moving from the participation programs of the past to involvement programs."

Required:

a. Discuss the job skill areas you expect robots to create an additional need for.
b. Explain why the cost accountant is or is not correct in questioning the classification of direct and indirect labor.
c. Describe the change in self-image the workers will have as a result of the mixture of duties.
d. Explain the meaning of the president's remark regarding participation and involvement.

C22–26 Internal Control over Payroll Procedures (L.O. 1)

Butler Company employs approximately 600 production workers and has the following payroll procedures. All hiring is performed by the factory supervisors, who make their decision after interviewing applicants. After the interview, the applicant is either hired or rejected. If the applicant is hired, a W-4 form is prepared indicating the number of exemptions claimed. This employee's Withholding Exemption Certificate serves as a notice to the payroll clerk that the employee has been hired; the hiring factory supervisor writes the hourly rate on the form and forwards it to the Payroll Department. The factory supervisors verbally inform the payroll clerks of any rate adjustments for employees under their supervision.

Near the entrance to the factory is a box containing blank time cards. At the beginning of the week, each production worker removes a blank card and fills in his or her name in pencil. Workers record their arrival and departure times on these cards daily.

At the end of the pay period, payroll clerks replace the completed time cards with blank cards. If a worker does not have a time card, it is assumed that he or she is no longer employed, and his or her name is removed from the payroll. The chief payroll accountant manually signs payroll checks. Payroll checks for the majority of employees are distributed at the Payroll Department. During the days on which payroll is paid, employees go to the Payroll Department to pick up their checks. Unfortunately, some employees wait in line 45 minutes or more to receive them. Not only does this represent lost production time, but it also presents a traffic problem because space is limited outside the Payroll Department window.

Payroll checks for employees working in critical assembly lines are given to the factory supervisors for distribution. The supervisors arrange for the delivery of checks for workers who are absent.

The payroll bank account is reconciled by the chief payroll accountant, who also prepares state and federal payroll tax reports.

Required:

Make suggestions for improving control over hiring practices and payroll procedures.

C22–27 (CMA) Behavioral Impact of Incentive Plans (L.O. 4)

Renslen Inc., a truck manufacturing conglomerate, has recently purchased two divisions, Meyers Service Company and Wellington Products Inc. Meyers provides maintenance service on large truck cabs for 18-wheeler trucks, and Wellington produces air brakes for the 18-wheeler trucks.

The employees at Meyers take pride in their work, as Meyers is proclaimed to offer the best maintenance service in the trucking industry. The management of Meyers, as a group, has received additional compensation from a 10 percent bonus pool based on income before taxes and bonus; Renslen plans to continue to compensate the Meyers management team on this basis as it is the same incentive plan used for all other Renslen divisions.

Wellington offers a high-quality product to the trucking industry and is the premium choice even when compared to foreign competition. The management team at Wellington strives for zero defects and minimal scrap costs; current scrap levels are at 2 percent. The incentive compensation plan for Wellington management has been a 1 percent bonus based on gross profit margin; Renslen plans to continue to compensate the Wellington management team on this basis.

Below are the condensed Income Statements for both divisions for this fiscal year ended May 31, 19X1.

	Renslen Inc. Divisional Income Statements For the Year Ended May 31, 19X1	
	Meyers Service Company	**Wellington Products Inc.**
Revenues	$4,000,000	$10,000,000
Cost of product	75,000	4,950,000
Salaries*	2,200,000	2,150,000
Fixed selling expenses	1,000,000	2,500,000
Interest expense	30,000	65,000
Other operating expense	278,000	134,000
Total expense	3,583,000	9,799,000
Income before taxes and bonus	$ 417,000	$ 201,000

*Each division has $1,000,000 of management salary expense that is eligible for the bonus pool.

Renslen has invited the management teams of all its divisions to an off-site management workshop in July where the bonus checks will be presented. Renslen is concerned that the different bonus plans at the two divisions may cause some heated discussion.

Required:

a. Determine the 19X1 bonus pool available for the management team at
   (1) Meyers Service Company
   (2) Wellington Products Inc.

b. Identify at least two advantages and at least two disadvantages to Renslen Inc. of the bonus pool incentive plan at
   (1) Meyers Service Company
   (2) Wellington Products Inc.

c. Having two different types of incentive plans for two operating divisions of the same corporation can create problems.
   (1) Discuss the behavioral problems that could arise within management for Meyers Service Company and Wellington Products by having different types of incentive plans.
   (2) Present arguments that Renslen can give to the management teams of both Meyers and Wellington to justify having two different incentive plans.

The Use of Costs in Pricing Decisions

After studying this chapter, you should be able to:

1. Explain the role of cost in the final pricing decision.

2. Discuss the variety of market conditions, ranging from a monopolistic market, in which a company has some control over the prices charged, to a perfectly competitive market, in which a company accepts the price established by the market.

3. Evaluate the various cost-based methods on which prices can be established, such as variable costs, differential costs, full costs, and conversion costs.

4. Apply the role of social costs and social responsibility in an organization's pricing strategy.

PRACTICAL APPLICATION BOX **Pricing Strategies for Manufacturers**

Companies should find out if their pricing strategies are being used properly. In using premium pricing, managers should consider more than adding a flat dollar amount. Instead, the premium price should result in a higher percentage return than the return on the standard model. Making a good product at a high premium price can be highly profitable. For example, Maytag's reputation for quality allows them to charge premium prices; this has yielded the company the highest return on investment in the indus-

try. Henry Ford used marginal pricing when he developed the moving assembly line. In marginal pricing the fixed cost content in the selling price is reduced to make the price more attractive, thus increasing volume. Marginal pricing is applicable in the growth stage when new technology provides an innovative company with an advantage over competitors. Overall, managers realize that the goal of pricing strategy is to maximize profits.

From: Thomas S. Dudick, "Pricing Strategies for Manufacturers," *Management Accounting*, November 1989, pp. 30–37.

Introduction

The first eight chapters of this book concern the collection of cost figures that managers need to determine sales prices. Although the accumulation of costs serves inventory valuation purposes, managers also use these data for pricing decisions. This chapter discusses ways of establishing the sales price according to various cost concepts and explains when each approach is most appropriate. For example, differential cost pricing may be appropriate for short-run, specialized situations, but it could be risky to use in the long run.

When a product's sales price is only one of many elements that determine its success or failure, price determination certainly warrants much of the manager's time and consideration. It is difficult to separate price determination from other market mix elements, such as advertising, product quality, and delivery terms. Management must decide whether to offer quantity discounts and under what terms. A pricing decision also includes studying the profitability of varying prices to stimulate sales in certain seasons of the year.

Influence of Various Parties (L.O. 1)

Because the pricing policy management establishes affects so many people both inside and outside the company, some conflict of interest among managers, salespersons, and customers is to be expected. To reflect each of these interests, a company may establish a pricing committee to study the market structure and data supplied. This committee should be aware of **suboptimization;** that is, departments that are not attempting to fulfill companywide goals but work toward their own departmental objectives instead. A company must also identify its interpretation of profit maximization; this is expressed as either a rate of return on capital or a specific dollar amount of net income. A company's interpretation of profit maximization should be in harmony with the market share it is trying to gain. For example, it may have to be satisfied with a lower profit in the short run to improve its chance of profit maximization in the long run.

A pricing decision must consider these conflicting interests:

Salespersons generally prefer as low a sales price as possible so the product is easy to sell. Because sales personnel must explain to prospective customers any differences from competitors' prices, companies should give the sales force information enabling them to explain these differences.

The company should also involve advertising's top managers in the pricing procedure because the price quoted can be a form of sales promotion. For example, a $0.98 or $0.99 price seems less expensive than $1.

Because customers help make up the market structure, the company should obtain a profile of their buying habits and the factors that motivate them. Managers should study the physical and social needs that customers satisfy when they purchase products.

Consumer Behavior

In analyzing consumer behavior, a key concern is the interpretation that customers place on the price of a product. Most customers can justify buying something only if they believe the purchase price is fair. As a result, they may view a price cut as a reduction in quality or an attempt by the company to dispose of outdated merchandise that few people desire.

Often, a lower price may not be the best answer if customers are trying to satisfy a social need such as status or prestige. In fact, customers may interpret a price increase as a quality improvement or as an increase in product demand, indicating that other customers believe this is a good product. Additionally, some customers may believe that a price rise means they should purchase the product before the limited supply is exhausted.

As mentioned in connection with the Robinson-Patman Amendment, the government influences pricing policies by designating some competitive practices as unfair. Even though local governments have some impact on pricing policies, state and federal governments have the largest effect. Certain industries, such as petroleum and agriculture, are subject to additional restrictions. Even though we cannot ignore these restrictions, other factors play a more important role in the pricing decision of most companies.

The established sales price must yield a fair return to all those handling the product. Conflict may arise, however, in trying to determine what a fair and adequate return is. One way is by estimating the optimum price range to charge customers and then working backward through the various distribution stages. The process obviously becomes more complex when using a wide distribution method involving several intermediaries. While the manufacturer usually prefers that several intermediaries distribute the product, a distributor may prefer to sell the product on an exclusive basis. Thus, managers must determine the distribution channel before reaching a pricing decision.

Because competitors help form the market structure in which the company operates, a study of the competitive situation helps determine which pricing strategy is most appropriate. Competitors do influence the upper limits of pricing. Usually companies should not set a price materially above their competitors unless they offer a higher quality service or product. We discuss the various market structures, such as perfect competition and monopoly, later in the chapter when we introduce the supply and demand concept.

Determinants of Pricing (L.O. 2)

For a price to be successful, it must not only consider the other elements in the marketing mix but also satisfy certain external and internal constraints. External factors include the influence of supply and demand, fads and trends, competition, and other market conditions. Internal factors include the cost of the product or service and the company's objectives. For a company to continue operations, the product's price clearly must cover all costs and yield a reasonable rate of return to investors if the manufacturer is a profit-making company.

External Determinants of Pricing

In addition to profitability and other internal considerations, accountants must consider the following external determinants of pricing before they begin an analysis of the cost studies:

1. The environment in which the company sells products.
2. The product's characteristics compared with those of competing products to evaluate the importance of brand loyalty and other factors affecting product demand.
3. The market structure including the number of competitors as well as the number of customers.
4. Customers' buying habits to better undertand the significance of price in the decision to buy.
5. The influence of legislation such as the Robinson-Patman Amendment; see Chapter 21.

Demand and Supply Curves

A **demand curve** expresses the relationship between the market price of the good and the quantity demanded. With all other variables constant *(ceteris paribus),* the quantity demanded of an economic good varies inversely with the price of the good. Thus, the higher the price, the lower the quantity demanded.

Before beginning production, management needs assurance that enough consumers will accept the price established to warrant production. We treat tastes, income, and the price of other goods as constants in determining the consumer's demand curve. A **change in the quantity demanded** refers to a movement along a given single demand curve, while a shift in a demand curve refers to a **change in demand.** This distinction is important to the pricing decision, because a change in quantity demanded is the result of a price change. A change in demand, however, refers to the effect of changes in variables other than the price on the quantity of the good demanded. For example, an increase in demand occurs when consumers become willing to buy more of a particular good at each possible price because their income has increased. On the other hand, a decrease in demand occurs and the demand curve shifts when consumers' taste for a product changes and they buy less of the product at each possible price.

Price Elasticity of Demand

The elasticity of demand expresses the relationship between customer behavior and price changes. **Price elasticity of demand** indicates how total revenue changes when a price change causes a change in quantity demanded. The elasticity concept measures the degree of responsiveness of quantity demanded to changes in the market price. When a price decrease causes quantity demanded to increase so much that total revenue increases, demand is called *elastic,* or greater than unity. However, we assume unitary elasticity if a price decrease causes no change in total revenue because the percentage cut in price is offset by a percentage rise in quantity. On the other hand, if the price decrease causes such a small increase in quantity demanded that total revenue decreases, demand is inelastic, or less than unity. When demand is called *inelastic,* it does not mean that consumers are unresponsive to price changes. Only when demand is perfectly inelastic will there be no change in the quantity demanded with a price change. We say demand is perfectly elastic if quantity demanded is infinitely responsive to a change in price.

We can best understand this relationship between customer behavior and price changes by determining an exact numerical measurement using the following formula, where Q represents quantity demanded, P represents the price of goods, and Δ represents a change:

$$\frac{(\Delta Q)/Q}{(\Delta P)/P}$$

For example, if the quantity demanded is very responsive to price changes, a given relative change in price causes a more than proportionate change in quantity demanded. If a small change in price results in a large change in the quantity demanded, the price elasticity of demand is high. If the formula results in an absolute value less than 1, or unity, the demand curve is inelastic, and total revenue increases when we raise the price. By analyzing elasticity of demand, managers can decide whether they can profitably raise or lower a price.

EXHIBIT 23–1

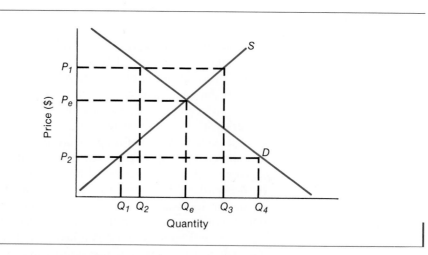

Because sellers react to higher prices by increasing the quantity of goods supplied, the **supply curve** illustrated in Exhibit 23–1 is upward sloping. Conversely, since consumers demand less at higher prices, the demand curve is downward sloping. Exhibit 23–1 shows the market determines the price for a perfectly competitive market, given the assumptions made earlier about consumers. If we initially assume a price of P_1 and quantity demanded is only Q_2, sellers have excess inventory since they are willing to offer Q_3 at this price. To avoid having this excess inventory, the market bids down the product's price. However, the cost of the product provides a floor below which the price usually will not fall. In a purely competitive market, price falls until **market equilibrium** occurs at the point where the quantities supplied and demanded are equal. Assume, instead, that initially the price is P_2 and the quantity that sellers are willing to supply is Q_1; this results in excess demand because consumers want to buy Q_4. Consumers' excess demand bids up the price to P_e.

Cross Elasticity of Demand

Cross elasticity of demand measures the extent to which various commodities relate to each other. The relationships in pricing decisions are those between substitute commodities and complementary commodities. The cross elasticity of demand is positive when commodities are substitutes for each other; hardcover and softcover books illustrate this situation. An increase in the price of hardcover books increases softcover book consumption; or a decrease in the price of hardcover books decreases softcover book consumption. The percentage changes in the price of hardcover books and the consumption of softcover books are in the same direction, whether price moves up or down. In either case, cross elasticity is positive. Commodities that are complementary to each other have negative cross elasticities. Tennis balls and tennis rackets are complementary products; high cross elasticity indicates close relationships.

Competitive Structures (L.O. 2)

One of the important external factors affecting pricing is the market structure in which a company operates. An individual company's demand differs from

EXHIBIT 23–2   Marginal Cost and Marginal Revenue for a Monopolist

Quantity	Average Revenue or Price	Total Revenue	Total Cost	Total Profit	Marginal Revenue (MR)		Marginal Cost (MC)
1	$300	$ 300	$ 170	$300	$250	>	$150
2	275	550	320	230	185	>	140
3	245	735	460	275	137	>	125
4	218	872	585	287	133	=	133
5	201	1,005	718	287	− 105	<	157
6	150	900	875	25	− 25	<	200
7	125	875	1,075	− 200			

the total market demand depending on the relationship of the sellers to each other. At one extreme is the monopolist whose company's demand is the same as the industry's because the monopolist is the only seller. At the other extreme is the pure, or perfect, competitor. The perfect competitor's output does not affect the market price because there are so many competing companies that no one company can sell enough of the industry output to significantly influence price. Therefore, a firm operating in perfect competition is a price taker, and the sales price is constant. In other markets, marginal revenue from each additional unit of sales declines, resulting in a curvilinear total revenue function. In a perfectly competitive market, the price elasticities of the industry determine the degree of difference between a company's elasticity and the industry's. Thus, in perfect competition the difference is infinite, while the difference is zero in a monopoly.

Monopoly

A market with only one seller is called a **monopoly,** which means that the company's demand is identical to the market demand for the products. However, for this to have any meaning, the monopolist must be assured that other companies will not enter the market regardless of the price of the monopolist's products. Even though there may be more than one seller, a monopoly exists if there are no close substitutes for the monopoly product.

Exhibit 23–2 shows the quantity sold of a monopolist's products varies inversely with the sales price. The change in the total revenue received from selling one more unit is called **marginal revenue (MR).** Exhibit 23–2 shows marginal revenue for any given quantity is less than the average revenue or price because, to sell an additional unit, we must reduce sales price. In the first elastic range of the demand curve, total revenue rises with quantity sold. When the quantity sold places the company in inelastic demand regions, total revenue reaches its maximum, which is five units in Exhibit 23–2.

Exhibit 23–2 also shows **marginal cost (MC),** the additional cost of producing one more unit. Marginal cost initially declines due to increasing economies of scale resulting from greater efficiencies of production as we produce more units. Eventually, the marginal costs increase at an increasing rate due to diseconomies of scale because inputs become scarce. Maximum profit equilibrium for a monopolist is where marginal revenue equals marginal cost. In Exhibit 23–2, this is a price of $201 that yields a total profit of $287; here marginal revenue and marginal cost are both equal at $133.

EXHIBIT 23–3   Profit Maximization under Monopoly

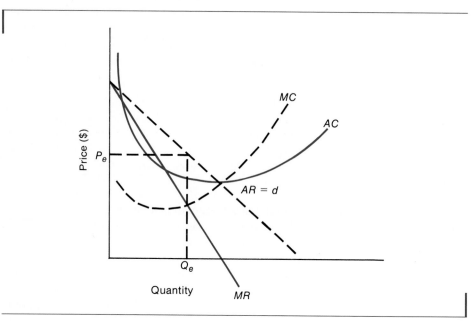

Law of Diminishing Returns. At some point in operations, diminishing returns set in and we cannot increase output except by increasing the marginal cost. The **law of diminishing returns** states that beyond some point, we obtain decreasing amounts of additional output when we add equal extra units of a varying input to a fixed amount of some other input. Stated in another manner, if we apply additional labor to a fixed amount of plant and equipment, eventually output will rise less proportionately to the increase in the number of workers employed. In Exhibit 23–2, marginal cost decreases with each additional unit until it reaches four units of output. Hence, the point of diminishing returns is four units. In the short run, management must work with a fixed capacity; as a result, costs rise sharply beyond the point of diminishing returns or decreasing cost. In the long run, when management has enough time to adjust its production facilities, it can produce at a capacity with the lowest average cost. Because of diminishing returns, producers usually require a higher price to make extra, higher-cost quality.

Profit Maximization in Monopoly. As seen in Exhibit 23–2, profit maximization for a monopolist is where marginal revenue equals marginal cost. This is not at the highest price possible, which is $300 for the monopolist in Exhibit 23–2. With a monopolist's downward sloping demand curve, as illustrated in Exhibit 23–3, marginal revenue (MR) is less than average revenue (AR) at any specific point. Maximum equilibrium occurs at the point where marginal cost intersects with marginal revenue. We determine equilibrium price (P_e) by going up the demand curve; quantity Q_e is sold at this point. As shown in Exhibit 23–3, we do not use average total cost to arrive at the monopolist's maximum equilibrium point. However, we cannot ignore total cost because a company must cover total cost to remain in operation in the long run. Note that the behavior of variable and fixed costs affects the shape of the average cost curve. As volume increases, we reach the point where we can add production only by increasing plant capacity, increasing fixed costs. Remember Chapter 3 emphasized that accountants assume a particular firm is operating within a relevant range of output where the revenue and cost functions are approximately linear.

Monopolistic Competition

The term **imperfect competition** refers to all market structures—such as monopoly, monopolistic competition, and oligopoly—that deviate from the purely competitive market model. **Monopolistic competition** is a market condition in which many small producers offer similar but not identical products. Even though monopolistic competition conditions do not involve as many companies as does perfect competition, there are enough firms so each has little or no control over the market price because each firm has a relatively small percentage of the total market. Sellers use packaging, trade names, and other sales promotions to differentiate their products in the minds of consumers. This market structure assumes that companies can easily enter the industry, since there are no significant barriers. If a monopolistic competitor changes output or price, the company need not fear retaliation from other companies in the industry. There is no mutual interdependence among the firms in the industry because of the large number of companies involved. As a result, each firm determines its policies without considering the possible reactions of rival firms.

However, a company does not have much freedom to change prices because the goods that competitors are selling are close substitutes and the cross elasticities of demand are high. For example, with high cross elasticities of demand, a change in price causes a relatively large change in quantity demanded because consumers often switch to another product. While product differentiation helps lessen some of this switching from one product to another, the number of sales gained by any individual company is small, due to the many companies in the industry. The result is that competition among companies in a monopolistically competitive market is more concerned with product differentiation than with price.

Profit Maximization in Monopolistic Competition. The demand curve for a monopolistic competitor, as shown in Exhibit 23–4, is more elastic at a given price than that of the entire industry. Profit maximization for a monopolistic competitor occurs at a price where marginal revenue (*MR*) equals marginal cost (*MC*), as shown in Exhibit 23–4. In the short run, the industry attracts new companies if profits exist. This causes the demand for an individual company's output to fall and become more elastic. In the struggle to keep its customers, a company usually increases its sales promotion, causing total cost to increase. This generally results in no economic profits because the average cost (*AC*) curve would be tangent to the demand curve.

Oligopoly

An **oligopoly** exists if the number of companies in the industry is small and little product differentiation exists. Because of the availability of close substitutes, each company closely watches the pricing strategy of its competitors. For example, a company knows that if it cuts its prices, competitors will match the price cut, resulting in a less favorable condition for all companies. On the other hand, if an oligopolist raises prices, competitors probably will not follow and the

EXHIBIT 23–4   Profit Maximization under Monopolistic Competition

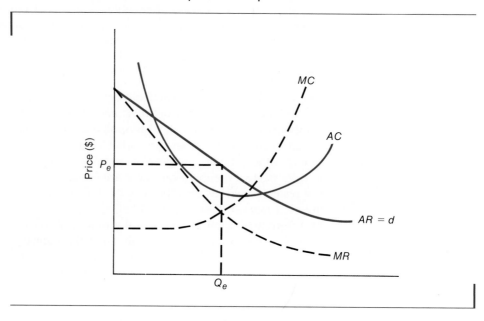

oligopolist will lose its share of the market. When faced with these conditions, sellers of homogeneous goods have a strong incentive to charge only the prevailing price. Generally, this price is more than marginal cost and is higher than that established in a perfectly competitive market. In the past, oligopolistic companies have been accused of tacitly agreeing to price their products at a specified figure, which leads to administered pricing. Before antitrust laws stopped such strategies, companies formed trusts, cartels, and mergers that collusively set prices.

Profit Maximizations in Oligopoly. Rather than use pricing as a marketing strategy, most oligopolists use other techniques; however, even these techniques have short-term effects because competitors rapidly move to counteract them. These close interactions make it difficult to generalize regarding the appearance of the oligopolist's demand curve. Assuming tacit agreement between companies, the demand curve could appear as in Exhibit 23–5. Line *DD* represents the demand curve for all sellers when they move prices together and share a total market. The more elastic line *dd* represents one company's demand curve when it acts alone in changing its price, resulting in sales lost to competitors.

The company's rivals match any price cut below Point *X* and the *DD* demand curve prevails. Conversely, at any point above *X*, *dd* prevails, because competitors do not match the company's price cuts. Because two different demand curves exist, there are different *MR* curves, as shown by the dotted lines in Exhibit 23–5. Significant shifts in the marginal cost (*MC*) curve do not change the price charged because of the discontinuity in the *MR* curve. This is the reason we often describe oligopolists' prices as sticky; they remain stable even with considerable cost changes.

EXHIBIT 23–5   Profit Maximization under Oligopoly

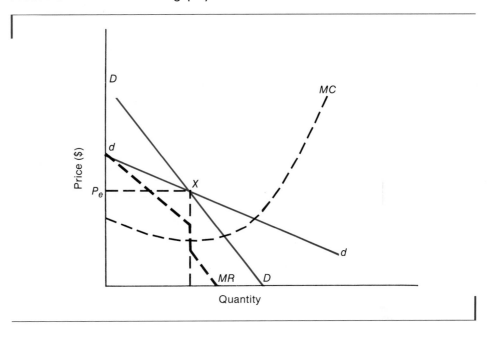

Perfect Competition

The market structures just described involve imperfect competition. The companies must compete for their market share because an individual company's market share is always uncertain and it cannot sell as much as it desires. In addition, in imperfect competition, a company never is certain of the marketing strategy of its competitors if it changes its prices. However, these conditions do not exist for a perfect competitor. There are so many producers in **perfect competition** that no one individual company has any influence on the market price. There is little need for nonprice competition, such as sales promotion, because the products sold are homogeneous and no consumer preference for a specific brand exists. While the monopolistic competitor uses packaging, trade names, and other means of sales promotion to differentiate its products in the consumers' minds, the perfect competitor does not. A perfect competitor accepts the price established in the market. Sellers, however, hoard products if the prices are too low and buyers do not buy if prices are too high.

In a perfectly competitive market, a random relationship exists between buyer and seller, as neither cares with whom they deal. We rarely find this market structure in practice, although some metal products and commodities markets resemble perfectly competitive situations. Instead, companies sell most products when the pricing decision is complex because product differentiation exists, if only in the consumer's mind.

In illustrating both the pure competitor's demand and the industry demand, Exhibit 23–6 indicates that the pure competitor cannot influence the market price

E X H I B I T 23–6   Pure or Perfect Competition

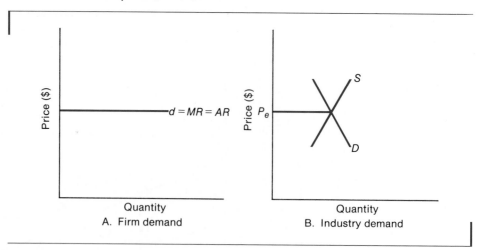

A. Firm demand

B. Industry demand

by changing output. In fact, the company's demand is a horizontal line of infinite elasticity at equilibrium because the pure competitor must take the market price for each product sold. The company's average revenue (*AR*) equals the market price. In addition, because companies sell all units at the same price, marginal revenue (*MR*) equals the equilibrium market price. The pricing decision that perfect competitors must make is not complex. They merely accept the price that competitors are asking because they do not control a large enough share of the market to influence prices.

Profit Maximization in Perfect Competition. Profit maximization for a perfect competitor is easy because all the competitor must do is find the output quantity that yields maximum profit and sell at that output with the given market price. Exhibit 23–7 shows the perfect competitor refers to its marginal cost curve (*MC*) because its point of profit maximization is where $P = MC = MR$. However, the company would not operate if average revenue (*AR*) lies below average variable costs (*AVC*), because then average revenue does not cover the differential cost per unit. The perfect competitor obtains its supply curve by referring to only that portion of its marginal cost curve above the lowest point of the company's average variable cost curve. By adding all the company supply curves horizontally, we determine the industry supply curve.

As stated earlier, a company operating in a perfectly competitive market does not have the power to influence price and, therefore, must accept the prevailing one. However, this does not mean that the cost accountant in this company is of no value to management. On the contrary, the cost accountant should prepare budgets showing profitability at different operating levels based on total costs and revenues. Management can use these budgets to determine optimum operations.

Even though the theory of the role of supply and demand in pricing is sound, often management may not know what the exact demand for its product is at each price offered because business conditions, the political environment, and the actions of competitors all affect demand. The executives responsible for the

EXHIBIT 23–7   Profit Maximization in Perfect Competition

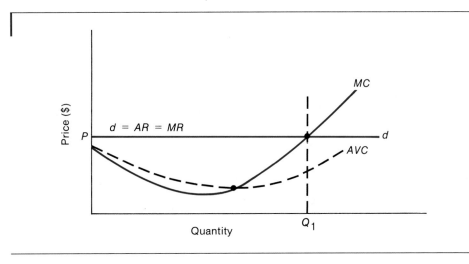

pricing decision do not know how consumers will react to these changing factors; thus, a good pricing policy is difficult to establish. In addition, the economist's demand curve assumes that all consumers have the same characteristics, when, in fact, different classes of consumers have varying characteristics. The relationship of customers to the pricing process is more complex than indicated by price elasticity and the law of demand, for each product has several demand curves representing different classes of potential customers. To best meet the needs of each class of customers, companies should consider offering different grades of each product.

Economic Profits

Economic profits involve both implicit and explicit costs and differ from accounting income. **Explicit costs** consist of payments for resources bought or rented by the company. **Implicit costs** are costs of self-owned, self-employed resources that do not require an outlay of cash. Economic (pure) profit is the excess revenue remaining after absorbing all explicit and implicit costs. Implicit costs include charges for owners' capital and risk taking. Economic profit is a return above a normal profit. **Normal profit** is the imputed return to capital which is the minimum amount of profit to keep the company in business in the long run. Economists consider normal profit to be part of total cost.

Accounting income, in contrast, is revenue less explicit expenses, based on actual transactions. The economists' concept of profit is less precise because they define expenses in broader terms. Using the accountant's concept of profit, there is no distinction between normal profit and economic profit.

Residual income, which Chapter 14 illustrates as a divisional performance measurement, is closely associated with economic profit. **Residual income** is divisional net income less the imputed interest on invested capital. Imputed interest is the cost of capital or the desired rate of return on divisional investment. This imputed interest charge is equivalent to the economist's normal profit.

Relationship among Demand, Supply, and Cost (L.O. 3)

The previous discussion considers demand-based pricing theory with little attention to the relationship between cost and price. We vividly display this relationship through examination of the familiar supply and demand curves. Economists believe that supply and demand determine price; costs, in turn, help determine the supply offered for sale. By matching supply, demand, price, and costs, we determine the products to manufacture, who produces them, and for which customers. Generally, the supply side expressed in dollars is the cost of production and distribution, and the demand side is the revenue obtained from that production and distribution.

Pricing considers the interests of both buyers and sellers because companies reducing the selling price without corresponding reductions in cost also reduce the supply of a given product. The product's cost forces a company to resist lowering the selling price, both in the short run and the long run. Certainly, regardless of the cost concept used, companies strive to keep cost to a minimum by adopting the most efficient methods of production.

While the relationship between cost and price exists, there is little agreement about how close this relationship actually is in practice. Managers generally consider costs as simply a floor below which price cannot fall. The difficulty is that opinions differ regarding how to measure costs. The long-run approach to pricing must consider different costs because its objective is not the same as that of short-run pricing. The price established for long-run purposes must cover full costs as well as a satisfactory return on the assets invested, while a short-run price tries to maximize the utilization of existing facilities. As discussed in Chapter 14, differential costs are relevant in a short-run, accept-or-decline decision.

A principal objective of a company is to earn a satisfactory return on the assets used. To do this, companies must provide products or services at a price that consumers accept. Earlier in the chapter, we discussed profit maximization for the different market structures. However profit maximization often ignores long-run survival because if the return on investment is too high, profits draw new companies into the industry. This increase in the number of companies supplying the product drives the price down and, hence, lowers the return on investment. In addition, companies earning such high returns are subject to the criticism that they do not have the public interest at heart. This can lead to public, political, or legal pressure for price reduction. As a result, some companies cover only their variable costs in the short run, attracting no new entrants. Conversely, investors refuse to place additional assets in a company if the return is too low.

While we recognize that a company's total revenue must exceed its total cost before generating a profit, the pricing procedure becomes more complex when separately setting selling prices for each product. A significant part of the complexity lies in deciding how much of indirect costs each product's price should cover. Generally, in a normal pricing situation, the selling price of a product should be high enough to recover (1) the direct costs traceable to the product, (2) a fair share of allocated indirect costs, and (3) a satisfactory profit. As discussed later, it may be more profitable for management to resort to other methods of price determination in a specialized pricing situation.

Return on Assets Employed

The pricing strategy used by some companies is to base the selling price on a desired rate of **return on assets employed.** The **return on total assets,** frequently called *return on investment* (ROI), is the ratio of net profit to total assets. In return on asset pricing, we divide the desired operating profit by the average assets employed to arrive at the planned return on asset percentage. Or instead, we can use the following formula in determining a percentage markup on cost in trying to generate a specified rate of return on assets employed. Assume that management wants to earn a 25 percent return on the $40 million assets employed and that annual costs total $16 million.

$$\text{Percentage markup on cost} = \frac{\text{Assets employed}}{\text{Total annual costs}} \times \begin{array}{c}\text{Desired rate of return}\\\text{on assets employed}\end{array}$$

$$\text{Percentage markup on cost} = \frac{\$40,000,000}{\$16,000,000} \times 25 \text{ percent} = 62.5 \text{ percent}$$

$$\text{Sales volume} = \begin{array}{c}\text{Total annual}\\\text{costs}\end{array} + \left(\begin{array}{c}\text{Total annual}\\\text{costs}\end{array} \times \begin{array}{c}\text{Percentage}\\\text{markup on}\\\text{costs}\end{array}\right)$$

$$\text{Sales volume} = \$16,000,000 + (\$16,000,000 \times 62.5 \text{ percent})$$

$$= \$16,000,000 + \$10,000,000 = \$26,000,000$$

Rather than being expressed as a percentage markup on cost, the desired rate of return on assets employed can be multiplied by the assets employed (25 percent × $40,000,000 = $10,000,000) and added to the total annual costs as follows:

$$\$10,000,000 + \$16,000,000 = \$26,000,000$$

We divide the units we expect to sell by the $26 million necessary sales volume to yield the unit sales price. This sales volume gives the following **total asset turnover:**

$$\text{Total asset turnover} = \frac{\text{Sales}}{\text{Total assets}} = \frac{\$26,000,000}{\$40,000,000} = .65 \text{ times}$$

A comparison of this turnover with the industry average may reveal that the company is not generating a sufficient volume of business for the size of its asset investment. The preceding turnover indicates that it takes more than one year for the company to completely turn over its assets. Since average turnovers vary considerably by industry, it is not appropriate to determine if this represents an efficient level of operations.

The percentage markup on cost formula ignores many complexities because we assume the assets employed to be static; in reality, this is rarely true. As volume increases, the assets used, such as cash and inventory, usually increase. A change in the product's sales price or cost can also cause a change in assets employed. For example, with higher prices, accounts receivable are higher. Decreases in cost and sales price have the opposite effect. Despite these complexities, a consideration of the assets used does give management an insight into more valid pricing.

Gross Margin Pricing

Even though the return on asset pricing method is more appropriate for decision making because it uses more information in calculating potential selling prices, we can apply the **gross margin pricing** method to arrive at a sales price. Gross margin pricing uses the following formula:

$$\text{Planned gross margin rate} = \frac{\text{Gross margin}}{\text{Revenue}}$$

The return on asset pricing method is a better method than gross margin pricing because it recognizes an amount that would be equivalent to the return needed to attract and/or compensate investors for the use of their funds. The long-run survival of an organization depends on its ability to earn a long-run return on investors' funds.

Cost-Plus Pricing Methods (L.O. 3)

The measurement of cost is especially important when the buyer has agreed to pay a price based on cost, such as government contracts that reimburse providers for their cost plus an allowance for profits. With cost-plus or backward-cost, a desired percentage for profit is added to the full cost of the product. However, determination of the desired profit percentage is often difficult. As illustrated previously, we may express the profit percentage as a percentage of the assets employed. Yet, the varying amount of assets required is a factor which must receive some attention.

Variable Cost Pricing

Variable cost pricing emphasizes the contribution margin by delineating the behavior of variable and fixed cost. One form of variable cost pricing involves adding a markup on variable costs to full costs. We carefully study cost-volume-profit relationships in determining variable cost formulas. Proponents of variable costing argue that this method allows management to determine prices for either the short run or the long run because it relates the effect of different prices to total fixed costs. However, there is a danger in focusing all attention on variable costs and contribution margin. Suppose a company has two products, A and B, for which monthly operating statements prepared on a variable costing basis show the following:

	Product A	Product B
Sales (1,000 units each)	$23,000	$16,000
Less variable expense	15,000	8,000
Contribution margin	$ 8,000	$ 8,000

Because Products A and B have identical contribution margins, there may be a temptation to treat them as equals in pricing. However, such an analysis of only contribution margin may lead to erroneous conclusions. If management can determine that these products require different effort and costs of marketing, executive analysis, and research and engineering, they should arrive at the cost by including these expenses. For example, assume that fixed manufacturing costs are $2,000 for each product; fixed marketing costs for the period are $3,000;

engineering costs, $1,000; and executive analysis, $2,000. The marketing staff estimates that it spends 60 percent of its time on Product A and 40 percent on Product B because of the unstable market demand for Product A. In addition, workers package Product A in a glass container. The engineering staff estimates that over the last several years it has spent 70 percent of its time in redesigning Product A's container. Despite these attempts to improve the container, there have been several lawsuits from customers for damages. Because managers normally spend many hours in consultation with the company's lawyers and in court trials, they believe they spend 75 percent of their time with Product A. As a result of this information, they developed the following analysis:

	Product A	Product B
Contribution margin	$8,000	$8,000
Fixed expenses:		
Manufacturing	$2,000	$2,000
Marketing	1,800 (60%)	1,200 (40%)
Engineering	700 (70%)	300 (30%)
Executive analysis	1,500 (75%)	500 (25%)
	$6,000	$4,000
Operating income	$2,000	$4,000
Cost per unit	$ 6	$ 4
Income per unit	2	4

This analysis shows why managers should not treat the products as equals. Even though the allocations may not be precise, they give management a better insight into the costs to use for pricing than does a contribution approach. Note, however, the allocations may change next period depending on the attention given to either of the products.

Contribution margin analysis also labels fixed costs as irrelevant and omits them from consideration in pricing. Assume that the company has determined the span of control for a supervisor is five direct labor workers employed. The company has received several bids of $2,000 each for processing 100 additional units per month. Because the present work force cannot handle any increase in workload, each 100-unit order requires one additional direct labor worker earning $900 monthly. Variable material and overhead amount to $8 per unit; supervisors earn $1,200 monthly.

As Exhibit 23–8 shows, contribution margin analysis generally does not include a charge for the supervisor until the company employs the 55th worker and adds the supervisor. However, we could argue that the supervisor's cost is really due to adding the 51st, 52nd . . . 55th worker as well and the 56th and 57th worker in the future. Contribution margin analysis could cause a company to reject profitable opportunities, as illustrated in Exhibit 23–8.

Differential Cost Pricing

Differential cost pricing (also called **marginal cost pricing**) focuses attention on the contribution to fixed costs and profit that an additional order generates. This method involves adding a markup on differential cost. The differential cost of an order is the increase in total costs resulting from the production of additional units. Differential cost pricing differs from variable cost pricing, which adds a markup on variable costs to full cost. Differential cost pricing includes both variable and fixed costs as differential cost on which a markup is determined. Differential cost pricing is appropriate for some specific situations,

EXHIBIT 23–8

Contribution margin approach

Worker Number	Revenue	Cost	Contribution	Decision
51	$2,000	$1,700	$300	Accept
52	2,000	1,700	300	Accept
53	2,000	1,700	300	Accept
54	2,000	1,700	300	Accept
55	2,000	2,900	(900)	Reject

Alternative approach

Worker Number	Revenue	Cost*	Profit	Decision
51	$2,000	$1,940	$60	Accept
52	2,000	1,940	60	Accept
53	2,000	1,940	60	Accept
54	2,000	1,940	60	Accept
55	2,000	1,940	60	Accept

*$900 per direct labor worker + $800 variable materials and overhead + ($1,200/5 supervisors' costs).

especially those of a short-run nature. The assertion that companies should base their sales price on marginal or differential cost so that marginal revenue equals marginal cost assumes that a company can estimate the demand curve for each of its products. Unfortunately, many companies lack this ability.

To illustrate differential cost pricing, assume the following product costs from accounting records:

	Product C	Product D
Direct material	$ 5	$ 5
Direct labor	6	2
Factory overhead:		
Variable	4	1
Differential fixed	3	2
Allocated fixed	3	2
Total production cost	$21	$12

The differential cost of material, labor, and factory overhead for Product C is $18 and $10 for Product D. With a 25 percent markup on differential cost, the sales price becomes:

	Product C	Product D
Markup on differential costs	$ 4.50 (25% × $18)	$ 2.50 (25% × $10)
Full cost	21.00	12.00
Sales price	$25.50	$14.50

Companies can appropriately use differential cost and variable cost pricing theories when they face difficult times and must improve profits by receiving some revenue more than variable or differential cost rather than no revenue at all. Such revenue makes some contribution to the fixed costs for which the company has already made a commitment. Admittedly, contribution margin is helpful in short-run pricing and profit planning because companies can compare the increase in cost resulting from a sale with the revenue increment to determine whether to accept the order.

With some even rarer short-run projects, it may be more profitable in the long run for the company to sell below variable costs. Generally, variable cost is the floor below which the sales price cannot fall. However, we can challenge this statement in some situations. For example, if a company has a skilled labor force that is difficult to replace, management might accept an order in which sales price is less than variable costs to receive some revenue to apply to existing wages and other costs. This approach might be more profitable in the long run than laying off the workers and running the risk of not being able to replace them.

Full-Cost Pricing

While we can set sales prices by adding a markup on differential cost or variable cost, full-cost pricing predominates. One of the purposes for cost accounting is to allocate elements of cost to arrive at a basis for deciding on the sales price. This **full-cost pricing** involves determining not only the product's direct costs but also the company's indirect costs that cannot be traced to one product line. We can use the allocation methods described in Chapter 4. However, there is no way to prove that one method is more correct than another because like all measurements, they are approximations. Admittedly, the full cost of any product involves cost allocations that we often base on judgment, opinion, and habit. Yet, allocations that attempt to meet the criteria discussed in Chapter 4 provide that each product is bearing an equitable share of the production costs incurred by the company. If management establishes a sales price of $28 for Product C and of $16 for Product D, the gross margin is 25 percent of the selling price. The $7 gross margin for Product C and the $4 gross margin for Product D is a 33⅓ percent mark-on ($7/$21 of Product C's full cost and $4/$12 of Product D's full cost) to the production cost.

Conversion Cost Pricing

The use of **conversion cost pricing** does not consider the material used in the product; instead, the emphasis is on the labor and factory overhead required, known as conversion cost. Companies mainly use conversion cost pricing when the customers furnish the material. The rationale behind this pricing theory is that companies can realize greater profits if they direct efforts to the products requiring less labor and overhead because they can produce and sell more units. Companies can effectively use this pricing theory if they have limited factory capacity when the capacity constraint is labor and overhead cost.

In the full-cost pricing example, Product D requires the same amount of material as Product C, but only $7 of direct labor and factory overhead, while Product C requires $16 direct labor and overhead. When using a 25 percent markup on conversion cost, the sales price for each product becomes the following:

	Product C	**Product D**
Full cost	$21.00	$12.00
Markup on conversion cost	4.00 (25% × $16)	1.75 (25% × $7)
Sales price	$25.00	$13.75

Using this strategy, each product generates the same profit per unit of scarce resource.

Standard Costs. A company can base its pricing decision on standard costs regardless of whether managers adopt the full-cost or variable cost approach. Standard costs represent the costs of efficient production methods at a normal capacity. However, before using standard costs as a basis for the pricing decision, managers should be certain that the standards established reflect current conditions. An advantage of this approach is that standard costs are usually broken down into fixed and variable components, and this is critical in many pricing decisions.

Direct Cost Pricing

When using the **direct cost pricing** theory, companies establish selling prices at a certain percentage above the direct, or traceable, costs incurred in manufacturing the product. This resembles the use of uniform gross profit percentages by merchandising companies. This pricing procedure has validity when the amount of indirect costs that should be equitably borne by each product line is essentially the same percentage of direct costs and when the assets employed by product lines are similar. Some managers believe that this method is more valid to apply in practice because it does not require that companies base prices on indirect costs. They believe that accountants cannot allocate indirect costs with a high degree of accuracy and that the pricing decision should not use indirect costs.

Product E illustrates direct cost pricing. With indirect costs of approximately 18 percent of direct costs and management wishing to earn a profit equal to 25 percent of total cost, the following calculation compares the direct cost pricing method with the full-cost pricing method.

	Product E	
	Direct Cost Pricing	**Full-Cost Pricing**
Direct costs	$17	$17
Indirect costs		3
Total costs		$20
Mark-on [18% + 25% + (25% × 18%) = 47%] ...	8 ($17 × 47%)	5 ($20 × 25%)
Selling price	$25	$25

We multiply total costs of $20 under the full-cost method by the desired profit percentage to arrive at a markup of $5 and a resulting sales price of $25. If, instead, we use the direct cost pricing method, the mark-on percentage must cover indirect costs plus the desired 25 percent profit. A 47 percent mark-on is as follows [18% + 25% + (25% × 18%)] = 47 percent. After applying this 47 percent mark-on to direct costs, we determine a $25 selling price, which is identical to that computed using the full-cost pricing method.

As stated earlier, direct cost pricing has validity if the cost characteristics of the various product lines are similar. Some managers might argue that even if their product lines do have different margins, the difference is offset because one product line's losses counterbalance gains on other product lines. However, this reasoning is faulty, for these differences only counterbalance each other if the sales quantities of each product line are in the proportion originally assumed when the sales prices were set. For example, if a company sells a larger proportion of the high-cost products and a smaller proportion of the low-cost products, overall company profits would be less than planned. In addition, the company may be unable to justify the sales price of each product line, because they sell some products for a price lower than their costs require, while other products have a higher price than required by cost. In the latter case, the company runs the risk of losing sales to competitors.

Evaluation of All Cost-Based Pricing Methods. There is little agreement about which costing theory is most appropriate for use in pricing, and we can criticize each method. Although the full-costing method does consider all production costs, it generally ignores marketing and administrative costs. The volume level at which companies calculate unit fixed costs also significantly affects full costs, as emphasized in previous illustrations. There is also a danger in using only differential costs or variable costs in pricing, because a company must cover all fixed or variable expenses to earn a profit. The marketing staff might be misled or tempted to cut prices to the point where they cover only variable costs; this results in underpricing and ultimate disaster for the company.

Certainly, if it sells a product for full cost plus a profit, the company should not base the sales price only on differential cost. Pricing includes much more than totaling the specific costs involved and adding a mark-on to these costs. Cost information only provides an estimate of the sales price. In fact, many companies merely accept the existing market price without any involved pricing decision. They realize that customers will not pay more than this price and there is no justification for charging less. While each of the costing theories presented is appropriate for specific pricing decisions, pricing strategy involves many considerations. Basing prices solely on one costing approach is risky; managers must consider other factors.

Regardless of the costing concept used, the relevant costs are the ones incurred in the future, not necessarily those of the past. A change in the plant equipment or facilities, for example, can affect the overhead cost of a product, and the development of more efficient methods of production reduces costs. Similarly, a change in the level of activity affects costs. In addition, the product's specifications may change, resulting in a corresponding change in cost. Even if the product remains the same, its cost may change. For example, a supplier may charge a higher price for material, or a company may sign a labor union contract calling for increased wages.

Inflation can cause future cost to vary from historical cost. Accountants must adjust historical costs to reflect different rates of inflation. If accountants expect the different cost components to increase by different percentages, more detailed calculations of future cost are necessary.

Even after conducting sophisticated analyses of the market structure and cost studies to arrive at the optimum price for a product or service, management should give attention to the profitability of price revisions. This phase of the pricing problem is almost a continual process; management should be constantly studying the changing market environment in which the product or service is offered for sale. For example, the effect of price changes in substitute and complementary products. More specifically, although golf balls and golf clubs are complementary products, they are substitute goods for tennis balls and rackets. A company may find it profitable to lower its price of golf clubs to improve the market for golf balls. However, if the sporting goods dealer is not careful, this price reduction can cause some sporting enthusiasts to switch from playing tennis to golf. Management thus should not assume that the optimum price will be static.

Social Responsibility and Pricing (L.O. 4)

Social Costs. The pricing method a company chooses may not consider its social costs; **social costs** are the outcome of an interaction of several complex economic, physical, and biological systems. Air and water pollution, soil erosion, and emissions of residual waste products are examples of social costs. An externality arises whenever a company's activities have a negative or positive impact on the environment for which the company is not held accountable. If the activities of a company lead to depletion of social resources, the result is a social cost. Conversely, if the activities lead to an increase in social resources, the result is a social benefit. We do not use the costs of the social benefits created by the production-related activities of a business enterprise in variable or differential cost pricing because they are not measured directly in monetary units.

It is generally agreed that perfect competition in all markets leads to maximum social welfare. If markets are highly competitive and consumers and producers rationally attempt to reach a maximum level of satisfaction, the market allocates available resources in a way that maximizes social welfare. If we manipulate private market prices, then marginal social costs do not equal the margin social benefit, and we do not achieve maximum social welfare. The indirect effects of this situation, referred to as **external economies or diseconomies,** are the social costs and social benefits not taken into account with the private marginal cost pricing rule.

Despite a lack of consensus about the definition of social costs and corporate social responsibility, generally we consider **social responsibility** the voluntary response of corporations to those needs of society that would not normally be met within the framework of the profit motive. The traditional view of corporate responsibility is that of pursuing profitability, with little or no concern for social needs. However, organizations are becoming increasingly aware that some obligations go beyond obeying laws and protecting self-interest. Many people agree that organizations have some social responsibility but disagree about the level of that responsibility. The following levels of social responsibility, beginning with a minimal social responsibility effort, reflect this differing opinion:

1. To make a profit and survive in business because this instituton has an economic responsibility. Most people agree that the corporation's responsibility in society extends beyond its obligation to earn a profit for the owners.
2. To obey laws given by society as part of the ground rules by which the business is to operate.
3. To assume entirely voluntary or discretionary responsibilities determined by management's desires.
4. To assume ethical responsibilities expected by society but not required by law.
5. To create public expectations in a voluntary setting and follow high standards of moral and social responsibility.

In the long run, socially responsible activities are in the self-interest of the organization. Further, organizations have the opportunity to create and maintain a favorable public image. Also, engaging in these activities may discourage governmental intervention and regulation. In addition to a lack of agreement regarding what is a socially responsible activity, these activities may divert the attention and resources of the organization to no one's advantage. Any organization's objective is to satisfy the economic goals of the firm's owners, and it may not be able to engage in socially responsive activities while fulfilling economic goals.

Summary

Even though pricing is a complicated procedure requiring an understanding of several factors, many companies allow managers who have no special training or experience to set prices. A dangerous consequence is that these managers often base pricing decisions strictly on intuition rather than on careful cost studies. Certainly a trade-off exists between the pricing data management desires and the cost of gathering these data. However, the time spent in examining cost and the effect of price changes on demand is usually worthwhile.

This chapter emphasizes that trial and error is not an adequate basis for developing a product's price. Companies need sophisticated analysis of full cost, differential cost, and elasticity of supply and demand—not just a slight consideration of the additional revenue and cost generated by a price change. While costs have a major influence on pricing decisions, companies cannot disregard their competitors and customers. Managers must consider the impact of a pricing decision on these influences, as well as on the profitability and survival of the company.

Pricing is a complex subject that involves many company employees, each of whom believes that a particular pricing theory is the most appropriate. Admittedly, for instance, there is difficulty in using full costing because a unit's full cost depends on the volume of sales and production. The volume of sales, however, is partially determined by the product's price. The numerous factors in a pricing decision, many of which are difficult to measure and quantify, add complexity. Accountants have both the responsibility and the challenge of providing cost studies that managers can use for guidance in this area.

The view that corporate responsibility is that of pursuing profitability, with little concern for social needs and completely ignoring social costs in pricing is no longer widely accepted. Today, many people believe that managers should not only abide by society's laws but also consider the effects of their decisions on the rest of society. Further, organizations should assume some obligation in solving some of society's problems in addition to earning a profit for their owners, and their pricing strategy should reflect this responsibility.

Important Terms and Concepts

suboptimization, 789
demand curve, 791
ceteris paribus, 791
change in quantity demanded, 791
change in demand, 791
price elasticity of demand, 791
supply curve, 792
market equilibrium, 792
cross elasticity of demand, 792
monopoly, 793
marginal revenue, 793
marginal cost, 793
law of diminishing returns, 794
imperfect competition, 795
monopolistic competition, 795

oligopoly, 795
perfect competition, 797
economic profit, 799
explicit and implicit costs, 799
normal profit, 799
residual income, 799
return on assets employed, 801
return on total assets, 801
total asset turnover, 801
gross margin pricing, 802
variable cost pricing, 802
differential cost pricing (marginal cost pricing), 803
full-cost pricing, 805

Problem for Self-Study

Sales Needed to Achieve Desired Return

Mattson Company provides the following financial data arranged in alphabetical order:

Cash	$ 50,000
Current liabilities	500,000
Fixed expenses	50,000
Merchandise inventory	130,000
Notes receivable	120,000
Plant and equipment	500,000
Stockholders' equity	300,000
Variable expenses	$8 per unit
Volume estimated for next year	10,000 units sold

Required:

a. Determine the total sales and unit sales price to satisfy management's objective of an income that equals a 15 percent return on its investment in total assets.
b. Express the desired income as a percentage of sales.
c. Compute the budgeted percentage of sales to total assets.
d. Assume the company sells 8,000 units instead of 10,000 units. What will be the income expressed as a percentage of total assets?

Solution to Problem for Self-Study

MATTSON COMPANY

a.

Assets

Cash	$ 50,000
Merchandise inventory	130,000
Notes receivable	120,000
Plant and equipment	500,000
Total	$800,000

Desired return on assets = 15% × $800,000 = $120,000

Sales = ($8 × 10,000 units) var. exp. + $50,000 fixed exp. + $120,000

Sales = $250,000

Unit sales price = $\dfrac{\$250,000}{10,000}$ = $25

b. $\dfrac{\$120,000}{\$250,000}$ = 48%

c. $\dfrac{\$250,000}{\$800,000}$ = 31.25%

d. Sales (8,000 units @ $25) = $200,000

Return on total assets = $\dfrac{\$200,000}{\$800,000} \times \dfrac{\$86,000^*}{\$200,000}$ = 10.75%

*	$200,000	Sales revenue
Less	64,000	Variable costs ($8 × 8,000)
	$136,000	
Less	50,000	Fixed costs
	$ 86,000	Income

Review Questions

1. Explain why you agree or disagree that managers should ask themselves, "Do I really know what my products cost?"

2. *a.* Why is the determination of a product's price so difficult?
   b. Name some external and internal factors that influence the pricing decision.

3. Define differential cost pricing and give an illustration of when it is in the company's best interest for management *not* to use this method.

4. *a.* Why is the use of differential cost analysis in short-term pricing considered a defensive planning technique?
   b. Why do unit differential costs sometimes establish the minimum sales price in short-run pricing decisions?

5. Assume a company sells products that differ only very slightly from competitors' products. Also, there are many competitors in this industry.

   a. Under these conditions how much influence will the company's cost have on the price it charges?
   b. What costs should the sale price at least cover in short-term price cutting situations experienced by this company?

6. *a.* Discuss the role of cost in pricing decisions.
   b. When would a company establish its sales price below variable cost?

7. How does the law of diminishing returns play a role in the pricing decision?

8. Discuss the relationship between demand, supply, and cost.

9. Describe several cost-plus pricing methods.

10. Social costs are not considered in differential cost pricing. Define these costs and their relationship to social responsibility.

CPA/CMA/CIA Multiple Choice Questions

1. (AICPA) Adly Corporation wishes to earn a 30 percent return on its $100,000 investment in equipment used to produce Product X. Based on estimated sales of 10,000 units of Product X next year, the costs per unit would be as follows:

Variable manufacturing costs	$5
Fixed selling and administrative costs . . .	2
Fixed manufacturing costs	1

   At how much per unit should Product X be priced for sale?

   a. $5.
   b. $8.
   c. $10.
   d. $11.

2. (AICPA) Nada Company established its pricing structure to yield a gross margin of 30 percent. The following data pertain to the year ended December 31, 19X1:

Sales	$1,000,000
Inventory, January 1, 19X1	500,000
Purchases	400,000
Inventory, per actual count at December 31, 19X1 . . .	80,000

   Nada is satisfied that all sales and purchases have been fully and properly recorded. How much might Nada reasonably estimate as a shortage in inventory at December 31, 19X1?

   a. $100,000.
   b. $120,000.
   c. $200,000.
   d. $276,000.

3. (AICPA) Aba Caterers quotes a price of $30 per person for a dinner party. This price includes the 6 percent sales tax and the 15 percent service charge. Sales tax is computed on the food plus the service charge. The service charge is computed on the food only. At what amount does Aba price the food?

   a. $23.70.
   b. $24.61.
   c. $25.50.
   d. $28.20.

4. (CIA) A product has a downward sloping demand curve and an upward sloping supply curve; a decrease in demand will have a:

   a. Price decreasing effect and a quantity increasing effect.
   b. Price increasing effect and a quantity decreasing effect.
   c. Price and quantity increasing effect.
   d. Price and quantity decreasing effect.

5. (CMA) If both the supply and the demand for a good increase, the market price will

   a. Rise only in the case of an inelastic supply function.
   b. Fall only in the case of an inelastic supply function.
   c. Not be predictable with only these facts.
   d. Rise only in the case of an inelastic demand function.
   e. Fall only in the case of an inelastic demand function.

6. (CIA) A company is considering selling 10,000 units of a new product that has the following estimated data:

	Per Unit
Revenue	$20.00
Direct materials	3.00
Direct labor	4.00
Variable factory overhead	2.00
Sales commission	1.00
Allocated fixed overhead	5.00

Adding the product will not increase total fixed costs, but will increase profits by:

   a. $ 50,000
   b. $100,000.
   c. $110,000.
   d. $140,000.

7. (AICPA) In the contribution margin approach to pricing, the price at which the income remains constant is equal to the price that covers

   a. Prime costs.
   b. Variable costs.
   c. Fixed costs.
   d. Fixed and variable costs plus the desired profit.

8. (CPA) Total profits will be maximized when:

   a. Total revenue equals total cost.
   b. Marginal revenue equals zero.
   c. Marginal cost equals average cost.
   d. Marginal cost equals marginal revenue.

9. (AICPA) Diva Company wants to establish a selling price that will yield a gross margin of 40 percent on sales of a product whose cost is $12.00 per unit. The selling price should be

   a. $16.80.
   b. $19.20.
   c. $20.00.
   d. $30.00.

10. (AICPA) Doe Company wants to sell a product at a gross margin of 20 percent. The cost of the product is $2. The selling price should be

    a. $1.60.
    b. $2.10.
    c. $2.40.
    d. $2.50.

Exercises

E23–1 Direct and Full-Cost Pricing (L.O. 3)

Indirect costs of a product manufactured by Jeakle Company amount to 60 percent of direct costs. Direct costs of the product are $10 for each unit. Management wishes to add a 25 percent markup on the cost basis used to arrive at the sales price.

Required:

a. Determine the sales price if direct cost pricing is used.
b. Determine the sales price if full-cost pricing is used.

E23–2 Contribution Margin and Pricing (L.O. 1)

The marketing personnel of Feaver Company conducted numerous market surveys to determine the most profitable price for its product. Based on these surveys, managers project the following sales volumes at the various prices:

> 27,500 units at $74 per unit
> 25,400 units at $74.50 per unit
> 21,000 units at $80.90 per unit
> 18,750 units at $89 per unit

Fixed costs of $450,000 would remain unchanged over the range of production capacities predicted for these prices. Forecasted variable expense is $42.25 per unit.

Required:

Determine the selling price that would maximize company income.

E23–3 Direct Cost Pricing and Full-Cost Pricing (L.O. 3)

Roke Company has determined the indirect cost of all its products is 75 percent of direct costs. Management wishes to earn a profit equal to 20 percent of total costs.

Required:

Compare the direct cost pricing method to the full-cost pricing method assuming the direct costs of a product are $25.

E23–4 Profit Maximization under Monopolistic Market (L.O. 2)

Arthur Company manufactures a variety of products, one of which was developed by a secret process and is enjoying a monopolistic market. Due to its technological nature, it is doubtful that a competitor can develop a substitute in the near future. Arthur Company will not begin production until an order is received.

The Marketing and Production Departments provide management with the following prices and the total costs for various quantities:

Quantity	Average Price	Total Cost
1	$350	$ 260
2	325	490
3	290	710
4	250	890
5	220	1,040
6	180	1,200

Required:

Determine the price at which profits are maximized.

E23–5 Using Cost as Basis for Sales Price (L.O. 1)

Warren, Inc., has estimated its fixed overhead to be $10,000 for a monthly planned production of 5,000 units. The unit cost is based on standards as follows:

Direct material	$5
Direct labor	3
Variable overhead	8

Required:

Compute the sales price assuming the following alternative markups are added to full cost to arrive at the sales price:

a. 10 percent markup on variable cost.
b. 5 percent markup on full cost.
c. 20 percent markup on conversion cost.

E23–6 Estimating Gross Margin with Sales Price Increase (L.O. 1)

Sales of Charles Alworth Company's principal product totaled $600,000 in 19X1. Cost of goods sold was as follows:

Direct material used	$180,000
Direct labor	60,000
Variable factory overhead	30,000
Fixed factory overhead	90,000

The company has received a price change from its supplier so that material prices will average 10 percent higher in 19X2. Managers have signed a labor union contract calling for an 8 percent wage increase. Variable factory overhead is applied on the basis of direct labor dollars. To earn the same rate of gross margin as in 19X1, the sales price will be increased. This sales price increase will result in a 6 percent decrease in the number of units sold.

Required:

Determine what 19X2 total sales must be to earn the same gross margin as in 19X1.

E23–7 Desired Sales and Asset Turnover (L.O. 3)

The following information is from Charles Mott Company:

Assets		Liabilities and Owners' Equity	
Cash	$ 75,000	Current liabilities	$380,000
Accounts receivable	125,000	Owners' equity	520,000
Inventory	192,000		
Property	508,000		

Fixed expenses: $98,500
Variable expenses: $8.25 per unit
Estimated volume for next year: 14,000 units sold

Required:

a. Calculate the sales the company must have if management wants an income equal to a 12 percent return on its investment in total assets. What unit sales price is needed to achieve this objective?
b. Compute the budgeted total asset turnover.
c. Calculate the desired income as a percentage of sales.
d. Assume the company sells 16,000 units instead of 14,000. What will be the return on total assets?

E23–8 Profit Maximization under Monopolistic Market (L.O. 2)

Basford Manufacturing, Inc., makes a variety of products, one of which was developed by a secret process and is enjoying a monopolistic market. Due to its technological nature, it is doubtful that a competitor can develop a substitute in the near future. Basford, Inc., will not begin production until an order is received.

The Marketing and Production Departments provide management with the following prices and the total costs for various quantities:

Quantity	Average Price	Total Cost
1	$525	$ 350
2	480	630
3	445	905
4	400	1,090
5	360	1,225
6	320	1,450
7	280	1,580

Required:

Determine the price at which profits are maximized.

Problems

P23–9 Price Decreases and Volume (L.O. 3)

After studying the following income statement for its product, management of Ott Company believes that a reduction in sales price may be justified:

Year Ending December 31, 19X1

Sales (100,000 units)		$500,000
Variable costs	$200,000	
Fixed costs	210,000	410,000
Income before taxes		$ 90,000

Required:

a. Calculate how much extra volume must be sold in 19X2 to yield an income equal to that earned in 19X1 if decreases of 8 percent, 12 percent, and 20 percent in selling prices become necessary.
b. Explain why successive price decreases of equal amounts require progressively larger increases in volume to equalize profits.
c. Discuss the factors management should study further before reducing the sales price.

P23–10 Sales Price to Achieve Objective (L.O. 1)

During the current year Jim Jamison Company sold 80 heating units for $200 each. Included in the costs were a $30 unit material cost and a $40 unit direct labor cost. Factory overhead is 100 percent of direct labor cost. Interest expense on a 12 percent bank loan is equivalent to $2 per unit, while federal and state income tax at a 35 percent rate equals $4.50 per unit.

Effective at mid-year, material costs decreased 10 percent, and direct labor increased 20 percent. Interest rates increased from 12 percent to 14 percent, equaling $2.50 per unit at the 14 percent rate.

Required:

a. Compute the sales price per unit that will produce the same ratio of gross profit expressed as a percentage of sales price assuming no change in the rate of overhead in relation to direct labor costs.

b. Compute the sales price per unit that will produce the same ratio of gross profit expressed as a percentage of sales price assuming that $10 of the overhead consists of fixed costs.

P23–11 Sales and Cash Breakeven Points (L.O. 1)

Perry Rental Service is in a wooded Idaho community that they believe is an ideal marketing setting for a chain saw rental operation. The company owns 18 chain saws, which are rented for $9 per hour to both contractors and homeowners. Oil and gasoline cost $3.50 per hour; repair and maintenance, $2.50 per hour; and the commission, $1 per hour. Insurance and depreciation average $60 and $140, respectively, per chain saw per year. Utilities on the rental office and adjacent maintenance building amount to $170 per month; rent on these two buildings is $250 per month; and insurance is $15 per month. Monthly salaries are $350.

Management determined 60 hours per chain saw per month to be the maximum demand in this geographical location. Perry owns all but four of the chain saws and plans to pay for these in monthly note payments within the year. Each chain saw costs $700, which is considered expensive for this type of tool, but the owner purchased a high-quality product thinking the higher price would be justified since the tools would likely be subject to harsh use.

Required:

a. Exclude the note payment on the chain saws and give the sales breakeven point and the cash breakeven point in hours per month per chain saw. Ignore any tax shield from noncash expenses.

b. Compute the average hours per month the company must rent the chain saws to meet all cash outlays required including the note payment on the four chain saws.

P23–12 Price Quotes (L.O. 3)

Camco, Inc., is a single product company that manufactures an insecticide, Radar. Radar is sold through national supermarket chains and drugstore chains. Recently another firm asked Camco, Inc., to submit a bid for a 5,000-pound order of a private brand insecticide. While the chemical compound of the private brand differs from Radar, the manufacturing process is very similar.

Under its typical manufacturing process, the company would subdivide the private brand into ten 500-pound units. Each unit requires 30 direct labor-hours and the following chemicals:

Chemicals	Quantity in Pounds
A-3	100
B-5	125
C-7	175
D-9	100

Camco also uses A-3 and B-5 in the production of Radar. However, Camco, Inc., does not carry C-7 and D-9 in its inventory and these chemicals will be purchased from Camco suppliers. Camco also has a chemical E-1 which is the by-product of Radar. E-1 can substitute for D-9 on a one-for-one basis and will not change the quality of the private brand. E-1 is sold to other chemical companies at current market price.

Chemists indicate that there are 1,500 pounds of a chemical called Cs left over from a discontinued product which can substitute for C-7 on a two-for-one basis. The salvage value of the 1,500 pounds of Cs is $530.

Inventory and relevant cost data for the chemicals in the private brand are as follows:

1.

Chemicals	Pounds in Inventory	Actual Price per Pound When Purchased	Current Market Price per Pound
A-3	1,200	$1.50	$1.70
B-5	1,300	2.00	1.80
C-7	0	0	2.10
D-9	0	0	0.95
E-1	1,100	0	0.50

2. Camco, Inc., pays its workers $5 an hour before overtime. If overtime is required, workers receive wages at time-and-a-half the regular rate. Based on its production schedule, Camco, Inc., can incur 500 additional direct labor-hours before it reaches the full capacity level at which overtime will be required.

3. Accountants determine the manufacturing overhead at the beginning of each year and use direct labor-hours as the base. The predetermined overhead rate for this year is as follows:

	Cost per Direct Labor-Hour
Variable manufacturing overhead	$3.25
Fixed manufacturing overhead	2.25
Total	$5.50

Required:

a. Compute the minimum bid (the bid will not increase or decrease its current profit) for Camco if this is a one-time order.

b. Determine the minimum bid for Camco, Inc., if there is a 40 percent markup on its manufacturing cost and the private brand will be a regular order in the future.

P23–13 Optimum Price Volume Alternatives (L.O. 3)

Yolande, Inc., is a record company. It manufactures cassette tapes, LPs, and CDs. The following interim financial statement is for last month:

Yolande, Inc.
Condensed Income Statement for April

	Cassette Tape	LP	CD	Total
Sales	$10,000	$8,000	$12,000	$30,000
Cost of goods sold	4,000	4,000	4,500	12,500
Gross margin	$ 6,000	$4,000	$ 7,500	$17,500
Marketing and administrative expenses:				
Variable	1,500	1,744	1,740	4,984
Fixed	3,000	2,400	3,600	9,000
Total marketing and administrative expenses ..	$ 4,500	$4,144	$ 5,340	$13,984
Income before taxes	$ 1,500	$ (144)	$ 2,160	$ 3,516

The fixed marketing and administrative expense is allocated to each product according to the predetermined rate established at the beginning of each year.

Although the manufacturing process of cassette tapes, LPs, and CDs are in the same plant, Yolande regards them as three independent units and each unit carries its own production cost, except the fixed overhead cost which is based on 80 percent capacity of full production.

	Cassette Tape	LP	CD
Full production capacity per month	1,800 units	1,800 units	1,800 units
Current production	1,200 units	1,600 units	1,200 units
Manufacturing cost per unit:			
Direct materials	$1.15	$0.90	$1.35
Direct labor	0.75	0.60	0.85
Variable manufacturing overhead	0.65	0.55	0.75
Fixed manufacturing overhead	0.65	0.45	0.80
Total manufacturing costs	$3.20	$2.50	$3.75
Variable marketing and administrative unit cost	1.20	1.09	1.45

The Marketing Department of Yolande just completed a market forecast. The following schedule indicates the relation between sales price and sales volume of each product line.

Cassette Tape		LP		CD	
Unit Price	Sales Volume	Unit Price	Sales Volume	Unit Price	Sales Volume
$ 6	1,500	$4	1,750	$ 8	1,600
7	1,370	5	1,600	9	1,300
8	1,250	6	1,550	10	1,200
9	1,100	7	1,400	11	1,100
10	900	8	1,200	12	950

Also in the report, the Marketing Department indicates that the prospects of increased sales for cassette tapes and CDs are good, but that the LP market will remain steady.

Required:

a. Indicate the unit selling price Yolande should select for each of its products for the rest of the year.

b. Assume the sales forecast of the next eight months is the same as April. Should Yolande shut down its LP Division temporarily for the rest of the year and reopen it next year?

P23–14 Net Present Value of Investment Opportunities (L.O. 1)

Auto Parts, Inc., is entering its 12th year of operations. The agenda for its upcoming monthly meeting of company executives includes consideration of several investment decisions. Management will give those attending a summary of the possibilities and instruct them to be prepared to discuss and defend their positions. The list follows:

1. Determination of the sales price for a new automotive part needs to be finalized. The following estimated probabilities of annual sales at previously suggested prices have been furnished by the sales manager. The part has a variable cost per unit of $12.

Sales in Units	Selling Price			
	$12	$13	$14	$15
40,000	—	—	5%	90%
50,000	—	40%	10	10
60,000	40%	20	45	—
70,000	60	40	40	—

2. Evaluation of two mutually exclusive plans for improving operating results:

   Plan A—Double volume through an intensive promotional effort. This will lower the profit margin to 3 percent of sales and require an additional investment of $100,000.

   Plan B—Eliminate some unprofitable products and improve efficiency by adding $350,000 in capital equipment. This will decrease sales volume by 5 percent but improve the profit margin to 6 percent.

   The current profit margin is 4 percent on net annual sales of $2,500,000. An investment of $400,000 is needed to finance these sales. The company uses return on investment to measure operating results.

3. Consideration of requests for short-term financing from three franchised dealers. The dealers have agreed to repay the loans within three years and to pay 6 percent of net income for the three-year period for the use of the funds. The following table summarizes by dealer the financing requested and the total remittances (principal plus 6 percent of net income) expected at the end of each year:

	Dealer		
	Adams	**Brock**	**Crane**
Financing requested	$100,000	$70,000	$40,000
Remittances expected at end of:			
Year 1	$ 30,000	$40,000	$30,000
Year 2	40,000	30,000	20,000
Year 3	60,000	20,000	10,000
	$130,000	$90,000	$60,000

The financing will be made available only if the annual beforetax return to Auto Parts, Inc., exceeds the required rate of 22 percent on investment. Discount factors (rounded) providing this rate of return: Year 1—0.8; Year 2—0.7; and Year 3—0.6.

Required:

a. Prepare a schedule computing the expected incremental income for each of the sales prices proposed for the new automotive part in item 1 on the list. Include the expected sales in units (weighted according to the sales manager's estimated probabilities), the expected total monetary sales, expected total variable costs, and expected incremental income.

b. Prepare schedules comparing Auto Parts, Inc.'s current rate of return on investment to the anticipated rates of return for each of the two plans in item 2.

c. Prepare a schedule to compute the net present value of the investment opportunities of financing Adams, Brock, and Crane. The schedule should determine whether the discounted cash flows expected from each dealer are more or less than Auto Parts, Inc.'s investment in loans in each.

P23–15 Using Standards for Pricing (L.O. 3)

Sales Company established the following standards five years ago; since that time several changes have been made in the production process:

Material (2 pounds @ $1 per pound)	$ 2
Direct labor (1 hour @ $10 per hour)	10
Factory overhead (1 hour @ $5 per hour)	5
Standard manufacturing cost per unit	$17

A normal capacity of 100,000 units was the basis for developing standards for factory overhead. Budgeted factory overhead costs in establishing the standards were

Variable factory overhead	$300,000
Fixed factory overhead	200,000
Total factory overhead	$500,000

The midyear financial statements indicate the following costs of manufacturing and selling 50,000 units:

Material	$ 250,000
Direct labor	650,000
Variable factory overhead	200,000
Fixed factory overhead	120,000
Advertising	25,000
Marketing salaries	50,000
Administrative supplies	16,000
Administrative salaries	30,000
Total expenses	$1,341,000

ATA Company offers to buy 10,000 units annually for three years for $18, FOB shipping point. These units represent a slight modification of Sales's present product.

Top management of Sales Company realizes that they are considering a drastic marketing step not only for its financial consequences but also for the manufacturing factors affected. The following estimate of the financial aspects of the proposal for the first 12 months supports a recommendation to accept ATA's offer. The sales proposal includes a 10 percent increase in marketing and administrative salaries since the ATA offer represents a 10 percent increase in sales volume; however, no other marketing or administrative expenses are included.

Sales Proposal
First 12 Months Results

Proposed sales (10,000 @ $18)		$180,000
Estimated costs and expenses:		
Production (10,000 @ $17)	$170,000	
Marketing salaries	5,000	
Administrative salaries	3,000	
Total estimated costs		178,000
Income		$ 2,000

Required:

a. Criticize the first year's financial analysis of the proposal prepared by Sales Company, listing any weaknesses you detect.

b. Prepare a more appropriate analysis for the first year of the ATA order, indicating if the order should be rejected.

P23–16 Determining Sales Price to Achieve Objectives (L.O. 1)

Kimberly Wells plans to establish a drapery company specializing in the manufacture of custom-made draperies and bedspreads, as well as purchased hardware parts, exclusively for the residential market of Butler County. The company will have manufacturing, display, and office space in a light industrial area occupied by similar businesses. Management expects very little walk-in trade; thus, location is important only from a general geographic standpoint.

After extensive research, Wells estimated the following sales and costs for the first year:

Total Market—United States (millions)

Drapery hardware	$ 334
Draperies	935
Bedspreads	534
Curtains	334
Total expected sales	$2,137
U.S. population	203,300,000
Butler County population	722,017

Management is confident that their company can capture 10 percent of the Butler County custom market, recognizing that custom drapes represent 20 percent of all drapery sales. From previous experience in this field, management expects that 10 percent of total hardware sales are for custom drapes. In addition, it expects 1 percent of all bedspread sales to be for the custom market. No curtains are custom made.

Drapery shops typically base the quoted price of their product on the estimated material and labor used to manufacture the product. Butler Drapery Shop has taken the following typical product and estimated its material and labor cost. Material and labor for custom bedspreads bear the same relationship to sales price as do drapery costs.

**Manufactured Items (Typical
Product 48″ × 84″
Lined Drapery Made of Satin)**

Direct material cost	$13.52
Labor cost	9.36
	$22.88
Markup	29.12
Sales price	$52.00

Less markup is realized on drapery hardware parts that are purchased since the material cost constitutes 50 percent of the sales price, while direct labor on such parts remains at 18 percent of sales price.

Management expects all other costs to total $19,100 for the year.

Required:

a. Develop a market forecast providing (1) the expected Butler County expenditures for drapery and curtain hardware, draperies, bedspreads, and curtains; (2) the portion of these expenditures which represents the custom-made market; and (3) Butler Drapery Shop's projected sales and expenses for the year.

b. Calculate the percentage the sales price must increase if management wishes to earn a 25 percent return on the $125,000 in assets employed in the company.

P23–17 Evaluating Cost Proposal (L.O. 3)

As auditor for one of the Air Force agencies, you are examining a proposal submitted by the Small Engines Company, classified as a small business. Small Engines Company performs contract work for both government agencies and private firms. The bid is being submitted under a cost-plus arrangement. They do not have a detailed cost accounting system, but their financial records have been audited by a CPA for the last two years and they were given a clean opinion by the auditors.

In submitting their bid initially, only the following financial report was attached.

Bid Submitted in 19X3

Direct cost:	
Parts and supplies	$ 5,000
Payroll, health, and welfare	1,500
Managers and assistant managers (all will be working	
only on this project)	3,500
Total direct costs	$10,000
General and administrative (12.5% × direct cost)	1,250
Total cost	$11,250
Total bid (cost + 10%)	$12,375

After examining the proposal, you believe that the financial information is not adequate to verify the general and administrative costs. You contact the firm's attorney who has the responsibility for negotiating the contract. When you ask for copies of the last year's certified financial statements, he is very reluctant to supply them. In fact, he says, "Why do you need them? You do not understand what the figures on these certified financial statements mean anyway." You tactfully explain to him that you have extensive accounting training and experience and believe that you are qualified to analyze them. Also, you remind him that you are both a CMA and a CPA and this provides credence of your ability. When these comments do not solicit the action desired, you remind the attorney that you have the authority to open this bidding up to completely competitive procedures rather than to selected small business organizations. This proves to be enough of an incentive that he forwards last year's income statement. In 19X2, the following three contracts were received by the company:

SMALL ENGINES COMPANY
Income Statement for Year Ended December 31, 19X2

	Repair Contract	Shipyard Contract	Brown Company Contract
Revenue	$12,000	$15,000	$18,000
Costs:			
Parts and supplies ..	$ 2,000	$ 3,600	$ 4,100
Payroll, health, and welfare	400	800	1,700
Managers and assistants	1,600	4,600	6,200
General and administrative	200	900	960
Total cost	$ 4,200	$ 9,900	$12,960
Operating income	$ 7,800	$ 5,100	$ 5,040

Required:

a. Indicate how you would verify the accuracy of the 12.5 percent general and administrative cost allocation in the bid.

b. Evaluate the accuracy of the 12.5 percent application rate.

P23–18 Use of Contribution Margin in Pricing Decisions (L.O. 3)

As a consultant strongly supportive of the contribution reporting concept, you are surprised to find that contribution reporting is not employed to a great extent at Spritt, Inc. Instead, you find that marketing, engineering, and administrative expenses are allocated in detail. When you ask Ann Brown, director of financial planning at Spritt, why contribution reporting is not employed more extensively, she indicates that while the concept is employed to some degree, management also believes that the profit after allocating marketing, administrative, and engineering expenses is very important. Management also believes an analysis of only contribution margin may lead a company to false conclusions, especially in pricing decisions.

When you press Brown for an explanation, she gives you the following monthly data for two of the firm's products:

	Totals
Sales—Product A (500 units)	$100,000
Sales—Product B (700 units)	210,000
Variable manufacturing cost—Product A	35,000
Variable manufacturing cost—Product B	87,500
Variable marketing and administrative—Product A	15,000
Variable marketing and administrative—Product B	52,500
Fixed manufacturing cost	40,000
Marketing (fixed)	20,000
Executive analysis (fixed)	42,000
Research and patents (fixed)	10,000

All four products processed use approximately the same amounts of floor space and supervision. However, of the hours spent in promoting these two products, the marketing staff estimates that 45 percent of their time is spent on Product A, 20 percent on Product B, and the remainder equally on the other two company products. A customer claims physical damage from using Product A. Consequently, management has spent many hours in consultation with their lawyers. In estimating the time spent on each product, management believes an allocation of 30 percent to Product A and 20 percent to Product B is appropriate. Because the customer claims Product A's glass container is defective, management is concerned there may be additional lawsuits unless changes are made. The engineering staff has been working on a new design for the container that management hopes to patent soon. However, the explosive nature of Product A will always present additional hazards, and it is doubtful that a container can be designed that is completely free of potential problems. Time sheets for the research department show 70 percent of their hours were spent in analyzing and testing Product A, while the remainder of the time was divided equally among the other three products.

Brown further believes that while marginal analysis is a very useful tool, its benefits are overemphasized. One reason for this, she says, is that too many costs are omitted because they are labeled as fixed and irrelevant. She describes the following situation which occurred recently in the Fabricating Department. When the Fabricating Department was employing two supervisors and 16 direct labor workers, several orders were received for processing 100 additional units per month. The revenue from each 100-unit order would amount to $1,000 monthly. Since the work force could not handle any increase in workload, one additional direct labor worker was required to handle each 100-unit increase. The supervisor will be added when the 24th worker is employed. Direct labor workers and supervisors earn $700 and $1,248 per month, respectively. Variable materials and overhead amount to $1 per finished unit.

Brown claims that the use of marginal analysis in this situation would have been a costly mistake. Instead, a total cost approach was used, further supporting her contention that fixed costs and allocated costs are indispensable in the operation of a business and that they should not be omitted from the accountant's analysis in pricing decisions.

Required:

a. Agree or disagree with Brown's contention that contribution reporting can lead to false conclusions. Support your position with financial analyses of Products A and B.
b. Prepare marginal and total cost analyses for use in making a decision as to whether to accept any one of eight additional 100-unit orders.

P23–19 (CMA) Using Costs in Bid Prices (L.O. 1)

Marcus Fibers Inc. specializes in the manufacture of synthetic fibers that the company uses in many products such as blankets, coats, and uniforms for police and firefighters. Marcus has been in business since 1975 and has been profitable each year since 1983. The company uses a standard cost system and applies overhead on the basis of direct labor hours.

Marcus has recently received a request to bid on the manufacture of 800,000 blankets scheduled for delivery to several military bases. The bid must be stated at full cost per unit plus a return on full cost of no more than 9 percent after income taxes. Full cost has been defined as including all variable costs of manufacturing the product, a reasonable amount of fixed overhead, and reasonable incremental administrative costs associated with the manufacture and sale of the product. The contractor has indicated that bids in excess of $25.00 per blanket are not likely to be considered.

In order to prepare the bid for the 800,000 blankets, Andrea Lightner, cost accountant, has gathered the information presented in the box about the costs associated with the production of the blankets.

Required:

a. Calculate the minimum price per blanket that Marcus Fibers Inc. could bid without reducing the company's net income.
b. Using the full cost criteria and the maximum allowable return specified, calculate Marcus Fibers Inc.'s bid price per blanket.
c. Without prejudice to your answer to Requirement b, assume that the price per blanket that Marcus Fibers Inc. calculated using the cost-plus criteria specified is greater than the maximum bid of $25.00 per blanket allowed. Discuss the factors that Marcus Fibers Inc. should consider before deciding whether or not to submit a bid at the maximum acceptable price of $25.00 per blanket.

Raw material	$1.50 per pound of fibers
Direct labor	$7.00 per hour
Direct machine costs*	$10.00 per blanket
Variable overhead	$3.00 per direct labor-hour
Fixed overhead	$8.00 per direct labor-hour
Incremental administrative costs	$2,500 per 1,000 blankets
Special fee**	$0.50 per blanket
Material usage	6 pounds per blanket
Production rate	4 blankets per direct labor-hour
Effective tax rate	40 percent

*Direct machine costs consist of items such as special lubricants, replacement of needles used in stitching, and maintenance costs. These costs are not included in the normal overhead rates.

**Marcus recently developed a new blanket fiber at a cost of $750,000. In an effort to recover this cost, Marcus has instituted a policy of adding a $0.50 fee to the cost of each blanket using the new fiber. To date, the company has recovered $125,000. Lightner knows that this fee does not fit within the definition of full cost as it is not a cost of manufacturing the product.

P23–20 Determining Optimal Pricing Alternative (L.O. 1)

William Grasty Investment Corporation completed the construction of a $2 million building last year. The building is on the outskirts of a major western city on an important highway leading into the city. The building was designed to appeal to a professional clientele such as doctors, dentists, lawyers, and accountants.

Even though tenants have different rates depending on the lease period and the options involved, the following average price of the space has been set, based on floor location:

Floor Style	Average Rate per Square Foot per Year	Square Feet Available
A	$8.00	71,000
B	7.50	100,000
C	6.50	80,000

The prices are higher than those of the competition, but management believes that its price is justified by product differentiation. The building offers its tenants free use of a health club so that they can exercise during lunch hours. A plush restaurant and bar on top of the building is open to the public for both lunch and dinner. Management believes that the convenience of a nice restaurant for business entertaining is an added attraction.

Even though the building is 10 miles from the nearest hospital, management believes that this should not be a great hindrance to the medical profession. In comparison to the office space located nearer the hospital, Grasty Investment's building is more plush. As its advertisements emphasize, occupants of the building avoid heavy downtown traffic. The building is in a higher income suburb where more of its proposed tenants live; management believes this is an added attraction.

Management has, however, been concerned with the average tenant roll for the first 12 months of operation. The projected overall occupancy rate for this period of time was 85 percent, although the actual rates never reached expectations. The actual average percentage of occupancy by floor style for the year was Style A, 70 percent; Style B, 75 percent; and Style C, 78 percent.

Management had hoped that by the second year of operations the occupancy rate would be approximately 95 percent; however, since the rate of increase of tenants moving into the building has been much slower than anticipated, the company believes that it must carefully study the problem. Management believes that the low occupancy rate may stem from several causes. One may be that the rates charged are not justified; the "extras" perceived by management may not be viewed as such by the clientele and do not warrant the higher rates. In addition, the selected target market may be too small. Members of the medical profession may so prefer the convenience of office space near the hospital with which they are affiliated that the plush surroundings are not inducement enough.

In addition, the company is faced with rising utility costs. Variable costs per square foot occupied for each floor style are expected to increase to $3.50, including utilities and newspaper advertising, for the second year. Fixed annual costs are expected to be $680,000 for the second year.

Management is also faced with the possibility that some of the present tenants may break their leasing agreements. These tenants include a snack bar, pharmacy, and hairstyling salon; their marketing plan is geared to having many people in the building. These three major tenants are upset because business is not as profitable as expected since the building has not been occupied faster. Each of the three has seriously threatened to move if the occupancy rate does not improve immediately. The hairstyling salon rents 1,500 square feet of Floor Style B; the snack bar and the pharmacy, 2,000 square feet, and 3,000 square feet, of Floor Style C, respectively.

Thus far, management has been able to postpone the move of these three tenants because of negotiation with a large government agency to lease one entire floor. This agency has offered to rent 10,000 square feet of Floor Style A at a $6.20 rate per square foot per year. Because of the extra traffic, the agency is also asking that Grasty Company provide additional janitorial service which will cost Grasty $2 per square foot. Management recognizes that the probability of the government agency leasing the building for a long period of time is much greater than for other clients. Variable costs of $3.50 per square foot are also expected for the space occupied by the government agency. In addition, if the government agency becomes a tenant, management expects an increased occupancy of 6 percent of total square footage of Floor Space A and 5 percent each in Floor Spaces B and C. These leases will be signed at the existing rates.

The vice president of finance argues that the company cannot afford a reduction in rate for the government agency. He believes even if the three tenants leasing the snack bar, pharmacy, and hairstyling salon do leave because the government agency does not sign a lease, he will be able to lease, at existing rates, 60 percent of the space that would be occupied by the government agency and 70 percent of the space lost if the three tenants move. To accomplish this, he plans to use a marketing agency to personally contact physicians and lawyers and explain the benefits of the building. The marketing agency will charge a flat fee of $5,000 plus 10 percent of the first year's rental fees for space that they sell.

The vice president of marketing has been trying for months to convince top management that the present promotion policy of only using newspaper advertising is inadequate. She agrees with using the services of the vice president of finance's agency to increase occupancy, but suggests the company also conduct a television advertising campaign involving 50 minutes of local television time which will cost $260 per minute. Data from a market survey conducted last month show that if both these promotion services are added, 80 percent of the space under consideration by the government agency and 78 percent of the space lost if the three tenants move would be occupied at existing rates. (Assume the increase in occupancy over the vice president of finance's proposal is the result of the television advertising campaign and the marketing agency fee will be the same as in the vice president of finance's recommendation.)

The president of Grasty Company disagrees with both vice presidents and with the rate reduction necessary for the government agency to move in. Instead, he proposes the following change in price for all tenants effective at the beginning of the second year.

Room Style	Average Rate per Square Foot per Year
A	$7.00
B	6.50
C	5.50

The president's forecast shows that this will result in the following average rates of occupancy for the second year: Style A, 82 percent; Style B, 90 percent; Style C, 95 percent. This additional volume would also increase the already profitable restaurant and bar.

Other members of the management team disagree with all plans thus far proposed and believe that a time lag between opening the offices and the desired occupancy levels should be expected for a building of this size. They argue that no change in rates should be made; instead, the company should wait and allow potential occupants to become more aware of the benefits this office building offers. These executives believe that if no change in the promotion policy or the price rates is made, the following rates of occupancy will be in effect: Style A, 70 percent; Style B, 76 percent; Style C, 80 percent.

Required:

a. Determine income before taxes from leasing activities using the following alternatives:
   (1) The government agency offer is accepted.
   (2) Vice president of finance's recommendation.
   (3) Vice president of marketing's recommendation.
   (4) President's recommendation for rate reduction.
   (5) Rate schedule stays the same allowing for a time lag.
b. Indicate any additional factors to be considered before a decision is made.

Cases

C23–21 Evaluating Pricing Policy (L.O. 3)

Dill Corporation was formed as a method of benefiting key employees of a national corporation. The employees invested in this company with the assurance that they would receive a high yield on their funds. For the first few years of its existence, the corporation showed a small but consistent growth with profitable operations. Various business ventures were continually suggested to Dill Corporation for consideration. After a venture was considered as being a good risk, having good growth possibilities, and being compatible with current operations, Dill would either buy an established company or set up a new company operating the new business as a division.

In the past few years, Dill Corporation has begun to show large losses despite tremendously increasing sales volume. At this time the corporation has four operating divisions: a service company, a brokerage and speciality division, a printing company, and a retail sales division. Each division was established as an independent company with a part-time bookkeeper.

After analysis, Dill management discovered that the retail sales operation appeared to be the cause of much of the loss. At this time a new manager was hired for the retail sales division, and an experienced accountant was hired to be the controller for the entire corporation. A primary job of the new accountant was to determine and correct the problems with the retail sales division because as sales in the division continued to increase, losses also became larger.

After much analysis, the controller discovered that salespersons were allowed to determine the discounts they would give their customers and to whom credit would be issued. In addition, the retail sales division kept a warehouse full of inventory although almost any product needed could be supplied by one of their local wholesalers usually on the same day. There were many cases of items being purchased which were in stock in the warehouse. Top management has informed the controller that the gross margin on the products sold by the retail division was supposed to average 40 percent on sales price; however, in studying a typical sale, the controller found the following:

$100	. . . .	Cost
40	. . . .	40 percent markup
$140	. . . .	Sales price

The manager of the retail sales division is hesitant to make any changes as he fears salespersons will quit if discounts are cut back and sales prices increased.

Required:

Suggest how to improve the profitability of the retail sales division.

C23–22 Management Philosophy and Its Effect on Pricing (L.O. 1)

Ben Boston Printing Press is constantly faced with a shortage of cash. The owner-managers are Mae Boston, her two sons, Ben and Tom, and their wives, Martha and Sally. Mae Boston supervises the bookbinders; Ben is the sales manager; Tom, the production manager; Martha, the payroll clerk-bookkeeper; and Sally, the supervisor of the layout operation. There are 12 people, excluding the family, employed full time. In addition, several skilled people are available to work part time, if needed. The 12 employees operate the company's various pieces of equipment.

Management is faced with pressing working capital needs. They believe part of their problem may be inadequate costing procedures. Management believes very strongly that they should never turn down business. Much of their work is custom orders that vary considerably in use of equipment and time. Ben, the sales manager, claims that he has no trouble getting orders; in fact, he says when he sees that volume will be down next week because of lack of orders, he hustles more orders.

None of the owners has had formal business training; however, they believe that their practical experience in the business is quite adequate. All family members are in supervisory roles and only if necessary do they assume direct labor positions.

The cash flow in and out is very erratic. The company is behind several months on payments for the printing presses. When there is a strong fear that the equipment may be repossessed, the owners hurry around and find enough cash to quiet the creditors temporarily. Often this means that when deliveries are made, their customers are given a chance to deduct 5 percent from the bill if they can immediately make cash payments.

The company claims that it cannot use a cost-based pricing system because it must meet competition. In addition, no cost figures are available. Their pricing strategy consists of referring to an eight-year-old industry price schedule classified by standard jobs. Then an additional fee is added to reflect whatever inflation they feel is necessary. After this total figure is determined, management asks itself whether that is the maximum the customer will bear. If it is not, the bid price is increased. If they believe they have priced themselves out of a job, they automatically reduce the bid price without reference to any other factor.

After the family contacts you concerning their needs, you visit the plant still undecided whether you will be able to help them, not yet agreeing to perform any consulting work. Then, early one morning, Tom calls you to plead for assistance. When you are able to calm Tom down, you find that he and Ben have had a big disagreement. Ben purchased a large hospitalization insurance policy for the company. This was purchased the day following his wife's visit to a neurosurgeon who scheduled back surgery for her in two weeks. Ben claims that the insurance agent assured him that the neurosurgery would be covered under their policy. When the facts are actually uncovered, you determine that the real reason Tom got so upset was because he had just received a call from an equipment creditor threatening to repossess one of his printing presses.

While drinking your morning coffee, you remember that the company's income statement from last month reported the following expenses, arranged in alphabetical order:

Accountant's fee	Miscellaneous expense
Advertising	Payroll taxes
Casual labor	Property insurance
Delivery expense	Rent expense
Depreciation expense	Repair expense
Employees' salaries	Supplies expense
Freight expense	Telephone expense
Interest expense (on current and past-due notes)	Utility expense

All of these were in addition to the salaries each family member earns. You feel that one of your first steps is to calculate the approximate cost of operating each machine per hour. This will become the basis for their pricing strategy. You gather the following data for two pieces of the company's total equipment, each requiring one machine operator:

Printing Press Cost—$7,770 (7-year life)

Monthly rent expense	$121.00
Monthly repairs	30.00
Machine operator	5.51 per hour
Payroll taxes, 9%	
Occupies 10% of floor space	
Present volume, 86 hours per momth	

Folder Cost—$1,500 (6-year life)

Machine operator	$ 5.51 per hour
Payroll taxes, 9%	
Monthly repairs	10.00
Occupies 12.5% of floor space	
Present volume, 22 hours per month	

The total monthly indirect overhead amounts to $3,472 based on a normal volume.

Required:

a. Comment on how the management philosophy of the company could be improved.
b. Cite any inherent problems that will be difficult to solve with the existing structure.
c. Assume that due to the hospitalization insurance crisis, the company needs a schedule showing the order in which monthly payments should be made. Prepare one.
d. Determine the hourly cost of operating the printing press and the folder.

C23–23 Identifying Social Responsibility Activities (L.O. 4)

Ann Watson earned a major in social work before deciding, at age 40, to return to school and major in cost accounting. After successfully completing the accounting program, she was hired in a large industrial firm as a cost accountant. While employed as a social worker, she became aware of programs undertaken by local industries that were designed to fulfill what the corporation considered its social responsibility. She also noticed, with regret, all the waste and smoke that these corporations dumped into the environment.

Although relatively satisfied with her new job as an accountant, Watson could not give up her concern for the environment while focusing so much attention on company cost and profit. She decided that, whenever the occasion arose, she would use her position to encourage the company to become more involved in community affairs.

Once, for example, when she was asked by the vice president at an office party if she thought the company was fulfilling its social responsibility, she had quickly remarked, "Indeed, no, because I believe this corporation, as well as others, should voluntarily respond to such needs of society as providing jobs in depressed areas of this city. The indigent population has problems in getting from one part of the city to another because of poor local transportation facilities." The vice president laughed and said, "Oh, forget that—this company fulfills its social responsibility by other means. Just last week we removed a high fence around the plant because some group argued that it was an eyesore; however, I hope we do not get fined since the zoning laws require a fence around the plant."

The vice president continued, "We also have installed antipollution devices on the factory smokestacks to reduce emissions to the standard established by state law. Also along with this concern for safety, we are requiring new employees to attend training programs so that they can operate the machinery more efficiently and safely." He listed these four additional projects that reflected the company's social responsibility: (1) contributing to the expense of a nationally known ballet company to perform in several programs in the community; (2) releasing two of its middle managers from their duties so they could actively participate in the local United Fund campaign; (3) adding a safety device to a product according to the recommendations of voluntary organizations that evaluate product safety; and (4) initiating a program to hire and train handicapped persons.

Later, Ann asked her supervisor why the vice president became so hostile when she suggested providing jobs in depressed areas. The supervisor related that the company tried to build a small labor-intensive subsidiary in a depressed part of the city several years ago to be staffed and managed by the indigent of that area. The plant closed after 18 months because of several misconceptions. One was that the company underestimated the time and money needed to establish the capitalist motivation in a culture to which it was alien; federal officials also gave less help than anticipated according to the company. Another reason was that the support from other businesses did not materialize; also the company couldn't get enough experienced managers with indigent backgrounds nor did they have much luck in convincing customers of the quality of its products. In addition, the community leaders who were attracted to this project soon found that their commitments to other civic activities prevented their spending as much time as earlier anticipated and they were, after all, less concerned about costs or meeting budgets.

In view of these recent events, Watson wonders if she should change her attitude regarding social responsibility to reflect a more practical approach.

Required:

a. Consider each of the seven programs itemized by the vice president and explain if it reflects the objective of social responsibility.
b. Explain why the labor-intensive plant in the depressed area failed.
c. Discuss the personal needs managers may have been trying to satisfy in establishing the plant in this depressed area.

CHAPTER 24

Revenue Variances, Material Mix and Yield Variances, and Labor Mix and Yield Variances

CHAPTER OBJECTIVES

After studying this chapter, you should be able to:

1. Explain how different levels of detail in variance analysis are appropriate and cost justified depending on the individual circumstance.

2. Prepare sales price, sales mix, and sales quantity variances for each product sold.

3. Calculate market size and market share variances that detail the sales quantity variance.

4. Determine material and labor mix and yield variances and interpret their meaning.

5. Describe the constraints involved with assumed substitution.

Introduction (L.O. 1)

One of cost accountants' prime responsibilities is assisting management in evaluating performance by determining variances between actual operations and planned operations. Chapters 11 and 12 describe how standard costing enables variances to be computed and interpreted for direct materials, direct labor, and factory overhead in the single product company and in the single ingredient product. This chapter applies standard cost and variance analysis and budgeting principles presented in earlier chapters to a multiproduct company and a multi-ingredient product.

In addition, we discuss the computation and analysis of the revenue variance, comprised of the sales price variance and the sales volume variance for the multiproduct company. The chapter also covers the direct materials and direct labor mix and yield variances for the multi-ingredient product; these are simply a further breakdown of the material and labor quantity variances studied in Chapters 11 and 12.

Revenue Variances for Multiproduct Companies (L.O. 2 and 3)

For planning purposes, a company that sells several products may assume that sales of its products occur in constant proportions. For example, a grocery may assume it sells two gallons of milk for every pound of steak. Management may intentionally use a low markup on one product (milk) to attract customers and increase sales of other products (such as steak) with higher contribution margins. Not only is the quantity of products sold important for management but also the relative mix of products.

A multiproduct company concentrates on a product-by-product analysis of sales price and sales volume. Companies often use sales price and sales volume variances to evaluate marketing performance. We determine the **sales price**

EXHIBIT 24–1

	Clevenger Company		
	Product A	**Product B**	**Total**
Budgeted unit sales price	$16	$20	—
Actual unit sales price	17	18	—
Standard variable cost per unit	12	12	—
Budgeted unit contribution margin	4	8	—
Budgeted sales volume	2,000 units	3,000 units	5,000 units
Budgeted sales mix percentage	40%	60%	100%
Actual sales volume	3,000 units	1,000 units	4,000 units
Actual sales mix percentage	75%	25%	100%
Total budgeted market for industry	12,500	10,000	
Budgeted market share	16%	30%	
Actual industry sales	6,000	5,000	
Actual market share	50%	20%	

variance by multiplying the difference between actual sales price and budgeted sales price times the actual quantity sold. The **sales volume variance** (also called **sales activity variance**) compares budgeted and actual quantity and mix.

To illustrate the revenue variances, assume Clevenger Company provides the estimated and actual results for its two product lines for the first quarter of the year as shown in Exhibit 24–1.

Based on an industry sales forecast, 12,500 units of Product A and 10,000 units of Product B will be sold this period. Management expects Product A sales of 2,000 units and Product B sales of 3,000 units. This is equivalent to a 16 percent share of Product A's market and a 30 percent share of Product B's market. Actual industry sales were 6,000 units of Product A and 5,000 units of Product B. This yields an actual market share of 50 percent (3,000/6,000 units) for Product A and 20 percent (1,000/5,000 units) for Product B.

Sales Price Variance

The sales price variance is computed as:

$$(\text{Actual sales price} - \text{Budgeted sales price}) \times \text{Actual quantity sold}$$

For Product A of Clevenger Company:

$$(\$17 - \$16) \times 3,000 = \$3,000 \text{ Favorable price variance}$$

For Product B of Clevenger Company:

$$(\$18 - \$20) \times 1,000 = \$2,000 \text{ Unfavorable price variance}$$

The sales price variance is favorable for Product A because of the $1 increase in sales price. Conversely, the sales price variance is unfavorable for Product B because there is a $2 per unit decrease in sales price. The sales price variance can be broken down by such causal factors as changes in quantity discount, early payment discount, and list price.

Sales Volume Variance

We are using contribution margin to calculate sales volume variances. Therefore, we can call this variance a **contribution margin variance.** We need a knowledge of cost behavior to determine contribution margin, which is revenue less variable costs. If costs cannot be broken down easily into their variable and fixed components, we compute a **gross margin variance.** We calculate the gross margin variance the same as the contribution margin variance except that we substitute gross margin for contribution margin in the formulas.

Weighted-Average Budgeted Contribution Margin. Before computing the sales volume variance, we must calculate the weighted-average budgeted contribution margin per unit. Using the information from Exhibit 24–1, the planned mix of 2 units of Product A (or 2,000) to 3 units of Product B (or 3,000) results in the following unit contribution margin for the product mix:

$$\frac{A}{2(\$4)} + \frac{B}{3(\$8)}$$

$$= \$8 + \$24 = \$32/5 = \$6.40 \text{ average budgeted contribution margin}$$

We compute the sales volume variance as follows:

Budgeted contribution margin:	
(5,000 units × $6.40)	$32,000
Actual contribution margin:	
Product A + Product B	
(3,000 units × $4) (1,000 units × $8) ...	20,000
Sales volume variance—unfavorable	$12,000

The sales volume variance is broken down into sales quantity and sales mix variances. We can subdivide the sales quantity variance into a market size variance and a market share variance. Other breakdowns of the sales mix variance include by geographic region or customer class.

Sales Mix Variance

The **sales mix variance** adjusts for the change in contribution margin because the company did not sell the products in the proportions anticipated in the master budget. Using the information from Exhibit 24–1, the sales mix variance is

Sales-mix variance =

$$\left[\left(\begin{array}{c}\text{Actual} \\ \text{sales-mix} \\ \text{percentage}\end{array} - \begin{array}{c}\text{Budgeted} \\ \text{sales-mix} \\ \text{percentage}\end{array}\right) \times \begin{array}{c}\text{Actual total} \\ \text{sales volume of all} \\ \text{products in units}\end{array}\right]$$

$$\times \text{ (Budgeted individual unit contribution margin}$$

$$- \text{ Budgeted average unit contribution margin)}$$

For Product A:

$$= [(75\% - 40\%) \times 4,000] \times (\$4 - \$6.40)$$
$$= (35\% \times 4,000) \times -\$2.40 = \qquad \$3,360 \text{ unfavorable}$$

For Product B:

$$= [(25\% - 60\%) \times 4,000] \times (\$8 - \$6.40)$$
$$= (-35\% \times 4,000) \times \$1.60 = \qquad 2,240 \text{ unfavorable}$$
$$\qquad\qquad\qquad\qquad\qquad\qquad\qquad \$5,600 \text{ unfavorable}$$

The sales mix variance measures the effect of changes from the budgeted average unit contribution margin combined with a change in the quantity of specific product lines. A sales mix variance provides useful information when a company sells multiple products because it captures the effect on income arising from a change in the mix of products sold. The overall sales mix variance just computed was unfavorable for two reasons: First, the company sold more units of Product A than budgeted, and Product A's $4 unit contribution margin is lower than the $6.40 average. Second, the company sold fewer units of Product B than planned, and Product B's $8 unit contribution margin is higher than the $6.40 average.

Sales Quantity Variance

We calculate the **sales quantity variance** by multiplying the difference between the actual units sold and the master fixed budget units by the weighted-average budgeted contribution margin per unit as follows:

Sales quantity variance = (Actual sales volume in units − Fixed budget volume in units) × Budgeted average unit contribution margin

For Product A in Exhibit 24–1:

(3,000 units − 2,000 units) × $6.40 budgeted contribution margin = $ 6,400 favorable

For Product B in Exhibit 24–1:

(1,000 units − 3,000 units) × $6.40 budgeted contribution margin =   12,800 unfavorable

Sales quantity variance, total $ 6,400 unfavorable

The sales quantity variance weights all units at the budgeted average contribution margin, showing the impact on profits of a change in physical volume.

Note that the sales quantity variance formula uses a fixed budget volume that we do not adjust to the actual volume achieved. (Chapter 9 discusses fixed and flexible budgeting concepts.) Because the physical volume used in flexible budgeting equals actual physical volume (except, possibly, where the flexible budget is prepared for standard capacity), we could express the sales quantity variance formula as:

(Flexible budget volume in units − Fixed budget volume in units) × Budgeted average unit contribution margin = Sales quantity variance

Thus, the actual sales volume in units is sometimes called the *flexible budget unit sales.*

Proof of Variances. We can prove the sales mix and the sales quantity variances by totaling them as follows to produce the sales volume variance:

Sales mix variance, total	$ 5,600	unfavorable
Sales quantity variance, total	6,400	unfavorable
Sales volume variance	$12,000	unfavorable

Market Size and Market Share Variances

We can further break down each product's sales quantity variance into market size and market share variances. We use budgeted average contribution margin for these two products; however, if we were analyzing only one product, we would use that individual product's contribution margin.

Market size variance = Budgeted market share percentage ×
(Actual industry sales volume in units − Budgeted industry sales volume in units) × Budgeted average contribution margin per unit

For Product A:
= .16 × (6,000 − 12,500) × $6.40
= .16 × 6,500 × $6.40
= $6,656 unfavorable

For Product B:
= .30 × (5,000 − 10,000) × $6.40
= $9,600 unfavorable

Market share variance = (Actual market share percentage − Budgeted market share percentage) × (Actual industry sales volume in units × Budgeted average contribution margin per unit)

For Product A:
= (.50 − .16) × (6,000 × $6.40)
= .34 × $38,400
= $13,056 favorable

For Product B:
= (.20 − .30) × (5,000 × $6.40)
= $3,200 unfavorable

	Product A	Product B
Market size variance	$ 6,656 unfavorable	$ 9,600 unfavorable
Market share variance	13,056 favorable	3,200 unfavorable
Sales quantity variance	$ 6,400 favorable	$12,800 unfavorable

Product A's total market size sharply decreased, but the company increased its share of Product A's market from 16 to 50 percent. However, Product B lost when its actual share of the total market was 20 percent and not the 30 percent budgeted. Product B's industry sales also suffered with a drop in sales from 10,000 budgeted to 5,000 actual sales.

Material and Labor Mix and Yield Variances for Multi-Ingredient Products (L.O. 4)

We can apply sales mix and quantity variances to production inputs. Many production procedures, especially process costing operations, use a recipe or formula to indicate the specifications for each class of material or labor ingredient. Management may vary the mix in an attempt to improve the yield. Or the price of an ingredient or labor class may increase, and management may respond by reducing the quantity of this specific ingredient or labor grade. In some cases, varying the mix does not affect the quantity of the resulting product; in other cases, it does. Although a product's specifications may allow changes in the various material and labor classes when a substitute becomes less costly, managers usually establish tolerance limits beyond which they cannot change the specifications.

Separation of Quantity Variance. Breaking the quantity variance for material and labor down into mix and yield variances can lead to better management control. We calculate price or rate variances for each type of material or each category of labor in the usual manner described in Chapter 11. The total material price variance is the sum of the price variances for all material types. On the other hand, the total labor rate variance is the sum of the rate variances for all labor classes.

Production Mix and Yield Variances

When a company uses several inputs to process its products and the inputs are partially substitutable for each other (for example, substituting beans for peas in vegetable soup), we can calculate mix and yield variances that identify the cost or savings of substituting one material for another. We compute a **mix variance** by comparing the standard formula to the standard cost of material or labor actually used. The resulting variance arises from mixing raw material or classes of labor in a ratio that differs from standard specifications. For example, the textile or chemical industry can mix different combinations of raw material and still yield a perfect product.

A **yield variance** results because the yield obtained differs from the one expected on the basis of material or labor input. A yield variance reflects the extra costs or savings incurred because we used more inputs than the original specifications or recipe called for. To make candy, for example, we cook sugar, corn syrup, cocoa, and milk to yield fudge. We expect a certain quantity of these raw materials to yield a specified number of pounds of fudge. A yield variance results if the actual output of fudge differs from that expected. Often an advantage created by a mix or yield variance cancels the disadvantage of the other variance. For example, the new mix may result in a favorable mix variance, but an unfavorable yield variance offsets it. Likewise, the advantages gained from a favorable yield variance may result in an unfavorable mix variance. Accountants usually consider a *labor yield* variance as the result of the quantity and/or the quality of the material handled.

Material Mix and Yield Variances

We can calculate production mix and yield variances in total for the batch of material or for each grade of material. Our calculations use the following data:

Standard ingredient mix

The standard ingredient mix for a certain type of sausage is

	Standard Pounds	Standard Price	Standard Cost
Meat A	250	$0.40	$100
Meat B	600	0.25	150
Meat C	50	0.88	44
Meal	200	0.18	36
Input	1,100		$330
Output	1,000		

Standard cost per pound of material input ($330/1,100 pounds) $0.30
Cost per pound of output ($330/1,000 pounds) $0.33

At the end of the month, the company determined that they used the following actual pounds of meat and meal to produce 40,000 pounds of sausage:

	Actual Quantity	Actual Cost per Pound	Actual Quantity at Standard Price
Meat A	9,900	$0.44	$ 3,960 (9,900 × $0.40)
Meat B	24,600	0.22	6,150 (24,600 × $0.25)
Meat C	2,400	0.93	2,112 (2,400 × $0.88)
Meal	8,100	0.17	1,458 (8,100 × $0.18)
	45,000		$13,680

In contemplating the mix variance, one realizes that the actual quantities used did not conform to the standard formula. For example, workers finished 40,000 pounds of sausage; if they had used the standard formula they would have used 10,000 pounds (250 pounds × 40 batches) of Meat A instead of the 9,900 pounds actually used.

To determine the mix variance, we calculate the budgeted mix quantity by determining the amount of each ingredient to use at budgeted mix. For example, Meat A includes 22.73% of the total material ingredients (250/1,100 pounds = 22.73%). If workers had applied this percentage to the total actual quantity, they should have used 22.73% × 45,000 = 10,229 pounds of Meat A. Exhibit 24–2 illustrates mix and yield variances in detail for each class of material using the diagram approach. Even through we are calculating individual mix and yield variances, we recognize that each input is related to the other. Part of the reason for developing these variances is to determine the effect of altering the mix on the total product output made up of all the ingredients. Exhibit 24–2 also illustrates the material price variances.

Total Material Mix and Yield Variances. Rather than compute individual mix and yield variances for each ingredient as shown in Exhibit 24–2, management may find total **material mix and yield variances** better meet their needs. In the following mix variance, we multiply the actual quantities used by the standard price per pound and then compare it to the actual quantities multiplied by the standard cost per pound of material input.

Total material mix variance

Actual quantity at standard price:

Meat A (9,900 pounds @ $0.40)	$3,960	
Meat B (24,600 pounds @ $0.25)	6,150	
Meat C (2,400 pounds @ $0.88)	2,112	
Meal (8,100 pounds @ $0.18)	1,458	$13,680
Actual quantity at standard input cost		
(45,000 pounds × $0.30)		13,500
Unfavorable material mix variance		$ 180

Total material yield variance

The total yield variance is

Actual input quantity at standard input cost (45,000 pounds × $0.30)	$13,500
Actual output quantity at standard output cost (40,000 pounds × $0.33)	13,200
Unfavorable material yield variance	$ 300

An alternative approach to computing material yield variances is to compare the expected loss from processing with the actual loss as follows:

Expected loss from processing	100/1,100 = 9.09%
Expected yield percent	100.00% − 9.09% = 90.91%
5,000 Actual loss	(45,000 − 40,000 pounds)
4,091 Expected loss	(9.09% × 45,000 pounds put into process)
909 × $0.33 cost per pound of output = $300 unfavorable yield variance	

Stated another way, the yield is unfavorable because we put 45,000 pounds into processing and expected to receive 40,909 (45,000 × 90.91%) of output. We only received 40,000 pounds, giving us an unplanned loss of 909 pounds.

Not separating the quantity variance into mix and yield variances would result in the following $480 unfavorable material quantity variance. This does not give managers adequate information for a multi-ingredient product.

EXHIBIT 24-2   Price, Mix, and Yield Variances

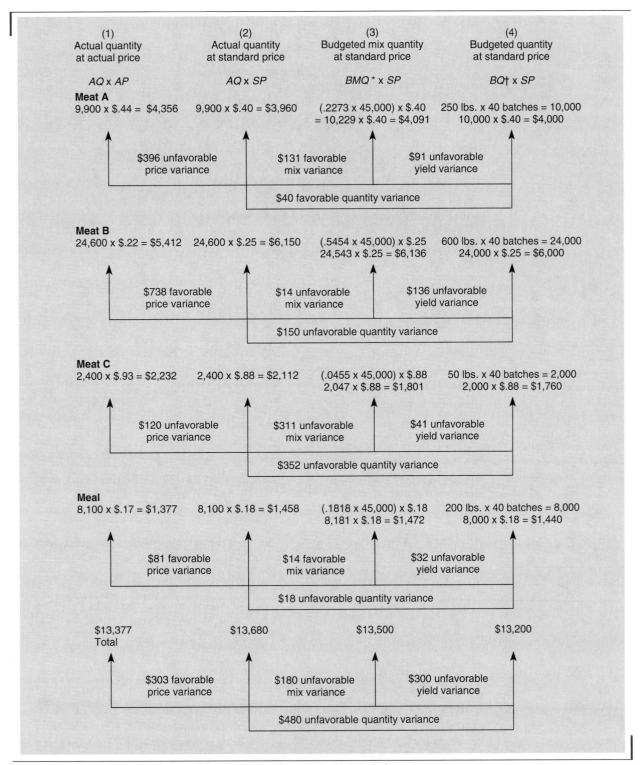

*Quantity that would have been used at budgeted mix
†Budgeted quantity using standard formula

$480 U materials quantity variance

Materials mix   Materials yield
variance   variance
$180 U $300 U

Materials quantity variance

Standard pounds		Actual pounds				
(10,000*	−	9,900)	× $.40	=	$ 40 F	
(24,000	−	24,600)	× $.25	=	150 U	
(2,000	−	2,400)	× $.88	=	352 U	
(8,000	−	8,100)	× $.18	=	18 U	
Total materials quantity variance					$480 U	

*250 pounds per batch x 40 batches.

Journalizing Material Mix and Yield Variances. If a company keeps its direct materials inventory at standard cost, accountants record a material price variance for each of the four materials at the time the company purchases the material, using the analysis presented in Chapter 11. Company accountants would make the following journal entry to record the material mix and yield variances:

Work in Process Inventory (40,000 pounds × $0.33)	13,200	
Material Mix Variance	180	
Material Yield Variance	300	
Direct Materials Inventory (kept at standard)		13,680

If, instead, a company keeps its Direct Materials Inventory at actual cost, the credit to Direct Materials Inventory is actual quantity used multiplied by the actual cost. Accountants would record a Material Price Variance at the time of purchase with this system.

Labor Mix and Yield Variances

Just as the previous example illustrates how to determine the material mix and yield variances comprising the material quantity variance, the following example illustrates how to separate the labor efficiency variance into labor mix and yield variances.

Standard Crew Mix. Assume a crew of employees performs operations in three different pay grades. A standard crew mix consists of 20 worker-hours distributed among the pay grades as follows:

Pay Grade	Hours	Standard Rate	Standard Cost
A2	6	$20	$120
C4	5	16	80
D5	9	24	216
	20		$416

Output: 400 gallons
Standard cost per crew ($416/20 hours) = $20.80

During the month, charges to the department included 570 hours of A2 at an actual rate of $20.40, 420 hours of C4 at an actual rate of $16.20, and 700 hours of D5 at an actual rate of $23.72, giving a total labor cost of $35,036 for 1,690 hours. For 32,000 gallons of the product finished during the month, we compute the **labor mix** and **labor yield variances** as shown in Exhibit 24–3 using the diagram approach.

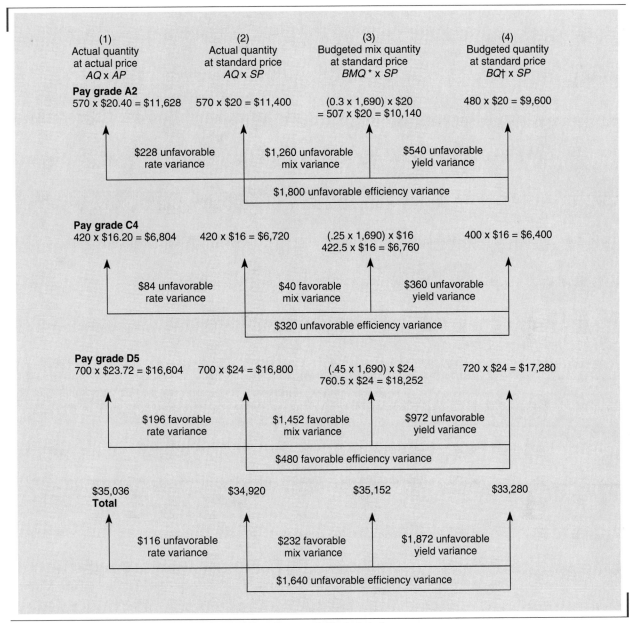

*Quantity that would have been used at budgeted mix
†Budgeted quantity using standard formula

We compute the labor mix variance similarly to the material mix variance. For example, of the 1,690 actual hours used, 30 percent (6/20 hours) should have been Pay Grade A2 hours or a total of 507 hours. Instead, the company employed 570 Grade A2 hours; they used a higher proportion of this more expensive pay grade than indicated by the crew formula. If they had followed the standard formula exactly for the 80 batches completed (32,000 gallons of output/ 400 gallons per batch = 80 batches), Pay Grade A2 hours should have totaled 80 × 6 hours = 480 hours. Using more A2 hours results in an unfavorable yield variance for Pay Grade A2 of $540. We calculate mix and yield variances similarly for the other pay grades. If we use total, rather than individual, mix and yield variances as shown in Exhibit 24–3, the computation is as follows:

Total labor mix variance

Actual Hours at Standard Rate

	Actual Hours	Standard Rate	Total Standard Cost for Actual Hours
A2	570	$20	$11,400
C4	420	16	6,720
D5	700	24	16,800
	1,690		$34,920

Actual hours at weighted standard cost:		
(1,690 actual hours × $20.80 standard hourly rate) ...	35,152	
Favorable labor mix variance	$ 232	

Total labor yield variance

Actual hours at standard cost		
(1,690 hours × $20.80)	$35,152	
Output at standard cost expressed in standard hours:		
$\frac{32,000}{400}$ = 80 batches × 20 hours = 1,600 hours		
1,600 hours × $20.80 standard hourly rate	33,280	
Unfavorable labor yield variance	$ 1,872	

Equation Approach to Computing Labor Rate Variance. The following illustrates the short-cut, equation approach for computing labor rate variances for each pay grade of labor. You may prefer the equation approach in Chapter 11 rather than the diagram approach in Exhibit 24–3.

Labor rate variance

Pay Grade	Actual Rate	Standard Rate	Rate Variance		Total Rate Variance
A2	$20.40	$20	$0.40 U*	$228 U*	$(0.40 × 570 hours)
C4	16.20	16	0.20 U	84 U	($0.20 × 420 hours)
D5	23.72	24	0.28 F	196 F	($0.28 × 700 hours)
				$116 U	

*U = Unfavorable; F = Favorable.

Journalizing Labor Rate, Mix, and Yield Variances. The following journal entry records the labor mix, labor yield, and labor price variances:

Work in Process Inventory	33,280	
Labor Yield Variance	1,872	
Labor Rate Variance	116	
Labor Mix Variance		232
Payroll		35,036

Assumed Substitutability of Material and Labor in Products

We assume substitutability of product inputs—that a company can substitute finished products in a sales mix. For example, we assume a company can substitute Meat C for Meat A or swap sale of Product B for Product A. However, we know there is a limit to this exchange. While Meat C may replace Meat A in limited amounts without changing the taste of sausage, there is an even greater limit to the amount of cheap meal that can be used instead of meat in sausage.

Assume instead we pay all classes of labor the same, all material inputs cost the same per pound, or all products sold had the same contribution margin. Under any of these conditions there would be no mix variance for that ingredient or product. For example, if the engineer and the janitor on a crew of workers earned the same wage per hour, the substitution of laborers would have no effect on the total cost of a job. We do know that other constraints prevent us from complete substitutability, however. The engineer can sweep the floor, but the janitor lacks the skills needed to perform an engineering task. Managers must remember these general concepts when interpreting mix and yield variances.

A question arises: Should we routinely calculate mix and yield variances? The answer depends on the opportunity management has for substitution between material ingredients and various skills of labor. If trade-off alternatives are available, cost/benefit analysis usually indicates that calculations are worthwhile because they provide insight that managers could not obtain through the quantity variance.

Summary

Chapter 11 introduces material and labor price and quantity variances, and Chapter 12 discusses factory overhead variances. Management may use additional revenue and cost variances to further pinpoint responsibility for other major sources of deviations from plans. Companies selling multiple products or using multiple material and labor inputs in their manufacturing process especially have supplementary sources of variances available.

Because products have different unit contribution margins, the mix of their sales affect net income. Companies may not sell products in the proportions anticipated by management. The sales mix variances capture the effect of these changes on net income. Likewise, the production mix variance reflects the extra cost or savings from substituting material and labor inputs. Yield variances measure the impact on costs and profits of a change in physical volume.

However, merely calculating the variance does not complete the cost accountant's full responsibility. More importantly, managers must understand the specific impact of the various factors measured before they can take appropriate corrective actions.

Important Terms and Concepts

sales price variance, 830
sales volume variance, 831
sales activity variance, 831
contribution margin variance, 831
gross margin variance, 832
sales mix variance, 832

sales quantity variance, 833
material mix variance, 836
material yield variance, 836
labor mix variance, 838
labor yield variance, 838

Problem for Self-Study

Material Price, Mix and Yield Variance, and Journal Entries

Ricketts, Inc., processes tomato-beef soup and sells it in 19-ounce cans. The standard input for material per batch is as follows:

	Pounds	Standard Price per Pound
Tomatoes	160	$0.70
Corn	115	0.20
Beef	100	0.975
Onion and seasonings	25	0.30
Input	400	
Output	375	

Some variations in ingredients to obtain the special flavor are permitted. The following materials were purchased during the month. Direct materials inventory is kept at standard.

Tomatoes	(16,000 pounds)	$11,840.00
Corn	(12,000 pounds)	2,160.00
Beef	(8,500 pounds)	8,797.50
Onion and seasonings	(2,400 pounds)	600.00

During the month, 30,000 cans of soup were filled with the following materials put in process:

Tomatoes	15,600
Corn	11,300
Beef	7,800
Onion and seasonings	2,300
	37,000

Required:

a. Compute a material purchase price variance for each of the materials and a total material mix and a total yield variance for the month. Indicate if the variance is favorable or unfavorable.

b. Prepare journal entries to record the issuance of material, the variances, and the disposition of variances.

Solution to Problem for Self-Study

RICKETTS, INC.

a.

	Pounds	Standard Cost
Tomatoes	160	$112.00
Corn	115	23.00
Beef	100	97.50
Onion and seasonings	25	7.50
Input	400	$240.00
Output	375	

Standard cost per pound of input: $240/400 = $0.60
Standard cost per pound of output: $240/375 = $0.64

Material purchase price variance

	Actual Pounds	Standard Price	Actual Price	Price Variance per Pound	Total Purchase Price Variance
Tomatoes	16,000	$0.70	$0.74	$0.04 U	$640 U
Corn	12,000	0.20	0.18	0.02 F	240 F
Beef	8,500	0.975	1.035	0.06 U	510 U
Onion and seasonings	2,400	0.30	0.25	0.05 F	120 F
					$790 U

Material mix variance

	Actual Quantity	Standard Price	Amounts
Tomatoes	15,600	$0.70	$10,920.00
Corn	11,300	0.20	2,260.00
Beef	7,800	0.975	7,605.00
Onion and seasonings	2,300	0.30	690.00
	37,000		$21,475.00

Actual quantity at standard input cost (37,000 lbs. × $0.60) 22,200.00

Favorable materials mix variance . . . . $ 725.00

Material yield variance

Actual quantity at standard input cost $22,200.00
Actual output at standard output cost (35,625* × $0.64) 22,800.00
Favorable material yield variance . . . . $ 600.00

*19 ounces × 30,000 cans = 570,000 ounces ÷ 16 oz. = 35,625 pounds.

Alternative way of computing yield variance

25/400 =   6.25% Expected loss from processing
2,312.5 =   Expected loss (6.25% × 37,000 materials put into process)
−1,375.0 =   Actual loss (37,000 − 35,625)
937.5 pounds × $0.64 = $600

b.

Direct Materials Inventory	22,607.50[†]	
Material Purchase Price Variance	790.00	
Accounts Payable		23,397.50
Work in Process Inventory	22,800.00	
Material Mix Variance		725.00
Material Yield Variance		600.00
Direct Materials Inventory		21,475.00
Material Yield Variance	600.00	
Materials Mix Variance	725.00	
Material Purchase Price Variance		790.00
Cost of Goods Sold		535.00

†Tomatoes	16,000 × $0.70 =	$11,200.00
Corn	12,000 × $0.20 =	2,400.00
Beef	8,500 × $0.975 =	8,287.50
Onion and seasonings	2,400 × $0.30 =	720.00
		$22,607.50

Review Questions

1. Discuss any constraints you see in the substitutability that we assume when calculating sales mix and production mix variances.

2. Assume a company makes a special vegetarian diet soup and all beans, carrots, celery, and onions cost the same per pound. Also the company prides itself on having an across-the-board pay scale so that all workers are paid the same per hour. How would this situation affect the company's production mix variances?

3. Assume a company has a planned mix of 5 units of Product X to 2 units of Product Y. The individual unit contribution margin for X is $6 and $13 for Y. What is the weighted-average budgeted contribution margin? How do you use the weighted-average budgeted contribution margin in variance analysis?

4. Should material mix and yield variances be routinely calculated for all companies?

5. What does the sales mix variance capture and how does this information assist management?

6. *a.* How would you determine how much detail is necessary and useful in decomposing variances down into the next higher level of detail?

   b. When should a cost accountant stop any further breakdown?

7. *a.* At a low level of analysis for sales variances, what variances would you compute?

   b. What types of variances would these low detailed variances be decomposed into at higher levels of analysis?

8. What would you review in a company to determine the cause of a *a* mix variance, and *b* yield variance?

9. Describe circumstances in which the overall sales mix variance would be unfavorable.

10. For what types of operations would material mix and labor yield variances be appropriate?

11. Assume you are making a product which has two ingredients, A and B, which are substitutable. The recipe for one batch of 10 gallons is 5 gallons of A at $6 a gallon and 5 gallons of B at $10 a gallon. At the end of the month, you find 500 gallons of finished products were made using 210 gallons of A costing $5.90 a gallon and 300 gallons of B costing $11 a gallon. What is the mix variance for each of the two products?

12. Using the data in Question 11, determine the price and yield variances for each of the ingredients.

CMA/CIA/AICPA Multiple Choice Questions

1. (CIA) Actual and budgeted information about the sales of a product for June follow:

	Actual	Budget
Units	8,000	10,000
Sales revenue	$92,000	$105,000

   The sales price variance for June was

   a. $8,000 favorable.
   b. $10,000 favorable.
   c. $10,500 unfavorable.
   d. $8,500 unfavorable.

2. (CIA) The Blue Company has failed to reach its planned activity level during its first two years of operation. The following table shows the relationship between units produced, sales, and normal activity for these years and the projected relationship for Year 3. All prices and costs have remained the same for the last two years and are expected to do so in Year 3. Income has been positive in both Year 1 and Year 2.

	Units Produced	Sales	Planned Activity
Year 1	90,000	90,000	100,000
Year 2	95,000	95,000	100,000
Year 3	90,000	90,000	100,000

Because Blue Company uses an absorption costing system, one would predict gross margin for Year 3 to be

a.   Greater than Year 1.
b.   Greater than Year 2.
c.   Equal to Year 1.
d.   Equal to Year 2.

3.   (CIA) The sales mix variance

a.   Measures the effect of the deviation from the budgeted average contribution margin per unit associated with a change in the quantity of a particular product.
b.   Would be favorable when a company sells less of the products bearing unit contribution margins higher than average.
c.   Would be an unfavorable 5 percent whenever a 5 percent decrease occurs in a company's overall sales volume.
d.   Would be unfavorable when a company sells less of the products bearing unit contribution margins lower than average.

4.   (CIA) A company sells two products, X and Y. The sales mix consists of a composite unit of 2 units of X for every 5 units of Y (2:5). Fixed costs are $49,500. The unit contribution margins for X and Y are $2.50 and $1.20, respectively. If the company has a profit of $22,000, the unit sales must have been

	Product X	Product Y
a.	5,000	12,500
b.	13,000	32,500
c.	23,800	59,500
d.	28,600	71,500

5.-6.   (CMA) Use the following data for these items:
Folsom Fashions sells a line of women's dresses. Folsom's performance report for November 19X1 is as follows:

	Actual	Budget
Dresses sold	5,000	6,000
Sales	$235,000	$300,000
Variable costs	145,000	180,000
Contribution margin	$ 90,000	$120,000
Fixed costs	84,000	80,000
Operating income	$ 6,000	$ 40,000

The company uses a flexible budget to analyze its performance and to measure the effect on operating income of the various factors affecting the difference between budgeted and actual operating income.

5.   The effect of the sales-volume variance on the contribution margin for November is

a. $30,000 unfavorable.
b. $18,000 unfavorable.
c. $20,000 unfavorable.
d. $15,000 unfavorable.
e. $65,000 unfavorable.

6.   The sales price variance for November is

a. $30,000 unfavorable.
b. $18,000 unfavorable.
c. $20,000 unfavorable.
d. $15,000 unfavorable.
e. $65,000 unfavorable.

7. (AICPA) Which of the following is the most probable reason a company would experience an unfavorable labor rate variance and a favorable labor efficiency variance?

   a. The mix of workers assigned to the particular job was heavily weighted toward the use of higher-paid, experienced individuals.
   b. The mix of workers assigned to the particular job was heavily weighted toward the use of new relatively low-paid, unskilled workers.
   c. Because of the production schedule, workers from other production areas were assigned to assist this particular process.
   d. Defective materials caused more labor to be used in order to produce a standard unit.

8. (AICPA) In the following budgeted profit/volume chart, EG represents a two-product company's profit path. EH and HG represent the profit paths of products 1 and 2, respectively.

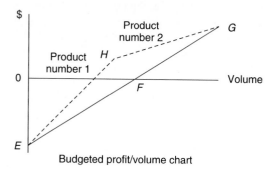

Budgeted profit/volume chart

Sales prices and cost behavior were as budgeted, actual total sales equaled budgeted sales, and there were no inventories. Actual profit was greater than budgeted profit. Which product had actual sales in excess of budget, and what margin does OE divided by OF represent?

	Product with Excess Sales	**OE/OF**
a.	No. 1	Contribution margin
b.	No. 1	Gross margin
c.	No. 2	Contribution margin
d.	No. 2	Gross margin

Exercises

E24–1 Market Size and Market Share Sales Variances (L.O. 3)

Norton Company is a leading low-cost and high-performance computer manufacturer in the personal computer industry. The average selling price of its PCs is $1,200 and the average variable production cost of a PC is $500. In preparing its 19X5 sales budget, the management expects that sales of its PC will reach 500,000 units. This is equivalent to a 20 percent share of the PC market. Based on an industry sales forecast, there will be 2,500,000 PCs sold in 19X5. At the end of 19X5, the actual sales figure indicates that Norton has sold 540,000 units and actual industry sales are 2,250,000 units.

Required:

Compute the market size and market share sales variances for Norton's PC.

E24–2 Sales Quantity and Sales Mix Variances (L.O. 2)

The First Company sells Products A and B whose sales prices are $6 and $12, respectively. The variable cost for Product A is $4 and $7 for Product B. Total fixed costs for the company are estimated at $30,000. Assume management plans to sell a total of 9,000 units with a planned mix of 1 unit of Product A to 2 units of Product B. Suppose, instead, that 8,000 units composed of 1,600 units of Product A and 6,400 units of Product B are actually sold.

Required:

Compute for each product the sales quantity and sales mix variances. Prove your answer.

E24–3 Journal Entries to Record Unit Material Yield, Mix, and Price Variances (L.O. 4)

Dean Company uses standard costing in its manufacturing process. The following is the standard mix of one unit of copper steel:

	Pounds	Standard Rate	Standard Cost
Copper	3	$2.00	$ 6.00
Iron	5	1.50	7.50
Carbon	2	1.00	2.00
	10		$15.50

In the month of June, Dean Company produced 1,000 units of copper steel and the material cost of each unit is as follows:

	Pounds	Total Cost
Copper	2.5	$ 7.50
Iron	6.0	7.50
Carbon	1.0	2.00
	9.5	$17.00

Required:

a. Determine the material yield, the material mix, and the material price variance per finished unit. Compute a total mix and total yield variance for the unit, but individual price variances for each material.

b. Prepare a journal entry to record the issuance of material and the material variances. The materials inventory is kept at actual cost.

E24–4 Sales Quantity, Sales Mix, Sales Price Variances (L.O. 2)

This year's budget for Brown, Inc., a multiproduct firm, is

	Product Lines			
	A	B	C	Total
Sales	$1,200,000	$900,000	$600,000	$2,700,000
Less: variable costs	588,000	390,000	430,000	1,408,000
Fixed costs allocated on direct labor dollars .	200,000	200,000	100,000	500,000
Income before taxes	$ 412,000	$310,000	$ 70,000	$ 792,000
Units	204,000	102,000	34,000	340,000

At year-end, you determine that total fixed costs and unit variable costs were exactly as budgeted, but the following units per product line were sold at these sales prices.

Product Line	Units	Unit Sales Price
A	175,000	$ 6.00
B	122,500	8.50
C	52,500	17.50
Total units	350,000	

Required:

a. Compute sales quantity variances and sales mix variances for each product line.
b. Prove your answer for Requirement *a.*
c. Compute sales price variances for each product.

E24–5 Material Price, Mix, and Yield Variances (L.O. 4)

Kitty Cat Company provides you with their standard material formula for cat food. Material is mixed in 525-pound batches. The standard input for material per batch is as follows:

	Pounds	Standard Price per Pound
Meal	100	$0.19
Fish parts	75	0.30
Horse meat	350	0.16
Input	525	
Output	500	

The cat food is packed in cans weighing 2 pounds; 21,000 cans were packed during the month. Meanwhile, workers put the following materials in process:

	Pounds	Total Cost
Meal	9,000	$1,800
Fish parts	6,200	2,046
Horse meat	28,800	4,032
	44,000	$7,878

Required:

a. Compute a material price variance, a material mix, and a yield variance for each of the materials for the month. Indicate if the variance is favorable or unfavorable. (Round the budgeted mix quantity percentage to two decimal places.)
b. Explain what you should do as the company's cost accountant in investigating the variance you determined in Requirement *a.*

Problems

P24–6 Material Price, Mix, and Yield Variances (L.O. 4)

Edsel Company is the leading sausage producer in the nation. In its beef sausage, it uses three grades of beef. The standard amount of each grade of beef in each 10-pound batch of sausage is as follows:

	Pounds	Standard Price per Pound	Standard Cost
Grade A	5	$4	$20
Grade B	3	2	6
Grade C	2	1	2
	10		$28

During March, Edsel produced 1,100 pounds of beef sausage; the actual amount of beef consumption and cost is as follows:

	Pounds	Total Cost
Grade A	450	$2,025
Grade B	320	800
Grade C	380	304
	1,150	$3,129

Required:

a. Compute a material price variance, a material mix, and a yield variance for each grade of beef for the month. Indicate if each is favorable or unfavorable.

b. Prepare the journal entry to record these variances for March.

P24–7 Sales Quantity, Mix, Price Variances (L.O. 2)

In December 19X1, Shoney Company's six-month operating budget forecast the following expenses in each of its product lines:

	Product Lines		
	A1	**B2**	**C3**
Unit sales price	$20	$15	$25
Unit variable expense	$ 5	$ 8	$10
Budgeted volume	2,500	3,000	2,000
Total fixed expenses	$60,000		

In July 19X2, the following actual operating results for the last six months are released:

	Product Lines		
	A1	**B2**	**C3**
Sales revenue	$52,650	$52,700	$57,200
Units sold	2,700	3,100	2,200

Required:

a. Determine sales quantity variances and sales mix variances for each product line assuming that actual variable costs were the same as budgeted.

b. Prove your answer to Requirement *a*.

c. Compute sales price variances for each product.

P24–8 Labor Rate, Mix, and Yield Variances (L.O. 4)

Felix Industries is the leading cordless telephone manufacturer in the Southwest. Its manufacturing process is performed by a crew of employees in different pay grades. A standard crew hour consists of 20 direct labor-hours distributed as follows:

Pay Grade	Hours	Standard Rate	Standard Cost
G7	4	$12	$ 48
G8	8	8	64
G9	8	6	48
	20		$160

Output: 5 cordless telephones

In April, Felix produced 500 cordless telephones. Actual hours and labor cost were

Pay Grade	Hours	Total Costs
G7	350	$ 4,900
G8	775	6,975
G9	950	6,650
	2,075	$18,525

Required:

a. Compute a labor rate, a labor mix, and a labor yield variance for each pay grade.

b. Prepare the journal entry to record these variances for April.

P24–9 Sales Quantity, Sales Mix, and Sales Price Variances (L.O. 2)

Wash Company produces three product lines, A, B, and C. Its budget for the next period is based on the following:

	Product Lines		
	A	B	C
Sales price	$8.00	$12.00	$10.00
Variable expenses	4.00	9.00	4.00
Budgeted volume	3,000	7,500	4,500
Total fixed expenses			$26,650

Required:

At the end of the period, you determine that Wash sold 12,000 units consisting of 2,000 of Product A, 4,000 of Product B, and 6,000 of Product C.

a. Determine the sales quantity and sales mix variance for each product line.
b. Prove your answer to Requirement *a.*
c. Compute sales price variances for each of the products assuming actual sales revenue was $12,000 for A, $64,000 for B, and $78,000 for C.

P24–10 Labor Rate, Mix, Yield Variances, and Journal Entries (L.O. 4)

To perform its production process, Town Company employs a crew of workers in different pay grades. A standard crew hour consists of 100 worker-hours distributed as follows:

Pay Grade	Hours	Standard Rate	Standard Cost
A	40	$ 8	$320
B	46	6	276
C	10	18	180
D	4	28	112
	100		$888

Output: 100 tons

During the month, charges to the department included 2,600 hours of Pay Grade A at a total cost of $19,500; 2,500 hours of Pay Grade B at a total cost of $17,250; 620 hours of Pay Grade C at a total cost of $10,633; and 250 hours of Pay Grade D at a total cost of $7,125. Workers produced 6,000 tons of finished goods during the month.

Required:

a. Compute individual labor rate, total labor mix, and labor yield variances.
b. Prepare the journal entry to record these variances and the direct labor cost.
c. Prepare calculations to determine if the company used more or less hours of Pay Grades A and D than specified in their labor crew formula. Indicate whether their use of each of these pay grades was favorable or unfavorable. Interpret the meaning of the favorable or unfavorable indication assuming the crew formula is correct.

P24–11 Materials, Yield, Mix, and Price Variances (L.O. 4)

Nectron Company has determined that, after allowing for normal processing losses, the standard mix of material used in producing a finished product is as follows:

Material X (6 gallons @ $4.00)	$24
Material R (16 gallons @ $1.50)	24
Material T (18 gallons @ $2.00)	36
Total	$84

During a given period, the actual cost per fully inspected unit was as follows:

Material X (8 gallons @ $4.10)	$32.80
Material R (14 gallons @ $1.40)	19.60
Material T (16 gallons @ $1.85)	29.60
Total	$82.00

Required:

a. Determine the material yield variance per finished unit.
b. Determine the material mix variance per finished unit.
c. Determine the material price variance per finished unit.
d. Prepare a journal entry to record the issuance of material and the material variances. The materials inventory is kept at actual cost.

P24–12 (CMA adapted) Material Price, Mix, and Yield Variances (L.O. 1)

The LAR Chemical Company manufactures a wide variety of chemical compounds and liquids for industrial uses. The standard mix for producing a single batch of 500 gallons of one liquid is as follows:

Liquid Chemical	Quantity (Gallons)	Cost per Gallon	Total Cost
Maxon	100	$2.00	$200
Salex	300	0.75	225
Cralyn	225	1.00	225
	625		$650

There is a 20 percent loss in liquid volume during processing due to evaporation. The finished liquid is put into 10-gallon bottles for sale. Thus, the standard material cost for a 10-gallon bottle is $13.

The actual quantities of direct materials and the respective cost of the materials placed in production during November were as follows:

Liquid Chemical	Quantity (Gallons)	Total Cost
Maxon	8,480	$17,384
Salex	25,200	17,640
Cralyn	18,540	16,686
	52,220	$51,710

A total of 4,000 bottles (40,000 gallons) was produced during November.

Required:

a. Calculate the total direct material variance for the liquid product for November and then further analyze the total variance into a:
  (1) Material price variance.
  (2) Material mix variance.
  (3) Material yield variance.
b. Explain how LAR Chemical Company could use each of the three material variances—price, mix, yield—to help control the cost of manufacturing this liquid compound.

P24–13 Labor Rate, Mix, and Yield Variances (L.O. 4)

Dunston Company's production process is performed by a crew of employees in different pay grades. A standard crew hour consists of 60 labor-hours distributed as follows:

Pay Grade	Hours	Standard Rate	Standard Cost
A	25	$ 8	$200
B	12	12	144
C	18	10	180
D	5	20	100
	60		$624
Output	100 tons		

During the month, charges to the department included 1,260 hours of Pay Grade A at a total cost of $10,332; 610 hours of B at a total cost of $7,076; 925 hours of C at a total cost of $9,620; and 265 hours of D at a total cost of $5,830. There were 5,000 tons of finished goods produced during the month.

Required:

Round budgeted mix quantity percents to two decimal places.

a. Compute a labor rate, a labor mix, and a labor yield variance for each pay grade.
b. Prepare the journal entry to record these variances and the direct labor cost.

P24–14 Material Price, Mix, and Yield Variances; and Journal Entries (L.O. 1)

In processing a specialty type of sausage, the Tucker Company experiences some loss. The standard product mix for a 100-pound batch is as follows:

> 20 pounds of Meat A @ $0.41 per pound
> 25 pounds of Meat B @ $0.80 per pound
> 30 pounds of Meat C @ $0.30 per pound
> 45 pounds of Meat D @ $0.60 per pound

The company records the material price variance at the time of purchase. Materials purchased were as follows:

> 1,480 pounds of Meat A = $ 666.00
> 1,550 pounds of Meat B =   1,209.00
> 1,750 pounds of Meat C =   577.50
> 3,000 pounds of Meat D =   1,650.00
> $4,102.50

In producing the 60 batches during the month, the following actual material quantities were put into production:

> 1,280 pounds of Meat A
> 1,490 pounds of Meat B
> 1,740 pounds of Meat C
> 2,650 pounds of Meat D

Required:

a. Determine individual material purchase price and total material mix and total yield variances.
b. Prepare journal entries to record the variances determined in Requirement *a* and the disposition of variances assuming all completed units are sold.

P24–15 Labor Rate, Mix, and Yield Variances (L.O. 4)

Gabriel Corporation is the leading toy manufacturer in the Southwest. The production process of one of its products, space guns, is performed by workers in the Assembly Department (AD), Inspection Department (ID), and Packaging Department (PD). Workers in these departments are in different pay grades. It requires 10 worker-hours to produce five space guns and the hours in each department are distributed as follows:

Department	Hours	Standard Rate	Standard Cost
AD	7	$8	$56
ID	2	9	18
PD	1	6	6
	10		$80

Output = 5 space guns

In the month of May, 5,000 space guns have been produced and the production cost in each department has been incurred as follows:

Department		Hours	Total Cost
AD	....	6,500	$45,500
ID	....	2,500	25,000
PD	....	1,150	8,050
		10,150	$78,550

Required:

a. Compute a labor rate, a labor mix, and a labor yield variance for each department.

b. Prepare the journal entry to record these variances.

P24–16 Material Price, Mix, and Yield Variances and Journal Entries (L.O. 4)

Anderson Company sells a chemical to industrial companies for cleaning purposes. Inspection of the chemical content is made at frequent intervals because some of the material is subject to evaporation. The standard product mix for a 50-gallon batch is as follows:

20 gallons of Chemical A @ $0.40 per gallon
5 gallons of Chemical B @ $0.80 per gallon
30 gallons of Chemical C @ $0.30 per gallon
5 gallons of Chemical D @ $0.60 per gallon

The company records the material price variance at the time of purchase. Materials purchased were as follows:

2,500 gallons of Chemical A @ $0.44 per gallon = $1,100.00
650 gallons of Chemical B @ $0.85 per gallon =   552.50
3,650 gallons of Chemical C @ $0.32 per gallon = 1,168.00
550 gallons of Chemical D @ $0.57 per gallon =   313.50

In producing the 120 batches during the month, the following actual material quantities were put into production:

2,450 gallons of Chemical A
540 gallons of Chemical B
3,620 gallons of Chemical C
475 gallons of Chemical D

Required:

a. Determine individual material purchase price variances, a total material mix variance, and a total yield variance.

b. Prepare journal entries to record the variances determined in Requirement *a* and the disposition of variances assuming all completed units are sold. Assume all variances are treated as period costs.

P24–17 (CMA) Labor Mix and Yield Variances (L.O. 1)

Landeau Manufacturing Company has a process cost accounting system. A monthly analysis compares the actual results with both a monthly plan and a flexible budget. Accountants establish the standard direct labor rates used in the flexible budget each year when the annual plan is formulated. These remain constant all year.

The standard direct labor rates in effect for the fiscal year ending June 30, 19X8, and the standard hours allowed for the output for April follow:

	Standard Direct Labor Rate per Hour	Standard Direct Labor-Hours Allowed for Output
Labor class III	$8	500
Labor class II	$7	500
Labor class I	$5	500

The wage rates for each labor class increased on January 1, 19X8, under the terms of a new union contract negotiated in December 19X7. Management did not revise the standard wage rates to reflect the new contract.

The actual direct labor-hours worked and the actual direct labor rates per hour experienced for April were as follows:

	Actual Direct Labor Rate per Hour	Actual Direct Labor-Hours
Labor class III	$8.50	550
Labor class II	$7.50	650
Labor class I	$5.40	375

Required:

a. Calculate the dollar amount of the total direct labor variance for April for the Landeau Manufacturing Company and analyze the total variance into the following components:
   (1) Direct labor rate variance.
   (2) Direct labor mix variance.
   (3) Direct labor performance (efficiency) variance.
b. Discuss the advantages and disadvantages of a standard cost system in which the standard direct labor rates per hour are not changed during the year to reflect such events as a new labor contract.

P24–18 (CMA) Sales, Material, Labor, Overhead, and Contribution Margin Variances (L.O. 2)

Allglow Company is a cosmetics manufacturer specializing in stage makeup. The company's best selling product is SkinKlear, a cream used under the stage makeup to protect the skin from frequent use of makeup. SkinKlear is packaged in three sizes—8 ounces, 1 pound, and 3 pounds—and regularly sells for $21 per pound. The standard cost per pound of SkinKlear, based on Allglow's normal monthly production of 8,000 pounds, is as follows:

Cost Item	Quantity	Standard Cost	Total Cost
Direct materials			
Cream base	9.0 oz.	$0.05/oz.	$0.45
Moisturizer	6.5 oz.	0.10/oz.	0.65
Fragrance	0.5 oz.	1.00/oz.	0.50
			$ 1.60
Direct labor*			
Mixing	0.5 hr.	$4.00/hr.	$2.00
Compounding	1.0 hr.	5.00/hr.	5.00
			7.00
Variable overhead† . . .	1.5 hr.	$2.10/hr.	3.15
Total standard cost per pound			$11.75

*Direct labor dollars include employee benefits.
†Applied on the basis of direct labor-hours.

Based on these standard costs, Allglow prepares monthly budgets. The budgeted performance and the actual performance for May 19X1, when the company produced and sold 9,000 pounds of SkinKlear, follow:

Contribution Report for SkinKlear
For May 19X1

	Budget	Actual	Variance
Units	8,000	9,000	1,000 F
Revenue	$168,000	$180,000	$12,000 F
Direct material	12,800	16,200	3,400 U
Direct labor	56,000	62,500	6,500 U
Variable overhead	25,200	30,900	5,700 U
Total variable costs	$ 94,000	$109,600	$15,600 U
Contribution margin	$ 74,000	$ 70,400	$ 3,600 U

Barbara Simmons, Allglow's president, was not pleased with these results; despite a sizable increase in the sales of SkinKlear, there was a decrease in the product's contribution to the overall profitability of the firm. Simmons has asked Allglow's cost accountant, Brian Jackson, to prepare a report that identifies the reasons why the contribution margin for SkinKlear has decreased. Jackson has gathered the following information to help in the preparation of the report:

May 19X1 Usage Report for SkinKlear

Cost Item	Quantity	Actual Cost
Direct materials		
Cream base	84,000 oz.	$ 4,200
Moisturizer	60,000 oz.	7,200
Fragrance	4,800 oz.	4,800
Direct labor		
Mixing	4,500 hr.	18,000
Compounding—Manual	5,300 hr.	26,500
Compounding—Mechanized	2,700 hr.	13,500
Compounding—Idle	900 hr.	4,500
Variable overhead		30,900
Total variable cost		$109,600

While doing his research, Jackson discovered that the manufacturing department had mechanized one of the manual operations in the compounding process on an experimental basis. The mechanized operation replaced manual operations that represented 40 percent of the compounding process.

The workers' inexperience with the mechanized operation caused increased usage of both the cream base and the moisturizer; however, Jackson believed these inefficiencies would be negligible if mechanization became a permanent part of the process and the workers' skills improved. The idle time in compounding was traceable to the fact that fewer workers were required for the mechanized process. During this experimental period, the idle time was charged to direct labor rather than overhead. The excess workers could either be reassigned or laid off in the future. Jackson also was able to determine that all of the variable manufacturing overhead costs over standard could be traced directly to the mechanization process.

Required:

a. Prepare an explanation of the $3,600 unfavorable variance between the budgeted and actual contribution margin for SkinKlear during May 19X1 by calculating the following variances:
   (1) Sales price variance.
   (2) Material price variance.
   (3) Material quantity variance.
   (4) Labor efficiency variance.
   (5) Variable overhead efficiency variance.
   (6) Variable overhead spending variance.
   (7) Contribution margin volume variance.
b. Allglow Company must decide whether or not the compounding operation in the SkinKlear manufacturing process that was mechanized on an experimental basis should continue to be mechanized. Calculate the variable cost savings that can be expected to arise in the future from the mechanization. Explain your answer.

25

Behavioral and Ethical Factors in Accounting Control

CHAPTER OBJECTIVES

After studying this chapter, you should be able to:

1. Explain the role of the cost accountant in utilizing informal organizations to achieve company goals.

2. Apply accounting control techniques and describe the role expectancy theory plays in accounting systems.

3. Contrast Theory X, Theory Y, and Theory Z management styles.

4. Relate the resistance to change, contingency theory, and adaptive responses to environmental uncertainty.

5. Discuss the ethics of cost accountants.

PRACTICAL
APPLICATION BOX

Using Marketing Techniques to Obtain Management Approval of Advanced Cost Accounting Systems

Accountants often use communication approaches appropriate for selling the need for standard accounting systems to management when they are actually trying to sell the need for *complex, customized systems*. Because many resources are required to develop and implement new automated equipment and computer information systems, such systems are difficult to obtain given scarce resources. That places accountants in positions of having to win management approval for expensive, yet intangible products that top management never sees and that most accountants have never used themselves. Accountants could borrow marketing techniques to justify expenditures. A first step is to determine whether managers recognize a need for the proposed system. A second step is evaluating the business environment by identifying all factors that may affect the purchasing decision. Overall, accountants are more likely to gain acceptance of a new accounting system if key decision makers perceive that a proposed system will satisfy their needs and also be cost effective.

From: Carolyn R. Stokes and Kay W. Lawrimore, "Selling a New Cost Accounting System," *Cost Management*, Fall 1989, pp. 129–34.

Introduction

Accountants do not operate in a behavioral vacuum. In addition to technical expertise, accountants must be knowledgeable about what motivates people and how they interpret and use accounting systems. Accountants' professional skills are applied within the context of an organization composed of individuals, each with different motives, attitudes, and needs.

This chapter discusses several theories for individual behavior. We discuss how the accountant and responsibility accounting systems can influence the behavior of others and stimulate employees and managers to perform in a manner that contributes to the success of the entire company.

Responsibility Accounting and Behavior (L.O. 1)

As ownership and management became separated, owners sought control over managers while managers sought control over subordinates. This created a situation in which interpersonal relations and communications between individuals and groups of individuals became more important. Along with this development, the complexity of technology and other environmental influences increased.

Responsibility accounting should facilitate the decentralization of decision making to utilize the expertise of all managers. However, managers may hesitate to give up some of their authority and areas of control. They find it very ego satisfying to have their own empires of control. Managers should recognize that although this is a natural tendency, this attitude is very dangerous because it places such a burden on a few individuals that they cannot carry out all company functions effectively. Often it is difficult in the early stages to detect a situation in which there are more tasks than individuals to adequately accomplish them. At this stage, management believes that it is taking advantage of a great opportunity to keep expenses down by not expanding human resources. This is when companies can benefit most from a responsibility accounting system because such a system requires defining and communicating overall goals to subunits as operational goals.

Goal Congruence

The responsibility accounting system should encourage managers to pursue objectives congruent with the overall goals of the company. This is **goal congruence;** that is, companies design goals and subgoals to encourage action consistent with top-management's objectives. In addition, employees should participate in establishing goals and standards of performance that ensure attainment of company objectives. Managers must be certain that employees understand not only the reasons for the standards but also how the standards affect each of them. Participation in selecting measures of goal achievement increases employees' acceptance of an evaluation program.

A difficult, but important, task of leaders is reconciling the values and goals of their group with the objectives of the company. Within each organization, several leaders hold the group together. However, for a leader to do this, the group must accept a common basis of beliefs or objectives. Managers who are not working toward common organizational goals can damage the company. For example, many companies evaluate managers on the profits of their divisions. Near the end of an accounting period, managers may realize that they must quickly cut costs to show a profit. They are, therefore, tempted to eliminate those costs totally under their control that do not require the approval of any other party. A manager may delay some needed machine repair and maintenance, for example, or avoid replacing needed personnel. Both of these actions are detrimental to the company's overall goals. Hiring and training new employees are necessary, and failing to make timely repairs may delay production or even cause permanent damage to a machine.

Formal and Informal Organization

Accountants should recognize that within each company is a network of both formal and informal relationships. The organization chart displays the **formal organization** structure that establishes lines of authority and responsibility. In contrast to informal relationships, the formal organization is larger and more stable. Communication between lines and levels of the organization, however, is not as frequent as in the informal organization and is usually written, not spoken. The **informal organization** is a network of personal and social relations not established or required by the formal organization. Managers cannot rescind informal organizations. They develop from the social interaction of employees, which means that they develop spontaneously as people associate with each other. Communications within an informal organization are more rapid and dynamic than those in formal relationships and consist mainly of oral messages. Informal organizations by their nature are unstable, subjective, and smaller. They often develop into formal relationships as they become larger, thereby giving rise to a new set of informal relationships. The emphasis within informal organizations is on people and their relationships. Formal organizations emphasize positions of authority and functions. Informal authority attaches to a person, while formal authority attaches to a position. Persons receive formal authority only by virtue of their positions.

Status within the informal organization may be more important to individuals than their positions in the formal organization, depending on an individual's sense of values. Formal status refers to the relation of supervisor and subordinate as designated by the chain of command of the formal organization in any company. Informal status refers to the social rank that others accord to someone because of their feelings toward the person. Informal status is the position that one has in a social system. The formal organization more clearly defines status based on one's position within the company. An individual's personality, age, seniority, technical competence, work location, and freedom to move about in his or her work area determine status within the informal organization. While status is an intangible state of mind, it serves the following functions: furnishes an incentive for more effective operations, provides for ranking and comparison, supplies a framework for cooperation and communication, and gives people a sense of responsibility.

Management should identify the leaders of the informal organizational network and obtain the support of these leaders. This process provides management an opportunity to communicate its operational goals to these leaders to gain their support and to ensure that the leaders' actions are consistent with the company's objectives. Managers increase their effectiveness if they invest time in talking to employees about companywide issues, as well as everyday matters. Informal communication not only facilitates decision making but also provides a way to express management concern for the well-being of employees.

Effective management requires an organizational atmosphere in which both the formal and informal organization can work together. If used properly, the informal organization can lighten the workload of the manager by filling in gaps in formal orders or in the manager's abilities.

Control Activities (L.O. 2)

A responsibility accounting system relates expenses to the manager responsible for them; therefore, the effectiveness of the system depends on control activities. Control activities compel events to conform to predetermined plans; thus, they involve the measurement and correction of activities of subordinates to ensure that plans occur within the time specified. Control takes two forms—positive and negative. Positive control is an attempt to ensure that a company reaches its objectives. Negative control is an attempt at preventing unwanted or undesirable activities. Control activities must thus involve the forces that both integrate and disrupt company activities. Effective managers emphasize the integrating forces and suppress and prevent the disrupting forces.

Control involves seeing not only that employees carry out a plan but also that companies meet their objectives with the resources committed. A plan lacks control if it needs more resources than were originally forecast. One of the objectives of **responsibility accounting** is to trace the costs incurred in such circumstances to the person responsible for the transaction. Responsibility accounting assumes all costs are controllable; however, the degree of control depends on the period in question as well as the level of management. Admittedly, some costs are more difficult to control than others, but all costs are controllable at some level at some time. For example, all costs are controllable by top management in the long run because management at this level has enough time to relieve itself of all commitments such as insurance, depreciation, and other costs of plant asset ownership. In addition, because a lower line supervisor does not have the necessary authority to determine which machine or building to purchase or lease, companies should not hold supervisors accountable for the depreciation or rent charges. Instead, higher levels of management are responsible for such costs.

An important aspect of control involves reporting on the progress of performance in meeting the objectives established. To do this, management should provide for effective communication of performance evaluations to the person responsible for meeting such objectives. This communication may include routine and special reports, which may be in written, oral, or graphic form. Reporting also includes other means of communication such as staff meetings and conferences, through which managers receive information as a basis for control of action. Control exists even if managers receive no information—as in management by exception—or if the variance from objectives is insignificant and does not warrant a report calling for action. The Theory X discussion later in the chapter presents management by exception more fully.

Insufficient controls can become an ever-growing problem. Employees readily sense such lack of control; this can seriously undermine their performance. To compound the problem, management may realize that control is insufficient, but be unable to determine exactly which factors are actually out of control. Lack of control breeds randomness. For example, if supervisors of a Mixing Department find that they can secure needed material without following the established procedures given in the company's manuals, Assembly Department supervisors will soon follow this pattern, too.

Accountants should prepare various types of information depending on management needs. If the primary objective is an evaluation of past events, the accountant provides information that is relatively objective and descriptive. If, on the other hand, management is choosing among several alternatives, accountants should provide information that describes each option to highlight differences among the choices. Accountants then need to provide differential analysis showing the forecasted consequences of each alternative. Because of the nature of this information, it is often subjective, reflecting hypothetical future conditions. Information needed for control involves fixing the responsibility for performance by measuring operations against some standard or objective. This information should be objectively and consistently defined.

Timely Control Reports

As accountants realize the importance of their role as communicators, they spend less time on the mechanical aspects of accounting and concentrate their attention on improving the clarity of their reports. Management should establish certain guidelines about preparing control reports.

Since availability of reports to managers on a timely basis is an important criterion for control, the plant's cost structure should allow periodic reports informing management of progress about standards. The plant reports of daily activities should, therefore, flow through the cost and accounting sections on a regular basis to keep the reports current.

Not only should accountants provide managers with timely reports, they must also relate the report to the user's needs and responsibilities. Generally, the closer a report is to the event, the more useful it is. In addition, the format of the reports should be consistent. When the report layout is changed, changes should be explained to recipients.

Responsibility for Variances

Control is more effective if employees detect variances as the work is in process rather than at the end of operations. Accountants can compile these variances in daily or weekly reports, expressed in physical terms, such as pounds or hours. Inspection at key production stages during operations can reveal spoilage and other losses. Reports to managers should avoid areas over which they have no control or authority. For example, a lower line supervisor usually has little voice in purchasing or leasing plant facilities. As a result, the reports this person receives should not focus on the rent or depreciation expense the cost center incurred. Above all, managers should not be held responsible for variances over which they have no control. The following report example illustrates this concept.

Assume a company has established the following per unit standards for material and labor in the Mixing Department based on 5,000 units normal capacity per period:

Material (3 gallons @ $5 per gallon)	$15
Labor (2 hours @ $10 per hour)	20

For the 5,200 units produced, a management consultant charged the Mixing Department supervisor with the following variances:

Net material variance:	
Actual material cost (16,100 gallons)	$82,110
Standard material cost at normal capacity	78,000
Unfavorable material variance	$ 4,110

Net labor variance:
Actual labor cost ($10.20 actual rate) $106,590
Standard labor cost at normal capacity   100,000
Unfavorable labor variance . . . . $ 6,590

Accountants circulated variance reports for each department throughout production management ranks. The Mixing Department supervisor believed further investigation was needed to explain the significant unfavorable variances. The purchasing agent revealed that all material suppliers faced shortages of the supplies needed and had increased their prices. Also, this shortage caused the Purchasing Department to order a lower-quality material that required an increase of 2 percent in Mixing Department handling and a 3 percent waste increase. Because the labor workers hired by the Personnel Department lacked training, the Mixing Department supervisor indicated these new recruits spent 100 hours learning the processing operations. Based on these facts, the report unfairly embarrassed the Mixing Department supervisor. An improved analysis of variances reveals the following:

Actual material cost and actual labor cost to make 5,200 units should not be compared to the standard cost to make the normal capacity of 5,000 units.

Instead, the Mixing Department supervisor should be held responsible for these two variances:

Material Quantity Variance
3 gallons × 5,200 units = 15,600 standard gallons × 103% = 16,068 standard gallons used due to lower quality of material
(16,100 actual gallons − 16,068) × $5 = $160 unfavorable material quantity variance

Labor Quantity Variance

102% × 10,400 = 10,608
                   − 100   hours in training
                  10,508   hours
                  10,450   actual hours ($106,590/$10.20 actual rate)
                      58   hours
                  $10.20
                 $591.60   favorable

The Purchasing Department should account for the following unfavorable material price variance and labor quantity variance even though market conditions may have made them justifiable.

Material Price Variance

$5.10   actual material price ($82,110/16,100 gallons)
 5.00   standard material price
$ .10   difference
×16,100 actual gallons
$1,610   unfavorable price variance

The Personnel Department or whatever cost center has the responsibility of hiring, matching skills with available positions, and employee training should bear the $1,000 cost of the 100 hours spent in training.

Labor Quantity Variance Due to Material Quality
The Purchasing Department should account for the $2,080 cost of the additional 208 hours (2% × 10,400 standard hours = 208) spent in handling the material due to the improper grade.

Regardless of how much attention accountants devote to the preparation of the reports, they waste much report preparation effort if they make no follow-up advice on inefficient performance. Unfortunately, accountants too frequently simply compile variances in reports, the cycle ends, and another one begins. Management misses a very important phase of the control process in these circumstances by not specifying the reasons for the variances from standards so the company can take corrective action. If employees see that management intends to do nothing about any variances, they tend to disregard the standards.

Concise Pattern. Because a report recipient has limited time to study the information, accountants should compile the report in the fewest possible words needed to convey the true picture. Explanations should be brief and to the point, omitting all unnecessary data. We should lay out the results in a clear and concise pattern. In addition, we should gear the report to the personality of the person reviewing it: Some managers want detailed analysis with tabulations of statistics; others want the facts in a simple form. Certainly, we should prepare these reports in terms that management understands. Regardless of whether executives have sales or production backgrounds, they should be able to interpret the accounting terminology.

Supportive Comments. While management may be aware that such factors as work stoppage, overtime, and extra help affect performance, they may not accurately know how efficient the operation is without supportive comments. Managers can use comments on both positive and negative performance as a guide to improve operations. Supportive comments should point out problem areas in a manner that the report users can understand. Reports with comments giving direction on how to improve performance and/or reinforce successful performance are of more value to the recipient than those that do not. Reports containing supportive comments play an important role in coordinating goals and in combining the varied interests of management.

Accountants realize that their responsibility for effective internal reporting also involves educating the report recipient. Recipients are more willing to study the data if they understand the purpose of the information. In addition, accountants recognize an obligation to educate report recipients regarding how they can more effectively use the data prepared.

Highlight Exceptions. Although it is management's responsibility to take corrective action to eliminate the factors causing cost variances, it is the accountant's duty to report the facts in such a manner that employees can control costs. The report should highlight areas requiring management action to improve performance. Reports should emphasize evidence of good performance, as well as performance below acceptable levels. For this reason, reports should compare actual performance for a cost or profit center to that center's planned performance. Accountants run a risk if they compare one cost center's actual performance to the actual operations of another cost center because the conditions under which they obtained these results are likely to differ considerably.

Determining which variances represent the exceptions that require management action can be complex. We use subjective judgment, hunches, and rules of thumb in distinguishing significant variances from insignificant variances. In some instances, a small variance may deserve management's attention and follow-up. Obviously, a 6 percent variance in a $5 million cost item warrants more attention than a 30 percent variance in a $15,000 cost. As a result, many companies use a rule of thumb incorporating both a dollar amount and a percentage. For example, investigate all variances exceeding $4,000 or 20 percent of standard cost, whichever is lower. Statistical tools can reduce the subjective element by separating those variances that are controllable from those that are the result of random events.

Cost-Benefit Analysis

Variance analysis is subject to the same cost-benefit analysis as other elements in the information system. Unfortunately, the interdependence of the sources of variances make such an analysis complex. For example, should companies hold supervisors responsible for the spoilage of material caused by a machine malfunction? On the one hand, the supervisor may not have control over the machine's operation and is not accountable. However, if the machine malfunction is the result of improper usage or lack of repairs and maintenance, an argument exists for holding the supervisor responsible. In addition, the supervisor is responsible for reporting machine malfunctions to the proper party. Interdependence also becomes a factor should the Purchasing Department order material that does not meet required specifications. Production workers then must cut or shape the material before they can use it in the manufacturing process. This becomes an even larger issue if it is difficult to determine exactly how much extra labor is involved. Thus, there is often an interrelationship between the process, people, and techniques involved in variance analysis.

This interdependence, in turn, makes it difficult to ascertain the cost and benefit associated with variance analysis. In deciding whether to investigate variances to discover their cause, accountants should consider the time needed for analysis. The search may involve conferences with production supervisors or workers, or it may focus on engineering or scientific issues. This search may be both costly and time-consuming.

There will always be a trade-off in data gathering between the cost of acquiring additional data and the benefit of these data. A system becomes too expensive when it produces more reports than management can or will use. This also has a detrimental effect on the morale of the employees who have prepared the reports. They cannot feel pride in their work when they see that it is not fulfilling a purpose. Accountants should strive to strike an optimum balance between the cost of the information and the benefits of this information. Companies should consult information users in evaluating these cost-benefit relationships, because they are aware of the internal and external constraints affecting their needs.

Accounting Controls

For the responsibility accounting system to provide an objective measure of an individual's performance, certain accounting controls should be in effect. Otherwise, there is no assurance that the performance feedback is valid and is a good basis for corrective action. Accounting controls involve methods and processes designed to protect assets and the reliability of financial records. A company normally has such control features as annual audits by independent accountants, fidelity bonds on their employees, electronic data processing equipment, organization charts detailing employee responsibility, and proofs and controls for documents and reports. Also included are procedures manuals, a system of budgets and standards, and an internal auditing staff. Chapters 9 and 10 discuss budgeting while Chapters 11 and 12 introduce standard costing. Next, we briefly discuss procedures manuals and internal auditing procedures.

Procedures Manual. An **accounting procedures manual** is of invaluable help, for it provides information about approving changes in accounting methods as well as detailed instructions for individual accounting procedures. It also includes both the chart of accounts for the accounting systems, including a general description of the account classifications, and methods for analyzing operating accounts. A procedures manual usually incorporates a schedule showing the departments responsible for specific report preparation, the report due dates, and the distribution dates. Inclusion of the summarizing procedures and closing schedules is helpful later for training new employees. Accountants may include the following information: cost determination for government contracts, standard form letters, conversion tables, table of equivalents, Financial Accounting Standards Board reporting requirements, and Securities and Exchange Commission and other government requirements concerning records and reports.

A procedures manual saves time because managers do not have to verbally repeat information and instructions. With written communication, there is also less chance of misunderstanding instructions. Managers have increased assurance that employees correctly understand and interpret instructions. An additional advantage of procedures manuals is that they assist new employees by providing them with information and clearer knowledge of what managers expect of them.

To have an effective procedures manual, the accounting department should make regular revisions, keeping the material current. Management should periodically distribute revisions to all persons affected by the changes. They must also generate enthusiasm so that personnel follow the manual. Personnel are more likely to accept and follow a clearly written and prepared manual. The internal auditing staff should conduct periodic audits to determine the degree of compliance with the procedures listed in the manual.

Internal Auditing. A company may also have its own **Internal Auditing** Department to review accounting, financial, and other operations as an independent appraisal activity. Since the Internal Auditing Department usually performs a staff function, it has no operating responsibilities and usually reports to the board of directors. Internal auditors make evaluations of the degree of compliance with managerial procedures, including whether the company is following accounting procedures, government regulations, and contractual obligations. They support this evaluation of the effectiveness of control by objective analyses, appraisals, and recommendations. Internal auditors distribute this information to management. While the Internal Auditing Department can make recommendations, only management can implement them. In addition, as employees, internal auditors do not have the external auditor's independence in fact and in appearance. External and internal auditors both appraise the effectiveness of internal control; however, internal auditors evaluate both accounting and administrative controls.

Traditional Accounting Model: Theory X (L.O. 3)

Theory X is the basis of the traditional accounting model and the controls it stresses. **Theory X** considers workers to be motivated solely by economic forces, innately lazy, and interested in doing as little work as possible. Because this theory presents workers as ordinarily inefficient and wasteful, it assumes that tight budgets and controls are necessary. It strongly emphasizes the use of accounting as an instrument to reduce and control costs. This model establishes the formal organization chart and the job title as the source of managerial authority.

Frederick W. Taylor's scientific management movement reflects these underlying ideas about human nature. This movement considered the employee as an additional part of the machine. Maximizing the productivity of the worker by increasing efficiency and reducing costs was a central concept of Taylor's. After publication in 1911 of Taylor's famous work, *The Principles of Scientific Management,* the movement flourished and rapidly became an important part of the business scene. Taylor and his successors studied factory costs in detail and stimulated the development of modern cost and management accounting. Their emphasis on control, segment responsibility, and accountability also affected cost accounting concepts.

The scientific management movement, however, has several drawbacks. For one thing, it allows the creation of many repetitive, nonmotivating jobs. As a result, in many large industrial plants today, there is much inattention and sometimes even conscious motivation to do a bad job. Bored workers may think of new, often destructive, ways to break the monotony. Even though persons with little education and little creative ability usually find assembly-line work acceptable, many people in these jobs are overqualified. Accountants contribute to the assembly-line problem by overemphasizing short-run unit costs and by not determining the cost of boredom-induced absenteeism and turnover. Instead, this cost is allocated to and hidden in general overhead.

The scientific method also fails to avoid distorted reporting. If accountants agree that the major purpose of cost accounting is to provide various levels of administration with data that facilitate decision making, they must also be certain that employees who can develop many ingenious ways of falsifying accounting reports to hide poor performance do not distort performance measurement. Such falsification often occurs in an organizational climate of fear and distrust in which the employees feel they must protect themselves. Employees can justify, to themselves at least, this falsification of accounting records if they do not understand the reporting system or feel that it is too strict. As discussed later in the chapter, the behavioral science approach and Theory Z help overcome some of the problems.

Spending Spree

We often see a similar distortion in the recurring government and business budget cycles, in which the measurement of performance against the budget influences the next budget. When expenditures are less than budgeted amounts, a tendency exists to revise the subsequent budget downward. When expenditures exceed the budgeted amount, companies often penalize managers. It usually takes a manager only one cycle to recognize the rules of this game. The manager then engages in excess spending the last few weeks of an appropriation year to avoid having budget cuts the next year. This cycle occurs because budgets often overemphasize specialized departments and not the total organization.

In organizations using the scientific management method, accountants often find themselves caught between the demands of two people or groups who exert conflicting pressures. Such incompatible expectations are frequent in the budgeting process. Production personnel, for example, usually believe that accountants should not include tight controls in budgets, while top management usually believes that the budget contains too much slack. Accountants recognize these conflicting positions, and hence often become defensive about their work, reverting to technical accounting jargon to confuse one faction or the other.

The reporting of unfavorable variances sometimes causes further breakdowns in the communication chain, especially if reports do not also publish the reasons for unfavorable variances. We discussed this in an earlier example involving the Mixing Department supervisor who used more material than the standard specifications allowed because the Purchasing Department ordered a cheaper grade of material than the standard specified. The Mixing Department showed an unfavorable material quantity variance. The company penalized the supervisor when, in fact, the Purchasing Department was at fault. Companies avoid such errors when they make clear the causes of unfavorable variances.

Emphasis on Punishment

The traditional practice in accounting and the scientific management approach is *management by exception,* which holds that control reports should only emphasize and highlight areas that vary significantly from the objective or standard. However, many times the exceptions studied are only unfavorable variances rather than also investigating exceptionally high favorable variances. The emphasis is on punishment rather than a combination of reward and punishment, which more effectively improves production. Workers striving for high performance often become quite anxious because management by exception highlights only their mistakes. They find themselves preoccupied with the number of times they have unfavorable variances rather than with their performance level over the long run. Employees highly interested in their work may suffer unnecessarily when management emphasizes deficiencies in their cost centers, especially if these are deficiencies over which they had no control. As a result, they doubt the validity of the standard or budget set by management and soon ignore it.

Behavioral Science Approach: Theory Y (L.O. 3)

As a result of these deficiencies in the traditional accounting model and scientific management approach, accountants conducted research studies analyzing the behavior of employees in a work group. These studies led to the behavioral science movement that utilizes a human relations approach. This human relations approach—often called the **Theory Y** concept—assumes that the average person learns to accept and to seek responsibility. Theory Y does not view workers as being lazy. In fact, this concept stresses that the expenditure of physical and mental effort in work is as natural as play or rest. This approach presumes that human beings exercise self-direction and self-control in the service of their objectives.

Behavioral scientists believe that employees earn authority; good leaders get someone to follow them because they deserve respect. By proving their ability, these leaders command the respect of the individuals following them. The traditional view of leadership, on the other hand, states that the source of authority is merely a person's position on the organization chart. The behavioral scientists attack the organization chart, however, saying that it does not reflect the way people really work together. They further believe that organization charts often unduly restrict or inhibit individual employees by forcing them into a preconceived mold.

The Hawthorne experiments of 1927 to 1932 and an awakened interest in human relations in the 1930s and 1940s spurred the **behavioral science movement.** The Hawthorne study revealed that the attitude of management toward employees affects efficiency and productivity more than do such material factors as rest periods, illumination, and money. The behavioral science approach supports the thesis that management involves getting tasks done with and through people, and that managers center their attention on interpersonal relations. This approach emphasizes the human aspect of management along with the principle that when people work together to accomplish group objectives, they understand each other. The focus of the behavioral science approach is on individuals and their motivations as sociopsychological beings.

Management by Objectives.   Closely aligned with the behavioral science approach is the **management by objectives process** that involves all levels of management. After top management establishes specific and measurable goals for the organization, employees then set job and personal goals congruent with the organizational goals. Together, employees and supervisors agree on the criteria for measuring performance. Periodically they review this performance so employees can take needed corrective action. A formal review at the end of the cycle follows these periodic evaluations.

In general, management has abandoned autocratic leadership for a human relations approach. Research in the social sciences has provided a better understanding of human behavior and acknowledges that people need to feel important and wanted. Even though employees do not always reveal their feelings in words, they do have a strong desire for psychological security, and they need a sense of belonging. The following sections describe the principal theories in behavioral science and their relationship to responsibility accounting.

Hierarchy of Needs

Abraham Maslow explained behavior by individuals seeking satisfaction through a hierarchy of needs. According to this theory, humans have definite categories of needs, arranged in a natural hierarchy of urgency. Maslow's general thesis is that all needs do not emerge at the same time. After satisfying one level of needs, an individual may then engage in other forms of behavior to satisfy needs at the next level. Maslow presented the following five basic categories of needs, in order of fulfillment priority: (1) physiological—including the need for food, water, oxygen, rest, and sex; (2) safety—need for a predictable and organized world; (3) belongingness and love—desire for affectionate relations with others and a recognized place in a group; (4) esteem—self-respect and achievement; (5) self-actualization—needs of individuals to become what they are capable of being.

According to **Maslow's hierarchy of needs,** in a work context, after satisfying basic lower-order needs, individuals can move from routine and boring jobs to those holding more potential for satisfying their higher-order needs. However, in evaluating Maslow's theory, one must ask whether an individual must completely satisfy a need before the next level need emerges. Maslow himself stated that needs are inseparable and interrelated. He also recognized that the hierarchy is not rigid; for example, a creative person may experience the self-actualization need long before partially satisfying lower-level needs.

Herzberg's Two-Factor Theory

Frederick Herzberg provided an alternative theory. According to Herzberg, those factors in the work environment providing job satisfaction do not necessarily also cause dissatisfaction. *Hygiene factors* include company personnel policies, salary, quality of working conditions, and technical supervision on the job. These are the characteristics of the work environment that cause dissatisfaction. Herzberg believed that employee dissatisfaction is likely when these factors are absent in the work situation; however, the presence of hygiene factors does not necessarily motivate employees—they only prevent dissatisfaction. *Motivators* are the job content factors producing satisfaction; these include job achievement, recognition of achievement, and responsibility for achievement. According to Herzberg's theory, the absence of motivational factors in the work situation does not bring about dissatisfaction. But when present, motivators relate to a high level of job satisfaction. Motivators involve intrinsic factors or the actual content of a job, not just extrinsic factors of the job environment.

According to Herzberg's findings, the factors that make people unhappy on a job are not the same as those that contribute to lasting satisfaction. Responsibility, advancement, and the nature of the job are the most important job conditions contributing to lasting satisfaction. However, there is an overlap of motivators and hygiene factors, and what is a motivator for one person may be a hygiene factor for another. The Herzberg model suggests the traditional methods of increasing wages and fringe benefits may not increase motivation. Instead, managers should give employees the opportunity for individual accomplishment associated with work.

Extrinsic and Intrinsic Rewards

The need satisfaction theories proposed by Maslow and Herzberg relate to the use of extrinsic and intrinsic rewards. **Extrinsic rewards** are tangible and measurable, such as salaries, fringe benefits, year-end bonuses, and carpeted offices. An organization's punishment and reward system influences individuals' extrinsic motivation. **Intrinsic rewards** are those internalized by the individual. They are intangible and consist of feelings of satisfaction and achievement that people receive from good performance. Participation and other intrinsic factors that lead to self-actualization are important motivational variables. This type of reward appeals to the higher-level needs of esteem and self-actualization. Intrinsic motivation is not visible nor so readily controllable by the organization. Through its information and control system, an organization must provide an environment in which an individual can relate intrinsic rewards to motivation.

Until recently, managers believed that extrinsic rewards had the most impact on motivation of individuals. Accordingly, they rewarded employees who performed well with a bonus in dollars or an increase in salary. However, more recent motivation research shows that extrinsic rewards, such as money, may not continue to motivate performance. After meeting the individual's basic needs, intrinsic rewards must be present for improved or greater performance because extrinsic rewards elicit less performance or possibly no additional improvement. Some individuals do not follow this pattern as they care for achieving nothing more than their basic needs. However, most individuals have an internal reward system needing activation also. For a person with a high achievement motive, extrinsic rewards are a measure of success and, therefore, may help to motivate performance.

Thus, opinions differ regarding the influence that an extrinsic reward, such as pay, has on motivating an employee. Maslow's theory is that money fulfills the lower-level physiological and safety needs. Herzberg's motivator-hygiene theory breaks rewards down into two categories: motivators and hygiene. By doing this he found that motivators such as job advancement and responsibility contribute to an individual's satisfaction and motivation but are unlikely to contribute to job dissatisfaction if they are absent. On the other hand, extrinsic rewards do not produce satisfaction, but an absence of extrinsic rewards can produce dissatisfaction.

The impact that extrinsic and intrinsic rewards have on performance depends on the performance expected, the task involved, the individuals and their needs at the given time, and the situation. Intrinsic rewards are not motivators for all people. Items that might be intrinsically rewarding to one individual may not be rewarding to another individual. The value that this satisfaction has differs from individual to individual. Therefore, employers cannot directly give intrinsic rewards. At best, they can provide opportunities allowing the individual to achieve these; but the individual must internalize these rewards.

Job Enrichment and Job Enlargement. Companies can use **job enrichment** in giving intrinsic rewards to employees by providing opportunities for personal growth and meaningful work experience. Job enrichment gives workers more autonomy and responsibility for planning, directing, and controlling their performance. It also allows the redesign of jobs to include a greater variety of work content. Companies qualitatively expand jobs by adding tasks that vary in levels of difficulty, such as found with increased specialization.

Even though job enlargement has the same purpose as job enrichment—that of reducing job monotony, increasing employee motivation, and providing opportunities for personal growth—**job enlargement** does not give the individual any more control over the job. Job enlargement expands the duties of the job, giving the job holder more duties of the same nature to perform. For example, employees rotate through similar jobs.

Reinforcement Theory. Because managers want to improve job performance, they seek various models and theories to explain human behavior and to effectively motivate employees. In their search, they may obtain some job improvement by making consequences contingent on job performance. A contingency is the link that connects job behavior with the consequences of that behavior. These contingencies are an important factor in reinforcement theory.

Reinforcement theory is the psychological theory that three elements—desired behavior, contingencies, and consequences—constitute a framework for motivating job performance. Thus, since a manager can use contingencies and consequences to influence behavior, this is called **behavior modification.** Even though reinforcement theory is sometimes manipulative and unethical, contingencies of reinforcement do influence job behavior and performance. It is useful for managers to recognize these concepts in creating work environments in which people can self-actualize. Reinforcement theory cannot force an employee to find a particular consequence reinforcing or rewarding. Instead, it requires that managers find behavior-contingency-consequence relationships that reinforce employee behavior.

Behavioral Research

The cycle of behavioral research has shifted from the individual to the complex organization and back to the individual. The increased acceptance by behavioral researchers that individuals comprise complex organizations and that certain key individual behavioral patterns determine the behavioral patterns for the entire organization caused this shift. Behavioral researchers have determined that by studying individual behavior in general and that of the key individuals in particular, they can determine the attitudes and actions of the entire organization. Organizations are self-selecting in the types of individuals they retain. The key individuals within an organization determine what types of individuals the organization self-selects.

Early research on human behavior first focused on individual motives, personality, and cognitive processes. The enterprises studied then were smaller than the organizations researched today. The focus of attention was the individual solving production and related problems. There was much less complexity and interaction in these smaller firms; thus, it was crucial to analyze individual behavior. The early research concerned relatively simple problems such as the relationship between workers and their manager; in most cases, the manager was also the owner.

Researchers directed their efforts to viewing large, complex organizations as information-processing entities that structured themselves to meeting the technological and environmental demands. The move to organizational research identified the need to adopt new types of organizations to respond effectively to dynamic environments. For a time much of the research focused on ways to make corporations more efficient and ways to increase the information processing capacity of corporations. Even though more information was available, decision making did not improve. Researchers overlooked that it is not the information capacity of the organization but the collective information capacity of the individual decision makers that determines an organization's success.

Evaluation of Human Relations Approach. We cannot deny the behavioral science thesis that management involves human behavior. Clearly, good leadership is important in effective management. However, the human relations approach leads to the manipulation of employees when organizations attempt to manage people's lives. Also, too much emphasis on human relations can make people feel sorry for themselves, and they can use their psychological problems as an excuse for poor performance. In addition, an overemphasis on behavioral science can distort individual responsibility and make it easy for people to slough off their duties. Rather than producing a desired good or service, a company may focus too much attention on individual employees and their relations.

Contingency Theory (L.O. 4)

Both the traditional and behavioral science approaches to control attempted to identify one best way. In the traditional approach, the emphasis was on the best management style; in the human relations phase, it was the one best leadership style. The **contingency theory** approach to control searches for conditions under which certain combinations of variables work best. Contingency theory has arisen in recognition that the organization should develop adaptive responses to environmental uncertainty and unpredictability. The contingency model hypothesizes three major contingencies that affect subunit performance: (1) factors internal to the subunit (internal factors); (2) interrelationships with other subunits (interdependency factors); and (3) interactions external to the firm (environmental factors). According to contingency theory, these three contingencies operate differentially across organizational subunits.

According to contingency theory, efficient organizational structures vary with organizational contextual factors such as environment, size, stage of maturity, and sophistication of technology. Contingency theory also further implies that certain managerial techniques, such as participative decision making or task directed leadership, are contingent on the organization's context and structure. Contingency theory's approach to the problem of influencing subordinate behavior is to focus on those organizational variables and relationships whose combination results in high performance.

The cost accountant's role is to develop information systems that are both flexible and elaborate enough to facilitate an adaptive response to both internal and external factors as they change. For a company operating in a stable external environment, an information system that relies on responsibility accounting, centralized authority, and rules to control decision makers is usually sufficient. However, as uncertainty increases, the organization becomes more complex to interact with the less stable environment. The end result is increased decentralization and a need for more information to control and coordinate the organization.

Expectancy Theory of Motivation

The expectancy model is a comprehensive performance model for organizations based on the contingency philosophy. This model plays a role in evaluating cost accounting systems. **Expectancy theory** holds that individuals have expectations about how well they will perform. Individuals believe that certain efforts will lead to specific performance levels. In addition, they have expectations that certain performance will lead to probable rewards. The theory gives insight into what motivates people and thereby enables the design of management accounting systems which encourages the motivation of individuals and assessment by a company to determine if it is using its individual potential.

In its basic format, the model stipulates that people have two sets of expectancies about any given task. The first set relates to the expectation that a given level of effort or performance (P) shall lead to the desired outcome (O). The subjects assign values to the various outcomes based on their personal desirability. These are valences (V). The subjects form expectancies that their efforts will lead to the required performance (P). The second set relates to the expectation that the desired outcome will lead to an intrinsic or extrinsic valence or both valences. According to expectancy theory, an individual's motivation is a multiplicative function of the sum of the ($E \rightarrow P$) expectancies (the expectancy that the individual's personal effort can result in the required performance), and the sum of the $[(P \rightarrow O)(V)]$ products (the expectancy that the required performance will result in perceived outcomes multiplied by the valence or attractiveness of these outcomes). This means that an individual's motivation to perform depends on both the expectancy of being able to perform properly and the expectancy of obtaining rewards of various values.

Thus, if managers discover what motivates people to perform in a certain way and which rewards employees value, they can act accordingly. If organizations can change or manipulate employees' expectancies about their efforts and performance, they achieve better results. After determining sources of motivation, the accounting system can deliver and measure these results. This represents the important implication of expectancy theory for accounting systems. It is an interactive situation. The knowledge gained from expectancy theory determines which variables to measure and what steps to take to motivate individuals. Not only can the accounting system determine the performance of individuals but it can also give feedback about whether management is focusing on the correct variables for motivation.

Managers also develop expectations about cost accounting systems subject to the rules of the expectancy theory. There can be a negative backlash when they hold unrealistically high expectations of the system. Before implementation of the system, managers have these expectations: very high, very low, or unsure of uses. Basing the success of the system on frequency of use and proportion of the management group using the system, the best success rate results when top management has very high expectations of the system. Expectancy theory explains that in any accounting system installation when top management—the senders—have very high expectations, employees widely use the system. Lower management—the receivers—bring their expectations of the system in line with top management. A system usually fails when top management has very low expectations. When top management is unsure, top management actually becomes the receiver, and the success of the system is based on lower management's expectations, which decline because of top management's uncertain position.

Accountants use expectancy theory in determining the level at which to set standards to generate optimum results. If they set standards so high that employees cannot attain them through reasonable effort, this lowers the expectancy that a given level of effort leads to the outcome. It also lowers the expectancy of intrinsic or extrinsic valences given the outcome. The result is lower motivation. On the other hand, if employees can easily achieve standards, the expectancy relating efforts to outcome is high but the expectancy relating rewards to outcome is low.

Behavioral Implications of Profit and Cost Centers (L.O. 4)

Some companies rely on the profit center as a motivational tool by giving specific levels of management a percentage of divisional profits. As Chapter 14 explained, a profit center is accountable for both revenues and costs, while a cost center is a segment responsible only for costs. The profit center concept recognizes that individual personal objectives dominate over corporate objectives because this concept allows individual managers more flexibility in setting goals within their own areas of responsibility. Some managers view profit centers as educational devices encouraging lower level management to focus on corporate objectives.

Managers of profit and cost centers should understand the accounting information they receive so they readily use it in their decision making. When managers consider the data too complicated or unfair, conflict results. Managers should know which costs are allocated and why they are assigned to a given center. It is also important that the information managers receive be clear and simple, representing their tasks. The data reporting results to profit or cost centers should be consistent. If not, managers spend much time just arguing over the inconsistencies in the numbers before them.

Suboptimization

Accountants must provide profit center managers with data about the total performance of the organization; otherwise, suboptimization and narrow-mindedness result. **Suboptimization** is a condition in which each segment benefits to the detriment of the overall company; this is just the opposite of goal congruence.

A company's reward system often encourages suboptimization. For example, assume a company annually awards bonuses to territory managers based on net income. The actual regional results are

	North	South	East	West	Total
			Territory (000s)		
Territory sales	$200	$350	$440	$690	$1,680
Territorial variable and fixed expenses	120	200	140	290	750
Segment margin	$ 80	$150	$300	$400	$ 930
Allocated companywide expenses (equally)	60	60	60	60	240
Net income	$ 20	$ 90	$240	$340	$ 690

Several behavioral problems are likely to develop in this situation because the reward system encourages each territory manager to focus attention solely on net income. The following factors explain why arbitrarily giving a bonus as a percentage of net income has dysfunctional consequences:

1. Normally territory managers cannot control companywide expenses that reduce segment net income. Also, allocating companywide expenses equally is probably unfair because one territory may receive more benefit from corporate activities than other territories; yet all regions receive equal assigned expense.

2. The territories may have very different potential markets and market shares; it may be much easier for some regions to increase sales and income.

3. Some territories may lease their facilities and have rent expense while others may own their plant and warehouses. Depending on the age of the facilities owned, significant differences in occupancy cost occur. For example, if the segment plant facilities are old, depreciation cost is likely to be much less than leasing expense.

4. The bonus system encourages territory managers to refrain from incurring such discretionary costs as preventive maintenance, research, and advertising that reduce short-run net income. Avoiding the incurrence of maintenance and promotion now may have detrimental long-run effects.

5. Overall, such reward systems encourage suboptimization and place an emphasis on the short run. The reward system gives territory managers an incentive to play short-term corporate games and engage in projects that only have a current benefit.

(The problem for self-study at the end of this chapter discusses cases where accounting systems reward competition, rather than cooperation.)

The use of larger computer facilities with their improved capabilities for centralized decision making may reverse a trend toward decentralization. Profit maximization may demand more centralized decision making. A change in decentralized profit responsibility could give segment managers responsibility for implementing a portion of a centrally derived profit decision. Thus, the profit goal for a segment may be much less than the maximum profit the segment could make if left to itself. This holistic approach may continue even to the point that top management expects certain profit centers to operate at a loss because maximization of overall profitability requires one segment to take a loss that another segment will more than make up. As an example, management may decide that to satisfy the overall company goals, a center must supply other parts of the business with materials or products at marginal cost and allow the company to take all the profit on resale.

Budgeted goals become substitutes for goal maximization. Whether a profit goal that is less than maximum will motivate a manager as effectively is questionable. Motivating individuals to enhance someone else's performance, rather than one's own directly measurable performance, is difficult. Because the success of the overall company depends on the willingness of individual segment managers and employees to make these sacrifices, corporate managers should take steps to make certain segment managers do not engage in suboptimization. Segment managers will more likely make such sacrifices if they trust corporate managers to repay their actions and restore equity in the future. Corporate managers earn this trust through their actions.

Theory Z (L.O. 3)

Rather than using either Theory X or Theory Y, more organizations are utilizing Theory Z as their model. Interpersonal skills are central to the Theory Z way of doing business. Trust, loyalty to a company, and a career-long commitment to one's job are the foundation of **Theory Z.** The idea is that productivity and trust go together. Theory Z supervisors trust workers to use their discretion in a manner consistent with the organization's goals. **Egalitarianism,** a central feature of Type Z organizations, implies that each person can apply discretion and can work autonomously without close supervision because each employee is trusted.

Employees Are Valuable Assets

Also, most Theory Z companies have well-developed philosophies that their employees are their most valuable assets. Management views workers as a resource rather than a cost. A Theory Z philosophy expresses concern for employees' needs and emphasizes cooperation and teamwork. Managers use downward delegation to achieve a greater span of control. Downward delegation requires respect for the feelings and human capacity of subordinates.

Theory Z companies avoid adversary relationships at all costs. Adversary positions usually develop when one or both parties take a position and try to prove they are right rather than approaching a problem with open minds. The Theory Z approach solves problems as a group, rather than encouraging a blame game. Theory Z organizations address the problem, not the personality.

For example, a typical slogan in a Theory Z company is *find waste.* Managers avoid using a slogan that says eliminate waste, implying that employees are deliberately inefficient. This attitude offends employees. Instead, Theory Z gives employees the opportunity and encouragement to find waste and provides them with the tools to help focus on the waste.

Openness Reduces Resistance to Change

Theory Z organizations encourage openness. Openness does not mean hostility; instead openness values a realistic appraisal of both problems and achievements. Leaders who frankly disagree with others and who go out of their way to create an atmosphere that welcomes differing opinions produces change. This openness reduces employee hostility to the introduction of labor-saving technology and to organizational changes. Business organizations are like humans because a top priority is survival. Companies also resist change and a rearrangement of their functions. Changes are often resisted not because of their precise nature, but *because* they are changes.

Theory Z evaluates employees according to a multitude of criteria rather than solely on individual bottom-line contribution. Personality and behavior, rather than output, is the key criterion in most Theory Z companies. In this way, employees do not feel that effectiveness and efficiency, which may sometimes be beyond their control, are the main criteria in the evaluation. A prevailing atmosphere of trust and respect for all people in the development and use of their maximum capabilities exists.

Input in Decision Making. A Theory Z manager does not make a decision until others who will be affected have had sufficient time to offer their views. Further, a Theory Z manager does not implement decisions until workers are willing to support the decision even though they may disagree with the manager's judgment. The Theory Z approach encourages group members to help each other develop job-relevant knowledge and skills by direct instruction, by providing feedback about behavior, and by serving as models of appropriate behavior.

Summary

The high esteem with which accountants are held indicates that many members of the profession have been especially effective in making assumptions about the behavior of people in an organization. Accountants recognize that it is impossible to adequately solve accounting problems without also considering the motivations, values, and behavior of the company's employees. This recognition is important because accounting systems operate in human organizations and these systems serve human purposes. The objective of these systems is to achieve coordination of company activities toward the accomplishment of the organization's goals.

Increased global competition requires managers to take more risks and for greater lengths of time. This requires team building and the development of management replacements to meet these demands. Because of these increased demands, management needs the support of a responsibility accounting system. This information system is beneficial because a company must define its overall goals and, in turn, communicate these objectives to each subunit in such a way that they thoroughly understand areas of responsibility. Responsibility accounting also permits effective utilization of the management by exception concept. However, the accountant should be certain that managers analyze both favorable and unfavorable significant deviations. A responsibility accounting system also provides an objective measure of an individual's performance. This performance feedback allows employees to take rapid corrective action.

Today's accountants recognize they need to understand human needs and aspirations before providing information to effectively motivate outstanding performance. The measuring and reporting techniques used by the accountant have a significant impact on the employee-superior relationship. Accounting reports emphasizing only unfavorable performance often lead the way for additional failure. Accountants should not only make management aware of poor performance but they should also provide them information for rewarding efficient production. Accountants and management should acknowledge that employees soon recognize that the internal reporting methods reflect the company's behavioral assumptions.

Theory Z emphasizes long-range survival by viewing employees and suppliers as vital assets, not replaceable adversaries. As managers treat employees with respect and trust, the organization moves to higher quality and productivity. These attitudes create a climate where employees benefit emotionally as well as financially from the success of the total organization. The rewards will be low labor turnover, low absenteeism, and increasing higher skill and loyalty in the employees. The quality of products and services increases and productivity of the organization improves steadily as complaints and other wasteful practices disappear.

Important Terms and Concepts

goal congruence, 857
formal organization, 858
informal organization, 858
responsibility accounting, 859
accounting procedures manual, 864
internal auditing, 864
Theory X, 865
Theory Y, 866
behavioral science movement, 867
management by objectives process, 867
Maslow's hierarchy of needs, 868

Herzberg's two-factor theory, 868
extrinsic and intrinsic rewards, 868
job enrichment, 869
job enlargement, 869
reinforcement theory, 870
behavior modification, 870
contingency theory, 871
expectancy theory, 871
suboptimization, 873
Theory Z, 874
egalitarianism, 875

Appendix 25–A Standards of Ethical Conduct (L.O. 5)

Cost accountants have responsibilities to their employing organizations, to others in the organizations, and to themselves. While their positions involve collecting, analyzing, and reporting operating information, their conduct must be ethical. Their ethics require that they exercise initiative and good judgment in providing management with information having a potentially adverse economic impact, such as reports about poor product quality, cost overruns, and abuses of company policy. Not only should they communicate to management their professional judgments or opinions but also favorable and unfavorable data. They should protect proprietary information as well as follow the chain of command. Controllers are responsible for internal control and for ensuring that employees follow company policies and enforce controls necessary to achieve the firm's objectives. Before proceeding with any questionable actions, controllers should determine whether they are violating professional standards, personal principles, or the company's code of ethics.

The following standards of ethical conduct and how to resolve these conflicts are from the National Association of Accountants' *Statement on Management Accounting,* 1983.

Standards of Ethical Conduct for Management Accountants

Management accountants have an obligation to the organizations they serve, their profession, the public, and themselves to maintain the highest standards of ethical conduct. In recognition of this obligation, the Institute of Certified Management Accountants and the National Association of Accountants have promulgated the following standards of ethical conduct for management accountants. Adherence to these standards is integral to achieving the Objective of Management Accounting. Management accountants shall not commit acts contrary to these standards nor shall they condone the commission of such acts by others within their organizations.

Competence
Management accountants have a responsibility to:

- Maintain an appropriate level of professional competence by ongoing development of their knowledge and skills.
- Perform their professional duties in accordance with relevant laws, regulations, and technical standards.
- Prepare complete and clear reports and recommendations after appropriate analysis of relevant and reliable information.

Confidentiality
Management accountants have a responsibility to:

- Refrain from disclosing confidential information acquired in the course of their work except when authorized, unless legally obligated to do so.
- Inform subordinates as appropriate regarding the confidentiality of information acquired in the course of their work and monitor their activities to assure the maintenance of that confidentiality.
- Refrain from using or appearing to use confidential information acquired in the course of their work for unethical or illegal advantage either personally or through third parties.

Integrity
Management accountants have a responsibility to:

- Avoid actual or apparent conflicts of interest and advise all appropriate parties of any potential conflict.

- Refrain from engaging in any activity that would prejudice their ability to carry out their duties ethically.
- Refuse any gift, favor, or hospitality that would influence or would appear to influence their actions.
- Refrain from either actively or passively subverting the attainment of the organization's legitimate and ethical objectives.
- Recognize and communicate professional limitations or other constraints that would preclude responsible judgment or successful performance of an activity.
- Communicate unfavorable as well as favorable information and professional judgments or opinions.
- Refrain from engaging in or supporting any activity that would discredit the profession.

Objectivity

Management accountants have a responsibility to:

- Communicate information fairly and objectively.
- Disclose fully all relevant information that could reasonably be expected to influence an intended user's understanding of the reports, comments, and recommendations presented.

Resolution of Ethical Conduct

In applying the standards of ethical conduct, management accountants may encounter problems in identifying unethical behavior or in resolving an ethical conflict. When faced with significant ethical issues, management accountants should follow the established policies of the organization bearing on the resolution of such conflict. If these policies do not resolve the ethical conflict, management accountants should consider the following courses of action:

- Discuss such problems with the immediate superior except when it appears that the superior is involved, in which case the problem should be presented initially to the next higher managerial level. If a satisfactory resolution cannot be achieved when the problem is initially presented, submit the issues to the next higher managerial level. If the immediate superior is the chief executive officer, or equivalent, the acceptable reviewing authority may be a group such as the audit committee, executive committee, board of directors, board of trustees, or owners. Contact with levels above the immediate superior should be initiated only with the superior's knowledge, assuming the superior is not involved.
- Clarify relevant concepts by confidential discussion with an objective advisor to obtain an understanding of possible courses of action.
- If the ethical conflict still exists after exhausting all levels of internal review, the management accountant may have no other recourse on significant matters than to resign from the organization and to submit an informative memorandum to an appropriate representative of the organization.

Except where legally prescribed, communication of such problems to authorities or individuals not employed or engaged by the organization is not considered appropriate.

Problem for Self-Study

Accounting Systems Rewarding Competition, Not Cooperation

Give examples and discuss why often the accounting system is set up to reward competition and not cooperation.

Solution to Problem for Self-Study

Accounting Systems Rewarding Competition, Not Cooperation

Accounting systems are often designed to promote or reward competition rather than cooperation. This is particularly true if they are designed in the traditional method. If the system is designed to reward individual segments or profitability only, each segment manager is going to use every resource available to have the best segment in the organization. Often this is at the expense of the other segments. Instead of having a cooperative, integrated organization, each segment tries to outdo the others.

Accounting systems are often set up to be used as control devices to detect unfavorable variances and to report them. This is based on a vertical system and competition among the components of a business to do well as compared with their own budget even if it may hurt another part of the company. An alternative is to use a more horizontal approach and encourage cooperation, not competition. This may be done by changing the matrix to consider other factors affecting variances.

Evaluations for employees are most often individually determined. This brings about competition among the individual employees. This is in contrast to evaluation of a team, with each member being responsible for, and evaluated on his/her particular share which has been specified. The team approach could bring about greater cooperation and cohesiveness.

Examples of procedures in traditional accounting that encourage competition rather than cooperation are the following:

1. Static budgets—These provide for specific sales, production costs, and operating expenses for the various units. The pressure is on to operate within the budget limits once these have been established. These budgets do not encourage cooperation. In other words, if a large savings in one unit would cause a small increase in another unit with a net savings for the total company, the action probably would not be implemented because of the unfavorable effect ensuing to the unit which would go over its budget. Instead, suboptimization occurs to the detriment of the company.

2. Time horizon of budgets—The time horizon of many budgets leads to competition as it is the measure of performance and road to upward mobility. The short run is seen as more important than the long run. What can and does happen is that a budget is used to reward those who stay within it and punish those who overrun. A segment may be operating within its budget, but the plant may be falling apart through neglect and nonexpenditure.

3. Responsibility accounting—Division managers are often evaluated on segment net income or return on investment. The accounting system does not provide for any recognition for lowering profits or increasing expenses of one unit in an effort to have the opposite effect on the total organization. Unusual environmental factors are not taken into consideration. Responsibility accounting does not recognize organizational interdependence but may increase interdepartmental conflict as segment managers seek to improve their own record or protect themselves from blame without regard to what happens elsewhere. Responsibility accounting systems are based on a closed systems logic; as a consequence, the computation of budget variances fails to recognize the dynamic interacting nature of organizational units which may or may not correspond to established cost centers. The system reflects a control over people because it is biased in the favor of performance evaluation over learning.

4. Transfer pricing—Encourages competition in the same way as responsibility accounting. The transferring division argues and receives permission to use transfer prices above market price. The receiving division would then be appropriately justified in complaining that it is not being treated fairly since as buyers they seek the lowest price. This policy creates an entire line of organization competition whereas

cooperation would produce better overall organizational attainment of goals. In firms where transfer pricing is in use and the bonus or incentive pay program is based on individual unit profits, there will be even more competition than cooperation between the profit centers. Each profit center manager attempts to attach the highest possible exit price while pushing hard for the lowest entry price. Again, the welfare of the total organizational operations is not the prevailing concern.

5. Standard cost system—This accounting system bears an implicit command to meet the standards. Although both favorable and unfavorable variances are exposed, the unfavorable ones get the most attention. Variance classification places primary emphasis on performance evaluation and ignores the learning aspect of deviations. As a result, managers do not have information about the underlying causes of system-wide variance. For example, the purchase of inferior material by the purchasing division may be accomplished to incur a favorable price variance. However, this would probably result in an unfavorable quantity variance in the production departments. This situation arises because departments are usually judged on the income of their own department. The impact of this occurrence is not readily known to higher management because each department's variances are computed independent of others. As a result, the individual department strives to increase income within its segment even though it may be detrimental to the organization as a whole. The overall effect is that no systemwide learning takes place.

6. Profit center concept (closely related to responsibility accounting)—Within the profit center, the aggressive manager who is actively seeking advancement will attempt to minimize internal costs for labor, materials, and metered goods or services. Some forms of metered services, such as preventive maintenance or equipment repairs, will be bypassed during an accounting period in an effort to hold costs down and improve short-term profits for the center. If the bonus plan is based on profit center profits, the manager will be rewarded for competing successfully although in the long run this competition is damaging for the firm.

7. The cost controllability criterion often ignores the fact that the underlying cause of a variation may be uncontrollable even though the cost itself is incurred within a cost center. An example of this would be a labor variance caused by improper workmanship in a prior department. Responsibility accounting defines controllability in terms of effects or outcomes rather than causes. Higher managers spend much time and effort on unnecessary investigations while lower managers spend time defending and blame shifting. Dysfunctional behavior aimed at looking good on measured variables will likely result because management by exception emphasizes negative performance more often than positive; subordinates are conditioned to associate managers with a negative event.

8. Charging inputs to departments at standard prices to protect these centers from cost fluctuations elsewhere creates artificial autonomy between segments and maintains the fiction of controllability. This procedure only keeps management from focusing properly on the sources of disturbances because each manager pays attention to only those variances which have a sizable impact on his or her department. When costs are charged at standard, the larger issue of how problems in one area affect others is ignored.

Accounting system design should incorporate behavioral considerations in the area of competition and cooperation. This is assumed to be a very difficult task to accomplish, considering the natural inclination of humanity to view everything on a "me first" basis.

Review Questions

1. Discuss ways that accountants influence the behavior of other individuals within the organization.

2. *a.* How are responsibility and control related?
   b. What dangers does a company face if it has insufficient control?

3. Describe a situation often encountered in business when a company's overall profitability will be maximized if one segment will take a loss which will be more than made up in another segment.

4. Which Theory (X, Y, or Z) supports the following: "Persons of integrity treat secretaries and executives with equal respect; they also approach subordinates with the same understanding and values that characterize their family relationships"? Discuss your answer.

5. Discuss the accountant's role in control functions. Before control can be effective, what steps must be taken?

6. Discuss how an accounting system based on the scorecard principles of responsibility accounting often promote competition as opposed to cooperation.

7. Discuss your reaction to this statement: Some companies claim they have participative decision making when in reality they are not truly participative; instead, early communication of any proposed changes helps to reduce uncertainty in the organization. Advance notice to employees concerning upcoming decisions gives them a chance to rationalize and accept the outcomes.

8. *a.* What are the underlying concepts of the traditional accounting model?
   b. What impact did the scientific management movement have on cost accounting concepts?

9. Define accounting control and give several examples.

10. Discuss the criteria that a good report must meet.

Exercises

E25–1 Top Management Behavior (L.O. 2)

Clifton Key, president, remarked casually to the data processing manager, Robert Knight, that it would be helpful if he had the printouts concerning the proposed capital expenditures by Friday. Key wanted to study them over the weekend before meeting with the equipment salespersons and the board of directors the following week.

Knight immediately called a halt to all programs being run so his staff could concentrate on having these reports for the president. This meant delaying the monthly income statement with its detailed cost of production reports comparing actual costs to standard costs for several days.

Knight and his staff worked overtime and were pleased that they were able to produce the reports for the president by Friday. However, on the following Tuesday, the fifth working day after the end of the month, when they normally delivered the income statements and budget comparisons to the president, the statements were incomplete. The data processing manager thought the president would understand the delay. He became upset after receiving an angry phone call asking for an explanation of the missing reports.

Required:

Explain what caused the problem. Could anything have prevented this situation from occurring?

E25–2 Expectancy Theory and Intrinsic Rewards (L.O. 4)

Expectancy theory requires the placing of values or weight on various outcomes based on the probability of their occurrence and the value or valence placed on the outcome by the person desiring such outcomes. This theory should act to motivate accountants to establish accounting systems based positively on rewarding appropriate behavior of participants. The influence of extrinsic and intrinsic rewards on motivation is another important factor in system design.

Required:

a. List the implications of expectancy theory for cost accounting systems.
b. Relate the impact of extrinsic and intrinsic rewards to performance.

E25–3 Behavioral Impact of Activities (L.O. 3)

Describe the behavioral impact of:

a. Systems that keep the pay and performance of workers secret from their co-workers.
b. Decentralized companies with divisions not sharing information with other divisions.
c. Avoiding the performance of a task rather than asking for explanations.

E25–4 High Achievers and Budget Level Difficulty (L.O. 2)

Assume you have recently completed research on budget performance that linked achievement to the level of performance. You found that people who are high achievers often choose moderate goals for themselves and avoid difficult tasks.

Further, your findings were that high achievers avoided operating under tight budgets based on ideal or theoretical standards unless there were commensurate rewards attached to these budgets. Also, your research indicated that monetary rewards do not motivate high achievers nearly as much as other people.

Required:

a. Give a possible reason why high achievers avoid choosing:
   (1) Simple tasks.
   (2) Difficult tasks.
b. Using Maslow's and Herzberg's findings, explain why money does not motivate individuals who are high achievers nearly as much as individuals who are not high achievers.

E25–5 Behavioral Research (L.O. 3)

For a time behavioral research focused on ways to make corporations more efficient and ways to increase the information processing capacity of corporations. More and more information was being made available, but decision making did not improve. Critics now argue that what was overlooked was it is not the information capacity of the organization but the collective information capacity of the individual decision makers that determined the organization's success. They contend that it does not seem reasonable to expect progress in any of the areas of interest in organizational development without progress in the understanding of human behavior. Further, behavioral research has to combine the study of complex organizations with the study of complex individual behavior to develop an adequate motivational theory. Thus, recent research has begun to include the study of individual behavior along with organizational structure and environmental variables.

Required:

Suggest why there is a reemphasis on individual behavior in behavioral research rather than on complex organizations.

E25–6 Traditional Concepts of Control (L.O. 2)

Traditionally, accountants used control techniques to meet the goals established by a few people at the top of the organization. Usually top management's principal objective was maximization of business profit. Further, these managers assumed that employees had the capacity to act in only limited ways and were not adaptive to specific situations. Further, employees were assumed to be motivated primarily by economic forces. In turn, the needs which the workers strive to satisfy were those at the bottom of the hierarchy of needs. Self-esteem and self-actualization were assumed not to be addressed. Work was an unpleasant task which employees avoided whenever possible; tight controls were needed to achieve any level of productivity. Thus, according to classical theories of control, the primary function of accounting is to achieve profit maximization. The accounting system serves as a control device reflecting unfavorable performance through unfavorable variances in comparing actual results to standards. The accounting system is designed to be objective and neutral in its evaluation since performance is compared against overall organizational goals. This comparison is viewed with a high degree of certainty and rationality because it is assumed that accountants have only one correct way to report financial data.

Required:

Contrast traditional concepts of control and modern cost control regarding employee behavior, the organization's objectives, and accounting's role.

E25–7 Control of Ordering Procedures (L.O. 2)

At the McLain Company the system for acquiring material requires that the supervisor of each cost center prepare a material requisition form when material is needed. This then becomes the source document for transferring cost to Work in Process Inventory. At the end of each week, one entry is made summarizing the material requisitions handled that week.

Don Lyerly, the supervisor of the Mixing Department, has become close friends with Mike Douglass, the storekeeper. In fact, they are seen golfing together almost every weekend. Lyerly is a good supervisor, but he has been heard to remark, "Preparing these material requisitions is a waste of my time; I should be handling all the emergencies that occur in my department." In fact, on several occasions in the past, he has picked up the phone and called in a material order to the storekeeper so that it could be delivered more rapidly than through the use of the normal material document flow. Lyerly has told Douglass to always cover for him and, if necessary, forge his signature on any required documents. Lyerly assumes this is what happens when he calls in an order.

Required:

Enumerate the dangers you see in the telephone ordering procedure used by the supervisor. Should this ever be allowed to occur and, if so, what follow-up procedures should be implemented?

E25–8 Behavioral Approaches to Integration and Differentiation (L.O. 4)

As companies decentralize by establishing independent and autonomous profit centers, they often sacrifice goal congruence in the interest of autonomy. Management accountants, especially those with behavioral backgrounds, suggest that this trade-off is not required; an approach can be used that enhances organizational differentiation and also facilitates organization integration.

Required:

a. Explain how the contingency theory of organizational structure and/or performance evaluation helps resolve the integration versus differentiation issue.
b. Suggest ways in which the expectancy theory of individual motivation and performance may present an alternative incentive scheme that will help achieve coordination and the necessary differentiation profit centers must have.

E25–9 Traditional Cost Data and Contemporary Control (L.O. 2)

Some critics argue that traditional cost data frequently does not fit contemporary concepts of control because these data often reflect the concepts of Taylor's management theories. Workers are viewed as being lazy, wasteful, and only motivated by economic rewards; the emotions of an individual are not given any consideration in the decision making process under this management theory. These critics believe Taylor was influenced by economic theory that was developed using a closed systems approach. Thus, they contend that traditional cost data do not fit contemporary concepts of control because they are essentially based on a closed systems concept of the organization. A closed systems organization is separated from the external environment and does not take into consideration the inevitable interaction that takes place between the system and its environment. The cost data generated by the traditional system are based on the conviction that the underlying input-output relationships are clear and predictable. In many organizational situations these relationships may be subject to constraints imposed by not only the task environment (relevant external environment) but also other subsystems within the organization. The techniques of collecting and reporting the traditional data assume complete objectivity on the part of the accounting system, but the choice of what data to collect, the manner of reporting, and the level to which such reports are made may all have a behavioral impact on the people subjected to such data. Critics argue that traditional cost data are geared to a single organizational goal of profit maximization. Yet, organizations have a multiplicity of objectives that cannot all be incorporated into a profit figure.

Required:

Discuss why traditional cost data often does not fit contemporary concepts of control.

E25–10 Rational Information Processing Behavior (L.O. 3)

A consultant to your company believes there are many factors affecting information processing behavior in organizations. She groups them into these four categories: nature and attributes of message received from information system, manager's personal qualities and attitudes, social interaction, and format and group decision function used.

Required:

Discuss briefly the three principal factors affecting rational information processing behavior in organizations for each of these four groups.

Problems

P25–11 Responsibility for Variances (L.O. 2)

Pallesen Company has adopted the following standards in the Mixing Department for its oil product:

	Per Unit
Material (2 gallons @ $3)	$ 6
Labor (5 hours @ $3)	15
Variable factory overhead (5 hours @ $2)	10
Fixed factory overhead (5 hours @ $4)	20
Normal capacity per quarter is 5,000 hours.	

Pallesen's major customer has been on strike much of the last quarter; as a result, Pallesen has cut production to 800 units rather than overstock inventory. The following actual costs are for the last quarter:

Material (2,300 gallons)	$ 7,475
Labor (4,250 hours)	13,175
Variable factory overhead	8,115
Fixed factory overhead	21,600

A machine operating improperly for three weeks caused estimated spoilage of 500 gallons. This material spoilage had no effect on the quantity of labor used. Pallesen purchased 2,500 gallons of material this quarter and used the LIFO inventory method.

All employees are hired and trained by the company's personnel department before being placed in the Mixing Department.

Required:

a. Calculate the variances for which the supervisor of the Mixing Department should be held responsible.

b. Calculate any variances for which other individuals should be held accountable.

P25–12 Behavioral Role of Cost Accountants in MBO (L.O. 4)

Management by objectives (MBO) is a participative process involving all management levels. This process measures and evaluates both segment and individual performance.

Required:

a. Describe briefly the process and the steps involved.

b. Explain to what degree the process suffers if some of these steps are omitted.

c. Discuss what problems you can identify with MBO.

d. Assume you are the chief cost accountant. What should be your role in the MBO process:
   (1) Within your own cost accounting department?
   (2) Within the entire organization?

e. Describe how the degree of goal congruence already achieved within an organization affects the successful implementation of the MBO process.

f. Discuss why an MBO system could stimulate interest in the products of the cost accounting system over a wider range of users.

P25–13 Preparation of Accounting Reports and Behavior of Users (L.O. 4)

Although more timely, complete, and reliable information can improve decision making, it often does not because the information system is treated independently from the personality characteristics of the report users and expectations regarding the future environment. Research shows some relationship between the level of the personality characteristics of authoritarianism, need for independence and flexibility, and individuals' reported perception of organizational climate and their attitude toward the accounting system. There is also support for the theory that anticipating the future effects on information and its use by recipients has an effect on decisions currently made by senders. For example, if a firm perceives information as being advantageous to the firm's future, then current financial reports reflect the optimistic assumptions made by financial statement preparers. The converse can be equally true as the perception of bad news can lead to less optimistic report preparation.

Required:

a. Describe the relationship you would expect to find between leadership patterns and personality characteristics with the use of accounting data.

b. Discuss reasons why the provision of more timely, complete, and reliable information may not improve decision making.

c. Give behavioral support for the position that anticipating the future effects on information and its use by recipients has an effect on decisions currently made by preparers of financial reports.

P25–14 Evaluating Reporting Procedure (L.O. 2)

Larry Bell, an employee at the Smith Company, is responsible for polishing a wheel and inserting it in the motor of a wall clock. Like all other productive employees at the company, Larry has an assigned operation that is not difficult to perform, but it does require some concentration. At the beginning of each day, Larry picks up one basket containing the unpolished wheels and another basket containing the partly assembled clocks. At the end of each day he turns in the clocks he assembled, as well as any unpolished wheels. He rarely ever completes the basket before the workday ends, but if he should, he can request another basket. No count is made of the partly assembled clocks or unpolished wheels placed in each basket given to Larry. However, at the end of each day when Larry turns in his day's production, the clocks in which he has placed a polished wheel are counted.

All production employees are paid on an hourly basis. Even though no employees are paid on a piece-rate basis, a comparison is made between actual and standard production. Standards were set several years ago by a team of engineers using time and motion studies. Standards were set for each job position, and each employee was then given a standard.

Department heads may use their discretion in the use of the standards. Some department heads prepare daily summaries as shown for June 15, 19X1, in the Assembly Department in which Larry Bell works. On June 15, Larry completed 280 units during the eight hours he worked. With a standard of 40 units per hour, the standard productive time of his output was seven hours (280 units/40 units) resulting in a loss of one hour. Data for the other employees in the Assembly Department are also given in the daily summary report presented.

These daily summaries may be posted on the departmental bulletin board or the department head may only use them when talking privately with individual employees. Daily summaries are then combined into weekly summaries in some departments. Other departments may prepare weekly or monthly summaries similar to the one illustrated for the Assembly Department. The plant superintendent receives monthly summaries for all production departments.

SMITH COMPANY
Assembly Department
June 15, 19X1

	Actual Output	Standard per Hour	Standard Productive Hours	Actual Hours	Variance Loss	Variance Gain
Larry Bell	280	40	7.00	8	1.00	
Carolyn Carr	400	50	8.00	7.5		0.50
Harold Douglass . . .	580	80	7.25	6.5		0.75
Herschel Ezell	450	60	7.5	8	0.50	
Kent Miller	405	90	4.5	5	0.50	

Required:

a. Rank the performance of the Assembly Department employees.
b. Assume you are a department head. How would you use the standards provided?
c. Assume you are a department head. What would you look for first in your summary, regardless of the time period?
d. Assume you are a department head. Do you see any need for keeping the reports after they are summarized? Explain.
e. Suggest any improvements in the reporting procedure of the company.

P25–15 Expectancy of Success and Rewards (L.O. 2)

Assume that you have recently completed a behavioral research budgeting study indicating that given the same reward structure, a manager's motivation to achieve a cost budget is lowest when the manager's probability of success of achieving the budget is low. Further, this probability is lowest when tight theoretical standards are used in the budgeting process. However, your research has not shown that difference exists between the level of a manager's motivation to achieve a cost budget through use of the following, given the same reward structure:

1. A budget of moderate difficulty using currently attainable standards.
2. An easy budget using liberal cost standards.

Your research also indicates that the attractiveness of the incentives attached to budgets may play a much greater role in determining the motivational force to achieve the cost budget than does the expectancy of successfully achieving the budgets.

Required:

a. Outline briefly the research findings.
b. Use the expectancy theory to explain why you think motivation was lowest with budgets based on theoretical standards given the same reward structure.
c. Explain the traditional belief about the motivational level of managers when their companies use currently attainable standards as opposed to liberal standards.
d. Discuss the relationship between theoretical standards and a nonparticipative, authoritative approach.
e. Discuss the impact that the following have on motivation disregarding the budget's level of difficulty, in view of this research:
    (1) Individual goals.
    (2) Budget objectives.
    (3) Manager's skill level.
f. Provide support for the view that a manager's risk of loss increases as the difficulty level of the budget decreases.
g. Discuss the importance of the attractiveness of incentives and budget level of difficulty, assuming other studies support your behavioral research findings.
h. Assume additional research supports your findings. What implications do these research studies have for the traditional belief that cost budgets of varying difficulty level play a very important role in motivating managers?

P25–16 (CMA) Behavior Modification and Reinforcement Theory (L.O. 4)

Peter Wilson is the Shipping Department manager of the Industrial Division of National Electric, a large manufacturer of electrical and electronics equipment sold only to wholesalers. Wilson has been with National for 15 years and currently manages 25 employees, including supervisors, transportation and shipping specialists, and hourly workers.

Wilson often deals directly with employees in his department rather than going through their supervisors. At times he even reprimands employees in the Finishing Department when shipping deadlines are endangered. Joe Sullivan, Finishing Department manager, has received several complaints from his employees concerning Wilson's behavior. These complaints generally concern Wilson's telling them what to do and specifically concern abusive behavior by Wilson.

Sullivan has asked Wilson to go through him when dealing with the Finishing Department employees, but Wilson usually says, "I have to correct these problem situations immediately and can't bother with the bureaucracy." When Wilson persisted in dealing directly with Finishing Department employees, Sullivan appealed to Fred Garrison, the Industrial Division manager.

Garrison had been aware of the Shipping Department supervisors' dissatisfaction with Wilson dealing directly with shipping employees and had overlooked the situation in deference to Wilson's experience and ability. Wilson's intrusion into the Finishing Department, however, was quite another matter, and Garrison was convinced that some action was necessary. Garrison decided to attempt to correct Wilson's actions through the use of behavior modification.

Required:

a. Explain the theory of behavior modification.
b. Define and distinguish between the following as they relate to behavior modification:
   (1) Positive reinforcement.
   (2) Negative reinforcement.
   (3) Punishment.
   (4) Extinction.
c. Give specific recommendations, consistent with behavior modification, that Fred Garrison could use in an attempt to correct Wilson's actions.
d. Discuss some of the basic criticisms of behavior modification.

P25–17 Kanban Squares (L.O. 4)

In a recent move to adopt newer manufacturing techniques Kreiger Company marked off kanban squares the size of one unit with yellow tape in the factory. An assembler at one table places a completed unit on the square within easy reach of the next assembler at the next table. No more units can be completed until the next assembler removes the unit from the kanban square.

This company also uses kanban squares to serve another purpose. Lights and a problem display board next to each workstation permit capture of problem causes. When assemblers do not have units in their kanban squares, they wait ten seconds for a unit to arrive. After ten seconds, they turn on a yellow light signaling a problem. The light tells subsequent assemblers that they are also going to be slowed down. The yellow light alerts the supervisor to find the real causes.

Kreiger management believes this is a better approach than the one often used by conventional manufacturing in which no one records the real causes. They argue that Kreiger workers have little reason to get embarrassed and go on the defensive. Rather than give each assembler the uncomfortable feeling of being blamed for most of the shutdowns, high costs, poor housekeeping, and bad quality products, assemblers have the opportunity to state the factor beyond their control that causes the slowdown. Assemblers explain the cause of the problem when the slowdown occurs, rather than trying to remember what the problem factor was several days later.

Kreiger also uses red lights throughout the production floor to signal major problems. With the adoption of the JIT concept, the Kreiger president reminded company management that job titles mean little and responsibilities blur when problems have to be fixed quickly. When a red light goes on, everyone must help to solve the problem before it becomes a disaster. As a result, engineers, plant managers, schedulers, and other salaried support production people are spending much less time in their offices. In fact, some of them are now suggesting that their offices, the computer, and computer staff should be moved closer to production operations. One advocate of the move made this observation: "We need to get the support people into the vacated space fast; otherwise, someone will revert to our 'old way' and fill the space with inventory again when no one is looking."

Required:

a. Explain why the company has a policy that no units can be completed until the next kanban square on the assembly line is empty.
b. Do you think the kanban light system asks the question, "Why can't you keep up?" so that workers become defensive and argue that they have too much work to do? Or do you view the light system as a way to give workers a chance to air their problems?
c. Give one advantage and one disadvantage you can see in moving:
   (1) Salaried support people's desks on the factory floor, intermingled with workstations.
   (2) The computer which supports manufacturing and its computer staff on the floor.

P25–18 Traditional and Contemporary Management Accounting (L.O. 3)

Traditional management accounting stresses clear lines of authority with information flowing in an upward direction and emphasizes the use of the accounting system as a control or watchdog tool. This is necessary because the work force available to carry out this task is considered to be indifferent to the goals of the organization, lazy, and economically motivated, thus requiring very close control through authority. In contrast, contemporary management accounting recognizes that an organization has many diverse goals reflective of the goals of the dominant members. Because the existence of these diverse goals is recognized, contemporary management accounting assumes that employees are motivated by a wide variety of economic, social, and psychological needs and drives. It further assumes that employees can adapt and are capable of solving problems and making decisions.

Required:

a. (1) Contrast the classical and modern views of behavior.
   (2) Explain how this difference affects the perceived decision-making approach.
b. Agree or disagree that the traditional cost accumulation system fits the contemporary behavioral cost concept.
c. Discuss what variables indicate if an organization has a management system that is authoritative or participative.
d. Support the idea that traditional management accounting has been influenced by economic theory.

P25–19 Corporate and Individual Goals (L.O. 1)

The president of Ferony Company has spent several hours reviewing the previous year's financial statement. He is concerned that earnings declined last year. Ferony experienced steady growth and excellent profit margins in its first eight years of operation, but in the last two years, its share of the market has remained stable. In view of these developments, the president has called a meeting of the top management team, the firm's four vice presidents. After studying historical data and predicting future sales, each member of the team presented his or her strategy for profit improvement.

The vice president of marketing suggested that the advertising approach be changed so that sales promotion is directed toward additional markets. He also recommended that additional funds be applied toward advertising so that a national television campaign can be included. He believes that this strategy can improve earnings enough so that an increase in sales price is unnecessary.

The vice president of finance disagrees with the vice president of marketing's approach. She believes an increase in sales price is justified since competitors' prices are already higher than Ferony's prices. In addition, she is skeptical about increasing the advertising budget, because she is doubtful about the short-run benefit. The financial vice president's concern is that the company's cash and short-term investment position will be jeopardized.

The vice president of marketing insists that even though many of the additional sales generated by the national television campaign would be credit sales, 95 percent of them would be collected within 90 days.

The vice president of engineering and research agrees that additional markets should be sought, but that product improvement is the answer. He suggests that the company conduct extensive tests for the purpose of making innovations in the company's product line. He believes that with these additional features, the company will be recognized as an industry leader.

The vice president of production is concerned about rising labor rates and believes that unless Ferony increases its labor rates, many of the skilled labor workers will look for work elsewhere. She agrees with the vice president of engineering and research that the product could be improved by incorporating new features and possibly by using a higher grade of material. In addition, she believes that time and motion studies would result in an improvement in the work flow.

The president has listened intently to each suggestion and agrees with many of these ideas, as he recognizes the need for increasing labor rates. However, he believes that company management should become more involved in civic activities; in fact, he has just been approached by the campaign manager for the United Fund Drive about volunteers. He believes additional study is required before a specific strategy is chosen.

Required:

State the implied corporate goals being expressed by each of the following and how these relate to their own personal goals:

a. Vice president of marketing.
b. Vice president of finance.
c. Vice president of engineering and research.
d. Vice president of production.
e. President.

P25–20 Evaluating Departmental Reports (L.O. 2)

Michael Flint has reason to reflect on the past 10 years with pride, as his company has grown from a small operation to its present stage of an industry leader. Much of the company success is due to Flint's management. As majority owner, he became familiar with all facets of operation. The rapport he developed with factory supervisors encouraged a constant interchange of ideas for product improvement.

As the company grew, Flint devoted more and more of his time to planning and policymaking, so factory supervisors became responsible for operations. Flint regretted this situation because he believed it resulted in a breakdown in communications. In addition, factory supervisors are not bringing all problems in operations to Flint's attention. As a result, Flint has asked a cost consultant to prepare a system of monthly reports that would provide him with more information than he can obtain from his limited direct observation. After the cost consultant spent many hours of study and discussion with Flint and his supervisors, she prepared the following sample of a departmental report. The supervisor in charge of each department will receive a copy of this report, as will Flint.

FLINT COMPANY
July 19X2

Supervisor *Harold Douglass*   Department *Mixing*

	July 19X2	June 19X2	Average for Last Six Months	July 19X1
Direct material cost	$20,000	$18,800	$18,000	$15,000
Scrap as a percent of material cost	5%	5.5%	6%	5.8%
Direct labor cost	$24,000	$24,600	$23,000	$22,300
Sales value of production	82,000	80,000	76,000	72,000
Allocated administrative cost .	6,000	5,800	5,400	5,000

Direct material cost represents a summary of the actual material used—obtained from material requisitions for each department.

Scrap as a percent of material cost represents the net cost of scrap (direct material cost less sales value of scrap recovered) expressed as a percentage of direct material cost.

Direct labor cost includes regular wages (regular hourly rate multiplied by actual hours worked) and overtime premiums. Individual supervisors are responsible for scheduling operations and top management expects them to keep overtime to a minimum.

Sales value of production represents the sales price of the production processed through the department. Actual sales price has increased an average of 10 percent each year due to the effect of inflation.

Allocated administrative cost represents the department's share of such costs as top management salaries, rent, and utilities for the administrative offices, and administrative staff salaries. The basis for allocation is floor space occupied by each department.

Currently, managers compare monthly figures to the previous month's results, the average for the last six months, and results for the same month in the preceding year. In addition, the consultant suggested that Flint compare individual departmental reports with those from other departments.

Required:

a. List any weaknesses in the departmental report suggested by the cost consultant.
b. Give any suggestions for improving the report.

P25–21 Participative Management (L.O. 1)

President David Morgan of Waco Company was meeting with several other top executives when the subject of participative and autocratic management was introduced. Morgan began bragging about the success his company had when participative management was implemented. In supporting his convictions, he said, "Let me tell you about our latest adoption of a new budgeting technique called zero-based budgeting. (This approach is discussed in Chapter 10.) Top management of our company left the decision whether to adopt this approach completely to the division controllers. After the approach was explained to the controllers, they voted on its adoption and have wholeheartedly supported it ever since."

However, the president's interpretation of participative management is somewhat biased. Division controllers received a letter from the vice president of finance inviting them to the headquarter's offices for a one-day seminar to learn about zero-based budgeting. The vice president indicated in the letter that he was extremely excited about this new approach, and he felt it offered the company many advantages.

Plans were made to bring in a nationally recognized consultant for a day to explain the theory of this new management tool. At noon the division controllers would vote on its adoption. If a positive vote was received, the consultant would spend the afternoon explaining the implementation of this budgeting technique.

The consultant was somewhat surprised by the questions he received during the morning session. He realized that if a positive vote was received, controllers would have the responsibility of selling the idea to the supervisors at their plants. A management by objective (MBO) system was in effect at all divisions in which each manager was given specific goals. However, the managers insisted that they were never given enough funds to fulfill these goals; as a result, they were reprimanded at year-end for having unfavorable variances. Repeatedly, managers asked the consultant if this new budgeting approach integrated objectives with funds. As one controller asked, "If you provide me with a certain sum of money on the condition that I promise to fulfill certain stated goals, will I be fussed at if I only achieve these goals and not those that are more stringent?" After the consultant convinced the controllers that indeed zero-based budgeting required the preparation of various levels of effort and the proposed expenditures to meet each level, the controllers voted unanimously to adopt the new system.

Required:

Agree or disagree with the president's contention that participative management is in effect, stating your reasons.

P25–22 Improved Analysis of Variance (L.O. 2)

Monroe Company manufactures batteries. It has established the following per unit standards for material and labor in Department 22, based on 1,000 units normal capacity per period:

Material (4 pounds @ $0.50 per pound)	$2.00
Labor (½ hour @ $8.40 per hour)	$4.20

During the period, Department 22 produced 1,200 batteries and the following variances were charged to the supervisor of this department. Since the cost accountant is on sick leave, other personnel who are not thoroughly familiar with standard cost have had to prepare these variances.

Net material variance:	
Actual material cost (5,160 pounds)	$3,354
Standard material cost at normal capacity	2,000
Unfavorable material variance	$1,354
Net labor variance:	
Actual labor cost ($8.40 actual rate)	$5,124
Standard labor cost at normal capacity	4,200
Unfavorable labor variance	$ 924

Variance reports for each department are combined on a report and circulated to all plant management levels. The supervisor of Department 22 believes that he has unfairly had to bear the brunt of embarrassment caused by these significant unfavorable variances. When he asked the Purchasing Department about the increase in material cost, he was told that all suppliers were faced with a shortage of the material needed and had increased their prices. Due to this shortage, the Purchasing Department also had to order a lower quality of material that required an increase of 5 percent in the handling and processing Department 22 had to perform and an increase in waste of 10 percent. The supervisor of Department 22 was also displeased with the labor workers that the Personnel Department had recently recruited, as these employees did not have the training necessary to immediately begin processing batteries. As a result, the supervisor had to spend 25 hours last period explaining the processing technique to these new recruits.

Required:

Prepare a variance report for Department 22 if you see any errors in the computations or the variances presented or if you believe a better analysis of variances should be presented.

Cases

C25–23 Difference in Management Styles (L.O. 3)

As owner and general manager of the Bruceton Manufacturing Company, Guy Bruceton feels that he runs a tight ship. Ever since he founded the company 20 years ago, he has insisted on tight budgets and has employed many cost control techniques. A standard cost system is in effect, and accountants report variances weekly to his two production supervisors, Bob Smith and Jane Jones.

Bruceton is quite proud of Smith's insistence that the standards should be tight. He has often heard Smith remark, "Remember, our workers will not produce unless they see that they have to." Smith believes the company should install even tighter controls if they are to survive in the future. Smith spends very little time talking with the employees under him. However, he has told them that any time they have a problem about either their jobs or their personal lives, they should feel free to come to him. Smith is a rather quiet, reserved individual who has said that he didn't want to be nosy and interfere in his employees' lives. Smith prepares most of his cost center's budgets himself rather than further increasing the workload of each of his supervisors. When he is in doubt concerning an issue, he seeks their advice.

Jones, on the other hand, disagrees with both Bruceton and Smith on several issues. In fact, Bruceton has called Jones in on several occasions to remind her of the image she should project to the employees reporting to her. Bruceton believes Jones's subordinates should call her "Ms. Jones" rather than "Jane," as this will remind the employees that she is their superior. Jones is an outgoing individual with a friendly personality. Bruceton has further reprimanded Jones several times for joking and laughing with subordinates. Jones has an open-door policy, and employees are often in her office discussing on-the-job problems as well as personal matters.

Jones spends much time at the end of the year explaining the budgeting procedure to supervisors, who further briefly explain the process to employees under them. Each supervisor prepares a budget for their respective cost center which Jones reviews and revises before forwarding it to Bruceton. If Jones revises a budget, she explains to the supervisor the reason for the necessary change.

Despite the number of times Bruceton has talked with Jones, he cannot honestly say he is disappointed with the performance of any of Jones's cost centers. In fact, there is little difference between the level of efficiency of the cost centers that report to Jones and those that report to Smith.

Required:

Explain why there is little difference in the efficiency level of Jones's and Smith's cost centers.

C25–24 Informal Organizations (L.O. 1)

When Ann Watts returned to the business environment as a cost accountant after taking off five years to raise her family, she vowed that she would not listen to office gossip. Her philosophy was that what you do not know, cannot hurt you. She is staying true to this vow and refuses to talk about the personal lives of co-workers when she has lunch with other employees.

However, she began to wonder if she was making a mistake trying to isolate herself from the office grapevine. She noticed that she seemed to have more trouble getting along with her co-workers and supervisors. Watts did not have the benefit of the behind-the-scene information about these people's personal lives. For instance, last week when she delivered last month's cost of goods manufactured statement to the controller, he was rude to her and began asking for explanations why direct material and direct labor costs had increased so drastically during the last quarter. When she was unable to give a concise answer, he immediately told her to have a detailed report on his desk by 8:00 the next morning.

By the time she arrived back at her office from this meeting, she was seriously considering resigning. Her secretary, noting the distraught look on her face, asked what was the matter. After Watts told her what had happened, the secretary remarked, "Oh, don't you know? His 16-year-old son wrecked the family car last night. While no one was badly hurt, he completely destroyed his new sports car."

This started Watts thinking that maybe she should become more a part of the group. Yet, she dreaded the thoughts of trying to separate herself from some of the obsessive gossipers she had seen around the company. However, Watts also remembered several other events that had left her with egg on her face.

Once, for example, when the vice president asked her at an office party how she liked the change in office dress code, she had quickly remarked, "I think it is completely old-fashioned not to allow the company's female professional staff to wear pant suits to their jobs. Further, I believe this is discrimination." Later, she learned that it was this vice president who had pressed so hard for the change in dress code to prohibit pant suits. His argument had been that the company paid these ladies a high enough salary to require that they dress accordingly. Most of the women employees had resented the change to a more formal dress code, but they had limited their verbal outbursts to discussions among themselves.

In view of these recent events, Watts questions her approach to the working environment and wonders if she should change her tactics regarding the informal communication system.

Required:

a. Compare the sources of power and authority for an informal organization with those of a formal organization.
b. Explain the factors that cause the development of informal organizations within the formal organization structure of companies.
c. Discuss ways an informal communication system can be beneficial to the management process in achieving the organization's goals.
d. Describe the ways formal and informal communication systems differ as to accuracy and speed of communication. What is the impact that communicaion has on employees?
e. Discuss (1) what employees can learn from office talk and (2) what its dangers are.
f. Explain why Ann Watts has or has not made an error in her approach to the informal work group.

C25–25 Behavioral Impact of Nonverbal Communications (L.O. 3)

Accountants communicate through a variety of channels; written messages and verbal exchanges appear as the most obvious. However, they also exhibit communication by their facial expressions, tone of voice, manner of dress, use of office space and decor, personal dress and appearance, and other nonverbal signals. When nonverbal signals accompany a verbal message, they may reinforce it or contradict the verbal message.

Sometimes the physical or nonverbal communication better reflects an individual's true feelings than either written or oral communication. This is probably true because most written or oral communication is a conscious effort by the individual; nonverbal is more of an unconscious response. The following accountants present barriers to effective communication by their nonverbal signals.

In meeting the recently hired staff lawyer, Accountant A says, "I am so glad to meet you. If you play tennis or golf, let's get together very soon." Due to the busy work schedule, Accountant A has remained seated behind a stack of reports on his desk and did not make eye contact with the lawyer.

As controller of the company, Accountant B has many subordinate staff accountants. However, she is a recent graduate of a master's program which introduced her to the merits of participative management. She prides herself on applying this concept throughout the accounting department. In her office operations, the following often occurs:

1. Accountant B often keeps subordinates waiting for conferences simply to prove her status.
2. Accountant B considers herself very intelligent and in conversation often helps subordinates and peers complete their sentences.
3. Recognizing that her time is very important, Accountant B accepts phone calls and other outside interruptions when in discussion with others.

Accountant C's most common body position when listening to a speaker is to sit with arms folded and legs crossed.

Accountant D addresses subordinates over a large, uncluttered desk, even though there are other chairs and tables available within the office.

Accountant E uses Accountant F's office as an exit since this is a closer route to the elevator than through the hall.

Required:

a. Describe the behavioral message given by each of these five accountants.
b. Discuss the impact of these behavioral messages on the organization's future and the receivers of these messages.
c. Suggest how each of these accountants can improve his or her communication process.

C25–26 Empire Building (L.O. 4)

When interviewing James Fain about the introduction of a new product line, he reports that now that he is nearing retirement, he seldom interferes with the business. Instead, he indicates that his son Bob is in charge of production while his other son Jim is in charge of sales. To minimize friction, the two sons have agreed not to interfere in each other's division operations. To secure this independence, the production division maintains a large stock of the finished products listed in the catalog. It can deliver most orders within a short time. The sales division accepts orders on products not listed in the catalog.

James also indicates that he relied heavily on Don Ward, his purchasing agent. Ward had joined the firm shortly after James purchased the company 20 years ago while his sons were still in high school. Ward had been very aggressive and hungry for power and status. He had impressed James with his eagerness to learn and follow instructions given by the owner. Thus, a unique relationship had developed in which Ward had provided James with inside information concerning employee morale and complaints. Ward served as a good sounding board for new ideas James had regarding employee benefits and scheduling. This devotion did not go unrewarded for James promoted Ward rapidly and was able to bypass the hierarchy. Ward soon won control over such allied functions as receiving, inventory control, stores, and production control. However, Ward had difficulty building a material management function, and Ward encountered several head-on clashes with the engineers. The more vocal engineers in the group soon resigned, and the matter settled down.

In discussing the organization changes that have occurred within the last five years, James noted the enlargement of the Systems Analyst Department. The Systems Analyst Department set out to capture the programmers—for five previous years, the programmers had significant expert power in the organization due to the implementation of the necessary new computer system. The programmers used this expert power to gain status, high salaries, and the right to flaunt bureaucratic rules and to exhibit a general arrogance. Others in the company resented the programmers, but since they needed their services, the programmers survived as an isolated social system in the organization. Later the function of the systems analyst emerged to challenge that of programmers, and territorial wars followed. As the programmers' position in the firm deteriorated, their department became a prime takeover candidate of the Systems Analyst Department. Hanging on as best they could, the programmers resorted to patterns to protect their power by developing protective myths and norms of secrecy. They also established elaborate recruiting and training policies by requiring all job applicants to possess a degree from a four-year college plus two years of on-the-job experience.

The supervisor of the Systems Analyst Department convinced top management that these expertise games the programmers played were costing the firm an extra $8,000 for each programmer hired. This results in the company purchasing skills not needed. Having passed this step, the systems analyst supervisor made the programmers' expertise substitutable by bringing in alternate programmers. The Programming Department was moved from next door to the computers housed on the second floor to an isolated office at the end of the third floor hall. Eventually, the systems analysts acquired the programmers.

In later conversations concerning written policies, James indicated that the maintenance workers refused to prepare policy manuals and records of repairs completed. They disregarded all maintenance directions and blueprints. He even suspected them of allowing these blueprints to disappear from the plants.

Maintenance workers prevented both production workers and supervisors from involving themselves in any way with machine repairs. Machine operators were not to learn anything about their machines' operations. Maintenance workers kept all maintenance and repair problems secret. They gave the machine operators no explanation for the source of any machine operating problem.

According to the president, as the organization has grown, the role of the secretaries in each department has grown, too. Many now have power to purchase and allocate supplies, allocate their services, and schedule work. James is convinced that the expanded role is saving the company many payroll dollars.

Overall, James believes that the company is in a much better shape than it was when he purchased it. Soon after the purchase, many of the production workers began complaining bitterly over the quality of cafeteria food. These workers insisted on having some of their peers meet personally with the president to explain their complaints. However, the president refused such a meeting because he felt he should fight authority with more authority. In addition, he had understood that the previous owner-president often compromised merely for the sake of peace, and he refused to follow that pattern. Instead, James exposed the wrongdoers, and told them to shape up or ship out. He added more supervision and control to increase the likelihood of proving misconduct. James believes he took the correct action because he has received no food complaints recently.

Required:

a. Discuss the impact on the firm by having the sons not interfering in each other's divisions.
b. Describe similarities between the maintenance workers and the systems analysts' actions.
c. Explain why the actions taken by the purchasing agent place a person in a very vulnerable position of power.
d. List problems that could easily develop in connection with the expanded role of the secretaries.
e. Comment on compromising for the sake of peace.
f. Identify the basic issue involved in the workers' complaints about the quality of food that occurred with the change in ownership-management.
g. Suggest alternative actions James Fain can take now.

C25–27 Profit Centers in the Evaluation System (L.O. 4)

According to Jay Doran, president of Baltimore Company, one reason morale is so high among employees is that the company adopted a stock option plan several years ago. Thus, key people can see the immediate impact of their personal efforts on company sales and earnings as well as on the stock price. He admits, however, that as the company has grown from 100 employees to 500, stock options have become less motivational.

Now the company relies more on the profit center concept as a motivational tool and pays a percentage of division profits to all employees from supervisors upward. With corporate objectives losing their importance as a motivational force, individual personal objectives are clearly becoming dominant. For instance, Doran explains, learning that the profits of a particular division exceeded the overall profitability of the total company is of more personal interest to its supervisor than is learning that the overall company profits were X percent during the previous quarter. In addition, Doran informs you that the profit center concept allows individuals to combat the feeling that as the company grows, they become smaller and smaller fish in a bigger and bigger pond. Doran further contends that employees favorably identify with profit centers psychologically—what the company calls their center does make a difference to the division managers.

The philosophy of Baltimore management is that profit centers are primarily educational devices to get lower-level management to think of corporate-level objectives. This method of training exposes supervisors to various environmental constraints, which they soon realize vary with management level. To illustrate his point, Doran presented the following partial organization chart:

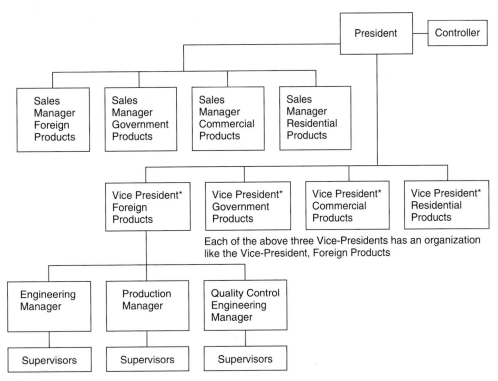

*Profit Centers

To reinforce this treatment of each product line serving as a profit center, Baltimore establishes prices for transfers of semifinished components between product lines. Where available, they use competitive outside market prices as the bases; otherwise, the sales managers impose a transfer price. When questioned as to how successful transfer pricing has been at Baltimore, Doran acknowledged that he has heard some grumbling from managers and vice presidents.

Even though Doran is the first to admit that he lacks accounting expertise, he believes that Baltimore has not made enough changes in the accounting system as the company has grown. For example, supervisors often have to wait a month after the quarter ends before receiving profit reports. Also, many of them do not understand how accountants allocate marketing and administrative costs to their departments or why in some quarters they have exceeded budget merely because the marketing and administrative expense allocations were larger than budgeted.

Annually, the president and the sales managers review the product lines and make sales projections and consider price levels. These individuals work closely with the controller in arriving at logical bases for allocating marketing and administrative expenses. From this analysis, the team forecasts profits for the product lines.

Required:

a. Discuss any existing factors that could lead to problems in the company's evaluation system. Give possible solutions to these problems.
b. Suggest improvements in the design of the accounting information system.

C25–28 Conflict in Management Philosophy (L.O. 3)

Jones Cannery is an intermediate-sized company located in a large, metropolitan city in the western United States. Jones has approximately $100 million worth of assets, after depreciation. The company cans vegetables and soup, purchasing vegetables from both local sources and farms located in the southeast. They deliver finished products to wholesalers via rail and trucks. Jones has its own transport truck delivery department.

Jones has been in business for approximately 50 years and has grown from a small, local, independent cannery to an intermediate-sized one. Jones has its own marketing company and markets its products through approximately 300 retail chain outlets. It also markets its products to the U.S. government, various state and municipal governments, other final consumers, and wholesalers.

Both the cannery and its marketing company are subsidiaries of a large diversified foods company with headquarters in the southern United States. Over the past few years, Jones, its marketing arm, and its parent company have all realized strong growth in all facets of operations.

Evolution of management dilemma. Along with Jones's growth, however, certain management difficulties have become apparent. Actually, the roots of these management problems originate in the company's development and history. Jones began its existence as a small cannery fighting for survival in a highly competitive atmosphere. The management philosophy of its early period was strictly the Puritan work ethic. Managers viewed workers as having an inherent dislike of work, with relatively little ambition and wanting security above all.

The management philosophy of the early period reflected a solid commitment to external control and the threat of punishment. In this period, top management strictly enforced management policies and directives. They often threatened to fire employees, and stiff tongue lashings were quite common. The task of management was to drive employees to get their work done, and the employees' only concern was to work as hard as necessary and keep their mouths shut.

However, as Jones began to grow and a larger company acquired the company, individuals with a more behavioristic approach to management were hired. As these managers replaced the old managers, the company began to face a very difficult and stressful period in its growth. Often, the younger managers found themselves subordinate to old managers who strongly disagreed with behavioral science methods. There was much tension as the older managers resisted change. People who were subordinate to the new managers but trained in the old ways also resisted change; this compounded the problem.

Some of the original managers who learned management techniques in the early, supervisor-dominated period are now top executives in the company. As Jones has grown and become a subsidiary of the large international foods company, however, the company recruited new executive talent to fill openings created by expansion and retirement. The new managers are young, and many have advanced graduate degrees. They are generally more liberal and particularly more behavioristically oriented than are any of the older executives from the early period. The problem resulting from the clash between the old and the new has reached dilemma proportions in the Finance/Accounting Department at Jones.

Problem in Accounting Department. The finance and accounting function at Jones has grown from just a few clerks working in different areas to two junior accountants, six accounting supervisors in charge of the various functional areas, two accounting managers, an assistant controller, and a controller. Mary Miller had been the controller for many years until her promotion to vice president for finance. She has been responsible for the growth and development of the accounting and finance function from its bare beginning. Miller is a CPA and believes in a strict disciplinary approach to management. She believes employees should keep their mouths shut and work hard. Further, she contends that employees need the motivation that the constant threat of either a tongue lashing or being fired provides. When Miller was controller, she developed two degreed accountants, James Key and Thelma Ezell, who became strong adherents of her method.

Key, a non-CPA, believes that competence and hard work are all that count and that just because one has a CPA certificate does not mean that one is either competent or a hard worker. Of course, he believes that Miller is an exceptional CPA.

Key, an assistant controller, strictly enforces deadlines. His employees must work considerable overtime if they do not meet deadlines. His idea of management by exception is to inform employees when they are making mistakes and let them know he will not tolerate mistakes. Further, he believes there is no reason to compliment or reward an employee for doing a good job. After all, that is what they get paid for.

Key's management by exception approach has been something of a disaster for the finance and accounting employees. Workers who are striving for high performance often become quite anxious because this management by exception policy highlights only their mistakes. They find themselves preoccupied with the number of times they make mistakes rather than with their performance level over the long run. Over the years this policy was in effect, there was considerable turnover in the Accounting Department. As many as three different employees occupied a single position during one six-week period. Morale has been quite low, and various employees have reported Key to the personnel director from time to time. This has resulted in practically no relief for the employees, however, since Miller, Key's mentor, has considerably more power at Jones Cannery than does the personnel director. Moreover, to impress top parent-company management, Key and Miller have traditionally set high standards that are difficult for the accounting and finance employees to meet. This has only served to increase anxiety and turnover and decrease morale. Miller's other disciple is Thelma Ezell, who is currently one of the two accounting managers. However, she is limited in her management function because of living in the shadow of Miller and Key. She highly admires them, believes in their methods, and feels the Finance/Accounting Department could not survive without them.

When the company promoted Miller to vice president a year ago, a major restructuring of the Accounting Department took place. Before the restructuring, many clerks and a credit manager, all of whom reported to Key, then called the accounting manager, made up the department. Miller was controller and Ezell worked for her. The restructuring organized the Accounting Department into functional areas. Supervisors were both appointed from within the company and hired from the outside. The company created two accounting manager positions and appointed Ezell to one of them. The position of assistant controller remained occupied by Key. However, an accountant from outside the cannery filled the vacant position of controller. For this position, top management in the parent company wanted an intelligent, experienced individual who possessed both an MBA degree and a CPA certificate. Further, they wanted a person who used modern management techniques. They hired Harold Douglas to fill this position. He had an MBA degree, was a CPA, represented the epitome of diplomacy and tact, and was an adherent of the behavioral management school. Almost immediately, Key began to resent that the company had brought in an outsider to fill the position for which he had worked so hard. However, Douglas charged ahead and began to introduce many new ideas relating to financial reports and the handling of employee discipline problems. He held management seminars for accounting supervisors and advanced management seminars for the managers and Key. He began to set realistic goals for the department and attempted to trim back overtime hours. Amidst all of this, Key continued to resist Douglas. He continually made uncomplimentary remarks, in the presence of Ezell and some of the supervisors, about Douglas and his methods. Ezell, still under the considerable influence of Key, began to develop a bad attitude toward Douglas. In Key's words, "Douglas is trying to turn us all into a bunch of psychiatrists. We're wasting so much time counseling employees that we're not getting any work done."

Key also began to work around Douglas by seeking Miller for advice rather than following the chain of command and going to Douglas. Douglas, displeased with Key, countered by stepping around Key in relaying instructions rather than going through Key, and often countermanded instructions that supervisors had received from Key. To make matters worse, a discipline problem arose one day concerning a female clerk who worked for one of the account supervisors. The supervisor counseled the clerk using Douglas's approach. Key, feeling that Douglas's approach was not severe enough and knowing Douglas was out of town at the time, called in the clerk after the supervisor had talked with her and gave her a thorough tongue lashing. Key then informed Miller, who became infuriated with the clerk and also called her in and gave her another tongue lashing and threatened to fire her. News of the treatment of the clerk spread through the office, and morale dropped considerably. Several employees complained to the initially involved supervisor. When Douglas returned, he found out about what had happened. This strained relations between Douglas and Key further. This clash of management philosophies has continued. Morale is at an all-time low in the accounting department, and several employees have resigned to seek employment elsewhere. The clash is also hindering progress toward greater automation of accounting systems.

Required:

a. Indicate the factors that have caused the management dilemma.
b. React to Key's comment that Douglas is trying to turn the management team into psychiatrists.
c. Suggest solutions to alleviate the conflict.

C25–29 Behavioral Needs of Employees in a Changing Environment (L.O. 4)

Edmond Office Equipment Company began operations 30 years ago, specializing in the development of typewriters. Over the years, the company has earned average profits of $150,000 on sales of nearly $1.5 million annually. However, in recent years, sales have fallen to less than $300,000, and the company has become unprofitable.

Dan Edmond, the founder and president, is very conservative and views small businesses as risky. As a result, the company had no debt for 15 years; retained earnings financed all growth. Interest on bond investments played a larger role in helping to meet the obligations incurred by the sales and production aspects of the business.

Bob Edmond, a nephew of the founder of the organization, is frustrated that his efforts to improve the company have not been successful. While he agrees that he has obtained valuable experience first as director of marketing and now as vice president of finance, he questions whether he should leave the organization or attempt other tactics to turn the company around. He admits that he feels some responsibility to the company his uncle founded, especially since no other family member has made a definite commitment to the firm.

This is the same philosophy held by Dan Edmond. He views the company as a family trust because his two sisters each hold 20 percent of the stock. Actual voting has never occurred, since Dan owns 35 percent of the stock with Bob holding 5 percent. Bob believes that it is up to him to determine the company's future as his uncle wishes to retire and does not have any children.

When first organized, the founder ran the company very informally as a one-person operation. This philosophy is still prevalent as the president continues to exert a high degree of dominance over management. Personnel evaluation is extremely informal. The president believes he should tell employees what to do in performing the job and then let them be on their own. However, he did agree several years ago to establishing the three major product lines as separate profit centers with each manager having a significant amount of authority within their centers. These three profit centers are office furniture and fixtures, office supplies, and automatic typing. Each profit center consists of a sales department, production department, a service department, and an administrative department.

When word processing began using sophisticated input/output devices for text, the demand for office products changed. Because Edmond hesitated to invest funds in this new development, the company lagged behind its competitors and many grabbed a large share of Edmond's market. As a result, two firms became dominant and barriers to entry for most segments were significant. Edmond's marketing policy was not very aggressive as they allowed the two dominant competitors to do the missionary work for word processing equipment while they followed up with those potential customers who required less costly automatic typing equipment. Edmond distributes most of its typewriters through independent local dealers. Foreign sales account for about 2 percent of total current sales, down from 18 percent five years ago. Bob believes this decline resulted because German manufacturers have developed the technology to manufacture similar or better devices and can more favorably compete because of decreased shipping costs and import duties.

Because the greatest decline in sales has occurred in the automatic typing division, the president decided to establish a task force from the three different profit centers to identify this division's problems and make recommendations to correct them. He appointed the following people to the task force:

From Office Supplies Division: John Brown, Personnel Director
Mary Smith, Budget Supervisor

From the Office Furniture and Fixture Division: Cindy Black, Administrative Department Manager

From the Automatic Typing Division: Bob Denton, Profit Center Manager
Jim Green, Assistant Profit Center Manager
Ann Strong, Salesperson
Louis Wells, Service Person

Bob believes that his firm's product does have advantages over competitors as the automated typewriter developed by the company engineers is more versatile and simpler to repair than the more advanced systems. However, the machine produced by Edmond does have one serious disadvantage—it is more difficult to learn to operate than competitors' products.

Employees' overall performance does not satisfy Bob. However, he places much of this blame on the lack of supervision and poor worker morale. He admits that it is hard to motivate employees when management is disenchanted also. Bob and his uncle have had several disagreements over the years about product development. Most of these stemmed from the uncle's unwillingness to fund a large capital commitment for new projects.

Bob worries that the professional scientists and engineers employed are not making sufficient progress in designing a new word processing system that will represent an improvement over those presently on the market. In talking with the automated typing profit center manager, he receives the following information:

1. There is widespread concern among these professionals that management may hire technical school graduates or individuals who have only received on-the-job training in this area from competing companies.
2. Engineers want competitive salaries and benefits.
3. Engineers wish to be treated as high-caliber professionals.
4. Several scientists have also expressed interest in gaining graduate education at a local university while employed.
5. These scientists want to be better qualified to publish some of their findings in technical journals.
6. Other professionals believe this graduate education will give them an opportunity for advancement in status and salary to higher management levels or positions within the research division.
7. Others express interest in attending conventions of other professional scientists where they can discuss their work.
8. However, many of them have complaints about the resources and laboratory facilities.
9. All professionals believe they must have their ideas recognized and the opportunities to see these ideas put to use.

10. Another point in which there is agreement is that they want the freedom to solve problems and manage their own work within the constraints of the organization.

11. Others stress the importance of a local environment that offers good libraries, colleges, art museums, and other cultural opportunities.

Bob has been searching for ways that the company can diversify and has narrowed the alternatives down to five new products related to office products. An additional alternative for Bob developed recently when he saw an old college classmate who has developed a different automatic typewriter. He is anxious for Bob to join him in forming a new company.

Required:

a. Enumerate the changes in the word processing industry that present threats and opportunities for the company.

b. Explain if the company could have changed its strategy within the last 20 years so it could have continued as a successful operation.

c. Describe the behavioral problems you see arising among the group members of the task force as a result of the composition of this group.

d. Discuss the contribution a person such as Mary Smith, the budget supervisor, could make in this task force.

e. Identify and discuss the specific needs expressed in the 11 issues by the scientists and engineers, using Maslow's and Herzberg's approaches.

Appendix Cases

C25–30A Recommendations for Ethical Situation (L.O. 5)

Victor, Inc., manufactures microcomputers with 60 percent of its sales made through personal sales calls. Salespersons receive a commission on each sale; however, successful sales often reflect many months of solicitation, entertaining, and promotional demonstrations. In this highly competitive market environment, salespersons also must travel extensively within the region searching for new clients.

Victor's most successful model, the Ap-IT, has been responsible for much of the company's growth within the last few years. However, two years ago, a major competitor introduced a more versatile microcomputer and Victor's sales have slowed down sharply. In fact, production management has begun manufacturing a more efficient model which they are introducing in the market. While Victor can use some of the Ap-IT model parts on the newer version, much of the material inventory is rapidly becoming obsolete. Unfortunately, Victor has a significant amount of this inventory in its parts warehouse.

Because of its dramatic impact on the entire company, you are surprised to hear the vice president's report to the officers of a local bank from whom a large note is outstanding. In this conversation, the vice president makes the assurance that Victor has no obsolete inventory. In your accounting records you have begun making provisions to write down the material and parts that are obsolete to their net realizable value. Just last week you had talked with the vice president, to whom you report directly, concerning the need for this write down and how detrimental it was going to be to the current period's financial statements. However, you recognize that this vice president's image and merit raise relates directly to the company's financial results.

In your position as controller, you also notice that travel and entertainment expenses have been increasing each month. In investigating the situation, you find documents needed to support reimbursement are often missing. According to company tradition, superiors of the employee requesting reimbursement are responsible for reviewing expenditures and signing the request. Despite your earlier request to the president to establish tightly written travel and entertainment policies, you remember that the company took no action on this matter. The company requires salespersons, as well as all other management personnel, to submit receipts for any traveling, food, and lodging expenses incurred. However, in reviewing expenditures and talking with the travel clerks, you gain the distinct impression that the line of least resistance is the general rule. Underpayments are likely to provoke cries of outrage from the managers requesting travel reimbursement while they accept overpayments in courteous silence. Travel clerks often find it difficult to evaluate when client entertaining is cost justified; thus, their philosophy is when in doubt, pay.

To further complicate the matter, evaluations from salespersons and other Marketing Department personnel are reviewed when the company considers travel clerks for raises and promotions. Naturally, those travel clerks that give the salespersons the least hassle in reimbursing their travel and entertainment claims receive higher evaluations.

As controller, you have also had difficulty in contacting travel clerks because of absences within the department. Victor, Inc., has a rule that should absences or lateness total five or more in any six-month period, employees must forfeit the entire 4 percent normal raise due at the next merit review. Victor counts a week's absence equally with a 10-minute lateness. Thus, workers in danger of accumulating a fifth absence within six months merely remain ill and away from work during their fourth absence until their first absence is more than six months old. There is a limit on how much younger workers can violate this rule because at some point their salary ceases and sickness benefits take over. This is usually sufficient to get the younger worker to return to work. Employees with 20 or more years of service, however, receive sickness benefits of 85 percent of normal salary.

These absences help explain why there is such a delay in recording travel expense. Several times within the last month, you have asked for an update on travel and entertainment expenses, only to find that the records are current through four weeks ago.

Required:

a. List the problems you are encountering as controller for the company.
b. Describe what you think is causing these problems.
c. Determine the ethical considerations you should recognize in this situation.
d. Recommend a course of action in this situation and give your reasons for selecting this action.

C25–31A Ethical Values and Corporate Espionage (L.O. 5)

Top management of Company A recognized that decision making involves much more than the use of quantitative accounting techniques to arrive at a presumably optimal choice. Instead, Company A accomplishes effective decision making through an interdisciplinary process which encompasses the value system of the participants. Humans mostly learn rather than inherit behavior. Behavior is the outcome of conscious and subconscious selection processes and must reflect both the limitations of human cognition and the complexity of our total environment.

Values may be thought of as the guidance system a person uses when confronted with a choice among alternatives. Individuals also view values as the desired ends and means to the end when an individual selects from among available alternatives. Ethics are the standards for decision making. People acquire values early in life and retain them throughout their existence. Their value base is in their religious and moral philosophy as well as in their philosophy for interacting with other individuals on a daily basis.

Company A top management recognized that value judgments are unavoidable in taking corrective action to ensure that the implemented choice has a result compatible with the original objective. They have spent much time discussing their obligation to employees in providing an environment that does not threaten individual value systems. In recruiting for managerial positions, Company A tried to secure information concerning candidates' involvement in religious and civic activities and the stability of their family backgrounds.

Several years ago, concern over the possibility of facing an ethics issue prompted management to act. Due to the sensitive nature of the topic, the president gathered information concerning value development in males and females. There is research supporting the hypothesis that females differ from males in the way they develop values. Females primarily value continuing relationships and the caring that supports them. Males tend to give priority to rules and systems of order that ensure greater control. Female managers involve themselves with the breach of caring after punishing a subordinate.

Even though management believed several people should develop the ethics policy, they also studied using a group decision-making process. Studies have shown that the collective behavior of a group is a direct consequence of individual decision procedures with the addition of a process for resolving conflict. While some conflict may be constructive, cooperative groups generally make better decisions than groups with extensive interpersonal conflict. Group members may react to interpersonal conflict by lowering their goals and shifting toward consensus. The group may force individuals to compromise to arrive at a consensus. To reduce conflict and dissent, groups frequently adopt decision rules for making a final choice.

The president appointed a group, composed of both men and women from a variety of backgrounds, to develop a written ethical policy. Much controversy arose in each of the ethics committee meetings; however, finally the group developed a written ethical policy. Even though the committee developed a long written ethics policy, it does not mention how far an employee may go to find out what the competition is up to.

For years high-tech companies have used questionable techniques to obtain competitors' secrets; now low-tech companies, such as Company A, began feeling the pressure to pursue competitor intelligence to keep their piece of the shrinking market. With the mounting competitive pressures, Company A became more aggressive in its marketing and planning strategy.

After several years of receiving periodic assignments to gather intelligence on material and labor costs, production volume, and other matters from competitors and potential acquisition targets, management gave Accountant X the general assignment to gather information on the competition.

Accountant X adopted cat-burglar tactics, even to the point of changing from business clothing to jeans and a ski mask for nighttime searches of competitors' trash where Accountant X found such information as secret merger plans. Combing through dumpsters in the dark and paying a trash hauler for access to his truck, Accountant X risked being crushed in a compactor. Accountant X became known within Company A as Director of Covert Activities.

Accountant X's drive to deliver what he thought Company A wanted led to counterspying. When top management discovered that Accountant X was selling Company A's secrets to competitors, the news shocked them. Their response was that they did not order the trash searches—that Accountant X was pretty much on his own. Further, top management added that "when you put good people on projects, you expect them to be ethical."

On discovery of the plot to sell Company A's corporate secrets, Accountant X admitted that no one forced him to spy on competitors. However, Accountant X strongly argued that if he hadn't been spying for Company A, he would never have considered going against them. Accountant X admitted that some of his actions to competitors were not ethical, but once you start to sacrifice what you believe, where do you stop?

Required:

a. Discuss what happens when an individual discovers a conflict between personal and organizational values.
b. Describe the dangers that employees placed in positions such as Accountant X will, in turn, raid their own companies' files and try to sell the contents to major competitors.
c. React to this statement: "Competitors' trash is fair game once it leaves their offices—that's why there are shredders."
d. Discuss what companies can do to guard against industry espionage.
e. Explain how anyone can consider actions of the group as effective because compromise is almost certain to be a requirement for group decision making.

f. List common decision rules that groups, such as Company A's ethics policy group, adopt to reduce conflict and dissent. Indicate advantages and disadvantages of each decision rule cited.

C25–32A (CMA) Ethics and Budgetary Slack (L.O. 5)

Norton Company, a manufacturer of infant furniture and carriages, is in the initial stages of preparing the annual budget for 19X2. Scott Ford has recently joined Norton's accounting staff and is interested to learn as much as possible about the company's budgeting process. During a recent lunch with Marge Atkins, sales manager, and Pete Granger, production manager, Ford initiated the following conversation:

Ford: "Since I'm new around here and am going to be involved with the preparation of the annual budget, I'd be interested to learn how the two of you estimate sales and production numbers."

Atkins: "We start out very methodically by looking at recent history, discussing what we know about current accounts, potential customers, and the general state of consumer spending. Then, we add that usual dose of intuition to come up with the best forecast we can."

Granger: "I usually take the sales projections as the basis for my projections. Of course, we have to make an estimate of what this year's closing inventories will be which is sometimes difficult."

Ford: "Why does that present a problem? There must have been an estimate of closing inventories in the budget for the current year."

Granger: "Those numbers aren't always reliable since Marge makes some adjustments to the sales numbers before passing them on to me."

Ford: "What kind of adjustments?"

Atkins: "Well, we don't want to fall short of the sales projections so we generally give ourselves a little breathing room by lowering the initial sales projection anywhere from 5 to 10 percent."

Granger: "So, you can see why this year's budget is not a very reliable starting point. We always have to adjust the projected production rates as the year progresses and, of course, this changes the ending inventory estimates. By the way, we make similar adjustments to expenses by adding at least 10 percent to the estimates; I think everyone around here does the same thing."

Required:

a. Marge Atkins and Pete Granger have described the use of budgetary slack.
  (1) Explain why Atkins and Granger behave in this manner, and describe the benefits they expect to realize from the use of budgetary slack.
  (2) Explain how the use of budgetary slack can adversely affect Atkins and Granger.
b. As a management accountant, Scott Ford believes that the behavior described by Marge Atkins and Pete Granger may be unethical and that he may have an obligation not to support this behavior. By citing the specific standards of competence, confidentiality, integrity, and/or objectivity from *Statements on Management Accounting Number 1C,* "Standards of Ethical Conduct for Management Accountants," explain why the use of budgetary slack may be unethical.

Capstone Case

Role of Behavioral Theory in New Business Operations

In May of the current year, Bill and Mary Powell purchased an 80-acre farm containing sand and rock pits. Previously, Bill and his brother, Sam, were in the gravel business together. However, they found the farm they jointly owned did not contain enough rock and sand to support two families. Additionally, each brother had an adult son who wanted to work with them.

Because of this inadequate rock and sand capacity, Bill purchased a different farm, and Powell Sand and Gravel Company began operations. Bill was confident that his willingness to work plus the dedication of his wife, Mary, would ensure successful operations. Mary quit her secretarial job and assumed the duties of the office manager for their company.

The company lacked the necessary equipment, forcing Bill to purchase expensive machinery. Since there was little differential cost in acquiring machinery larger than they presently needed, Bill and Mary purchased excess capacity initially. They bought an expensive loader on lease-purchase and purchased two new trucks. They also built a wash plant and completed expensive welding. Thus, the company incurred heavy start-up costs even though the Powells were unable to purchase all the equipment they believed they needed.

Fortunately, there was little rain during the summer months and operations made steady progress. There were eight nonfamily members employed during the summer months. When some of these employees were not digging sand and gravel from the company farm, they used the company trucks to haul dirt for another company. This company paid Powell Sand and Gravel a flat fee per truckload. Initial operations pleased the couple because they were able to meet all current obligations as they came due.

However, in October, the Powells found operations increasingly difficult with their limited equipment. They had to cut their payroll to four employees because their equipment was inadequate to rapidly extract gravel materials from the ground to sell. Mary and Bill's adult married son continues to work with them; the company pays him per truckload delivered. They believe they need more money to purchase a drag line and additional machinery to obtain the gravel deeper in the ground. Sam and Bill's brother, Mark, owns and operates a successful concrete plant and is anxious to buy more than 20,000 truckloads of gravel annually. However, without the drag line, Bill Powell believes it will be difficult to fill this demand.

A competing company in their community is going out of business having run out of gravel and sand material on its property. Bill and Mary believe this is an ideal time to capture the market, but consider it impossible without a loan to purchase additional equipment. Even though winter is approaching, Bill believes that if they can get materials out of the ground, their trucks can deliver sand and gravel even in cold weather. However, whenever the temperature drops below 35 degrees, contractors are unable to pour concrete and there is little demand for sand and gravel.

This hard-working couple indicate they have investigated alternative uses of their present equipment and found that they could use their two trucks only for hauling gravel to brother Mark's company. For the last two months, Mark has loaned Bill his company's drag line on the days when his workers do not need the equipment. Mark charges them a daily fee which all parties believe is reasonable. They subtract this fee from the charge for the gravel Bill's employees deliver to Mark's company. However, because of pride and determination to make their own business a success, both Mary and Bill feel reluctant to depend on borrowing Mark's drag line. They believe they can survive on their own without counting on family favors.

Analysis of their records reveals these expenses for monthly sales of $18,000: labor, $5,500; gas, $3,250; house and plant utilities, $1,640; and telephone, $224. All sales are cash sales.

Bill and Mary now owe the following:

- Land and house—balance of loan is $85,000; 5 years remaining on mortgage, paying $1,000 principal and interest per month.
- Note from local bank—$145,000 (secured by farm, but not secured by equipment) due in November, currently paying only interest expense; Bill and Mary think their bank will renew the note; they owe $1,200 per month in interest; the company has kept up to date on paying the bank note interest.

- $25,000 Truck—owe $9,000, paying $750 monthly on principal and interest.
- $115,000 Machinery and equipment on a lease-purchase—paying $3,000 principal and interest per month.
- $65,000 Excavator on a lease-purchase—paying $1,400 principal and interest per month; the Powells will lose their $7,245 down payment if they send this excavator back to the leasing company; however, the excavator can no longer get deep enough in the ground to obtain any gravel. The large excavator has many attachments in addition to the bucket which they purchased. There is also a drill attachment for winter operations.

Mary and Bill believe a $345,000 loan would allow them to consolidate other loans, buy the two loaders and two drag lines needed, and have some working capital left over. They think they would pay the same interest rate on this $345,000 loan as the bank is presently charging. The couple believe they can arrange for the loan to extend over a longer time period.

Even though Mary and Bill believe their bank will grant the loan, brother Mark has somewhat reluctantly agreed to loan them the money if the bank loan is unavailable. When pressed for present alternatives, Mary and Bill admit that they are aware of a $16,000 used loader for sale for which the repayment period is one year. By borrowing the brother's drag line and purchasing the used loader, they could operate on a marginal basis for a short period. However, maintenance problems associated with the used loader concern Bill.

Required:

a. Discuss the extent to which contingency theory affects this decision.
b. Identify the contingency factors involved.
c. Explain how you see Maslow's hierarchy of needs in operation.
d. Calculate the present monthly cash flow for Powell Sand and Gravel Company on $18,000 monthly sales.
e. Identify the serious mistakes the Powells made.
f. Discuss what alternatives you think are available for the company and give the justifications/advantages of choosing each alternative.
g. Advise the owners based on the limited information you have. Do you believe they should incur additional debt to purchase the additional equipment? Support your answer and advice.
h. Suggest steps Bill and Mary can take immediately.
i. Describe additional data the company needs before making a final decision.

QUANTITATIVE MODELS FOR PLANNING AND CONTROL

26

Gantt Charts, PERT, and Decision Tree Analysis

CHAPTER OBJECTIVES

After studying this chapter, you should be able to:

1. Prepare graphs and networks for use in planning and controlling processes where there are time flows.

2. Compare actual and budgeted time and cost for each activity so the resulting variance reflects the impact one activity's delay has on the overall project.

3. Provide, through decision tree analysis, a systematic framework for analyzing a sequence of interrelated decisions.

4. Apply the time value of future earnings by discounting the expected value of future decisions.

Introduction

Increasingly, cost accountants are devoting more attention to furnishing management and other interested parties with data they can use in cost control and planning rather than emphasizing cost accumulation and determination. Cost accounting now considers the predictive ability of data rather than solely emphasizing the past. Accountants are integrating control models within the cost accounting system for monitoring actual results against plans to provide feedback for corrective action. This involvement in managerial planning and control has led to the use of Gantt charts, Program Evaluation and Review Technique (PERT), and decision tree analysis.

Gantt Charts (L.O. 1)

One aid to planning that is simple to prepare is a **Gantt chart,** a bar chart with time shown on the horizontal axis and the duration of the task represented as a bar running from the starting date to the ending date. Industry uses Gantt charts as a method of recording progress toward goals. On a given date, a Gantt chart easily shows how expected performance of a specific task compares with actual performance, which tasks should be in progress on a specific date, and how close to completion a task should be on a given date.

Control Device

Gantt charts are a control technique because they readily allow the comparison of actual production with scheduled production to identify variations and initiate corrective action. As shown in Exhibit 26–1, a Gantt chart involves (1) identifying and showing the sequence of activities and (2) scheduling the work by

EXHIBIT 26–1

Gantt Chart—Each Block Represents One Workweek Beginning on Monday and Ending on Friday

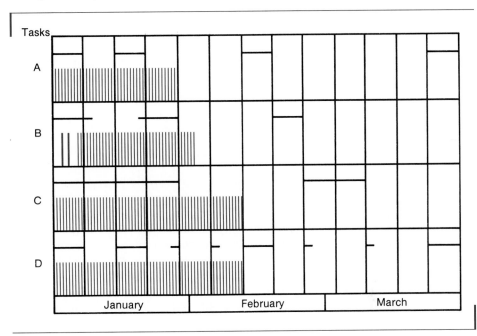

periods. The Y-axis of a Gantt chart represents the tasks or activities workers must perform, while the X-axis represents the time available for work. The horizontal broken line represents work scheduled by periods within the departments. The short vertical broken lines represent work unfinished or carried over from previous periods. The large shaded bar line is a summation of the individual horizontal broken lines and represents cumulative work to be performed.

Exhibit 26–1 divides time into weeks for each month. Management schedules Task A for the first and third weeks of January, the middle of February, and the last week of March. The four horizontal lines show this scheduled work for Task A. When added, these lines represent four weeks of cumulative work; the heavy horizontal line indicates this work. On examination, the chart shows that management could schedule additional jobs during the second and fourth weeks of January. The workers have no backlog of work to complete on Task A, because there are no short vertical lines as there are for Task B.

Advantages of Gantt Charts

Gantt charts provide a visual display of planned utilization of facilities so managers can make appropriate revisions to obtain better use of resources. After managers study the horizontal broken lines illustrating when work is scheduled, they can plan additional tasks for the time periods represented by breaks in the horizontal lines. The heavy bold line representing cumulative work assists managers in computing total work-hours required for each task as well as in scheduling repairs and maintenance. Gantt charts also alert managers to areas in which large variations in planned and actual performance exist so they can reallocate resources.

Network Models (L.O. 1)

Even though Gantt charts are simple systematic tools for planning, they fail to indicate which tasks workers must complete before beginning others. This failure results because all activities are arranged vertically on a Gantt chart. Network models provide for this aspect of planning. Program Evaluation Review Technique (PERT) is one of the more sophisticated planning and control devices.

Program Evaluation Review Technique

Program Evaluation Review Technique (PERT) is a systematic procedure for using network analysis to plan and measure actual progress toward scheduled events. The United States military developed PERT for the Polaris program to aid in controlling this large-scale project. Generally, organizations use PERT for exceptional projects whose managers have limited experience. The **critical path method (CPM)** developed by industry closely relates to PERT.

As illustrated in Exhibit 26–2, PERT diagrams are free-form, network diagrams showing each activity as an arrow between events. A network for **PERT-Time analysis** contains a sequence of arrows showing interrelationships among activities with time being the basic element in these activities. A circle represents an **event,** indicating the beginning or completion of a task. Events are discrete points, numbered for identification, that consume no resources. Arrows represent **activities** or tasks to be accomplished to go from one event to the next. An activity consumes resources and has a duration over time starting at one event and ending with the occurrence of the next event. We show activities from left to right in the necessary order of their accomplishment. Workers must complete

EXHIBIT 26–2   Network for PERT-Time

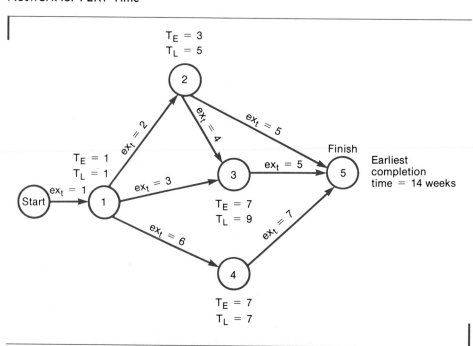

all the activities leading to an event before the event occurs. This explains why an event at the head of the arrow should have a higher number, if possible, than an event at the end of the arrow.

Expected Activity Time. After developing the network diagram, managers make an estimate of the time needed to complete each activity. We base the **expected activity time** on the 1–4–1 three-estimate method, a weighted average of the shortest time, the average time, and the longest time. We weight the shortest and the longest times, one; and the average time, four. The formula for time estimations is

$$ex_t = \text{\frac{1}{6}} \text{ (optimistic time } + 4 \text{ most likely time } + \text{ pessimistic time)}$$

Exhibit 26–2 shows only the expected time (ex_t); to illustrate, the expected time of the activity beginning at 1 and ending at 4 is computed as: optimistic time = 3 weeks; most likely estimate = 6 weeks; pessimistic estimate = 9 weeks

$$\frac{3 + 4(6) + 9}{6} = 6 \text{ weeks } ex_t$$

We compute the expected times for the other activities similarly and write them on the upper sides of the arrows in Exhibit 26–2. Rather than expressing time in weeks, daily units can express the time estimates.

Critical Path. We can determine the longest duration for completion of the entire project using a PERT network. The **critical path** is this longest path. Managers can reduce the total time of the project only by shortening the critical path. The reason this path is critical is that if any activity on the path takes longer than expected, a delay in the entire project occurs. Every network has at least one critical path. To find the critical path, we compute the cumulative expected activity time along each of the paths. In Exhibit 26–2, the cumulative paths are

Paths	Cumulative Expected Activity Time (in weeks)
0-1-2-5	1 + 2 + 5 = 8
0-1-2-3-5	1 + 2 + 4 + 5 = 12
0-1-3-5	1 + 3 + 3* + 5 = 12
0-1-4-5	1 + 6 + 7 = 14†

*Time lag of three weeks waiting until completion of activity 2–3.
†Critical path with cumulative activity time of 14 weeks.

Slack. Paths that are not critical have **slack time**; however, activities along the critical path do not. The slack associated with an event is the amount of time a company can delay the event without affecting the completion of the project. The larger the amount of slack, the less critical the activity, and vice versa. Slack is the difference between the latest allowable time that a worker may complete an event and the earliest expected time. Exhibit 26–2 also indicates the earliest completion time. The **earliest completion time** (T_E) is the cumulative time of the event. In Exhibit 26–2, the T_E of event 2 is three weeks (1 + 2), the duration of activity 0-1 and 1-2. The T_E for event 3 is more complex because it has two cumulative paths, one along path 0-1-2-3 (seven weeks) and the other along the path 0-1-3 (four weeks). When an event has more than one cumulative path, the longest completion time of any path is the T_E for that event. This means the earliest completion time for event 3 is seven weeks. Note that this causes a time lag for path 0-1-3-5 as production cannot leave event 3 until week seven. Exhibit 26–2 indicates the T_E for all other events.

After computing the earliest completion time for all events, we determine the **latest completion time** (T_L). The T_L on the critical path equals the T_E because there is no slack on this path. We compute the other events' latest completion times by working backwards through the network. For instance, the T_L for event 3 is nine weeks, the latest completion time for event 5, the event that follows it, and the five weeks of activity 3-5 ($14 - 5 = 9$ weeks). If an event has several activities flowing from it, there may be several latest completion times. However, the minimum of these times is the T_L for that event. Slack now can be computed using the following formula:

$$S = T_L - T_E$$

The slack at event 2 is two weeks ($S = 5 - 3 = 2$ weeks). This allows management to delay event 2 up to two weeks without delaying the overall project's expected completion time of 14 weeks. However, if a noncritical activity uses more than its expected time, we must recompute the slack time for subsequent events. For example, if activity 1–2 takes three weeks instead of the estimated two weeks, event 2's slack time has been reduced one week, for a total slack of one week.

Flexibility with Slack. Slack introduces flexibility into the network because it serves as a buffer for events not located on the critical path. When time lags appear on the critical path, managers can transfer materials, labor, and equipment to the problem areas. However, managers must be alert to the effect of these transfers on other paths, because they have made little or no progress if transfers in turn create problems on other paths.

Crashing. Not only does information about slack time allow management to continually monitor a project's status but these data may also serve as a guide in rescheduling tasks to shorten the overall project's completion time. In Exhibit 26–2, event 3 has two weeks of slack. If these weeks represent idle resources, it may be possible to use these resources in critical events and cut the 14-week completion time of the project. Of course, there are limits to transferring idle resources, depending on the task's specifications. Activity time may also be reduced by hiring more labor, overtime, or acquiring more equipment. **Crashing** is what we call these efforts designed to complete the project ahead of schedule. However, when managers use crashing, the project's variable costs increase. Crashing the network means finding the minimum cost for completing the project in minimum time to achieve an optimum trade-off between time and cost. Determining the appropriate trade-off is referred to as *PERT-Cost analysis.*

PERT-Cost Analysis

PERT-Cost analysis of the trade-off between time and cost is essential to determine the cost effectiveness of crashing. We use the same type of network illustrated in Exhibit 26–2 for PERT-Time as employed in PERT-Cost. However, we include two estimated times, a crash time and a normal expected time, for each activity. Exhibit 26–3 indicates the expected time (ex_i) from Exhibit 26–2 along with the crash time (cr_i) for each activity. If the activity is as shown in 1-3 and 3-5 in Exhibit 26–3 and managers cannot crash it, there is no difference in these times and we can omit the crash time.

EXHIBIT 26–3   Network for PERT-Cost

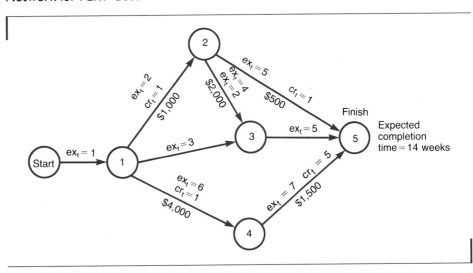

We estimate the costs of completing the activity under normal expected conditions and under crash conditions. A comparison of these two cost projections results in the determination of the *differential,* or *incremental, crash cost* for each activity that managers can crash. For example, the expected cost of activity 2-5 is $18,000 requiring five weeks. If instead, workers complete the activity in one week and management projects the cost at $20,000, the result is $500 differential cost per week [($20,000 − $18,000) ÷ (5 − 1 week)]. In Exhibit 26–3, differential crash cost per week is written below the arrow for each activity. Note that activities 1-3 and 3-5 have no differential crash cost because managers cannot crash either of these activities.

In PERT-Cost analysis of the trade-off between time and cost, managers study the status of the project. Assume that the project illustrated in Exhibits 26–2 and 26–3 has a normal cost of $100,000, shown as follows, if no crashing occurs:

No activities crashed

Paths	Cumulative Expected Weeks
0-1-2-5	8
0-1-2-3-5	12
0-1-3*-5	12
0-1-4-5	14†

*Time lag as cannot leave event 3 until week 7.
†Critical path—14 weeks for project completion.
$100,000—project cost.

In studying trade-offs, the company should crash first the critical activity with the lowest differential cost on the critical path. Even though activity 2-5 has the lowest differential cost ($500) in the network, it is not on the critical path. Crashing activity 2-5 will not shorten the overall project's completion time until managers first crash another activity. Crashing activity 2-5 would only increase slack time from 6 to 10 weeks on this path. Instead, activity 4-5, with a differential cost of $1,500, is the one to crash because its differential cost is lowest of those activities on the critical path. However, managers can only shorten it two weeks before paths 0-1-2-3-5 and 0-1-3-5 also become critical. This results in the following status analysis showing that crashing reduced project time by two weeks but increased cost $3,000 (2 weeks $\times$ $1,500). Now we have three critical paths and we can shorten the schedule only by reducing the length of all of them.

First Iteration.

	Activity 4-5 Crashed Two Weeks
Paths	**Cumulative Expected Weeks**
0-1-2-5	8
0-1-2-3-5	12*
0-1-3-5	12 (still cannot leave event 3 until week 7)
0-1-4-5	12*

*Critical paths—12 weeks for project completion.
$100,000 + 2 ($1,500) = $103,000 project cost.

Second Iteration. A next iteration is to shorten activity 1-2 by one week because this activity has the lowest differential cost on path 0-1-2-3-5.

This also reduces the time on path 0-1-3-5 since now the project can leave event 3 at the sixth week of operation. However, this does not shorten overall project completion time until further crashing of activities occurs.

Thus, there is no overall time savings unless additional crashing occurs on path 0-1-4-5. You might have started in a different order or used a different combination from that illustrated in this second and third iteration. The important factor is to arrive at the final overall project time of 9 weeks.

	Activity 1-2 Crashed One Week
Paths	**Cumulative Expected Weeks**
0-1-2-5	7
0-1-2-3-5	11
0-1-3-5	11 (now can leave event 3 at week 6)
0-1-4-5	12*

*Critical path—12 weeks for project completion.
$103,000 + $1,000 = $104,000 project cost.

Third Iteration. A next iteration involves shortening activity 2-3 by two weeks and activity 1-4 by three weeks. By crashing activity 2-3 there is no longer a time lag at event 3 for path 0-1-3-5 since the project can leave event 3 at the fourth week now. By crashing these two activities, overall project cost has increased with extra weeks saved, as the following illustrates:

	Activity 2-3 Crashed Two Weeks and Activity 1-4 Crashed Three Weeks
Paths	**Cumulative Expected Weeks**
0-1-2-5	7
0-1-2-3-5	9*
0-1-3-5	9* (now can leave event 3 at week 4)
0-1-4-5	9*

*Critical paths—9 weeks for project completion.
$104,000 + 2 ($2,000) + 3 ($4,000) = $120,000 project cost.

Even though we further crash paths 0-1-4-5 and 0-1-2-5, we cannot reduce overall project time because there is no further reduction in paths 0-1-3-5 and 0-1-2-3-5. We cannot crash the remaining activities along these paths. This results in a final trade-off of crashing four activities and finishing the project in nine weeks, or five weeks earlier, at a minimum crash cost of $20,000, or total project cost of $120,000.

Deciding When to Crash

In deciding whether the company should proceed at the normal pace or attempt a crash program, we should compare the total differential cost of the crash program ($20,000 in our example) with the cost savings or benefits of the crash program. If we expect the contribution margin earned to be $6,000 a week, we should undertake the crash program because the $30,000 ($6,000 × 5 weeks) exceeds the $20,000 differential cost. If, however, the additional contribution profits the company expects to receive by completing the project early does not exceed $20,000, the company should follow the normal schedule.

Construction contracts may include penalties for failing to complete the project by a specified time. We can compare these penalties to differential cost in determining if crashing is profitable. For example, assume these penalties were in effect for the preceding case presented in Exhibit 26–3: no penalty if completed within 9 weeks, $5,000 penalty for a 12-week completion, and $15,000 for a 14-week completion. We should undertake crashing to reduce the project from 14 weeks to 12 weeks because the differential cost is $3,000 ($103,000 cost for 12 weeks − $100,000 normal cost for 14 weeks), which is less than the $10,000 penalty increase from $5,000 to $15,000. However, we cannot financially justify avoiding completely a penalty because it costs us $17,000 ($120,000 − $103,000) to reduce completion time from 12 weeks to 9 weeks. This $17,000 differential cost exceeds the $5,000 penalty we would save.

Variance Analysis and PERT-Cost (L.O. 2)

The PERT-Cost network may display expected and actual time and cost so managers can direct immediate attention to time slippage of the activities on the critical path. Comparison of actual time and costs with budgeted figures can reveal variances for each activity so management may direct corrective action. Penalties are also a factor in analyzing variances for each activity.

We illustrate variance analysis using the previous example in which we plan to crash activity 4-5 by 2 weeks to avoid the $15,000 penalty with total planned completion time of 12 weeks and a $5,000 penalty incurred. We assume project costs to occur evenly over time.

Assume activity 2-5, which is not on the critical path, requires seven weeks instead of the expected five weeks at a total actual cost of $5,500. Although this does not affect overall project completion time because this path had available slack, it does increase activity costs such as rental of plant facilities and labor costs. Assume management budgeted in advance that the differential cost of extending completion per week on activity 2-5 was $100. Assume further that the normal cost to complete activity 2-5 in five weeks was $5,000.

The variances for activity 2-5 are

Actual cost	$5,500
Normal cost	5,000
Net unfavorable variance	$ 500

This net unfavorable variance can be broken down into a **spending variance** and an **activity time variance** reflecting the cost of extending completion. The spending variance reflects price and quantity variances for direct material, direct labor, and overhead. We compute the spending variance similarly as using variable (flexible) budgeting. While the flexible budgeting approach, first presented in Chapter 9, adjusts for actual units produced or hours worked, the PERT-Cost budget adjusts for the time required to complete the activity. Activity 2-5's variances are

Unfavorable activity time variance (2 weeks × $100 cost of extending completion per week)	$200
Unfavorable spending variance ($5,500 actual cost − $5,200 which is $5,000 normal cost for five weeks + $200 additional cost for the extra two weeks)	300
Total unfavorable variance	$500

Assume instead that activity 4-5, which management planned to crash two weeks down to five weeks, required seven weeks at an actual cost of $21,000. These two weeks could not be made up elsewhere on the critical path so the overall project required 14 weeks which resulted in a $15,000 penalty. Assume that the normal cost for activity 4-5 was $20,000 with the differential cost of extending completion per week on this activity of $1,000. The following variances result:

Actual cost ($21,000 + $10,000 penalty increase)	$31,000
Normal cost adjusted for planned crashing [$20,000 + (2 × $1,500 weekly differential cost of crashing)]	23,000
Net unfavorable variance	$ 8,000

Three variances comprise the net unfavorable variance. By computing a **project time variance,** the activity manager is less likely to focus attention only on activity 4-5, but to recognize the impact of the delay on the overall project. Recognizing a project time variance discourages the tendency to suboptimize, which is choosing actions that are in one activity's best interest but not for the benefit of the overall project. The $8,000 net variance comprises the following:

Unfavorable project time variance which is the penalty increase	$10,000	
Unfavorable spending variance ($21,000 − $20,000 normal cost)	1,000	$11,000
Favorable activity time variance which is the differential cost to shorten two weeks that were saved (2 weeks × $1,500)		3,000
Net unfavorable variance		$ 8,000

The computation of a project time variance may also motivate activity managers to search for ways to speed up completion time especially if time has slipped on other activities. Assume instead that even though activity 4-5 required seven weeks instead of the crash time of five weeks, workers could make up the two weeks on activity 1-4. The normal cost of activity 1-4 for six weeks was $10,000 with the weekly differential cost of extending this activity, $2,000. Workers complete activity 1-4 in four weeks at a cost of $15,000. The variances for activity 4-5 are identical to those in the previous example; variances for activity 1-4 are

Normal cost	$10,000
Actual cost ($15,000 − $10,000 penalty increase saved)	5,000
Net favorable variance	$ 5,000

Favorable project time variance (the penalty increase)	$10,000	
Favorable spending variance [$15,000 actual cost − $18,000 normal cost adjusted for shortening two weeks which is $10,000 + (2 × $4,000 weekly differential cost to crash)] . . .	3,000	$13,000
Unfavorable activity time variance (the differential cost to crash two weeks: 2 × $4,000)		8,000
Net favorable variance		$ 5,000

This analysis shows that it cost $8,000 to shorten the activity 1-4 completion time, but the company saved the $10,000 penalty increase. This indicates we made a correct decision because the increased cost was more than offset by the penalty saved.

If there had been a time slippage on activities on separate critical paths and the overall project time had extended to 14 weeks, a $15,000 penalty would have been in effect. Under these conditions, we would allocate the $10,000 penalty increase between the activities failing to meet their budgeted time. While the accountant must use professional judgment in making the allocation, a general guideline is that the allocation should result in both an unfavorable project time and activity time variance for the activities having a time slippage.

Decision Tree Analysis (L.O. 3)

Another method with potential as a decision-making tool is **decision tree analysis.** Decision trees provide a systematic framework for analyzing a sequence of interrelated decisions the manager may make over time. This technique expresses decision making in a sequence of acts, events, and consequences under the assumption that the projects management considers today often have strong implications for future profitability. In turn, the relationship between the investment decision managers must make at present and the results of that decision in the future is complex. Stemming from the present investment decisions are alternative scenarios that depend on the occurrence of future events and the consequences of those events. Decision tree analysis encourages the study and understanding of these scenarios.

Advantages of Decision Tree Analysis

The decision tree can clarify for management the choices, risks, monetary gains, objectives, and information needs involved in an investment problem. In comparison with other analytical tools, a decision tree may be a more effective means of presenting the relevant information. Regardless of its size, a decision tree always combines action choices with different possible events or results of action that chance or other uncontrollable circumstances partially affect.

Managers should make today's decisions by considering the anticipated effect these decisions and the outcome uncertain events can have on future decisions and goals. Today's decisions affect tomorrow's decisions both directly and indirectly, and decision tree analysis allows management to focus on this relationship. Managers can use analytical techniques, such as discounted cash flow and present value methods, to obtain a better picture of the impact of future events and decision alternatives. Use of a decision tree permits management to consider various alternatives with greater ease and clarity. The interactions among present decision alternatives and uncertain events and their possible payoffs become clearer. Because decision trees present no new financial data, they do not show anything that management does not already know. The advantage is this concept presents data in a manner that enables systematic analysis and better decisions.

Weaknesses of Decision Tree Analysis

A decision tree does not give management the answer to an investment problem. Instead, it helps management determine which alternative yields the greatest expected monetary gain at any particular choice point, given the information and the alternatives important to the decision. A decision tree does not identify all possible events nor does it list all the decisions that must be made on a subject under analysis. The business environment does not restrict the number of possible choices to two or three. However, it is impossible to analyze all the implications of every act into the indefinite future and take them formally into account in selecting a decision strategy. We include only those decisions and events or results that are important to management and have consequences they wish to compare. With more than a small number of choices, decision tree analysis by hand becomes tedious and complicated. The use of computers is especially suitable when studying the effect of variations in figures and/or the events involved continue for some time. The interactions of such decisions with the objectives of other parts of the business organization would be too complicated to compute manually.

Decision tree analysis treats uncertain alternatives as if they were discrete, well-defined possibilities. For example, we often assume uncertain situations depend basically on a single variable, such as the level of demand or the success or failure of a development project. While cash flow may depend solely on demand in some situations, it may also depend on several independent or partially related variables subject to such chance influences as cost, demand, yield, and economic climate.

Requirements for Decision Tree Preparation

Making a decision tree requires the following steps, which this chapter illustrates later:

1. Identification of the points of decision and the alternatives available at each point.
2. Determination of the points of uncertainty and the type or range of alternative outcomes at each point.
3. Estimates of the probabilities of different events or results of actions.
4. Estimates of the costs and gains of various events and actions.
5. Analysis of the alternative values in choosing a course of action.

Investment problems like those in the following example are appropriate for the application of the decision tree. The management of Tucker Industries must decide whether to build a small plant or a large one to manufacture a new product with a market life of 12 years. The company's managers are uncertain about the size of the market for their product. The company grew rapidly between 1980 and 1987; however, the last few years have seen only small market gains.

If the market for this new product turns out to be large, present management will be able to push the company into a new period of profitable growth. Consequently, the Research and Development Department, particularly the development project engineer, argues that building a large plant will enable the company to exploit the first major product development the department has produced in several years. However, if the company builds a big plant, it must incur fixed costs with it whatever the market demand. If demand is low in the first years, the fixed costs of operating a large plant will result in unprofitable operations. A large plant costs $4.8 million, while a small plant costs $3.2 million with expansion costing an additional $2.4 million later.

The marketing manager supports the large plant because of fear that competitors will enter the market with equivalent products if Tucker is unable to fill the demand for the new product. Further, the marketing manager is confident that the company's sales personnel will be aggressive enough to promote the product sufficiently. Ideas for an exhaustive advertising campaign are already on the drawing board.

The controller is wary of large, unneeded plant capacity. This officer favors building a small plant and expanding it in two years if demand is high during the introductory period. However, the controller recognizes that later expansion to meet high-volume demand involves a total plant cost greater than the cost of a large plant built initially. In addition, a large plant is more efficient to operate than an expanded plant.

After consultation, top management arrives at the following marketing estimates:

	Initially	Long-term
Initially low demand and long-term high:	20%	60%
Initially high demand and continued high:	40%	
Initially low demand and continued low:	10%	40%
Initially high demand and long-term low:	30%	

Management estimates an initial high demand of 70 percent (40 + 30); if it is high initially, there is a 57 percent (40/70) conditional probability that demand will continue at a high level. Comparing 57 percent with 40 percent, a high initial sales level increases the estimated chance of high sales in later periods. On the other hand, there is a 30 percent (20 + 10) chance that sales will be low initially; the chances are 33 percent (10/30) that initial low sales will lead to low sales in the later period, and a 67 percent (20/30) chance that initial low sales will lead to high demand after the first two years. However, if Tucker experiences an initial low demand with a small plant, management has agreed there will be no expansion. Based on these projections, management estimates a 60 percent chance of a large market in the long run and a 40 percent chance of a low demand in the long run.

The accounting staff arrives at the following estimated cash flows:

1. Small plant:

   a. With expansion after two years and continuous high demand, annual $600,000 cash flow for the first two years and annual cash flows of $1 million thereafter would result.

   b. With expansion after two years and high demand not sustained, estimated annual cash flows of $280,000 from year three onward would result.

   c. With initially high and sustained demand and no expansion, $600,000 annual cash flows would be the yield for the first two years. Competition would cause this to drop to $480,000 in the long run when other companies are attracted by the high demand.

   d. With initially high demand and low long-term demand and no expansion, $600,000 annual cash flows for the first two years and $350,000 a year thereafter.

   e. With initially low demand and high long-term demand and no expansion, $350,000 annual cash flows for the first two years increasing to $480,000 per year thereafter.

    f. With a continuous low demand, annual net cash flows of $350,000 would be the yield.

2. Large plant:

    a. With an initially low demand and long-term high demand, $200,000 cash flows each for the first two years and $1.2 million annually thereafter since this large plant is more costly to operate than the small plant for the first 2 years, but more efficient to operate for the last 10 years than would be a small, expanded plant.

    b. With continuous high demand, $1.2 million annual cash flows would be the yield.

    c. With continuous low demand, only $200,000 annual cash flows because of high fixed costs and inefficiencies.

    d. With initially high but long-term low demand, $600,000 cash flow for each of the first two years and $200,000 for each of the next years.

The decision tree shown in Exhibit 26–4 incorporates the preceding data. This decision tree indicates the **action** or **decision points (forks)** by square nodes and the **chance event forks** by round ones. There is no single way to diagram a decision problem: rather than use squares and circles, we could place the terms *act* and *event* above or below the appropriate fork. However, all variations of the shape of the tree rarely change the order of the acts and events from left to right. While Tucker management knew all the information in Exhibit 26–4 before preparing the decision tree, its use leads to better decisions by encouraging executives to engage in a more systematic analysis. The decision tree shows management which decision today will contribute most to its long-term goals.

Roll-Back Concept (L.O. 4)

The next step in the analysis uses the **roll-back concept.** Briefly, the roll-back method involves: (1) proceeding from right to left on each terminal point, (2) finding the total expected value at every chance event, and (3) choosing that course of action with the highest expected value. At the time of deciding whether to build a large or small plant (Decision 1), management does not involve itself with Decision 2. Also, as in initially building a large plant, it may not even have to make a second decision. Exhibit 26–5 illustrates this analysis. Using the maximum expected total cash flow as the criterion, and rolling back to Decision 2, we see that the company would expand the plant *if* it had the option. The total expected value of the expansion alternative is $263,000 ($4,504,000 − $4,241,000) more than the no-expansion alternative over the 10-year life remaining. (We ignore discounting future profits now and introduce them later.)

Even though the present issue is how to make Decision 1, we start at Decision 2 using the roll-back concept. By putting a monetary value on Decision 2, management can compare the gain from building a small plant (the upper branch) to initially building a large plant (the lower branch). The $4,504,000 net expected value from expansion with Decision 2 is its **position value.** Thus, if you repeated Decision 2 again and again, you would expect annually to get a $1 million yield 57 percent of the time and a $280,000 yield 43 percent of the time. It is

EXHIBIT 26-4

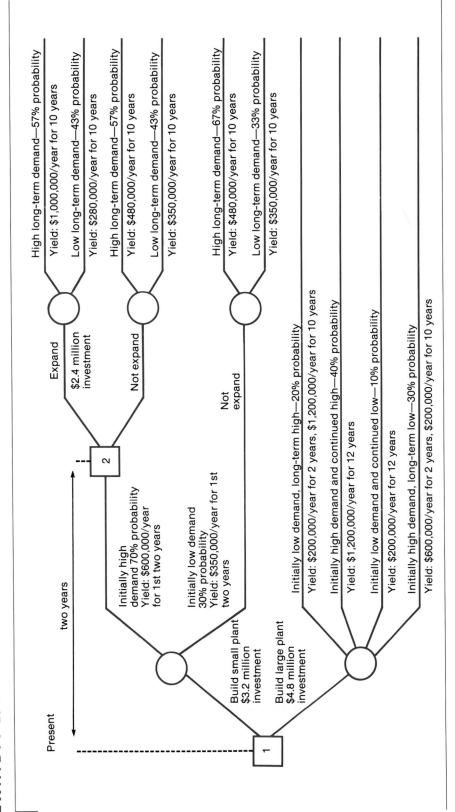

EXHIBIT 26–5　　Expected Value of Decision 2

Choice	Chance Event	(1) Probability	(2) Total Yield (10 Years)		(1) × (2) Expected Value
Expand	High long-term demand	.57	$10,000,000		$5,700,000
	Low long-term demand	.43	2,800,000		1,204,000
				Total	$6,904,000
				Less expansion cost	2,400,000
				Net	$4,504,000
Not expand	High long-term demand	.57	$ 4,800,000		$2,736,000
	Low long-term demand	.43	3,500,000		1,505,000
				Total	$4,241,000
				No expansion cost	–0–
				Net	$4,241,000

worth $4,504,000 for Tucker management to get to the position where it can make Decision 2. Given this value, management can ask, what is the best action at Decision 1?

Exhibit 26–6 compiles the cash flows for Decision 1. In the top half are the yields for a small plant, including the Decision 2 position value of $4,504,000 plus a $1.2 million yield for the two years before Decision 2. In the lower half are the yields for 12 years for various events if Tucker builds a large plant. These yields are the annual cash flow from Exhibit 26–4 multiplied by the appropriate number of years. We obtain the following comparison when we reduce these yields by their probabilities:

Build small plant:
$$(\$5,704,000 \times .70) + (\$5,500,000 \times .20) +$$
$$(\$4,200,000 \times .10) - \$3,200,000 = \$2,312,800$$
Build large plant:
$$(\$12,400,000 \times .20) + (\$14,400,000 \times .40) +$$
$$(\$2,400,000 \times .10) + (\$3,200,000 \times .30) - \$4,800,000 = \$4,640,000$$

The choice that maximizes expected total cash yield at Decision 1 is to build the large plant initially.

Discounted Expected Value of Decisions (L.O. 4)

Because the time between successive decision stages on a decision tree may be long, we must consider the time value of future earnings. We weight the differences in immediate cost or revenue against differences in value at the next stage. We can place the two alternatives on a Decision 2 basis if the value assigned to the next stage is discounted by an appropriate percentage. This is similar to the

EXHIBIT 26-6

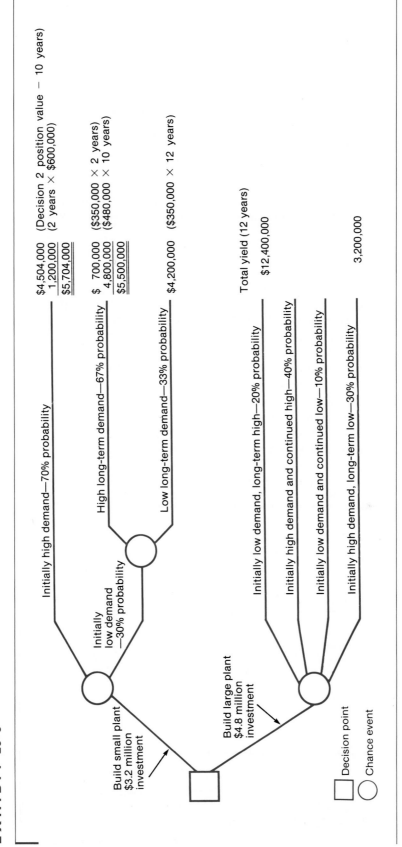

Build small plant
$3.2 million
investment

Build large plant
$4.8 million
investment

Initially high demand—70% probability

Initially
low demand
—30% probability

High long-term demand—67% probability

Low long-term demand—33% probability

Initially low demand, long-term high—20% probability

Initially high demand and continued high—40% probability

Initially low demand and continued low—10% probability

Initially high demand, long-term low—30% probability

$4,504,000   (Decision 2 position value — 10 years)
 1,200,000   (2 years × $600,000)
$5,704,000

$ 700,000   ($350,000 × 2 years)
 4,800,000   ($480,000 × 10 years)
$5,500,000

$4,200,000   ($350,000 × 12 years)

Total yield (12 years)

$12,400,000

3,200,000

☐ Decision point
◯ Chance event

EXHIBIT 26–7   Decision 2 with Discounting

	Yield	Present Value
Expand—High demand	$1,000,000/year for 10 years	$5,650,000 ($1,000,000 × 5.65)
Expand—Low demand	$ 280,000/year for 10 years	$1,582,000 ($280,000 × 5.65)
Not expand—High demand	$ 480,000/year for 10 years	$2,712,000 ($480,000 × 5.65)
Not expand—Low demand	$ 350,000/year for 10 years	$1,977,500 ($350,000 × 5.65)

use of a discount rate in the present value or discounted cash flow techniques and makes allowance for the cost of capital. We discount both cash flows and position value.

Accounting for Time

Using a 12 percent discount rate applied to the cash flows from Exhibit 26–4, we can obtain Exhibit 26–7 data. When considering the time value of money, we first prepare the decision tree as in Exhibit 26–4; Exhibit 26–7 is the next step. (There is no need to prepare the analysis illustrated earlier in Exhibits 26–5 and 26–6.) We discount the cash flow for all 10 years, including the first year's cash flow. The figures in the present value column represent the present value at the time of making Decision 2, not at the time of making Decision 1. (Remember that if a large plant is built initially, there is no Decision 2.)

Exhibit 26–8 uses the same approach as previously illustrated in Exhibit 26–5; however, we now use discounted yield figures to arrive at a **discounted expected value.** Since the discounted expected value of the no-expansion alternative is higher, the $2,396,165 becomes the position value of Decision 2.

We repeat the same analytical procedure used previously for Decision 1 in Exhibit 26–9; however, now we incorporate discounting. We treat the Decision 2

EXHIBIT 26–8   Discounted Expected Value of Decision 2

Choice	Chance Event	(1) Probability	(2) Present Value Yield		(1) × (2) Discounted Expected Value
Expand	High long-term demand	.57	$5,650,000		$3,220,500
	Low long-term demand	.43	1,582,000		680,260
				Total	$3,900,760
				Less expansion cost	2,400,000
				Net	$1,500,760
Not expand	High long-term demand	.57	$2,712,000		$1,545,840
	Low long-term demand	.43	1,977,500		850,325
				Total	$2,396,165
				No expansion cost	–0–
				Net	$2,396,165

EXHIBIT 26–9 Decision I Analysis

Choice	Chance Event	(1) Probability	Yield		(2) Discounted Value of Yield	(1) × (2) Discounted Expected Yield
Build small plant	Initially high demand	.70	$600,000/year, 2 years	$1,014,000	($600,000 × 1.690)	$2,046,621
			Decision 2 value: $2,396,165 at end of 2 years	1,909,744	($2,396,165 × .797)	
				$2,923,744		
	Initially low demand, high long-term	.20	$350,000/year, 2 years	$ 591,500	($350,000 × 1.690)	550,684
			$480,000/year, 10 years	2,161,920	[$480,000 × (6.194 − 1.690)]	
				$2,753,420		
	Continuous low demand	.10	$350,000/year, 12 years	$2,167,900	($350,000 × 6.194)	216,790
					Total	$2,814,095
					Less investment	3,200,000
					Net	$ (385,905)
Build large plant	Initially low demand, high long-term	.20	$200,000/year, 2 years	$ 338,000	($200,000 × 1.690)	$1,148,560
			$1,200,000/year, 10 years	5,404,800	[$1,200,000 × (6.194 − 1.690)]	
				$5,742,800		
	Continuous high demand	.40	$1,200,000/year, 12 years	$7,432,800	($1,200,000 × 6.194)	2,973,120
	Continuous low demand	.10	$200,000/year, 12 years	$1,238,800	($200,000 × 6.194)	123,880
	Initially high demand, low long-term	.30	$600,000/year, 2 years	$1,014,000	($600,000 × 1.690)	574,440
			$200,000/year, 10 years	900,800	[$200,000 × (6.194 − 1.690)]	
				$1,914,800		
					Total	$4,820,000
					Less investment	4,800,000
					Net	$ 20,000

position value of $2,396,165 at the time of Decision 1 as if it were a lump sum received at the end of the two years. Note that the discount rate of 0.797 comes from Table A, present value of $1 for two years, at a 12 percent rate, shown in the Appendix to this book. Again, we assume a 12 percent discount rate with the cash flow for all years discounted, including the first year's cash flow. We discount cash flows for years 3 through 12 to the present by a factor derived by subtracting 1.690, the factor for 12 percent, 2 years, in Table B in the Appendix from 6.194, the factor for 12 percent, 12 years, in Table B. The large-plant alternative is again the preferred decision based on the discounted expected cash flow. The margin of difference of $405,905 ($20,000 + $385,905) is smaller than the $2,327,200 ($4,640,000 − $2,312,800) obtained without discounting.

Other Factors to Consider

We must consider the expected monetary gains along with the risks. Because managers have different viewpoints toward risk, they draw different conclusions about the various alternatives. The controller will likely see the uncertainty surrounding the decision in a much different light than will the marketing manager or the development project engineer. A major investment might also pose risk to an individual's job and career. While one individual may stand to gain much from a project's success and lose little from its failure, others in the company may be risking much if a project fails. The types of risks and how individuals regard them from a personal viewpoint affect not only the assumptions they make but also the strategy they follow in handling risks.

Top management should jointly consider the political environment when selecting plant size. They should ask what risks and prospects are at stake. Is it a possible bankruptcy or an opportunity for large profit increases and job stability? Is it a major career opportunity? The individuals who bear the risks—whether employees, stockholders, managers, or the community—and the numbers affected, assume significance. In addition, the character of the risk that each person bears merits evaluation. How disastrous would a failure be to individuals as well as to the company and the community's economy? Whether the risk is once in a lifetime, insurable, or unique is important. The decision tree does not eliminate these risks; however, it shows management what decision makes the largest contribution to long-term goals.

Summary

This chapter presents several techniques and analyses that prove helpful in planning complex projects and in investment analysis. Gantt charts are a simple control technique that compares scheduled and actual production. However, Gantt charts are inadequate for sophisticated projects requiring an understanding of what tasks to complete before beginning others. Network models, such as PERT, show interrelationships among activities. Use of a PERT network determines a project's critical path so managers can prevent delaying overall completion time. Paths that are not critical have slack and thus provide some flexibility for managers. Slack time also serves as a guide in rescheduling tasks to shorten the project's overall completion time. Managers use PERT-Cost analysis in deciding whether crashing the project is economically feasible.

Decision tree analysis clarifies choices and risks and the related profits of long-term investment alternatives. Because decision trees present financial data in a systematic manner, the relationships and consequences of present decision alternatives and uncertain events and their possible payoffs become clearer. Certainly, decision tree analysis does not provide the single, accurate solution to an investment decision. Instead, the objective is to assist managers in assessing which alternative at any particular choice point yields the greatest expected monetary gain given the information available and alternatives to the decision. In using decision tree analysis, we recognize that we must consider the expected monetary gains along with the risks. Further, we realize that members of the management team view these risks differently. Unless we recognize these differences initially, those who must assist in making the decision by supplying data and analyses, and those who are operating the plant and promoting the product, will view the decision in conflicting ways. The criteria for success may be vastly different.

Important Terms and Concepts

Problem for Self-Study

Critical Path and Slack Time

Rim Company's management provides the following activities and their related expected completion times in building a complex missile:

Activity	Expected Completion Time (In Months)
0-1	2
1-2	3
1-3	4
1-4	4
2-3	2
3-5	3
4-6	9
5-6	1

Required:

a. Develop a PERT network for the listed activities.
b. Identify the critical path.
c. Indicate on the PERT network the earliest completion time and the latest completion time.
d. Determine how many days the following events can be delayed without extending the time of the overall project:
   (1) Event 4.
   (2) Event 5.

Solution to Problem for Self-Study

RIM COMPANY

a. and c.

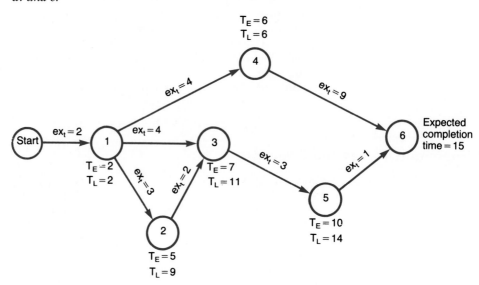

b.

Paths	Cumulative Expected Time (In Months)
0-1-4-6	2 + 4 + 9 = 15*
0-1-3-5-6	2 + 4 + 1† + 3 + 1 = 11
0-1-2-3-5-6	2 + 3 + 2 + 3 + 1 = 11

*Critical path.
†Time lag at Event 3.

d. (1) Slack on Event 4 = None since this is the critical path.
   (2) Slack on Event 5 = 4.

Review Questions

1. Identify two ways that PERT is superior to Gantt chart techniques for complex projects.

2. Discuss how PERT can be used in planning a complex project.

3. Should management analyze time slippage on all activities?

4. Define the term *critical path* and explain why it is considered critical.

5. What is slack and how can management utilize it?

6. *a.* What is the purpose of decision tree analysis?
   b. List three advantages and three weaknesses of decision tree analysis.

7. Discuss some of the factors that must be considered in decision making that decision tree analysis does not incorporate.

8. What is meant by crashing the network and what is the differential crash cost of an activity?

9. What is the advantage of holding an activity manager responsible for a project time variance?

10. If an activity has a favorable spending variance, what does this indicate?

11. How can the time value of future earnings be used in decision tree analysis?

12. Define the roll-back concept; discuss how it is used in decision tree analysis.

CPA/CMA/CIA Multiple Choice Questions

1. (CIA) The legal department of a firm prepared the decision tree below for a possible patent infringement suit.

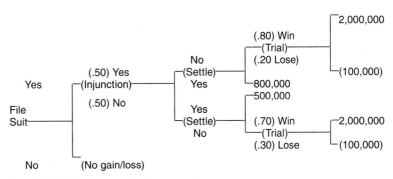

   Based on the decision tree, the firm should

   a. Not file the suit.
   b. File suit; settle if injunction granted.
   c. File suit; settle if injunction not granted.
   d. Carry suit to trial.

2. (CMA) The use of a decision tree is appropriate for decision making under conditions of

   a. Uncertainty and risk.
   b. Uncertainty and subjective likelihoods.
   c. Uncertainty and objective likelihoods.
   d. Certainty.
   e. Risk.

3. (CIA) Which of the following would appear on a PERT network diagram but not on a Gantt or bar chart?

   a. The critical path.
   b. Each activity in the project.
   c. Project completion time.
   d. Slack time.

4. (CMA) AceCo has completed the following PERT-Time diagram for a project. The number between nodules is the expected time required to complete the task before the next nodule can be started.

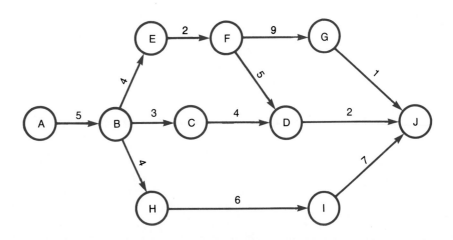

The length of the critical path for this project is

   a. 21.
   b. 14.
   c. 52.
   d. 18.
   e. Some amount other than those given above.

5. (CIA) The decision tree for an oil company preparing to test drill at a new site is shown below. Event probabilities are shown in parentheses; payoffs (in $ million) are shown in brackets.

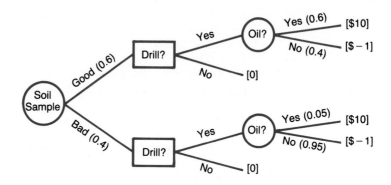

Given that the soil sample could misrepresent the possibility for oil production, the expected payoff for this tree is:

   a. $3.18 (million).
   b. $4.5 (million).
   c. $9 (million).
   d. $10 (million).

6. (CIA) The following diagram represents various project activities and the sequencing requirement in days. Define the critical path.

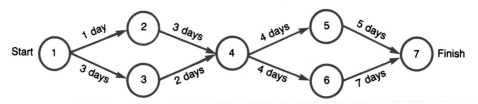

   a. Path 1-2-4-5-7.
   b. Path 1-2-4-6-7.
   c. Path 1-3-4-5-7.
   d. Path 1-3-4-6-7.

7. (CIA) When using the critical path method, which of the following best describes the effect of a delay along the critical path?

   a. The delay affects only a single event.
   b. Activities not on the critical path are unaffected.
   c. The total time along the critical path is increased by the amount of the delay.
   d. The slack time of the single event following the delay is reduced by the amount of the delay.

8. (CIA) The Gantt chart below shows that the project is

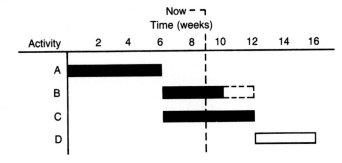

a. Complete.
b. Ahead of schedule.
c. On schedule.
d. Behind schedule.

9. (CMA) Program evaluation and review technique (PERT) is used on many projects to estimate project completion time. Assume that the following two-activity network exists for a project.

Activity	Mean Time	Variance of Time
A-B . . .	11 days	6 days
B-C . . .	7 days	3 days

Assume that total time is normally distributed and $P(\pm 1.96Z) = 95\%$, $P(\pm 1.65Z) = 90\%$, $P(\pm 1.00Z) = 68\%$.

The probability that the project will be completed in 21 days is

a. 0.84.
b. 0.34.
c. 0.67.
d. 0.95.
e. Some probability other than those given above.

10. (AICPA) Gandy Company is considering a proposal to introduce a new product, RLX. An outside marketing consultant prepared the following payoff probability distribution describing the relative likelihood of monthly sales volume levels and related income (loss) for RLX:

Monthly Sales Volume	Probability	Income (Loss)
6,000	.10	$ (70,000)
12,000	.20	10,000
18,000	.40	60,000
24,000	.20	100,000
30,000	.10	140,000

The expected value of the monthly income from RLX is

a. $ 48,000.
b. $ 53,000.
c. $ 60,000.
d. $240,000.

11. (AICPA) In a program evaluation review technique (PERT) system, activities along the critical path

a. Follow the line of best fit.
b. Have a slack of zero.
c. Have a positive slack.
d. Intersect at a corner point described by the feasible area.

Exercises

E26–1 Analyzing Progress on PERT-Cost Network (L.O. 1)

The cost accounting staff at Vermont, Inc., has prepared the following PERT-Cost network with expected time (ex_t) noted for all activities. The actual time (ac_t) for the three activities completed is also noted on the network. The budgeted (*Bud*) cost for each activity and the actual (*Act*) cost incurred is indicated for the completed activities. Actual time and cost incurred are shown for activities 2-6 and 3-5 that are partially completed.

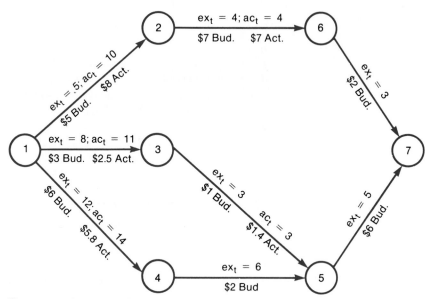

Time expressed in weeks, dollars in millions.

Required:

a. Determine the critical path, indicating the time for all paths.
b. Compute the budgeted cost of completing the project.
c. Indicate which activities need management's immediate attention and why this attention is needed.

E26–2 Gantt Charts (L.O. 1)

Metalworks, Inc., received four orders for specially designed gears. Each gear must go through two departments in sequence, Hobbing and Machining. The supervisors estimated the time required for each order. Expressed in days, these times are

	Orders			
	1	2	3	4
Hobbing	4	7	5	8
Machining	3	2	5	9

There is no backlog in the departments on orders in process. To minimize time in departments, select the shortest times for orders in both departments. Then schedule first the order requiring the least amount of hobbing time. Schedule last the order requiring the least amount of machining time. Repeat this rule for each sequence until all orders are sequenced.

Required:

a. Develop a Gantt chart for the four orders. Move each order from one department to the next minimizing the total time required to complete all orders.

b. Determine how long it will take to complete work on all four orders.

E26–3 Critical Path and Slack (L.O. 1)

Ace Construction Company developed the following network for building complex equipment. Your assistance in using the program evaluation review technique is required.

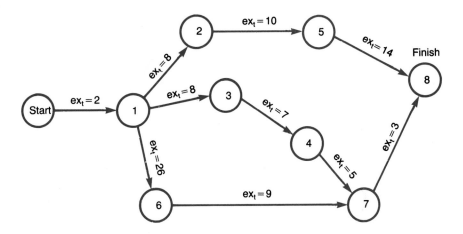

Required:

a. Determine the critical path.

b. Determine the latest time for reaching Event 4.

c. Assume all other paths operate on schedule but path segment 4-7 has an unfavorable time variance of 10. What is the effect on the critical path?

d. Compute the earliest time for reaching event 5 via path 0-1-2-5.

E26–4 PERT-Time Network and Expected Completion Time (L.O. 1)

Mason, Inc.'s project requires the following sequence of activities:

$$0\text{-}1, \ 1\text{-}2, \ 1\text{-}3, \ 1\text{-}4, \ 2\text{-}5, \ 3\text{-}5, \ 4\text{-}7, \ 5\text{-}6, \ 5\text{-}8, \ 6\text{-}7, \ 7\text{-}8$$

Required:

a. Draw a PERT-Time network for these activities.

b. Identify the paths on this network.

c. Determine the expected completion time for a limited number of these events as follows:

Activity	Optimistic	Most Likely	Pessimistic
0-1	2	4	9
1-2	1	3	5
1-3	2	3	7
1-4	4	6	11

E26–5 Determine Critical Path, Slack Time (L.O. 2)

Lens Construction, Inc. has contracted to complete a complex machine and has asked for assistance in analyzing the project. Using the Program Evaluation Review Technique, the following network has been developed:

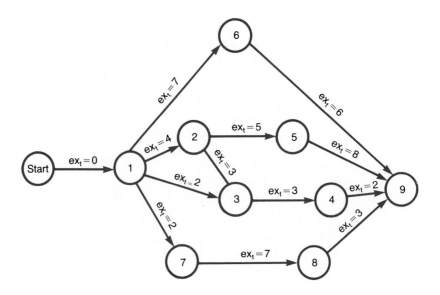

Required:

a. Identify the paths and indicate the critical path.
b. Determine the earliest time for reaching Event 9 via path 1-7-8-9.
c. Determine the latest time for reaching Event 9 via path 1-6-9.
d. Assume all other paths operate on schedule but path segment 1-6 has an unfavorable time variance of two. What is the effect on the critical path?
e. Define slack time.
f. Identify the latest time for leaving Event 6.

E26–6 Developing PERT Network with T_E and T_L (L.O. 1)

Cabincraft, Inc., management is making plans for a complex missile and will need the following activities. The expected completion time for each of these activities is:

Activity	Estimated Completion Time in Weeks
0-1	2
1-2	4
1-3	3
1-4	7
2-5	6
3-5	8
4-6	2
5-6	3
6-7	4
6-8	5
7-8	5

Required:

a. Develop a PERT network for these activities indicating the earliest completion time and the latest completion time.
b. Identify the critical path(s).

E26–7 PERT Network and Critical Path (L.O. 1)

In building a PERT-Time network, management of Markhaum, Inc., listed the events to finish the projects. They next arrived at the following activities leading to these events:

	Time Estimates in Weeks		
Activity	**Optimistic**	**Most Likely**	**Pessimistic**
0-1	3.0	3.5	7.0
1-2	4.0	6.0	8.0
1-3	0.8	1.9	3.6
1-4	2.0	2.5	6.0
2-3	0.3	4.5	5.7
3-5	0.8	1.8	4.0
4-6	1.8	4.6	9.8
5-6	0.2	1.0	1.8

Required:

a. Construct the PERT network.
b. Determine the expected completion times for all activities.
c. Determine the critical path.

Problems

P26–8 Crashing from a Prepared PERT-Cost Network (L.O. 1)

P. McMickle hires engineers to work closely with their management accountants in preparing PERT-Cost analyses. From their experience, they have determined they require the following activities displayed on the PERT network for construction of a machine. Along with each activity is its estimated normal time (ex_t), the crash time for each activity (cr_t), and the related additional cost required to meet the crash time expressed per week. The normal cost is $10,000.

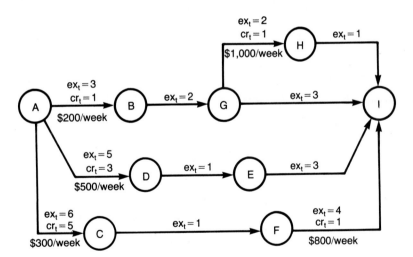

Required:

a. Identify all paths and the time involved on each path; determine the critical path.
b. Determine the minimum time in which the machine could be installed, and the costs incurred to achieve this earlier installation.

P26–9 Determining Expected Activity Time for PERT Network (L.O. 1)

Dormitory, Inc., provides the following data regarding a large construction project:

Estimates of Expected Completion Time Expressed in Weeks

Activities	Optimistic	Most Likely	Pessimistic
0-1	7	8	15
1-2	4	6	8
1-3	2	3	10
1-5	1	2	9
2-4	3	4	11
3-7	7	8	21
5-6	6	7	14
4-7	1	2	3
4-8	4	5	18
6-8	1	2	9
7-8	3	4	5

Required:

a. Determine the expected time for each activity.
b. Draw a PERT-Time network for the listed activities showing the earliest time (T_E) and the latest time (T_L) for each event.
c. Identify the paths indicating the critical one(s).

P26–10 PERT-Cost with Variance Analysis (L.O. 2)

Jenkins Company is the general contractor for a missile project, and management estimated the time to complete each activity under normal conditions. In their planning, they studied the extra cost of an activity exceeding its normal time, which would require additional equipment rental, salaries, and plant usage. Also in their analysis, they forecasted the cost and time required if any activity was crashed. The following data are a result of this study:

Activity	Expected Time in Weeks	Crash Time in Weeks	Normal Cost	Differential Cost to Shorten Each Week	Additional Cost of Extending Completion by One Week
Start-1 . .	3	—	$ 400	—	—
1-2	5	4	360	$ 800	$700
1-3	5	4	280	225	400
2-4	5	4	200	300	150
2-5	4	3	3,150	1,000	600
3-5	8	5	1,120	250	100
4-6	5	4	300	400	180
5-6	4	3	450	200	120

Jenkins Company agreed in the contract with the defense agency to a penalty clause stating that if the missile was completed within 17 weeks, there would be no penalty; if within 18 weeks, Jenkins would pay $400 penalty; if within 19 weeks, a penalty of $1,000; and if within 20 weeks, a penalty of $1,800. Project costs are assumed to occur evenly over time.

Required:

a. Prepare a PERT network analysis showing the expected and crash times and the differential cost per week.
b. Determine the critical path.
c. Calculate by how much time the company should shorten the project to save all or part of the penalty. Show calculations to support your answer.

   Consider situations d *through* f *independently assuming management planned to crash the project for a planned completion of 18 weeks.*

d. Indicate the variances involved if activity 2-5 is completed within six weeks at a cost of $4,600. Assume management did not plan to crash activity 2-5.
e. Assume management planned to crash activity 5-6 one week to avoid an additional penalty, but that it fails to complete the activity in the three weeks and, instead,

requires four weeks for an actual cost of $420. Also assume that this lost week cannot be made up on other activities along the critical path. What are the variances involved?

f. (1) Assume that even though management planned to crash activity 1-3 one week, they were unable to achieve this objective, and activity 1-3 was completed in five weeks at a cost of $360. However, the week lost is regained through speeding up completion of activity 3-5 to seven weeks, at an actual cost of $1,400. What are the variances for activity 1-3 and activity 3-5?

(2) Explain if it was profitable to speed up completion of activity 3-5 under these circumstances.

P26–11 Adjusting Cash Flow for Time Value of Money (L.O. 4)

Spece, Inc., presently sells a line of hand tools. Production has been fairly even over the last several years with competition increasing. Many of Spece's competitors have expanded their line of tools, but Spece has continued with its present style and variety.

However, management is worrying that it may need to upgrade its product line, either now or in three years. At the end of three years, if no upgrading is performed presently, management must again face this decision. The cost of upgrading the product line is forecasted to be $15,000 regardless of when it occurs.

A team of marketing experts has analyzed short-run and long-run market conditions and worked with the accountants to arrive at expected cash yields for the next eight years. After much study, the team initially believes that there are two alternatives:

1. Do not upgrade the product line now: There is a 20 percent probability for an initial successful market environment for the next three years; the annual cash flow for the next three years under these circumstances would be $4,000. If, however, conditions are not favorable, an unsuccessful market will yield an annual cash flow for the next eight years of $2,000, since if the initial market environment is unsuccessful, they will not upgrade their product line.

    If the initial market is successful, management can either:

    a. Upgrade the product line. There is a 40 percent probability of a successful market with cash flows of $10,000 annually for five years. If the market is unsuccessful, annual cash flows are expected to be $2,000 for the five years.

    b. Not upgrade the product line: There is a 30 percent probability of a successful market with cash flows of $6,000 annually for five years. If instead, an unsuccessful market exists, annual cash flow is predicted to be $1,000 for the five years.

2. Upgrade the product line now: If the market is successful, in both the short run and the long run (a 40 percent probability), a $14,000 annual cash flow for the eight years under study is expected. With an unsuccessful market, $3,000 is the forecasted annual cash flow for the eight years.

Required:

a. Draw a decision tree; adjust the cash flows for the time value of money using a discount rate of 10 percent.

b. Indicate the course of action you would advise.

P26–12 Short-Run Decision Tree Analysis (L.O. 3)

Wheat, Inc., a large chemical manufacturer, has been selling a plastic material known as Romac to industrial users for several years. Presently, Wheat has 35 percent of the market; two other large competitors have captured the remainder. Romac is basically a modification of another plastic material, Cocmel; however, Romac's characteristics make it superior in many respects, even though Romac's price averages $1.50 per pound higher. Wheat, Inc.'s initial tests of Romac showed that waste could be reduced significantly with the use of Romac rather than Cocmel. Recently, however, several university studies reveal that this claim is unfounded. In view of the publicity given these independent studies, Wheat management is concerned about whether its present $5 price per pound can be maintained. Marketing research indicates that an appropriate strategy is to attempt to capture more of the Cocmel market by emphasizing the flexibility of Romac and giving less attention to possible waste reduction. Attempts are also being made to find other plastic materials for which Romac can be used as a substitute. After careful study, four possible pricing alternatives are suggested:

1. Reduce price of Romac to $4 per pound.
2. Reduce price to $4.50.
3. Maintain price at $5; Wheat expects to sell 42,000 pounds of Romac at this level.
5. Raise price to $5.20 and attempt product differentiation; Wheat expects to sell 30,000 pounds of Romac at this level.

In view of the oligopoly market environment, any reduction in price will be matched by competitors. However, if Wheat raises its price to $5.20 or maintains its present $5 price, its two competitors probably will not follow and Wheat will lose some of the Romac market unless it is able to establish more product differentiation.

If Wheat lowers Romac's price to $4, there is a 60 percent probability that competitors will charge $4; a 30 percent chance they will charge $4.50; and a 10 percent chance they will continue to charge $5.

If, instead, Wheat lowers Romac's price to $4.50, there is a 15 percent probability that competitors will charge $4; a 50 percent chance they will charge $4.50; and a 35 percent chance they will continue to charge $5. If Wheat lowers Romac's price to $4 or $4.50 and Romac competitors continue to charge $5, 70,000 pounds are expected to be sold per year.

Price retaliation by Cocmel producers is expected if Wheat and its Romac competitors reduce Romac's price. If Wheat charges $4 or $4.50 for Romac and its competitors charge $4, there is a 40 percent probability that Cocmel producers will charge $2.50. Wheat's sales of Romac are then expected to be 45,000 annually. A 35 percent probability exists that Cocmel producers will charge $3.25; at this level, Wheat expects Romac sales of 48,000. There is a 25 percent chance that a $3.50 price will continue to be charged by Cocmel producers. Wheat's annual sales are expected to be 58,000 at this level.

If Wheat charges $4 or $4.50 for Romac and its competitors charge $4.50 for Romac, there is a 20 percent probability Cocmel producers will charge $2.50 for Cocmel; Wheat's sales of Romac are expected to be 50,000 annually. A 50 percent probability exists that Cocmel producers will charge $3.25, and Wheat's annual sales of Romac will be 55,000 at this level. Finally, there is a 30 percent chance Cocmel producers will continue to charge $3.50; Wheat's annual sales of Romac are expected to be 60,000 pounds at this level.

For simplicity, assume a $3 variable cash cost per pound and cash annual fixed costs of $50,000 at all anticipated sales volumes.

Regardless of the pricing arrangement chosen, the market for Romac is not expected to be stable beyond two years.

Required:

Prepare decision tree analysis using estimated cash flow for two years to determine the preferred pricing strategy. Indicate the expected value for two years and the preferred strategy.

P26–13 PERT-Cost with Variance Analysis and Crashing Limitations (L.O. 2)

In planning for the construction of a project, Houston, Inc., also estimates the cost if an activity exceeds its normal time as well as the feasibility of crashing an activity. The following results of this study indicate that some activities cannot be crashed while other activities must be crashed in their entirety rather than partially.

Activity	Expected Time in Weeks	Crash Time in Weeks	Normal Cost	Differential Cost to Shorten Each Week	Additional Cost of Extending Completion by One Week
A-B ...	7	2*	4,000	500	400
A-C ...	6	1	900	100	150
A-D ...	3	1	1,800	400	100
B-E ...	8	—	1,000	?	200
C-E ...	4	3*	750	800	100
D-G ...	4	1	600	200	300
E-F ...	2	—	400	—	500
F-H ...	6	—	500	—	300
G-H ...	4	3	200	50	80

*Cannot be partially crashed.

Management agrees to pay the buyer a $4,000 penalty if the project is completed in 23 weeks; a $2,000 penalty if within 20 weeks; and no penalty if completion occurs within 16 weeks. Project costs are assumed to occur evenly over time.

Required:

a. Prepare a PERT network analysis showing the expected and crash times and the differential cost per week.
b. Determine the critical path.
c. Show calculations to support your decision as to how much time the project should be crashed to save all or part of the penalty.
d. Assume that activity A-D requires 6 weeks at a cost of $2,600. Determine the variances.

P26–14 Decison Tree: Expected Value of Perfect Information (L.O. 3)

Janet Humphreys, Inc., manufactures and sells nationally a carbonated soft drink. A strong market has recently been slacking off, and management credits this slump to the increasing popularity of diet sodas. Janet Humphreys, Inc., has not entered the diet drink market but is in the process of developing a low-calorie version of its cola.

Marketing personnel have been considering potential strategies. If the diet cola is introduced nationally, a large amount of money and many hours of effort will be required for a full, nationwide advertising and distribution campaign. Since Janet Humphreys, Inc., will be entering the market later than its competitors, additional promotion will be required; in addition, there is some risk in a nationwide introduction because of Humphrey's later market entrance. After assessing the market, management arrives at two reasonable alternative strategies:

1. Immediately introduce the diet drink nationwide without a test campaign. Humphreys will decide whether to stop production of the diet drink 18 months later.
2. Limit the introduction to a 10-state area. Based on the result of this test campaign, Humphreys will decide whether to introduce the low-calorie drink nationally.

If $50 million in revenues are generated in the 18-month period, management will consider the national introduction a success. If revenues are $20 million or less for the period, management will consider the campaign unsuccessful. Variable expenses are expected to be 70 percent of sales. Fixed expenses are expected to total $8 million for the period regardless of the result of the campaign. Management estimates there is a 40 percent chance of Strategy 1 being successful.

There is the possibility that the test results will indicate that Janet Humphreys, Inc., should conduct a nationwide promotion and distribution campaign, when, in fact, a nationwide campaign will be unsuccessful. Conversely, the test result may indicate that Humphreys should not conduct a nationwide promotion and distribution campaign when, in fact, a nationwide campaign will be successful.

Required:

a. Prepare a decision tree identifying all alternatives and possible outcomes.

b. Determine the expected monetary value of the first strategy.

c. Assuming the test campaign can perfectly predict whether or not a nationwide campaign will be successful, use expected monetary value as the decision criterion to calculate the maximum dollar amount Humphreys should be willing to pay for perfect information.

d. Identify and discuss at least three criticisms of using the expected monetary value criterion for decision problems.

P26–15 Short-Run Decision Tree Analysis (L.O. 3)

After a period of intense competition, Key, Inc., has won a contract to produce a new motor suitable for military equipment. The contract specifies the purchase of 50,000 motors per year at $50 each for a period of two years and allows Key to subcontract production. The company is uncertain whether the contract will be renewed after the second year; thus, the company has no guarantee of revenue from this type motor after the second year. There is a possibility of a commercial market developing, but it is so uncertain that management believes it should not presently consider this market at all.

For this reason, Key, Inc., does not believe that a viable alternative is to expand present facilities. This decision was strongly influenced by the fact that there is some idle capacity now as well as decreasing sales of its commercial No. 12 motor. After careful study, management arrives at the following four alternatives:

1. Rent plant facilities within the community and run production on one shift. Management believes it has a 40 percent chance of being able to rent a vacant factory. If this space can be occupied, annual cash cost is expected to be $1.6 million. If, instead, a one-story building is renovated, annual cash cost is expected to be $1.8 million. A 25 percent probability exists for Key's being able to lease this. Finally, a 35 percent probability exists for Key to lease a two-story building. The arrangement of this building is not as desirable thus causing increased costs of handling; annual cash cost is expected to be $2.1 million for the building. These three potential sites are presently under lease; but Key, Inc., lawyers have contacted the owners, and each has expressed an interest in possible subleasing.

2. Employ a third shift using present facilities. Annual cash cost is estimated to be $1.7 million.

3. Subcontract the manufacture of parts and establish a simple assembly line. The costs associated with this strategy depend on the future demand of the commercial No. 12 motors. If demand increases (20 percent probability), there will be no idle capacity for production of military motors, and the entire production of the military motors must be subcontracted. Annual cash cost of both the subcontracting and the assembly is expected to be $1.5 million. If the No. 12 motor's market remains steady (a 30 percent probability), some departments can be relocated within existing plant facilities, thus allowing space for the military motor assembly. Annual cash cost associated with this alternative is estimated to be $1.61 million. If the market declines (estimated 50 percent probability), space will not be a problem. Considering all factors, the annual cash cost is expected to be $1.78 million.

4. Halt production of No. 12 commercial motors and keep two labor shifts. The workers and machines presently producing No. 12 motors could be easily switched to the production of the military motors. Total annual cash cost is expected to be $1.87 million.

Required:

Prepare decision tree analysis using estimated cash flow for two years to determine the preferred alternative. Indicate the expected value for two years and the preferred alternative.

P26–16 PERT Network and Slack Time (L.O. 1)

In planning the activities necessary to construct a large building, Utah Company arrived at the following activities and expected completion times:

Activity	Expected Completion Time (In Weeks)
0-1	1
1-2	2
1-3	2
1-4	7
2-3	1
3-5	8
3-6	12
4-5	10
5-7	13
6-7	6

Required:

a. Develop a PERT network for the listed activities.
b. Identify the critical path.
c. Indicate on the PERT network the earliest completion time and the latest completion time.
d. Determine the slack time on Path 0-1-4-5-7.

P26–17 PERT-Cost Analysis (Continuation of P26–16) (L.O. 1)

The management of Utah Company, mentioned in P26–16, has determined that some of the activities can be crashed. The crash time in weeks and the related total differential cost to achieve the crash program follow. The cost of the project following the normal schedule is $600,000.

Activity	Crash Time	Total Differential Cost
0-1	NC	—
1-2	1	$ 1,000
1-3	NC	—
1-4	1	24,000
2-3	NC	—
3-5	5	15,000
3-6	8	16,000
4-5	8	24,000
5-7	NC	—
6-7	2	1,000

NC = No change in time or cost is possible.

Required:

a. Prepare a PERT network showing (or insert in the network prepared in P26–16) the expected and crash time and the differential cost per week.
b. Indicate the minimum time in which the project could be completed and the costs incurred to achieve this earlier opening.
c. Compute the minimum additional contribution to profits needed to justify completing the project early.

P26–18 Weaknesses of Decision Tree: Adjusting Cash Flow for Time Value of Money (L.O. 3)

As a consultant for Yale Company, you have been asked to assist in its decision regarding the optimal size of plant facilities expansion. In talking with you, members of top management, who are all in their 50s and 60s, are quick to emphasize that they want some conventional decision tools used to answer this investment problem rather than some "cute, way-out approach," such as decision tree analysis. Later, in talking with younger management personnel on lower levels, you begin to understand the significance of top management's remark regarding decision tree analysis. These younger managers had recently used it as a scientific tool to support the main argument another problem involved, only to be strongly rebuffed by top management.

Yale has recently developed a new product with an expected life of 10 years. Present manufacturing facilities are inadequate to produce the product, so Yale must decide how much to expand the present plant. Market research believes it has reliable tests indicating that the domestic market alone is sufficient to require a 20,000-square-foot expansion. Data concerning an export market are less accurate; however, marketing personnel believe that if demand is high in the export market, a 40,000-square-foot expansion is warranted. Management is faced with the immediate decision of whether to expand by 20,000 square feet now with a possible later 20,000-square-foot expansion, or to expand 40,000 square feet initially. Management is in agreement that there is not enough space available in the present site to exceed a total 40,000-square-foot expansion.

Bids from local contractors have averaged $75 per square foot; however, if a second expansion of 20,000 square feet is undertaken, the price is expected to be $120 per square foot for this additional space. This price is estimated to reflect inflation as well as additional costs due to remodeling the first expansion. If the smaller expansion is undertaken, it will be four years before a second expansion is made, if at all.

Market research studies indicate there is a 60 percent chance that the initial demand will be high. Management agrees that if the initial demand is low, there is complete assurance that the long-term demand will also be low, and they will not expand. They believe there is a 50 percent chance that if initial demand is high it will continue, while only a 10 percent chance that a low long-term demand will follow a high-demand initial market. The projections of net annual cash flow follow.

You are convinced that decision tree analysis is appropriate and believe that you can demonstrate this to top management.

Years 1–4	Demand Level	Annual Cash Flow
1. Small expansion	High	$300,000
2. Small expansion	Low	200,000
3. Large expansion	High	700,000
4. Large expansion	Low	100,000
Years 5–10		
1. Small expansion with later additional expansion	High	600,000
2. Small expansion with later additional expansion	Low	200,000
3. Small expansion, no further expansion	High	400,000
4. Small expansion, no further expansion	Low	250,000
5. Large initial expansion	High	700,000
6. Large initial expansion	Low	100,000

Required:

a. Discuss potential reasons for top management's resistance to decision tree analysis.
b. Give the weaknesses or limitations of decision tree analysis.
c. Draw a decision tree; adjust the cash flow for the time value of money using a discount rate of 14 percent. Discount the cash flow for all years.
d. Indicate the course of action you would advise.
e. Discuss other factors that could affect your decision.

P26–19 Decision Tree Using Discounted Expected Yield (L.O. 4)

After two years of study, Kingsberry Company's engineering staff presented a proposal for an expansion installation of their computer-based control system. The present system has been in operation for four years and cash savings are being achieved. The expected cost of the new system is $1.2 million. A reduction in labor costs and less material waste are the claimed advantages. The equipment needed for the expansion can be purchased and installed quickly because the supplier is anxious to further test the system in an actual application. The supplier's bid of $1.2 million represents a reduced price for this on-site testing; the price will be $1.4 million in one year. Possible technical malfunctions, as well as uncertain product demand, have convinced several Kingsberry vice presidents that additional engineering studies should be conducted. The vice president of production suggests that action be postponed until the Tire Industry Association completes both its one-year study of the technical capacities of the system and a forecast of market demand; cost of this survey to Kingsberry will be $25,000. The marketing vice president argues that more reliance could be placed on analysis conducted by an independent research team than on that from industry studies; the cost of an independent research team's analysis will be $40,000. However, all vice presidents agree that cost studies and probabilities of various events should be carefully estimated since the investment is substantial. They are also in agreement that one of the three alternatives must be chosen. After many hours of study, the following data are obtained:

	Probability
Postpone expansion and use industry studies:	
Weak initial market, negative technical studies	30%
Strong initial market, positive technical studies	70
Postpone expansion and hire independent research team:	
Weak initial market, negative technical studies	35%
Strong initial market, positive technical studies	65

If the expansion is made in year one, there is a 55 percent chance of an initial weak market and many technical problems and a 45 percent chance of an initial strong market and limited technical malfunctions. Using either the industry study or the independent research study, it will be one year before the results can be examined and the machine installed. The system's impact is expected to extend eight years from the present, regardless of the date of installation. Probabilities for long-term market demand are given below for the three different alternatives:

Market Based on Industry Study or for Immediate Expansion	Percent
Weak long-term after a weak initial	70
Strong long-term after a weak initial	30
Weak long-term after strong initial	20
Strong long-term after strong initial	80
Market Based on Independent Study	**Percent**
Weak long-term after a weak initial	60
Strong long-term after weak initial	40
Weak long-term after strong initial	25
Strong long-term after strong initial	75

The annual cash savings for the weak and strong markets by years is as follows:

	Annual Cash Savings			
	Year 1		**Years 2–8**	
Market	**Without Expansion**	**With Expansion**	**Without Expansion**	**With Expansion**
Weak	$40,000	$200,000	$ 50,000	$240,000
Strong	$75,000	$450,000	$100,000	$580,000

Required:

a. Using a 10 percent discount rate for the cash flow, prepare a decision tree; discount the cash flow for all years.

b. Indicate the course of action you would advise.

P26–20 Short-Run and Long-Run Decision Tree Analysis (L.O. 3)

Early, Inc., management is faced with the decision whether to build a small plant or a large one to manufacture BTX, a new chemical with a market life of 10 years.

Uncertainty exists among management regarding how large the market for their product will be. As a result, the size of the building to house plant operations is undecided. The cost accountant argues that the company will run too much risk with high overhead if it initially builds a large-scale plant costing $3.5 million. The accountant argues instead that a small plant costing $2 million should be built now with an agreement to make a decision at the end of three years regarding a plant addition. Engineers estimate the addition will cost $2 million later giving a total plant cost of $4 million.

Marketing personnel forecast a 60 percent probability of an initial high demand. Conservative managers agree that there is a 40 percent probability of an initial low demand.

This capital investment decision is critical, other managers agree, because of its impact on later years. Due to the nature of the product, all personnel agree that the initial market reaction will determine market success in later years. Long-run contracts will be secured from customers so that the probability for an initial high or low demand also represents long-term market demand.

After consultation, top management arrives at the following forecasted yields:

	Market Demand	Annual Yield for First 3 Years	Annual Yield for Remainder
Small plant built initially and expanded	High	$ 500,000	$1,000,000
Small plant built initially and not expanded	High	500,000	500,000
Small plant built initially and not expanded	Low	300,000	300,000
Large plant built initially	High	1,000,000	1,000,000
Large plant built initially	Low	200,000	200,000

Required:

a. Prepare a decision tree analysis indicating the preferred alternative.

b. Assume an accounting consultant advises management to consider the time value of money since the chemical market life is expected to be 10 years. Using a 15 percent discount rate for the cash flow, discount the cash flow for all years. Prepare only whatever additional analysis you might need using relevant analysis from Requirement *a*.

c. Indicate the course of action you would advise reconciling any difference between the analysis in Requirements *a* and *b*.

P26–21 (CMA) Payoff Table and Decision Tree Analysis (L.O. 3 and 4)

Steven Company has been producing component parts and assemblies for use in the manufacture of microcomputers and microcomputer peripheral equipment for 10 years. The company plans to introduce a magnetic tape cartridge back-up unit for IBM-compatible microcomputers in the near future.

Steven's Research and Development (R&D) and Market Research Departments have been working on this project for an extended period and the combined development costs incurred to date amount to $1.5 million. R&D designed several alternative back-up units. Three of the designs were approved for development into prototypes, and from these only one will be manufactured and sold. Market Research has determined that the appropriate selling price would be $400 per unit, regardless of the model selected.

The estimated demand schedule for three different market situations follows. These three demand levels are the only ones the company considers feasible, and other demand levels are not expected to occur. Steven can meet all demand levels because its fixed plant currently is below full capacity.

	Unit Sales	Probability of Occurrence
Light demand	20,000	25%
Moderate demand	80,000	60
Heavy demand	120,000	15

Steven's accounting and engineering staffs have worked together to develop manufacturing cost estimates for each of the three model designs. Costs for the three models follow. Manufacturing overhead, 40 percent of which is variable, is applied to Steven's products using a plantwide application rate of 250 percent of direct labor-dollars.

	Model A	**Model B**	**Model C**
Unit costs:			
Direct materials	$150	$100	$114
Direct labor	40	50	48
Manufacturing overhead	100	125	120
Total unit costs	$290	$275	$282

	Model A	**Model B**	**Model C**
Other costs:			
Tooling and advertising	$3,000,000	$4,500,000	$4,100,000
Incurred development costs	1,500,000	1,500,000	1,500,000

Steven has decided to employ an expected value model in its analysis to reach a decision as to which of the three prototypes it will manufacture and sell.

Required:

a. Develop a payoff table to determine the expected monetary value for each of the three models Steven Company could manufacture. Based on your analysis, identify the prototype model Steven should manufacture and sell.

b. Steven Company's costs for a back-up unit design that was not developed into a prototype were estimated as follows.

Unit costs:	
Direct materials	$130
Direct labor	46
Manufacturing overhead	115
Total unit costs	$291

Other costs:	
Tooling and advertising	$4,000,000
Incurred development costs	1,500,000

If this design had been developed by Steven into a viable model, it would have sold for $400 and had the same expected demand as the other models. Steven's management eliminated this model from consideration because it was considered an inadmissable act (i.e., the calculation of its payoff would have been irrelevant). Explain why the model design was considered an inadmissable act, thus making the calculation of its payoff irrelevant.

c. Steven Company could have employed a decision tree model in this situation. Explain how the decision tree model could have been employed in making this decision. (No calculations are required.)

Case

C26–22 Behavioral Impact of PERT Diagrams (L.O. 1)

Chicago, Inc., has recently been awarded a bid for a complex machine. Prior to submitting the bid, the vice president of research and the vice president of engineering prepared a PERT chart showing the network of activities required to complete the tasks. They also estimated the crash time and costs involved with each activity. The construction is quite detailed involving the coordination of three different production departments. In addition, Chicago, Inc., has never manufactured a machine similar to this so that the two vice presidents had to use their best judgment in arriving at the times required for each task.

In accepting the bid the buyer indicates that the machine must be completed within the crash time. In fact, in talking with the company president, the buyer offers to pay

$1,000 a day for any days that the machine is completed in advance of the crash time. The company president promises the buyer that he will check into this matter.

After formal receipt of the bid, the three production managers whose departments will be involved in the construction are called together for a meeting. The two vice presidents who were responsible for preparing the PERT chart and bids present the data. The Machining Department manager begins asking specific questions as to the type of molds and materials that will be needed. The research vice president tries unsuccessfully to convey to her the specific grade of material that was included in the bid. The Finishing Department manager is equally concerned about the time allotted for the molds and paint to dry. In the midst of this confusion, the pattern department manager realizes that only two weeks were estimated for the design of the machine. He is especially worried that the skill level of personnel presently employed will be inadequate for this duty. Finally after trying to communicate his concern to the vice presidents he remarks, "I wish I had known about this machine construction three weeks ago because I would have given Karen Jones the raise she wanted; then I would have had a better chance of retaining her. She has resigned to work as a draft person for a competitor."

The two vice presidents become perplexed as well as annoyed with all the questions and worries expressed. In concluding the meeting, the vice presidents warn the department managers that they must "live with the PERT-Cost chart," and that all their necks are "on the line." They further inform the Production Department managers that the president is expected to put pressure on all of them to finish before the crash time because of the $1,000-a-day offer for early completion.

Required:

a. Identify what has caused the confusion and concern expressed by the department managers.
b. Explain why you do or do not expect the machine to be completed by the crash time.

CHAPTER 27

Linear Programming and the Cost Accountant

CHAPTER OBJECTIVES

After studying this chapter, you should be able to:

1. Apply linear programming techniques to cost accounting issues either through computer usage or manually.

2. Interpret linear programming solutions.

3. Use linear programming to maximize profits with specific constraints.

4. Understand model formulation in linear programming to minimize cost.

Introduction

As the problems of management become more complex, it becomes urgent to have more accurate information. For accountants to satisfy this need, they must have expertise in the use of quantitative tools. One of the major benefits of using such tools is the low expense involved in calculating the impact of change on a proposed course of action. One of the best-known operations research models used in the business environment is linear programming.

Linear Programming Defined (L.O. 1)

Linear programming is a mathematical approach to maximizing profits or minimizing costs by finding a feasible combination of available resources that accomplishes either objective. Linear programming recognizes that resources are not only limited but also have alternative uses. Linear programming is a powerful planning tool, but it is complex and usually requires a computer to derive solutions.

We can apply linear programming to the following business-related problems:

1. Allocating resources (e.g., assigning jobs to machines) to maximize profits.

2. Selecting product ingredients (e.g., blending chemical products) to minimize costs.

3. Assigning personnel, machines, and other business components (e.g., scheduling flight crews).

4. Scheduling output to balance demand, production, and inventory levels.

5. Determining transportation rules to minimize distribution cost.

Accountants should possess basic knowledge of linear programming; that is, they should recognize problems that they can analyze using linear programming. The ideal situation is for the accountant to understand the mathematics involved and be able to communicate with operations researchers and mathematicians. In this chapter, however, we take the position that the accountant should focus on drafting and formulating the models and then analyzing the solution obtained. This approach leaves the technical details to the operations researchers. If you desire a solid understanding of linear programming, consult books on quantitative models.

Effects of Constraints (L.O. 1)

The focus in linear programming is on scarce resources. Managers face few challenges in decision making if there are unlimited resources; selecting a course of action to achieve a specific objective in this situation is relatively easy. Unfortunately, most managers make few decisions involving unlimited resources because production and marketing constraints affect their choice of action.

Constraints Absent

Assume, for example, that a company has unlimited resources and its aim is to maximize profits. Its manufacturing facilities can be used to produce either of two products, A or B. Assume further that the entire output of either product can be sold, and the contribution margin per machine-hour is as follows:

	Product	
	A	B
Unit sales price	$10.00	$4.50
Unit variable cost	8.00	3.00
Unit contribution margin	$ 2.00	$1.50
Machine-hours required per unit	1	4
Contribution margin per machine-hour	$2.00	$0.375

Since the company can sell all it manufactures, the obvious decision is to use all available capacity in manufacturing Product A, because it has the higher contribution per hour of capacity.

Constraints Present

Unfortunately, most business problems are not this simple. Assume, instead, that the manufacturer has a total of 1,000 machine-hours available per period (a production constraint) and that it can sell only 600 units of Product A and 500 units of Product B (a marketing constraint). In this simple situation with few constraints, the decision is to produce as many units of the more profitable Product A as the company can sell. The company uses the remaining machine time to produce Product B. The maximum contribution to fixed costs and income is $1,350 by producing 600 units of Product A and 100 units of Product B to fully utilize the 1,000 machine-hours.

Product A—600 units @ $2 contribution margin per unit	.	$1,200
Product B—100 units @ $1.50 contribution margin per unit		150
Maximum contribution margin		$1,350

Since we assume fixed costs to be the same whether we manufacture Product A or B, fixed costs are irrelevant and ignored in the calculation. In addition, even though Product A's $2 unit contribution margin is higher than Product B's $1.50 contribution margin, the contribution margin per hour is important. This results because the limit of 1,000 machine-hours is a scarce resource.

Linear Programming Terms (L.O. 2)

The previous example introduced production and marketing constraints. However, these simple data do not need linear programming analysis. In many situations, we cannot obtain the solution so readily and need linear programming to find the optimal combination of resources that maximizes profits or minimizes costs. The purpose of linear programming is to find a mix of the products that yields the **objective function,** or the factor to maximize or minimize. In this example, the objective function is to maximize total contribution margin which, in turn, maximizes profit. In other uses of linear programming, the objective function might be to minimize costs. The **constraints** determine limitations on the feasible solution. Constraints are the conditions that restrict the optimal value of the objective function. In this example, the following three constraints are present: a 600-unit maximum sales demand for Product A, a 500-unit maximum sales demand for Product B, and a total of 1,000 available machine-hours. The optimal feasible solution represents all the possible combinations of Product A and Product B that the company can manufacture and sell. We use the following mathematical symbols in linear programming equations:

$$\geq \text{ equal to or greater than}$$
$$\leq \text{ equal to or less than}$$
$$= \text{ equal to}$$

Linear Programming Requirements (L.O. 2)

In summary, the following requirements must be present in a decision situation to employ linear programming:

1. Express the objective function and the limitations as mathematical equations or inequalities because we base the decision on a determinate solution.

2. Specify the objective function; it is either a profit-maximizing or cost-minimizing function.

3. Specify and quantify the constraints because resources are limited. Constraints must also be consistent and define a feasible region for a solution. The constraints cannot be specified so there is no solution for every value of the objective function.

4. The objective function and the constraints must be linear and continuous.

5. Both the objective function and the constraints must be independent and known with certainty.

6. The objective function and all constraints must be a function of a prespecified set of quantitative variables, and these variables must be interrelated. They generally represent resources that must be combined to produce one or more products.

Solution Methods (L.O. 3 and 4)

The following solution methods are available for linear programming problems:

1. *Graphic method:* The easiest technique, but limited to simple problems. The basic rule is that the optimum solution lies at the extreme point of feasible combinations of products without going beyond the constraints.

2. *Simplex method:* Managers more commonly use this technique because it is very effective. The simplex method is a stepwise process that approaches an optimum solution. It is an algorithm to move from a possible solution to another solution which is at least as good. We reach the optimum solution when we cannot find a better solution. Many computer facilities have linear programming packages available that use the simplex algorithm to find the optimal solution.

Graphic Method

When a linear programming involves only two variables, we use a two-dimensional graph to determine the optimal solution.

Maximizing Profits. Exhibit 27–1 illustrates the **graphic method** where the *x*-axis represents the number of Product A units and the *y*-axis represents the number of Product B units. The combination of Products A and B that results in the largest contribution margin attainable within the limits set by the constraints will maximize profits. In the example presented in Exhibit 27–1, this can be stated algebraically:

$$CM = \$2.00 \text{ A} + \$1.50 \text{ B}$$

Three Constraints Plotted. The constraints can also be expressed algebraically as follows:

Sales demand for Product A: $A \leq 600$
Sales demand for Product B: $B \leq 500$
Machine-hours available: $1A + 4B \leq 1,000$

In addition, we need the following obvious statements so we do not mathematically determine negative quantities of products:

$$A \geq 0 \qquad B \geq 0$$

We first plot the constraints. If we devote all 1,000 machine-hours to the production of A, we can produce 1,000 units of A, but we do not manufacture any Product B. If, instead, we devote all the hours to manufacturing Product B, we can produce 250 B units (1,000 hours/4 hours per Product B), but no Product A. We determine the maximum limits of production possibilities by connecting these points. All combinations of Products A and B that we can manufacture, fully utilizing the machine-hours limitation of 1,000 hours, lie along this line. We next plot the marketing constraints, a 600-unit sales demand for Product A and 500 units for Product B. However, in Exhibit 27–1, the marketing constraint that sales demand for Product B will not exceed 500 units is redundant since the production constraint indicates that we can manufacture only 250 units of Product B with the 1,000 machine-hours available. We do not connect lines for

EXHIBIT 27–1   Graphic Solution Depicting Profit Maximization, Three Constraints Plotted, Products A and B

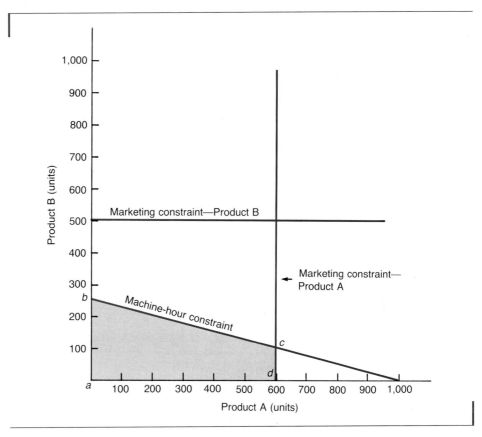

Product A's and Product B's marketing constraint because they each involve only one product.

We establish the boundaries of the feasible area of combination after plotting all constraints. In Exhibit 27–1, this area is a polygon with four corners labeled *a*, *b*, *c*, and *d*. Within this feasible area, many combinations of Products A and B exist that we can manufacture and sell. For example, the following are a few of these combinations available:

Units of A	Units of B
0	250
200	200
400	150
600	100

Even though many combinations of Products A and B satisfy the production and marketing constraints, one combination maximizes the contribution margin. According to mathematical laws, the best feasible solution is at one of the four corner points. (As discussed later, the optimal solution may be at more than one corner point; in this case, any point on the line joining these two points is also optimal.) As a result, we test all corner point variables to find the combination that maximizes profits.

| Corner Point | Combination | | Contribution Margin |
	Units of A	Units of B	$2.00 A + $1.50 B =
a	0	0	($2 × 0) + ($1.50 × 0) = $0
b	0	250	($2 × 0) + ($1.50 × 250) = $375
c	600	100	($2 × 600) + ($1.50 × 100) = $1,350*
d	600	0	($2 × 600) + ($1.50 × 0) = $1,200

*Optimum.

The company maximizes profits at corner c representing 600 units of A and 100 units of B, giving a total contribution margin of $1,350.

Objective Functions Plotted. Instead of the trial and error method of working with the coordinates of the corners of the polygon, we can plot **objective function lines** as Exhibit 27–2 illustrates. We can determine the slope of the objective function line from the two products' contributions as follows using the total contribution margin equation:

$$CM = \$2.00 \text{ A} + \$1.50 \text{ B}$$

To find the slope reflecting the rate of change of B for one additional A, divide by the coefficient of B and then transfer B to the left side of the equation:

EXHIBIT 27–2   Graphic Solution Depicting Profit Maximization, Objective Functions Plotted, Products A and B

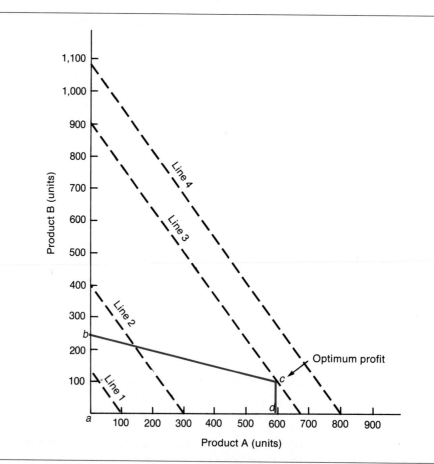

$$\frac{CM}{\$1.50} = \frac{\$2.00}{\$1.50}A + B$$

$$B = \frac{CM}{\$1.50} - \frac{\$2.00}{\$1.50}A$$

Thus, the slope of the objective function is a negative $2.00/$1.50 or − ⁴⁄₃. In our example, Product A contributes $2 per unit and Product B contributes $1.50 per unit. Therefore, one unit of A equals one and one third units of Product B. If we connect any of two quantities of Products A and B in the ratio of A, 1 and B, ⁴⁄₃ (or A, ³⁄₄; B, 1), we can calculate many product combinations, each having the same marginal contribution. Exhibit 27–2 shows the following four lines drawn.

Line	Units of Product A ($2.00 CM/Unit)	Units of Product B ($1.50 CM/Unit)
1	100	133
2	300	400
3	675	900
4	800	1,066

Along Line 1, any combination of Products A and B yields a total contribution margin of $200; along Line 2, the total contribution is $600; along Line 3, a $1,350 contribution margin; and along Line 4, a $1,600 contribution margin. These lines illustrate that as the objective function lines move out from the point of origin, the total contribution margin increases. We realize the optimum profit when we can draw no further lines without going beyond the constraints. The optimum profit occurs in Exhibit 27–2 at corner *c*. If the objective function is optimized at two corner points, any point on the line joining these two points is also optimal. Even though along line 4 the $1,600 contribution margin is greater than at corner *c*, the combinations of Products A and B along this line are outside the constraints.

Four Constraints Plotted.   The previous example involving Products A and B is less complex than many business problems because we limited the constraints. For example, if a company's labor-hours per period are divided into two departments and each product requires varying amounts of time in each department, the solution is not as obvious. A linear programming model can determine how many units of each product should be produced each period to obtain the maximum profit.

Consider a company that manufactures regular and super products in its Mixing and Finishing Departments. There are 400 hours of mixing capacity and 240 hours of finishing capacity each day. Regular products require 2 hours of mixing and 0.8 hour of finishing per unit. If the company devotes all production facilities to manufacturing regular products, the maximum daily output is 200 units (400/2 hours per regular product) in the Mixing Department and 300 units (240/0.8 hours per regular product) in the Finishing Department. Super products, however, require 1¼ hours of mixing and one hour of finishing per unit. If, instead, they devote all facilities to processing the super products, maximum daily output of super products in the Mixing Department is 320 units (400/1.25 hours per super product) and 240 units (240/1 hour per super product) in the Finishing Department. In addition to these constraints, there is such a critical shortage of material used in processing super products that the company must limit production to a maximum of 180 units per day. Management worries that this shortage exists because market demand is sufficient for the company to sell all it produces. (In effect, there is no marketing constraint for super products.) However, sales forecasts indicate the company can sell a maximum of 150 units of regular products daily. The following summarizes these constraints and the contribution margin per unit:

	Regular Products	Super Products
Mixing—Maximum daily output	200 units	320 units
Finishing—Maximum daily output	300 units	240 units
Material shortage constraint	—	180 units
Marketing constraint	150 units	—
Unit contribution margin	$5	$3

The objective is to find the combination of regular and super products that maximizes the following profit function:

Let R = number of units of regular product.
Let S = number of units of super product.
$$CM = \$5R + \$3S$$

Exhibit 27–3 plots these constraints:

Production hours constraints: Mixing: $2R + 1.25S \leq 400$

Finishing: $0.8R + 1S \leq 240$

Material shortage constraint: $S \leq 180$

Marketing constraint: $R \leq 150$

Additionally: $R \geq 0$

$S \geq 0$

As shown in Exhibit 27–3, the area of feasible production combinations is a polygon with six corners denoted by a, b, c, d, e, and f. Contributions at each of these corners are as follows:

EXHIBIT 27–3   Graphic Solution Depicting Profit Maximization, Four Constraints Plotted, Regular and Super Products

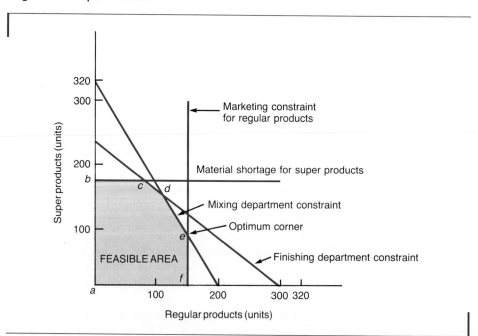

Corner Point	Regular Units	Super Units	$CM = \$5R + \$3S$
a	–0–	–0–	$0
b	–0–	180	$540
c	80	180	$940
d	100	160	$980
e	150	80	$990*
f	150	–0–	$750

*Optimum.

If, instead, we plot objective function lines, the slope is $-\frac{5}{3}$ indicating that 1 unit of regular product equals $1\frac{2}{3}$ units of super product. Exhibit 27–4 plots the objective function lines for the regular and the super products. Along Line 1, the contribution margin is $500; along Line 2, $752; and along Line 3, $990, which is the largest margin that the company can earn within production constraints. Note how close Line 3 comes to corner *d* since the contribution margin at corner *d* is $980, which is $10 less than at corner *e*. We could argue that either corner *d* or *e* is the optimum combination.

Minimizing Costs. We can also use linear programming to select product ingredients that minimize costs. For example, assume that to produce a more beautiful green for its golf course, a country club plans to spread at least 4,800 pounds of fertilizer and 5,600 pounds of special chemicals on the soil. However, club management is able to buy only fertilizer and chemicals in a mixture, not in a pure form.

A dealer has offered to sell management 100-pound bags of Mixture A at $2 each which contains the equivalent of 30 pounds of fertilizer and 70 pounds of chemicals. Mixture B is also available in 100-pound bags at $4 each; it contains the equivalent of 80 pounds of fertilizer and 20 pounds of chemicals.

EXHIBIT 27–4   Graphic Solution Depicting Profit Maximization, Objective Functions Plotted, Regular and Super Products

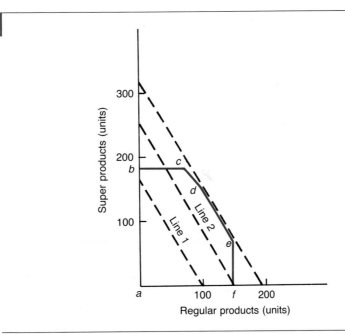

The objective is to find the combination of Mixtures A and B that satisfies the chemical and fertilizer requirements and also minimizes cost.

$$\text{Let } A = \text{Bags of Mixture A}$$
$$\text{Let } B = \text{Bags of Mixture B}$$

The following summarizes these constraints and the cost per bag of mixture:

$$\text{Minimize: } \$2A + \$4B$$

Subject to: Fertilizer requirements: $30A + 80B \geq 4{,}800$
Chemical requirements: $70A + 20B \geq 5{,}600$
Additionally: $A \geq 0$
$B \geq 0$

After plotting these constraints in Exhibit 27–5, the feasible area has three corners denoted as a, b, and c. Note that this solution differs from the linear programming exhibits shown earlier in the chapter because cost minimization is the objective. Its feasible area lies beyond the constraints rather than within the constraints as shown in previous exhibits. Cost at each of these corners is as follows:

Corner Point	Bags of Mixture *A*	Bags of Mixture *B*	Cost = $2*A* + $4*B*
a	0	280	$1,120
b	71	34	$ 142 + $136 = $278*
c	160	0	$ 320

*Optimal.

E X H I B I T   27–5   Graphic Solution Depicting Cost Minimization, Two Constraints Plotted, Mixtures A and B

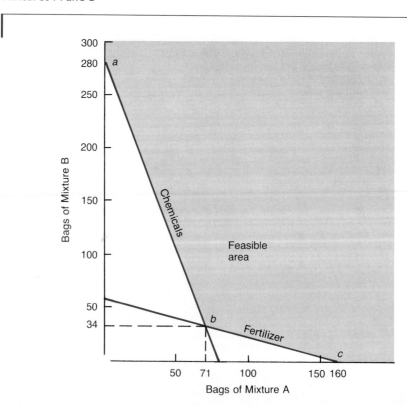

As shown in Exhibit 27–5, the club minimizes cost by purchasing 71 bags of Mixture A and 34 bags of Mixture B.

Simplex Method

The graphic approach works best when there are only two products involved, therefore requiring only a two-dimensional treatment. We use the **simplex method** to solve more complex problems involving many cost centers and products.

Maximizing Profits. We use matrix algebra in the simplex method to reach an optimum solution. We arrange the equations that form the constraints in a matrix of coefficients and manipulate them as a group with matrix algebra. Even though it is too detailed to describe extensively in this book, the simplex method basically involves solving sets of simultaneous equations where the number of unknowns in each set is equal to the number of constraints.

We must take the following steps before applying the method. (Note that the first two steps are identical to those used with the graphic method.)

1. Establish the relationships for the constraints or inequalities. The set of constraints for the super and regular product is

$$\text{Mixing: } 2R + 1.25S \le 400$$
$$\text{Finishing: } 0.8R + 1S \le 240$$
$$\text{Material shortage: } S \le 180$$
$$\text{Marketing: } R \le 150$$

Both R and S must be zero or positive values:

$$R \ge 0; S \ge 0$$

2. Establish the objective function. The company expects a contribution of $5 and $3 for each unit of regular product and super product respectively, thus:

$$CM = \$5R + \$3S$$

3. Change the set of inequalities into a set of equations by introducing slack variables. By adding an arbitrary variable to one side of the inequality, an equality results. This arbitrary variable is called a **slack variable** because it takes up the slack in the inequality. The resulting equalities from the four inequalities introduced earlier are

$$2R + 1.25S + s_1 = 400$$
$$0.8R + 1S + s_2 = 240$$
$$S + s_3 = 180$$
$$R + s_4 = 150$$

Maximize: $CM = \$5R + \$3S + 0s_1 + 0s_2$

Slack variable s_1 represents unused mixing hours; s_2, unused finishing hours; s_3, unused material; and s_4, unused marketing demand. Because the slack variables do not contribute to profits, we do not add them to the profit equation. In tabular format this is

Solution Variable	Solution Values	s_1	s_2	s_3	s_4	R	S
		0	0	0	0	5	3
	400	1	0	0	0	2	1.25
	240	0	1	0	0	0.8	1
	180	0	0	1	0	0	1
	150	0	0	0	1	1	0

Z
$C_j - Z_j$

The tableau results from rewriting the equations of the problem. Row 1 results from the first constraint written as:

$$400 = 2R + 1.25S + 1s_1 + 0s_2$$

Row 2 results from the second constraint written as:

$$240 = 0.8R + 1S + 0s_1 + 1s_2$$

After the tableau is manipulated using the simplex algorithm, the final solution tableau is generated by a computer program:

C_j	Solution Variable	Solution Values	s_1 $C_j 0$	s_2 0	s_3 0	s_4 0	R 5	S 3	
0	s_2	40	-0.8	1	0	0.8	0	0	
0	s_3	100	-0.8	0	1	1.6	0	0	
3	S	80	0.8	0	0	-1.6	0	1	
5	R	150	0	0	0	1	1	0	Profit
		Z_j	2.4	0	0	0.2	5	3	990
		$C_j - Z_j$	-2.4	0	0	-0.2	0	0	

Reading the solution value, the optimal solution is 80 units of super product and 150 units of regular products with an optimal value of $Z = 990$, from:

$$Z = 5R + 3S + 0s_1 + 0s_2$$
$$Z = 5(150) + 3(80) = 990$$

Sensitivity Analysis. This final tableau is the key to sensitivity analysis because we use its data to calculate how much the contribution margin can vary, if at all, without changing the optimal solution. The term **sensitivity analysis** describes how sensitive the linear programming optimal solution is to a change in any one number. Sensitivity analysis answers what-if questions about the effect of changes in prices or variable costs; changes in value; addition or deletion of constraints, such as available machine-hours; and changes in industrial coefficients, such as the labor-hours required in manufacturing a specific unit. An exhaustive treatment of sensitivity analysis is beyond the scope or intent of this chapter; however, a discussion of shadow prices is appropriate.

Shadow Price. The preceding output produced with the linear programming computer package provides additional information of economic significance. In the last row of the table ($C_j - Z_j$) is the amount of profit which the company will add if they add one unit of the variable j to the solution. This measure of the contribution foregone by failing to have one more unit of scarce capacity in a specific incident is a **shadow price**. Earlier, slack variables s_1 and s_2 were added to convert the constraints into equalities as follows:

Mixing: $2R + 1.25S + s_1 = 400$
Finishing: $0.8R + 1S   + s_2 = 240$

The tableau indicates that increasing slack variable s_1 by 1 unit will make Z increase by $2.40 from $990 to $992.40. If we increase the right side of the constraint from 400 to 401, this is the same as adding a negative one unit of s_1 and will increase Z by $+$2.40. This number, -2.4, is the shadow price or dual price of s_1, the slack variable in the first constraint. This represents the maximum amount we should pay for an additional unit of the resource described in the first constraint. Thus, shadow prices facilitate the calculation of the potential-variation in contribution margin from expanding capacity and alleviating the constraint.

The value in the s_2 column, $C_j - Z_j$ row, is -0 representing the shadow price of s_2, and the opposite of the amount Z increases with every additional unit of Finishing Department resource. Since in the solution, we already have enough finishing capacity to make 40 additional units, no gain would occur if we added more finishing resources.

We need caution in interpreting shadow prices because these variations in the right side of the constraints produce the shadow price change in the objective function only within a certain range of their optimal values. Shadow prices are effective quantifications of opportunity cost only if the products and idle capacity do not change. In our example, if all regular products or all super products become the optimal solution, the shadow prices would change.

Summary

As the emphasis in cost accounting shifts even more from providing costs for inventory valuation to determining relevant costs for decision making and internal planning, we need new techniques. The information needed is not easily available using conventional cost accounting techniques. Thus, accountants must be familiar with such quantitative tools as linear programming. However, cost accountants seldom have full responsibility for the development and use of linear programming models. Instead, the primary concern of cost accountants is in determining objective function coefficients. In addition, the cost accountant's focus should be on recognizing situations in which linear programming may be applicable and then obtaining any needed operations research assistance in solving the problem. Certainly, linear programming is a powerful management tool, but it is complex and usually requires the use of a computer.

Important Terms and Concepts

linear programming, 949
objective function, 951
constraints, 951
graphic method, 952
objective function lines, 954

simplex method, 959
slack variable, 959
sensitivity analysis, 960
shadow price, 960

Problem for Self-Study

Reynolds, Inc., manufactures Products A and B. The contribution margin for Product A is $2.25 and $1.25 for Product B. One unit of A requires two hours of machining time and one unit of B requires four hours. There is a limit of 20,000 hours of machining time and 18,000 hours of finishing time available. One unit of A requires 2.25 hours of finishing time; B requires 2 hours. In addition, both units require a direct material that is difficult to obtain. One unit of A requires 1.25 gallons and one unit of B requires 2 gallons. Company purchases of the material are limited to 15,000 gallons.

Required:

Use the graphic method to determine the optimal combination of A and B for the firm to maximize contribution margin.

Solution to Problem for Self-Study

Product	Machining	Finishing	Direct Material	Contribution Margin
A	2	2.25	1.25	$2.25
B	4	2	2	1.25
Constraints	20,000	18,000	15,000	

Examine the constraints:

$$\text{Machining:} \quad 2A \quad + 4B \le 20,000$$
$$\text{Finishing:} \quad 2.25A + 2B \le 18,000$$
$$\text{Direct material: } 1.25A + 2B \le 15,000$$

$$CM = \$2.25A + \$1.25B$$

if B = 0:

$$\text{Machining:} \quad 2A \le 20,000$$
$$A \le 10,000$$
$$\text{Finishing:} \quad 2.25A \le 18,000$$
$$A \le 8,000$$
$$\text{Direct material: } 1.25A \le 15,000$$
$$A \le 12,000$$

if A = 0:

$$\text{Machining:} \quad 4B \le 20,000$$
$$B \le 5,000$$
$$\text{Finishing:} \quad 2B \le 18,000$$
$$B \le 9,000$$
$$\text{Direct material: } 2B \le 15,000$$
$$B \le 7,500$$

These values determine the limits of the constraint equations depicted on the graph:

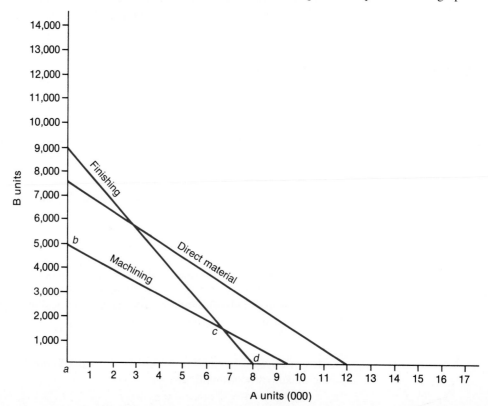

Determine the contribution margin for each corner point using the equation

$$CM = \$2.25A + \$1.25B$$

Table of Corner Point Contribution Margin Values

Corner Point	A Value	B Value	Contribution Margin
a	–0–	–0–	–0–
b	–0–	5,000	$ 6,250.00
c	6,666	1,500	16,873.50
d	8,000	–0–	18,000.00*

*Optimal solution.

Review Questions

1. To use linear programming, what requirements must be satisfied?
2. What is the major benefit of using models to represent real-world situations?
3. Define linear programming.
4. How are resources regarded in a linear programming model?
5. Give three applications of linear programming.
6. Define the term *objective function* and give an example.
7. What are constraints in linear programming, and how do they affect the decision?
8. Give three examples of constraints encountered in business problems.
9. Contrast the two solution methods used with linear programming.
10. How is the area of feasible combinations determined? Where is the optimal solution located?
11. How is the slope of objective function lines determined and how is the optimum profit determined with their use?
12. Discuss the relationship between sensitivity analysis and shadow prices.

CPA/CMA/CIA Multiple Choice Questions

1.–3. (CMA) The following data apply to these items.

Jarten Company manufactures and sells two products. Demand for the two products has grown to such a level that Jarten can no longer meet the demand with its facilities. The company can work a total of 600,000 direct labor-hours annually using three shifts. A total of 200,000 hours of machine time is available annually. The company plans to use linear programming to determine a production schedule that will maximize its net return.

The company spends $2 million in advertising and promotion, and incurs $1 million for general and administrative costs. The unit sales price for Model A is $27.50; Model B sells for $75 each. The unit manufacturing requirement and unit cost data are as shown below. Overhead is assigned on a machine hour (MH) basis.

	Model A		Model B	
Raw material		$ 3		$ 7
Direct labor	1.0 DLH @ $8	8	1.5 DLH @ $8	12
Variable overhead	0.5 MH @ $12	6	2.0 MH @ $12	24
Fixed overhead	0.5 MH @ $4	2	2.0 MH @ $4	8
		$19		$51

1. The objective function that would maximize Jarten's net income is

   a. 10.50A + 32.00B.
   b. 8.50A + 24.00B.

    c. 27.50A + 75.00B.
    d. 19.00A + 51.00B.
    e. 17.00A + 43.00B.

2. The constraint function for the direct labor is

    a. 1A + 1.5B ≤ 200,000.
    b. 8A + 12B ≤ 600,000.
    c. 8A + 12B ≤ 200,000.
    d. 1A + 1.5B ≤ 4,800,000.
    e. 1A + 1.5B ≤ 600,000.

3. The constraint function for the machine capacity is

    a. 6A + 24B ≤ 200,000.
    b. $\dfrac{1}{0.5}A + \dfrac{1.5}{2.0}B \le 800{,}000.$
    c. 0.5 A + 2B ≤ 200,000.
    d. (0.5 + .5)A + (2 + 2)B ≤ 200,000.
    e. (0.5 × 1) + (1.5 × 2.00) ≤ (200,000 × 600,000).

4. (AICPA) Bolton Company produces a food product in 50 gallon batches. The basic ingredients used are Material X costing $8 per gallon, and Material Y costing $12 per gallon. No more than 16 gallons of X can be used, and at least 18 gallons of Y must be used. How would the objective function (minimization of product cost) be expressed?

    a.   8X + 12Y.
    b.   8X + 18Y.
    c. 16X + 18Y.
    d. 16X + 34Y.

5. (CMA) The process of evaluating the effect of changes in variables such as sales price or labor wage rates on the optimum solution in a linear programming application is called

    a. Simplex method analysis.
    b. Iterative analysis.
    c. Regression analysis.
    d. Sensitivity analysis.
    e. Matrix analysis.

6. (CIA) The data below were gathered on two different machine centers and two products.

	Production Hours per Unit		
	A	B	Hours Available
Machine Center 1	2.5	4	60
Machine Center 2	6	3	70
Contribution per unit	$4	$5	

    Which item would be part of a linear programming formulation of this problem?

    a. Maximize: Contribution ≥ 4A + 5B.
    b. Subject to: A ≤ 0.
    c. Subject to: 2.5A + 4B ≤ 60.
    d. Subject to: 4A + 5B ≤ 130.

7. (CMA) One limitation of the linear programming technique is that it is effective only for

    a. Two product situations.
    b. Manufacturing resource constraint situations.

    c. Straight-line relationship situations.

    d. Income maximization situations.

    e. Cost minimization situations.

8. (CIA) A company prints sheet music which is sold nationally to local music stores. The company is investigating the replacement of its current printing press with one of two new presses. The following data relate to the two new printing presses:

Per Unit	Press X	Press Y
Sales price	$3.95	$3.95
Paper	0.25	0.50
Ink	0.25	0.50
Labor	1.00	1.50
Variable overhead*	1.00	0.50
Fixed overhead*	0.50	0.25

*Applied on the basis of machine hours.

The company's facilities will only accommodate one printing press and no expansion of the facilities is planned. Ample market exists for all sheet music produced. If machine hours are limited next year with Press X requiring twice as many machine-hours per unit of music as Press Y, the company should base the replacement decision upon the following contribution margins for Presses X and Y, respectively:

    a. $0.95 and $0.70.

    b. $0.95 and $1.40.

    c. $1.45 and $0.95.

    d. $1.45 and $1.90.

Exercises

E27–1 Linear Programming and Minimum Cost (L.O. 4)

To produce a more durable, beautiful green for its golf course, Civic Country Club is advised to spread at least 9,600 pounds of special chemicals and 10,000 pounds of fertilizer. However, club management is only able to buy the fertilizer and chemicals in a mixture, not in a pure form.

A dealer has offered 100-pound bags of Mixture X at $6 each which contains the equivalent of 20 pounds of fertilizer and 16 pounds of chemicals. Mixture Y is also available in 100-pound bags, at $9 each; it contains the equivalent of 50 pounds of fertilizer and 50 pounds of chemicals.

Required:

Express the relationships as inequalities. How many bags of Mixture X and Mixture Y should the club buy to obtain the required fertilizer and chemicals at minimum cost? Solve graphically with Mixture X on the vertical axis.

E27–2 Graphic Solution (L.O. 1)

Management of Richard Company is analyzing the requirements for producing chemicals on idle machines during March and April. Based on past results, the production of 1 gallon of Boxa requires 3 hours of labor in March; 4 hours of labor in April, $2 in cash, and 4.5 hours of machine time. To produce 1 gallon of Doxa, 2 hours of labor are required in March, 6 hours of labor in April, $2.25 in cash, and 9 hours of machine time. Available for the production of these chemicals are 600 labor-hours in March, 2,100 labor-hours in April, $450 cash, and 1,350 machine-hours. The contribution margin is $2 per gallon of Boxa and $3 per gallon of Doxa.

Required:

a. Using graphic techniques, determine how the company should divide its production between Boxa and Doxa for the two-month period to maximize profits. Express the relationships in mathematical form and indicate the total contribution margin.

b. Determine which of the requirements is not a true constraint.

E27–3 Algebraic Expressions (L.O. 2)

Gleim Company manufactures Products A and B; each requires two processes, mixing and grinding. The contribution margin is $5 for Product A and $8 for Product B. One unit of A requires two hours of mixing and three hours of grinding time. One unit of B requires three hours of mixing and two hours of grinding time. There are 60 hours of mixing available daily and 48 hours of grinding available. The following graph shows the maximum number of units of each product that may be processed in the two departments.

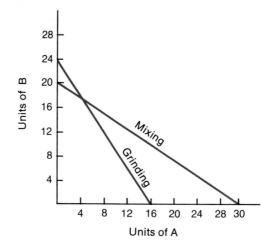

Required:

a. Give the objective function expressed algebraically.

b. Give the production constraint expressed algebraically.

c. Consider the constraints (restrictions) on processing and determine which combination of Products A and B maximizes the total contribution margin.

E27–4 Profit-Maximizing Schedule (L.O. 3)

The graph on page 967 for White, Inc., presents the constraint functions for a machine manufacturing company whose production problem can be solved by linear programming. The company earns $50 for each calculator sold and $20 for each typewriter sold.

Required:

What is the profit-maximizing production schedule? Provide support for your answer.

E27–5 Linear Programming and Minimum Cost (L.O. 4)

Southern Rose Gardens is advised to spread at least 4,000 pounds of nitrogen and 9,600 pounds of fertilizer. However, management is only able to buy the nitrogen and fertilizer in a mixture, not in a pure form.

A dealer has offered to sell 100-pound bags of Mixture A at $8 each which contains the equivalent of 20 pounds of nitrogen and 80 pounds of fertilizer. Mixture B is also available in 100-pound bags, at $5 each; it contains the equivalent of 40 pounds of nitrogen and 60 pounds of fertilizer.

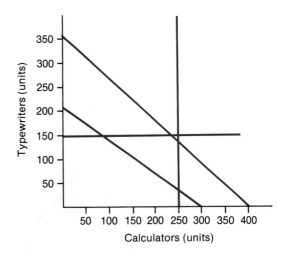

Required:

Express the relationships as inequalities. How many bags of Mixture A and Mixture B should the gardens buy to obtain the required nitrogen and fertilizer at minimum cost? Solve graphically.

E27–6 Expressing Objective Function and Constraints (L.O. 2)

Griffin, Inc., produces three items. Estimates of next year's sales prices and costs are as follows:

	Products		
	A	**B**	**C**
Market demand for a year	4,000 units	2,000 units	1,000 units
	Per Unit		
Sales price	$450	$250	$300
Direct material	300 pounds at $1 per pound	50 pounds at $2 per pound	100 pounds at $2 per pound
Direct labor	2 hours at $10 per hour	4 hours at $12 per hour	5 hours at $10 per hour
Variable overhead	$50	$20	$10
Fixed overhead	$40	$60	$30

Capacity available within the company:
  Direct material handling facilities—900,000 pounds per year
  Direct labor* ($10 per hour labor)—7,500 hours per year
  Direct labor* ($12 per hour labor)—10,000 hours per year
*$12 labor can be substituted for $10 labor, but not vice versa.

Required:

a. Express the objective function algebraically.
b. Express all the constraints involved for the three products algebraically.

E27–7 Maximizing a Production Schedule (L.O. 3)

The Shell Corporation manufactures and sells two grades, A and B, of a single wood product. Each grade must be processed through three phases—mixing, fitting, and finishing—before it is sold. The following unit information is provided:

	A	B
Selling price	$18.00	$12.00
Direct materials	0.85	2.00
Direct labor	7.30	5.60
Variable overhead	1.15	1.80
Fixed overhead	0.60	0.30
Materials requirements in pounds	5	4
Labor requirements in hours:		
Mixing	2	5
Fitting	4	3
Finishing	1	6

Only 3,000 pounds per week can be obtained. The Mixing Department has 1,000 hours of labor available each week; the Fitting Department, 800 hours; and the Finishing Department, 980 hours. No overtime is allowed.

Contract commitments require the company to make 220 units of A per week. In addition, company policy is to produce at least 60 additional units of A and 40 units of B each week to actively remain in each of the three markets. Because of competition, only 150 units of B can be sold each week.

Required:

Formulate and label the linear objective function and the constraint functions necessary to maximize the contribution margin.

Problems

P27–8 Graphic Linear Programming (L.O. 3)

Jacksonville Corporation manufactures Products A and B. The daily production requirements are as follows:

Product	Contribution Margin per Unit	Hours Required per Unit per Department		
		Mixing	Plating	Finishing
A	$10	1.5	2.0	1.2
B	5	2.5	1.5	.5
Total hours per day per department		18,000	12,000	6,000

Daily sales demand expected for A is 6,500 units; for B, 9,000 units.

Required:

a. Indicate the objective function in determining daily production of each unit.
b. Set linear equations for the constraints.
c. Determine the optimal solution using the graphic method.

P27–9 Graphic Solution (L.O. 2)

Evans, Inc., can produce Parts A and B on either of two machines. When using Machine 1, workers need eight minutes to make Part A, and six minutes for Part B. The comparable times on Machine 2 are 10 minutes for Part A and 4 minutes for Part B. During each working day, 72 minutes are available on Machine 1 and 80 minutes on Machine 2. Daily marketing demands are not expected to exceed 12 units of Part A and 7 units of Part B.

Required:

a. Formulate and label the linear objective function and the constraint functions necessary to maximize the contribution margin, assuming the contribution margin for Part A is $9 and $12 for Part B.

b. Use the graphic solution to find the product mix which optimizes contribution margin.

P27–10 Maximum and Minimum Production Constraints (L.O. 3)

Smith Company manufactures Products A and B through two processing operations. The company may produce either Product B exclusively or various combinations of both products except that Product B must equal or exceed 50 units per day. A shortage of material has limited production of Product A to 100 units per day. Assume all relationships between capacity and production are linear, and that all the data and relationships are deterministic rather than probabilistic. The following constraints are given:

	Hours Required to Produce One Unit		Unit Contribution Margin
	Process 1	Process 2	
Product A	4	5	$3
Product B	2	3	$5
Total capacity, hours per day	800	750	

Required:

Using graphic techniques, determine how many units of each product the company should produce to maximize profits. Express the relationships in mathematical form and indicate the total contribution margin. (Graph Product A on the *X*-axis for consistency.)

P27–11 Expressing Objective Function (L.O. 2)

The Cannon Company produces and sells Products X, Y, and Z. The company has such limited production capacity that only 2,500 direct labor-hours and 24,000 pounds of direct materials are available each month. All three products use the same type of direct material which costs $2 per pound. Direct labor is paid at the rate of $6 per hour.

A consultant suggests that the company consider using linear programming for determining optimum product mix. Based on prior years' operations, the accountants gather the following data concerning each product which includes expected sales prices and labor and material costs by product line. Costs for variable overhead and fixed overhead are assumed to be the same for each product line since approximately the same quantity of each product was produced and sold last year.

Price and Cost Information (per Unit)			
	X	Y	Z
Selling price	$25.00	$30.00	$40.00
Direct labor	9.00	12.00	15.00
Direct materials	8.00	6.00	10.00
Variable overhead	5.00	5.00	5.00
Fixed overhead	1.00	1.00	1.00

Required:

Formulate and label the linear objective function and the constraint functions necessary to maximize contribution margin. Use X, Y, and Z to represent units of the three products.

P27–12 Graphic Linear Programming (L.O. 3)

Barbara Johnston Corporation manufactures Products A and B. The daily production requirements are as follows:

Product	Contribution Margin per Unit	Hours Required per Unit per Department		
		Machining	Plating	Finishing
A	$ 6	2	5.0	1.5
B	15	4	2.5	1.0
Total hours per day per department		16,000	20,000	15,000

Maximum daily demand is expected to be 13,000 units for A and 7,000 units for B.

Required:

a. Indicate the objective function in determining daily production of each unit.
b. Set linear equations for the constraints.
c. Determine the optimal solution using the graphic method.

P27–13 Graphic Solution with Varying Condition (L.O. 2)

Dean Pipkin, Inc. manufactures two products, Regular and Super. Each product must be processed in each of three departments: Fabricating, Assembling, and Finishing. The hours needed to produce one unit per department and the maximum possible hours per department follow:

	Production Hours per Unit		Maximum Capacity Hours
	Regular	Super	
Fabricating	3	5.25	1,050
Assembling	6.4	4	1,600
Finishing	6	5	1,800

Other restrictions: Regular ≥ 75
Super   ≥ 50

The objective is to maximize profits; unit contribution margin is $8—Regular and $6—Super.

Required:

a. Calculate the most profitable number of units of Regular products and Super products to manufacture, given the objective and constraints. Determine your answer by utilizing the graphic solution method. (Graph regular product on *X*-axis.)
b. Indicate your answer to Requirement *a* if there were no minimum restrictions on the products and the direct material cost for Regular products has been reduced $2 per unit due to quantity buying.

P27–14 Production Constraints and Optimum Combination (L.O. 3)

Disk Company manufactures two products, Regular and Super. Each product must pass through two processing operations. All materials are introduced in the Mixing Department. There are no work in process inventories. Either one product exclusively or various combinations of both products may be produced subject to the following constraints:

	Mixing Dept.	Spinning Dept.	Contribution Margin per Unit
Hours required to produce one unit of			
Regular	6.25 hours	2 hours	$5.00
Super	8 hours	1.5 hours	$4.00
Total capacity, hours per day	2,500	600	

A shortage of technical labor has limited Super production to 250 units per day. There are no constraints on the production of Regular products other than the hour constraints in the previous schedule. Assume that all relationships between capacity and production are linear, and that all the above data and relationships are deterministic rather than probabilistic.

Required:

a. Identify the production constraints for the Mixing Department and the Spinning Department, given the objective to maximize total contribution margin.
b. Identify the labor constraint for production of Super products, given the objective to maximize total contribution margin.
c. Indicate the objective function of the data presented.
d. Graphically determine the optimum combination to maximize contribution analysis.

P27–15 Graphic Linear Programming (L.O. 2)

Johns Corporation manufactures Products A and B. The daily production requirements are

	Contribution Margin		Hours Required per Unit per Department		
Product	Per Unit		Machining	Plating	Finishing
A	$ 8		5	3	2.5
B	12		2	6	2.0
Total hours per day in department			10,000	12,000	8,000

Maximum daily demand is expected to be 1,500 units for A and 3,000 units for B.

Required:

a. Indicate the objective function in determining daily production of each unit.
b. Set linear equations for the constraints.
c. Determine optimal solution using the graphic method.

P27–16 Linear Programming Techniques (L.O. 3)

The following information was furnished for the Ray Company's two products, tables and chairs:

	Maximum Daily Capacities in Units			
	Shaping Department	Sanding Department	Sales Price per Unit	Variable Cost per Unit
Tables	300	250	$75	$45
Chairs	225	150	20	14

Any combination of tables and chairs can be produced as long as the maximum capacity of the department is not exceeded because the daily capacities of each department represent the maximum production for either product assuming each department devoted full time to that product. For example, the company can shape 300 tables and no chairs or shape 225 chairs and no table or some combination of the two products. Shortages of skilled labor prohibit the production of more than 200 tables per day. The company used the preceding production information to develop the following graph:

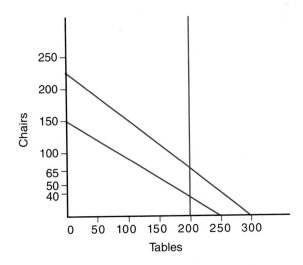

Required:

a. Comparing the information in the table with the graph, identify and list the graphic location (coordinates) of the:
   (1) Shaping department's capacity.
   (2) Production limitation for tables because of the labor shortage.
   (3) Area of feasible production combinations.
b. Determine the total contribution margin of each of the points of intersections of lines bounding the feasible production area, identifying the best production alternative.

P27–17 Linear Programming Techniques (L.O. 2)

Britt Company furnished the following information for its two products, Deluxe and Super motors:

| | Maximum Daily Capacities in Units | | | |
	Fabricating Department	Finishing Department	Sales Price per Unit	Variable Cost per Unit
Deluxe	60	90	$30	$20
Super	100	80	40	25

Any combination of Deluxe and Super can be produced as long as the maximum capacity of the department is not exceeded because the daily capacities of each department represent the maximum production for either product assuming each department devoted full time to that product. For example, the company can finish 90 Deluxe motors and no Super motors or 80 Super motors and no Deluxe motors per day, or some combination of the two products. Material shortages prohibit the production of more than 60 Super motors per day. The company used the preceding production information to develop the following graph:

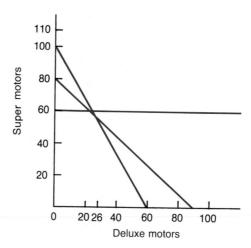

Required:

a. Comparing the information in the table with the graph in the figure, identify and list the graphic location (coordinates) of the:
   (1) Finishing department's capacity.
   (2) Production limitation for Super motors because of the materials shortage.
   (3) Area of feasible production combinations.
b. Compute the total contribution margin of each of the points of intersections of lines bounding the feasible production area identifying the best production alternative.

P27–18 (CMA adapted) Formulating Objective and Constraint Functions (L.O. 2 and 3)

Leastan Company manufactures a line of commercial and residential carpeting. Two grades of fiber—heavy-duty and regular—are in both types of carpeting. The mix of the two grades differs in each type of carpeting, with the commercial grade using a greater amount of heavy-duty fiber.

Leastan will introduce a new line of carpeting in two months to replace the current line. The present fiber in stock will not be used in the new line. Management wants to exhaust the present stock of regular and heavy-duty fiber during the last month of production.

Data on the current lines of commercial residential carpeting are as follows:

	Commercial	Residential
Selling price per roll	$1,000	$800
Production specifications per roll of carpet:		
Heavy-duty fiber	80 pounds	40 pounds
Regular fiber	20 pounds	40 pounds
Direct labor-hours	15 hours	15 hours
Standard cost per roll of carpet:		
Heavy-duty fiber ($3 per pound)	$240	$120
Regular fiber ($2 per pound)	40	80
Direct labor ($10 per pound)	150	150
Variable manufacturing overhead (60% of direct labor cost)	90	90
Fixed manufacturing overhead (120% of direct labor cost)	180	180
Total standard cost per roll	$700	$620

Leastan has 42,000 pounds of heavy-duty fiber and 24,000 pounds of regular fiber in stock. All fiber not used in the manufacture of the present types of carpeting during the last month of production can be sold as scrap at $0.25 a pound.

There is a maximum of 10,500 direct labor-hours available during the month. The labor force can work on either type of carpeting.

Sufficient demand exists for the present line of carpeting so that all quantities produced can be sold.

Required:

a. Calculate the number of rolls of commercial carpet and residential carpet Leastan Company must manufacture during the last month of production to completely exhaust the heavy-duty and regular fiber still in stock.

b. Explain how Leastan Company can manufacture these quantities of commercial and residential carpeting during the last month of production.

c. A member of Leastan Company's cost accounting staff has stated that linear programming should be used to determine the number of rolls of commercial and residential carpeting to manufacture during the last month of production.

   (1) Explain why linear programming should be used in this application.

   (2) Formulate the objective and constraint functions so that this application can be solved by linear programming.

APPENDIX

T A B L E A: Present Value of $1

Years Hence	1%	2%	4%	6%	8%	10%	12%	14%	15%	16%	18%	20%	22%	24%	25%	26%	28%	30%	35%	40%	45%	50%
1	0.990	0.980	0.962	0.943	0.926	0.909	0.893	0.877	0.870	0.862	0.847	0.833	0.820	0.806	0.800	0.794	0.781	0.769	0.741	0.714	0.690	0.667
2	0.980	0.961	0.925	0.890	0.857	0.826	0.797	0.769	0.756	0.743	0.718	0.694	0.672	0.650	0.640	0.630	0.610	0.592	0.549	0.510	0.476	0.444
3	0.971	0.942	0.889	0.840	0.794	0.751	0.712	0.675	0.658	0.641	0.609	0.579	0.551	0.524	0.512	0.500	0.477	0.455	0.406	0.364	0.328	0.296
4	0.961	0.924	0.855	0.792	0.735	0.683	0.636	0.592	0.572	0.552	0.516	0.482	0.451	0.423	0.410	0.397	0.373	0.350	0.301	0.260	0.226	0.198
5	0.951	0.906	0.822	0.747	0.681	0.621	0.567	0.519	0.497	0.476	0.437	0.402	0.370	0.341	0.328	0.315	0.291	0.269	0.223	0.186	0.156	0.132
6	0.942	0.888	0.790	0.705	0.630	0.564	0.507	0.456	0.432	0.410	0.370	0.335	0.303	0.275	0.262	0.250	0.227	0.207	0.165	0.133	0.108	0.088
7	0.933	0.871	0.760	0.665	0.583	0.513	0.452	0.400	0.376	0.354	0.314	0.279	0.249	0.222	0.210	0.198	0.178	0.159	0.122	0.095	0.074	0.059
8	0.923	0.853	0.731	0.627	0.540	0.467	0.404	0.351	0.327	0.305	0.266	0.233	0.204	0.179	0.168	0.157	0.139	0.123	0.091	0.068	0.051	0.039
9	0.914	0.837	0.703	0.592	0.500	0.424	0.361	0.308	0.284	0.263	0.225	0.194	0.167	0.144	0.134	0.125	0.108	0.094	0.067	0.048	0.035	0.026
10	0.905	0.820	0.676	0.558	0.463	0.386	0.322	0.270	0.247	0.227	0.191	0.162	0.137	0.116	0.107	0.099	0.085	0.073	0.050	0.035	0.024	0.017
11	0.896	0.804	0.650	0.527	0.429	0.350	0.287	0.237	0.215	0.195	0.162	0.135	0.112	0.094	0.086	0.079	0.066	0.056	0.037	0.025	0.017	0.012
12	0.887	0.788	0.625	0.497	0.397	0.319	0.257	0.208	0.187	0.168	0.137	0.112	0.092	0.076	0.069	0.062	0.052	0.043	0.027	0.018	0.012	0.008
13	0.879	0.773	0.601	0.469	0.368	0.290	0.229	0.182	0.163	0.145	0.116	0.093	0.075	0.061	0.055	0.050	0.040	0.033	0.020	0.013	0.008	0.005
14	0.870	0.758	0.577	0.442	0.340	0.263	0.205	0.160	0.141	0.125	0.099	0.078	0.062	0.049	0.044	0.039	0.032	0.025	0.015	0.009	0.006	0.003
15	0.861	0.743	0.555	0.417	0.315	0.239	0.183	0.140	0.123	0.108	0.084	0.065	0.051	0.040	0.035	0.031	0.025	0.020	0.011	0.006	0.004	0.002
16	0.853	0.728	0.534	0.394	0.292	0.218	0.163	0.123	0.107	0.093	0.071	0.054	0.042	0.032	0.028	0.025	0.019	0.015	0.008	0.005	0.003	0.002
17	0.844	0.714	0.513	0.371	0.270	0.198	0.146	0.108	0.093	0.080	0.060	0.045	0.034	0.026	0.023	0.020	0.015	0.012	0.006	0.003	0.002	0.001
18	0.836	0.700	0.494	0.350	0.250	0.180	0.130	0.095	0.081	0.069	0.051	0.038	0.028	0.021	0.018	0.016	0.012	0.009	0.005	0.002	0.001	0.001
19	0.828	0.686	0.475	0.331	0.232	0.164	0.116	0.083	0.070	0.060	0.043	0.031	0.023	0.017	0.014	0.012	0.009	0.007	0.003	0.002	0.001	
20	0.820	0.673	0.456	0.312	0.215	0.149	0.104	0.073	0.061	0.051	0.037	0.026	0.019	0.014	0.012	0.010	0.007	0.005	0.002	0.001		
21	0.811	0.660	0.439	0.294	0.199	0.135	0.093	0.064	0.053	0.044	0.031	0.022	0.015	0.011	0.009	0.008	0.006	0.004	0.002	0.001		
22	0.803	0.647	0.422	0.278	0.184	0.123	0.083	0.056	0.046	0.038	0.026	0.018	0.013	0.009	0.007	0.006	0.004	0.003	0.001	0.001		
23	0.795	0.634	0.406	0.262	0.170	0.112	0.074	0.049	0.040	0.033	0.022	0.015	0.010	0.007	0.006	0.005	0.003	0.002	0.001			
24	0.788	0.622	0.390	0.247	0.158	0.102	0.066	0.043	0.035	0.028	0.019	0.013	0.008	0.006	0.005	0.004	0.003	0.002	0.001			
25	0.780	0.610	0.375	0.233	0.146	0.092	0.059	0.038	0.030	0.024	0.016	0.010	0.007	0.005	0.004	0.003	0.002	0.001	0.001			
26	0.772	0.598	0.361	0.220	0.135	0.084	0.053	0.033	0.026	0.021	0.014	0.009	0.006	0.004	0.003	0.002	0.002	0.001				
27	0.764	0.586	0.347	0.207	0.125	0.076	0.047	0.029	0.023	0.018	0.011	0.007	0.005	0.003	0.002	0.002	0.001	0.001				
28	0.757	0.574	0.333	0.196	0.116	0.069	0.042	0.026	0.020	0.016	0.010	0.006	0.004	0.002	0.002	0.002	0.001	0.001				
29	0.749	0.563	0.321	0.185	0.107	0.063	0.037	0.022	0.017	0.014	0.008	0.005	0.003	0.002	0.002	0.001	0.001	0.001				
30	0.742	0.552	0.308	0.174	0.099	0.057	0.033	0.020	0.015	0.012	0.007	0.004	0.003	0.002	0.001	0.001	0.001	0.001				
40	0.672	0.453	0.208	0.097	0.046	0.022	0.011	0.005	0.004	0.003	0.001	0.001										
50	0.608	0.372	0.141	0.054	0.021	0.009	0.003	0.001	0.001	0.001												

TABLE B: Present Value of $1 Received Annually for N Years

Years (N)	1%	2%	4%	6%	8%	10%	12%	14%	15%	16%	18%	20%	22%	24%	25%	26%	28%	30%	35%	40%	45%	50%
1	0.990	0.980	0.962	0.943	0.926	0.909	0.893	0.877	0.870	0.862	0.847	0.833	0.820	0.806	0.800	0.794	0.781	0.769	0.741	0.714	0.690	0.667
2	1.970	1.942	1.886	1.833	1.783	1.736	1.690	1.647	1.626	1.605	1.566	1.528	1.492	1.457	1.440	1.424	1.392	1.361	1.289	1.224	1.165	1.111
3	2.941	2.884	2.775	2.673	2.577	2.487	2.402	2.322	2.283	2.246	2.174	2.106	2.042	1.981	1.952	1.923	1.868	1.816	1.696	1.589	1.493	1.407
4	3.902	3.808	3.630	3.465	3.312	3.170	3.037	2.914	2.855	2.798	2.690	2.589	2.494	2.404	2.362	2.320	2.241	2.166	1.997	1.849	1.720	1.605
5	4.853	4.713	4.452	4.212	3.993	3.791	3.605	3.433	3.352	3.274	3.127	2.991	2.864	2.745	2.689	2.635	2.532	2.436	2.220	2.035	1.876	1.737
6	5.795	5.601	5.242	4.917	4.623	4.355	4.111	3.889	3.784	3.685	3.498	3.326	3.167	3.020	2.951	2.885	2.759	2.643	2.385	2.168	1.983	1.824
7	6.728	6.472	6.002	5.582	5.206	4.868	4.564	4.288	4.160	4.039	3.812	3.605	3.416	3.242	3.161	3.083	2.937	2.802	2.508	2.263	2.057	1.883
8	7.652	7.325	6.733	6.210	5.747	5.335	4.968	4.639	4.487	4.344	4.078	3.837	3.619	3.421	3.329	3.241	3.076	2.925	2.598	2.331	2.108	1.922
9	8.566	8.162	7.435	6.802	6.247	5.759	5.328	4.946	4.772	4.607	4.303	4.031	3.786	3.566	3.463	3.366	3.184	3.019	2.665	2.379	2.144	1.948
10	9.471	8.983	8.111	7.360	6.710	6.145	5.650	5.216	5.019	4.833	4.494	4.192	3.923	3.682	3.571	3.465	3.269	3.092	2.715	2.414	2.168	1.965
11	10.368	9.787	8.760	7.887	7.139	6.495	5.937	5.453	5.234	5.029	4.656	4.327	4.035	3.776	3.656	3.544	3.335	3.147	2.757	2.438	2.185	1.977
12	11.255	10.575	9.385	8.384	7.536	6.814	6.194	5.660	5.421	5.197	4.793	4.439	4.127	3.851	3.725	3.606	3.387	3.190	2.779	2.456	2.196	1.985
13	12.134	11.343	9.986	8.853	7.904	7.103	6.424	5.842	5.583	5.342	4.910	4.533	4.203	3.912	3.780	3.656	3.427	3.223	2.799	2.468	2.204	1.990
14	13.004	12.106	10.563	9.295	8.244	7.367	6.628	6.002	5.724	5.468	5.008	4.611	4.265	3.962	3.824	3.695	3.459	3.249	2.814	2.477	2.210	1.993
15	13.865	12.849	11.118	9.712	8.559	7.606	6.811	6.142	5.847	5.575	5.092	4.675	4.315	4.001	3.859	3.726	3.483	3.268	2.825	2.484	2.214	1.995
16	14.718	13.578	11.652	10.106	8.851	7.824	6.974	6.265	5.954	5.669	5.162	4.730	4.357	4.033	3.887	3.751	3.503	3.283	2.834	2.489	2.216	1.997
17	15.562	14.292	12.166	10.477	9.122	8.022	7.120	6.373	6.047	5.749	5.222	4.775	4.391	4.059	3.910	3.771	3.518	3.295	2.840	2.492	2.218	1.998
18	16.398	14.992	12.659	10.828	9.372	8.201	7.250	6.467	6.128	5.818	5.273	4.812	4.419	4.080	3.928	3.786	3.529	3.304	2.844	2.494	2.219	1.999
19	17.226	15.678	13.134	11.158	9.604	8.365	7.366	6.550	6.198	5.877	5.316	4.844	4.442	4.097	3.942	3.799	3.539	3.311	2.848	2.496	2.220	1.999
20	18.046	16.351	13.590	11.470	9.818	8.514	7.469	6.623	6.259	5.929	5.353	4.870	4.460	4.110	3.954	3.808	3.546	3.316	2.850	2.497	2.221	1.999
21	18.857	17.011	14.029	11.764	10.017	8.649	7.562	6.687	6.312	5.973	5.384	4.891	4.476	4.121	3.963	3.816	3.551	3.320	2.852	2.498	2.221	2.000
22	19.660	17.658	14.451	12.042	10.201	8.772	7.645	6.743	6.359	6.011	5.410	4.909	4.488	4.130	3.970	3.822	3.556	3.323	2.853	2.498	2.222	2.000
23	20.456	18.292	14.857	12.303	10.371	8.883	7.718	6.792	6.399	6.044	5.432	4.925	4.499	4.137	3.976	3.827	3.559	3.325	2.854	2.499	2.222	2.000
24	21.243	18.914	15.247	12.550	10.529	8.985	7.784	6.835	6.434	6.073	5.451	4.937	4.507	4.143	3.981	3.831	3.562	3.327	2.855	2.499	2.222	2.000
25	22.023	19.523	15.622	12.783	10.675	9.077	7.843	6.873	6.464	6.097	5.467	4.948	4.514	4.147	3.985	3.834	3.564	3.329	2.856	2.499	2.222	2.000
26	22.795	20.121	15.983	13.003	10.810	9.161	7.896	6.906	6.491	6.118	5.480	4.956	4.520	4.151	3.988	3.837	3.566	3.330	2.856	2.500	2.222	2.000
27	23.560	20.707	16.330	13.211	10.935	9.237	7.943	6.935	6.514	6.136	5.492	4.964	4.524	4.154	3.990	3.839	3.567	3.331	2.856	2.500	2.222	2.000
28	24.316	21.281	16.663	13.406	11.051	9.307	7.984	6.961	6.534	6.152	5.502	4.970	4.528	4.157	3.992	3.840	3.568	3.331	2.857	2.500	2.222	2.000
29	25.066	21.844	16.984	13.591	11.158	9.370	8.022	6.983	6.551	6.166	5.510	4.975	4.531	4.159	3.994	3.841	3.569	3.332	2.857	2.500	2.222	2.000
30	25.808	22.396	17.292	13.765	11.258	9.427	8.055	7.003	6.566	6.177	5.517	4.979	4.534	4.160	3.995	3.842	3.569	3.332	2.857	2.500	2.222	2.000
40	32.835	27.355	19.793	15.046	11.925	9.779	8.244	7.105	6.642	6.234	5.548	4.997	4.544	4.166	3.999	3.846	3.571	3.333	2.857	2.500	2.222	2.000
50	39.196	31.424	21.482	15.762	12.234	9.915	8.304	7.133	6.661	6.246	5.554	4.999	4.545	4.167	4.000	3.846	3.571	3.333	2.857	2.500	2.222	2.000

980

Budget—*Cont.*
period, 300
production
profit pl[...]
progr[...]
pr[...]

INDEX